THE AMERICAN COMMONWEALTH

A Liberty*Classics* Edition

James Bryce

JAMES BRYCE

THE AMERICAN COMMONWEALTH

With an Introduction by Gary L. McDowell

V O L U M E I I

Liberty Fund
Indianapolis
1995

This is a Liberty*Classics* Edition published by Liberty Fund, Inc., a foundation established to encourage study of the ideal of a society of free and responsible individuals.

The cuneiform inscription that serves as our logo and as the design motif for our endpapers is the earliest-known written appearance of the word "freedom" (*amagi*), or "liberty." It is taken from a clay document written about 2300 B.C. in the Sumerian city-state of Lagash.

Frontispiece: James Bryce, 1906, Chief Secretary for Ireland. From H. A. L. Fisher, *James Bryce: Viscount Bryce of Dechmont, O.M.*, vol. 1 (London: Macmillan, 1927). Front cover: *The County Election* (detail) by George Caleb Bingham. 1851–1852. Oil on canvas, 35-7/16 × 48-3/4″. The Saint Louis Art Museum.

Liberty Fund, Inc.
8335 Allison Pointe Trail, Suite 300
Indianapolis, Indiana 46250-1687
(317) 842-0880

Library of Congress Cataloging-in-Publication Data

Bryce, James Bryce, Viscount, 1838–1922.
  The American commonwealth / James Bryce.
    p.   cm.
  Includes bibliographical references and index.
  ISBN 0-86597-116-1 (set : hardcover : alk. paper).—ISBN
0-86597-117-X (set : pbk. : alk. paper).—ISBN 0-86597-118-8 (vol.
1 : hardcover : acid-free paper).—ISBN 0-86597-119-6 (vol. 1 :
paperback : acid-free paper).—ISBN 0-86597-120-X (vol. 2 :
hardcover : acid-free paper).—ISBN 0-86597-121-8 (vol. 2 :
paperback : acid-free paper)
    1. United States—Politics and government.   2. State governments—
United States.   3. United States—Social conditions.   I. Title.
JK246.B9   1995
320.473—dc20   95-11187

10 9 8 7 6 5 4 3 2 1

Contents

──────────── V O L U M E I ────────────

Introductory

P A R T I

The National Government

P A R T I I

The State Governments

Appendix

──────────── V O L U M E I I ────────────

P A R T I I I

The Party System

P A R T   I V

Public Opinion

P A R T V

Illustrations and Reflections

P A R T V I

Social Institutions

Appendix I

Appendix II

Appendix III

Appendix IV

PART III

THE PARTY SYSTEM

C H A P T E R   5 3

Political Parties and Their History

In the preceding chapters I have endeavoured to describe the legal frame-
work of American government as it exists both in the nation and in the
states. Beginning from the federal and state constitutions we have seen what
sort of a structure has been erected upon them as a foundation, what methods
of legislation and administration have been developed, what results these
methods have produced. It is only occasionally and incidentally that we
have had to consider the influence upon political bodies and methods of
those extra-legal groupings of men called political parties. But the spirit and
force of party has in America been as essential to the action of the machinery
of government as steam is to a locomotive engine; or, to vary the simile,
party association and organization are to the organs of government almost
what the motor nerves are to the muscles, sinews, and bones of the human
body. They transmit the motive power, they determine the directions in
which the organs act. A description of them is therefore a necessary
complement to an account of the Constitution and government; for it is into
the hands of the parties that the working of the government has fallen. Their
ingenuity, stimulated by incessant rivalry, has turned many provisions of
the Constitution to unforeseen uses, and given to the legal institutions of
the country no small part of their present colour.

To describe the party system is, however, much harder than it has been
to describe those legal institutions. Hitherto we have been on comparatively
firm ground, for we have had definite data to rely upon, and the facts set
forth have been mostly patent facts which can be established from books
and documents. But now we come to phenomena for a knowledge of which
one must trust to a variety of flying and floating sources, to newspaper
paragraphs, to the conversation of American acquaintances, to impressions
formed on the spot from seeing incidents and hearing stories and anecdotes,

the authority for which, though it seemed sufficient at the time, cannot always be remembered. Nor have I the advantage of being able to cite any previous treatise on the subject;[1] for though the books and articles dealing with the public life of the United States may be counted by hundreds, I know of no author who has set himself to describe impartially the actual daily working of that part of the vast and intricate political machine which lies outside the Constitution, nor, what is more important still, the influences which sway the men by whom this machine has been constructed and is daily manipulated. The task, however, cannot be declined; for it is that very part of my undertaking which, even though imperfectly performed, may be most serviceable to the student of modern politics. A philosopher in Germany, who had mastered all the treatises on the British Constitution, perused every statute of recent years, and even followed through the newspapers the debates in Parliament, would know far less about the government and politics of England than he might learn by spending a month there conversing with practical politicians, and watching the daily changes of sentiment during a parliamentary crisis or a general election.

So, too, in the United States, the actual working of party government is not only full of interest and instruction, but is so unlike what a student of the federal Constitution could have expected or foreseen, that it is the thing of all others which anyone writing about America ought to try to portray. In the knowledge of a stranger there must, of course, be serious gaps. But since no native American has yet essayed the task of describing the party system of his country, it is better that a stranger should address himself to it, than that the inquiring European should have no means of satisfying his curiosity. And a native American writer, even if he steered clear of partisanship, which I think he might, for in no country does one find a larger number of philosophically judicial observers of politics, would suffer from his own familiarity with many of those very things which a stranger finds perplexing. Thus European and even American readers may find in the sort of perspective which a stranger gets of transatlantic phenomena some compensation for his necessarily inferior knowledge of details.

In America the great moving forces are the parties. The government counts for less than in Europe, the parties count for more; and the fewer

---

[1] Since the first edition of this book was published, many works on the subject have appeared, some of great merit. Among them are M. Ostrogorski's *Democracy and the Organization of Political Parties;* Professor Morse's *History of Political Parties in the U.S.;* Professor Jesse Macy's *Party Organization and Machinery;* Professor Henry Jones Ford's *Rise and Growth of American Politics.*

have become their principles and the fainter their interest in those principles, the more perfect has become their organization. The less of nature the more of art; the less spontaneity the more mechanism. But before I attempt to describe this organization, something must be said of the doctrines which the parties respectively profess, and the explanation of the doctrines involves a few preliminary words upon the history of party in America.

Although the early colonists carried with them across the sea some of the habits of English political life, and others may have been subsequently imitated from the old country, the parties of the United States are pure home growths, developed by the circumstances of the nation. The English reader who attempts, as Englishmen are apt to do, to identify the great American parties with his own familiar Whigs and Tories, or even to discover a general similarity between them, had better give up the attempt, for it will lead him hopelessly astray. Here and there we find points of analogy rather than of resemblance, but the moment we try to follow out the analogy it breaks down, so different are the issues on which English and American politics have turned.

In the United States, the history of party begins with the Constitutional Convention of 1787 at Philadelphia. In its debates and discussions on the drafting of the Constitution there were revealed two opposite tendencies, which soon afterwards appeared on a larger scale in the state conventions, to which the new instrument was submitted for acceptance. These were the centrifugal and centripetal tendencies—a tendency to maintain both the freedom of the individual citizen and the independence in legislation, in administration, in jurisdiction, indeed in everything except foreign policy and national defence, of the several states; an opposite tendency to subordinate the states to the nation and vest large powers in the central federal authority.

The charge against the Constitution that it endangered states' rights evoked so much alarm that some states were induced to ratify only by the promise that certain amendments should be added, which were accordingly accepted in the course of the next three years. When the machinery had been set in motion by the choice of George Washington as president, and with him of a Senate and a House of Representatives, the tendencies which had opposed or supported the adoption of the Constitution reappeared not only in Congress but in the president's cabinet, where Alexander Hamilton, secretary of the treasury, counselled a line of action which assumed and required the exercise of large powers by the federal government, while Jefferson, the secretary of state, desired to practically restrict its action to foreign affairs. The advocates of a central national authority had begun to receive the name of

Federalists, and to act pretty constantly together, when an event happened which, while it tightened their union, finally consolidated their opponents also into a party. This was the creation of the French Republic and its declaration of war against England. The Federalists, who were shocked by the excesses of the Terror of 1793, counselled neutrality, and were more than ever inclined to value the principle of authority, and to allow the federal power a wide sphere of action. The party of Jefferson, who had now retired from the administration, were pervaded by sympathy with French ideas, were hostile to England whose attitude continued to be discourteous, and sought to restrict the interference of the central government with the states, and to allow the fullest play to the sentiment of state independence, of local independence, of personal independence. This party took the name of Republicans or Democratic Republicans, and they are the predecessors of the present Democrats. Both parties were, of course, attached to republican government—that is to say, were alike hostile to a monarchy. But the Jeffersonians had more faith in the masses and in leaving things alone, together with less respect for authority, so that in a sort of general way one may say that while one party claimed to be the apostles of liberty, the other represented the principle of order.

These tendencies found occasions for combating one another, not only in foreign policy and in current legislation, but also in the construction and application of the Constitution. Like all documents, and especially documents which have been formed by a series of compromises between opposite views, it was and is susceptible of various interpretations, which the acuteness of both sets of partisans was busy in discovering and expounding. While the piercing intellect of Hamilton developed all those of its provisions which invested the federal Congress and president with far-reaching powers, and sought to build up a system of institutions which should give to these provisions their full effect, Jefferson and his coadjutors appealed to the sentiment of individualism, strong in the masses of the people, and, without venturing to propose alterations in the text of the Constitution, protested against all extensions of its letter, and against all the assumptions of federal authority which such extensions could be made to justify. Thus two parties grew up with tenets, leaders, impulses, sympathies, and hatreds, hatreds which soon became so bitter as not to spare the noble and dignified figure of Washington himself, whom the angry Republicans assailed with invectives the more unbecoming because his official position forbade him to reply.[2]

---

[2] In mockery of the title he had won from public gratitude a few years before, he was commonly called by them "the stepfather of his country."

At first the Federalists had the best of it, for the reaction against the weakness of the old Confederation which the Union had superseded disposed sensible men to tolerate a strong central power. The president, though not a member of either party, was, by force of circumstances, as well as owing to the influence of Hamilton, practically with the Federalists. But during the presidency of John Adams, who succeeded Washington, they committed grave errors. When the presidential election of 1800 arrived, it was seen that the logical and oratorical force of Hamilton's appeals to the reason of the nation told far less than the skill and energy with which Jefferson played on their feelings and prejudices. The Republicans triumphed in the choice of their chief, who retained power for eight years (he was reelected in 1804), to be peaceably succeeded by his friend Madison for another eight years (elected in 1808, reelected in 1812), and his disciple Monroe for eight years more (elected in 1816, reelected in 1820). Their long-continued tenure of office was due not so much to their own merits, for neither Jefferson nor Madison conducted foreign affairs with success, as to the collapse of their antagonists. The Federalists never recovered from the blow given in the election of 1800. They lost Hamilton by death in 1804. No other leader of equal gifts appeared, and the party, which had shown little judgment in the critical years 1810–14, finally disappears from sight after the second peace with England in 1815.

One cannot note the disappearance of this brilliant figure, to Europeans the most interesting in the earlier history of the Republic, without the remark that his countrymen seem to have never, either in his lifetime or afterwards, duly recognized his splendid gifts. Washington is, indeed, a far more perfect character. Washington stands alone and unapproachable, like a snow peak rising above its fellows into the clear air of morning, with a dignity, constancy, and purity which have made him the ideal type of civic virtue to succeeding generations. No greater benefit could have befallen the Republic than to have such a type set from the first before the eye and mind of the people. But Hamilton, of a virtue not so flawless, touches us more nearly, not only by the romance of his early life and his tragic death, but by a certain ardour and impulsiveness, and even tenderness of soul, joined to a courage equal to that of Washington himself. Equally apt for war and for civil government, with a profundity and amplitude of view rare in practical soldiers or statesmen, he stands in the front rank of a generation never surpassed in history, a generation which includes Burke and Fox and Pitt and Grattan, Stein and Hardenberg and William von Humboldt, Wellington and Napoleon. Talleyrand, who seems to have felt for him something as near affection as that cold heart could feel, said, after knowing all the famous men of the time, that only Fox and Napoleon were Hamilton's equals, and that he had divined Europe, having never seen it.

This period (1788–1824) may be said to constitute the first act in the drama of American party history. The people, accustomed hitherto to care only for their several commonwealths, learn to value and to work their new national institutions. They become familiar with the Constitution itself, as partners get to know, when disputes arise among them, the provisions of the partnership deed under which their business has to be carried on. It is found that the existence of a central federal power does not annihilate the states, so the apprehensions on that score are allayed. It is also discovered that there are unforeseen directions, such for instance as banking and currency and internal communications, through which the federal power can strengthen its hold on the nation. Differences of view and feeling give rise to parties, yet parties are formed by no means solely on the basis of general principles, but owe much to the influence of prominent personalities, of transient issues, of local interests or prejudices. The small farmers and the Southern men generally follow the Republican standard borne aloft by the great state of Virginia, while the strength of the Federalists lies in New England and the Middle states, led sometimes by Massachusetts, sometimes by Pennsylvania. The commercial interests were with the Federalists, as was also the staid solid Puritanism of all classes, headed by the clergy. Someone indeed has described the struggle from 1796 to 1808 as one between Jefferson, who was an avowed freethinker, and the New England ministers; and no doubt the ministers of religion did in the Puritan states exert a political influence approaching that of the Presbyterian clergy in Scotland during the seventeenth century. Jefferson's importance lies in the fact that he became the representative not merely of democracy, but of local democracy, of the notion that government is hardly wanted at all, that the people are sure to go right if they are left alone, that he who resists authority is prima facie justified in doing so, because authority is prima facie tyrannical, that a country where each local body in its own local area looks after the objects of common concern, raising and administering any such funds as are needed, and is interfered with as little as possible by any external power, comes nearest to the ideal of a truly free people. Some intervention on the part of the state there must be, for the state makes the law and appoints the judges of appeal; but the less one has to do with the state, and a fortiori the less one has to do with the less popular and more encroaching federal authority, so much the better. Jefferson impressed this view on his countrymen with so much force and such personal faith that he became a sort of patron saint of freedom in the eyes of the next generation, who used to name their children after him,[3] and to give dinners and deliver high-flown speeches on his birthday, a festival only second in importance to the immortal Fourth of July. He had borrowed from the revolutionists of France even their theatrical ostentation of simplicity. He rejected the ceremonial with which Washington had sustained the chief magistracy of the nation, declaring that to him there was no majesty but that of the people.

As New England was, by its system of local self-government through the town meeting, as well as by the absence of slavery, in some respects the most democratic part of the United States, it may seem surprising that it should have been a stronghold of the Federalists. The reason is to be found partly in its Puritanism, which revolted at the deism or atheism of the French revolutionists, partly in the interests of its shipowners and merchants, who desired above all things a central government which, while strong enough to make and carry out treaties with England and so secure the development of American commerce, should be able also to reform the currency of the country and institute a national banking system. Industrial as well as territorial interests were already beginning to influence politics. That the mercantile and manufacturing classes, with all the advantages given them by their wealth, their intelligence, and their habits of cooperation, should have been vanquished by the agricultural masses, may be ascribed partly to the fact that the democratic impulse of the War of Independence was strong among the citizens who had grown to manhood between 1780 and 1800, partly to the tactical errors of the Federalist leaders, but largely also to the skill which Jefferson showed in organizing the hitherto undisciplined battalions of Republican voters. Thus early in American history was the secret revealed, which Europe is only now discovering, that in free countries with an extended suffrage, numbers without organization are helpless and with it omnipotent.

I have ventured to dwell on this first period, because being the first it shows the origin of tendencies which were to govern the subsequent course of party strife. But as I am not writing a history of the United States I pass by the particular issues over which the two parties wrangled, most of them long since extinct. One remark is however needed as to the view which

---

[3] It is related of a New England clergyman that when, being about to baptize a child, he asked the father the child's name, and the father replied, "Thomas Jefferson," he answered in a loud voice, "No such unchristian name: John Adams, I baptize thee," with the other sacramental words of the rite.

each took of the Constitution. Although the Federalists were in general the advocates of a loose and liberal construction of the fundamental instrument, because such a construction opened a wider sphere to federal power, they were ready, whenever their local interests stood in the way, to resist Congress and the executive, alleging that the latter were overstepping their jurisdiction. In 1814 several of the New England states, where the opposition to the war then being waged with England was strongest, sent delegates to a convention at Hartford, which, while discussing the best means for putting an end to the war and restricting the powers of Congress in commercial legislation, was suspected of meditating a secession of trading states from the Union. On the other hand, the Republicans did not hesitate to stretch to their utmost, when they were themselves in power, all the authority which the Constitution could be construed to allow to the executive and the federal government generally. The boldest step which a president has ever taken, the purchase from Napoleon of the vast territories of France west of the Mississippi which went by the name of Louisiana, was taken by Jefferson without the authority of Congress. Congress subsequently gave its sanction. But Jefferson and many of his friends held that under the Constitution even Congress had not the power to acquire new territories to be formed into states. They were therefore in the dilemma of either violating the Constitution or losing a golden opportunity of securing the Republic against the growth on its western frontier of a powerful and possibly hostile foreign state. Some of them tried to refute their former arguments against a lax construction of the Constitution, but many others avowed the dangerous doctrine that if Louisiana could be brought in only by breaking down the walls of the Constitution, broken they must be.[4]

The disappearance of the Federal party between 1815 and 1820 left the Republicans masters of the field. But in the United States if old parties vanish, nature quickly produces new ones. Sectional divisions soon arose among the men who joined in electing Monroe in 1820, and under the influence of the personal hostility of Henry Clay and Andrew Jackson (chosen president in 1828), two great parties were again formed (about 1830) which some few years later absorbed the minor groups. One of these two parties carried on, under the name of Democrats, the dogmas and

---

[4] It is now generally held that the Constitution does permit the federal government to acquire the new territory, and Congress to form states out of it. Many of the Federalist leaders warmly opposed the purchase, but the farseeing patriotism of Hamilton defended it.

See upon this subject the so-called Insular Cases, 1900–1901, 182 U.S. Reports, pp. 222, 244, and 540, and 183 U.S. Reports, p. 151.

traditions of the Jeffersonian Republicans. It was the defender of states' rights and of a restrictive construction of the Constitution; it leant mainly on the South and the farming classes generally, and it was therefore inclined to free trade. The other section, which called itself at first the National Republican, ultimately the Whig party, represented many of the views of the former Federalists, such as their advocacy of a tariff for the protection of manufactures, and of the expenditure of public money on internal improvements. It was willing to increase the army and navy, and like the Federalists found its chief, though by no means its sole, support in the commercial and manufacturing parts of the country, that is to say, in New England and the Middle states. Meantime a new question far more exciting, far more menacing, had arisen. In 1819, when Missouri applied to be admitted into the Union as a state, a sharp contest broke out in Congress as to whether slavery should be permitted within her limits, nearly all the Northern members voting against slavery, nearly all the Southern members for. The struggle might have threatened the stability of the Union but for the compromise adopted next year, which, while admitting slavery in Missouri, forbade it for the future north of lat. 36° 30'. The danger seemed to have passed, but in its very suddenness there had been something terrible. Jefferson, then over seventy, said that it startled him "like a fire-bell in the night." After 1840 things grew more serious, for whereas up till that time new states had been admitted substantially in pairs, a slave state balancing a free state, it began to be clear that this must shortly cease, since the remaining territory out of which new states would be formed lay north of the line 36° 30'. As every state held two seats in the Senate, the then existing balance in that chamber between slave states and free states would evidently soon be overset by the admission of a larger number of the latter. The apprehension of this event, with its probable result of legislation unfriendly to slavery, stimulated the South to the annexation of Texas, and the war with Mexico which led to further annexations, and made them increasingly sensitive to the growth, slow as that growth was, of Abolitionist opinions at the North. The question of the extension of slavery west of the Missouri River had become by 1850 the vital and absorbing question for the people of the United States, and as in that year California, having organized herself without slavery, was knocking at the doors of Congress for admission as a state, it had become an urgent question which evoked the hottest passions, and the victors in which would be victors all along the line. But neither of the two great parties ventured to commit itself either way. The Southern Democrats hesitated to break with those Democrats of the Northern states who sought to restrict slavery. The Whigs of the North, fearing to alienate the South by any decided action against the growing pretensions of the slaveholders, temporized and suggested compromises which practically served the cause of slavery. Anxious to save at all hazards the Union as it had hitherto stood, they did not perceive that changes of circumstances and feeling were making this effort a hopeless one, and that in trying to keep their party together they were losing hold of the people, and alienating from themselves the men who cared for principle in politics. That this was so presently appeared. The Democratic party had by 1852 passed almost completely under the control of the slaveholders, and was adopting the dogma that Congress enjoyed under the Constitution no power to prohibit slavery in the Territories. This dogma obviously overthrew as unconstitutional the Missouri Compromise of 1820. The Whig leaders discredited themselves by Henry Clay's compromise scheme of 1850, which, while admitting California as a free state, appeased the South by the Fugitive Slave law. They received a crushing defeat at the presidential election of 1852; and what remained of their party finally broke in pieces in 1854 over the bill for organizing Kansas as a Territory in which the question of slaves or no slaves should be left to the people, a bill which of course repealed the Missouri Compromise. Singularly enough, the two great orators of the party, Henry Clay and Daniel Webster, both died in 1852, wearied with strife and disappointed in their ambition of reaching the presidential chair. Together with Calhoun, who passed away two years earlier, they are the ornaments of this generation, not indeed rising to the stature of Washington or Hamilton, but more remarkable than any, save one, among the statesmen who have followed them. With them ends the second period in the annals of American parties, which, extending from about 1820 to 1856, includes the rise and fall of the Whig party. Most of the controversies which filled it have become matter for history only. But three large results, besides the general democratization of politics, stand out. One is the detachment of the United States from the affairs of the Old World. Another is the growth of a sense of national life, especially in the Northern and Western states, along with the growth at the same time of a secessionist spirit among the slaveholders. And the third is the development of the complex machinery of party organization, with the adoption of the principle on which that machinery so largely rests, that public office is to be enjoyed only by the adherents of the president for the time being.

The Whig party having begun to fall to pieces, the Democrats seemed for the moment, as they had been once before, left in possession of the field. But this time a new antagonist was quick to appear. The growing boldness of the slave owners had begun to alarm the Northern people when they were startled by the decision of the Supreme Court, pronounced in the case of the slave Dred Scott, which laid down the doctrine that Congress had no power to forbid slavery anywhere, and that a slaveholder might carry his slaves with him where he pleased, seeing that they were mere objects of property, whose possession the Constitution guaranteed.[5] This completed the formation out of the wrecks of the Whigs and Know-Nothings, or "American party," together with the Free Soilers and "Liberty" party, of a new party, which in 1856 had run Fremont as its presidential candidate and taken the name of Republican. At the same time an apple of discord was thrown among the Democrats. In 1860 the latter could not agree upon a candidate for president. The Southern wing pledged themselves to one man, the Northern wing to another; a body of hesitating and semi-detached politicians put forward a third. Thus the Republicans through the divisions of their opponents triumphed in the election of Abraham Lincoln, presently followed by the secession of eleven slave states.

The Republican party, which had started by proclaiming the right of Congress to restrict slavery and had subsequently denounced the Dred Scott decision, was of course throughout the Civil War the defender of the Union and the assertor of federal authority, stretched, as was unavoidable, to lengths previously unheard of. When the war was over, there came the difficult task of reconstructing the now reconquered slave states, and of securing the position in them of the lately liberated Negroes. The outrages perpetrated on the latter, and on white settlers in some parts of the South, required further exertions of federal authority, and made the question of the limit of that authority still a practical one, for the old Democratic party, almost silenced during the war, had now reappeared in full force as the advocate of states' rights, and the watchful critic of any undue stretches of federal authority. It was found necessary to negative the Dred Scott decision and set at rest all questions relating to slavery and to the political equality of the races by the adoption of three important amendments to the Constitution. The troubles of the South by degrees settled down as the whites regained possession of the state governments and the Northern troops were withdrawn. In the presidential election of 1876 the war question and Negro question had become dead issues, for it was plain that a large and

---

[5] This broad doctrine was not necessary for the decision of the case, but delivered as an *obiter dictum* by the majority of the court.

increasing number of the voters were no longer, despite the appeals of the Republican leaders, seriously concerned about them.

This election marks the close of the third period, which embraces the rise and overwhelming predominance of the Republican party. Formed to resist the extension of slavery, led on to destroy it, compelled by circumstances to expand the central authority in a way unthought of before, that party had now worked out its programme and fulfilled its original mission. The old aims were accomplished, but new ones had not yet been substituted, for though new problems had appeared, the party was not prepared with solutions. Similarly the Democratic party had discharged its mission in defending the rights of the reconstructed states, and criticizing excesses of executive power; similarly it too had refused to grapple either with the fresh questions which had begun to arise since the war, or with those older questions which had now reappeared above the subsiding flood of war days. The old parties still stood as organizations, and still claimed to be the exponents of principles. Their respective principles had, however, little direct application to the questions which confronted and divided the nation. A new era was opening which called either for the evolution of new parties, or for the transformation of the old ones by the adoption of tenets and the advocacy of views suited to the needs of the time. But this fourth period, which began with 1876, has not yet seen such a transformation, and we shall therefore find, when we come to examine the existing state of parties, that there is an unreality and lack of vital force in both Republicans and Democrats, powerful as their organizations are.

The foregoing sketch, given only for the sake of explaining the present condition of parties, suggests some observations on the foundations of party in America.

If we look over Europe we shall find that the grounds on which parties have been built and contests waged since the beginning of free governments have been in substance but few. In the hostility of rich and poor, or of capital and labour, in the fears of the haves and the desire of the have-nots, we perceive the most frequent ground, though it is often disguised as a dispute about the extension of the suffrage or some other civic right. Questions relating to the tenure of land have played a large part; so have questions of religion; so too have animosities or jealousies of race; and of course the form of government, whether it shall be a monarchy or a republic, has sometimes been in dispute. None of these grounds of quarrel substantially affected American parties during the three periods we have been examining. No one has ever advocated monarchy, or a restricted suffrage, or a unified instead of a federal republic. Nor down to 1876 was there ever any party which could promise more to the poor than its opponents. In 1852 the Know-Nothing party came forward as the organ of native American opinion against recent immigrants, then chiefly the Irish (though German immigration had begun to swell from 1849 onwards), and the not unnatural tendency to resent the power of foreign-born voters has sometimes since appeared in various parts of the country. But as this 'American' party, for a time powerful by the absorption of many of the Whigs, failed to face the problem of slavery, and roused jealousy by its secret organization, it soon passed away, though it deserves to be remembered as a force disintegrating the then existing parties. The complete equality of all sects, with the complete neutrality of the government in religious matters, has fortunately kept religious passion outside the sphere of politics. The only exceptions to be noted are the occasionally recurring (though latterly less vehement) outbreaks of hostility to the Roman Catholic church. Nor would these outbreaks have attained political importance but for the strength added to them by the feeling of the native against the foreigner. They have been most serious at times when and in places where there has been an influx of immigrants from Europe large enough to seem to threaten the dominance of American ideas and the permanence of American institutions.

Have the American parties then been formed only upon narrow and local bases, have they contended for transient objects, and can no deeper historical meaning, no longer historical continuity, be claimed for them?

Two permanent oppositions may, I think, be discerned running through the history of the parties, sometimes openly recognized, sometimes concealed by the urgency of a transitory question. One of these is the opposition between a centralized or unified and a federalized government. In every country there are centrifugal and centripetal forces at work, the one or the other of which is for the moment the stronger. There has seldom been a country in which something might not have been gained, in the way of good administration and defensive strength, by a greater concentration of power in the hands of the central government, enabling it to do things which local bodies, or a more restricted central government, could not do equally cheaply or well. Against this gain there is always to be set the danger that such concentration may weaken the vitality of local communities and authorities, and may enable the central power to stunt their development. Sometimes needs of the former kind are more urgent, or the sentiment of the people tends to magnify them; sometimes again the centrifugal forces obtain the upper hand. English history shows several such alternations. But in America the federal form of government has made this permanent and natural opposition specially conspicuous. The salient feature of the Constitution is the effort it makes to establish an equipoise between the force which would carry the planet states off into space and the force which would draw them into the sun of the national government. There have always therefore been minds inclined to take sides upon this fundamental question, and a party has always had something definite and weighty to appeal to when it claims to represent either the autonomy of communities on the one hand, or the majesty and beneficent activity of the national government on the other. The former has been the watchword of the Democratic party. The latter was seldom distinctly avowed, but was generally in fact represented by the Federalists of the first period, the Whigs of the second, the Republicans of the third.

The other opposition, though it goes deeper and is more pervasive, has been less clearly marked in America, and less consciously admitted by the Americans themselves. It is the opposition between the tendency which makes some men prize the freedom of the individual as the first of social goods, and that which disposes others to insist on checking and regulating his impulses. The opposition of these two tendencies, the love of liberty and the love of order, is permanent and necessary, because it springs from differences in the intellect and feelings of men which one finds in all countries and at all epochs. There are always persons who are struck by the weakness of mankind, by their folly, their passion, their selfishness; and these persons, distrusting the action of average mankind, will always wish to see them guided by wise heads and restrained by strong hands. Such guidance seems the best means of progress, such restraint the only means of security. Those on the other hand who think better of human nature, and have more hope in their own tempers, hold the impulses of the average man to be generally towards justice and peace. They have faith in the power of reason to conquer ignorance, and of generosity to overbear selfishness. They are therefore disposed to leave the individual alone, and to entrust the masses with power. Every sensible man feels in himself the struggle between these two tendencies, and is on his guard not to yield wholly to either, because the one degenerates into tyranny, the other into an anarchy out of which tyranny will eventually spring. The wisest statesman is he who best holds the balance between them.

Each of these tendencies found among the fathers of the American Republic a brilliant and characteristic representative. Hamilton, who had a low opinion of mankind, but a gift and a passion for large constructive statesmanship, went so far in his advocacy of a strong government as to be suspected of wishing to establish a monarchy after the British pattern. He has left on record his opinion that the free Constitution of England, which he admired in spite of the faults he clearly saw, could not be worked without its corruptions.[6] Jefferson carried further than any other person set in an equally responsible place has ever done, his faith that government is either needless or an evil, and that with enough liberty, everything will go well. An insurrection every few years, he said, must be looked for, and even desired, to keep government in order. The Jeffersonian tendency long remained, like a leaven, in the Democratic party, though in applying Jeffersonian doctrines the slaveholders stopped when they came to a black skin. Among the Federalists, and their successors the Whigs, and the more recent Republicans, there has never been wanting a full faith in the power of freedom. The Republicans gave an amazing proof of it when they bestowed the suffrage on the Negroes. Neither they nor any American party has ever professed itself the champion of authority and order. That would be a damaging profession. Nevertheless it is rather towards what I may perhaps venture to call the Federalist-Whig-Republican party than towards the Democrats that those who have valued the principle of authority have been generally drawn. It is for that party that the Puritan spirit, not extinct in America, has felt the greater affinity, for this spirit, having realized the sinfulness of human nature, is inclined to train and control the natural man by laws and force.

The tendency that makes for a strong government being akin to that which makes for a central government, the Federalist-Whig-Republican party, which has, through its long history, and under its varying forms and names, been the advocate of the national principle, found itself for this reason also led, more frequently than the Democrats, to exalt the rights and powers of government. It might be thought that the same cause would have made the Republican party take sides in that profound opposition which we perceive today in all civilized peoples, between the tendency to enlarge the sphere of legislation and state action, and the doctrine of laissez faire. So far, however, this has not happened. There may seem to be more in the character and temper of the Republicans than of the Democrats that leans towards state interference. But when the question arises in a concrete instance neither party is much more likely than the other to oppose such interference. Federal

---

[6] David Hume had made the same remark, natural at a time when the power of Parliament was little checked by responsibility to the people.

control has been more frequently and further extended through legislation passed by Republican Congresses. But that has happened largely because the Republicans have, since the Civil War, possessed majorities much more often than have the Democrats, so that when the need for legislation arose, it fell to the former to meet that need. Neither party has thought out the subject in its general bearings; neither has shown any more definiteness of policy regarding it than the Tories and the Liberals have done in England.

American students of history may think that I have pressed the antithesis of liberty and authority, as well as that of centrifugal and centripetal tendencies, somewhat too far in making one party a representative of each through the first century of the Republic. I do not deny that at particular moments the party which was usually disposed towards a strong government resisted and decried authority, while the party which specially professed itself the advocate of liberty sought to make authority more stringent. Such deviations are however compatible with the general tendencies I have described. And no one who has gained even a slight knowledge of the history of the United States will fall into the error of supposing that order and authority mean there what they have meant in the monarchies of continental Europe.

The Parties of Today

There are now two great and several minor parties in the United States. The great parties are the Republicans and the Democrats. What are their principles, their distinctive tenets, their tendencies? Which of them is for tariff reform, for the further extension of civil service reform, for a spirited foreign policy, for the regulation of railroads and telegraphs by legislation, for changes in the currency, for any other of the twenty issues which one hears discussed in the country as seriously involving its welfare?

This is what a European is always asking of intelligent Republicans and intelligent Democrats. He is always asking because he never gets an answer. The replies leave him in deeper perplexity. After some months the truth begins to dawn upon him. Neither party has, as a party, anything definite to say on these issues; neither party has any clean-cut principles, any distinctive tenets. Both have traditions. Both claim to have tendencies. Both have certainly war cries, organizations, interests enlisted in their support. But those interests are in the main the interests of getting or keeping the patronage of the government. Distinctive tenets and policies, points of political doctrine and points of political practice, have all but vanished. They have not been thrown away, but have been stripped away by time and the progress of events, fulfilling some policies, blotting out others. All has been lost, except office or the hope of it.

The phenomenon may be illustrated from the case of England, where party government has existed longer and in a more fully developed form than in any other part of the Old World.[1] The essence of the English parties has lain in the existence of two sets of views and tendencies which divide

---

[1] English parties are however not very ancient; they date only from the struggle of the Stuart kings with the Puritan and popular party in the House of Commons, and did not take regular shape as Whigs and Tories till the reign of Charles II.

the nation into two sections, the party, let us say, though these general terms are not very safe, and have been less applicable in recent years than they were down to 1874, of movement and the party of standing still, the party of liberty and the party of order. Each section believes in its own views, and is influenced by its peculiar tendencies, recollections, mental associations, to deal in its own peculiar way with every new question as it comes up. The particular dogmas may change: doctrines once held by Whigs alone may now be held by Tories also; doctrines which Whigs would have rejected seventy years ago may now be part of the orthodox programme of the Liberal party. But the tendencies have been permanent and have always so worked upon the various fresh questions and problems which have presented themselves during the last two centuries, that each party has had not only a brilliant concrete life in its famous leaders and zealous members, but also an intellectual and moral life in its principles. These principles have meant something to those who held them, so that when a fresh question arose it was usually possible to predict how each party, how even the average members of each party, would regard and wish to deal with it. Thus even when the leaders have been least worthy and their aims least pure, an English party has felt itself ennobled and inspirited by the sense that it had great objects to fight for, a history and traditions which imposed on it the duty of battling for its distinctive principles. It is because issues have never been lacking which brought these respective principles into operation, forcing the one party to maintain the cause of order and existing institutions, the other that of freedom and what was deemed progress, that the two English parties have not degenerated into mere factions. Their struggles for office have been redeemed from selfishness by the feeling that office was a means of giving practical effect to their doctrines.

But suppose that in Britain all the questions which divide Tories from Liberals were to be suddenly settled and done with. Britain would be in a difficulty. Her free government has so long been worked by the action and reaction of the ministerialists and the opposition that there would probably continue to be two parties. But they would not be really, in the true old sense of the term, Tories and Liberals; they would be merely Ins and Outs. Their combats would be waged hardly even in name for principles, but only for place. The government of the country, with the honour, power, and emoluments attached to it, would still remain as a prize to be contended for. The followers would still rally to the leaders; and friendship would still bind the members together into organized bodies; while dislike and suspicion would still rouse them against their former adversaries. Thus not only the leaders, who would have something tangible to gain, but even others, who had only their feelings to gratify, would continue to form political clubs, register voters, deliver party harangues, contest elections, just as they do now. The difference would be that each faction would no longer have broad principles—I will not say to invoke, for such principles would probably continue to be invoked as heretofore—but to insist on applying as distinctively its principles to the actual needs of the state. Hence quiet or fastidious men would not join in party struggles; while those who did join would no longer be stimulated by the sense that they were contending for something ideal. Loyalty to a leader whom it was sought to make prime minister would be a poor substitute for loyalty to a faith. If there were no conspicuous leader, attachment to the party would degenerate either into mere hatred of antagonists or into a struggle over places and salaries. And almost the same phenomena would be seen if, although the old issues had not been really determined, both the parties should have so far abandoned their former position that these issues did not divide them, but each professed principles which were, even if different in formal statement, practicably indistinguishable in their application.

This, which conceivably may happen in England under her new political conditions, is what has happened with the American parties. The chief practical issues which once divided them have been settled. Some others have not been settled, but as regards these, the professions of the two parties so far agree that we cannot now speak of any conflict of principles.

When life leaves an organic body it becomes useless, fetid, pestiferous; it is fit to be cast out or buried from sight. What life is to an organism, principles are to a party. When they which are its soul have vanished, its body ought to dissolve, and the elements that formed it be regrouped in some new organism:

> The times have been
> That when the brains were out the man would die.

But a party does not always thus die. It may hold together long after its moral life is extinct. Guelfs and Ghibellines warred in Italy for nearly two centuries after the emperor had ceased to threaten the pope, or the pope to befriend the cities of Lombardy. Parties go on contending because their members have formed habits of joint action, and have contracted hatreds and prejudices, and also because the leaders find their advantage in using these habits and playing on these prejudices. The American parties now continue to exist, because they have existed. The mill has been constructed, and its machinery goes on turning, even when there is no grist to grind. But this is not wholly the fault of the men; for the system of government requires and implies parties, just as that of England does. These systems are made to be worked, and always have been worked, by a majority; a majority must be cohesive, gathered into a united and organized body: such a body is a party.

When an ordinary Northern Democrat was asked, say about 1880, to characterize the two parties, he used to say that the Republicans were corrupt and incapable, and would cite instances in which persons prominent in that party, or intimate friends of its leaders, had been concerned in frauds on the government or in disgraceful lobbying transactions in Congress. In 1900 he was more likely to allege that the Republican party is the party of the rich, influenced by the great corporations, whereas the Democrats are the true friends of the people. When you press him for some distinctive principles separating his own party from theirs, he may perhaps refer to Jefferson, and say that the Democrats are the protectors of states' rights and of local independence, and the Republicans hostile to both. If you go on to inquire what bearing this doctrine of states' rights has on any presently debated issue he may admit that, for the moment, it has none, but will insist that should any issue involving the rights of the states arise, his party will be, as always, the guardian of American freedom.

This is nearly all that can be predicated about the Democratic party. If a question involving the rights of a state against the federal authority were to emerge, its instinct would lead it to array itself on the side of the state rather than of the central government, supposing that it had no direct motive to do the opposite. Seeing that at no point from the outbreak of the war down to 1913, except in the Fifty-third Congress (1893–95), has it possessed a majority in both houses of Congress as well as the president in power, its devotion to this principle has not been tested, and might not resist the temptation of any interest the other way. However, this is matter of speculation, for at present the states fear no infringement of their rights. So conversely of the Republicans. Their traditions ought to dispose them to support federal power against the states, but their action in a concrete case would probably depend on whether their party was at the time in condition to use that power for its own purposes. If they were in a minority in Congress, they would be little inclined to strengthen Congress against the states. The simplest way of proving or illustrating this will be to run quickly through the questions of present practical interest.

One of those which most interests the people, though of course not all the people, is the regulation or extinction of the liquor traffic. On this neither party has committed or will commit itself. The traditional dogmas of neither cover it, though the Northern Democrats have been rather more disposed to leave men to themselves than the Republicans, and rather less amenable to the influence of ethical sentiment. Practically for both parties the point of consequence is what they can gain or lose. Each has clearly something to lose. The drinking part of the population is chiefly foreign. Now the Irish are mainly Democrats, so the Democratic party in the North has often feared to offend them. The Germans are mainly Republican, so the Republicans are equally bound over to caution.[2] It is true that though the parties, as parties, have been, in almost all states, neutral or divided, Temperance men are, in the North and West,[3] generally Republicans, whiskey-men and saloonkeepers generally Democrats. The Republicans therefore more frequently attempt to conciliate the anti-liquor party by flattering phrases. They suffer by the starting of a Prohibitionist candidate, since he draws more voting strength away from them than he does from the Democrats.

Free Trade *v.* Protection is another burning question, and has been so since the early days of the Union. The old controversy as to the constitutional right of Congress to impose a tariff for any purpose but that of raising revenue, has been laid to rest, for whether the people in 1788 meant or did not mean to confer such a power, it has been exerted for so many years, and on so superb a scale, that no one now doubts its legality. Before the war the Democrats were advocates of a tariff for revenue only, i.e., of free trade. A few of them still hold that doctrine in its fulness, but as the majority, though they have frequently declared themselves to favour a reduction of the present system of import duties, have not been clear upon the general principle, the party trumpet has given an uncertain sound. Moreover, Pennsylvania is Protectionist on account of its iron industries; several Southern states have leanings that way for the same reason, or because they desire high import duties on their own products, on sugar for instance, or on timber. Unwilling to alienate the Democrats of such districts, the party has generally sought to remain unpledged, or, at least, in winking with one eye to the men of the Northwest and Southeast who desired to

---

[2] Race counts for much less in politics than it did in the last century.

[3] The Southern Negroes have usually voted for the Republicans, but were frequently opposed to restrictions on the sale of liquor. On the other hand, the better class of Southern whites, who are of course Democrats, are largely Temperance men, and many states have now either prohibited the sale of liquor or have adopted a local option system, under which each county decides whether it will be "wet" or "dry" (i.e., permit or forbid the sale of intoxicants).

reduce the tariff, it was tempted to wink with the other to the iron men of Pittsburg and the sugar men of the Far South.

This division, however, did not prevent the Democratic party from passing in 1913 an act which largely reduced protective duties. It did not, however, any more than the Republicans, avow pure free trade principles, and though the Republicans have been heretofore the high tariff party, many among them have latterly shown themselves quite as desirous of seeing reductions made in the present rates as are the "revisionist" section of the Democrats.[4]

Civil service reform long received the lip service of both parties, a lip service expressed by both with equal warmth, and by the average professional politicians of both with equal insincerity. Such reforms as have been effected in the mode of filling up places, have been forced on the parties by public opinion, rather than carried through by either, or else were due to the enlightened views of individual presidents. None of the changes made— and they are perhaps the most beneficial of recent changes—has raised an issue between the parties. The best men in both parties support the Civil Service Commission and would extend the scheme still further; the worst men in both would gladly get rid of it.

The regulation by federal authority of railroads carrying on commerce between the states has attracted great attention for many years. Neither party has had anything distinctive to say upon it in the way either of advocacy or of condemnation. Both have asserted that it is the duty of railways to serve the people, and not to tyrannize over or defraud them, so the Interstate Commerce Acts passed in and since 1887 with this view cannot be called party measures. The discussion of the subject continues, and while some have urged that it is impossible effectively to regulate interstate railroad traffic without regulating all railroad traffic, a few have gone so far as to suggest that the national government ought to acquire all the railroads of the country. But neither party is committed to a particular line of policy. So also both profess themselves eager to restrain the abuse of their powers by corporations, and to put an end to monopolies.

Finances have on the whole been well managed, and debt paid off with surprising speed. But there have been, and are still, serious problems raised by the condition of the currency. In 1896 the great majority of the Democratic party pledged itself to the free coinage of silver; but a section important by

---

[4] The protective tariff has struck its roots so deep and rallied so many interests to its support that in the presidential elections of 1904 and 1908 the general issue of "tariff for revenue only" was not raised at all, though there was some talk among Republicans, and far more among Democrats, of tariff revision.

its social and intellectual influence seceded and ran a candidate of its own. The schism has been healed by the dropping of the free silver issue, and a Currency Act was passed in 1913,[5] the working of which will be closely watched. The matter is not now a party issue.

As regards the extension and government of territories outside the North American continent, the Democratic party did not approve the acquisition of the Philippines, and has announced an intention to withdraw therefrom as soon as conveniently may be, but there has been no controversy between it and the Republicans over the administrative policy to be followed there and in Puerto Rico.

It is the same as regards questions belonging to the sphere of state politics, such as woman suffrage, or ballot reform, or child labour, or an eight-hour law, or convict labour. Neither party has any distinctive attitude on these matters; neither is more likely, or less likely, than the other to pass a measure dealing with them. It is the same with regard to the general doctrine of laissez faire as opposed to governmental interference. Neither Republicans nor Democrats can be said to be friends or foes of state interference: each will advocate it when there seems a practically useful object to be secured, or when the popular voice seems to call for it. It is the same with foreign policy. Both parties are practically agreed not only as to the general principles which ought to rule the conduct of the country, but as to the application of these principles, and this has been shown even in a matter which raised so many difficult questions as the condition of Mexico has done since the fall of President Diaz. The party which opposes the president may at any given moment seek to damage him by defeating some particular proposal he has made, but this it will do as a piece of temporary strategy, not in pursuance of any settled doctrine.

Yet one cannot say that there is today no difference between the two great parties. There is a difference of spirit or sentiment perceptible even by a stranger when, after having mixed for some time with members of the one he begins to mix with those of the other, and doubtless more patent to a native American. It resembles (though it is less marked than) the difference of tone and temper between Tories and Liberals in England. The intellectual

---

[5] *Publisher's Note:* Lord Bryce is apparently referring to the Federal Reserve Act of 1913. The last "Currency Act" was passed by Congress in 1908; but in 1913—the decade indicated in the text—Congress enacted the Federal Reserve Act. Prominent political leaders of the period, including Woodrow Wilson, William Jennings Bryan, and Carter Glass (the act's chief sponsor), frequently used the term "Currency Act" when referring to the Federal Reserve Act. See, for example, Paolo Coletta, *William Jennings Bryan*, 3 vols. (Lincoln: University of Nebraska Press, 1964–69), 2: 126–39.

view of a Democrat of the better sort has been not quite the same as that of his Republican compeer. Each of course thinks meanly of the other; but while the Democrat has generally deemed the Republican "dangerous" (i.e., likely to undermine the Constitution), the Republican was more apt to think the Democrat (at least in the North) low toned or reckless. So in England your Liberal used to fasten on stupidity as the characteristic fault of the Tory, while the Tory suspected the morals and religion more than he despised the intelligence of the Radical. But these statements, generally true of Democrats and Republicans from the time of the Civil War till near the end of the century, have latterly been less applicable. There is still a contrast between the larger and more radical wing of the Democratic party and the older school of Republicans, but the conservative section of the Democrats differ very little from the conservative Republicans; and there are radical Republicans whose views are shared by plenty of Democrats. This approximation seems to indicate that the time for a reconstruction of parties is approaching; but party organizations are strong things, and often interfere with the course of natural evolution.

It cannot be charged on the American parties that they have drawn towards one another by forsaking their old principles. It is time that has changed the circumstances of the country, and made those old principles inapplicable. An eminent journalist remarked to me in 1908 that the two great parties were like two bottles. Each bore a label denoting the kind of liquor it contained, but each was empty. This at any rate may be said, that the parties may seem to have erred rather by having clung too long to outworn issues, and by neglecting to discover and work out new principles capable of solving the problems which now perplex the country. In a country so full of change and movement as America new questions are always coming up, and must be answered. New troubles surround a government, and a way must be found to escape from them; new diseases attack the nation, and have to be cured. The duty of a great party is to face these, to find answers and remedies, applying to the facts of the hour the doctrines it has lived by, so far as they are still applicable, and when they have ceased to be applicable, thinking out new doctrines conformable to the main principles and tendencies which it represents. This is a work to be accomplished by its ruling minds, while the habit of party loyalty to the leaders powerfully serves to diffuse through the mass of followers the conclusions of the leaders and the reasonings they have employed.

"But," the European reader may ask, "is it not the interest as well as the duty of a party thus to adapt itself to new conditions? Does it not, in failing to do so, condemn itself to sterility and impotence, ultimately, indeed, to supersession by some new party which the needs of the time have created?"

This is what usually happens in Europe. Probably it will happen in the long run in America also, unless the parties adapt themselves to the new issues, just as the Whig party fell in 1852–57 because it failed to face the problem of slavery. That it happens more slowly may be ascribed partly to the completeness and strength of the party organizations, which make the enthusiasm generated by ideas less necessary, partly to the growing prominence of "social" and "labour" as well as economic questions, on which both parties are equally eager to conciliate the masses, and equally unwilling to proclaim definite views, partly to the fact that several questions on which the two great parties still hesitate to take sides are not presently vital to the well-being of the country. Something is also due to the smaller influence in America than in Europe of individual leaders. English parties, which hesitate long over secondary questions, might hesitate longer than is now their practice over vital ones also, were they not accustomed to look for guidance to their chiefs, and to defer to the opinion which the chiefs deliver. And it is only by courage and the capacity for initiative that the chiefs themselves retain their position.

Composition of the Parties

The less there is in the tenets of the Republicans and Democrats to make their character intelligible to a European reader, so much the more desirable is it to convey some idea of what may be called their social and local, their racial and ecclesiastical complexions.

The Republican party was formed between 1854 and 1856 chiefly out of the wrecks of the Whig party, with the addition of the Abolitionists and Free Soilers, who, disgusted at the apparent subservience to the South of the leading Northern Whigs, had for some time previously acted as a group by themselves, though some of them had been apt to vote for Whig candidates. They had also recruits from the Free Soil Democrats, who had severed themselves from the bulk of the Democratic party, and some of whom claimed to be true Jeffersonians in joining the party which stood up against the spread of slavery.[1] The Republicans were therefore from the first a Northern party, more distinctly so than the Federalists had been at the close of the preceding century, and much more distinctly so than the Whigs, in whom there had been a pretty strong Southern element.

The Whig element brought to the new party solidity, political experience, and a large number of wealthy and influential adherents. The Abolitionist element gave it force and enthusiasm, qualities invaluable for the crisis which came in 1861 with the secession of all save four of the slaveholding states. During the war, it drew to itself nearly all the earnestness, patriotism, religious and moral fervour, which the North and West contained. It is still, in those regions, the party in whose ranks respectable, steady, pious, well-conducted men are to be looked for. If you find yourself dining with one

---

[1] The name Republican was given to the new party, not without the hope of thereby making it easier for these old school Democrats to join it, for in Jefferson's day his party had been called Republican.

of "the best people" in any New England city, or in Philadelphia, or in Cincinnati, Cleveland, Chicago, or Minneapolis, you assume that the guest sitting next you is a Republican, almost as confidently as in English county society you would assume your neighbour to be a Tory; that is to say, you may sometimes be wrong, but in four cases out of five you will be right. In New York the presumption is weaker, though even there you will be right three times out of five. One may say that all over the North, the merchants, manufacturers, and professional men of the smaller perhaps even more than of the larger towns, have tended to be Republicans. So too have the farmers, particularly in the upper Mississippi Valley, although there, as well as on the Pacific coast, the growth of what is called "radicalism" has occasionally strengthened the Democratic vote. The working class in the cities is divided, but the more solid part of it, the church-goers and total abstainers, are generally Republicans, while some are inclined to socialism. A number, still considerable, though of course daily diminishing, are veterans of the Civil War; and these naturally rally to the old flag. When turning southwards one reaches the borders of the old slave states, everything is changed. In Baltimore the best people are so generally Democrats that when you meet a Republican in society you ask whether he is not an immigrant from New England. This is less markedly the case in Kentucky and Missouri, but in Virginia, or the Carolinas, or the Gulf states, very few men of good standing belong to the Republican party, which consists of the lately enfranchised Negroes, of a certain number of whites, seldom well regarded, who organize and use the Negro vote, and who in the years that followed the war were making a good thing for themselves out of it; of a number of federal officials (a number very small when the Democrats are in power), who have been put into federal places by their friends at Washington, on the understanding that they are to work for the party, and of a few stray people, perhaps settlers from the North, who have not yet renounced their old affiliations. It is not easy for an educated man to remain a Republican in the South, not only because the people he meets in society are Democrats, but because the Republican party managers are apt to be black sheep.

In such Middle states as New York and New Jersey, to which one may for this purpose add Ohio and Indiana, and on the Pacific slope, the parties are nearly balanced, and if one regards state as well as national elections, the majority of votes is seen to sway now this way now that, as the circumstances of the hour, or local causes, or the merits of individual candidates, may affect the popular mind. Pennsylvania is now, as she has been since 1860, a Republican state, owing to her interest in a protective tariff. New York, whose legislature has been often Republican, is in presidential elections still to be deemed doubtful. In all these states, the better sort of people are mostly Republicans. It is in that party you look to find the greater number of the philanthropists, the men of culture, the financial magnates and other persons of substance who desire to see things go on quietly, with no shocks given to business confidence by rash legislation. These are great elements of strength. They were gained for the Republican party by its earlier history, which drew into it in the days of the war those patriotic and earnest young men who are now the leading elderly men in their respective neighbourhoods. Against them there was for a time (1884–96) to be set the tendency of a section of the Republican party, a section small in numbers but including some men of character and intelligence, to break away, or, as it is called, "bolt" from the party platform and "ticket." This section explained its conduct by declaring that the great claims which the party gained on the confidence of the country by its resistance to slavery and its vigorous prosecution of the war had been forfeited by maladministration since the war ended, and by the scandals which had gathered round some of its conspicuous figures. If intelligence and cultivation dispose their possessors to desert at a critical moment, the party would have been stronger without this element, for, as everybody knows, a good party man is he who stands by his friends when they are wrong. That group was mostly reabsorbed into the Republican ranks. But somewhat later another tendency to division appeared in the disposition of some Republicans, especially in the Northwest, to go faster and further, especially in economic legislation, than the moneyed men wished to follow. No open schism has so far resulted, but the antagonism of tendency is manifest.

The Democratic party has suffered in the North and West from exactly the opposite causes to the Republican. It was long discredited by its sympathy with the South, and by the opposition of a considerable section within it (the so-called Copperheads) to the prosecution of the war. This shadow hung heavy over it till the complete pacification of the South and growing prominence of new questions began to call men's minds away from the war years. From 1869 to 1885 it profited from being in opposition. Saved from the opportunity of abusing patronage, or becoming entangled in administration jobs, it was able to criticize freely the blunders or vices of its opponents. It may however be doubted whether its party managers were, take them all in all, either wiser or purer than those whom they criticized, nor do they seem to have inspired any deeper trust in the minds of impartial citizens. When, as has several times happened, the Democrats have obtained a majority in the House of Representatives, their legislation was not higher in aim or more judicious in the choice of means than that which Republican Congresses have produced. Hence the tendency to fall away from the Republican ranks of 1872–96 enured to the benefit of the Democrats less than might have been expected. In 1896 the emergence of the free silver question as a burning issue produced a serious breach in the party, the consequences of which, though it was to outward appearance healed in the presidential nomination of 1904 did not for some time disappear. The Democratic party includes not only nearly all the talent, education, and wealth of the South, together with the great bulk of the Southern farmers and poorer whites, but also a respectable minority of good men in the Middle states and the Northwest, and a slightly smaller minority in the rural parts of New England.[2]

In these last-mentioned districts its strength lies chiefly in the cities, a curious contrast to those earlier days when Jefferson was supported by the farmers and Hamilton by the townsfolk.[3] But the large cities have now a population unlike anything that existed in those distant days, a vast ignorant fluctuating mass of people, many of them only recently admitted to citizenship, who have little reason for belonging to one party rather than another, but are attracted some by the name of the Democratic party, some by the fact that it is not the party of the well-to-do, some by the leaders belonging to their own races who have risen to influence in its ranks. The adhesion of this mob gives the party a slight flavour of rowdyism, as its old associations used to give it, to a Puritan palate, a slight flavour of irreligion. Not so long ago, a New England deacon—the deacon is in America the type of solid respectability—would have found it as hard to vote for a Democratic candidate as an English archdeacon to vote for a Yorkshire Radical. But these old feelings are wearing away. A new generation of voters has arisen which never saw slavery, and which cares little about Jefferson for good or for evil. This generation takes parties as it finds them. Even among the older voters there has been a sensible change within the recent years. Many of the best Republicans, who remembered the Democrats as the party of which a strong section sympathized with the slaveholders

---

[2] In the presidential elections of 1904 and again in 1908 two Southern states were carried by the Republicans.

[3] Jefferson regarded agriculture as so much the best occupation for citizens that he was alarmed by the rumour that the codfish of the Northeastern coasts were coming down to the shores of Virginia and Carolina, lest the people of those states should "be tempted to catch them, and commerce, of which we have already too much, receive an accession."

before the war, and disapproved of the war while it was being waged, looked with horror on the advent to power of a Democratic president. The country, however, has not been ruined by Mr. Cleveland, either then or in his second term, but went on much as before, its elements of good and evil mixed and contending, just as under Republican administrations. The alarm which the moneyed classes felt in 1896 had nothing to do with the old controversies, and the association with the Democratic party of the states where slavery prevailed no longer creates any real prejudice against it in Northern minds.

Race differences have played a considerable part in the composition of the parties, but it is a diminishing part, because in the second and still more in the third generation a citizen is an American first and foremost and loses quickly the race consciousness which his father or grandfather had. Besides the native Americans, there were till about 1890 men of five nationalities in the United States—British, Irish, Germans, Scandinavians, French Canadians.[4] Of these, however, the English and Scotch lose their identity almost immediately, being absorbed into the general mass of native citizens. Though very numerous, they have hitherto counted for nothing politically, because English immigrants have either been indifferent to political struggles or have voted from the same motives as an average American. They have to some slight extent remained British subjects, not caring for the suffrage, and those who have adopted the United States as their country have seldom exerted their voting power as a united body.

Far otherwise with the Irish. They retain their national spirit and disposition to act together into the second, rarely however into the third, generation; they are a factor potent in federal and still more potent in city politics. Now the Irish have hitherto been nearly all Democrats. The exodus from Ireland, which had been considerable as far back as 1842, swelled in 1847 (the year after the famine) to vast proportions; and was from the first a source of help to the Democratic party, probably because the latter was less Protestant in sentiment than the Whig party, and was already dominant in the city of New York, where the Irish first became a power in politics. The aversion to the Negro which they soon developed, made them, when the Republican

[4] There have entered since 1890 large masses of Poles, Czechs, Italians, Russian Jews, Slovaks and other Slavs from the Austro-Hungarian monarchy, Magyars, Roumans, Greeks, Syrians, and Armenians (as to all of which see Chapter 92); but though these newer elements have increased rapidly of late years, no one of them can be said to have affected the composition of the parties over the country at large. In New York City the Jews (of whom there are about 400,000 adult males) were at first mostly Democrats, and the Italians mostly Republicans. These new immigrants are most numerous in the great cities and in the mining regions.

party arose, its natural enemies, for the Republicans were, both during and after the war, the Negro's patrons. Before the war ended the Irish vote had come to form a large part of the Democratic strength, and Irishmen were prominent among the politicians of that party: hence newcomers from Ireland have generally enlisted under its banner. Of late years, however, there have been plenty of Irishmen, and indeed of Irish leaders and bosses, among the Republicans of the great cities; and statesmen of that party often sought to "placate" and attract the Irish vote in ways too familiar to need description. It is now, except in a few cities, far less of a solid vote, Irish immigration having much declined.

The German immigration, excluding of course the early German settlements in Pennsylvania, began rather later than the Irish; and as there was some jealousy between the two races, the fact that the Irish were already Democrats when the Germans arrived, may be one reason why the latter have been more inclined to enrol themselves as Republicans, while another was to be found in the fact that German exiles of 1849 were naturally hostile to slavery. The Germans usually become farmers in the Middle and Western states, where, finding the native farmers mainly Republicans, they imitated the politics of their neighbours. That there are many German Democrats in the great cities may be ascribed to the rather less friendly attitude of the Republicans to the liquor traffic, for the German colonist is faithful to the beer of his fatherland, and, in the case of the Roman Catholic Germans, to the tacit alliance which subsisted in many districts between the Catholic Church and the Democrats. The Germans are a cohesive race, keeping up national sentiment by festivals, gymnastic societies, processions, and national songs, but as they take much less keenly to politics, and are not kept together by priests, their cohesion is more short-lived than that of the Irish. The American-born son of a German is already completely an American in feeling as well as in practical aptitude. The German vote over the whole Union may be roughly estimated as five-ninths Republican, four-ninths Democratic. But it is even more true of the Germans than of the Irish that in the twentieth century they have been ceasing to constitute a "solid vote" in the older sense of the term, and before 1930 politicians may have left off thinking of either race as a distinct voting entity.

The Scandinavians—Swedes and Norwegians, with a few Danes and a handful of Icelanders—now form a large element among the farmers of the Upper Mississippi states, particularly Wisconsin, Minnesota, and the Dakotas. So far as can be judged from the short experience the country has of them, for their immigration did not begin to swell till after the middle of the nineteenth century, they Americanize even more readily than their Teutonic cousins from the southern side of the Baltic. However, both Swedes and Norwegians are still so far clannish that in these states both parties find it worth while to run for office now and then a candidate of one or other, or candidates of both, of these nationalities, in order to catch the votes of his or their compatriots.[5] Nine-tenths of them were Republicans, until the rise of the so-called "People's Party," which for the time detached a good many; and some of these have passed into the Democratic ranks. Like the Germans, they came knowing nothing of American politics, but the watchful energy of the native party workers enlisted them under a party banner as soon as they were admitted to civic rights. They make perhaps the best material for sober and industrious agriculturists that America receives, being even readier than the Germans to face hardship, and more content to dispense with alcoholic drinks.

The French Canadians are numerous in New England, and in one or two other Northern states, yet not numerous enough to tell upon politics, especially as they frequently remain British subjects. Their religion disposes those who become citizens to side with the Democratic party, but they can hardly be said to constitute what is called "a vote," and occasionally "go Republican."

In the northern half of the country, the Negroes are not generally an important element, but their vote in New York, Ohio, and Indiana is large enough to be worth having whenever the state is doubtful. Gratitude for the favour shown to their race has kept them mostly but not exclusively Republicans. They are seldom admitted to a leading place in party organizations, but it is found expedient in presidential contests to organize a "coloured club" to work for the candidate among the coloured population of a town. In states like Maryland, Kentucky, and Missouri, where there are plenty of white Republicans, they have voted steadily Republican, unless paid to abstain. In the further South, their mere numbers would have enabled them, were they equal to the whites in intelligence, wealth, and organization, not merely to carry congressional seats, but even in some states to determine a presidential election. But in these three respects they are unspeakably inferior. At first, under the leadership of some white adventurers, mostly of

---

[5] There has been some slight jealousy between Swedes and Norwegians, so that where they are equally strong it is not safe to put forward a candidate of either race without placing on the same ticket a candidate of the other also. But where the population of either race is too small to support a church or a social institution of its own, they fraternize for this purpose, feeling themselves much nearer to one another than they are to any other element.

the "carpetbagger" class, they went almost solid for the Republican party; and occasionally, even since the withdrawal of Federal troops, they have turned the balance in its favour. Presently, however, the Democrats gained the upper hand; and most of the Negroes, losing faith in their former bosses, and discouraged by finding themselves unfit to cope with a superior race, either ceased to vote or found themselves prevented by the whites from doing so. Latterly the seven Southern states have so altered their constitutions as to exclude nine-tenths of the Negroes from the suffrage.[6]

Religion comes very little into American party except when, as sometimes has happened, the advance of the Roman Catholic church and the idea that she exerts her influence to secure benefits for herself, causes an outburst of Protestant feeling.[7] Roman Catholics are usually Democrats, because, except in Maryland, which is Democratic anyhow, they are mainly Irish.[8] Congregationalists and Unitarians, being presumably sprung from New England, are apt to be Republicans. Presbyterians, Methodists, Baptists, Episcopalians, have no special party affinities. They are mostly Republicans in the North, Democrats in the South. The Mormons fight for their own hand, and in Utah, Idaho, and Arizona have been wont to cast their votes, under the direction of their hierarchy, for the local party which promised to interfere least with them. Lately in Idaho a party found it worth while to run a Mormon candidate.

The distribution of parties is to some extent geographical. While the South casts a solid Democratic vote, and the strength of the Republicans lies in the Northeast and Northwest, the intermediate position of the Middle states corresponds to their divided political tendencies. The reason is that in America colonization has gone on along parallels of latitude. The tendencies of New England reappear in northern Ohio, northern Illinois, Michigan, Wisconsin, Minnesota, giving the Republicans a predominance in this vast and swiftly growing Western population, which it takes the whole weight of the solid South to balance. This geographical opposition does not, however, betoken a danger of political severance. The material interests of the agriculturists of the Northwest are not different from those of the South: free trade, for instance, will make as much and no more difference to the wheat grower of Illinois as to the cotton grower of Texas,

---

[6] See further as to the Negroes, Chapters 94 and 95.

[7] As recently in the formation of the American Protective Association, which became for a time a political factor in parts of the Northwest.

[8] In 1904 and 1908, however, it was believed that the bulk of the Roman Catholics, at any rate in New York, supported the Republican candidates.

to the ironworkers of Tennessee as to the ironworkers of Pennsylvania. And the existence of an active Democratic party in the North prevents the victory of either geographical section from being felt as a defeat by the other.

This is an important security against disruption. And a similar security against the risk of civil strife or revolution is to be found in the fact that the parties are not based on or sensibly affected by differences either of wealth or of social position. Their cleavage is not horizontal according to social strata, but vertical. This would be less true if it were stated either of the Northern states separately, or of the Southern states separately: it is true of the Union taken as a whole. It might cease to be true if the new socialist or labour parties were to grow till it absorbed or superseded either of the existing parties. The same feature has characterized English politics as compared with those of most European countries, and has been a main cause of the stability of the English government and of the good feeling between different classes in the community.[9]

---

[9] Since 1886 the vast majority of the rich, a proportion probably larger than at any previous time, has in England belonged to one of the two historic parties. But this phenomenon may not be permanent.

Further Observations on the Parties

Besides the two great parties which have divided America for thirty years, there are two or three lesser organizations or factions needing a word of mention. About 1820–30 there was a period when one of the two great parties having melted away, the other had become split up into minor sections.[1] Parties were numerous and unstable, new ones forming, and after a short career uniting with some other, or vanishing altogether from the scene. This was a phenomenon peculiar to that time, and ceased with the building up about 1832 of the Whig party, which lasted till shortly before the Civil War. But De Tocqueville, who visited America in 1831–32, took it for the normal state of a democratic community, and founded upon it some bold generalizations. A stranger who sees how few principles now exist to hold each of the two great modern parties together will be rather surprised that they have not shown more tendency to split up into minor groups and factions.

What constitutes a party? In America there is a simple test. Any section of men who nominate candidates of their own for the presidency and vice-presidency of the United States are deemed a national party. Adopting this test we shall find that there are now two or three national parties in addition to the Republicans and Democrats.

The first minor party was that of the Greenbackers, who arose soon after the end of the Civil War. They demanded a large issue of greenbacks (i.e, paper money, so called from the colour of the notes issued during the war), alleging that this must benefit the poorer classes, who will obviously be richer when there is more money in the country. It may seem incredible

---

[1] The same phenomenon reappeared at the break-up of the Whigs between 1852 and 1857, and from a like cause.

that there should still be masses of civilized men who believe that money is value, and that a liberal issue of stamped paper can give the poor more bread or better clothes. If there were a large class of debtors, and the idea was to depreciate the currency and let them then pay their debts in it, one could understand the proposal. Such a depreciation existed during and immediately after the Civil War. As wages and prices had risen enormously, people were receiving more money in wages, or for goods sold, than they had received previously, while they were paying fixed charges, such as interest on mortgage debts, in a depreciated paper currency. Thus the small farmers were on the whole gainers, while creditors and persons with fixed incomes were losers. It is true that both farmers and working men were also paying more for whatever they needed, food, clothes, and lodging; still they seemed to have felt more benefit in receiving larger sums than they felt hardship in paying out larger sums. Those who called for a great increase of paper money did not profess to wish to depreciate the currency; nor were they to any great extent supported by a debtor class to which a depreciated currency would be welcome, as a debased coinage served the momentary occasions of mediæval kings. But the recollections of the war time with its abundant employment and high wages clung to many people, and were coupled with a confused notion that the more money there is in circulation so much the more of it will everybody have, and so much the better off will he be, so much the more employment will capital find for labour, and so much the more copious will be the fertilizing stream of wages diffused among the poor.[2]

The Greenback party, which at first called itself Independent, held a national nominating convention in 1876, at which nineteen states were represented, and nominated candidates for president and vice-president, issuing an emphatic but ungrammatical denunciation of the financial policy of the Republican and Democratic parties. They again put forward candidates in 1880 and 1884, but made a poor show in the voting and presently melted away, some of those who had supported it presently going to recruit the Populist party.

The various Labour or Socialist parties are composed, not of agriculturists like the Greenbackers, but chiefly of working men in cities and mining districts, including many of the recent immigrants. It is not easy to describe

---

[2] The matter is further complicated by the fact that the national banknotes issued by the national banks are guaranteed by government bonds deposited with the U.S. Treasury, bonds on which the national government pays interest. The Greenbackers desired to substitute greenbacks, or so-called "fiat money," for these banknotes as a circulating medium.

the precise tenets of a Labour party, for it includes persons of very various views, some who would be called in Europe pronounced Collectivists, others who wish to restrain the action of railway and telegraph companies and other so-called "monopolists," and of course many who, while dissatisfied with existing economic conditions, and desiring to see the working classes receive a larger share of the good things of the world, are not prepared to say in what way these conditions can be mended and this result attained. Speaking generally, the reforms advocated by the leaders of the Labour party have included the "nationalization of the land," the imposition of a progressive income tax,[3] the taking over of railroads and telegraphs by the national government, the prevention of the immigration of Chinese and of any other foreign labourers who may come under contract, the restriction of all so-called monopolies, the forfeiture of railroad land grants, the increase of the currency, the free issue of inconvertible paper, and, above all, the statutory restriction of hours of labour. But it must not be supposed that all the leaders, much less all the followers, adopt all these tenets; nor has it been always easy to say who are to be deemed its leaders. It shows a tendency to split up into factions. Its strength has lain in the trade unions of the operative class, and for a time in the enormous organization or league of trade unions that was known as the Knights of Labour; and it is therefore warmly interested in the administration of the various state laws which affect strikes and the practice of boycotting by which strikes often seek to prevail. It has much support from the recent immigrants who fill the great cities, especially the socialistically inclined sections of the Germans, Jews, Poles, Czechs, and other Austro-Hungarian Slavs.

The Labour party did not run a presidential candidate till 1888, and was then divided, so that its strength could not be well estimated. But it has been wont to put forward candidates in state and city elections when it saw a chance. It ran Mr. Henry George for mayor of New York City in 1886, and obtained the unexpected success of polling 67,000 votes against 90,000 given to the regular Democratic, and 60,000 to the regular Republican candidate;[4] but this success was not sustained in the contest for the governorship of the state of New York in 1887, when a vote of only 37,000

---

[3] This was demanded by the Greenback national convention in its platforms of 1880 and 1884, and by the Farmers' Alliance in 1890; but less than might be expected has been heard of it in America. Its adoption in the Canton of Vaud in Switzerland caused some of the wealthier inhabitants to quit the canton, and in Zürich after it has been raised to a pretty high figure people found that any further rise would be deleterious, so the increase stopped.

[4] In 1874 when a Labour candidate was first run for the New York mayoralty he obtained only between 3,000 and 4,000 votes.

was cast by the Labour party in the city. In 1892 one section, calling itself the Socialist Labour Party, ran a presidential candidate, but obtained only 21,164 votes, 17,956 of which came from New York, the rest from Pennsylvania, New Jersey, Massachusetts, and Connecticut. In 1900 the party which has since called itself Socialist was founded. Both these parties sometimes put forward candidates in state or city elections. The Socialists are a somewhat incalculable force in state and city politics, seldom strong enough to carry their own candidates, but sometimes able to defeat one of the regular parties by drawing away a part of its voters, or to extort a share of the offices for some of their nominees. It is only in some states, chiefly Northern states, that candidates of this complexion appear at all.

The Prohibitionists, or opponents of the sale of intoxicating liquors, have since 1872 regularly held a national convention for the nomination of a presidential candidate, and put out a ticket, i.e., nominated candidates for president and vice-president. The action of this party has been most frequent in the state legislatures, because the whole question of permitting, restricting, or abolishing the sale of intoxicants is a matter for the states and not for Congress. However, the federal government raises a large revenue by its high import duty on wines, spirits, and malt liquors, and also levies an internal excise. As this revenue was for some years before 1890 no longer needed for the expenses of the national government, it was proposed to distribute it among the states, or apply it to some new and useful purpose, or to reduce both customs duties and the excise. The fear of the first or second of these courses, which would give the manufacture and sale of intoxicants a new lease of life, or of the third, which would greatly increase their consumption, was among the causes which induced the Prohibitionists to enter the arena of national politics; and they further justify their conduct in doing so by proposing to amend the federal Constitution for the purposes of prohibition, and to stop the sale of intoxicants in the Territories and in the District of Columbia, which are under the direct control of Congress.[5]

---

[5] The Prohibitionist platform of 1892, issued by their national convention, contained the following passage:

"The liquor traffic is a foe to civilization, the arch enemy of popular government, and a public nuisance. It is the citadel of the forces that corrupt politics, promote poverty and crime, degrade the nation's home life, thwart the will of the people, and deliver our country into the hands of rapacious class interests. All laws that under the guise of regulation legalize and protect this traffic, or make the government share in its ill-gotten gains, are 'vicious in principle and powerless as a remedy.' We declare anew for the entire suppression of the manufacture, sale, importation, exportation, and transportation of alcoholic liquors as a beverage by Federal and State legislation, and the full powers of the government should be exerted to secure this result." In 1908 their convention declared one of its principles to be "the submission by congress to the several States

Their running a candidate for the presidency has been more a demonstration than anything else, as they cast a comparatively weak vote, many even of those who sympathize with them preferring to support one or other of the great parties rather than throw away a vote in the abstract assertion of a principle. One ought indeed to distinguish between the Prohibitionists proper, who wish to stop the sale of intoxicants altogether, and the Temperance men, who are very numerous among Republicans in the North and Democrats in the South, and who, while ready to vote for local option and a high licence law, disapprove the attempt to impose absolute prohibition by general legislation.[6] The number of persons who are both thoroughgoing Prohibitionists and pure Prohibitionists, that is to say, who are not also Republicans or Democrats, is small, far too small, even when reinforced by a section of the "Temperance men," and by discontented Republicans or Democrats who may dislike the "regular" candidates of their party, to give the Prohibition ticket a chance of success in any state. The importance of the ticket lies in the fact that in a doubtful state it may draw away enough votes from one of the "regular" candidates to leave him in a minority. Mr. Blaine probably suffered in this way in the election of 1884, most of the votes cast for the Prohibitionist candidate having come from quondam Republicans. On the other hand, a case may be imagined in which the existence of an outlet or safety-valve, such as a Prohibitionist ticket, would prevent the "bolters" from one party from taking the more dangerous course of voting for the candidate of the opposite party. Latterly the party vote has been too small to make much difference.

The strength of the Prohibitionist party lies in the religious and moral earnestness which animates it and makes it for many purposes the successor and representative of the Abolitionists of forty years ago. Clergymen were prominent in its conventions, and women took an active part in its work.

---

of an amendment to the Constitution prohibiting the manufacture, sale, importation, exportation, or transportation of alcoholic liquors for beverage purposes."

One might have expected the Prohibitionists to advocate the repeal of the protective tariff on manufactured goods so as to make it necessary to maintain customs duties and an excise on intoxicants for the purposes of the National government. But this would imply that these beverages might still be consumed, which is just what the more ardent spirits in the temperance party refuse to contemplate. In 1892 they said: "Tariff should be levied only as a defence against foreign governments which lay tariff upon or bar out our products from their markets, revenue being incidental."

[6] Many state legislatures have "placated" the Temperance men by enacting that "the hygienics of alcohol and its action upon the human body" shall be a regular subject of instruction in the public schools. Whether this instruction does more good or harm is a controverted point, as to which see the report for 1890 of the U.S. Commissioner of Education.

Partly from its traditions and temper, partly because it believes that women would be on its side in elections, it advocates the extension to them of the electoral franchise. But it has latterly lost much of its political importance, though temperance has advanced both in the diffusion of its principles and in practice.

A spirit of discontent with the old parties, and vague wish to better by legislation the condition of the agriculturists, caused the growth of what was called at first the Farmers' Alliance Party, and thereafter the People's Party, or "Populists." In 1889 and 1890 it rose suddenly to importance in the West and South, and secured some seats from Western states in the Fifty-second and succeeding Congresses. Its platform agreed in several points with those of the Greenbackers and Labour men, but instead of seeking to "nationalize" the land, it desired to reduce the taxation on real estate and to secure (among other benefits) loans from the public treasury to farmers at low rates of interest. It ran a candidate at the presidential election of 1892 (carrying four states and obtaining one electoral vote in each of two others), but has since then so much declined, that in 1908 only 29,108 votes were cast for the candidate whom it nominated. Although the economic and social conditions of agricultural life in America are likely from time to time to produce similar outbreaks of dissatisfaction, with impatient cries for unpractical remedies, the tendency has of recent years been towards the formation of parties professing views of a more or less Collectivist type. In 1900, 1904, 1908, and 1912 a party calling itself Socialist and another calling itself Socialist Labour ran candidates for the presidency; and in 1908 there also appeared an "Independence Party," which denounced the Republican and Democratic parties alike. Of these minor new parties the largest vote was in 1912 cast by the Socialist, 901,873. In 1904 its vote had been 402,321. In 1912 the new Progressive party ran its candidates.

The advocates of woman suffrage cannot be reckoned a national party, because the question is one for the states, and because women have no vote in presidential elections (save in ten states). In 1884 a woman was nominated, but did not go to the poll.[7]

Though the group which went by the name of Mugwumps has disappeared, it had a temporary significance which entitles it to the meed of a melodious tear.[8] At the presidential election of 1884 a section of the Republican party,

---

[7] See further as to women's suffrage, Chapter 99.

[8] The name is said to be formed from an Indian word denoting a chief or aged wise man, and was applied by the "straight-out" Republicans to their bolting brethren as a term of ridicule. It was

more important by the intelligence and social position of the men who composed it than by its numbers, "bolted" (to use the technical term) from their party, and refused to vote for Mr. Blaine. Some simply abstained, some, obeying the impulse to vote which is strong in good citizens in America, voted for Mr. St. John, the Prohibitionist candidate, though well aware that this was practically the same thing as abstention. The majority, however, voted against their party for Mr. Cleveland, the Democratic candidate; and it seems to have been the transference of their vote which turned the balance in New York State, and thereby determined the issue of the whole election in Mr. Cleveland's favour. They were therefore not to be reckoned as a national party, according to the American use of the term, because they did not run a ticket of their own, but supported a candidate started by one of the regular parties. The only organization they formed consisted of committees which held meetings and distributed literature during the election, but dissolved when it was over. They maintained no permanent party machinery; and did not act as a distinct section, even for the purposes of agitation, at subsequent presidential elections. Some of them have since been absorbed (especially in New England and New York) into the Democratic party, others have returned to their old affiliations. They were not so much a section as a tendency, persons in whom a growing disposition to a detached independence was for the time embodied. The tendency is now chiefly conspicuous in municipal politics, where it has given birth to Good Government Clubs and other civic associations intended to purify the administration of cities.

The Mugwumps bore no resemblance to any British party. The tendency which called them into being is discernible chiefly in New England and in the cities of the Eastern states generally, but it affects some few persons scattered here and there all over the North and West as far as California. In the South (save in such border cities as St. Louis and Louisville) there were none, because the Southern men who would, had they lived in the North, have taken to Mugwumpism, were in the South Democrats. There did not in 1884 seem to be in the Democratic party, either in North or South, as much material for a secession similar to that of the "bolters" of that year as was then shown to exist among the Republicans. In 1893, however, an enormous "swing-over" in New York State of votes usually Democratic to the Republican side, provoked by the nomination of a man deemed tainted

---

then taken up by the latter as a term of compliment; though the description they used formally in 1884 was that of "Independent Republicans."

to an important judicial office, showed that the Mugwump element or tendency was to be reckoned with, at least in the Northeastern states, by both parties alike, and in 1896 (as already remarked) many of the richer and more influential gold Democrats "bolted" the party ticket and ran a presidential ticket of their own.

The reader must be reminded of one capital difference between the Republican and Democratic parties and the minor ones which have just been mentioned. The two former are absolutely coextensive with the Union. They exist in every state, and in every corner of every state. They exist even in the Territories, though the inhabitants of Territories have no vote in federal elections. But the four minor parties that held conventions in the elections of and since 1900, did not attempt to maintain organizations all over the Union.[9] The Populists, though for the moment strong in the West, had no importance in the Atlantic states. Where these minor parties are strong, or where some question has arisen which keenly interests them, they may run their man for state governor or mayor, or will put out a ticket for state senators or assemblymen; or they will take the often more profitable course of fusing for the nonce with one of the regular parties, giving it their vote in return for having the party nominations to one or more of the elective offices assigned to their own nominee.[10] This helps to keep the party going, and gives to its vote a practical result otherwise unattainable.

Is there not, then, some European may ask, a Free Trade party? Not in the American sense of the word "party." The Democratic party used to stand for a "tariff for revenue only," and there are still more advocates of a low rate of duties in that party than among their opponents. But there is no political organization which devotes itself to the advocacy of free trade by the usual party methods, much less does anyone think of starting candidates either for the presidency or for Congress upon a pure anti-protectionist platform.

Why, considering the reluctant hesitancy which the old parties have been apt to show in taking up a clear and distinctive attitude upon new questions, and formulating definite proposals regarding them, and considering also that in the immense area of the United States, with its endless variety of economic interests and social conditions, we might expect local diversities of aim and view which would here and there crystallize, and so give rise to many local

[9] In 1912 the Socialist party was the only minor party for which votes were cast in every state. The Prohibitionists obtained votes in forty states, and the Socialist Labour in twenty.

[10] The Labour men and latterly the Socialists did this pretty frequently, the Prohibitionists scarcely ever. As to the Progressive party in the presidential election of 1912, see p. 849, *post*.

parties—why are not the parties far more numerous? Why, too, are the parties so persistent? In this changeful country one would look for frequent changes in tenets and methods.

One reason is, that there is at present a strong feeling in America against any sentiment or organization which relies on or appeals to one particular region of the country. Such localism or sectionalism is hateful, because, recalling the disunionist spirit of the South which led to the war, it seems anti-national and unpatriotic. By the mere fact of its springing from a local root, and urging a local interest, a party would set all the rest of the country against it. As a separately organized faction seeking to capture the federal government, it could not succeed against the national parties, because the Union as a whole is so vast that it would be outvoted by one or other of them. But if it is content to remain a mere opinion or demand, not attacking either national party, but willing to bestow the votes it can control on whichever will meet its wishes, it is powerful, because the two great parties will bid against one another for its support by flatteries and concessions. For instance, the question which has interested the masses on the Pacific coast is that of excluding Chinese immigrants, and latterly the Japanese also, because they compete for work with the whites and bring down wages. Now if the "anti-Mongolians" of California, Washington, and Oregon were to create a national party, based on this particular issue, they would be insignificant, for they would have little support over five-sixths of the Union. But by showing that the attitude of the two great parties on this issue will determine their own attitude toward these parties, they control both, for as each desires to secure the vote of California, Washington, and Oregon, each vies with the other in promising and voting for anti-Asiatic legislation. The position of the Irish extremists was similar, except of course that they are a racial and not a geographical "section." Their power, which Congress has sometimes recognized in a way scarcely compatible with its dignity or with international courtesy, lay in the fact that as the Republicans and Democrats are nearly balanced, the congressional leaders of both desired to "placate" this faction, for which neither had a sincere affection. An Irish party, or a German party, or a Roman Catholic party, which should run its candidates on a sectional platform, would stand self-condemned in American eyes as not being genuinely American. But so long as it is content to seek control over parties and candidates, it exerts an influence out of proportion to its numbers, and checked only by the fear that if it demanded too much, native Americans might rebel, as they did in the famous Know-Nothing or "American" party of 1853–58. The same fate would befall a party based upon some trade interest, such as protection to a particular sort of manufactures, or the stimulation of cattle breeding as against sheep. Such a party might succeed for a time in a state, and might dictate its terms to one or both of the national parties; but when it attempted to be a national party it would become ridiculous and fall.

A second cause of the phenomenon which I am endeavouring to explain may be found in the enormous trouble and expense required to found a new national party. To influence the votes, even to reach the ears, of nearly one hundred millions of people, is an undertaking to be entered on only when some really great cause fires the national imagination, disposes the people to listen, persuades the wealthy to spend freely of their substance. It took six years of intense work to build up the Republican party, which might not even then have triumphed in the election of 1860, but for the split in the ranks of its opponents. The attempt made in 1872 to form a new independent party out of the discontented Republicans and the Democrats failed lamentably. The Independent Republicans of 1884 did not venture to start a programme or candidate of their own, but were prudently satisfied with helping the Democratic candidate, whom they deemed more likely than the Republican nominee to give effect to the doctrine of civil service reform which they were advocating.

The case of these Independents, or Mugwumps, is an illustrative one. For many years past there had been complaints that the two old parties were failing to deal with issues that had grown to be of capital importance, such as the tariff, the currency, the improvements of methods of business in Congress, the purification of the civil service and extinction of the so-called Spoils System. These complaints, however, have not come from the men prominent as practical statesmen or politicians in the parties, but from outsiders, and largely from the men of intellectual cultivation and comparatively high social standing. Very few of such men took an active part in "politics," however interested they might be in public affairs. They were amateurs as regards the practical work of "running" ward meetings and conventions, of framing "tickets," and bringing up voters to the poll, in fact of working as well as organizing that vast and complicated machinery which an American party needs. Besides, it is a costly machinery, and they did not see where to find the money. Hence they recoiled from the effort, and aimed at creating a sentiment which might take concrete form in a vote, given for whichever of the parties seemed at any particular time most likely to adopt, even if insincerely, the principles, and push forward, even if reluctantly, the measures which the Independents advocate.

Why, however, does it so seldom happen that the professional politicians, who "know the ropes," and know where to get the necessary funds, more frequently seek to wreck a party in order to found a new one more to their mind? Because they are pretty well satisfied with the sphere which existing parties give them, and comprehend from their practical experience how hazardous such an experiment would be.

These considerations may help to explain the remarkable cohesion of parties in America, and the strength of party loyalty, a phenomenon more natural in Europe, where momentous issues inflame men's passions, and where the bulk of the adherents are ignorant men, caught by watchwords and readily attracted to a leader, than in a republic where no party has any benefit to promise to the people which it may not as well get from the other, and where the native voter is a keen-witted man, with little reverence for the authority of any individual. There is however another reason flowing from the character of the American people. They are extremely fond of associating themselves, and prone to cling to any organization they have once joined. They are sensitive to any charge of disloyalty. They are gregarious, each man more disposed to go with the multitude and do as they do than to take a line of his own,[11] and they enjoy "campaigning" for its own sake. These are characteristics which themselves require to be accounted for, but the discussion of them belongs to later chapters. A European is surprised to see prominent politicians supporting, sometimes effusively, a candidate of their own party whom they are known to dislike, merely because he is the party candidate. There is a sort of military discipline about party life which has its good as well as its bad side, for if it sometimes checks the expression of honest disapproval, it also restrains jealousy, abashes self-seeking, prevents recrimination.

Each of the American parties has usually been less under the control of one or two conspicuous leaders than are British parties. So far as this is due to the absence of men whose power over the people rests on the possession of brilliant oratorical or administrative gifts, it is a part of the question why there are not more such men in American public life, why there are fewer striking figures than in the days of Jefferson and Hamilton, of Webster and Calhoun. It is however also due to the peculiarities of the Constitution. The want of concentration of power in the legal government is reflected in the structure of the party system. The separation of the legislative from the ex-

---

[11] That is to say, they respect the authority of the mass, to which they themselves belong, though seldom that of individual leaders. See *post*, Chapter 85, "The Fatalism of the Multitude."

ecutive department lowers the importance of leadership in parties, as it weakens both these departments. The president, who is presumably among the leading men, cannot properly direct the policy of his party, still less speak for it in public, because he represents the whole nation. His ministers cannot speak to the people through Congress. In neither house of Congress is there necessarily any person recognized as the leader on either side. As neither house has the power over legislation and administration possessed by such an assembly as the French or Italian Chamber, or the English House of Commons, speeches delivered or strategy displayed in it do not tell upon the country with equal force and directness. There remains the stump, and it is more by the stump than in any other way that an American statesman speaks to the people. But what distances to be traversed, what fatigues to be encountered before he can be a living and attractive personality to the electing masses! An English statesman leaves London at two o'clock, and speaks in Birmingham, or Leeds, or Manchester, the same evening. In a few years, every great town knows him like its own mayor, while the active local politicians who frequently run up from their homes to London hear him from the galleries of the House of Commons, wait on him in deputations, are invited to the receptions which his wife gives during the season. Even railways and telegraphs cannot make America a compact country in the same sense that Britain is.

From the Civil War till the end of last century, neither Republicans nor Democrats leaned on and followed any one man as Mr. Gladstone and Lord Beaconsfield, as before them Lords Derby, John Russell, and Palmerston, as still earlier Sir Robert Peel and Lord Melbourne, were followed in England. No one since Mr. Seward exercised even so much authority as Mr. Bright did when out of office, or as Gambetta did in France, or as Mr. Parnell in Ireland, over the sections of opinion which each of these eminent men has represented.

How then are the parties led in Congress and the country? Who directs their policy? Who selects their candidates for the most important posts? These are questions which cannot be adequately answered till the nature of the party machinery has been described. For the moment I must be content to suggest the following as provisional answers:

The most important thing is the selection of candidates. This is done in party meetings called conventions. When a party has any policy, it is settled in such a convention and declared in a document called a platform. When it has no policy, the platform is issued none the less. Party tactics in Congress are decided on by meetings of the party in each house of Congress called caucuses. Leaders have of course much to do with all three processes.

But they often efface themselves out of respect to the sentiment of equality, and because power concealed excites less envy.

How do the parties affect social life? At present not very much, at least in the Northern and Middle states, because it is a comparatively slack time in politics. Your dining acquaintances, even your intimate friends, are not necessarily of the same way of voting as yourself, and though of course political views tend to become hereditary, there is nothing to surprise anyone in finding sons belonging to different parties from their fathers. In the South, where the recollections of the great struggle are kept alive by the presence of a Negro voting power which has had to be controlled, things are different; and they were different in the North till the passions of civil strife had abated.

So far, I have spoken of the parties only as national organizations, struggling for and acting on or through the federal government. But it has already been observed (Chapter 46) that they exist also as state and city organizations, contending for the places which states and cities have to give, seeking to control state legislatures and municipal councils. Every circumscription of state and local government, from the state of New York with its nine millions of inhabitants down to the "city" that has just sprung up round a railway junction in the West, has a regular Republican party organization, confronted by a similar Democratic organization, each running its own ticket (i.e., list of candidates) at every election, for any office pertaining to its own circumscription, and each federated, so to speak, to the larger organizations above it, represented in them and working for them in drilling and "energizing" the party within the area which is the sphere of its action.

What have the tenets of such national parties as the Republicans and Democrats to do with the politics of states and cities? Very little with those of states, because a matter for federal legislation is seldom also a matter for state legislation. Still less with those of cities or counties. Cities and counties have not strictly speaking any political questions to deal with; their business is to pave and light, to keep the streets clean, maintain an efficient police and well-barred prisons, administer the poor law and charitable institutions with integrity, judgment, and economy. The laws regulating these matters have been already made by the state, and the city or county authority has nothing to do but administer them. Hence at city and county elections the main objects ought to be to choose honest and careful men of business. It need make no difference to the action of a mayor or school trustee in any concrete question whether he holds Democratic or Republican views.

However, the habit of party warfare has been so strong as to draw all elections into its vortex; nor would either party feel safe if it neglected the means of rallying and drilling its supporters, which state and local contests supply. There is this advantage in the system, that it stimulates the political interest of the people, which is kept alive by this perpetual agitation. But the multiplicity of contests has the effect of making politics too absorbing an occupation for the ordinary citizen who has his profession or business to attend to; while the result claimed by those who in England defend the practice of fighting municipal elections on party lines, viz., that good men are induced to stand for local office for the sake of their party, is the last result desired by the politicians, or expected by anyone. It is this constant labour which the business of politics involves, this ramification of party into all the nooks and corners of local government, that has produced the class of professional politicians, of whom it is now time to speak.

The Politicians

Institutions are said to form men, but it is no less true that men give to institutions their colour and tendency. It profits little to know the legal rules and methods and observances of government, unless one also knows something of the human beings who tend and direct this machinery, and who, by the spirit in which they work it, may render it the potent instrument of good or evil to the people. These men are the politicians.[1]

What is one to include under this term? In England it usually denotes those who are actively occupied in administering or legislating, or discussing administration and legislation. That is to say, it includes ministers of the Crown, members of Parliament (though some in the House of Commons and the majority in the House of Lords care little about politics), a few leading journalists, and a small number of miscellaneous persons, writers, lecturers, organizers, agitators, who occupy themselves with trying to influence the public. Sometimes the term is given a wider sweep, being taken to include all who labour for their political party in the constituencies, as, e.g., the chairmen and secretaries of local party associations, and the more active committeemen of the same bodies. The former, whom we may call the inner-circle men, are professional politicians in this sense, and in this sense only, that politics is the main though seldom the sole business of their lives. But at present extremely few of them make anything by it in the way of money. A handful hope to get some post; a somewhat larger number find that a seat in Parliament enables them to push their financial undertakings or make them at least more conspicuous in the commercial world. But the gaining of a livelihood does not come into the view of the great majority at

---

[1] In America (Canada as well as the United States) people do not say "politicians," but "the politicians," because the word indicates a class with certain defined characteristics.

all. The other class, who may be called the outer circle, are not professionals
in any sense, being primarily occupied with their own avocations; and none
of them, except here and there an organizing secretary, or registration agent,
and here and there a paid lecturer, makes any profit out of the work.[2] The
phenomena of France and Italy and Germany are generally similar, that is
to say, those who devote their whole time to politics are a very small class,
those who make a living by it an even smaller one.[3] Of all the countries of
Europe, Greece is that in which persons who spend their life in politics
seem to bear the largest proportion to the whole population; and in Greece
the pursuit of politics is usually the pursuit of place.

To see why things are different in the United States, why the inner circle
is much larger both absolutely and relatively to the outer circle than in
Europe, let us go back a little and ask what are the conditions which develop
a political class. The point has so important a bearing on the characteristics
of American politicians that I do not fear to dwell somewhat fully upon it.

In self-governing communities of the simpler kind—for one may leave
absolute monarchies and feudal monarchies on one side—the common affairs
are everybody's business and nobody's special business. Some few men by
their personal qualities get a larger share of authority, and are repeatedly
chosen to be archons, or generals, or consuls, or burgomasters, or landam-
mans, but even these rarely give their whole time to the state, and make
little or nothing in money out of it. This was the condition of the Greek
republics, of early Rome,[4] of the cities of mediæval Germany and Italy, of
the cantons of Switzerland till very recent times.

When in a large country public affairs become more engrossing to those
who are occupied in them, when the sphere of government widens, when
administration is more complex and more closely interlaced with the
industrial interests of the community and of the world at large, so that there
is more to be known and to be considered, the business of a nation falls

---

[2] Of course now and then a man who has worked hard for his party is rewarded by a place.
Barristers who have spent their substance in contesting seats have a better chance of judgeships,
and there are usually five or six practising counsel in the House of Commons who are supposed
to contemplate the possibility of their obtaining legal office. But these cases are so few as to
make no practical difference.

[3] The number of persons who live off politics by getting places or by manipulating finance is said
to have increased in France of late years. But it cannot be very large even now.

[4] The principal business in life of Cincinnatus was to till his fields, and a dictatorship a mere
interlude. When I waited on the president of the Republic of Andorra, one of the oldest states in
Europe, in 1873, I found him in a red shirt with his coat off wielding a flail on the floor of his
barn.

into the hands of the men eminent by rank, wealth, and ability, who form a sort of governing class, largely hereditary. The higher civil administration of the state is in their hands; they fill the chief council or legislative chamber and conduct its debates. They have residences in the capital, and though they receive salaries when actually filling an office, and have opportunities for enriching themselves, the majority possess independent means, and pursue politics for the sake of fame, power, or excitement. Those few who have not independent means can follow their business or profession in the capital, or can frequently visit the place where their business is carried on. This was the condition of Rome under the later republic,[5] and of England and France till quite lately—indeed it is largely the case in England still—as well as of Prussia and Sweden.[6]

Let us see what are the conditions of the United States.

There is a relatively small leisured class of persons engaged in no occupation and of wealth sufficient to leave them free for public affairs. So far as such persons are to be found in the country, for some are to be sought abroad, they are to be found in a few great cities.

There is no class with a sort of hereditary prescriptive right to public office, no great families whose names are known to the people, and who, bound together by class sympathy and ties of relationship, help one another by keeping offices in the hands of their own members.

The country is a very large one, and has its political capital in a city without trade, without manufactures, without professional careers. Even the seats of state governments are often placed in comparatively small towns.[7] Hence a man cannot carry on his gainful occupation at the same time that he attends to "inner-circle" politics.

Members of Congress and of state legislatures are invariably chosen from the places where they reside. Hence a person belonging to the leisured class of a great city cannot get into the House of Representatives or the legislature of his state except as member for a district of his own city.

---

[5] Rome in the later days of the Republic had practically become a country, that is to say, the range of her authority and the mass of her public business were much greater than in any of the Greek cities, even in Athens in the days of Pericles. The chances of making illicit gains were enormous, but confined to a small number of persons.

[6] Norway, the most democratic of the monarchical countries of Europe, is the one which has probably the smallest class of persons continuously occupied with politics.

[7] E.g., the seat of government for Maryland is Annapolis, not Baltimore; for Ohio, Columbus, not Cincinnati; for Illinois, Springfield, not Chicago; for California, Sacramento, not San Francisco; for Washington Territory, Olympia, not Seattle or Walla Walla; for Louisiana, Baton Rouge, not New Orleans.

The shortness of terms of office, and the large number of offices filled by election, make elections very frequent. All these elections, with trifling exceptions, are fought on party lines, and the result of a minor one for some petty local office, such as county treasurer, affects one for a more important post, e.g., that of member of Congress. Hence constant vigilance, constant exertions on the spot, are needed. The list of voters must be incessantly looked after, newly admitted or newly settled citizens enrolled, the active local men frequently consulted and kept in good humour, meetings arranged for, tickets (i.e., lists of candidates) for all vacant offices agreed upon. One election is no sooner over than another approaches and has to be provided for, as the English sporting man reckons his year by "events," and thinks of Newmarket after Ascot, and of Goodwood after Newmarket.

Now what do these conditions amount to? To this—a great deal of hard and dull election and other local political work to be done. Few men of leisure to do it, and still fewer men of leisure likely to care for it. Nobody able to do it in addition to his regular business or profession. Little motive for anybody, whether leisured or not, to do the humbler and local parts of it (i.e., so much as concerns the minor elections), the parts which bring neither fame nor power.

If the work is to be done at all, some inducement, other than fame or power, must clearly be found. Why not, someone will say, the sense of public duty? I will speak of public duty presently; meantime let it suffice to remark that to rely on public duty as the main motive power in politics is to assume a commonwealth of angels. Men such as we know them must have some other inducement. Even in the Christian church there are other than spiritual motives to lead its pastors to spiritual work; nor do all poets write because they seek to express the passion of their souls. In America we discover a palpable inducement to undertake the dull and toilsome work of election politics. It is the inducement of places in the public service. To make them attractive they must be paid. They are paid, nearly all of them, memberships of Congress[8] and other federal places, state places (including memberships of state legislatures), city and county places. Here then—and to some extent even in humbler forms, such as the getting of small contracts or even employment as labourers—is the inducement, the remuneration for political work performed in the way of organizing and electioneering. Now add that besides the paid administrative and legislative places which a

---

[8] Though, as observed in a previous chapter, the payment of members of Congress does not seem to have any marked effect in lowering the type of members. It is the offices rather than legislative posts that sustain the professional class.

democracy bestows by election, judicial places are also in most of the states elective, and held for terms of years only; and add further, that the holders of nearly all those administrative places, federal, state, and municipal, which are not held for a fixed term, are liable to be dismissed, as indeed many still are so liable and are in practice dismissed, whenever power changes from one party to another,[9] so that those who belong to the party out of office have a direct chance of office when their party comes in. The inducement to undertake political work we have been searching for is at once seen to be adequate, and only too adequate. The men needed for the work are certain to appear because remuneration is provided. Politics has now become a gainful profession, like advocacy, stockbroking, the dry goods trade, or the getting up of companies. People go into it to live by it, primarily for the sake of the salaries attached to the places they count on getting, secondarily in view of the opportunities it affords of making incidental and sometimes illegitimate gains. Every person in a high administrative post, whether federal, state, or municipal, and, above all, every member of Congress, has opportunities of rendering services to wealthy individuals and companies for which they are willing to pay secretly in money or in money's worth. The better officials and legislators—they are the great majority, except in large cities—resist the temptation. The worst succumb to it, and the prospect of these illicit profits renders a political career distinctly more attractive to an unscrupulous man.

We find therefore that in America all the conditions exist for producing a class of men specially devoted to political work and making a livelihood by it. It is work much of which cannot be done in combination with any other kind of regular work, whether professional or commercial. Even if the man who unites wealth and leisure to high intellectual attainments were a frequent figure in America, he would not take to this work; he would rather be a philanthropist or cultivate arts and letters. It is work which, steadily pursued by an active man, offers an income. Hence a large number of persons are drawn into it, and make it the business of their life; and the fact that they are there as professionals has tended to keep amateurs out of it.

There are, however, two qualifications which must be added to this statement of the facts, and which it is best to add at once. One is that the mere pleasure of politics counts for something. Many people in America as

[9] The progress of the civil service reform movement has greatly reduced the number of federal officers dismissed on a change of administration; and a similar reduction is going on in some states and cities.

well as in England undertake even the commonplace work of local canvassing and organizing for the sake of a little excitement, a little of the agreeable sense of self-importance, or from that fondness for doing something in association with others which makes a man become secretary to a cricket club or treasurer of a fund raised by subscription for some purpose he may not really care for. And the second qualification is that pecuniary motives operate with less force in rural districts than in cities, because in the former the income obtainable by public office is too small to induce men to work long in the hope of getting it. Let it therefore be understood that what is said in this chapter refers primarily to cities, and of course also to persons aiming at the higher federal and state offices; and that I do not mean to deny that there is plenty of work done by amateurs as well as by professionals.

Having thus seen what are the causes which produce professional politicians, we may return to inquire how large this class is, compared with the corresponding class in the free countries of Europe, whom we have called the inner circle.

In America the inner circle, that is to say, the persons who make political work the chief business of life, for the time being, includes:

Firstly. All members of both houses of Congress.

Secondly. All federal officeholders except the judges, who are irremovable, and who have sometimes taken no prominent part in politics.

Thirdly. A large part of the members of state legislatures. How large a part, it is impossible to determine, for it varies greatly from state to state. I should guess that in New York, Pennsylvania, New Jersey, California, Maryland, and Louisiana, half (or more) of the members were professional politicians; in Ohio, Virginia, Illinois, Texas, perhaps less than half; in Georgia, Kentucky, Iowa, Minnesota, Oregon, not more than one-third; in Massachusetts, Vermont, and some other states, perhaps even less. But the line between a professional and nonprofessional politician is too indefinite to make any satisfactory estimate possible.

Fourthly. Nearly all state officeholders, excluding all judges in a very few states, and many of the judges in the rest.

Fifthly. Nearly all holders of paid offices in the greater and in many of the smaller cities, and many holders of paid offices in the counties. There are, however, great differences in this respect between different states, the New England states and the newer states of the Northwest, as well as some Southern states, choosing many of their county officials from men who are not regularly employed on politics, although members of the dominant party.

Sixthly. A large number of people who hold no office but want to get one, or perhaps even who desire work under a municipality. This category includes, of course, many of the "workers" of the party which does not command the majority for the time being, in state and municipal affairs, and which has not, through the president, the patronage of federal posts. It also includes many expectants belonging to the party for the time being dominant, who are earning their future places by serving the party in the meantime.[10]

All the above may fairly be called professional or inner-circle politicians, but of their number I can form no estimate, save that it must be counted by hundreds of thousands, inasmuch as it practically includes nearly all state and local and most federal officeholders as well as most expectants of public office.[11]

It must be remembered that the "work" of politics means in America the business of winning nominations (of which more anon) and elections, and

---

[10] But, as already observed, there are also in the rural districts and smaller towns many workers and expectants who do not look for places.

[11] The inner circle may in England be roughly taken to include:

Members of the House of Lords, say	80
Members of the House of Commons	670
Editors, and chief writers on leading newspapers, say	300
Expectant candidates for House of Commons, say	450
Persons who in each constituency devote most of their time to politics, e.g., secretaries of political associations, registration agents, etc., say	2500
	4000

Comparatively few newspapers are primarily political, and in many constituencies (e.g., Irish and Highland counties) there are very few persons occupied in political work. I do not, therefore, think this estimate too low.

In the United States there are now out of the whole number of federal offices about 100,000 which may be said to attract aspirants to endeavour to gain them by political work. Allowing one expectant for each office (a small allowance), and assuming the state and local offices bestowed as the reward for political services to be one and a half times as numerous as the above federal offices (they are, of course, more numerous), and allowing one expectant to each such office, we should have a total of over $100,000 + 150,000 \times 2 = 500,000$, a little less than one-third of the total number employed in railway work. Deducting from this total those who, though they work for office, do not make such work their main business, and those who work with no special eye to office, we should still have a very large total, doubtless over 250,000 of persons whose chief occupation and livelihood lies in politics.

that this work is incomparably heavier and more complex than in England, because:

(1) The voters are a larger proportion of the population; (2) the government is more complex (federal, state, and local) and the places filled by election are therefore far more numerous; (3) elections come at shorter intervals; (4) the machinery of nominating candidates is far more complete and intricate; (5) the methods of fighting elections require more technical knowledge and skill; (6) ordinary private citizens do less election work, seeing that they are busier than in England, and the professionals exist to do it for them.

I have observed that there are also plenty of men engaged in some trade or profession who interest themselves in politics and work for their party without any definite hope of office or other pecuniary aim. They correspond to what we have called the outer-circle politicians of Europe. It is hard to draw a line between the two classes, because they shade off into one another, there being many farmers or lawyers or saloonkeepers, for instance, who, while pursuing their regular calling, bear a hand in politics, and look to be some time or other rewarded for doing so. When this expectation becomes a considerable part of the motive for exertion, such an one may fairly be called a professional, at least for the time being, for although he has other means of livelihood, he is apt to be impregnated with the habits and sentiments of the professional class.

The proportion between outer-circle and inner-circle men is in the United States a sort of ozonometer by which the purity and healthiness of the political atmosphere may be tested. Looking at the North only, for I have no tolerable data as to the South, and excluding congressmen, the proportion of men who exert themselves in politics without pecuniary motive is largest in New England, in the country parts of New York, in northern Ohio, and the Northwestern states, while the professional politicians most abound in the great cities—New York, Philadelphia, Brooklyn, Boston, Baltimore, Buffalo, Cincinnati, Louisville, Chicago, St. Louis, New Orleans, San Francisco. This is because these cities have the largest masses of ignorant voters, and also because their municipal governments, handling large revenues, offer the largest facilities for illicit gains.

I shall presently return to the outer-circle men. Meantime let us examine the professionals somewhat more closely; and begin with those of the humbler type, whose eye is fixed on a municipal or other local office, and seldom ranges so high as a seat in Congress.

As there are weeds that follow human dwellings, so this species thrives best in cities, and even in the most crowded parts of cities. It is known to the Americans as the "ward politician," because the city ward is the chief sphere of its activity, and the ward meeting the first scene of its exploits. A statesman of this type usually begins as a saloon- or barkeeper, an occupation which enables him to form a large circle of acquaintances, especially among the "loafer" class who have votes but no reason for using them one way more than another, and whose interest in political issues is therefore as limited as their stock of political knowledge. But he may have started as a lawyer of the lowest kind, or lodginghouse keeper, or have taken to politics after failure in storekeeping. The education of this class is only that of the elementary schools. If they have come after boyhood from Europe, it is not even that. They have of course no comprehension of political questions or zeal for political principles; politics mean to them merely a scramble for places or jobs. They are usually vulgar, sometimes brutal, not so often criminal, or at least the associates of criminals. It is they who move about the populous quarters of the great cities, form groups through whom they can reach and control the ignorant voter, pack meetings with their creatures.

Their methods and their triumphs must be reserved for a later chapter. Those of them who are Irish, an appreciable though diminishing proportion in a few cities, have seldom Irish patriotism to redeem the mercenary quality of their politics. They are too strictly practical for that, being regardful of the wrongs of Ireland only so far as these furnish capital to be used with Irish voters. Their most conspicuous virtues are shrewdness, a sort of rough good-fellowship with one another, and loyalty to their chiefs, from whom they expect promotion in the ranks of the service. The plant thrives in the soil of any party, but its growth is more vigorous in whichever party is for the time dominant in a given city.

English critics, taking their cue from American pessimists, have often described these men as specimens of the whole class of politicians. This is misleading. The men are bad enough both as an actual force and as a symptom. But they are confined to a few great cities, those eleven or twelve I have already mentioned; it is their achievements there, and particularly in New York, where the mass of ignorant immigrants is largest, that have made them famous.

In the smaller cities, and in the country generally, the minor politicians are mostly native Americans, less ignorant and more respectable than these last-mentioned street vultures. The barkeeping element is represented among them, but the bulk are petty lawyers, officials, federal as well as state and county, and people who for want of a better occupation have turned office-seekers, with a fair sprinkling of storekeepers, farmers, and newspaper men. The great majority have some regular avocation, so that they are by no means wholly professionals. Law is of course the business which best fits in with politics. They are only a little below the level of the class to which they belong, which is what would be called in England the lower middle, or in France the *petite bourgeoisie*, and they often suppose themselves to be fighting for Republican or Democratic principles, even though in fact concerned chiefly with place hunting. It is not so much positive moral defects that are to be charged on them as a slightly sordid and selfish view of politics and a laxity in the use of electioneering methods.

These two classes do the local work and dirty work of politics. They are the rank and file. Above them stand the officers in the political army, the party managers, including the members of Congress and chief men in the state legislatures, and the editors of influential newspapers. Some of these have pushed their way up from the humbler ranks. Others are men of superior ability and education, often college graduates, lawyers who have had practice, less frequently merchants or manufacturers who have slipped into politics from business. There are all sorts among them, creatures clean and unclean, as in the sheet of St. Peter's vision, but that one may say of politicians in all countries. What characterizes them as compared with the corresponding class in Europe is that their whole time is more frequently given to political work, that most of them draw an income from politics and the rest hope to do so, that they come more largely from the poorer and less cultivated than from the higher ranks of society, and that they include but few men who have pursued any of those economical, social, or constitutional studies which form the basis of politics and legislation, although many are proficients in the arts of popular oratory, of electioneering, and of party management.

They show a high average level of practical cleverness and versatility, and a good deal of legal knowledge. They are usually correct in life, for intoxication as well as sexual immorality is condemned by American more severely than by European opinion, but are often charged with a low tone, with laxity in pecuniary matters, with a propensity to commit or to excuse jobs, with a deficient sense of the dignity which public office confers and the responsibility it implies. I shall elsewhere discuss the validity of these charges, and need only observe here that even if the years since the Civil War have furnished some grounds for accusing the class as a whole, there are many brilliant exceptions, many leading politicians whose honour is as stainless and patriotism as pure as that of the best European statesmen. In this general description I am simply repeating what nonpolitical Americans themselves say. It is possible that with their half-humorous tendency to exaggerate they dwell too much on the darker side of their public life. My own belief is that things are healthier than the newspapers and common talk lead a traveller to believe, and that the blackness of the worst men in the large cities has been allowed to darken the whole class of politicians as the smoke from a few factories will darken the sky over a whole town. However, the sentiment I have described is no doubt the general sentiment. "Politician" is a term of reproach, not merely among the "superfine philosophers" of New England colleges, but among the better sort of citizens over the whole Union. "How did such a job come to be perpetrated?" I remember once asking a casual acquaintance who had been pointing out some scandalous waste of public money. "Why, what can you expect from the politicians?" was the surprised answer.

Assuming these faults to exist, to what causes are they to be ascribed? Granted that politics has to become a gainful profession, may it not still be practised with as much integrity as other professions? Do not the higher qualities of intellect, the ripe fruits of experience and study, win for a man ascendency here as in Europe? Does not the suspicion of dishonour blight his influence with a public which is itself at least as morally exacting as that of any European country? These are questions which can be better answered when the methods of party management have been described, the qualities they evoke appreciated, their reaction on men's character understood.

It remains to speak of the nonprofessional or outer-circle politicians, those who work for their party without desiring office. These men were numerous and zealous shortly before and during the Civil War, when the great questions of the exclusion of slavery from the Territories and the preservation of the Union kindled the enthusiasm of the noblest spirits of the North, women as well as men. No country ever produced loftier types of dauntless courage and uncompromising devotion to principle than William Lloyd Garrison and his fellow workers in the Abolitionist cause. Office came to Abraham Lincoln, but he would have served his party just as earnestly if there had been no office to reward him.[12] Nor was there any want of high-souled patriotism in the South. The people gave their blood freely, and among the

---

[12] Lincoln was never a professional politician, for he continued to practise as a lawyer till he became president: but he was so useful to his party that for some years before 1860 he had been obliged to spend a great part of his time in political work, and probably some would have called him a professional.

leaders there were many who offered up fine characters as well as brilliant talents on an altar which all but themselves deemed unhallowed. When these great issues were finally settled, and the generation whose manhood they filled began to pass away, there was less motive for ordinary citizens to trouble themselves about public affairs. Hence the professional politicians had the field left free; and as they were ready to take the troublesome work of organizing, the ordinary citizen was contented to be superseded, and thought he did enough when he went to the poll for his party. Still there are districts where a good deal of unpaid and disinterested political work is done. In some parts of New England, New York, and Ohio, for instance, citizens of position bestir themselves to rescue the control of local elections from the ward politicians. In the main, however, the action of the outer circle consists in voting, and this the ordinary citizen does more steadily and intelligently than anywhere in Europe, unless perhaps in Switzerland. Doubtless much of the work which outer-circle politicians do in Europe is in America done by professionals. But that lively interest in politics which the English outer circle feels and which is not felt by the English public generally, is in America felt by almost the whole of the nation, that is to say, by the immense majority of native white Americans, and even by the better sort of immigrants, or, in other words, the American outer circle comes far nearer to including the whole nation than does the outer circle of England. Thus the influence which counterworks that of professionals is the influence of public opinion expressing itself constantly through its countless voices in the press, and more distinctly at frequent intervals by the ballot box. I say "counterworks," because, while in Europe the leaders and still more the average legislators share and help to make public opinion, in the United States the politician stands rather outside, and regards public opinion as a factor to be reckoned with, much as the sailor regards the winds and currents that affect his course. His primary aim, unless he be exceptionally disinterested, is place and income; and it is in this sense that he may be described as a member of a definite profession.

Why the Best Men Do
Not Go Into Politics

But," someone will say, who has read the reasons just assigned for the development of a class of professional politicians, "you allow nothing for public spirit. It is easy to show why the prize of numerous places should breed a swarm of office-seekers, not so easy to understand why the office-seekers should be allowed to have this arena of public life in a vast country, a free country, an intelligent country, all to themselves. There ought to be patriotic citizens ready to plunge into the stream and save the boat from drifting towards the rapids. They would surely have the support of the mass of the people who must desire honest and economical administration. If such citizens stand aloof, there are but two explanations possible. Either public life must be so foul that good men cannot enter it, or good men must be sadly wanting in patriotism."

This kind of observation is so common in European mouths as to need an explicit answer. The answer is twofold.

In the first place, the arena is not wholly left to the professionals. Both the federal and the state legislatures contain a fair proportion of upright and disinterested men, who enter chiefly, or largely, from a sense of public duty, and whose presence keeps the mere professionals in order. So does public opinion, deterring even the bad men from the tricks to which they are prone, and often driving them, when detected in a serious offense, from place and power.

However, this first answer is not a complete answer, for it must be admitted that the proportion of men of intellectual and social eminence who enter public life is smaller in America than it was in each of the free countries of Europe. Does this fact indicate a want of public spirit?

It is much to be wished that in every country public spirit were the chief motive propelling men into public life. But is it so anywhere now? Has it been so at any time in a nation's history? Let anyone in England, dropping for the moment that self-righteous attitude of which Englishmen are commonly accused by foreigners, ask himself how many of those whom he knows as mixing in the public life of his own country have entered it from motives primarily patriotic, how many have been actuated by the love of fame or power, the hope of advancing their social pretensions or their business relations. There is nothing necessarily wrong in such forms of ambition; but if we find that they count for much in the public life of one country, and for comparatively little in the public life of another, we must expect to find the latter able to reckon among its statesmen fewer persons of eminent intelligence and energy.

Now there are several conditions present in the United States, conditions both constitutional and social, conditions independent either of political morality or of patriotism, which make the ablest citizens less disposed to enter political life than they would otherwise be, or than persons of the same class are in Europe. I have already referred to some of these, but recapitulate them shortly here because they are specially important in this connection.

The want of a social and commercial capital is such a cause. To be a federal politician you must live in Washington, that is, abandon your circle of home friends, your profession or business, your local public duties. But to live in Paris or London is of itself an attraction to many Englishmen and Frenchmen.

There is no class in America to which public political life comes naturally, scarcely any families with a sort of hereditary right to serve the state. Nobody can get an early and easy start on the strength of his name and connections, as still happens in several European countries.

In Britain or France a man seeking to enter the higher walks of public life has more than five hundred seats for which he may stand. If his own town or county is impossible he goes elsewhere. In the United States he cannot. If his own district is already filled by a member of his own party, there is nothing to be done, unless he will condescend to undermine and supplant at the next nominating convention the sitting member. If he has been elected and happens to lose his own renomination or reelection, he cannot reenter Congress by any other door. The fact that a man has served gives him no claim to be allowed to go on serving. In the West, rotation has been the rule. No wonder that, when a political career is so precarious, men of worth and capacity hesitate to embrace it. They cannot afford to be thrown out of their life's course by a mere accident.[1]

Politics have been since the Civil War less interesting or at any rate less exciting, than they have in Europe during the same period. The two kinds of questions which most attract eager or ambitious minds, questions of foreign policy and of domestic constitutional change, were generally absent, happily absent. Currency and tariff questions and financial affairs generally, internal improvements, the regulation of railways and so forth, are important, no doubt, but to some minds not fascinating. How few people in the English or French legislatures have mastered them, or would relish political life if it dealt with little else! There are no class privileges or religious inequalities to be abolished. Religion, so powerful a political force in Europe, is outside politics altogether.

In most European countries there has been for many years past an upward pressure of the poorer or the unprivileged masses, a pressure which has seemed to threaten the wealthier and more particularly the landowning class. Hence members of the latter class have had a strong motive for keeping tight hold of the helm of state. They have felt a direct personal interest in sitting in the legislature and controlling the administration of their country. This has not been so in America. Its great political issues have not been class issues. On the contrary there has been, till within the last few years, so great and general a sense of economic security, whether well or ill founded I do not now inquire, that the wealthy and educated have been content to leave the active work of politics alone.

The division of legislative authority between the federal Congress and the legislatures of the states further lessens the interest and narrows the opportunities of a political career. Some of the most useful members of the English Parliament have been led to enter it by their zeal for philanthropic schemes and social reforms. Others enter because they are interested in foreign politics or in commercial questions. In the United States foreign politics and commercial questions belong to Congress, so no one will be led by them to enter the legislature of his state. Social reforms and philanthropic enterprises belong to the state legislatures, so no one will be led by them to enter Congress. The limited sphere of each body deprives it

---

[1] The tendency in Switzerland to reelect the same men to the legislature and to public office has doubtless worked as much for good in politics there as the opposite tendency works for evil in the United States. Men who have supported measures which their constituency disapproves are often reelected because they are thought honest and capable. The existence of the *referendum* facilitates this.

of the services of many active spirits who would have been attracted by it had it dealt with both these sets of matters, or with the particular set of matters in which their own particular interest happens to lie.

In America there are more easy and attractive openings into other careers than in most European countries. The development of the great West, the making and financing of railways, the starting of industrial or mercantile enterprises in the newer states, offer a tempting field to ambition, ingenuity, and self-confidence. A man without capital or friends has a better chance than in Europe, and as the scale of undertakings is vaster, the prizes are more seductive. Hence much of the practical ability which in the Old World goes to parliamentary politics or to the civil administration of the state, goes in America into business, especially into railways and finance. No class strikes one more by its splendid practical capacity than the class of railroad men. It includes administrative rulers, generals, diplomatists, financiers, of the finest gifts. And in point of fact (as will be more fully shown later) the railroad kings have of late years swayed the fortunes of American citizens more than the politicians.

The fascination which politics have for many people in England is largely a social fascination. Those who belong by birth to the upper classes like to support their position in county society by belonging to the House of Commons, or by procuring either a seat in the House of Lords, or the lord-lieutenancy of their county, or perhaps a post in the royal household. The easiest path to these latter dignities lies through the Commons. Those who spring from the middle class expect to find by means of politics an entrance into a more fashionable society than they have hitherto frequented. Their wives will at least be invited to the party receptions, or they may entertain a party chieftain when he comes to address a meeting in their town. Such inducements scarcely exist in America. A congressman, a city mayor, even a state governor, gains nothing socially by his position. There is indeed, except in a few large cities with exclusive sets, really nothing in the nature of a social prize set before social ambition, while the career of political ambition is even in those cities wholly disjoined from social success. The only exception to this rule occurs in Washington, where a senator or cabinet minister enjoys *ex officio* a certain social rank.[2]

---

[2] It is the same in some, though by no means in all, of the cantons of Switzerland. Office carries little or no social consideration with it. In some cantons the old families have so completely withdrawn or become so completely shut out from public office, federal or cantonal, that it would be assumed that a politician was necessarily a plebeian. I remember to have been told in Bern of a foreign diplomatist who, walking one day with one of the old patricians of the city, stopped at the door of the government offices. "Where are you going?" asked the patrician. "To see one of your ministers on business." "You don't mean that you are going to speak to one of the *canaille!*"

None of these causes is discreditable to America, yet, taken together, they go far to account for the large development of the professional element among politicians. Putting the thing broadly, one may say that in America, while politics are relatively less interesting than in Europe and lead to less, other careers are relatively more interesting and lead to more.[3]

It may however be alleged that I have omitted one significant ground for the distaste of "the best people" for public life, viz., the bad company they would have to keep, the general vulgarity of tone in politics, the exposure to invective or ribaldry by hostile speakers and a reckless press.

I omit this ground because it seems insignificant. In every country a politician has to associate with men whom he despises and distrusts, and those whom he most despises and distrusts are sometimes those whose so-called social rank is highest—the sons or nephews of great nobles. In every country he is exposed to misrepresentation and abuse, and the most galling misrepresentations are not the coarse and incredible ones, but those which have a semblance of probability, which delicately discolour his motives and ingeniously pervert his words. A statesman must soon learn, even in decorous England or punctilious France or polished Italy, to disregard all this, and rely upon his conscience for his peace of mind, and upon his conduct for the respect of his countrymen. If he can do so in England or France or Italy, he may do so in America also. No more there than in Europe has any upright man been written down, for though the American press is unsparing, the American people are shrewd, and sometimes believe too little rather than too much evil of a man whom the press assails. Although therefore one hears the pseudo-European American complain of newspaper violence, and allege that it keeps him and his friends from doing their duty by their country, and although it sometimes happens that the fear of newspaper attacks deters a good citizen from exposing some job or jobber, still I could not learn the name of any able and high-minded man of whom it could be truly said that through this cause his gifts and virtues had been reserved for private life. The roughness of politics has, no doubt, some influence on the view which wealthy Americans take of a public career, but these are just the Americans who think that European politics are worked, to use the common phrase, "with kid gloves," and they are not the class most inclined anyhow to come to the front for the service of the nation. Without denying that there is recklessness in the American press, and a want of refinement

---

was the reply. The minister was, as Swiss statesmen generally are, a perfectly respectable man; but to a Bernese Junker his being a minister was enough to disparage him.

[3] This is true even of eminence in letters or art. A great writer or eloquent preacher is relatively more honoured and valued in America than in England.

in politics generally, I do not believe that these phenomena have anything like the importance which European visitors are taught, and willingly learn, to attribute to them. Far more weight is to be laid upon the difficulties which the organization of the party system, to be described in the following chapters, throws in the way of men who seek to enter public life. There is, as we shall see, much that is disagreeable, much that is even humiliating, in the initial stages of a political career, and doubtless many a pilgrim turns back after a short experience of this Slough of Despond.

To explain the causes which keep so much of the finest intellect of the country away from national business is one thing, to deny the unfortunate results would be quite another. Unfortunate they certainly are. But the downward tendency observable since the end of the Civil War seems to have been arrested. When the war was over, the Union saved, and the curse of slavery gone forever, there came a season of contentment and of lassitude. A nation which had surmounted such dangers seemed to have nothing more to fear. Those who had fought with tongue and pen and rifle, might now rest on their laurels. After long-continued strain and effort, the wearied nerve and muscle sought repose. It was repose from political warfare only. For the end of the war coincided with the opening of a time of swift material growth and abounding material prosperity, in which industry and the development of the West absorbed more and more of the energy of the people. Hence a neglect of the details of politics by the better class of voters such as had never been seen before. Later years have brought a revival of interest in public affairs, and especially in the management of cities. There is more speaking and writing and thinking, practical and definite thinking, upon the principles of government than at any previous epoch. Good citizens are beginning to put their hands to the machinery of government; and those who do so are, more largely than formerly, young men, who have not contracted the bad habits which the practice of politics engendered among many of their elders, and who will in a few years have become an even more potent force than they are now.[4] If the path to Congress and the state legislatures and the higher municipal offices were cleared of the stumbling blocks and dirt heaps which now encumber it, cunningly placed there by the professional politicians, a great change would soon pass upon the composition of legislative bodies, and a new spirit be felt in the management of state and municipal as well as of national affairs.

[4] This seems to be even more true in 1914 than it was when first written in 1894.

C H A P T E R   5 9

Party Organizations

The Americans are, to use their favourite expression, a highly executive people, with a greater ingenuity in inventing means, and a greater promptitude in adapting means to an end, than any European race. Nowhere are large undertakings organized so skilfully; nowhere is there so much order with so much complexity; nowhere such quickness in correcting a suddenly discovered defect, in supplying a suddenly arisen demand.

Government by popular vote, both local and national, is older in America than in continental Europe. It is far more complete than even in England. It deals with larger masses of men. Its methods have engaged a greater share of attention, enlisted more inventive skill in their service, than anywhere else in the world. They have therefore become more elaborate and, so far as mere mechanism goes, more perfect than elsewhere.

The greatest discovery ever made in the art of war was when men began to perceive that organization and discipline count for more than numbers. This discovery gave the Spartan infantry a long career of victory in Greece, and the Swiss infantry a not less brilliant renown in the later Middle Ages. The Americans made a similar discovery in politics between 1820 and 1840. By degrees, for even in America great truths do not burst full-grown upon the world, it was perceived that the victories of the ballot box, no less than of the sword, must be won by the cohesion and disciplined docility of the troops, and that these merits can only be secured by skilful organization and long-continued training. Both parties flung themselves into the task, and the result has been an extremely complicated system of party machinery, firm yet flexible, delicate yet quickly set up and capable of working well in the roughest communities.[1] Strong necessity, long practice, and the fierce

[1] Since the earlier editions of this book appeared, a careful and instructive study of U.S. political party machinery has been published by M. Ostrogorski in a work entitled *Democracy and the Organization of Political Parties*.

749

competition of the two great parties, have enabled this executive people to surpass itself in the sphere of electioneering politics. Yet the principles are so simple that it will be the narrator's fault if they are not understood.

One preliminary word upon the object of a party organization. To a European politician, by which I mean one who knows politics but does not know America, the aims of a party organization, be it local or general, seem to be four in number:

Union—to keep the party together and prevent it from wasting its strength by dissensions and schisms

Recruiting—to bring in new voters, e.g., immigrants when they obtain citizenship, young men as they reach the age of suffrage, newcomers, or residents hitherto indifferent or hostile

Enthusiasm—to excite the voters by the sympathy of numbers, and the sense of a common purpose, rousing them by speeches or literature

Instruction—to give the voters some knowledge of the political issues they have to decide, to inform them of the virtues of their leaders, and the crimes of their opponents

These aims, or at least the first three of them, are pursued by the party organizations of America with eminent success. But they are less important than a fifth object which has been little regarded in Europe, though in America it is the mainspring of the whole mechanism. This is the selection of party candidates; and it is important not only because the elective places are far more numerous than in any European country, but because they are tenable for short terms, so that elections frequently recur. Since the parties, having of late had few really distinctive principles, and therefore no well-defined aims in the direction of legislation or administration, exist practically for the sake of filling certain offices, and carrying on the machinery of government, the choice of those members of the party whom the party is to reward, and who are to strengthen it by the winning of the offices, becomes a main end of its being.

There are three ways by which in self-governing countries candidates may be brought before electors. One is for the candidate to offer himself, appealing to his fellow citizens on the strength of his personal merits, or family connections, or wealth, or local influence. This was the practice in most British constituencies till our own time; and seems to be the practice over parliamentary Europe still. It was not uncommon in the Southern states before the Civil War. Another is for a group or junto of influential men to put a candidate forward, intriguing secretly for him or openly recommending him to the electors. This also largely prevailed in England, where, in counties, four or five of the chief landowners used to agree as to the one of themselves who should stand for the county, or perhaps chose the eldest son of a duke or marquis as the person whom rank designated.[2] So in Scotch boroughs a knot of active bailies and other citizens combined to bring out a candidate, but generally kept their action secret, for "the clique" was always a term of reproach. The practice is common in France now, where the committees of each party recommend a candidate.

The third system is that in which the candidate is chosen neither by himself nor by the self-elected group, but by the people themselves, i.e., by the members of a party, whether assembled in mass or acting through representatives chosen for the purpose. This plan offers several advantages. It promises to secure a good candidate, because presumably the people will choose a suitable man. It encourages the candidate, by giving him the weight of party support, and therefore tends to induce good men to come forward. It secures the union of the party, because a previous vote has determined that the candidate is the man whom the majority prefer, and the minority are therefore likely, having had their say and been fairly outvoted, to fall into line and support him. This is the system which now prevails from Maine to California, and is indeed the keystone of transatlantic politics. But there is a further reason for it than those I have mentioned.

That no American dreams of offering himself for a post unless he has been chosen by his party, or some section thereof, is due not to the fact that few persons have the local preeminence which the social conditions of Europe bestow on the leading landowners of a neighbourhood, or on some great merchants or employers in a town, nor again to the modesty which makes an Englishman hesitate to appear as a candidate for Parliament until he has got up a requisition to himself to stand, but to the notion that the popular mind and will are and must be all in all, that the people must not only create the office-bearer by their votes, but even designate the persons for whom votes may be given. For a man to put himself before the voters is deemed presumptuous, because an encroachment on their right to say whom they will even so much as consider. The theory of popular sovereignty requires that the ruling majority must name its own standard-bearers and servants, the candidates, must define its own platform, must in every way express its own mind and will. Were it to leave these matters to the initiative of candidates offering themselves, or candidates put forward by

---

[2] Thus in Mr. Disraeli's novel of *Tancred* the county member, a man of good birth and large estates offers to retire in order to make room for the oldest son of the duke when he comes of age. This would not happen nowadays, unless of course the duke were a party leader, and the county member desired to be rewarded by a peerage.

an unauthorized clique, it would subject itself to them, would be passive instead of active, would cease to be worshipped as the source of power. A system for selecting candidates is therefore not a mere contrivance for preventing party dissensions, but an essential feature of matured democracy.

It was not however till democracy came to maturity that the system was perfected. As far back as the middle of the eighteenth century it was the custom in Massachusetts, and probably in other colonies, for a coterie of leading citizens to put forward candidates for the offices of the town or colony, and their nominations, although clothed with no authority but that of the individuals making them, were generally accepted. This lasted on after the Revolution, for the structure of society still retained a certain aristocratic quality. Clubs sprang up which, especially in New York State, became the organs of groups and parties, brought out candidates, and conducted election campaigns; while in New England the clergy and the men of substance continued to act as leaders. Presently, as the democratic spirit grew, and people would no longer acquiesce in self-appointed chiefs, the legislatures began to be recognized as the bodies to make nominations for the higher federal and state offices. Each party in Congress nominated the candidate to be run for the presidency, each party in a state legislature the candidate for governor, and often for other posts also. This lasted during the first two or three decades of the nineteenth century, till the electoral suffrage began to be generally lowered, and a generation which had imbibed Jeffersonian principles had come to manhood, a generation so filled with the spirit of democratic equality that it would recognize neither the natural leaders whom social position and superior intelligence indicated, nor the official leadership of legislative bodies. As party struggles grew more bitter, a party organization became necessary, which better satisfied the claims of petty local leaders, which knit the voters in each district together and concentrated their efforts, while it expressed the absolute equality of all voters, and the right of each to share in determining his candidate and his party platform. The building up of this new organization was completed for the Democratic party about the year 1835, for the Whig party not till some years later. When the Republican party arose about 1854, it reproduced so closely, or developed on lines so similar, the methods which experience had approved, that the differences between the systems of the two great parties are now unimportant, and may be disregarded in the sketch I have to give.

The essential feature of the system is that it is from bottom to top strictly representative. This is because it has power, and power can flow only from the people. An organization which exists, like the political associations of Britain, almost entirely for the sake of canvassing, conducting registration, diffusing literature, getting up courses of lectures, holding meetings and passing resolutions, has little or no power. Its object is to excite, or to persuade, or to manage such business as the defective registration system of the country leaves to be fulfilled by voluntary agencies. So too in America the committees or leagues which undertake to create or stimulate opinion have no power, and need not be strictly representative. But when an organization which the party is in the habit of obeying, chooses a party candidate, it exerts power, power often of the highest import, because it practically narrows the choice of a party, that is, of about a half of the people, to one particular person out of the many for whom they might be inclined to vote.[3] Such power would not be yielded to any but a representative body, and it is yielded to the bodies I shall describe because they are, at least in theory, representative, and are therefore deemed to have the weight of the people behind them.

[3] The rapid change in the practice of England in this point is a curious symptom of the progress of democratic ideas and usages there. As late as the general elections of 1868 and 1874, nearly all candidates offered themselves to the constituency, though some professed to do so in pursuance of requisitions emanating from the electors. In 1880 many—I think most—Liberal candidates in boroughs, and some in counties, were chosen by the local party associations, and appealed to the Liberal electors on the ground of having been so chosen. In 1885 and at every subsequent election, all or nearly all new Liberal candidates were so chosen, and a man offering himself against the nominee of the association was denounced as an interloper and traitor to the party. The same process has been going on in the Tory party, though more slowly. The influence of the locally wealthy, and also that of the central party office, remains somewhat greater among the Tories, but in course of time choice by representative associations will doubtless become the rule. This subject has been excellently treated in Mr. A. L. Lowell's *Government of England,* which see.

The main difference which still exists between British and American practice is that in Britain the sitting member is always understood to have a presumptive claim to be adopted as the party candidate. Unless he has become personally unpopular, or has failed to support his party, he is almost certain to be renominated, whereas in the United States no such presumptive claim is recognized.

CHAPTER 60

The Machine

The organization of an American party consists of two distinct, but intimately connected, sets of bodies, the one permanent, the other temporary. The function of the one is to manage party business, of the other to nominate party candidates.[1]

The first of these is a system of managing committees. In some states every election district has such a committee, whose functions cover the political work of the district. Thus in country places there is a township committee, in cities a ward committee. There is a committee for every city, for every district, and for every county. In other states it is only the larger areas, cities, counties, and congressional or state assembly districts that have committees. There is, of course, a committee for each state, with a general supervision of such political work as has to be done in the state as a whole. There is a national committee for the political business of the party in the Union as a whole, and especially for the presidential contest.[2] The whole country is covered by this network of committees, each with a sphere of action corresponding to some constituency or local election area, so that the proper function of a city committee, for instance, is to attend to elections for city offices, of a ward committee to elections for ward offices, of a district committee to elections for district offices. Of course the city committee, while supervising the general conduct of city elections, looks to each ward organization to give special attention to the elections in its own ward; and the state committee will in state elections expect similar help

---

[1] The system described in this chapter has been recently much modified, but as no new system has yet taken its place over the whole country, it is best to let the chapter stand, while adding a note at the end.

[2] Within the state committees and national committee there is almost always a small executive committee in practical control.

754

from, and be entitled to issue directions to, all bodies acting for the minor areas—districts, counties, townships, cities, and wards—comprised in the state. The smaller local committees are in fact autonomous for their special local purposes, but subordinate in so far as they serve the larger purposes common to the whole party. The ordinary business of these committees is to raise and apply funds for election purposes and for political agitation generally, to organize meetings when necessary, to prepare lists of voters, to disseminate political tracts and other information, to look after the press, to attend to the admission of immigrants as citizens and their enrolment on the party lists.[3] At election times they have also to superintend the canvass, to procure and distribute tickets at the polls (unless this is, under recent legislation, done by a public authority), to allot money for various election services, to see that voters are brought up to the poll; but they are often aided, or virtually superseded, in this work by "campaign committees" specially created for the occasion. Finally, they have to convoke at the proper times those nominating assemblies which form the other parallel but distinct half of the party organization.

These committees are permanent bodies, that is to say, they are always in existence and capable of being called into activity at short notice. They are reappointed annually by the primary (hereinafter described) or convention (as the case may be) for their local area, and of course their composition may be completely changed on a reappointment. In practice it is but little changed, the same men continuing to serve year after year, because they hold the strings in their hands, because they know most and care most about the party business. In particular, the chairman is apt to be practically a permanent official, and (if the committee be one for a populous area) a powerful and important official, who has large sums to disburse and quite an army of workers under his orders. The chairmanship of the organizing committee of the county and city of New York, for instance, is a post of great responsibility and influence, in which high executive gifts find a worthy sphere for their exercise.

One function and one only—besides that of adopting platforms—is beyond the competence of these committees—the choice of candidates. That belongs to the other and parallel division of the party organization, the nominating assemblies.

Every election district, by which I mean every local area or constituency

---

[3] The business of registration is undertaken by the public authority for the locality, instead of being, as in England, partially left to the action of the individual citizen or of the parties.

which chooses a person for any office or post, administrative, legislative, or judicial, has a party meeting to select the party candidate for that office. This is called nominating. If the district is not subdivided, i.e., does not contain any lesser districts, its meeting is called a primary. A primary has two duties. One is to select the candidates for its own local district offices. Thus in the country a township primary[4] nominates the candidates for township offices, in a city a ward primary nominates those for ward offices (if any). The other duty is to elect delegates to the nominating meetings of larger areas, such as the county or congressional district in which the township is situated, or the city to which the ward belongs. The primary is composed of all the party voters resident within the bounds of the township or ward. They are not too numerous, for in practice the majority do not attend, to meet in one room, and they are assumed to be all alike interested. But as the party voters in such a large area as a county, congressional district, or city, are too numerous to be able to meet and deliberate in one room, they must act through representatives, and entrust the choice of candidates for office to a body called a nominating convention.[5] This body is composed of delegates from all the primaries within its limits, chosen at those primaries for the sole purpose of sitting in the convention and of there selecting the candidates.

Sometimes a convention of this kind has itself to choose delegates to proceed to a still higher convention for a larger area. The greatest of all nominating bodies, that which is called the national convention and nominates the party candidate for the presidency, is entirely composed of delegates from other conventions, no primary being directly represented in it. As a rule, however, there are only two sets of nominating authorities, the primary which selects candidates for its own petty offices, the convention composed of the delegates from all the primaries in the local circumscriptions of the district for which the convention acts.

A primary, of course, sends delegates to a number of different conventions, because its area, let us say the township or ward, is included in a number of different election districts, each of which has its own convention. Thus the same primary will in a city choose delegates to at least the following conventions, and probably to one or two others:[6] (a) To the city convention,

---

[4] I take township and ward as examples, but in parts of the country where the township is not the unit of local government (see Chapter 48 *ante*), the local unit, whatever it is, must be substituted.

[5] Sometimes, however, a primary is held for a whole congressional district or city. As to recent changes in the primary system, see note at end of this chapter. All that is said here must be taken as subject to what is said hereafter regarding the new statutory primaries created in many states.

[6] There may be also a county convention for county offices, and a judicial district convention for judgeships, but in a large city or county the county convention delegates may also be delegates

which nominates the mayor and other city officers; (*b*) to the assembly district convention, which nominates candidates for the lower house of the state legislature; (*c*) to the senatorial district convention, which nominates candidates for the state senate; (*d*) to the congressional district convention, which nominates candidates for Congress; (*e*) to the state convention, which nominates candidates for the governorship and other state offices. Sometimes, however, the nominating body for an assembly district is a primary and not a convention. In New York City the assembly district is the unit, and each of the thirty districts has its primary.

This seems complex: but it is a reflection of the complexity of government, there being everywhere three authorities, federal, state, and local (this last further subdivided), covering the same ground, yet the two former quite independent of one another, and the third for many purposes distinct from the second.

The course of business is as follows. A township or ward primary is summoned by the local party managing committee, who fix the hour and place of meeting, or if there be not such a committee, then by some permanent officer of the organization in manner prescribed by the bye-laws. A primary for a larger area is usually summoned by the county committee. If candidates have to be chosen for local offices, various names are submitted and either accepted without a division or put to the vote, the person who gets most votes being declared chosen to be the party candidate. He is said to have received the party nomination. The selection of delegates to the various conventions is conducted in the same way. The local committee has usually prepared beforehand a list of names of persons to be chosen to serve as delegates, but any voter present may bring forward other names. All names, if not accepted by general consent, are then voted on. At the close of the proceedings the chairman signs the list of delegates chosen to the approaching convention or conventions, if more than one, and adjourns the meeting *sine die*.

The delegates so chosen proceed in due course to their respective conventions, which are usually held a few days after the primaries, and a somewhat longer period before the elections for offices.[7] The convention is summoned by the managing committee for the district it exists for, and

---

to the congressional convention, perhaps also to the state assembly district and senatorial district conventions.

[7] In the case of elections to the presidency and to the governorship of a state the interval between the nominating convention and the election is much longer—in the former case nearly four months.

The procedure described here is that of state and local conventions. For national nominating conventions, see Chapter 69 *post*.

when a sufficient number of delegates are present, someone proposes a temporary chairman, or the delegate appointed for the purpose by the committee of the district for which the convention is being held "calls the meeting to order" as temporary chairman. This person names a committee on credentials, which forthwith examines the credentials presented by the delegates from the primaries, and admits those whom it deems duly accredited. Then a permanent chairman is proposed and placed in the chair, and the convention is held to be "organized," i.e., duly constituted. The managing committee have almost always arranged beforehand who shall be proposed as candidates for the party nominations, and their nominees are usually adopted. However, any delegate may propose any person he thinks fit, being a recognized member of the party, and carry him on a vote if he can. The person adopted by a majority of delegates' votes becomes the party candidate, and is said to have "received the nomination." The convention sometimes, but not always, also amuses itself by passing resolutions expressive of its political sentiments; or if it is a state convention or a national convention, it adopts a platform, touching on, or purporting to deal with, the main questions of the day. It then, having fulfilled its mission, adjourns *sine die*, and the rest of the election business falls to the managing committee. It must be remembered that primaries and conventions, unlike the local party associations of England, are convoked but once, make their nominations, and vanish. They are swans which sing their one song and die.

The national convention held every fourth year before a presidential election needs a fuller description, which I shall give presently. Meantime three features of the system just outlined may be adverted to.

Every voter belonging to the party in the local area for which the primary is held, is presumably entitled to appear and vote in it. In rural districts, where everybody knows everybody else, there is no difficulty about admission, for if a Democrat came into a Republican primary, or a Republican from North Adams tried to vote in the Republican primary of Lafayetteville, he would be recognized as an intruder and expelled. But in cities where people do not know their neighbours by headmark, it becomes necessary to have regular lists of the party voters entitled to a voice in the primary. These are made up by the local committee, which may exclude persons whom, though they call themselves Republicans (or Democrats, as the case may be), it deems not loyal members of the party. The usual test is, Did the claimant vote the party ticket at the last important election, generally the presidential election, or that for the state governorship? If he did not, he may be excluded. Sometimes, however, the local rules of the party require everyone admitted to the list of party voters to be admitted by the votes of the existing members, who may reject him at their pleasure, and also exact from each member two pledges, to obey the local committee, and to support the party nominations, the breach of either pledge being punishable by expulsion. In many primaries voters supposed to be disagreeably independent are kept out either by the votes of the existing members or by the application of these strict tests. Thus it happens that three-fourths or even four-fifths of the party voters in a primary area may not be on the list and entitled to raise their voice in the primary for the selection of candidates or delegates. Another regulation, restricting nominations to those who are enrolled members of the regular organization, makes persons so kept off the list ineligible as party candidates.

Every member of a nominating meeting, be it a primary or a convention of delegates, is deemed to be bound by the vote of the majority to support the candidate whom the majority select, whether or no an express pledge to that effect has been given. And in the case of a convention, a delegate is generally held to bind those whom he represents, i.e., the voters at the primary which sent him. Of course no compulsion is possible, but long usage and an idea of fair play have created a sentiment of honour (so-called) and party loyalty strong enough, with most people and in all but extreme cases, to secure for the party's candidate the support of the whole party organization in the district.[8] It is felt that the party must be kept together, and that he who has come into the nominating meeting hoping to carry his own candidate must abide by the decision of the majority. The vote of a majority has a sacredness in America not yet reached in Europe.

As respects the freedom left to delegates to vote at their own pleasure or under the instructions of their primary, and to vote individually or as a solid body, the practice is not uniform. Sometimes they are sent up to the nominating convention without instructions, even without the obligation to "go solid." sometimes they are expressly directed, or it is distinctly understood by them and by the primary, that they are to support the claims of a particular person to be selected as candidate, or that they are at any rate to vote all together for one person. Occasionally they are even given a list arranged in order of preference, and told to vote for A. B., failing him for C. D., failing him for E. F., these being persons whose names have

---

[8] The obligation is however much less strict in the case of municipal elections, in which party considerations sometimes count for little.

already been mentioned as probable candidates for the nomination. This, however, would only happen in the case of the greater offices, such as those of member of Congress or governor of a state. The point is in practice less important than it seems, because in most cases, whether there be any specific and avowed instruction or not, it is well settled beforehand by those who manage the choice of delegates what candidate any set of delegates are to support, or at least whose lead they are to follow in the nominating convention.

Note further how complex is the machinery needed to enable the party to concentrate its force in support of its candidates for all these places, and how large the number of persons constituting the machinery. Three sets of offices, municipal or county, state, federal, have to be filled; three different sets of nominating bodies are therefore needed. If we add together all the members of all the conventions included in these three sets, the number of persons needed to serve as delegates will be found to reach a high total, even if some of them serve in more than one convention. Men whose time is valuable will refuse the post of delegate, gladly leaving to others who desire it the duty of selecting candidates for offices to which they seldom themselves aspire. However, as we shall see, such men are but rarely permitted to become delegates, even when they desire the function.

"Why these tedious details?" the European reader may exclaim. "Of what consequence can they be compared to the Constitution and laws of the country?" Patience! These details have more significance and make more difference to the working of the government than many of the provisions of the Constitution itself. The mariner feels the trade winds which sweep over the surface of the Pacific and does not perceive the coral insects which are at work beneath its waves, but it is by the labour of these insects that islands grow, and reefs are built upon which ships perish.

Note on Recent Legislation Regarding Primaries

Soon after 1890 the sins of the machine, and the abuse of the system of nomination by primaries and conventions described in this and succeeding chapters, led to an effort to cure those abuses and to secure the ordinary citizen in his freedom of selecting candidates for office by bringing party nominations under the authority of the law and surrounding them with safeguards similar to those which surround elections. Thus statutes have been enacted in nearly all the states which deal to a greater or less extent with the times and manner of holding primary meetings for the nomination of party candidates for office and of delegates for party conventions.

Oklahoma, the latest of the new states of the Union, entered the Union with a constitution containing four important constitutional provisions on the subject of primary elections. (See these in Appendix to Vol. I.)

The regulations imposed upon the holding of these party meetings differ widely in the several states. They range from minor provisions concerning the dates of primaries, the preparation of the ballots, and the regularization of the methods of counting, up to sweeping and drastic measures, such as are found in Oregon and Wisconson, for instance, requiring the nomination of nearly all party candidates (including United States senators) at public primaries conducted under official supervision.

It would be impossible to give within moderate compass a full account of these statutes for they vary from state to state and are often complicated in their provisions. Moreover, they are frequently changed. All that can be done here is to summarize the tendencies they disclose, and to indicate briefly those features in the system of party nomination which are now being made subject to legislative interference.

Many laws fix the dates on which primaries should be held for all the political parties and also prescribe conditions as to the times at which the primaries and conventions shall be summoned.

The determination of who may vote at a primary and who are to be deemed legitimate and regular members of a particular party entitled to vote at its primaries is a vexed question on which no uniformity of practice exists. Broadly speaking there are two systems. Under the "open primary" plan the use of the so-called "Australian" secret ballot enables the voter to vote a party primary ticket without declaring to which party he belongs, though, to prevent him from voting for more than one party at a primary, it is generally provided that ballots cast for any person as candidate for a nomination are to be counted for that person only as a candidate of the party upon whose ticket his name is written. In Wisconsin, for instance, the primary is secret, and the voter may cast his ballot as he pleases. Under the "closed primary" plan the voter is subjected to some test determining his party affiliation, and can vote only for the candidates of that party. In some states he is required to enrol himself as a member of some particular party if he wishes to take part in the proceedings of the primary. So in California, under a statute of 1909, the voter must declare the political party with which he intends to affiliate, otherwise he cannot vote at the primary; and it is provided that at the primary he shall receive the ballot of that party and of no other. So in Minnesota the voter must declare his allegiance before he receives the party ballot. In some states he must even announce his intention to support the party at the election next following; in some he must bind himself to support the persons nominated at the primary (so in Louisiana and Texas). Other states allow the authorities of the party themselves to fix the test of membership in a party which shall qualify the person to cast a primary vote.

Many states have a separate official ballot for each party at the primary, but others are content to regulate the colour, size, etc., of the party ballot.

Those states which require all parties to hold their primaries on the same day generally require them to use the same polling place and official ballot boxes.

The conduct of primaries is now generally placed under the supervision of regular officials being the same as those who conduct the elections: and the hours of opening and closing the primary, as well as the particular method of voting at it are prescribed.

The official expenses of primaries are borne by the same public authority which bears the general election expenses.

For the prevention of corruption and other offences at primaries the usual precautions against bribery and fraudulent voting at elections are prescribed.

The extent to which the primaries are used for the nomination of candidates varies from state to state. In general it is only delegates to conventions and members of political committees who are required to be selected by ballot. Sometimes it is left to the local committee of the party to determine whether or not the primary shall be used for nomination to local offices. The laws of Wisconsin, Oregon, Nebraska, and several other states require the primary to be used for the nomination of United States senators, who, of course, have to be elected by the legislature, and of all other officers except presidential electors, school superintendents and certain judicial persons.

Many legal questions have arisen and many decisions have been delivered upon these enactments when it has been alleged that provisions of a particular primary law are unconstitutional.

The further extension of the principle of legislative control over the operations of political parties has become a leading question in the politics of not a few states. Oregon, Wisconsin, Minnesota, and Oklahoma might seem to have gone as far as it is possible to go in this direction, but, as has already been observed, many states are continuing to make experiments in the matter. A succinct account of the condition of legislation on the subject in 1908 may be found in a Report of the Connecticut State Commissioners of January 1909. In 1914 every state had laws under which some candidates were nominated in direct primaries, and a majority had established statewide direct primaries applicable to all or nearly all offices except (in a few cases) judgeships.

Regarding the practical value of these primary laws as a means of relieving the good average citizen from the yoke of party machines, opinion has not yet settled itself. The new laws were disliked, and in some states opposed, by the professional politicians; and this naturally confirmed the reformers in their expectation of good results. In some states, however, it is alleged that the professionals have succeeded in manipulating the new system so as practically to reestablish their own control, although, of course, at the cost of more trouble to themselves than they had previously to take. In other states this does not seem to have happened; and the voters think themselves more free than formerly. The extreme complexity of some primary laws, and the long and elaborately constructed ballot placed before the voter, do give ground for the apprehension that the professional politicians may lay hold of and work a system which, in some of its forms, no one but an expert can master. And it is also feared that the expense of working primaries, which are practically another set of elections, may prove a heavy burden both on the public revenue, so far as it is chargeable thereon, and upon the candidates, who will have to spend money in a good many ways, some perhaps illegitimate. As President Lowell says (*Public Opinion and Popular Government,* p. 150): "Under the usual system of direct primaries a special organization to solicit the nomination is normally a necessity, even when the only question is between the rival ambitions of individuals. Such an organization is very expensive and can hardly be undertaken unless the candidate or his friends are prepared to spend money freely. The contests for nomination at the direct primaries in Wisconsin in 1909 are said to have cost the candidates $802,659."

That provision of many of these laws which requires a voter at a primary to declare himself beforehand a member of the political party, or even binds him to support the primary's nominee, seems in itself objectionable, but has in some states been thought needed as a protection against tricks. May it not, however, be thought that such a provision unduly limits the voter's freedom? Why should the citizen be obliged to put himself into a sheep pen and feel himself bound legally, or, if not legally, yet to some extent morally, to support a particular party candidate at a future election? Who can tell what persons may be selected, or what further light may be thrown on the records of those persons, or what aspect the issues will have assumed on the following day?

Apart, however, from this objection, Europeans whose habit of regarding party organization as a purely voluntary matter and parties as fluid and changing, not solid and permanent entities, makes them averse to any legal recognition of parties as concrete and authoritative bodies existing within the community, are disposed to ask whether these laws may not be a sort of counsel of despair, an abandonment by the good citizens of their old hope of extinguishing or superseding the machine altogether by the voluntary and unfettered action of the voters themselves. Were those citizens who have no interest except in good government, those who value their party only because it is a means of giving effect to their views of the true needs and aims of the nation, to take hold themselves, and by their own constant presence and activity make meetings for the nomination of candidates serve their proper purpose of selecting those men whom they feel to be their best men, this recourse to state regulation and supervision might be dispensed with. In Britain, however, parties are so much less organized and so much less powerful as organizations than they are in the United States that the reflections which occur to an English mind may be deemed inapplicable to American conditions; and it is plain that in many states the reformers hold these primary laws to be a long step toward the overthrow of the machine and of the evils associated with its action.

Pending further experience of the working of these measures, the variety of which gives ground for hope that one form may ultimately approve itself as the best, all that it seems safe to say is that the rapid adoption by one state after another of the plan of invoking the law to restore to voters their freedom in the choice of candidates shows that the evils of the old system have become widely recognized, and that the spirit of reform, now thoroughly awakened, will doubtless persist until some solid and lasting improvements have been secured.

C H A P T E R   6 1

What the Machine Has to Do

The system I have described is simple in principle, and would be simple in working if applied in a European country where elective offices are few. The complexity which makes it puzzle many Americans, and bewilder all Europeans, arises from the extraordinary number of elections to which it is applied, and from the way in which the conventions for different election districts cross and overlap one another. A few instances may serve to convey to the reader some impression of this profusion of elections and intricacy of nominating machinery.

In Europe a citizen rarely votes more than twice or thrice a year, sometimes less often, and usually for only one person at a time. Thus in England any householder, say at Manchester or Liverpool, votes once a year for a town councillor (if there is a contest in his ward); once in four (on an average) for a member of the House of Commons.[1] Allowing for the frequent cases in which there is no municipal contest in his ward, he will not on an average vote more than one and a half times each year. It is much the same in Scotland, nor do elections seem to be more frequent in France, Germany, or Italy, or even perhaps in Switzerland.

In the United States, however, the number of elective offices is so enormous and the terms of office usually so short that the voter is not only very frequently called upon to go to the polls, but has a very large number of candidates placed before him from among whom he must choose those whom he prefers.[2] Moreover, besides the voting at the regular election, he

---

[1] He may also vote once a year for guardians of the poor, but this office is usually so little sought that the election excites slight interest and comparatively few persons vote. If he goes to a vestry meeting he may, in places where there is a select vestry, vote for its members.

[2] Speaking generally the ordinary citizen has to vote for five sets of offices, viz., federal, state, district, county, city, the federal elections coming once in two years (Congress) and once in four

ought also to vote at primaries, i.e., to vote to select the candidates from among whom he is subsequently to choose those whom he desires to have as officers; while in many states the law now fixes the day and manner in which he ought to do so. And as if this was not burden enough, he has also, in a good many states, to vote also on a number of legislative propositions which the law requires to be submitted to him for his decision instead of their being left to state legislatures or city councils. As Professor Beard well observes:[3]

> The glaring absurdity of this system can best be illustrated by concrete examples, which bring home the details of the voters' task. I have before me the ballot for the thirteenth and thirty-fourth wards of the sixth congressional district of Chicago in 1906. It is two feet and two inches by eighteen and one-half inches; and it contains 334 names distributed with more or less evenness as candidates for the following offices:

> State treasurer, state superintendent of public instruction, trustees of the University of Illinois, representatives in Congress, state senator, representatives in the state Assembly, sheriff, county treasurer, county clerk, clerk of the probate court, clerk of the criminal court, clerk of the circuit court, county superintendent of schools, judge of the county court, judge of the probate court, members of the board of assessors, member of the board of review, president of the board of county commissioners, county commissioners (ten to be elected on general ticket), trustees of the sanitary district of Chicago (three to be elected), clerk of the municipal court, bailiff of the municipal court, chief justice of the municipal court, judges of the municipal court (nine to be elected), judges of the municipal court for the four-year term (nine to be elected), judges of the municipal court for the two-year term (nine to be elected).

> In Sioux City, Iowa, the following nine elections were held in 1908:

> January 21. Special election on the commission plan of government.
> February 24. City primary. Regular biennial election. Candidates nominated for eighteen city offices.
> March 9. School election. Regular annual. Two directors and a school treasurer

---

(presidential election) and the others at longer or shorter (usually short) intervals according to the laws of the particular state. Even a single city election may present a very complicated problem to the voter.

[3] *Political Science Quarterly,* Vol. XXIV. p. 598. Professor Beard's article entitled *The Ballot's Burden* contains many valuable facts and remarks on the way in which the complexity of nominating and election machinery destroys that freedom of the citizen which it was originally meant to secure.

elected. A tax proposition to appropriate $60,000 for a school-house fund also voted on.

March 30. City election. Regular biennial. Eight officers and a council of ten elected, each voter voting for eleven candidates.

May 28. Special election on traction franchise. Franchise defeated.

June 2. Regular biennial election. Candidates nominated for twenty-eight different national, state and local offices.

August 11. Second special election on traction franchise.

November 3. General election. Regular. Forty-three officials voted for, including thirteen presidential electors, twelve state officers, one congressman, one state senator, two state representatives, nine county and five township officers. Amendment to state constitution also voted on.

November 17. Special election on the Perry Creek and the Bacon Creek conduit and the gas franchise.

Surely the people of the United States believe, with the inhabitants of Lilliput, "that the common size of human understandings is fitted to some station or other, and that Providence never intended to make the management of public affairs a mystery."

It is not only the elections that bother us. The primaries, whether under the convention or direct nomination systems are, if possible, more complicated; and, as everybody knows, whoever controls the primaries controls the strategic point in our whole election system. If all of the voters, moved by the appeals of the good government people and stung by the taunts of the bosses, were to appear at the primaries of their parties, they would not be able to change the actual operation of the nomination system; for the preliminary work of the nominations, owing to the intricacies of the process, must be done by the experts—a fact too often overlooked by those who advocate direct nominations as a cure for boss rule. Within the cycle of four years, every party voter in every election district in New York City, with minor variations, must vote from one to four times for the following party candidates:

(1) Members of the city committee; (2) members of the county committee; (3) members of the assembly district committee; (4) delegates to an aldermanic district convention; (5) delegates to a municipal court district convention; (6) delegates to a borough convention; (7) delegates to a city convention; (8) delegates to a county convention; (9) delegates to a judicial district convention; (10) delegates to an assembly district convention; (11) delegates to a senatorial district convention; (12) delegates to a congressional district convention; (13) delegates to an assembly district convention.

The best way to demonstrate the colossal task set before the bewildered New York voter is to describe an actual primary ballot—the Democratic ballot for the thirty-second assembly district. It is eight and one-half inches by two feet four inches. It contains the names of 835 candidates: 417 for members of the county general committee, 104 for delegates to the county convention, 40 for delegates to the first district municipal court convention, 65 for delegates to the second district municipal court convention, 104 for delegates to the thirty-second assembly district convention and 105 for delegates to the thirty-fourth, thirty-fifth and thirty-sixth aldermanic district conventions.

Let us now take another illustration from Massachusetts, and regard the system from another side by observing how many sets of delegates a primary will have to send to the several nominating conventions which cover the local area to which the primary belongs.[4]

A Massachusetts primary will choose the following sets of persons, including committee-men, candidates, and delegates:

1. Ward and city committees in cities, and town committees in towns.[5]
2. In cities, candidates for common council and board of aldermen, so in towns, candidates for town officers, *i.e.* selectmen, school committee, overseers of poor, town clerk and treasurer, assessors of taxes, etc.
3. In cities, delegates to a convention to nominate city officers.
4. Delegates to a convention to nominate county officers.
5. Candidates for representatives to State legislature, or delegates to a convention to nominate the same.
6. Delegates to a convention for nominating candidates for State Senate.
7. Delegates to a convention for nominating candidates for State Governor's council.
8. Delegates to a convention for nominating candidates for State offices (*e.g.* Governor, Lieutenant-Governor, etc.).

The above are annual. Then every two years—

9. Delegates to a congressional district convention for nominating candidates for representatives to Congress.

Then every four years—

10. Delegates to a district convention for nominating other delegates (corresponding to the members of Congress) to the national Presidential Convention of the party; and

---

[4] I owe the following list, and the explanatory note at the end of the volume, to the kindness of a friend in Massachusetts (Mr. G. Bradford of Boston), who has given much attention to the political methods of his country.

[5] A "town" in New England is the unit of rural local government corresponding to the township of the Middle and Western states. See Chapter 48 *ante*.

11. Delegates to a general convention for nominating four delegates at large (corresponding to United States senators) to national Presidential Convention.[6]

In New York City many posts have recently been made appointive, yet at the November elections there were in 1908 eighty-six candidates for the offices to be filled by election. In 1909 when a mayor was to be chosen, there were eighty-one candidates, although the party lists had been so far united that a good many of the candidates on several of these lists were the same. The ballot paper was 3 feet $9\frac{1}{2}$ inches long and 15 inches wide and had eighteen columns of candidates besides a nineteenth in which the voter might place the names, under the respective offices, of the persons he desired to vote for who were not on the printed lists of candidates. So at Chicago in the November election of 1908, there were on the ballot paper (exclusive of the names of presidential electors) the names of 195 candidates, nominated to fill 46 posts in the state and the county, as well as the municipal judgeships, but no other city offices. However, I need not weary the reader with further examples, for the facts above stated are fairly illustrative of what goes on over the whole Union.

It is hard to keep one's head through this mazy whirl of offices, elections, and primaries or nominating conventions. In America itself one finds few ordinary citizens who can state the details of the system, though these are of course familiar to professional politicians.

The first thing that strikes a European who contemplates this organization is the great mass of work it has to do. In Ohio, for instance, there are, if we count in such unpaid offices as are important in the eyes of politicians, on an average more than twenty offices to be filled annually by election. Primaries or conventions have to select candidates for all of these. Managing committees have to organize the primaries, 'run' the conventions, conduct the elections. Here is ample occupation for a class of professional men.

What are the results which one may expect this abundance of offices and elections to produce?

Where the business is that of selecting delegates and, in the particular state, the selection of candidates is made by the older kind of primaries and conventions, it will be hard to find an adequate number of men of any mark or superior intelligence to act as delegates. The bulk will be persons unlikely to possess, still more unlikely to exercise, a careful or independent judgment. The functions of delegate being in the case of most conventions humble and

---

[6] See further the note to this chapter in the Appendix.

uninteresting, because the offices are unattractive to good men, persons whose time is valuable will not, even if they do exist in sufficient numbers, seek it. Hence the best citizens, i.e., the men of position and intelligence, will leave the field open to inferior persons who have any private or personal reason for desiring to become delegates. I do not mean to imply that there is necessarily any evil in this as regards most of the offices, but mention the fact to explain why few men of good social position think of the office of delegate, except to the national convention once in four years, as one of trust or honour.

If on the other hand the new statutory primaries have in the particular state superseded conventions, then the attendance at these primaries and the choice of candidates there is a serious task thrown on the voter for which his knowledge of the persons from whom candidates are to be selected may be quite inadequate. As Professor Beard remarks:

> The direct nomination device will duplicate the present complicated mechanism and render it necessary to have abler experts who understand not only the mysteries of the regular election law but the added mysteries of the primary law as well. . . . The primary law is in most States a booklet of no mean proportions and taken in connection with the ordinary election law is enough to stagger the experienced student to say nothing of the inexperienced voter for whose guidance it is devised.

The number of places to be filled by election being very large, ordinary citizens will find it hard to form an opinion as to the men best qualified for the offices. Their minds will be distracted among the multiplicity of places. In large cities particularly, where people know little about their neighbours, the names of most candidates will be unknown to them, and there will be no materials, except the recommendation of a party organization, available for determining the respective fitness of the candidates put forward by the several parties. Most of the elected officials are poorly paid. Even the governor of a great state may receive no more than $5,000 to $8,000 a year, the lower officials much less. The duties of most offices require no conspicuous ability, but can be discharged by any honest man of good sense and business habits. Hence they will not (unless where they carry large fees or important patronage) be sought by persons of ability and energy, because such persons can do better for themselves in private business; it will be hard to say which of many candidates is the best; the selection will rouse little stir among the people at large.

Those who have had experience of public meetings know that to make them go off well, it is as desirable to have the proceedings prearranged as it is to have a play rehearsed. You must select beforehand not only your chairman, but also your speakers. Your resolutions must be ready framed; you must be prepared to meet the case of an adverse resolution or hostile amendment. This is still more advisable where the meeting is intended to transact some business, instead of merely expressing its opinion; and when certain persons are to be selected for any duty, prearrangement becomes not merely convenient but indispensable in the interests of the meeting itself, and of the business which it has to dispatch. "Does not prearrangement practically curtail the freedom of the meeting?" Certainly it does. But the alternative is confusion and a hasty unconsidered decision. Crowds need to be led; if you do not lead them they will go astray, will follow the most plausible speaker, will break into factions and accomplish nothing. Hence if a primary is to discharge properly its function of selecting candidates for office or a number of delegates to a nominating convention, it is necessary to have a list of candidates or delegates settled beforehand. And for the reasons already given, the more numerous the offices and the delegates, and the less important the duties they have to discharge, so much the more necessary is it to have such lists settled; and so much the more likely to be accepted by those present is the list proposed. On the other hand the new statutory primary intended to secure the freedom of the voter is also so complex a matter that preliminary steps must be taken by experts familiar with the law and practice governing it.

The reasons have already been stated which make the list of candidates put forth by a primary or by a nominating convention carry great weight with the voters. They are the chosen standard-bearers of the party. A European may remark that the citizens are not bound by the nomination; they may still vote for whom they will. If a bad candidate is nominated, he may be passed over. That is easy enough where, as in England, there are only one or two offices to be filled at an election, where these few offices are important enough to excite general interest, and where therefore the candidates are likely to be men of mark. But in America the offices are numerous, they are mostly unimportant, and the candidates are usually obscure. Accordingly guidance is not merely welcome, but essential. Even in England the voters may in large boroughs know little of the names submitted and be puzzled how to cast his vote, and the party as a whole votes for the person who receives the party nomination from the organization authorized to express the party view. Hence the high importance attached to "getting the nomination" which in so many places is equivalent to an election; hence the care bestowed on constructing the nominating machinery;

hence the need for prearranging the lists of delegates to be submitted to the primary, and of candidates to come before the convention.

I have sought in this chapter first to state how the nominating machine is constituted, and what work it has to do, then to suggest some of the consequences which the quantity and nature of that work may be expected to entail. We may now go on to see how in practice the work turns out to be done.

C H A P T E R   6 2

How the Machine Works

Nothing seems fairer or more conformable to the genius of democratic institutions than the system I have described, whereby the choice of party candidates for office is vested in the mass of the party itself. A plan which selects the candidate likely to command the greatest support prevents the dissension and consequent waste of strength which the appearance of rival candidates of the same party involves; while the popular character of that method excludes the dictation of a clique, and recognizes the sovereignty of the people. It is a method simple, uniform, and agreeable throughout to its leading principle.

To understand how it actually works one must distinguish between two kinds of constituencies or voting areas. One kind is to be found in the great cities—places whose population exceeds, speaking roughly, 100,000 souls, of which there were in 1910 fifty in the United States. The other kind includes constituencies in small cities and rural districts. What I have to say will refer chiefly to the Northern states—i.e., the former free states, because the phenomena of the Southern states are still exceptional, owing to the vast population of ignorant Negroes, among whom the whites, or rather the better sort of whites, still stand as an aristocracy.

The tests by which one may try the results of the system of selecting candidates are two. Is the choice of candidates for office really free—i.e., does it represent the unbiased wish and mind of the voters generally? Are the offices filled by men of probity and capacity sufficient for the duties?

In the country generally, i.e., in the rural districts and small cities, both these tests are tolerably well satisfied. It is true that many of the voters do not attend the primaries. The selection of delegates and candidates is left to be made by that section of the population which chiefly interests itself in politics; and in this section local attorneys and office-seekers have much influence. The persons who seek the post of delegate, as well as those who seek office, are seldom the most energetic and intelligent citizens; but that is because these men have something better to do. An observer from Europe who looks to see men of rank and culture holding the same place in state and local government as they do in England, especially rural England, or in Italy, or even in parts of rural France and Switzerland, will be disappointed. But democracies must be democratic. Equality will have its perfect work; and you cannot expect citizens who are pervaded by its spirit to go cap in hand to their richer neighbours begging them to act as delegates, or city or county officials, or congressmen. This much may be said, that although there is in America no difference of rank in the European sense, superior wealth or intelligence does not prejudice a man's candidature, and in most places improves its chances. If such men are not commonly chosen, it is for the same reason which makes them comparatively scarce among the town councillors of English municipalities.

In these primaries[1] and conventions the business is always prearranged— that is to say, the local party committee come prepared with their list of delegates or candidates. This list is usually, but not invariably, accepted, or if serious opposition appears, alterations may be made to disarm it and preserve the unity of the party. The delegates and candidates chosen are generally the members of the local committee, their friends or creatures. Except in very small places, they are rarely the best men. But neither are they the worst. In moderately sized communities men's characters are known, and the presence of a bad man in office brings on his fellow citizens evils which they are not too numerous to feel individually. Hence tolerable nominations are made, the general sentiment of the locality is not outraged; and although the nominating machinery is worked rather in the name of the people than by the people, the people are willing to have it so, knowing that they can interfere if necessary to prevent serious harm.

In large cities the results are different because the circumstances are different. We find there, besides the conditions previously enumerated— viz., numerous offices, frequent elections, universal suffrage, an absence of stimulating issues—three others of great moment:

A vast population of ignorant immigrants;
The leading men all intensely occupied with business;

---

[1] The reference here is to primaries of the older type. Though they are being largely superseded by the newer directly nominating primaries, a knowledge of both systems is still necessary. It was indeed the abuse of the old primaries which led to the statutes creating the new ones.

Communities so large that people know little of one another, and that the interest of each individual in good government is comparatively small.

Anyone can see how these conditions affect the problem. The immigrants are entitled to obtain a vote after three or four years' residence at most (often less), but they are not fit for the suffrage.[2] They know nothing of the institutions of the country, of its statesmen, of its political issues. Those especially who come from Central and Southern Europe bring little knowledge of the methods of free goverment, and from Ireland they used to bring a suspicion of all government. Incompetent to give an intelligent vote, but soon finding that their vote has a value, they fall into the hands of the party organizations, whose officers enrol them in their lists, and undertake to fetch them to the polls. I was long ago taken to watch the process of citizen-making in New York. Droves of squalid men, who looked as if they had just emerged from an emigrant ship, and had perhaps done so only a few weeks before, for the law prescribing a certain term of residence is frequently violated, were brought up to a magistrate by the ward agent of the party which had captured them, declared their allegiance to the United States, and were forthwith placed on the roll.[3] Such a sacrifice of common sense to abstract principles has seldom been made by any country. Nobody pretends that such persons are fit for civic duty, or will be dangerous if kept for a time in pupilage, but neither party will incur the odium of proposing to exclude them. The real reason for admitting them, besides democratic theory, has been either that the locally dominant party expected to gain their votes,[4] or that neither of the parties wished to incur such odium as might attach to those who seemed to be debarring residents from full civic rights. It is an afterthought to argue that they will sooner become good citizens by being immediately made full citizens. A stranger must not presume to say that the Americans have been imprudent, but he may doubt whether the possible ultimate gain compensates the direct and certain danger.

[2] Federal law prescribes a residence of five years as the prerequisite for naturalization, but the laws of not a few Western states enable a vote to be acquired in a shorter term by one who is not a United States citizen. See Chapter 28 *ante*. And in some states, persons who have not completed their five years are often fraudulently naturalized.

[3] Things are better now than they were then, but even now there is no security that the recently arrived immigrant possesses the qualifications required for the giving of an intelligent vote. It is even alleged that many of the immigrants (especially Italians) brought over to be employed on railroad-making and other similar works come under what are virtually contracts to cast their votes in a particular way, and do so cast them, possibly returning to Europe after some months or years, richer by the payment they have received for their votes as well as for their labour.

[4] At one time a speedy admission to citizenship was adopted as an inducement to immigrants, but this motive has ceased to have force in most states.

In these great transatlantic cities, population is far less settled and permanent than in the cities of Europe. In New York, Chicago, St. Louis, Minneapolis, San Francisco, a very small part of the inhabitants are natives of the city, or have resided in it for twenty years. Hence they know but little of one another, or even of those who would in Europe be called the leading men. There are scarcely any old families, families associated with the city,[5] whose name recommends one of their scions to the confidence of his fellow citizens. There are few persons who have had any chance of becoming generally known, except through their wealth; and the wealthy have neither time nor taste for political work. Political work is a bigger and heavier affair than in small communities; hence ordinary citizens cannot attend to it in addition to their regular business. Moreover, the population is so large that an individual citizen feels himself a drop in the ocean. His power of affecting public affairs by his own intervention seems insignificant. His pecuniary loss through overtaxation, or jobbery, or malversation, is trivial in comparison with the trouble of trying to prevent such evils.

As party machinery is in great cities most easily perverted, so the temptation to pervert it is there strongest, because the prizes are great. The offices are well paid, the patronage is large, the opportunities for jobs, commissions on contracts, pickings, and even stealings, are enormous. Hence it is well worth the while of unscrupulous men to gain control of the machinery by which these prizes may be won.[6]

Such men, the professional politicians of the great cities, have two objects in view. One is to seize the local city and county offices. A great city of course controls the county in which it is situate. The other is so to command the local party vote as to make good terms with the party managers of the state, and get from them a share in state offices, together with such legislation as is desired from the state legislature, and similarly to make good terms with the federal party managers, thus securing a share in federal offices, and the means of influencing legislation in Congress. How do the city professionals move towards these objects?

There are two stages in an election campaign. The first is to nominate

---

[5] In a few of the older cities some such families still exist, but their members do not often enter "politics."

[6] Although what is here stated is generally true of machines in large cities, there may be, even in such cities, districts inhabited by well-to-do people, in which the political organizations, being composed of men of good character and standing, are honestly worked. The so-called "brownstone districts" in New York City have, I believe, fair machines.

the candidates you desire; the second to carry them at the polls. The first of these is often the more important, because in many cities the party majority inclines so decidedly one way or the other (e.g., most districts of New York City are steadily Democratic, while Philadelphia is Republican), that nomination is in the case of the dominant party equivalent to election. Now to nominate your candidates you must, above all things, secure the primaries. They require and deserve unsparing exertion, for everything turns upon them.[7]

The first thing is to have the kind of primary you want. Now the composition of a primary is determined by the roll or "check list," as it is called, of ward voters entitled to appear in it. This is prepared by the managing committee of the ward, who are naturally desirous to have on it only such men as they can trust or control. They are aided in securing this by the rules requiring members to be admitted by the votes of those already on the list, and exact from persons admitted a pledge to obey the committee, and abide by the party nominations.[8] Men of independent temper often refuse this pledge, and are excluded. Many of the ward voters do not apply for admission. Of those who do apply and take the pledge, some can be plausibly rejected by the primary on the ground that they have on some recent occasion failed to vote the party ticket. Thus it is easy for an active committee to obtain a subservient primary, composed of persons in sympathy with it or obedient to it. In point of fact the rolls of membership of many primaries are largely bogus rolls. Names of former members are kept on when these men have left the district or died; names are put on of men who do not belong to the district at all, and both sets of names are so much "voting stock," applicable at the will and needs of the local party managers,

---

[7] The two paragraphs that follow refer to primaries of the older type, the primary under the laws recently passed in nearly all states being simply an election of candidates by the whole body either of the voters of each party separately or of the voters of both parties voting together.

[8] The rules of the Tammany Hall (Democratic) organization in New York City for many years past made the consent of a majority of the members of each primary necessary to the admission of a new member. A similar system prevails among the Republicans in that city. "The organization of the twenty-four Republican primaries (one for each Assembly district) is as complicated, and the access to membership as difficult, as that of any private club." Now, however, under the New York primary law of 1899 a person desiring to qualify to vote at a primary has to enrol himself on the general registration days, declaring on the enrolment form that he is in general sympathy with the party which he has designated by his mark at the foot of the paper, that he intends to support the nominees of such party for state and national offices generally at the next general election, and that he has not since the last preceding first of January enrolled as a member of any other party. No one not then enrolled may vote at a party primary.

who can admit the latter to vote, and "recognize" men personating the former. In fact, their control of the lists enables them to have practically whatever primary they desire.[9]

The next thing is to get the delegates chosen whom you wish for. The committee when it summons the primary settles in secret conclave the names of the delegates to be proposed, of course selecting men it can trust, particularly officeholders bound to the party which has put them in, and "workers" whom the prospect of office will keep faithful. When the meeting assembles a chairman is suggested by the committee and usually accepted. Then the list of delegates, which the committee has brought down cut and dry, is put forward. If the meeting is entirely composed of professionals, officeholders, and their friends, it is accepted without debate. If opponents are present, they may propose other names, but the official majority is almost always sufficient to carry the official list, and the chairman is prepared to exert, in favour of his friends, his power of ruling points of order. In extreme cases a disturbance will be got up, in the midst of which the chairman may plausibly declare the official list carried, or the meeting is adjourned in the hope that the opposition will not be at the trouble of coming next time, a hope likely to be realized, if the opposition consists of respectable citizens who dislike spending an evening in such company. Sometimes the professionals will bring in roughs from other districts to shout down opponents, and if necessary threaten them. One way or another the "regular" list of delegates is almost invariably carried against the "good citizens." When however there are two hostile factions of professionals, each anxious to secure nominations for its friends, the struggle is sharper and its issue more doubtful. Fraud is likely to be used on both sides; and

[9] In 1880 it was computed that out of 58,000 Republican voters in New York City not more than 6,000, or 8,000 at most, were members of the Republican organization, and entitled to vote in a primary.

The numbers present in the old-fashioned primaries were sometimes very small. "At the last Republican primaries in New York City only 8 per cent of the Republican electors took part. In only eight out of twenty-four districts did the percentage exceed 10, in some it was as low as 2 per cent. In the Twenty-first Assembly District Tammany Primary, 116 delegates, to choose an Assembly candidate, were elected by less than fifty voters. In the Sixth Assembly District County Democracy Primary, less than 7 per cent of the Democratic voters took part, and of those who did, sixty-nine in number, nearly one-fourth were election officers. The primary was held in a careless way in a saloon while card-playing was going on."—Mr. A. C. Bernheim in *Pol. Science Quarterly* for March 1888.

A trustworthy correspondent wrote to me from Philadelphia in 1894. "There is probably an average of 150 Republican voters to an election district. The average attendance at primaries is said to be about 12, which is approximately the number of party servants necessary to manage the meeting under party rules."

fraud often provokes violence.[10] It is a significant illustration of the difference between the party system in America and Europe that in the former foul play is quite as likely, and violence more likely, to occur at party nominating meetings than in the actual elections where two opposing parties are confronted.

The scene now shifts to the nominating convention, which is also summoned by the appropriate committee. When it is "called to order" a temporary chairman is installed, the importance of whose position consists in his having (usually) the naming of a committee on credentials, or contested seats, which examines the titles of the delegates from the various primaries to vote in the convention. Being himself in the interest of the professionals, he names a committee in their interest, and this committee does what it can to exclude delegates who are suspected of an intention to oppose the candidates whom the professionals have prearranged. The primaries have almost always been so carefully packed, and so skilfully "run," that a majority of trusty delegates has been secured; but sometimes a few primaries have sent delegates belonging to another faction of the party, or to some independent section of the party, and then there may be trouble. Occasionally two sets of delegates appear, each claiming to represent their primary. The dispute generally ends by the exclusion of the Independents or of the hostile faction, the committee discovering a flaw in their credentials, but sometimes, though rarely, the case is so clear that they must be admitted. In doubtful cases a partisan chairman is valuable, for, as it is expressed, "he is a solid 8 to 7 man all the time." When the credentials have been examined the convention is deemed to be duly organized, a permanent chairman is appointed, and the business of nominating candidates proceeds. A spokesman of the professionals proposes A. B. in a speech, dwelling on his services to the party. If the convention has been properly packed, he is nominated by acclamation. If there be a rival faction represented, or if independent citizens who dislike him have been sent up by some primary which the professionals have failed to secure, another candidate is proposed and a vote taken. Here also there is often room for a partial chairman to influence the result; here,

---

[10] For a remarkable instance in Baltimore see the report of United States Civil Service Commissioner Roosevelt made to the president, May 1, 1891. "Pudding ballots" (composed of six or seven ballots folded together as if one) were profusely used at these primary elections in the various wards of Baltimore. One of the witnesses examined, an employee of the Custom House, testified as follows: "Each side cheats as much as it can in the primaries. Whoever gets two judges wins. I do just the same as they do. They had two judges." . . . Q. "How do you do your cheating?" A. "Well, we do our cheating honourably. If they catch us at it, it's all right: it's fair. I even carried the box home with me on one occasion . . . I have broken up more than one election."

as in the primary, a tumult or a hocus pocus may in extreme cases be got up to enable the chairman to decide in favour of his allies.

Americans are, however, so well versed in the rules which govern public meetings, and so prepared to encounter all sorts of tricks, that the managers do not consider success certain unless they have a majority behind them. This they almost certainly have; at least it reflects discredit on their handling of the primaries if they have not. The chief hope of an opposition therefore is not to carry its own candidate but so to frighten the professionals as to make them abandon theirs, and substitute some less objectionable name. The candidate chosen, who, ninety-nine times out of a hundred, is the person predetermined by the managers, becomes the party nominee, entitled to the support of the whole party. He has received "the regular nomination." If there are other offices whereto nominations have to be made, the convention goes on to these, which being despatched, it adjourns and disappears forever.

I once witnessed such a convention, a state convention, held at Rochester, New York, by the Democrats of New York State, at that time being under the control of the Tammany Ring of New York City. The most prominent figure was the famous Mr. William M. Tweed, then in the zenith of his power. There was, however, little or nothing in the public proceedings from which an observer could learn anything of the subterranean forces at work. During the morning, a tremendous coming and going and chattering and clattering of crowds of men who looked at once sordid and flashy, faces shrewd but mean and sometimes brutal, vulgar figures in good coats forming into small groups and talking eagerly, and then dissolving to form fresh groups, a universal *camaraderie*, with no touch of friendship about it; something between a betting ring and the flags outside the Liverpool Exchange. It reminded one of the swarming of bees in tree boughs, a ceaseless humming and buzzing which betokens immense excitement over proceedings which the bystander does not comprehend. After some hours all this settled down; the meeting was duly organized; speeches were made, all dull and thinly declamatory, except one by an eloquent Irishman; the candidates for state offices were proposed and carried by acclamation; and the business ended. Everything had evidently been prearranged; and the discontented, if any there were, had been talked over during the swarming hours.

After each of the greater conventions it is usual to hold one or more public gatherings, at which the candidates chosen are solemnly adopted by the crowd present, and rousing speeches are delivered. Such a gathering, called a "ratification" meeting, has no practical importance, being attended only by those prepared to support the nominations made. The candidate is now launched, and what remains is to win the election.

The above may be thought, as it is thought by many Americans, a travesty of popular choice. Observing the forms of consulting the voters, it substantially ignores them, and forces on them persons whom they do not know, and would dislike if they knew them. It substitutes for the party voters generally a small number of professionals and their creatures, extracts prearranged nominations from packed meetings, and calls this consulting the pleasure of the sovereign people.[11]

Yet every feature of the machine is the result of patent causes. The elective offices are so numerous that ordinary citizens cannot watch them, and cease to care who gets them. The conventions come so often that busy men cannot serve in them. The minor offices are so unattractive that able men do not stand for them. The primary lists are so contrived that only a fraction of the party get on them; and of this fraction many are too lazy or too busy or too careless to attend. The mass of the voters are ignorant; knowing nothing about the personal merits of the candidates, they are ready to follow their leaders like sheep. Even the better class, however they may grumble, are swayed by the inveterate habit of party loyalty, and prefer a bad candidate of their own party to a (probably no better) candidate of the other party. It is less trouble to put up with impure officials, costly city government, a jobbing state legislature, an inferior sort of congressman, than to sacrifice one's own business in the effort to set things right. Thus the machine works on, and grinds out places, power, and the opportunities for illicit gain to those who manage it.

[11] It was a perception of these facts and a growing discontent with their results that suggested the new primary laws above referred to.

Rings and Bosses

This is the external aspect of the machine; these the phenomena which a visitor taken round to see a number of primaries and nominating conventions would record. But the reader will ask, How is the machine run? What are the inner springs that move it? What is the source of the power the committees wield? What force of cohesion keeps leaders and followers together? What kind of government prevails among this army of professional politicians?

The source of power and the cohesive force is the desire for office, and for office as a means of gain. This one cause is sufficient to account for everything, when it acts, as it does in these cities, under the condition of the suffrage of a host of ignorant and pliable voters.

Those who in great cities form the committees and work the machine are persons whose chief aim in life is to make their living by office. Such a man generally begins by acquiring influence among a knot of voters who live in his neighbourhood, or work under the same employer, or frequent the same grog shop or beer saloon, which perhaps he keeps himself. He becomes a member of his primary, attends regularly, attaches himself to some leader in that body, and is forward to render service by voting as his leader wishes, and by doing duty at elections. He has entered the large and active class called, technically, "workers," or more affectionately, "the boys." Soon he becomes conspicuous in the primary, being recognized as controlling the votes of others—"owning them" is the technical term—and is chosen delegate to a convention. Loyalty to the party there and continued service at elections mark him out for further promotion. He is appointed to some petty office in one of the city departments, and presently is himself nominated for an elective office. By this time he has also found his way on to the ward committee, whence by degrees he rises to sit on the central committee, having carefully nursed his local connection and surrounded himself with a band of adherents, who are called his "heelers," and whose loyalty to him in the primary, secured by the hope of "something good," gives weight to his words. Once a member of the central committee he discovers what everybody who gets on in the world discovers sooner or later, by how few persons the world is governed. He is one of a small knot of persons who pull the wires for the whole city, controlling the primaries, selecting candidates, "running" conventions, organizing elections, treating on behalf of the party in the city with the leaders of the party in the state. Each of this knot, which is probably smaller than the committee, because every committee includes some ciphers put on to support a leader, and which may include one or two strong men not on the committee, has acquired in his upward course a knowledge of men and their weaknesses, a familiarity with the wheels, shafts, and bands of the party machine, together with a skill in working it. Each can command some primaries, each has attached to himself a group of dependents who owe some place to him, or hope for some place from him. The aim of the knot is not only to get good posts for themselves, but to rivet their yoke upon the city by garrisoning the departments with their own creatures, and so controlling elections to the state legislature that they can procure such statutes as they desire, and prevent the passing of statutes likely to expose or injure them. They cement their dominion by combination, each placing his influence at the disposal of the others, and settle all important measures in secret conclave.

Such a combination is called a ring.

The power of such a combination is immense, for it ramifies over the whole city. There are, in New York City, for instance, more than forty thousand persons employed by the city authorities (without counting the eleven thousand school teachers), the large majority dismissible by their superiors at short notice and without cause assigned. Of the large number employed by the national government in the customhouse, post office, and other branches of the federal service,[1] many are similarly dismissible by the proper federal authority; and there are also state servants, responsible to and dismissible by the state authority. If the same party happens to be supreme in city politics, in the federal government, and in the state government, all this army of employees is expected to work for the party leaders of the city,

---

[1] The state of things under which rings first developed was worse, because then everybody was dismissible. Now many federal posts and (in some places) some city posts have been brought under civil service rules, but there are still a great many officials who are expected to work for the party.

in city primaries, conventions, and elections, and is virtually amenable to the orders of these leaders.[2] If the other party holds the reins of federal government and state government, then the city wire-pullers have at any rate their own ten thousand or more, while other thousands swell the army of "workers" for the opposite party. Add those who expect to get offices, and it will be seen how great and how disciplined a force is available to garrison the city and how effective it becomes under strict discipline. Yet it is not larger than is needed, for the work is heavy. *Tantae molis erat Romanam condere gentem.*

In a ring there is usually some one person who holds more strings in his hand than do the others. Like them he has worked himself up to power from small beginnings, gradually extending the range of his influence over the mass of workers, and knitting close bonds with influential men outside as well as inside politics, perhaps with great financiers or railway magnates, whom he can oblige, and who can furnish him with funds. At length his superior skill, courage, and force of will make him, as such gifts always do make their possessor, dominant among his fellows. An army led by a council seldom conquers; it must have a commander in chief, who settles disputes, decides in emergencies, inspires fear or attachment. The head of the ring is such a commander. He dispenses places, rewards the loyal, punishes the mutinous, concocts schemes, negotiates treaties. He generally avoids publicity, preferring the substance to the pomp of power, and is all the more dangerous because he sits, like a spider, hidden in the midst of his web. He is a boss.

Although the career I have sketched is that whereby most bosses have risen to greatness, some attain it by a shorter path. There have been brilliant instances of persons stepping at once on to the higher rungs of the ladder in virtue of their audacity and energy, especially if coupled with oratorical power. The first theatre of such a man's successes may have been the stump rather than the primary; he will then become potent in conventions, and either by hectoring or by plausible address, for both have their value, spring into popular favour, and make himself necessary to the party managers. It

---

[2] Assuming, as one usually may, that the city leaders are on good terms with the federal and state party managers.

Federal statutes and civil service rules made under them now provide that no person in the public service shall be compelled to contribute service or money for political purposes; and that persons in the competitive service shall take no active part in political campaigns, or use official authority or influence for the purpose of interfering with an election or controlling the result thereof. These rules, however, do not cover the whole field, and it is believed that they are not always observed.

is of course a gain to a ring to have among them a man of popular gifts, because he helps to conceal the odious features of their rule, gilding it by his rhetoric, and winning the applause of the masses who stand outside the circle of workers. However, the position of the rhetorical boss is less firmly rooted than that of the intriguing boss, and there have been instances of his suddenly falling to rise no more.

A great city is the best soil for the growth of a boss, because it contains the largest masses of manageable voters as well as numerous offices, and plentiful opportunities for jobbing. But a whole state sometimes falls under the dominion of one intriguer. To govern so large a territory needs high abilities; and the state boss is always an able man, somewhat more of a politician, in the European sense, than a city boss need be. He dictates state nominations, and through his lieutenants controls state and sometimes congressional conventions, being in diplomatic relations with the chief city bosses and local rings in different parts of the state. His power over them mainly springs from his influence with the federal executive and in Congress. He is usually, almost necessarily, a member of Congress, probably a senator, and can procure, or at any rate can hinder, such legislation as the local leaders desire or dislike. The president cannot ignore him, and the president's ministers, however little they may like him, find it worth while to gratify him with federal appointments for persons he recommends, because the local votes he controls may make all the difference to their own prospects of getting some day a nomination for the presidency. Thus he uses his congressional position to secure state influence, and his state influence to strengthen his federal position. Sometimes, however, he is rebuffed by the powers at Washington and then his state thanes fly from him. Sometimes he quarrels with a powerful city boss, and then honest men come by their own.

It must not be supposed that the members of rings, or the great boss himself, are wicked men. They are the offspring of a system. Their morality is that of their surroundings. They see a door open to wealth and power, and they walk in. The obligations of patriotism or duty to the public are not disregarded by them, for these obligations have never been present to their minds. A state boss is usually a native American and a person of some education, who avoids the grosser forms of corruption, though he has to wink at them when practised by his friends. He may be a man of personal integrity.[3] A city boss is often of foreign birth and humble origin; he has

---

[3] So too a rural boss is often quite pure, and blameworthy rather for his intriguing methods than for his aims.

grown up in an atmosphere of oaths and cocktails. Ideas of honour and purity are as strange to him as ideas about the nature of the currency and the incidence of taxation. Politics is merely a means for getting and distributing places. "What," said an ingenuous delegate at one of the national conventions at Chicago in 1880, "what are we here for except the offices?" It is no wonder if he helps himself from the city treasury and allows his minions to do so. Sometimes he does not rob, and like Clive, wonders at his own moderation. And even the city boss improves as he rises in the world. Like a tree growing out of a dust heap, the higher he gets, the cleaner do his boughs and leaves become. America is a country where vulgarity is sealed off more easily than in England, and where the general air of good nature softens the asperities of power. Some city bosses are men from whose decorous exterior and unobtrusive manners no one would divine either their sordid beginnings or their noxious trade. As for the state boss, whose talents are probably greater to begin with, he must be of very coarse metal if he does not take a polish from the society of Washington.

A city ring works somewhat as follows. When the annual or biennial city or state elections come round, its members meet to discuss the apportionment of offices. Each may desire something for himself, unless indeed he is already fully provided for, and anyhow desires something for his friends. The common sort are provided for with small places in the gift of some official, down to the place of a policeman or doorkeeper or messenger, which is thought good enough for a common "ward worker." Better men receive clerkships or the promise of a place in the customhouse or post office to be obtained from the federal authorities. Men still more important aspire to the elective posts, seats in the state legislature, a city aldermanship or commissionership, perhaps even a seat in Congress. All the posts that will have to be filled at the coming elections are considered with the object of bringing out a party ticket, i.e., a list of candidates to be supported by the party at the polls when its various nominations have been successfully run through the proper conventions. Some leading man, or probably the boss himself, sketches out an allotment of places; and when this allotment has been worked out fully, it results in a slate, i.e., a complete draft list of candidates to be proposed for the various offices.[4] It may happen that the

---

[4] A pleasant story is told of a former boss of New York State, who sat with his vassals just before the convention, preparing the slate. There were half a dozen or more state offices for which nominations were to be made. The names were with deliberation selected and set down, with the exception of the very unimportant place of state prison inspector. One of his subordinates ventured to call the attention of the boss to what he supposed to be an inadvertence, and asked who was

slate does not meet everybody's wishes. Some member of the ring or some local boss—most members of a ring are bosses each in his own district, as the members of a cabinet are heads of the departments of state, or as the cardinals are bishops of dioceses near Rome and priests and deacons of her parish churches—may complain that he and his friends have not been adequately provided for, and may demand more. In that case the slate will probably be modified a little to ensure good feeling and content; and it will then be presented to the convention.

But there is sometimes a more serious difficulty to surmount. A party in a state or city may be divided into two or more factions. Success in the election will be possible only by uniting these factions upon the same nominees for office. Occasionally the factions may each make its list and then come together in the party convention to fight out their differences. But the more prudent course is for the chiefs of each faction to arrange matters in a private conference. Each comes wishing to get the most he can for his clansmen, but feels the need for a compromise. By a process of "dickering" (i.e., bargaining by way of barter), various offers and suggestions being made all round, a list is settled on which the high contracting parties agree. This is a deal, or trade, a treaty which terminates hostilities for the time, and brings about "harmony." The list so settled is now a slate, unless some discontented magnate objects and threatens to withdraw. To do so is called "breaking the slate." If such a "sorehead" persists, a schism may follow, with horrible disaster to the party; but usually a new slate is prepared and finally agreed upon. The accepted slate is now ready to be turned by the machine into a ticket, and nothing further remains but the comparatively easy process of getting the proper delegates chosen by packed primaries, and running the various parts of the ticket through the conventions to which the respective nominations belong. Internal dissension among the chiefs is the one great danger; the party must at all hazards be kept together, for the power of a united party is enormous. It has not only a large but a thoroughly trained and disciplined army in its officeholders and office-seekers; and it can concentrate its force upon any point where opposition is threatened to the regular party nominations.[5] All these officeholders and office-seekers

---

to be the man for that place, to which the great man answered, with an indulgent smile, "I guess we will leave *that* to the convention."

[5] As for instance by packing the primaries with its adherents from other districts, whom a partisan chairman or committee will suffer to come in and vote.

These remarks all refer to the old-fashioned primaries. The new statutory primary, as already observed, is a different thing, whose defects, as well as its merits, are different.

have not only the spirit of self-interest to rouse them, but the bridle of fear to check any stirrings of independence. Discipline is very strict in this army. Even city politicians must have a moral code and moral standard. It is not the code of an ordinary unprofessional citizen. It does not forbid falsehood, or malversation, or ballot stuffing, or "repeating." But it denounces apathy or cowardice, disobedience, and above all, treason to the party. Its typical virtue is "solidity," unity of heart, mind, and effort among the workers, unquestioning loyalty to the party leaders, and devotion to the party ticket. He who takes his own course is a kicker or bolter; and is punished not only sternly but vindictively. The path of promotion is closed to him; he is turned out of the primary, and forbidden to hope for a delegacy to a convention; he is dismissed from any office he holds which the ring can command. Dark stories are even told of a secret police which will pursue the culprit who has betrayed his party, and of mysterious disappearances of men whose testimony against the ring was feared. Whether there is any foundation for such tales I do not undertake to say. But true it is that the bond between the party chiefs and their followers is very close and very seldom broken. What the client was to his patron at Rome, what the vassal was to his lord in the Middle Ages, that the "heelers" and "workers" are to their boss in these great transatlantic cities. They render a personal feudal service, which their suzerain repays with the gift of a livelihood; and the relation is all the more cordial because the lord bestows what costs him nothing, while the vassal feels that he can keep his post only by the favour of the lord.

European readers must again be cautioned against drawing for themselves too dark a picture of the boss. He is not a demon. He is not regarded with horror even by those "good citizens" who strive to shake off his yoke. He is not necessarily either corrupt or mendacious, though he grasps at place, power, and wealth. He is a leader to whom certain peculiar social and political conditions have given a character dissimilar from the party leaders whom Europe knows. It is worth while to point out in what the dissimilarity consists.

A boss needs fewer showy gifts than a European demagogue. His special theatre is neither the halls of the legislature nor the platform, but the committee-room. A power of rough and ready repartee, or a turn for florid declamation, will help him; but he can dispense with both. What he needs are the arts of intrigue and that knowledge of men which teaches him when to bully, when to cajole, whom to attract by the hope of gain, whom by appeals to party loyalty. Nor are so-called social gifts unimportant. The lower sort of city politicians congregate in clubs and barrooms; and as much of the cohesive strength of the smaller party organizations arises from their being also social bodies, so also much of the power which liquor dealers exercise is due to the fact that "heelers" and "workers" spend their evenings in drinking places, and that meetings for political purposes are held there. Of the 1,007 primaries and conventions of all parties held in New York City preparatory to the elections of 1884, 633 took place in liquor saloons.[6] A boss ought therefore to be hail fellow well met with those who frequent these places, not fastidious in his tastes, fond of a drink and willing to stand one, jovial in manners, and ready to oblige even a humble friend.

The aim of a boss is not so much fame as power, and not so much power over the conduct of affairs as over persons. Patronage is what he chiefly seeks, patronage understood in the largest sense in which it covers the disposal of lucrative contracts and other modes of enrichment as well as salaried places. The dependants who surround him desire wealth, or at least a livelihood; his business is to find this for them, and in doing so he strengthens his own position.[7] It is as the bestower of riches that he holds his position, like the leader of a band of condottieri in the fifteenth century.

The interest of a boss in political questions is usually quite secondary. Here and there one may be found who is a politician in the European sense, who, whether sincerely or not, purports and professes to be interested in some principle or measure affecting the welfare of the country. But the attachment of the ringster is usually given wholly to the concrete party, that is to the men who compose it, regarded as officeholders or office-seekers; and there is often not even a profession of zeal for any party doctrine. As a noted politician once happily observed, "There are no politics in politics." Among bosses, therefore, there is little warmth of party spirit. The typical boss regards the boss of the other party much as counsel for the plaintiff regards counsel for the defendant. They are professionally opposed, but not necessarily personally hostile. Between bosses there need be no more enmity

---

[6] Where primary laws are in force, primaries are no longer held in saloons.

[7] "A Boss is able to procure positions for many of his henchmen on horse railroads, the elevated roads, quarry works, etc. Great corporations are peculiarly subject to the attack of demagogues, and they find it greatly to their interest to be on good terms with the leader in each district who controls the vote of the assemblyman and alderman; and therefore the former is pretty sure that a letter of recommendation from him on behalf of any applicant for work will receive most favourable consideration. The leader also is continually helping his supporters out of difficulties, pecuniary and otherwise: he lends them a dollar now and then, helps out, when possible, such of their kinsmen as get into the clutches of the law, gets a hold over such of them as have done wrong and are afraid of being exposed, and learns to mix bullying judiciously with the rendering of service."—Mr. Theodore Roosevelt, in an article in the *Century* magazine for November 1886.

than results from the fact that the one has got what the other wishes to have. Accordingly it sometimes happens that there is a good understanding between the chiefs of opposite parties in cities; they will even go the length of making a joint "deal," i.e., of arranging for a distribution of offices whereby some of the friends of one shall get places, the residue being left for the friends of the other.[8] A well-organized city party has usually a disposable vote which can be so cast under the directions of the managers as to effect this, or any other desired result. The appearance of hostility must, of course, be maintained for the benefit of the public; but as it is for the interest of both parties to make and keep these private bargains, they are usually kept when made, though of course it is seldom possible to prove the fact.

The real hostility of the boss is not to the opposite party, but to other factions within his own party. Often he has a rival leading some other organization, and demanding, in respect of the votes which that organization controls, a share of the good things going. The greatest cities can support more than one faction within the same party; thus New York has long had three Democratic organizations, two of which are powerful and often angrily hostile. If neither can crush the other, it finds itself obliged to treat, and to consent to lose part of the spoils to its rival. Still more bitter, however, is the hatred of boss and ring towards those members of the party who do not desire and are not to be appeased by a share of the spoils, but who agitate for what they call reform. They are natural and permanent enemies; nothing but the extinction of the boss himself and of bossdom altogether will satisfy them. They are moreover the common enemies of both parties, that is, of bossdom in both parties. Hence in ring-governed cities professionals of both parties will sometimes unite against the reformers, or will rather let their opponents secure a place than win it for themselves by the help of the "independent vote." Devotion to "party government," as they understand it, can hardly go farther.

This great army of workers is mobilized for elections, the methods of which form a wide and instructive department of political science. Here I refer only to their financial side, because that is intimately connected with the machine. Elections need money, in America a great deal of money. Where, then, does the money come from, seeing that the politicians themselves belong to, or emerge from, a needy class?

The revenues of a ring, that is, their collective, or, as one may say, corporate revenues, available for party purposes, flow from five sources.

---

[8] In one great state it was recently well understood that the Democratic boss of the chief city and the Republican boss of the state were in the habit of trading offices with one another.

I. The first is public subscriptions. For important elections such as the biennial elections of state officers, or perhaps for that of the state legislature, a "campaign fund," as it is called, is raised by an appeal to wealthy members of the party. So strong is party feeling that many respond, even though they suspect the men who compose the ring, disapprove its methods, and have no great liking for the candidates.

II. Contributions are sometimes privately obtained from rich men and especially from corporations (though statutes are now attempting to prevent this) who, though not directly connected with the ring, may expect something from its action. Contractors, for instance, have an interest in getting pieces of work from the city authorities. Railroad men have an interest in preventing state legislation hostile to their lines. Both, therefore, may be willing to help those who can so effectively help them. This source of income is only available for important elections. Its incidental mischief in enabling wealth to control a legislature through a ring is serious.

III. An exceptionally audacious ring will sometimes make an appropriation from the city or (more rarely) from the state treasury for the purposes not of the city or the state, but of its own election funds. It is not thought necessary to bring such an appropriation into the regular accounts to be laid before the public; in fact, pains are taken to prevent the item from appearing, and the accounts have often to be manipulated for that purpose. The justification, if any, of conduct not authorized by the law, must be sought in precedent, in the belief that the other side would do the same, and in the benefits which the ring expects to confer upon the city it administers. It is a method of course available only when ring officials have the control of public funds, and cannot be resorted to by an opposition.

IV. A tax used to be levied upon the officeholders of the party, varying from one to four or even five per cent upon the amount of their annual salaries. The aggregate annual salaries of the city officials in New York City amounted to $11,000,000, and those of the two thousand five hundred federal officials, who, if of the same party, might also be required to contribute,[9] to $2,500,000. An assessment at two per cent on these amounts would produce over $220,000 and $50,000 respectively, quite a respectable sum for election expenses in a single city.[10] Even policemen in cities, even

---

[9] Federal officials would, as a rule, contribute only to the fund for federal elections; but when the contest covered both federal and city offices, the funds would be apt to be blended.

   The totals of salaries of officials now are of course far larger, but as it is impossible to ascertain today on how much of them an assessment is paid, the figures in the text have been allowed to stand.

[10] To make the calculation complete we should have to reckon in also the (comparatively few) state officials and assessments payable by them.

office boys and workmen in federal dockyards, have been assessed by their party. As a tenant had in the days of feudalism to make occasional money payments to his lord in addition to the military service he rendered, so now the American vassal must render his aids in money as well as give knightly service at the primaries, in the canvass, at the polls. His liabilities are indeed heavier than those of the feudal tenant, for the latter could relieve himself from duty in the field by the payment of scutage, while under the machine a money payment never discharges from the obligation to serve in the army of "workers." Forfeiture and the being proclaimed as "nithing," are, as in the days of the Anglo-Norman kings, the penalty for failure to discharge the duties by which the vassal holds. Efforts which began with an order issued by President Hayes in 1877 applying to federal offices have been made to prevent by administrative action and by legislation the levying of this tribute on federal officials, but it is believed that the evil has not yet been extirpated. Indeed, some officials do not wait to be "assessed," but think they "earn merit" (as the Buddhists say) by sending in their contributions ultroneously before any suggestion reaches them.

V. Another useful expedient has been borrowed from European monarchies in the sale of nominations and occasionally of offices themselves.[11] A person who seeks to be nominated as candidate for one of the more important offices, such as a judgeship or a seat in the state Senate, or in Congress, is often required to contribute to the election fund a sum proportioned to the importance of the place he seeks, the excuse given for the practice being the cost of elections; and the same principle is occasionally applied to the gift of nonelective offices, the right of appointing to which is vested in some official member of a ring—e.g., a mayor. The price of a nomination for a seat in the state legislature is said to run from $500 up to $1,000, and for one of the better judgeships as high as $5,000; but this is largely matter of conjecture.[12] Of course much less will be given if the prospects of

---

[11] As judicial places were sold under the old French monarchy, and commissions in the army in England till 1872.

[12] "A judgeship," said (writing in 1883) Mr. F. W. Whitridge, "costs in New York about $15,000; the district attorneyship the same; for a nomination to Congress the price is about $4000, though this is variable; an aldermanic nomination is worth $1500, and that for the Assembly from $600 to $1500. The amount realized from these assessments cannot be exactly estimated but the amount raised by Tammany Hall, which is the most complete political organization, may be fixed very nearly at $125,000 (£25,000). This amount is collected and expended by a small executive committee who keep no accounts and are responsible only to each other."—Article "Assessments" in *Amer. Cyclop. of Political Science*. In 1887, the City Chamberlain of New York estimated the average minimum assessment levied on a candidate for mayor at $20,000, for comptroller at $10,000, for district attorney at $5,000. However, in 1887 the Democratic rings in New York

carrying the election are doubtful: the prices quoted must be taken to represent cases where the party majority makes success certain. Naturally, the salaries of officials have to be raised in order to enable them to bear this charge, so that in the long run it may be thrown upon the public; and an eminent boss of New York City defended, before a committee of the legislature, the large salaries paid to aldermen, on the ground that "heavy demands were made on them by their party."[13]

City demanded $25,000 for the nomination to the comptrollership, and $5,000 for that to a state senatorship. The salary of the comptroller is $10,000 for three years, that of Senator $1,500 for two years, i.e., the senatorial candidate was expected to pay $2,000 more than his total salary, a fact suggestive of expectations of gain from some other source.

[13] "Before a committee of the New York legislature the county clerk testified that his income was nearly $80,000 a year, but with refreshing frankness admitted that his own position was practically that of a figurehead, and that all the work was done by his deputy on a small fixed salary. As the county clerk's term is three years, he should nominally receive $240,000, but as a matter of fact two-thirds of the money probably goes to the political organizations with which he is connected."—Mr. T. Roosevelt in *Century* magazine for November 1886. A county officer answered the same committee, when they put what was meant to be a formal question as to whether he performed his public duties faithfully, that he did so perform them whenever they did not conflict with his political duties(!), meaning thereby, as he explained, attending to his local organizations, seeing politicians, "fixing" primaries, bailing out those of his friends who were summoned to appear before a justice of peace, etc.

CHAPTER 64

Local Extension of Rings and Bosses

To determine the extent to which the ring and boss system sketched in the preceding chapters prevails over the United States would be difficult even for an American, because it would require a minute knowledge of the local affairs of all the states and cities. Much more, then, is it difficult for a European. I can do no more than indicate generally the results of the inquiries I have made, commending the details of the question to some future investigator.

It has been pointed out that rings and bosses are the product not of democracy, but of a particular form of democratic government, acting under certain peculiar conditions. They belong to democratic government, as the old logicians would say, not *simpliciter* but *secundum quid*: they are not of its essence, but are merely separable accidents. We have seen that these conditions are:

The existence of a Spoils System (= paid offices given and taken away for party reasons);
Opportunities for illicit gains arising out of the possession of office;
The presence of a mass of ignorant and pliable voters;
The insufficient participation in politics of the "good citizens."

If these be the true causes or conditions producing the phenomenon, we may expect to find it most fully developed in the places where the conditions exist in fullest measure, less so where they are more limited, absent where they do not exist.

A short examination of the facts will show that such is the case.

It may be thought that the Spoils System is a constant, existing everywhere, and therefore not admitting of the application of this method of concomitant variations. That system does no doubt prevail over every state of the Union, but it is not everywhere an equally potent factor, for in some cities the offices are much better paid than in others, and the revenues which their occupants control are larger. In some small communities the offices, or most of them, are not paid at all. Hence this factor also may be said to vary.

We may therefore say with truth that all of the four conditions above named are most fully present in great cities. Some of the offices are highly paid; many give facilities for lucrative jobbing; and the unpaid officers are sometimes the most apt to abuse these facilities. The voters are so numerous that a strong and active organization is needed to drill them; the majority so ignorant as to be easily led. The best citizens are engrossed in business and cannot give to political work the continuous attention it demands. Such are the phenomena of New York, Philadelphia, Chicago, Pittsburgh, Minneapolis, St. Paul, St. Louis, Cincinnati, San Francisco, and New Orleans. In these cities ring-and-bossdom has attained its amplest growth, overshadowing the whole field of politics.

Of the first two of these I need not speak in detail here, proposing to refer to their phenomena in later chapters, but Chicago, often shockingly misgoverned, has latterly improved and seems likely to improve further under the vigilant action of a group of public-spirited citizens. As regards certain other cities, I subjoin some remarks with which I was favoured in 1887 by leading citizens resident therein, in reply to interrogatories which I addressed to them; and have in each case added a few words to bring the story down through more recent years. Knowing how apt a stranger is to imagine a greater uniformity than exists, I desire to enable the reader to understand to what extent the description I have given is generally true, and with what local diversities its general truth is compatible. And as the remarks quoted illustrate the phenomena of city misgovernment in general, they have the interest which belongs to original and contemporaneous historical authorities.

Cincinnati (Ohio), population in 1890, 296,908, in 1910, 364,463:

> Our Ring is in a less formal shape than is sometimes seen, but dishonest men of both parties do in fact combine for common profits at the public expense. As regards a Boss, there is at this moment an interregnum, but some ambitious men are observed to be making progress towards that dignity. Rings are both the effect and the cause of peculation. They are the result of the general law of combination to further the interest of the combiners.
>
> Where a Ring exists it can always exclude from office a good citizen known to be hostile to it. But a good easy man who will not fight and will make a reputable figurehead may be an excellent investment.

The large cities are the great sufferers from the Spoils System, because in them power gives the greatest opportunity for profit and peculation. In them also it is easy to make a more or less open combination of keepers of tippling shops and the "bummers," etc., who congregate in them. Here, too, is the natural home of the class of vagabonds who will profess devotion to the party or the man who will pay them, and who combine to levy blackmail upon every candidate, and in turn are ready to stuff ballot-boxes, to buy votes, to "repeat," etc. These scoundrels "live by politics" in their way, and force their services upon more prominent men, till there comes to be a sort of "solidarity" in which men of national reputation find themselves morally compromised by being obliged to recognize this sort of fraternity, and directly or indirectly to make themselves responsible for the methods of these "henchmen" and followers. They dare not break with this class because its enmity would defeat their ambitions, and the more unscrupulous of them make fullest use of the co-operation, only rendering a little homage to decency by seeking to do it through intermediaries, so as not too disgustingly to dirty their own hands.

In such a condition of things the cities become the prey of the "criminal class" in politics, in order to ensure the discipline and organization in State and national politics which are necessary to the distinguished leaders for success. As a result it goes almost without saying that every considerable city has its rings and its actual or would-be bosses. There are occasional "revolutions of the palace," in which bosses are deposed, or "choked off," because they are growing too fat on the spoils, and there is no such permanence of tenure as to enable the uninitiated always to tell what boss or what ring is in power. They do not publish an *Almanach de Gotha*, but we feel and know that the process of plunder continues. A man of genius in this way, like a Tweed or a Kelly, comes occasionally to the front, but even in the absence of a ruler of this sort the ward politicians can always tell where the decisive influences reside.

The *size* of the city in which the system reaches full bloom depends upon its business and general character. Small towns with a proportionately large manufacturing population are better fields for rings than more homogeneous communities built up as centres of mercantile trade. The *tendency* however is to organize an official body of "workers" in even the smallest community; and the selfishness of man naturally leads to the doctrine that those who do the work shall live by it. Thus, from the profits of "rotation in office" and the exercise of intrigue and trick to get the place of the present incumbent, there is the *facilis descensus* to regarding the profits of peculation and the plunder of the public as a legitimate corrective for the too slow accumulation from legal pay. Certain salaries and fees in local offices are notoriously kept high, so that the incumbent may freely "bleed" for party use, or, what is the same thing, for the use of party "bummers." Thus we have had clerks of courts and sheriffs getting many times as much pay as the judges on the bench, etc. From this, jobbing in contracts, bribery, and unblushing stealing are reached by such easy steps that perhaps the local politician is hardly conscious of the progress in his moral education.

It would not be fitting to insert here equally free comments on the conditions of today. But in 1912 Cincinnati was described by competent observers as suffering from the old evils, and it is no secret that she had been long ruled by a boss of eminent capacity.

St. Louis (Missouri), population in 1890, 451,770; in 1910, 687,029:

> There are always Rings in both parties more or less active according to circumstances.
>
> Two or perhaps three men are the recognized Bosses of the Democratic party (which is in the majority), one man of the Republican.
>
> The Rings are the cause of both peculation and jobbery, although St. Louis has had no "big steal."
>
> A good citizen seeking office would be excluded by the action of the Rings in our large cities, except in times of excitement, when good people are aroused to a proper sense of duty. [1]

In 1909 St. Louis had no recognized boss, and had enjoyed for some years an exceptionally good mayor. There was, however, a good deal of ring power, acting on or through the city councils. Attempts were being made in 1912 to enact a new charter.

Louisville (Kentucky), population in 1880, 161,129; in 1910, 223,928:

> It can hardly be said that there is a regular Ring in Louisville. There are corrupt combinations, but they are continually shifting. The higher places in these combinations are occupied by Democrats, these being the ruling party, but they always contain some Republicans.
>
> The only Boss there is in Louisville today is the Louisville Gas Company. It works mainly through the Democratic party, as it is easier to bribe the "Republican" negroes into the support of Democratic candidates than white Democrats to support Republicans.
>
> There is very little peculation in Kentucky now—no great disclosure for over five years; but there is a great deal of jobbery.
>
> The effect of the combinations is of course towards excluding good and capable men from office and to make room for mere favourites and local politicians. [2]

In 1909 Louisville was stated to be suffering from rings, but in a

---

[1] My correspondent wrote in 1892 that the above remarks were still equally applicable. Both parties remained under a despotic ring rule.

[2] The condition of Louisville was described as substantially the same in 1893.

comparatively mild form. A civic uprising in 1906 had given her for three years an upright and capable mayor.

Minneapolis (Minnesota), population in 1890, 164,738:

There has been for several years past a very disreputable Ring, which has come into power by capturing the machinery of the Democratic party, through (1) diligent work in the ward caucuses; (2) by its active alliance with the liquor dealers, gamblers, and so forth, and the support of "lewd fellows of the baser sort," regardless of national political preferences; (3) by a skilful and plausible championship of "labor" and a capture of the labor vote.

The Boss of this gang is thoroughly disliked and distrusted by the responsible and reputable element of his party in Minnesota, but they tolerate him on account of his popularity and because they cannot break him down. He has operated chiefly through control of the police system. Instead of suppressing gambling houses, for example, he, being a high official, has allowed several of them to run under police protection, himself sharing in their large gains. Until recently the liquor saloon licences have been $500 (£100) a year. He and the heads of the police department have allowed a number of places to retail liquor somewhat secretly outside the police patrol limits, within which we restrict the liquor traffic, and from these illicit publicans the Ring has collected large sums of money.

The Ring has seemed to control the majority in the Common Council, but the system of direct taxation and of checking expenditure is so open, and the scrutiny of the press and public so constant, that there has been little opportunity for actual plunder. In the awarding of contracts there is sometimes a savour of jobbery, and several of the councilmen are not above taking bribes. But they have been able to do comparatively little mischief; in fact, nothing outrageous has occurred outside of the police department. The Ring has lately obtained control of the (elective) Park Board, and some disreputable jobs have resulted. So there have been malpractices in the department of health and hospitals, in the management of the water system and in the giving away of a street railway franchise. But we are not a badly-plundered city by any means; and we have just succeeded in taking the control of the police out of the hands of the Ring officials and vested it in a Metropolitan Police Board, with excellent results. Two of the Ring are now under indictment of the county grand jury for malpractices in office.

In 1910, population 301,408, things had improved in Minneapolis. A trustworthy correspondent wrote in 1909:

Old party lines, while not exactly obliterated, have become indistinct in all elections, whether municipal, state, or national. In fact the hold of the party over its members has become a very uncertain thing and consequently the control of the party machinery no longer suffices to bring victory at the polls. No one boss or political ring can frame a set of candidates and force it on a party since the voters have now a direct vote upon all candidates for office, except those elected for the State, at which, under the primary law, it is a common practice for voters belonging to the minority party to participate in the nomination of the candidates in the majority party. The practice is contrary to law, and to indulge in it the voter must forego the right of taking part in the nomination of candidates of his own party. The Voters' League, which attempts to prevent the election of incompetent men to the city Councils and to the Board of County Commissioners by publishing the records of all candidates for office and by making recommendations to voters irrespective of party conditions, has also been a force in local politics.

Minneapolis has no real political boss. There have been political rings, and these still exist, but in a modified form. The real power in politics in the city is believed to be in the hands of some prominent corporations.

St. Paul, population in 1890, 133,156, in 1910, 214,744:

There is no regular Ring in St. Paul. It has for many years been in the hands of a clique of municipal Democratic politicians, who are fairly good citizens, and have committed no very outrageous depredations. The city is run upon a narrow partisan plan, but in its main policies and expenditures the views of leading citizens as formulated in the Chamber of Commerce almost invariably prevail.

The Rings of Western cities (adds my informant) are not deliberately organized for plunder or jobbery. They grow out of our party politics. Certain of the worse elements of a party find that their superior diligence and skill in the manipulation of precinct and ward caucuses put them in control of the local machinery of their party organization. The success of their party gives them control of municipal affairs. They are generally men who are not engaged in successful trade or professional life, and make city politics their business. They soon find it profitable to engage in various small schemes and jobs for profit, but do not usually perpetrate anything very bold or bad.

I have taken the two cities of Minneapolis and St. Paul because they illustrate the differences which one often finds between places whose population and other conditions seem very similar. The centres of these two cities are only ten miles apart; their suburbs have begun to touch; they will soon be, in a material sense, one city. Minneapolis is younger, and has grown far more rapidly, and the manufacturing element in its population is larger. But in most respects it resembles its elder sister—they are extremely jealous of one another—so closely that an Old World observer who has not realized the swiftness with which phenomena come and go in the West is surprised to find the political maladies of the one so much graver than those of the other.

It has been seen how things stood in 1887. In 1893 they had changed for the better in both cities. The boss of Minneapolis had vanished, and the party opposed to that he had adorned was in power. The municipal administration, if not free from reproach, was comparatively free from scandals. St. Paul showed a marked improvement. A mayor had been elected on a "reform ticket," and the municipal clique formerly dominant had been broken up. But no one could feel sure that these gains would be preserved.

In 1909 Minneapolis having (as above reported) done much to reform her ways, it was stated that the situation in St. Paul had changed much less. The former political clique still held power. A boss had for some time been reigning, but the police administration was described as efficient. Such are the vicissitudes of cities.

The great city of San Francisco, capital of the "Pacific slope," with a population in 1910 of 416,912 people, was for years ruled by a formidable boss who, through an energetic lieutenant, commanded the fire department of the city, and used its 350 paid employees as a sort of prætorian guard. He controlled the city elections, dominated the officials, was a power in state politics, tampered with the administration of the criminal law. At last steps were taken to have him and his grand vizier indicted for peculation, whereupon they both fled to Canada, and the city escaped the yoke. But the conditions which produced bossdom remaining, it fell before long under a still worse yoke. In 1907 there was a local revolution, due to the discovery of corruption on the part of prominent officials for which two were imprisoned, but the phenomena of that uprising and the events that have followed cannot yet be with propriety described in these pages. In 1913 there was an honest government.

Pittsburg, population (in 1910) 533,905, has had a chequered history. No city has been more swayed by bosses of ability and audacity. Lately a strong and able mayor gave it a good administration, the results of which have tended to raise the standard which the people expect; but whether that standard will be maintained seems still doubtful. In 1910 several members of the city government were convicted of corruption.

In cities of the second rank (say from 10,000 to 100,000 inhabitants) some of the same mischiefs exist, but on a smaller scale. The opportunities for jobbing are limited. The offices are moderately paid. The population of new immigrants, politically incompetent, and therefore easily pervertible, bears a smaller ratio to the native Americans. The men prominent by their wealth or capacity are more likely to be known to the mass of the voters, and may have more leisure to join in local politics. Hence, although we find rings in many of these cities, they are less powerful, less audacious, less corrupt. There are, of course, differences between one city and another, differences sometimes explicable by its history and the character of its population. A very high authority wrote to me in 1887 from Michigan, a state above the average:

> I have heard no charge of the reign of Bosses or Rings for the "purposes of peculation" in any of the cities or towns of Michigan or Indiana, or indeed in more than a few of our cities generally, and those for the most part are the large cities. In certain cases rings or bosses have managed political campaigns for partisan purposes, and sometimes to such an extent, say in Detroit, that good citizens have been excluded from office or have declined to run. But robbery was not the aim of the rings. In not a few of our cities the liquor-saloon keepers have combined to "run politics" so as to gain control and secure a municipal management friendly to them. That is in part the explanation of the great uprising of the Prohibition party.

Detroit (population in 1910, 465,766) was described in 1909 as improving steadily, owing to an aroused public sentiment for good government which is forcing higher standards on the professional politicians.

Denver, now a city of 213,381, has obtained an unenviable notoriety for the prevalence of corrupt influences in its politics, but the administration of its affairs seems to be efficient.

The cities of New York State seem to suffer more than those of New England or the West. Albany (a place of 100,000 people) has long groaned under its rings, but as the seat of the New York legislature it is a focus of intrigue. Buffalo (with 400,000) has a large population of foreign origin and obeys a boss. Rochester and Troy are ruled by local cliques; the latter is full of fellows who go to serve as "repeaters" at Albany elections. Syracuse is smaller and said to be more pure than Rochester, but has of late years shown some serious symptoms of the same disease. Cleveland is a larger place than any of these, but having, like the rest of northern Ohio, a better quality of population, its rings have never carried things with a high hand, nor stolen public money, and it is fortunate in having a strong nonpolitical commercial organization of good citizens who keep an eye on the city government. The same may be said to such New England cities as Providence, Augusta, Hartford, Worcester, Lowell, though neither Boston nor New Haven have been free from rings. The system more or less exists in all these, but the bosses have not ventured to exclude respectable outsiders from office, nor have they robbed the city, debauched the legislature, retained their power by election frauds after the manner of their great models in New York and Philadelphia. And this seems to hold true also of the Western and Southern cities of moderate size. A seaside suburb of one great Eastern city once produced a singularly audacious boss, who combined that position with those of head of the police and superintendent of the principal Sunday school. He had tampered freely with the election returns, giving his support sometimes to one party sometimes to another, and had apparently been able to "turn over" the vote of the place at his pleasure. A rising of the "good citizens" at last succeeded in procuring his conviction and imprisonment for election offences.

As regards Ohio a judicious authority said:

> Rings are much less likely to exist in the smaller cities, though a population of 30,000 or 40,000 may occasionally support them. We should hardly find them in a city below 10,000: any corruption there would be occasional, not systematic.

As regards Missouri I am informed that:

> We have few or no rings in cities under 60,000 inhabitants. The smaller cities are not favourable to such kinds of control. Men know one another too well. There is no large floating irresponsible following as in large cities.

A similar answer from Kentucky adds that rings have nevertheless been heard of in cities so small as Lexington when it had 22,000 inhabitants and Frankfort with less than half that population. In these three states the facts seem to be still much as formerly stated.

In quite small towns and in the rural districts—in fact, whenever there is not a municipality, but government is either by a town meeting and selectmen or by township or county officials—the dangerous conditions are reduced to their minimum. The new immigrants are not generally planted in large masses but scattered among the native population, whose habits and modes of thinking they soon acquire. The Germans and Scandinavians who settle in the country districts have been among the best of their race, and form a valuable element. The country voter, whether native or foreign, is exposed to fewer temptations than his brother of the city, and is less easy either to lead or to drive. He is parsimonious, and pays his county or town officials on a niggardly scale. A boss has therefore no occupation in such a place. His talents would be wasted. If a ring exists in a small city it is little more than a clique of local lawyers who combine to get hold of the local offices, each in his turn, and to secure a seat for one of themselves in the state legislature, where there may be pickings to be had. It is not easy to draw the line between such a clique, which one may find all the world over, and a true ring; but by whichever name we call the weed, it does little harm to the crop. Here and there, however, one meets with a genuine boss even in these seats of rural innocence. I know a New England town, with a population of about ten thousand people, which was long ruled by such a local wire-puller. I do not think he stole. But he had gathered a party of voters round him, by whose help he carried the offices, and got a chance of perpetrating jobs which enriched himself and supplied work for his supporters. The circumstances, however, are exceptional. Within the taxing area of the town there lie many villas of wealthy merchants, who do business in a neighbouring city, but are taxed on their summer residences here. The funds which this town has to deal with were therefore much larger than would be the case in most towns of its size, while many of the rich taxpayers are not citizens here, but vote in the city where they live during the winter.[3] Hence they could not go to the town meeting to beard the boss, but had to grin and pay while they watched his gambols.

Speaking generally, the country places and the smaller cities are not ring-ridden. There is a tendency everywhere for the local party organizations to fall into the hands of a few men, perhaps of one man. But this happens not so much from an intent to exclude others and misuse power, as because the work is left to those who have some sort of interest in doing it, that, namely, of being themselves nominated to an office. Such persons are seldom professional office-seekers, but lawyers, farmers, or storekeepers, who are glad to add something to their income, and have the importance, not so contemptible in a village, of sitting in the state legislature. Nor does much harm result. The administration is fairly good; the taxpayers are not robbed. If a leading citizen, who does not belong to the managing circle, wishes to get a nomination, he will probably succeed; in fact, no one will care to exclude him. In many places there is a nonparty "citizens' committee" which takes things out of the hands of the two organizations by running as candidates respectable men irrespective of party. Such candidates generally succeed if the local party managers have offended public sentiment by bad nominations. In short, the materials for real ring government do not exist, and its methods are inapplicable, outside the large cities. No one needs to fear it, or does fear it.

---

[3] It will be remembered that in the United States, though a man may pay taxes on his real estate in any number of states or counties or cities, he can vote, even in purely local elections or on purely local matters, in one place only—that in which he is held to reside. In this respect the principle of "no taxation without representation" has been ignored.

What has been said refers chiefly to the Northern, Middle, and Western states. The circumstances of the South are different, but they illustrate equally well the general laws of ring growth. In the Southern cities there is scarcely any population of European immigrants. The lowest class consists of Negroes and "poor whites." The Negroes are ignorant, and would be dangerously plastic material in the hands of unscrupulous wire-pullers, as was amply shown after the Civil War. But they have hitherto mostly belonged to the Republican party, and the Democratic party has so completely regained its ascendency that the bosses who controlled the Negro vote can do nothing. In most parts of the South the men of ability and standing have interested themselves in politics so far as to dictate the lines of party action. Their position when self-government was restored and the carpetbaggers had to be overthrown forced them to exertion. Sometimes they use or tolerate a ring, but they do not suffer it to do serious mischief, and it is usually glad to nominate one of them, or anyone whom they recommend. The old traditions of social leadership survive better in the South than in the North, so that the poorer part of the white population is more apt to follow the suggestions of eminent local citizens and to place them at its head when they will accept the position. Moreover, the South is a comparatively poor country. Less is to be gained from office (including membership of a legislature), either in the way of salary or indirectly through jobbing contracts or influencing legislation. The prizes in the profession of politics being fewer, the profession is not prosecuted with the same earnestness and perfection of organization. There are, however, some cities where conditions similar to those of large Northern cities reappear, and there ring-and-bossdom reappears also. New Orleans is the best example— it has a strong ring— and in Arkansas and Texas, where there never was a plantation aristocracy like that of the slave states on the Atlantic coast, rings are pretty numerous, though, as the cities are small and seldom rich, their exploits attract little attention. That in Galveston fell when the commission form of city government was adopted.

Spoils

An illustration of Oxenstjerna's dictum regarding the wisdom with which the world is governed may be found in the fact that the greatest changes are often those introduced with the least notion of their consequence, and the most fatal those which encounter least resistance. So the system of removals from federal office which began in the days of Andrew Jackson, though disapproved of by several among the leading statesmen of the time, including Clay, Webster, and Calhoun, excited comparatively little attention in the country, nor did its advocates foresee a tithe of its far-reaching results.

The Constitution of the United States vests the right of appointing to federal offices in the president, requiring the consent of the Senate in the case of the more important, and permitting Congress to vest the appointment of inferior officers in the president alone, in the courts, or in the heads of departments. It was assumed that this clause gave officials a tenure at the pleasure of the president, i.e., that he had the legal right of removing them without cause assigned. But the earlier presidents considered the tenure as being practically for life or during good behaviour, and did not remove, except for some solid reason, persons appointed by their predecessors. Washington in his eight years displaced only nine persons, and all for cause, John Adams nine in four years, and those not on political grounds. Jefferson in his eight years removed thirty-nine, but many of these were persons whom Adams had unfairly put in just before quitting office; and in the twenty years that followed (1808–28) there were but sixteen removals. In 1820, however, a bill was run through Congress fixing four years as the term for a large number of the more important offices, and making those terms expire shortly after the inauguration of a president. This was ominous of evil, and called forth the displeasure of both Jefferson and Madison. The president, however, and his heads of departments, did not remove, so the tenure of good behaviour generally remained. But a new era began with the hot and heady Jackson, who reached the presidential chair in 1829. He was a rough Westerner, a man of the people, borne into power by a popular movement, incensed against all who were connected with his predecessor, a warm friend and a bitter enemy, anxious to repay services rendered to himself. Penetrated by extreme theories of equality, he proclaimed in his message that rotation in office was a principle in the Republican creed, and obeyed both his doctrine and his passions by displacing five hundred postmasters in his first year, and appointing partisans in their room. The plan of using office as a mere engine in partisan warfare had already been tried in New York, where the stress of party contests had led to an early development of many devices in party organization; and it was a New York adherent of Jackson, Marcy, who, speaking in the Senate in 1832, condensed the new doctrine in a phrase that has become famous—"To the victor belong the spoils."[1]

From 1828 till a few years ago the rule with both parties has been that on a change of president nearly all federal offices, from the embassies to European courts down to village postmasterships, are deemed to be vacant. The present holders may of course be continued or reappointed (if their term has expired); and if the new president belongs to the same party as his predecessor, many of them will be; but they are not held to have either a legal or a moral claim. The choice of the president or departmental head has been absolutely free, no qualifications, except the citizenship of the nominee, being required, nor any check imposed on him, except that the Senate's consent is needed to the more important posts.[2]

The want of knowledge on the part of the president and his ministers of the persons who applied for places at a distance, obliged them to seek information and advice from those who, belonging to the neighborhood, could give it. It was natural for the senators from a state or the representative in Congress from a district within which a vacant office lay, to recommend to the president candidates for it, natural for the president or his ministers

---

[1] Before 1820 Governor Clinton complained "of an organized and disciplined corps of Federal officials interfering in State elections." Marcy's speech was a defence of the system of partisan removals and short terms from the example of his own state. "They [the New York politicians] when contending for victory avow the intention of enjoying the fruits of it. They see nothing wrong in the rule that to the victor belong the spoils of the enemy."

[2] See on this subject, Chap. 5, in Vol. 1.

The act of 1820 as extended by subsequent legislation applies to more than 6,000 offices. Its mischief, however, was not confined to the legal vacating of these posts, but has lain largely also in establishing a custom applying to a far larger number of minor places.

to be guided by this recommendation, of course, in both cases, only when they belonged to the same party as the president. Thus the executive became accustomed to admit the rights the politicians claimed, and suffered its patronage to be prostituted to the purpose of rewarding local party service and conciliating local party support. Now and then a president, or a strong minister controlling the president, has proved restive; yet the usage continues, being grounded on the natural wish of the executive to have the goodwill and help of the senators in getting treaties and appointments confirmed, and on the feeling that the party in every district must be strengthened by a distribution of good things, in the way which the local leader thinks most serviceable. The essential features of the system are, that a place in the public service is held at the absolute pleasure of the appointing authority; that it is invariably bestowed from party motives on a party man, as a reward for party services (whether of the appointee or of someone who pushes him); that no man expects to hold it any longer than his party holds power; and that he has therefore the strongest personal reasons for fighting in the party ranks. Thus the conception of office among politicians came to be not the ideal one, of its involving a duty to the community, nor the "practical" one, of its being a snug berth in which a man may live if he does not positively neglect his work, but the perverted one, of its being a salary paid in respect of party services, past, present, and future.

The politicians, however, could hardly have riveted this system on the country but for certain notions which had become current among the mass of the people. "Rotation in office" was, and indeed by most men still is, held to be conformable to the genius of a democracy. It gives every man an equal chance of power and salary, resembling herein the Athenian and Florentine system of choosing officers by lot. It is supposed to stimulate men to exertion, to foster a laudable ambition to serve the country or the neighbourhood, to prevent the growth of an official caste, with its habits of routine, its stiffness, its arrogance. It recognizes that equality which is so dear to the American mind, bidding an official remember that he is the servant of the people and not their master, like the bureaucrats of Europe. It forbids him to fancy that he has any right to be where he is, any ground for expecting to stay there. It ministers in an odd kind of way to that fondness for novelty and change in persons and surroundings which is natural in the constantly moving communities of the West. The habit which grew up of electing state and city officers for short terms tended in the same direction. If those whom the people itself chose were to hold office only for a year or two, why should those who were appointed by federal authority have a more stable tenure? And the use of patronage for political purposes was further justified by the example of England, whose government was believed by the Americans of Jackson and Van Buren generation to be worked, as it had been largely worked, by the Patronage Secretary of the Treasury in his function of distributing places to members of the House of Commons, and honours (such as orders, and steps in the peerage) to members of the House of Lords, ecclesiastical preferments to the relatives of both.[3]

Another and a potent reason why the rotation plan commended itself to the Americans is to be found in the belief that one man is as good as another, and will do well enough any work you set him to, a belief happily expressed by their old enemy King George III when he said that "every man is good enough for any place he can get." In America a smart man is expected to be able to do anything that he turns his hand to, and the fact that a man has worked himself into a place is some evidence of his smartness. He is a "practical man." This is at bottom George III's idea; if you are clever enough to make people give you a place, you are clever enough to discharge its duties, or to conceal the fact that you are not discharging them. It may be added that most of these federal places, and those which come most before the eyes of the ordinary citizen, require little special fitness. Any careful and honest man does fairly well for a tide-waiter or a lighthouse keeper. Able and active men had no great interest in advocating appointment by merit or security of tenure, for they seldom wanted places themselves; and they had, or thought they had, an interest in jobbing their poor relatives and unprosperous friends into the public service. It is true that the relative or friend ran the risk of being turned out. But hope is stronger than fear. The prospect of getting a place affects ten people for one who is affected by the prospect of losing it, for aspirants are many and places relatively few.

Hitherto we have been considering federal offices only, the immense majority whereof are such petty posts as those of postmaster in a village, customhouse officer at a seaport, and so forth, although they also include clerkships in the departments at Washington, foreign ambassadorships and consulates, and governorships of the Territories. The system of rotation had however laid such a hold on the mind of the country that it soon extended itself over state offices and city offices also, in so far as such offices

---

[3] Now of course the tables have been turned, and the examples of the practically irremovable English civil service and of the competitive entrance examinations in England are cited against the American system.

remained appointive, and were not, like the higher administrative posts and (in most of the states and the larger cities) the judicial offices, handed over to popular election. Thus, down to that very recent time of which I shall speak presently, appointment by favour and tenure at the pleasure of the appointer became the rule in every sphere and branch of government, national, state, and municipal. It may seem strange that a people so eminently practical as the Americans acquiesced in a system which perverts public office from its proper function of serving the public, destroys the prospect of that skill which comes with experience, and gives nobody the least security that he will gain a higher post, or even retain the one he holds, by displaying conspicuous efficiency. The explanation is that administration used to be conducted in a happy-go-lucky way, that the citizens, accustomed to help themselves, relied very little on their functionaries, and did not care whether they were skilful or not, and that it was so easy and so common for a man who fell out of one kind of business to take to and make his living by another that deprivation seemed to involve little hardship. However, the main reason was that there was no party and no set of persons specially interested in putting an end to the system, whereas there soon came to be a set specially concerned to defend it. It developed, I might almost say created, the class of professional politicians, and they maintained it, because it exactly suited them. That great and growing volume of political work to be done in managing primaries, conventions, and elections for the city, state, and national governments, whereof I have already spoken, and which the advance of democratic sentiment and the needs of party warfare evolved from 1820 down to about 1850, needed men who should give to it constant and undivided attention. These men the plan of rotation in office provided. Persons who had nothing to gain for themselves would soon have tired of the work. The members of a permanent civil service would have had no motive for interfering in politics, because the political defeat of a public officer's friends would have left his position the same as before, and the civil service not being all of one party, but composed of persons appointed at different times by executives of different hues, would not have acted together as a whole. Those, however, whose bread and butter depend on their party may be trusted to work for their party, to enlist recruits, look after the organization, play electioneering tricks from which ordinary party spirit might recoil. The class of professional politicians was therefore the first crop which the Spoils System, the system of using public office as private prize of war, bore. Bosses were the second crop. In the old Scandinavian poetry the special title of the king or chieftain is "the giver of rings." He attracts followers and rewards the services, whether of the warrior or the skald, by liberal gifts. So the boss wins and holds power by the bestowal of patronage. Places are the guerdon of victory in election warfare; he divides this spoil before as well as after the battle, promising the higher elective offices to the strongest among his fighting men, and dispensing the minor appointive offices which lie in his own gift, or that of his lieutenants, to combatants of less note but equal loyalty. Thus the chieftain consolidates, extends, fortifies his power by rewarding his supporters. He garrisons the outposts with his squires and henchmen, who are bound fast to him by the hope of getting something more, and the fear of losing what they have. Most of these appointive offices are too poorly paid to attract able men; but they form a stepping-stone to the higher ones obtained by popular election; and the desire to get them and keep them provides that numerous rank and file which the American system requires to work the machine. In a country like England office is an object of desire to a few prominent men, but only to a few, because the places which are vacated on a change of government are less then sixty in all, while vacancies in other places happen only by death or promotion. Hence an insignificant number of persons out of the whole population have a personal pecuniary interest in the triumph of their party. In England, therefore, one has what may be called the general officers and headquarters staff of an army of professional politicians, but few subalterns and no privates. And in England most of these general officers are rich men, independent of official salaries. In America the privates are proportioned in number to the officers. They are a great host. As nearly all live by politics, they are held together by a strong personal motive. When their party is kept out of the spoils of the federal government, as the Democrats were out from 1861 till 1885, they have a second chance in the state spoils, a third chance in the city spoils; and the prospect of winning at least one of these two latter sets of places maintains their discipline and whets their appetite, however slight may be their chance of capturing the federal offices.

It is these spoilsmen who have depraved and distorted the mechanism of politics. It is they who pack the primaries and run the conventions so as to destroy the freedom of popular choice, they who contrived and executed the election frauds which disgrace some states and cities—repeating and ballot stuffing, obstruction of the polls, and fraudulent countings in.[4]

---

[4] The fact that in Canada the civil service is permanent has doubtless much to do with the absence of such a regular party machine as the United States possess.

In making every administrative appointment a matter of party claim and personal favour, the system has lowered the general tone of public morals, for it has taught men to neglect the interests of the community, and made insincerity ripen into cynicism. Nobody supposes that merit has anything to do with promotion, or believes the pretext alleged for an appointment. Politics has been turned into the art of distributing salaries so as to secure the maximum of support from friends with the minimum of offence to opponents. To this art able men have been forced to bend their minds; on this presidents and ministers have spent those hours which were demanded by the real problems of the country.[5] The rising politician must think of obscure supporters seeking petty places as well as of those greater appointments by which his knowledge of men and his honesty deserve to be judged. It is hardly a caricature in Mr. Lowell's satire when the intending presidential candidate writes to his maritime friend in New England,

> If you git me inside the White House,
> Your head with ile I'll kinder 'nint,
> By gittin' you inside the light-house,
> Down to the end of Jaalam pint.

After this, it seems a small thing to add that rotation in office has not improved the quality of the civil service. Men selected for their services at elections or in primaries have not proved the most capable servants of the public. As most of the posts they fill need nothing more than such ordinary business qualities as the average American possesses, the mischief has not come home to the citizens generally, but it has sometimes been serious in the higher grades, such as the departments at Washington and some of the greater customhouses.[6] Moreover, the official is not free to attend to his official duties. More important, because more influential on his fortunes, is the duty to his party of looking after its interests at the election, and his duty to his chiefs, the boss and ring, of seeing that the candidate they favour gets the party nomination. Such an official, whom democratic theory seeks to remind of his dependence on the public, does not feel himself bound to the public, but to the city boss or senator or congressman who has procured his appointment. Gratitude, duty, service, are all for the patron. So far from

---

[5] President Garfield said "one third of the working hours of senators and representatives is scarcely sufficient to meet the demands in reference to the appointments to office. . . . With a judicious system of civil service the business of the departments could be better done at half the cost."

[6] Sometimes the evil was so much felt that a subordinate of experience was always retained for the sake of teaching those who came in by political favour how to carry on the work.

making the official zealous in the performance of his functions, insecurity of tenure has discouraged sedulous application to work, since it is not by such application that office is retained and promotion won. The administration of some among the public departments in federal and city government is more behind that of private enterprises than is the case in European countries; the ingenuity and executive talent which the nation justly boasts, are least visible in national or municipal business. In short, the civil service is not in America, and cannot, under the system of rotation, become a career. Place-hunting is the career, and an office is not a public trust, but a means of requiting party services, and also, under the method of assessments previously described, a source whence party funds may be raised for election purposes.

Some of these evils were observed as far back as 1853, when an act was passed by Congress requiring clerks appointed to the departments at Washington to pass a qualifying examination.[7] Neither this nor subsequent legislative efforts in the same direction produced any improvement, for the men in office who ought to have given effect to the law were hostile to it. Similar causes defeated the system of competitive examination, inaugurated by an act of Congress in 1871, when the present agitation for civil service reform had begun to lay hold of the public mind. Mr. Hayes (1877–81) was the first president who seems to have honestly desired to reform the civil service, but the opposition of the politicians, and the indifference of Congress, which had legislated merely in deference to the pressure of enlightened opinion outside, proved too much for him. A real step in advance was, however, made in 1883, by the passage of the so-called Pendleton Act, which instituted a board of civil service commissioners (to be named by the president), directing them to apply a system of competitive examinations to a considerable number of offices in the departments at Washington, and a smaller number in other parts of the country. President Arthur named a good commission, and under the rules framed by it progress was made. The action of succeeding presidents has been matter of some controversy; but while admitting that less has been done in the way of reform than might have been desired, it is no less true that much more has been done than it would have been safe to expect in 1883. Both Mr. Cleveland and Mr. Roosevelt largely extended the scope of the act. In the so-called "classified service," to which the examination system is applied,

---

[7] To have made places tenable during good behaviour would have been open to the objection that it might prevent the dismissal of incompetent men against whom no specific charge could be proved.

some removals for political reasons have from time to time been made, but the percentage of such removals is far smaller than in the unclassified service. Honest efforts have been made by recent presidents to prevent the intrusion of politics and to enforce the rule that civil servants in the classified service shall not take an active part in campaigns.

The act of 1883 originally applied to only 14,000 posts. It has since been so extended that now out of 367,794 employees in the civil service, 234,940 are subject to competitive examination under civil service rules. Of those not subject to examination, 9,105 are presidential appointees, 7,202 of whom are first, second and third class postmasters, 37,712 are fourth class postmasters, and the bulk of the remainder minor employees, largely labourers.[8] The salaries of those covered by the act amount to very much more than half of the total sum paid in salaries by the government. Its moral effect, however, has been even greater than this proportion represents, and entitles it to the description given of it at the time as "a sad blow to the pessimists." Public sentiment is more and more favourable, and though the lower sort of "professionals" were incensed at so great an interference with their methods, and Congress now and then (as in the case of the census bill of 1909) shows imperfect sympathy with the principle, all, or nearly all, the leading men in both parties seem now disposed to support it. It strengthens the hands of any president who may desire reform, and has stimulated the civil service reform movement in states and municipalities. Between 1883 and 1910 seven states (New York, Massachusetts, Wisconsin, Illinois, Colorado, New Jersey and Ohio) had adopted the merit system, which has also been adopted by nearly one hundred cities. Nevertheless, there remain a great many posts, even in the higher national civil service, within the spoils category which is European countries would be permanent nonpolitical posts.

Some time must yet pass before the result of these changes upon the purification of politics can be fairly judged. It is for the present enough to say that while the state of things above described was generally true both of federal and of state and city administration from 1830 till 1883, there is now reason to hope that the practice of appointing for short terms, and of refusing to reappoint, or of dismissing in order to fill vacancies with political adherents, has been shaken. Nor can it be doubted that the extension of examinations will tend more and more to exclude mere spoilsmen from the public service.

[8] Report of Civil Service Commission for 1909.

CHAPTER 66

Elections and Their Machinery

I cannot attempt to describe the complicated and varying election laws of the different states. But the methods of conducting elections have so largely influenced the development of machine politics, and the recent changes in them have made so much stir and seem likely to have such considerable results, that the subject must not pass unnoticed.

All expenses of preparing the polling places and of paying the clerks and other election officers who receive and count the votes, are borne by the community, not (as in Britain) by the candidates.

All elections, whether for city, state, or federal offices, are in all states conducted by ballot, which, however, was introduced, and was long regarded, not so much as a device for preventing bribery or intimidation, but rather as the quickest and easiest mode of taking the votes of a multitude. Secrecy had not been specially aimed at, nor in point of fact generally secured.

An election is a far more complicated affair in America than in Europe. The number of elective offices is greater, and as terms of office are shorter, the number of offices to be voted for in any given year is much greater. To save the expense of numerous distinct pollings, it was long usual, though by no means universal, to take the pollings for a variety of offices at the same time, that is to say, to elect federal officials (presidential electors and congressmen), state officials, county officials, and city officials on one and the same day and at the same polling booths. Presidential electors are chosen only once in four years, congressmen once in two. But the number of state and county and city places to be filled is so large that a voter seldom goes to the polling booth without having to cast his vote for at least eight or ten persons, candidates for different offices, and sometimes he may vote for thirty or more.

This gave rise to the system of slip tickets. A slip ticket is a list, printed on a long strip of paper, of the persons standing in the same interest, that is to say, recommended by the same party or political group for the posts to be filled up at any election.[1] For many years, the universal practice was for each such voting ticket to be printed and issued by a party organization, and to be then distributed at the polling booths by the party agents to the voters and placed by them in the box. The voter usually voted the ticket as he received it, that is to say, he voted *en bloc* for all the names it contained. It was indeed open to him to modify it by striking out certain names ("scratching") and writing in others, or by placing over a name a bit of paper, gummed at the back for the purpose (called a "paster"), on which was printed the name of some other candidate. But the always potent tendency to vote the party list as a whole was naturally stronger when that whole list found itself on the same piece of paper in the voter's hands than it would have been had the paper contained in alphabetical order the names of all the candidates whomsoever, making it necessary to pick and choose among them. This, however, was the least of the evils incident to the system. When (as often happened) the two great parties had bad names on their respective state or city tickets, the obvious remedy was the formation of a "citizens' " or "independent" organization to run better men. The heavy expense of printing and distributing the tickets was a serious obstacle to the making of such independent nominations, while the "regular" ticket distributers did all in their power to impede the distribution of these "independent tickets," and generally to confuse and mislead the independent voter. The expenses which the regular parties had to bear were made by their leaders a pretext for levying "election assessments" on candidates, and thereby (see *ante,* p. 791) of virtually selling nominations. And, finally, the absence of secrecy, for the voter could be followed by watchful eyes from the moment when he received the party ticket from the party distributer till he dropped it into the box, opened a wide door to bribery and intimidation. A growing sense of these mischiefs roused at length the zeal of reformers. In 1885 a bill for the introduction of a really secret ballot was presented to the legislature of Michigan, and in 1888 such a measure, resembling in its outlines the ballot laws of Australia and those of the United Kingdom, was enacted in Massachusetts. The unprecedented scale on which money was illegitimately used in the presidential election of 1888 provoked general

---

[1] A ticket includes more names or fewer, according to the number of offices to be filled, but usually more than a dozen, and often far more.

alarm, and strengthened the hands of reformers so much that secret, or, as they are called, "Australian," official ballot laws are now in force in all the states except Georgia and South Carolina; but in Tennessee and North Carolina the ballot law is not statewide, i.e., applies to certain counties only. Missouri and New Jersey have halfway measures embodying certain features of the Australian system.[2] It may cause surprise that the Southern states, communities which lived in alarm at the large Negro vote, did not sooner seize so simple a method of virtually excluding the bulk of that vote, but the reason is doubtless to be found in the fact that a secret ballot, unaccompanied by provisions for illiterate voters, would have excluded many whites also. Georgia and South Carolina may probably ere long follow their sisters in the enactment of secret ballot laws, and the strength of the movement is witnessed by the fact that in eleven states provisions on the subject have been embodied in the constitutions.

The new laws of these forty-six states are of varying merit. Nearly all the laws provide for the official printing of the voting papers, for the inclusion of the names of all candidates upon the same paper, so that the voter must himself place his mark against those he desires to support, and for the depositing of the paper in the box by the voter in such manner as to protect him from observation. Thus secrecy has been nearly everywhere secured, and while independent candidates have a better chance, a heavy blow has been struck at bribery and intimidation. The practice of "peddling" the ballots at the polling place by the agents of the parties, which had reached portentous dimensions in New York, has in most places disappeared, while the extinction of the head of expenses incurred for this purpose, as well as for ballot printing, has diminished the pretext for levying assessments. Elections are far more orderly than they were, because more secret, and because the attendant crowd of those who peddle and hang about the polls, disposed to turbulence and ready for intimidation, has been much reduced. And it is an incidental gain that the most ignorant class of voters, who in the North are usually recent immigrants, have been in some states deprived of their votes, in others stimulated (as happened to the more intelligent Negroes in parts of the South) to improve their education, and fit themselves to vote. Even where provision is made for the voting of illiterates, a certain disgrace, which citizens desire to escape, attaches to him who is forced to have recourse to this provision. No one proposes to revert to the old system, nor has the ingenuity of artful politicians succeeded, to any great extent, in evading the salutary provisions of the new statutes.

---

[2] West Virginia permits the voter to choose between the open, sealed, or secret ballot.

So much for what may be called the machinery of voting. There are, however, several other questions that may be asked regarding an election system. One is, whether it is honestly carried out by the officials? To this question no general answer can be given, because there are the widest possible differences between different states; differences due chiefly to the variations in their election laws, but partly also to the condition of the public conscience. In some states the official conduct of elections is now believed to be absolutely pure, owing, one is told, to the excellence of a minutely careful law. In others, frauds, such as ballot stuffing and false counting, are said to be common, not only in city, but also in state and more rarely in federal elections. I have no data to determine how widely frauds prevail, for their existence can rarely be proved, and they often escape detection. They are sometimes suspected where they do not exist. It is however clear that in some states they are frequent enough to constitute a serious reproach.[3]

Another question is: Does the election machinery prevent intimidation, bribery, personation, repeating, and the other frauds which the agents of candidates or parties seek to perpetrate? Here, too, there are great differences between one state and city and another, differences due both to the laws and to the character of the population. Of intimidation there is now but little, save in a few cities, where roughs, or occasionally even the police, are said to molest a voter supposed to belong to the other party, or to be inclined to desert their own party. But till the enactment of the secret ballot laws, it sometimes happened that employers endeavoured to send their workingmen to the polls in a body in order to secure their votes; and the dislike to this was one of the motives which won popular favour for these laws. Repeating and personation are not rare in dense populations, where the agents and officials do not, and cannot, know the voters' faces; and these frauds are sometimes organized on a grand scale by bringing bands of roughs from one city to another.

---

[3] They were specially frequent, and are not extinct, in some of the Southern states, having been there used before recent amendments to the state constitutions had debarred the vast majority of the Negroes from the suffrage. It was here that the use of "tissue ballots" was most common. I was told in San Francisco that elections had become more pure since the introduction of glass ballot boxes, which made it difficult for the presiding officials to stock the ballot box with voting papers before the voting began in the morning. After the election of 1893, nearly one hundred election officers in New York City, about twenty-five in Brooklyn, and a good many in the smaller cities were indicted for offences against the election laws, and especially for permitting "repeaters" to vote, for accompanying voters into the booth on a false pretence of their blindness or physical incapacity, and for cheating in the counting of the votes. Many were convicted. Repeating has been profusely practised in New York and (it is said) largely by professional criminals, in some subsequent elections. However the official management of elections has there and elsewhere improved.

Bribery is a sporadic disease, but often intense when it occurs. Most parts of the Union are pure, as pure as Scotland, where since 1868 there has been only one election petition for alleged bribery. Other parts are no better than the small boroughs of Southern England were before the Corrupt Practices Act of 1883.[4] No place, however, not even the poorest ward in New York City, sinks below the level of such constituencies as Yarmouth or Sandwich used to be in England. Bribery is seldom practised in America in the same way as it used to be at Rome, by distributing small sums among a large mass of poor electors, or even, as in many English boroughs, among a section of voters (not always the poorest) known to be venal, and accustomed to reserve their votes till shortly before the close of the poll. The American practice has been to give sums of from $20 to $50 to an active local "worker," who undertakes to bring up a certain number of voters, perhaps twenty or thirty, whom he "owns" or can get at. He is not required to account for the money, and spends a comparatively small part of it in direct bribes, though something in drinks to the lower sort of elector. This kind of expenditure belongs to the category rather of paid canvassing than of bribery, yet sometimes the true European species occurs. In a New Hampshire rural town not long ago, $10 were paid to each of two hundred doubtful voters. In some districts of New York the friends of a candidate will undertake, in case he is returned, to pay the rent of the poorest voters who occupy tenement houses, and the candidate subsequently makes up the amount.[5] The expenses of congressional and presidential elections are often heavy, and though the larger part goes in organization and demonstrations, meetings, torchlight processions, and so forth, a part is likely to go in some illicit way. A member of Congress for a poor district in a great city told me that his expenses ran from $8,000 up to $10,000, which is just about what

---

[4] The British general election of 1880 gave rise to no less than ninety-five petitions impugning returns on the ground of some form of corruption, and many were sustained. After the election of 1886 there was not a single petition. After that of 1892 there were ten petitions alleging corrupt practices, and in three of these the election was declared void on the ground of such practices. More recent elections have brought very few petitions, and the boroughs in which bribery still exists are probably less than a dozen. This improvement must, however, be partly ascribed to the Redistribution Act of 1885, which extinguished the small boroughs.

[5] At an election in Brooklyn, a number of coloured voters sat (literally) on the fence in front of the polling booths, waiting to be bought, but were disappointed, the parties having agreed not to buy them. There is a good deal of bribery among the coloured voters in some of the cities, e.g., in those of Kentucky and Southern Ohio, and in Philadelphia.

When there is a real issue before the voters, bribery diminishes. In the mayoralty contest of 1886, in New York, the usually venal classes went straight for the Labour candidate, and would not be bought.

a parliamentary contest used to cost in an English borough constituency of equal area. In America the number of voters in a congressional district is more than five times as great as in an average English constituency, but the official expenses of polling booths and clerks are not borne by the candidate. In a corrupt district along the Hudson River above New York I have heard of as much as $50,000 being spent at a single congressional election, when in some other districts of the state the expenses did not exceed $2,000. In a presidential election great sums are spent in doubtful, or, as they are called, "pivotal," states. Indiana was "drenched with money" in 1880, much of it contributed by great corporations, and a large part doubtless went in bribery. What part ever does go it is the harder to determine, because elections are rarely impeached on this ground, both parties tacitly agreeing that bygones shall be bygones. The election of 1888 was one of the worst on record, so large was the expenditure in doubtful states. In that year well-informed Americans came to perceive that bribery at elections was a growing evil in their country, though even now they think it less noxious than either bossism or election frauds.

This alarm has favoured the movement for the enactment of laws against corrupt practices. More than half the states have now passed such statutes. New York requires every candidate and the treasurer of every political committee to file an itemized statement of receipts and expenditure. Every payment exceeding $5 must be accounted for in detail; and expenditures are restricted to certain purposes. The provisions vary from state to state; on the whole they seem to be working for good. The practice, so general in America, of conducting elections by a party committee, which makes its payments on behalf of all the candidates running in the same interests, renders it more difficult than it is in Britain to fix a definite limit to the expenditure, either by a candidate himself or upon the conduct of the election. However, some of the new laws attempt this, fixing a low scale for "campaign expenditures," and imposing severe penalties on the receiver as well as giver of any bribe, whether to vote or to refrain from voting, a form in which bribery seems to be pretty frequent. Other but much lighter penalties are imposed on the practice of treating. It seems probable that the blow struck at electoral corruption by the secret ballot laws will be followed up by a general limitation of expenditures. Another important advance has been made by a federal law which requires the publication of the sums received by party committees in federal elections, and by another which seeks to end the pernicious habit into which large corporations had fallen of making contributions, usually kept secret, to party campaign expenditure.

On the whole the shadows have not darkened; the presidential election of 1912 cost relatively less than preceding contests had done for many years. The Republican National Committee returned its total receipts at $904,828, while those of the Democratic National Committee were $1,159,446, and those of the Progressive National Committee $676,672. These figures, however, do not include the sums received and expended by state committees, part of which went to the conduct of the national campaign.

It is always difficult to estimate the exact value of laws which propose to effect by mechanical methods reforms which in themselves are largely moral. This much, however, may be said, that while in all countries there is a proportion (varying from age to age and country to country) of good men who will act honourably whatever the law, and similarly a proportion of bad men who will try to break or evade the best laws, there is also a considerable number of men standing between these two classes, whose tendency to evil is not too strong to be repressed by law, and in whom a moral sense is sufficiently present to be capable of stimulation and education by a good law. Although it is true that you cannot make men moral by a statute, you can arm good citizens with weapons which improve their chances in the unceasing conflict with the various forms in which political dishonesty appears. The value of weapons, however, depends upon the energy of those who use them. These improved ballot acts and corrupt practices acts need to be vigorously enforced, for the disposition, of which there have been some signs, to waive the penalties they impose, and to treat election frauds and other similar offences as trivial matters, would go far to nullify the effect to be expected from the statutes.

Strong arguments have been adduced in favour of another reform in election laws, viz., the trial of contested elections, not, as now, by the legislative body to which the candidate claims to have been chosen, but by a court of law. The determinations of a legislature are almost invariably coloured by party feeling, and are usually decided by a party majority in favour of the contestant whose admission would increase their strength. Hence they obtain little respect, while corrupt or illegal practices do not receive their due condemnation in the avoidance of the election they have tainted. Against these considerations there must be set the danger that the judges who try such cases may sometimes show, or be thought to show, political partisanship, and that the credit of the bench may thus suffer. The experience of England, where disputed parliamentary elections have since 1867 been tried by judges of the superior courts, and municipal elections since 1883 by county court judges, does not wholly dispose of this apprehension; for it happens every now and then that judges are accused of partiality, or at least of an unconscious bias. Still, British opinion prefers the present system to the old one under which committee of the House of Commons tried election petitions. In the United States the validity of the election of an executive officer sometimes comes before the courts, and the courts, as a rule, decide such cases with fairness. The balance of reason and authority seems to lie with those who, like ex-Speaker Reed, have advocated the change. It was proposed as a constitutional amendment by the legislature of New York to the voters in 1892, but rejected. Latterly it seems to have dropped out of sight.

Not satisfied, however, with the purification of election methods, some few reformers go further, and have proposed to render the ballot box a more complete representation of the will of the people by making voting compulsory. The idea is not quite new; in some Greek states citizens were compelled to attend the assembly; similar provisions were to be found in parts of the United States in last century, while in modern Switzerland several cantons fine electors who fail to vote at elections or when laws are proposed under a referendum. The Swiss evidence as to the merits of the plan is not uniform. In St. Gallen, for instance, where it was introduced so far back as 1835, it seems to have worked well, while in Solothurn it proved ineffective, and was ultimately abolished. On the whole, however, the effect would seem to have been to bring out a comparatively heavy vote, sometimes reaching 83 and even 84 per cent of the registered electors, though it deserves to be noticed that the cantons in which the plan exists are, speaking generally, those in which political life is anyhow most active.[6] In the United States, however, abstention from voting does not appear to be a very serious, and certainly is not a growing, evil. City and state elections sometimes fail to draw even three-fourths of the voters to the polls; but in the presidential election of 1880, a year coinciding with that of the national census, and therefore suitable for investigation, 84 per cent of the qualified voters in the whole United States actually tendered their votes, while of the remaining 16 per cent fully three-fourths can be accounted for by illness, old age, necessary causes of absence, and, in the case of the Southern Negroes, intimidation, leaving not more than 4 per cent out of the total number of voters who may seem to have stayed away from pure indifference.[7] This

---

[6] I quote from a paper by M. Simon Deploige in the Belgian *Revue Générale* for March 1893. The plan is now being tried in Belgium.

[7] The subject is examined with care and acuteness by Professor A. B. Hart in his *Practical Essays on American Government*.

was a good result as compared with Germany, or with the United Kingdom, where 77 per cent is considered a pretty high proportion to secure, though at some recent British elections the figure has gone above 80 per cent. In the presidential election of 1892 the total number of votes cast showed only about half the increase on 1888 which the estimated growth of population ought to have given. This abstention, however, may have been largely due not to indifference, but to an unwillingness in one party to support the party candidate. In the election of 1900 the percentages varied much in different states, but do not seem to have reached on an average, 80 per cent. In 1912 the total popular vote was about a million and a half more than in 1900. The increased proportion of the population of aliens and disfranchised Negroes makes it difficult to form an estimate.

The plan of compelling men to vote on pain of being fined or incurring some disability is not likely to be adopted, and one of the arguments against it is indicated by the cause suggested for the abstentions of 1892. It is not desirable to deprive electors displeased by the nomination of a candidate of the power of protesting against him by declining to vote at all. At present, when bad nominations are made, independent voters can express their disapproval by refusing to vote for these candidates. Were voting compulsory, they would probably, so strong is party spirit, vote for these bad men rather than for their opponents, not to add that the opponents might be equally objectionable. Thus the power of party leaders and of the machine generally might be increased. I doubt, however, whether such a law as suggested could, if enacted, be effectively enforced; and it is not well to add another to the list of half-executed statutes.

The abuse of the right of appointing election officers can hardly be called a corrupt practice; yet it has in some places and notably in New York City, caused serious mischiefs. There elections were for a time under the control of the Police Board, but this plan gave rise to great abuses, and now elections have by statute been placed in charge of a special board of four commissioners, two of whom must be Republicans, two Democrats, there being also in each district four election inspectors, again two Republicans and two Democrats, with a ballot clerk from each party.[8] The selection of shops or other buildings as polling places is made by the board on the recommendation of the parties, each being allowed a half share.

[8] This statutory recognition of party as a qualification for office is not unusual in America, having been found necessary to ensure an approach to equality of distribution between the parties of the posts of election officers, for the fairness of whose action it was essential that there should be some sort of guarantee.

The particular form of evil here described, now checked in some states, still flourishes like a green bay tree in others. But on the whole, as will have been gathered from this chapter, the record of recent progress is encouraging, and not least encouraging in this, that the less honest politicians themselves have been forced to accept and pass measures of reform which public opinion, previously apathetic or ignorant, had been aroused by a few energetic voices to demand.

CHAPTER 67

Corruption

No impression regarding American politics is more generally diffused in Europe than that contained in the question which the traveller who has returned from the United States becomes so weary of being asked, "Isn't everybody corrupt there?" It is an impression for which the Americans themselves, with their airy way of talking about their own country, their fondness for broad effects, their enjoyment of a good story and humorous pleasure in exaggerations generally, are largely responsible. European visitors who, generally belonging to the wealthier classes, are generally reactionary in politics, and glad to find occasion for disparaging popular government, eagerly catch up and repeat the stories they are told in New York or San Francisco. European readers take literally the highly coloured pictures of some American novels and assume that the descriptions there given of certain men and groups "inside politics"—descriptions legitimate enough in a novel—hold true of all men and groups following that unsavoury trade. Europeans, moreover, and Englishmen certainly not less than other Europeans, have a useful knack of forgetting their own shortcomings when contemplating those of their neighbours; so you may hear men wax eloquent over the depravity of transatlantic politicians who will sail very near the wind in giving deceptive pledges to their own constituents, who will support flagrant jobs done on behalf of their own party, who will accept favours from, and dine with, and receive at their own houses, financial speculators and members of the legislature whose aims are just as base, and whose standard is just as low as those of the worst congressman that ever came to push his fortune in Washington.

I am sensible of the extreme difficulty of estimating the amount of corruption that prevails in the United States. If a native American does not know—as few do—how deep it goes nor how widely it is spread, much less can a stranger. I have, however, submitted the impressions I formed to the judgment of some fair-minded and experienced American friends, and am assured by them that these impressions are substantially correct; that is to say, that they give a view of the facts such as they have themselves formed from an observation incomparably wider than that of a European traveller could be.

The word "corruption" needs to be analyzed.[1] It is used to cover several different kinds of political unsoundness.

One sense, the most obvious, is the taking or giving of money bribes. Another sense is the taking or giving of bribes in kind, e.g., the allotment of a certain quantity of stock or shares in a company, or of an interest in a profitable contract, or of a land grant. The offence is essentially the same as where a money bribe passes, but to most people it does not seem the same, partly because the taking of money is a more unmistakable selling of one's self, partly because it is usually uncertain how the bribe given in kind will turn out, and a man excuses himself by thinking that its value will depend on how he develops the interest he has obtained. A third sense of the word includes the doing of a job, e.g., promising a contractor that he shall have the clothing of the police or the cleaning of the city thoroughfares in return for his political support; giving official advertisements to a particular newspaper which puffs you; promising a railroad president, whose subscription to party funds is hoped for, to secure the defeat of a bill seeking to regulate the freight charges of his road or threatening its land grants. These cases shade off into those of the last preceding group, but they seem less black, because the act done is one which would probably be done anyhow by someone else from no better motive, and because the turpitude consists not in getting a private gain but in misusing a public position to secure a man's own political advancement. Hence the virtue that will resist a bribe will often succumb to these temptations.

There is also the sense in which the bestowal of places of power and profit from personal motives is said to be a corrupt exercise of patronage. Opinion has in all countries been lenient to such action when the place is given as a reward of party services, but the line between a party and a personal service cannot be easily drawn.

Then, lastly, one sometimes hears the term stretched to cover insincerity

---

[1] The term "graft" has within the present century established itself as that which technically describes the corrupt taking of money by public officials, and its frequent use testifies not to a spread of the malady, but rather to the growing sensitiveness of the public conscience and the more earnest efforts to abate the evil.

in professions of political faith. To give pledges and advocate measures which one inwardly dislikes and deems opposed to the public interest is a form of misconduct which seems far less gross than to sell one's vote or influence, but it may be, in a given instance, no less injurious to the state.

Although these two latter sets of cases do not fall within the proper meaning and common use of the word "corruption," it seems worthwhile to mention them, because derelictions of duty which a man thinks trivial in the form with which custom has made him familiar in his own country, where perhaps they are matter for merriment, shock him when they appear in a different form in another country. They get mixed up in his mind with venality, and are cited to prove that the country is corrupt and its politicians profligate. A European who does not blame a minister for making a man governor of a colony because he has done some backstairs parliamentary work, will be shocked at seeing in New York someone put into the customhouse in order that he may organize primaries in the district of the congressman who has got him the place. English members of Parliament condemn the senator who moves a resolution intended to "placate" the Irish vote, while they forget their own professions of ardent interest in schemes which they think economically unsound but likely to rouse the flagging interest of the agricultural labourer. Distinguishing these senses in which the word "corruption" is used, let us attempt to inquire how far it is chargeable on the men who compose each of the branches of the American federal and state government.

No president has ever been seriously charged with pecuniary corruption. The presidents have been men very different in their moral standard, and sometimes neither scrupulous nor patriotic, but money or money's worth they have never touched for themselves, great as the temptations must have been to persons with small means and heavy expenses. They have doubtless often made bad appointments from party motives, have sought to strengthen themselves by the use of their patronage, have talked insincerely and tolerated jobs; but all these things have also been done within the last thirty years by sundry English, French, and Italian prime ministers, some of whom have since been canonized.

The standard of honour maintained by the presidents has not always been maintained by the leading members of recent administrations, several of whom have been suspected of complicity in railroad jobs, and even in frauds upon the revenue. They may not have, probably they did not, put any part of the plunder into their own pockets, but they have winked at the misdeeds of their subordinates, and allowed the party funds to be replenished, not by direct malversation, yet by rendering services to influential individuals or corporations which a strict sense of public duty would have forbidden. On the other hand, it is fair to say that there seems to be no case since the war—although there was a bad case in President Buchanan's cabinet just before the war—in which a member of the cabinet has received money, or its equivalent, as a price of either an executive act or an appointment, while inferior officials, who have been detected in so doing (and this occasionally happens), have been dismissed and disgraced.[2]

Next, as to Congress. It is particularly hard to discover the truth about Congress, for few of the abundant suspicions excited and accusations brought against senators or members of the House have been, or could have been, sifted to the bottom. Among nearly five hundred men there will be the clean and the unclean. The opportunities for private gain are large, the chances of detection small; few members keep their seats for five or six successive congresses, and one-third are changed every two years, so the temptation to make hay while the sun shines is all the stronger.

There are several forms which temptation takes in the federal legislature. One is afforded by the position a member holds on a committee. All bills and many resolutions are referred to some one of the committees, and it is in the committee-room that their fate is practically decided. In a small body each member has great power, and the exercise of power (as observed already)[3] is safeguarded by little responsibility. He may materially advance a bill promoted by an influential manufacturer, or financier, or railroad president. He may obstruct it. He may help, or may oppose, a bill directed against a railroad or other wealthy corporation, which has something to gain or lose from federal legislation.[4] No small part of the business of Congress is what would be called in England private business; and although the individual railroads which come directly into relation with the Federal government are not numerous—the great transcontinental lines which have received land grants or other subventions are the most important—questions affecting these roads have frequently come up and have involved large

---

[2] The so-called Whisky Ring of 1875 and the Star Route gang of a later time are perhaps the most conspicuous instances of malpractices in the civil service. Some gross instances of misconduct on the part of minor officers in the New York custom office were discovered in 1909.

[3] See Chap. 15 in Vol. I. on the committees of Congress.

[4] I remember to have heard of the governor of a Western Territory who, when he came East, used to borrow money from the head of a great railway which traversed his Territory, saying he would oblige the railway when it found occasion to ask him. His power of obliging included the right to veto bills passed by the Territorial legislature. This governor was an ex-boss of an Eastern state whom his party had provided for by bestowing the governorship on him.

amounts of money. The tariff on imports opens another enormous sphere in which legislative intervention affects private pecuniary interests; for it makes all the difference to many sets of manufacturers whether duties on certain classes of goods are raised, or maintained, or lowered. Hence the doors of Congress are besieged by a whole army of commercial or railroad men and their agents, to whom, since they have come to form a sort of profession, the name of lobbyists is given.[5] Many congressmen are personally interested, and lobby for themselves among their colleagues from the vantage ground of their official positions.

Thus a vast deal of solicitation and bargaining goes on. Lobbyists offer considerations for help in passing a bill which is desired or in stopping a bill which is feared. Two members, each of whom has a bill to get through, or one of whom desires to prevent his railroad from being interfered with while the other wishes the tariff on an article which he manufactures kept up, make a compact by which each aids the other. This is logrolling: You help me to roll my log, which is too heavy for my unaided strength, and I help you to roll yours. Sometimes a member brings in a bill directed against some railroad or other great corporation, merely in order to levy blackmail upon it. This is technically called a strike. An eminent railroad president told me that for some years a certain senator regularly practised this trick. When he had brought in his bill he came straight to New York, called at the railroad offices, and asked the president what he would give him to withdraw the bill. That the Capitol and the hotels at Washington are a nest of such intrigues and machinations, while Congress is sitting, is admitted on all hands; but how many of the members are tainted no one can tell. Sometimes when money passes it goes not to the member of Congress himself, but to some boss who can and does put pressure on him. Sometimes, again, a lobbyist will demand a sum for the purpose of bribing a member who is really honest, and, having ascertained that the member is going to vote in the way desired, will keep the sum in his own pocket. Bribery often takes the form of a transfer of stocks or shares, nor have even free passes on railroads been scorned by some of the more needy legislators. The abuse on this head had grown so serious that the bestowal of passes was forbidden [on interstate lines] by federal statute in 1887 and is now forbidden by the constitutions of many states.[6] In 1883 portions of a correspondence in the

---

[5] See *ante*, Note (B) to Chap. 16 in Appendix to Vol. I.

[6] All lines traversing the territory of more than one state are subject to the power of Congress to "regulate commerce." As to free passes, see the instructive remarks of the Interstate Commerce Commission in their First Report. The grant by the state of free passes on railways to members of the chambers has led to abuses in Italy.

years 1876–78 between Mr. Huntington, one of the proprietors and directors of the Central (now Southern) Pacific Railroad, who then represented that powerful corporation at Washington, and one of his agents in California, were published; and from these it appeared that the company, whose land grants were frequently threatened by hostile bills, and which was exposed to the competition of rival enterprises, which (because they were to run through Territories) Congress was asked to sanction, defended itself by constant dealings with senators and representatives—dealings in the course of which it offered money and bonds to those whose support it needed.[7]

It does not seem, from what one hears on the spot, that money is often given, or, I should rather say, it seems that the men to whom it is given are few in number. But considerations of some kind pretty often pass,[8] so that corruption in both the first and second of the above senses must be admitted to exist and to affect a portion, though only a small portion of Congress.[9] A position of some delicacy is occupied by eminent lawyers who sit in Congress and receive retainers from powerful corporations whose interests may be affected by congressional legislation, retainers for which they are often not expected to render any forensic service.[10] There are various ways in which members of Congress can use their position to advance their personal interests. They have access to the executive, and can obtain favours from it; not so much because the executive cares what legislation they pass, for it has little to do with legislation, but that the members of the cabinet are on their promotion, and anxious to stand well with persons whose influence covers any considerable local area, who may perhaps be even able to control the delegation of a state in a nominating

---

[7] Mr. Huntington comments freely on the character of various members of both houses, and describes not only his own operations, but those of Mr. Scott, his able and active opponent, who had the great advantage of being able to command passes on some railways running out of Washington. In one letter he uses a graphic and characteristic metaphor: "Scott has switched off (i.e., off the Central Pacific track and on to his own railroad track) Senators S. and W., but you know they can be switched back with the proper arrangements when they are wanted."

The Report of the U.S. Pacific Railway Commission says of these transactions, "There is no room for doubt that a large portion of the sum of $4,818,000 was used for the purpose of influencing legislation and of preventing the passage of measures deemed to be hostile to the interests of the company, and for the purpose of influencing elections."—Report, p. 84.

[8] The president of a great Western railroad told me that congressmen used to come to the company's office to buy its land, and on seeing the price list would say, "But isn't there a discount? Surely you can give the land cheaper to a friend. You know I shall be your friend in Congress," and so forth.

[9] Among the investigations which disclosed the existence of bribery among members of Congress, the most prominent since that of 1856–57 are those of the Credit Mobilier and the Pacific Mail cases.

[10] See Vol. I., p. 109, note.

convention. Hence a senator or congressman may now and then sway the executive towards a course it would not otherwise have taken, and the resulting gain to himself, or to some person who has invoked his influence, may be an illicit gain, probably not in the form of money, but as a job out of which something may be made. Again, it has been hitherto an important part of a member's duty to obtain places for his constituents in the federal civil service. There are still many such places not subject to the civil service rules. Here there has lain a vast field, if not for pecuniary gain, for appointments are not sold, yet for the gratification of personal and party interests. Nor does the mischief stop with the making of inferior appointments, for the habit of ignoring public duty which is formed blunts men's sense of honour, and makes them more apt to yield to some grosser form of temptation. Similar causes produced similar effects during last century in England, and it is said that the French legislature now suffers from the like malady, members of the chamber being incessantly occupied in wheedling or threatening the executive into conferring places or decorations upon their constituents.

The rank and file of the federal civil service attain a level of integrity as high as that of England or Germany. The state civil service is comparatively small, and in most states one hears little said against it; yet cases of defaulting state treasurers are not uncommon. Taking one part of the country with another, a citizen who has business with a government department, such as the customs or excise, or with a state treasurer's office, or with a poor-law or school authority, has as much expectation of finding honest men to deal with as he has of finding trustworthy agents to conduct a piece of private commercial business. Instances of dishonesty are more noticed when they occur in a public department, but they seem to be little (if at all) more frequent.[11]

It is hard to form a general judgment regarding the state legislatures, because they differ so much among themselves. Those of Massachusetts, Vermont, and several of the Northwestern states, such as Michigan, are pure, i.e., the members who would take a bribe are but few, and those who would push through a job for some other sort of consideration a comparatively small fraction of the whole.[12] Even in the Northwest, however, a wealthy man has great advantages in securing a federal senatorship at the hands of the legislature.[13] Some states, including New York and Pennsylvania, have

[11] There have, however, been some serious cases of malpractice in the customs at the seaports.
[12] The new Western legislatures vary greatly from time to time. Sometimes they are quite pure; the next election under some demagogic impulse may bring in a crowd of mischievous adventurers.
[13] Colorado some while ago and more recently Illinois are instances.

so bad a name that people profess to be surprised when a good act passes, and a strong governor is kept constantly at work vetoing bills corruptly obtained. Several causes have contributed to degrade the legislature of New York State. The Assembly having but 150 members, and the Senate 51, each member is worth buying. There are in the state, besides New York, several considerable ring-governed cities whence bad members come. There are also immensely powerful corporations, such as the great railroads which traverse it on their way to the West. Great corporations are the bane of state politics, for their management is secret, being usually in the hands of one or two capitalists, and their wealth is so large that they can offer bribes at which ordinary virtue grows pale. They have, moreover, in many cases this excuse, that it is only by the use of money they can ward off the attacks constantly made upon them by demagogues or blackmailers. The Assembly includes many honest men, and a few rich men who do not need a *douceur*, but the proportion of tainted men is large enough to pollute the whole lump. Of what the bribetaker gets he keeps a part for himself, using the rest to buy the doubtful votes of purchaseable people; to others he promises his assistance when they need it, and when by such logrolling he has secured a considerable backing, he goes to the honest men, among whom, of course, he has a considerable acquaintance, puts the matter to them in a plausible way—they are probably plain farmers from the rural districts—and so gains his majority. Each great corporation keeps an agent at Albany, the capital of the state, who has authority to buy off the promoters of hostile bills, and to employ the requisite professional lobbyists. Such a lobbyist, who may or may not be himself a member, bargains for a sum down, $5,000 or $10,000, in case he succeeds in getting the bill in question passed or defeated, as the case may be; and when the session ends he comes for his money, and no questions are asked. This sort of thing now goes on, or has lately gone on, in several other states, though nowhere on so grand a scale. Virginia, Maryland, California, Illinois, Missouri, are all more or less impure; Louisiana, under the influence of its lottery company (now happily at an end), was even worse than New York.[14] But the lowest point was reached in some of the Southern states shortly after the war, when, the Negroes having received the suffrage, the white inhabitants were still excluded as rebels, and the executive government was conducted by Northern carpetbaggers under the protection of Federal troops. In some states the treasury was pilfered; huge state debts were run up; Negroes voted farms to themselves;

---

[14] The New York legislature has been believed to have improved of late years, and probably may be improving, though a grave case of corruption was unearthed in 1909–10.

all kinds of robbery and jobbery went on unchecked. South Carolina, for instance, was a perfect Tartarus of corruption, as much below the Hades of Illinois or Missouri as the heaven of ideal purity is above the ordinary earth of Boston and Westminister.[15] In its legislature there was an old darkey, jet black and with venerable white hair, a Methodist preacher, and influential among his brother statesmen, who kept a stall for legislation, where he dealt in statutes at prices varying from $100 to $400. Since those days there has been a peaceful revolution for the better at the South, but some of its legislative bodies have still much leeway to make up.

Of city governments I have spoken in previous chapters. They are usually worse when the population begins to exceed 100,000, and includes a large proportion of recent immigrants. They are generally pure in smaller places, that is to say, they are as pure as those of an average English, French, or German city.

The form which corruption usually takes in the populous cities is the sale of "franchises" (especially monopolies in the use of public thoroughfares)— a frequent and scandalous practice[16]—the jobbing of contracts, and the bestowal of places upon personal adherents, both of them faults not unknown in large European municipalities, and said to be specially rife in Paris, though no rifer than under Louis Napoleon, when the reconstruction of the city under Prefect Haussman provided unequalled opportunities for the enrichment of individuals at the public expense. English small local authorities, and even, though much more rarely, town councils, do some quiet jobbery. No European city has, however, witnessed scandals approaching those of New York, where the public was in 1869–70 robbed on a vast scale, and accounts were systematically cooked to conceal the thefts,[17] or the malversations that occurred in connection with the Philadelphia City Hall and with the erection of the Pennsylvania State Capitol at Harrisburg.

On a review of the whole matter, the following conclusions may be found not very wide of the truth.

Bribery exists in Congress, but is confined to a few members, say 5 per cent of the whole number. It is more common in the legislatures of a few, but only a few, states, practically absent from the higher walks of the federal civil service, rare among the chief state officials, not frequent among

---

[15] Τόσσον ἔνερθ' Ἀΐδεω ὅσον οὐρανός ἐστ' ἀπὸ γαίης: Iliad VIII, 16.

[16] A notorious case is the sale by the New York aldermen of the right to lay a tramway in Broadway. Nearly the whole number were indicted and some were punished by imprisonment.

[17] See Chapter 88 *post*.

the lower officials, unknown among the federal judges, rare among state judges.[18]

The taking of other considerations than money, such as a share in a lucrative contract, or a railway pass, or a "good thing" to be secured for a friend, prevails among legislators to a somewhat larger extent. Being less coarsely palpable than the receipt of money, it is thought more venial. One may roughly conjecture that from 15 to 20 per cent of the members of Congress and perhaps rather more of an average state legislature would allow themselves to be influenced by inducements of this kind.

Malversation of public funds occurs occasionally in cities, rarely among federal or state officers.

Jobbery of various kinds, i.e., the misuse of a public position for the benefit of individuals, is not rare, and in large cities common. It is often disguised as a desire to render some service to the party, and the same excuse is sometimes found for a misappropriation of public money.

Patronage is usually dispensed with a view to party considerations or to win personal support. But this remark is equally true of England and France, the chief difference being that owing to the short terms and frequent removals the quantity of patronage is relatively greater in the United States.

If this is not a bright picture, neither is it so dark as that which most Europeans have drawn, and which the loose language of many Americans sanctions. What makes it seem dark is the contrast between the deficiencies which the government shows in this respect, and the excellence, on the one hand of the frame of the Constitution, on the other of the tone and sentiment of the people. The European reader may, however, complain that the picture is vague in its outlines. I cannot make it more definite. The facts are not easy to ascertain, and it is hard to say what standard one is to apply to them. In the case of America men are inclined to apply an ideal standard, because she is a republic, professing to have made a new departure in politics, and setting before her a higher ideal than most European monarchies. Yet it must be remembered that in a new and large country, where the temptations are enormous and the persons tempted have many of them no social position to forfeit, the conditions are not the most favourable to virtue. If, recognizing the fact that the path of the politician is in all countries thickly set with snares, we leave ideals out of sight and try America by the

---

[18] Senators were often charged with buying themselves into the Senate: but, so far as I could ascertain, it did not often happen that a candidate for the Senate directly bribed members of the state legislature, though frequently he made heavy contributions to the party election fund, used to defray the election expenses of the members of the party dominant in the state legislature.

average concrete standard of Europe, we shall find that while her legislative bodies fall much below the level of purity maintained in England and Germany, and also below that of France and Italy, the body of her higher federal officials, in spite of the evils flowing from an uncertain tenure, is not, in point of integrity, at this moment markedly inferior to the administrations of most European countries. This is perhaps less generally true of most of the state officials; and it certainly cannot be said of those who administer the business of the larger cities, for the standard of purity has there sunk to a point lower than that which the municipalities of any European country show.

The War Against Bossdom

It must not be supposed the inhabitants of ring-ruled cities tamely submit to their tyrants. The Americans are indeed, what with their good nature and what with the preoccupation of the most active men in their private business, a long-suffering people. But patience has its limits, and when a ring has pushed paternal government too far, an insurrection may break out. Rings have generally the sense to scent the coming storm, and to avert it by making two or three good nominations, and promising a reduction of taxes. Sometimes, however, they hold on their course fearless and shameless, and then the storm breaks upon them.

There are several forms which a reform movement or other popular rising takes. The recent history of great cities supplies examples of each. The first form is an attack upon the primaries.[1] They are the key of a ring's position, and when they have been captured their batteries can be turned against the ring itself. When an assault upon the bosses is resolved upon, the first thing is to form a committee. It issues a manifesto calling on all good citizens to attend the primaries of their respective wards, and there vote for delegates opposed to the ring. The newspapers take the matter up, and repeat the exhortation. As each primary is held, on the night fixed by the ward committee of the regular (that is, the ring) organization, some of the reformers appear at it, and propose a list of delegates, between whom and the ring's list a vote of the members of the primary is taken. This may succeed in some of the primaries, but rarely in a majority of them; because (as explained in a previous chapter) the rolls seldom or never include the whole party voters of the ward, having been prepared by the professionals

---

[1] The remarks that follow must be taken subject to the alterations recently introduced, in many states, by the new primary laws. I allow these remarks to stand because they describe what existed before those laws, and still exist in states that have not adopted them.

in their own interest. Sometimes only one-fourth or one-fifth of the voters are on the primary roll, and these are of course the men on whom the ring can rely. Hence, even if the good citizens of the district, obeying the call of patriotism and the reform committee, present themselves at the primary, they may find so few of their number on the roll that they will be outvoted by the ringsters. But the most serious difficulty is the apathy of the respectable, steady-going part of the population to turn out in sufficient numbers. They have their engagements of business or pleasure to attend to, or it is a snowy night and their wives persuade them to stay indoors. The well-conducted men of small means are an eminently domestic class, who think they do quite enough for the city and the nation if they vote at the polls. It is still more difficult to induce the rich to interest themselves in confessedly disagreeable work. They find themselves at a primary in strange and uncongenial surroundings. Accustomed to be treated with deference in their countinghouse or manufactory, they are jostled by a rough crowd, and find that their servants or workmen are probably better known and more influential than they are themselves. They recognize by sight few of the persons present, for, in a city, acquaintance does not go by proximity of residence, and are therefore at a disadvantage for combined action, whereas the professional politicians are a regiment where every private in each company knows his fellow private and obeys the officers. Hence, the best, perhaps the only chance of capturing a primary is by the action of a group of active young men who will take the trouble of organizing the movement by beating up the members of the party who reside in the district, and bearding the local bosses in the meeting. It is a rough and toilsome piece of work, but young men find a compensation in the fun which is to be had out of the fight; and when a victory is won, theirs is the credit. To carry a few primaries is only the first step. The contest has to be renewed in the convention, where the odds are still in favour of the professionals, who "know the ropes" and may possibly outwit even a majority of reform delegates. The managing committee is in their hands, and they can generally secure a chairman in their interests. Experience has accordingly shown that this method of attacking the machine very rarely succeeds; and though the duty of attending the primaries continues to be preached, the advice shares the fate of most sermons. Once in a way, the respectable voter will rouse himself, but he cannot be trusted to continue to do so year after year. He is like those citizen-soldiers of ancient Greece who would turn out for a summer inroad into the enemy's country, but refused to keep the field through the autumn and winter.

A second expedient, which may be tried instead of the first, or resorted to after the first has been tried and failed, is to make an independent list of nominations and run a separate set of candidates. If this strategy be resolved on, the primaries are left unheeded; but when the election approaches, a committee is formed which issues a list of candidates for some or all of the vacant offices in opposition to the "regular" list issued by the party convention, and conducts the agitation on their behalf. This saves all trouble in primaries or conventions, but involves much trouble in elections, because a complete campaign corps has to be organized, and a campaign fund raised.[2] Moreover, the average voter, not having followed politics closely enough to comprehend his true duty and interest, and yielding to his established party habits, inclines, especially in state and federal elections, to vote the "regular ticket." He starts with a certain prejudice against those who are "troubling Israel" by dividing the party, because he sees that in all probability the result will be not to carry the independent ticket, but to let in the candidates of the opposite party. Hence the bolting independents can rarely hope to carry so large a part of their own party with them as to win the election. The result of their action will rather be to bring in the candidates of the other side, who may be no better than the men on the ticket of their own ring. Accordingly, reformers have become reluctant to take this course, for though it has the merit of relieving their feelings, it exposes them to odium, involves great labour, and effects nothing more than may be obtained by one or other of the two methods which I have next to describe.

The third plan is to abstain from voting for the names on your party ticket to which you object. This is scratching. You are spared the trouble of running candidates of your own, but your abstention, if the parties are nearly balanced, causes the defeat of the bad candidates whom your own party puts forward, and brings in those of the other party. This is a good plan when you want to frighten a ring, and yet cannot get the more timid reformers to go the length of voting either an independent ticket or the ticket of the other party. It is employed when a ring ticket is not bad all through, but contains some fair names mingled with some names of corrupt or

---

[2] "To run an anti-machine candidate for mayor it is necessary to organize a new machine at an expense of from $60,000 to $100,000 (£12,000 to £20,000), with a chance of his being 'sold out' then by the men who are hired to distribute his ballots."—Mr. J. B. Bishop in the paper on "Money in City Elections," written in 1887. Now that the new laws of nearly all states provide for official voting papers, the last-mentioned risk has disappeared, but the expense of getting up a new election organization is still heavy. Someone has said that the difference between running as a regular candidate and running on your own account as an independent candidate is like the difference between travelling by railway and making a new railway of your own to travel by.

dangerous men. You scratch the latter and thereby cause their defeat; the others, receiving the full strength of the party, are carried.

If, however, indignation against a dominant ring has risen so high as to overcome the party predilections of ordinary citizens, if it is desired to administer condign and certain punishment to those who have abused the patience of the people, the reformers will take a more decided course. They urge their friends to vote the ticket of the opposite party, either entire or at least all the better names on it, thus ensuring its victory. This is an efficient method, but a desperate one, for you put into power a ring of the party which you have been opposing all your life, and whose members are possibly quite as corrupt as those of the ring which controls your own party. The gain you look for is not therefore the immediate gain of securing better city government, but the ultimate gain of raising the general practice of politics by the punishment of evildoers. Hence, whenever there is time to do so, the best policy is for the reformers to make overtures to the opposite party, and induce them by the promise of support to nominate better candidates than they would have nominated if left to themselves. A group of bolters afraid of being called traitors to their party, will shrink from this course; and if they are weak in numbers, their approaches may be repulsed by the opposition. But the scheme is always worth trying, and has several times been crowned with success. By it the reforming party among the Democrats of Baltimore once managed to defeat their ring in an election of judges. They settled in conference with the Republicans a nonpartisan ticket, which gave the Republicans (who were a minority) a better share of the bench than they could have got by fighting alone, and which substituted respectable Democrats for the objectionable names on the regular Democratic ticket. A similar combination of the reform Republicans in Philadelphia with the Democrats, who in that city are in a permanent minority, led to the defeat of the Republican Gas Ring (whereof more in a later chapter). This method has the advantage of saving expense, because the bolters can use the existing machinery of the opposite party, which organizes the meetings and circulates the literature. It is on the whole the most promising strategy, but needs tact as well as vigour on the part of the independent leaders. Nor will the opposite party always accept the proffered help. Sometimes it fears the gifts of the Greeks, sometimes it hopes to win unhelped, and therefore will not sacrifice any of its candidates to the scruples of the reformers. Sometimes its chiefs dislike the idea of reform so heartily as to prefer defeat at the hands of a ring of the other party to a victory which might weaken the hold of professionals upon the machine and lead to a general purification of politics.

If the opposite party refuses the overtures of the reformers who are "kicking" against their own machine, or will not purify the ticket sufficiently to satisfy them, there remains the chance of forming a third party out of the best men of both the regular organizations, and starting a third set of candidates. This is an extension and improvement of the first of the four enumerated methods, and has the greater promise of success because it draws votes from both parties instead of from one only. It has been frequently employed of late years in cities, generally of the second order, by running what is called a "citizens' ticket."

Of course bolters who desert their own party at a city election do not intend permanently to separate themselves from it. Probably they will vote its ticket at the next state or presidential election. Their object is to shake the power of their local boss, and if they cannot overthrow the ring, at least to frighten it into better behavior. This they often effect. After the defeat of some notorious candidates, the jobs are apt to be less flagrant. But such repentances are like those of the sick wolf in the fable, and experience proves that when the public vigilance has been relaxed, the ringsters of both parties return to their wallowing in the mire.

The difficulties of getting good citizens to maintain a steady war against the professionals have been found so great, and in particular the attempt to break their control of the primaries has so often failed, that remedies have been sought in legislation. Not a few states have extended the penalties attached to bribery and frauds at public elections to similar offences committed at primaries and nominating conventions, deeming these acts to be, as in fact they are, scarcely less hurtful to the community when practised at purely voluntary and private gatherings than when employed at elections, seeing that the average electors follow the regular nomination like so many sheep: it is the candidate's party label, not his own character, that is voted for. And now, as already observed, by the laws regulating primaries passed in almost every state, bribery or any sort of fraud practised at a primary election is made an offence punishable as if it was a final election.[3] Similar provisions protect the delegate to a convention from the candidate, the candidate from the delegate, and the party from both. Minnesota led the way by a set of stringent regulations, making the annulment or destruction of any ballots cast at a party meeting held for the purpose of choosing either candidates or delegates, or the wrongfully preventing persons from voting who are entitled to vote, or personation, or "any other fraud or wrong tending to defeat or affect the result of the election," a misdemeanour

---

[3] See note on primary laws to Chapter 60 *ante*.

punishable by a fine not exceeding $3,000, or three years' imprisonment, or both penalties combined.[4] Europeans are surprised that legislation should not only recognize parties, but should actually attempt to regulate the internal proceedings of a political party at a perfectly voluntary gathering of its own members, a gathering whose resolutions no one is bound to obey or regard in any way. But it was because the machine had succeeded in nullifying the freedom of the voter that statutes were framed to protect even his voluntary action as a member of a party. That such a plan should be tried at all is a phenomenon to be seriously pondered by those who are accustomed to point to America as the country where the principle of leaving things alone has worked most widely and usefully; and it is the strongest evidence of the immense vigour of these party organizations, and of the authority their nominations exert, that reformers, foiled in the effort to purify them by appeals to the conscience and public spirit of the voter himself, should be driven to invoke the arm of the law.

The struggle between the professional politicians and the reformers has been going on in the great cities, with varying fortune, since 1870. As illustrations of the incidents that mark it will be found in subsequent chapters, I will here say only that in the onslaughts on the rings, which most elections bring round, the reformers, though they seldom capture the citadel, often destroy some of the outworks, and frighten the garrison into a more cautious and moderate use of their power. After an election in which an "independent ticket" has received considerable support, the bosses are disposed to make better nominations, and, as an eminent New York professional (the late Mr. Fernando Wood) said, "to pander a little to the moral sense of the community." Every campaign teaches the reformers where the enemy's weak points lie, and gives them more of that technical skill which has hitherto been the strength of the professionals. It is a warfare of volunteers against disciplined troops, but the volunteers, since they are fighting for the taxpayers at large, would secure so great a preponderance of numbers, if they could but move the whole body of respectable citizens, that their triumph will evidently depend in the long run upon their own constancy and earnestness. If their zeal does not flag; if they do not suffer themselves to be disheartened by frequent repulses; if, not relying too absolutely on any one remedy, they attack the enemy at every point, using every social and educational as well as legal appliance, the example of their disinterested public spirit, as well as the cogency of their arguments, cannot fail to tell

[4] Statutes of Minnesota of 1887, Chapter IV, §§ 99–105. It is significant that these sections apply only to cities of 5,000 inhabitants or upwards.

on the voters; and no boss, however adroit, no ring, however strongly entrenched, will be able to withstand them. The war, however, will not be over when the enemy has been routed. Although much may be done by legislative remedies, such as new election laws, new provisions against corruption, a reconstruction of the frame of city government, and a purification of the civil service, there are certain internal and, so to speak, natural causes of mischief, the removal of which will need patience and unremitting diligence. In great cities—for it is throughout chiefly of cities that we have to think—a large section of the voters will, for many years to come, be comparatively ignorant of the methods of free government which they are set to work. They will be ignorant even of their own interests, failing to perceive that wasteful expenditure injures those who do not pay direct taxes, as well as those who do. Retaining some of the feelings which their European experience has tended to produce, they will distrust appeals coming from the best-educated classes, and be inclined to listen to loose-tongued demagogues. Once they have joined a party they will vote at the bidding of its local leaders, however personally unworthy.[5] While this section remains numerous, rings and bosses will always have materials ready to their hands. There is, however, reason to expect that with the progress of time this section will become relatively smaller. And even now, large as it is, it could be overthrown and bossdom extirpated, were the better citizens to maintain unbroken through a series of elections that unity and vigour of action of which they have at rare moments, and under the impulse of urgent duty, shown themselves capable. In America, as every-where else in the world, the commonwealth suffers more often from apathy or shortsightedness in the richer classes, who ought to lead, than from ignorance or recklessness in the humbler classes, who are generally ready to follow when they are wisely and patriotically led.

[5] Says Mr. Roosevelt: "Voters of the labouring class in the cities are very emotional: they value in a public man what we are accustomed to consider virtues only to be taken into account when estimating private character. Thus if a man is open-handed and warm-hearted, they consider it as being a fair offset to his being a little bit shaky when it comes to applying the eighth commandment to affairs of state. In the lower wards (of New York City), where there is a large vicious population, the condition of politics is often fairly appalling, and the [local] boss is generally a man of grossly immoral public and private character. In these wards many of the social organizations with which the leaders are obliged to keep on good terms are composed of criminals or of the relatives and associates of criminals. . . . The president of a powerful semi-political association was by profession a burglar, the man who received the goods he stole was an alderman. Another alderman was elected while his hair was still short from a term in the State prison. A school trustee had been convicted of embezzlement and was the associate of criminals."
—*Century* magazine for November 1886.

C H A P T E R   6 9

National Nominating Conventions

In every American election there are two acts of choice, two periods of contest. The first is the selection of the candidate from within the party by the party; the other is the struggle between the parties for the post. Frequently the former of these is more important, more keenly fought over, than the latter, for there are many districts in which the predominance of one party is so marked that its candidate is sure of success, and therefore the choice of a candidate is virtually the choice of the officer or representative.

Preceding chapters have described the machinery which exists for choosing and nominating a candidate. The process was similar, and, subject to the variations introduced by the recent primary laws, is still similar in every state of the Union, and through all elections to office, from the lowest to the highest, from that of common councilman for a city ward up to that of president of the United States. But, of course, the higher the office, and the larger the area over which the election extends, the greater are the efforts made to secure the nomination, and the hotter the passions it excites. The choice of a candidate for the presidency is so striking and peculiar a feature of the American system that it deserves a full examination.

Like most political institutions, the system of nominating the president by a popular convention is the result of a long process of evolution.

In the first two elections, those of 1789[1] and 1792, there was no need for nominations of candidates, because the whole nation wished and expected George Washington to be elected. So too, when in 1796 Washington declared his retirement, the dominant feeling of one party was for John Adams, that

---

[1] The president is now always chosen on the Tuesday after the first Monday in the November of an even year, whose number is a multiple of four (e.g., 1880, 1884, 1888), and comes into office in the spring following; but the first election was held in the beginning of 1789, because the Constitution had been then only just adopted.

of the other for Thomas Jefferson, and nobody thought of setting out formally what was so generally understood.

In 1800, however, the year of the fourth election, there was somewhat less unanimity. The prevailing sentiment of the Federalists went for reelecting Adams, and the small conclave of Federalist members of Congress which met to promote his interest was deemed scarcely necessary. The (Democratic) Republicans, however, while united in desiring to make Jefferson president, hesitated as to their candidate for the vice-presidency, and a meeting of Republican members of Congress was therefore called to recommend Aaron Burr for this office. It was a small meeting and a secret meeting, but it is memorable not only as the first congressional caucus but as the first attempt to arrange in any way a party nomination.

In 1804 a more regular gathering for the same purpose was held. All the Republican members of Congress were summoned to meet; and they unanimously nominated Jefferson for president, and George Clinton of New York for vice-president. So in 1808 nearly all the Republican majority in both houses of Congress met and formally nominated Madison and Clinton. The same course was followed in 1812, and again in 1816. But the objections which were from the first made to this action of the party in Congress, as being an arrogant usurpation of the rights of the people—for no one dreamed of leaving freedom to the presidential electors—gained rather than lost strength on each successive occasion, so much so that in 1820 the few who met made no nomination,[2] and in 1824, out of the Democratic members of both houses of Congress summoned to the "nominating caucus," as it was called, only sixty-six attended, many of the remainder having announced their disapproval of the practice.[3] The nominee of this caucus came in only third at the polls, and this failure gave the *coup de grâce* to a plan which the levelling tendencies of the time, and the disposition to refer everything to the arbitrament of the masses, would in any case have soon extinguished. No congressional caucus was ever again held for the choice of candidates.

A new method, however, was not at once discovered. In 1828 Jackson was recommended as candidate by the legislature of Tennessee and by a number of popular gatherings in different places, while his opponents

---

[2] It was not absolutely necessary to have a nomination, because there was a general feeling in favour of reelecting Monroe. The sentiments which suggested 'rotation' in office as proper for less important posts did not include places of such importance as those of president or state governor.

[3] The whole number was then 261, nearly all Democratic Republicans, for the Federalist party had been for some time virtually extinct.

accepted, without any formal nomination, the then president, J. Q. Adams, as their candidate. In 1831, however, assemblies were held by two great parties (the Anti-Masons and the National Republicans, afterwards called Whigs) consisting of delegates from most of the states; and each of these conventions nominated its candidates for the presidency and vice-presidency. A third "national convention" of young men, which met in 1832, adopted the Whig nominations, and added to them a series of ten resolutions, constituting the first political platform ever put forth by a nominating body. The friends of Jackson followed suit by holding their national convention which nominated him and Van Buren. For the election of 1836, a similar convention was held by the Jacksonian Democrats, none by their opponents. But for that of 1840, national conventions of delegates from nearly all the states were held by both Democrats and Whigs, as well as by the (then young and very small) party of the Abolitionists. This precedent has been followed in every subsequent contest, so that the national nominating conventions of the great parties are now as much a part of the regular machinery of politics as the rules which the Constitution itself prescribes for the election. The establishment of the system coincides with and represents the complete social democratization of politics in Jackson's time. It suits both the professionals, for whom it finds occupation and whose power it secures, and the ordinary citizen who, not having time himself to attend to politics, likes to think that his right of selecting candidates is duly recognized in the selection of candidates by delegates whom he is entitled to vote for. But the system was soon seen to be liable to fall under the control of selfish intriguers and therefore prejudicial to the chances of able and independent men. As early as 1844 Calhoun refused to allow his name to be submitted to a nominating convention, observing that he would never have joined in breaking down the old congressional caucus had he foreseen that its successor would prove so much more pernicious.

Thus from 1789 till 1800 there were no formal nominations; from 1800 till 1824, nominations were made by congressional caucuses; from 1824 to 1840, nominations irregularly made by state legislatures and popular meetings were gradually ripening towards the method of a special gathering of delegates from the whole country. This last plan has held its ground since 1840, but its workng is beginning to be affected by the new plan of primary votings.[4]

Its perfection, however, was not reached at once. The early conventions

[4] See last paragraph of this chapter.

were to a large extent mass meetings.[5] The later and present ones are regularly constituted representative bodies, composed exclusively of delegates, each of whom has been duly elected at a party meeting in his own state, and brings with him his credentials. It would be tedious to trace the process whereby the present system was created, so I shall be content with describing it in outline as it now stands.

The Constitution provides that each state shall choose as many presidential electors as it has persons representing it in Congress, i.e., two electors to correspond to the two senators from each state, and as many more as the state sends members to the House of Representatives. Thus Delaware and Idaho have each three electoral votes, because they have each only one representative besides their two senators. New York has thirty-nine electoral votes; two corresponding to its two senators, thirty-seven corresponding to its thirty-seven representatives in the House.

Now in the nominating convention each state is allowed twice as many delegates as it has electoral votes, e.g., Delaware and Idaho have each six delegates, New York has seventy-eight. The delegates are chosen by local conventions in their several states, viz., two for each congressional district by the party convention of that district, and four for the whole state (called delegates-at-large) by the state convention. As each convention is composed of delegates from primaries, it is the composition of the primaries which determines that of the local conventions, and the composition of the local conventions which determines that of the national. To every delegate there is added a person called his "alternate," chosen by the local convention at the same time, and empowered to replace him in case he cannot be present in the national convention. If the delegate is present to vote the alternate is silent; if from any cause the delegate is absent, the alternate steps into his shoes.

Respecting the freedom of the delegate to vote for whom he will, there have been differences both of doctrine and of practice. A local convention or state convention may instruct its delegates which aspirant[6] shall be their first choice, or even, in case he cannot be carried, for whom their subsequent votes shall be cast. Such instructions are frequently given, and still more

---

[5] In 1856 the first Republican convention, which nominated Frémont, was rather a mass meeting than a representative body, for in so many states there was not a regular organization of the new party. So was the seceding Republican convention which met at Cincinnati in 1872 and nominated Greeley.

[6] I use throughout the term "aspirant" to denote a competitor for the nomination, reserving the term "candidate" for the person nominated as the party's choice for the presidency.

frequently implied, because a delegate is often chosen expressly as being
the supporter of one or other of the aspirants whose names are most
prominent. But the delegate is not absolutely bound to follow his instructions.
He may vote even on the first ballot for some other aspirant than the one
desired by his own local or state convention. Much more, of course, may
he, though not so instructed, change his vote when it is plain that that
aspirant will not succeed. His vote is always a valid one, even when given
in the teeth of his instructions; but how far he will be held censurable for
breaking them depends on a variety of circumstances. His motives may be
corrupt; perhaps something has been given him. They may be pardonable;
a party chief may have put pressure on him, or he may desire to be on the
safe side, and go with the majority. They may be laudable; he really seeks
to do the best for the party, or has been convinced by facts lately brought
to his knowledge that the man for whom he is instructed is unworthy. Where
motives are doubtful, it may be charitable, but it is not safe, to assume that
they are of the higher order. Each "state delegation" has its chairman, and
is expected to keep together during the convention. It usually travels together
to the place of meeting; takes rooms in the same hotel; has a recognized
headquarters there; sits in a particular place allotted to it in the convention
hall; holds meetings of its members during the progress of the convention
to decide on the course which it shall from time to time take. These
meetings, if the state be a large and doubtful one, excite great interest, and
the sharp-eared reporter prowls round them, eager to learn how the votes
will go. Each state delegation votes by its chairman, who announces how
his delegates vote; but if his report is challenged, the roll of delegates is
called, and they vote individually. Whether the votes of a state delegation
shall be given solid for the aspirant whom the majority of the delegation
favours, or by the delegates individually according to their preferences, is
a point which has excited bitter controversy. The present practice of the
Republican party (so settled in 1876 and again in 1880) allows the delegates
to vote individually, even when they have been instructed by a state
convention to cast a solid vote. The Democratic party, on the other hand,
sustains any such instruction given to the delegation, and records the vote
of all the state delegates for the aspirant whom the majority among them
approve. This is the so-called unit rule. If, however, the state convention
has not imposed the unit rule, the delegates vote individually.

For the sake of keeping up party life in the Territories and in the federal
District of Columbia, delegates from them have been admitted to the
national convention, although the Territories and District (and of course the
transmarine possessions) have no votes in a presidential election. Such

delegates still attend from Hawaii and Alaska and the District; and even from Puerto Rico and the Philippine Islands. Delegations of states which are known to be in the hands of the opposite party, and whose preference of one aspirant to another will not really tell upon the result of the presidential election, are admitted to vote equally with the delegations of the states sure to go for the party which holds the convention.[7] This arrangement is justified on the ground that it sustains the interest and energy of the party in states where it is in a minority. But it permits the choice to be determined by districts whose own action will in no wise affect the election itself, and the delegates from these districts are apt to belong to a lower class of politicians, and to be swayed by more sordid motives than those who come from states where the party holds a majority.[8]

So much for the composition of the national convention; we may now go on to describe its proceedings.

It is held in the summer immediately preceding a presidential election, usually in June or July, the election falling in November. A large city is always chosen, in order to obtain adequate hotel accommodation, and easy railroad access. Formerly, conventions were commonly held in Baltimore or Philadelphia, but since the centre of population has shifted to the Mississippi Valley, Cincinnati, St. Louis, Denver, Minneapolis, and especially Chicago, have become the favourite spots.

Business begins by the "calling of the convention to order" by the chairman of the national party committee. Then a temporary chairman is nominated, and, if opposed, voted on; the vote sometimes giving an indication of the respective strength of the factions present. Then the secretaries and the clerks are appointed, and the rules which are to govern the business are adopted. After this, the committees, particularly those on credentials and resolutions, are nominated, and the convention adjourns till their report can be presented.

The next sitting usually opens, after the customary prayer, with the appointment of the permanent chairman, who inaugurates the proceedings

---

[7] In the Republican National Convention of 1908 an attempt was made to reduce the number of delegates from the states where the party is weak by proposing that every state should have four delegates-at-large and one additional delegate for every 10,000 Republican votes polled at the last preceding presidential election. This plan, which would have greatly reduced the representation in the convention of nearly all the Southern states, was rejected by a vote of 506 to 470.

[8] Although the large majority of the delegates in the conventions of the two great parties belong to the class of professional politicians, there is always a minority of respectable men who do not belong to that class, but have obtained the post owing to their interest in seeing a strong and honest candidate chosen. The great importance of the business draws men of talent and experience from most parts of the country.

with a speech. Then the report of the committee on resolutions (if completed) is presented. It contains what is called the platform, a long series of resolutions embodying the principles and programme of the party, which has usually been so drawn as to conciliate every section, and avoid or treat with prudent ambiguity those questions on which opinion within the party is divided. Any delegate who objects to a resolution can move to strike it out or amend it; but it is generally "sustained" in the shape it has received from the practised hands of the committee.

Next follows the nomination of aspirants for the post of party candidate. The roll of states is called, and when a state is reached to which an aspirant intended to be nominated belongs, a prominent delegate from that state mounts the platform, and proposes him in a speech extolling his merits, and sometimes indirectly disparaging the other aspirants. Another delegate seconds the nomination, sometimes a third follows; and then the roll call goes on till all the states have been despatched, and all the aspirants nominated.[9] The average number of nominations is seven or eight; it rarely exceeds twelve.[10] In 1908 there were only eight at the Republican, three at the Democratic, convention, and it was well understood in each case that only one person had a chance of success.

Thus the final stage is reached, for which all else has been but preparation— that of balloting between the aspirants. The clerks call the roll of states from Alabama to Wyoming, and as each is called the chairman of its delegation announces the votes, e.g., six for A, five for B, three for C, unless, of course, under the unit rule, the whole vote is cast for that one aspirant whom the majority of the delegation supports. When all have voted, the totals are made up and announced. If one competitor has an absolute majority of the whole number voting, according to the Republican rule, a majority of two-thirds of the number voting, according to the Democratic rule, he has been duly chosen, and nothing remains but formally to make his nomination unanimous. If, however, as has happened often, no one obtains the requisite majority, the roll is called again, in order that individual delegates and delegations (if the unit rule prevails) may have the opportunity of changing their votes; and the process is repeated until some one of the aspirants put forward has received the required number of votes. Sometimes many roll calls take place. In 1852 the Democrats nominated Franklin Pierce

---

[9] Nominations may however be made at any subsequent time.

[10] However, in the Republican Convention of 1888, fourteen aspirants were nominated at the outset, six of whom were voted for on the last ballot. Votes were given at one or other of the ballotings for nineteen aspirants in all.

on the forty-ninth ballot, and the Whigs General Scott on the fifty-third. In 1880, thirty-six ballots were taken before General Garfield was nominated. But, in 1835, Martin Van Buren; in 1844, Henry Clay; in 1868 and 1872, Ulysses S. Grant; in 1888 Mr. Cleveland, were unanimously nominated, the three former by acclamation, the latter on the first ballot. In 1884 Mr. Blaine was nominated by the Republicans on the fourth ballot, Mr. Cleveland by the Democrats on the second; in 1888, Mr. Harrison on the eighth. In 1896 Mr. McKinley was nominated on the first ballot and Mr. Bryan on the fifth. In 1892 both Mr. Harrison (then president) and Mr. Cleveland were nominated on the first ballot, each of them by an overwhelming majority. Similarly in 1904 both Mr. Roosevelt and Mr. Parker and in 1908 both Mr. Taft and Mr. Bryan were each of them nominated on the first ballot. Thus it sometimes happens that the voting is over in an hour or two, while at other times it may last for days. In 1912 Mr. Taft was nominated by the Republicans on the first ballot after an embittered struggle over the credentials of certain delegates. Three hundred forty-three delegates abstained from voting and a month later held a convention of their own, at which a new party, called Progressive, was formed, and Mr. Roosevelt was nominated for the presidency. At the Democratic convention in the same year Mr. Woodrow Wilson was nominated on the forty-sixth ballot.

When a candidate for the presidency has been thus found, the convention proceeds similarly to determine its candidate for the vice-presidency. The inferiority of the office, and the exhaustion which has by this time overcome the delegates, make the second struggle a less exciting and protracted one. Frequently one of the defeated aspirants is consoled by this minor nomination, especially if he has retired at the nick of time in favour of the rival who has been chosen. The work of the convention is then complete,[11] and votes of thanks to the chairman and other officials conclude the proceedings. The two nominees are now the party candidates, entitled to the support of the party organizations and of loyal party men over the length and breadth of the Union.

Entitled to that support, but not necessarily sure to receive it. Even in America, party discipline cannot compel an individual voter to cast his ballot for the party nominee. All that the convention can do is to recommend the candidate to the party; all that opinion can do is to brand as a kicker or bolter whoever breaks away; all that the local party organization can do is to strike the bolter off its lists. But how stands it, the reader will ask, with

---

[11] Except for the idle formality of appointing a committee to notify to the candidate his selection.

the delegates who have been present in the convention, have had their chance of carrying their man, and have been beaten? Are they not held absolutely bound to support the candidate chosen?

This is a question which has excited much controversy. The constant impulse and effort of the successful majority have been to impose such an obligation on the defeated minority, and the chief motive which has prevented it from being invariably formally enforced by a rule or resolution of the convention has been the fear that it might precipitate hostilities, might induce men of independent character, or strongly opposed to some particular aspirant, to refuse to attend as delegates, or to secede early in the proceedings when they saw that a person whom they disapproved was likely to win.

At the Republican National Convention at Chicago in June 1880 an attempt was successfully made to impose the obligation by the following resolution, commonly called the "Ironclad Pledge":

"That every member of this convention is bound in honour to support its nominee, whoever that nominee may be, and that no man should hold his seat here who is not ready so to agree."

This was carried by 716 votes to 3. But at the Republican National Convention at Chicago in June 1884, when a similar resolution was presented, the opposition developed was strong enough to compel its withdrawal; and in point of fact, several conspicuous delegates at that convention strenuously opposed its nominee at the subsequent presidential election, themselves voting, and inducing others to vote, for the candidate of the Democratic party.

The general tendency towards a reform of the nominating system as a whole has recently led to the enactment in fifteen states of laws enabling the voters of each party to declare at a primary state election their preference for a particular aspirant as the candidate of their party, and requiring the delegates chosen by the party to give their votes in the party convention accordingly. Should this method of ascertaining the wishes of the majority of each party come to prevail over the whole Union, the present convention system will be profoundly changed. There will then be practically an election of candidates by the people. Great efforts will of course be made in every state to win for one or other among the party aspirants the position of party candidate, but the character of those efforts will be different. There will be more public meetings, at many of which the aspirants will doubtless present their respective claims. There may possibly be less underground intrigue. Time alone can shew how the new plan will work, and whether it will eliminate all aspirants except those who possess conspicuous popular gifts.

The Nominating Convention at Work

We have examined the composition of a national convention and the normal order of business in it. The more difficult task remains of describing the actual character and features of such an assembly, the motives which sway it, the temper it displays, the passions it elicits, the wiles by which its members are lured or driven to their goal.

A national convention has two objects, the formal declaration of the principles, views, and practical proposals of the party, and the choice of its candidates for the executive headship of the nation.

Of these objects the former has in critical times, such as the two elections preceding the Civil War, been of great importance. In the Democratic Convention at Charleston in 1860, a debate on resolutions led to a secession, and to the break-up of the Democratic party,[1] and in 1896 there were contests in both conventions over the treatment to be given to the currency question, the struggle being especially warm among the Democrats. So in 1908 a short but significant debate arose in the Republican convention over amendments of a "radical" character. But, with such occasional exceptions as last hereinbefore mentioned, the adoption of platforms, drafted in a somewhat vague and pompous style by the committee, has been almost a matter of form. Some observations on these enunciations of doctrine will be found in another chapter.[2]

The second object is of absorbing interest and importance, because the

---

[1] The national conventions of those days were much smaller than now, nor were the assisting spectators so numerous.

[2] Chapter 83. The nearest English parallel to an American "platform" is to be found in the addresses to their respective constituencies issued at a general election by the prime minister (if a member of the House of Commons) and the leader of the opposition in that House. Such addresses, however, do not formally bind the whole party, as an American platform does.

presidency is the great prize of politics, the goal of every statesman's ambition. The president can by his veto stop legislation adverse to the wishes of the party he represents. The president is the supreme dispenser of patronage.

One may therefore say that the task of a convention is to choose the party candidate. And it is a task difficult enough to tax all the resources of the host of delegates and their leaders. Who is the man fittest to be adopted as candidate? Not even a novice in politics will suppose that it is the best man, i.e., the wisest, strongest, and most upright. Plainly, it is the man most likely to win, the man who, to use the technical term, is most "available." What a party wants is not a good president but a good candidate. The party managers have therefore to look out for the person likely to gain most support, and at the same time excite least opposition. Their search is rendered more troublesome by the fact that many of them, being themselves either aspirants or the close allies of aspirants, are not disinterested, and are distrusted by their fellow searchers.

Many things have to be considered. The ability of a statesman, the length of time he has been before the people, his oratorical gifts, his "magnetism," his family connections, his face and figure, the purity of his private life, his "record" (the chronicle of his conduct) as regards integrity—all these are matters needing to be weighed. Account must be taken of the personal jealousies and hatreds which a man has excited. To have incurred the enmity of a leading statesman, of a powerful boss or ring, or of an influential newspaper, is serious. Several such feuds may be fatal.

Finally, much depends on the state whence a possible candidate comes. Local feeling leads a state to support one of its own citizens; it increases the vote of his own party in that state, and reduces the vote of the opposite party. Where the state is decidedly of one political colour, e.g., so steadily Republican as Vermont, so steadily Democratic as Maryland, this consideration is weak, for the choice of a Democratic candidate from the former, or of a Republican candidate from the latter, would not make the difference of the state's vote. It is therefore from a doubtful state that a candidate may with most advantage be selected; and the larger the doubtful state the better. California, with her ten electoral votes, is just worth "placating"; Indiana, with her fifteen votes, more so; New York, with her thirty-nine votes, most so of all. Hence an aspirant who belongs to a great and doubtful state is prima facie the most eligible candidate.

Aspirants hoping to obtain the party nomination from a national convention may be divided into three classes, the two last of which, as will appear presently, are not mutually exclusive, viz.:

Favourites   Dark Horses   Favourite Sons

A favourite is always a politician well known over the Union, and drawing support from all or most of its sections. He may be a man who has distinguished himself in Congress, or in some high executive post, or in the politics of some state so large that its politics are matter of knowledge and interest to the whole nation. He is usually a person of conspicuous gifts, whether as a speaker, or a party manager, or an administrator. The drawback to him is that in making friends he has also made enemies.

A dark horse is a person not very widely known in the country at large, but known rather for good than for evil. He has probably sat in Congress, been useful on committees, and gained some credit among those who dealt with him in Washington. Or he has approved himself a safe and assiduous party man in the political campaigns of his own and neighbouring states, yet without reaching national prominence. Sometimes he is a really able man, but without the special talents that win popularity. Still, speaking generally, the note of the dark horse is respectability, verging on colourlessness; and he is therefore a good sort of person to fall back upon when able but dangerous favourites have proved impossible. That native mediocrity rather than adverse fortune has prevented him from winning fame is proved by the fact that the dark horses who have reached the White House, if they have seldom turned out bad presidents, have even more seldom turned out distinguished ones.

A favourite son is a politician respected or admired in his own state, but little regarded beyond it. He may not be, like the dark horse, little known to the nation at large, but he has not fixed its eye or filled its ear. He is usually a man who has sat in the state legislature; filled with credit the post of state governor; perhaps gone as senator or representative to Washington, and there approved himself an active promoter of local interests. Probably he possesses the qualities which gain local popularity—geniality, activity, sympathy with the dominant sentiment and habits of his state; or while endowed with gifts excellent in their way, he has lacked the audacity and tenacity which push a man to the front through a jostling crowd. More rarely he is a demagogue who has raised himself by flattering the masses of his state on some local questions, or a skilful handler of party organizations who has made local bosses and spoilsmen believe that their interests are safe in his hands. Anyhow, his personality is such as to be more effective with neighbours than with the nation, as a lamp whose glow fills the side chapel of a cathedral sinks to a spark of light when carried into the nave.

A favourite son may be also a dark horse; that is to say, he may be well known in his own state, but so little known out of it as to be an unlikely candidate. But he need not be. The types are different, for as there are favourite sons whom the nation knows but does not care for, so there are dark horses whose reputation, such as it is, has not been made in state affairs, and who rely very little on state favour.

There are seldom more than two, never more than three favourites in the running at the same convention. Favourite sons are more numerous—it is not uncommon to have four or five, or even six, though perhaps not all these are actually started in the race. The number of dark horses is practically unlimited, because many talked of beforehand are not actually started, while others not considered before the convention begins are discovered as it goes on. This happened in the leading and most instructive case of James A. Garfield, who was not voted for at all on the first ballot in the Republican Convention of 1880, and had, on no ballot up to the thirty-fourth, received more than two votes. On the thirty-sixth[3] he was nominated by 399. So, in 1852, Pierce was scarcely known to the people when he was sprung on the convention. So, in 1868, Horatio Seymour, who had been so little thought of as a candidate that he was chairman of the Democratic Convention, was first voted for on the twenty-second ballot. He refused to be nominated, but was induced to leave the chair and nominated on that very ballot.

To carry the analysis farther, it may be observed that four sets of motives are at work upon those who direct or vote in a convention, acting with different degrees of force on different persons. There is the wish to carry a particular aspirant. There is the wish to defeat a particular aspirant, a wish sometimes stronger than any predilection. There is the desire to get something for one's self out of the struggle—e.g., by trading one's vote or influence for the prospect of a federal office. There is the wish to find the man who, be he good or bad, friend or foe, will give the party its best chance of victory. These motives cross one another, get mixed, vary in relative strength from hour to hour as the convention goes on and new possibilities are disclosed. To forecast their joint effect on the minds of particular persons and sections of a party needs wide knowledge and eminent acuteness. To play upon them is a matter of the finest skill.

[3] In 1860 the Democratic Convention at Charleston nominated Mr. Douglas on the fifty-seventh ballot.

The proceedings of a nominating convention can be best understood by regarding the three periods into which they fall: the transactions which precede the opening of its sittings; the preliminary business of passing rules and resolutions and delivering the nominating speeches; and, finally, the balloting.

A president has scarcely been elected before the newspapers begin to discuss his probably successor. Little, however, is done towards the ascertainment of candidates till about a year before the next election, when the factions of the chief aspirants prepare to fall into line, newspapers take up their parable in favour of one or other, and bosses begin the work of "subsoiling," i.e., manipulating primaries and local conventions so as to secure the choice of such delegates to the next national convention as they desire. In most of the conventions which appoint delegates, the claims of the several aspirants are canvassed, and the delegates chosen are usually chosen in the interest of one particular aspirant. The newspapers, with their quick sense of what is beginning to stir in men's thoughts, redouble their advocacy, and the "boom" of one or two of the probable favourites is thus fairly started. Before the delegates leave their homes for the national convention, most of them have fixed on their candidate, many having indeed received positive instructions as to how their vote shall be cast. All appears to be spontaneous, but in reality both the choice of particular men as delegates, and the instructions given, are usually the result of untiring underground work among local politicians, directed, or even personally conducted, by two or three skilful agents and emissaries of a leading aspirant, or of the knot which seeks to run him. Sometimes the result of the convention turns on the skill shown in sending up "handpicked" delegates.

Four or five days before the day fixed for the opening of the convention the delegations begin to flock into the city where it is to be held. Some come attended by a host of friends and camp followers, and are received at the depot (railway terminus) by the politicians of the city, with a band of music and an admiring crowd. Thus Tammany Hall, the famous Democratic club of New York City, came six hundred strong to Chicago in July 1884, filling two special trains.[4] A great crowd met it at the station, and it marched, following its boss, from the cars to its headquarters at the Palmer House, in procession, each member wearing his badge, just as the retainers of Earl Warwick the kingmaker used to follow him through the streets of London

---

[4] The boss of Tammany was an object of special curiosity to the crowd, being the most illustrious professional in the whole United States.

with the bear and ragged staff upon their sleeves. Less than twenty of the six hundred were delegates; the rest ordinary members of the organization, who had accompanied to give it moral and vocal support.[5]

Before the great day dawns many thousands of politicians, newspapermen, and sightseers have filled to overflowing every hotel in the city, and crowded the main thoroughfares so that the streetcars can scarcely penetrate the throng. It is like a mediæval pilgrimage, or the mustering of a great army. When the chief delegations have arrived the work begins in earnest. Not only each large delegation, but the faction of each leading aspirant to the candidacy, has its headquarters, where the managers hold perpetual session, reckoning up their numbers, starting rumours meant to exaggerate their resources, and dishearten their opponents, organizing raids upon the less experienced delegates as they arrive. Some fill the entrance halls and bars of the hotels, talk to the busy reporters, extemporize meetings with tumultuous cheering for their favourite. The common "worker" is good enough to raise the boom by these devices. Meanwhile, the more skilful leaders begin (as it is expressed) to "plough around" among the delegations of the newer Western and Southern states, usually (at least among the Republicans) more malleable, because they come from regions where the strength of the factions supporting the various aspirants is less accurately known, and are themselves more easily "captured" by bold assertions or seductive promises. Sometimes an expert intriguer will "break into" one of these wavering delegations, and make havoc like a fox in a hen roost. "Missionaries" are sent out to bring over individuals; embassies are accredited from one delegation to another to endeavour to arrange combinations by coaxing the weaker party to drop its own aspirant, and add its votes to those of the stronger party. All is conducted with perfect order and good humour, for the least approach to violence would recoil upon its authors; and the only breach of courtesy is where a delegation refuses to receive the ambassadors of an organization whose evil fame has made it odious.

It is against etiquette for the aspirants themselves to appear in the convention,[6] whether from some lingering respect for the notion that a man must not ask the people to choose him, but accept the proffered honour, or on the principle that the attorney who conducts his own case has a fool for

---

[5] The two other Democratic organizations of New York City, the County Democracy and Irving Hall, came each in force—the one a regiment of five hundred, the other of two hundred.

[6] Oddly enough, the only English parallel to this delicate reserve is to be found in the custom which forbids a candidate for the representation in Parliament of the University of Oxford to approach the university before or during the election.

a client. But from Washington, if he is an official or a senator, or perhaps from his own home, or possibly even from his room in the city, each aspirant keeps up hourly communication with his managers in the convention, having probably a private telegraph or telephone wire laid on for the purpose. Not only may officials, including the president himself, become aspirants, but federal officeholders may be, and very largely are, delegates, especially among the Southern Republicans when that party is in power.[7] They have the strongest personal interest in the issue; and the heads of departments can, by promises of places, exert a potent influence. One hears in America, just as one used to hear in France under Louis Napoleon or Marshal MacMahon, of the "candidate of the Administration."

As the hour when the convention is to open approaches, each faction strains its energy to the utmost. The larger delegations hold meetings to determine their course in the event of the man they chiefly favour proving "unavailable." Conferences take place between different delegations. Lists are published in the newspapers of the strength of each aspirant. Sea and land are compassed to gain one influential delegate, who "owns" other delegates. If he resists other persuasions, he is "switched on" to the private wire of some magnate at Washington, who "talks to him," and suggests inducements more effective than those he has hitherto withstood. The air is thick with tales of plots and treasons, so that no politician trusts his neighbour, for rumour spares none.

At length the period of expectation and preparation is over, and the summer sun rises upon the fateful day to which every politician in the party has looked forward for three years. Long before the time (usually 11 A.M.) fixed for the beginning of business, every part of the hall, erected specially for the gathering—a hall often large enough to hold from ten to fifteen thousand persons—is crowded.[8] The delegates—who in 1912 were 1,078 in the Republican Convention and 1,086 in the Democratic—are a mere drop in the ocean of faces. Eminent politicians from every state of the Union, senators and representatives from Washington not a few, journalists and reporters, ladies, sightseers from distant cities, as well as a swarm of partisans from the city itself, press in; some semblance of order being kept by the sergeant-at-arms and his marshals. Some wear devices, sometimes the badge of their state, or of their organization; sometimes the colours or emblem of their favorite aspirant. Each state delegation has its allotted place

---

[7] Not to add that many Southern Republican delegates are supposed to be purchasable.

[8] Admission is of course by ticket, and the prices given for tickets to those who, having obtained them, sell them, run high, up to $30, or even $50.

marked by the flag of the state floating from a pole, or a board bearing its name raised aloft; but leaders may be seen passing from one group to another, while the spectators listen to the band playing popular airs, and cheer any well-known figure that enters.

When the assembly is "called to order," a prayer is offered—each day's sitting begins with a prayer by some clergyman of local eminence,[9] the susceptibilities of various denominations being duly respected in the selection—and business proceeds according to the order described in last chapter. First come the preliminaries, appointment of committees and chairmen, then the platform, and probably on the second day, but perhaps later, the nominations and balloting, the latter sometimes extending over several days. There is usually both a forenoon and an afternoon session.

A European is astonished to see nearly one thousand men prepare to transact the two most difficult pieces of business an assembly can undertake, the solemn consideration of their principles, and the selection of the person they wish to place at the head of the nation, in the sight and hearing of twelve or fourteen thousand other men and women. Observation of what follows does not lessen the astonishment. The convention presents in sharp contrast and frequent alternation, the two most striking features of Americans in public—their orderliness and their excitability. Everything is done according to strict rule, with a scrupulous observance of small formalities which European meetings would ignore or despise. Points of order almost too fine for a parliament are taken, argued, decided on by the chair, to whom everyone bows. Yet the passions that sway the multitude are constantly bursting forth in storms of cheering or hissing at an allusion to a favourite aspirant or an obnoxious name, and five or six speakers often take the floor together, shouting and gesticulating at each other till the chairman obtains a hearing for one of them. Of course it depends on the chairman whether or no the convention sinks into a mob. A chairman with a weak voice, or a want of prompt decision, or a suspicion of partisanship, may bring the assembly to the verge of disaster, and it has more than once happened that when the confusion that prevailed would have led to an irregular vote which might have been subsequently disputed, the action of the manager acting for the winning horse has, by waiving some point of order or consenting to an adjournment, saved the party from disruption. Even in the noisiest scenes good sense, with a feeling for the need of fair play—fair play according to the rules of the game, which do not exclude some dodges repugnant to an

---

[9] I have heard in such a prayer thanks returned to the Almighty for having secured the nomination of a particular candidate at a previous sitting of the convention and the request preferred that He would make sure the election of that candidate.

honourable man—will often reassert itself, and pull back the vehicle from the edge of the precipice.

The chief interest of the earlier proceedings lies in the indications which speeches and votings give of the relative strength of the factions. Sometimes a division on the choice of a chairman, or on the adoption of a rule, reveals the tendencies of the majority, or of influential leaders, in a way which sends the chances of an aspirant swiftly up or down the barometer of opinion. So when the nominating speeches come, it is not so much their eloquence that helps a nominee as the warmth with which the audience receives them, the volume of cheering and the length of time, perhaps an hour or more, during which the transport lasts. As might be guessed from the size of the audience which he addresses, an orator is expected to "soar into the blue empyrean" at once. The rhetoric is usually pompous and impassioned, but few are those who can make themselves heard by the whole of the multitude. To read a speech, even a short speech, from copious notes, is neither irregular nor rare.

While forenoon and evening, perhaps even late evening, are occupied with the sittings of the convention, canvassing and intrigue go on more briskly than ever during the rest of the day and night. Conferences are held between delegations anxious to arrange for a union of forces on one candidate.[10] Divided delegations hold meetings of their own members, meetings often long and stormy, behind closed doors, outside which a curious crowd listens to the angry voices within, and snatches at the reports which the dispersing members give of the result. Sometimes the whole issue of the convention hinges on the action of the delegates of a great state, which, like New York, under the unit rule, can throw seventy-eight votes into the trembling scale. It may even happen, although this is against a well-settled custom, that a brazen aspirant himself goes the round of several delegations and tries to harangue them into supporting him.

Sometimes it is well known beforehand whom the convention will nominate. One aspirant may be so generally popular with the whole party that the delegates have nothing to do but register a foregone conclusion. Or it may happen that the leaders of the party have reached an agreement which a majority of the delegates can be relied on to carry out. Such cases,

---

[10] In the Democratic Convention of 1884 it was understood that the choice of Mr. Cleveland, the leading favourite, would depend on the action of the delegation of New York State, not only, however, because it cast the largest vote, but because it was his own state, and because it was already foreseen that the presidential election would turn on the electoral vote of New York. Thus the struggle in the convention came to be really a duel between Mr. Cleveland and the boss of Tammany, with whom Mr. Cleveland had at an earlier period in his career "locked horns."

however, have hitherto been infrequent, and in what follows I describe the more usual phenomenon of a struggle between contending factions and aspirants prolonged until the moment comes for the convention to decide.

As it rarely happens that any aspirant is able to command at starting a majority of the whole convention, the object of his friends is to arrange a combination whereby he may gather from the supporters of other aspirants votes sufficient to make up the requisite majority, be it two-thirds, according to the Democratic rule, or a little more than a half, according to the Republican. Let us take the total number of votes at 1,000—a trifle below the figure in 1912. There are usually two aspirants commanding each from 280 to 350, one or two others with from 50 to 120, and the rest with much smaller figures, 20 to 40 each. A combination can succeed in one of two ways: (*a*) one of the stronger aspirants may pick up votes, sometimes quickly, sometimes by slow degrees, from the weaker candidates, sufficient to overpower the rival favourite; (*b*) each of the strongest aspirants may hold his forces so well together that after repeated ballotings it becomes clear that neither can win against the resistance of the other. Neither faction will, however, give way, because there is usually bitterness between them, because each would feel humiliated, and because each aspirant has so many friends that his patronage will no more than suffice for the clients to whom he is pledged already. Hence one or other of the baffled favourites suddenly transfers the votes he commands to some one of the weaker men, who then so rapidly "develops strength" that the rest of the minor factions go over to him, and he obtains the requisite majority.[11] Experience has so well prepared the tacticians for one or other of these issues that the game is always played with a view to them. The first effort of the managers of a favourite is to capture the minor groups of delegates who support one or other of the favourite sons and dark horses. Not till this proves hopeless do they decide to sell themselves as dear as they can by taking up and carrying to victory a dark horse or perhaps even a favourite son, thereby retaining the pleasure of defeating the rival favourite, while at the same time establishing a claim for themselves and their faction on the aspirant whom they carry.[12]

[11] Suppose A and B, favourites, to have each 330 votes. After some ballotings, A's friends, perceiving they cannot draw enough of the votes commanded by C, D, and F (who have each 70), and of G and H (who have each 30) to win, give their 330 votes to F. This gives him so considerable a lead that C, D, and G go over to him on the next ballot; he has then 570, and either wins at once (Republican rule) or will win next ballot (Democratic rule).

[12] It will be understood that while the favourites and favourite sons are before the convention from the first, some of the dark horses may not appear as aspirants till well on in the balloting. They may be persons who have never been thought of before as possible candidates. There is therefore always a great element of exciting uncertainty.

It may be asked why a dark horse often prevails against the favourites, seeing that either of the latter has a much larger number of delegates in his favour. Ought not the wish of a very large group to have so much weight with the minor groups as to induce them to come over and carry the man whom a powerful section of the party obviously desires? The reason why this does not happen is that a favourite is often as much hated by one strong section as he is liked by another, and if the hostile section is not strong enough to keep him out by its unaided vote, it is sure to be able to do so by transferring itself to some other aspirant. Moreover, a favourite has often less chance with the minor groups than a dark horse may have. He has not the charm of novelty. His "ins and outs" are known; the delegations weighed his merits before they left their own state, and if they, or the state convention that instructed them, decided against him then, they are slow to adopt him now. They have formed a habit of "antagonizing" him, whereas they have no hostility to some new and hitherto inconspicuous aspirant.

Let us now suppose resolutions and nominating speeches despatched, and the curtain raised for the third act of the convention. The chairman raps loudly with his gavel,[13] announcing the call of states for the vote. A hush falls on the multitude, a long deep breath is drawn, tally books are opened and pencils grasped, while the clerk reads slowly the names of state after state. As each is called, the chairman of its delegation rises and announces the votes it gives, bursts of cheering from each faction in the audience welcoming the votes given to the object of its wishes. Inasmuch as the disposition of most of the delegates has become known beforehand, not only to the managers, but to the public through the press, the loudest welcome is given to a delegate or delegation whose vote turns out better than had been predicted.

In the first scene of this third and decisive act the favourites have, of course, the leading parts. Their object is to produce an impression of overwhelming strength, so the whole of this strength is displayed, unless, as occasionally happens, an astute manager holds back a few votes. This is also the bright hour of the favourite sons. Each receives the vote of his state, but each usually finds that he has little to expect from external help, and his friends begin to consider into what other camp they had better march over. The dark horses are in the background, nor is it yet possible to say which (if any) of them will come to the front.

The first ballot seldom decides much, yet it gives a new aspect to the

---

[13] The gavel is a sort of auctioneer's hammer used by a chairman to call the attention of the meeting to what he is saying or to restore order. That used at a national convention is then made of pieces of wood from every state.

battlefield, for the dispositions of some groups of voters who had remained doubtful is now revealed, and the managers of each aspirant are better able to tell, from the way in which certain delegations are divided, in what quarters they are most likely to gain or lose votes on the subsequent ballots. They whisper hastily together, and try, in the few moments they have before the second ballot is upon them, to prepare some new line of defence or attack.

The second ballot, taken in the same way, sometimes reveals even more than the first. The smaller and more timid delegations, smitten with the sense of their weakness, despairing of their own aspirant, and anxious to be on the winning side, begin to give way; or if this does not happen on the second ballot, it may do so on the third. Rifts open in their ranks, individuals or groups of delegates go over to one of the stronger candidates, some having all along meant to do so, and thrown their first vote merely to obey instructions received or fulfil the letter of a promise given. The gain of even twenty or thirty votes for one of the leading candidates over his strength on the preceding ballot so much inspirits his friends, and is so likely to bring fresh recruits to his standard, that a wily manager will often, on the first ballot, throw away some of his votes on a harmless antagonist that he may by rallying them increase the total of his candidate on the second, and so convey the impression of growing strength.

The breathing space between each ballot and that which follows is used by the managers for hurried consultations. Aides-de-camp are sent to confirm a wavering delegation, or to urge one which has been supporting a now hopeless aspirant to seize this moment for dropping him and coming over to the winning standard. Or the aspirant himself, who, hundreds of miles away, sits listening to the click of the busy wires, is told how matters stand, and asked to advise forthwith what course his friends shall take. Forthwith it must be, for the next ballot is come, and may give the battlefield a new aspect, promising victory or presaging irretrievable defeat.

Anyone who has taken part in an election, be it the election of a pope by cardinals, of a town clerk by the city council, of a fellow by the dons of a college, of a schoolmaster by the board of trustees, of a pastor by a congregation, knows how much depends on generalship. In every body of electors there are men who have no minds of their own; others who cannot make up their minds till the decisive moment, and are determined by the last word or incident; others whose wavering inclination yields to the pressure or follows the example of a stronger colleague. There are therefore chances of running in by surprise an aspirant whom few may have desired, but still fewer have positively disliked, chances specially valuable when controversy has spent itself between two equally matched competitors, so that the majority are ready to jump at a new suggestion. The wary tactician awaits his opportunity; he improves the brightening prospects of his aspirant to carry him with a run before the opposition is ready with a counter move; or if he sees a strong antagonist, he invents pretexts for delay till he has arranged a combination by which that antagonist may be foiled. Sometimes he will put forward an aspirant destined to be abandoned, and reserve till several votings have been taken the man with whom he means to win. All these arts are familiar to the convention manager, whose power is seen not merely in the dealing with so large a number of individuals and groups whose dispositions he must grasp and remember, but in the cool promptitude with which he decides on his course amid the noise and passion and distractions of twelve thousand shouting spectators. Scarcely greater are the faculties of combination and coolness of head needed by a general in the midst of a battle, who has to bear in mind the position of every one of his own corps and to divine the positions of those of the enemy's corps which remain concealed, who must vary his plan from hour to hour according to the success or failure of each of his movements and the new facts that are successively disclosed, and who does all this under the roar and through the smoke of cannon.

One balloting follows another till what is called "the break" comes. It comes when the weaker factions, perceiving that the men of their first preference cannot succeed, transfer their votes to that one among the aspirants whom they like best, or whose strength they see growing. When the faction of one aspirant has set the example, others are quick to follow, and thus it may happen that after thirty or forty ballots have been taken with few changes of strength as between the two leading competitors, a single ballot, once the break has begun, and the column of one or both of these competitors has been "staggered," decides the battle.

If one favourite is much stronger from the first than any other, the break may come soon and come gently, i.e., each ballot shows a gain for him on the preceding ballot, and he marches so steadily to victory that resistance is felt to be useless. But if two well-matched rivals have maintained the struggle through twenty or thirty ballots, so that the long strain has wrought up all minds to unwonted excitement, the break, when it comes, comes with fierce intensity, like that which used to mark the charge of the Old Guard. The defeat becomes a rout. Battalion after battalion goes over to the victors, while the vanquished, ashamed of their candidate, try to conceal themselves by throwing away their colours and joining in the cheers that acclaim the conqueror. In the picturesquely technical language of politicians, it is a stampede.

To stampede a convention is the steadily contemplated aim of every manager who knows he cannot win on the first ballot.[14] He enjoys it as the most dramatic form of victory, he values it because it evokes an enthusiasm whose echo reverberates all over the Union, and dilates the party heart with something like that sense of supernatural guidance which Rome used to have when the cardinals chose a pope by the sudden inspiration of the Holy Spirit. Sometimes it comes of itself, when various delegations, smitten at the same moment by the sense that one of the aspirants is destined to conquer, go over to him all at once.[15] Sometimes it is due to the action of the aspirant himself. In 1880 Mr. Blaine, who was one of the two leading favourites, perceiving that he could not be carried against the resistance of the Grant men, suddenly telegraphed to his friends to transfer their votes to General Garfield, till then a scarcely considered candidate. In 1884 General Logan, also by telegraph, turned over his votes to Mr. Blaine between the third and fourth ballot, thereby assuring the already probable triumph of that favourite.

When a stampede is imminent, only one means exists of averting it, that of adjourning the convention so as to stop the panic and gain time for a combination against the winning aspirant. A resolute manager always tries this device, but he seldom succeeds, for the winning side resists the motion for adjournment, and the vote which it casts on that issue is practically a vote for its aspirant, against so much of "the field" as has any fight left in it. This is the most critical and exciting moment of the whole battle. A dozen speakers rise at once, some to support, some to resist the adjournment, some to protest against debate upon it, some to take points of order, few of which can be heard over the din of the howling multitude. Meanwhile, the managers who have kept their heads rush swiftly about through friendly delegations, trying at this supreme moment to rig up a combination which may resist the advancing tempest. Tremendous efforts are made to get the second favourite's men to abandon their chief and "swing into line" for

---

[14] To check stampeding the Republican Convention of 1876 adopted a rule providing that the roll call of states should in no case be dispensed with. This makes surprise and tumult less dangerous. (See Stanwood's useful *History of Presidential Elections*.) With the same view the Republican Convention of 1888 ruled that no vote given on any balloting should be changed before the end of that balloting. The impulse to "jump on the bandwagon" is strong in moments of excitement.

[15] Probably a dark horse, for the favourite sons, having had their turn in the earlier ballotings, have been discounted, and are apt to excite more jealousy among the delegates of other states.

some dark horse or favourite son, with whose votes they may make head till other factions rally to them.

> In vain, in vain, the all-consuming hour
> Relentless falls—

The battle is already lost, the ranks are broken and cannot be rallied, nothing remains for brave men but to cast their last votes against the winner and fall gloriously around their still waving banner. The motion to adjourn is defeated, and the next ballot ends the strife with a hurricane of cheering for the chosen leader. Then a sudden calm falls on the troubled sea. What is done is done, and whether done for good or for ill, the best face must be put upon it. Accordingly the proposer of one of the defeated aspirants moves that the nomination be made unanimous, and the more conspicuous friends of other aspirants hasten to show their good humour and their loyalty to the party as a whole by seconding this proposition. Then, perhaps, a gigantic portrait of the candidate, provided by anticipation, is hoisted up, a signal for fresh enthusiasm, or a stuffed eagle is carried in procession round the hall.

Nothing further remains but to nominate a candidate for the vice-presidency, a matter of small moment now that the great issue has been settled. This nomination is frequently used to console one of the defeated aspirants for the presidential nomination, or is handed over to his friends to be given to some politician of their choice. If there be a contest, it is seldom prolonged beyond two or three ballots. The convention is at an end, and in another day the whole host of exhausted delegates and camp followers, hoarse with shouting, is streaming home along the railways.[16]

The fever heat of the convention is almost matched by that of the great cities, and indeed of every spot over the Union to which there runs an electric wire. Every incident, speech, vote, is instantly telegraphed to all the cities. Crowds gather round the newspaper offices, where frequent editions are supplemented by boards displaying the latest bulletins. In Washington, Congress can hardly be kept together, because every politician

---

[16] Should the plan of presidential primaries, referred to at the end of Chapter 69, be generally adopted, the conditions under which a convention works will be materially changed. When one aspirant has obtained at the primaries a majority of all the votes cast, the convention will have nothing to do but ratify a selection already made by the party, and then adopt a platform. Should no aspirant have secured an absolute majority, it will be so difficult for anyone who has not received a large measure of popular support at the primaries to get himself chosen that the field of choice, which has heretofore included men who had been scarcely considered before the convention met, will be sensibly narrowed.

is personally interested in every move of the game. When at last the result is announced, the partisans of the chosen candidate go wild with delight; salvos of artillery are fired off, processions with bands parade the streets, ratification meetings are announced for the same evening, "campaign clubs" bearing the candidate's name are organized on the spot. The excitement is of course greatest in the victor's own state, or in the city where he happens to be resident. A crowd rushes to his house, squeezes his hand to a quivering pulp, congratulates him on being virtually president, while the keen-eyed reporter telegraphs far and wide how he smiled and spoke when the news was brought. Defeated aspirants telegraph to their luckier rival their congratulations on his success, promising him support in the campaign. Interviewers fly to prominent politicians, and cross-examine them as to what they think of the nomination. But in two days all is still again, and a lull of exhaustion follows till the real business of the contest begins some while later with the issue of the letter of acceptance, in which the candidate declares his views and outlines his policy.

C H A P T E R   7 1

The Presidential Campaign

A presidential election in America is something to which Europe can show nothing similar. Though the issues which fall to be decided by the election of a chamber in France or Italy, or of a House of Commons in England, are often far graver than those involved in the choice of A or B to be executive chief magistrate for four years, the commotion and excitement, the amount of "organization," of speaking, writing, telegraphing, and shouting, is incomparably greater in the United States. It is only the salient features of these contests that I shall attempt to sketch, for the detail is infinite.

The canvass usually lasts about four months. It begins soon after both of the great parties have chosen their candidate, i.e., before the middle of July; and it ends early in November, on the day when the presidential electors are chosen simultaneously in and by all the states. The summer heats and the absence of the richer sort of people at the seaside or mountain resorts keep down the excitement during July and August; it rises in September, and boils furiously through October.

The first step is for each nominated candidate to accept his nomination in a letter, sometimes as long as a pamphlet, setting forth his views of the condition of the nation and the policy which the times require. Such a letter is meant to strike the keynote for the whole orchestra of orators. It is, of course, published everywhere, extolled by friendly and dissected by hostile journals. Together with the "platform" adopted at the national party convention, it is the official declaration of party principles, to be referred to as putting the party case, no less than the candidate himself, before the nation.

While the candidate is composing his address, the work of organization goes briskly forward, for in American elections everything is held to depend on organization. A central or national party committee nominated by the national convention, and consisting of one member from each state, gets it members together and forms a plan for the conduct of the canvass. It raises money by appealing to the wealthy and zealous men of the party for subscriptions, and, of course, presses those above all who have received something in the way of an office or other gratification from the party[1] or who expect something from its action. The chairman of this committee is an important personage, who exercises great power and upon whose abilities much may depend. The treasurer is also always a prominent man, in whom both energy and discretion are required. It communicates with the leading statesmen and orators of the party, and arranges in what district of the country each shall take the stump. It issues shoals of pamphlets, and forms relations with party newspapers. It allots grants from the "campaign fund" to particular persons and state committees, to be spent by them for "campaign purposes," an elastic term which may cover a good deal of illicit expenditure. Enormous sums are gathered and disbursed by this committee, and the accounts submitted do not, as may be supposed, answer all the questions they suggest. The committee directs its speakers and its funds chiefly to the doubtful states, those in which eloquence or expenditure may turn the balance either way. There are seldom more than six or seven such states at any one election, possibly fewer.

The efforts of the national committee are seconded not only by a congressional committee[2] and by state committees, but by an infinite number of minor organizations over the country, in the rural districts no less than in the cities. Some of these are permanent. Others are created for the election alone; and as they contemplate a short life, they make it a merry one. These "campaign clubs," which usually bear the candidates' names, are formed on every imaginable basis, that of locality, of race, of trade or profession, of university affiliation. There are Irish clubs, Italian clubs, German clubs,

---

[1] As a statute now forbids the levying of assessments for party purposes on members of the federal civil service, it is deemed prudent to have no federal official on this committee, lest in demanding subscriptions from his subordinates he should transgress the law.

Large contributions used to be made by the great manufacturing and other corporations, partly because those who managed them thought their corporate interests involved in the success of one party, partly (it has been alleged) because they hoped to receive certain favors from the party to which they were giving pecuniary aid. The practice has now been forbidden by a statute enacted by Congress in 1907.

[2] In 1908 both parties, under the provisions of a statute, returned the money collected by their respective national committees for election purpose. The Republican return was $1,655,518; the Democratic was $620,644. These were deemed unusually small sums.

Scandinavian clubs, Polish clubs, coloured (i.e., Negro) clubs, Orange clubs. There are young men's clubs, lawyers' clubs, dry-goods clubs, insurance men's clubs, shoe and leather clubs. There are clubs of the graduates of various colleges. Their work consists in canvassing the voters, making up lists of friends, opponents, and doubtfuls, getting up processions and parades, holding meetings, and generally "booming all the time."

This is mostly unpaid labour. But there are also thousands of paid agents at work, canvassing, distributing pamphlets or leaflets, lecturing on behalf of the candidate. It is in America no reproach to a political speaker that he receives a fee or a salary. Even men of eminence are permitted to receive not only their travelling expenses, but a round sum. Formerly a candidate, unless possessed of popular gifts, did but little speaking. Latterly he has been expected to take the field and stay in it fighting all the time, a terrible strain on health and voice. He is of course chiefly seen in the doubtful states, where he speaks for weeks together twice or thrice on most days, filling up the intervals with "receptions" at which he has to shake hands with hundreds of male callers, and be presented to ladies scarcely less numerous.[3] The leading men of the party are, of course, pressed into the service. Even if they dislike and have opposed the nomination of the particular candidate, party loyalty and a lively sense of favours to come force them to work for the person whom the party has chosen. An eminent Irishman or an eminent German used to be deemed especially valuable for a stumping tour, because he influenced the vote of his countrymen. Similarly each senator is expected to labour assiduously at his own state, where presumably his influence is greatest, and any refusal to do so is deemed a pointed disapproval of the candidate.

The committees print and distribute great quantities of campaign literature, pamphlets, speeches, letters, leaflets, and one can believe that this printed matter is more serviceable than it would be in England, because a larger part of the voters live in quiet country places, and like something to read in the evening. Even novelettes are composed in the interests of a candidate, wherein lovers talk about tariffs under the moon. Sometimes a less ingenuous use is made of the press. On the very eve of the election of 1880, too late for a contradiction to obtain equal publicity, a forged letter, purporting to come from Mr. Garfield, and expressing views on Chinese immigration and labour, distasteful to the Pacific states, was lithographed and scattered broadcast over California, where it told heavily against him.

[3] Sometimes he stumps along a line of railroad, making ten-minute speeches from the end platform of the last car.

Most constant and effective of all is the action of the newspapers. The chief journals have for two or three months a daily leading article recommending their own and assailing the hostile candidate, with a swarm of minor editorial paragraphs bearing on the election. Besides these there are reports of speeches delivered, letters to the editor with the editor's comments at the end, stories about the candidates, statements as to the strength of each party in particular states, counties, and cities. An examination of a few of the chief newspapers during the two months before a hotly contested election showed that their "campaign matter" of all kinds formed between one-half and one-third of the total letterpress of the paper (excluding advertisements), and this, be it remembered, every day during those two months. The most readable part of this matter consists in the reports of the opinion of individual persons, more or less prominent, on the candidate. You find, for instance, a paragraph stating that the Rev. Dr. A., president of such and such a college, or Mr. B., the philanthropist who is head of the Y Z Bank, or ex-Governor C., or Judge D., has said he thinks the candidate a model of chivalric virtue, or fit only for a felon's cell, as the case may be, and that he will vote for or against him accordingly.[4] Occasionally the prominent man is called on by an interviewer and gives a full statement of his views, or he writes to a young friend who has asked his advice in a private letter, which is immediately published. The abundance of these expressions or citations of the opinions of private citizens supplies a curious evidence of the disposition of some sections in a democracy to look up to its intellectual and moral leaders. For the men thus appealed to are nearly all persons eminent by their character, ability, learning, or success in business; the merely rich man is cited but rarely, and as if his opinion did not matter, though of course his subscription may. Judges and lawyers, university dignitaries and literary men, are, next to the clergy,[5] the persons most often quoted.

The function of the clergy in elections is very characteristic of the country

---

[4] Sometimes a sort of amateur census is taken of the persons occupied in one place in some particular employment, as, of the professors in a particular college, or even of the clerks in a particular store, these being taken as samples of store clerks or professors generally; and the party organ triumphantly claims that three-fourths of their votes will be cast for its candidate. Among the "throbs of Connecticut's pulse," I recollect an estimate of the "proclivities" of the workmen in the Willimantic mills in that state.

[5] An eminent Unitarian clergyman having written a letter condemning a candidate, the leading organ of that candidate in sneering at it, remarked that after all Dr. Clarke's coachman's vote was as good as Dr. Clarke's; to which it was rejoined by a hostile journalist that hundreds of voters would follow Dr. Clarke, and hundreds more be offended at this disrespectful reference to him.

and the occasion. They used during the period from 1820 to 1856 to give politics a wide berth, for not only would their advocacy of any particular cause have offended a section among their flocks, but the general sentiment condemned the immixture in politics of a clerical element. The struggle against slavery, being a moral issue, brought them into more frequent public activity. Since the close of that struggle they have again tended to retire. However, the excitement of a presidential election suspends all rules; and when questions affecting the moral character of the candidates are involved, clerical intervention is deemed natural. Thus in the contest of 1884, the newspapers were full of the opinions of clergymen. Sermons were reported if they seemed to bear upon the issue. Paragraphs appeared saying that such and such a pastor would carry three-fourths of his congregation with him, whereas the conduct of another in appearing at a meeting on behalf of the opposing candidate was much blamed by his flock. Not many ministers actually took the platform, though there was a general wish to have them as chairmen. But one, the late Mr. Henry Ward Beecher, did great execution by his powerful oratory, artillery all the more formidable because it was turned against the candidate of the party to which he had through his long life belonged. Nor was there any feature in the canvass of that same candidate more remarkable than the assembly of 1,018 clergymen of all denominations (including a Jewish rabbi), which gathered at the Fifth Avenue Hotel in New York, to meet him and assure him of their support on moral grounds, immediately before the election day.[6]

From a class usually excluded from politics by custom to a class excluded by law, the transition is easy. Women as a rule (setting aside the four woman suffrage Western states) keep as much aloof from electoral contests in America as in continental Europe, and certainly more than in England, for I have never heard of their forming an organization to canvass the voters of a district in America, as the (Conservative) Primrose League and the Women's Liberal Associations do in England. Nor are women appointed delegates from any ward primary,[7] as they have lately been in some places

---

[6] One of the clerical speakers spoke of the opposite candidate as receiving the support of "rum, Romanism, and rebellion." This phrase, eagerly caught up, and repeated by hostile newspapers, incensed the Roman Catholics of New York, and was believed to have turned the election against the candidate in whose interest the alliteration was invented. Nothing so dangerous as a friend.

[7] Women, however, have often appeared as delegates at the conventions of the Prohibition party; and there have been instances in which they have been admitted as delegates to a Republican state convention in Massachusetts.

In 1904 several women were alternate delegates to the Republican National Convention from Wyoming, Colorado, and Idaho, and in 1908 one woman came as an "alternate" from Colorado to the Republican convention.

in England. However, the excitement of a close struggle sometimes draws even women into the vortex. Receptions are tendered by the ladies of each party to the candidate, and are reported in the public press as politically significant, while among the letters which appear in the newspapers not a few bear female signatures.

Speaking and writing and canvassing are common to elections all over the world. What is peculiar to America is the amazing development of the "demonstration" as a means for raising enthusiasm. For three months, processions, usually with brass bands, flags, badges, crowds of cheering spectators, are the order of the day and night from end to end of the country. The Young Men's Pioneer club of a village in the woods of Michigan turns out in the summer evening; the Democrats or Republicans of Chicago or Philadelphia leave their business to march through the streets of these great cities many thousands strong.

When a procession is exceptionally large, it is called a parade. In New York City, on the 29th of October 1884, the businessmen who supported Mr. James Gillespie Blaine held such a demonstration. They were organized by profession or occupation: the lawyers, 800 strong, forming one battalion, the dry-goods men another, the produce exchange a third, the bankers a fourth, the brokers a fifth, the jewellers a sixth, the petroleum exchange a seventh, and so on *ad infinitum*. They started from the Bowling Green near the south end of Manhattan Island, and marched right up the city along Broadway to Madison Square, where Mr. Blaine reviewed and addressed them. Rain fell incessantly, and the streets were deep with mud, but neither rain above nor mud below damped the spirits of this great army, which tramped steadily along, chanting various "campaign refrains," such as

Five, Five, Five Cent Fare;[8]

but most frequently

Blaine, Blaine, James G. Blaine,
We don't care a bit for the rain,
O—O—O—O—HI—O.[9]

There were said to have been 25,000 businessmen in this parade, which was followed soon after by another more miscellaneous Blaine parade of

[8] Mr. Cleveland had, as governor of New York State, vetoed as unconstitutional a bill establishing a uniform fare of 5 cents on the New York City elevated railroads. This act was supposed to have alienated the working men and ruined his presidential prospects.

[9] In the state elections held in Ohio shortly beforehand, the Republicans had been victorious, and the omen was gladly caught up.

60,000 Republicans, as well as (of course) by counter parades of Democrats. A European, who stands amazed at the magnitude of these demonstrations, is apt to ask whether the result attained is commensurate with the money, time, and effort give to them. His American friends answer that, as with advertising, it is not to be supposed that shrewd and experienced men would thus spend their money unless convinced that the expenditure was reproductive. The parade and procession business, the crowds, the torches, the badges, the flags, the shouting, all this pleases the participants by making them believe they are effecting something; it impresses the spectators by showing them that other people are in earnest, it strikes the imagination of those who in country hamlets read of the doings in the great city. In short, it keeps up the "boom," and an American election is held to be, truly or falsely, largely a matter of booming.

If the cynical visitor smiles at these displays, he is constrained to admire the good humour and good order which prevail. Neither party in the Northern, Middle, and Western states dreams of disturbing the parades or meetings of the other. You might believe, from the acclamations which accompany a procession, that the whole population was with it, for if opponents are present they do not hoot or hiss, and there are always enough sympathizers to cheer. During the hotly contested elections of 1880 and 1896, hardly any collisions or disturbances reported from California to Maine. Even in Virginia, Maryland, Missouri, where the old Southern party is apt to let its angry passions rise against the Negroes and their white Republican allies, the breaches of order were neither numerous nor serious. Over five-sixths of the Southern states perfect quiet prevailed. It is true that one party could there count on an overwhelming majority, so that there was no excuse for the one to bully nor any inducement for the other to show fight. The elections of 1904 and 1908 were even more tranquil. If any disturbances occurred anywhere in the latter year no notice of them found its way into the press.

The maxim that nothing succeeds like success is nowhere so cordially and consistently accepted as in America. It is the cornerstone of all election work. The main effort of a candidate's orators and newspapers is to convince the people that their side is the winning one, for there are sure to be plenty of voters anxious to be on that side, not so much from any advantage to be gained for themselves as because reverence for "the people" makes them believe that the majority are right. Hence the exertions to prove that the Germans, or the Irish, or the working men are going for candidate X or candidate Y. Hence the reports of specimen canvasses showing that 70 per cent of the clerks in a particular bank or 80 per cent of the professors in a particular theological college have declared themselves for X. Hence the announcements of the betting odds for a particular candidate, and the assertion that the supporters of the other man who had put large sums on him are now beginning to hedge.[10] But the best evidence to which a party can appeal is its winning minor elections which come off shortly before the great presidential one. In three states, Vermont, Maine, and Oregon, the choice of a governor and other state officers takes place in September, i.e., within two months of the presidential contest. If the state is a safe one for the Republicans or the Democrats (as the case may be), the votes cast are compared with those cast at the last preceding similar election, and the inference drawn that one or other party is gaining. If it is a doubtful state the interest is still more keen, and every nerve is strained to carry an election whose issue will presage, and by presaging contribute to, success in the presidential struggle. Possibly the candidate or some of his ablest speakers stump this state; probably also it is drenched with money. The inferences from such a contest may be thought uncertain, because state elections are always complicated with local questions, and with the character of the particular candidates for state offices. But it is a maxim among politicians that in a presidential year local issues vanish, the voters being so warmed with party spirit that they go solid for their party in spite of all local or personal obstacles. The truth of this view was illustrated by the fact that Ohio used often to return a majority of Democrats to Congress and had a Democratic majority in her own legislature, but for several elections gave a majority for the presidential candidate of the Republican party. The eagerness shown to carry the October elections in this great and often doubtful state used to be scarcely second to that displayed in the presidential contest. She has now (and Indiana likewise) put her fall elections later, and makes them coincide (every second term) with the presidential election, in order to avoid the tremendous strain which they had been forced to bear. Before this change it was often made an argument why the party should select its candidate from Ohio, that this would give a better chance of winning the preliminary canter, and thereby securing the advantage of a presageful victory.[11]

---

[10] There is a great deal of betting on elections, so much that bribery is often alleged to be practised by those who are heavily involved. The constitutions or statutes of some states make it an offence to give or take a bet on an election. In the campaigns of 1904 and 1908 the odds were from the first on one candidate, and after a little fluctuation during a few weeks, rose slowly but steadily in his favour till the end. This happened also in 1912.

[11] There is a touch of superstition in the value set in America upon the first indications of the popular sentiment, like that which made the Romans attach such weight to the vote of the century

So far I have described the contest as one between two parties and two candidates only. But it is sometimes complicated by the appearance of other minor parties and minor candidates who, although they have no chance of success, affect the main struggle by drawing off strength from one side or the other. In the elections of 1880–92 the Prohibitionist party and the Greenback party each held a national convention, nominated candidates for presidency and vice-presidency, and obtained at the polls a number of votes far too small to carry any single state, and therefore, of course, too small to choose any presidential electors, but sufficient to affect, perhaps to turn, the balance of strength between Republicans and Democrats in two or three of the doubtful states. The Prohibitionist candidate drew most of his votes from the Republican side; a Greenbacker from the Democratic: and so more recently the appearance of a Populist or Socialist candidate has been supposed to injure the Democratic prospects. Hence there was apt to be a sort of tacit alliance during the campaign between the Republican organs and the Labour or Socialist party, between the Democratic organs and the Prohibitionist; and conversely much ill blood between Republicans and Prohibitionists, between Democrats and Labour men. Anyone can see what an opening for intrigue is given by these complications, and how much they add to the difficulty of predicting the result of the contest. The area of that contest is a continent, and in the various regions of the continent forces different in nature and varying in strength are at work.

---

first called up to vote in the *comitia centuriata*. It was selected by lot, perhaps not merely because the advantage of calling first a century which he might know to be favourable to his own view or candidate was too great a one to be left to the presiding magistrate, but also because its declaration was thus deemed to be an indication of the will of the gods who governed the lot.

The Issues in Presidential Elections

U pon what does a presidential election turn? The presidential candidate has a double character. He is put forward as being individually qualified for the great place of executive head of the nation, because he is a man of integrity, energy, firmness, intellectual power, experience in affairs. He is also recommended as a prominent member of a great national party, inspired by its traditions, devoted to its principles, and prepared to carry them out not only in his properly executive capacity, but, what is more important, as the third branch of the legislature, armed with a veto on bills passed by Congress. His election may therefore be advocated or opposed either on the ground of his personal qualities or of his political professions and party affiliations. Here we have a marked difference between the American and European systems, because in England, and perhaps still more in France, Belgium, and Italy, elections turn chiefly on the views of the parties, secondarily on the character of individual leaders, seeing that the leaders are not chosen directly by the people, but are persons who have come to the top in the legislatures of those countries, or have been raised to office by the Crown. In America, therefore, we have a source of possible confusion between issues of two wholly distinct kinds—those which affect the personal qualifications of the candidate, and those which regard the programme of his party.

Whether, in any given presidential election, the former or the latter class of issues are the more conspicuous and decisive, depends partly on the political questions which happen to be then before the people, partly on the more or less marked individuality of the rival candidates. From about 1850 down to 1876, questions, first of the extension of slavery, then of its extinction, then of the reconstruction of the Union, had divided the nation, and made every contest a contest of principles and of practical measures. Since the controversies raised by the war have been settled, there were, till the free silver question emerged in 1896, few real differences of political principle between the parties, and questions of personal fitness therefore became relatively more important. Now that both currency issues and those raised by the war with Spain have subsided, the qualities of the candidates seem again tending to be potent factors.

The object of each party naturally is to put forward as many good political issues as it can, claiming for itself the merit of having always been on the popular side. Anyone who should read the campaign literature of the Republicans would fancy that they were opposed to the Democrats on many important points. When he took up the Democratic speeches and pamphlets he would be again struck by the serious divergences between the parties, which, however, would seem to arise, not on the points raised by the Republicans, but on other points which the Republicans had not referred to. In other words, the aim of each party is to force on its antagonist certain issues which the antagonist rarely accepts, so that although there is a vast deal of discussion and declamation on political topics, there are few on which either party directly traverses the doctrines of the other. Each pummels, not his true enemy, but a stuffed figure set up to represent that enemy. During the presidential elections after that of 1876, the Republicans sought to force to the front the issue of protection versus free trade, which the Democrats sometimes hesitated to accept, having avowed Protectionists within their own ranks, and knowing that the bulk of the nation was (at most) prepared only for certain reductions in the tariff. Thus while Republican orators were advocating a protective tariff on a thousand platforms, hardly a Democrat ventured to refer to the subject except by saying that he would not refer to it. Both sides declared against monopolists and the power of corporations. Both professed to be the friends of civil service reform, though neither cared for it. Both promised to protect the rights of the Americans all over the world, to withstand Bismarck in his attacks on American bacon—this was in 1884—and to rescue American citizens from British dungeons. Both, however, were equally zealous for peace and goodwill among the nations, and had no idea of quarrelling with any European power. These appeals and professions made no great impression upon the voters. The American, like the Englishman, usually votes with his party, right or wrong, and when there is little distinction of view between the parties it becomes all the easier to stick to your old friends. The Republican party still had much support from those who remembered that it had saved the Union in the days of Secession. The Democratic party commanded a solid South.

The election of 1888 was remarkable for the fact that the victory of the party which had been defeated in 1884 was mainly due to a personal intrigue, a secret "deal," which was believed to have turned over from the Democrats to the Republicans the thirty-six electoral votes of New York State. In the contest of 1892 the Democrats imitated the Republican tactics of 1884 by attacking the latter party upon an issue (that of the Federal Elections or so-called "Force" Bill) which the Republicans had carefully avoided, and which they refused to accept. The protective tariff did on this occasion raise a definite issue and materially affect the result. But as regards currency questions, profound and important as they were, the "platforms" of the two great parties differed but slightly, and neither could command the allegiance to its platform of the whole of its rank and file. In particular the strange spectacle was presented of a candidate avowing strong and clear views, who found himself in this weighty matter more in accordance with the bulk of his Republican opponents than with a large section of his Democratic supporters.

In the election of 1896 the section last referred to carried the Democratic Convention and nominated its candidate, so the contest turned upon the free silver issue. Here there was an economic question of capital importance, which divided the Republicans from the "regular" Democrats, for a part of the Democratic party, differing from the majority on the currency, had broken away and nominated its own candidates for presidency and vice-presidency. On this occasion campaign oratory and literature were directed to a tangible issue. Economic doctrines were forcibly argued; the intelligence of the electors was appealed to; the contest was splendidly stimulating and educative. In 1900 something similar happened, though the currency was then a less prominent issue. In 1904 that issue had disappeared. Both then and in 1908 there was a less sharp opposition of contending doctrines, and on many points the parties were practically agreed, though one stated its views in more "radical" terms than the other, and the Democrats kept almost silent on tariff questions while the Republicans talked of cautiously revising a scale of duties which they lauded as beneficial.

When political controvery is languid, personal issues come to the front. They are in one sense small, but not for that reason less exciting. Whoever has sat in any body of men, from a college debating society up to a legislative chamber, knows that no questions raise so much warmth, and are debated with so much keenness as questions affecting the character and conduct of individual men. They evoke some of what is best and much of what is worst in human nature. In a presidential election it is impossible to avoid discussing the personal merits of the candidates, because much depends on those merits. It has also proved impossible to set limits to the discussion. Unmitigated publicity is a condition of eminence in America; and the excitement in one of these contests rises so high that (at elections in which personal issues are prominent) the canons of decorum which American custom at other times observes, are cast aside by speakers and journalists. The air is thick with charges, defences, recriminations, till the voter knows not what to believe.

These censures are referable to three classes.[1] One used to include what was called the candidate's "war record." To have been disloyal to the Union in the hour of its danger was a reproach. To have fought for the North, still more to have led a Northern regiment or division, covered a multitude of sins. It is the greatest of blessings for America that she fights so seldom, for in no country do military achievements carry a candidate farther, not that the people love war, for they do not, but because success in a sphere so remote from their ordinary life touches their imagination, marks a man out from his fellows, associates his name with their passionate patriotism, gives him a claim on the gratitude, not of a party, but of the nation as a whole. His prowess in repulsing the British troops at New Orleans made Andrew Jackson twice president, in spite of grave faults of temper and judgment. Some Indian skirmishes fixed the choice of the Whig party in 1840 upon William H. Harrison, though his competitor for the nomination was Henry Clay. Zachary Taylor was known only by his conduct of the Mexican war, when he was elected by the same party in 1848. The failure of General Grant as president in his first term, a failure which those who most heartily recognized his honour and patriotism could not deny, did not prevent his reelection in 1872; and the memory of his services came near to giving him a third nomination in 1880.

More serious, however, than the absence of a war record, have been charges of the second class—those impeaching the nominee's personal integrity. These few candidates used to escape. Few men can have passed years in a state legislature or state or city office, or Congress, without coming into contact with disreputable persons, and occasionally finding themselves in situations capable of being misrepresented. They may have

---

[1] This and the two following paragraphs are allowed to stand in the text because they describe what happened in earlier elections and might possibly, given similar conditions, happen again. But what is said in them does not apply to the contests from 1888 onwards, for in these there have been comparatively few and slight attacks upon the character of candidates.

The inquiry into a candidate's honesty is pursued so keenly that even his property tax returns are scrutinized to found charges of his having endeavoured to evade the law. Such a charge played a great part in a recent presidential contest.

walked warily, they may not have swerved from the path of rectitude, but they must have been tempted to do so, and it requires no great invention to add details which give a bad look to the facts. As some men of note, from whom better things had been expected, have lapsed, a lapse by a man of standing seems credible. It was therefore an easy task for the unscrupulous passions which a contest rouses to gather up rumours, piece out old though unproved stories of corruption, put the worst meaning on doubtful words, and so construct a damning impeachment, which will be read in party journals by many voters who never see the defence. The worst of this habit of universal invective is that the plain citizen, hearing much which he cannot believe, finding foul imputations brought even against those he has reason to respect, despairs of sifting the evidence, and sets down most of the charges to malice and "campaign methods," while concluding that the residue is about equally true of all politicians alike. The distinction between good and bad men may for many voters be practically effaced, and the spectacle be presented of half the honest men supporting for the headship of the nation a person whom the other half declare to be a knave. Extravagant abuse produces a reaction, and makes the honest supporters of a candidate defend even his questionable acts. And thus the confidence of the country in the honour of its public men was lowered.

Less frequent, but more offensive, have sometimes, though happily rarely, been the charges made against the private life of a candidate, particularly in his relations with women. American opinion is highly sensitive on this subject. Nothing damages a man more than a reputation for irregularity in these relations; nothing therefore opens a more promising field to slander, and to the coarse vulgarity which is scarcely less odious, even if less mendacious, than slander itself.

Though these have been the chief heads of attack, there is nothing in the life or habits of a candidate out of which materials for a reproach might not be drawn. Of one it is said that he is too fond of eating; of another that though he rents a pew in Dr. Y—'s church, he is more frequently seen in a Roman Catholic place of worship; of a third that he deserted his wife twenty-five years ago; of a fourth that he is an atheist. His private conversations may be reported; and when he denies the report, third persons are dragged in to refute his version. Nor does criticism stop with the candidate himself. His leading supporters are arraigned and dissected. A man's surroundings do no doubt throw some light upon him. If you are shown into a library, you derive an impression from the books on the shelves and the pictures on the wall; much more then may you be influenced by the character of a man's personal friends and political associates. But such methods of judging must be applied cautiously. American electioneering has now and then carried them beyond reasonable limits.

These personal issues do not always come to the front. The candidates may both be free from any reasonable possibility of reproach. This tends to be more and more the case; and there have in fact been few attacks on personal character in recent elections—practically none in 1908 and 1912.

Obviously, both the integrity and the abilities of the rival candidates deserve to be carefully weighed by the electors and ought to affect the result, for the welfare of the country may be profoundly affected by them. The personal qualities of a president generally make more difference to the United States than the personal qualities of a prime minister do to Britain. Sometimes, however, this quite proper regard to the personal merits or demerits of the candidates has tended to draw attention away from political discussions, and has thereby lessened what may be called the educational value of the campaign. A general election in England seems better calculated to instruct the masses of the people in the principles as well as the practical issues of politics, than the longer and generally hotter presidential contest in America. The average intelligence of the voter (excluding the Negroes) is higher in America than in Britain, and his familiarity not only with the passwords and catchwords of politics, but with the structure of his own government, is much greater. But in Britain the contest is primarily one of programmes and not of persons. The leaders on each side are freely criticized, and most people are largely influenced by their judgment of the prime minister, and of the person who will become prime minister if the existing ministry be dismissed. Still the men are almost always overshadowed by the principles which they respectively advocate, and as invective and panegyric have already been poured for years, there is little inducement to rake up or invent tales against them. Controversy turns on the needs of the country, and on the measures which each party puts forward; attacks on a ministry are levelled at their public acts instead of their private characters. Americans who watch general elections in England say that they find in the speeches of English candidates more appeal to reason and experience, more argument and less sentimental rhetoric, than in the discourses of their own campaign orators. To such a general judgment there are, of course, many exceptions. The campaign of 1896 was highly educative, and those of 1904, 1908, and 1912, turning largely on economic questions, were similarly valuable. There have always been in the United States public speakers such as Mr. Henry Ward Beecher was in the days of the Civil War, whose vigorous thinking has been in the highest degree instructive as well as stimulative; and the oratory of English candidates is probably, regarded as mere oratory, less effective than that of the American stump.

An examination of the causes which explain this difference belongs to another part of this book. Here I will only remark that the absence from British elections of flags, uniforms, torches, brass bands, parades, and all the other appliances employed in America, for making the people "enthuse," leaves the field more free for rational discussion. Add to this that whereas the questions discussed on British platforms during the last two generations have been mainly questions needing argument, such as that of the corn laws in the typical popular struggle which Cobden and Bright and Villiers led, the most exciting theme for an American speaker during a whole generation was one—the existence and extension of slavery—which specially called for emotional treatment. Such subjects as the regulation of the tariff, competing plans of liquor legislation, currency and labour questions of controlling or abolishing trusts, are so difficult to sift thoroughly before a popular audience that election speakers were long tempted to evade them or to deal in sounding commonplaces. Latterly, however, the growing gravity of the problems which the customs tariff and the national currency present, has induced a noteworthy change, a change strikingly apparent in 1896; and although these complex economic topics are often handled with little knowledge and in a declamatory way, it is a real gain that the popular mind should be constantly directed to them and forced to think seriously about them.

If the presidential contest may seem to have usually done less for the formation of political thought and diffusion of political knowledge than was to be expected from the immense efforts put forth and the intelligence of the voters addressed, it nevertheless rouses and stirs the public life of the country. One can hardly imagine what the atmosphere of American politics would be without this quadrennial storm sweeping through it to clear away stagnant vapours, and recall to every citizen the sense of his own responsibility for the present welfare and future greatness of his country. Nowhere does government by the people through the people for the people take a more directly impressive and powerfully stimulative form than in the choice of a chief magistrate by fifteen millions of citizens voting on one day.

Further Observations on Nominations and Elections

Several questions may have occurred to the European reader who has followed the foregoing account of presidential nominations and elections.

The most obvious is—How comes it that a system of nomination by huge party assemblies has grown up so unlike anything which the free countries of Europe have seen?

The nominating convention is the natural and legitimate outgrowth of two features of the Constitution, the restricted functions of Congress and the absolute sovereignty of the people. It was soon perceived that under the rule of party, a party must be united on its candidate in order to have a prospect of success. There was therefore need for a method of selecting the candidate which the whole of a party would recognize as fair and entitled to respect. At first the representatives of the party in Congress assumed the right of nomination. But it was presently felt that they were not entitled to it, for they had not been chosen for any such purpose, and the president was not constitutionally responsible to them, but rather set up to check them. When the congressional caucus had been discredited, the state legislatures tried their hands at nominations; but acting irregularly, and with a primary regard to local sentiment, they failed to win obedience. The self-authorized and sometimes secret action of both these sets of persons caused resentment. It began to be held that whom the people were to elect the people must also nominate. Thus presently the tumultuous assemblies of active politicians were developed into regular representative bodies, modelled after Congress, and giving to the party in each state exactly the same weight in nominating as the state possessed in voting. The elaborate nominating scheme of primaries and conventions which was being constructed for the purpose of city, state, and congressional elections, was applied to the election of a president, and the national convention was the result. We may call it an effort of nature to fill the void left in America by the absence of the European parliamentary or cabinet system, under which an executive is called into being out of the legislature by the majority of the legislature. In the European system no single act of nomination is necessary, because the leader of the majority comes gradually to the top in virtue of his own strength.[1] In America there must be a single and formal act: and this act must emanate from the people, since it is to them that the party leader, when he becomes chief magistrate, will be responsible. There is not quite so strong a reason for entrusting to the convention the function of declaring the aims and tenets of the party in its platform, for this might properly be done by a caucus of the legislature. But as the president is, through his veto power, an independent branch of the legislature, the moment of nominating him is apt for a declaration of the doctrines whereof the party makes him the standard-bearer.

What have been the effects upon the public life of the country of this practice of nomination by conventions? Out of several I select two. Politics have turned largely upon the claims of rival personalities. The victory of a party in a presidential election depends upon its being unanimous in its support of a particular candidate. It must therefore use every effort to find, not necessarily the best man, but the man who will best unite it. In the pursuit of him, it is distracted from its consideration of the questions on which it ought to appeal to the country, and may form its views on them hastily or loosely. The convention is the only body authorized to declare the tenets and practical programme of the party. But the duty of declaring them is commonly overshadowed by the other duty of choosing the candidate, which naturally excites warmer feelings in the hearts of actual or potential officeholders. Accordingly delegates are chosen by local conventions rather as the partisans of this or that aspirant than as persons of political ability or moral weight; and the function of formulating the views of the party may be left to, and ill discharged by, men of an inferior type.

[1] The nearest parallel to the American nominating system is the selection of their leader by the opposition in the House of Commons, of which there have been only three instances, the choice of Lord Hartington by the Liberal members in that House in 1875, on which occasion the other candidates withdrew before a vote was needed; the choice of Sir Henry Campbell-Bannerman by the same party in 1898, on which occasion no other candidate appeared; and the choice of Mr. Law by the Tory party in 1911. The selection of a prime minister is the act of the Crown. If he sits in the House of Commons, he naturally leads it; if in the other house, he chooses one of his colleagues to lead in the Commons.

A further result will have been foreseen by those who have realized what these conventions are like. They are monster meetings. Besides the thousand delegates, there are some twelve to fifteen thousand spectators on the floor and in the galleries, while at Chicago in 1860, there were also thousands on the roof. It goes without saying that such a meeting is capable neither of discussing political questions and settling a political programme, nor of deliberately weighing the merits of rival aspirants for the nomination. Its platform must be presented to it cut and dry, and this is the work of a small committee. In choosing a candidate, it must follow a few leaders.[2] And what sort of leaders do conventions tend to produce? Two sorts—the intriguer and the declaimer. There is the man who manipulates delegates and devises skilful combinations. There is also the orator, whose physical gifts, courage, and readiness enable him to browbeat antagonists, overawe the chairman, and perhaps, if he be possessed of eloquence, carry the multitude away in a fit of enthusiasm. For men of wisdom and knowledge, not seconded by a commanding voice and presence, there is no demand, and little chance of usefulness, in these tempestuous halls.

Why, however, it may also be asked, should conventions be so pre-eminently tempestuous, considering that they are not casual concourses, but consist of persons duly elected, and are governed by a regular code of procedure? The reason may be found in the fact that in them are united the two conditions which generate excitement, viz., very large numbers and important issues to be determined. In no other modern assemblies[3] do these conditions concur. Modern deliberative assemblies are comparatively small— the House of Representatives has only 435 members; the French Chamber 584; while in the British House of Commons there is sitting space for only 400. Large popular gatherings, on the other hand, such as mass meetings, are excitable in virtue of their size, but have nothing to do but pass resolutions, and there is seldom controversy over these, because such meetings are attended only by those who agree with the summoners. But a national convention consists of about one thousand delegates, as many alternates, and some fourteen thousand spectators. It is the hugest mass

[2] Hamilton had acutely remarked in 1788 that the larger an assembly the greater is the power of a few in it. See Vol. I, p. 172.

[3] In the ancient world the assemblies of great democratic cities like Athens or Syracuse presented both these conditions; they had large numbers present, and almost unlimited powers. But they were at any rate permanent bodies, accustomed to meet frequently, composed of men who knew one another, who respected certain leaders, and applauded the same orators. The American convention consists of men who come together once only in their lives, and then for a week or less.

meeting the world knows of. Not only, therefore, does the sympathy of numbers exert an unequalled force, but this host, larger than the army with which the Greeks conquered at Marathon, has an issue of the highest and most exciting nature to decide, an issue which quickens the pulse even of those who read in cold blood afterwards how the votes fell as the roll of states was called, and which thrills those who see and listen, and, most of all, those who are themselves concerned as delegates, with an intensity of emotion surpassing, in proportion to the magnitude of the issue, that which attends the finish of a well-contested boat race. If you wish to realize the passionate eagerness of an American convention, take the House of Commons or the French Chamber during a division which is to decide the fate of a ministry, and a policy, and raising the numbers present twenty-fold, imagine the excitement twenty-fold hotter. Wanting those wonderful scenes which a great debate and division in Parliament provide the English with, America has evolved others not less dramatic. The contrast between the two countries is perhaps most marked in this, that in Parliament the strife is between two parties, in an American convention between the adherents of different leaders belonging to the same party. We might have expected that in the more democratic country more would turn upon principles, less upon men. It is exactly the other way. The struggle in a convention is over men, not over principles.

These considerations may serve to explain to a European the strange phenomena of a convention. But his inquiry probably extends itself to the electoral campaign which follows. "Why," he asks, "is the contest so much longer, more strenuous, and more absorbing than the congressional elections, or than any election struggle in Europe, although Europe is agitated by graver problems than now occupy America? And why does a people externally so cool, self-contained, and unimpulsive as the American work itself up into a fever of enthusiasm over an issue which may not be permanently important between two men, neither of whom will do much good or can do much harm?"

The length of the contest is a survival. The Americans themselves regret it, for it sadly interrupts both business and pleasure. It is due to the fact that when communication was difficult over a rough and thinly settled country, several months were needed to enable the candidates and their orators to go round. Now railways and telegraphs have drawn the continent so much together that five or six weeks would be sufficient. That the presidential election is fought more vehemently than congressional elections seems due to its coming only half as often; to the fact that the president is the dispenser of federal patronage, and to the habit, formed in days when the president was the real head of the party, and his action in foreign affairs might be of transcendent importance, of looking on his election as the great trial of party strength. Besides, it is the choice of one officer by the whole country, a supreme political act in which every voter has a share, and the same share; an act which fills the whole of the party in all of the states with the sense that it is feeling and thinking and willing as one heart and mind. This simultaneity of effort, this concentration of interest upon one person and one polling day, gives to the struggle a sort of tension not to be looked for where a number of elections of different persons are going on in as many different spots, nor always at the same time. In congressional elections each constituency has to think first of itself and its own candidate. In the presidential elections all eyes are fixed on the same figure; the same personal as well as political issue is presented to the nation. Each polling district in a state, each state in the Union, emulates every other in the efforts it puts forth to carry the party ticket.

To explain why the hardheaded self-possessed Americans go so wild with excitement at election times is a more difficult task. See what the facts are: From Abraham Lincoln's reelection in 1864 down to the end of the nineteenth century there had not been a single presidential candidate (always excepting General Grant) of whom his friends could say that he had done anything to command the gratitude of the nation. Some of these candidates had been skilful party leaders, others had served with credit in the Civil War. None could be called distinguished in the sense in which, I will not say, Hamilton, Jefferson, Marshall, Webster, but J. Q. Adams, Clay, Benton, Calhoun, Seward, Stanton, and Chase, were distinguished men. To avoid recent events let us go back to Mr. Blaine and Mr. Cleveland in the election of 1884. One had been Speaker of the House, and was a skilful debater in Congress, an effective speaker on a platform, a man socially attractive, never forgetting a face or a service. The other had made a shrewd and upright mayor of Buffalo and governor of New York State. Compare the services rendered to the country by them, or by any other candidate of recent times, with those of Mazzini, Garibaldi, Cavour, and Victor Emmanuel to Italy, of Bismarck and Moltke to Germany, even of Thiers and Gambetta to France in her hour of peril. Yet the enthusiasm shown for Mr. Blaine (who seems to have drawn out the precious fluid at a higher temperature than his rival), the demonstrations made in his honour wherever he appeared, equalled anything done, in their several countries, for these heroes of Italy, Germany, or France. As for England, where two great political leaders, towering far above their fellows, have of late years excited the warmest admiration and the bitterest dislike from friends and foes, imagine eight hundred English barristers turning out from the Temple and Lincoln's Inn to walk in slow procession from London Bridge to South Kensington, shouting themselves hoarse for Gladstone or Disraeli!

In attempting an explanation, I will take the bull by the horns, and ask whether the world is right in deeming the Americans a cool and sober people? The American is shrewd and keen, his passion seldom obscures his reason; he keeps his head in moments when a Frenchman, or an Italian, or even a German, would lose it. Yet he is also of an excitable temper, with emotions capable of being quickly and strongly stirred. That there is no contradiction between these qualities appears from the case of the Scotch, who are both more logical and more cautious in affairs than the English, but are also more enthusiastic, more apt to be swept away by a passionate movement.[4] Moreover, the Americans like excitement. They like it for its own sake, and go wherever they can find it. They surrender themselves to the enjoyment of this pleasure the more willingly because it is comparatively rare, and relieves the level tenor of their ordinary life. Add to this the further delight which they find in any form of competition. The passion which in England expresses itself in the popular eagerness over a boat race or a horse race, extends more widely in America to every kind of rivalry and struggle. The presidential election, in which two men are pitted against one another over a four months' course for the great prize of politics, stirs them like any other trial of strength and speed; sets them betting on the issue, disposes them to make efforts for a cause in which their deeper feelings may be little engaged.

These tendencies are intensified by the vast area over which the contest extends, and the enormous multitude that bears a part in it. The American imagination is peculiarly sensitive to the impression of great size. "A big thing" is their habitual phrase of admiration. In Europe, antiquity is what chiefly commands the respect of some minds, novelty what rouses the interest of others. Beyond the Atlantic, the sense of immensity, the sense that the same thought and purpose are animating millions of other men in sympathy with himself, lifts a man out of himself, and sends him into transports of eagerness and zeal about things intrinsically small, but great through the volume of human feeling they have attracted. It is not the

---

[4] Sir Walter Scott remarks of Edinburgh, early in the eighteenth century, that its mob was one of the fiercest in Europe. The history of the Covenant from 1638 downwards is full of episodes which indicate how much more excitable is Scotch than English blood.

profoundity of an idea or emotion, but its lateral extension which most quickly touches the American imagination. For one man who can feel the former, a hundred are struck by the latter; and he who describes America must remember that he has always to think first of the masses.

These considerations may help to explain the disproportion that strikes a European between the merits of the presidential candidate and the blazing enthusiasm which he evokes. It is not really given to him as an individual, it is given to the party personified in him, because he bears its banner, and its fervour is due, not even so much to party passion as to the impressionist character of the people, who desire to be excited, desire to demonstrate, desire, as English undergraduates say, "to run with the boats," and cheer the efforts of the rowers. As regards the details of the demonstrations, the parades and receptions, the badges and brass bands and triumphal arches, anyone can understand why the masses of the people—those who in Europe would be called the lower-middle and working classes—should relish these things, which break the monotony of their lives, and give them a sense of personal participation in a great movement. Even in London, least externally picturesque among European cities, when the working men turn out for a Hyde Park meeting they come marshalled in companies under the banners of their trade unions or other societies, carrying devices, and preceded by music. They make a somewhat scrubby show, for England does not know how to light up the dullness of her skies and streets by colour in costume or variety in design. But the taste for display is there as it is in human nature everywhere. In England, the upper class is shy of joining in any such "functions," even when they have a religious tinge. Its fastidiousness and sense of class dignity are offended. But in America, the sentiment of equality is so pervading that the rich and cultivated do not think of scorning the popular procession; or if some do feel such scorn, they are careful to conceal it. The habit of demonstrating with bands and banners and emblems was formed in days when the upper class was very small, and would not have dreamt of standing aloof from anything which interested the crowd; and now, when the rich and cultivated have grown to be as numerous, and, in most respects, as fastidious as the parallel class in Europe, the habit is too deeply rooted to be shaken. Nobody thinks of sneering. To do as the people do is a tribute to the people's majesty. And the thousand lawyers who shout "James G. Blaine, O-h-i-o," as they march through the October mud of Broadway, have no more sense that they are making themselves ridiculous than the European noble who backs with repeated obeisances out of the presence of his sovereign.

Types of American Statesmen

As trees are known by their fruits, and as different systems of government evidently tend to produce different types of statesmanship, it is pertinent to our examination of the American party system to inquire what are the kinds of statesmen which it engenders and ripens to maturity. A democracy, more perhaps than any other form of government, needs great men to lead and inspire the people. The excellence, therefore, of the methods democracy employs may fairly enough be tested by the excellence of the statesmen whom these methods call forth. Europeans are wont to go farther, and reason from the character of the statesmen to the character of the people, a convenient process, because it seems easier to know the careers and judge the merits of persons than of nations, yet one not universally applicable. In the free countries of Europe, the men who take the lead in public affairs may be deemed fair specimens of its best talent and character, and fair types, possibly of the virtues of the nation, though the temptations of politics are great, certainly of its practical gifts. But in two sorts of countries one cannot so reason from the statesmen to the masses. In despotic monarchies the minister is often merely the king's favourite, who has risen by unworthy arts, or, at any rate, not by merit. And in a democracy where birth and education give a man little advantage in the race, a political career may have become so unattractive as compared with other pursuits that the finest or most ambitious spirits do not strive for its prizes, but generally leave them to men of the second order.

This second case is, as we have seen, to some extent the case of America. We must not therefore take her statesmen as types of the highest or strongest American manhood. The national qualities come out fully in them, but not always in their best form. I speak of the generations that have grown up since the great men of the Revolution epoch died off. Some of those men were the peers of the best European statesmen of the time: one of them rises in moral dignity above all his European contemporaries. The generation to which J. Q. Adams, Jackson, Webster, Clay, Calhoun, and Benton belonged is less impressive, perhaps because they failed to solve a question which may have been too hard for anyone to solve. Yet the men I have mentioned were striking personalities who would have made a figure in any country. Few of the statesmen of the third or Civil War period enjoyed more than a local reputation when it began, but in its course several of them developed remarkable powers, and one became a national hero. The fourth generation is now upon the stage, and it is too soon to attempt to conjecture the place they will hold in the judgment of posterity. Only a few who belong to it have as yet won high fame. The times, it is remarked, are comparatively quiet. What is wanted is not so much an impassioned popular leader nor a great philosophic legislator as men who will administer the affairs of the nation with skill and rectitude, and who, fortified by careful study and observation, will grapple with the economic problems which the growth of the country makes urgent. While admitting this, we must also ascribe something to the character of the party system which, as we have seen, is unfavourable to the development of the finest gifts. Let us note what are the types which that system displays to us.

In such countries as England, France, Germany, and Italy there is room and need for five sorts of statesmen. Men are wanted for the management of foreign and colonial policy, men combining the talents of a diplomatist with a wide outlook over the world's horizon. The needs of social and economic reform, grave in old countries with the mistakes of the past to undo, require a second kind of statesman with an aptitude for constructive legislation. Thirdly there is the administrator who can manage a department with diligence and skill and economy. Fourthly comes the parliamentary tactician, whose function it is to understand men, who frames cabinets and is dexterous in humouring or spurring a representative assembly.[1] Lastly we have the leader of the masses, who, whether or no he be a skilful parliamentarian, thinks rather of the country than of the chamber, knows how to watch and rouse the feelings of the multitude, and rally a great party to the standard which he bears aloft. The first of these has no need for

[1] Englishmen will think of the men who framed the new Poor Law of 1834 as specimens of the second class, of Sir G. C. Lewis as a specimen of the third, of Lord Palmerston as a specimen of the fourth. The aptitudes of the third and fourth were united in Sir Robert Peel.

eloquence; the second and third can get on without it; to the fourth it is almost, yet not absolutely, essential; it is the life breath of the fifth.[2]

Let us turn to America. In America there are few occasions for the first sort of statesman, while the conditions of a federal government, with its limited legislative sphere, are unfavourable to the second, as frequently changing cabinets are to the third. It is chiefly for persons of the fourth and fifth classes we must look. Persons of those classes we shall find, but in a different shape and guise from what they would assume in Europe. American politics seem at this moment to tend to the production of two types, the one of whom may be called *par excellence* the man of the desk or of the legislature, the other the man of the convention and the stump. They resemble the fourth and fifth of our European types, but with instructive differences.

The first of these types is usually a shrewd, cool, hardheaded man of business. He is such a man as one would find successful in the law or in commerce if he had applied his faculties to those vocations. He has mostly been, is often still, a practising counsel and attorney. He may lack imagination and width of view; but he has a tight grip of facts, a keen insight into men, and probably also tact in dealing with them. That he has come to the front shows him to possess a resolute and tenacious will, for without it he must have been trodden down in the fierce competition of a political career. His independence is limited by the necessity of keeping step with his party, for isolated action counts for little in America, but the tendency to go with one's party is so inbred there that a man feels less humiliated by waiving his private views than would be the case in Europe. Such compliance does not argue want of strength. As to what is called "culture," he has often at least a susceptibility to it, with a wish to acquire it which, if he has risen from humble beginnings, may contrast oddly with the superficial roughness of his manner. He is a ready and effective rather than a polished speaker, and is least agreeable when, forsaking the solid ground of his legal or administrative knowledge, he attempts the higher flights of eloquence.

Such a man does not necessarily make his first reputation in an assembly. He may begin as governor of a state or mayor of a large city, and if he earns a reputation there, can make pretty sure of going on to Congress if he desires it. In any case, it is in administration and the legislative work which deals with administration that he wins his spurs. The sphere of local

[2] It need hardly be said that the characteristic attributes of these several types are often found united in the same person; indeed no one can rise high who does not combine at least two of the four latter.

government is especially fitted to develop such talents, and to give that peculiar quality I have been trying to describe. It makes able men of affairs; men fit for the kind of work which needs the combination of a sound business head and the power of working along with others. One may go further and say, that this talent is the sort of talent which during the last half century has been most characteristic of the American people. Their greatest achievements have lain in the internal development of their country by administrative shrewdness, ingenuity, promptitude, and an unequalled dexterity in applying the principle of association, whether by means of private corporations or of local public or quasi-public organisms. These national characteristics reappear in federal politics, not always accompanied by the largeness of vision and mastery of the political and economic sciences which that wider sphere demands.

The type I describe is less brilliant than those modern Europe has learned to admire in men like Bismarck or Cavour, perhaps one may add, Tisza or Minghetti or Castelar. But then the conditions required for the rise of the last-named men do not exist in America, nor is her need for them pressing. America would have all she wants if such statesmen as I have described were more numerous; and if a philosophic mind, capable of taking in the whole phenomena of transatlantic society, and propounding comprehensive solutions for its problems, were more common among the best of them. Persons of this type have hitherto been most frequently found in the Senate, to which they usually rise from the House of Representatives or from a state legislature. They are very useful there; indeed, it is they who have given it that authority which it long enjoyed but is now fast losing.

The other kind of statesman is the product of two factors which give to American politics their peculiar character, viz., an enormous multitude of voting citizens and the existence of a wonderful network of party organizations for the purpose of selecting and carrying candidates for office. To move the masses, a man must have the gifts of oratory; to rule party committees, he must be a master of intrigue. The stump and the committee room are his sphere. There is a great deal of campaign speaking to be done at state elections, at congressional elections, above all, in presidential campaigns. It does not flow in such a perennial torrent as in England, for England has since 1876 become the most speech-flooded country in the world, but it is more copious than in France, Italy, or Germany. The audiences are less ignorant than those of Europe, but their critical standard is not higher; and whereas in England it is Parliament that forms most speakers and creates the type of political oratory, Congress renders no such service to America.

There is therefore, I think, less presumption in America than in Europe that the politician who makes his way by oratory is a man either of real eloquence or of vigorous thinking power. Able, however, he must be. He is sure to have fluency, a power of touching either the emotions or the imagination, a command of sonorous rhetoric. Probably he has also humour and a turn for quick retort. In fact, he must have the arts—we all know what they are—which please the multitude; arts not blamable in themselves, but needing to be corrected by occasional appearances before a critical audience. These arts joined to a powerful voice and a forcible personality will carry a man far. If he can join to them a ready and winning address, a geniality of manner if not of heart, he becomes what is called magnetic. Now, magnetism is among the highest qualities which an American popular leader can possess. Its presence may bring him to the top. Its absence may prevent him from getting there. It makes friends for him wherever he goes. It immensely enhances his powers in the region of backstairs politics.

For besides the visible work on the stump, there is the invisible work of the committee-room, or rather of the inner conclave, whose resolves are afterwards registered in the committee, to be still later laid before the convention. The same talent for intrigue which in monarchies or oligarchies is spent within the limits of a court or a knot of ruling families, here occupies itself with bosses and rings and leaders of political groups. To manipulate these men and groups, to know their weaknesses, their ambitions, their jealousies, to play upon their hopes and fears, attaching some by promises, entrapping others through their vanity, browbeating others into submission, forming combinations in which each partisan's interest is so bound up with that of the aspiring statesman that he is sure to stand faithfully by his chief—all this goes a long way to secure advancement under the party system.

It may be thought that between such aptitudes and the art of oratory there is no necessary connection. There are intriguers who are nothing but intriguers, useless on the stump or on the platform of a convention; and such a man does occasionally rise to national prominence. First he gains command of his own state by a dexterous use of patonrage; then he wins influence in federal politics by being able to dispose of his state vote in federal elections; finally he forces his way into the Senate, and possibly even aspires to the presidential chair, deluded by his own advancement, and by the applause of professionals who find in success sufficient evidence of worthiness. Recent instances of such careers are not wanting. But they are exceptions due to the special conditions of exceptionally demoralized states.

Speaking generally, oratory is essential to distinction. Fluent oratory, however, as distinguished from eloquence, is an art which most able men can acquire with practice. In popularly governed countries it is as common as it is worthless. And a link between the platform and the committee-room is found in the quality of magnetism. The magnetic man attracts individuals just as he captivates masses. Where oratory does not need either knowledge or reflection, because the people are not intent upon great questions, or because the parties evade them, where power of voice and skill in words, and ready sympathy with the feelings and prejudices of the crowd, are enough to command the ear of monster meetings, there the successful speaker will pass for a statesman. He will seem a fit man to put forward for high office, if he can but persuade the managers to run him; and therefore the other side of his activity is spent among and upon the managers.

It sometimes happens that the owner of these gifts is also a shrewd, keen, practical man, so that the first type is blended with the second. Nor is there anything to prevent the popular speaker and skilled intriguer from also possessing the higher attributes of statesmanship. This generation has seen the conjunction both in America and in France. But the conjunction is rare; not only because these last-named attributes are themselves rare, but because the practice of party intrigue is unfavourable to their development. It narrows a man's mind and distorts his vision. His eye, accustomed to the obscurity of committee-rooms, cannot range over the wide landscape of national questions. Habits of argument formed on the stump seldom fit a man to guide a legislature. In none of the greatest public men that have adorned America do we discern the features of the type just sketched. Hamilton was no intriguer, though he once executed a brilliant piece of strategy.[3] Neither was Clay or Webster. Jefferson, who added an eminent talent for party organization and management to his powers as a thinker and writer, was no speaker; and one might go through the whole list without finding one man of the first historic rank in whom the art of handling committees and nominating conventions was developed to that pitch of excellence which it has now reached in the hands of far inferior men. National conventions offer the best field for the display of the peculiar kind of talent which this type of statesman exhibits. To rouse delegates and one thousand spectators needs powerful lungs, a striking presence, address, and courage. A man capable enough in Congress may fail in this arena. But less than half the

---

[3] In agreeing that the national capital should be placed in the South in return for the support of two Southern men to his plan for the settlement of the public debt.

work of a convention is done on the public stage. Delegates have to be seen in private, combinations arranged, mines laid and those of the opponent discovered and countermined, a distribution of the good things in the gift of the party settled with swarms of hungry aspirants. Easy manners, tact, and suppleness, a reputation for remembering and requiting good turns and ill turns—in fact, many of the qualities which make a courtier—are the qualities which the intrigues of a convention require, develop, and perfect.

Besides such causes inherent in the present party system as check the growth of first-class statesmen more rare than might be expected from the vastness of the nation and its boundless energy, there are two others which spring from the constitutional arrangements of the country. One is the disconnection of Congress from the executive. How this works to prevent true leadership has been already explained.[4] Another is the existence of states, each of which has a political life and distinct party organization of its own. Men often rise to eminence in a state without making their mark in national politics. They may become virtual masters of the state either in a legitimate way by good service to it or in an illegitimate way as its bosses. In either case they have to be reckoned with when a presidential election comes round, and are able, if the state be a doubtful one, to dictate their terms. Thus they push their way to the front without having ever shown the qualities needed for guiding the nation; they crowd out better men, and they make party leadership and management even more of a game than the Spoils System and the convention system have tended to make it. The state vote comes to be in national politics what the ward vote is in city politics, a commodity which a boss or ring can dispose of; the man who can influence it has a power greater than his personal merits entitle him to; and the kind of skill which can make friends of these state bosses and bring them into a "pool" or working combination becomes valuable, if not essential, to a national party leader. In fact, the condition of things is not wholly unlike that of England in the middle of the eighteenth century, when a great boroughmonger like the Duke of Newcastle was a power in the country, who must be not only consulted and propitiated at every crisis, but even admitted to a ministry if it was to secure a parliamentary majority. When a crisis rouses the nation, the power of these organization-mongers or vote-owners vanishes, just as that of the English boroughowning magnate was checked on like occasions, because it is only when the people of a state are listless that their boss is potent. Unable to oppose a real wish of the masses,

---

[4] See Chaps. 21, 25, and 26 in Vol. 1.

he can use their vote only by professing obedience while guiding it in the direction of the men or the schemes he favours.

This remark suggests another. I have remarked that among statesmen of the former of the two types described, there are always ability and integrity sufficient for carrying on the regular business of the country. Men with those still higher gifts which European nations look for in their prime ministers (though they do not always find them) have indeed never been absent, but they have been comparatively rare. The Americans admit the fact, but explain it by arguing that there has been no crisis needing those gifts. Whether this is true may be doubted. Men of constructive statesmanship were surely needed in the period after the Civil War; and it is possible that a higher statesmanship might have averted the war itself. The Americans, however, maintain that when the hour comes, it brings the man. It brought Abraham Lincoln. When he was nominated by the famous convention of 1860 his name had been little heard of beyond his own state. But he rose at once to the level of the situation, and that not merely by virtue of strong clear sense, but by his patriotic steadfastness and noble simplicity of character. If this was luck, it was just the kind of luck which makes a nation hopeful of its future, and inclined to overlook the faults of the methods by which it finds its leaders.

What the People Think of It

The European reader who has followed thus far the description I have attempted to give of the working of party politics, of the nominating machine, of the Spoils System, of elections and their methods, of venality in some legislative and municipal bodies, may have been struck by its dark lines. He sees in this new country evils which savour of Old World corruption, even of Old World despotism. He is reminded sometimes of England under Sir Robert Walpole, sometimes of Russia under the czar Nicholas I. Assuming, as a European is apt to do, that the working of political machinery fairly reflects the temper, ideas, and moral standard of the governing class, and knowing that America is governed by the whole people, he may form a low opinion of the people. Perhaps he leaps to the conclusion that they are corrupt. Perhaps he more cautiously infers that they are heedless. Perhaps he conceives that the better men despair of politics and wash their hands of it, while the mass of the people, besotted with a self-confidence born of their rapid material progress, are blind to the consequences which the degradation of public life must involve. All these views one may hear pronounced by persons who have visited the United States, and of course more confidently by persons who have not. It is at any rate a plausible view that whatever public opinion there may be in America upon religion, or morality, or literature, there can be little public opinion about politics, and that the leading minds, which in all countries shape and direct opinion, have in America abdicated that function, and left the politicians to go their own way.

Such impressions are far from the truth. In no country is public opinion stronger or more active than in the United States; in none has it the field so completely to itself, because aristocracies like those of Europe do not exist, and because the legislative bodies are relatively less powerful and less independent. It may seem a paradox to add that public opinion is on the whole wholesome and upright. Nevertheless, this also is true.

Here we are brought face to face with the cardinal problem of American politics. Where political life is all-pervading, can practical politics be on a lower level than public opinion? How can a free people which tolerates gross evils be a pure people? To explain this is the hardest task which one who describes the United States sees confronting him. Experience has taught me, as it teaches every traveller who seeks to justify when he returns to Europe his faith in the American people, that it is impossible to get Englishmen at any rate to realize the coexistence of phenomena so unlike those of their own country, and to draw the inferences which those phenomena suggest to one who has seen them with his own eyes. Most English admirers of popular government, when pressed with the facts, deny them. But I have already admitted them.

To present a just picture of American public opinion one must cut deeper than the last few chapters have done, and try to explain the character and conditions of opinion itself beyond the Atlantic, the mental habits from which it springs, the organs through which it speaks. This is what I propose to do in the chapters which follow. Meanwhile it is well to complete the survey of the actualities of party politics by stating in a purely positive, or as the Germans say "objective," way, what the Americans think about the various features of their system portrayed in these last chapters, about spoils and the machine, about corruption and election frauds. I omit attempts at explanation; I seek only to sum up the bare facts of the case as they strike one who listens to conversation and reads the newspapers.

Corruption. Most of it the people, by which I mean not the masses but all classes of the people, do not see. The proceedings of Congress excite less interest than those of legislative chambers do in France or England. Venality occurs chiefly in connection with private legislation, and even in Washington very little is known about this, the rather as committees deliberate with closed doors. Almost the only persons who possess authentic information as to what goes on in the Capitol are railroad men, land speculators, and manufacturers who have had to lobby in connection with the tariff. The same remark applies, though less forcibly, to the venality of certain state legislatures. A farmer of western New York may go through a long life without knowing how his representative behaves at Albany. Albany is not within his horizon.[1]

---

[1] This remark does not apply to the malversations of officials in cities like New York or Philadelphia. These nobody can help knowing.

The people see little and they believe less. True, the party newspapers accuse their opponents, but the newspapers are always reviling somebody; and it is because the words are so strong that the tale has little meaning. For instance, in a hard fought presidential contest charges affecting the honour of one of the candidates were brought against him by journals supporting the other candidate, and evidence tendered in support of them. The immense majority of his supporters did not believe these charges. They read their own newspapers chiefly, which pooh-poohed the charges. They could not be at the trouble of sifting the evidence, against which their own newspapers offered counter arguments, so they quietly ignored them. I do not say that they disbelieved. Between belief and disbelief there is an intermediate state of mind.

The habit of hearing charges promiscuously bandied to and fro, but seldom probed to the bottom, makes men heedless. So does the fact that prosecutions frequently break down even where there can be little doubt as to the guilt of the accused. A general impression is produced that things are not as they should be, yet the line between honest men and dishonest men is not sharply drawn, because those who are probably honest are attacked, and those who are almost certainly dishonest escape punishment. The state of mind of the average citizen is a state rather of lassitude than of callousness. He comes to think that politicians have a morality of their own, and must be judged by it. It is not his morality; but because it is professional, he does not fear that it will infect other plain citizens like himself.

Some people shrug their shoulders and say that politicians have always been so. Others, especially among the cultivated classes, will tell you that they wash their hands of the whole affair. "It is only the politicians—what can you expect from the politicians?" Leaving out the cynics on the one side, and the perfectionist reformers on the other, and looking at the bulk of ordinary citizens, the fair conclusion from the facts is that many do not realize the evil who ought to realize it and be alarmed, and that those who do realize it are not sufficiently alarmed. They take it too easily. Yet now and then when roused they will inflict severe penalties on the receivers of bribes, as they did on the New York aldermen who were bribed to grant the right of laying a streetcar line in Broadway. The givers of bribes are apt to be more leniently dealt with.

Election Frauds. As these are offences against popular government and injure the opposite party, they excite stronger, or at least more general disapproval than do acts of venality, from which only the public purse suffers. No one attempts to palliate them; but proof is difficult, and punishment therefore uncertain. Legislative remedies have been tried, and fresh ones are constantly being tried. If people are less indignant than they would be in England, it is because they are less surprised. There is one exception to the general condemnation of the practice. In the Southern states Negro suffrage produced, during the few years of "carpetbagging" and military government which followed the war, incredible mischief. When these states recovered full self-government, and the former "rebels" were readmitted to the suffrage, the upper class of the white population "took hold" again, and in order, as they expressed it, "to save civilization," resolved that come what might the Negro and white Republican vote should not, by obtaining a majority in the state legislatures, be in a position to play these pranks further. The Negroes were at first roughly handled or, to use the technical term, "bulldozed," but as this excited anger at the North, it was found better to attain the desired result by manipulating the elections in various ways, "using no more fraud than was necessary in the premises," as the pleaders say. As few of the Negroes are fit for the suffrage, these services to civilization have been leniently regarded even at the North, and are justified at the South by men quite above the suspicion of personal corruption.

The Machine. The perversion of rings and bosses of the nominating machinery of primaries and conventions excites a disgust which is proportioned to the amount of fraud and trickery employed, an amount not great when the "good citizens" make no counter exertions. The disgust is often mingled with amusement. The boss is a sort of joke, albeit an expensive joke. "After all," people say, "it is our own fault. If we all went to the primaries, or if we all voted an independent ticket, we could make an end of the boss." There is an odd sort of fatalism in their view of democracy. If a thing exists in a free country, it has a right to exist, for it exists by the leave of the people, who may be deemed to acquiesce in what they do not extinguish. Nevertheless, the disgust rose high enough to enable the reformers to secure the enactment of the new primary laws, which represent a real effort to smash the machine.

The Spoils System. As to spoils and favouritism in patronage, I have already explained why the average citizen tolerates both. He has been accustomed to think rotation in office a recognition of equality, and a check on the growth of that old bugbear, an "aristocracy of officeholders." Favouritism seemed natural, and competitive examinations pedantic. Usage sanctioned a certain amount of jobbery, so you must not be too hard on a man who does no more than others have done before him.

The conduct, as well as the sentiment, of the people is so much better than the practice of politicians that it is hard to understand why the latter are judged so leniently. No ordinary citizen, much less a man of social standing and high education, would do in his private dealings what many politicians do with little fear of disgrace. The career of the latter is not destroyed, while the former would lose the respect of his neighbours, and probably his chances in the world. Europe presents no similar contrast between the tone of public and that of private life.

There is, however, one respect in which a comparison of the political morality of the United States with that of England does injustice to the former.

The English have two moralities for public life, the one conventional or ideal, the other actual. The conventional finds expression not merely in the pulpit, but also in the speeches of public men, in the articles of journalists. Assuming the normal British statesman to be patriotic, disinterested, truthful, and magnanimous, it treats every fault as a dereliction from a well-settled standard of duty, a quite exceptional dereliction which disentitles the culprit to the confidence even of his own party, but does not affect the generally high tone of British political life. The actual morality, as one gathers it in the lobbies of the legislative chambers, or the smoking rooms of political clubs, or committee-rooms at contested elections, is a different affair. It regards (or lately regarded) the bribery of voters as an offence only when detection has followed; it assumes that a minister will use his patronage to strengthen his party or himself; it smiles at election pledges as the gods smiled at lovers' vows; it defends the abuse of parliamentary rules; it tolerates equivocations and misleading statements proceeding from an official even when they have not the excuse of state necessity. It is by this actual standard that Englishmen do in fact judge one another; and he who does not sink below it need not fear the conventional ideality of press and pulpit.

Perhaps this is only an instance of the tendency in all professions to develop a special code of rules less exacting than those of the community at large. As a profession holds some things to be wrong, because contrary to its etiquette, which are in themselves harmless, so it justifies other things in themselves blamable. In the mercantile world, agents play sad tricks on their principals in the matter of commissions, and their fellow merchants are astonished when the courts of law compel the ill-gotten gains to be disgorged. At the University of Oxford, everybody who took a Master of Arts degree was, until 1871, required to sign the Thirty-nine Articles of the Church of England. Hundreds of men signed who did not believe, and admitted that they did not believe, the dogmas of this formulary; but nobody thought the worse of them for a solemn falsehood. We know what latitude, as regards truth, a "scientific witness," honourable enough in his private life, permits himself in the witness box. Each profession indulges in deviations from the established rule of morals, but takes pains to conceal these deviations from the general public, and continues to talk about itself and its traditions with an air of unsullied virtue. What each profession does for itself most individual men do for themselves. They judge themselves by themselves, that is to say, by their surroundings and their own past acts, and thus erect in the inner forum of conscience a more lenient code for their own transgressions than that which they apply to others. A fault which a man has often committed seems to him slighter than one he has refrained from and sees others committing. Often he gets others to take the same view. "It is only his way," they say; "it is just like Roger." The same thing happens with nations. The particular forms in which faults like corruption, or falsehood, or unscrupulous partisanship have appeared in the recent political history of a nation shock its moral sense less than similar offences which have taken a different form in some other country.

Each country, while accustomed to judge her own statesmen, as well as her national behaviour generally, by the actual standard, and therefore to overlook many deflections from the ideal, always applies the conventional or absolute standard to other countries. Europeans have done this to America, subjecting her to that censorious scrutiny which the children of an emigrant brother receive on their return from aunts and uncles.

How then does America deal with herself?

She is so far lenient to her own defects as to judge them by her past practice; that is to say, she is less shocked by certain political vices, because these vices are familiar, than might have been expected from the generally high tone of her people. But so far from covering things up as the English do, professing a high standard, and applying it rigorously to other countries, but leniently to her own offspring, she gives an exceptionally free course to publicity of all kinds, and allows writers and speakers to paint the faults of her politicians in strong, not to say exaggerated, colours. Such excessive candour is not an unmixed gain. It removes the restraint which the maintenance of a conventional standard imposes. There is almost too little of make-believe about Americans in public writing, as well as in private talk, and their dislike to humbug, hypocrisy, and what they call English pharisaism, not only tends to laxity, but has made them wrong in the eyes of the Old World their real moral sensitiveness. Accustomed to see constant lip service rendered to a virtue not intended to be practised, Europeans naturally assume that things are in the United States several shades darker than they are painted, and interpret frankness as cynicism. Were American politics judged by the actual and not the conventional standard of England, the contrast between the demerits of the politicians and the merits of the people would be less striking.

Supplementary Note to Editions of 1910 and 1914

REMARKS ON THE GROWTH OF PARTY: ITS PERVERSIONS AND THE REMEDIES APPLIED

It may be well to add here a few further observations, suggested by recent events, on the party system.

The government of the United States, and of every state, and of every city, was originally intended and expected to be conducted by the people as a whole through their elected representatives, who, being the best and wisest, were to act for the whole people in their common interest. But, within a few years of its establishment, the government, both in the nation and in the states, and subsequently in the cities also, was seized upon by party, which has ever since controlled it and worked it, so that no other way of working it has even been thought of, or can now be easily imagined. Out of party there naturally grew the machine, i.e., an elaborate system of party organization created for the purpose of selecting candidates and securing their election by the people. The machine is the offspring of two phenomena, both natural, though both unforeseen. One was the deficiency of public zeal among the citizens, a deficiency not indeed more marked here than in other countries but here more unfortunate. The other was the excess of private zeal among the politicians, who perceived that public work could be turned to private gain. Thus the Spoils System sprang into being, office being the prize of party victory.

But the action of these factors was mightily increased by the influence of democratic theory pushed to extremes. The doctrine of human equality was taken to imply that one man was just as good as another for public office. The doctrine of popular sovereignty was applied by giving the election of nearly all officials in state, county, and city to the voters and by choosing the officials for very short terms. The consequence of this was that it became impossible for the voters, in such large communities as states and great cities, to know who were the fittest men to choose for the large number of elective offices. Hence the action and power of the machine became inevitable. Since the voters could not possibly select the numerous candidates needed, it stepped in and selected them. Since the incessant elections required a great deal of work, it stepped in and conducted the elections.

These evils grew with the increasing size of the communities and the increasing wealth of the country, which threw into the hands of legislatures and officials immense opportunities for bestowing favours on unscrupulous groups of men bent on gain. It is easy for such men to influence a legislature, and it was well worth their while to do so.

At last a point was reached at which the evils aroused the public conscience and were felt to be injuring the whole community. How were they to be dealt with? Human intelligence, by a sort of natural law, chooses the path of least resistance, and instead of trying to root out an evil altogether, oftens seeks to discover some expedient which will get round the evil and avoid its worst consequences. So in this instance the voters, instead of destroying the machine or setting it right by ejecting the professionals and making a party organization truly represent the whole party and the principles the party stands for, resorted to the plan of creating statutory primaries, that is to say, of duplicating elections by holding a party election to choose candidates as preliminary to the general election for choosing officials. Already, instead of trying to reform the legislatures, which had largely lost public confidence by their subservience to the machine and to powerful private interests, they had limited the powers and shortened the sittings of the legislatures; and were turning to the state governor whenever he happened to be a strong and upright man, encouraging him to lead and restrain the legislature so far as his legal powers went. And now at last they have begun to supersede the legislature by taking to themselves the direct power of lawmaking through the institution of the referendum and the initiative, these being in their essence an effort to get rid, not only of the evils incident to the selfishness of legislatures and their amenability to improper influences, but also of party itself, as a force which divides the people and prevents them from taking the shortest way to accomplish their will.

All this beautiful series of constitutional developments in state and city government has evolved itself naturally and logically within little more than a century. The constant element in the series has been democractic theory, i.e., the faith in unlimited and direct popular choice and the doctrine that one man is as fit for public office as another. These doctrines, largely abstract in their origin, rooted themselves in mens' minds, under conditions which made them seem reasonable, in small communities, where the citizens were nearly on a level in education and intelligence, and where the questions of government that arose were within the range of an ordinary man's knowledge. When such notions came to be applied to hugh communities like the states and the vast modern cities, their inapplicability was manifest, while at the same time the need for an organization to work the party system became more evident. Improvements in the representative system might have seemed to be the obvious remedy, but unfortunately the same changes had so injured, and at last discredited, the legislatures of states and cities that the efforts for reform took a different line.

Since 1894, when the preceding chapters on the party system were last revised, public opinion has become more impatient of the rule of the machine, and more sensitive to scandals, while "good citizens" have begun to show more activity in their campaign for purity. "Boss rule" seems to be losing its hold in some of the cities, and the tendency to emancipate them from the state legislatures and stimulate the inhabitants to frame better schemes of government and take a more constant interest in their working has gained ground. Accordingly, although the facts set forth above are still so far generally true that the statements can properly be allowed to stand, it may safely be said that the sky is brighter in 1914 than it was in 1894.

PART IV

PUBLIC OPINION

The Nature of Public Opinion

In no country is public opinion so powerful as in the United States: in no country can it be so well studied. Before I proceed to describe how it works upon the government of the nation and the states, it may be proper to consider briefly how it is formed, and what is the nature of the influence which it everywhere exercises upon government.

What do we mean by public opinion? The difficulties which occur in discussing its action mostly arise from confounding opinion itself with the organs whence people try to gather it, and from using the term, sometimes to denote everybody's views, that is, the aggregate of all that is thought and said on a subject, sometimes merely the views of the majority, the particular type of thought and speech which prevails over other types.

The simplest form in which public opinion presents itself is when a sentiment spontaneously rises in the mind and flows from the lips of the average man upon his seeing or hearing something done or said. Homer presents this with his usual vivid directness in the line which frequently recurs in the *Iliad* when the effect produced by a speech or event is to be conveyed: "And thus anyone was saying as he looked at his neighbour." This phrase describes what may be called the rudimentary stage of opinion. It is the prevalent impression of the moment. It is what any man (not every man) says, i.e., it is the natural and the general thought or wish which an occurrence evokes. But before opinion begins to tell upon government, it has to go through several other stages. These stages are various in different ages and countries. Let us try to note what they are in England or America at the present time, and how each stage grows out of the other.

A businessman reads in his newspaper at breakfast the events of the preceding day. He reads that Prince Bismarck has announced a policy of protection for German industry, or that Mr. Henry George has been nominated for the mayoralty of New York. These statements arouse in his mind sentiments of approval or disapproval, which may be strong or weak according to his previous predilection for or against protection or Mr. Henry George, and of course according to his personal interest in the matter. They rouse also an expectation of certain consequences likely to follow. Neither the sentiment nor the expectation is based on processes of conscious reasoning—our businessman has not time to reason at breakfast—they are merely impressions formed on the spur of the moment. He turns to the leading article in the newspaper, and his sentiments and expectations are confirmed or weakened according as he finds that they are or are not shared by the newspaper writer. He goes down to his office in the train, talks there to two or three acquaintances, and perceives that they agree or do not agree with his own still faint impressions. In his business office he finds his partner and a bundle of other newspapers which he glances at; their words further affect him, and thus by the end of the day his mind is beginning to settle down into a definite view, which approves or condemns Prince Bismarck's declaration or the nomination of Mr. George. Meanwhile a similar process has been going on in the minds of others, and particularly of the journalists, whose business it is to discover what people are thinking. The evening paper has collected the opinions of the morning papers, and is rather more positive in its forecast of results. Next morning the leading journals have articles still more definite and positive in approval or condemnation and in prediction of consequences to follow; and the opinion of ordinary minds, hitherto fluid and undetermined, has begun to crystallize into a solid mass. This is the second stage. Then debate and controversy begin. The men and the newspapers who approve Mr. George's nomination argue with those who do not; they find out who are friends and who opponents. The effect of controversy is to drive the partisans on either side from some of their arguments, which are shown to be weak; to confirm them in others, which they think strong; and to make them take up a definite position on one side. This is the third stage. The fourth is reached when action becomes necessary. When a citizen has to give a vote, he votes as a member of a party; his party prepossessions and party allegiance lay hold on him, and generally stifle any individual doubts or repulsions he may feel. Bringing men up to the polls is like passing a steam roller over stones newly laid on a road: the angularities are pressed down, and an appearance of smooth and even uniformity is given which did not exist before. When a man has voted, he is committed: he has thereafter an interest in backing the view which he has sought to make prevail. Moreover, opinion, which may have been manifold till the polling, is thereafter generally twofold only. There is a view which has triumphed and a view which has been vanquished.

In examining the process by which opinion is formed, we cannot fail to note how small a part of the view which the average man entertains when he goes to vote is really of his own making. His original impression was faint and perhaps shapeless; its present definiteness and strength are mainly due to what he has heard and read. He has been told what to think, and why to think it. Arguments have been supplied to him from without, and controversy has imbedded them in his mind. Although he supposes his view to be his own, he holds it rather because his acquaintances, his newspapers, his party leaders all hold it. His acquaintances do the like. Each man believes and repeats certain phrases, because he thinks that everybody else on his own side believes them, and of what each believes only a small part is his own original impression, the far larger part being the result of the commingling and mutual action and reaction of the impressions of a multitude of individuals, in which the element of pure personal conviction, based on individual thinking, is but small.

Everyone is of course predisposed to see things in some one particular light by his previous education, habits of mind, accepted dogmas, religious or social affinities, notions of his own personal interest. No event, no speech or article, ever falls upon a perfectly virgin soil: the reader or listener is always more or less biased already. When some important event happens, which calls for the formation of a view, these preexisting habits, dogmas, affinities, help to determine the impression which each man experiences, and so far are factors in the view he forms. But they operate chiefly in determining the first impression, and they operate over many minds at once. They do not produce variety and independence; they are soon overlaid by the influences which each man derives from his fellows, from his leaders, from the press.

Orthodox democratic theory assumes that every citizen has, or ought to have, thought out for himself certain opinions, i.e., ought to have a definite view, defensible by arguments, of what the country needs, of what principles ought to be applied in governing it, of the men to whose hands the government ought to be entrusted. There are persons who talk, though certainly very few who act, as if they believed this theory, which may be compared to the theory of some ultra-Protestants that every good Christian has or ought to have, by the strength of his own reason, worked out for himself from the Bible a system of theology. But one need only try the experiment of talking to that representative of public opinion whom the

Americans call "the man in the cars," to realize how uniform opinion is among all classes of people, how little there is of that individuality in the ideas of each individual which they would have if he had formed them for himself, how little solidity and substance there is in the political or social beliefs of nineteen persons out of every twenty. These beliefs, when examined, mostly resolve themselves into two or three prejudices and aversions, two or three prepossessions for a particular leader or section of a party, two or three phrases or catchwords suggesting or embodying arguments which the man who repeats them has not analyzed. It is not that these nineteen persons are incapable of appreciating good arguments, or are unwilling to receive them. On the contrary, and this is especially true of the working classes, an audience is usually pleased when solid arguments are addressed to it, and men read with most relish the articles or leaflets, supposing them to be smartly written, which contain the most carefully sifted facts and the most exact thought. But to the great mass of mankind in all places, public questions come in the third or fourth rank among the interests of life, and obtain less than a third or a fourth of the leisure available for thinking. It is therefore rather sentiment than thought that the mass can contribute, a sentiment grounded on a few broad considerations and simple trains of reasoning; and the soundness and elevation of their sentiment will have more to do with their taking their stand on the side of justice, honour, and peace, than any reasoning they can apply to the sifting of the multifarious facts thrown before them, and to the drawing of the legitimate inferences therefrom.

It may be suggested that this analysis, if true of the uneducated, is not true of the educated classes. It is less true of that small class which in Europe specially occupies itself with politics; which, whether it reasons well or ill, does no doubt reason. But it is substantially no less applicable to the commercial and professional classes than to the working classes; for in the former, as well as in the latter, one finds few persons who take the pains, or have the leisure, or indeed possess the knowledge, to enable them to form an independent judgment. The chief difference between the so-called upper, or wealthier, and humbler strata of society is that the former are less influenced by sentiment and possibly more influenced by notions, often erroneous, of their own interest. Having something to lose, they imagine dangers to their property or their class ascendency. Moving in a more artificial society, their sympathies are less readily excited, and they more frequently indulge the tendency to cynicism natural to those who lead a life full of unreality and conventionalisms.

The apparent paradox that where the humbler classes have differed in opinion from the higher, they have often been proved by the event to have been right and their so-called betters wrong (a fact sufficiently illustrated by the experience of many European countries during the last half-century[1]), may perhaps be explained by considering that the historical and scientific data on which the solution of a difficult political problem depends are really just as little known to the wealthy as to the poor. Ordinary education, even the sort of education which is represented by a university degree, does not fit a man to handle these questions, and it sometimes fills him with a vain conceit of his own competence which closes his mind to argument and to the accumulating evidence of facts. Education ought, no doubt, to enlighten a man; but the educated classes, speaking generally, are the property-holding classes, and the possession of property does more to make a man timid than education does to make him hopeful. He is apt to underrate the power as well as the worth of sentiment; he overvalues the restraints which existing institutions impose; he has a faint appreciation of the curative power of freedom, and of the tendency which brings things right when men have been left to their own devices, and have learnt from failure how to attain success. In the less-educated man a certain simplicity and openness of mind go some way to compensate for the lack of knowledge. He is more apt to be influenced by the authority of leaders; but as, at least in England and America, he is generally shrewd enough to discern between a great man and a demagogue, this is more a gain than a loss.

While suggesting these as explanations of the paradox, I admit that it remains a paradox. But the paradox is not in the statement, but in the facts. Nearly all great political and social causes have made their way first among the middle or humbler classes. The original impulse which has set the cause in motion, the inspiring ideas that have drawn men to it, have no doubt come from lofty and piercing minds, and minds generally belonging to the cultivated class. But the principles and precepts these minds have delivered have waxed strong because the masses have received them gladly, while the wealthiest and educated classes have frowned on or persecuted them.

---

[1] It may be said that this has been so because the movements of the last century have been mostly movements in a democratic direction, which obtained the sympathy of the humbler classes because tending to break down the power and privilege which the upper classes previously enjoyed. This observation, however, does not meet all the cases, among which may be mentioned the attitude of the English working classes towards Italy from 1848 onwards, as well as their attitude in the American Civil War from 1861 to 1865, and in the Eastern Question from 1876 onwards, for in none of these instances had they any personal interest. I purposely take cases far back in the past.

The most striking instance of all is to be found in the early history of Christianity.

The analysis, however, which I have sought to give of opinion applies only to the nineteen men out of twenty, and not to the twentieth. It applies to what may be called passive opinion—the opinion of those who have no special interest in politics, or concern with them beyond that of voting, of those who receive or propagate, but do not originate, views on public matters. Or, to put the same thing in different words, we have been considering how public opinion grows and spreads, as it were, spontaneously and naturally. But opinion does not merely grow; it is also made. There is not merely the passive class of persons; there is the active class, who occupy themselves primarily with public affairs, who aspire to create and lead opinion. The processes which these guides follow are too well known to need description. There are, however, one or two points which must be noted, in order to appreciate the reflex action of the passive upon the active class.

The man who tries to lead public opinion, be he statesman, journalist, or lecturer, finds in himself, when he has to form a judgment upon any current event, a larger measure of individual prepossession, and of what may be called political theory and doctrine, than belongs to the average citizen. His view is therefore likely to have more individuality, as well as more intellectual value. On the other hand, he has also a stronger motive than the average citizen for keeping in agreement with his friends and his party, because if he stands aloof and advocates a view of his own, he may lose his influence and his position. He has a past, and is prevented, by the fear of seeming inconsistent, from departing from what he has previously said. He has a future, and dreads to injure it by severing himself ever so little from his party. He is accordingly driven to make the same sort of compromise between his individual tendencies and the general tendency which the average citizen makes. But he makes it more consciously, realizing far more distinctly the difference between what he would think, say, and do, if left to himself, and what he says and does as a politician, who can be useful and prosperous only as a member of a body of persons acting together and professing to think alike.

Accordingly, though the largest part of the work of forming opinion is done by these men—whom I do not call professional politicians, because in Europe many of them are not solely occupied with politics, while in America the name of professionals must be reserved for another class—we must not forget the reaction constantly exercised upon them by the passive majority. Sometimes a leading statesman or journalist takes a line to which he finds that the mass of those who usually agree with him are not responsive. He perceives that they will not follow him, and that he must choose between isolation and a modification of his own views. A statesman may sometimes venture on the former course, and in very rare cases succeed in imposing his own will and judgment on his party. A journalist, however, is almost invariably obliged to hark back if he has inadvertently taken up a position disagreeable to his clientèle, because the proprietors of the paper have their circulation to consider. To avoid so disagreeable a choice, a statesman or a journalist is usually on the alert to sound the general opinion before he commits himself on a new issue. He tries to feel the pulse of the mass of average citizens; and as the mass, on the other hand, look to him for initiative, this is a delicate process. In European countries it is generally the view of the leaders which prevails, but it is modified by the reception which the mass give it; it becomes accentuated in the points which they appreciate; while those parts of it, or those ways of stating it, which have failed to find popular favour, fall back into the shade.

This mutual action and reaction of the makers or leaders of opinion upon the mass, and of the mass upon them, is the most curious part of the whole process by which opinion is produced. It is also that part in which there is the greatest difference between one free country and another. In some countries, the leaders count for, say, three-fourths of the product, and the mass for one-fourth only. In others we may find these proportions reversed. In some countries the mass of the voters are not only markedly inferior in education to the few who lead, but also diffident, more disposed to look up to their betters. In others the difference of intellectual level between those who busy themselves with politics and the average voter is far smaller. Perhaps the leader is not so well instructed a man as in the countries first referred to; perhaps the average voter is better instructed and more self-confident. Where both of these phenomena coincide, so that the difference of level is inconsiderable, public opinion will evidently be a different thing from what it is in countries where, though the constitution has become democratic, the habits of the nation are still aristocratic. This is the difference between America and the countries of Western Europe.

Government by Public Opinion

We talk of public opinion as a new force in the world, conspicuous only since governments began to be popular. Statesmen, even in the last generation, looked on it with some distrust or dislike. Sir Robert Peel, for instance, in a letter written in 1820, speaks with the air of a discoverer, of "that great compound of folly, weakness, prejudice, wrong feeling, right feeling, obstinacy, and newspaper paragraphs, which is called public opinion."

Yet opinion has really been the chief and ultimate power in nearly all nations at nearly all times. I do not mean merely the opinion of the class to which the rulers belong. Obviously the small oligarchy of Venice was influenced by the opinion of the Venetian nobility, as the absolute czar is influenced now by the opinion of his court and his army. I mean the opinion, unspoken, unconscious, but not the less real and potent, of the masses of the people. Governments have always rested and, special cases apart, must rest, if not on the affection, then on the reverence or awe, if not on the active approval, then on the silent acquiescence, of the numerical majority. It is only by rare exception that a monarch or an oligarchy has maintained authority against the will of the people. The despotisms of the East, although they usually began in conquest, did not stand by military force but by popular assent. So did the feudal kingdoms of mediaeval Europe. So do the despotisms of the sultan (so far, at least, as regards his Mussulman subjects), of the shah, and of the Chinese emperor. The cases to the contrary are chiefly those of military tyrannies, such as existed in many of the Greek cities of antiquity, and in some of the Italian cities of the Renaissance, and such as exist now in the so-called republics of Central and South America. That even the Roman Empire, that eldest child of war and conquest, did not rest on force but on the consent and goodwill of its subjects is shown by the smallness of its standing armies, nearly the whole of which were employed against frontier enemies, because there was rarely any internal revolt or disturbance to be feared. Belief in authority, and the love of established order, are among the strongest forces in human nature, and therefore in politics. The first supports governments *de jure*, the latter governments *de facto*. They combine to support a government which is *de jure* as well as *de facto*. Where the subjects are displeased, their discontent may appear perhaps in the epigrams which tempered the despotism of Louis XV in France, perhaps in the sympathy given to bandits like Robin Hood, perhaps in occasional insurrections like those of Constantinople under the Eastern emperors. Of course, where there is no habit of combination to resist, discontent may remain for some time without this third means of expressing itself. But, even when the occupant of the throne is unpopular, the throne as an institution is in no danger so long as it can command the respect of the multitude and show itself equal to its duties.

In the earlier or simpler forms of political society public opinion is passive. It acquiesces in, rather than supports, the authority which exists, whatever its faults, because it knows of nothing better, because it sees no way to improvement, probably also because it is overawed by some kind of religious sanction. Human nature must have something to reverence, and the sovereign, because remote and potent and surrounded by pomp and splendour, seems to it mysterious and half divine. Worse administrations than those of Asiatic Turkey and Persia at this moment can hardly be imagined, yet the Mohammedan population show no signs of disaffection. The subjects of Darius and the subjects of Theebaw obeyed as a matter of course. They did not ask why they obeyed, for the habit of obedience was sufficient. They could, however, if disaffected, have at any moment overturned the throne, which had only, in both cases, an insignificant force of guards to protect it. During long ages the human mind did not ask itself— in many parts of the world does not even now ask itself—questions which seem to us the most obvious. Custom, as Pindar said, is king over all mortals and immortals, and custom prescribed obedience. When in any society opinion becomes self-conscious, when it begins to realize its force and question the rights of its rulers, that society is already progressing, and soon finds means of organizing resistance and compelling reform.

The difference, therefore, between despotically governed and free countries does not consist in the fact that the latter are ruled by opinion and the former by force, for both are generally ruled by opinion. It consists rather in this, that in the former the people instinctively obey a power which they do not know to be really of their own creation, and to stand by their own permission; whereas in the latter the people feel their supremacy, and consciously treat their rulers as their agents, while the rulers obey a power which they admit to have made and to be able to unmake them—the popular will. In both cases force is seldom necessary, or is needed only against small groups, because the habit of obedience replaces it. Conflicts and revolutions belong to the intermediate stage, when the people are awakening to the sense that they are truly the supreme power in the state, but when the rulers have not yet become aware that their authority is merely delegated. When superstition and the habit of submission have vanished from the whilom subjects, when the rulers, recognizing that they are no more than agents for the citizens, have in turn formed the habit of obedience, public opinion has become the active and controlling director of a business in which it was before the sleeping and generally forgotten partner. But even when this stage has been reached, as has now happened in most civilized states, there are differences in the degree and mode in and by which public opinion asserts itself. In some countries the habit of obeying rulers and officials is so strong that the people, once they have chosen the legislature or executive head by whom the officials are appointed, allow these officials almost as wide a range of authority as in the old days of despotism. Such people have a profound respect for government as government, and a reluctance, due either to theory or to mere laziness, perhaps to both, to interfere with its action. They say, "That is a matter for the administration; we have nothing to do with it;" and stand as much aside or submit as humbly as if the government did not spring from their own will. Perhaps they practically leave themselves, as did the Germans of Bismarck's day, in the hands of a venerated monarch and a forceful minister, giving these rulers a free hand so long as their policy moves in accord with the general sentiment of the nation, and maintains its glory. Perhaps while frequently changing their ministries, they nevertheless yield to each ministry, and to its executive subordinates all over the country, an authority great while it lasts, and largely controlling the action of the individual citizen. This seems to be still true of France. There are other countries in which, though the sphere of government is strictly limited by law, and the private citizen is little inclined to bow before an official, the habit has been to check the ministry chiefly through the legislature, and to review the conduct of both ministry and legislature only at long intervals, when an election of the legislature takes place. This has been, and to some extent is still, the case in Britain. Although the people rule, they rule not directly, but through the House of Commons, which they choose only once in four or five years, and which may, at any given moment, represent rather the past than the present will of the nation.

I make these observations for the sake of indicating another form which the rule of the people may assume. We have distinguished three stages in the evolution of opinion from its unconscious and passive into its conscious and active condition. In the first it acquiesces in the will of the ruler whom it has been accustomed to obey. In the second conflicts arise between the ruling person or class, backed by those who are still disposed to obedience, on the one hand, and the more independent or progressive spirits on the other; and these conflicts are decided by arms. In the third stage the whilom ruler has submitted, and disputes are referred to the sovereign multitude, whose will is expressed at certain intervals upon slips of paper deposited in boxes, and is carried out by the minister or legislature to whom the popular mandate is entrusted. A fourth stage would be reached, if the will of the majority of the citizens were to become ascertainable at all times, and without the need of its passing through a body of representatives, possibly even without the need of voting machinery at all. In such a state of things the sway of public opinion would have become more complete, because more continuous, than it is in those European countries which, like France, Italy, and Britain, look chiefly to parliaments as exponents of national sentiment. The authority would seem to remain all the while in the mass of the citizens. Popular government would have been pushed so far as almost to dispense with, or at any rate to anticipate, the legal modes in which the majority speaks its will at the polling booths; and this informal but direct control of the multitude would dwarf, if it did not supersede, the importance of those formal but occasional deliverances made at the elections of representatives. To such a condition of things the phrase, "rule of public opinion," might be most properly applied, for public opinion would not only reign but govern.

The mechanical difficulties, as one may call them, of working such a method of government are obvious. How is the will of the majority to be ascertained except by counting votes? How, without the greatest inconvenience, can votes be frequently taken on all the chief questions that arise? No country has yet surmounted these inconveniences, though little Switzerland with its referendum and initiative has faced and partially dealt with some of them, and some of the American states are treading in the same path. But what I desire to point out is that even where the machinery for weighing or measuring the popular will from week to week or month to month has not been, and is not likely to be, invented, there may nevertheless be a disposition on the part of the rulers, whether ministers or legislators, to act as if it existed; that is to say, to look incessantly for manifestations of current popular opinion, and to shape their course in accordance with their reading of those manifestations. Such a disposition will be accompanied by a constant oversight of public affairs by the mass of the citizens, and by a sense on their part that they are the true governors, and that their agents, executive and legislative, are rather servants than agents. Where this is the attitude of the people on the one hand and of the persons who do the actual work of governing on the other, it may fairly be said that there exists a kind of government materially, if not formally, different from the representative system as it presented itself to European thinkers and statesmen of the last generation. And it is to this kind of government that democratic nations seem to be tending.

The state of things here noted will find illustration in what I have to say in the following chapters regarding opinion in the United States. Meanwhile a few remarks may be hazarded on the rule of public opinion in general.

The excellence of popular government lies not so much in its wisdom— for it is as apt to err as other kinds of government—as in its strength. It has been compared, ever since Sir William Temple, to a pyramid, the firmest based of all buildings. Nobody can be blamed for obeying it. There is no appeal from its decisions. Once the principle that the will of the majority, honestly ascertained, must prevail, has soaked into the mind and formed the habits of a nation, that nation acquires not only stability, but immense effective force. It has no need to fear discussion and agitation. It can bend all its resources to the accomplishment of its collective ends. The friction that exists in countries where the laws or institutions handed down from former generations are incompatible with the feelings and wishes of the people has disappeared. A key has been found that will unlock every door.

On the other hand, such a government is exposed to two dangers. One, the smaller one, yet sometimes troublesome, is the difficulty of ascertaining the will of the majority. I do not mean the difficulty of getting all citizens to vote, because it must be taken that those who do not vote leave their will in the hands of those who do, but the difficulty of obtaining by any machinery yet devised a quite honest record of the results of voting. Where the issues are weighty, involving immense interests of individual men or groups of men, the danger of bribery, of force, and still more of fraud in taking and counting votes, is a serious one. When there is reason to think that ballots have been tampered with, the value of the system is gone; and men are remitted to the old methods of settling their differences.

The other danger is that minorities may not sufficiently assert themselves. Where a majority has erred, the only remedy against the prolongation or repetition of its error is in the continued protests and agitation of the minority, an agitation which ought to be conducted peaceably, by voice and pen, but which must be vehement enough to rouse the people and deliver them from the consequences of their blunders. But the more complete the sway of majorities is, so much the less disposed is a minority to maintain the contest. It loses faith in its cause and in itself, and allows its voice to be silenced by the triumphant cries of its opponents. How are men to acquiesce promptly and loyally in the decision of a majority, and yet to go on arguing against it? How can they be at once submissive and aggressive? That conceit of his own goodness and greatness which intoxicates an absolute monarch besets a sovereign people also, and the slavishness with which his ministers approach an Oriental despot may reappear in the politicians of a Western democracy. The duty, therefore, of a patriotic statesman in a country where public opinion rules, would seem to be rather to resist and correct than to encourage the dominant sentiment. He will not be content with trying to form and mould and lead it, but he will confront it, lecture it, remind it that it is fallible, rouse it out of its self-complacency. Unfortunately, courage and independence are plants which a soil impregnated with the belief in the wisdom of numbers does not tend to produce; nor is there any art known to statesmen whereby their growth can be fostered.

Experience has, however, suggested plans for lessening the risks incident to the dominance of one particular set of opinions. One plan is for the people themselves to limit their powers, i.e., to surround their own action and the action of their agents with restrictions of time and method which compel delay. Another is for them so to parcel out functions among many agents that no single one chosen indiscreetly, or obeying his mandate overzealously, can do much mischief, and that out of the multiplicity of agents differences of view may spring which will catch the attention of the citizens.

The temper and character of a people may supply more valuable safeguards. The country which has worked out for itself a truly free government must have done so in virtue of the vigorous individuality of its children. Such an individuality does not soon yield even to the pressure of democratic conditions. In a nation with a keen moral sense and a capacity for strong emotions, opinion based on a love of what is deemed just or good will resist the multitude when bent on evil; and if there be a great variety of social conditions, of modes of life, of religious beliefs, these will prove centres of resistance to a dominant tendency, like rocks standing up in a river, at which he whom the current sweeps downwards may clutch. Instances might be cited even from countries where the majority has had every source of strength at its command—physical force, tradition, the all but universal persuasions and prejudices of the lower as well as of the higher classes—in which small minorities have triumphed, first by startling and then by leavening and convincing the majority. This they have done in virtue of that intensity of belief which is oftenest found in a small sect or group, not because it is small, but because if its belief were not intense it would not venture to hold out at all against the adverse mass. The energy of each individual in the minority makes it in the long run a match for a majority huger but less instinct with vitality. In a free country more especially, ten men who care are worth a hundred who do not.

Such natural compensations as this occur in the physical as well as in the spiritual and moral world, and preserve both. But they are compensations on which the practical statesman cannot safely rely, for they are partial, they are uncertain, and they probably tend to diminish with the progress of democracy. The longer public opinion has ruled, the more absolute is the authority of the majority likely to become, the less likely are energetic minorities to arise, the more are politicians likely to occupy themselves, not in forming opinion, but in discovering and hastening to obey it.

CHAPTER 78

How Public Opinion Rules in America

It was observed in last chapter that the phrase "government by public opinion" is most specifically applicable to a system wherein the will of the people acts directly and constantly upon its executive and legislative agents. A government may be both free and good without being subject to this continuous and immediate control. Still this is the goal toward which the extension of the suffrage, the more rapid diffusion of news, and the practice of self-government itself, necessarily lead free nations; and it may even be said that one of their chief problems is to devise means whereby the national will shall be most fully expressed, most quickly known, most unresistingly and cheerfully obeyed. Delays and jerks are avoided, friction and consequent waste of force are prevented, when the nation itself watches all the play of the machinery and guides its workmen by a glance. Towards this goal the Americans have marched with steady steps, unconsciously as well as consciously. No other people now stands so near it.

Of all the experiments which America has made, this is that which best deserves study, for her solution of the problem differs from all previous solutions, and she has shown more boldness in trusting public opinion, in recognizing and giving effect to it, than has yet been shown elsewhere. Towering over presidents and state governors, over Congress and state legislatures, over conventions and the vast machinery of party, public opinion stands out, in the United States, as the great source of power, the master of servants who tremble before it.

For the sake of making clear what follows, I will venture to recapitulate what was said in an earlier chapter as to the three forms which government has taken in free countries. First came primary assemblies, such as those of the Greek republics of antiquity, or those of the early Teutonic tribes, which have survived in a few Swiss cantons. The whole people met, debated current questions, decided them by its votes, chose those who were to carry out its will. Such a system of direct popular government is possible only in small communities, and in this day of large states has become a matter rather of antiquarian curiosity than of practical moment.

In the second form, power belongs to representative bodies, parliaments and chambers. The people in their various local areas elect men, supposed to be their wisest or most influential, to deliberate for them, resolve for them, choose their executive servants for them. They give these representatives a tolerably free hand, leaving them in power for a considerable space of time, and allowing them to act unchecked, except in so far as custom, or possibly some fundamental law, limits their discretion. This is done in the faith that the chamber will feel its responsibility and act for the best interests of the country, carrying out what it believes to be the wishes of the majority, unless it should be convinced that in some particular point it knows better than the majority what the interests of the country require. Such a system has long prevailed in England, and the English model has been widely imitated on the continent of Europe and in the British colonies.

The third is something between the other two. It may be regarded either as an attempt to apply the principle of primary assemblies to large countries, or as a modification of the representative system in the direction of direct popular sovereignty. There is still a legislature, but it is elected for so short a time and checked in so many ways that much of its power and dignity has departed. Ultimate authority is not with it, but with the people, who have fixed limits beyond which it cannot go, and who use it merely as a piece of machinery for carrying out their wishes and settling points of detail for them. The supremacy of their will is expressed in the existence of a constitution placed above the legislature, although capable of alteration by a direct popular vote. The position of the representatives has been altered. They are conceived of, not as wise and strong men chosen to govern, but as delegates under specific orders to be renewed at short intervals.

This is the form established in the United States. Congress sits for two years only. It is strictly limited by the Constitution, and by the coexistence of the state governments, which the Constitution protects. It has (except by way of impeachment) no control over the federal executive, which is directly named by and responsible to the people. So, too, the state legislatures sit for short periods, do not appoint the state executives, are hedged in by the prohibitions of the state constitutions. The people frequently legislate directly by enacting or altering a constitution. The principle of popular sovereignty could hardly be expressed more unmistakably. Allowing for the differences to which the vast size of the country gives rise, the mass of the citizens may be deemed as directly the supreme power in the United States as the Assembly was at Athens or Syracuse.[1] The only check on the mass is that which they have themselves imposed, and which the ancient democracies did not possess, the difficulty of changing a rigid constitution. And this difficulty is serious only as regards the federal Constitution.

As this is the most developed form of popular government, so is it also the form which most naturally produces what I have called government by public opinion. Popular government may be said to exist wherever all power is lodged in and issues from the people. Government by public opinion exists where the wishes and views of the people prevail, even before they have been conveyed through the regular law-appointed organs, and without the need of their being so conveyed. As in a limited monarchy the king, however powerful, must act through certain officers and in a defined legal way, whereas in a despotism he may act just as he pleases, and his initial written on a scrap of paper is as sure of obedience as his full name signed to a parchment authenticated by the Great Seal or the countersignature of a minister, so where the power of the people is absolute, legislators and administrators are quick to catch its wishes in whatever way they may be indicated, and do not care to wait for the methods which the law prescribes. This happens in America. Opinion rules more fully, more directly, than under the second of the systems described above.

A consideration of the nature of the state governments as of the national government will show that legal theory as well as popular self-confidence gives birth to this rule of opinion. Supreme power resides in the whole mass of citizens. They have prescribed, in the strict terms of a legal document, the form of government. They alone have the right to change it, and that only in a particular way. They have committed only a part of their sovereignty to their executive and legislative agents, reserving the rest to themselves. Hence their will, or in other words, public opinion, is constantly felt by these agents to be, legally as well as practically, the controlling authority. In England, Parliament is the nation, not merely by a legal fiction, but because the nation looks to Parliament only, having neither reserved any authority to itself nor bestowed any elsewhere. In America, Congress is not the nation, and does not claim to be so.

The ordinary functions and business of government, the making of laws, the imposing of taxes, the interpretation of laws and their execution, the administration of justice, the conduct of foreign relations, are parcelled out

[1] Rome is a somewhat peculiar case, because she left far more power to her nonrepresentative Senate and to her magistrates than the Greek democracies did to their councils or officials. See Chap. 25 in Vol. I.

among a number of bodies and persons whose powers are so carefully balanced and touch at so many points that there is a constant risk of conflicts, even of deadlocks. Some of the difficulties thence arising are dealt with by the courts, as questions of the interpretation of the Constitution. But in many cases the intervention of the courts, which can act only in a suit between parties, comes too late to deal with the matter, which may be an urgent one; and in some cases there is nothing for the courts to decide, because each of the conflicting powers is within its legal right. The Senate, for instance, may refuse the measures which the House thinks necessary. The president may veto bills passed by both houses, and the houses may not have a two-thirds majority to pass them over his veto. Congress may urge the president to adopt a certain course of action, and the president may refuse. The president may propose a treaty to the Senate and the Senate may reject it. In such cases there is a stoppage of governmental action which may involve loss to the country. The master, however, is at hand to settle the quarrels of his servants. If the question be a grave one, and the mind of the country clear upon it, public opinion throws its weight into one or other scale, and its weight is decisive. Should opinion be nearly balanced, it is no doubt difficult to ascertain, till the next election arrives, which of many discordant cries is really the prevailing voice. This difficulty must, in a large country, where frequent plebiscites are impossible, be endured; and it may be well, when the preponderance of opinion is not great, that serious decisions should not be quickly taken. The general truth remains that a system of government by checks and balances specially needs the presence of an arbiter to incline the scale in favour of one or other of the balanced authorities, and that public opinion must therefore be more frequently invoked and more constantly active in America than in other countries.

Those who invented this machinery of checks and balances were anxious not so much to develop public opinion as to resist and build up breakwaters against it. No men were less revolutionary in spirit than the heroes of the American Revolution. They had made a revolution in the name of Magna Charta and the Bill of Rights: they were penetrated by a sense of the dangers incident to democracy. They conceived of popular opinion as aggressive, revolutionary, unreasoning, passionate, futile, and a breeder of mob violence. We shall presently inquire whether this conception has been verified. Meantime be it noted that the efforts made in 1787 to divide authority and, so to speak, force the current of the popular will into many small channels instead of permitting it to rush down one broad bed, have really tended to exalt public opinion above the regular legally appointed organs of government. Each of these organs is too small to form opinion, too narrow to express it, too weak to give effect to it. It grows up not in Congress, not in state legislatures, not in those great conventions which frame platforms and choose candidates, but at large among the people. It is expressed in voices everywhere. It rules as a pervading and impalpable power, like the ether which, as physicists say, passes through all things. It binds all the parts of the complicated system together and gives them whatever unity of aim and action they possess.

There is also another reason why the opinion of the whole nation is a more important factor in the government of the United States than anywhere in Europe. In Europe there has always been a governing class, a set of persons whom birth, or wealth, or education has raised above their fellows, and to whom has been left the making of public opinion together with the conduct of administration and the occupancy of places in the legislature. The public opinion of Germany, Italy, France, and England has been substantially the opinion of the class which wears black coats and lives in good houses, though in the two latter countries it has begun of late years to be affected by the opinion of the classes socially lower. Although the members of the British Parliament now obey the mass of their constituents when the latter express a distinct wish, still the influence which plays most steadily on them and permeates them is the opinion of a class or classes and not of the whole nation. The class to which the great majority of members of both houses belong (i.e., the landowners and the persons occupied in professions and in the higher walks of commerce) is the class which chiefly forms and expresses what is called public opinion. Even in these days of vigilant and exacting constituencies one sees many members of the House of Commons the democratic robustness or provincial crudity of whose ideas melts like wax under the influence of fashionable dinner parties and club smoking rooms. It is a common complaint that it is hard for a member to "keep touch" with the opinion of the masses.

In the United States public opinion is the opinion of the whole nation, with little distinction of social classes. The politicians, including the members of Congress and of state legislatures, are, perhaps not (as Americans sometimes insinuate) below, yet certainly not above the average level of their constituents. They find no difficulty in keeping touch with outside opinion. Washington or Albany may corrupt them, but not in the way of modifying their political ideas. They do not aspire to the function of forming opinion. They are like the Eastern slave who says "I hear and obey." Nor is there any one class or set of men, or any one "social layer," which more than another originates ideas and builds up political doctrine for the mass. The opinion of the nation is the resultant of the views, not of a number of

classes, but of a multitude of individuals, diverse, no doubt, from one
another, but, for the purposes of politics far less diverse than if they were
members of groups defined by social rank or by property.

The consequences are noteworthy. Statesmen cannot, as in Europe, declare
any sentiment which they find telling on their friends or their opponents in
politics to be confined to the rich, or to the governing class, and to be
opposed to the general sentiment of the people. In America you cannot
appeal from the classes to the masses. What the employer thinks, his
workmen think.[2] What the wholesale merchant feels, the retail storekeeper
feels, and the poorer customers feel. Divisions of opinion are vertical and
not horizontal. Obviously this makes opinion more easily ascertained, while
increasing its force as a governing power, and gives the people, that is to
say, all classes in the community, a clearer and stronger consciousness of
being the rulers of their country than European peoples have. Every man
knows that he is himself a part of the government, bound by duty as well
as by self-interest to devote part of his time and thoughts to it. He may
neglect this duty, but he admits it to be a duty. So the system of party
organizations already described is built upon this theory; and as this system
is more recent, and is the work of practical politicians, it is even better
evidence of the general acceptance of the doctrine than are the provisions
of constitutions. Compare European countries, or compare the other states
of the New World. In the so-called republics of Central and South America
a small section of the inhabitants pursue politics, while the rest follow their
ordinary avocations, indifferent to elections and pronunciamentos and
revolutions. In Germany, and in the German and Slavonic parts of the
Austro-Hungarian monarchy, people think of the government as a great
machine which will go on, whether they put their hand to it or not, a few
persons working it, and all the rest paying and looking on. The same thing
is largely true of republican France, and of semi-republican Italy, where
free government is still a novelty, and local self-government in its infancy.
Even in England, though the eighty years that have passed over her since
the great Reform Act have brought many new ideas with them, the ordinary
voter is still far from feeling, as the American does, that the government is
his own, and he individually responsible for its conduct.

---

[2] Of course I do not include questions specially relating to labour, in which there may be a direct
conflict of interests. Nor is it to be denied that the wealthiest men, especially financiers, have
become more of a class, holding views of their own on questions affecting capital, than they
were some decades ago.

CHAPTER 7 9

Organs of Public Opinion

How does this vague, fluctuating, complex thing we call public opinion—omnipotent yet indeterminate, a sovereign to whose voice everyone listens, yet whose words, because he speaks with as many tongues as the waves of a boisterous sea, it is so hard to catch—how does public opinion express itself in America? By what organs is it declared, and how, since these organs often contradict one another, can it be discovered which of them speak most truly for the mass? The more completely popular sovereignty prevails in a country, so much the more important is it that the organs of opinion should be adequate to its expression, prompt, full, and unmistakable in their utterances. And in such European countries as England and France, it is now felt that the most successful party leader is he who can best divine from these organs what the decision of the people will be when a direct appeal is made to them at an election.

I have already observed that in America public opinion is a power not satisfied with choosing executive and legislative agents at certain intervals, but continuously watching and guiding those agents, who look to it, not merely for a vote of approval when the next general election arrives, but also for directions which they are eager to obey, so soon as they have learnt their meaning. The efficiency of the organs of opinion is therefore more essential to the government of the United States than even to England or to France.

An organ of public opinion is, however, not merely the expression of views and tendencies already in existence, but a factor in further developing and moulding the judgment of the people. Opinion makes opinion. Men follow in the path which they see others treading; they hasten to adopt the view that seems likely to prevail. Hence every weighty voice, be it that of a speaker, or an association, or a public meeting, or a newspaper, is at once

929

the disclosure of an existing force and a further force influencing others. This fact, while it multiplies the organs through which opinion is expressed, increases the difficulty of using them aright, because every voice seeks to represent itself as that of the greater, or at least of a growing number.

The press, and particularly the newspaper press, stands by common consent first among the organs of opinion. Yet few things are harder than to estimate its power, and state precisely in what that power consists.

Newspapers are powerful in three ways—as narrators, as advocates, and as weathercocks. They report events, they advance arguments, they indicate by their attitude what those who conduct them and are interested in their circulation take to be the prevailing opinion of their readers. In the first of these regards the American press is the most active in the world. Nothing escapes it which can attract any class of readers. It does not even confine itself to events that have happened, but is apt to describe others which may possibly have happened, however slight the evidence for them: *pariter facta atque infecta canebat*. This habit affects its worth as an historic record and its influence with sober-minded people. Statesmen may be heard to complain that once an untrue story has been set flying they cannot efface the effect however complete the contradiction they may give it; and injustice is thus frequently done. Sometimes, of course, there is deliberate misrepresentation. But more often the erroneous statements are the natural result of the high pressure under which the newspaper business is carried on. The appetite for news, and for highly spiced or "sensational" news, is enormous, and journalists working under keen competition and in unceasing haste are disposed to take their chance of the correctness of the information they receive.

Much harm there is, but sometimes good also. It is related of an old barrister that he observed: "When I was young I lost a good many causes which I ought to have won, and now, that I have grown old and experienced, I win a good many causes which I ought to lose. So, on the whole, justice has been done." If in its heedlessness the press often causes pain to the innocent, it does a great and necessary service in exposing evildoers, many of whom would escape were it never to speak except upon sufficient evidence. It is a watchdog whose noisy bark must be tolerated, even when the person who approaches has no bad intent. No doubt charges are so promiscuously and often so lightly made as to tell less than they would in a country where the law of libel was more frequently appealed to. But many abuses are unveiled, many more prevented by the fear of publicity.

Although the leading American newspapers contain far more nonpolitical matter than those of Europe, they also contain, especially of course before any important election, more domestic political intelligence than any, except perhaps two or three, of the chief English journals. Much of it is inaccurate, but partisanship distorts it no more than in Europe, perhaps less. The public has the benefit of hearing everything it can wish, and perhaps more than it ought to wish, to know about every occurrence and every personality. The intelligence is not quite of the same kind as in England or France. There are fewer reports of speeches, because fewer speeches of an argumentative nature are made, but more of the schemes and doings of conventions and political cliques, as well as of the sayings of individuals.

As the advocates of political doctrines, newspapers are of course powerful, because they are universally read and often ably written. They are accused of unfairness and vituperation, but I doubt if there is any marked difference in this respect between their behaviour and that of European papers at a time of excitement. Nor could I discover that their arguments were any more frequently than in Europe addressed to prejudices rather than to reason; indeed they are less markedly party organs than are those of Britain. In America, however, a leading article carries less weight of itself, being discounted by the shrewd reader as the sort of thing which the paper must of course be expected to say, and is effective only when it takes hold of some fact (real or supposed), and hammers it into the public mind. This is what the unclean politician has to fear. Mere abuse he does not care for, but constant references to and comments on misdeeds of which he cannot clear himself tell in the long run against him.

The influence attributed to the press is evidenced not only by the posts (especially foreign legations) frequently bestowed upon the owners or editors of leading journals, but by the current appeals made to good party men to take in only stanch party papers, and by the threats to "read out" of the party journals which show a dangerous independence. Nevertheless, if the party press be estimated as a factor in the formation of opinion, whether by argument or by authority, it must be deemed less powerful in America than in Europe, because its average public is shrewder, more independent, less readily impressed by the mysterious "we." I doubt if there be any paper by which any considerable number of people swear; and am sure that comparatively few quote their favourite journal as an oracle in the way many persons still do in England. The vast area of the republic and the absence of a capital prevent any one paper from winning its way to predominance, even in any particular section of the country. Herein one notes a remarkable contrast to the phenomena of the Old World. Although the chief American newspapers are, regarded as commercial properties, "bigger things" than those of Europe, they do not dominate the whole press as a few journals do in most European countries. Or, to put the same thing differently, in England, and much the same may be said of France and Germany, some twenty newspapers cover nine-tenths of the reading public, whereas in America any given twenty papers would not cover one-third.

In those cities, moreover, where one finds really strong papers, each is exposed to a severer competition than in Europe, for in cities most people look at more than one newspaper. The late Mr. Horace Greeley, who for many years owned and edited the *New York Tribune*, is probably the only case of an editor who, by his journalistic talent and great self-confidence, acquired such a personal influence over multitudes of readers as to make them watch for and follow his deliverances. He was to the later Whig party and the earlier Republican party much what Katkoff was to the National party in Russia between 1870 and 1880, and had, of course, a far greater host of readers.

It is chiefly in its third capacity, as an index and mirror of public opinion, that the press is looked to. This is the function it chiefly aims at discharging; and public men feel that in showing deference to it they are propitiating, and inviting the commands of, public opinion itself. In worshipping the deity you learn to conciliate the priest. But as every possible view and tendency finds expression through some organ in the press, the problem is to discover which views have got popular strength behind them. Professed party journals are of little use, though one may sometimes discover from the way they advance an argument whether they think it will really tell on the opposite party, or use it only because it falls within their own programme. More may therefore be gleaned from the independent or semi-independent journals, whereof there are three classes: papers which, like two or three in the great cities, generally support one party, but are apt to fly off from it when they disapprove its conduct, or think the people will do so; papers which devote themselves mainly to news, though they may give editorial aid to one or other party according to the particular issue involved; and papers not professedly, or primarily political. Of this last class the most important members are the religious weeklies, to whose number and influence few parallels can be discovered in Europe. They are mostly either neutral or somewhat loosely attached to their party, usually the Republican party, because it began as the Free Soil party, and includes, in the North, the greater number of serious-minded people. It is only on great occasions, such as a presidential election, or when some moral issue arises, that they discuss current politics at length. When they do, great is their power, because they are deemed to be less "thirled" to a party or a leader, because they speak from a moral standpoint, and because they are read on Sunday, a time of leisure, when their seed is more likely to take root. The other weekly and monthly magazines used to deal less with politics than did the three leading English monthlies, but some of them are now largely occupied with political or politico-social topics, their influence seems to grow with the increasing amount of vigorous writing they contain.

During presidential contests much importance is attributed to the attitude of the leading papers of the great cities, for the revolt of anyone from its party—as, for instance, the revolt of several Republican papers during the election of 1884 and that of many Democratic papers in 1896—indicates discontent and danger. Where a schism exists in a state party, the bosses of one or other section will sometimes try to capture and manipulate the smaller country papers so as to convey the impression that their faction is gaining ground. Newspapers take more notice of one another, both by quoting from friendly sheets and by attacking hostile ones, than is usual in England, so that any incident or witticism which can tell in a campaign is at once taken up and read in a day or two in every city from Detroit to New Orleans.

The Americans have invented an organ for catching, measuring, and indicating opinion, almost unknown in Europe, in their practice of citing the private deliverances of prominent men. Sometimes this is done by publishing a letter, addressed not to the newspaper but to a friend, who gives it the publicity for which it was designed. Sometimes it is announced how the prominent man is going to vote at the next election. One may often notice short paragraphs stating that Judge So-and-So, or Dr. Blank, an eminent clergyman, is going to "bolt" the presidential or state ticket of his party; and perhaps the reasons assigned for his conduct follow. Of the same nature, but more elaborate, is the interview, in which the prominent man unbosoms himself to a reporter, giving his view of the political position in a manner less formal and obtrusive but not less effective than that of a letter to the editor. Sometimes, at the editor's suggestion, or of his own motion, a brisk reporter waits on the leading citizen and invites the expression of his views, which is rarely refused, though, of course, it may be given in a guarded and unsatisfying way. Sometimes the leading citizen himself, when he has a fact on which to comment, or views to communicate, sends for the reporter, who is only too glad to attend. The plan has many conveniences, among which is the possibility of disavowing any particular phrase as one which has failed to convey the speaker's true meaning. All these devices serve to help the men of eminence to impress their ideas on the public, while they show that there is a part of the public which desires such guidance.

Taking the American press all in all, it seems to serve the expression, and subserve the formation, of public opinion more fully than does the press of any part of the European continent, and not less fully than that of England. Individual newspapers and those who write in them may enjoy less power than is the case in some countries of the Old World; but if this be so, the cause is to be found in the fact that the journals lay themselves out to give news rather than views, that they are less generally bound to a particular party, and that readers are, except at critical moments, less warmly interested in politics than are educated Englishmen, because other topics claim a relatively larger part of their attention. The American press may not be above the moral level of the average good citizen—in no country does one either expect or find it to be so—but it is above the level of the machine politicians in the cities. In the war waged against these worthies the bolder and stronger newspapers have on occasion given powerful aid to the cause of reform by dragging corruption to light.

While believing that a complete picture of current opinion can be more easily gathered from American than from English journals, I do not mean to imply that they supply all a politician needs. Anyone who has made it his business to feel the pulse of his own must be sensible that when he has been travelling abroad for a few weeks, he is sure, no matter how diligently he peruses the leading home papers of all shades, to "lose touch" of the current sentiment of the country in its actuality. The journals seem to convey to him what their writers wish to be believed, and not necessarily what the people are really thinking; and he feels more and more as weeks pass the need of an hour's talk with four or five discerning friends of different types of thought, from whom he will gather how current facts strike and move the minds of his countrymen. Every prudent man keeps a circle of such friends, by whom he can test and correct his own impressions better than by the almost official utterances of the party journals. So in America there is much to be learnt from conversation with judicious observers outside politics and typical representatives of political sections and social classes, which the most diligent study of the press will not give, not to add that it occasionally happens that the press of a particular city may fall, for a time, under potent local influences which prevent it from saying all that ought to be said.

Except during electoral campaigns, public meetings play a smaller part in the political life of the United States than in that of Western Europe. Meetings were, of course, more frequent during the struggle against slavery than they need be in these quieter times, yet the difference between European and American practice cannot be wholly due to the more stirring questions which have latterly roused Europeans. A meeting in America is usually held for some practical object, such as the selection of candidates or the creation of an organization, less often as a mere demonstration of opinion and means of instruction. When instruction is desired, the habit is to bring down a man of note to give a political lecture, paying him from $75 to $100, or perhaps even $150, nor is it thought unbecoming for senators and ex-senators to accept such fees. The meetings during an election campaign, which are numerous enough, do not always provide argumentative speaking, for those who attend are assumed to be all members of one party, sound already, and needing nothing but an extra dose of enthusiasm; but since first the protective tariff and thereafter silver and the currency became leading issues, the proportion of reasoning to declamation has increased. Members of Congress do not deliver such annual discourses to their constituents as it has become the fashion for members of the House of Commons to deliver in England; and have indeed altogether an easier time of it as regards speaking, though a far harder one as regards the getting of places for their constituents. American visitors to England seem surprised and even a little edified when they find how much meetings are made to do there in the way of eliciting and cultivating opinion among the electors. I have often heard them praise the English custom, and express the wish that it prevailed in their own country.

As the ceaseless desire of every public man is to know which way the people are going, and as the polls are the only sure index of opinion, every election, however small, is watched with close attention. Now elections are in the United States as plentiful as revolutions in Peru. The vote cast for each party in a city, or state legislature district, or congressional district, or state, at the last previous election, is compared with that now cast, and inferences drawn as to what will happen at the next state or presidential election. Special interest attaches to the state pollings that immediately precede a presidential election, for they not only indicate the momentary temper of the particular voters but tell upon the country generally, affecting that large number who wish to be on the winning side. As happens in the similar case of what are called "by-elections" to the House of Commons in England, too much weight is generally attributed to these contests, which are sometimes, though less frequently than in England, decided by purely local causes. Such elections, however, give the people opportunities of expressing their displeasure at any recent misconduct chargeable to a party, and sometimes lead the party managers to repent in time and change their course before the graver struggle arrives.

Associations are created, extended, and worked in the United States more quickly and effectively than in any other country. In nothing does the executive talent of the people better shine than in the promptitude wherewith the idea of an organization for a common object is taken up, in the instinctive discipline that makes everyone who joins in starting it fall into his place, in the practical, businesslike turn which the discussions forthwith take. Thus in 1884, the cattlemen of the farther West, finding difficulties in driving their herds from Texas to Wyoming and Montana, suddenly convoked a great convention in Chicago which presented a plan for the establishment of a broad route from South to North, and resolved on the steps proper for obtaining the necessary legislation. Here, however, we are concerned with associations only as organs for focussing and propagating opinion. The greater ones, such as the temperance and total abstinence societies, ramify over the country and constitute a species of political organization which figures in state and even in presidential contests. Nearly every "cause," philanthropic, economic, or social, has something of the kind. Local associations or committees are often formed in cities to combat the machine politicians in the interests of municipal reform; while every important election calls into being a number of "campaign clubs," which work while the struggle lasts, and are then dissolved. For these money is soon forthcoming; it is more plentiful than in Europe, and subscribed more readily for political purposes.

Such associations have great importance in the development of opinion, for they rouse attention, excite discussion, formulate principles, submit plans, embolden and stimulate their members, produce that impression of a spreading movement which goes so far towards success with a sympathetic and sensitive people. *Possunt quia posse videntur* is doubly true in America as regards the spectators as well as the actors, because the appearance of strength gathers recruits as well as puts heart into the original combatants. Unexpected support gathers to every rising cause. If it be true that individuality is too weak in the country, strong and self-reliant statesmen or publicists too few, so much the greater is the value of this habit of forming associations, for it creates new centres of force and motion, and nourishes young causes and unpopular doctrines into self-confident aggressiveness. But in any case they are useful as indications of the tendencies at work and the forces behind these tendencies. By watching the attendance at the meetings, the language held, the amount of zeal displayed, a careful observer can discover what ideas are getting hold of the popular mind.

One significant difference between the formation and expression of opinion in the United States and in Europe remains to be noted. In England and Wales over half of the population was in 1911 to be found in sixty cities with a population exceeding 50,000. In France opinion is mainly produced in, and policy, except upon a few of the broadest issues, dictated by, the urban population, though its number falls much below that of the rural. In America the cities with a population exceeding 50,000 inhabitants were in 1910 one hundred and nine with an aggregate population of about 24,500,000, little more than 25 percent of the total population. The number of persons to the square mile was in 1911 618 in England and Wales, and was in the continental United States (1910), 30.9. Hence those influences formative of opinion which city life produces, the presence of political leaders, the influence they personally diffuse, the striking out and testing of ideas in conversation, may tell somewhat less on the American than on the English people, crowded together in their little island, and would tell much less but for the stronger social instincts of the Americans and the more general habit of reading daily newspapers.

In endeavouring to gather the tendencies of popular opinion, the task of an American statesman is in some respects easier than that of his English compeer. As social distinctions count for less in America, the same tendencies are more generally and uniformly diffused through all classes, and it is not necessary to discount so many special points of difference which may affect the result. As social intercourse is easier, and there is less *gêne* between a person in the higher and one in the humbler ranks, a man can better pick up in conversation the sentiments of his poorer neighbours. Moreover, the number of persons who belong to neither party, or on whom party allegiance sits loosely, is relatively smaller than in England, so the unpredictable vote—the doubtful element which includes those called in England "armchair politicians"—does not so much disturb calculations. Nevertheless, the task of discerning changes and predicting consequences is always a difficult one, in which the most skilful observers may err. Public opinion does not tell quite so quickly or quite so directly upon legislative bodies as in England, not that legislators do not wish to know it, but that the interposition of the machine acts to some extent as a sort of nonconductor. The din of voices is incessant, the parties are in many places nearly balanced. There are frequent small changes from which it would be rash to infer any real movement of opinion, even as he who comes down to the beach must watch many wavelets break in ripples on the sand before he can tell whether the tide be ebbing or flowing.

It may be asked how, if the organs of public opinion give so often an uncertain sound, public opinion can with truth be said not only to reign but to govern. The answer is that a sovereign is not the less a sovereign because his commands are sometimes misheard or misreported. In America everyone listens for them. Those who manage the affairs of the country obey to the best of their hearing. They do not, as has been heretofore the case in Europe, act on their own view, and ask the people to ratify: they take the course which they believe the people at the moment desire. Leaders do not, as sometimes still happens in England, seek to force or anticipate opinion; or if they do, they suffer for the blunder by provoking a reaction. The people must not be hurried. A statesman is not expected to move ahead of them; he must rather seem to follow, though if he has the courage to tell the people that they are wrong, and refuse to be the instrument of their errors, he will be all the more respected. Those who fail because they mistake eddies and cross currents for the main stream of opinion, fail more often from some personal bias, or from vanity, or from hearkening to a clique of adherents, than from want of materials for observation. A man who can disengage himself from preconceptions, who is in genuine sympathy with his countrymen, and possesses the art of knowing where to look for typical manifestations of their sentiments, will find the organs through which opinion finds expression more adequate as well as more abundant in America than they are in any other country.

National Characteristics as Moulding Public Opinion

As the public opinion of a people is even more directly than its political institutions the reflection and expression of its character, it is convenient to begin the analysis of opinion in America by noting some of those general features of national character which give tone and colour to the people's thoughts and feelings on politics. There are, of course, varieties proper to different classes, and to different parts of the vast territory of the Union; but it is well to consider first such characteristics as belong to the nation as a whole, and afterwards to examine the various classes and districts of the country. And when I speak of the nation I mean the native Americans. What follows is not applicable to the recent immigrants from Europe, and, of course, even less applicable to the Southern Negroes.

The Americans are a good-natured people, kindly, helpful to one another, disposed to take a charitable view even of wrongdoers. Their anger sometimes flames up, but the fire is soon extinct. Nowhere is cruelty more abhorred. Even a mob lynching a horse thief in the West has consideration for the criminal, and will give him a good drink of whisky before he is strung up. Cruelty to slaves was rare while slavery lasted, the best proof of which is the quietness of the slaves during the war when all the men and many of the boys of the South were serving in the Confederate armies. As everybody knows, juries are more lenient to offences of all kinds but one, offences against women, than they are anywhere in Europe. The Southern "rebels" were soon forgiven; and though civil wars are proverbially bitter, there have been few struggles in which the combatants did so many little friendly acts for one another, few in which even the vanquished have so quickly buried their resentments. It is true that newspapers and public speakers say hard things of their opponents; but this is a part of the game, and is besides a way of relieving their feelings: the bark is sometimes the louder in order that a bite may not follow. Vindictiveness shown by a public man excites general disapproval, and the maxim of letting bygones be bygones is pushed so far that an offender's misdeeds are often forgotten when they ought to be remembered against him.

All the world knows that they are a humorous people. They are as conspicuously the purveyors of humour to the nineteenth century as the French were the purveyors of wit to the eighteenth. Nor is this sense of the ludicrous side of things confined to a few brilliant writers. It is diffused among the whole people; it colours their ordinary life, and gives to their talk that distinctively new flavour which a European palate enjoys. Their capacity for enjoying a joke against themselves was oddly illustrated at the outset of the Civil War, a time of stern excitement, by the merriment which arose over the hasty retreat of the Federal troops at the battle of Bull Run. When William M. Tweed was ruling and robbing New York, and had set on the bench men who were openly prostituting justice, the citizens found the situation so amusing that they almost forgot to be angry. Much of President Lincoln's popularity, and much also of the gift he showed for restoring confidence to the North at the darkest moments of the war, was due to the humorous way he used to turn things, conveying the impression of not being himself uneasy, even when he was most so.

That indulgent view of mankind which I have already mentioned, a view odd in a people whose ancestors were penetrated with the belief in original sin, is strengthened by this wish to get amusement out of everything. The want of seriousness which it produces may be more apparent than real. Yet it has its significance; for people become affected by the language they use, as we see men grow into cynics when they have acquired the habit of talking cynicism for the sake of effect.

They are a hopeful people. Whether or no they are right in calling themselves a new people, they certainly seem to feel in their veins the bounding pulse of youth. They see a long vista of years stretching out before them, in which they will have time enough to cure all their faults, to overcome all the obstacles that block their path. They look at their enormous territory with its still only half-explored sources of wealth, they reckon up the growth of their population and their products, they contrast the comfort and intelligence of their labouring classes with the condition of the masses in the Old World. They remember the dangers that so long threatened the Union from the slave power, and the rebellion it raised, and see peace and harmony now restored, the South more prosperous and contented than at any previous epoch, perfect good feeling between all sections of the country. It is natural for them to believe in their star. And this sanguine temper makes them tolerant of evils which they regard as transitory, removable as soon as time can be found to root them up.

They have unbounded faith in what they call the people and in a democratic system of government. The great states of the European continent are distracted by the contests of republicans and monarchists, and of rich and poor—contests which go down to the foundations of government, and in France are further embittered by religious passions. Even in England the ancient Constitution is always under repair, and while many think it is being ruined by changes, others hold that still greater changes are needed to make it tolerable. No such questions trouble American minds, for nearly everybody believes, and everybody declares, that the frame of government is in its main lines so excellent that such reforms as seem called for need not touch those lines, but are required only to protect the Constitution from being perverted by the parties. Hence a further confidence that the people are sure to decide right in the long run, a confidence inevitable and essential in a government which refers every question to the arbitrament of numbers. There have, of course, been instances where the once insignificant minority proved to have been wiser than the majority of the moment. Such was eminently the case in the great slavery struggle. But here the minority prevailed by growing into a majority as events developed the real issues, so that this also has been deemed a ground for holding that all minorities which have right on their side will bring round their antagonists, and in the long run win by voting power. If you ask an intelligent citizen why he so holds, he will answer that truth and justice are sure to make their way into the minds and consciences of the majority. This is deemed an axiom, and the more readily so deemed because truth is identified with common sense, the quality which the average citizen is most confidently proud of possessing.

This feeling shades off into another, externally like it, but at bottom distinct—the feeling not only that the majority, be it right or wrong, will and must prevail, but that its being the majority proves it to be right. This idea, which appears in the guise sometimes of piety and sometimes of fatalism, seems to be no contemptible factor in the present character of the people. It will be more fully dealt with in a later chapter.

The native Americans are an educated people, compared with the whole mass of the population in any European country except Switzerland, parts of Germany, Norway, Iceland, and Scotland; that is to say, the average of knowledge is higher, the habit of reading and thinking more generally diffused, than in any other country. They know the Constitution of their own country, they follow public affairs, they join in local government and learn from it how government must be carried on, and in particular how discussion must be conducted in meetings, and its results tested at elections. The town meeting was for New England the most perfect school of self-government in any modern country. In villages, men used to exercise their minds on theological questions, debating points of Christian doctrine with no small acuteness. Women in particular, pick up at the public schools and from the popular magazines far more miscellaneous information than the women of any European country possess, and this naturally tells on the intelligence of the men. Almost everywhere one finds women's clubs in which literary, artistic, and social questions are discussed, and to which men of mark are brought to deliver lectures.

That the education of the masses is nevertheless a superficial education goes without saying. It is sufficient to enable them to think they know something about the great problems of politics; insufficient to show them how little they know. The public elementary school gives everybody the key to knowledge in making reading and writing familiar, but it has not time to teach him how to use the key, whose use is in fact, by the pressure of daily work, almost confined to the newspaper and the magazine. So we may say that if the political education of the average American voter be compared with that of the average voter in Europe, it stands high; but if it be compared with the functions which the theory of the American government lays on him, which its spirit implies, which the methods of its party organization assume, its inadequacy is manifest. This observation, however, is not so much a reproach to the schools, which at least do what English schools omit—instruct the child in the principles of the Constitution—as a tribute to the height of the ideal which the American conception of popular rule sets up.

For the functions of the citizen are not, as has hitherto been the case in Europe, confined to the choosing of legislators, who are then left to settle issues of policy and select executive rulers. The American citizen is virtually one of the governors of the Republic. Issues are decided and rulers selected by the direct popular vote. Elections are so frequent that to do his duty at them a citizen ought to be constantly watching public affairs with a full comprehension of the principles involved in them, and a judgment of the candidates derived from a criticism of their arguments as well as a recollection of their past careers. The instruction received in the common schools and from the newspapers, and supposed to be developed by the practice of primaries and conventions, while it makes the voter deem himself capable of governing, does not completely fit him to weigh the real merits of statesmen, to discern the true grounds on which questions ought to be decided, to note the drift of events and discover the direction in which parties are being carried. He is like a sailor who knows the spars and ropes of the ship and is expert in working her, but is ignorant of geography and navigation; who can perceive that some of the officers are smart and others dull, but cannot judge which of them is qualified to use the sextant or will best keep his head during a hurricane.

They are a moral and well-conducted people. Setting aside the *colluvies gentium* which one finds in Western mining camps, and which popular literature has presented to Europeans as far larger than it really is, setting aside also the rabble of a few great cities and the Negroes of the South, the average of temperance, chastity, truthfulness, and general probity is somewhat higher than in any of the great nations of Europe. The instincts of the native farmer or artisan are almost invariably kindly and charitable. He respects the law; he is deferential to women and indulgent to children; he attaches an almost excessive value to the possession of a genial manner and the observance of domestic duties.

They are also—and here again I mean the people of native American stock, especially in the Eastern and Middle states, on the whole, a religious people. It is not merely that they respect religion and its ministers, for that one might say of Russians or Sicilians, not merely that they are assiduous churchgoers and Sunday school teachers, but that they have an intelligent interest in the form of faith they profess, are pious without superstition, and zealous without bigotry. The importance which some still, though all much less than formerly, attach to dogmatic propositions, does not prevent them from feeling the moral side of their theology. Christianity influences conduct, not indeed half as much as in theory it ought, but probably more than it does in any other modern country, and far more than it did in the so-called ages of faith.

Nor do their moral and religious impulses remain in the soft haze of self-complacent sentiment. The desire to expunge or cure the visible evils of the world is strong. Nowhere are so many philanthropic and reformatory agencies at work. Zeal outruns discretion, outruns the possibilities of the case, in not a few of the efforts made, as well by legislation as by voluntary action, to suppress vice, to prevent intemperance, to purify popular literature.

Religion apart, they are an unreverential people. I do not mean irreverent—

far from it; nor do I mean that they have not a great capacity for hero worship, as they have many a time shown. I mean that they are little disposed, especially in public questions—political, economical, or social—to defer to the opinions of those who are wiser or better instructed than themselves. Everything tends to make the individual independent and self-reliant. He goes early into the world; he is left to make his way alone; he tries one occupation after another, if the first or second venture does not prosper; he gets to think that each man is his own best helper and adviser. Thus he is led, I will not say to form his own opinions, for even in America few are those who do that, but to fancy that he has formed them, and to feel little need of aid from others towards correcting them. There is, therefore, less disposition than in Europe to expect light and leading on public affairs from speakers or writers. Oratory is not directed towards instruction, but towards stimulation. Special knowledge, which commands deference in applied science or in finance, does not command it in politics, because that is not deemed a special subject, but one within the comprehension of every practical man. Politics is, to be sure, a profession, and so far might seem to need professional aptitudes. But the professional politician is not the man who has studied statesmanship, but the man who has practised the art of running conventions and winning elections.

Even that strong point of America, the completeness and highly popular character of local government, contributes to lower the standard of attainment expected in a public man, because the citizens judge of all politics by the politics they see first and know best—those of their township or city—and fancy that he who is fit to be selectman, or county commissioner, or alderman, is fit to sit in the great council of the nation. Like the shepherd in Virgil, they think the only difference between their town and Rome is in its size, and believe that what does for Lafayetteville will do well enough for Washington. Hence when a man of statesmanlike gifts appears, he has little encouragement to take a high and statesmanlike tone, for his words do not necessarily receive weight from his position. He fears to be instructive or hortatory, lest such an attitude should expose him to ridicule; and in America ridicule is a terrible power. Nothing escapes it. Few have the courage to face it. In the indulgence of it even this humane race can be unfeeling.

They are a busy people. I have already observed that the leisured class is relatively small, is in fact confined to a few Eastern cities. The citizen has little time to think about political problems. Engrossing all the working hours, his avocation leaves him only stray moments for this fundamental duty. It is true that he admits his responsibilities, considers himself a member of a party, takes some interest in current events. But although he would reject the idea that his thinking should be done for him, he has not leisure to do it for himself, and must practically lean upon and follow his party. It astonished me in 1870 and 1881 to find how small a part politics play in conversation among the wealthier classes and generally in the cities. Since 1896 there has been a livelier and more constant interest in public affairs; yet even now business matters so occupy the mind of the financial and commercial classes, and athletic competitions the minds of the uneducated classes and of the younger sort in all classes, that political questions are apt, except at critical moments, to fall in the background.[1] In a presidential year, and especially during the months of a presidential campaign, there is, of course, abundance of private talk, as well as of public speaking, but even then the issues raised are largely personal rather than political in the European sense. But at other times the visitor is apt to feel—more, I think, than he feels anywhere in Britain—that his host has been heavily pressed by his own business concerns during the day, and that when the hour of relaxation arrives he gladly turns to lighter and more agreeable topics than the state of the nation. This remark is less applicable to the dwellers in villages. There is plenty of political chat round the store at the cross roads, and though it is rather in the nature of gossip than of debate, it seems, along with the practice of local government, to sustain the interest of ordinary folk in public affairs.[2]

The want of serious and sustained thinking is not confined to politics. One feels it even more as regards economical and social questions. To it must be ascribed the vitality of certain prejudices and fallacies which could scarcely survive the continuous application of such vigorous minds as one finds among the Americans. Their quick perceptions serve them so well in business and in the ordinary affairs of private life that they do not feel the need for minute investigation and patient reflection on the underlying principles of things. They are apt to ignore difficulties, and when they can

---

[1] The increased space given to athletics and games of all sorts in the newspapers marks a change in public taste no less striking here than it is in Britain. As it is equally striking in the British colonies, one may take it as a feature common to the modern English-speaking world, and to that world only, for it is scarcely discernible in continental Europe.

[2] The European country where the common people best understand politics is Switzerland. That where they talk most about politics is, I think, Greece. I remember, for instance, in crossing the channel which divides Cephalonia from Ithaca, to have heard the boatmen discuss a recent ministerial crisis at Athens during the whole voyage with the liveliest interest and apparently some knowledge.

no longer ignore them, they will evade them rather than lay siege to them according to the rules of art. The sense that there is no time to spare haunts an American even when he might find the time, and would do best for himself by finding it.

Someone will say that an aversion to steady thinking belongs to the average man everywhere. True. But less is expected from the average man in other countries than from a people who have carried the doctine of popular sovereignty further than it has ever been carried before. They are tried by the standard which the theory of their government assumes. In other countries statesmen or philosophers do, and are expected to do, the solid thinking for the bulk of the people. Here the people are supposed to do it for themselves. To say that they do it imperfectly is not to deny them the credit of doing it better than a European philosopher might have predicted.

They are a commercial people, whose point of view is primarily that of persons accustomed to reckon profit and loss. Their impulse is to apply a direct practical test to men and measures, to assume that the men who have got on fastest are the smartest men, and that a scheme which seems to pay well deserves to be supported. Abstract reasonings they dislike, subtle reasonings they suspect; they accept nothing as practical which is not plain, downright, apprehensible by an ordinary understanding. Although openminded, so far as willingness to listen goes, they are hard to convince, because they have really made up their minds on most subjects, having adopted the prevailing notions of their locality or party as truths due to their own reflection.

It may seem a contradiction to remark that with this shrewdness and the sort of hardness it produces, they are nevertheless an impressionable people. Yet this is true. It is not their intellect, however, that is impressionable, but their imagination and emotions, which respond in unexpected ways to appeals made on behalf of a cause which seems to have about it something noble or pathetic. They are capable of an ideality surpassing that of Englishmen or Frenchmen.

They are an unsettled people. In no state of the Union is the bulk of the population so fixed in its residence as everywhere in Europe; in some it is almost nomadic. Except in the more stagnant parts of the South, nobody feels rooted to the soil. Here today and gone tomorrow, he cannot readily contract habits of trustful dependence on his neighbours. Community of interest, or of belief in such a cause as temperance, or protection for native industry, unites him for a time with others similarly minded, but congenial spirits seldom live long enough together to form a school or type of local opinion which develops strength and becomes a proselytizing force. Perhaps this tends to prevent the growth of variety in opinion. When a man arises with some power of original thought in politics, he is feeble if isolated, and is depressed by his insignificance, whereas if he grows up in favourable soil with sympathetic minds around him, whom he can in prolonged intercourse permeate with his ideas, he learns to speak with confidence and soars on the wings of his disciples. One who considers the variety of conditions under which men live in America may certainly find ground for surprise that there should be so few independent schools of opinion.

But even while an unsettled, they are nevertheless an associative, because a sympathetic people. Although the atoms are in constant motion, they have a strong attraction for one another. Each man catches his neighbour's sentiment more quickly and easily than happens with the English. That sort of reserve and isolation, that tendency rather to repel than to invite confidence, which foreigners attribute to the Englishman, though it belongs rather to the upper and middle class than to the nation generally, is, though not absent, yet less marked in America.[3] It seems to be one of the notes of difference between the two branches of the race. In the United States, since each man likes to feel that his ideas raise in other minds the same emotions as in his own, a sentiment or impulse is rapidly propagated and quickly conscious of its strength. Add to this the aptitude for organization which their history and institutions have educed, and one sees how the tendency to form and the talent to work combinations for a political or any other object has become one of the great features of the country. Hence, too, the immense strength of party. It rests not only on interest and habit and the sense of its value as a means of working the government, but also on the sympathetic element and instinct of combination ingrained in the national character.

They are a changeful people. Not fickle, for they are if anything too tenacious of ideas once adopted, too fast bound by party ties, too willing to pardon the errors of a cherished leader. But they have what chemists call low specific heat; they grow warm suddenly and cool as suddenly; they are liable to swift and vehement outbursts of feeling which rush like wildfire across the country, gaining glow, like the wheel of a railway car, by the

---

[3] I do not mean that Americans are more apt to unbosom themselves to strangers, but that they have rather more adaptiveness than the English, and are less disposed to stand alone and care nothing for the opinion of others. It is worth noticing that Americans travelling abroad seem to get more easily into touch with the inhabitants of the country than the English do: nor have they the English habit of calling those inhabitants—Frenchmen, for instance, or Germans—"the natives."

accelerated motion. The very similarity of ideas and equality of conditions which makes them hard to convince at first makes a conviction once implanted run its course the more triumphantly. They seem all to take flame at once, because what has told upon one, has told in the same way upon all the rest, and the obstructing and separating barriers which exist in Europe scarcely exist here. Nowhere is the saying so applicable that nothing succeeds like success. The native American or so-called Know-Nothing party had in two years from its foundation become a tremendous force, running, and seeming for a time likely to carry, its own presidential candidate. In three years more it was dead without hope of revival. Now and then, as for instance in the elections of 1874–75, and again in those of 1890, there comes a rush of feeling so sudden and tremendous, that the name of tidal wave has been invented to describe it.

After this it may seem a paradox to add that the Americans are a conservative people. Yet anyone who observes the power of habit among them, the tenacity with which old institutions and usages, legal and theological formulas, have been clung to, will admit the fact. Moreover, prosperity helps to make them conservative. They are satisfied with the world they live in, for they have found it a good world, in which they have grown rich and can sit under their own vine and fig tree, none making them afraid. They are proud of their history and of their Constitution, which has come out of the furnace of civil war with scarcely the smell of fire upon it. It is little to say that they do not seek change for the sake of change, because the nations that do this exist only in the fancy of alarmist philosophers. There are nations, however, whose impatience of existing evils, or whose proneness to be allured by visions of a brighter future, makes them underestimate the risk of change, nations that will pull up the plant to see whether it has begun to strike root. This is not the way of the Americans. They are no doubt ready to listen to suggestions from any quarter. They do not consider that an institution is justified by its existence, but admit everything to be matter for criticism. Their keenly competitive spirit and pride in their own ingenuity have made them quicker than any other people to adopt and adapt inventions. Telephones were in use in every little town over the West, while in the city of London men were just beginning to wonder whether they could be made to pay. The Americans have doubtless of late years become, especially in the West, an experimental people, so far as politics and social legislation are concerned, and there is today less reverence for the national Constitution itself than there was in the generation that fought through the Civil War. The growing discontent with existing social conditions, the growing resentment at the power which the possessors of great wealth have been able to exercise, have disposed many persons to desire changes in political arrangements under which such things are possible.

Yet we may still say that as respects the fundamentals of their government, the American people are still a conservative people, in virtue both of the deep instincts of their race and of that practical shrewdness which recognizes the value of permanence and solidity in institutions. They are conservative in their fundamental beliefs, in the structure of their governments, in their social and domestic usages. They are like a tree whose pendulous shoots quiver and rustle with the lightest breeze, while its roots enfold the rock with a grasp which storms cannot loosen.

C H A P T E R   8 1

Classes as Influencing Opinion

These are some of the characteristics of American opinion in general, and may, if I am right in the description given, be discovered in all classes of the native white population. They exist, however, in different measure in different classes, and the above account of them needs to be supplemented by some remarks on the habits and tendencies of each class. I do not, of course, propose to describe the present opinions of classes, for that would require an account of current political questions: my aim is merely to state such general class characters as go to affect the quality and vigour of opinion. Classes are in America by no means the same thing as the greater nations of Europe. One must not, for political purposes, divide them as upper and lower, richer and poorer, but rather according to the occupations they respectively follow and the conditions of life that constitute their environment. Their specific characters, as a naturalist would say, are less marked even in typical individuals than would be the case in Europe, and are in many individuals scarcely recognizable. Nevertheless, the differences between one class and another are sufficient to produce distinctly traceable influences on the political opinion of the nation, and to colour the opinions, perhaps even to determine the political attitude, of the district where a particular class predominates.

I begin with the farmers, because they are, if not numerically the largest class, at least the class whose importance is most widely felt. As a rule they are owners of their land; and as a rule the farms are small, running from forty or fifty up to three hundred acres. In a few places, especially in the West, large landowners let farms to tenants, and in some parts of the South one finds big plantations cultivated by small tenants, often Negroes. But far more frequently the owner tills the land and the tiller owns it. The proportion of hired labourers to farmers is therefore very much smaller than in England, partly because farms are usually of a size permitting the farmer and his family to do much of the work by themselves, partly because machinery is more extensively used, especially in the level regions of the West. The labourers, or, as they are called, the "hired men," do not, taking the country as a whole, form a social stratum distinct from the farmers, and there is so little distinction in education or rank between them that one may practically treat employer and employed as belonging to the same class.

The farmer is a keener and more enterprising man than in Europe, with more of that commercial character which one observes in Americans, far less anchored to a particular spot, and of course subject to no such influences of territorial magnates as prevail in England, Germany, or Italy. He has now, in such states as Illinois and Wisconsin, realized what applied science can do for agriculture. He is so far a businessman as sometimes to speculate in grain or bacon. Yet he is not free from the usual defects of agriculturists. He is obstinate, tenacious of his habits, not readily accessible to argument. His way of life is plain and simple, and he prides himself on its simplicity, holding the class he belongs to to be the mainstay of the country, and regarding city folk with a mixture of suspicion and jealousy, because he deems them as inferior to himself in virtue as they are superior in adroitness, and likely to outwit him. Sparing rather than stingy in his outlays, and living largely on the produce of his own fields, he has so little ready money that small sums appear large to him; and as he fails to see why everybody cannot thrive and be happy on $1,500 a year, he thinks that figure a sufficient salary for a county or district official, and regulates his notions of payment for all other officials, judges included, by the same standard. To belong to a party and support it by his vote, seems to him part of a citizen's duty, but his interests in national politics are secondary to those he feels in agriculturists' questions, particularly in the great war against monopolies and capitalists, which the power and in some cases the tyranny of the railroad companies has provoked in the West. Naturally a grumbler, as are his brethren everywhere, finding his isolated life dull, and often unable to follow the causes which depress the price of produce, he is the more easily persuaded that his grievances are due to the combinations of designing speculators. The agricultural newspaper to which he subscribes is of course written up to his prejudices, and its adulation of the farming class confirms his belief that he who makes the wealth of the country is tricked out of his proper share in its prosperity. Thus he now and then makes desperate attempts to right himself by legislation, lending too ready an ear to politicians who promise him redress by measures possibly unjust and usually unwise.

In his impatience with the regular parties, he has been apt to vote for those who call themselves a people's or farmer's party, and who dangled before him the hope of getting "cheap money," of reducing the expenses of legal proceedings, and of compelling the railroads to carry his produce at unremunerative rates. However, after all said and done, he is an honest, kindly sort of man, hospitable, religious, patriotic: the man whose hard work has made the West what it is. It is chiefly in the West that one must now look for the well-marked type I have tried to draw, yet not always in the newer West; for, in regions like northern Minnesota, Wisconsin, and Dakota, the farming population is mainly foreign—Scandinavian and German—while the native Americans occupy themselves with trading and railroad management. However, the Scandinavians and Germans acquire in a few years many of the characteristics of the native farmer, and follow the political lead given by the latter. In the early days of the Republic, the agriculturists were, especially in the middle and the newer parts of the Southern states, the backbone of the Democratic party, sturdy supporters of Jefferson, and afterwards of Andrew Jackson. When the opposition of North and South began to develop itself and population grew up beyond the Ohio, the pioneers from New England who settled in that country gave their allegiance to the Whig party; and in the famous "log cabin and hard cider" campaign, which carried the election of General Harrison as president, that worthy, taken as a type of the hardy backwoodsman, made the Western farmer for the first time a noble and poetical figure to the popular imagination. Nowadays he is less romantic, yet still one of the best elements in the country. He stood by the Union during the war, and gave his life freely for it. For many years afterwards his vote now carried the Western, and especially the Northwestern states for the Republican party, which is to him still the party which saved the Union and protected the Negro.

The shopkeepers and small manufacturers may be said to form a second class, though in the smaller towns, of the West especially, their interests are so closely interwoven with those of the cultivators, and their way of life so similar, that there is little special to remark about them. In the larger towns they are sharper and more alive to what is passing than the rural population, but their intellectual horizon is not much wider. A sort of natural selection carries the more ambitious and eager spirits into the towns, for the native American dislikes the monotony and isolation of a farm life with its slender prospect of wealth. To keep a store in a "corner lot" is the ambition of the keen-witted lad. The American shopkeeper, it need hardly be said, has not the obsequiousness of his European congener, and is far from fancying that retail trade has anything degrading about it. He is apt to take more part in local politics than the farmer, but less apt to become a member of a state legislature, because he can seldom leave his store as the farmer can at certain seasons leave his land. He reads more newspapers than the farmer does, and of course learns more from current talk. His education has been better, because city schools are superior to country ones. He is perhaps not so certain to go solid for his party. He has less ground of quarrel with the railroads, but if connected with a manufacturing industry, is of course more likely to be interested in tariff questions, or, in other words, to be a Protectionist. His occupation, however, seldom gives him any direct personal motive for supporting one party more than another, and he has less of that political timidity which Europeans take to be the note of the typical bourgeois than the retail dealer of France or England.

The working men, by which I mean those who toil with their hands for wages, form a less well-marked class than is the case in most parts of Europe, and have not so many subclasses within their own body, though of course the distinction between skilled and unskilled labour makes itself felt, and one may say, speaking generally, that all unksilled labourers are comparatively recent immigrants. The native workpeople are of course fairly educated; they read the daily newspapers, while their women may take a weekly religious journal and a weekly or monthly magazine; many of them, especially in the smaller cities, belong to a congregation in whose concerns they are generally interested. Many are total abstainers. Their wives have probably had a longer schooling and read more widely than they do themselves. In the smaller towns both in New England and the West, and even in some of the large cities, such as Philadelphia and Chicago, the better part of them own the houses they live in, wooden houses in the suburbs with a little verandah and a bit of garden, and thus feel themselves to have a stake in the country. Their womankind dress with so much taste that on Sunday, or when you meet them in the steam cars, you would take them for persons in easy circumstances. Till the latter part of last century, strikes were less frequent than in England, nor, in spite of the troubles of recent years, has there hitherto existed any general sense of hostility to employers. This is due partly to the better circumstances of the workmen, partly to the fact that the passage from the one class to the other is easy and frequent. Thus, notwithstanding the existence of so-called Labour parties, and the recent creation of a vast organization embracing all trades over the whole Union, there has been less of collective class feeling and class action among workmen than in England,[1] certainly much less than in France or Germany. Politicians have of late years begun to pose as the special friends of the working man. Although in a country where the popular vote is omnipotent there seems something absurd in assuming that the working man is weak and stands in need of special protection, still the great power of capital, the illegitimate means by which that power acts upon legislatures, the growing disparities of fortune, and the fact that rich men bear less than their due share of taxation, have furnished a basis for labour agitation. While contributing as many recruits to the army of professional politicians as do the other classes, the wage-earning class is no more active in political work than they are, and furnishes few candidates for state or federal office. Till recently little demand was made for the representation of labour as labour either in Congress or in state legislatures. There are of course many members who have begun life as operatives; but very few in Congress (though some in the state legislatures) whose special function or claim it is to be the advocates of their whilom class. Such progress as Communistic or Socialistic movements have made has been chiefly among the immigrants from Central Europe, Germans, Slavs, and Italians, with a smaller contingent of Irish and Swedish support, but it is not easy to say how great this progress is, for the educated classes had known and cared very little about the growth of new doctrines among the workers until the recent outbreak of Anarchist violence at Chicago in 1886 turned all eyes upon a new source of peril to civilization. One question, however, which never fails to excite the workmen is the introduction of cheap foreign labour, and the bringing in of workmen to fill the place of strikers. A statute forbids the landing in the country of persons coming under a contract to work. In the Pacific states the feeling against the Chinese, who took lower wages, often one-half of what whites obtain, was for a time not merely the prime factor in Californian state politics, but induced the Senate to ratify treaties and Congress to pass acts, the last one extremely stringent, forbidding their entry. One trade, however, the Chinese are permitted to follow, and have now almost monopolized, that of washermen—one cannot say, washerwomen. Even a small city rarely wants its Chinese laundry. The

---

[1] An experienced American friend writes me: "Although immigrants from Great Britain are the best of all our immigrants, English workmen are more apt to stir up trouble with their employers than those of any other race. Employers say that they fear their English workmen, because they are generally suspicious, and disbelieve in the possibility of anything but hostility between men and masters."

entry, early in the present century, of a large number of Japanese, roused similar antagonism, and led to negotiations with the government of Japan by which the influx was stopped.

It will be gathered from what I have said that there is no want of intelligence or acuteness among the working people. For political purposes, and setting apart what are specifically called labour questions, there is really little difference between them and other classes. Their lights are as good as those of farmers or traders, their modes of thinking similar. They are, however, somewhat more excitable and more easily fascinated by a vigorous personality, as the success of General Benjamin F. Butler among the shoemakers of his Massachusetts district proved. A powerful speaker with a flow of humour and audacity will go farther with them than with the more commercially minded shopkeeper, or the more stolid agriculturist, if indeed one can call any American stolid.

The ignorant masses of such great cities as New York, Cincinnati, Chicago, San Francisco, together with the dangerously large "tramp" class, are hardly to be reckoned with the working class I have been describing, but answer better to what is called in England "the residuum." They are no longer Irish and Germans, for these races have moved upward in the social scale, but chiefly Poles and other Slavs, Italians, Negroes, and such native Americans as have fallen from their first estate into drink and penury. The most recent immigrants can hardly be said to possess political opinions, for they have not had time to learn to know the institutions of their new country. But as to the earlier incomers, and especially the Irish, Germans, and Scandinavians, one may note three sentiments which have affected them, besides adhesion to the party which snapped them up when they landed, or which manipulates them by leaders of their own race. One of these sentiments is religious sympathy. Such of them as are Roman Catholics are ready to stand by whichever party may obtain the favour, or be readiest to serve the interests, of their church.[2] Another is the protection of the liquor traffic. The German loves his beer, and deems a land where this most familiar of pleasures is unattainable no land of freedom, while the Irishman stands by a trade in which his countrymen are largely engaged. And, thirdly, the American-Irish were for a time largely swayed by dislike of England, which has made them desire to annoy her, and if possible to stir up a quarrel between her and the land of their adoption. This feeling began to decline

---

[2] Those of the German immigrants who remain in the great cities instead of going West, seem to be mostly Catholics, at least in name; as are also the Poles, Czechs, and Slovaks.

after 1886, and is now confined to a comparatively small part of the population of Irish origin.

The European reader must not suppose that this lowest section of the labouring class is wholly composed of immigrants, nor that all of the city-dwelling immigrants belong to it, for there are many foreigners whose education and skill places them at once on a level with the native American workmen.[3] Its importance in politics arises less from its number, than from the cohesion, in every great city, of so much of it as is massed there. Being comparatively ignorant, and for the most part not yet absorbed into the American population, it is not moved by the ordinary political forces, nor amenable to the ordinary intellectual and moral influences, but "goes solid" as its leaders direct it, a fact which gives these leaders exceptional weight, and may enable them, when parties are nearly balanced, to dictate their terms to statesmen. The disposition to truckle to the forces of disorder, and to misuse the power of pardoning offenders, which prominent state officials have sometimes evinced, is due to the fear of the so-called "Labour vote," a vote which would have much less power were the suffrage restricted to persons who have resided fifteen or twenty years in the country. Nevertheless the immigrants are not so largely answerable for the faults of American politics as the stranger might be led by the language of many Americans to believe. There is a disposition in the United States to use the immigrants, and especially the Irish, much as the cat is used in the kitchen to account for broken plates and food which disappears. The cities have no doubt suffered from the immigrant vote. But New York was not an Eden before the Irish came; and would not become an Eden were they all return to green Erin, or move on to arid Arizona.

The capitalist class consists of large merchants, manufacturers, bankers, and railroad men, with a few great land speculators and directors of trading or carrying companies. How much capacity and energy, how much wealth and influence there is in this small class everybody knows. It includes the best executive ability of the country, and far more ability than is devoted to the public service of the state. Though such persons do not, and hardly could, hold aloof from politics—some of them are indeed zealous party men—their interest lies chiefly in using politics for their own purposes, and especially in resisting the attacks with which they are threatened, sometimes by the popular movement against monopolists and great corporations, sometimes by men anxious to reduce the present high tariff which the

---

[3] As to the recent emigrants, see Chapter 92 post.

manufacturers declare to be essential to their industries. One-half of the capitalists are occupied in preaching laissez faire as regards railroad control, the other half in resisting it in railroad rate matters, in order to have their goods carried more cheaply, and in tariff matters in order to protect industries threatened with foreign competition. Yet they manage to hold well together. Their practical talent does not necessarily imply political insight, any more than moral elevation, nor have they generally the taste or leisure to think seriously about the needs of the state. In no country does one find so many men of eminent capacity for business, shrewd, inventive, forcible, and daring, who have so few interests and so little to say outside the sphere of their business knowledge.

But the wealthy have many ways of influencing opinion and the course of events. Some of them own, others find means of inspiring, newspapers. Many are liberal supporters of universities and colleges, and it is alleged that they occasionally discourage the promulgation, by college teachers, of opinions they dislike. Presidents of great corporations have armies of officials under their orders, who cannot indeed be intimidated, for public opinion would resent that, yet may be suffered to know what their superior thinks and expects. Cities, districts of country, even states or territories, have much to hope or fear from the management of a railway, and good reason to conciliate its president. Moreover, as the finance of the country is in the hands of these men and every trader is affected by financial changes, as they control enormous joint-stock enterprises whose shares are held and speculated in by hosts of private persons of all ranks, their policy and utterances are watched with anxious curiosity, and the line they take determines the conduct of thousands not directly connected with them. A word from several of the great financiers would go a long way with leading statesmen. They are for the most part a steadying influence in politics, being opposed to sudden changes which might disturb the money market or depress trade, and especially opposed to complications with foreign states. They are therefore *par excellence* the peace party in America, for though some might like to fish in troubled waters, the majority would have far more to lose than to gain.

There remains the group of classes loosely called professional men, of whom we may dismiss the physicians as neither bringing any distinctive element into politics, nor often taking an active interest therein, and the journalists, because they have been considered in treating of the organs of opinion, and the clergy as inhibited by public feeling from direct immixture in political strife. In the antislavery and Free Soil struggles, ministers of religion were prominent, as they are now in the temperance movement, and indeed will always be when a distinctly moral issue is placed before the country. But in ordinary times, and as regards most questions, they find it prudent to rest content with inculcating such sound principles as will elevate their hearers' views and lead them to vote for the best men. Some few, however, of exceptional zeal or unusually well-assured position do appear on political platforms, and, like the late Mr. Henry Ward Beecher, justify their courage by their success. The Roman Catholic prelates have great influence with their flocks, but are so sensible of the displeasure which its exercise would cause among the native Americans as to be guarded in political action, allowing themselves a freer hand in promoting temperance or other moral causes. Some of them have been among the most prominent and influential figures in the country.

The lawyers, who are both barristers and attorneys in one, there being no such distinction of the profession into two branches as exists in Britain and France, are of all classes that which has most to do with politics.[4] From their ranks comes a large part, probably a half, and apparently the better half, of the professional politicians. Those who do not make politics a business have usually something to do with it, and even those who have little to do with it enjoy opportunities of looking behind the scenes. The necessities of their practice oblige them to study the federal Constitution and the constitution of their own state, as well as to watch current legislation. It is therefore from the legal profession that most of the leading statesmen have been drawn, from the days of Patrick Henry, John Jay, and John Adams down to those of Abraham Lincoln and the presidential candidates of the last generation. Hence both in great cities and in small ones the lawyer is favourably placed for influencing opinion. If he be a man of parts, he is apt to be the centre of local opinion, as Lincoln was in Springfield, where he practised law and made his reputation.[5] When in some great community like New York or Boston a demonstration is organized, some distinguished advocate, such as Charles O'Conor was in New York, such as Rufus Choate was in Boston, used to be selected for the oration of the day, because he had the power of speech, and because everybody knew him. Thus the lawyers, if less powerful in proportion to their numbers than the capitalists, are perhaps equally powerful as a whole, since more numerous

---

[4] An account of the American bar will be found in a later chapter.

[5] I have heard townsmen of the great president describe how the front of his house used to be a sort of gathering place on summer evenings where his racy talk helped to mould the opinion of the place.

and more locally active. Of course it is only on a very few professional questions that they act together as a class. Their function is to educate opinion from the technical side, and to put things in a telling way before the people. Whether the individual lawyer is or is not a better citizen than his neighbours, he is likely to be a shrewder one, knowing more about government and public business than most of them do, and able at least to perceive the mischiefs of bad legislation, which farmers or shopkeepers may faintly realize. Thus on the whole the influence of the profession makes for good, and though it is often the instrument by which harm is wrought, it is as often the means of revealing and defeating the tricks of politicians, and of keeping the wholesome principles of the Constitution before the eyes of the nation. Its action in political life may be compared with its function in judicial proceedings. Advocacy is at the service of the just and the unjust equally, and sometimes makes the worse appear the better cause, yet experience shows that the sifting of evidence and the arguing of points of law tend on the whole to make justice prevail.

There remain the men of letters and artists, an extremely small class outside a few Eastern cities, and the teachers, especially those in colleges and universities. The influence of literary men has been felt more through magazines than through books, for native authorship suffered severely, till the enactment of the Copyright Act of 1891, from the deluge of cheap English reprints. That of the teachers tells primarily on their pupils and indirectly on the circles to which those pupils belong, or in which they work when they have left college. For a long time, and especially during the struggle between free trade and protection and in the earlier days of the municipal reform movement in the latter part of last century, "college professors" used to be denounced by the professional politicians as unpractical, visionary, pharisaical, "kid-gloved," "high-toned," "un-American," the fact being that an impulse towards the improvement of party methods, civil service reform and tariff reform, was coming from the universities, and was felt in the increased political activity of the better educated youth. The new generation of lawyers, clergymen, and journalists, of teachers in the higher schools and indeed of businessmen also, many of whom now receive a university education, have been inspired by the universities, at first chiefly by the older and more highly developed institutions of the Eastern states, but latterly by the universities of the West also, with a more serious and earnest view of politics than has prevailed among the richer classes since the strain of the Civil War passed away. Their horizon has been enlarged, their patriotism tempered by a sense of national shortcomings, and quickened by a higher ideal of national well-being. The confidence that all other prosperity will accompany material prosperity, the belief that good instincts are enough to guide nations through practical difficulties, errors which led astray so many worthy people in the last generation, are being dispelled, and a juster view of the great problems of democratic government presented. The seats of learning and education are at present among the most potent forces making for progress and the formation of sound opinion in the United States, and they increase daily in the excellence of their teachers no less than in the number of their students.

Before quitting this part of the subject a few general observations are needed to supplement or sum up the results of the foregoing inquiry.

There is in the United States no such general opposition as in continental Europe of richer and poorer classes, no such jealousy or hostility as one finds in France between the bourgeoisie and the operatives, not even that touch of antagonism which may now be noted in Australia. Class distinctions do exist for the purposes of social intercourse. But it is only in the larger cities that the line is sharply drawn between those who call themselves gentlemen and those others to whom, in talk among themselves, the former set would refuse this epithet.

There is no one class or set of men whose special function it is to form and lead opinion. The politicians certainly do not. Public opinion leads them.

Still less is there any governing class. The class whence most officeholders come corresponds, as respects education and refinement, to what would be called the lower middle class in Europe. But officeholders are not governors.

Such class issues as now exist or have recently existed, seldom, or to a small extent, coincide with issues between the two great parties. They are usually toyed with by both parties alike, or if such a question becomes strong enough to be made the basis of a new party, such a party will usually stand by itself apart from the two old and regular organizations.

In Europe, classes have become factors in politics either from interest or from passion. Legislation or administration may have pressed hardly on a class, and the class has sought to defend and emancipate itself. Or its feelings may have been wounded by past injury or insult, and it may seek occasions for revenge. In America the latter cause has never existed, and till recently neither was the former apparent, though of late years complaints have been made that the law deals unfairly with labour unions.[6] Hence

---

[6] Those who argue that legislation is unjust to the working man have usually blamed it less for what it did than for what it omitted or did not prevent. Any statute which bore harshly on any

classes are not prime factors in American politics or in the formation of native political opinion. In the main, political questions proper have held the first place in a voter's mind, and questions affecting his class the second.[7] The great strikes which have of late years convulsed large sections of the country, and the labour agitation which has accompanied them, have brought new elements of class passion and class interest upon the scene.

The nation is not an aggregate of classes. They exist within it, but they do not make it up. You are not struck by their political significance as you would be in any European country. The people is one people, although it occupies a wider territory than any other nation, and is composed of elements from many quarters.

Even education makes less difference between various sections of the community than might be expected. One finds among the better instructed many of those prejudices and fallacies to which the European middle classes are supposed peculiarly liable. Among the less instructed of the native Americans, on the other hand, there is a comprehension of public affairs, a shrewdness of judgment, and a generally diffused interest in national welfare, exceeding that of the humbler classes in Europe. They have shown, and notably on several occasions within the present century, a power of responding to the appeals made to them by a highminded and curageous leader which has startled and quelled the machine politicians, and cheered the hearts of those who have faith in popular government.

This is the strong point of the nation. This is what gives buoyancy to the vessel of the state, enabling her to carry with apparent ease the dead weight of ignorance which European immigration continues to throw upon her decks.

---

class as a class would in America be repealed forthwith. There is at present in some states an agitation for altering the law which restrains what is called coercive "picketing" or molestation in labour disputes, and also for providing some more complete compensation for accidents.

[7] There are exceptions—e.g., tariff questions are foremost in the minds of manufacturers, the exclusion of Oriental labourers in those of California working men, transportation grievances often in those of farmers.

Local Types of Opinion—East, West, and South

Both the general tendencies and the class tendencies in the development of public opinion which I have attempted to sketch, may be observed all over the vast area of the Union. Some, however, are more powerful in one region, others in another, while the local needs and feelings of each region tend to give a particular colour to its views and direction to its aims. One must therefore inquire into and endeavour to describe these local differences, so as, by duly allowing for them, to correct what has been stated generally with regard to the conditions under which opinion is formed, and the questions which evoke it.

In an earlier chapter I have classified the states into five groups, the Northeastern or New England states, the Middle states, the Northwestern states, the Southern states, and the states of the Pacific slope. For the purposes of our present inquiry there is no material difference between the first two of these groups, but the differences between the others are significant. It is needless to add that there are, of course, abundance of local differences within these divisions. Pennsylvania, for instance, is for many purposes unlike Ohio. Georgia stands on a higher level than Louisiana. Idaho is more raw than Illinois. To go into these minor points of divergence would involve a tedious discussion, and perhaps confuse the reader after all, so he must be asked to understand that this chapter endeavours to present only the general aspect which opinion wears in each section of the country, and that what is said of a section generally, is not meant to be taken as equally applicable to every state within it.

In the Eastern states the predominant influence is that of capitalists, manufacturers, merchants—in a word, of the commercial classes. The East finds the capital for great undertakings all over the country, particularly for the making of railroads, the stock of which is chiefly held by Eastern investors, and the presidents whereof often have their central office in New York, though the line may traverse the Western or Southern states. The East also conducts the gigantic trade with Europe. It ships the grain and the cattle, the pork and the petroleum, it finances the shipping of much of the cotton, it receives and distributes nearly all the manufactured goods that Europe sends, as well as most of the emigrants from the ports of the Old World.[1] The arms of its great bankers and merchants stretch over the whole Union, making those commercial influences which rule in their own seat potent everywhere. Eastern opinion is therefore the most quickly and delicately sensitive to financial movements and to European influences, as well as the most firmly bound to a pacific policy. As in the beginning of the century, trade interests made Massachusetts and Connecticut anxious to avoid a breach with England, to whose ports their vessels plied, so now, though the shipping which enters Eastern ports is chiefly European (British, Norwegian, German, French), the mercantile connections of American and European merchants and financiers are so close that an alarm of war might produce widespread disaster.

The East is also, being the oldest, the best educated and if no longer the most intellectually active yet perhaps the most intellectually polished, quarter of the country.[2] Not only does it contain more men of high culture, but the average of knowledge and thought (excluding the mob of the great cities and some backward districts in the hills of Pennsylvania) is higher than elsewhere. Its literary men and eminent teachers labour for the whole country, and its cities, which show the lowest element of the population in their rabble, show also the largest number of men of light and leading in all professions. Although very able newspapers are published in the West as well as in the East, still the tone of Eastern political discussion is more generally dignified and serious than in the rest of the Union. The influences of Europe, which, of course, play first and chiefly upon the East, are, so far as they affect manners and morality, by no means an unmixed good. But in the realm of thought Europe and its criticism are a stimulative force, which corrects any undue appreciation of national virtues, and helps forward sound views in economics and history. The leisured and well-read class to

---

[1] Some Germans and Italians enter by New Orleans or the ports of Texas.

[2] The percentage of persons able to read and write is as high in some of the Western states, such as Iowa and Nebraska, as in New England, but this may be because the recent immigrants depress the level of New England.

be found in some Eastern cities is as cosmopolitan in tone as can be found anywhere in the world, yet has not lost the piquancy of its native soil. Its thought appropriates what is fresh and sound in the literature or scientific work of Germany, England, and France more readily than any of those countries seems to learn from each of the others. These causes, added to the fact that the perversions of party government have been unusually gross among the irresponsible masses that crowd these very cities, has roused a more strenuous opposition to the so-called "machine" than in other parts of the country. The Eastern voter is less bound to his party, more accustomed to think for himself, and to look for light, when he feels his own knowledge defective, to capable publicists. When, either in federal or state or city politics, an independent party arises, repudiating the bad nominations of one or both of the regular organizations, it is here that it finds its leaders and the greatest part of its support. There has also been in New England something of the spirit of Puritanism, cold and keen as glacier air, with its high standard of public duty and private honour, its disposition to apply the maxims of religion to the conduct of life, its sense, much needed in this tenderhearted country, that there are times when Agag must be hewn in pieces before the Lord in Gilgal. If the people of New England and rural New York had been left unpolluted by the turbid flood of foreign immigration, they would be the fittest of any in the world for a pure democratic government. Evils there would still be, as in all governments, but incomparably less grave than those which now tax the patriotism of the party which from these states holds up the banner of reform for the whole Union.

It is impossible to draw a line between the East and the West, because the boundary is always moving westward. In 1870 Ohio was typically Western in character; now it has as much in common with Connecticut or New York as with Kansas or Minnesota. The most distinctive elements in the Western states are the farming class, which here attains its greatest strength, and the masses of Germans and Scandinavians, who fill whole districts, often outnumbering the native Americans. For many years these immigrants contributed so much more largely to the voting than to the thinking power of the newer states, that their presence was one of the main reasons why the political power of the West exceeded its political capacity. They are honest, industrious, and worthy people, the parents of good American citizens, useful men to clear the woods and break up the prairie, and now, having learnt the institutions of the country, they are no longer behind their native born neighbors in political intelligence, nor less ready to try experiments in legislation and in the reform of election methods. The predominance of the agricultural interest has the faults and merits indicated in the account already given of the farming class. Western opinion is politically unenlightened, still dislikes theory, and holds the practical man to be the man who, while discerning keenly his own interest, discerns nothing else beyond the end of his nose. It has boundless confidence in the future of the country, of the West in particular, of its own state above all, caring not much for what the East thinks, and still less for the judgment of Europe. It feels sure everything will come right, and thinks "cheap transportation" to be the one thing needful. Reckless in enterprises, it is stingy in paying its officials, judges included. Good-natured and indulgent to a fault, it is nevertheless displeased to hear that its senator lives in luxury at Washington. Its townsfolk are so much occupied in pushing their towns, between whose newspapers there is a furious rivalry—they hate one another as Athens hated Thebes, or Florence, Pisa—its rich men in opening up railroads, its farmers in their household and field toil, labour being scarce and dear, that politics were for a long time left to the politicians, who, however, were not the worst specimens of their class, and the ordinary voter stuck steadily to his party, disliking "independents" and "bolters." Now, however, the wave of what is called "radicalism" which has from time to time surged up along and beyond the Mississippi, has brought a keener interest into political reform and legislative work, and that splendid energy which the Western men showed when, in the Civil War days, their stourthearted, large-limbed regiments poured down to Southern battlefields has thrown more of itself than it had done since those days, into plans for improving the methods of politics and curbing what is held to be the excessive power of combined wealth. The Western man is no more disposed than formerly to listen to philosophical reasonings, or trouble himself about coming dangers, but his sentiment as well as his interest has been so enlisted in these plans, that he is not likely soon to drop them.

The West may be called the most distinctively American part of America, because the points in which it differs from the East are the points in which America as a whole differs from Europe. But the character of its population differs in different regions, according to the parts of the country from which the early settlers came. Now the settlers have generally moved along parallels of latitude, and we have therefore the curious result that the characteristics of the older states have propagated themselves westward in parallel lines, so that he who travels from the Atlantic to the Rocky Mountains will find fewer differences to note than he who, starting from Texas, travels north to Manitoba. Thus northern Ohio was filled from New England and western

New York, and in its turn colonized northern Illinois, Michigan, and much of the farther Northwest. Southern Ohio and Illinois, together with a great part of Indiana, were peopled from Virginia and Kentucky, and the somewhat inferior quality of these early settlers is still traceable. Missouri was colonized from the slave states, and retains traces of their character.[3] Kansas lies just west of Missouri, but it received in the days of the Free Soil struggle many Puritan immigrants from the free states, and shows, though it used to be called the state of "cranks," a high type of political intelligence. The Scandinavians are chiefly in Wisconsin and Minnesota, and the two Dakotas, the Germans numerous in Iowa also, and indeed all over these newer states, including Texas. So far back as 1870 Milwaukee was a German rather than an American city,[4] and in 1890 it appeared that there were townships in Wisconsin in which the tax lists had for years been kept in German, and counties in which a paid interpreter was required to enable the business of the courts to be transacted. Oklahoma, into which settlers have swarmed from all parts of the Northwest as well as the Southwest, is preeminently the land of sanguine radicalism and experimental legislation. New Mexico and Arizona were, till Congress in 1910 passed an act for their admission as states, still Territories, and the former has a large Mexican element. Yet over them, too, the network of party organization has been spread, though, of course, the sparser population feeds a feebler political life.

The Pacific slope, as its inhabitants call it, geographically includes the states of Oregon and Washington, but Oregon and Washington resemble the Northwestern states in so many respects that she may better be classed therewith. California and Nevada on the other hand, to whom we may now add Arizona, are distinctly peculiar. They are more Western than the states I have just been describing, with the characteristics of those states intensified and some new features added. They are cut off by deserts and barren mountain ranges from the agricultural part of the Mississippi basin, nor is population ever likely to become really continuous across this wilderness. Mining industries play a larger part in them than in any other state, except Colorado. Their inhabitants are unsettled and fluctuating, highly speculative, as one may expect those who mine and gamble in mining stocks to be.

---

[3] In Oregon there is a district which was settled by people from Kentucky and Tennessee, rather exceptionally, for the outflow of these states seldom moved so far to the north. The descendants of these immigrants are now less prosperous and enterprising than those of the men who came from the free states.

[4] Asking my way about the streets, I found German more helpful than English. In the same year it was noticeable that in Wisconsin the paper money (then alone in use) had got a marked smell from the use of skins and furs by the newly arrived Swedes and Norwegians.

They used to be chiefly occupied with questions of their own, such as Oriental immigration, the management of the great Central and Southern Pacific railroad system, which has been accused of dominating the trade and industries of California; and the reconcilement of the claims of miners and agriculturists to the waters of the rivers, which each set seeks to appropriate, and which the former claims the right to foul. Now forces and tendencies, generally similar, are at work on both sides of the Rocky Mountains, and so are the issues which occupy men's minds. Yet public opinion is here, in spite of the proverbial shrewdness, energy, and hardihood of the men of the Pacific, somewhat more fitful and gusty, less amenable to the voice of sober reason, and less deferential to the authority of statesmen, or even of party than anywhere else in the Union. "Interests," such as those of a great mine-owning group, or of a railroad, are immensely powerful, and the reactions against them not less so.

Of the South, the solid South, as it is often called, because its presidential vote has since 1876 been cast almost entire for the Democrats, some account will be found in three later chapters, one sketching its history since the war ended, two others describing the condition of the Negro and his relations to the whites. Here, therefore, I will speak only of the general character of political opinion and action in the former slave states. The phenomena they present are unexampled. Equality before the law is in theory absolute and perfect, being secured by the federal Constitution. Yet the political subjection of a large part (in one state a majority) of the population is no less complete.

There are three orders of men in the South.

The first is the upper or educated class, including the children of the planting aristocracy which ruled before the Civil War, together with the Northern men who have since 1865 settled in the towns for the purposes of trade or manufacture. Of this order more than nine-tenths—those in fact who have survived from the old aristocracy, together with those who have since arisen from the humbler class, and with most of the newer arrivals— belong to the Democratic party. Along with the high spirit and self-confidence which belong to a ruling race, these Southern men showed an enlargement of view and an aptitude for grasping decided and continuous lines of policy, in fact, a turn for statesmanship as contrasted with mere politics, which was less common in the North, because less favoured by the conditions under which ambition has in the North to push its way. The Southern man who entered public life had a more assured position than his rival from a Northern state, because he represented the opinion of a united body who stood by him, regarding him as their champion, and who expected from him less subservience to their instructions. He did not need to court so assiduously the breath of popular favour. He was not more educated or intelligent; and had lived in a less stimulating atmosphere. But he had courage and a clear vision of his objects, the two gifts essential for a statesman; while the united popular impulse behind him supplied a sort of second patriotism. The element of gain entered somewhat less into Southern politics, partly because the country is poor and though the South begins to be commercialized, the sensitiveness on the "point of honour" and a flavour of punctiliousness in manners, recall the olden time. Opinion in the slave states before the war, in spite of the divisions between Democrats and Whigs, was generally bold, definite, and consistent, because based on a few doctrines. It was the opinion of a small class who were largely occupied with public affairs, and fond of debating them upon first principles and the words of the federal constitution. It has preserved this quality, while losing its old fierceness and better recognizing the conditions under which it must work in a federal republic. On the other hand, the extreme strength of party feeling, due to the extreme sensitiveness regarding the Negro, has prevented the growth of independent opinion, and of the tendency which in the North is called Mugwumpism. And although the leading statesmen are not inferior to those whom the North sends to Washington, the total number of thoughtful and enlightened men is, in proportion to the population, smaller than in the Northeast, smaller even than in such Western states as Illinois or Ohio.

I have used the past tense in describing these phenomena, because the South is changing, and the process is now scarcely swifter in the West than in those parts of Tennessee, North Carolina, Georgia, and Alabama where the coal and iron deposits have recently been opened up. Most parts, however, are still thinly settled by whites, and so poor that a traveller finds it hard to understand how, when still poorer, the people managed to resist for four years the armies of the wealthy and populous North. There is therefore less eagerness and hopefulness than in the West, less searching discussion and elaborate organization than in the East, less of everything that is characteristically democratic. The machine has, in some states, been brought to no such terrible perfection as in the North, because the need of it was not felt where one party was sure of victory, and because talent or social position usually designated the men to be selected as candidates, or the men whose voice would determine the selection. Of late years, however, the aristocratic element in Southern politics has grown weaker, and merits that were deemed characteristic of Southern statesmen are more rarely seen. Those who regret that there has not been, since the Civil War generation died out, a stronger group of leaders sent from the South to Washington, attribute the fact to the superior attractions of a business career in a region which is growing and developing so fast and to the departure of some of the ablest intellects to Northern cities where they expect to find a larger field for their talents.

The second order consists of those who used to be called the mean whites. Their condition strengthens the impression of half civilization which the rural districts of the South produce upon the traveller, and which comes painfully home to him in the badness of the inns. While slavery lasted, these whites were, in the lowlands of the planting states, a wretched, because economically superfluous, class. There was no room for them as labourers, because the slaves did the work on the plantations; they had not the money to purchase land and machinery for themselves, nor the spirit to push their way in the towns, while the system of large slave-worked properties made, as the latifundia did long ago in Italy, the cultivation of small farms hopeless, and the existence of a thriving free peasantry impossible. The planters disliked these whites and kept them off their estates as much as possible; the slaves despised them, and called them "poor white trash." In South Carolina and the Gulf states, they picked up a wretched livelihood by raising some vegetables near their huts, and killing the wild creatures of the woods, while a few hung round the great houses to look out for a stray job. Shiftless, ignorant, improvident, with no aims in the present nor hopes for the future, citizens in nothing but the possession of votes, they were a standing reproach to the system that produced them, and the most convincing proof of its economic as well as moral failure. In the northerly slave states, they were better off, and in the highlands of Western Virginia, Kentucky, Tennessee, and North Carolina, where there were few or no slaves, they had, along with much rudeness and ignorance, the virtues of simple mountaineers. Their progress since the war has been marked, both near the mining and manufacturing towns, which give work and furnish markets, and in the cotton-bearing uplands, where many have acquired farms and prospered as tillers of the soil. Everywhere, however, they remain, in point of education and enlightenment, behind the small farmers or artisans of the North and West. Before the war they followed, as a matter of course (except in the mountains, where the conditions were different), the lead of the planting class, not more out of deference to it than from aversion to the Negroes. The less a man had to be proud of, the more proud was he of his colour. Since the war, they have been no less anxious than their richer neighbours to exclude the Negroes from any share in the government. But they are no longer mere followers. They have begun to think and act for themselves; and, though one of the first signs of independence was shown in the acceptance of the impracticable projects that were for a time advocated by the Farmers' Alliance, they have become a body which has views, and with whose views it is necessary to reckon.

The Negroes constitute nearly one-third of the population of the old slave states, and in two states (Mississippi and South Carolina) they are in a majority, being nearly equal to the whites in Louisiana and Georgia. Though their presence is the dominant factor in Southern politics, they cannot be said to form or influence opinion; and it is not their votes, but the efforts made to prevent them from voting, that have influenced the course of events. I reserve for subsequent chapters an account of their singular positions.

Remembering that of the whole population of the Union, nearly one-third is in the Southern states, and that the majority of that one-third, viz., the lower part of the poor whites and nearly all the Negroes, has no political knowledge or capacity, nothing that can be called rational opinion, and remembering also the large mass of recently arrived and ignorant immigrants, it will be seen how far the inhabitants of the United States are from being a democracy enlightened through and through. If one part of the people is as educated and capable as that of Switzerland, another is as ignorant and politically untrained as that of Russia.

Of the four divisions of the country above described, the West (including Oregon and Washington) has already the largest vote, and since it grows faster than the others, will soon be indisputably sovereign. But as it grows, it loses some of its distinctive features, becoming more like the East, and falling more and more under Eastern influences, both intellectual and financial. It must not therefore be supposed that what is now typically Western opinion will be the reigning opinion of the future. The Pacific states will in time be drawn closer to those of the Mississippi Valley, losing something of such specific quality as they still possess; and centres of literary activity, such as now exist chiefly in the Atlantic states, will be more and more scattered over the whole country. Opinion will therefore be more homogeneous, or at least less local, in the future than it has been in the past; even as now it is less determined by local and state influences than it was in the earlier days of the Republic.

The Action of Public Opinion

The last few chapters have attempted to explain what are the conditions under which opinion is formed in America, what national qualities it reflects, how it is affected by class interests or local circumstances, as well as through what organs it manifests itself. We must now inquire how it acts, and for this purpose try to answer three questions.

By whom is public opinion formed? i.e., by the few or by the many?

How does it seek to grasp and use the legal machinery which the constitutions (federal and state) provide?

What means has it of influencing the conduct of affairs otherwise than through the regular legal machinery?

It may serve to illustrate the phenomena which mark the growth of opinion in America if we compare them with those of some European country. As Britain is the country in which public opinion has been longest and with least interruption installed in power, and in which the mass of the people are more largely than elsewhere interested in public affairs,[1] Britain supplies the fittest materials for a comparison.

In Britain political supremacy belongs to the householder voters, who number (over the whole United Kingdom) about 7,500,000, being rather less than two-thirds of the adult male population. Public opinion ought in theory to reside in them. Practically, however, as everybody knows, most of them have little that can be called political opinion. It is the creation and possession of a much smaller number.

An analysis of public opinion in Britain will distinguish three sets of persons—I do not call them classes, for they do not coincide with social

---

[1] Always excepting Switzerland, Norway, and Greece, whose conditions are, however, too dissimilar from those of America to make a comparison profitable.

grades—those who make opinion, those who receive and hold opinion, those who have no opinions at all.

The first set consists of practical politicians (i.e., a certain number of members of the Lower House and a smaller fraction of members of the Upper, together with men taking an active part in local party organizations), journalists and other public writers, and a small fringe of other persons, chiefly professional men, who think and talk constantly about public affairs. Within this set of men, who are to be counted by hundreds rather than by thousands, it is the chiefs of the great parties who have the main share in starting opinion, the journalists in propagating it. Debates in Parliament do something, and the speeches which custom, recent, but strong and increasing, requires the leaders to deliver up and down the country, and which are of course reported, replace Parliament when it is not sitting. The function of the dozen best thinkers and talkers in each party is now not merely, as in the last generation, to know and manage Parliament, to watch foreign affairs, and prepare schemes of domestic legislation, but to inspire, instruct, stimulate, and attach the outside public. So too members of the houses of Parliament find that the chief utility of their position lies in its enabling them to understand the actualities of politics better than they could otherwise do, and to gain a hearing outside for what they may have to say to their fellow countrymen. This small set of persons constitutes what may be called the working staff of the laboratory; it is among them, by the reciprocal action and reaction on one another of the chiefs, the followers, and the press, that opinion receives its first shape.[2]

The second set of persons consists of those who watch public affairs with a certain measure of interest. When an important question arises, they look at the debates in Parliament or some platform deliverance by a leader, and they have at all times a notion of what is passing in the political world. They now and then attend a public meeting. They are not universally, but

---

[2] Small as it may still seem to an American, the class that forms public opinion has been steadily widening in England. Last century it consisted only of the then ruling class—the great families—the houses of Parliament, a certain number of lawyers, with a very few journalists and clergymen, and a sort of fringe of educated men and monied men brought into relations with the rulers. This was the England which allowed George III to alienate and lose the North American colonies. Even then, no doubt, the mass of voters outside (extremely small when compared with the numbers of today) counted for something, for there was always a possibility of their interfering when some feeling spread among them, one or other of the parties being ready to stimulate and use such a feeling, and a general election enabling it to find expression in the counties and in a few of the boroughs. When the Reform Bill of 1832 enlarged the suffrage, and almost extinguished the pocket boroughs, what had been the ruling class sank into being merely the officeholding class; and now, though it died hard, its monopoly of office is departing as its monopoly of sitting in Parliament did in 1832.

now pretty largely, enrolled as members of some political association. When an election arrives they go to vote of their own accord. They talk over politics after dinner or coming into town by a suburban train. The proportion of such persons is larger in the professional classes (and especially among the lawyers) than in the mercantile, larger in the upper mercantile than among the working men of the towns, larger among skilled than unskilled artisans, larger in the North than in the South, larger among the town workmen than among the newly enfranchised agricultural labourers. It varies in different parts of the country, and is perhaps relatively smaller in London than in other cities. If still less than a third of the total number of voters, it is nevertheless an increasing proportion.[3]

The third set includes all the rest of the voters. Though they possess political power, and are better pleased to have it, they do not really care about it—that is to say, politics occupy no appreciable space in their thoughts and interests. Some of them vote at elections because they consider themselves to belong to a party, or fancy that on a given occasion they have more to expect from the one party than from the other; or because they are brought up on election day by someone who can influence them. The number who vote tends to increase with the importation of party into municipal and other local contests; and from the same cause some now enrol themselves in party associations. Others will not take the trouble to go to the polls. No one, except on the stump, can attribute independent political thinking to this mass of persons, because their knowledge and interest, though growing under the influence of the privileges they enjoy, are still slight. Many have not even political prepossessions, and will stare or smile when asked to which party they belong. They count for little except at elections, and then chiefly as instruments to be used by others. So far as the formation or exercise of opinion goes, they may be left out of sight.[4]

It is obviously impossible to draw a sharp line between the second set

---

[3] In Chapter 57 *ante*, I have attempted to distinguish an inner and outer circle of persons who take an active part in political work. What I here call the first or opinion-making set would lie almost wholly within the inner circle, and would be much smaller than that circle.

[4] What is said here cannot of course be proved, but will commend itself to anyone who, knowing a large constituency, compares the number of persons who attend public meetings at an election and can be trusted to come of themselves to the polls with the total number of voters on the lists. In the London constituencies I doubt if more than 10 per cent of the nominal voting strength show their interest in either of these ways. From 25 to 35 per cent do not even vote. The voting proportion is much larger in the northern and west Midland towns and in Scotland. In the old days of small constituencies, when it might have been supposed that the restriction of the franchise would have made it more prized, inexperienced candidates were always struck by the small percentage, out of those whom they personally canvassed, who seemed to care about politics, or even deemed themselves steady party men.

and the third, or to estimate their relative numbers, because when politics are dull many persons subside into indifference whom the advent of a crisis may again arouse. And of course there are plenty of people in the second set who though interested in politics, have no sort of real knowledge or judgment about them. Such considerations, however, do not touch the point of the present analysis, which is to distinguish between the citizens who originate opinion (the first set), those who hold and somewhat modify it (the second set), and those who are rather to be deemed, and then only when they come to the poll, mere ballot markers. The first set do the thinking; they scatter forth the ideas and arguments. The second set receive and test what is set before them. What their feeling or judgment approves they accept and give effect to by their votes; what they dislike or suspect is refused and falls dead, or possibly sets them the other way. The measure of the worth of a view or proposal—I do not mean its intrinsic worth, but its power of pleasing the nation—is however not merely the breadth of the support it obtains, but also the zeal which it inspires in those who adopt it. Although persons in the second set usually belong to one or other party,[5] and are therefore prima facie disposed to accept whatever comes from their party leaders, yet the degree of cordiality with which they accept indicates to a leader how their minds are moving, and becomes an element in his future calculations. Thus the second set, although rather receptive than creative, has an important function in moulding opinion, and giving it the shape and colour it finally takes when it has crystallized under the influence of a party struggle. The third set can scarcely be called a factor in the formation of opinion, except in so far as one particular proposal or cry may sometimes prove more attractive to it than another. It has some few fixed ideas or prejudices which a statesman must bear in mind, but in the main it is passive, consisting of persons who either follow the lead of members of the first or second set, or who are so indifferent as to refuse to move at all.

The United States present different phenomena. There what I have called the first set is extremely small. The third set is relatively smaller than in Britain, and but for the recent immigrants and the Negroes would be insignificant. It is in the second set that opinion is formed as well as tested, created as well as moulded. Political light and heat do not radiate out from

---

[5] The increasingly party character of municipal contests tends to draw an always larger number of persons from the third class into the second, because being dragged up to vote at a municipal election they acquire, if not opinions, at least the habit of party action and of repeating party cries.

a centre as in England. They are diffused all through the atmosphere, and are little more intense in the inner sphere of practical politicians than elsewhere. The ordinary citizens are interested in politics, and watch them with intelligence, the same kind of intelligence (though a smaller quantity of it) as they apply to their own business. They are forced by incessant elections to take a more active part in public affairs than is taken by any European people. They think their own competence equal to that of their representatives and officebearers; and they are not far wrong. They do not therefore look up to their statesmen for guidance, but look around to one another, carrying to its extreme the principle that in the multitude of counsellors there is wisdom.

In America, therefore, opinion is not made but grows. Of course it must begin somewhere; but it is often hard to say where or how. As there are in the country a vast number of minds similar in their knowledge, beliefs, and attitude, with few exceptionally powerful minds applying themselves to politics, it is natural that the same idea should often occur to several or many persons at the same time, that each event as it occurs should produce the same impression and evoke the same comments over a wide area. When everybody desires to agree with the majority, and values such accord more highly than the credit of originality, this tendency is all the stronger. An idea once launched, or a view on some current question propounded, flies everywhere on the wings of a press eager for novelties. Publicity is the easiest thing in the world to obtain; but as it is attainable by all notions, phrases, and projects, wise and foolish alike, the struggle for existence— that is to say, for public attention—is severe.

I do not, of course, deny that here, as everywhere else in the world, some one person or group must make a beginning, but seek to point out that, whereas in Europe it is patent who does make the beginning, in America a view often seems to arise spontaneously, and to be the work of many rather than of few. The individual counts for less, the mass counts for more. In propagating a doctrine not hitherto advocated by any party the methods used are similar to those of England. A central society is formed, branch societies spring up over the country, a journal (perhaps several journals) is started, and if the movement thrives, an annual convention of its supporters is held, at which speeches are made and resolutions adopted. If any striking personality is connected with the movement as a leader, as Garrison was with Abolitionism, he cannot but become a sort of figurehead. Yet it happens more rarely in America than in England that an individual leader gives its character to a movement, partly because new movements less often begin among, or are taken up by, persons already known as practical politicians.

As regards opinion on the main questions of the hour, such as the extension of slavery long was, and questions affecting railways, trusts, the currency, the tariff, are now, it rises and falls, much as in any other country, under the influence of events which seem to make for one or other of the contending views. There is this difference between America and Europe, that in the former speeches seem to influence the average citizen less, because he is more apt to do his own thinking; newspaper invective less, because he is used to it; current events rather more, because he is better informed of them. Party spirit is probably no stronger in America than in England, so far as a man's thinking and talking go, but it tells more upon him when he comes to vote.

An illustration of what has been said may be found in the fact that the proportion of persons who actually vote at an election to those whose names appear on the voting list is larger in America than in Europe. In some English constituencies this percentage is from 60 to 70 per cent, though at exciting moments it is larger than this, taking the country as a whole. At the general election of 1910 it exceeded 80 per cent. In America 80 per cent may be a fair average, taking presidential elections, which call out the heaviest vote, and in some recent contests this proportion was exceeded. Something may be ascribed to the more elaborate local organization of American parties; but against this ought to be set the fact that the English voting mass includes not quite two-thirds, the American nearly the whole, of the adult male population, and that the English voters are the more solid and well-to-do part of the population.

Is there, then, in the United States, no inner sphere of thinkers, writers, and speakers, corresponding to what we have called the "first set" in England?

There are individual men corresponding to individuals in that English set, and probably quite as numerous. There are journalists of great ability, there are a few literary men, clergymen and teachers, a good many lawyers, some businessmen, some few politicians. But they are isolated and unorganized, and do not constitute a class. Most of them are primarily occupied with their own avocations, and have only spare time to give to political thinking or writing. They are nearly all resident in or near the Eastern and four or five of the largest Western cities, and through many large tracts of country scarce any are to be found. In England the profession of opinion-making and leading is the work of specialists; in America, except as regards the few journalists and statesmen aforesaid, of amateurs. As the books of amateurs have merits which those of professional book writers are apt to want, so something is gained by the absence of the professional element from American political opinion. But that which these amateurs produce is less coherent, less abundant, and less promptly effective upon the mass of the citizens than the corresponding English product. In fact, the individual Americans whom we are considering can (except the journalists and statesmen aforesaid) be distinguished from the mass of citizens only by their superior intellectual competence and their keener interest in public affairs. (Of the "professional politicians" there is no question, because it is in the getting and keeping of places that these gentlemen are occupied.) We may therefore repeat the proposition, that in America opinion does not originate in a particular class, but grows up in the nation at large, though, of course, there are leading minds in the nation who have more to do with its formation than the run of their fellow citizens. A good instance of the power such men may exercise is afforded by the success of the civil service reform movement, which began among a few enlightened citizens in the Eastern states, who by degrees leavened, or were thought to be leavening, the minds of their fellows to such an extent that the politicians were forced, sorely against the grain, to bring in and pass the appropriate legislation. Other instances may be found in the swift success obtained by those who advocated the secret or "Australian" ballot, a measure not specially desired by the "politicians," and in the spread of the recent legislation establishing statutory primaries, which was advocated in the West by a comparatively small number of reformers and then found support from a large body of citizens who had come to dislike the machine and its ways.

An illustration of a different kind, but not less striking, was the victory of the agitation for international copyright. A few literary men, seconded after a while by a very few publishers, had for weary years maintained what seemed a hopeless struggle for the extension to foreign authors of the right to acquire copyright in America, theretofore reserved to citizens only. These men were at first ridiculed. People asked how they could expect that the nation, whose chief reading was in European books, sold very cheap because the author received no profit, would raise the price of these books against itself? Neither Republicans nor Democrats had anything to gain by passing the bill, and Congress, by large majorities, rejected or refused to advance (which came to the same thing) every bill presented to it. The agitators, however, persevered, receiving help from a sympathetic press, and so worked upon the honour and good sense of the people that Congress at last came round. The hostile interests fought hard, and extorted some concessions. But in 1891 the bill was passed.[6]

We may now ask in what manner opinion, formed or forming, is able to influence the conduct of affairs?

The legal machinery through which the people are by the constitution (federal and state) invited to govern is that of elections. Occasionally, when the question of altering a state constitution comes up, the citizen votes directly for or against a proposition put to him in the form of a constitutional amendment; but otherwise it is only by voting for a man as candidate that he can (except of course in the states which have adopted the initiative and referendum) give expression to his views, and directly support or oppose some policy. Now, in every country, voting for a man is an inadequate way of expressing one's views of policy, because the candidate is sure to differ in one or more questions from many of those who belong to the party. It is especially inadequate in the United States, because the strictness of party discipline leaves little freedom of individual thought or action to the member of a legislature, because the ordinary politician has little interest in anything but the regular party programme, and because in no party are the citizens at large permitted to select their candidate, seeing that he is found for them and forced on them by the professionals of the party organization. While, therefore, nothing is easier than for opinion which runs in the direct channel of party to give effect to itself frequently and vigorously, nothing is harder than for opinion which wanders out of that channel to find a legal and regular means of bringing itself to bear upon those who govern either as legislators or executive officers. This is the weak point of the American party system, perhaps of every party system, from the point of view of the independent-minded citizen, as it is the strong point from that of the party manager. A body of unorganized opinion is therefore helpless in the face of compact parties. It is obliged to organize. When organized for the promotion of a particular view or proposition it has in the United States three courses open to it.

The first is to capture one or other of the great standing parties, i.e., to persuade or frighten that party into adopting this view as part of its programme, or, to use the technical term, making it a plank of the platform, in which case the party candidates will be bound to support it. This is the most effective course, but the most difficult; for a party is sure to have

---

[6] "Never despair of America!" was the exclamation of an eminent literary man (the late Mr. R. W. Gilder), who had been one of the most active promoters of the measure.

something to lose as well as to gain by embracing a new dogma. Why should such parties as those of America have lately been troubling themselves with taking up new questions, unless they are satisfied they will gain thereby? Their old dogmas are indeed worn threadbare, but have been hitherto found sufficient to cover them.

The second course is for the men who hold the particular view to declare themselves a new party, put forward their own programme, run their own candidates. Besides being costly and troublesome, this course would be thought ridiculous where the view or proposition is not one of first-rate importance, which has already obtained wide support. Where however it is applicable, it is worth taking, even when the candidates cannot be carried, for it serves as an advertisement, and it alarms the old party, from which it withdraws voting strength in the persons of the dissidents.

The third is to cast the voting weight of the organized promoters of the doctrine or view in question into the scale of whichever party shows the greatest friendliness, or seems most open to conversion. As in many states the regular parties are pretty equally balanced, even a comparatively weak body of opinion may decide the result. Such a body does not necessarily forward its own view, for the candidates whom its vote carries are nowise pledged to its programme.[7] But it has made itself felt, shown itself a power to be reckoned with, improved its chances of capturing one or other of the regular parties, or of running candidates of its own on some future occasion. When this transfer of the solid vote of a body of agitators is the result of a bargain with the old party which gets the vote, it is called "selling out"; and in such cases it sometimes happens that the bargain secures one or two offices for the incoming allies in consideration of the strength they have brought. But if the new group be honestly thinking of its doctrines and not of the offices, the terms it will ask will be the nomination of good candidates, or a more friendly attitude towards the new view.

These are the ways in which either the minority of a party, holding some doctrine outside the regular party programme, or a new group aspiring to be a party, may assert itself at elections. The third is applicable wherever the discipline of the section which has arisen within a party is so good that

[7] The practice of interrogating candidates with a view to obtain pledges from them to vote in a particular sense is less used in America than in England. The rigour of party discipline, and the fact that business is divided between the federal and the state legislatures may have something to do with this difference. However, American candidates are sometimes pressed during election meetings by questions and demands from groups advocating moral reforms, such as liquor prohibition.

its members can be trusted to break away from their former affiliation, and vote solid for the side their leaders have agreed to favour. It is a potent weapon, and liable to be abused. But in a country where the tide runs against minorities and small groups it is most necessary. The possibility of its employment acts as a check on the regular parties, disposing them to abstain from legislation which might irritate any body of growing opinion and tend to crystallize it as a new organization, and making them more tolerant of minor divergences from the dogmas of the orthodox programme than their fierce love of party uniformity would otherwise permit.

So far we have been considering the case of persons advocating some specific opinion or scheme. As respects the ordinary conduct of business by officials and legislators, the fear of popular displeasure to manifest itself at the next elections is, or course, the most powerful of restraining influences. Under a system of balanced authorities, such fear helps to prevent or remove deadlocks as well as the abuse of power by any one authority. A president (or state governor) who has vetoed bills passed by Congress (or his state legislature) is emboldened to go on doing so when he finds public opinion on his side; and Congress (or the state legislature) will hesitate, though the requisite majority may be forthcoming, to pass these bills over the veto. A majority in the House of Representatives, or in a state legislative body, which has abused the power of closing debate by the "previous question" rule, may be frightened by expressions of popular disapproval from repeating the offence. When the two branches of a legislature differ, and a valuable bill has failed, or when there has been vexatious filibustering, public opinion fixes the blame on the party primarily responsible for the loss of good measures or public time, and may punish it at the next election. Thus, in many ways and on many occasions, though not so often or so fully as is needed, the vision of the polls, seen some months or even years off, has power to terrify and warn selfish politicians. As the worth of courts of law is to be estimated not merely by the offences they punish and the causes they try, but even more by the offences from which the fear of penalties deters bad men, and by the payments which the prospect of a writ extracts from reluctant debtors, so a healthy and watchful public opinion makes itself felt in preventing foolish or corrupt legislation and executive jobbery. Mischief is checked in America more frequently than anywhere else by the fear of exposure, or by newspaper criticisms on the first stage of a bad scheme. And, of course, the frequency of elections—in most respects a disadvantage to the country—has the merit of bringing the prospect of punishment nearer.

It will be asked how the fear is brought home, seeing that the result of a coming election must usually be uncertain. Sometimes it is not brought home. The erring majority in a legislature may believe they have the people with them, or the governor may think his jobs will be forgotten. Generally, however, there are indications of the probable set of opinion in the language held by moderate men and the less partisan newspapers. When some of the organs of the party which is in fault begin to blame it, danger is in the air, for the other party is sure to use the opening thus given to it. And hence, of course, the control of criticism is most effective where parties are nearly balanced. Opinion seems to tell with special force when the question is between a legislative body passing bills or ordinances, and a president, or governor, or mayor, vetoing them, the legislature recoiling whenever they think the magistrate has got the people behind him. Even small fluctuations in a vote produce a great impression on the minds of politicians.

The constancy or mutability of electoral bodies is a difficult phenomenon to explain, especially where secret voting prevails, and a dangerous one to generalize on. The tendency of the electoral vote in any constituency to shift from Tory to Whig or Whig to Tory, used in England to be deemed to indicate the presence of a corrupt element. It was a black mark against a borough. In America it sometimes deserves the same interpretation, for there are corruptible masses in not a few districts. But there are also cases in which it points to the existence of an exceptionally thoughtful and unprejudiced element in the population, an element which rejects party dictation, and seeks to cast its vote for the best man. The average American voter is more likely to consider himself attached to a party than the English, and is, I think, less capricious, and therefore if a transfer of votes from one party to the other does not arise from some corrupt influence, it betokens serious disapproval on the part of the bolters. In the United States fluctuations are most frequent in some of the less sober and steady Western states, and in some of the most enlightened, such as New York and Massachusetts. In the former the people may be carried away by a sudden impulse; in the latter there is a section which judges candidates more by personal merits than by party professions.

These defects which may be noted in the constitutional mechanism for enabling public opinion to rule promptly and smoothly, are, in a measure, covered by the expertness of Americans in using all kinds of voluntary and private agencies for the diffusion and expression of opinion. Where the object is to promote some particular cause, associations are formed and federated to one another, funds are collected, the press is set to work, lectures are delivered. When the law can profitably be invoked (which is often the case in a country governed by constitutions standing above the legislature), counsel are retained and suits instituted, all with the celerity and skill which long practice in such work has given. If the cause has a moral bearing, efforts are made to enlist the religious or semireligious magazines, and the ministers of religion.[8] Deputations proceed to Washington or to the state capital, and lay siege to individual legislators. Sometimes a distinct set of women's societies is created, whose action on and through women is all the more powerful because the deference shown to the so-called weaker sex enables them to do what would be resented in men. Once in Iowa, when a temperance ticket was being run at the elections, parties of ladies gathered in front of the polling booths and sang hymns all day while the citizens voted. Everyone remembers what was called the "Women's Whisky War" when, in several Western states, bands of women entered the drinking saloons and, by entreaties and reproaches, drove out the customers. In no country has any sentiment which touches a number of persons so many ways of making itself felt; though, to be sure, when the first and chief effort of every group is to convince the world that it is strong, and growing daily stronger, great is the difficulty of determining whether those who are vocal are really numerous or only noisy.

For the promotion of party opinion on the leading questions that divide or occupy parties, there exist, of course, the regular party organizations, whose complex and widely ramified mechanism has been described in an earlier chapter. Opinion is, however, the thing with which this mechanism is at present least occupied. Its main objects are the selection of the party candidates and the conduct of the canvass at elections. Traces of the other purpose remain in the practice of adopting, at state and national conventions, a platform, or declaration of principles and views, which is the electoral manifesto of the party, embodying the tenets which it is supposed to live for. A convention is a body fitted neither by its numbers nor its composition for the discussion and sifting of political doctrines; but, even if it were so fitted, that is not the work to which its masters would set it. A "platform" is invariably prepared by a small committee, and usually adopted by the general committee, and by the convention, with little change. Its tendency is neither to define nor to convince, but rather to attract and to confuse. It is a mixture of denunciation, declamation, and conciliation. It reprobates

---

[8] In Philadelphia, during a struggle against the city boss, the clergy were requested to preach election sermons.

the opposite party for their past misdeeds, and "views with alarm" their present policy. It repeats the tale of the services which the party of those who issue it has rendered in the past, is replete with sounding democratic generalities, and attempts so to expand and expound the traditional party tenets as to make these include all sound doctrines, and deserve the support of all good citizens. Seldom in recent years have either platforms or the process that produces them had a powerful influence on the maturing and clarification of political opinion. However, in such times as that which immediately preceded the Civil War, and again in the silver struggle of 1896, conventions have recorded the acceptance of certain vital propositions, and rejection of certain dangerous proposals, by one or other of the great parties, and they may again have to do so, not to add that an imprudent platform may lay a party open to damaging attacks. When any important election comes off, the party organization sends its speakers out on stumping tours, and distributes a flood of campaign literature. At other times opinion moves in a different plane from that of party machinery, and is scarcely affected by it.

One might expect that in the United States the thoughts of the people would be more equally and uniformly employed on politics than in European countries. The contrary is the case. Opinion, no doubt, is always alive and vigilant, always in process of formation, growth, and decay. But its activity is less continuous and sustained than in Europe, because there is a greater difference between the spring tide of a presidential campaign year and the neap tides of the three off years than there is between one year and another under the European system of chambers which may be dissolved and ministries which may be upset at any moment. Excitement at one time is succeeded by exhaustion at another. America suffers from a sort of intermittent fever—what one may call a quintan ague. Every fourth year there come terrible shakings, passing into the hot fit of the presidential election; then follows what physicians call "the interval"; then again the fit. In Europe the persons who move in what I have called the inner sphere of politics, give unbroken attention to political problems, always discussing them both among themselves and before the people. As the corresponding persons in America are not organized into a class, and to some extent not engaged in practical politics, the work of discussion has been left to be done, in the three "off years," by the journalists and a few of the more active and thoughtful statesmen, with casual aid from such private citizens as may be interested. Now many problems require uninterrupted and what may be called scientific or professional study. Foreign policy obviously presents such problems. The shortcomings of modern England in the conduct of foreign affairs have been not unreasonably attributed to the fact that, while the attention of her statesmen is constantly distracted from them by domestic struggles, her people have not been accustomed to turn their eyes abroad except when some exciting event, such as the Egyptain troubles of 1882–85 or the Bulgarian massacre of 1876, forces them to do so. Hence a state like Germany, where a strong throne keeps a strong minister permanently in power for a long period, obtains advantages which must be credited not wholly to the wisdom of the statesmen but also to the difficulties under which their rivals in more democratic countries labour. America has had few occasions for giving her attention to foreign affairs, but some of her domestic problems are such as to demand that careful observation and unbroken reflection which neither her executive magistrates, nor her legislatures, nor any leading class among her people now give.

Those who know the United States and have been struck by the quantity of what is called politics there, may think that this description underrates the volume and energy of public political discussion. I admit the endless hubbub, the constant elections in one district or another, the paragraphs in the newspapers as to the movements or intentions of this or that prominent man, the reports of what is doing in Congress and in the state legislatures, the decisions of the federal courts in constitutional questions, the rumours about new combinations, the revelations of ring intrigues, the criticisms on appointments. It is nevertheless true that in proportion to the number of words spoken, articles printed, telegrams sent, and acts performed, less than is needed is done to form serious political thought, and bring practical problems towards a solution. I once travelled through Transylvania with Mr. Leslie Stephen in a peasant's wagon, a rude, long, low structure filled with hay. The roads were rough and stony, the horses jangled their bells, the driver shouted to the horses and cracked his whip, the wheels clanked, the boards rattled, we were deafened and shaken and jolted. We fancied ourselves moving rapidly so long as we looked straight in front, but a glance at the trees on the roadside showed that the speed was about three miles an hour. So the pother and din of American politics keep the people awake, and give them a sense of stir and motion, but the machine of government carries them slowly onward. Fortunately they have no need to hurry. It is not so much by or through the machinery of government as by their own practical good sense, which at last finds a solution the politicians may have failed to find, that the American people advance. When a European visitor dines with a company of the best citizens in such a city as Chicago or

Boston, Cleveland or Baltimore, he is struck by the acuteness, the insight, the fairness with which the condition and requirements of the country are discussed, the freedom from such passion or class feeling as usually clouds equally able Europeans, the substantial agreement between members of both the great parties as to the reforms that are wanted, the patriotism which is so proud of the real greatness of the Union as frankly to acknowledge its defects, the generous appreciation of all that is best in the character or political methods of other nations. One feels what a reserve fund of wisdom and strength the country has in such men, who so far from being aristocrats or recluses, are usually the persons whom their native fellow townsmen best know and most respect as prominent in business and in the professions. In ordinary times the practical concern of such men with either national or local politics is no greater, possibly less, than that of the leaders of business in an English town towards its municipal affairs. But when there comes an uprising against the bosses, it is these men who are called upon to put themselves at the head of it; or when a question like that of civil service reform has been before the nation for some time, it is their opinion which strikes the keynote for that of their city or district, and which shames or alarms the professional politicians. Men of the same type, though individually less conspicuous than those whom I take as examples, are to be found in many of the smaller towns, especially in the Eastern and Middle states, and as time goes on their influence grows. Much of the value of this most educated and reflective class in America consists in their being no longer blindly attached to their party, because more alive to the principles for which parties ought to exist. They may be numerically a small minority of the voters, but as in many states the two regular parties command a nearly equal normal voting strength, a small section detached from either party can turn an election by throwing its vote for the candidate, to whichever party he belongs, whom it thinks capable and honest. Thus a comparatively independent group wields a power in elections altogether disproportionate to its numbers, and by a sort of side wind can not only make its hostility feared, but secure a wider currency for its opinions. What opinion chiefly needs in America in order to control the politicians is not so much men of leisure, for men of leisure may be dilettantes and may lack a grip of realities, but a more sustained activity on the part of the men of vigorously independent minds, a more sedulous effort on their part to impress their views upon the masses, and a disposition on the part of the ordinary well-meaning but often inattentive citizens to prefer the realities of good administration to outworn party cries.

The Tyranny of the Majority

The expression "tyranny of the majority" is commonly used to denote any abuse by the majority of the powers which they enjoy, in free countries under and through the law, and in all countries outside the law. Such abuse will not be tyrannous in the sense of being illegal, as men called a usurper like Dionysius of Syracuse or Louis Napoleon in France a tyrant, for in free countries whatever the majority chooses to do in the prescribed constitutional way will be legal. It will be tyrannous in the sense of the lines

> O it is excellent
> To have a giant's strength, but it is tyrannous
> To use it like a giant.

That is to say, tyranny consists in the wanton and improper use of strength by the stronger, in the use of it to do things which one equal would not attempt against another. A majority is tyrannical when it decides without hearing the minority, when it suppresses fair and temperate criticism on its own acts, when it insists on restraining men in matters where restraint is not required by the common interest, when it forces men to contribute money to objects which they disapprove and which the common interest does not demand, when it subjects to social penalties persons who disagree from it in matters not vital to the common welfare. The element of tyranny lies in the wantonness of the act, a wantonness springing from the insolence which sense of overwhelming power breeds, or in the fact that it is a misuse for one purpose of authority granted for another. It consists not in the form of the act, which may be perfectly legal, but in the spirit and temper it reveals, and in the sense of injustice and oppression which it evokes in the minority.

Philosophers have long since perceived that the same tendencies to a wanton or unjust abuse of power which exist in a despot or a ruling oligarchy may be expected in a democracy from the ruling majority, because they are tendencies incidental to human nature.[1] The danger was felt and feared by the sages of 1787, and a passage in the *Federalist* (No. 50) dwells on the safeguards which the great size of a federal republic, and the diverse elements of which it will be composed, offer against the tendency of a majority to oppress a minority.

Since Tocqueville dilated upon this as the capital fault of the American government and people, Europeans, already prepared to expect to find the tyranny of the majority a characteristic sin of democratic nations, have been accustomed to think of the United States as disgraced by it, and on the strength of this instance have predicted it as a necessary result of the growth of democracy in the Old World. It is therefore worth while to inquire what foundation exists for the reproach as addressed to the Americans of today.

We may look for signs of this tyranny in three quarters: firstly, in the legislation of Congress; second, in the constitutions and statutes of the states; third, in the action of public opinion and sentiment outside the sphere of law.

The federal Constitution, which has not only limited the competence of Congress but hedged it round with many positive prohibitions, has closed some of the avenues by which a majority might proceed to abuse its powers. Freedom of speech, freedom of religion, opportunities for debate, are all amply secured. The power of taxation, and that of regulating commerce, might conceivably be used to oppress certain classes of persons, as, for instance, if a prohibitory duty were to be laid on certain articles which a minority desired and the majority condemned the use of. But nothing of the sort has been attempted. Whatever may be thought of the expediency of the present tariff, which, no doubt, favours one class, it cannot be said to oppress any class. In its political action, as, for instance, during the struggle over slavery, when for a while it refused to receive Abolitionist petitions, and even tried to prevent the transmission by mail of Abolitionist matter, and again during and after the war in some of its reconstruction measures, the majority, under the pressure of excitement, exercised its powers harshly and unwisely. But such political action is hardly the kind of action to which the charge we are examining applies.

---

[1] The comparison of the majority to a monarch is as old as Aristotle. μόναρχς ὁ δῆμος γίνεται (*Polit.* iv. 4, 26). ὥσπερ τυράννῳ τῷ δήμῳ χαριζόμενοι (*Ibid.* ii. 12, 4). In Greek cities, where the respect for law was weak, a triumphant party frequently overrode the law, just as the tyrants did.

In the states, a majority of the citizens may act either directly in enacting (or amending) a constitution, or through their legislature by passing statutes. We might expect to find instances of abuse of power more in the former than in the latter class of cases, because though the legislature is habitually and the people of the state only intermittently active, the legislatures have now been surrounded by a host of constitutional limitations which a tyrannical majority would need some skill to evade. However, one discovers wonderfully little in the state constitutions now in force of which a minority can complain. These instruments contain a great deal of ordinary law and administrative law. If the tendency to abuse legislative power to the injury of any class were general, instances of it could not fail to appear. One does not find them. There are some provisions strictly regulating corporations, and especially railroads and banks, which may perhaps be unwise, and which in limiting the modes of using capital apply rather to the rich than to the masses. But such provisions cannot be called wanton or oppressive.

The same remark applies to the ordinary statutes of the states, so far as I have been able to ascertain their character. They can rarely be used to repress opinion or its expression, because the state constitutions contain ample guarantees for free speech, a free press, and the right of public meeting. For the same reason, they cannot encroach on the personal liberty of the citizen, nor on the full enjoyment of private property. In all such fundamentals the majority has prudently taken the possible abuse of its power out of the hands of the legislature.

When we come to minor matters, we are met by the difficulty of determining what is a legitimate exercise of legislative authority. Nowhere are men agreed as to the limits of state interference. Some few think that law ought not to restrict the sale of intoxicants at all; many more that it ought not to make the procuring of them, for purposes of pleasure, difficult or impossible. Others hold that the common welfare justifies prohibition. Some deem it unjust to tax a man, and especially an unmarried man, for the support of public schools, or at any rate of public schools other than elementary. To most Roman Catholics it seems unjust to refuse denominational schools a share of the funds raised by taxing, among other citizens, those who hold it a duty to send their children to schools in which their own faith is inculcated. Some think a law tyrannical which forbids a man to exclude others from ground which he keeps waste and barren, while others blame the law which permits a man to reserve, as they think, tyrannically, large tracts of country for his own personal enjoyment. So any form of state establishment or endowment of a particular creed or religious body will by some be deemed an abuse, by others a wise and proper use of state authority. Remembering such differences of opinion, all I can say is that even those who take the narrower view of state functions will find little to censure in the legislation of American states. They may blame the restriction or prohibition of the sale of intoxicants. They may think that the so-called "moral legislation" for securing the purity of literature, and for protecting the young against various temptations, attempts too much. They may question the expediency of the legislation intended for the benefit of working men. But there are few of these provisions which can fairly be called wanton or tyrannical, which display a spirit that ignores or tramples on the feelings or rights of a minority. The least defensible statutes are perhaps those which California has aimed at the Chinese (who are not technically a minority since they are not citizens at all), and those by which some Southern states have endeavoured to accentuate the separation between whites and Negroes, forbidding them to be taught in the same schools or colleges or to travel in the same cars.

We come now to the third way in which a majority may tyrannize, i.e., by the imposition of purely social penalties, from mere disapproval up to insult, injury, and boycotting. The greatest of Athenian statesmen claimed for his countrymen that they set an example to the rest of Greece in that enlightened toleration which does not even visit with black looks those who hold unpopular opinions, or venture in any wise to differ from the prevailing sentiment. Such enlightenment is doubtless one of the latest fruits and crowns of a high civilization, and all the more to be admired when it is not the result of indifference, but coexists with energetic action in the field of politics or religion or social reform.

If social persecution exists in the America of today, it is only in a few dark corners. One may travel all over the North and West, mingling with all classes and reading the newspapers, without hearing of it. As respects religion, so long as one does not openly affront the feelings of one's neighbours, one may say what one likes, and go or not go to church. Doubtless a man, and still more a woman, will be better thought of, especially in a country place or small town, for being a church member and Sunday school teacher. But no one is made to suffer in mind, body, or estate for simply holding aloof from a religious or any other voluntary association. He would be more likely to suffer in an English village. Even in the South, were a stricter standard of orthodoxy is maintained among the clergy of the Protestant bodies than in the North or West, a layman may think as he pleases. It is the same as regards social questions, and of course as regards politics. To boycott a man for his politics, or even to discourage his shop in the way not uncommon in some parts of rural England and Ireland, would excite indignation in America; as the attempts of some labour organizations to boycott firms resisting strikes have aroused strong displeasure. If in the South a man took to cultivating the friendship of Negroes and organizing them in clubs, or if in the Far West a man made himself the champion of the Indians, he might find his life become unpleasant, though one hears little of recent instances of the kind. In any part of the country he who should use his rights of property in a hard or unneighbourly way, who, for instance, should refuse all access to a waterfall or a beautiful point of view, would be reprobated and sent to Coventry. I do not know of such cases; perhaps the fear of general disapproval prevents their arising.

In saying that there is no social persecution, I do not deny that in some places, as, for instance, in the smaller towns of the West, there may sometimes have been too little allowance for difference of tastes and pursuits, too much disposition to expect every family to conform to the same standard of propriety, and follow the same habits of life. A person acting, however innocently, without regard to the beliefs and prejudices of his neighbours might be talked about, and perhaps looked askance upon. Many a man used to the variety of London or Washington would feel the monotony of Western life, and the uniform application of its standards, irksome and even galling. But, so far as I could ascertain, he would have nothing specific to complain of. And these Western towns become every day more like the cities of the East. Taking the country all in all, it is hard to imagine more complete liberty than individuals or groups enjoy either to express and propagate their views, or to act as they please within the limits of the law, limits which, except as regards the sale of intoxicants, are drawn as widely as in Western Europe.

In the earlier half of last century it was very different. Congress was then as now debarred from oppressive legislation. But in some Northern states the legislatures were not slow to deal harshly with persons or societies who ran counter to the dominant sentiment. The persecution by the legislature of Connecticut, as well as by her own townsfolk, of Miss Prudence Crandall, a benevolent Quakeress who had opened a school for Negro children, is a well-remembered instance. A good many rigidly Puritanic statutes stood unrepealed in New England, though not always put in force against the transgressor. In the slave states laws of the utmost severity punished whosoever should by word or act assail the "peculiar institution." Even more tyrannical than the laws was the sentiment of the masses. In Boston a mob, a well-dressed mob, largely composed of the richer sort of people, hunted Garrison for his life through the streets because he was printing an Abolitionist journal; a mob in Illinois shot Elijah Lovejoy for the same offence; and as late as 1844 another Illinois crowd killed Joseph Smith, the Mormon prophet, who, whatever may be thought of his honesty or his doctrines, was as much entitled to the protection of the laws as any other citizen. In the South, as everyone knows, there was a reign of terror as regards slavery. Anyone suspected of Abolitionism might think himself lucky if he escaped with tar and feathers, and was not shot or flogged almost to death. This extreme sensitiveness was of course confined to a few burning questions; but the habit of repressing by law or without law obnoxious opinions was likely to spread, and did spread, at least in the South, to other matters also. As regards thought and opinion generally over the Union, Tocqueville declares:

> Je ne connais pas de pays où il règne, en général, moins d'indépendance d'esprit et de véritable liberté de discussion qu'en Amerique. La majorité trace un cercle formidable autour de la pensée. Au dedans de ces limites, l'écrivain est libre, mais malheur a lui s'il ose en sortir! Ce n'est pas qu'il ait à craindre un auto-da-fé, mais il est en butte à des dégoûts de tout genre et à des persécutions de tous les jours. La carrière politique lui est fermée: il a offensé la seule puissance qui ait la faculté de l'ouvrir. On lui refuse tout, jusqu'à la gloire.—Vol. ii, ch. 7.

He ascribes not only the want of great statesmen, but the low level of literature, learning, and thought, to this total absence of intellectual freedom.

It is hard for anyone who knows the Northern states now to believe that this can have been a just description of them so lately as 1832. One is tempted to think that Tocqueville's somewhat pessimistic friends in New England, mortified by the poverty of intellectual production around them, may have exaggerated the repressive tendencies in which they found the cause of that poverty. We can now see that the explanation was erroneous. Freedom does not necessarily increase fertility. As they erred in their diagnosis, they may have erred in their observation of the symptoms.

Assuming, however, that the description was a just one, how are we to explain the change to the absolute freedom and tolerance of today, when every man may sit under this own vine and fig tree and say and do (provided he drink not the juice of that vine) what he pleases, none making him afraid?

One may suspect that Tocqueville, struck by the enormous power of general opinion, may have attributed too much of the submissiveness which he observed to the active coercion of the majority, and too little to that tendency of the minority to acquiescence which will be discussed in the next succeeding chapter. Setting this aside, however, and assuming that the majority did in those days really tyrannize, several causes may be assigned for its having ceased to do so. One is the absence of violent passions. Slavery, the chief source of ferocity, was to the heated minds of the South a matter of life or death; Abolitionism seemed to many in the North a disloyal heresy, the necessary parent of disunion. Since the Civil War there has been no crisis calculated to tempt majorities to abuse their legal powers. Partisanship has for years past been more intense in Great Britain—not to say Ireland—and France than in America. When Tocqueville saw the United States, the democratic spirit was in the heyday of its youthful strength, flushed with self-confidence, intoxicated with the exuberance of its own freedom. The first generation of statesmen whose authority had restrained the masses, had just quitted the stage. The anarchic teachings of Jefferson had borne fruit. Administration and legislation, hitherto left to the educated classes, had been seized by the rude hands of men of low social position and scanty knowledge. A reign of brutality and violence had set in over large regions of the country. Neither literature nor the universities exercised as yet any sensible power. The masses were so persuaded of their immense superiority to all other peoples, past as well as present, that they would listen to nothing but flattery, and their intolerance spread from politics into every other sphere. Our European philosopher may therefore have been correct in his description of the facts as he saw them: he erred in supposing them essential to a democratic government. As the nation grew, it purged away these faults of youth and inexperience, and the stern discipline of the Civil War taught it sobriety, and in giving it something to be really proud of, cleared away the fumes of self-conceit.

The years which have passed since the war have been years of immensely extended and popularized culture and enlightenment. Bigotry in religion and in everything else has been broken down. The old landmarks have been removed: the habits and methods of free inquiry, if not generally practised, have at least become superficially familiar; the "latest results," as people call them, of European thought have been brought to the knowledge of native Americans more fully than to the masses of Europe. At the same time, as all religious and socio-religious questions, except those which relate to education, are entirely disjoined from politics and the state, neither those who stand by the old views, nor those who embrace the new, carry that bitterness into their controversies which is natural in countries where religious questions are also party questions, where the clergy are a privileged and salaried order, where the throne is held bound to defend the altar, and the workman is taught to believe that both are leagued against him. The influence of these causes will, it may be predicted, be permanent. Should passion again invade politics, or should the majority become convinced that its interests will be secured by overtaxing the few, one can imagine the tendency of fifty years ago reappearing in new forms. But in no imaginable future is there likely to be any attempt to repress either by law or by opinion the free exercise and expression of speculative thought on morals, on religion, and indeed on every matter not within the immediate range of current politics.

If the above account be correct, the tyranny of the majority is no longer a blemish on the American system, and the charges brought against democracy from the supposed example of America are groundless. As tyranny is one of those evils which tends to perpetuate itself, those who had been oppressed revenging themselves by becoming oppressors in their turn, the fact that a danger once dreaded has now disappeared is no small evidence of the recuperative forces of the American government, and the healthy tone of the American people.

The Fatalism of the Multitude

One feature of thought and sentiment in the United States needs special examination because it has been by most observers either ignored or confounded with a phenomenon which is at bottom quite different. This is a fatalistic attitude of mind, which, since it disposes men to acquiesce in the rule of numbers, has been, when perceived, attributed to or identified with what is commonly called the tyranny of the majority. The tendency to fatalism is never far from mankind. It is one of the first solutions of the riddle of the earth propounded by metaphysics. It is one of the last propounded by science. It has at all times formed the background to religions. No race is naturally less disposed to a fatalistic view of things than is the Anglo-American, with its restless self-reliant energy,

Nil actum reputans dum quid restaret agendum,

its slender taste for introspection or meditation. Nevertheless even in this people the conditions of life and politics have bred a sentiment or tendency which seems best described by the name of fatalism.

In small and rude communities, every free man, or at least every head of a household, feels his own significance and realizes his own independence. He relies on himself, he is little interfered with by neighbours or rulers.[1] His will and his action count for something in the conduct of the affairs of the community he belongs to, yet common affairs are few compared to those in which he must depend on his own exertions. The most striking pictures of individualism that literature has preserved for us are those of the

---

[1] The kind of self-reliant attitude I am seeking to describe is quite a different thing from the supposed "state of nature" in which a man has no legal relations with his fellows. It may exist (as in early Rome) among the members of a community closely united by legal ties.

Homeric heroes, and of the even more terrible and self-reliant warriors of the Norse sagas, men like Ragnar Lodbrog and Egil, son of Skallagrim, who did not regard even the gods, but trusted to their own might and main. In more developed states of society organized on an oligarchic basis, such as were the feudal kingdoms of the Middle Ages, or in socially aristocratic countries such as most parts of Europe have remained down to our own time, the bulk of the people are no doubt in a dependent condition, but each person derives a certain sense of personal consequence from the strength of his group and of the person or family at the head of it. Moreover, the upper class, being the class which thinks and writes, as well as leads in action, impresses its own type upon the character of the whole nation, and that type is still individualistic, with a strong consciousness of personal free will, and a tendency for each man, if not to think for himself, at least to value and to rely on his own opinion.

Let us suppose, however, that the aristocratic structure of society has been dissolved, that the old groups have disappeared, that men have come to feel themselves members rather of the nation than of classes, or families, or communities within the nation, that a levelling process has destroyed the ascendency of birth and rank, that large landed estates no longer exist, that many persons in what was previously the humbler class have acquired possession of property, that knowledge is easily accessible and the power of using it not longer confined to the few. Under such conditions of social equality the habit of intellectual command and individual self-confidence will have vanished from the leading class, which creates the type of national character, and will exist nowhere in the nation.

Let us suppose, further, that political equality has gone hand in hand with the levelling down of social eminence. Every citizen enjoys the same right of electing the representatives and officials, the same right of himself becoming a representative or an official. Everyone is equally concerned in the conduct of public affairs, and since no man's opinion, however great his superiority in wealth, knowledge, or personal capacity, is legally entitled to any more weight than another's, no man is entitled to set special value on his own opinion, or to expect others to defer to it; for pretensions to authority will be promptly resented. All disputes are referred to the determination of the majority, there being no legal distinction between the naturally strong and the naturally weak, between the rich and the poor, between the wise and the foolish. In such a state of things the strong man's self-confidence and sense of individual force will inevitably have been lowered, because he will feel that he is only one of many, that his vote or voice counts for no more than that of his neighbour, that he can prevail, if at all, only by keeping himself on a level with his neighbour and recognizing the latter's personality as being every whit equal to his own.

Suppose, further, that all this takes place in an enormously large and populous country, where the governing voters are counted by so many millions that each individual feels himself a mere drop in the ocean, the influence which he can exert privately, whether by his personal gifts or by his wealth, being confined to the small circle of his town or neighbourhood. On all sides there stretches round him an illimitable horizon; and beneath the blue vault which covers that horizon there is everywhere the same busy multitude with its clamour of mingled voices which he hears close by. In this multitude his own being seems lost. He has the sense of insignificance which overwhelms us when at night we survey the host of heaven and know that from even the nearest star this planet of ours is invisible.

In such a country, where complete political equality is strengthened and perfected by complete social equality, where the will of the majority is absolute, unquestioned, always invoked to decide every question, and where the numbers which decide are so vast that one comes to regard them as one regards the largely working forces of nature, we may expect to find certain feelings and beliefs dominant in the minds of men.

One of these is that the majority must prevail. All free government rests on this belief, for there is no other way of working free government. To obey the majority is, therefore, both a necessity and a duty, a duty because the alternative would be ruin and the breaking up of laws.

Out of this dogma there grows up another which is less distinctly admitted, and indeed held rather implicitly than consciously, that the majority is right. And out of both of these there grows again the feeling, still less consciously held, but not less truly operative, that it is vain to oppose or censure the majority.

It may seem that there is a long step from the first of these propositions to the second and third; and that, in fact, the very existence of a minority striving with a majority implies that there must be many who hold the majority to be wrong, and are prepared to resist it. Men do not at once abandon their views because they have been outvoted; they reiterate their views, they reorganize their party, they hope to prevail, and often do prevail in a subsequent trial of strength.

All this is doubtless involved in the very methods of popular government. But it is, nevertheless, true that the belief in the rights of the majority lies very near to the belief that the majority must be right. As self-government is based on the idea that each man is more likely to be right than to be wrong, and that one man's opinion must be treated as equally good with another's, there is a presumption that when twenty thousand vote one way and twenty-one thousand another, the view of the greater number is the better view. The habit of deference to a decision actually given strengthens this presumption, and weaves it into the texture of every mind. A conscientious citizen feels that he ought to obey the determination of the majority, and naturally prefers to think that which he obeys to be right. A citizen languidly interested in the question at issue finds it easier to comply with and adopt the view of the majority than to hold out against it. A small number of men with strong convictions or warm party feeling will, for a time, resist. But even they feel differently towards their cause after it has been defeated from what they did while it had still a prospect of success. They know that in the same proportion in which their supporters are dismayed, the majority is emboldened and confirmed in its views. It will be harder to fight a second battle than it was to fight the first, for there is (so to speak) a steeper slope of popular disapproval to be climbed. Thus, just as at the opening of a campaign, the event of the first collisions between the hostile armies has great significance, because the victory of one is taken as an omen and a presage by both, so in the struggles of parties success at an incidental election works powerfully to strengthen those who succeed, and depress those who fail, for it inspires self-confidence or self-distrust, and it turns the minds of waverers. The very obscurity of the causes which move opinion adds significance to the result. So in the United States, when the elections in any state precede by a few weeks a presidential contest, their effect has sometimes been so great as virtually to determine that contest by filling one side with hope and the other with despondency. Those who prefer to swim with the stream are numerous everywhere, and their votes have as much weight as the votes of the keenest partisans. A man of convictions may insist that the arguments on both sides are after the polling just what they were before. But the average man will repeat his arguments with less faith, less zeal, more of a secret fear that he may be wrong, than he did while the majority was still doubtful; and after every reassertion by the majority of its judgment, his knees grow feebler till at last they refuse to carry him into the combat.

The larger the scale on which the majority works, the more potent are these tendencies. When the scene of action is a small commonwealth, the individual voters are many of them personally known to one another, and the causes which determine their votes are understood and discounted. When it is a moderately sized country, the towns or districts which compose it are not too numerous for reckoning to overtake and imagination to picture them, and in many cases their action can be explained by well-known reasons which may be represented as transitory. But when the theatre stretches itself to a continent, when the number of voters is counted by many millions, the wings of imagination droop, and the huge voting mass ceases to be thought of as merely so many individual human beings no wiser or better than one's own neighbours. The phenomenon seems to pass into the category of the phenomena of nature, governed by far-reaching and inexorable laws whose character science has only imperfectly ascertained, and which she can use only by obeying. It inspires a sort of awe, a sense of individual impotence, like that which man feels when he contemplates the majestic and eternal forces of the inanimate world. Such a feeling is even stronger when it operates, not on a cohesive minority which had lately hoped, or may yet hope, to become a majority, but on a single man or small group of persons cherishing some opinion which the mass disapproves. Thus out of the mingled feelings that the multitude will prevail, and that the multitude, because it will prevail, must be right, there grows a self-distrust, a despondency, a disposition to fall into line, to acquiesce in the dominant opinion, to submit thought as well as action to the encompassing power of numbers. Now and then a resolute man will, like Athanasius, stand alone against the world. But such a man must have, like Athanasius, some special spring of inward strength; and the difficulty of winning over others against the overwhelming weight of the multitude will, even in such a man, dull the edge of hope and enterprise. An individual seeking to make his view prevail, looks forth on his hostile fellow countrymen as a solitary swimmer, raised high on a billow miles from land, looks over the countless waves that divide him from the shore, and quails to think how small the chance that his strength can bear him thither.

This tendency to acquiescence and submission, this sense of the insignificance of individual effort, this belief that the affairs of men are swayed by large forces whose movement may be studied but cannot be turned, I have ventured to call the fatalism of the multitude. It is often confounded with the tyranny of the majority, but is at bottom different, though, of course, its existence makes abuses of power by the majority easier, because less apt to be resented. But the fatalistic attitude I have been seeking to describe does not imply any compulsion exerted by the majority. It may rather seem to soften and make less odious such an exercise of their power, may even dispense with that exercise, because it disposes a minority to submit without the need of a command, to renounce spontaneously its own view and fall in with the view which the majority has expressed. In the fatalism of the multitude there is neither legal nor moral compulsion; there is merely a loss of resisting power, a diminished sense of personal responsibility and of the duty to battle for one's own opinions, such as has been bred in some peoples by the belief in an overmastering fate. It is true that the force to which the citizen of the vast democracy submits is a moral force, not that of an unapproachable Allah, nor of the unchangeable laws of matter. But it is a moral force acting on so vast a scale, and from causes often so obscure, that its effect on the mind of the individual may well be compared with that which religious or scientific fatalism engenders.

No one will suppose that the above sketch is intended to apply literally to the United States, where in some matters legal restrictions check a majority, where local self-government gives the humblest citizen a sphere for public action, where individualism is still in many forms and directions so vigorous. An American explorer, an American settler in new lands, an American man of business pushing a great enterprise, is a being as bold and resourceful as the world has ever seen. All I seek to convey is that there are in the United States signs of such a fatalistic temper, signs which one must expect to find wherever a vast population governs itself under a system of complete social and political equality, and which may grow more frequent as time goes on.

There exist in the American Republic several conditions which specially tend to create such a temper.

One of these is the unbounded freedom of discussion. Every view, every line of policy, has its fair chance before the people. No one can say that audience has been denied him, and comfort himself with the hope that, when he is heard, the world will come round to him. Under a repressive government, the sense of grievance and injustice feeds the flame of resistance in a persecuted minority. But in a country like this, where the freedom of the press, the right of public meeting, the right of association and agitation have been legally extended, and are daily exerted, more widely than anywhere else in the world, there is nothing to awaken that sense. He whom the multitude condemns or ignores has no further court of appeal to look to. Rome has spoken. His cause has been heard and judgment has gone against him.

Another is the intense faith which the Americans have in the soundness of their institutions, and in the future of their country. Foreign critics have said that they think themselves the special objects of the care of Divine

Providence. If this be so, it is matter neither for surprise nor for sarcasm. They are a religious people. They are trying, and that on the largest scale, the most remarkable experiment in government the world has yet witnessed. They have more than once been surrounded by perils which affrighted the stoutest hearts, and they have escaped from these perils into peace and prosperity. There is among pious persons a deep conviction—one may often hear it expressed on platforms and from pulpits with evident sincerity—that God has specially chosen the nation to work out a higher type of civilization than any other state has yet attained, and that this great work will surely be brought to a happy issue by the protecting hand that has so long guided it. And, even when the feeling does not take a theological expression, the belief in what is called the "mission of the Republic" for all humanity is scarcely less ardent. But the foundation of the Republic is confidence in the multitude, in its honesty and good sense, in the certainty of its arriving at right conclusions. Pessimism is the luxury of a handful; optimism is the private delight, as well as public profession, of nine hundred and ninety-nine out of every thousand, for nowhere does the individual associate himself more constantly and directly with the greatness of his country.

Now, such a faith in the people, and in the forces that sway them, disposes a man to acquiescence and submission. He cannot long hold that he is right and the multitude wrong. He cannot suppose that the country will ultimately suffer because it refuses to adopt what he urges upon it. As he comes of an energetic stock, he will use all proper means to state his views, and give them every chance of prevailing. But he submits more readily than an Englishman would do, ay, even to what an Englishman would think an injury to his private rights. When his legal right has been infringed, he will confidently proceed to enforce at law his claim to redress, knowing that even against the government a just cause will prevail. But if he fails at law, the sense of his individual insignificance will still his voice. It may seem a trivial illustration to observe that when a railway train is late, or a waggon drawn up opposite a warehouse door stops the streetcar for a few minutes, the passengers take the delay far more coolly and uncomplain-ingly than Englishmen would do. But the feeling is the same as that which makes good citizens bear with the tyranny of bosses. It is all in the course of nature. Others submit; why should one man resist? What is he that he should make a fuss because he loses a few minutes, or is taxed too highly? The sense of the immense multitude around him presses down the individual; and, after all, he reflects, "things will come out right" in the end.

It is hard adequately to convey the impression which the vastness of the country and the swift growth of its population make upon the European traveller. I well remember how it once came on me after climbing a high mountain in an Eastern state. All around was thick forest; but the setting sun lit up peaks sixty or seventy miles away, and flashed here and there on the windings of some river past a town so far off as to seem only a spot of white. I opened my map, a large map, which I had to spread upon the rocks to examine, and tried to make out, as one would have done in England or Scotland, the points in the view. The map, however, was useless, because the whole area of the landscape beneath me covered only two or three square inches upon it. From such a height in Scotland the eye would have ranged from sea to sea. But here when one tried to reckon how many more equally wide stretches of landscape lay between this peak and the Mississippi, which is itself only a third of the way across the continent, the calculation seemed endless and was soon abandoned. Many an Englishman comes by middle life to know nearly all England like a glove. He has travelled on all the great railroads; there is hardly a large town in which he has not acquaintances, hardly a county whose scenery is not familiar to him. But no American can be familiar with more than a small part of his country, for his country is a continent. And all Americans live their life through under the sense of this prodigious and daily growing multitude around them, which seems vaster the more you travel, and the more you realize its uniformity.

We need not here inquire whether the fatalistic attitude I have sought to sketch is the source of more good or evil. It seems at any rate inevitable; nor does it fail to produce a sort of pleasure, for what the individual loses as an individual he seems in a measure to regain as one of the multitude. If the individual is not strong, he is at any rate as strong as anyone else. His will counts for as much as any other will. He is overborne by no superiority. Most men are fitter to make part of the multitude than to strive against it. Obedience is to most sweeter than independence; the Roman Catholic church inspires in its children a stronger affection than any form of Protestantism, for she takes their souls in charge, and assures them that, with obedience, all will be well.

That which we are presently concerned to note is how greatly such a tendency as I have described facilitates the action of opinion as a governing power, enabling it to prevail more swiftly and more completely than in countries where men have not yet learned to regard the voice of the multitude as the voice of fate. Many submit willingly; some unwillingly, yet they submit. Rarely does anyone hold out and venture to tell the great majority of his countrymen that they are wrong.

Moreover, public opinion acquires a solidity which strengthens the whole body politic. Questions on which the masses have made up their minds pass out of the region of practical discussion. Controversy is confined to minor topics, and however vehemently it may rage over these, it disturbs the great underlying matters of agreement no more than a tempest stirs the depths of the Atlantic. Public order becomes more easily maintained, because individuals and small groups have learned to submit even when they feel themselves aggrieved. The man who murmurs against the world, who continues to preach a hopeless cause, incurs contempt, and is apt to be treated as a sort of lunatic. He who is too wise to murmur and too proud to go on preaching to unheeding ears, comes to think that if his doctrine is true, yet the time is not ripe for it. He may be in error; but if he is right, the world will ultimately see that he is right even without his effort. One way or another he finds it hard to believe that this vast mass and force of popular thought in which he lives and moves can be ultimately wrong. *Securus judicat orbis terrarum*.

Wherein Public Opinion Fails

Without anticipating the criticism of democratic government to be given in a later chapter, we may wind up the examination of public opinion by considering what are its merits as a governing and overseeing power, and, on the other hand, what defects, due either to inherent weakness or to the want of appropriate machinery, prevent it from attaining the ideal which the Americans have set before themselves. I begin with the defects.

The obvious weakness of government by opinion is the difficulty of ascertaining it. English administrators in India lament the impossibility of learning the sentiments of the natives, because in the East the populations, the true masses, are dumb. The press is written by a handful of persons who, in becoming writers have ceased to belong to the multitude, and the multitude does not read. The difficulties of Western statesmen are due to an opposite cause. The populations are highly articulate. Such is the din of voices that it is hard to say which cry prevails, which is swelled by many, which only by a few, throats. The organs of opinion seem almost as numerous as the people themselves, and they are all engaged in representing their own view as that of the "people." Like other valuable articles, genuine opinion is surrounded by many counterfeits. The one positive test applicable is that of an election, and an election can at best do no more than test the division of opinion between two or three great parties, leaving subsidiary issues uncertain, while in many cases the result depends so much on the personal merits of the candidates as to render interpretation difficult. An American statesman is in no danger of consciously running counter to public opinion, but how is he to discover whether any particular opinion is making or losing way, how is he to gauge the voting strength its advocates can put forth, or the moral authority which its advocates can exert? Elections cannot be further multiplied, for they are too numerous already. The referendum, or plan of submitting a specific question to the popular vote, is the logical resource, but it is troublesome and costly to take the votes of millions of people over an area so large as that of one of the greater states; much more then is this method difficult to apply in federal matters. This is the first drawback to the rule of public opinion. The choice of persons for offices is only an indirect and often unsatisfactory way of declaring views of policy, and as the elections at which such choices are made come at fixed intervals, time is lost in waiting for the opportunity of delivering the popular judgment.

The framers of the American Constitution may not have perceived that in labouring to produce a balance, as well between the national and state governments as between the executive and Congress, in weakening each single authority in the Government by dividing powers and functions among each of them, they were throwing upon the nation at large, that is, upon unorganized public opinion, more work than it had ever discharged in England, or could duly discharge in a country so divided by distances and jealousies as the United States then were. Distances and jealousies have been lessened. But as the progress of democracy has increased the self-distrust and submission to the popular voice of legislators, so the defects incident to a system of restrictions and balances have been aggravated. Thus the difficulty inherent in government by public opinion makes itself seriously felt. It can express desires, but has not the machinery for turning them into practical schemes. It can determine ends, but is less fit to examine and select means. Yet it has weakened the organs by which the business of finding appropriate means ought to be discharged.

American legislatures are bodies with limited powers and sitting for short terms. Their members are less qualified for the work of constructive legislation, than are those of most European chambers. They are accustomed to consider themselves delegates from their respective states and districts, responsible to those districts, rather than councillors of the whole nation labouring for its general interests; and they have no executive leaders, seeing that no official sits either in Congress or in a state legislature. Hence if at any time the people desire measures which do not merely repeal a law or direct an appropriation, but establish some administrative scheme, or mark out some positive line of financial policy, or provide some body of rules for dealing with such a topic as bankruptcy, railroad or canal communications, the management of public lands, and so forth, the people cannot count on having their wishes put into tangible workable shape. When members of Congress or of a state legislature think the country desires legislation, they begin to prepare bills, but the want of leadership and of constructive skill often prevents such bills from satisfying the needs of the case, and a timidity which fears to go beyond what opinion desires, may retard the accomplishment of the public wish; while, in the case of state legislatures, constructive skill is seldom present. Public opinion is slow and clumsy in grappling with large problems. It looks at them, talks incessantly about them, complains of Congress for not solving them, is distressed that they do not solve themselves. But they remain unsolved. Vital decisions have usually hung fire longer than they would have been likely to do in European countries. The war of 1812 seemed on the point of breaking out over and over again before it came at last. The absorption of Texas was a question of many years. The extension of slavery question came before the nation in 1819; after 1840 it was the chief source of trouble; year by year it grew more menacing; year by year the nation was seen more clearly to be drifting towards the breakers. Everybody felt that something must be done. But it was the function of no one authority in particular to discover a remedy, as it would have been the function of a cabinet in Europe. I do not say the sword might not in any case have been invoked, for the temperature of Southern feeling had been steadily rising to war point. But the history of 1840–60 leaves an impression of the dangers which may result from fettering the constitutional organs of government, and trusting to public sentiment to bring things right. Some other national questions, less dangerous, but serious, are now in the same condition. The currency question has been an incessant source of disquiet, and it is now many years since the campaign against trusts began. The question of reducing the surplus national revenue puzzled statesmen and the people at large longer than a similar question would be suffered to do in Europe, and when solved in 1890 by the passage of the dependent pension bill, was solved to the public injury in a purely demagogic or electioneering spirit. I doubt whether any European legislature would have so openly declined the duty of considering the interests of the country, and abandoned itself so undisguisedly to the pursuit of the votes of a particular section of the population. And the same thing holds, *mutatis mutandis*, of state governments. In them also there is no set of persons whose special duty it is to find remedies for admitted evils. The structure of the government provides the requisite machinery neither for forming nor for guiding a popular opinion, disposed of itself to recognize only broad and patent facts, and to be swayed only by such obvious reasons as it needs little reflection to follow. Admirable practical acuteness, admirable ingenuity in inventing and handling machinery, whether of iron and wood or of human beings, coexist, in the United States, with an aversion to the investigation of general principles as well as to trains of systematic reasoning.[1] The liability to be caught by fallacies, the inability to recognize facts which are not seen but must be inferentially found to exist, the incapacity to imagine a future which must result from the unchecked operation of present forces, these are indeed the defects of the ordinary citizen in all countries, and if they are conspicuous in America, it is only because the ordinary citizen, who is more intelligent there than elsewhere, is also more potent.

It may be replied to these observations, which are a criticism as well upon the American frame of government as upon public opinion, that the need for constructive legislation is small in America, because the habit of the country is to leave things to themselves. This is not really the fact. A great state has always problems of administration to deal with; these problems do not become less grave as time runs on, and the hand of government has for years past been more and more invoked in America for many purposes thought to be of common utility with which legislation did not formerly intermeddle.

There is more force in the remark that we must remember how much is gained as well as lost by the slow and hesitating action of public opinion in the United States. So tremendous a force would be dangerous if it moved rashly. Acting over and gathered from an enormous area, in which there exist many local differences, it needs time, often a long time, to become conscious of the preponderance of one set of tendencies over another. The elements both of local difference and of class difference must be (so to speak) well shaken up together, and each part brought into contact with the rest, before the mixed liquid can produce a precipitate in the form of a practical conclusion. And in this is seen the difference between the excellence as a governing power of opinion in the whole Union, and opinion within the limits of a particular state. The systems of constitutional machinery by which public sentiment acts are similar in the greater and in the smaller area; the constitutional maxims practically identical. But public opinion, which moves slowly, and, as a rule, temperately, in the field of national affairs, is sometimes hasty and reckless in state affairs. The population of a state may be of one colour, as that of the Northwestern states is preponderantly agricultural, or may contain few persons of education and political knowledge, or may fall under the influence of a demagogue or a clique, or may be possessed by some local passion. Thus its opinion may

---

[1] To say this is not to ignore the influence exercised on the national mind by the "glittering generalities" of the Declaration of Independence; nor the theoretical grounds taken up for and against states' rights and slavery, and especially the highly logical scheme excogitated by Calhoun.

want breadth, sobriety, wisdom, and the result be seen in imprudent or unjust measures. The constitution of California of 1879, the legislation of Illinois, Iowa, and Wisconsin, which beginning with the Granger movement has from time to time annoyed and harassed the railroads without establishing a useful control over them, the tampering with their public debts by several states, are familiar instances of follies, to use no harder name, which local opinion approved, but which would have been impossible in the federal government, where the controlling opinion is that of a large and complex nation, and where the very deficiencies of one section or one class serve to correct qualities which may exist in excess in some other.

The sentiment of the nation at large, being comparatively remote, acts but slowly in restraining the vagaries or curing the faults of one particular state. The dwellers on the Pacific coast care very little for the criticism of the rest of the country on their anti-Hindu or anti-Japanese violence; Pennsylvania and Virginia disregarded the best opinions of the Union when they so dealt with their debts as to affect their credit; those parts of the South in which homicide goes unpunished, except by the relatives of the slain, are unmoved by the reproaches and jests of the more peaceable and well-regulated states. The fact shows how deep the division of the country into self-governing commonwealths goes, making men feel that they have a right to do what they will with their own, so long as the power remains to them, whatever may be the purely moral pressure from those who, though they can advise, have no title to interfere. And it shows also, in the teeth of the old doctrine that republicanism was fit for small communities, that evils peculiar to a particular district, which might be ruinous in that district if it stood alone, become less dangerous when it forms part of a vast country.

We may go on to ask how far American opinion succeeds in the simpler duty, which opinion must discharge in all countries, of supervising the conduct of business, and judging the current legislative work which Congress and other legislatures turn out.

Here again the question turns not so much on the excellence of public opinion as on the adequacy of the constitutional machinery provided for its action. That supervision and criticism may be effective, it must be easy to fix on particular persons the praise for work well done, the blame for work neglected or ill-performed. Experience shows that good men are the better for a sense of their responsibility and ordinary men useless without it. The free governments of Europe and the British colonies have gone on the principle of concentrating power in order to be able to fix responsibility. The American plan of dividing powers, eminent as are its other advantages, makes it hard to fix responsibility. The executive can usually allege that it had not received from the legislature the authority necessary to enable it to grapple with a difficulty; while in the legislature there is no one person or group of persons on whom the blame due for that omission or refusal can be laid. Suppose some gross dereliction of duty to have occurred. The people are indignant. A victim is wanted, who, for the sake of the example to others, ought to be found and punished, either by law or by general censure. But perhaps he cannot be found, because out of several persons or bodies who have been concerned, it is hard to apportion the guilt and award the penalty. Where the sin lies at the door of Congress, it is not always possible to arraign either the Speaker or the dominant majority, or any particular party leader. Where a state legislature or a city council has misconducted itself, the difficulty is greater, because party ties are less strict in such a body, proceedings are less fully reported, and both parties are apt to be equally implicated in the abuses of private legislation. Not uncommonly there is presented the sight of an exasperated public going about like a roaring lion, seeking whom it may devour, and finding no one. The results in state affairs would be much worse were it not for the existence of the governor with his function of vetoing bills, because in many cases, knowing that he can be made answerable for the passage of a bad measure, he is forced up to the level of a virtue beyond that of the natural man in politics. This tendency to look to him has recently tended to increase his power; and the disposition to seek a remedy for municipal misgovernment in enlarging the functions of the mayor illustrates the same principle.

Although the failures of public opinion in overseeing the conduct of its servants are primarily due to the want of appropriate machinery, they are increased by its characteristic temper. Quick and strenuous in great matters, it is heedless in small matters, overkindly and indulgent in all matters. It suffers weeds to go on growing till they have struck deep root. It has so much to do in looking after both Congress and its state legislature, a host of executive officials, and perhaps a city council also, that it may impartially tolerate the misdoings of all till some important issue arises. Even when jobs are exposed by the press, each particular job seems below the attention of a busy people or the anger of a good-natured people, till the sum total of jobbery becomes a scandal. To catch and to hold the attention of the people is the chief difficulty as well as the first duty of an American reformer.

The long-suffering tolerance of public opinion towards incompetence and misconduct in officials and public men generally, is a feature which has struck recent European observers. It is the more remarkable because nowhere is executive ability more valued in the management of private concerns, in which the stress of competition forces every manager to secure at whatever price the most able subordinates. We may attribute it partly to the good nature of the people, which makes them overlenient to nearly all criminals, partly to the preoccupation with their private affairs of the most energetic and useful men, who therefore cannot spare time to unearth abuses and get rid of offenders, partly to an indifference induced by the fatalistic sentiment which I have already sought to describe. This fatalism acts in two ways. Being optimistic, it disposes each man to believe that things will come out right whether he "takes hold" himself or not, and that it is therefore no great matter whether a particular ring or boss is suppressed. And in making each individual man feel his insignificance, it disposes him to leave to the multitude the task of setting right what is everyone else's business just as much as his own. An American does not smart under the same sense of personal wrong from the mismanagement of his public business, from the exaction of high city taxes and their malversation, as an Englishman would in the like case. If he suffers, he consoles himself by thinking that he suffers with others, as part of the general order of things, which he is no more called upon than his neighbours to correct.

It may be charged as a weak point in the rule of public opinion, that by fostering this habit it has chilled activity and dulled the sense of responsibility among the leaders in political life. It has made them less eager and strenuous in striking out ideas and plans of their own, less bold in propounding those plans, more sensitive to the reproach, even more feared in America than in England, of being a crotchet-monger or a doctrinaire. That new or unpopular ideas are more frequently started by isolated thinkers, economists, social reformers, than by statesmen, may be set down to the fact that practical statesmanship indisposes men to theorizing. But in America the practical statesman is apt to be timid in advocacy as well as infertile in suggestion. He seems to be always listening for the popular voice, always afraid to commit himself to a view which may turn out unpopular. It is a fair conjecture that this may be due to his being by his profession a far more habitual worshipper as well as observer of public opinion, than will be the case with men who are by profession thinkers and students, men who are less purely Americans of today, because under the influence of the literature of past times as well as of contemporary Europe. Philosophy, taking the word to include the historical study of the forces which work upon mankind at large, is needed by a statesman not only as a consolation for the disappointments of his career, but as a corrective to the superstitions and tremors which the service of the multitude implants.

The enormous force of public opinion is a danger to the people themselves, as well as to their leaders. It no longer makes them tyrannical, but it fills them with an undue confidence in their wisdom, their virtue, and their freedom. It may be thought that a nation which uses freedom well can hardly have too much freedom; yet even such a nation may be too much inclined to think freedom an absolute and all-sufficient good, to seek truth only in the voice of the majority, to mistake prosperity for greatness. Such a nation, seeing nothing but its own triumphs, and hearing nothing but its own praises, seems to need a succession of men like the prophets of Israel to rouse the people out of their self-complacency, to refresh their moral ideals, to remind them that the life is more than meat, and the body more than raiment, and that to whom much is given of them shall much also be required. If America has no prophets of this order, she fortunately possesses two classes of men who maintain a wholesome irritation such as that which Socrates thought it his function to apply to the Athenian people. These are the instructed critics who exert a growing influence on opinion through the higher newspapers, and by literature generally, and the philanthropic reformers who tell more directly upon the multitude, particularly through the churches. Both classes combined may not as yet be doing all that is needed. But the significant point is that their influence represents not an ebbing but a flowing tide. If the evils they combat exist on a larger scale than in past times, they, too, are more active and more courageous in rousing and reprehending their fellow countrymen.

Wherein Public Opinion Succeeds

I n the examination of the actualities of politics as well as of forms of government, faults are more readily perceived than merits. Everybody is struck by the mistakes which a ruler makes, or by evils which a constitution fails to avert, while less praise than is due may be bestowed in respect of the temptations that have been resisted, or the prudence with which the framers of the government have avoided defects from which other countries suffer. Thus the general prosperity of the United States and the success of their people in all kinds of private enterprises, philanthropic as well as gainful, throws into relief the blemishes of their government, and makes it the more necessary to point out in what respects the power of public opinion overcomes those blemishes, and maintains a high level of good feeling and well-being in the nation.

The European observer of the working of American institutions is apt to sum up his conclusions in two contrasts. One is between the excellence of the Constitution and the vices of the party system that has laid hold of it, discovered its weak points, and brought in a swarm of evils. The Fathers, he says, created the Constitution good, but their successors have sought out many inventions.[1] The other contrast is between the faults of the political class and the merits of the people at large. The men who work the machine are often selfish and unscrupulous. The people, for whose behoof it purports to be worked, and who suffer themselves to be "run" by the politicians, are honest, intelligent, fair-minded. No such contrast exists anywhere else in the world. Either the politicians are better than they are in America, or the people are worse.

---

[1] Though some at least of the faults of the party system are directly due to the structure of the Constitution.

The causes of this contrast, which to many observers has seemed the capital fact of American politics, have been already explained. It brings out the truth, on which too much stress cannot be laid, that the strong point of the American system, the dominant fact of the situation, is the healthiness of public opinion, and the control which it exerts. As Abraham Lincoln said in his famous contest with Douglas, "With public sentiment on its side, everything succeeds; with public sentiment against it, nothing succeeds."

The conscience and common sense of the nation as a whole keep down the evils which have crept into the working of the Constitution, and may in time extinguish them. Public opinion is a sort of atmosphere, fresh, keen, and full of sunlight, like that of the American cities, and this sunlight kills many of those noxious germs which are hatched where politicians congregate. That which, varying a once famous phrase, we may call the genius of universal publicity, has some disagreeable results, but the wholesome ones are greater and more numerous. Selfishness, injustice, cruelty, tricks, and jobs of all sorts shun the light; to expose them is to defeat them. No serious evils, no rankling sore in the body politic, can remain long concealed, and when disclosed, it is half destroyed. So long as the opinion of a nation is sound, the main lines of its policy cannot go far wrong, whatever waste of time and money may be incurred in carrying them out. It was observed in the last chapter that opinion is too vague and indeterminate a thing to be capable of considering and selecting the best means for the end on which it has determined. The counterpart of that remark is that the opinion of a whole nation, a united and tolerably homogeneous nation, is, when at last it does express itself, the most competent authority to determine the ends of national policy.[2] In European countries, legislatures and cabinets sometimes take decisions which the nation, which had scarcely thought of the matter till the decision has been taken, is ultimately found to disapprove. In America, men feel that the nation is the only power entitled to say what it wants, and that, till it has manifested its wishes, nothing must be done to commit it. It may sometimes be long in speaking, but when it speaks, it speaks with a weight which the wisest governing class cannot claim.

The frame of the American government has assumed and trusted to the

---

[2] The distinction between means and ends is, of course, one which it is hard to draw in practice, because most ends are means to some larger end which embraces them. Still if we understand by ends the main and leading objects of national policy, including the spirit in which the government ought to be administered, we shall find that these are, if sometimes slowly, yet more clearly apprehended in America than in Europe, and less frequently confounded with subordinate and transitory issues.

activity of public opinion, not only as the power which must correct and remove the difficulties due to the restrictions imposed on each department, and to possible collisions between them, but as the influence which must supply the defects incidental to a system which works entirely by the machinery of popular elections. Under a system of elections one man's vote is as good as another, the vicious and ignorant have as much weight as the wise and good. A system of elections might be imagined which would provide no security for due deliberation or full discussion, a system which, while democratic in name, recognizing no privilege, and referring everything to the vote of the majority, would in practice be hasty, violent, tyrannical. It is with such a possible democracy that one has to contrast the rule of public opinion as it exists in the United States. Opinion declares itself legally through elections. But opinion is at work at other times also, and has other methods of declaring itself. It secures full discussion of issues of policy and of the characters of men. It suffers nothing to be concealed. It listens patiently to all the arguments that are addressed to it. Eloquence, education, wisdom, the authority derived from experience and high character, tell upon it in the long run, and have, perhaps not always their due influence, but yet a great and growing influence. Thus a democracy governing itself through a constantly active public opinion, and not solely by its intermittent mechanism of elections, tends to become patient, tolerant, reasonable, and is more likely to be unembittered and unvexed by class divisions.

It is the existence of such a public opinion as this, the practice of freely and constantly reading, talking, and judging of public affairs with a view to voting thereon, rather than the mere possession of political rights, that gives to popular government that educative and stimulative power which is so frequently claimed as its highest merit. Those who, in the last generation, were forced to argue for democratic government against oligarchies or despots, were perhaps inclined, if not to exaggerate the value of extended suffrage and a powerful legislature, at least to pass too lightly over the concomitant conditions by whose help such institutions train men to use liberty well. History does not support the doctrine that the mere enjoyment of power fits large masses of men, any more than individuals or classes, for its exercise. Along with that enjoyment there must be found some one or more of various auspicious conditions, such as a direct and fairly equal interest in the common welfare, the presence of a class or group of persons respected and competent to guide, an absence of religious or race hatreds, a high level of education, or at least of intelligence, old habits of local self-government, the practice of unlimited free discussion. In America it is not simply the habit of voting but the briskness and breeziness of the whole atmosphere of public life, and the process of obtaining information and discussing it, of hearing and judging each side, that form the citizen's intelligence. True it is that he would not gain much from this process did it not lead up to the exercise of voting power: he would not learn so much on the road did not the polling booth stand at the end of it. But if it were his lot, as it is that of the masses in some European countries, to exercise his right of suffrage under few of these favouring conditions, the educational value of the vote would become comparatively small. It is the habit of breathing as well as helping to form public opinion that cultivates, develops, trains the average American. It gives him a sense of personal responsibility stronger, because more constant, than exists in those free countries of Europe where he commits his power to a legislature. Sensible that his eye ought to be always fixed on the conduct of affairs, he grows accustomed to read and judge, not indeed profoundly, sometimes erroneously, usually under party influences, but yet with a feeling that the judgment is his own. He has a sense of ownership in the government, and therewith a kind of independence of manner as well as of mind very different from the demissness of the humbler classes of the Old World. And the consciousness of responsibility which goes along with this laudable pride, brings forth the peaceable fruits of moderation. As the Greeks thought that the old families ruled their households more gently than upstarts did, so citizens who have been born to power, born into an atmosphere of legal right and constitutional authority, are sobered by their privileges. Despite their natural quickness and eagerness, the native Americans are politically patient. They are disposed to try soft means first, to expect others to bow to that force of opinion which they themselves recognize. Opposition does not incense them; danger does not, by making them lose their heads, hurry them into precipitate courses. In no country does a beaten minority take a defeat so well. Admitting that the blood of the race counts for something in producing that peculiar coolness and self-control in the midst of an external effervescence of enthusiasm, which is the most distinctive feature of the American masses, the habit of ruling by public opinion and obeying it counts for even more. It was far otherwise in the South before the war, but the South was not a democracy, and its public opinion was that of a passionate class.

The best evidence for this view is to be found in the educative influence of opinion on newcomers. Anyone can see how severe a strain is put on democratic institutions by the influx every year of nearly a million of untrained Europeans. Being in most states admitted to full civic rights before they have come to shake off European notions and habits, these strangers enjoy political power before they either share or are amenable to American opinion.[3] They follow blindly leaders of their own race, are not moved by discussion, exercise no judgment of their own. This lasts for some years, probably for the rest of life with those who are middle-aged when they arrive. It lasts also with those who, belonging to the more backward races, remain herded together in large masses, and makes them a dangerous element in manufacturing and mining districts. But the younger sort, when, if they be foreigners, they have learnt English, and when, dispersed among Americans so as to be able to learn from them, they have imbibed the sentiments and assimilated the ideas of the country, are thenceforth scarcely to be distinguished from the native population. They are more American than the Americans in their desire to put on the character of their new country. This peculiar gift which the Republic possesses of quickly dissolving and assimilating the foreign bodies that are poured into her, imparting to them her own qualities of orderliness, good sense, and a willingness to bow to the will of the majority, is mainly due to the all-pervading force of opinion, which the newcomer, so soon as he has formed social and business relations with the natives, breathes in daily till it insensibly transmutes him. Their faith, and a sentiment of resentment against England, long kept among the Irish a body of separate opinion, which for a time resisted the solvent power of its American environment. But the public schools finished the work of the factory and the newspapers. The Irish immigrant's son is now an American citizen for all purposes.

It is chiefly the faith in publicity that gives to the American public their peculiar buoyancy, and what one may call their airy hopefulness in discussing even the weak points of their system. They are always telling you that they have no skeleton closets, nothing to keep back. They know, and are content that all the world should know, the worst as well as the best of themselves. They have a boundless faith in free inquiry and full discussion. They admit the possibility of any number of temporary errors and delusions. But to suppose that a vast nation should, after hearing everything, canvassing everything, and trying all the preliminary experiments it has a mind to, ultimately go wrong by mistaking its own true interests, seems to them a sort of blasphemy against the human intelligence and its Creator.

They claim for opinion that its immense power enables them to get on with but little government. Some evils which the law and its officers are in

---

[3] As to recent immigrants, see further in Chapter 92.

other countries required to deal with are here averted or cured by the mere force of opinion, which shrivels them up when its rays fall on them. As it is not the product of any one class, and is unwilling to recognize classes at all, for it would stand self-condemned as un-American if it did, it discourages anything in the nature of class legislation. Where a particular section of the people, such, for instance, as the Western farmers or the Eastern operatives, think themselves aggrieved, they clamour for the measures thought likely to help them. The farmers legislated against the railroads, the labour party asks an eight-hour law. But whereas on the European continent such a class would think and act as a class, hostile to other classes, and might resolve to pursue its own objects at whatever risk to the nation, in America national opinion, which everyone recognizes as the arbiter, mitigates these feelings, and puts the advocates of the legislation which any class demands upon showing that their schemes are compatible with the paramount interest of the whole community. To say that there is no legislation in America which, like the class legislation of Europe, has thrown undue burdens on the poor, while jealously guarding the pleasures and pockets of the rich, is to say little, because where the poorer citizens have long been a numerical majority, invested with political power, they will evidently take care of themselves. But the opposite danger might have been feared, that the poor would have turned the tables on the rich, thrown the whole burden of taxation upon them, and disregarded in the supposed interest of the masses what are called the rights of property. Not only has this not been attempted—it has been scarcely even suggested (except, of course, by professed Collectivists as part of a reconstruction of society), and it excites no serious apprehension. There is nothing in the machinery of government that could do more than delay it for a time, did the masses desire it. What prevents it is the honesty and common sense of the citizens generally, who are convinced that the interests of all classes are substantially the same, and that justice is the highest of those interests. Equality, open competition, a fair field to everybody, every stimulus to industry, and every security for its fruits, these they hold to be the self-evident principles of national prosperity.

If public opinion is heedless in small things, it usually checks measures which, even if not oppressive, are palpably selfish or unwise. If before a mischievous bill passes, its opponents can get the attention of the people fixed upon it, its chances are slight. All sorts of corrupt or pernicious schemes which are hatched at Washington or in the state legislatures are abandoned because it is felt that the people will not stand them, although they could be easily pushed through those not too scrupulous assemblies.

There have been instances of proposals which took people at first by their plausibility, but which the criticism of opinion riddled with its unceasing fire till at last they were quietly dropped. It was in this way that President Grant's attempt to annex San Domingo failed. He had made a treaty for the purpose, which fell through for want of the requisite two-thirds majority in the Senate, but he persisted in the scheme until at last the disapproval of the general public, which had grown stronger by degrees and found expression through the leading newspapers, warned him to desist. After the war, there was at first in many quarters a desire to punish the Southern leaders for what they had made the North suffer. But by degrees the feeling died away, the sober sense of the whole North restraining the passions of those who had counselled vengeance; and, as everyone knows, there was never a civil war or rebellion, whichever one is to call it, followed by so few severities.

Public opinion often fails to secure the appointment of the best men to places, but where undivided responsibility can be fixed on the appointing authority, it prevents, as those who are behind the scenes know, countless bad appointments for which politicians intrigue. Considering the power of party managers over the federal executive, and the low sense of honour and public duty as regards patronage among politicians, the leading posts are filled, if not by the most capable men, yet seldom by bad ones. The judges of the Supreme Court, for instance, are, and have always been, men of high professional standing and stainless character. The same may be, though less generally, said of the upper federal officials in the North and West. That no similar praise can be bestowed on the exercise of federal patronage in the Southern states since the war, is an illustration of the view I am stating. As the public opinion of the South (that is to say, of the whites who make opinion there) was steadily hostile to the Republican party, which commanded the executive during the twenty years from 1865 to 1885, the Republican party managers were indifferent to it, because they had nothing to gain or to lose from it. Hence they made appointments without regard to it. Northern opinion knows comparatively little of the details of Southern politics and the character of officials who act there, so that they might hope to escape the censure of their supporters in the North. Hence they jobbed their patronage in the South with unblushing cynicism, using federal posts there as a means not merely of rewarding party services, but also of providing local white leaders and organizers to the coloured Southern Republicans. Their different behaviour there and in the North therefore showed that it was not public virtue, but the fear of public opinion, that was making their

Northern appointments on the whole respectable, while those in the South were at that time so much the reverse. The same phenomenon has been noticed in Great Britain. Jobs are frequent and scandalous in the inverse ratio of the notice they are likely to attract.[4]

In questions of foreign policy, opinion is a valuable reserve force. When demonstrations are made by party leaders intended to capture the vote of some particular section, the native Americans only smile. But they watch keenly the language held and acts done by the State Department (Foreign Office), and, while determined to support the president in vindicating the rights of American citizens, would be found ready to check any demand or act going beyond their legal rights which could tend to embroil them with a foreign power. There is still a touch of spread-eagleism and an occasional want of courtesy and taste among public speakers and journalists when they refer to other countries; and there is a determination in all classes to keep European interference at a distance. But among the ordinary native citizens one finds (I think) less obtrusive selfishness, less chauvinism, less cynicism in declaring one's own national interests to be paramount to those of other states, than in any of the great states of Europe. Justice and equity are more generally recognized as binding upon nations no less than on individuals. Whenever humanity comes into question, the heart of the people is sound. The treatment of the Indians reflects little credit on the Western settlers who have come in contact with them, and almost as little on the federal government, whose efforts to protect them have been often foiled by the faults of its own agents, or by its own want of promptitude and foresight. But the wish of the people at large has always been to deal generously with the aborigines, nor have appeals on their behalf, such as those made by the late Mrs. Helen Jackson, ever failed to command the sympathy and assent of the country.

Throughout these chapters I have been speaking chiefly of the Northern states and chiefly of recent years, for America is a country which changes fast. But the conduct of the Southern people, since their defeat in 1865, illustrates the tendency of underlying national traits to reassert themselves when disturbing conditions have passed away. Before the war the public

---

[4] It has often been remarked that posts of the same class are more jobbed by the British executive in Scotland than in England, and in Ireland than in Scotland, because it is harder to rouse Parliament, which in Great Britain discharges much of the function which public opinion discharges in America, to any interest in an appointment made in one of the smaller countries. In Great Britain a minister making a bad appointment has to fear a hostile motion (though Parliament is overlenient to jobs) which may displace him; in the United States a president is under no such apprehension. It is only to opinion that he is responsible.

opinion of the slave states, and especially of the planting states, was practically the opinion of a class—the small and comparatively rich landowning aristocracy. The struggle for the defence of their institution had made this opinion fierce and intolerant. To a hatred of the Abolitionists, whom it thought actuated by the wish to rob and humiliate the South, it joined a misplaced contempt for what it deemed the moneygrubbing and peace-at-any-price spirit of the Northern people generally. So long as the subjugated states were ruled by arms, and the former "rebels" excluded by disfranchisement from the government of their states, this bitterness remained. When the restoration of self-government, following upon the liberation of the Confederate prisoners and the amnesty, had shown the magnanimity of the North, its clemency, its wish to forget and forgive, its assumption that both sides would shake hands and do their best for their common country, the hearts of the Southern men were conquered. Opinion went round. Frankly, one might almost say cheerfully, it recognized the inevitable. It stopped those outrages on the Negroes which the law had been unable to repress. It began to regain "touch" of, it has now almost fused itself with, the opinion of the North and West. No one Southern leader or group can be credited with this; it was the general sentiment of the people that brought it about. Still less do the Northern politicians deserve the praise of the peacemakers, for many among them tried for political purposes to fan or to rekindle the flame of suspicion in the North. It was the opinion of the North generally, more liberal than its guides, which dictated not merely forgiveness, but the restoration of equal civic rights. Nor is this the only case in which the people have proved themselves to have a higher and a truer inspiration than the politicians.

It has been observed that the all-subduing power of the popular voice may tell against the appearance of great statesmen by dwarfing aspiring individualities, by teaching men to discover and obey the tendencies of their age rather than rise above them and direct them. If this happens in America, it is not because the American people fail to appreciate and follow and exalt such eminent men as fortune bestows upon it. It has a great capacity for loyalty, even for hero worship. "Our people," said an experienced American publicist to me, "are in reality hungering for great men, and the warmth with which even pinchbeck geniuses, men who have anything showy or taking about them, anything that is deemed to betoken a strong individuality, are followed and glorified in spite of intellectual emptiness, and perhaps even moral shortcomings, is the best proof of the fact." Henry Clay was the darling of his party for many years, as Jefferson, with less of personal fascination, had been in the preceding generation. Daniel Webster retained the devotion of New England long after it had become clear that his splendid intellect was mated to a far from noble character. A kind of dictatorship was yielded to Abraham Lincoln, whose memory is cherished almost like that of Washington himself. Whenever a man appears with something taking or forcible about him, he becomes the object of so much popular interest and admiration that those cooler heads who perceive his faults, and perhaps dread his laxity of principle, reproach the proneness of their less discerning countrymen to make an idol out of wood or clay. The career of Andrew Jackson is a case in point, though it may be hoped that the intelligence of the people would estimate such a character more truly today than it did in his own day. I doubt if there be any country where a really brilliant man, confident in his own strength, and adding the charm of a striking personality to the gift of popular eloquence, would find an easier path to fame and power, and would exert more influence over the minds and emotions of the multitude. Such a man, speaking to the people with the independence of conscious strength, would find himself appreciated and respected.

Controversy is still bitter, more profuse in personal imputations than one expects to find it where there are no grave issues to excuse excitement. But in this respect also there is an improvement. Partisans are reckless, but the mass of the people lends itself less to acrid partisanship than it did in the times just before the Civil War, or in those first days of the Republic which were so long looked back to as a sort of heroic age. Public opinion grows more temperate, more mellow, and assuredly more tolerant. Its very strength disposes it to bear with opposition or remonstrance. It respects itself too much to wish to silence any voice.

PART V

ILLUSTRATIONS & REFLECTIONS

[This Part contains some illustrations, drawn from recent American history, of the working of political institutions and public opinion, together with observations on several political questions for which no suitable place could be found in the preceding Parts.]

The Tammany Ring in New York City

Although I have described in previous chapters the causes which have induced the perversion and corruption of democratic government in great American cities, it seems desirable to illustrate more fully, from passages in the history of two such cities, the conditions under which those causes work and the forms which that perversion takes. The phenomena of municipal democracy in the United States are the most remarkable and least laudable which the modern world has witnessed; and they present some evils which no political philosopher, however unfriendly to popular government, appears to have foreseen, evils which have scarcely showed themselves in the cities of Europe, and unlike those which were thought characteristic of the rule of the masses in ancient times. I take New York and Philadelphia as examples because they are older than Chicago, Pittsburgh, and St. Louis, larger than Boston and Baltimore. And I begin with New York, because she displayed on the grandest scale phenomena common to American cities, and because the plunder and misgovernment from which she has suffered have become specially notorious over the world.

From the end of the eighteenth century the state and (somewhat later) the city of New York were, more perhaps than any other state or city, the seat of intrigues and the battleground of factions. Party organizations early became powerful in them, and it was by a New York leader—Marcy, the friend of President Jackson—that the famous doctrine of "the Spoils to the Victors" was first formulated as already the practice of New York politicians. These factions were for a long time led, and these intrigues worked, by men belonging to the upper or middle class, to whom the emoluments of office were desirable but not essential. In the middle of the century, however, there came a change. The old native population of the city was more and more swollen by the immigration of foreigners: first of the Irish, especially from 1846 onwards; then also of the Germans from 1849 onwards; finally of Polish and Russian Jews, as well as of Italians and of Slavs from about 1883 onwards. Already in 1870 the foreign population, including not only the foreign both but a large part of their children who, though born in America, were still virtually Europeans, constituted a half or perhaps even a majority of the inhabitants; and the proportion of foreigners has since then grown still larger.[1] These newcomers were as a rule poor and ignorant. They knew little of the institutions of the country, and had not acquired any patriotic interest in it. But they received votes. Their numbers soon made them a power in city and state politics, and all the more so because they were cohesive, influenced by leaders of their own race, and not, like the native voters, either disposed to exercise, or capable of exercising, an independent judgment upon current issues. From among them there soon emerged men whose want of book-learning was overcome by their natural force and shrewdness, and who became apt pupils in those arts of party management which the native professional politicians had already brought to perfection.

While these causes were transferring power to the rougher and more ignorant element in the population, the swift developments of trade which followed the making of the Erie Canal and opening up of railway routes to the West, with the consequent expansion of New York as a commercial and financial centre, had more and more distracted the thoughts of the wealthier people from local politics, which required more time than busy men could give, and seemed tame compared with that struggle over slavery, whereon, from 1850 to 1865, all patriotic minds were bent. The leading men, who fifty years earlier would have watched municipal affairs and perhaps borne a part in them, were now so much occupied with their commercial enterprises or their legal practice as to neglect their local civic duties, and saw with unconcern the chief municipal offices appropriated by persons belonging to the lower strata of society.

Even had these men of social position and culture desired to retain a hold in city politics, the task would not have been easy, for the rapid growth of New York, which from a population of 108,000 in 1820 had risen to

---

[1] In 1870, 44 per cent of the population of New York were of foreign birth; in 1890, 42 per cent; in 1900, 37 per cent; in 1910, 40.4 per cent. The percentage of persons who were practically foreigners was and is of course much greater, because it includes many of the sons born in the United States of persons still imperfectly Americanized. It is true that some of the recent immigrants do not for a time obtain votes, but against this must be set the fact that the proportion of adults is much larger among the immigrants than in the whole population.

209,000 in 1830, to 813,000 in 1860, and to 942,000 in 1870, brought in swarms of strangers who knew nothing of the old residents, and it was only by laboriously organizing these newcomers that they could be secured as adherents. However laborious the work might be, it was sure to be done, because the keenness of party strife made every vote precious. But it was work not attractive to men of education, nor suited to them. It fell naturally to those who themselves belonged to the lower strata, and it became the source of the power they acquired.

Among the political organizations of New York the oldest and most powerful was the Tammany Society. It is as old as the federal government, having been established under the name of the Columbian Society in 1789, just a fortnight after Washington's inauguration, by an Irish American called William Mooney, and its purposes were at first social and charitable rather than political. In 1805 it entitled itself the Tammany Society, adopting, as is said, the name of an Indian chief called Tammanend or Tammany, and clothing itself with a sort of mock Indian character. There were thirteen tribes, with twelve "sachems" under a grand sachem, a "sagamore" or master of ceremonies, and a "wiskinski" or doorkeeper. By degrees, and as the story goes, under the malignant influence of Aaron Burr, it took a strongly political tinge as its numbers increased. Already in 1812 it was a force in the city, having become a rallying centre for what was then called the Republican and afterwards the Democratic party; but the element of moral aspiration does not seem to have become extinct, for in 1817 it issued an address deploring the spread of the foreign game of billiards among young men of the upper classes. At one time, too, it possessed a sort of natural history museum, which was ultimately purchased by the well-known showman, P. T. Barnum. Till 1822 it had been governed by a general meeting of its members, but with its increased size there came a representative system; and though the Society proper continued to be governed and its property held by the "sachems," the control of the political organization became vested in a general committee consisting of delegates elected at primary meetings throughout the city, which that organization was now beginning to overspread. This committee, originally of thirty-three members, numbered seventy-five in 1836, by which time Tammany Hall had won its way to a predominant influence on city politics. Of the present organization I shall speak later.

The first sachems had been men of some social standing, and almost entirely native Americans. The general democratization, which was unfortunately accompanied by a vulgarization, of politics that marked the time of Andrew

Jackson, lowered by degrees the character of city politicians, turning them into mere professionals whose object was lucre rather than distinction or even power. This process told on the character of Tammany, making it more and more a machine in the hands of schemers, and thus a dangerous force, even while its rank and file consisted largely of persons of some means, who were interested as direct taxpayers in the honest administration of municipal affairs. After 1850, however, the influx from Europe transformed its membership while adding to its strength. The Irish immigrants were, both as Roman Catholics and in respect of such political sympathies as they brought with them, disposed to enter the Democratic party. Tammany laid hold of them, enrolled them as members of its district organizations, and rewarded their zeal by admitting a constantly increasing number to posts of importance as district leaders, committeemen, and holders of city offices. When the Germans arrived, similar efforts were made to capture them, though with a less complete success. Thus from 1850 onwards Tammany came more and more to lean upon and find its chief strength in the foreign vote. Of the foreigners who have led it, most have been Irish. Yet it would be wrong to represent it, as some of its censors have done, as being predominantly Irish in its composition. There have always been and are now a vast number of native Americans among the rank and file, as well as a few conspicuous among its chiefs. It contains many Germans, possibly one-half of the German voters who can be reckoned as belonging to any party. And today the large majority of the Russian and Polish Jews (very numerous in some parts of the city), of the Czechs and other Austro-Hungarian Slavs, and possibly also of the Italians, obey its behests, even if not regularly enrolled as members. For the majority of these immigrants are Democrats, and Tammany has been and is the standard bearer of the Democratic party in the city. It has had rivals and enemies in that party. Two rival machines (now long since extinct)—Mozart Hall, formerly led by Mr. Fernando Wood, and the "County Democracy," guided for some years by the late Mr. Hubert O. Thompson—at different times confronted, and sometimes even defeated it; while at other times "making a deal" with it for a share in municipal spoils. Once, as we shall presently see, it incurred the wrath of the best Democrats of the city. Still it has on the whole stood for and been at most times practically identified with the Democratic party, posing on the Fourth of July as the traditional representative of Jeffersonian principles; and it has in that capacity grown from the status of a mere private club to be an organization commanding a number of votes which used to be sufficient not only to give it the mastery of the city but even to turn the balance in the great State of New York, and thereby, perhaps, to determine the result of a presidential election.

I must, however, return to those early days when Tammany was young and comparatively innocent, days when the machine system and the Spoils System were still but half developed, and when Chancellor Kent could write (in 1835), that "the office of assistant alderman could be pleasant and desirable to persons of leisure, of intelligence, and of disinterested zeal for the wise and just regulation of the public concerns of the city"! In 1834 the mayoralty was placed in the direct gift of the people. In 1842 all restrictions on the suffrage in the city were removed, just before the opening of an era when they would have been serviceable. In 1846 the new constitution of the state transferred the election of all judges to the people. In 1857 the state legislature, which had during the preceding twenty years been frequently modifying the municipal arrangements, enacted a new charter for the city. The practice of New York state had been to pass special laws regulating the frame of government for each of its cities, instead of having one uniform system for all municipalities. It was an unfortunate plan, for it went far to deprive New York of self-government by putting her at the mercy of the legislature at Albany, which, already corrupt, has been apt to be still further corrupted by the party leaders of the city, who could usually obtain from it such statutes as they desired. As I am not writing a municipal history of New York, but merely describing the action in that history of a particular party club, no more need be said of the charter and statutes of 1857 than that they greatly limited the powers of the Common Council. The chief administrative functions were vested in the mayor and the heads of various departments, while the power of raising and appropriating revenues was divided between a body called the Board of Supervisors and the legislature. Of the heads of the departments, some were directly chosen by the people, others appointed by the mayor, who himself held office for two years. To secure for their adherents some share in the offices of a city with a large Democratic majority, the legislature, then controlled by the Republicans, created a number of new boards for city administration, most of these members were to be appointed by the governor of the state. The police of the city in particular, whose condition had been unsatisfactory, were now placed under such a board, wholly independent of the municipal authorities, a change which excited strong local opposition and led to a sanguinary conflict between the old and the new police.

This was the frame of municipal government when the hero who was to make Tammany famous appeared upon the scene. The time was ripe, for the lowest class of voters, foreign and native, had now been thoroughly organized and knew themselves able to control the city. Their power had been shown in the success of a demagogue, the first of the city demagogues, named Fernando Wood, who by organizing them had reached the mayoral chair from beginnings so small that he was currently reported to have entered New York as the leg of an artificial elephant in a travelling show. This voting mob were ready to follow Tammany Hall. It had become the Acropolis of the city; and he who could capture it might rule as tyrant.[2]

William Marcy Tweed was born in New York in 1823, of a Scotch father and an American mother. His earliest occupation was that of a chairmaker—his father's trade; but he failed in business, and first became conspicuous by his energy in one of the volunteer fire companies of the city, whereof he was presently chosen foreman. These companies had a good deal of the club element in them, and gave their members many opportunities for making friends and becoming known in the district they served. Tweed had an abounding vitality, free and easy manners, plenty of humour, though of a coarse kind, and a jovial, swaggering way which won popularity for him among the lower and rougher sort of people. His size and corpulency made it all the easier for him to support the part of the genial good fellow; and it must be said to his credit, that though he made friends lightly, he was always loyal to his friends. Neither shame nor scruples restrained his audacity. Forty years earlier these qualities would no more have fitted him to be a popular leader than Falstaff's qualities would have fitted him to be the chancellor of King Henry V; and had anyone predicted to the upper classes of New York that the boisterous fireman of 1845, without industry, eloquence, or education, would in 1870 be ruler of the greatest city in the western world, they would have laughed him to scorn. In 1850, however, Tweed was elected alderman, and soon became noted in the Common Council, a body already so corrupt (though the tide of immigration had only just begun to swell) that they were commonly described as the forty thieves. He came out of it a rich man, and was presently sent to Washington as member for a district of the city. In the wider arena of Congress, however, he cut but a poor figure. He seems to have spoken only once, and then without success. In 1857 he began to repair his fortunes, shattered at the national capital, by obtaining the post of public school commissioner in New York, and soon afterwards he was elected to the Board of Supervisors,

---

[2] The nature and modes of action of rings in general have been described in Part III, Chapters 59–65. See also as to city government, Chapters 50–52 in Part II.

of which he was four times chosen president. There his opportunities for jobbery and for acquiring influence were much enlarged. "Heretofore his influence and reputation had both been local, and outside of his district he had hardly been known at all. Now his sphere of action embraced the whole city, and his large figure began to loom up in portentous magnitude through the foul miasma of municipal politics."[3]

Tweed was by this time a member of Tammany Hall, and in 1863 he was elected permanent chairman of the general committee. Not long after he and his friends captured the inner stronghold of the Tammany Society, a more exclusive and hitherto socially higher body; and he became grand sachem, with full command both of the Society, with its property and traditional influence, and of the political organization. This triumph was largely due to the efforts of another politician, whose fortunes were henceforward to be closely linked with Tweed's, Mr. Peter B. Sweeny, a lawyer of humble origin but with some cultivation and considerable talent. The two men were singularly unlike, and each fitted to supply the other's defects. Sweeny was crafty and taciturn, unsocial in nature and saturnine in aspect, with nothing to attract the crowd, but skilful in negotiation and sagacious in his political forecasts. He was little seen, preferring to hatch his schemes in seclusion; but his hand was soon felt in the arrangement by which the hostility of Mozart Hall, the rival Democratic organization, was removed, its leader Fernando Wood, obtaining a seat in Congress, while Tammany was thus left in sole sway of the Democratic vote of the city. The accession of Mozart Hall brought in another recruit to the Tammany group, Mr. A. Oakey Hall. This person was American by origin, better born and educated than his two associates. He was a lawyer by profession, and had occasionally acted as a lobbyist at Albany, working among the Republican members, for he then professed Republican principles—as Mr. Sweeny had worked occasionally among the Democrats. He had neither the popular arts, such as they were, of Tweed nor the stealthy astuteness of Sweeny, and as he never seemed to take himself seriously, he was not taken seriously by others. But he was quick and adroit, he had acquired some influence among the Mozart Hall faction; and his position as member of a well-known legal firm seemed to give a faint tinge of respectability to a group which stood sadly in need of that quality. He had been elected district attorney (public prosecutor) in 1862, by a combination of Mozart Hall with the Republicans (having been previously assistant district attorney), and had

[3] Mr. C. F. Wingate in the *North American Review*, No. CCXLV (1874), p. 368.

thus become known to the public. A fourth member was presently added in the person of Richard B. Connolly, who had become influential in the councils of Tammany. This man had been an auctioneer, and had by degrees risen from the secretaryship of a ward committee to be, in 1851, elected county clerk (although not then yet naturalized as a citizen), and in 1859 state senator. His friends, who had seen reason to distrust his exactness as a counter of votes, called him Slippery Dick. His smooth manner and insinuating ways inspired little confidence, nor do his talents seem to have gone beyond a considerable skill in figures, a skill which he was soon to put to startling uses. Another man of importance, who was drawn over from the Mozart Hall faction, was Albert Cardozo, a Portuguese Jew, only twenty-six years of age, but with legal talents only less remarkable than the flagrant unscrupulousness with which he prostituted them to party purposes. He was now, through Tammany influence, rewarded for this adhesion by being elected to one of the chief judgeships of the city; and two other equally dishonest minions of the Tweed group were given him as colleagues in the persons of George Barnard and John H. McCunn.

In 1865 Tweed and the other Tammany chiefs, to whom fortune and affinity of aims had linked him, carried for the mayoralty one of their number, Mr. John T. Hoffman, a man of ability, who might have had a distinguished career had he risen under better auspices; and at the election of 1868 they made a desperate effort to capture both the state and the city. Frauds of unprecedented magnitude, both in the naturalizing of foreigners before the election and in the conduct of the election itself, were perpetrated. The average number of persons naturalized by the city courts had been, from 1856 to 1867, 9,200. In 1868 this number rose to 41,000, and the process was conducted with unexampled and indecent haste by two of the judges whom Tammany had just placed on the bench to execute its behests. False registrations, repeating on a large scale, and fraudulent manipulation of the votes given rolled up for Tammany a majority sufficient to secure for its friend Hoffman the governorship of the state. The votes returned as cast in New York City were 8 per cent in excess of its total voting population. The vacancy caused by Hoffman's promotion was filled by the election of Mr. Hall. Thus at the beginning of 1869 the group already mentioned found itself in control of the chief offices of the city, and indeed of the state also.[4] Hall was mayor; Sweeny was city chamberlain, that is to say, treasurer of

---

[4] "On the 1st of January, 1869," said Mr. Tilden, "when Mr. A. Oakey Hall became mayor, the Ring became completely organized and matured." Pamphlet entitled *The New York City Ring: Its Origin, Maturity, and Fall,* New York, 1873.

the city and county; Tweed was street commissioner and president of the Board of Supervisors; Connolly, comptroller, and thus in charge of the city finances. Meanwhile their nominee, Hoffman, was state governor, able to veto any legislation they disliked, while on the city bench they had three apt and supple tools in Cardozo, Barnard, and McCunn. Other less conspicuous men held minor offices, or were leagued with them in managing Tammany Hall, and through it, the city. But the four who have been first named stood out as the four ruling spirits of the faction, to all of whom, more or less, though not necessarily in equal measure, the credit or discredit for its acts attached; and it was to them primarily, though not exclusively, that the name of the Tammany Ring came to be thenceforth applied.[5]

Having a majority in the state legislature, the ring used it to procure certain changes in the city charter which, while in some respects beneficial, as giving the city more control over its own local affairs, also subserved the purposes of its actual rulers. The elective Board of Supervisors was abolished, and its financial functions transferred to the recorder and aldermen. The executive power was concentrated in the hands of the mayor, who also obtained the power of appointing the chief municipal officers, and that for periods varying from four to eight years. He exercised this power (April 1870) by appointing Tweed commissioner of public works, Sweeny commissioner of parks, and (in pursuance of a subsequent enactment) Connolly comptroller. In a new board, called the Board of Apportionment, and composed of the mayor (Hall), the comptroller (Connolly), the commissioner of public works (Tweed), and the president of the board of parks (Sweeny), nearly all authority was now practically vested, for they could levy taxes, appoint the subordinate officials, lay down and enforce ordinances.[6] Besides his power of appointing heads of departments, the mayor had the right to call for reports from them in whatever form he pleased, and also the sole right of impeachment, and he had further, in conjunction with the comptroller, to allow or revise the estimate the board was annually to submit, and to fix the salary of the civil judges. the undisguised supremacy which this new

---

[5] Elaborate and unsparing portraits of these four gentlemen and of the three ring judges, as well as of some minor ringsters, may be found in Mr. Wingate's article in the *North American Review* for October 1874 (No. CCXLV). His analysis of their characters and conduct seems to have evoked from them no contradictions, and certainly gave rise to no legal proceedings. Reference may also be made for the history of the ring generally to the collected speeches of Mr. Samuel J. Tilden (see especially the speech of Nov. 2nd, 1871, in Mr. Bigelow's edition), and to those of Mr. Henry D. Clinton (published as a pamphlet in 1872), as well as to Mr. Tilden's pamphlet already cited.

[6] *North American Review* for Jan. 1875 (No. CCXLVI, pp. 172–75).

arrangement, amounting almost to dictatorship (purchased, as was believed, by gross bribery conducted by Tweed himself in the state legislature at Albany), conferred upon the quattuorvirate was no unmixed advantage, for it concentrated public attention on them, and in promising them impunity it precipitated their fall.

In the reign of the ring there is little to record beyond the use made by some of them of the opportunities for plunder, which this control of the municipal funds conferred. Plunder of the city treasury, especially in the form of jobbing contracts, was no new thing in New York, but it had never before reached such colossal dimensions. Two or three illustrations may suffice.

Large schemes of street-opening were projected, and for this purpose it became necessary to take and pay compensation for private property, and also, under the state laws, to assess betterment upon owners whose property was to be benefited. Sweeny, who knew something of the fortunes amassed in the rebuilding of Paris under the prefecture of Baron Haussmann, and was himself an admirer (and, as was said, an acquaintance) of Louis Napoleon, was credited with knowing how to use public improvements for private profit. Under the auspices of some members of the ring, commissioners for the carrying out of each improvement were appointed by the ring judges—in the famous case of the widening of Broadway by Cardozo in a perfectly novel manner. Those members and their friends then began quietly to purchase property in the spots which were eventually taken by the commissioners, and extravagant compensation was thereupon awarded to them, while other owners, who enjoyed no secret means of predicting the action of the commissioners, received for similar pieces of land far smaller sums, the burden of betterment also being no less unequally distributed as between the ringsters and other proprietors. In this way great sums passed from the city to those whom the ring favoured, in certain cases with commissions to some of its members.[7] Among the numerous contracts by which the city treasury was depleted, not a few were afterwards discovered to have been given for printing to three companies in which Tweed and his intimates were interested. Nearly $3,000,000 were paid to them within two years for city printing and stationery. Other contracts for wood-paving and concrete were hardly less scandalous.

The claims outstanding against the Board of Supervisors, previous to 1870, furnished another easy and copious source of revenue, for under a

---

[7] Details may be read in *North American Review*, No. CCXLVI, pp. 131–35.

statute which the ring had procured these claims, largely fraudulent or fictitious, were to be examined and audited by an *ad interim* board of audit composed of the mayor, the comptroller, and Tweed. The board delegated the duties of auditing to an ex-bankrupt creature of Tweed's named Watson, who had been appointed city auditor, and who went to work with such despatch that in three and a half months he had presented warrants for claims to the amount of $6,312,000 to the members of the *ad interim* board—for the board itself seems to have met only once—on whose signature these bills were accordingly paid out of the city treasury.[8] Subsequent investigation showed that from 65 to 85 per cent of the bills thus passed were fictitious, and of the whole Tweed appears to have received 24 per cent. But all the other financial achievements of the ring pale their ineffectual fires beside those connected with the erection and furnishing of the county courthouse. When designed in 1868 its cost was estimated at $250,000. Before the end of 1871 a sum variously estimated at from $8,000,000 to $13,000,000 (£1,600,000 to £2,600,000) had been expended upon it, and it was still unfinished. This was effected, as was afterwards proved in judicial proceedings, by the simple method of requiring the contractors, many of whom resisted for a time, to add large sums to their bills, sums which were then appropriated by Tweed, Connolly, and their minions or accomplices.[9] Nothing could have been more direct or more effective. The orders were given by Tweed, the difference between the real and the nominal charge was settled by the contractor with him or with the auditor, and the bills, passed and signed by the members of the Board of Supervisors or Board of Apportionment (as the case might be), were approved by the auditor Watson and were paid out of the city funds at the bank. The proceeds were then duly divided, his real charges, or perhaps a little more, going to the contractor, and the rest among the boss and his friends.

Under such a system there was nothing surprising in the growth of the city debt. Fresh borrowing powers as well as taxing powers had been obtained from the state legislature, and they were freely used. According to the published report of the committee which subsequently investigated the city finances, the bonded debt of the city rose from $36,293,000 at the beginning of 1869, to $97,287,000 in September 1871; that is, by $61,000,000. Adding to this the floating debt incurred during the same two

---

[8] *North American Review*, July 1875 (No. CCXLVII, pp. 116–20).

[9] Among the items in the bills for fitting up and furnishing the courthouse (amounting to more than $6,000,000, besides more than $2,000,000 for repairs), the items of $404,347 for safes, and $7,500 for thermometers were found amusing when eventually disclosed.

years and eight months, viz., $20,000,000, the total price which the city paid for the privilege of being ruled by Tammany during those thirty-two months reached $81,000,000, or more than twice the amount of the debt as it stood in 1868.[10] And for all this there was hardly anything in the way of public improvements to show.

What, it may be asked, did the people of New York, and in particular the taxpayers at whose expense these antics were proceeding, think of their rulers, and how did they come to acquiesce in such a government, which, not content with plundering them, had degraded justice itself in the person of the ring judges, and placed the commerce and property of the city at the mercy of unscrupulous and venal partisans? I was in New York in the summer of 1870, and saw the ring flourishing like a green bay tree. Though the frauds just described were of course still unknown, nobody had a word of respect for its members. Tweed, for instance, would never have been invited to any respectable house. I was taken to look at Justices Barnard and Cardozo as two of the most remarkable sights of the city; and such indeed they were. I inquired why such things were endured, not merely patiently, but even with a sort of amused enjoyment, as though the citizens were proud of having produced a new phenomenon the like whereof no other community could show. It was explained to me that these things had not come suddenly, but as the crown of a process of degredation prolonged for some fifteen years or more which had made corruption so familiar as to be no longer shocking. The respectable leaders of the Democratic party had, with few exceptions, winked at the misdeeds of those who commanded a vote which they needed for state and national purposes. The press had been largely muzzled by lavish payments made to it for advertising, and a good many minor journals were actually subsidized by the ring. The bench, though only partially corrupt, was sufficiently in league with the ring for the sanction which the law required from it in certain cases to be unavailable as a safeguard. As for the mass of citizens, on whose votes this structure of iniquity had been reared, nearly half of them were practically strangers to America, amenable to their own clubs and leaders, but with no sense of

---

[10] I take these figures from the report of Mr. Andrew H. Green (then comptroller of the city) made in October 1874. Of the unliquidated debt claims, many of which were then still outstanding, the report says: "Only a small proportion of this monstrous legacy of corruption and misgovernment was free from evidence of the most ingeniously and diabolically contrived frauds. For three years the million-headed hydra has been struggling to force the doors of the treasury. It has bought, bribed, and brought to its aid by the offer of a division of profits in case of success, the fraud, the craft, and the greed of the most unscrupulous lawyers, legislators, and plotters in the community. It has tainted the press and dictated political nominations." (p. 7.)

civic duty to their new country nor likely to respond to any appeals from its statesmen. Three-fourths or more of them paid little or nothing in the way of direct taxes and did not realize that the increase of civil burdens would ultimately fall upon them as well as upon the rich. Moreover, the ring had cunningly placed on the payrolls of the city a large number of persons rendering comparatively little service, who had become a body of janizaries, bound to defend the government which paid them, working hard for it at elections, and adding, together with the regular employees, no contemptible quota to the total Tammany vote.[11] As for the boss, those very qualities in him which repelled men of refinement made him popular with the crowd.

I asked what under such circumstances the respectable citizens proposed to do. My friends raised their eyebrows. One, of a historical turn, referred to the experience of Rome in the days of Clodius and Milo, and suggested the hiring of gladiators.

"These be thy gods, O Democracy: these are the fruits of abstract theory in politics. It was for this then that the yoke of George the Third was broken and America hailed as the dayspring of feeedom by the peoples of Europe— that a robber should hold the keys of the public treasury, and a ruffian be set to pollute the seat of justice." So might the shade of Alexander Hamilton have spoken, if permitted to revisit, after seventy years, the city his genius had adorned. Yet it was not such a democracy as Jefferson had sought to create and Hamilton to check that had delivered over to Tweed and to Barnard the greatest city of the Western world. That was the work of corruptions unknown to the days of Jefferson and Hamilton, of the Spoils System, of election frauds, of the gift of the suffrage to a host of ignorant strangers, and above all of the apathy of those wealthy and educated classes, without whose participation the best-framed government must speedily degenerate.

In the autumn of 1870 the ring seemed securely seated. Tweed, the master spirit, was content to scoop in money, and enjoy the licentious luxury which it procured him; though some declared that he had fixed his eyes upon the American legation in London. Sweeny preferred the substance to the ostentation of power; and Connolly's tastes were as vulgar as Tweed's, without the touch of open-handedness which seemed to palliate the latter's

---

[11] Mr. Tilden (*Origin and Fall of the New York Ring*) observes that the ring had at its disposal "the whole local government machinery, with its expenditure and patronage and its employment of at least 12,000 persons, besides its possession of the police, its influence on the judiciary, its control of the inspectors and canvassers of the elections."

greed. Cardozo, however, had his ambitions, and hungered for a place on the supreme federal bench; while Hall, to whom no share in the booty was ever traced, and who may not have received any, was believed to desire to succeed Hoffman as governor of the state, when that official should be raised by the growing influence of Tammany to the presidency of the United States. No wonder the ring was intoxicated by the success if had already won. It had achieved a fresh triumph in reelecting Hall as mayor at the end of 1870; and New York seemed to lie at its feet.

Its fall came suddenly; and the occasion sprang from a petty personal quarrel. A certain O'Brien, conspicuous as a leader in a discontented section of the Democratic party, was also personally sore because he had received an office below his hopes, and cherished resentment against Sweeny, to whom he attributed his disappointment. A henchman of his named Copeland, employed in the auditor's office, happened to find there some accounts headed "county liabilities" which struck him as suspicious. He copied them and showed them to O'Brien, who perceived their value, and made him copy more of them, in fact a large part of the fraudulent accounts relating to the furnishing of the court house. Threatening the ring, with the publication of these compromising documents, O'Brien tried to extort payment of an old claim he had against the city; but after some haggling the negotiations were interrupted by the accidental death of Watson, the auditor. Ultimately O'Brien carried his copies to the New York *Times*, a paper which had already for some months past been attacking Tammany with unwonted boldness. On the 8th of July, 1871, it exposed the operations of the ring; and denounced its members, in large capitals, as thieves and swindlers, defying them to sue it for libel. Subsequent issues contained extracts from the accounts copied by Copeland; and all were summed up in a supplement, published on July 29th and printed in German as well as English, which showed that a sum of nearly $10,000,000 in all had been expended upon the courthouse, whose condition everybody could see, and for armoury repairs and furnishings. Much credit is due to the proprietor of the *Times*, who resisted threats and bribes offered him on behalf of the ring to desist from his onslaught and perhaps even more to the then editor, the late Mr. Louis J. Jennings, whose conduct of the campaign was full of fire and courage. The better classes of the city were now fully aroused, for the denials or defences of the mayor and Tweed found little credence. On September 4th a meeting of citizens was held, and a committee of seventy persons, many of them eminent by ability, experience, or position, formed to investigate the frauds charged, which by this time had drawn the eyes of the whole state and country. It is needless to recount the steps by which Connolly, the person most directly implicated, and the one whom his colleagues sought to make a scapegoat of, was forced to appoint as deputy an active and upright man (Mr. A. H. Green), whose possession and examination of the records in the comptroller's office proved invaluable. The leading part in the campaign was played by Mr. Samuel J. Tilden, chairman of the Democratic party in the state, afterwards governor of the state, and in 1876 candidate for the federal presidency against Mr. Hayes. Feeling acutely the disgrace which the ring had brought upon the Democratic party, he was resolved by pursuit and exposure to rid the party of them and their coterie once for all; and in this he was now seconded by all the better Democrats. But much was also due to the brilliant cartoons of Mr. Thomas Nast, whose rich invention and striking drawing presented the four leading members of the ring in every attitude and with every circumstance of ignominy.[12] The election for state offices held in November was attended by unusual excitement. The remaining members of the ring, for Connolly was now extinct and some of the minor figures had taken to flight, faced in boldly, and Tweed in particular, cheered by his renomination in the Democratic state convention held shortly beforehand, and by his reelection to the chairmanship of the general committee of Tammany, now neither explained nor denied anything, but asked defiantly in words which in New York have passed into a proverb, "What are you going to do about it?" His reliance on his own district of the city, and on the Tammany masses as a whole, was justified, for he was reelected to the state senate and the organization gave his creatures its solid support. But the respectable citizens, who had for once been roused from their lethargy, and who added their votes to those of the better sort of Democrats and of the Republican party, overwhelmed the machine, notwithstanding the usual election frauds undertaken on its behalf. Few of the ring candidates survived, and the ring itself was irretrievably ruined. Public confidence returned, and the price of real estate advanced. Sweeny forthwith announced his withdrawal from public life, and retired to Canada. The wretched Connolly was indicted and found so few friends that he remained in jail for six weeks before he could procure bail. Tweed, though dispirited by the murder of his boon-companion, the notorious Fisk (who had been carrying through the scandalous Erie

---

[12] Tweed felt the sharpness of the weapon. He said once: "I don't care a straw for your newspaper articles; my constituents don't know how to read, but they can't help seeing them damned pictures"; and indeed there was always a crowd round the window in which *Harper's Weekly* (then admirably edited by the late Mr. George William Curtis) was displayed.

railroad frauds by the help of the ring judges), stood his ground with characteristic courage, and refused to resign the office to which the mayor had appointed him. However, in December he was arrested,[13] but presently released on insignificant bail by Judge Barnard. The state assembly, in which the reformers had now a majority, soon afterwards took steps to impeach Barnard, McCunn, and Cardozo. Cardozo resigned; the other two were convicted and removed from the bench. The endless delays and minute technicalities of the courts of New York protracted Tweed's trial till January 1873, when, after a long hearing, the jury were discharged because unable to agree. He was thereupon rearrested, and upon his second trial in November, when special efforts had been made to secure a trustworthy jury, was found guilty and sentenced to twelve years' imprisonment. After a while the court of appeals released him, holding the sentence irregular, because cumulative; he was then rearrested in a civil suit by the city, escaped, was caught in Spain, identified by a caricature, and brought back to prison, where he died in 1876. Hall was thrice tried. On the first occasion the death of a juryman interrupted the proceedings; on the second the jury disagreed; on the third he obtained a favourable verdict. Connolly fled the country and died in exile. None of the group, nor of Tweed's other satellites, ever again held office.

This was the end of the Tweed Ring. But it was not the end of Tammany. Abashed for the moment, the stooping earthward while the tempest swept by, that redoubtable organization never relaxed its grip upon the New York masses. It was only for a few months that the tempest cleared the air. The "good citizens" soon forgot their sudden zeal. Neglecting the primaries, where indeed they might have failed to effect much, they allowed nominations to fall back into the hands of spoilsmen, and the most important city offices to be fought for by factions differing only in their names and party badges, because all were equally bent upon selfish gain. Within five years from the overthrow of 1871, Tammany was again in the saddle, and the city government practically in the nomination of Mr. John Kelly, tempered by the rival influence of the ex-prize fighter Morrissey. In 1876 a vigorous pen, reviewing the history of the preceding eight years, and pointing out how soon the old mischiefs had reappeared, thus described the position:

> A few very unscrupulous men, realizing thoroughly the changed condition of affairs, had organized the proletariat of the city; and, through the form of suffrage,

---

[13] When asked on being committed to state his occupation and creed, he answered that he was a statesman, and of no religion.

had taken possession of its government. They saw clearly the facts of the case, which the doctrinaires, theorists, and patriots studiously ignored or vehemently denied. They knew perfectly well that New York City was no longer a country town, inhabited by Americans and church-goers, and officered by deacons. They recognized the existence of a very large class which had nothing, and availed themselves of its assistance to plunder those who had something. The only way to meet them effectually and prevent a recurrence of the experience is for the friends of good government equally to recognize facts and shape their course accordingly. The question then is a practical one.

If New York, or any other great city in America which finds itself brought face to face with this issue, were an independent autonomy,—like Rome or many of the free cities of the Middle Ages,—the question would at once be divested of all that which in America makes if difficult of solution. Under these circumstances the evil would run its course, and cure itself in the regular and natural way. New York would have a Cæsar within six months. Whether he came into power at the head of the proletariat or seized the government as the conservator of property would make no difference. The city would instinctively find rest under a strong rule. The connection which exists, and necessarily can never be severed, between the modern great city and the larger State, closes this natural avenue of escape. New York City is tied to New York State, and must stumble along as best it may at its heels. It is guaranteed a government republican in form, and consequently a radical remedy for the evil must be found within that form, or it cannot be found at all, and the evil must remain uncured.

The thing sought for then is to obtain a municipal government, republican in form, in which property, as well as persons, shall be secured in its rights, at the cost of a reasonable degree only of public service on the part of the individual citizen. The facts to be dealt with are few and patent. On the one side a miscellaneous population, made up largely of foreigners, and containing an almost preponderating element of vice, ignorance, and poverty, all manipulated by a set of unscrupulous professional politicians; on the other a business community, engrossed in affairs, amassing wealth rapidly, and caring little for politics. Between the two the usual civic population, good and bad, intent on pleasure, art, literature, science, and all the myriad other pursuits of metropolitan life. The two essential points are the magnitude and the diversified pursuits of the population, and its division into those who have and those who have not.

Bearing these facts, which cannot be changed, in mind, then a few cardinal principles on which any successful municipal government, republican in form, must rest, may safely be formulated. In the first place, the executive must be strong and responsible; in the second place, property must be entitled to a representation as well as persons; in the third place, the judiciary must be as far removed as possible from the political arena. In other words, justice must be made as much as possible to descend from above. Curiously enough, each of these principles, instead of being a novelty, is but a recurrence to the ancient ways.[14]

These counsels, and many others like them, were not taken to heart. Since 1871 the frame of municipal government was frequently tinkered with. A comprehensive scheme of reform, proposed by a strong commission which Governor Tilden appointed in 1876, failed to be carried; and though great progress has been made in the way of better ballot and election laws and some progress in the way of civil service reform, the Spoils System still throve, repeaters still voted in large numbers, and election returns could still be manipulated by those who control the city government. There have been some excellent mayors, such as Mr. Hewitt, for the catastrophe of 1871 has never been forgotten by Tammany, whose chieftains sometimes find it prudent to run reputable candidates. No more Barnards or Cardozos have disgraced the bench, for the bar association is vigorous and watchful; and when very recently a judge who had been too subservient to a suspected state boss was nominated by the influence of that gentleman to one of the highest judicial posts in the state, the efforts of the association, well supported in the city, procured his defeat by an overwhelming majority.

Nevertheless, Tammany has held its ground; and the august dynasty of bosses goes on. When Mr. John Kelly died some time ago, the sceptre passed to the hands of the not less capable and resolute Mr. Richard Croker, once the keeper of a liquor saloon, and for some short time the holder of a clerkship under Tweed himself.[15] Mr. Croker, like Lorenzo de' Medici in Florence, held no civic office, but, as chairman of the Tammany subcommittee on organization, controlled all city officials, while, by the public avowal of the Speaker of the House of Assembly, during the session of 1893, "all legislation (i.e., in the state legislature at Albany) emanated from Tammany Hall, and was dictated by that great statesman, Richard Croker.[16] Ultimately Mr. Croker, like the emperors Diocletian and Charles V, abdicated the crown. He retired to the enjoyment of an estate and a racing stud in Ireland, and Mr. Charles F. Murphy reigned in his stead.

[14] *North American Review* for October 1876 (No. CCLIII, p. 421), an unsigned article.

[15] Full details regarding the career of Mr. Croker, of his henchman, Police Justice Patrick Divver, and of other Tammany "braves" of that day, may be found in an article in the *Atlantic Monthly* for February 1894, by Mr. H. C. Merwin, and more fully in the "Annual Records" of assemblymen and senators from New York City, published by the City Reform Club.

[16] Mr. D. G. Thompson, *Politics in a Democracy*, p. 127, an odd little book which purports to defend Tammany by showing that it gives the New York masses the sort of government they desire and deserve.

The reader will expect some further words to explain how the Tammany of today is organized, by what means it holds its power, and what sort of government it gives the city.

Each of the thirty-five "assembly districts" in the boroughs of Manhattan and Bronx annually elects a certain number of members, varying from 60 to 270, to sit on the general committee of Tammany Hall, which has long claimed to be, and at present is, the "regular" Democratic organization of the city. The committee is thus large, numbering several thousand persons, and on it there also sit the great chiefs who are above taking district work. Each district has also a "leader" who is always on the general committee; and the thirty-five leaders form the executive committee of the Hall, which has also other committees, including that on finance, whereof Mr. Croker was chairman. Each election district has, moreover, a district committee, with the "leader" (appointed by the assembly district leader) as chairman and practically as director. This committee appoints a captain for every one of the voting precincts into which the district is divided. There are about 1,100 such precincts, and these 1,100 captains are held responsible for the vote cast in their respective precincts. The captain is probably a liquor seller, and as such has opportunities of getting to know the lower class of voters. He has often some small office, and usually some little patronage, as well as some money, to bestow. In each of the thirty-five districts there is a party headquarters for the committee and the local party work, and usually also a clubhouse, where party loyalty is cemented over cards and whiskey, besides a certain number of local "associations," called after prominent local politicians, who are expected to give an annual picinic, or other kind of treat, to their retainers. A good deal of social life, including dances and summer outings, goes on in connection with these clubs.[17]

Such an organization as this, with its tentacles touching every point in a vast and amorphous city, is evidently a most potent force, especially as this force is concentrated in one hand—that of the boss of the Hall. He is practically autocratic; and under him these thousands of officers, controlling probably nearly 200,000 votes, move with the precision of a machine.[18] However, it has been not only in this mechanism, which may be called a legitimate method of reaching the voters, that the strength of Tammany has

[17] Full and clear descriptions may be found in Mr. H. C. Merwin's article already cited, and in Mr. Thompson's book, pp. 66 *sqq.*

[18] The highest total vote ever cast in New York was 285,000 (in 1892). In the city election of 1890 Tammany polled 116,000 votes; out of 216,000 cast in 1892 the Tammany candidate for mayor had 173,000, there being, however, no other Democratic candidate.

lain. Its control of the city government gave it endless opportunities of helping its friends, of worrying its opponents, and of enslaving the liquor dealers. Their licenses were at its mercy, for the police could proceed against or wink at breaches of the law, according to the amount of loyalty the saloonkeeper shows to the Hall. From the contributions of the liquor interest a considerable revenue was raised; more was obtained by assessing officeholders, down to the very small ones; and, perhaps, most of all by blackmailing wealthy men and corporations, who found that the city authorities have so many opportunities of interfering vexatiously with their business that they preferred to buy them off and live in peace.[19] The worst form of this extortion was the actual complicity with criminals which consists in sharing the profits of crime. A fruitful source of revenue, roughly estimated at $1,000,000 a year has been derived, when the party was supreme at Albany, from legislative blackmailing in the legislature, or, rather, from undertaking to protect the great corporations from the numerous "strikers," who threaten them there with bills. A case has been mentioned in which as much as $60,000 was demanded from a great company; and the president of another is reported to have said (1893): "Formerly we had to keep a man at Albany to buy off the 'strikers' one by one. This year we simply paid over a lump sum to the Ring, and they looked after our interests." But of all their engines of power none was so elastic as their command of the administration of criminal justice. The mayor appointed the police justices, now called city magistrates, usually selecting them from certain Tammany workers, sometimes from the criminal class, not often from the legal profession. These justices were often Tammany leaders in their respective districts.[20] Said a distinguished publicist of those days:

> The police captain of the precinct, the justice of the police court, and the district leader of the Tammany organization are all leagued together to keep the poor in subjection and prevent the rich from interfering. Their means of annoyance for a poor man are endless. They can arrest him on small pretences, prevent his getting employment from the city, or city contractors, pursue him for allowing his goods to remain on the sidewalk, and for not cleaning off the snow promptly, tax him heavily, or let him go free. All these means of persecution are freely resorted to, so that the poor, and especially the foreign poor, are really as much in subjection to Tammany as the Italians to the Camorra. The source of it all is

---

[19] An Investigating Committee of the New York State Senate cast a scorching light on this so-called "Police Protective Tariff," as to which see also an article in the *Forum* for August 1894, by Mr. J. B. Leavitt.

[20] *Atlantic Monthly, ut supra*.

the character of the mayor. He appoints the police commissioners, and the commissioners appoint the captains, and he appoints the police justices also, and is responsible for their quality. When the act under which the present justices act was under consideration in the legislature, the proviso that all appointees should be lawyers of a certain standing at the bar was stricken out, so that the mayor has a completely free hand in selection, and the result is that most of those dealers, gamblers, or simple adventurers, who have lived from the age of twenty by holding small offices, such as doorkeepers or clerks of the minor city courts.

Now there is in the moral sphere of city government nothing so important as what I may call the administration of petty justice, that is, justice among the poor, ignorant, and friendless, the class who cannot pay lawyers or find bail, and especially that very large class in the cities on our eastern coast, of poor foreigners who know nothing of our laws and constitutions, and to whom the police magistrate or the police captain represent the whole government of the country, Federal, State, and municipal, who accept without a murmur any sentence which may be pronounced on them, or any denial of justice which may overtake them. They get all their notions of the national morality, and really their earliest political training, from their contact with these officers and with the district "leader." Upon their experience with these people it depends very much what kind of citizens they will become, they and their children after them. Well, one of the very first lessons they learn is that they can have no standing in court unless they are members of the Tammany Society, or as simple voters they have a "pull," that is, some sort of occult influence with the magistrate. In default of this their complaints are dismissed, and they are found guilty and sent up to "the Island," or held in bail which they cannot procure, or in some manner worsted.[21]

With such sources of power it is not surprising that Tammany Hall should have commanded the majority of the lower and the foreign masses of New York, though it has never been shown to hold an absolute majority of all the voters of the city. Its local strength is fairly well proportioned to the character of the local population; and though there are plenty of native Americans among the rank and file as well as among the leaders, still it has been from the poorer districts, inhabited by Jews, Irish, Germans, Italians, Bohemians, that its heaviest vote has come.[22] These poor people do not support it because it is vicious. They like it and think it a good thing; it satisfies their instincts of combination and good fellowship; it is often all the government they know. Mr. Merwin puts the attitude of the better sort

---

[21] Mr. E. L. Godkin in *Annals of the Amer. Acad. of Polit. Science* for May 1894, p. 17.
[22] An instructive examination of the vote by districts which brings this result clearly out is given by Mr. Thompson, pp. 79–91.

of Tammany adherents, and particularly of the native American, when he writes:

> The Tammany man dislikes and despises the Anglomania of what is called "society" in New York; he distrusts the people who compose "society" and believes them at heart out of sympathy with American principles, whereas Tammany in his view is a concrete protest against monarchy and monarchical arrangements of society. He considers that Tammany is, on the whole, a good body, that it gives New York a good government, that it stands for what is manly and patriotic. It troubles him somewhat that a few of the leaders are said to be acquiring ill-gotten gains; and if the scandal increases he will overthrow those leaders and appoint others in their stead. Meanwhile Tammany is his party, his church, his club, his totem. To be loyal to something is almost a necessity of all incorrupt natures, and especially of the Celtic nature. The Tammany man is loyal to Tammany.
>
> In truth there is very little in New York to suggest any higher ideal. What kind of a spectacle does the city present to a man working his way up from poverty to wealth,—to one, for instance, who began as a "tough," and ends as a capitalist? The upper class—at least the richer class, the class chiefly talked about in the papers—is, with exceptions, of course, given over to material luxury and to ostentation. It is without high aims, without sympathy, without civic pride or feeling. It has not even the personal dignity of a real aristocracy. Its sense of honour is very crude. And as this class is devoted to the selfish spending, so the business class is devoted to the remorseless getting of money.[23]

To this description of the attitude of the Tammany rank and file it may be added that, as few of them pay any direct taxes, they have no sense of the importance of economy in administration. True it is that they ultimately pay, through their rent and otherwise, for whatever burdens are laid on the city. But they do not perceive this—and as the lawyers say, *De non apparentibus et non existentibus eadem est ratio*. The government of the rich by the manipulation of the votes of the poor is a new phenomenon in the world; and where the rich have little contact with the poor, and the poor little respect for the rich, happy results can hardly be expected. Apart from the abuse of the minor criminal justice, apart from the blackmailing of innocent men as well as of offenders, apart from the impunity which the payment of blackmail secures to some forms of vice,[24] apart from such lapses from virtue as that of the aldermen who sold the right of laying a

---

[23] *Atlantic Monthly, ut supra.*

[24] Great credit is due to a courageous clergyman who at some personal risk succeeded in exposing this system, and helped thereby to obtain the appointment of the investigating committee.

railroad in Broadway—twenty-two out of the twenty-four were indicted for bribery—the actual administration of the city injured and offended the ordinary citizen less than might have been expected. The police force, often as they were made the engine of extortion or the accomplice in vice, are an efficient force, though harsh in their methods, and they keep life and property secure.[25] The fire department is well managed; the water supply is copious; the public schools have been usually, though not invariably, "kept out of politics." If the government has been wasteful in details, it was seldom conspicuously extravagant; and the rulers who grew rich through it have done so by indirect methods, and not out of the city treasury. Scandals like those of Tweed's time have not recurred. The city debt was reduced between 1876 and 1894 to $104,000,000, though it must be added that the swift increase of the wealth of the city enabled a rate of taxation moderate for the United States ($1.85 to $1.79 on the valuation of property) to produce an immense revenue.[26] Considering what by origin, by training, by environment, and by tastes and habits, are the persons who rule the city through Tammany—considering the criminal element among them and their close association with the liquor saloons, it may excite surprise that the government, corrupt as it has been, was not also more wasteful.[27]

Those who have grasped the singular condition of New York and its population, will find it less surprising that this government should have proved itself so hard to overthrow. In 1890 a great effort to overthrow it was made. A section of the Democrats leagued itself with the Republicans to bring out what was understood to be "a joint ticket," while the independent reformers blessed the alliance, and endorsed its candidates.[28] Success had been hoped for; but Tammany routed its adversaries by 23,000 votes. It

[25] The senate committee elicited the fact—already indeed suspected—that an applicant for employment in the police must pay for appointment, and an officer must contribute a large sum either to the ring or to the police commissioners for promotion. The New York police are a brave and active force, but long custom is said to have made the overlooking breaches of the law for a consideration seem to them a venial fault.

[26] "The increase in the assessed valuation of property (real and personal) in New York City is annually about $70,000,000; and in 1893 reached the unprecedented sum of $105,254,253."— *City Government in the U.S.*, by Mr. Alfred R. Conkling, New York, 1894.

[27] "The city is governed today by three or four men of foreign birth who are very illiterate, are sprung from the dregs of the foreign population, have never pursued any regular calling, were entirely unknown to the bulk of the residents only five years ago, and now set the criticisms of the intelligent and educated classes at defiance."—*Annals of the Amer. Acad., ut supra.*

[28] Being in New York during the election, I spent some hours in watching the voting in the densely peopled tenement-house districts and thus came to realize better than figures can convey how largely New York is a European city, but a European city of no particular country, with elements of ignorance and squalor from all of them.

turned out that about 30,000 Republicans had not voted—some because their bosses, secretly friendly to Tammany, did not canvass them, some because they did not care to vote for anything but a Republican ticket, some out of sheer indifference and laziness. This proved that strongly entrenched as Tammany is, Tammany could be overthrown if the "good citizens" were to combine for municipal reform, setting aside for local purposes those distinctions of national party which have nothing to do with city issues. The rulers of "the wigwam," as Tammany is affectionately called, do not care for national politics, except as a market in which the vote they control may be sold. That the citizens of New York should continue to rivet on their necks the yoke of a club which is almost as much a business concern as one of their own dry-goods stores, by dividing forces which, if united, would break the tyranny that has lasted for two generations—this indeed seems strange, yet perhaps no stranger than other instances of the power of habit, of laziness, of names and party spirit. In 1894, Tammany was defeated, and the improved government that for some years followed made the "better element" see more clearly what they might gain by reform. Victory came at last in 1902, by which time Greater New York, consisting of four boroughs added to the old city, had come into being under the new charter. In the two succeeding elections candidates for the mayoralty supported by Tammany were successful; but these elections are too near the time at which I write to be proper subjects for discussion here. Suffice it to say that the mayors between 1902 and 1913 gave the city a much purer and more efficient administration than it had enjoyed before, and that in 1913 a split in the party due to a quarrel between the boss and the governor of the state brought upon Tammany a crushing disaster. Although there are departments of the government, such as the police and the police magistrates, that may still be open to grave criticism, the sky of New York was in 1914 brighter than it had been for many years, bright enough to encourage the hope that the clouds which remain will ultimately pass away.

The Philadelphia Gas Ring

Philadelphia, though it has not maintained that primacy among American cities which in the days of the Revolution was secured to it by its population and its central position, is still one of the greatest cities in America, with a population of about a million.[1] Though the element of recent immigrants is much smaller than in New York or Boston or Chicago,[2] the old Quaker character has died out, or remains perceptible only in a certain air of staid respectability which marks the city as compared with the luxury of New York and the tumultuous rush of Chicago. It has of late years been strongly Republican in its politics, partly because that party obtained complete ascendency during the war, partly because Pennsylvania is a Protectionist state, owing to her manufacturing industries, and Philadelphia, as the stronghold of protection, is attached to the party which upholds those doctrines. During the Civil War the best citizens were busily absorbed in its great issues, and both then and for some time after, welcomed all the help that could be given to their party by any men who knew how to organize the voters and bring them up to the polls; while at the same time their keen interest in national questions made them inattentive to municipal affairs. Accordingly, the local control and management of the party fell into the hands of obscure citizens, men who had their own ends to serve, their own fortunes to make, but who were valuable to the party because they kept it in power through their assiduous work among the lower class of voters. These local leaders formed combinations with party managers in the state legislature which sits at Harrisburg, the capital of Pennsylvania, and with a clique managed from Washington by a well-known senatorial family,

---

[1] In 1910 it was 1,549,008.

[2] Only 24 per cent of the people of Philadelphia are of foreign birth, whereas in Boston the percentage is 35 and in Chicago nearly 42.

which for a long time controlled the Pennsylvania vote in Republican National Conventions and in Congress. They were therefore strongly entrenched, having powerful allies, both in state politics and in federal politics. Since they commanded the city vote, both these sets of politicians were obliged to conciliate them; while the commercial interests of Philadelphia in the maintenance of a protective tariff pressed so strongly on the minds of her leading merchants and manufacturers as to make them unwilling to weaken the Republican party in either state or city by any quarrel with those who commanded the bulk of its heavy vote.

The obscure citizens of whom I have spoken had begun by acquiring influence in the primaries, and then laid their hands on the minor, ultimately also on the more important, city offices. They sometimes placed men of good social standing in the higher posts, but filled the inferior ones, which were very numerous, with their own creatures. The water department, the highway department, the tax department, the city treasurer's department, the county commissioner's office, fell into their hands. A mayor appointed by them filled the police with their henchmen till it became a completely partisan force. But the centre of their power was the Gas Trust, administered by trustees, one of whom, by his superior activity and intelligence, secured the command of the whole party machinery, and reached the high position of recognized boss of Philadelphia. This gentleman, Mr. James M'Manes, having gained influence among the humbler voters, was appointed one of the Gas Trustees, and soon managed to bring the whole of that department under his control. It employed (I was told) about two thousand persons, received large sums, and gave out large contracts. Appointing his friends and dependants to the chief places under the Trust, and requiring them to fill the ranks of its ordinary workmen with persons on whom they could rely, the boss acquired the control of a considerable number of votes and of a large annual revenue. He and his confederates then purchased a controlling interest in the principal horsecar (street tramway) company of the city, whereby they became masters of a large number of additional voters. All these voters were of course expected to act as "workers," i.e., they occupied themselves with the party organization of the city, they knew the meanest streets and those who dwelt therein, they attended and swayed the primaries, and when an election came round, they canvassed and brought up the voters. Their power, therefore, went far beyond their mere voting strength, for a hundred energetic "workers" mean at least a thousand votes. With so much strength behind them, the Gas Ring, and Mr. M'Manes at its head, became not merely indispensable to the Republican party in the city, but in fact its chiefs, able therefore to dispose of the votes of all those who were employed permanently or temporarily in the other departments of the city government—a number which one hears estimated as high as twenty thousand.[3] Nearly all the municipal offices were held by their nominees. They commanded a majority in the Select Council and Common Council. They managed the nomination of members of the state legislature. Even the federal officials in the customhouse and post office were forced into a dependent alliance with them, because their support was so valuable to the leaders in federal politics that it had to be purchased by giving them their way in city affairs. There was no getting at the Trust, because "its meetings were held in secret, its published annual report to the city councils was confused and unintelligible, and (as was subsequently proved) actually falsified."[4] Mr. M'Manes held the payrolls under lock and key, so that no one could know how many employees there were, and it was open to him to increase their number to any extent. The city councils might indeed ask for information, but he was careful to fill the city councils with his nominees, and to keep them in good humour by a share of whatever spoil there might be, and still more by a share of the patronage.

That so vast and solid an edifice of power, covering the whole of a great city, should be based on the control of a single department like the Gas Trust may excite surprise. But it must be remembered that when a number of small factions combine to rule a party, that faction which is a little larger, or better organized, or better provided with funds, than the others, obtains the first place among them, and may keep it so long as it gives to the rest a fair share of the booty, and directs the policy of the confederates with firmness and skill. Personal capacity, courage, resolution, foresight, the

---

[3] The ballot did not protect these voters. Prior to the introduction of the so-called "Australian" ballot in 1891 it was generally possible for the presiding election officer to know how each man voted.

[4] See *Report of the Committee of One Hundred*, published November 1884. A leading citizen of Philadelphia, from whom I have sought an explanation of the way in which the Gas Trust had managed to entrench itself, writes me as follows: "When in 1835 gas was first introduced in Philadelphia, it was manufactured by a private company, but the city reserved the right to buy out the stockholders. When this was done, in 1841, with the object of keeping the works 'out of politics,' the control was vested in a board of twelve, each serving for three years. These were constituted trustees of the loans issued for the construction and enlargement of the works. Their appointment was lodged in the hands of the city councils; but when, on more than one occasion, the councils endeavoured to obtain control of the works, the courts were appealed to and decided that the board, as trustees for the bondholders, could not be interfered with until the last of the bonds issued under this arrangement had matured and had been paid off. Thirty-year loans under these conditions were issued until 1855, so that it was not until 1885 that the city was able to break within the charmed circle of the Trust."

judicious preference of the substance of power to its display, are qualities whose union in one brain is so uncommon in any group of men that their possessor acquires an ascendency which lasts until he provokes a revolt by oppression, or is seen to be leading his party astray. And by the admission even of his enemies, Mr. M'Manes possessed these qualities. His origin was humble, his education scanty, but he atoned for these deficiencies by tact and knowledge of the world, with a quietly decorous demeanour veiling an imperious will. He knew how to rule without challenging opposition by the obtrusion of his own personality, nor does he seem to have used his power to plunder the city for his own behoof. The merit of the system was that it perpetuated itself, and in fact grew stronger the longer it stood. Whenever an election was in prospect, the ward primaries of the Republican party were thronged by the officers and workpeople of the Gas Trust and other city departments, who secured the choice of such delegates as the ring had previously selected in secret conclave. Sometimes, especially in the wards inhabited by the better sort of citizens, this "official list" of delegates was resisted by independent men belonging to the Republican party; but as the chairman was always in the interest of the ring, he rarely failed so to jockey these independents that even if they happened to have the majority present they could not carry their candidates. Of course it seldom happened that they could bring a majority with them, while argument would have been wasted on the crowd of employees and their friends with which the room was filled, and who were bound, some by the tenure of their office, others by the hope of getting office or work, to execute the behests of their political masters. The delegates chosen were usually officeholders, with a sprinkling of public works contractors, liquor dealers, always a potent factor in ward politics, and office expectants. For instance, the convention of 13th January 1881, for nominating a candidate for mayor, consisted of 199 delegates, 86 of whom were connected with some branch of the city government, 9 were members of the city councils, 5 were police magistrates, 4 constables, and 23 policemen, while of the rest some were employed in some other city department, and some others were the known associates and dependants of the ring. These delegates, assembled in convention of the party, duly went through the farce of selecting and voting for persons already determined on by the ring as candidates for the chief offices. The persons so selected thereby became the authorized candidates of the party, for whom every good party man was expected to give his vote. Disgusted he might be to find a person unknown, or known only for evil, perhaps a fraudulent bankrupt, or a broken-down bar keeper, proposed for his acceptance, but his only alternative being to vote for the Democratic nominee, who was probably no better, he submitted, and thus the party was forced to ratify the choice of the boss. The possession of the great city offices gave the members of the ring the means not only of making their own fortunes, but of amassing a large reserve fund to be used for "campaign purposes." Many of these offices were paid by fees and not by salary. Five officers were at one time in the receipt of an aggregate of $223,000, or an average of $44,600 each. One, the collector of delinquent taxes, received nearly $200,000 a year. Many others had the opportunity, by giving out contracts for public works on which they received large commissions, of enriching themselves almost without limit, because there was practically no investigation of their accounts.[5] The individual official was of course required to contribute to the secret party funds in proportion to his income, and while he paid in thousands of dollars from his vast private gains, assessments were levied on the minor employees down to the very policemen. On one occasion each member of the police force was required to pay $25, and some afterwards a further tax of $10, for party purposes. Anyone who refused, and much more, of course, anyone who asserted his right to vote as he pleased, was promptly dismissed. The fund was spent in what is called "fixing things up," in canvassing, in petty bribery, in keeping barrooms open and supplying drink to the workers who resort thither, and, at election times, in bringing in armies of professional personators and repeaters from Washington, Baltimore, and other neighbouring cities, to swell the vote for the ring nominees. These men, some of them, it is said, criminals, others servants in the government departments in the national capital, could of course have effected little if the election officials and the police had looked sharply after them. But those who presided at the voting places were mostly in the plot, being ring men and largely city employees, while the police— and herein not less than in their voting power lies the value of a partisan police—had instructions not to interfere with the strangers, but allow them to vote as often as they please, while hustling away keen-eyed opponents.[6]

This kind of electioneering is costly, for secrecy must be well paid for,

---

[5] In the suit subsequently instituted against the gas trustees, it was shown that in six years the trust had in cash losses, illegal transactions, and manufacturing losses due to corrupt management, involved the city in an expense of three and a half millions of dollars (about £700,000). These were the figures so far as ascertained in November 1884.—*Report of the Committee of One Hundred*, p. ii.

[6] A policeman is by law forbidden to approach within thirty feet of the voter. Who was to see that the law was observed when the guardians of the law broke it: according to the proverb, If water chokes, what is one to drink next?

and in other ways also the ring was obliged to spend heavily. Regarding each municipal department chiefly as a means of accumulating subservient electors, it was always tempted to "create new voting stock" (to use the technical expression), i.e., to appoint additional employees. This meant additional salaries, so the taxpayers had the satisfaction of knowing that the sums they paid went to rivet on their necks the yoke of the bosses, just as a Greek tyrant exacted from the citizens money to hire the mercenaries who garrisoned the Acropolis. And there was of course a vast deal of peculation in nearly all the departments; because clerks who had it in their power to disclose damaging secrets had little to fear, either from a superior or from the councilmen who had procured their appointment. Thus the debt of the city rose rapidly. In 1860 it stood at about $20,000,000 (£4,000,000). In 1881 it had reached $70,000,000 (£14,000,000). Taxation rose in proportion, till in 1881 it amounted to between one-fourth and one-third of the net income from the property on which it was assessed, although that property was rated at nearly its full value.[7] Yet withal the city was badly paved, badly cleansed, badly supplied with gas (for which a high price was charged), and with water.[8] That such a burden should have been borne, with so little to show for it, was all the more surprising, because in Philadelphia there is a larger number of well-to-do working people, owning the houses they lived in, than in any other city of the Union.[9] It might have been expected, therefore, that since the evils of heavy rating and bad administration pressed directly on an unusually large number of electors, the discontent would have been universal, the demand for reform overwhelming.[10]

But how was reform to be effected? Three methods presented themselves. One was to proceed against the gas trustees and other peculators in the courts of the state. But to make out a case the facts must first be ascertained, the accounts examined. Now the city departments did not publish all their accounts, or published them in a misleading and incomplete form. The powers which should have scrutinized them and compelled a fuller disclosure, were vested in the councils of the city, acting by their standing committees. But these councils were mainly composed of members or nominees of the

---

[7] I take these facts from an interesting paper on the *Form of Municipal Government for Philadelphia*, by Mr. John C. Bullit, Philadelphia, 1882.

[8] See Chapter 51, p. 570 of Vol. I.

[9] There were in Philadelphia in 1886, 90,000 individual owners of real estate, constituting more than a majority of all the votes ever cast in an election.

[10] During a considerable part of the time the enormous annual expenditure for "city improvements" was defrayed out of fresh loans, so the citizens did not realize the burden that was being laid on them.

ring, who had a direct interest in suppressing inquiry, because they either shared the profits of dishonesty, or had placed their own relatives and friends in municipal employment by bargains with the peculating heads of departments. They therefore refused to move, and voted down the proposals for investigation made by a few of their more public-spirited colleagues.[11]

Another method was to turn out the corrupt officials at the next election. The American system of short terms and popular elections was originally due to a distrust of the officials, and expressly designed to enable the people to recall misused powers. The astuteness of professional politicians had, however, made it unavailable. Good citizens could not hope to carry candidates of their own against the tainted nominees of the ring, because the latter having the "straight" or "regular" party nominations would command the vote of the great mass of ordinary party men, so that the only effect of voting against them would at best be to let in the candidates of the opposite, i.e., the Democratic, party. Those candidates were usually no better than the Republican ring nominees, so where was the gain? And the same reason, joined to party hostility, forbade good Republicans to vote for Democratic candidates. The Democrats, to be sure, might have taken advantage of Republican discontent by nominating really good men, who would in that case have been carried by the addition of the Republican "bolting" vote to the regular Democratic vote. But the Democratic wire-pullers, being mostly men of the same stamp as the Gas Ring, did not seek a temporary gain at the expense of a permanent disparagement of their own class. Political principles are the last thing which the professional city politician cares for. It was better worth the while of the Democratic chiefs to wait for their turn, and in the meantime to get something out of occasional bargains with their (nominal) Republican opponents, than to strengthen the cause of good government at the expense of the professional class.[12]

The third avenue to reform lay through the action of the state legislature. It might have ordered an inquiry into the municipal government of Philadel-

---

[11] A friend in Philadelphia writes me: "It might be thought that the power of election vested in the councils would enable the latter to control the trustees, but when 'politics' invaded the trust, a vicious circle speedily established itself, and the trust controlled the councils. Its enormous pay-roll enabled it to employ numerous 'workers' in each of the 600 or 700 election divisions of the city, and aspirants for seats in the councils found it almost impossible to obtain either nomination or election without the favour of the trust. Thus the councils became filled with its henchmen or 'heelers,' submissive to its bidding, not only in the selection of trustees to fill the four yearly vacancies, but in every detail of city government with which the leaders of the trust desired to interfere. It is easy to understand the enormous possibilities of power created by such a position."

[12] It was generally believed in February 1881, that the Democratic bosses had made a bargain (for valuable consideration) with the Gas Ring not to nominate Mr. Hunter, the reformers' candidate, for the receivership of taxes.

phia, or passed a statute providing for the creation of a better system. But this avenue was closed even more completely than the other two by the control which the city ring exercised over the state legislature. The Pennsylvania House of Representatives was notoriously a tainted body, and the Senate no better, or perhaps, as some think, worse. The Philadelphia politicians, partly by their command of the Philadelphia members, partly by the other inducements at their command, were able to stop all proceedings in the legislature hostile to themselves, and did in fact, as will appear presently, frequently balk the efforts which the reformers made in that quarter. It was enough for their purpose to command one house; indeed, it was practically enough to command the committee of that one house to which a measure is referred. The facilities for delay are such that a reforming bill can be stifled without the need of open opposition.

This was the condition of the Quaker City with its 850,000 people; these the difficulties reformers had to encounter. Let us see how they proceeded.

In 1870, a bill was passed by the state legislature at Harrisburg, at the instigation of the city ring, then in the first flush of youthful hope and energy, creating a Public Buildings Commission for the city of Philadelphia, a body with an unlimited term of office, with power to enlarge its numbers, and fill up vacancies among its members, to tax the city and to spend the revenue so raised on buildings, practically without restriction or supervision. When this act, which had been passed in one day through both houses, without having been even printed, came to the knowledge of the better class of citizens, alarm arose, and an agitation was set on foot for its abrogation. A public meeting was held in March 1871, a committee formed, with instructions to proceed to Harrisburg, and have the act repealed. The committee went to Harrisburg and urged members of both houses to support a repealing bill introduced into the state Senate. In May this bill passed the Senate, in which there was then a Democratic majority, five Republican members voting for it. However, a committee of the (Republican) House of Representatives reported against the repeal, influenced by interested persons from Philadelphia, and (as is generally believed) influenced by arguments weightier than words; so the Commission was maintained in force. The incident had, however, so far roused a few of the better class of Republicans, that they formed a Municipal Reform Association, whose career has been summarized for me by an eminent citizen of Philadelphia, in the words which follow:

The Association laboured earnestly to check the tide of misgovernment. Its task was a difficult one, for the passions aroused by the war were still vigorous, the reconstruction in progress in the South kept partisanship at a white heat, and fealty to party obligations was regarded as a sacred duty by nearly all classes. Consequently it had no newspaper support to depend upon, and as a rule it met with opposition from the leaders of both political organizations. Moreover, the laws regulating the registry of voters and the conduct of elections had been so framed as to render fraud easy and detection difficult. Undeterred by these obstacles, the Association set itself vigorously to work; it held public meetings, it issued addresses and tracts, it placed tickets in the field consisting of the better candidates of either party, and when neither had made passable nominations for an office it put forward those of its own. It continued in active existence for three or four years, and accomplished much of what it set out to do. Occasionally it succeeded in defeating specially objectionable candidates, and in electing better men to the city councils; the increase in the public debt was checked, the credit of the city was improved, and economy began to be practised in some of the departments; salaries were substituted for fees in the public offices; the election laws were revised and honest elections became possible; prosecutions were instituted against offenders, and enough convictions were secured to serve as a wholesome warning. The services of the Association were especially apparent in two directions. It contributed largely to the agitations which secured the calling of a convention in 1873 to revise the State constitution, it had a salutary influence with the convention, and it aided in obtaining the ratification of the new constitution by the people. Still more important was its success in arousing the public conscience, and in training a class of independent voters who gradually learned to cast their ballots without regard to so-called party fealty. It thus opened the way for all subsequent reforms, and when its members, wearied with its thankless task, one by one withdrew, and the Association disbanded, they could feel that not only was the condition of the city materially improved, but that their successors in the Sisyphæan labour would have a lighter burden and a less rugged ascent to climb. One important result of the attention which they had drawn to municipal mismanagement was the passage of an act of legislature, under which, in 1877, the governor of the State appointed a commission of eleven persons to devise a plan for the government of cities. This commission made a report proposing valuable improvements, and submitted it, with a bill embodying their suggestions, to the State legislature in 1878. The legislature, however, at the bidding of the Rings, for Pittsburg and other cities have their Rings as well as Philadelphia, smothered the bill, and all efforts to pass it failed till 1885.

In the course of 1880, the horizon began to clear.[13] Several honest and

---

[13] In the narrative which follows I have derived much assistance from a little book by Mr. George Vickers, entitled *The Fall of Bossism* (Philadelphia, 1883) which, with some oddities of style, contains a great many instructive details of the doings of the bosses and the reform campaign. Some information as to ring methods in Philadelphia may also be gathered from a lively satire published anonymously, entitled *Solid for Mulhooly* (New York, 1881).

outspoken men who had found their way into the two councils of the city, denounced the prevailing corruption, and by demands of inquiry began to rouse the citizens. A correspondent of a New York paper obtained facts about the management of the Gas Trust which, when published, told seriously on opinion. At the November election, while Philadelphia cast a heavy vote in favour of General Garfield as Republican candidate for the presidency, and for the Republican nominees for the offices of state auditor general, and judge of the state Supreme Court, she returned as city controller, a young Democrat, who having, with the help of the Municipal Reform Association, found his way into that office at the last preceding election, had signalized himself by uprightness and independence. The Republican bosses did their utmost against him, but the vote of independents among the Republicans, joined to that of the Democratic party (whose bosses, although secretly displeased with his conduct, did not openly throw him over), carried him in. Thirteen days afterwards, under the impulse of this struggle, an energetic citizen convened a meeting of leading merchants to set on foot a movement for choosing good men at the elections due in February 1881. This meeting created a committee of one hundred businessmen, including a large number of persons bearing the oldest and most respected names in Philadelphia. All were Republicans, and at first they endeavoured to effect their purposes by means, and within the limits of, the Republican party. They prepared a declaration of principles, containing their programme of municipal reform, and resolved to support no candidate who would not sign it. Soon the time came for making nominations for the three offices to be filled up, viz., those of mayor, receiver of taxes, and city solicitor. For mayor, the "regular" Republican party, controlled by Mr. M'Manes, nominated Mr. Stokley, who was then in office, a man against whom no fraud could be charged, but whose management of the police force and subservience to the boss had made him suspected by earnest reformers. At first, in the belief that he was prepared to subscribe their declaration, the One Hundred gave him their nomination; but when it turned out that he, influenced by the ring, refused to do so, they withdrew their "indorsement," and perceived that the time had come for a bolder course. Since they must resist the ring Republicans, they invited the cooperation of the Democratic party in choosing a good man. The novelty of the circumstances, and the opportunity of doing a good stroke for their party and their city at once, brought to the front the best element among the Democrats. Overruling their bosses by a sudden movement, the Democratic convention nominated Mr. King for the mayoralty, a bold and honest man, whom, though a Democrat, the Committee of One Hundred promptly accepted. For the not less important office of receiver of taxes, the One Hundred had nominated Mr. Hunter, a Republican, who had approved his public spirit by upright service in the common council. The ring Republicans had taken for their candidate an unknown man, supposed to be a creature of Mr. M'Manes; and everything now turned on the conduct of the Democratic nominating convention. It was strongly urged by the feeling of the people to accept Mr. Hunter. But the Democratic bosses had no mind to help a reformer, and even among the better men, the old dislike to supporting a person belonging to the opposite party was strong. A passionate struggle in the Democratic convention, round whose doors a vast and eager crowd had gathered, resulted in the carrying by a small majority of a regular party candidate named M'Grath against Mr. Hunter. Thereupon the delegates who supported Hunter seceded, and marched, escorted and cheered by excited crowds, to the rooms of the One Hundred, where they organized themselves afresh as an independent convention, and nominated Hunter. Immense enthusiasm was evoked in both parties by this novel and unexpectedly bold action. Independent Democrats organized clubs and committees in Hunter's cause, and the movement spread so fast that ten days before the election, M'Grath retired, leaving the regular Democrats free to cast their votes for the Republican Hunter, along with the Democratic King. Only one chance was now left to the Gas Ring—the lavish expenditure of money, and the resort to election frauds. They assessed the police, about 1,300 in number, $20 a head to replenish the campaign fund, levying assessments on the other city departments also. Preparations for repeating and ballot box stuffing were made as in former days, but the energy of the One Hundred, who, while they issued a circular to clergymen of all denominations requesting them to preach sermons on the duty of electors, issued also notices threatening prosecution against anyone guilty of an election fraud, and organized a large force of volunteer citizens to look after the police, so much frightened the ringsters and their dependents, that the voting was conducted with fairness and purity. The excitement on the polling day was unprecedented in municipal politics, and the success of the reform candidates who were chosen, King by a majority of six thousand, Hunter by twenty thousand, was welcomed with transports of joy. Astræa had returned—the "City of Independence" was again a city of freedom.

The Committee of One Hundred, to whose efforts the victory was mainly due, was kept on foot to carry on and perfect the work of reform. It recommended candidates at the spring and fall elections during the three years that followed, obtaining for them a measure of success encouraging, no doubt, yet less complete than had been expected. It retained counsel to aid in a suit instituted against the gas trustees, which resulted in disclosing scandalous waste and fraud, and has led to a great improvement in the management of that department. It induced the state legislature to reduce the salaries of a number of overpaid officials, and to place on a permanent basis the salaries of judges which had hitherto been voted annually. The mayor, whom it had carried in 1881, stopped the assessment of the police for "campaign purposes," and rigidly restrained them from joining in the nominating conventions or interfering with voters at the polls. The tax office was reorganized by the new receiver, and the income which its employees depleted turned into the city treasury. The system of banking city monies, which had been used for political purposes, was reformed under an ordinance of the city councils, secured by the efforts of the committee. The lists of voters, which had been carelessly and sometimes corruptly made up, were set to rights, and capable men appointed assessors instead of the ward politicians, often illiterate, to whom this duty had been previously entrusted. An inspector of highways was engaged by the committee to report cases in which contractors were failing to do the work in repairing streets and drains for which they were paid, and frauds were unearthed by which the city had been robbed of hundreds of thousands of dollars. Gross abuses in the management of the city almshouse and hospital were revealed; a new administration was installed, which in its first year saved the city $80,000, while the conviction and imprisonment of the chief offenders struck wholesome terror into evildoers in other departments. Finally, the committee undertook the prosecution of a large number of persons accused of fraud, repeating, personation, violence, tampering with ballot boxes, and other election offences, and by convicting some and driving others from the city, so much reduced these misdemeanours that in the end of 1883 the city elections were pronounced to show a clean bill of health.[14]

Work so various and so difficult cost the members of the Committee of One Hundred, who were nearly all men actively engaged in business, and had passed a self-denying ordinance binding themselves to accept no personal political advantage, an infinitude of time and trouble. Accordingly, when they found that the candidates, whom they had recommended at the election of February 1884, had been rejected in favour of other candidates, who

---

[14] The committee observe in the report that the party organization of the city, in nearly every instance, did its utmost by supplying bail, employing counsel, and rendering other assistance to protect the culprits, who were regarded as sufferers for the sake of their party.

made similar professions of reform, but seemed less likely, from their past history, to fulfil those professions, they determined to wind up and dissolve the committee. It had done great things and its failure to carry its candidates at this last election was due partly to the intrusion into municipal politics of the national issue of the protective tariff (the most burning of all questions to Philadelphians), partly to that languor which creeps over voters who fancy that by doing their duty strenuously for some years they have mortally wounded the power of corruption and need not keep up the fight till it is stone dead.

The situation was thus shortly afterwards summed up by competent writers:

> The committee of One Hundred fought the Ring at every point and at all points for city and county officers, the council, and the legislature, the plan being to unite for the nominations of the two great parties and endorse one or the other of the candidates, or even nominate candidates of their own. They sent tickets to every citizen, and created the class of "vest-pocket voters"—men who come to the polls with their tickets made up, to the confusion of "the boys." They changed for a while the complexion of councils, elected a reform mayor and receiver of taxes, caused the repeal of the infamous Delinquent Tax Collections Bill, and the equally notorious and obnoxious Recorder's Bill, and generally made a more decent observance of the law necessary throughout the city. In its nature, however, the remedy was esoteric and revolutionary, and therefore necessarily ephemeral. It could not retain the spoils system and thereby attract the workers. Its candidates, when elected, often betrayed it and went over to the regulars, who, they foresaw, had more staying qualities. Its members became tired of the thankless task of spending time and money in what must be a continuous, unending battle. The people became restive, and refused their support to what jarred on their conservative ideas and what they were pleased to call the dictation of an autocratic, self-constituted body. The cry was raised: "Who made thee a ruler and judge over us?"

> In 1883 the committee's candidate for controller was defeated in a pitched battle, and the following spring the reform mayor was beaten by over 7000 votes by the most advanced type of a machine politician, who has since been impeached by his own party in Common Council for pecuniary malfeasance.[15]

Since 1884 there have been many changes in the city administration, which I touch on but briefly, because it is to the Gas Ring episode that this

---

[15] Mr. E. P. Allinson and Mr. B. Penrose, in an article on "City Government in Philadelphia." For a history of earlier municipal government in the city, reference may be made to the treatise, "Philadelphia, 1681–1887," of the same authors.

chapter is devoted. A bill for reforming municipal government by the enactment of a new city charter, approved by the One Hundred, came before the state legislature in 1883. It was there smothered by the professionals at the instance of the Gas Ring. When it reappeared in the legislature of 1885 circumstances were more favourable. The relations between the state boss of Pennsylvania and the city ring headed by Boss M'Manes were strained. The state boss seems, while wishing to cripple the city ring by cutting off some of its patronage, to have thought that it would be well to conciliate the good citizens of Philadelphia by giving his powerful support to a reform measure. He was the more drawn to this course because the mayor of Philadelphia, whose appointing power would be enlarged by the bill, was, although not a "high-class politician," far from friendly to the Gas Trust. Long discussions of the bill in the press and at meetings had produced some effect even on the state legislature at Harrisburg; nor was there wanting in that body a small section of good members willing to help reform forward. Many leaders and most newspapers had in the course of the discussions been led to commit themselves to an approval of the bill, while not expecting it to pass. Thus, in 1885, the opposition in the legislature ceased to be open and direct, and came to turn on the question when the bill, if passed, should take effect. Its promoters prudently agreed to let its operation be delayed till 1887; and having thus "squared" some of their opponents, and outmanœuvred others, they ran it through. Public opinion and a righteous cause counted for something in this triumph, but even public opinion and righteousness might have failed but for the feud between Mr. M'Manes and the state boss.

The new city charter did some good. By bringing gas management under the control of the city executive, it extinguished the separate gas trust, and therewith quenched the light of Mr. M'Manes, who ceased to be formidable when his patronage departed, and thereafter became "a black number," free to devote his interest to theological questions, for he was a champion of orthodoxy in his church. Municipal administration gained by the concentration of power and responsibility in the mayor and the executive heads of departments whom he appoints. The councils, however, remained bad bodies, few of the members respected, many of them corrupt. They continued to be nominated by a clique of machine politicians, and this clique they obeyed, paying some regard to the interests of their respective wards, but none to those of the city. Reformers thought that to give them a salary might lessen their temptations, since it seemed impossible to raise their tone. In the stead of Mr. M'Manes, the state boss (a man even less trusted by the good citizens) reigned for a time through his lieutenants; and so tight was his grip of the city, that when, in 1890, the suspicions he aroused had provoked a popular uprising which overthrew his nominee for the state governorship, turning over to the other party some thirty thousand votes, he was still able to hold Philadelphia—rich, educated, staid, pious Philadelphia—by a large majority. Elections continued to be tainted with fraud and bribery; the politicians still refused the enactment of adequate laws for a secret ballot and the publication of election expenses. A menacing power was wielded by the great local corporations, including the railroad and streetcar companies. Whether by the use of money, or, as is thought more probable, by influencing the votes of their employees, or by both methods, these corporations seemed to hold the councils in the hollow of their hands. One of them secured from the city legislature, at a merely nominal figure, a public franchise, which, while it made the streets more dangerous, added to the market price of its stock about $6,600,000. And this was done by a two-thirds majority over the veto of the mayor, in the teeth of an active agitation conducted by the most worthy citizens. Against scandals like this the best city charter furnishes little protection. They can be cured only by getting upright councils, and these again can be secured only by having free instead of cooked nominations, honest elections, and a far more constantly active interest in the welfare of city than the mass of the voters have hitherto evinced. Philadelphia is not the only city in which private corporations have proved more than a match for public interests, and in which such corporations have netted immense profits, that ought to have gone to reduce the burdens of the people.[16]

Against these evils strenuous campaigns have been from time to time conducted by various associations of "good citizens," some permanent, some formed for a special occasion. These associations, of which it is enough to say that they have been worthy successors of the Committee of One Hundred, have included nearly all those whom high personal character is united to a sense of public duty. But their members have hitherto formed so small a proportion of the voters that it is only when some glaringly bad candidate is nominated or outrageous job perpetrated that their efforts tell in an election. In 1912, however, they gained a sudden victory, carrying as mayor a veteran reformer who had been one of the foremost fighters in February 1881.

The history of all these efforts and of the failure to effect any thorough

---

[16] It was stated by the Municipal League that the city had in recent years lost as much as $50,000,000 by improvident grants of valuable franchises to street railroad companies.

and permanent improvement in municipal conditions in this great city would stretch to a volume, were it given with the fulness needed to explain why the forces that make for misgovernment have proved so exceptionally strong. The episode I have selected is enough for the present purpose.

The European reader may have found four things surprising in the foregoing narrative—the long-suffering of the taxpayers up till 1881; the strength of party loyalty, even in municipal affairs where no political principle is involved; the extraordinary efforts required to induce the voters to protect their pockets by turning a gang of plunderers out of office; and the tendency of the old evils to reappear as soon as the ardour of the voters cools. He will be all the more surprised when he learns that most of the corrupt leaders in Philadelphia have been not men of foreign birth, but Americans born and bred, and that in none of the larger cities was the percentage of recent immigrants so small. The general causes of municipal misgovernment have been already set forth, but it may be well to repeat that the existence of universal suffrage in a gigantic city imposes a vast amount of work on those who would win an election. Nothing but a very complete and very active ward organization, an organization which knows every house in every street, and drops upon the new voter from Europe as soon as residence and the oath have made him a citizen, can grapple with the work of bringing up these multitudes to the poll. It was their command of this local organization, their practice in working it, the fact that their employees were a trained and disciplined body whose chief business was to work it—services in the gas or water or some other department being a mere excuse for paying the "workers" a salary—that gave the Gas Ring and its astute head their hold upon the voting power of the city, which all the best Republicans, with frequent aid from the Democrats, found it so hard to shake. It was the cohesion of this organization, the indifference of the bulk of its members to issues of municipal policy and their responsiveness to party names and cries, that enabled the henchmen of the state boss to reestablish a selfish tyranny and with impunity to sacrifice the interests of the city to those of rich and vote-controlling corporations.

The moral of the whole story is, however, best given in the words of four eminent Philadelphians. I multiply testimonies because Philadelphia is a peculiarly instructive instance of the evils which everywhere infect municipal government. Her social and economic conditions are far more favourable than those of New York or Chicago, and the persistence of those evils in her is, therefore, a more alarming symptom than the grosser scandals which have disgraced those cities with their masses of recent immigrants.

Two of them wrote me as follows in 1888. One said:

Those who study these questions most critically and think the most carefully fear more for the Republic from the indifference of the better classes than the ignorance of the lower classes. We hear endless talk about the power of the Labour vote, the Irish vote, the German vote, the Granger vote, but no combination at the ballot box today is as numerous or powerful as the stay-at-home vote. The sceptre which is stronger to command than any other is passed by unnoticed, not because outworn in conflict, but because rusted and wasted in neglect. The primary, the caucus, and the convention are the real rulers of America, and the hand which guides these is the master. Here again the stay-at-home vote is still more responsible. In New York City in 1885 there were 266,000 voters; of these 201,000 voted at the regular election and between 20,000 and 25,000 voted at the primary. This proportion would hold good the country over, and it appears that one out of every four does not vote at all, and nine out of every ten do not attend the primaries. It can therefore easily be seen that it is very easy to control the primaries, and granting strong party fealty how difficult it is to run an independent ticket against the machine.

The other, Mr. Henry C. Lea, the distinguished historian, said:

Your expression of surprise at the mal-administration of Philadelphia is thoroughly justified. In existing social conditions it would be difficult to conceive of a large community of which it would appear more safe to predicate judicious self-government than ours. Nowhere is there to be found a more general diffusion of property or a higher average standard of comfort and intelligence—nowhere so large a proportion of landowners bearing the burden of direct taxation, and personally interested in the wise and honest expenditure of the public revenue. In these respects it is almost an ideal community in which to work out practical results from democratic theories. I have often speculated as to the causes of failure without satisfying myself with any solution. It is not attributable to manhood suffrage, for in my reform labours I have found that the most dangerous enemies of reform have not been the ignorant and poor but men of wealth, of high social position and character, who had nothing personally to gain from political corruption, but who showed themselves as unfitted to exercise the right of suffrage as the lowest proletariat, by allowing their partisanship to enlist them in the support of candidates notoriously bad who happened by control of party machinery to obtain the "regular" nominations.

The nearest approach which I can make to an explanation is that the spirit of party blinds many, while still more are governed by the mental inertia which renders independent thought the most laborious of tasks, and the selfish indolence which shrinks from interrupting the daily routine of avocations. In a constituency so enormous the most prolonged and strenuous effort is required to oppose the ponderous and complicated machinery of party organization, which is always in the hands of professional politicians who obtain control over it by a process of natural selection, and who thus are perfectly fitted for the work. Recalcitrants are raw militia who take the field with overwhelming odds against them, both in numbers and discipline. Even though they may gain an occasional victory, their enthusiasm exhausts itself and they return to more congenial labours, while the "regular" is always on duty, and knows, with Philip II, that time and he can overcome any other two.

A third wrote in 1893:

The great majority of the voters take no interest in local politics. They refuse to attend the party primaries, and can rarely be induced to do more than spend a few minutes once a year in voting at city elections. Many refuse to vote at all, or yield only to corrupt inducements or to the solicitations of interested friends. The result is that combinations of unworthy leaders and mercenary henchmen are enabled to control the nominating conventions of both parties; and when election day comes, the people can do nothing but choose between two tickets dictated by equally corrupt men and nominated by similar methods.

A fourth, writing in 1894, observed:

The most characteristic feature of the situation is the supremacy of the Republican party, which has an immense majority in the city. Politically, therefore, the controlling party managers and the class from which reform leaders might be expected to come are in accord (manufacturing interests being the most important); and the advantages to be derived by persons in business in a large way from standing well with the managers of the dominant party are sufficiently great to check in no small degree individual inclination to strive for better conditions. As elsewhere in America, it is not the natural leaders in the community, the men who have succeeded in business or in the professions, who are party leaders, but men who are of no importance in any other connection. This fastens upon us an impersonal rule, those who exercise it not being influenced by public opinion, which would certainly act as a restraint upon men of standing. . . . The councils are dominated by the party managers who nominated them, and corporations who pay wages, in one way or another, to a considerable portion of the members.

When these comments were written Philadelphia was erecting a magnificent city hall, the loftiest building of its kind in the United States, with a tower, 510 feet in height, which far overtops Cologne Cathedral and the Pyramid of Cheops and St. Peter's at Rome. The thoughts of the traveller who is taken to admire it naturally turn to what goes on beneath its ample roof, and he asks whether the day will arrive when Philadelphian voters will take to heart the painful lessons of the past, and when the officials who reign in this municipal palace will become worthy of so superb a dwelling and of the city where the Declaration of Independence and the federal Constitution first saw the light. His Philadelphian friends reply that such a day will doubtless arrive. But though the situation was better in 1913 than it had been for many a long year, they have seen too many disappointments to feel sure that Astræa has "come to stay."

Kearneyism in California

I. The Character of California

What America is to Europe, what Western America is to Eastern, that California is to the other Western states. The characteristics of a new and quickly developed colonial civilization are all strongly marked. It is thoroughly American, but most so in those points wherein the Old World differs from the New. Large fortunes are swiftly made and not less swiftly spent. Changes of public sentiment are sudden and violent. The most active minds are too much absorbed in great business enterprises to attend to politics; the inferior men are frequently reckless and irresponsible; the masses are impatient, accustomed to blame everything and everybody but themselves for the slow approach of the millennium, ready to try instant, even if perilous, remedies for a present evil.

These features belong more or less to all the newer and rougher commonwealths. Several others are peculiar to California—a state on which I dwell the more willingly because it is in many respects the most striking in the whole Union, and has more than any other the character of a great country, capable of standing alone in the world. It has a superb climate, noble scenery, immense wealth in its fertile soil as well as in its minerals and forests. Nature is nowhere more imposing nor her beauties more varied.

It grew up, after the cession by Mexico and the discovery of gold, like a gourd in the night. A great population had gathered before there was any regular government to keep it in order, much less any education or social culture to refine it. The wildness of that time passed into the blood of the people, and has left them more tolerant of violent deeds, more prone to interferences with, or supersessions of, regular law, than are the people of most parts of the Union.

The chief occupation of the first generation of Californians was mining, an industry which is like gambling in its influence on the character, with its sudden alternations of wealth and poverty, its long hours of painful toil relieved by bouts of drinking and merriment, its life in a crowd of men who have come together from the four winds of heaven, and will scatter again as soon as some are enriched and others ruined, or the gold in the gulch is exhausted. Moreover, mining in this region means gambling, not only in camps among the miners, but among townsfolk in the shares of the mining companies. Californians of all classes have formed the habit of buying and selling in the mining exchanges, with effects on the popular temper both in business and in politics which everyone can understand. Speculation becomes a passion, patient industry is distasteful; there is bred a recklessness and turbulence in the inner life of the man which does not fail to express itself in acts.

When California was ceded to the United States, land speculators bought up large tracts under Spanish titles, and others, foreseeing the coming prosperity, subsequently acquired great domains by purchase, either from the railways which had received land grants, or directly from the government. Some of these speculators, by holding their lands for a rise, made it difficult for immigrants to acquire small freeholds, and in some cases checked the growth of farms. Others let their land on short leases to farmers, who thus came into a comparatively precarious and often necessitous condition; others established enormous farms, in which the soil is cultivated by hired labourers, many of whom are discharged after the harvest—a phenomenon rare in the United States, which, as everybody knows, is a country of moderately sized farms, owned by persons who do most of their labour by their own and their children's hands. Thus the land system of California presents features both peculiar and dangerous, a contrast between great properties, often appearing to conflict with the general weal, and the sometimes hard pressed small farmer, together with a mass of unsettled labour thrown without work into the towns at certain times of the year.[1]

Everywhere in the West the power of the railways has excited the jealousy of the people. In California, however, it has roused most hostility, because no state has been so much at the mercy of one powerful corporation. The Central Pacific Railway, whose main line extends from San Francisco to

---

[1] "Latifundia perdunt Californiam," someone said to me in San Francisco.

Ogden in Utah, where it meets the Union Pacific and touches the Denver and Rio Grande system, had been up till 1877, when my narrative begins, the only route to the Mississippi Valley and Atlantic,[2] and therefore possessed immense influence over the trade of the whole state. It was controlled by a small knot of men who had risen from insignificance to affluence, held nearly all the other railway lines in California, employed an enormous number of clerks and workmen, and made the weight of their hand felt wherever their interest was involved. Alike as capitalists, as potentates, and as men whose rise to gigantic wealth seemed due as much to the growth of the state as to their own abilities, and therefore to come under the principle which is called in England that of the "unearned increment," they excited irritation among the farming and trading class, as well as among the labourers. As great fortunes have in America been usually won by unusual gifts, any envy they can excite is tempered by admiration for the ability shown in acquiring them. The common people felt a kind of pride in the late Mr. A. T. Stewart, and feel it now even in that flagrant "monopolist," Mr. Jay Gould. But while these particular railway magnates were men of talent, there were also in California millionaires who had grown rich merely by lucky speculation. They displayed their wealth with a vulgar and unbecoming ostentation. They did not, as rich men nearly always do in the Atlantic states, bestow a large part of it on useful public objects. There was therefore nothing to break the wave of suspicious dislike.

Most of the Western states have been peopled by a steady influx of settlers from two or three older states. Minnesota, for instance, and Iowa have grown by the overflow of Illinois and Ohio, as well as by immigration direct from Europe. But California was filled by a sudden rush of adventurers from all parts of the world. They came mostly via Panama, for there was no transcontinental railway till 1869, and a great many came from the Southern states. This mixed multitude, bringing with it a variety of manners, customs, and ideas, formed a society more mobile and unstable, less governed by fixed beliefs and principles, than one finds in such Northwestern communities as I have just mentioned. Living far away from the steadying influences of the Eastern states, the Californians have developed, and are proud of having done so, a sort of Pacific type, which, though differing but slightly from the usual Western type, has less of the English element than one discovers in the American who lives on the Atlantic side of the Rocky

---

[2] There are now four other transcontinental lines, but two of them lie far to the north, and another belongs to the same group of men who have controlled the Central Pacific.

Mountains. Add to this that California is the last place to the west before you come to Japan. That scum which the westward moving wave of emigration carries on its crest is here stopped, because it can go no farther. It accumulates in San Francisco, and forms a dangerous constituent in the population of that great and growing city—a population perhaps more mixed than one finds anywhere else in America, for Frenchmen, Italians, Portuguese, Greeks, and the children of Australian convicts abound there, side by side with Negroes, Germans, and Irish. Of the Chinese one need not speak; for, though they numbered in 1880 some twelve thousand, have a large quarter to themselves, and have given rise to the dominant question in Pacific coast politics, they do not themselves join in any political movement, but mingle as little with the whites as oil with water.

California, more than any other part of the Union, is a country by itself, and San Francisco a capital. Cut off from the more populous parts of the Mississippi Valley by an almost continuous desert of twelve hundred miles, across which the two daily trains move like ships across the ocean, separated from Oregon on the north by a wilderness of sparsely settled mountain and forest, it grew up in its own way and acquired a sort of consciousness of separate existence. San Francisco dwarfed the other cities, for in those days Los Angeles had not risen to importance, and was a commercial and intellectual centre and source of influence for the surrounding regions, more powerful over them than is any Eastern city over its neighbourhood. It was a New York which has got no New England on one side of it, and no shrewd and orderly rural population on the other, to keep it in order. Hence both state and city were, and in a sense still are, less steadied by national opinion than any other state or city within the wide compass of the Union.

These facts in Californian history must be borne in mind in order to understand the events I am about to sketch.[3] They show how suited is her soil to revolutionary movements. They suggest that movements natural here are much less likely to arise in other parts of the Union.

---

[3] The narrative which follows does not profess to be complete, for the difficulty of procuring adequate data was very great. When I visited San Francisco in 1881, and again in 1883, people were unwilling to talk about the Kearney agitation, feeling, it seemed to me, rather ashamed of it, and annoyed that so much should have been made of it (more they declared than it deserved) in the Eastern states. When I asked how I could learn the facts in detail, they answered, "Only by reading through the files of the newspapers for the years 1877–80 inclusive." Some added that there were so many lies in the newspapers that I would not have got at the facts even then. Failing this method, I was obliged to rely on what I could pick up in conversation. I have, however, derived some assistance from a brilliant article by Mr. Henry George, who was than a resident of San Francisco, published in the New York *Popular Science Monthly* for August 1880.

II. The Sand Lot Party

In 1877 California was suffering from "hard times." The severe commercial depression which began the Eastern states in 1873, and touched the lowest point about 1876, had reached the Pacific coast, and was aggravated there by a heavy fall in mining stocks. The great bonanza finds some years before had ushered in a period of wild speculation. Everybody gambled in stocks from railroad kings down to maidservants. Stocks had now fallen, and everybody was hard hit. The railroad kings could stand their losses, but the clerks and shop assistants and workmen suffered, for their savings were gone and many were left heavily in debt, with their houses mortgaged and no hope of redemption. Trade was bad, work was scarce, and for what there was of it the Chinese, willing to take only half the ordinary wages, competed with the white labourer. The mob of San Francisco, swelled by disappointed miners from the camps and labourers out of work, men lured from distant homes by the hope of wealth and ease in the land of gold, saw itself on the verge of starvation, while the splendid mansions of speculators, who fifteen years before had kept little shops, rose along the heights of the city, and the newspapers reported their luxurious banquets. In the country the farmers were scarcely less discontented. They too had "gone into stocks," their farms were mortgaged, and many of them were bankrupt. They complained that the railroads crushed them by heavy freight rates, and asked why they, the bone and sinew of the country, should toil without profit, while local millionaires and wealthy Eastern bondholders drew large incomes from the traffic which the plough of the agriculturist and the pickaxe of the miner had created.

Both in the country and in the city there was disgust with politics and the politicians. The legislature was composed almost wholly either of office-seekers from the city or of petty country lawyers, needy and narrow-minded. Those who had virtue enough not to be "got at" by the great corporations had not intelligence enough to know how to resist their devices. It was a common saying in the state that each successive legislature was worse than its predecessor. The meeting of the representatives of the people was seen with anxiety, their departure with relief. Some opprobrious epithet was bestowed upon each. One was "the legislature of a thousand drinks"; another "the legislature of a thousand steals." County government was little better; city government was even worse. The judges were not corrupt, but most of them, as was natural considering the scanty salaries assigned to them, were inferior men, not fit to cope with the counsel who practised before them.

Partly owing to the weakness of juries, partly to the intricacies of the law and the defects of the recently adopted code, criminal justice was halting and uncertain, and malefactors often went unpunished. It became a proverb that you might safely commit a murder if you took the advice of the best lawyers.

Neither Democrats nor Republicans had done, nor seemed likely to do, anything to remove these evils or to improve the lot of the people. They were only seeking (so men thought) places or the chance of jobs for themselves, and could always be bought by a powerful corporation. Working men must help themselves; there must be new methods and a new departure. Everything, in short, was ripe for a demagogue. Fate was kind to the Californians in sending them a demagogue of a mean type, noisy and confident, but with neither political foresight nor constructive talent.

Late in 1877 a meeting was called in San Francisco to express sympathy with the men then on strike at Pittsburg in Pennsylvania. Their riotous violence, which had alarmed the respectable classes all over America, had gratified the discontented railroad operatives of California, then meditating a strike of their own against a threatened reduction of wages. Some strong language used at this meeting, and exaggerated by the newspapers, frightened the businessmen into forming a sort of committee of public safety, with the president of the famous Vigilance Committee of 1856, a resolute and capable man, at its head. Persons enrolled by it paraded the streets with sticks for some days to prevent any attack on the Chinese, but it was soon perceived that there was no real danger, and the chief result of the incident was further irritation of the poorer classes, who perceived that the rich were afraid of them, and therefore disposed to deal harshly with them. Shortly after came an election of municipal officers and members of the state legislature. The contest, as is the custom in America, brought into life a number of clubs and other organizations, purporting to represent various parties or sections of a party, and among others a body calling itself the "Workingmen's Trade and Labour Union," the secretary of which was a certain Denis Kearney.[4] When the election was over, Kearney declared that he would keep his union going, and form a working man's party. He was Irish by birth, and though in business as a drayman, had some experience as a sailor, and held a master's certificate. He had borne a good character for industry and steadiness till some friend "put him into stocks," and the loss of what he hoped to gain is said to have first turned him to agitation. He had gained some faculty

---

[4] See note in the Appendix at the end of this volume.

in speaking by practice at a Sunday debating club called the Lyceum of Self Culture. A self-cultivating lyceum sounds as harmless as a social science congress, but there are times when even mutual improvement societies may be dangerous. Kearney's tongue, loud and violent, soon gathered an audience. On the west side of San Francisco, as you cross the peninsula from the harbour towards the ocean, there was a large open space, laid out for building, but not yet built on, covered with sand, and hence called the Sand Lot. Here the mob had been wont to gather for meetings; here Kearney formed his party. At first he had mostly vagabonds to listen, but one of the two great newspapers took him up. These two, the *Chronicle* and the *Morning Call*, were in keen rivalry, and the former, seeing in this new movement a chance of going ahead, filling its columns with sensational matter, and increasing its sale among working men, went in hot and strong for the Sand Lot party. One of its reporters is credited with having dressed up Kearney's speeches into something approaching literary form, for the orator was an imperfectly educated man, with ideas chiefly gathered from the daily press. The advertisement which the *Chronicle* gave him by its reports and articles, and which he repaid by advising working men to take it, soon made him a personage; and his position was finally assured by his being, along with several other speakers, arrested and prosecuted on a charge of riot, in respect of inflammatory speeches delivered at a meeting on the top of Nob Hill, one of the steep heights which make San Francisco the most picturesque of American cities. The prosecution failed, and Kearney was a popular hero. Clerks and the better class of citizens now began to attend his meetings, though many went from mere curiosity, as they would have gone to a circus: the W.P.C. (Workingman's Party of California) was organized as a regular party, embracing the whole state of California, with Kearney for its president. The gathering on the Sand Lot to which all those "eager for new things," as the discontented class were of old time called, flocked every Sunday afternoon to cheer denunciations of corporations and monopolists, and to "resolute" against the rich generally, became a centre of San Francisco politics, and through the reports of some newspapers and the attacks of others, roused the people of the entire state. The *Morning Call* had now followed the lead of the *Chronicle*, trying to outbid it for the support of the working men. There was nothing positive, nothing constructive or practical, either in these tirades or in the programme of the party, but an open-air crowd is not critical, and gives the loudest cheers to the strongest language. Kearney was not without shrewdness and address: he knew how to push himself to the front, and win the reputation of rugged honesty: he always dressed as a workman and ran for no office, and while denouncing politicians as thieves and capitalists as bloodsuckers, while threatening fire and the halter if the demands of the people were not granted, he tried to avoid direct breaches of the law. On one occasion he held a gathering beside the mansions of the Central Pacific magnates on Nob Hill, pointed to them and to a bonfire which marked the place of the meeting, and while telling the people that these men deserved to have their houses burned, abstained from suggesting that the torch should be applied then and there. Another time he bade the people wait a little till his party had carried their candidate for the governorship of the state: "Then we shall have the control of the militia and the armouries; then we can go down to the Pacific Mail Company's dock and turn back the steamers that come in bringing the Chinese."[5] Immense enthusiasm was evoked by these harangues. He was crowned with flowers; he was, when released from prison on one occasion, drawn in triumph by his followers in his own dray; newspaper reporters thronged around to interview him; prominent politicians came to seek favours from him on the sly. Discontent among the working class was the chief cause that made the new party grow, for grow it did; and though San Francisco was the centre of its strength, it had clubs in Sacramento and the other cities, all led by the San Francisco convention which Kearney swayed. But there were further causes not to be passed over. One was the distrust of the officials of the state and the city. The municipal government of San Francisco was far from pure. The officials enriched themselves, while the paving, the draining, the lighting were scandalously neglected; corruption and political jobbery had found their way even into school management, and liquor was sold everywhere, the publicans being leagued with the heads of the police to prevent the enforcement of the laws. Another was the support given to their countryman by the Irish, here a discontented and turbulent part of the population, by the lower class of German immigrants, and by the longshoremen, also an important element in this great port, and a dangerous element (as long ago as Athens) wherever one finds them. The activity of the *Chronicle* counted for much, for it was ably written, went everywhere, and continued to give a point and force to Kearney's harangues, which made them more effective in print than even his voice had made them to the listening crowds. Some think that the monied classes at this juncture ought to have bought up the *Chronicle* (supposing they could have

---

[5] In an earlier agitation this company's yard was attacked, but the only person killed was a lad (one of the special constables defending it) whose gun burst.

done so secretly), and its then editor and proprietor has been much maligned
if he would have refused to be bought up.[6] The newspapers certainly played
a great part in the movement; they turned the Workingman's Party into a
force by representing it to have already become one. Most important of all,
however, was the popular hatred of the Chinese. This is so strong in
California that any party which could become its exponent rode on the crest
of the wave. The old parties, though both denouncing Chinese immigration
in every convention they held, and professing to legislate against it, had
failed to check it by state laws, and had not yet obtained federal laws
prohibiting it. They had therefore lost the confidence of the masses on this
point, while the Sand Lot party, whose leaders had got into trouble for the
ferocity of their attacks on the Chinese, gained that confidence, and became
the "anti-Mongolian" party *par excellence*. Like Cato with his *Delenda est
Carthago*, Kearney ended every speech with the words, "And whatever
happens, the Chinese must go."

Meanwhile, where were the old parties, and what was their attitude to
this new one? It is so hard in America to establish a new movement outside
the regular party lines, that when such a movement is found powerful we
may expect to find that there exist special causes weakening these lines.
Such forces existed in California. She lies so far from the Atlantic and
Mississippi states, and has been so much occupied with her own concerns—
even the War of Secession did not interest her as it did the country east of
the Rocky Mountains—that the two great national parties have had a
comparatively weak hold on the people. The Chinese question and the
railroad question dwarfed the regular party issues. Neither party had shown
itself able to deal with the former—both parties were suspected of having
been tampered with on the latter. Both had incurred the discredit which
follows every party in hard times, when the public are poor, and see that
their taxes have been ill-spent. The Sand Lot party drew its support chiefly
from the Democrats, who here, as in the East, have the larger share of the
rabble: hence its rise was not unwelcome to the Republicans, because it
promised to divide and weaken their old opponents; while the Democrats,

---

[6] This editor became subsequently famous over America by his "difficulties" with a leading Baptist
minister of San Francisco. He had shot this minister in the street from behind the blind of a
carriage, and thereby made him so popular that the W.P.C. carried him for their candidate for
the mayoralty. The blood feud, however, was not settled by this unintended service, for the
clergyman's son went soon after to the *Chronicle* office and slew the editor. The young man was
tried, and, of course, acquitted. He had only done what the customary law of primitive peoples
requires. It survives in Albania, and is scarcely extinct in Corsica.

hoping ultimately to capture it, gave a feeble resistance. Thus it grew the faster, and soon began to run a ticket of its own at city and state elections. It carried most of the city offices, and when the question was submitted to the people whether a new constitution should be framed for California, it threw its vote in favour of having one and prevailed.

"The hoodlums"[7] and other ragamuffins who had formed the audience at the first Sand Lot meetings could not have effected this. But the W.P.C. now got a heavy vote in San Francisco from the better sort of workingmen, clerks, and small shopkeepers. In the rural districts they had still more powerful allies. The so-called Granger movement had spread from the upper Mississippi states into California, and enlisted the farmers in a campaign against the railroads and other "monopolists" and corporations. To compel a reduction of charges for goods and passengers, to prevent the railroad from combining with the Panama Steamship Company, to reduce public expenditure, to shift more taxation on to the shoulders of the rich, and generally to "cinch" capital—these were the aims of the Granger party; nor will anyone who knows California think them wholly unreasonable. The only way to effect them was by a new constitution, not only because some could not have been attained under the then existing constitution (passed in 1849 and amended in several points subsequently), but also because the people have more direct control over legislation through a convention making a constitution than they have over the action of a legislature. The delegates to a convention go straight from the election to their work, have not time to forget, or to devise means of evading, their pledges, are less liable to be "got at" by capitalists. They constitute only one house, whereas the legislature has two. There is no governor to stand in the way with his veto. The rarity and importance of the occasion fixes public attention. Thus a new constitution became the object of the popular cry, and a heavy vote in favour of having it was cast by the country farmers as well as by decent working people in the towns just because it promised a new departure and seemed to get behind the old parties. As often happens, the "good citizens," who ought to have seen the danger of framing a new constitution at a time of such excitement, were apathetic and unorganized.

Next came, in the summer of 1878, the choice of delegates to the convention which was to frame the new constitution. The Workingman's Party carried many seats in the convention, but its nominees were ignorant

---

[7] The term "hoodlums" denotes those who are called in Australia "larrikins," and in Liverpool "corner boys," loafing youths of mischievous proclivities.

men, without experience or constructive ideas.[8] Among the lawyers, who secured a large representation, there were some so closely bound by business ties to the great corporations as to be disposed to protect the interests of these corporations, as well as those of the legal profession. In justice to many of them it must be added that their respect for the principles of the common law and for sound constitutional doctrine led them to do their best to restrain the wild folly of their colleagues. However, the workingmen's delegates, together with the more numerous and less corruptible delegates of the farmers, got their way in many things and produced that surprising instrument by which California is now governed.

III. The New Constitution

An able Californian writer gives the following account of the Constitution of 1879:

> The new Constitution adopted in May, 1879 made radical changes in almost every department of the Government. It completely changed the judicial system, and thereby rendered necessary an alteration of almost all the laws relating to civil and criminal procedure. It revolutionized the working, and to a great extent the scope of the legislative department, lopping off special and local legislation, and obliging the objects heretofore obtained by such legislation to be covered by general law. As a part of this revolution, it required a new plan of county, township, and city organization, with the idea partly of forcing the same general laws upon all local governments, and partly of investing such local governments with power to legislate for themselves. But the main underlying spirit of the new instrument was an attack upon capital under the specious name of opposition to monopolies. To use an expressive Californian phrase, capital, and especially accumulated capital, wherever it was found, was to be "cinched."[9] With this object in view, cheap labour was to be driven out of the country, and corporations so restricted and hampered in their operations as to be unable to make large profits. The cry was that there were unjust discriminations on the part of railroads, and extortionate rates on the part of water and gas companies; that vicious

---

[8] Anecdotes were still current three years afterwards of the ignorance of some of the delegates. When the clause prohibiting any "law impairing the obligation of contracts" (taken from the federal Constitution) was under discussion, a San Francisco delegate objected to it. An eminent lawyer, leader of the Californian bar, who recognized in the objector a little upholsterer who used to do jobs about his house, asked why. The upholsterer replied, that he disapproved altogether of contracts, because he thought work should be done by hiring workmen for the day.

[9] "Cinching" is drawing tight the girths of a horse.

practices were indulged in by mining corporations; that fair day's wages for fair day's labour could not be obtained; that rich men rolled in luxury, and that poor men were cramped with want. It may be admitted that there were some grounds for these complaints. But it does not follow that capital was any more tyrannical or corporations more unconscionable than by their very nature they are compelled to be.[10]

Some of the above points, and particularly the changes in local government and in the judicial system, lie outside the scope of the present narrative, and I therefore confine myself to inquiring how far the objects aimed at by the Sand Lot party were attained through the constitution whose enactment it had secured. They and the Grangers, or farmers' party, which made common cause with them, sought to deal with four questions in which lay the grievances chiefly complained of by discontented Californians. These were:

The general corruption of politicians, and bad conduct of state, county, and city government
Taxation, alleged to press too heavily on the poorer classes
The tyranny of corporations, especially railroads
The Chinese

Let us see what remedies the constitution applied to each of these. The cry of the Sand Lot party had been: "None but honest men for the offices." To find the honest men, and, having found them, to put them in offices and keep them there, is the great problem of American politics. The contributions made to its solution by the convention of 1879 were neither novel nor promising. Its main results may be summed up under the four heads above-mentioned.[11]

1. It restricts and limits in every possible way the powers of the state legislature, leaving it little authority except to carry out by statutes the provisions of the constitution. It makes "lobbying," i.e., the attempt to corrupt a legislator, and the corrupt action of a legislator, felony.
2. It forbids the state legislature or local authorities to incur debts beyond a certain limit, taxes uncultivated land equally with cultivated, makes sums due on mortgage taxable in the district where the mortgaged

[10] Mr. Theodore H. Hittell in the *Berkeley Quarterly* for July 1880.
[11] As to the nature of state constitutions in general, and the restrictions they now impose on legislatures, see Chapters 37 *sqq.* in Volume II.

property lies, authorizes an income tax, and directs a highly inquisitorial scrutiny of everybody's property for the purposes of taxation.

3. It forbids the "watering of stock," declares that the state has power to prevent corporations from conducting their business so as to "infringe the general well-being of the State"; directs the charges of telegraph and gas companies, and of water-supplying bodies, to be regulated and limited by law; institutes a railroad commission with power to fix the transportation rates on all railroads and examine the books and accounts of all transportation companies.

4. It forbids all corporations to employ any Chinese, debars them from the suffrage (thereby attempting to transgress the Fifteenth Amendment of the federal Constitution), forbids their employment on any public works, annuls all contracts for "coolie labour," directs the legislature to provide for the punishment of any company which shall import Chinese, to impose conditions on the residence of Chinese, and to cause their removal if they fail to observe these conditions.

It also declares that eight hours shall constitute a legal day's work on all public works.

When the constitution came to be submitted to the vote of the people, in May 1879, it was vehemently opposed by the monied men, who of course influence, in respect of their wealth, a far larger number of votes than they themselves cast. Several of the conservative delegates had, I was told, abstained from putting forth their full efforts to have the worst proposals rejected by the convention in the belief that when the people came to consider them, they would ensure the rejection of the whole instrument. Some of its provisions were alleged to be opposed to the Constitution of the United States, and therefore null. Others were denounced as ruinous to commerce and industry, calculated to drive capital out of the country. The struggle was severe, but the Granger party commanded so many rural votes, and the Sand Lot party so many in San Francisco (whose population is nearly a third of that of the entire state), that the constitution was carried, though by a small majority, only 11,000 out of a total of 145,000 citizens voting. Of course it had to be enacted as a whole, amendment being impossible where a vote of the people is taken.

The next thing was to choose a legislature to carry out the constitution. Had the same influences prevailed in this election as prevailed in that of the constitutional convention, the results might have been serious. But fortunately there was a slight reaction, now that the first and main step seemed to have been taken. The Republicans, Democrats, and Sand Lot party all ran "tickets," and owing to this division of the working men's and the Granger vote between Kearneyite candidates and the Democrats, the Republicans secured a majority, though a small one. Now the Republicans are in California, as they would themselves say, the moderate or conservative party, or as their opponents said, the party of the rich and the monopolists. Their predominance made the legislature of 1880 a body more cautious than might have been expected. Professing hearty loyalty to the new constitution, the majority showed this loyalty by keeping well within the letter of that instrument, while the working men and farmer members were disposed to follow out by bold legislation what they called its spirit. Thus the friends and the enemies of the constitution changed places. Those who had opposed it in the convention posed as its admirers and defenders; while those who had clamoured for and carried it now began to wish that they had made its directions more imperative. The influence and the money of the railroad and the other great corporations were of course brought into play, despite the terrors of a prosecution for felony, and became an additional "conservative force" of great moment.

Thus a series of statutes was passed which gave effect to the provisions of the constitution in a form perhaps as little harmful as could be contrived, and certainly less harmful than had been feared when the constitution was put to the vote. Many bad bills, particularly those aimed at the Chinese, were defeated, and one may say generally the expectations of the Sand Lot men were grievously disappointed.

While all this was passing, Kearney had more and more declined in fame and power. He did not sit either in the constitutional convention or in the legislature of 1880. The mob had tired of his harangues, especially as little seemed to come of them, and as the candidates of the W.P.C. had behaved no better in office than those of the old parties. He had quarrelled with the *Chronicle*. He was, moreover, quite unfitted by knowledge or training to argue the legal, economical, and political questions involved in the new constitution, so that the prominence of these questions threw him into the background. An anti-Chinese agitation, in which the unemployed marched about San Francisco, calling on employers to discharge all Chinese workmen, caused some alarm in the winter of 1879–80, but Kearney was absent at the time, and when he returned his party was wavering. Even his prosecution and imprisonment on what seems to have been a somewhat trivial charge gave only a brief revival to his popularity. The W.P.C. was defeated in a city election in March 1880 by a combination of the better class of Democrats with the Republicans, and soon after expired.

When I was in San Francisco in the fall of 1881, people talked of Kearney as a spent rocket. Some did not know whether he was in the city. Others said that the capitalists had rendered him harmless by the gift of a new dray and team. Not long afterwards he went East, and mounted the stump on behalf of the Labour party in New York. He proved, however, scarcely equal to his fame, for mob oratory is a flower which does not always bear transplantation. Though he lived till 1906, he was never again a leading figure in California politics, and was, indeed, in 1883, no longer deemed a force to be regarded. And now, as the Icelandic sagas say, he is out of the story.

After the session of 1880, Californian politics resumed their old features. Election frauds are said to have become less frequent since glass ballot boxes were adopted, whereby the practice of stuffing a box with papers before the voters arrive in the morning has been checked. But the game between the two old parties goes on as before. What remained of the Sand Lot group was reabsorbed into the Democratic party, out of which it had mainly come, and to which it had strong affinities. The city government of San Francisco is much what it was before the agitation—a few years later, under Boss Buckley, it was even worse—nor does the legislature seem to be any purer or wiser. When the railroad commission had to be elected, the railroad magnates managed so to influence the election, although it was made directly by the people, that two of the three commissioners chosen were, or soon afterwards came, under their influence, while the third was a mere declaimer. None of them possessed the practical knowledge of railway business needed to enable them to deal, in the manner contemplated by the constitution, with the oppressions alleged to be practised by the railroads; and the complaints of those oppressions seemed in 1883 to be as common as formerly. I enquired in that year why the railroad magnates had not been content to rely on certain provisions of the federal Constitution against the control sought to be exerted over their undertaking. The answer was that they had considered this course, but had concluded that it was cheaper to capture a majority of the commission. The passing of the Interstate Commerce Act by Congress was expected to bring about a change in the situation, but that act disappointed its promoters; and the tyranny of the Southern Pacific Railroad (as it is now called, for it has absorbed the Central Pacific line) remained severe. In July 1894, when the dispute between the Pullman Company and their employees in Illinois gave rise to a railway strike over large parts of the West, the mobs which attacked the depots and wrecked the trains in California seem to have been regarded by the mass of the people with a sympathy which can be attributed to nothing but the general hostility felt to the railroad company which had so long lain like an incubus on the state.

Some of the legislation framed under the Constitution of 1879 was soon pronounced by the supreme court of the state invalid, as opposed to that instrument itself or to the federal Constitution. So far as the condition of the people at large was affected, it is not so much to the constitution as to the general advance in prosperity that they owe what they have gained. However, the restrictions imposed on the legislature (as regards special legislation) and on local authorities (as regards borrowing and the undertaking of costly public works) have proved beneficial. Congress passed statutes stopping Chinese immigration, and the subsequent influx of Japanese labourers was reduced in 1908 to small dimension. The net result of the whole agitation was to give the monied classes in California a fright; to win for the state a bad name throughout America, and, by checking for a time the influx of capital, to retard her growth just when prosperity was reviving over the rest of the country; to worry, without seriously crippling, the great corporations, and to leave the working classes and farmers where they were. No great harm was done, and the constitution, pruned and trimmed by the courts, and frequently amended, usually in a 'radical' sense, ultimately came to work tolerably. Since those days, other states have enacted constitutions no less rash and no less drastic in some of their provisions.

IV. Observations on the Movement

I would leave the reader to draw a moral for himself, were he not likely to err, as I did myself, till corrected by my Californian friends, by thinking the whole movement more serious than it really was.

It rose with surprising ease and swiftness. The conditions were no doubt exceptionally favourable. No other population in America furnished so good a field for demagogy. But the demagogue himself was not formidable. He did not make the movement, but merely rode for a moment on the crest of the wave. Europeans may say that a stronger man, a man with knowledge, education, and a fierce tenacity of fibre, might have built up a more permanent power, and used it with a more destructive effect. But Californians say that a strong man would not have been suffered to do what Kearney did with impunity. Kearney throve—so they allege—because the solid classes despised him, and felt that the best thing was to let him talk himself out and reveal his own hollowness.

The movement fell as quickly as it rose. This was partly due, as has been said, to the incompetence of the leader, who had really nothing to propose and did not know how to use the force that seemed to have come to his hands. Something, however, must be set down to the credit of the American party system. The existing parties are so strong, and are spread over so wide an area, that it is very difficult to create a new party. Resting on a complex local organization, and supported by the central organization for the purposes of federal politics, they can survive a temporary eclipse in a particular state, while a new party cannot count itself permanent till it has established some such organization, central as well as local. This may operate badly in keeping old parties alive, when they deserve to die. But it operates well in checking the growth or abridging the life of mischievous local factions. That fund of good sense, moreover, which lies at the bottom of nearly every native American mind, soon produces a reaction against extreme measures. When the native voters, especially those who owned even a little property, had relieved their minds by voting for the new constitution, they felt they had gone far enough in the direction of change, and at the election of a legislature voted for moderate men. Support from this class having been withdrawn, the Sand Lot rabble ceased to be dangerous; and although threats of violence were abundant, and sometimes bloodthirsty, there was very little sedition or disorder.

Every stump orator in the West says a great deal more than he means, and is promptly discounted by his hearers. The populace of San Francisco has now and again menaced the Chinese quarter and the docks of the Pacific Mail Steamship Company, which brought the Chinese over, until Congress checked them. Once the Chinese armed in defence of Chinatown, and twice during these agitations a committee of public safety was formed to protect the banks and keep order in the streets. But many people doubt whether order was really endangered. The few attacks made on Chinese stores were done by small bands of hoodlums, who disappeared at the sight of the police. The police and militia seem to have behaved well all through. Moreover, any serious riot would in San Francisco be quelled speedily and severely by the respectable classes, who would supersede the municipal authority if it seemed to fear, or to be secretly leagued with, the authors of sedition. Even the meetings of the various political parties were scarcely ever disturbed or "bulldozed" by their opponents. When the Kearneyites once or twice molested Democratic meetings, they were so promptly repelled, that they desisted for the future.

There was very little of conscious or constructive communism or socialism in the movement. Kearney told the working men that the rich had thriven at their expense, and talked of hanging thieves in office, and burning the houses of capitalists. But neither he nor any other demagogue assailed the institution of property. The farmers, whose vote carried the new constitution, owned their farms, and would have recoiled from suggestions of agrarian socialism. And in fact the new constitution, although it contains provisions hostile to capital, "is anything but agrarian or communistic, for it entrenches vested rights, especially in land, more thoroughly than before. . . . It is anything but a working man's Constitution; it levies a poll tax without exemption; disfranchises a considerable portion of the floating labour vote; prevents the opening of public works in emergencies, and in various ways which working men, even in their present stage of enlightenment, may easily see, sacrifices the interests of the labouring classes, as well as the capitalists, to what the landowners regard as their interests."[12] A solitary Parisian communist who was elected to the convention "exercised no influence, and was expelled from the party for refusing to support the new Constitution." There were some rich men, and lawyers connected with the great corporations, among the candidates and supporters of the Sand Lot party. Others of the same class who tried secretly to use it had probably their selfish ends to serve, but would have been less willing to increase its strength had they regarded it as an attack on property in general. Theoretical Communism has not yet much hold upon native Americans, while its practical application does not commend itself to farmers who own their land and workmen who own their houses. The belief which prevailed in the Eastern states that the movement had a communistic character was therefore a mistaken one.

More mischief would have been done but for the existence of the federal Constitution. It imposed a certain check on the convention, who felt the absurdity of trying to legislate right in the teeth of an overruling instrument. It has been the means of upsetting some of the clauses of the Constitution of 1879, and some of the statutes passed by the legislature under them, and has discouraged attempts to pass others.

On the whole, not much evil has been wrought, at least not much compared with what was feared in the state itself, and believed in the East to have resulted. The better sort of Californians two years after were no longer alarmed, but seemed half ashamed and half amused when they recollected the scenes I have described. They felt somewhat as a man feels

[12] Mr. H. George, in *Popular Science Monthly* for August 1880.

when he awakes unrefreshed after a night of bad dreams. He fears at first that his parched tongue and throbbing head may mean that he has caught a fever. But when he has breakfasted and is again immersed in work, these sensations and apprehensions disappear together. After all, said the lawyers and bankers of San Francisco, we are going on as before, property will take care of itself in this country, things are not really worse so far as our business is concerned.

Neither are things better. It is natural to suppose that a shock, however short, must make a difference to a community, and affect its future fortunes. If this shock has so affected California, the results are not yet apparent. Though the new constitution has not altered the economic condition of the workmen and farmers, it might have been thought that the crisis, which suddenly startled this busy and (in San Francisco) luxurious society, would rouse good citizens to a more active interest in politics, make them see the necessity of getting better men into the offices and the legislature, and, indeed, of purifying public life altogether. But these consequences do not seem to have followed. In the stress and hurry of Californian life, impressions pass swiftly away. Good citizens are disposed to stand aside; and among the richer there are those who look forward to a time when, having made their fortunes, they will go East to spend them. San Francisco in particular continued to be deplorably misgoverned, and has passed from the tyranny of one ring to that of another, with no change save in the persons of those who prey upon her, and in the fact that there is now a well organized Labour party which in 1909 carried its candidate for mayor. The earthquake of 1906 was incidentally the means of unveiling corruptions which led to a temporary purification of city politics; but there was presently a relapse. It may be that another social and political shock is in store for the Golden State, a shock which, now that socialistic doctrines have made more progress, might be more violent than that of 1879, yet still within legal limits, for there seems no danger, in spite of such outbreaks as marked the great railway strikes of 1894, of mere mob law and anarchy. The forces at the disposal of order are always the stronger. It may on the other hand be that as society settles down from the feverish instability of these early days, as the mass of the people acquire a more enlightened view of their true interests, as those moral influences which count for so much in America assert their dominion more widely, the present evils will slowly pass away. The president of the Vigilance Committee of 1856 told me that all he had seen happen in San Francisco, since the days when it was a tiny Spanish mission station, made him confident that everything would come out straight. Probably he is right.

American experience shows that the optimists generally are. But as respects the municipal government of this great city his prophecy was in 1910 still awaiting fulfillment.

EPILOGUE TO THIS AND THE TWO LAST PRECEDING CHAPTERS

The illustrations given in these three chapters of perversions of popular government carry their moral with them, and only a few parting comments are needed.

Neither of the two great political parties has had in respect of the events narrated a better record than its rival. If the Tammany Ring sheds little lustre upon the Democrats of New York, the Gas Ring of Philadelphia is no more creditable to the Republicans of Pennsylvania.

Both in New York and in Philadelphia there was nothing truly political in the character and career of the rings. Tammany had been for thirty years a selfish combination of men who had purely personal ends to serve; and Tweed in particular was a mere vulgar robber. So the Gas Ring strove and throve, and its successors have striven and thriven, solely to secure patronage and gain to their respective members. True indeed it is that neither in New York nor in Philadelphia could the rings have won their way to power without the connivance of chiefs among the national parties, who needed the help of the vote the rings controlled; true also that that vote would never have become so large had not many citizens looked on the rings as the "regular" organizations, and heirs of the local party traditions. But neither ring had ever any distinctive principles or proposals; neither ever appealed to the people on behalf of a doctine or a scheme calculated to benefit the masses. Lucre, with office as a means to lucre, was their only aim, the party for the sake of the party their only watchword.

What, then, are the salient features of these two cases, and what the lessons they enforce? They are these. The power of an organization in a multitude; the facility with which the administrative machinery of government may be made the instrument of private gain; the disposition of the average respectable citizen to submit to bad government rather than take the trouble of overthrowing it. These are not wholly new phenomena, but they are hardly such as would have been looked for in the United States; and not one of them was feared when Tocqueville wrote.

Very different, and far less discreditable to those concerned, was the case of California. The movement which gave birth to the new constitution was a legitimate political movement. It was crude in its aims, and tainted with demagogism in its methods. But it was evoked by real evils; and it sought, however ignorantly, the public good. Kearney had no sordid personal ends to serve, and gained for himself nothing more solid than notoriety. His agitation was essentially the same as that which has appeared in the Western states under the forms of Grangerism, the Farmers' Alliance, and Populism, an effort to apply political remedies to evils, real or supposed, which are mainly economic rather than political, and only a part of which legislation can remove. Similar movements must from time to time be expected; all that can be hoped is to keep them within constitutional lines, and prevent them from damaging the credit and retarding the prosperity of the states they affect. Nothing is more natural than that those who suffer from hard times and see that a few men grow rich while the vast majority remain poor should confound the mischiefs which arise from state or city maladministration and from the undue power which the laws have permitted corporations to acquire with other hardships due to the constitution of human nature and the conditions of the world we live in, and should, possessing the whole power of the state, strike out wildly at all three at once. In a country so little restrained by ancient traditions or deference to the educated class as is Western America, a country where the aptitude for politics is so much in advance of economic wisdom, it is less surprising that these storms should sometimes darken the sky than that they should uproot so little in their course.

CHAPTER 91

The Home of the Nation

There are three points wherein the territories which constitute the United States present phenomena new in the annals of the world. They contain a huge people whose blood is becoming mixed in an unprecedented degree by the concurrent immigration of numerous European races. We find in them, besides the predominant white nation, ten millions of men belonging to a dark race, thousands of years behind in its intellectual development, but legally equal in political and civil rights. And thirdly, they furnish an instance to which no parallel can be found of a vast area, including regions very dissimilar in their natural features, occupied by a population nearly the whole of which speaks the same tongue, and all of which lives under the same institutions. Of these phenomena the first two, already more than once referred to, are dealt with in later chapters. The third suggests to us thoughts and questions which cannot pass unnoticed. No one can travel in the United States without asking himself whether this immense territory will remain united or be split up into a number of independent communities; whether, even if it remain united, diverse types of life and character will spring up within it; whether and how far climatic and industrial conditions will affect those types, carrying them farther from the prototypes of Europe. These questions, as well as other questions regarding the future local distribution of wealth and population, open fields of inquiry and speculation too wide to be here explored. Yet some pages may well be given to a rapid survey of the geographical conditions of the United States, and of the influence those conditions have exerted and may, so far as can be foreseen, continue to exert on the growth of the nation, its political and economical development. Beginning with a few observations first on the orography of the country and then upon its meteorology, we may consider how mountain ranges and climate have hitherto affected the movement of colonization and the main stream of political history. The chief natural sources of wealth may next be mentioned, and their possible effect indicated upon the development of population in particular areas, as well as upon the preservation of the permanent unity of the Republic.

One preliminary remark must not be omitted. The relation of geographical conditions to national growth changes, and with the upward progress of humanity the ways in which Nature moulds the fortunes of man are always varying. Man must in every stage be for many purposes dependent upon the circumstances of his physical environment. Yet the character of that dependence changes with his advance in civilization. At first he is helpless, and, therefore, passive. With what Nature gives in the way of food, clothing, and lodging he must be content. She is strong, he is weak; so she dictates his whole mode of life. Presently, always by slow degrees, but most quickly in those countries where she neither gives lavishly nor yet presses on him with a discouraging severity, he begins to learn how to make her obey him, drawing from her stores materials which his skill handles in such wise as to make him more and more independent of her. He defies the rigours of climate; he overcomes the obstacles which mountains, rivers, and forests place in the way of communications; he discovers the secrets of the physical forces and makes them his servants in the work of production. But the very multiplication of the means at his disposal for profiting by what Nature supplies brings him into ever closer and more complex relations with her. The variety of her resources, differing in different regions, prescribes the kind of industry for which each spot is fitted; and the competition of nations, growing always keener, forces each to maintain itself in the struggle by using to the utmost every facility for production or for the transportation of products. Thus certain physical conditions, whether of soil or of climate, of accessibility of inaccessibility, or perhaps of such available natural forces as waterpower, conditions of supreme importance in the earlier stages of man's progress, are now of less relative moment, while others, formerly of small account, have received their full significance by our swiftly advancing knowledge of the secrets of Nature and mastery of her forces. It is this which makes the examination of the influence of physical environment on the progress of nations so intricate a matter; for while the environment remains, as a whole, constant, its several parts vary in their importance from one age to another.[1] A certain severity of climate, for instance, which

---

[1] Navigable rivers, for instance, were at one time the main channels of commerce, so that towns were founded and prospered in respect of the advantages they gave. The extension of railways diminished their importance, and many great cities now owe their growth to their having become

retarded the progress of savage man, has been found helpful to semi-civilized man, in stimulating him to exertion, and in maintaining a racial vigour greater than that of the inhabitants of those hotter regions where civilization first arose. And thus in considering how man's lot and fate in the western continent have been affected by the circumstances of that continent, we must have regard not only to what he found on his arrival there, but to the resources which have been subsequently disclosed. Nor can this latter head be exhausted, because it is impossible to conjecture what still latent forces or capacities may be revealed in the onward march of science, and how such a revelation may affect the value of the resources now known to exist or hereafter to be explored.

It is only on a very few salient points of this large and complex subject that I shall touch in sketching the outlines of North American geography and noting some of the effects on the growth of the nation attributable to them.

The territory of the United States extends nearly 3,000 miles east and west from the Bay of Fundy to the mouth of the Columbia River, and 1,400 miles north and south from the Lake of the Woods to the Gulf of Mexico at Galveston. Compared with Europe, the physical structure of this area of 3,025,000 square miles[2] (excluding Alaska) is not only larger in scale, but far simpler. Instead of the numerous peninsulas and islands of Europe, with the bold and lofty chains dividing its peoples from one another, we find no isles (except Long Island) of any size on the two coasts of the United States, only one large peninsula (that of Florida), and only two mountain systems. Not only the lakes and rivers, but the plains also, and the mountain ranges, are of enormous dimensions. The coast presents a smooth outline. No great inlets, such as the Mediterranean and the Baltic, pierce the land and cut off one district from another, furnishing natural boundaries behind which distinct nations may grow up.

This vast area may be divided into four regions—two of level country, two, speaking roughly, of mountain. Beginning from the Atlantic, we find a strip which on the coast is nearly level, and then rises gradually westwards

---

centres where trunk lines meet. The discovery of means of cheaply transmitting electric power has given to flowing water a new commercial value, which however is greatest where the streams are too rapid for navigation.

[2] The area of China, the country with which the United States is most fit to be compared, since India and the Russian Empire are inhabited by many diverse races, speaking wholly diverse tongues, is estimated at 1,336,000 square miles; and the population, the estimates of which range from 280,000,000 to 350,000,000, may possibly be, in A.D. 2000, equalled by that of the United States.

into an undulating country. It varies in breadth from thirty or forty miles in the north to two hundred and fifty in the south, and has been called by geographers the Atlantic Plain and Slope. Behind this strip comes a range, or rather a mass of generally parallel ranges, of mountains. These are the Alleghenies, or so-called "Appalachian system," in breadth from one hundred to two hundred miles, and with an average elevation of from two to four thousand feet, some few summits reaching six thousand. Beyond them, still further to the west, lies the vast basin of the Mississippi and its tributaries, 1,100 miles wide and 1,200 miles long. Its central part is an almost unbroken plain for hundreds of miles on each side the river, but this plain rises slowly westward in rolling undulations into a sort of plateau, which, at the foot of the Rocky Mountains, has attained the height of 5,000 feet above the sea. The fourth region consists of the thousand miles that lie between the Mississippi basin and the Pacific. It includes three not entirely disconnected mountain ranges, the Rockies, the Sierra Nevada (continued northwards in the Cascade Range), and the much lower Coast Range (or rather series of roughly parallel ranges), which runs along the shore of the ocean. This region is generally mountainous, though within it there are some extensive plateaux and some wide valleys. Most of it is from 4,000 to 8,000 feet above the sea, with many summits exceeding 14,000, though none reaches 15,000. A considerable part of it, including the desert of Nevada, does not drain into the ocean, but sees its feeble streams received by lakes or swallowed up in the ground.

Before we consider how these natural divisions have influenced, and must continue to influence, American history, it is well to observe how materially they have affected the climate of the continent, which is itself a factor of prime historical importance. Two points deserve special notice. One is the great extent of temperate area which the continent presents. As North America is crossed by no mountain chains running east and west, corresponding to the Alps and Pyrenees in Europe, or to the Caucasus, Himalaya, and Altai in Asia, the cold winds of the north sweep down unchecked over the vast Mississippi plain, and give its central and southern parts, down to the Gulf of Mexico, winters cooler than the latitude seems to promise, or than one finds in the same latitudes in Europe. Nor ought the influence of the neighbouring seas to pass unregarded. Europe has, south of the narrow Mediterranean, a vast reservoir of heat in the Sahara: North America has the wide stretch of the Gulf of Mexico and the Caribbean Sea, with no region both hot and arid beyond. Thus Tennessee and Arkansas, in the latitude of Andalusia and Damascus, have a winter like that of Edinburgh twenty degrees further to the north; and while the summer of Minnesota, in latitude 45°, is as hot as that of Bordeaux or Venice in the same latitude, the winter is far more severe. Only the lowlands along the Atlantic coast as far north as Cape Hatteras have a high winter as well as summer temperature, for they are warmed by the hot water of the Gulf Stream, just as the extreme northeastern coast is chilled by the Polar current which washes it. The hilly country behind these southern Atlantic lowlands—the western parts of the two Carolinas, northern Georgia and Alabama—belongs to the Appalachian system, and is high enough to have cool and in parts even severe winters.

The other point relates to the amount of moisture. The first two of our four regions enjoy an ample rainfall. So do the eastern and the central parts of the Mississippi basin. When, however, we reach the centre of the continent, some four hundred miles west of the Mississippi, the air grows dry, and the scanty showers are barely sufficient for the needs of agriculture. It is only by the help of irrigation that crops can be raised all along the east foot of the Rocky Mountains and in the valleys of the fourth region, until we cross the Sierra Nevada and come within two hundred miles of the Pacific. In much of this Rocky Mountain region, therefore, stock rearing, or "ranching," as it is called, takes the place of tillage, though the recently invented methods of "dry farming" have enlarged the cultivable area. In some districts there is not enough moisture even to support grass. Between the Rocky Mountains and the Sierra Nevada there lie vast deserts, the largest that which stretches westward from the Great Salt Lake,[3] a desert of clay and stones rather than of sand, bearing only alkaline plants with low, prickly shrubs, and, apparently, destined to remain, save in some few spots where brooks descend from the mountains,[4] eternally sterile and solitary. Lofty as these environing mountains are, they bear scarce any perpetual snow, and no glaciers at all south of the fortieth parallel of north latitude.[5] The great peaks of Colorado lie little further south than the Pennine Alps, which they almost equal in height, but it is only in nooks and hollows turned away from the sun that snow lasts through the summer, so scanty is the winter snowfall and so rapidly does evaporation proceed in the dry air. That same general north and south direction of the American mountain ranges, which

---

[3] Similar but smaller deserts occur in Idaho and southeastern Oregon, and also in the extreme southwest. Part of the desert of Southern California is, like part of the Sahara and the valley of the Jordan and the Dead Sea, beneath the level of the ocean.

[4] In Central Colorado, when snow falls, it does not melt but disappears by evaporation, so dry is the air. Sir J. D. Hooker has (in his *Himalayan Journals*) noted the same phenomenon in Tibet.

[5] There is a small glacier on Mount Shasta.

gives cool winters to the Southern states, cuts off the westborne rainclouds from the Pacific, and condemns one-half or more of our fourth region to aridity. On the other hand, northwestern California, with the western parts of Oregon and Washington, washed by the Japan current, enjoy both a moderate and a humid—in some places very humid—climate, which, along the Pacific coast north of latitude 43°, resembles that of southwestern England.

Reserving for the moment a consideration of the wealth-producing capacities of the regions at whose physical structure and climate we have glanced, let us note how that structure and climate have affected the fortunes of the people.

Whoever examines the general lines of a nation's growth will observe that its development has been guided and governed by three main factors. The first is the preexisting character and habits of the race out of which the nation grows. The second is the physical aspect of the land the nation is placed in, and the third embraces the international concomitants of its formation—that is to say, the pressure of other nations upon it, and the external political circumstances which have controlled its movement, checking it in one direction or making it spread in another. The first of these factors may, in the case of the American people, be assumed as known, for their character and habits were substantially English.[6] To the second I will return presently. The third factor has been in the United States so unusually simple that one may dismiss it in a few sentences. In examining the origin of such nations as the German or French or Russian or Swiss or Spanish, one must constantly have regard to the hostile or friendly races or powers which acted on them; and these matters are, for the earlier periods of European history, often obscure. About America we know everything, and what we know may be concisely stated. The territory now covered by the United States was, from a political point of view, practically vacant when discovered in the end of the sixteenth century; for the aborigines, though their resistance was obstinate in places, and though that resistance did much to form the character of the Western pioneers, may be left out of account as a historical force. This territory was settled from three sides,

[6] There were doubtless other influences, especially Dutch; and the Scoto-Irish element differed somewhat from the English. But these are, after all, relatively small, not ten per cent, so to speak, of the whole. Far more important than the diverse elements of blood were the conditions of colonial, and especially of frontier, life which moulded the young nation, repeating in the period between 1780 and 1820 many of the phenomena which had accompanied the first settlements of the seventeenth century.

east, south, and west, and by three European peoples. The Spaniards and French occupied points on the coast of the Gulf. The Spaniards took the shores of the Pacific. The English (reckoning among the English the cognate Dutchmen and Swedes) planted a series of communities along the Atlantic coast. Of these three independent colonizations, that on the Gulf was feeble, and passed by purchase to the Anglo-Americans in 1803 and 1819. That on the Pacific was still more feeble, and also passed, but by conquest, to the Anglo-Americans in 1848. Thus the occupation of the country has been from its eastern side alone (save that California received her immigrants by sea between 1847 and 1867), and the march of the people has been steadily westward and southwestward. They have spread where they would. Other powers have scarcely affected them. Canada, indeed, bounds them on the north, but not till about 1890 did they begin to settle in the rich wheat lands of her Northwest, while from 1860 onwards there has been a considerable immigration from eastern Canada into the bordering parts of the United States. Like the Spaniards in South America, like the British in Australia, like the Russians in Siberia, the Anglo-Americans have had a free field; and we may pass from the purely political or international factor in the development of the nation to consider how its history has been affected by those physical conditions which have been previously noted.

The English in America were, when they began their march, one people, though divided into a number of autonomous communities; and, to a people already advanced in civilization, the country was one country, as if destined by nature to retain one and undivided whatever nation might occupy it.

The first settlements were in the region described above as the Atlantic Plain and Slope. No natural boundary, whether of water or mountain or forest, divided the various communities. The frontier line which bounded each colony was an artificial line—a mere historical accident. So long as they remained near the coast, nature opposed no obstacle to their cooperation in war, nor to their free social and commercial intercourse in peace. When, however, they had advanced westwards as far as the Alleghenies, these mountains barred their progress, not so much in the North, where the valley of the Hudson and Mohawk gave an easy path inland, as in Pennsylvania, Virginia, and Carolina. The dense, tangled, and often thorny underwood, even more than the high steep ridges, checked the westward movement of population, prevented the settlers from spreading out widely, as the Spaniards dispersed themselves over Central and South America, and helped, by inducing a comparatively dense population, to build up compact commonwealths on the Atlantic coast. So, too, the existence of this rough and, for a long time, almost impassable mountain belt, tended to cut off those who had crossed it into the western wilderness from their more polished parent stock, to throw them on their own resources in the struggle with the fierce aborigines of Kentucky and Ohio, and to give them that distinctive character of frontiersmen which was so marked a feature of American history during the first half of the nineteenth century, and has left deep traces on the Western men of today.

When population began to fill the Mississippi basin the essential physical unity of the country became more significant. It suggested to Jefferson, and it led Congress to approve, the purchase of Louisiana from Napoleon, for those who had begun to occupy the valleys of the Ohio and Tennessee rivers felt that they could not afford to be cut off from the sea to which these highways of commerce led. Once the stream of migration across, and around the southern extremity of, the Alleghenies had begun to flow steadily, the settlers spread out in all directions over the vast plain, like water over a marble floor. The men of the Carolinas and Georgia filled Alabama, Mississippi, and Arkansas; the men of Virginia and Kentucky filled southern Indiana, southern Illinois, and Missouri; the men of New England, New York, and Ohio filled Michigan, northern Illinois, Wisconsin, Iowa, and Minnesota. From the source to the mouth of the Mississippi there was nothing to break them up or keep them apart. Every Western state, except where it takes a river as a convenient boundary, is bounded by straight lines, because every state is an artificial creation. The people were one, and the wide featureless plain was also one. It has been cut into those huge plots we call states, not because there were physical or racial differences requiring divisions, but merely because political reasons made a federal seem preferable to a unitary system. As the size of the plain showed that the nation would be large, so did the character of the plain promise that it would remain united. When presently steamers came to ply upon the rivers, each part of the vast level was linked more closely to the others; and when the network of railways spread itself out from the East to the Mississippi, the Alleghenies practically disappeared. They were no longer a barrier to communication. Towns sprang up in their valleys; and now the three regions, which have been described as naturally distinct, the Atlantic slope, the Alleghenies, and the Mississippi basin, have become, economically and socially as well as politically, one country, though the dwellers in the wilder parts of the broad mountain belt still lag far behind their neighbours of the eastern and western lowlands.

When, however, the swelling tide of emigration reached the arid lands at the eastern base of the Rocky Mountains, its course was for a time stayed. This fourth region of mountain and desert, lying between the prairies of the Mississippi affluents and the Pacific Ocean, was, except its coast line, a practically unknown land till its cession by Mexico in 1846, and the inner and higher parts of it remained unexplored for some twenty years longer. As it was mostly dry and rugged, there was little to tempt settlers, for vast tracts of good land remained untouched in the central Mississippi plain. Many years might have passed before it began to fill up, but for the unexpected finding of gold in California. This event at once drew in thousands of settlers; and fresh swarms followed as other mines, principally of silver, began to be discovered in the inland mountain ranges; till at last for the difficult and dangerous wagon tract there was substituted a railway, completed in 1869, over mountains and through deserts from the Missouri to the Pacific. Had the Americans of 1850 possessed no more scientific resources than their grandfathers in 1790, the valleys of the Pacific coast, accessible only by sea round Cape Horn, or across the Isthmus of Panama, would have remained isolated from the rest of the country, with a tendency to form a character and habits of their own, and possibly disposed to aim at political independence. This, however, the telegraph and the railways have prevented. Yet the Rocky Mountains have not, like the Alleghenies, disappeared. The populous parts of California, Oregon, and Washington still find that range and the deserts a far more effective barrier than are the lower and narrower ridges on the eastern side of the continent. The fourth region remains a distinct section of the United States, both geographically and to some extent in its social and industrial aspects. All this was to be expected. What need not have happened, and might even have been thought unlikely, was the easy acquisition by the Anglo-Americans of California, Oregon, and Washington, regions far removed from the dominions which the Republic already possessed. Had the competition for unappropriated temperate regions been half as keen in 1840 as it was fifty years later for tropical Africa (a less attractive possession) between Germany, France, and Britain, some European power might have pounced upon these territories. They might then have become and remained a foreign country to the United States, and have had few and comparatively slight relations with the Mississippi basin. It is not nature, but the historical accident which left them in the hands of a feeble power like Mexico, that has made them now, and, so far as can be foreseen, for a long future, members of the great federation.

In the southeast as well as in the west of the North American continent, climate has been a prime factor in determining the industrial and political history of the nation. South of the thirty-fifth parallel of latitude, although the winters are cool enough to be reinvigorative, and to enable a race drawn from Northern Europe to thrive and multiply,[7] the summers, are, in the lowest grounds, too hot for such a race to sustain hard open-air work, or to resist the malaria of the marshy coast lands. Thus when very soon after the settlement of Virginia, and for nearly two centuries afterwards, natives of the tropics were imported from Africa and set to till the fields, this practice was defended on the ground of necessity, though the districts in which white people cannot work have now been shown to be very few indeed. By this African labour large crops of tobacco, cotton, rice, and sugar were raised, and large profits made; so that, while in the Northeastern states slavery presently died out, and the Negroes themselves declined in numbers, all the wealth and prosperity of the South came to depend upon slave labour, and slavery became intertwined with the pecuniary interests as well as the social habits of the ruling class. Thus a peculiar form of civilization grew up, so dissimilar from that of the Northern half of the country, that not even the large measure of state independence secured under the federal Constitution could enable the two sections to live together under the same government. Civil war followed, and for a time it seemed as if the nation were to be permanently rent in twain. Physical differences—differences of climate, and of all those industrial and social conditions that were due to climate—were at the bottom of the strife. Yet Nature herself fought for imperilled unity. Had the seceding states been divided from the Northern states by any natural barrier, such as a mountain range running from east to west across the continent, the operations of the invading armies would have been incomparably more difficult. As it was, the path into the south lay open, and the great south-flowing rivers of the West helped the invader. Had there not existed, in the Allegheny Mountains, a broad belt of elevated land, thrusting into the revolted territory a wedge of white population which, as it did not own slaves (for in the mountains there were scarce any), did not sympathize with secession, and for the most part actively opposed it, the chances of the Southern Confederates would have been far greater. The Alleghenies interrupted the cooperation of their Eastern and Western armies, and furnished recruits as well as adherents to the North; and it need hardly be added that the climatic conditions of the South made its white population

---

[7] New Orleans is in the same latitude as Delhi, whence the children of Europeans have to be sent home in order that they may grow up in health.

so much smaller, and on the whole so much poorer, than that of the North, that exhaustion came far sooner. He who sees the South even today, when it has in many places gained vastly since the war, is surprised not that it succumbed, but that it was able so long to resist.

With the extinction of slavery, the political unity of the country was secured, and the purpose of nature to make it the domain of a single people might seem to have been fulfilled. Before we inquire whether this result will be a permanent one, so far as physical causes are concerned, another set of physical conditions deserves to be considered, those conditions, namely, of earth and sky, which determine the abundance of useful products, that is to say, of wealth, and therethrough, of population also.

The chief natural sources of wealth are fertile soils, mineral deposits, and standing timber.[8] Of these three the last is now practically confined to three districts—the hills of Maine, the Alleghenies, and the ranges of the Pacific coast, especially in Washington, with a few spots in the Rockies, and the Sierra Nevada. Elsewhere, though there is a great deal of wooded country, the cutting and exporting of timber, or, as it is called beyond the Atlantic, "lumber," is not (except perhaps in Michigan) an important industry which employs or enriches many persons. It is, moreover, one which constantly declines, for the forests perish daily before fires and the axe far more swiftly than nature can renew them.

As no nation possesses so large an area of land available for the sustenance of man, so also none of the greatest nations can boast that out of its whole domain, so large a proportion of land is fit for tillage or for stock-rearing. If we except the stony parts of New England and eastern New York, where the soil is thinly spread over crystalline rocks, and the sandy districts which cover a considerable area in Virginia and North Carolina, nearly the whole of the more level tracts between the Atlantic and the Rocky Mountains is good agricultural land, while in some districts, especially on the upper Mississippi, this land has proved remarkably rich. Which soils will in the long run turn out most fertile, cannot yet be predicted. The prairie lands of the Northwest have needed least labour and have given the largest returns to their first cultivators; but it is doubtful whether this superiority will be maintained when protracted tillage has made artificial aids necessary, as has already happened in not a few places. Some of the soils in the Eastern and

---

[8] I omit the fisheries, because their commercial importance is confined to three districts, the coasts of Maine and Massachusetts, the rivers of Washington and parts of Alaska, and the seal-bearing Pribyloff Isles. The sea fisheries of the Pacific coast (Washington, Oregon, and California) are still not fully developed.

Southern states are said to improve with cultivation, being rich in mineral constituents. Not less rich than the Mississippi prairies, but far smaller in area, are the arable tracts of the Pacific slope, where, in Washington especially, the loam formed by the decomposition of the trappean rocks is eminently productive. In the inner parts of the Rocky Mountain region and between the Rockies and the Pacific coast, lie many plains and valleys of great natural fertility, but dependent, so deficient is the rainfall, upon an artificial supply of water. The construction of irrigation works, and the sinking of artesian wells has, since 1890, brought large areas under cultivation, the discovery of dry farming methods promises to make available others where irrigation cannot be employed, and it is probable that much more may still be done to reclaim tracts which were not long ago deemed hopelessly sterile. The Mormon settlements on the east and to the south of Great Salt Lake were the first considerable districts to be thus reclaimed by patient industry.

In estimating mineral resources, it is well to distinguish between mines of gold, silver, copper, and lead on the one hand, and those of coal and iron on the other. The former are numerous, and have given vast wealth to a few lucky speculators. In some parts of the Rockies and the ranges linking them to the Sierra Nevada, the traveller saw, even as early as 1881, silver mining claims staked out on every hill. But these mines are uncertain in their yield; and the value of silver is subject to great fluctuations. The growth of electrical industries has of late years enhanced the importance of copper, also a metal the price of which oscillates violently. Coal and iron present a surer, if less glittering gain, and they are needed for the support of many gigantic undertakings. Now, while gold, silver, and lead are chiefly found in the Rocky Mountain and Sierra Nevada system, copper mainly in the West and on Lake Superior, the greatest coal and iron districts[9] are in Pennsylvania and Ohio, and along the line of the Alleghenies southwards into Alabama. It is chiefly in the neighbourhood of coal deposits that manufactures develop, yet not exclusively, for the waterpower available along the foot of the New England hills led to the establishment of many factories there, which still remain and flourish under changed conditions, receiving their coal, however, largely by sea from Nova Scotia. Mineral oils, first largely exploited in Pennsylvania, and then in Ohio, have been discovered in many other regions, and most recently in Texas, Oklahoma, and California.

---

[9] There are other smaller coal districts, including one in Washington, on the shores of Puget Sound.

What has been the result of these conditions, and what do they promise?

First: An agricultural population in the Mississippi basin already great, and capable of reaching dimensions from which imagination recoils, for though the number of persons to the square mile will be less than in Bengal or Egypt, where the peasants' standard of comfort is incomparably lower than that of the American farmer, it may be as dense as in the most prosperous agricultural districts of Europe.

Secondly: An industrial population now almost equalling the agricultural,[10] concentrated chiefly in the Northeastern states and along the skirts of the Alleghenies, and in large cities springing up here and there where (as at Chicago, Cleveland, Minneapolis, and St. Louis) commerce plants its centres of exchange and distribution. This industrial population grows far more swiftly than the agricultural, and the aggregate value of manufactured products increases faster from census to census than does that of the products of the soil.

Thirdly: A similar but very much smaller agricultural and industrial population along the Pacific, five-sixths of it within eighty miles of the coast.

Fourthly: Between the Mississippi basin and this well-peopled Pacific shore a wide and very thinly inhabited tract, sometimes quite arid, and therefore a wilderness, sometimes showing grass-bearing hills with sheep or cattle, and a few ranchmen upon the hill slopes, more rarely valleys which irrigation has taught to wave with crops. And here and there through this tract, redeeming it from solitude, there will lie scattered mining towns, many of them quick to rise and almost as quick to vanish, but others destined, if placed in the centre of a mining district, to maintain a more permanent importance.

Thus the enormous preponderance of population will be on the eastern side of the continental watershed. It was so in 1910—five millions on the Pacific side out of a total continental population of nearly ninety-two millions—it is likely to remain so. The face of the nation will be turned eastward; and, to borrow a phrase of Lowell's, the front door of their house will open upon the Atlantic, the back door upon the Pacific. Faint and few, so far as we can now predict, though far greater than at this moment, and likely to increase rapidly after the opening of the Panama Canal, will be the

---

[10] The population inhabiting cities of 8,000 people and upwards was in 1910 still only 38.74 per cent of the total population (though in the North Atlantic division it reached 68.35 per cent). But a large part of those engaged in mining or manufactures may be found in places below that limit of population.

relations maintained with Eastern Asia and Australia across the vast expanse of that ocean compared with those that must exist with Europe, to which not only literature and social interests, but commerce also, will bind America by ties growing always closer and more numerous.

That the inhabitants of this territory will remain one nation is the conclusion to which, as already observed, the geography of the continent points. Considerations of an industrial and commercial kind enforce this forecast. The United States, with nearly all the vegetable staples of the temperate zone, and many that may be called subtropical, has within its borders a greater variety of products, mineral as well as vegetable, than any other country, and therefore a wider basis for internal interchange of commodities. Free Trade with other countries, desirable as it may be, is of less consequence where a vast home trade, stretching across a whole continent, has its freedom secured by the Constitution. The advantages of such freedom to the wheat and maize growers of the West, to the cotton and rice and sugar planters of the Gulf States, to the orange growers of Florida and the vine and fruit growers of California, to the cattle men of the West and the horse breeders of Kentucky and Idaho, to the lumbermen of Maine and Washington, to the coal and iron men of Pennsylvania and the Allegheny states, to the factories of New England, both employers and workmen, as well as to the consuming populations of the great cities, are so obvious as to constitute an immense security against separatist tendencies. Such advantages, coupled with the social and political forces discussed in other chapters, are now amply sufficient to hold the Pacific states to the Union, despite the obstacles which nature has interposed. In earlier stages of society these obstacles might well have proved insurmountable. Had communication been as difficult in the middle of the nineteenth century as it was in the sixteenth, the inhabitants of the Pacific coast might have formed a distinct nationality and grown into independent states; while in the inner recesses of the wide mountain land other and probably smaller communities would have sprung up, less advanced in culture, and each developing a type of its own. But the age we live in favours aggregation. The assimilative power of language, institutions, and ideas, as well as of economic and industrial forces, is enormous, especially when this influence proceeds from so vast a body as that of the American people east of the Rocky Mountains, compared to which the dwellers on the western slope are still but few. The failure of the Mormon attempt to found a state is an instance to show how vain is the effort to escape from these influences; for even without an exertion of the military power of the United States, they must soon, by the natural process of colonization, have been absorbed into its mass. There is, accordingly, no such reason to expect detachment now as there might have been had neither railroads nor telegraphs existed, and California been accessible only round Cape Horn or across the Isthmus. Now seven great trunk lines cross the continent; and though much of the territory which lies between the populous margin of the Pacific and the cities of Colorado, Nebraska, and Dakota is and must remain wild and barren, many settlements, mining, pastoral, and even agricultural, have begun to spring up in this intervening space, and the unpeopled gaps are narrowing day by day. Especially along the line of the more northerly railroads, population, though it must always be sparse, may become practically continuous. A close observer can, however, detect some differences in character between Californians and the Americans of the Eastern and Mississippi states; and it is possible, though perhaps hardly probable, that when immigration has ceased, and the Pacific coasts and valleys are peopled by the great grandchildren of Californians and Oregonians, this difference may become more marked, and a Pacific variety of the American species be discernible.

We have so far been proceeding on the assumption that the inhabitants of the United States will be in the future what they have been during the last three generations. It must, however be admitted that two agents are at work which may create differences between those who occupy different parts of the country greater than any which now exist. One of these is immigration from Europe, whereof I will only say that reasons have been given in a later chapter for doubting whether it will substantially alter the people in any section of the country, so strong is the assimilative power which the existing population exerts on the newcomers.[11] Large as it has been, it has nowhere yet affected the English spoken; and one may indeed note that though there are marked differences of pronunciation there are, as respects the words, hardly any dialectic variations over the vast area of the Union. The other is climate. Now climatic influences seem to work but slowly on a national type already moulded and, so to speak, hammered into a definite shape by many centuries. The English race is, after all, a very recent arrival in America. Few, indeed, of the progenitors of the present dwellers in the South have been settled there for two centuries; that is to say, the present generation is at most only the sixth on which the climate has had time to tell. It is therefore quite possible that, when five or six more centuries have passed, the lowlanders of the Gulf states may, under the

[11] See Chapter 92.

enervating heat of their summers, together with the desistance from physical exertion which that heat compels, have become different from what they now are; though the comparative coolness and consequent reinvigorative powers of the winters, and the infiltration into their population of newcomers from the hardier North, will be influences working in the contrary direction.[12] The moral and social sentiments predominant in a nation, and the atmosphere of ideas it breathes, tend, as education is more and more diffused, and the movements of travel to and fro become constantly brisker, to be more and more powerful forces in producing similarity of character, and similarity of character tells on the man's whole life and constitution.

A like question has been raised regarding the whole people of the United States as compared with the European stocks whence they sprung. The climate of their new country is one of greater extremes of heat and cold, and its air more generally stimulative, than are the climate and air of the British Isles, or even of Germany and Scandinavia. That this climate should, given sufficient time, modify the physical type of a race, and therewith even its intellectual type, seems only natural. Arctic winters and scanty nutriment have, in nine centuries, markedly reduced the stature of the Norwegians who inhabit Iceland, a country which has received practically no admixture of foreign blood, while the stern conditions of their lonely life have given them mental and moral habits distinguishable from those of the natives of modern Norway. But the problem is an obscure one, for many elements besides climate enter into it; and history supplies so few cases in point, that the length of time required to modify a physical type already settled for centuries is matter for mere conjecture. There have been many instances of races from cold or damp countries settling in warmer or dryer ones; but in all of these there has been also a mixture of blood, which makes it hard to say how much is to be attributed to climatic influences alone. What can be stated positively is, that the English race has not hitherto degenerated physically in its new home; in some districts it may even seem to have improved. The tables of life-insurance companies show that the average of life is as long as in Western Europe. People walk less and climb mountains less than they do in England, but quite as much physical strength and agility are put forth in games, and these are pursued with as much ardour. It was noted in the War of Secession that the percentage of recoveries from wounds

---

[12] The malarial fevers might tell in the same direction, but science has done so much to diminish their prevalence that this deleterious influence counts for less today than it did through last century. Of the Negroes, the race more naturally fitted for these Gulf lowlands, I shall speak in a later chapter.

was larger than in European wars, and the soldiers in both armies stood well the test of the long marches through rough and sometimes unhealthy regions to which they were exposed, those, perhaps, faring best who were of the purest American stock, i.e., who came from the districts least affected by recent immigration.[13] It has, however, already been remarked that the time during which physical conditions have been able to work on the Anglo-American race is much too short to enable any but provisional conclusions to be formed; and for the same reason it is premature to speculate upon the changes in character and intellectual tastes which either the natural scenery of the American continent, and in particular its vast central plain, or the occupations and economic environment of the people, with their increasing tendency to prefer urban to rural life, may in the course of ages produce. The science of ethnographic sociology is still only in its infancy, and the working of the causes it examines is so subtle that centuries of experience may be needed before it becomes possible to determine definite laws of national growth.

Let us sum up the points in which physical conditions seem to have influenced the development of the American people, by trying to give a short answer to the question, What kind of a home has Nature given to the nation?

She has furnished it with resources for production, that is, with potential wealth, ampler and more varied than can be found in any other country—an immense area of fertile soil, sunshine and moisture fit for all the growths of the temperate, and even a few of the torrid, zone, a store of minerals so large as to seem inexhaustible.

She has given it a climate in which the foremost races of mankind can thrive and (save in a very few districts) labour, an air in most regions not only salubrious, but more stimulating than that of their ancient European seats.

She has made communication easy by huge natural watercourses, and by the general openness and smoothness of so much of the continent as lies east of the Rocky Mountains.

In laying out a vast central and almost unbroken plain, she has destined the largest and richest region of the country to be the home of one nation, and one only. That the lands which lie east of this region between the Alleghenies and the Atlantic, and those which lie west of it between the

---

[13] Some valuable remarks on this subject will be found in Professor N. S. Shaler's interesting book, *Nature and Man in America*, from which I take these facts regarding life insurance and the experience of the Civil War.

Rocky Mountains and the Pacific, are also occupied by that one nation is due to the fact that before the colonization of the central region had gone far, means of communication were invented which made the Alleghenies cease to be a barrier, and that before the Pacific coast had been thickly settled, the rest of the country was already so great in population, wealth, and power that its attraction was as irresistible as the Moon finds the attraction of the Earth to be.

Severing its home by a wide ocean from the old world of Europe on the east, and by a still wider one from the half old, half new, world of Asia and Australasia on the west, she has made the nation sovereign of its own fortunes. It need fear no attacks nor even any pressure from the military and naval powers of the eastern hemisphere, and it has little temptation to dissipate its strength in contests with them. It has no doubt a strong neighbour on the North, but a friendly one, linked by many ties of interest as well as kinship, and not likely ever to become threatening. It had on the South neighbours who might have been dangerous, but fortune favoured it by making one of them hopelessly weak, and obliging the other, strong as she was, to quit possession at a critical moment. Thus is it left to itself as no great state has ever yet been in the world; thus its citizens enjoy an opportunity never before granted to a nation, of making their country what they will to have it.

These are unequalled advantages. They contain the elements of immense defensive strength, of immense material prosperity. They disclose an unrivalled field for the development of an industrial civilization. Nevertheless, students of history, knowing how unpredictable is the action of what we call moral causes, that is to say, of emotional and intellectual influences as contrasted with those rooted in physical and economic facts, will not venture to base upon the most careful survey of the physical conditions of America any bolder prophecy than this, that not only will the state be powerful and the wealth of its citizens prodigious, but that the nation will probably remain one in its government, and still more probably one in speech, in character, and in ideas.

C H A P T E R   9 2

The Latest Phase of Immigration

Since the fifth, sixth, and seventh centuries of the Christian Era, when vast displacements of population took place in Europe and Western Asia, carrying many Teutonic and Slavonic tribes out of their ancient seats into the territories of the Roman Empire, no age has seen migrations of the races of men comparable in magnitude to those which have since 1845 poured like a flood into the United States.[1] These new settlers have come from all parts of Europe except France, which few leave, and Spain, whose emigrants go to the Spanish-speaking parts of the New World. Latterly some have come from the Levant also.

The immigration falls into three periods, or rather consists of three successive streams, each of which brought on the scene a new race or group of races, while the former streams still continued to flow, though with a diminished volume.

Ever since the beginning of the nineteenth century there had been a steady but slender influx of settlers, which did not exceed 20,000 per annum until 1820. From that number it rose slowly with the prosperity of the country, and latterly with the cheaper and more rapid transportation by steam vessels, till 1842, when 100,000 entered. With the years 1845–46, the time of the terrible famine in Ireland, begins the first or Irish period of the full rush of immigration.[2] In the ten years 1845–55, more than 1,250,000 people came

[1] Upon the subject of the new immigrants the reader may be referred to Mr. J. R. Commons' book, *Races and Immigrants in America,* to Professor Steiner's books, *On the Trail of the Immigrant* and *The Immigrant Tide,* and to the reports of the Bureau of Immigration. Some interesting facts and suggestive views may also be found in Professor W. Z. Ripley's lecture entitled "The European Population of the United States."

[2] The Bureau of Immigration (Report for 1909) estimates that from 1776 to 1820 only 250,000 immigrants arrived, and from 1820 to 1909, 26,852,723.

from Ireland to the United States. The largest number was in 1851, when 221,253 landed. Thenceforward the flow was generally large, varying greatly, but seldom below 30,000 and sometimes as high as 80,000. Of late years it has tended to decrease, and in 1913 was only 27,876; the total from 1820 to 1909, inclusive, being 4,218,107, a number equal to the whole population of Ireland in 1909. Upon the top of this Celtic immigration there soon after came a second great wave, and this time from the Teutonic parts of Europe. The arrivals from Germany rose suddenly in 1852 from 72,000 to 145,000, and in 1854 reached 215,000, a number only once thereafter exceeded, viz., in 1882, when the total was 250,000. Since 1894 there has been a decline, and in 1913 only 34,329 immigrants came from Germany. The total number from 1820 till 1909 was 5,320,312.

Somewhat later began the inrush from the three Scandinavian countries. Insignificant till 1849, the number suddenly rose in 1866 to 13,000, and thereafter reached from 30,000 to 50,000 during many years, the highest tide-mark being 105,000 in 1882. In 1913 the number was 32,267, and the total from 1820 to 1909 is given as 1,896,139.

All this time the immigration from the rest of Europe had been trifling, except of course that from Great Britain, whence there came a steady though never copious stream. But in 1880 the theretofore small flow from the Austro-Hungarian monarchy rose swiftly, and in 1882 there was also an increase from Italy and Russia. The great prosperity then reigning in the United States was causing a strong indraught, and the immigration from all quarters reached a volume not equalled thereafter till 1907. From 1882 onwards other parts also of Europe have been affected; and after 1890, as the arrivals from Ireland and Germany began slowly to decline, Central and Southern Europe became the main source of the gigantic flood of new immigrants, whose total numbered in 1882, 789,000 and in 1913, 1,197,892. Czechs, Poles, Slovaks, Croats, Serbs, Magyars, Finns, Russians—these last nearly all Jews—Slovenes, Roumans (mostly from Transylvania), and Greeks, with a smaller number of Armenians, Syrians, and Bulgarians, have (taken together) latterly far outnumbered the entering Teutons, as the Italians have far outnumbered the Irish. It is computed that over eight millions in all entered between 1900 and the end of 1909, and that over thirty millions have entered in the seventy years between 1840 and 1913, twice what the total white population of the United States was in the former year.

The population of the United States was in 1840 almost wholly—perhaps as to seven-eighths—of British origin, i.e., roughly two-thirds Teutonic and one-third Celtic. Now it is a remarkable fact that in the immigration of the next fifty years, 1840–90, the Teutonic and Celtic elements which entered corresponded pretty nearly to the proportions which those two elements bore to one another in the population of 1840, Teutons, including Germans, Scandinavians, and English from the Teutonic parts of Britain, constituting about two-thirds, Irish about one-third, of the whole. Thus the racial composition of the American people as a whole was not markedly altered during that half-century, the proportion of Teutons to Celts remaining about the same. Neither was the proportion of religious persuasions much altered, for though nearly all the Irish and many Germans were Roman Catholics, all the Scandinavians, nearly all the English, and a majority of the Germans were Protestants.

Far otherwise is it with the third influx. New elements, hitherto unrepresented in the American people, and unlike either the Teuton or the Celt, have now been added. The American people of the future will be an amalgam from a much greater number of component elements than had entered into it theretofore. Moreover, these new accretions, except the Jews, Greeks, some of the Roumans, the Finns, and the Armenians, belong almost wholly to the Roman Church, so that if the children of the immigrants remain connected with that church, its share of the population will be relatively larger.

The chief causes of great migrations have in time past been four: (1) war; (2) political or religious oppression; (3) the desire of a growing population to find fresh land to cultivate; (4) the movement of labour from regions where it is abundant and cheap to regions where it is scarce and dear. Of these four, the first has not been operative in the present case, and the second only as respects Jews and Armenians. It is the third, and latterly even more markedly the fourth cause, that have brought about this vast outflow from the Old World to the New. The stirring of men's minds out of their fixed and ancient ways has reached even the illiterate peasantry of backward regions, and made them desire to better their condition. But the outflow has been accelerated and increased by two facts without precedent in earlier times. One is the extraordinary cheapness and swiftness of transportation by sea, the other the facilities which modern methods of advertising have enabled steamship companies to use, and which they have strenuously used, to induce the peasants of the most secluded corners of Europe to seek new homes beyond the ocean.[3] Some indeed come, not to

[3] Regarding the methods by which immigrants are induced to come, the following passage is found in the Report for 1909 of the Commissioner General of Immigration, p. 112:

"The peasants of Southern and Eastern Europe have for a number of years supplied a rich

settle, but to earn money and return. Yet these also help the movement, for those immigrants, especially Italians and Austro-Hungarian Slavs, who return home with their earnings after working for some months or a year in America, scatter abroad tales of the high wages they have gained, and thus excite the curiosity and eagerness of their neighbours. So the impulse spreads, and more and more are drawn from their humble homes to the Western Land of Promise.

The quality of the earlier immigrants, Irish and Teutonic, is too well known to need description. Many were uneducated, the Scandinavians probably least so, but they were intelligent peasants, of strong stocks, industrious, energetic, and capable of quickly accommodating themselves to the conditions of their new land and blending with its people. The Slavs and Italians from Central and Southern Europe are also peasants, and also industrious.[4] But they, and nearly all others of the newly arrived races, arrive more largely illiterate than the Germans or Irish, and are on a lower grade of civilization. The Jews and Greeks are more frequently small traders than agriculturists, but are also illiterate, and very clannish, less inclined than any other group to mix with native Americans or other immigrants. This third stream of newcomers, taken in all its elements, is, therefore, socially below the two earlier ones, and in every way more alien to American habits and standards.

It was the increase of this new flood that led to the passing of immigration laws more stringent than had previously been thought needful, laws which have established a system of rigorous tests for admission, following on a law forbidding labourers to be imported under a contract to work if there are any persons in the United States who are unemployed in the particular kind of work. Under the present laws an average number slightly exceeding one per cent are annually rejected. A growing zeal for sanitary measures and an alarm at the entrance of many persons likely to prove undesirable citizens had much to do with this legislation, but something must also be ascribed to the desire of the labour unions to keep out as many as possible

---

harvest to the promoter of immigration. The promoter is usually a steamship ticket agent, employed on a commission basis, or a professional money lender, or a combination of the two. His only interest is the wholly selfish one of gaining his commission and collecting his usury. He is employed by the steamship lines large and small without scruple, and to the enormous profit of such lines. The more aliens they bring over the more are there to be carried back if failure meets the tentative immigrant, and the more are likely to follow later if success is his lot. Whatever the outcome, it is a good proposition for the steamship line."

[4] Often they might have done better to stay at home. Greeks have been leaving fertile Thessaly, where a good deal of land lies untilled, to plant themselves in the slums of Chicago.

of those who come as competitors for labour, willing to take lower wages than those received by the workmen who were already American citizens.[5] Public opinion did not wish to see the established standard of wages and living reduced.

The difference between these recent immigrants and the Germans and Scandinavians who preceded them appears in this also, that whereas the former started at once for the land, and set themselves to fell the woods or till the prairies of the West, the bulk of the later comers have either, like the Jews and Greeks, flocked into the cities and taken to the life of retail trading or of handicrafts and petty industries there, or have, like the Slovaks and Poles and Italians, found occupation in the mining districts or in railway construction and other forms of unskilled work.[6] Today most of the hard, rough toil of the country is everywhere done by recent immigrants from Central or Southern Europe, or (to a smaller extent in the North and scarcely at all in the West) by Negroes. The Irish and the urban part of the German population have risen in the scale, and no longer form the bottom stratum.

Few indeed among the Slavonic or Italian immigrants have either the knowledge of the country or the enterprise or the capital needed to take up a farm, small as is the capital needed even now, when land is not so abundant as in 1890. But already one hears of Poles and Finns in New England and Bohemians in Iowa, and a few Russians (not Jewish) in one or two places settling down to cultivate little plots of ground, and doubtless the number of those who spread out in this way will go on increasing. At present, however, it is chiefly in New York and the country all round it, in Chicago and in the mining regions of Pennsylvania and the West, such for instance as Colorado, that the traveller is struck by the presence of a

---

[5] In 1913, 19,938 aliens (about 1.7 per cent of the total number seeking admission) were turned back, nearly a half because likely to become a public charge, a little over a fifth because afflicted with a contagious disease, most of the residue because coming in under a contract to labour.

[6] "The competition of races is the competition of standards of living. . . . The race with lowest necessities displaces others. The textile industry of New England was originally operated by the educated sons and daughters of American stock. The Irish displaced many of them, then the French Canadians completed the displacement. Then, when the children of the French had begun to acquire a higher standard, contingents of Portuguese, Greeks, Syrians, Poles, and Italians entered to prevent a rise. . . . Branches of the clothing industry in New York began with English and Scotch tailors then were captured by Irish and Germans, then by Russian Jews, and lastly by Italians; while in Boston the Portuguese took a share, and in Chicago the Poles, Bohemians, and Scandinavians. Almost every great manufacturing and mining industry has experienced a similar substitution of races. As rapidly as a race rises in the scale of living and through organization begins to demand higher wages and resist the pressure of long hours and over-exertion, the employers substitute another race, and the process is repeated."—*Races and Immigrants in America*, pp. 152, 153.

population obviously non-American and not even West European. The Jews, who occupy a large district in New York, and seem likely to remain a city-dwelling folk, form nearly one-fourth of its population. Both they and the Italians are numerous in Boston, though that ancient home of Puritanism is now rather an Irish than an American city.[7] In parts of New Jersey and southern New York one may in asking one's way along the roads find hardly anyone who can speak either English or German. So in Pennsylvania the Bible Society distributes copies of the New Testament in forty-two languages, while forty-nine are said to be spoken in New York City. In Chicago there are fourteen groups, of not less than ten thousand persons each, speaking foreign languages. The foreign-born and their offspring constituted in 1910[8] more than one-third of the total population of the country and rather more than half of the white population of the Northern and Western states, for it need hardly be said that there has been practically no immigration into the Southern states either of Celts, Teutons, or Slavs, though a little of Italians into Louisiana and of Germans into Texas. The older South (Virginia and the Carolinas) is the most purely English part of the United States.

A certain part of this recent immigration is transitory. Italians and Slovaks, for instance, after they have by thrift accumulated a sum which is large for them, return to their native villages, and carry back with them new notions and habits which set up a ferment among the simple rustics of a Calabrian or North Hungarian Valley.[9] For the United States the practice has the double advantage of supplying a volume of cheap unskilled labour when employment is brisk and of removing it when employment becomes slack, so that the number of the unemployed, often very large when a financial crisis has brought bad times, is rapidly reduced, and there is more work for the permanently settled part of the labouring class. It is the easier to go backwards and forwards, because two-thirds among all the races, except the Jews, are men, either unmarried youths or persons who have left their wives behind. (Many, however, bring out their wives afterwards.) Nor are there many children. Four-fifths of the whole who enter are stated to be between fourteen and forty-five years of age.

Between those of the new immigrants who work in mines or on the

---

[7] In New York 78.6 per cent and in Chicago 77.5 per cent of the population was in 1910 of foreign extraction, and out of a population of over seventeen millions in thirty of the greatest cities, 65.5 per cent were either foreign-born or the children of foreign-born persons.

[8] The census figures of 1910 gave the foreign-born white population at 12,873,990 and the native white population of foreign parentage at 18,137,417 out of a total population of 91,972,266.

[9] Interesting instances of the influence of these returned immigrants may be found in Professor Steiner's books above referred to.

construction of public works and the native Americans there is very little contact and practically no admixture. Even in the cities the Italians and the Jews keep to themselves, often occupying poor quarters exclusively their own. Sometimes, however, a group of Magyars or Czechs, working on a quarry or in a factory, will awaken the kindly interest of their neighbours who may, perhaps, build a chapel for them and gather their growing boys into a Young Men's Christian Association. On the whole, however, they seem to be left pretty much to the mercies, not always tender, of their employers. The condition of many who toil in the coal mines and iron furnaces of Pennsylvania is described as wretched. But they earn as much in two months as they would have earned in a year at home. Thus the outdraught from Europe continues, and has now excited so much disquiet in Hungary, as threatening a scarcity of labour, that the government has been taking steps to discourage the departure of the peasants.[10]

That the recent immigrants should contribute largely to the crime of the districts where they abound is only natural, for everywhere it is from the poorest and least educated class that the largest proportion of offenders come. Fourteen per cent of the aliens over ten years of age in New York State are illiterate. This fact, their strange tongues, and, for the first few years, a certain want of finish in their personal habits, have created among native Americans a prejudice against them which is not altogether just, for the great majority are, when they come, simple, honest folk, who, having heard of America as the land of freedom and prosperity, are prepared to love it and to serve it by hard and patient work.

The more ignorant, and especially those who go to seek employment in mines, quarries, and railroad construction, do not apply for citizenship. In 1906 a statute was passed placing the naturalization of alien immigrants under the supervision of the Bureau of Immigration, and providing, among other things, that the applicant for naturalization must be neither an anarchist nor a polygamist, must intend to make the United States his home, and must be able to speak English. Adherence to anarchist or polygamist opinions is indeed also made one of the grounds for refusing entrance to an immigrant. The object of the law was, however, not merely to exclude undesirable persons from citizenship, but to prevent persons who might desire to return to their country of origin with the character of American citizens, from acquiring that character and the protection abroad which it implies. The

---

[10] Some years ago building operations in Budapest came almost to a standstill owing to the departure of a large number of workers.

early immigrants, Irish, Germans, and Scandinavians, usually applied for and obtained citizenship very soon after their arrival. The political organizations laid hold of them and got them enrolled, desiring their votes. The more recent immigrants, and especially the Italians and Slavs, show less desire, and have not been looked after by the parties with the same assiduity. In 1900 more than half of the immigrants of those races were still aliens. It is generally the more ignorant, and especially those who do not settle on the land, who so remain. The Jewish immigrants, ignorant as they often are, are keen-witted, and as they mean to stay in America, they appreciate the advantage of becoming citizens at once. Numbering in New York about a million all told, they are already a power in politics. Many have joined Tammany Hall, and as they are even more cohesive than the Irish, their share in the control of that organization promises to be a large one.

Not a few of the immigrants have brought with them from Russia or Eastern Germany or Poland, the tenets of Socialism, and some few the doctrines of a revolutionary anarchism. The murder of President McKinley by such an one (born, however, in America), together with the inflammatory harangues delivered by adherents of this extreme creed, have done much to draw on them, even on those who nowise deserve it, the suspicion of native Americans.

If the influence in politics of the new immigrants has as yet been slender in proportion to their numbers, this is not merely because many of them still remain nonvoters, but also because they have not had time to learn to care about political topics. Those Southern Italians, for instance, who vote are said to be generally led to do so by pecuniary inducements. The first question which really lays hold on and appeals directly to the newcomer from strange lands, the first thing that brings him into direct touch with American life, is a labour dispute. Little as he has known of such matters before, a leader of his own race and tongue can easily draw him into a labour union, and when he is in it, and especially when a strike begins, no one can be more ardent or combative. Some unions have racial sections, which debate in their own language, and soon master the facts of the situation. If they are led by one not of their own race, he is usually an Irishman, such is the Irish aptitude for leadership. Employers who have brought together foreigners and put their faith in them as strikebreakers have sometimes been wofully disappointed. Indeed, the Pole or Slovak follows a militant chief more blindly than a native American would. He has less to lose, and his standard of comfort is so low that the privations of a strike affect him less.

In enquiring how far these newest comers are intermingling with the preexisting population, one must carefully distinguish between the original immigrants and their children born in the United States. The latter attend the common schools—in places where truancy laws are enforced—mix with the native inhabitants, grow up speaking English, and mostly forget their own language before they reach manhood. So far from desiring to remember it and to cling to their old nationality, they are eager to cast it away and to become in every sense Americans. Often they treat their parents, because foreign-born, with a sort of contempt. However slight may be their social contact with their native neighbours, they receive the same instruction, they tend to form the same habits of life, they read the same newspapers, they frequent the same public entertainments, and the more capable rise before long into positions where they are not merely units in a herd of workers "bossed" by an American or Irish foreman, but have a chance of forcing their own way upward. Exactly how far they intermarry outside their own race is not easy to say, but we may safely assume that those who have been born in the United States, or, entering very young, have grown up under American influences, find their race no insurmountable obstacle to alliances with those of native stock. There are more men than women among them, and the men try to marry into a social stratum a little above their own, a native American girl, if possible, or an Irish one. In such a land as the United States distinctions of race, unless marked by distinctions of colour, count for little.

Both as respects social admixture, however, and as respects propensity to crime, one must emphasize the difference between immigrants settling in large cities, or in mining regions, and those who are scattered out into smaller cities or country districts. In the latter they soon tend to mingle with the other residents, and the children grow up under similar and fairly wholesome conditions. But in such places as New York or Chicago they keep to themselves, often in streets inhabited entirely by those of the same race. It is difficult for parents who must themselves toil all day long to retain any control over children who enjoy the license and are exposed to the temptations of a vast city. Accordingly, the percentage of juvenile crime among the children of the foreign-born is more than twice as great as it is among children of native white parents.[11] This is so easily explicable by the conditions under which they live that it need not be taken to indicate moral inferiority. It has often happened that when people of rude and simple habits come into a more civilized environment they lose their best native qualities

---

[11] Commons, *Races and Immigrants,* p. 170.

and acquire the vices of civilization before its virtues. Out of this transitory phase the children of the immigrants may ere long pass.

Of the East Asiatic races that have entered the United States on the Pacific side of the continent it has not been necessary to speak in this chapter, because their immigration has been stopped. Statutes passed at the urgent instance of Californian workingmen, who disliked the competition of Chinese coolies, exclude all Chinese, except persons of the educated class, such as merchants, students, and travellers for pleasure; while under an arrangement made with the Japanese government in 1908, the influx of Japanese labourers, which was rising rapidly, has also been stopped. In 1910 there were in the United States 56,756 foreign-born Chinese, and it is possible that the number may increase slightly by illicit importation on the frontiers of Mexico and Canada. In 1910 there were 67,744 foreign-born Japanese; and since then many have departed and scarce any have arrived. Neither they, nor Chinese, nor Malays, nor Hindus, can be naturalized, but the children of these races, born in the United States, are born citizens, and may vote if registered, so any large addition to their numbers is all the more deprecated. It is needless to add that they remain quite distinct from the white inhabitants. The feeling against the entrance of the yellow races, less strong against the Chinese than it was in 1880, and qualified among the employers by the desire to have plenty of steady labour, is still strong enough to maintain the policy of exclusion, and does not seem likely to disappear in any period which can at present be foreseen. A like feeling exists in Australia and has there dictated an even more rigid warning off of all Asiatics. The humanitarian sentiment towards other races which was so strong in the middle of last century has visibly declined. No one, except a fruit grower who wants Japanese labourers for his orchards, openly complains of the exclusion,[12] and the all too frequent outrages perpetrated by whites upon men of a different colour excite less censure than they would have done in the last generation.

Two large questions remain to be considered. The first is, Will European immigration continue from 1910 till 1960 on a scale similar to that of the years 1860 to 1910, during which more than twenty millions have arrived? To answer this question we must consider two sets of facts: first, the capacity of Europe to send emigrants out, and secondly the attractiveness for immigrants of the United States.

---

[12] Or a well-to-do householder who suffers from the difficulty of obtaining domestic service, which, while great everywhere, is greatest on the Pacific coast.

It has already been noted that the number coming from Ireland now averages only about one-sixth of what it was from 1847 to 1854. The Ireland of 1910 has about half as many people as she had in 1845, and her agricultural conditions are so much more favourable now than they were then that the motives for expatriation are less. It is therefore probable that henceforth fewer Irishmen will leave their country. So also as to Germany. She sends out from one-fourth to one-fifth of the number that came in the years between 1881 and 1891. The drop in Norse and Swedish immigration is less marked, but it averaged from 1905 to 1909 less than a half of what it was between 1880 and 1893. One may fairly conclude such surplus population as there was when the large outflow began has now been drained off, so that what will in future depart will be merely any natural excess of population beyond those for whom there is opportunity enough at home. In the Scandinavian countries, especially in Sweden, a scarcity of labour has begun to be felt, and the government deplores even such emigration as still continues.

As respects the new sources of migration—Italy, Austria-Hungary, and Russia—no decline is yet evident, and the fluctuations which are recorded seem to depend on the state of the labour market in America. But it may be assumed that what has happened in Ireland, Germany, and Scandinavia will presently happen in Southeastern Europe also. The large outflow of peasants will leave more land available for the next generation. Wages will rise as labour grows scarcer, so there will be less reason for emigrating. As these countries were not overpopulated in the sense in which Ireland was overpopulated in 1840, the overflow which marked the years from 1890 to 1910 can hardly last much longer, unless, indeed, the sluices be raised in Russia. From that vast multitude of peasants new Slavonic millions might come, were the government to permit their departure. At present they emigrate mostly to Siberia.

The other side of the question relates to the attraction which America has exercised. Will the prospects of comfort and freedom she offers continue to stir the hopes of the European peasantry as they have done? Land is in the fertile West already scarcer and higher in price than it was, and virgin land is almost unattainable, except in the limited areas which are being made available by irrigation or by the new processes of dry farming. Those who leave Europe to till the soil elsewhere have now quite as great, if not greater, allurements in Canada or Argentina, and many who might formerly have gone to the United States are now seeking one or other of those countries. On the other hand, there is still a great demand for unskilled labour in the mine and the quarry and the forest, as well as for the construction of railroads. This is likely to continue for many a year to come, though every now and then a passing depression of trade may intervene to throw multitudes out of work.

It may therefore be expected that the natives of those parts of Europe, such as Russia, Poland, and South Italy, where wages are lowest and conditions least promising, will continue their movement to the United States until there is a nearer approach to an equilibrium between the general attractiveness of life for the poorer classes in the Old World and in the New. But the stream is likely to diminish in volume, as the outflow from a reservoir diminishes with the falling level of the water within. We must not expect the forty years from 1910 to 1950 to show an addition of twenty millions coming from without to the population of the United States, as did the forty years from 1870 to 1910.

The vast majority of the immigrants enter by the port of New York, and are on their arrival sent to Ellis Island, a rocky islet in the Hudson River, where they are inspected by officers of the Immigration Bureau before being permitted to proceed to their several destinations. In the great hall where they are penned together like sheep, there are a number of iron staircases, by which the immigrants mount from the ground floor to the floor above where they are inspected under the stringent provisions of the law. The spectator, as he stands listening to the incessant tramp, tramp of the feet of the men, women, and children as their shoes ring upon these iron steps, seems to hear the races of the Old World marching like an army into the New, and thinks of the tribes from Northern Europe who climbed the steep rock-paths over the Alpine passes whence they descended into the Roman Empire. Those came as conquerors; these come as humble suppliants for entrance into the land of a people rich and strong. But their coming cannot but affect that people. There were in the United States only forty-eight millions of white people, when the ten millions from Central and Southern Europe who have arrived since 1885 began to enter, an addition to the nation such as no nation ever received before. These ten millions, whose children are now counted by millions more, have indeed hardly yet begun to blend with the older population. But they must ultimately do so. Already they tell on the social and economic life of the country. Long before the end of the century their blood will have been largely mingled with that of the Anglo-American and Irish and German inhabitants. Thus the reflection is forced upon us, What changes in the character and habits of the American people will this influx of new elements make—elements wholly diverse not only in origin but in ideas and traditions, and scarcely less diverse from the

Irish and Teutonic immigrants of previous years than from the men of predominantly English stock who inhabited the country before the Irish or the Continental Teutons arrived?

This is the crucial question to which every study of the immigrant problem leads up. It is a matter of grave import for the world, seeing that it is virtually a new phenomenon in world history, because no large movement of the races of mankind from one region of the earth to another has ever occurred under conditions at all resembling these. But it is primarily momentous for the United States, and that all the more so because these new immigrants go to swell the class which already causes some disquietude, the class of unskilled labourers, the poorest, the most ignorant, and the most unsettled part of the population.

In the United States the uneasiness which this invasion excites takes shape in the question so often on men's lips, Will the new immigrants be good Americans? In the most familiar sense of these words the enquiry can be easily answered. If by the words "good Americans" is meant "patriotic Americans," patriotic they will be. They will be proud of America, loyal to the flag, quick to discard their European memories and sentiments, eager to identify themselves with everything distinctive of their new country. Within a few years the Italian or the Magyar, the Pole or the Rouman deems himself an American even if he be not yet a citizen. Much more do his children glory in the flag under which they were born. So far as politics are concerned, the unity and the homogeneity of the nation will not ultimately suffer.

Neither is there ground for apprehending any decline in the intellectual quality or practical alertness of the composite people of the future. Nearly all the instreaming races are equal in intelligence to the present inhabitants. Of the acuteness of Jews and Greeks and Italians it is superfluous to speak. One is told that the children of these stocks are among the brightest in the public schools, and that in New York they use the public libraries more than any others do. So, too, the Poles and the Czechs are naturally gifted races, quite as apt to learn as are the Germans, even if less solid and persistent. Than the Armenians there is no abler race in the world. A blending of races has often in past times been followed by an increase in intellectual fertility. It is possible that from among the Jews and Poles with their musical faculty, or the Italians with their artistic faculty, there may arise those who, stimulated by the new opportunities that surround them here, will carry the creative power of the country to a higher level of production in those branches of art than it has yet reached.

Whether the ethical quality of the nation will be affected, it is more difficult to conjecture. Of the races that are now entering, some have suffered in their birthland from economic and political conditions unfavourable to veracity and courage. Others, banded together against authority, have become prone to violence. But there are others, the Piedmontese and Lombards for instance, who come of a manly and industrious stock. The Czechs and the Poles, the Magyars and the Slovenes, do not appear to one who has seen them in their European homes to have less than their Teutonic neighbours of the virtues that belong to simple peasant folk. If the new immigrants or their children are found to sink below the average of conduct in the class they enter and show themselves more disorderly or dishonest than the native American, this will happen, not because the races are naturally more criminal, but rather because the conditions under which they begin life in their new country are unfavourable. The immigrant is cut loose from his old ties and from the influences that restrained him. He is far from his parents and his priest. He has no longer the public opinion of his neighbours to regard, no longer any disapproval of the local magnate to fear. He does not see round him the signs of a vigilant, even if oppressive, public authority which were conspicuous in his native village. In the rough, unsettled, perhaps homeless, life he leads, a tossing atom in a seething crowd who toil for employers with whom they have no healthy human relation, propensities towards evil are apt to spring into activity, and the softer feelings as well as the sense of duty to perish from inanition. The immigrant's child is in one way better placed, for he is influenced by his American school teachers and school companions, but in another way worse, because the traditions and habits of the simple life of rural Europe have for him faded away altogether, if indeed he ever knew them. He starts in life as an American, but without the fundamental ideas and ingrained traditions of the New Englander or Virginian of the old stock, for these ideas and sentiments do not go with the language and the right to vote. Whether his religion will cling to him remains to be seen. Its power is at any rate likely to be weaker, perhaps least weak among the Jews, whom their faith and their habits hold apart. Though they also are divided into sects some of which render slight or no obedience to the Mosaic law, they show much less tendency to blend with the rest of the population than do the other races. How long the Greeks and the Armenians will be kept distinct by loyalty to their ancient churches I will not venture to predict. Among all the immigrants the grasp of religion seems to loosen; many are lost to their church in the second and even more in the third generation.

So far we have been considering the influence of the immigrant on

American society as a member of it, not so much in the way of influencing others, as in that of constituting one of a body whose conduct forms a part of the average conduct of the inhabitants of the country.

There is, however, another aspect of the matter, really different though apt to be confounded with that already considered. It is this, What difference to the national type of character will be produced by the infusion of these new strains of blood? Before the year 1950 arrives, the children and grandchildren of the immigrants who have entered since 1885 will be distinguished from other Americans only by their surnames, and sometimes by their features and complexion.[13] They will no longer be Poles or Italians or Slovaks, but Americans. They will have intermarried with the original Anglo-Americans, and with other immigrants, so that the generation born in 1950 will contain racial elements quite diverse from any that were present a century before. In some parts of the country these racial elements may be so largely represented, that prima facie one would expect them to be traceable in the physical and mental characteristics of the inhabitants. When a stream of whitish hue receives a reddish stream with even one-third its volume, it runs thenceforth with water of an altered tint. Will something similar happen to the people of the United States?

Here let us pause to note a significant factor in the situation. It has been observed since about 1870 that the fecundity of the original Anglo-American race tends to decline. Benjamin Franklin considered six children to constitute the normal American family. The average is now slightly above two children, and the percentage of childless marriages much larger than formerly. Birth-rate statistics show that whereas the number of births to the thousand of population is in Hungary about 40, in Germany 36, in England and Scotland, Norway and Denmark 30, it is in Massachusetts and Michigan only 25, in Rhode Island and Connecticut 24. In some states of the Union it is doubtless higher than in these four. But in all the Northern states it is much smaller among native-born Americans than among the immigrants. In Massachusetts the birth rate of the foreign-born is three times as large as that among the native-born, and the decline in fecundity among American-born as compared with foreign-born all over the Union is indubitable. Thus we have the fact, not only that far more than half the total white population was in 1910 either foreign or the offspring of foreigners, but the further fact, that at least twice as many children were then being born to the foreign-born as to the

---

[13] Even surnames are often changed so as no longer to denote racial origin. I remember a case of a German named Klein, one of whose sons became Cline and another Little. Poles frequently change the spelling of their names or drop them and take new ones.

native-born. Should immigration continue on a large scale, and should this disparity in the fertility of the foreign and the native stocks also continue, the white population, which was in 1840 almost wholly Anglo-American, and in 1910 half native and half foreign, may in 1950 be three-fourths or more of foreign blood, i.e., three-fourths of all the inhabitants of the United States may be the offspring of those who have entered America since 1840.

Two qualifying facts may deserve mention. One is that a large part, possibly one-half, of these three-fourths of foreign stock to be expected in 1950 may probably be the descendants of those who have come from the United Kingdom, from Germany, and from Scandinavia, and the smaller part, perhaps 15 to 25 per cent of the total white population, the children of immigrants from Central and Southern Europe. The other is that the fecundity of the foreign stock already shows signs of declining in their new American environment. It is certainly greater among the immigrants than among their offspring born in the United States. The latter seem to be caught by the desire to reach a higher standard of living and rise in the social scale, a desire apt to express itself, among the ambitious, in taking a native American or an Irish wife. Thus, in the second generation, families tend to be smaller; and so by 1950 the birth rate of the children of foreigners may have sunk to the native American level.

Be these things as they may—and of course all forecasts must be speculative where the data are still so imperfect—the problem confronts us: What will be the result on the American people of this infusion we see beginning of a great volume of new blood drawn from races unlike the original Anglo-American stock?

In the problem there are two factors. One is the hereditary race character, by which an average Italian or Jew or Pole is born different from the average American of British ancestry. As racial quality shows itself in the lines of the face and the colour of hair and eyes, so is it also distinguishable in certain intellectual and emotional traits. The virtues and the faults of a Tuscan are not quite the same as those of a Prussian.

The other factor is the environment in which a child grows up to manhood and by which his character is moulded. An Italian or Polish infant, brought up in an American family and mixing during youth only with Americans, may in manhood still retain some racial traits, but they will be far less marked than if he had grown up in Naples or Krakow among people of his own nation. What is the relative importance of these two factors, heredity and environment? When ten or twelve millions of Italians, Poles, and other "new immigrants" have intermarried with Americans, will their offspring give evidence in physical and mental quality of a diverse element brought into the nation, or will the social forces at work which are moulding all persons born in America overlay and end by obliterating these racial differences?

(1) Scientific students are so far from agreed as to many of the phenomena of hereditary transmission that while stating that side of the problem, I will not venture to discuss it. But the other side is within the field of any observer who gives steady attention to the facts. So let us note some facts that show what in the United States the power of environment is capable of effecting.

The climate and food in North America are different from those that have helped to form in past centuries the type of each of these European races. Some observers claim to have already discovered among the American-born children of certain among the immigrant stocks, such as Jews and Southern Italians, physical divergences, particularly in skull form, from the normal European characteristics of the race as examined in the foreign-born parents of these children.[14] The enquiry is still incomplete, but some sort of divergence may well be expected after there has been time enough for the new conditions to work, and if physical structure is affected in the way which the observations made on Jews and Italians indicate, much more may mental changes follow.

(2) The immigrants belong to so many different races that no one race can in the long run maintain any distinctive type. Even should the first generation born in the United States tend to marry each within its own race, the next generation will not; and before the end of the twentieth century all will have been commingled, and the blood of the nation of that time will have been the product of many different strains. So the intellectual and moral character of the future American, whether or no altered by qualities added from these new races, will not bear a mark distinctive of any one of them. Large as may be the contribution of all the immigrants taken together, the contribution of each taken separately will be too small to leave a permanent trace. Neither the four and a half millions of Irishmen nor the five million of Germans who have come since 1845, though they may

---

[14] Reference may be made to an interesting report on this subject published by the Immigration Commission (Senate Document No. 208 of 1910) in which the conclusion is drawn from a large number of measurements made of Sicilians and Jews in New York that the long skulls of the former race are growing shorter and wider in the children of the immigrants than are the skulls of their parents, while the round skulls of the Jewish children are growing longer than those of their parents, both tending to approximate to the "cephalic index" characteristic of native Americans. But a far larger body of data is needed before any conclusions can be safely formed.

possibly have modified the national character, have added anything that can be called distinctively Irish or distinctively German.

(3) The point in which the present case of race fusion most differs from all preceding cases, is in the immense assimilative potency of the environment. Never before did less advanced races come into a country and people which possessed a like capacity for permeating newcomers with its ways of thinking, its tastes, its habits of life. The American type of civilization, whether in its material and economic, or in its social and political aspect, is at least as distinctive as any the Old World can show. The effigy and device—so to speak—which the American die impresses on every kind of metal placed beneath its stamp, is sharp and clear. The schools, the newspapers, the political institutions, the methods of business, the social usages, the general spirit in which things are done, all grasp and mould and remake a newcomer from the first day of his arrival, and turn him out an American far more quickly and more completely than the like influences transform a stranger into a citizen in any other country. Nowhere is life so intense; nowhere are men so proud of the greatness and prosperity of their country. These things strengthen the assimilative force of American civilization, because here the ties that held the stranger to the land of his birth are quickly broken and soon forgotten. His transformation is all the swifter and more thorough because it is a willing transformation.

Even, therefore, should another ten millions pour in from Southern and Eastern Europe, even should this infusion of new blood affect the quality of the nation in some way not yet to be foreseen, the type seems destined to stand, retaining the features that make it distinctively American. Changes in national character there will of course be, for a nation is always changing, even if it receives no accretions from without. It changes with the events that befall it and the influences that play on it from age to age. As the Americans of 1850, who had not yet been affected by immigration, were different from those of 1750, so the Americans of A.D. 2000 will in any case be different from those of 1900, nor will it be then possible to determine how much of the difference should be ascribed to the addition of new racial elements, how much to the working of other economic and moral causes. Thus the problem of ascertaining the effect of the commingling of a group of widely diverse and less advanced racial stocks with a stock and a civilization of unusual assimilative power may be no nearer solution then than it is now.

If the incoming of these masses of uneducated European peasants should, as some fear, be followed by a decline, either generally or in the places where they chiefly settle, of respect for the law and of the ethical standards generally, the cause will lie not so much in any moral inferiority of the immigrants as in the unfavourable conditions which surround them and their offspring in a land with whose people they have little in common, and where most of them are huddled together in the slums of vast cities, having lost one set of guiding influences before they have gained another. In these conditions there does lie a danger, and it is the greater because the aggregation of multitudes of men in huge industrial centres where the social relations that in former generations linked the poorer to the richer and more educated scarcely exist today, is itself a phenomenon of serious import. Grave and urgent, therefore, is the need for efforts to reach and befriend the immigrants and to form in their children high ideals of American citizenship. Much is already being done. The teachers in the schools of some of the cities realize the need and are devoting themselves in a worthy spirit to the work. So, too, in many places the churches, wisely avoiding whatever savours of proselytism, as well as the university and neighbourhood "settlements" and the Young Men's Christian Associations, are trying to get hold of the neglected strangers and help them to "find themselves" in their unfamiliar surroundings. Yet much more needs to be done, for in these cities and in the mining regions the opportunities of natural and wholesome human contact between the educated class and these new elements in the labouring class are but scanty.

That there is ground for anxiety in the presence of this vast and growing multitude of men ignorant and liable to be misled cannot be denied. One often hears the wish expressed that it had been found possible to withhold electoral power from them till they had lived long enough in the country to imbibe its spirit and be familiar with its institutions. While sharing this anxiety, I must add that it is least felt by those who know the immigrants best. The public-spirited and warmhearted men and women who work among them are not despondent. They declare that the immigrants respond quickly to any touch of personal kindness, and that not a few soon show themselves nowise inferior to other persons in the same grade of life. Great is the stimulative and educative as well as the assimilative power of the American environment.

The South Since the War

Though in the preceding chapters I have sought, so far as possible, to describe the political phenomena of America in general terms, applicable to all parts of the Union, it has often been necessary to remind the reader that the conditions of the Southern states, both political and social, are in some respects exceptional, one may almost say, abnormal. The experience of this section of the country has been different from that of the more populous and prosperous North, for the type of its civilization was till thirty years ago determined by the existence of slavery. It has suffered, and has been regenerated, by a terrible war. It is still confronted by a peculiar and menacing problem in the presence of a mass of Negroes much larger than was the whole population of the Union in 1800, persons who, though they are legally and industrially members of the nation, are still virtually an alien element, unabsorbed and unabsorbable. In the present chapter I propose to sketch in brief outline the fortunes of the Southern states since the war, and their present economic and social condition, reserving for the two chapters which follow an equally succinct account of the state of the coloured population, and their relations, present and prospective, to the whites.

The history and the industrial situation of the Southern states cannot be understood without a comprehension of their physical conditions. That part of them which lies east of the Mississippi consists of two regions. There is what may be called the plantation country, a comparatively level, low, and fertile region, lying along the coast of the Atlantic and the Gulf of Mexico, and stretching up the basin of the Mississippi River. And there is the highland region, a long, broad tongue of elevated land stretching down from the north into this level plantation country, between the thirty-ninth and the thirty-third parallels of north latitude. Although the mountain country encloses within its network of parallel ridges many fertile valleys, while upon its outer slopes, where they sink to the plain, there is plenty of good land, the greater part of its area is covered by thick forests, or is too steep and rough for tillage. To men with capital and to the better sort of settlers generally, it was uninviting, and thus while the rest of the South was being occupied and brought under cultivation, it long remained thinly peopled and in many districts quite wild, with scarcely any roads and no railways. As the soil was not fit for tobacco, cotton, rice, or sugar, the planters had no motive to bring slave labour into it, not to add that the winter cold made it no fit dwelling place for the swarthy children of the tropics. Hence this region was left to be slowly and sparsely peopled by the poorest of the whites, and a race of small farmers and woodmen grew up. They were rude and illiterate, cut off from the movements of the world, and having little in common with the inhabitants of the low country east and west of them, yet hardy and vigorous, with the virtues, and some of the fierceness, of simple mountaineers, honest among themselves, and with a dangerously keen sense of personal honour, but hostile to the law and its ministers. While the whole cultivation of the plain country of Virginia, the Carolinas, Georgia, Tennessee, and Kentucky was done by Negroes, and these states, more particularly Virginia and the Carolinas, were ruled by an oligarchy of wealthy planters, Negroes were scarcely to be seen in the mountains of eastern Kentucky, western Virginia, North Carolina, and eastern Tennessee, and the scanty white population of these mountains had no influence on the conduct of public affairs. Hence when the Civil War broke out, this race of hillmen, disliking slavery, and having no love for the planters, adhered to the Union cause, and sent thousands of stalwart recruits into the Union armies. Even today, though, as we shall presently see, it has been much affected by the running of railways through it, the opening of mines and the setting up of iron works, the mountain land of the South remains unlike the plain country both in the character of its inhabitants and in the physical conditions which have created that character, conditions which, as will appear in the sequel, are an important factor in the so-called Negro problem.

Excluding these highlanders—and excluding also the three border states which did not secede, Maryland, Kentucky, and Missouri—there were at the end of the war three classes of persons in the South. There was the planting aristocracy, which the war had ruined. The elder men had seen their estates laid waste, such savings as they possessed exhausted, their whole Negro property, estimated (over the whole country) at nearly $20,000,000, gone from them into freedom. Of the younger men, a large part had fallen in the field. All, old and young, had no capital left with which to work the estates that still remained in their hands. Land and Negroes had been their only wealth, for there were practically no manufactures and little commerce, save at the half dozen seaports; credit was gone; and everything, even the railroads, was in ruins. Thus the country was, as a whole, reduced to poverty, and the old plantation life broken up forever.

The second class consisted of the poor or, as they were often called, "mean" whites, who, in the lowlands and outside the few cities, included all the white population below the level of the planters. On them, too, slavery had left its hateful stamp. Considering themselves above field labour, for which in any case they were little disposed in the hot regions along the Atlantic and the Gulf coasts, they contracted habits of idleness and unthrift; they were uneducated, shiftless, unenterprising, and picked up their living partly by a languid cultivation of patches of land, and by hunting, partly by hanging about the plantations in a dependent condition, doing odd jobs and receiving occasional aid. To them the war brought good, for not only was labour dignified by the extinction of slavery, but their three or four years of service in the Confederate armies called out their finer qualities and left them more of men than it found them. Moreover with the depression of the planting oligarchy their social inferiority and political subservience became less marked.

The third class were the Negroes, then about four millions in number, whose sudden liberation threw a host of difficulties upon the states where they lived, and upon the federal government, which felt responsible not only for the good order of the reconquered South, but in a special manner for those whose freedom its action had procured. They were—even the majority of the (comparatively few) free blacks in the towns—illiterate, and scarcely more fit to fend for themselves and guide their course as free citizens than when they or their fathers had been landed from the slave ship.

In this state of things, three great problems presented themselves to the federal government whose victorious armies were occupying the South. How should the state governments in the states that had seceded and been conquered be reestablished? What provision should be made for the material support and protection in personal freedom of the emancipated slaves? To what extent should not merely passive but also active civil rights—that is to say, rights of participating in the government as electors or officials—be granted to these freedmen?

The solution of these problems occupied twelve eventful years from 1865 to 1877, and constitutes one of the most intricate chapters in American history. I must refrain from discussing either the party conflicts at Washington, or the subtle legal questions that were raised in Congress and in the courts, and be content with touching on the action taken by the federal and state governments so far and only so far as it affected the relations of the Negroes and the whites.

The first action was taken by the Southern states themselves. Conformably to his amnesty proclamation of 1863, President Lincoln had recognized new state governments, loyal to the Union, in Tennessee and Louisiana, as he had previously done in Arkansas. When the war had ended, the other reconquered states (except Texas) took a course similar to that which the loyalists of those states had taken. The white inhabitants, except those excluded by the terms of President Johnson's amnesty proclamation of May 1865, chose conventions; these conventions enacted new constitutions; and under these constitutions, new state legislatures were elected. These legislatures promptly accepted the amendment (the thirteenth) to the federal Constitution by which (in 1865) slavery had been abolished, and then went on to pass laws for the regulation of Negro labour and against vagrancy, laws which, though represented, and probably in good faith, as necessary for the control of a mass of ignorant beings suddenly turned adrift, with no one to control them and no habits of voluntary industry or thrift, kept the Negroes in a state of inferiority, and might have been so worked as to reduce a large part of them to practical servitude. This was a false move, for it excited alarm and resentment at the North; and it was accompanied by conflicts here and there between the whites, especially the disbanded Confederate soldiers, and the coloured people; conflicts the more regrettable because the slaves had, during the war, behaved excellently towards the defenceless white women and children on the plantations, and had given their former masters little or nothing to revenge. It was, therefore, in a suspicious temper that Congress approached the question of the resettlement of the South. The victors had shown unexampled clemency to the vanquished, but they were not prepared to kiss and be friends in the sense of at once readmitting those whom they deemed and called "rebels" to their old full constitutional rights. Slavery, which at the beginning of the war they had for the most part disclaimed the purpose to abolish, had now become utterly detestable to them, and the Negro an object of special sympathy. They felt bound to secure for him, after all they had done and suffered, the amplest protection. It might perhaps have been wiser to revert to the general maxims of American statesmanship, and rely upon the natural recuperative forces and the interest which the South itself had in reestablishing order and just government. But the Northern leaders could not be expected to realize how completely the idea of another revolt had vanished from the minds of the Southern people, who, in a characteristically American fashion, had already accepted the inevitable, perceiving that both slavery and the legal claim to secede were gone forever. And these leaders—more particularly those who sat in Congress—were goaded into more drastic measures than reflection might have approved by the headstrong violence of President Andrew Johnson, who, as a Southern states' rights man of the old type, had announced that the states were entitled to resume their former full rights of self-government, and who, while stretching his powers to effect this object, had been denouncing Congress in unmeasured terms. Very different might have been the course of events had the patient wisdom of Lincoln lived to guide the process of resettlement.

Under the influence of these sentiments, Congress refused to allow the members elected from the reconquered states to take their seats, and enacted a statute establishing a Freedmen's Bureau, armed with large powers for the oversight and support of the liberated Negroes. Passed in 1865, and in 1866 continued for two years longer, this act practically superseded the legislation of the reconquered states regarding the coloured people. Congress then passed and proposed for acceptance by the states (June 1866) an amendment (the fourteenth) to the federal Constitution, which conferred citizenship, state as well as federal, on all persons born or naturalized in the United States and subject to the jurisdiction thereof, forbade legislation by a state abridging the privileges or immunities of a citizen of the United States, and provided for reducing the representation in Congress of any state in proportion to the number of its citizens excluded from the suffrage. As all danger of a return of slavery had already vanished, it was a tremendous forward move to put this pressure upon the Southern states to confer full voting rights upon their Negroes. These states, however, would probably have done well to accept the amendment, and might perhaps have accepted it had they realized what was the temper of the party dominant at the North. But they complained of the proposal to cut down representation in respect of excluded citizens, arguing that there were Northern states where colour was a ground of exclusion, and which, nevertheless, would suffer much less than the Southern states because the number of their coloured residents was far smaller; and they also resented a provision of the amendment which disqualified from voting or office all persons who having ever taken an oath to support the Constitution of the United States had been concerned in "insurrection or rebellion against the same." Accordingly all these states, except Tennessee, rejected the amendment. This further stimulated the anger and suspicion of Congress, which proceeded (March 2, 1867) to pass the so-called Reconstruction Act (a bill "to provide efficient governments for the insurrectionary States") designed to create legitimate governments in the states not yet readmitted to the Union (ignoring the governments set up by the white inhabitants), and to determine the conditions proper for their readmission. By this act these states, that is, the whole seceding South except Tennessee, were divided into five military districts, each to be governed by a brigadier-general of the Federal army, until such time as a state convention should have framed a new constitution, the Fourteenth Amendment have been ratified and the state have been duly readmitted. The delegates to each convention were to be elected by all the male citizens, excluding such as, having previously sworn to support the federal Constitution, had been concerned in the late rebellion; and it was to these same voters that the new constitution when framed was to be submitted for ratification. This provision, while it admitted the Negroes to be voters and delegates to the conventions, debarred from both functions most of the leading whites, and left the conventions to be "run" by those few whites who had remained faithful to the Union, and by adventurers who had come from the North in the track of the Federal armies. The Reconstruction Act was duly carried out; conventions were held; constitutions granting equal suffrage to all, blacks and whites, were enacted, and new state governments installed accordingly, in which, however, the leading white men of each state, since not yet pardoned, could obtain no place either as legislators or as officials. By this procedure, six states were in 1868 readmitted to Congress, as having satisfied the conditions imposed, and the remaining states within the two years following. In July 1868, the Fourteenth Amendment became a part of the Constitution, having been accepted by three-fourths of the states, and in March 1870, the Fifteenth Amendment, forbidding the voting right of citizens to be "denied or abridged an account of race, colour, or previous condition of servitude," also became by similar acceptance part of the Constitution and binding on all the states. With this, and with the passing in 1870 and 1871 of penal laws, commonly called the Force Acts, intended to protect the Negroes in the exercise of the suffrage, the direct interference of the federal legislature ended. In 1872, by the general Amnesty Act, it readmitted the great bulk of the ex-Confederates to full political rights.

Meanwhile, how had things been going in the Southern states themselves? All the leading whites having been disqualified from voting or taking part in the government, the only factors or forces left were:

First, such whites as had adhered to the Union throughout the war—in most states neither a numerous nor an influential body
Secondly, a vast mass of Negroes suddenly set free, and absolutely

destitute, not only of political experience, but even of the most
rudimentary political ideas

Thirdly, men sent down from the North as agents of the Freedmen's
Bureau, or otherwise in connection with the federal government, and
persons who had come of themselves in the hope of profiting by such
opportunities for enrichment as the abnormal conditions of the country
might create

The voting strength was, of course, with the Negroes, especially in South
Carolina and the Gulf states (except Texas); and a certain number were
chosen to sit in the legislatures and to fill the less important offices. In the
legislatures of South Carolina and Mississippi, they formed the majority;
and from the latter state they sent one of themselves to the federal Senate.
But leadership, of course, fell to the whites, who alone were capable of it,
and chiefly to those white adventurers whose scanty stock of portable
property won for them the name of "carpetbaggers." They organized the
Negroes for elections, state and local, they tampered with the electoral lists
and stuffed the ballot boxes,[1] they "ran" the legislatures. They pounced
upon the lucrative places, satisfying Negro claims with posts of less
consequence,[2] they devised the various methods by which taxation was
increased, debt rolled up, offices created and lavishly paid, frauds of every
kind perpetrated for the benefit of themselves and their friends. Such a
saturnalia of robbery and jobbery has seldom been seen in any civilized
country, and certainly never before under the forms of free self-government.
The coloured voters could hardly be blamed for blindly following the guides
who represented to them the party to which they owed their liberty; and as
they had little property, taxation did not press upon them nor the increase
of debt alarm them. Those among the Negroes to whom the chief profit
accrued were the preachers, who enjoyed a sort of local influence, and could
sometimes command the votes of their fellows, and the legislators, who
were accustomed, in South Carolina, for instance, to be paid a few dollars
for every bill they passed.[3] But nine-tenths of the illicit gains went to the

---

[1] Sometimes the beautifully simple plan was adopted of providing the ballot box, carefully locked
and sealed at its proper aperture, with a sliding side.

[2] In South Carolina, in 1875, according to the trustworthy evidence of Governor Chamberlain, two
hundred persons had been appointed justices of the peace, with a certain civil as well as criminal
jurisdiction, who could neither read nor write.

[3] An anecdote is told of an old Negro in North Carolina who, being discovered counting the fees
he had received for his vote in the legislature, said with a chuckle, "I have been sold eleven times
in my life, and this is the first time I ever got the money."

whites. Many of them were persons of infamous character who ultimately saved themselves from justice by flight. For the time they enjoyed absolute impunity, without even that check which public opinion imposes on the worst rulers when they themselves belong to the district which they rule.

The position of these adventurers was like that of a Roman provincial governor and his suite in the later days of the Republic, or an English official in the East Indies in the earlier days of the Company's conquests, save that they had less to fear from subsequent prosecution than Verres, and less from a parliamentary enquiry than the companions of Clive. The very securities with which the federal system surrounds state autonomy contributed to encourage their audacity. The national government was not responsible, because the whole machinery of state government was in form complete and to all outward appearance in normal action. But as voting power lay with those who were wholly unfit for citizenship, and had no interest, as taxpayers, in good government, as the legislatures were reckless and corrupt, the judges for the most part subservient, the Federal military officers bound to support what purported to be the constitutional authorities of the state, Congress distant and little inclined to listen to the complaints of those whom it distrusted as rebels,[4] greed was unchecked and roguery unabashed. The methods of plunder were numerous. Every branch of administration became wasteful. Public contracts were jobbed, and the profits shared. Extravagant salaries were paid to legislators; extravagant charges allowed for all sorts of work done at the public cost. But perhaps the commonest form of robbery, and that conducted on the largest scale, was for the legislature to direct the issue of bonds in aid of a railroad or other public work, these bonds being then delivered to contractors who sold them, shared the proceeds with the governing ring, and omitted to execute the work. Much money was however taken in an even more direct fashion from the state treasury or from that of the local authority; and as not only the guardians of the public funds, but even, in many cases, the courts of law, were under the control of the thieves, discovery was difficult and redress unattainable. In this way the industrious and property-holding classes saw the burdens of the state increase, with no power of arresting the process. In North Carolina, $14,000,000 worth of railroad bonds were issued, and no railway made. In Alabama, the state debt rose in four years from

---

[4] Nearly the whole representation in Congress of these states was in the hands of the then ruling Republican party. The Southern members were largely accomplices in the local misgovernment here described, nearly half of them being carpetbaggers from the North, while few of the Northern members had any knowledge of it, some perhaps not caring to enquire.

$8,356,000 to $25,503,000, with little or nothing to show for it. In Mississippi, the state levy had been ten cents on the $100 of assessed value of lands. In 1874 it had risen to fourteen times that rate. In South Carolina, the state debt leapt in four years from $5,407,000 to $18,515,000, and Governor Moses, not content with his share of the plunder, openly sold his pardons, of which he granted 457 in two years. But the climax was reached in Louisiana, where, in a single year, the state debt was increased fourfold, and the local debt twofold, while in four years' time the total state and city indebtedness was rolled up by the sum of $54,000,000, all of which went to the spoilers, and nothing to permanent improvements.

Whether owing to those amiable traits in the national character which often survive the sterner virtues, or to the fact that the thieves were too busy filling their pockets to have leisure for other outrages, this misgovernment was accompanied by less oppression and cruelty than might have been expected. Some such acts there doubtless were, particularly in the rougher districts of the extreme Southwest; and in several states the dominant faction, not satisfied with the presence of Federal troops, sought to preserve order by creating bodies of state guards or state police, or a Negro militia. In Mississippi the coloured people were enrolled in a "Loyal League." Unlike the federal civil officials, who were often disreputable and unscrupulous partisans, sometimes most improperly combining the headship of the local Republican organization with an office demanding impartiality,[5] the federal military officers, though their conduct was sometimes impugned, seem on the whole to have behaved with uprightness and good sense, making their military control as gentle as such a thing ever can be. Nor did the Negroes, untutored as they were, and jubilant in their new freedom, show the turbulence or the vindictiveness which might have been looked for in a less kindly race. Nevertheless, disorders broke out. A secret combination, called the Ku Klux Klan, said to have been originally formed in Tennessee by youths for purposes of amusement, spread rapidly through the country, and became credited with the numerous petty outrages which, during 1868, and the following years, were perpetrated upon Negroes, and (less frequently) upon whites supposed to be in sympathy with Negroes, in the rural South. Many of these outrages were probably the work of village ruffians who had no connection with any organization, still less any political motive. But the impossibility of discovering those who committed them, and the absence of

---

[5] In Louisiana, for instance, the Federal marshal, who was entitled to call on the Federal troops to aid him, was for a time chairman of the Republican State Committee.

any local efforts to repress them, showed the profound discontent of the better class of whites with the governments which the coloured vote had installed, while unfortunately confirming Congress in its suspicion of the former rebels as being still at heart enemies of the Union and the Negro. No open resistance to the Federal troops was attempted; but neither their activity nor the penal laws passed by Congress were effective in checking the floggings, house-burnings, and murders which during these years disgraced some districts. Meanwhile, the North grew weary of repression, and began to be moved by the accounts that reached it of "carpetbag government." A political reaction, due to other causes, had made itself felt in the North; and the old principle of leaving the states to themselves gained more and more upon the popular mind, even within the still dominant Republican party. Though some of its prominent leaders desired, perhaps not without a view to party advantage, to keep down the South, they were overborne by the feeling, always strong in America, that every community to which self-government has been granted must be left to itself to work out its own salvation, and that continued military occupation could not be justified where no revolt was apprehended. The end came in 1876–77. Between 1869 and 1876 the whites had in every Southern state, except South Carolina, Florida, and Louisiana, regained control of the government, and in 1876 those three states were also recovered.[6] The circumstances were different, according to the character of the population in each state. In some a union of the moderate white Republicans with the Democrats, brought about by the disgust of all property holders at the scandals they saw and at the increase to their burdens as taxpayers, had secured legitimately chosen majorities, and ejected the corrupt officials. In some the same result was attained by paying or otherwise inducing the Negroes not to go to the polls, or by driving them away by threats or actual violence. Once possessed again of a voting majority, the whites, all of whom had by 1872 been relieved of their disabilities, took good care, by a variety of devices, legal and extra-legal, to keep that majority safe; and in no state has their control of the government been since shaken. President Hayes withdrew, in 1877, such Federal troops as were still left at the South, and none have ever since been despatched thither.

This sketch has been given, not so much because it is a curious phase in the history of democracy, and one not likely ever to recur, either in the

---

[6] Those states in which the whites first recovered control, such as Georgia, have generally fared best subsequently. They have had less debt to carry, and commercial confidence was sooner restored.

United States or elsewhere, as because it has determined and explained the whole subsequent course of events and the present attitude, whereof more anon, of the Southern people. That Congress made some mistakes is proved by the results. Among those results must be reckoned not merely the load of needless debt imposed upon the Southern states, and the retardation of their recovery from the losses of the war, but the driving of all their respectable white citizens into the Democratic party and their alienation from the Republicans of the North, together with the similar aggregation of the Negroes in the Republican party, and consequent creation of a so-called "colour line" in politics. Habits of lawlessness have moreover been perpetuated among the whites, and there was formed in both parties the pernicious practice of tampering with elections, sometimes by force and sometimes by fraud, a practice which strikes at the very root of free popular government.

But was the great and capital act of the Republican party when it secured the grant of the suffrage to the Negroes *en bloc* one of those mistakes? To nearly all Europeans such a step seemed and still seems monstrous. No people could be imagined more hopelessly unfit for political power than this host of slaves; and their unfitness became all the more dangerous because the classes among whom the new voters ought to have found guidance were partly disfranchised and partly forced into hostility. American eyes, however, saw the matter in a different light. To them it has been an axiom, that without the suffrage there is no true citizenship, and the Negro would have appeared to be scarcely free had he received only the private and passive, and not also the public and active, rights of a citizen. "I realized in 1867," said General Wade Hampton, one of the most distinguished leaders of the South, "that when a man had been made a citizen of the United States, he could not be debarred from voting on account of his colour. Such exclusion would be opposed to the entire theory of republican institutions."[7] It is true that there were Northern states, such as even the New England Connecticut and the half New England Ohio, as well as Michigan and Pennsylvania, in which persons of colour were so debarred.[8] But the Abolitionist movement and the war had given an immense stimulus to the abstract theory of human rights, and had made the Negro so much an object of sympathy to the Northern people, that these restrictions were vanishing before the doctrine of absolute democratic equality and the rights of man as man. There was,

---

[7] *North American Review* for March 1879.

[8] Connecticut as late as 1865 and Ohio as late as 1867 declined to extend equal suffrage to Negroes.

moreover, a practical argument of some weight. The gift of the suffrage presented itself to the Northern statesmen as the alternative to continuance of military government. Without the suffrage, the Negro might have been left defenceless and neglected, unimproved and unimproving. In the words of another eminent Southern statesman, Mr. Justice Lamar, "In the unaccustomed relation into which the white and coloured people of the South were suddenly forced, there would have been a natural tendency on the part of the former masters, still in the possession of the land and intelligence of the country and of its legislative power, to use an almost absolute authority, and to develop the new freedman according to their own idea of what was good for him. This would have resulted in a race distinction, and in such incidents of the old system as would have discontented the negro and dissatisfied the general sentiment of the country. If slavery was to be abolished, there could be nothing short of complete abolition, free from any of the affinities of slavery; and this would not have been effected so long as there existed any inequality before the law. The ballot was therefore a protection of the negro against any such condition, and enabled him to force his interests upon the consideration of the South."[9]

The American view that "the suffrage is the sword and shield of our law, the best armament that liberty offers to the citizen," does not at once commend itself to a European, who conceives that every government is bound to protect the unenfranchised equally with the enfranchised citizen. But it must be remembered that in the United States this duty is less vigilantly performed than in England or Germany, and that there were special difficulties attending its performance under a federal system, which leaves the duty, save where federal legislation is involved, to the authorities of the several states.

It has been usual to charge those who led Congress with another and less noble motive for granting electoral rights to the Negroes, viz., the wish to secure their votes for the Republican party. Motives are always mixed; and doubtless this consideration had its weight. Yet it was not a purely selfish consideration. As it was by the Republican party that the war had been waged and the Negro set free, the Republican leaders were entitled to assume that his protection could be secured only by their continued ascendancy. That ascendancy was not wisely used. But the circumstances were so novel and perplexing, that perhaps no statesmanship less sagacious than President Lincoln's could have handled them with success.

[9] *North American Review* for March 1879.

With the disappearance of the carpetbag and Negro governments, the third era in the political history of the South since the war began. The first had been that of exclusively white suffrage; the second, that of predominantly Negro suffrage. In the third, universal suffrage and complete legal equality were soon perceived to mean in practice the full supremacy of the whites. To dislodge the coloured man simply as a coloured man from his rights was impossible, for they were secured by the federal Constitution which prevails against all state action. The idea of disturbing them by formal legislative action was scarcely entertained. But the more they despaired of getting rid of the amendment, the more resolved were the Southern people to prevent it from taking any effect which could endanger their supremacy. They did not hate the Negro, certainly not half so much as they hated his white leaders by whom they had been robbed. "We have got," they said, "to save civilization," and if civilization could be saved only by suppressing the coloured vote, they were ready to suppress it. This was the easier, because, while most of the carpetbaggers had fled, nearly all the respectable whites of the South, including those who had been Whigs before the war and who had opposed secession, were now united in the New Democratic, or rather anti-Negro, party. A further evidence of the power of the motives which have swayed them may be found in the fact that nearly every Northern man who has of late years gone South for commercial purposes, has before long ranged himself with this anti-Negro party, whatever his previous "affiliations" may have been.

The modes of suppression have not been the same in all districts and at all times. At first there was a good deal of what is called "bulldozing," i.e., rough treatment and terrorism, applied to frighten the coloured men from coming to or voting at the polls. Afterwards, the methods were less harsh. Registrations were so managed as to exclude Negro voters, arrangements for polling were contrived in such wise as to lead the voter to the wrong place so that his vote might be refused; and, if the necessity arose, the Republican candidates were counted out, or the election returns tampered with. "I would stuff a ballot box," said a prominent man, "in order to have a good, honest government"; and he said it in good faith, and with no sense of incongruity. Sometimes the local Negro preachers were warned or paid to keep their flocks away. More humorous devices were not disdained, as when free tickets to a travelling circus were distributed among the Negroes, and the circus paid to hold its exhibition at a place and hour which prevented them from coming to vote. South Carolina enacted an ingenious law providing that there should be eight ballot boxes for as many posts to be filled at the election, that a vote should not be counted unless placed in the proper box, and that the presiding officer should not be bound to tell the voter which was the proper box in which each vote ought to be deposited. Illiterate Negroes so often voted in the wrong box, the boxes being frequently shifted to disconcert instructions given beforehand, that a large part of their votes were lost, while the illiterate white was apt to receive the benevolent and not forbidden help of the presiding officer.

Notwithstanding these impediments, the Negro long maintained the struggle, valuing the vote as the symbol of his freedom, and fearing to be reenslaved if the Republican party should be defeated. Leaders and organizers were found in the federal officeholders, of course all Republicans, a numerous class—Mr. Nordhoff, a careful and judicious observer, says there were in 1875 three thousand in Georgia alone—and a class whose members virtually held their offices on condition of doing their political work; being liable to be removed if they failed in their duty, as the sultan used to remove a vali who sent up too little money to Stamboul. After 1884, however, when the presidency of the United States passed to a Democrat, some of these officeholders were replaced by Democrats and the rest became less zealous. It was, moreover, already by that time clear that the whites, being again in the saddle, meant to stay there, and the efforts of the Republican organizers grew feebler as they lost hope. Their friends at the North were exasperated, not without reason, for the gift of suffrage to the Negroes had resulted in securing to the South a larger representation in Congress and in presidential elections than it enjoyed before the war, or would have enjoyed had the Negroes been left unenfranchised. They argued, and truly, that where the law gives a right, the law ought to secure the exercise thereof; and when the Southern men replied that the Negroes were ignorant, they rejoined that all over the country there were myriads of ignorant voters, mostly recent immigrants whom no one thought of excluding. Accordingly in 1890, having a majority in both houses of Congress and a president of their own party, the Republican leaders introduced a bill subjecting the control of federal elections to officers to be appointed by the president, in the hope of thus calling out a full Negro vote, five-sixths of which would doubtless have gone to their party. The measure appeared to dispassionate observers quite constitutional, and the mischief it was designed to remedy was palpable. It excited, however, great irritation at the South, uniting in opposition to it nearly all whites of every class, while no corresponding enthusiasm on its behalf was evoked at the North. It passed the House, but was dropped in the Senate under the threat of an obstructive resistance by the (then Democratic) minority. Secure, however, as the dominance of the whites seemed to be against either Northern legislation or Negro revolt, the Southern people remained uneasy and sensitive on the subject, and have been held together in a serried party phalanx by this one colour question, to the injury of their political life, which is thus prevented from freely developing on the lines of the other questions that from time to time arise. So keen is their recollection of the carpetbag days, so intense the alarm at any possibility of their return, that internal dissensions, such as those which the growth of the Farmers' Alliance party and (later) of the Populist party evoked, were seldom permitted to give Republican candidates a chance of a seat in Congress or of any considerable state office.

These remarks apply to the true South, and neither to the mountain regions, where, owing to the absence of the Negro element, there is, save in the wider valleys, still a strong Republican party, nor to the border states, Maryland, West Virginia, Kentucky, and Missouri, in which the coloured voters are not numerous enough to excite alarm. When it is desired to eliminate their influence on elections, a common plan is to bribe them. In Louisville one is told that quite a small payment secures abstention. To induce them to vote for a Democrat is, to their credit be it said, much more costly.

This horror of Negro supremacy is the only point in which the South cherishes its old feelings. Hostility to the Northern people has virtually disappeared. No sooner was Lee's surrender at Appomattox Court House known over the country, than the notion of persisting in efforts for secession and the hope of maintaining slavery expired. With that remarkable power of accepting an accomplished fact which in America is compatible with an obstinate resistance up to the moment when the fact becomes accomplished, the South felt that a new era had arrived to which they must forthwith adapt themselves. They were not ashamed of the war. They were and remain proud of it, as one may see by the provisions made by not a few states for celebrating the birthday of General Robert E. Lee or of ex-President Jefferson Davis, and by the zeal with which the monuments of the Civil War and its battlefields are cared for. Just because they felt that they had fought well, they submitted with little resentment, and it became a proverb among them that the two classes which still cherished bitterness were the two classes that did not fight—the women and the clergy. Even when fresh hostility was aroused by the reconstructive action of Congress in 1866 and 1867, and the abuses of carpetbag rule, no one dreamt of renewing the old struggle. Not, however, till the whites regained control, between 1870 and 1876, did the industrial regeneration of the country fairly begin. Two discoveries coincided with that epoch which have had an immense effect in advancing material prosperity, and changing the current of men's thoughts. The first was the exploration of the mineral wealth of the highland core of the country. In the western parts of Virginia and North Carolina, in the eastern parts of Tennessee, the northern parts of Georgia and Alabama, both coal and iron, not to speak of other minerals, have been found in enormous quantities, and often in such close juxtaposition that the production of pig iron and steel can be carried on with exceptional cheapness. Thus, Northern capital has been drawn into the country; Southern men have had a new field for enterprise, and have themselves begun to accumulate capital; prosperous industries have been created, and a large working-class population, both white and coloured, has grown up in many places, while the making of new railways has not only given employment to the poorer classes, but has stimulated manufacture and commerce in other directions. The second discovery was that of the possibility of extracting oil from the seeds of the cotton plant, which had formerly been thrown away, or given to hogs to feed on. The production of this oil has swelled to great proportions, making the cultivation of cotton far more profitable, and has become a potent factor in the extension of cotton cultivation and the general prosperity of the country. Most of the crop now raised, which usually exceeds eleven millions of bales, and in 1908 exceeded thirteen and a half millions (being more than thrice that which was raised, almost wholly by slave labour, before the war), is now raised by white farmers; while the mills which spin and weave it into marketable goods are daily increasing and building up fresh industrial communities. The methods of agriculture have been improved; and new kinds of cultivation introduced: the raising of fruit, for instance (in Florida particularly of oranges), has become in certain districts a lucrative industry. Nor has the creation of winter health resorts in the beautiful mountain land of North Carolina, and further south in South Carolina, Georgia, and Florida, been wholly without importance, for the Northern people who flock thither learn to know the South, and themselves diffuse new ideas among the backward population of those districts. Thus from various causes there has come to be a sense of stir and movement and occupation with practical questions, and what may be called a commercialization of society, which has, in some places, transformed Southern life. Manual labour is no longer deemed derogatory by the poorer whites (who are less of a distinct class than they used to be), nor commerce by the sons of the old planting aristocracy. Farmers no doubt complain, as they do everywhere in the

United States; yet it is a good sign that the average size of farms has been, in the Southeastern states, decreasing, the number of farmers and also the number of owners increasing, while the number of tenants who paid their rent in money instead of in kind almost doubled between 1880 and 1890. As capital, which used to be chiefly invested in slaves, has increased and become more generally diffused, it is more and more placed in permanent improvements, and especially in city buildings. Cities indeed have largely grown and are still growing, especially of course in the mining regions; and in the cities a new middle class has sprung up, formed partly by the elevation of the poorer class and partly by the depression of the old planting class, which has made the contrast between the social equality of Northern and the aristocratic tone of Southern society far less marked than it was before the war.

While slavery lasted the South was, except of course as regarded the children of planters and of the few merchants, an illiterate country. Even in 1870 the Southeastern states had only 30 per cent of their population of school age enrolled as school attendants, and the South Central and Western states only 34 per cent. The Reconstruction constitutions of 1867–70 contained valuable provisions for the establishment of schools; and the rise of a new generation, which appreciates the worth of education and sees how the North has profited by it, has induced a wholesome activity. The percentage of children enrolled to school age population has risen steadily.[10] It is no doubt true that the sum expended on schools is very unequal in the various states—Arkansas, for instance, spent in 1910–11 more than Mississippi or North Carolina, though her population is smaller than that of either of those states; true, also, that the expenditure is much less than in the North or West—Washington, for instance, spends more than twice as much as Arkansas, with very little more wealth; true, further, that the average number of days the schools were kept was in 1910–11 smaller in the Southern states (130.6 in the Southeastern states, 127.8 in the South Central, as compared with 179.8 in the Northeastern states). Still the progress is great, when one considers the comparative poverty of the Southern states, and the predominantly rural character of their very sparse population.

Anyone seeking to disparage the South need not want for points to dwell upon. He might remark that illiteracy is far more common than in the North or West; that there is little reading even among those who can read—one

---

[10] Report of the Commissioner of Education for 1912. "School age" is taken in the United States as covering the years from 5 to 18 inclusive.

need only walk through the streets of a Southern city and look into the few bookstores to be convinced of this—and far less of that kind of culture which is represented by lecture courses or by literary and scientific journals and societies. He would observe that hotels, railway stations, refreshment rooms, indeed all the material appliances of travelling comfort in which the North shines, are still on a lower level, and that the scattered population so neglects its roads that they are in some places impassable. Life, he might say, is comparatively rough, except in a few of the older cities, such as Richmond and Charleston; it has in many regions the character of border life in a half-settled country. And above all, he might dilate upon the frequency of homicide, and the small value that seems to be set upon human life, if one may judge from the imperfect and lenient action of the courts, which, to be sure, is often supplemented by private vengeance. Yet to the enumeration of these and other faults born of slavery and the spirit which slavery fostered, it would be rightly answered that the true way to judge the former slave states, is to compare them as they are now with what they were when the war ended. Everywhere there is progress; in some regions such progress, that one may fairly call the South a new country. The population is indeed unchanged, for it is only lately that settlers have begun to come from the North, and no part of the United States has within the present century received so small a share of European immigration.[11] Slavery was a fatal deterrent while it lasted, and of late years the climate, the presence of the Negro, and the notion that work was more abundant elsewhere, have continued to deflect in a more northerly direction the stream that flows from Europe. But the old race, which is, except in Texas (where there is a small Mexican and a larger German element) and in Louisiana, a pure English and Scoto-Irish race, full of natural strength, has been stimulated and invigorated by the changed conditions of its life. It has made great advances in almost every direction. Schools are better and more numerous. The roads are being improved. Cotton mills are rising in some places, iron-works in others. It sees in the mineral and agricultural resources of its territory a prospect of wealth and population rivalling those of the Middle and Western states. It has recovered its fair share of influence in the national government. It has no regrets over slavery, for it recognizes the barbarizing influence that slavery exerted. Neither does it cherish any dreams of

[11] In North Carolina in 1910 the foreign-born were only .4 of the population, in Mississippi 1.2, in Georgia 1.1. That the newcomers from Southern and Central Europe who now furnish the bulk of Old World immigration do not enter the South is deemed by its inhabitants to be an advantage.

separation. It has now a pride in the Union as well as in its state, and is in some ways more fresh and sanguine than the North, because less cloyed by luxury than the rich are there, and less discouraged by the spread of social unrest than the thoughtful have been there. But for one difficulty the South might well be thought to be the most promising part of the Union, that part whose advance is likely to be swiftest, and whose prosperity will be not the least secure.

This difficulty, however, is a serious one. It lies in the presence of ten millions of Negroes.

Present and Future of the Negro[1]

The total coloured population of the United States was in 1900, 8,840,789, and in 1910 it was 9,828,294, a number far greater than that of the English people in the reign of Queen Anne, and one which might anywhere but in North America be deemed to form a considerable nation. Of this total, probably nine millions are in the old slave states, and it is of these only that the present chapter will speak.[2] To understand their distribution in these states, the reader will do well to recall what was said in the last preceding chapter regarding the physical features of the South, for it is by those features that the growth of the coloured population in the various regions of the country has been determined. Though man is of all animals, except perhaps the dog, that which shows the greatest capacity for supporting all climates from Borneo to Greenland, it remains true that certain races of men thrive and multiply only in certain climates. As the races of Northern Europe have been hitherto unable to maintain themselves in the torrid zone, so the African race, being of tropical origin, dwindles away wherever it has to encounter cold winters. In what used to be called the border states— Maryland, Kentucky, and Missouri—the coloured element increases but slowly.[3] In West Virginia, East Kentucky, East Tennessee, and Western

---

[1] This chapter, which presents a general view of the Southern Negro and his relations with the whites, is supplemented by the chapter next following, which comments upon such changes in the situation as have occurred during the last sixteen years and contains the latest conclusions I have been able to form on the subject.

[2] The total white population of these states was, in 1910, 20,547,420, and the coloured 8,749,427.

[3] Kentucky showed a small decrease from 1880 to 1890, an increase in 1900, but a decrease in 1910. There was from 1890 to 1900 an absolute decrease of coloured population in eight other states—Maine (from 1870, though not from 1890, to 1900), Nebraska, North Dakota, South Dakota, Oregon, Vermont, Nevada, California, and New Mexico. From 1900 to 1910 there were small absolute decreases in New Hampshire, Connecticut, and Maryland.

North Carolina, the Negro is practically unknown in the highest and coolest spots, and in the other parts of that elevated country has scarcely been able to hold his own. It is in the low warm regions that lie near the Gulf Stream and the Gulf of Mexico, and especially in the sea islands of South Carolina and on the banks of the lower Mississippi that he finds the conditions which are at once most favourable to his development and most unfavourable to that of the whites. Accordingly it is the eight states nearest the Gulf—South Carolina, Georgia, Florida, Alabama, Mississippi, Louisiana, Arkansas, and Texas—that contain more than half the Negro population, which in two of them, South Carolina and Mississippi, exceeds the number of the whites. In Louisiana, where the two races were equal in 1890, the whites had in 1910 a majority of 227,212. These eight states showed an increase of the coloured population, from 1880 to 1890, at the rate of 18.4 per cent,[4] while in the rest of the South the rate was only 5.1 per cent; from 1900 to 1910 the rate was 14.6. It is thus clear that the Negro center of population is more and more shifting southward, and that the African is leaving the colder, higher, and drier lands for regions more resembling his ancient seats in the Old World.

A not less important question is the proportion between the Negroes and the whites. In 1790 the Negroes were 19.3 per cent or nearly one-fifth of the whole population of the Union. In 1880 they were 13.1 per cent; in 1890, 11.9 per cent; in 1910, 10.7 per cent. The rate of increase of the Negro population of the whole country from 1900 to 1910 was 11.2 per cent, while that of the whites was 22.3. Even in the former slave states (which receive very few immigrants from Europe) the increase of the whites during that decade was 25.1, that of the Negroes only 11.1 per cent, or about one-half the rate shown by the whites,[5] while in the eight black states mentioned above the percentage of increase of the white population is 27.4, that of the Negroes only 14.6. It thus appears that except in certain parts of these eight states, where physical conditions favourable to the growth of the coloured population prevail, the whites increase everywhere faster than the Negroes, and the latter constitute a relatively decreasing element.[6] This fact,

---

[4] It was still greater in Arkansas (46.7 per cent), Florida (31.2 per cent), and Texas (24.1 per cent), but the Negroes have been in these three states much less numerous than the whites, and the increase was probably largely due to Negro immigration from other states.

[5] West Virginia, Oklahoma, and Arkansas were the southern states which in 1910 showed a higher rate of increase of coloured than of white people. In South Carolina, Louisiana, and Texas the Negro race was about two-thirds behind in rate of increase, while in three South Atlantic and South Central States the actual number of Negroes had decreased in the decade.

[6] That which specially tends to keep down the Negro increase is the very large mortality among the children.

suspected previously was placed beyond doubt by the census of 1890. It is the dominating fact of the political and social situation.

Of the economic and industrial state of the whole nine millions it is hard to speak in general terms, so different are the conditions which different parts of the country present. In one point only are those conditions uniform. Everywhere, alike in the border states and in the farthest South, in the cities, both great and small, and in the rural districts, the coloured population constitute the poorest and socially lowest stratum, corresponding in this respect to the new immigrants in the Northern states, although, as we shall presently observe, they are far more sharply and permanently divided than are those immigrants from the classes above them. They furnish nine-tenths of the unskilled labour, and a still larger proportion of the domestic and hotel labour. Some, a comparatively small but possibly growing number, have found their way into the skilled handicrafts, such as joinery and metal work; and many are now employed in the mines and iron foundries of Southeastern Tennessee and Northern Alabama, where they receive wages sometimes equal to those paid to the white workmen, and are even occasionally admitted to the same trade unions.[7] In textile factories they are deemed decidedly inferior to the whites; the whirr of the machinery is said to daze them or to send them to sleep. On the other hand, they handle tobacco better than the whites, and practically monopolize the less skilled departments of this large industry, though not cigar making, for which Spaniards or Cubans are deemed best. In the cities much of the small retail trade is in their hands, as are also such occupations as those of barber (in which however they are said to be yielding to the whites), shoe-black, street vendor of drinks or fruit, together with the humbler kinds of railway service. In the rural districts the immense majority are either hired labourers or tenants of small farms, the latter class becoming more numerous the further south one goes into the hot and malarious regions, where the white man is less disposed to work on his own land. Of these tenants many—and some are both active and thrifty—cultivate upon a system of crop-sharing, like that of the *métayers* in France. Not a few have bought plots of land, and work it for themselves. Of those who farm either their own land or that for which they pay rent, an increasing number are raising crops for the market, and steadily improving their condition. Others, however, are content with getting from the soil enough food to keep their families; and this is more

---

[7] The average pay per day of the skilled white labourer is usually much higher, but not double that of the coloured. A large employer of labour in Virginia assured me some time ago that he paid some of his Negroes (iron-workers) as much as $4.50 per day. He added that they worked along with the whites, and drank less.

especially the case in the lower lands along the coast, where the population is almost wholly black, and little affected by the influences either of commerce or of the white race. In these hot lowlands the Negro lives much as he lived on the plantations in the old days, except that he works less, because a moderate amount of labour produces enough for his bare subsistence. No railway comes near him. He sees no newspaper. He is scarcely at all in contact with anyone above his own condition. Thus there are places, the cities especially, where the Negro is improving industrially, because he has to work hard and comes into constant relation with the whites; and other places, where he need work very little, and where, being left to his own resources, he is in danger of relapsing into barbarism. These differences in his material progress in different parts of the country must be constantly borne in mind when one attempts to form a picture of his present intellectual and moral state.

The phenomena he presents in this latter aspect are absolutely new in the annals of the world. History is a record of the progress towards civilization of races originally barbarous. But that progress has in all previous cases been slow and gradual. In the case of the chief Asiatic and European races, the earlier stages are lost in the mists of antiquity. Even the middle and later stages, as we gather them from the writings of the historians of antiquity and from the records of the Dark and Middle Ages, show an advance in which there is nothing sudden or abrupt, but rather a process of what may be called tentative development, the growth and enlargement of the human mind resulting in and being accompanied by a gradual improvement of political institutions and of the arts and sciences. In this process there are no leaps and bounds; and it is the work, not of any one race alone, but of the mingled rivalry and cooperation of several. Utterly dissimilar is the case of the African Negro, caught up in and whirled along with the swift movement of the American democracy. In it we have a singular juxtaposition of the most primitive and the most recent, the most rudimentary and the most highly developed, types of culture. Not greater is the interval which separates the chipped flints of the Stone Age from the Maxim gun of today. A body of savages is violently carried across the ocean and set to work as slaves on the plantations of masters who are three or four thousand years in advance of them in mental capacity and moral force. They are treated like horses or oxen, are kept at labour by the lash, are debarred from even the elements of education, have no more status before the law, no more share in the thought or the culture of their owner than the sheep which he shears. The children and grandchildren of those whom the slaveship brought to the plantation remain like their parents, save indeed that they have learnt a new and highly developed tongue and have caught up so much of a new religion as comes to them through preachers of their own blood. Those who have housework to do, or who live in the few and small towns, pick up some knowledge of white ways, and imitate them to the best of their power. But the great mass remain in their notions and their habits much what their ancestors were in the forests of the Niger or the Congo. Suddenly, even more suddenly than they were torn from Africa, they find themselves, not only freed, but made full citizens and active members of the most popular government the world has seen, treated as fit to bear an equal part in ruling, not themselves only, but also their recent masters. Rights which the agricultural labourers of England did not obtain till 1885 were in 1867 thrust upon these children of nature, whose highest form of pleasure had hitherto been to caper to the strains of a banjo.

This tremendous change arrested one set of influences that were telling on the Negro, and put another set in motion. The relation of master and servant came to an end, and with it the discipline of compulsory labour and a great part of such intercourse as there had been between the white and the black races. Very soon the whites began to draw away from the Negro, who became less a friend in fact the more he was an equal in theory. Presently the mixture of blood diminished, a mixture which may have been doing something for the blacks in leavening their mass—only slightly on the plantations, but to some extent in the towns and among the domestic servants—with persons of superior capacity and talent. On the other hand, there were immediately turned on the freedman a volume of new forces which had scarcely affected him as a slave. He had now to care for himself, in sickness and in health. He might go where he would, and work as much or as little as he pleased. He had a vote to give, or to sell. Education became accessible; and facilities for obtaining it were accorded to him, first by his Northern liberators, and thereafter, though insufficiently, by his old masters also. As he learned to read and to vote, a crowd of modern American ideas, political, social, religious, and economic, poured in upon him through the newspapers. No such attempt has ever been made before to do for a race at one stroke what in other times and countries Nature has spent centuries in doing. Other races have desired freedom and a share in political power. They have had to strive, and their efforts have braced and disciplined them. But these things were thrust upon the Negro, who found himself embarrassed by boons he had not thought of demanding.

To understand how American ideas work in an African brain, and how

American institutions are affecting African habits, one must consider what are the character and gifts of the Negro himself.

He is by nature affectionate, docile, pliable, submissive, and in these respects most unlike the Red Indian, whose conspicuous traits are pride and a certain dogged inflexibility. He is seldom cruel or vindictive—which the Indian often is—nor is he prone to violence, except when spurred by lust or drink. His intelligence is rather quick than solid; and though not wanting in a sort of shrewdness, he shows the childishness as well as the lack of self-control which belongs to the primitive peoples. A nature highly impressionable, emotional, and unstable is in him appropriately accompanied by a love of music, while for art he has—unlike the Red Indian—no taste or turn whatever. Such talent as he has runs to words; he learns languages easily and speaks fluently, but shows no capacity for abstract thinking, for scientific inquiry, or for any kind of invention. It is, however, not so conspicuously on the intellectual side that his weakness lies, as in the sphere of will and action. Having neither foresight nor "roundsight," he is heedless and unthrifty, easily elated and depressed, with little tenacity of purpose, and but a feeble wish to better his condition. Sloth, like that into which the Negroes of the Antilles have sunk, cannot be generally charged upon the American coloured man, partly perhaps because the climate is less enervating and nature less bountiful. Although not so steady a workman as is the white, he is less troublesome to his employers, because less disposed to strike. It is by his toil that a large part of the cotton, rice, and sugar crop of the South is now raised. But anyone who knows the laborious ryot or coolie of the East Indies is struck by the difference between a race on which ages of patient industry have left their stamp and the volatile children of Africa.

Among the modes or avenues in and by which the influences of white America are moulding the Negro, five deserve to be specially noted, those of the schools, of the churches, of literature, of industry, and of business or social relations.

Looking merely at the figures, elementary education would seem to have made extraordinary progress. In the former slave states there were, in 1907–8, 54.36 per cent of the coloured population of school age enrolled on the books of some school, the percentage of white pupils to the white population of school age in the same states being 70.34, and the percentage of enrolments to population over the whole United States 69.32.[8] In these states the coloured people were in 1910 33.1 per cent of the total population,

[8] *Report of the Commissioner of Education for 1908–9.*

and the coloured pupils 31.47 per cent of the total school enrolments. A smaller percentage of them than of white children is, therefore, on the books of the schools; but when it is remembered that in 1865 only an infinitesimally small percentage were at school at all, and that in many states it was a penal offence to teach a Negro to read, the progress made is remarkable. Between 1877 and 1908, while the white pupils in the common schools of the South increased 156 per cent, the coloured pupils increased 191 per cent. It must not, however, be concluded from these figures that nearly the whole of the coloured population are growing up possessed even of the rudiments of education. The ratio of attendance to school enrolment was, indeed, in 1908 almost as good for the Negroes as for the whites (62.18 against 66.13), the Negroes, both parents and children, having a desire for instruction. But the school terms are so short in most of the Southern states that a good many of whites and a far larger number of coloured children receive too little teaching to enable them to read and write with ease. Thus out of the Negroes in the old slave states over ten years of age, nearly 33.4 per cent were in 1910 returned as illiterates. That the amount of higher education—secondary, collegiate, or university education—obtained by the Negroes is not only absolutely small, but incomparably smaller than that obtained by the whites, is no more than might be expected from the fact that they constitute the poorest part of the population. The total number of institutions of this description was in 1908 as follows:[9]

Normal and Industrial schools,	53, with 17,711 pupils.
Secondary schools,	35, with 8,774 pupils.
Universities and colleges,[10]	47, with 18,859 pupils.
Schools of theology,	14, with 792 pupils.
Schools of law,	3, with 93 pupils.
Schools of medicine, dentistry, pharmacy,	3, with 789 pupils.

These universities are, of course, on a comparatively humble scale, and most of them might rather be called secondary schools. The grants made by the state governments nearly all go to elementary education, and the institutions which provide higher education for the Negro are quite unequal to the demands made upon them. Swarms of applicants for admission have to be turned away from the already overcrowded existing upper and normal schools and colleges; and thus the supply of qualified teachers for the

---

[9] *Report of the Commissioner of Education for 1908–9.* It is of course to be remembered that Negroes go rather more largely than formerly to professional schools in the North.

[10] Including preparatory and primary departments of universities.

coloured schools is greatly below the needs of the case. The total number is at present only 33,000, with 1,800,000 pupils to deal with. In the white schools, with 4,692,927 pupils, there are 116,539 teachers, a proportion (about 1 teacher to 40 pupils) obviously much too low, and too low even if we allow for the difference between enrolment and attendance. But the proportion in the coloured schools is lower still (1 to 55), and the teachers themselves are less instructed. The need for secondary and normal schools is, therefore, still urgent, though much has been and is being done by Northern benevolence for this admirable purpose.[11] There is something pathetic in the eagerness of the Negroes, parents, young people, and children, to obtain instruction. They seem to think that the want of it is what keeps them below the whites, just as in the riots which broke out in South Carolina during Sherman's invasion, the Negro mob burnt a library at Columbia because, as they said, it was from the books that "the white folks got their sense." And they have a notion (which, to be sure, is not confined to them) that it is the want of book-learning which condemns the vast bulk of their race to live by manual labor, and that, therefore, by acquiring such learning they may themselves rise in the industrial scale.

In the days of slavery, religion was practically the only civilizing influence which told upon the plantation hands. But religion, like everything else that enters the mind, is conditioned by the mental state of the recipient. Among the Negroes, it took a highly emotional and sensational form, in which there was little apprehension of doctrine and still less of virtue, while physical excitement constantly passed into ecstasy, hysterics, and the other phenomena which accompany what are called in America camp meetings. This form it has hitherto generally retained. The evils have been palpable, but the good has been greater than the evil; and one fears to conjecture what this vast mass of Africans might have been had no such influence been at work to soften and elevate them, and to create a sort of tie between them and their masters. Christianity, however, has been among the Negroes as it often was in the Dark Ages and as it is in some countries even today, widely divorced from morality. The Negro preachers, the natural and generally the only leaders of their people, are (doubtless with noble exceptions) by no means a model class, while through the population at large religious belief and even religious fervour are found not incompatible with great laxity in sexual

---

[11] Among the great benefactions whose income is applied for the education of the coloured people special mention may be made of the Peabody Fund, the John F. Slater Fund, and the Daniel Hand Fund, all of which seem to be very wisely administered. I find the total annual sum given by the North to normal and collegiate education among the Negroes estimated at a million dollars.

relations and a proneness to petty thefts. Fortunately, here also there is evidence of improvement. The younger pastors are described as being more rarely lazy and licentious than were those of the older generation; their teaching appeals less to passion and more to reason. As it is only coloured preachers who reach Negro congregations, the importance of such an improvement can hardly be overestimated. There is, of course, an enormous difference between the coloured churches in the cities, especially those of the border states, where one finds a comparatively educated clergy and laity, with ideas of decorum modelled on those of their white neighbors, and the pure Negro districts further south,[12] in some of which, as in parts of Louisiana, not merely have the old superstitions been retained, but there have been relapses into the Obeah rites and serpent worship of African heathendom. How far this has gone no one can say. There are parts of the lower Mississippi valley as little explored, so far as the mental and moral condition of the masses is concerned, as are the banks of the Congo and the Benué.

From what has been said of the state of education, it will have been gathered that the influence of books is confined to extremely few, and that even of newspapers to a small fraction of the coloured people. Nevertheless, the significance of whatever forms the mind of that small fraction must not be underestimated. The few thousands who read books or magazines, the few tens of thousands who see a daily paper, acquire the ideas and beliefs and aspirations of the normal white citizen, subject of course to the inherent differences in race character already referred to. They are in a sense more American than the recent immigrants from Central Europe and from Italy, who are now a substantial element in the population of the Middle and Western states. Within this small section of the coloured people are the natural leaders of the millions who have not yet attained to what may be called the democratic American consciousness. And the number of those upon whom books and newspapers play, in whom democratic ideas stimulate

---

[12] This is noted by Mr. Bruce in his book, *The Plantation Negro as a Freeman,* which presents a striking, though perhaps too gloomy a picture, of the condition of the race.

   Dr. Curry, who knew the South thoroughly, and admirably administered the Slater Fund, says, "One of the chief drawbacks to civilization in the negro race is the exceeding difficulty of giving a predominant ethical character to his religion. In the Black Belt, religion and virtue are often considered as distinct and separable things. The moral element, good character, is eliminated from the essential ingredients of Christianity, and good citizenship, womanliness, honesty, truth, chastity, cleanliness, trustworthiness, are not always of the essence of religious obligation. An intelligent, pious, courageous ministry is indispensable to any hopeful attempt to lift up the negro race."—*Atlantic Monthly* for June 1892, p. 732.

discontent with the present inferiority of their people, is steadily, and in some districts, rapidly increasing. The efforts of those who are best fitted to lead have been hitherto checked by the jealousy which the mass is apt to feel for those who rise to prominence; but this tendency may decline, and there will be no reason for surprise if men of eloquence and ambition are one day found to give voice to the sentiments of their brethren as Frederick Douglass did.[13]

The influence of industry is another name for the influence of self-help. As a slave, the Negro was no doubt taught to give steady, though unintelligent, labour; and this was probably a step forward from his condition in Africa. But labour all of it performed under supervision, and none of it followed by any advantage to the labourer except relief from the lash, labour whose aim was to accomplish not the best possible but the least that would suffice, did nothing to raise the character or to train the intelligence. Every day's work that the Negro has done since he became a freedman has helped him. Most of the work is rough work, whether on the land or in the cities, and is done for low wages. But the number of those who, either as owners or as tenant farmers, raise their own crops for the market, and of those who are finding their way into skilled employments, is an always increasing number. To raise crops for the market is an education in thrift, foresight, and business aptitude, as well as in agriculture; to follow a skilled industry is to train the intelligence as well as the hand, and the will as well as the intelligence. The provision for the instruction of the young Negroes in any handicraft is still quite inadequate, though such institutions at Hampton and Tuskegee have set admirable examples,[14] and the need of means for imparting it is even more urgent than is that of secondary schools. It is satisfactory to know that the necessity is beginning to be recognized, and some effort made to provide industrial training. The first person to point out that it was the thing most needful, was the founder of Hampton, one of the noblest characters of his time, the late General S. C. Armstrong.

Against the industrial progress of the Negro there must be set two depressing phenomena. One is the increase of insanity, marked since emancipation, and probably attributable to the increased facilities which freedom has given for obtaining liquor, and to the stress which independence

---

[13] I remember to have listened to a striking speech by a Negro in Richmond in which he appealed to the historic glories of the State of Virginia, and sought to rouse the audience by reminding them that they too were Virginians.

[14] The report of the Commissioner of Education, 1908–9, indicated that 23,160 pupils were receiving industrial training in schools above the elementary grades.

and education have imposed on the undeveloped brain of a backward race. The other, not unconnected with the former, is the large amount of crime. Most of it is petty crime, chiefly thefts of hogs and poultry, but there are also a good many crimes against women. Seventy per cent of the convicts in Southern jails are Negroes;[15] and though one must allow for the fact that they are the poorest part of the population and that the law is probably more strictly enforced against them than against the whites, this is a proportion double that of their numbers.[16] Even in the District of Columbia more than half the arrests are among the coloured people, though they are only one-third of the inhabitants.

The most potent agency in the progress of the humbler and more ignorant sections of a community has always been their intercourse with those who are more advanced. In the United States it is by their social commixture with the native citizens that European immigrants become so quickly assimilated, the British in two or three years, the Germans and Scandinavians in eight or ten. But the precondition of such commixture is the absence of race repulsion and especially the possibility of intermarriage. In the case of the American Negro, the race repulsion exists, and fusion by intermarriage is deemed impossible. The day of his liberation was also the day when the whites began to shun intercourse with him, and when opinion began to condemn, not merely regular marriage with a person of colour, for that had been always forbidden, but even an illicit union.

To understand the very peculiar phenomena which mark the relations of the two races, one must distinguish between the Northern and Southern states.

In the North there was before the war a marked aversion to the Negro and a complete absence of social intercourse with him. The Negroes were, of course, among the poorest and least educated persons in the community. But the poorest white looked down upon them just as much as the richest; and in many states they enjoyed no political rights. The sympathy felt for them during the Civil War, the evidence of courage and capacity for discipline they gave as soldiers in the Federal Army, and the disposition to protect them which the Republican party showed during the Reconstruction

[15] The South is still far behind the North in matters of prison management. Convicts, and sometimes white as well as coloured convicts, are in many states hired out to private employers or companies for rough work, and very harshly treated.

[16] Note, however, that in the rest of the Union (North East, North Central, and West), the proportion of prisoners in the jails is much higher among the foreign-born than in the population at large, doubtless because they are the poorest class.

period, modified this aversion; and in the North they are not subject to any legal disabilities. They are occasionally admitted to some inferior political office, or even to a seat in a state legislature. The Women's Christian Temperance Union receives them as members, and so does the Grand Army of the Republic, though they are grouped in distinct "posts." People sometimes take pleasure in going out of their way to compliment them. A coloured student was once chosen by his companions at Harvard University to be the "class orator" of the year; and I know of cases in which the lawyers of a city have signed memorials recommending a coloured barrister for appointment to an important federal office. Nevertheless, there is practically no social intermixture of white and coloured people. Except on the Pacific coast, a Negro never sits down to dinner with a white man, in a railway refreshment room. You never encounter him at a private party. He is not received in a hotel of the better sort, no matter how rich he may be. He will probably be refused a glass of soda water at a drug store. He is not shaved in a place frequented by white men, not even by a barber of his own colour. He worships in a church of his own. No native white woman would dream of receiving his addresses. Kindly condescension is the best he can look for, accompanied by equality of access to a business or profession. Social equality is utterly out of his reach, and in many districts he has not even equality of economic opportunity, for the white labourer may refuse to work with him and his colour may prove a bar to his obtaining employment except of the lowest kind.

In the South, on the other hand, the whites had before the war no sense of personal repulsion from the Negro. The domestic slave was in the closest relation with his master's family. Sometimes he was his master's trusted friend. The white child grew up with the black child as its playmate. The legal inequality was so immense that familiarity was not felt to involve any disturbance of the attitude of command. With emancipation there must needs come a change; but the change would have come more gently, and left a better relation subsisting, had it not been for the unhappy turn which things took in the Reconstruction period under the dominance of the Negro vote. The white people were then thoroughly frightened. They thought that the aim of the North was to force them to admit not only the civic but the social equality of the freedmen, and they resolved, if one can apply the language of deliberate purpose to what was rather an unconscious and uncontrollable impulse, to maintain the social inferiority of the Negro as well as to exclude him from political power. They declare that they know him better and like him better than the Northern people do. That there is not among the educated whites of the South any hostility to the race as a race is true enough. The sons of the planters, and of the better class generally, have kindly recollections of their former slaves, and get on well with their Negro servants and workmen; while among the freedmen, now comparatively few, there is still a loyal attachment to the children of their former masters. The poor whites, however, dislike the Negroes, resent the slightest assumption of equality on the part of the latter,[17] and show their hatred by violence, sometimes even by ferocity, when any disturbance arises or when a Negro fugitive has to be pursued. Except so far as it is involved in domestic service, the servants in the South being nearly all Negroes, there is now little intercourse between whites and blacks. In many states the law requires the railroad and even the streetcar companies to provide separate cars for the latter, though there are cities, such as Baltimore and Washington, where the same cars are used by both races. In most parts of the South a person of colour cannot enter a public refreshment room used by the whites except as the servant of a white; and one may see the most respectable and, possibly, even educated coloured woman, perhaps almost white, forced into the coloured car among rough Negroes, while the black nurse in charge of a white child is admitted to the white car. The two races are everywhere taught in distinct schools and colleges, though in one or two places Negroes have been allowed to study in the medical or law classes. They worship in different churches. Though the Negroes read the ordinary papers, they also support their own distinct organs. They have distinct Young Men's Christian Associations. With some exceptions in the case of unskilled trades, they are not admitted to trade unions.[18] In concert halls and theatres, if the coloured are admitted at all, it is to an inferior part of the chamber. They are, however, sometimes called to serve on juries. Civil justice is mostly fairly administered as between the races, but not criminal justice. In most parts of the South a white man would run little more risk of being hanged for the murder of a Negro than a Mussulman in Turkey for the murder of a Christian.

Under so complete a system of separation, it is clear that the influence of social intercourse between whites and blacks, an influence to which the domestic slaves before the war owed much, now counts for little. But the question of the attitude of the whites has another side. It means more than the suspension of a civilizing agency. Some Southern observers say that the

---

[17] A Virginian observed to me, "Our whites don't molest the negroes so long as the negroes don't presume!"

[18] Their unions were however admitted to the federation of the Knights of Labor. Sometimes there is a coloured union acting in conjunction with a white one.

coloured generation which has grown up since the war, and which has been
in less close touch with the white people than were the slaves and freedmen
of the last generation, is less friendly to them. It has lost the instinctive
sense of subservience and dependence, and its more educated members feel
acutely the contrast between their legal equality and their inequality in every
other respect. The lower class are also often unfriendly, prone to suspicion
and violence. In this situation there lie possibilities of danger. The strained
relations of the races appear most frequently in the lynchings of Negroes.
It is extremely hard to ascertain the truth of the reports regarding these
lawless acts. But there can be no doubt that over the South and, to a smaller
extent, in the North also, Negroes accused of assassinating white men, or
of outraging white women or children are frequently seized by white mobs
and summarily killed; that occasionally, though probably not often, an
innocent man perishes, and that the killing is sometimes accompanied by
circumstances of revolting cruelty. Now and then the culprit is burned alive.
Often his body, after he has been hanged, is riddled with bullets, a piece
of barbarism akin to the Eastern habit of mutilating the corpses of the slain.
The excuses offered for these acts are that white women, especially in
sparsely inhabited regions, are in considerable danger from the lust of brutal
Negroes, and that the swift apprehension and slaughter of the culprit not
only strikes greater dread than the regular process of justice, but does not
gratify the Negro's enjoyment of the pomp and ceremony of a formal trial
before a judge. It is also declared, and with truth, that whites also are
lynched, though not so frequently and in a less atrocious way,[19] that the
Negroes themselves occasionally lynch a Negro, that it is hard for the
executive authority, with no force except the militia at its command, to
protect prisoners and repress disorder, and that the lynchings are the work
of a comparatively small and rude part of the white population; the better
citizens disapproving, but being unable or unwilling to interfere.

Whatever palliations may be found in these circumstances—and it is quite
true that in a thinly peopled and unpoliced country white women do stand
in serious risk—there can be no doubt that the practice of lynching has a
pernicious effect on the whites themselves, accustoming them to cruelty,
and fostering a spirit of lawlessness which tells for evil on every branch of
government and public life. Were the Negroes less cowed by the superior

---

[19] There was, however, an instance some years ago, in which the party which was hunting for a
white murderer announced their intention of burning him. I do not know whether he was caught.
I have even read in the newspapers of a case in which a crowd allowed two women to flog a
third to death, but this was in a wild mountain region. All the parties were whites.

strength and numbers of the whites, reprisals, now rare, would be more frequent. Yet even in a race with so little vindictiveness or temper, terrible mischief is done. The tendency to accept the leadership of the whites, and to seek progress rather by industrial and educational than by political efforts has been damped, and the establishment of good feeling and a sense of public security retarded. The humble Negro shuns contact with the whites, not knowing when some band of roughs may mishandle him; and sometimes a lynching is followed by a sudden rush of coloured emigration from the state or district where it has happened.[20] The educated and aspiring Negro resents the savage spirit shown towards his colour, though he feels his helplessness too keenly to attempt any action which could check it.

This social repulsion and its consequences present a painful contrast to the effect of the four previous influences we have examined. As respects their intelligence, their character, their habits of industry, the coloured people are in most states making real progress. It is a progress very unequal as regards the different regions of the country, and perhaps may not extend to some districts of the so-called black belt, which stretches from the coast of South Carolina across the Gulf states. It is most evident in the matter of education, less evident as respects religion and the influence of literature. Its economic results are perceptible in the accumulation of property by city workmen, in the acquisition of small farms by rural cultivators, in the slow, but steady, increase in the number of coloured people in the professions of medicine, law, and literature. Were it accompanied by a growth of good feeling between whites and Negroes, and a more natural and friendly intercourse between them in business and in social matters, the horizon would be bright, and the political difficulties, which I shall presently describe, need not cause alarm. This intercourse is, however, conspicuously absent. The progress of the coloured people has been accompanied by the evolution of social classes within their own body. Wealthy and educated Negroes, such as one may now find in cities like Baltimore, Louisville, Richmond, Atlanta, and New Orleans, have come to form a cultured group, who are looked up to by the poorer class.[21] But these cultured groups are

---

[20] When the Territory of Oklahoma was opened for settlement, Negroes flocked in from Missouri and Arkansas hoping to obtain better security for themselves by their presence in considerable numbers.

[21] The mulattoes or quadroons are, as a rule, more advanced than the pure blacks, and are alleged to avoid intermarriage with the latter. Now and then, however, a pure black may be found of remarkable intelligence. Such a one, a Louisiana farmer, who read and talked with sense and judgment about the Greek philosophers, is described in the graphic and instructive sketches called *Studies in the South.—Atlantic Monthly* for February 1882.

as little in contact with their white neighbours as are the humblest coloured labourers, perhaps even less so. No prospect is open to them, whatever wealth or culture they may acquire, of finding an entrance into white society, and they are made to feel in a thousand ways that they belong to a caste condemned to perpetual inferiority. Their spokesmen in the press have latterly so fully realized the position as to declare that they do not seek social equality with the whites, that they are quite willing to build up a separate society of their own, and seek neither intermarriage nor social intercourse, but that what they do ask is equal opportunity in business, the professions, and politics, equal recognition of the worth of their manhood, and a discontinuance of the social humiliations they are now compelled to endure.

From this attempt to sketch the phenomena of the present, I proceed to consider the future. The future has two problems to solve. One is political; the other social. How is the determination of the whites to rule to be reconciled with the possession by the Negroes of equal rights of suffrage? How can the social severance or antagonism of the two races—by whichever term we are to describe it—the haughty assertion of superiority by the whites and the suppressed resentment of the more advanced among the coloured people, be prevented from ripening into a settled distrust and hostility which may affect the peace and prosperity of the South for centuries to come?

The methods whereby the Negroes have been prevented from exercising the rights of suffrage vested in them by law have been described in the last preceding chapter. These means became less violent as the Negroes more and more acquiesced in their exclusion; but whether violent or pacific, they were almost uniformly successful. In the so-called border states, the whites have been in so great a majority that they do not care to interfere with the coloured vote, except now and then by the use of money. Through the rest of the South the Negro came to realize that he would not be permitted to exercise any influence on the government; and his interest in coming to the polls declined accordingly. The main cause of this resolve of the whites to keep power entirely in their own hands is the alarm they feel at the possibility of Negro domination. A stranger, whether from the North or from Europe, thinks this alarm groundless. He perceives that the whites have not only the habit of command, but also nearly all the property, the intelligence, and the force of character which exist in the country. He reminds his Southern hosts that the balance even of numbers is inclining more and more in their favour; and that the probability of Northern intervention on behalf of the excluded

Negro voter has become, since the failure of the Federal Elections Bill of 1890, extremely slight, while the other conditions of 1867 can never recur. On this point, however, the Southern man is immovable. To him it is a simple question of self-preservation. "We like the negro," said a leader among them to me some years ago; "we know he must stay; we desire to treat him well. But if he votes, we must vote him, or outvote him."

The results of the policy followed were unfortunate. The Negroes, naturally docile and disposed to follow the lead of their white employer or neighbour, felt themselves suspected, and lived in a terror of being stripped of the civic rights which they were not suffered to exercise, like the terror which for a time possessed them of being thrown back into slavery. So far as they voted at all they mostly clung together, and voted solid, intimidating or boycotting anyone of their number who was supposed to be a "bolter." The whites, accustomed to justify their use of force or fraud by the plea of necessity, became callous to electoral malpractices. The level of purity and honesty in political methods, once comparatively high, declined; and the average Southern conscience grew to be no more sensitive than is that of professional politicians in Northern cities. Nor was the mischief confined to elections. The existence of this alarm has, by making the South regard the Negro as the capital question in national as well as state politics, warped the natural growth of political opinion and political parties upon all those other current questions which engage the mind of the people, and has to that extent retarded their reabsorption into the general political life of the Republic.

These evils were generally recognized. Out of the various remedies that were proposed for their cure, three deserve to be specially noted.

The first was (as proposed in the bill of 1890) to give protection to the coloured voter by the action of federal officers backed by federal troops. This could, of course, be done under the Constitution at federal elections only, and would not cover the equally important state and local elections. It would, moreover (as the discussions of 1890 showed), provoke great exasperation at the South, and might lead to breaches of the peace, from which the Negroes would be the chief sufferers. The whole South would resist it, and no small part of the Northern people would dislike it.

A second and opposite remedy was to repeal the Fifteenth Amendment to the federal Constitution, and leave each state free to exclude Negroes from the suffrage. This plan, although sometimes put forward by men of ability, was even more impracticable than the preceding one. A majority of three-fourths of the states could not possibly be secured for the repeal of a provision which the Northern people regard as sealing one of the main results of the Civil War.

The third suggested scheme was to limit the suffrage by some educational or even some pecuniary qualification—although American sentiment dislikes a property qualification, calculated to exclude many or most of the Negroes, not as Negroes, but because they were ignorant or poor. Such a scheme, though proposed by Gen. Wade Hampton in South Carolina as far back as 1867, was not tried until 1890, when Mississippi, by her constitution of that year,[22] provided that a person applying to be registered as a voter "shall be able to read any section of the Constitution, or be able to understand the same when read to him, or to give a reasonable interpretation thereof."

The advantages of such a method are obvious, and have suggested its adoption in a British colony where the presence of a large coloured population raised a problem not dissimilar to that we have been examining.[23] Recognizing the need of knowledge and intelligence for the due exercise of political power, it excludes a large mass of confessedly incompetent persons, while leaving the door open for those Negroes whose instructed capacity brings them up to the level of the bulk of the whites, and who, in some places, may be now from one-fifth to one-fourth of the whole Negro population. Thus it may operate, not only as an improvement in the electoral body, but as an incentive to educational progress.

The obstacles to the adoption of the plan were, however, serious. One was that in disfranchising their Negroes for want of education, most Southern states would have also to disfranchise that part of their white population, which was below any educational standard high enough to exclude the mass of Negroes. The percentage of illiterates to the whole population over ten years of age was in 1890 in the Southeastern states 14.5 and in the Southwestern 15. To expect these voters (about 1,412,000) to disfranchise themselves for the sake of excluding Negroes was to expect too much. The other was that every limitation of the suffrage might diminish *pro tanto* (Amendment XIV) a state's representation in federal elections, thereby weakening its influence in federal affairs and mortifying its self-esteem. The state of Mississippi, while facing, as it safely might, this possibility, evaded

[22] There was one Negro member in the convention that enacted this constitution, which was never (be it noted) submitted to the popular vote.

[23] In Cape Colony the Franchise and Ballot Act of 1892 raised the (previously very low) property qualification for the suffrage, and provided (§ 6) that no person shall be registered as an elector "unless he is able to sign his name and write his address and occupation." These provisions disqualify the great bulk of the native coloured people, few of whom have, as may be supposed, any interest in politics.

the former difficulty by the ingenious loophole under which the registering officials may admit whites who, though illiterate, are able to give a "reasonable interpretation" of any section of the state constitution. Such whites have, one is told, been able to satisfy the officials far more generally than have the Negroes. And if this particular section happens to be put to them, their common sense will find its interpretation obvious. Other states have since 1890 tried other methods, which are mentioned in the following chapter.

Even graver than the political difficulties which have been described is the social problem raised by the coexistence on the same soil, under the same free government, of two races so widely differing that they do not intermingle. Social disparity or social oppression cuts deeper than any political severance; and time, so far from curing the mischief, seems during the last thirty or forty years to have aggravated it. Politics leave untouched large parts of the field of human life, even in the United States; and the political inferiority of the coloured race, since it is the result of their retarded intellectual development, seems in accord with nature. Social inferiority, which is felt at every moment, and which reduces or destroys the sense of human brotherhood, is a more serious matter.

This problem is, moreover, a new one in history, for the relations of the ruling and subject races of Europe and Asia supply no parallel to it. Whoever examines the records of the past will find that the continued juxtaposition of two races has always been followed either by the disappearance of the weaker or by the intermixture of the two. Where race antagonisms still remain, as in parts of Eastern Europe, and on a far larger scale in Asia, one may expect a similar solution to be ultimately reached. In Transylvania, for instance, Saxons, Magyars, and Roumans stand apart from one another, all three, but especially the two latter, mutually suspicious and politically hostile. So further east one finds strong religious antagonisms (not without serious attendant evils), such as those of Sunnis, Shiahs, and Christians in Western Asia, or of Hindus and Mussulmans in India, antagonisms, however, which only partially coincide with race differences, and have thrown the latter quite into the shade. In all such cases, however, though one race or religion may be for the moment dominant, there is no necessary or permanent distinction between them; and there is, if the religious difficulty can be overcome, a possibility of intermarriage. Other cases may be suggested where a fusion is improbable, as between the British and the natives in India, or the colonists and the natives in South Africa. But the European rulers of India are a mere handful in comparison with the natives, nor do they settle in India so as to form a part of its permanent population. In New Zealand, the Maoris, hitherto a diminishing body, though now just maintaining their numbers, live apart on their own lands, but seem likely to be ultimately absorbed by the whites. In western South America the Spanish settlers have, in some regions, very largely mingled their blood with that of the native Indians, and may ultimately become as much blent with the latter as has befallen in Mexico. The peculiar feature of the race problem as it presents itself in the United States is, that the Negroes are in many districts one-third or even one-half of the population, are forced to live in the closest local contiguity with the whites, and are for the purposes of industry indispensable to the latter, yet are so sharply cut off from the whites by colour and all that colour means, that not merely a mingling of blood, but any social approximation, is regarded with horror, and perpetual severance is deemed a law of nature.

From such a position what issue? One hears little said in America of any possible issue, partly because the nation is tired of the whole subject, which has, in one form or another, vexed it ever since the early days of last century, partly because every plan that has been suggested is open to patent objections. Several, however, may deserve to be mentioned.

Even long before the war, and often since, it has been proposed that the Negroes should be retransported to Africa. The petty and stagnant Republic of Liberia owes its origin to the idea that it might furnish a home for Afro-American freedmen, and a centre whence they might be dispersed in larger and larger numbers through their ancient home. But in 1910 the more or less civilized population of Liberia of American origin was only some 18,000, the million of other inhabitants being aborigines, and the badly administered state was unable to pay its way.

There are two fatal objections to the plan of exporting the Southern Negroes to Africa. One is that they will not go; the other that the whites cannot afford to let them go. There is nothing to attract them in the prospect of being uprooted from their homes in a country where the comforts of civilization are attainable by industry, and thrown upon a new shore, already occupied by savages of whose very languages, except in the few spots where English is spoken, they are ignorant.[24] The Southern whites, so far from encouraging, would resist their departure; for it would mean the loss of the labour by which more than half the crops of the South are raised, and a

---

[24] A variation of this suggestion has been that while the pure blacks should be exported to Africa, the (usually more advanced) mulattoes and quadroons might go to reclaim the Antilles. See *An Appeal to Pharaoh;* New York, 1890.

great part of her mining and iron-working industries carried on. Much of the country might, for a time at least, remain untilled and useless were the Negro to disappear; for of the introduction of coolie labour from India there can be no talk in a nation which has so strictly forbidden the entrance of Chinese. The Negro, in short, is essential to the material prosperity of the South, and his departure would mean ruin to it. Even now, the Atlantic states do what they can to prevent their coloured labourers from leaving them to go west.[25]

Apart from these obstacles, the transference of many millions of people from one continent to another is beyond the horizon of the possible. Their annual increase exceeds 200,000, quite as large a number as could be, in a single year, conveyed to and provided for in Africa. How many emigrant ships, and at what cost, would be needed even for this, not to speak of the far larger expenses needed to keep them from starving till they had begun to scatter themselves through the interior of Africa! To proceed by transporting even 200,000 a year, would be to try to empty a running stream by a ladle. The notion of such a solution has been abandoned by all sensible men in America, though here and there a belated voice repeats it.

Easier seems the alternative plan of setting apart for the coloured people certain districts of the country, such as, for instance, the southern part of the Atlantic coast region and the lowlands of the Gulf, and moving them into these districts from the rest of the country, as Oliver Cromwell drove the wild Irish into Connaught. But neither does this solution find any favour in America. No state would consent to see even a part of its territory cut off and allotted to the Negroes, to be by them administered in their own way. The rest of the country would hardly admit a purely black state to be represented in Congress and to vote in presidential elections on equal terms. And in many parts of the South, which are better suited for whites than for Negroes, and in which, therefore, the white population is now much larger, the leading industries would suffer severely from the removal of Negro labour. Northern Alabama, for instance, is in point of climate a region well fitted for whites. But the iron works there employ great numbers of Negroes who are found efficient, and whose place might not be easily filled. Virginia is, in the main, a white state. But not only the growing of tobacco, but also its preparation for the market, is a Negro industry; and it would be no simple matter to find white workpeople to do it equally well and cheaply.

---

[25] Some states punish with fines or imprisonment anyone entering the state for the purpose of endeavouring to draw the Negroes to states further west.

This scheme, therefore, may also be dismissed as outside the range of practical politics.

There remains the suggestion that the method by which race antagonisms have been so often removed in the past in the Old World, and to some extent (as, for instance, in Mexico) in the New World also, may eventually be applied in the United States; that is to say, that the two races may be blent by intermarriage into one. To some Europeans, and to a very few old survivors of the Abolitionist party in the North, this solution appears possible and even natural. To all Southern sentiment it is shocking. I have never met a Southern man, whether born there or an incomer from the North, who would even discuss the possibility of such a general commixture of whites and blacks as Brazil has begun to show or as exists in some Mussulman countries. In no Southern state can such a marriage be legally contracted; and what is more remarkable, in every Southern state such unions are excessively rare. Even at the North, where the aversion to Negro blood is now less strong, "miscegenation," as they call it, is deemed such a disgrace to the white who contracts it that one seldom hears of its occurrence. Enlightened Southern men, who have themselves no dislike to the black race, justify this horror of intermarriage by arguing that no benefit which might thereby accrue to the Negroes could balance the evil which would befall the rest of the community. The interests of the nation and of humanity itself would, in their view, suffer by such a permanent debasement of the Anglo-American race as would follow. Our English blood is suffering enough already, they say, from the intrusion of inferior stock from continental Europe; and we should be brought down to the level of San Domingo were we to have an infusion from Africa added. This is the argument to which reason appeals. That enormous majority which does not reason is swayed by a feeling so strong and universal that there seems no chance of its abating within any assignable time. Revolutions in sentiment are, no doubt, conceivable, but they are more rare than revolutions in politics.

We arrive, therefore, at three conclusions:

I. The Negro will stay in North America.
II. He will stay locally intermixed with the white population.
III. He will stay socially distinct, as an alien element, unabsorbed and unabsorbable.

His position may, however, change from what it is now.

He may more and more draw southwards into the lower and hotter regions along the coasts of the Atlantic and the Gulf of Mexico. Whether in the more northerly states, such as Maryland and Missouri, he will decrease, may be doubtful. But it is certainly in those southerly regions that his chief future increase may be expected. In other words, he will be a relatively smaller, and probably much smaller, element than at present in the whole population north of latitude 36°, and a relatively larger one south of latitude 33°, and east of longitude 94° W.

This change would have both its good and its evil side. It may involve less frequent occasions for collision between the two races, and may dispose the Negroes, where they are comparatively few, to acquiesce less reluctantly in white predominance. But it will afford scantier opportunities for the gradual elevation of the race in the districts where they are most numerous. Contact with the whites is the chief condition for the progress of the Negro. Where he is isolated, or where he greatly outnumbers the whites, his advance will be retarded, although nothing has yet occurred to justify the fear that he will, even along the Gulf coast, or in the sea islands of Carolina, sink to the level of the Haytian.

The Negro may, indeed, in time he doubtless will, though more rapidly in some regions than in others, continue to advance in education, intelligence, and wealth, as well as in habits of thrift and application. Such progress may seem an unmixed good. Yet it can hardly fail to be accompanied in that small minority who advance most quickly, by a growing discontent with the social disabilities imposed upon the race. It will give them greater capacity for organization, possibly greater tenacity and courage, than they now possess; and these very things might, by alarming the whites, tend to widen the chasm between the races. Whether the coloured people will be any better able to give effect to any resentment they may feel, is doubtful, so great is the disparity in strength. But they might be more embittered, and this embitterment, reacting upon white sentiment, might retard the working of those healing influences which the progress of civilization generally brings in its train. Already one hears the younger whites of the South talk of the growing "uppishness" and impertinence of the Negro, as things to be resented and punished.

That sense of haughty superiority which other nations note in the English has in their Indian dominions done much to destroy the happy effects of the enormous social and economic improvements which the rule of Britain has effected. A young indigo planter, or a lieutenant only just released from school at home, will treat with wanton insolence or contumely natives of the highest caste, perhaps of dignified social position and ancient lineage; and though government punishes these offences in the rare cases when they are brought to its knowledge, the sentiment of Anglo-Indian society scarcely condemns them. Thus the very classes whom rank and education might have been expected to render loyal to British authority are alienated. When similar tendencies appear in the Anglo-American of the South, the Englishman, who knows how not a few of his own countrymen behave to the ancient and cultivated races of the East whom they have conquered, feels that he is not entitled to sit in judgment.

I do not suggest that there is any present political danger to the Republic, or even to any particular Southern state, from the phenomena here described. But the evil of these things is to be measured not merely by any such menace to political stability as they may involve, but also by the diminution of happiness which they cause, by the passions hurtful to moral progress they perpetuate, by the spirit of lawlessness they evoke, by the contempt for the rights of man as man which they engender. In a world already so full of strife and sorrow it is grievous to see added to the other fountains of bitterness a scorn of the strong for the weak, and a dread by the weak of the strong, grounded on no antagonism of interests, for each needs the other, but solely on a difference in race and colour.

Be these evils what they may—and serious as they seem to an observer from without, they are in most parts of the South not keenly felt in daily life—legislation and administration can do comparatively little to remove them. It is, indeed, to be wished that lynching should be sternly repressed— some of the Southern state governors are doing what they can for that purpose—and that the state statutes or local regulations enforcing separation of blacks from whites in travelling or in places of public resort should be at least modified, for they press hardly on the educated Negroes. But the real change to which the friends of the South and of the Negro look forward is a change in the feelings of the white people, and especially of the ruder and less educated part of them. The political troubles I have described have been tending to pass away under altered political conditions. For the social difficulty, rooted deep in the characters of the two races, none but moral remedies have any promise of potency, and the working of moral remedies, sure as we believe it to be, is always slow. Neither will compulsive measures quicken that working. In the United States, above all other countries, one must place one's hopes on what physicians call the healing power of Nature, and trust that the forces which make not only for equality, but also for peace and goodwill among men, will in due time reduce these evils, as they have reduced many others. There is no ground for despondency to anyone who remembers how hopeless the extinction of slavery seemed in 1820 or even in 1850 and who marks the progress which the Negroes have made since their sudden liberation. Still less is there reason for impatience, for questions like this have in some countries of the Old World required ages for their solution. The problem which confronts the South is one of the great secular problems of the world, presented here under a form of peculiar difficulty. And as the present differences between the African and the European are the product of thousands of years, during which one race was advancing in the temperate, and the other remaining stationary in the torrid zone, so centuries may pass before their relations as neighbours and fellow-citizens have been duly adjusted.

Further Reflections on
the Negro Problem

The position of the Negro race in the United States is so peculiar and raises so many questions of the gravest social and economic kind that although the last preceding chapter has been revised and adapted to the changes that have occurred since it was first written, it seems proper to devote some additional pages to a consideration of those aspects of the subject which strike the observer of today.[1]

The changes of the last seventeen years have not affected the main features of the situation. The larger any problem is and the more deeply rooted in the past are the factors which determine it, the more slowly do those main features alter. There has, however, been not only an ampler but also a more temperate discussion of the whole matter during the last decade than there ever was before. This discussion has been turned into new channels by the material development of the South, and has revealed in new lights the spirit that now pervades the Southern people.

The recovery of the South from the abyss of ruin into which the Civil War had thrown large sections of it, and especially Virginia, South Carolina, and Georgia, began a little before 1880 and has proceeded with growing speed. The assessed valuation of taxable property in the former slave states was in 1900 just what it had been in 1860, so long was the time needed to repair the losses of the long struggle. That recovery is now visible in all directions, in the bringing of new lands under cultivation, in the opening of mines, in the creation of iron and steel works, in the extension of cotton

---

[1] Among recent books to which reference may be made upon the topics dealt with in this chapter are Mr. Ray S. Baker's *Following the Color Line*, Mr. Stone's *American Race Problem*, Mr. E. G. Murphy's *Present South* and *Basis of Ascendancy*, Dr. Booker T. Washington's *Story of the Negro*, and Professor Albert Hart's *The Southern South*. See also the *U.S. Census Bulletin, No. 8*.

and other factories, in the rising value of real estate, and the parallel increase of the revenues of states and cities, in the foundation of agricultural and technical schools, and the expenditure of larger and larger sums upon public instruction, in the building of new railroads and the consolidation of many small lines into a few great systems which give a quicker and better service. The growth of population has not been so marked as in the Northern and Western states, but that is largely because very few immigrants from the Old World have hitherto come to the South, except into Texas. For some time past the backward people who dwell in the Allegheny highlands have begun to move downwards into the manufacturing and mining regions. And latterly a movement has begun, evident, though not yet large, of native Americans migrating from those parts of the North and West in which good farming land has become scarcer and dearer. The stream which ran to the West for so many years is now no longer able to spread itself out there, and tending to flow southward. Thus the increase of population is in the South of a wholesome kind, and it promises to continue.

A result of this progress is to be seen in the cheerful and hopeful spirit now visible. Men feel that they have turned the corner, and expect an expanding prosperity. Legislatures are more willing to spend money on education; and legislation is more enlightened, though in some states it still lags behind the progress of the North. This brighter view of things has affected the Southern view of the Negro. Between 1870 and 1900 his presence was to many persons a sort of nightmare. All sorts of absurd dangers were predicted; all sorts of absurd expedients for getting rid of him propounded. A calmer and saner view now prevails. The evils of the Reconstruction period are not forgotten, but as no one thinks they will ever recur, men can discuss the situation quietly and reasonably, feeling that as the Negro cannot be eliminated, the whites must learn to live with him and turn his presence to the best account.

Whatever cause the whites may have had for alarm twenty or thirty years ago, when the Negroes were supposed to be increasing faster than the whites, has now vanished. They show in each census a smaller percentage not only of the whole population of the Union, but even of the former slave states. In 1910 the percentage of Negroes to the whole population of the United States was 10.9; in 1880 it was 13.1.

This is attributable partly to a slightly declining birth rate, but more to the still high rate of Negro mortality. Infants are carelessly or ignorantly treated, and much havoc is wrought by diseases which, like tuberculosis, are the result of bad sanitary conditions.

The old controversy as to the capacity of the Negro for progress still rages. But about the fact that he has progressed there can be no dispute. What are the figures? When emancipated in 1862–65 the ex-slaves had no property at all. In 1910 they were cultivating as owners or tenants 893,384 farms. They owned in the sixteen Southern states 218,467 farms; and their aggregate property was estimated as being in 1910 between $400,000,000 and $500,000,000 (£80,000,00 to £100,000,000). Their churches are stated to own property to the value of $56,000,000, raised almost entirely by themselves.

So late as 1900 there were only two Negro banks in the United States; in 1909 there were believed to be fifty.[2]

They have entered all the professions. In 1900 there were more than 22,000 Negro teachers in schools and colleges, more than 15,000 ministers of religion, more than 1,700 physicians and surgeons, more than 700 lawyers. The numbers are doubtless now much larger. About two hundred Negro newspapers are now published, besides weekly and monthly magazines. Many Negroes are filling official posts with credit, and not a few have earned the respect and confidence of their white neighbours.

Their progress in education has been no less remarkable. At the date of emancipation probably less than 10 per cent of the freedmen could read and write. In 1870 the percentage of illiterate Negro adult males was 83.5. In 1910 it had fallen to 33.3. This is naturally by no means so great a reduction as among the Southern whites of native parentage, among whom the illiterates had sunk in 1910 to 7.7 per cent. But it represents an immense advance, when the conditions of a backward country and a very poor population are considered.[3] The Negroes have a remarkable desire for instruction, and their churches have since 1880 contributed $10,000,000 to give to their schools aid over and above the support from public funds. The attendance at the universities and colleges and technical schools has continued to grow steadily.[4]

That this progress should have been very unequal in different parts of the country, and that it should leave sections of the population still far behind, is no more than was to be expected. That natural differentiation of the

---

[2] *The Story of the Negro*, Vol. II, p. 204. It may be added that the industrial progress would doubtless have been still greater but for the prevalence of tuberculosis and other preventable diseases which depress the efficiency of the race.

[3] Nowhere in the South is school attendance compulsory, and the provision of schools for Negro children is still inadequate in most parts of the country. There is an urgent need for more and better educated teachers.

[4] The imperfection of the statistics, owing to the neglect of some institutions to supply statements, makes it impossible to give complete figures on this subject.

stronger from the weaker, of the brighter from the duller, which goes on in every community began among the Negroes as soon as the extinction of slavery started the normal social processes by which communities develop. The kidnapped unfortunates who were brought from Africa in slave ships had belonged to different Negro tribes in different stages of civilization, and to different ranks and classes in the same tribe, for few if any of these tribes were in that lowest kind of savagery which knows no ranks at all. The hold of the slaveship jumbled them all together, and the plantation life of toil, enforced by the whip, pressed them all down to the same level, though the few who obtained freedom soon showed an aptitude to rise. As soon as that pressure was removed, natural inequalities of capacity began to have their legitimate effect in raising some faster than others. Fortunate accidents of environment, the help of friendly free Negroes, the benevolent encouragement of a white ex-master or neighbour, the accident of admission to a school, heightened the action of the advantages which those who were born more capable possessed; until now, after nearly fifty years of freedom, social classes have begun to form, and the gap between the best-educated Negroes practising a profession or conducting a large business and the ignorant field labourer has become a wide one. Inequalities have reappeared, although those which we find among the American Negroes today are different from those that existed between their African ancestors before the heavy roller of servitude had passed over the captives.

Though a large part of the coloured population is still ignorant and backward, especially in the hottest parts of the Gulf states and along the costs of South Carolina and Georgia, the general advance is by no means confined to the townsfolk. On the contrary, one is often told that the least desirable Negroes are the lower class who live in the cities, while the most solid and industrious are the small farm owners and the artisans in the villages. There has certainly been a real and general progress among these better classes. It is visible in the better houses they inhabit, in the better method of cultivation some of them employ, in the figures that record the savings they place in the banks. Nor should the instances be forgotten in which the Negro has shown his capacity to do things for himself in a practical way. At Calhoun in Alabama there were lately nearly one hundred who had bought or were buying farms, having saved $80,000 for the purpose. The purely Negro town of Mound Bayou in the Mississippi delta, with a population of 2,000, is well governed, orderly, and prosperous, and there is a cooperative organization called the Farmers' Improvement Society in Texas, whose members have helped one another forward in many ways till they came to own 71,000 acres of land and were able to erect an agricultural college to give farm training to their children. There are many associations among the Negroes, both cooperative and charitable, and by them much good has been effected. Though there are some whites, politicians and others, who, taking their notion of the coloured people from the illiterate plantation labourers and the shiftless criminal loafers of the cities, deny that the Negro has advanced, and though there are others who think that he is advancing more than is compatible with white ascendancy, still the majority of the educated white people in the South see, recognise, and gladly recognise, that the standard of industry, thrift, and education is rising and that it is for the benefit of the South as a whole hardly less than for the Negroes that it should rise. Steady and efficient labour is one of the most urgent needs of the country. The more the Negro advances, the more he acquires; the larger become his wants, so much the better is his labour; the more industrious and educated he is, the less prone is he to vagrancy and to crime. It is among the ruder and more ignorant sort of white people that nearly all of the opposition to the education of the coloured is to be found.

But all the Southern whites, however they may otherwise differ, agree in desiring to eliminate the Negro as a factor in politics. In 1890, Mississippi led the way in this direction by her new constitution. Six other states have followed in her steps, viz., South Carolina, North Carolina, Alabama, Virginia, Louisiana, and Georgia. In the new constitutional provisions of these states, intended to exclude the bulk of the Negroes, there is not a word regarding "race, colour, or previous condition of servitude," as a ground of discrimination, so the Fifteenth Amendment to the federal Constitution is not directly infringed. The aim in view, an aim frankly avowed and justified, has been attained by provisions requiring the person who applies to be registered as a voter to have paid his taxes and to prove his possession of an educational or property qualification. Such tests (low as they were fixed), while excluding the bulk of the Negroes, would exclude a good many whites also, so it became necessary to open some other door through which whites with neither education nor property might enter. This was done in North Carolina and Louisiana by the so-called "grandfather clause" which admitted anyone whose father or grandfather had been a voter before 1867, while several other states granted registration to war veterans or their descendants.[5] Things were so arranged that by one door or another

[5] In 1910 Oklahoma amended her constitution by inserting the following provision: "No person shall be registered as an elector or vote in any election, unless he be able to read and write any section of the Constitution of the State, but no person who was on January 1st, 1866, or at any

nearly all the whites could find their way in, while the control of registration by white officials made it easy to exclude Negroes whose claim was at all doubtful, or whom it was desired to keep out. In Alabama it was estimated that only 5 per cent of the Negroes would under her new constitution keep the suffrage, and in Louisiana the number was reduced from 130,000 to 5,300. In the remaining four of the states that seceded, viz., Tennessee, Arkansas, Florida, and Texas, no constitutional change has been deemed needful. In them the Negroes are a smaller part of the population, and have not been in practice a voting force. Any attempt on their part to assert themselves would be promptly checked.

The broad result of these measures has been to reduce the number of coloured electors on the register in the states aforesaid to an average roughly conjectured at not more than 10 per cent of the total number of adult males. It is larger in some states and in some districts of each state than in other states and districts, and no one seems to know exactly how large it is in any given area. Of those who might get their names on the register very many do not care to do so—where, for instance, a poll tax is required, they omit to pay it. And of those comparatively few Negroes who are on the register, many do not in fact vote, partly from heedlessness, partly because they know that in federal elections, and to a large extent in state elections also, their votes would make no difference, except in the rare case of a division in the dominant Democratic party. That party is so strong in nearly all the Southern states[6] that the voting or abstention of the coloured voters, now everywhere so unimportant, could seldom affect the result of an election.

Under these conditions the Negroes have ceased to take much interest in politics. The are generally reckoned as belonging to the Republican party, but the organization of that party is kept up not so much in the hope of carrying elections as for the sake of securing representation in the national

---

time prior thereto, entitled to vote under any form of government or who at that time resided in some foreign nation, and no lineal descendant of such person, shall be denied the right to vote because of his inability so to read and write sections of such Constitution."

The enactment of such a provision in Oklahoma, which was not a state till 1907, and in which there were never any slaves except a few belonging to the Red Indians who were its only inhabitants till long after the Civil War, is the more remarkable because the Negroes are a small minority of the population.

It has been alleged, with what truth I know not, that irregularities occurred in the taking of the popular vote on this question; and the result seemed to excite surprise.

[6] This is less true of Missouri, Kentucky, Tennessee, and North Carolina than of the states further south.

convention of the party and establishing a claim to some federal offices, objects which may be legitimate in themselves, but from the attainment of which the ordinary Negro has nothing to gain. He is accordingly supposed to have lost such interest in politics as he once evinced, and to accept without complaints that civic passivity to which his race has been reduced.

With this result the whites are doubly, nay, trebly, satisfied. They are relieved from any fear of Negro dominance. They declare that the Negro is growing to be more industrious, orderly, and generally useful now when he has dropped all thoughts of politics, and they add that friendly relations between the races have become easier, because, as the Negro is no longer challenging equality, they are less called upon to proclaim superiority.

It is easy to call these disfranchising provisions evasions of the Fifteenth Amendment which was intended by its framers to secure the vote to the Negroes on the same terms as the whites. But the state of things in the period between 1873 and the adoption of these new constitutions, a period during which, first by violence and afterwards by various tricks and devices, the Negroes were over almost the whole South practically deprived of their legal voting power, was worse than is the present legal exclusion of the great majority of them. It was demoralizing to the whites;[7] it exacerbated feeling between the races; and as the Negroes were gaining nothing in those years by their nominal right to the suffrage, they have lost little by its curtailment. This is so generally understood by the people of the North that few have protested against the disfranchisement, and no attempt has been made to restore the boon which the nation was in 1870 supposed to be bestowing.

Among the leaders of the Negroes themselves there is a difference of view and policy on the matter. Some, bitterly resenting the disfranchising provisions, try to keep up an opposition to them, although they see little or no prospect of getting them repealed. Others think it better to accept facts which they are powerless to alter, consoling themselves by the reflection that provisions which make the suffrage depend on education and property tend to stimulate the Negro to raise himself to the tests prescribed for active

---

[7] Thoughtful men among the whites felt this. Mr. J. A. Hamilton, in his pamphlet *Negro Suffrage and Congressional Representation*, quotes among other deliverances to this effect the following words of Mr. Clarence Poe of North Carolina: "There is nothing more uncontrollable than lawlessness. Sow the wind and reap the whirlwind. Wink at your election officer's thievery in times of stress and peril and next you may have election thievery to aid in plundering schemes or to save the rings and cliques to which the election officer belongs. Give rein to mob violence at a time when you think such action justifiable, and you will find your reward in a popular contempt for the restraint of law."

citizenship. The bulk of the coloured people who live on the plantations take no interest in the matter. Among the more educated, the authority of Dr. Booker Washington has gone some way to commend the policy of preferring industrial progress to political agitation; not to add that it is hard to see what agitation could accomplish. It would not rouse the Republican party at the North, for since 1890 they have concluded that it is better to leave the South alone, while so far as state legislation is concerned, it might actually darken the prospects of the Negro by exciting more alarm and hostility in the breasts of the less kindly among the whites.[8]

Although the coloured people are not directly a factor in Southern politics, because few of them are allowed to vote, their presence has had indirect effects. The qualifications for the suffrage introduced to disfranchise them have, in some states, incidentally disfranchised a few of the poorer and more ignorant whites. For the purposes of the apportionment of representation among the states, all the Negroes, the disfranchised included, are reckoned, and thus contribute to make representation larger than it would otherwise be in the very states which have by their constitutions cut down the number of coloured voters.[9] The resentment which is felt by those Negroes who live in the North at the action of the Southern Democrats has ensured their sturdy support of the Republican party in states like Indiana, Ohio, and New York, where they constitute an appreciable vote. The disquiet which the presence of the black man causes in the South holds the vast bulk of the Southern whites together in the Democratic party, and has so far frustrated the efforts frequently made to build up a solid party of Southern white Republicans. Thus someone has observed, with the exaggeration deemed needed to enforce a neglected truth, that the Negro, powerless as he is, still dominates

[8] It is not, however, to be supposed that any Negro leaders undervalue the suffrage or have expressed an approval of the enactments which withhold it from the great mass of their race. Speaking of the aim of the Tuskegee Agricultural Institute, Dr. Booker Washington writes, "We did not seek to give our people the idea that political rights were not valuable or necessary, but rather to impress upon them that economic efficiency was the foundation for every kind of success" (*The Story of the Negro*, Vol. II, p. 292). "It ought to be clearly recognized that in a republican form of government if any group of people is left permanently without the franchise, it is placed at a serious disadvantage. I do not object to restrictions being placed on the use of the ballot, but if any portion of the population is prevented from taking part in the government by reason of these restrictions, they should have held out before them the incentive of securing the ballot in proportion as they grow in property-holding, intelligence, and character" (Vol. II, p. 370).

[9] It has been sometimes proposed by Northern politicians to exclude these disfranchised Negroes from the computation in the manner contemplated by the Fourteenth Amendment to the federal Constitution, but this has not been done. There would be vehement opposition, and any political gain would not be worth the trouble.

the South, for his presence is never forgotten, and makes many things different from what they would otherwise be.

No person of colour has for a long time past sat in Congress, nor in the legislature of any Southern state, though now and then one may find his way into a Northern state legislature. A few hold small county offices in the South, and a few have been appointed by presidents to federal posts, such as collectors of ports or postmasters, in the South.[10]

The difficulty of correctly describing the social relations of blacks and whites in the South is due not only to the very different accounts which different observers, often prejudiced, have given, but also the great diversities between the various parts of the population and various regions of a wide country, stretching from the Potomac to the Rio Grande. But some salient facts may be stated as almost universally true.

The absolute social separation of the two races continues everywhere just as described in the last preceding chapter. Rarely does any person of colour sit down to meat in a white man's house, or is in any other way recognized as an equal. The Southern whites conceive absolute separation to be essential in order, as many of them say, to assert and emphasize inequality, and, as all of them say, utterly to bar intermarriage. To the question whether so stringent an enforcement is necessary, the invariable reply is that nothing less would suffice to avert the fatal danger of an intermixture of blood. How much illicit intermixture goes on cannot be determined, but the number of light-coloured Negroes shows how large it must have been. It has by no means ceased.

In all states, though happily not in all parts of any state, there is friction between the races. In the North it exists chiefly between members of the labouring class. White working men and their labour unions generally refuse to work with coloured men, and the entrance to employment is so largely closed to them that one may say that the large majority of the Northern Negroes are confined to unskilled or unsettled avocations. In the Southern states the friction is perhaps less marked, and is least when one element, whether black or white, is in a large majority, less also in the rural districts than in the cities, where the Negro workpeople are supposed to be less submissive, where the proportion of bad characters among them is largest, and where the white workingmen are most rude and suspicious, the jealousy of labour competition being added to the jealousy of colour.[11] It is in these

---

[10] A good many are employed in the federal departments at Washington, some of these having entered by competition.

[11] Serious trouble arose in Georgia in 1909–10 over the attempt of a railway company to promote Negro firemen to be locomotive engineers.

cities that race quarrels and race riots such as those which unhappily occurred in Wilmington, North Carolina, in 1898, and in Atlanta, in 1906, are most to be feared. In 1910, a prize fight which took place in Nevada between a white man and a Negro in which the latter prevailed produced outbreaks of race enmity all over the country (including New York City). In the conflicts and riots at least one white man and nine or ten (by some accounts many more) Negroes were killed.

The extreme form of race friction is seen in lynching, a practice not confined to the South, though more common there than in the West, and more frequently attended by circumstances of horror. As some lynchings are not reported, and some are falsely reported, it is hard to determine the number that happen, but apparently they are becoming less frequent,[12] and they are more and more condemned by the opinion of the best citizens.

Deplorable as the practice is, and seriously as it aggravates race friction, because every instance, even if it seems excusable under the particular circumstances, is apt to be followed by a crop of minor outrages, still one must not ascribe it solely to racial hatred, for whites also are lynched, though less frequently. It is largely the outcome of a defective administration of criminal justice. Homicide often, in some regions usually, goes unpunished, because courts are weak or partial, juries fail to convict, even in clear cases, while the extreme technicalities of procedure, coupled with the timidity of state judges, permit legal points to be taken by which trials are protracted, cases are appealed on trivial grounds, and the carrying out of sentences is in one way or another delayed until somehow or other the criminal escapes altogether. This distrust of the regular organs and regular processes of law is the most fertile parent of these constant resorts to violent and illegal methods of punishment.[13]

The racial antagonism which breaks out in lynching has produced in many parts of the South an atmosphere of suspicion and disquiet on the part of the whites, of suspicion and terror on the part of the Negroes. This is less noticeable in those agricultural districts which are almost entirely black,

---

[12] Professor Cutler, who has carefully examined the subject, gives the total number of persons lynched in the United States from 1882 to 1903 at 3,337, of whom 1,997 were killed in the Southern, 363 in the Western, and 105 in the Eastern states. The largest number in any one year was 235 in 1892. More than one-third of the persons lynched were whites. In 1903 the number (for the whole United States) is given as 86, in 1907 as 63, only 2 of these in the North. At Coatesville in Pennsylvania a Negro was in 1911 lynched by being burnt to death, and nobody was punished.

[13] Upon this subject, see p. 14 of the Address of Mr. Taft (since president) to the Pennsylvania State Bar Association delivered in 1906; and also a paper by Professor J. W. Garner entitled *Crime and Judicial Inefficiency* (Annals of Amer. Acad. of Polit. Science, 1907).

than in the towns. Yet it has borne its part in producing an inflow of Negroes from rural districts to the larger cities as well as from the South generally toward the North. In many places planters, even those who treat their workpeople kindly, complain of the difficulty of getting Negro labour, though it is almost the only labour that can be hired for field work. Wages have been tending to rise, but it is said that with the more backward Negroes the result is not always good, for they work less regularly when they can earn as much by fewer days of toil.

This has excited so restless and migratory a spirit that several Southern states have passed laws intended to keep the Negro on the soil by throwing difficulties in the way of his going out of the state, while bills have been introduced to exclude him from mechanical trades in order that he may stick to farm labour. Sometimes, like the ryot of India, he falls into the toils of the usurious money lender; and in all his disputes, legal or extra legal, with the whites, the chances are against him. It is also alleged that when he works on the system of receiving part of the produce of the farm, he is sometimes cozened out of his proper share by his landlord, or, if he works for wages, is held in a sort of servitude through the debts he is forced to incur for the articles supplied to him by the employer. This peonage (as it is called) is facilitated by law and in some places has grown to be a system which, where employers and creditors are harsh in enforcing their claims, makes the Negro more unrestful and drives him away from the plantations to the cities or even into the North. Yet he is often no better off at the North, where the white labourers may refuse to work with him, and where he has no more chance than in the South of receiving, except in very exceptional cases, any sort of social recognition from any class of whites, while in the cities everywhere he is met by the competition of the generally more diligent and more intelligent whites. So the Negro is after all better off in the South and on the land than anywhere else; and in the South, where the need for labourers is great and he is not generally discriminated against in business matters, a wider door is open to him both in town and in country.

At the bottom of all the labour question there stands the fact that, as compared with the white man, whether he be a native or an Italian or Polish immigrant, the average Negro is an inefficient worker. He cannot be depended to come regularly to his work, and he does less in a given time. He plies his shovel with less vigour than an Irishman, and he is not so steady as a Chinaman. He has a still unchecked liking for vagrancy, and the Negro vagrant is prone to crime; these after all are the faults that depress him in the struggle for life. All that can be said is that they are the natural result of the previous conditions, that he is less lazy in the United States than in the West Indies, and that he is improving steadily if slowly— improving in the way which is surest, viz., by his own exertions and by the example of a few of the best among his own race. A solid ground of hope lies in the fact that the evils described will naturally diminish as he grows more efficient, and that with the extension of agricultural and manual instruction, his labour will doubtless become more efficient.

Broadly speaking, there are two tendencies at work among the Southern whites, which correspond to the two classes of which Southern society consists.

The lower and more ignorant whites, including both the descendants of those who before the war were called "mean whites," and those who have come down out of the mountains where the people had remained comparatively rude, dislike the Negroes, desiring to thrust them down and to keep them down, and, so far as they legally can, to deny them civil rights as well as social opportunities. With this class, the jealousy of labour competition has reinforced the repulsion of colour sentiment. From this class come not only the lynchings but the petty outrages practised on the weaker race; and it is in order to capture the votes of this class, which is unwilling to pay for Negro education and will sometimes boycott a white woman who devotes herself to teaching the Negroes, that anti-Negro harangues are delivered and anti-Negro bills are introduced by politicians of the less worthy type. The enmity is more collective than personal, for even where prejudice and jealousy are strongest, there are often friendly relations between individual white men of this class and their Negro neighbours, and although men of the kind described are not generally amenable to humanitarian appeals, yet those democratic doctrines which are engrained in the American mind have a certain power even over them, restraining impulses toward tyranny which might in other countries be irresistible. They might wish that the Negro was not a citizen at all, but as he is a citizen even when not a voter, his citizenship cannot be ignored.

The cultivated and progressive white people of the South, including most, though not quite all, of the leading businessmen and professional men, and many of the large landowners, cherish more kindly feelings. There are of course optimists and pessimists among them. Some, noting the progress which the Negro has already made, expect much from the effects of education and sympathetic help. Others, struck by the inferior quality of most Negro labour, think he will not in any assignable time be equal to the white as a skilled or reliable workman. But all agree in recognizing that as he is there and his labour is indispensable they must make the best of the position by giving him instruction, especially of an industrial kind, and by helping him to rise. Accordingly they advocate more liberal grants for Negro schools, and do their best to secure practical equality of civil rights and an administration of the law honestly impartial as between the races. They dislike lynching just as much as people in the North do. After the lamentable outbreak at Atlanta in September 1906, the best white citizens formed a committee for the protection of the Negroes, and this developed into the Atlanta Civil League, under the influence of which conditions showed a marked improvement. The same wish to secure protection for the Negro has been conspicuous among the most energetic and thoughtful white men in other cities.

As this opposition of two classes and two tendencies in the South is the key to the present position, so the best prospect for the future lies in the increase of the more enlightened class and the growing strength of the more friendly sentiment they represent. But it must be remembered that upon some things all Southern whites are agreed. They all dread intermarriage. They all deem absolute social separation as necessary to prevent mixture of blood. They all wish to keep strong drink away from the Negro,[14] and most of them are willing even to forego, for that purpose, facilities for getting it themselves. They all desire to prevent the Negro vote from being a factor in politics, though some would concede the suffrage to the few who have education and property. And they would all alike resent the slightest interference by the national government in any matter which concerns their state legislation, political or social, upon questions affecting the coloured race.

When one comes to speak of the views and attitude of the Negroes themselves, it is necessary to premise that only a small percentage have any views at all. Even among those who can read and write, the number with sufficient knowledge or intelligence to comprehend the whole situation is small. The average Negro is a naturally thoughtless, lighthearted, kindly, easygoing being, whose interests in life are of the most elementary order, and whose vision is limited to the few miles around his house. When he had a vote, he used it, unless influenced by a white employer or patron, at the bidding of a local leader of his own race, probably a preacher. In those

[14] See upon this subject an article by the Rev. Dr. White of Atlanta in the *South Atlantic Quarterly*, April 1908.

cities where it is worth buying, he is said to be ready to sell it. In some places, and especially where outrages have recently occurred, he lives in terror of violence from the ruder whites. But he has no racial enmity to the whites, and on the contrary is naturally deferential and submissive, responding quickly to any kindness shown to him, dangerous only when he is one of a mob, and trebly dangerous when the mob is drunk.

Among the small class of educated and reflective Negroes one may distinguish two tendencies. Reference has already been made to the opposite views of those who counsel acquiescence in, and of those who would agitate against, the restriction of the suffrage to a small section of their race. The divergence of views, however, goes further. There are those led by Dr. Booker Washington, who see no use in resisting patent facts, and therefore hold that all the Negro can at present do, and the most effective thing that, with a view to the future, he could in any case do, is to raise himself in intelligence, knowledge, industry, thrift, whatever else makes for self-help and self-respect. When he has gained these things, when he is felt to be a valuable part of the community, his colour will not exclude him from the opportunities of advancement which business presents, nor from the suffrage, nor from a share in public office. Complaints of injustice, well grounded as many of them may be, will profit little, and may even rouse further antagonism, but industrial capacity and the possession of property are sure to tell.

Others there are, such as Professor Du Bois,[15] who find it hard to practise this patience; and some are beginning to organize themselves in a more aggressive spirit for common help and protection. The only political power they can exert is through the votes of the Negroes in some Northern states, and it has not yet been shown that these will follow any leaders of the type described. They can, however, both in North and South, act together for trade purposes, can patronize stores kept by members of their race, and in other ways render material aid and make their presence felt.

One thing is now common to both these sections of the educated men of colour—a growing sense of race solidarity and a perception that instead of seeking favours from the whites or trying to cling to their skirts, the Negro must go his own way, make his own society, try to stand on his own feet, in the confidence that the more he succeeds in doing this, the more respected will he be. This race consciousness finds expression in various organizations

---

[15] His book, *The Souls of Black Folk,* presents in a striking manner the hardship of the coloured man's lot.

which have been formed among the Negroes for helping themselves, as well as in appeals, not always, however, responded to, to give their patronage by preference to members of the race in business relations and in professional work.

This feeling of race consciousness has in most places included, and now more and more includes, the people of mixed blood, about whom a word may be said. Whereas in Spanish and Portuguese countries persons who are not evidently black are reckoned as white, in the United States any trace of African blood marks a man as a Negro and subjects him to the disabilities attaching to the race. In Latin America whoever is not black is white; in Teutonic America whoever is not white is black. The number of this mixed population, though it cannot be exactly ascertained, is estimated at not quite one-third of the total coloured population, that is, about three millions. The proportion is largest in the Northern and Middle states, smallest in South Carolina, Georgia, and the Gulf states. While in some far Southern districts it does not reach one-fifth, there are parts of Missouri, Kentucky, Virginia, and Maryland where it is two-fifths. All these persons, even if there be only an eighth or a sixteenth of Negro blood, and there be nothing in face or accent to indicate their origin, are held to belong to the Negro race.[16] To what extent children continue to be born from parents of different races no one knows. In eleven Northern and Western states, as well as in all the Southern and in Arizona, intermarriage is illegal, and in some states a punishable offence, but illicit connections are said to be still frequent, though some state laws have tried to repress this practice also by penalties. One-eighth is in some states taken as the infusion which makes a man legally a Negro; but less than that would affect him socially. There is much controversy, and so far no scientific certainty because no adequate data, regarding the physiological effect of race mixture. The common view holds the mixed race to be superior in intelligence but rather inferior in physical stamina to the pure black. It dwells on the fact that nearly all the Negroes who have risen to distinction have been mulattoes. But there are men of large experience who think differently.[17] In some cities, especially in the North, mulattoes and quadroons are said to have formerly looked down on the pure blacks, and sought to create an exclusive society of their own. But

[16] The laws of some states treat a man with at least one-eighth of Negro blood as a Negro; others speak merely of "visible admixture."

[17] The authorities of Hampton Institute report that their pure black pupils pass just as high in the examinations as do the mulattoes. If the latter are frequently quicker, the former are more persevering.

that racial consciousness to which I have already referred has been drawing all sections of the African race together, disposing the lighter coloured, since they can get no nearer to the whites, to identify themselves with the mass of those who belong to their own stock.

Among these light-coloured people, it is on those who, knowing their white relatives by sight, and forced to feel that persons by nature their cousins—perhaps even their brothers or sisters—are placed above them on a level to which they cannot climb, that the sense of social inequality presses most cruelly. But it presses on every educated Negro. He may have studied at a Northern university, may have associated there in a friendly if not intimate way with white students, may have passed his examinations with equal credit.[18] In face and figure he may be scarcely distinguishable from them. But in after life an impassable barrier will stand between him and them. That under such conditions there should be bitterness can excite no surprise. The wonder rather is that not more bitterness finds expression; and this may be ascribed partly to the simple faith and religious resignation which lie deep in the Negro character, partly also to the fact that the coloured people have from childhood grown up accustomed to it, so that the contrast becomes keenly painful only to a few. It is fortunate that the African race is not naturally sullen or vindictive, and that its gaiety of temper finds many alleviations for the trials of life.

Whoever, revisiting a country after a long interval, seeks to form a sound judgment on the changes that are passing, does well to check the statistical facts by his personal impressions and his personal impressions by the statistical facts. As regards the position of the Negroes, the facts that can be expressed in figures are generally encouraging. They must be growing more industrious, because they own far more land, and their total property has increased much faster than their numbers. Their sanitary condition is still in many places deplorable, but the efforts which are being made to reduce disease, and particularly tuberculosis, offer a prospect of improvement. Educationally too there is visible progress, not merely in the reduction of illiteracy, but in the increased proportion who receive industrial training and in the number who enter occupations requiring a cultivated intelligence. The statistics of crime are still regrettably high, but it must be remembered that the poorest part of a population is always that from which by far the largest

---

[18] At one large and flourishing state university of the North, seeing some ten or fifteen coloured students graduate, I was told that they were treated with due courtesy by their fellow students and in no way discriminated against, but it was added that if there had been in the university hundreds instead of tens of them, things would have been different.

proportion of offenders comes, and offences committed by Negroes are in some parts of the country more constantly and severely dealt with than those committed by whites. Lynchings are less frequent. The prohibition of the use of intoxicating drinks, which has now been enacted in nearly every state of the South, will, if strictly carried out, do much to diminish both the volume of Negro crime and the risks of violent white revenge.

When one turns from the tangible facts to the less tangible impressions which the traveller receives, the strongest among these is the sense of a revival of life and energy among the whites over nearly all the South. The spirit of this generation is a different spirit from that of the generation which fought, and largely perished, in the Civil War; but it retains some measure of the dignity and largeness of view which adorned the old Southern aristocracy. And although sectionalism is passing away, the Southern men of today have along with their pride in the Union a special pride in their own land, and a Southern patriotism of their own, like the Scottish patriotism which Scotsmen superadd to the allegiance they owe to the United Kingdom. This love of the South is an inspiring motive. It not merely spurs men to the development of the material resources of a region whose wealth in such resources is scarcely even yet appreciated, but it makes them strive to build up a community with high standards in public and private life, and with an intellectual culture abreast of that of the older Northern states. There have been many evidences (notably in the progress of the temperance movement and of the Laymen's Missionary Movement) of the strength of moral and religious sentiment in the South. Such an enlargement of view and sense of what befits a great people naturally disposes the best citizens to a more generous and sympathetic treatment of the Negro and a wiser handling of the Negro question as a whole than was possible in the days immediately following the Reconstruction period. Thus one finds among the most thoughtful Southern men, the men whose moral leadership is recognized, a more hopeful and cheerful spirit than formerly, a spirit which sees that justice and tenderness toward the weak and backward race will make for the good of the stronger race also.

Nor is this more friendly attitude visible only among the leaders of thought. Although the mass of the poorer and more ignorant whites remain suspicious and unfriendly, the visitor discerns all through the educated class in the South a greater disposition to be indulgent to the Negroes, to protect and to help them in their difficult, upward path. This is most visible where there is evident activity and prosperity—one is struck by it in North Carolina, for instance. Nor is the reason hard to find, for when people feel themselves advancing, their hearts expand, and when they are busy they cease to brood gloomily over a problem which has been for many years a sort of obsession in many parts of the country. They feel with Senator John Sharp Williams of Mississippi when he said, "In the face of this great problem it would be well that wise men think more, that good men pray more, and that all men talk less and curse less." So lately spoke another eminent Southerner, "Not another word about the negro problem. Get to work."

Thus if we compare 1870 with 1890 and 1890 with 1910, there are grounds for hope. But if we regard the actual state of things, and note how slowly changes for the better have been moving, we shall realize how much remains to be done. As the pessimist, fixing his eye only on existing evils, fails to allow for the forces which are tending to lessen them, so the optimist, who sees these forces at work, is always in danger of expecting them to work too quickly. In such a case as this, where the scale is enormous because in the South nearly ten millions of black men are scattered over nearly a million of square miles, and where the real improvement to be effected, that from which all the rest must spring, is an improvement in the character and habits which a race has formed during thousands of years, progress must needs be slow.

It was observed in the last preceding chapter that forecasts are unusually difficult in a case to the phenomena of which no parallel can be found. All prediction must rest on an observation of similar facts observed before elsewhere and on the historical development those facts have taken. Now, though there have been endless instances in history of the contact of advanced and backward races, none of these instances present phenomena sufficiently resembling those of the South to enable us to conjecture the future from the past.

The case most nearly resembling that of the Southern states is to be found in South Africa at the present day. There we see a large population of black people, the settled part of whom enjoy private civil rights equal to those of the whites, while in one part of the country (Cape Colony) a small number, who have attained a certain standard of education and property, enjoy political rights also. There, as in the South, we note a complete social separation between the races, with no prospect of any fusion between them, and a tendency also on the part of the ruder section of the whites to dislike the blacks and treat them scornfully. The outlook in South Africa is in so far darker than it is in the Southern states that the Kafir population immensely outnumbers the whites, and, though the bulk of it still remains in a tribal condition, far behind the American Negroes in point of education, it is naturally of a more vigorous character and more martial spirit than are most of the latter. However, the native problem in South Africa is still so far from being solved that one can only begin to conjecture the forms it is likely to take when the Kafirs become more civilized. It is in an earlier phase than the American problem, and does not help us toward a solution of the latter.

That latter was never more tersely and forcibly stated than by the late Mr. Henry W. Grady of Atlanta when he said:[19]

> The problem of the South is to carry on within her body politic two separate races, equal in civil and political rights, and nearly equal in numbers. She must carry these races in peace, for discord means ruin. She must carry them separately, for assimilation means debasement. She must carry them in equal justice, for to this she is pledged in honour and in gratitude. She must carry them even unto the end, for in human probability she will never be quit of either.

All that whoever wishes to forecast the future of the Southern Negroes can do is to study the forces actually at work in the South and try to form an estimate of the power they will respectively exert hereafter. Those forces are curiously intertwined, and while some promise to work for the bettering of existing conditions, others may work for their worsening. Many of the wiser minds in the South think that their combined effect will on the whole be for good. Some, however, think otherwise. The best way of stating the case is to present each view separately, and the more hopeful view may come first. I give it in the five paragraphs that follow.

The growing material prosperity of the South, a prosperity likely to increase still further, will make the labour of the Negro more and more needed, and will therefore make the Southern whites feel more and more anxious to retain him, to encourage him, to improve the quality of his work.

The Negro will share in this prosperity; and as his material condition improves, as he is better housed and clothed and acquires a taste for the comforts of life, he will be more industrious and more efficient. Thus will he become more self-respecting; and therewith also more respected. In becoming more educated, and especially better trained for industrial pursuits, the Negro will not only be able to hold his own in handicrafts, even in those which at present he seems in danger of losing, but will generally begin to awaken to the duties and responsibilities of citizenship. As he will be more eager to qualify himself for the suffrage, by reaching the prescribed

---

[19] These words of a brilliant Southerner, too soon lost to his country, are quoted from Professor Hart's *Southern South*, p. 151.

standard of knowledge and property, so there will be less objection to his enjoying the suffrage when it is perceived that he has grown fitter for it.

As more and more among the coloured people rise to the level which the more advanced have now reached, and as they form higher aims in life than physical enjoyment and amusement, they will gain more self-control and steadiness of purpose. Crime will tend to diminish, and the occasions for friction between the races will be fewer.

As Negro society becomes more settled, and more of the more ambitious and capable men rise to positions of influence in the occupations of merchants and bankers, lawyers and physicians, the educated African will feel less discontented and less resentful at his social isolation from the whites, because he will have a better society of his own. To stand well in that society will be a legitimate subject for pride. His nascent race consciousness will then take the direction not of antagonism to the whites, but of showing what the African can do when he has got his chance, and the current that might have been dangerous in one channel will be harmless and fertilizing in another.

The growing agricultural and industrial progress of the whole South, accompanied by a scarcely less marked educational progress, will reduce both the enmity and the suspicion which now fill the breasts of so many of the ruder and more ignorant Southern whites. Men are more kindly when they are more comfortable. When they come to be occupied with pushing themselves forward in the world as are native Americans in the North, they will not let the presence of the Negro darken their sky and embitter their feelings as he has done for the last forty years. The memories of the Reconstruction period will in time pass away. People will see the present as it is and not in the light of a dismal past. The best part of the South has already recovered its old life and spring; and as this renovation spreads among the hitherto backward classes, they too will come to see the African and the difficulties his presence causes with a calmer and less unfriendly eye, and will recognize that harshness or scorn toward a weaker race tells harmfully on the stronger itself, as everyone now recognizes that slavery hurt the character of the slaveholder more than it did that of the slave.

Against these sanguine anticipations let us set a pessimist's view of the probabilities, though Southern pessimism finds its grounds less in philosophic or historical reasonings than in an instinctive race antagonism which is quite compatible with kindliness to the individual Negro. These also must be stated, and as far as possible in the words of the men who hold them.

If the Negro shares in the prosperity of the South, if he grows richer and enters the professions more largely, he will become more "uppish," will be quicker to claim social equality and more resentful of its denial. What the whites deem his insolence will provoke the reprisals from them. This will increase the tension between the two colours. And as the upper section of the Negroes find that all their advance in knowledge and material well-being brings them socially no nearer to the whites, their feelings will grow more bitter and the relations of the races more strained.

So too, assuming that race consciousness grows among the coloured people, may it not lead them to organize themselves in a way calculated to alarm and provoke the whites? The desire of the bulk of the whites to "keep down" the Negro and make him "know his place," may be unchristian. But it exists, and any display of increasing strength on the part of the weaker race will aggravate it.

This tendency may show itself especially where the suffrage is concerned. If the Negroes so advance in property and in the capacity to pass the education tests now prescribed as to make them constitute, in some states, or counties, or cities, one-half or even one-third or one-fourth of the voters, the old alarms regarding their political influence will recur, possibly with increased force, because they will be more intelligent and better organized than they were before 1890, when electoral rights began to be withdrawn. If such a largely increased body of coloured voters should possess the franchise, the politics of the South will be disturbed and warped by the presence of a body likely to vote all together as a race irrespective of the ordinary political issues, and bartering their votes (not necessarily for money) to one party or the other as temporary advantage suggests. Probably an effort would under such circumstances be made to devise new methods for excluding at least the bulk of the coloured men; but such methods would seem more objectionable and would excite more resistance when applied to educated persons than they have done as applied in recent years to the ignorant multitude which has little or no property.

The difficulties attendant on competition in the labour market which have already caused trouble in a few places or trades are likely to be aggravated as a larger number of Negroes enter the more skilled employments. Though white workmen are deemed more efficient, the difference in efficiency is less than the difference in the wages paid to the Negroes, who at present accept much less than whites will. Irritation may follow similar to that which arose when Chinese content with lower wages competed with Americans in California and with Australians in Victoria and New South Wales. In those countries the Chinese were at last excluded. But the African cannot be prevented from seeking to improve his position merely because his competition will displease the white.

Already it is a thing without precedent in the world's annals that two races enjoying equal civil and to some extent equal political rights should live side by side in close juxtaposition yet never intermingling, one of them stronger than the other and under constant temptation to abuse its strength. The more completely the weaker race absorbs the civilization of the stronger race and rises to its level, the more extraordinary will the situation become. Can anything but trouble be expected?

Though it is right to let the pessimist's case be fully stated, and though his gloomy prognostications cannot be dismissed as visionary, for there may be an element of future conflict in the strengthening of African race consciousness, still the more hopeful of these two views of the situation will commend itself to one who compares the present with the past and who notes that the best men in the South, the men whose intimate knowledge and freedom from prejudice gives weight to their judgment, incline to the hopeful side. The matter may be summed up by these final observations.

The white population increases faster than the Negro not only over the whole Union, but in the South. The Negro therefore is not a political danger.

The Negro is needed as a labourer, and the more he advances, the more useful is his labour to a country which urgently needs labour. To treat the Negro fairly and help him to progress is therefore the interest of the whites.

The question whether the races can live peaceably together is at bottom a moral question, a question of good feeling, of humanity, of the application of the principles of the Gospel. Race antagonism is no doubt a strong sentiment. Many a time it has shown its formidable power. Yet it may decline under the influence of reason and good feeling. In 1810 slavery existed over nearly the whole of the American continent and its islands. Those whom it shocked were few, and still fewer contemplated its abolition. Even so late as 1860 it was defended on principle and defended out of the Bible. When the sentiment of a common humanity has so grown and improved within a century as to destroy slavery everywhere, may it not be that a like sentiment will soften the bitterness of race friction also? It is at any rate in that direction that the stream of change is running.

Foreign Policy and
Territorial Extension

So far I have had to say nothing, and now I need say but little, of a subject which would have been constantly obtruding itself had we been dealing with any country in Europe. To every country in Europe foreign relations are a matter of primary importance. The six great powers of that continent all think it necessary to protect themselves against one another by armies, fleets, and alliances. Great Britain, seeking no extension of territory and comparatively safe from attack at home, has many colonies and one vast dependency to protect, and is drawn by them, far more than by her European position, into the tangled web of Old World diplomacy. To all these powers, and not less to the minor ones, the friendly or hostile attitude of the others is matter of vital consequence. Not only, therefore, must immense sums be spent on warlike preparations, but a great establishment of officials must be maintained and no small part of the attention of the administration and the legislature be given to the conduct of the international relations of the state. These relations, moreover, constantly affect the internal politics of the country; they sometimes cause the triumph or the defeat of a party; they influence financial policy; they make or mar the careers of statesmen.

In the United States, nothing of the kind. From the Mexican war of 1845, down to the Spanish war of 1898, external relations very rarely, and then only to a slight extent, affected internal political strife. As they did not occupy the public mind they did not lie within the sphere of party platforms or party action. We have hitherto found no occasion to refer to them save in describing the functions of the Senate; and I mention them now as the traveller did the snakes in Iceland, only to note their absence, and to indicate some of the results ascribable to thereto.

Though the chief and obvious cause of this striking contrast between the great western Republic and the powers of Europe is to be found in her geographical position on a continent where, since she bought out France and Spain, she has had only two neighbours, one comparatively weak on the south and one naturally friendly on the north, much must also be set down to the temper and convictions of the people. They are, and have usually been, pacific in their views, for the unjustifiable, because needless, war with Mexico was the work of the slaveholding oligarchy and opposed to the general sentiment of the people. They have no lust of conquest, possessing already as much land as they want. They have always been extremely jealous of a standing army, the necessary support of ambitious foreign policies. They have been so much absorbed by and interested in the development of their material resources as to care very little for what goes on in other countries. As there is no military class, so also there is no class which feels itself called on to be concerned with foreign affairs, and least of all is such a class to be found among the politicians. Even leading statesmen are often strangely ignorant of European diplomacy, much more the average senator or congressman. And into the mind of the whole people there has sunk deep the idea that all such matters belong to the bad order of the Old World; and that the true way for the model Republic to influence that world is to avoid its errors, and set an example of pacific industrialism.

This view of the facts may appear strange to those who remember that the area of the United States proper, which in 1783 was about one million square miles, is now something over three and a half millions.[1] All this added territory, however, except the cessions made by Mexico in 1847, came peaceably by way of purchase or (in the case of Texas) voluntary union; and all (with the possible exception of Alaska) consists of regions which naturally cohere with the original Republic, and ought to be united with it. The limits of what may be called natural expansion have now (subject to what will be said presently) been reached; and the desire for annexation is no stronger than at any preceding epoch, while the interest in foreign relations generally has not increased. For a time a sort of friendship was professed for Russia, more for the sake of teasing England than from any real sympathy with a despotic monarchy very alien to the American spirit. But at present absolute neutrality and impartiality as regard the Old World is observed; and a remarkable proof of the desire to abstain from engagements affecting it was given, when the United States government declined to ratify the International Act of the Berlin Conference of 1885

---

[1] As to the new transmarine dominions, see next chapter.

regulating the Congo Free State, although its minister at Berlin had taken part in the deliberations of the conference by which that act was prepared. And it was after much delay and some hesitation that they ratified (in 1892) even the Brussels International Slave Trade Act.[2]

Such abstinence from Old World affairs is the complement to that declaration of a purpose to prevent any European power from attempting to obtain a controlling influence in New World affairs which was made by President Monroe in his message of 1823. The assertion is less needed now than it was in Monroe's day, because the United States have grown so immensely in strength that no European power can constitute a danger to them. It would no doubt lead the government to consider international questions arising even in South America as much more within the scope of their influence than any, not directly affecting their own citizens, which might arise in the Old World, but the occasions for applying such a principle are comparatively few, and are not likely to involve serious difficulties with any European power.

The notion that the United States ought to include at least all the English- and French-speaking communities of North America is an old one. Repeated efforts were made before and during the War of Independence to induce Canada, Nova Scotia, and even the Bermuda Islands to join the revolted colonies. For many years afterwards the view continued to be expressed that no durable peace with Great Britain could exist so long as she retained possessions on the North American continent. When by degrees that belief died away, the eyes of ambitious statesmen turned to the South. The slaveholding party sought to acquire Cuba and Puerto Rico, hoping to turn them into slave states; and President Polk even tried to buy Cuba from Spain. After the abolition of slavery, attempts were made under President Johnson in 1867 to acquire St. Thomas and St. John's from Denmark, and by President Grant (1869–73) to acquire San Domingo—an independent republic—but the Senate frustrated both. Apart from these incidents, the United States showed no desire to extend its territories, save by the purchase of Alaska, from the Mexican war down to 1898.

The results of the general indifference to foreign politics are in so far unfortunate that they have often induced carelessness in the choice of persons to represent the United States at European courts, the ambassador to Great Britain being usually the only one who has really important negotiations to

---

[2] In 1906 the U.S. government signed, though with some reservations, the general act of the Algeciras Conference for regulating the affairs of Morocco.

conduct, and cause very inadequate appropriations to be voted for the support of such envoys. In other respects her detachment has been for the United States an unspeakable blessing. A very small army sufficed, and it was employed chiefly in the Far West for the repression of Indian troubles, troubles which have now come to an end. In 1890 the army consisted of about 25,000 privates and a little over 2,000 officers. The officers, admirably trained at West Point, the famous military academy which has maintained its high character and its absolute freedom from political affiliations since its first foundation, have been largely occupied in scientific or engineering work. Only a small navy seemed to be required—a fortunate circumstance, because the navy yards have sometimes given rise to administrative scandals. The cry sometimes raised for a large increase in the United States fleet surprised and still surprises European observers; for the power of the United States to protect her citizens abroad is not to be measured by the number of vessels or guns she possesses, but by the fact that there is no power in the world which will not lose far more than it can possibly gain by quarrelling with a nation which could, in case of war, so vast are its resources, not only create an armoured fleet but speedily equip swift vessels to attack the commerce of its antagonist. The possession of powerful armaments is apt to inspire a wish to use them. For many years no cloud rose on the external horizon, and one may indeed say that the likelihood of a war between the United States and any of the great naval powers has appeared too slight to be worth considering.

The freedom of the country from militarism of spirit and policy here described conduced not only to the slightness of a branch of expenditure which European states find almost insupportable, but also to the exemption of this Republic from a source of danger which other republics have found so serious—the ambition of successful generals, and the interference of the army in political strifes. Strong and deep-rooted as are the constitutional traditions of the United States, there have been moments, even in her history, when the existence of a great standing army might have menaced or led to civil war. Patriotism has not suffered, as Europeans sometimes fancy it must suffer, by long-continued peace. Manliness of spirit has not suffered because so few embrace the profession of arms; and the internal politics of the country, already complicated enough, are relieved from those further complications which the intrusion of issues of foreign policy bring with them. It need hardly be added that those issues are the very issues which a democracy, even so intelligent a democracy as that of the United States, is least fitted to comprehend, and which its organs of government are least fitted to handle with promptitude and success. Fortunately, the one principle to which the people have learnt to cling in foreign policy is, that the less they have of it the better; and though aspiring politicians sometimes try to play upon national pride by using arrogant language to other powers, or by suggesting schemes of annexation, such language is generally reprobated, and such schemes are usually rejected.

To state this tendency of national opinion does not, however, dispose of the question of territorial expansion; for nations are sometimes forced to increase their dominions by causes outside their own desires or volitions. The possibilities that lie before America of such expansion deserve a brief discussion.

Occupying the whole width of their continent from ocean to ocean, the Americans have neighbours only on the north and on the south. It is only in these directions that they could extend themselves by land; and extension on land is, if not easier, yet more tempting than by sea. On the north they touch the great Canadian confederation with its nine provinces, also extending from the Atlantic to the Pacific, and bound together by transcontinental railways. Its population is rapidly increasing, especially in the Northwest, and although legally subject to the British Crown and legislature, it is admittedly mistress of its own destinies. It was at one time deemed a matter of course that the United States would seek to annex Canada, peaceably if possible, but if not, then by force of arms. Even so late as 1864, Englishmen were constantly told that the first result of the triumph of the Federal armies in the War of Secession would be to launch a host flushed with victory against the Canadian Dominion, because when the passion for war has been once roused in a nation, it clamours for fresh conquests. Many were the arguments from history by which it was sought to convince Britain that for her own safety she ought to accede to the wily suggestions which Louis Napoleon addressed to her, deliver the slave states from defeat and herself from a formidable rival. Since those days Canada has become a far more tempting prize, for part of her northwestern territories between Lake Superior and the Rocky Mountains, then believed to be condemned to sterility by their climate, has proved to be one of the richest wheat-growing districts on the continent. The power of the United States is now far greater than in 1865, nor would it be easy for Britain and Canada effectively to defend a frontier so long and so naturally weak as is that which separates the dominion from its neighbours on the south. Yet today the possibility of absorbing Canada is seldom mentioned in the United States. Were it ever to come about, it would come about at the wish and by the act of the Canadians themselves, not as the result of any external force.

There are several reasons for this. One is the growing friendliness of the Americans to Britain. Considering how much commoner than love is hatred, or at least jealousy, between nations, considering the proverbial bitterness of family quarrels, and considering how intense was the hatred felt in the United States towards England in the earlier part of last century,[3] rekindled by the unhappy war of 1812, kept alive by the sensitiveness of the one people and the arrogance of the other, imprinted afresh on new generations in America by silly schoolbooks and Fourth of July harangues, inflamed anew by the language of a section of English society during the Civil War, it is one of the remarkable events of our time that a cordial feeling should now exist between the two chief branches of the English race. The settlement of the Alabama claims has contributed to it. The democratization of Britain and the growth of literature and science in America have contributed to it. The greater respect which Europeans have come to show to America has contributed to it. The occasional appearance of illustrious men who, like Dr. Phillips Brooks and Mr. J. R. Lowell, become dear to both countries, has counted for something. But the ocean steamers have done perhaps most of all, because they have enabled the two peoples to know one another. Such unfriendly language towards Britain as still appears in the American press has been chiefly due to the wish to gratify a (now small) section of the Irish population and will vanish when the last traces of enmity in Ireland to England have passed away. Thus the old motives for an attack upon Canada are gone. But there is reason to think that even if Canada were separated from the British Empire, the Americans would not be eager to bring her into the Union. They would not try to do so by force, because that would be contrary to their doctrines and habits. They have a well-grounded aversion, strengthened by their experience of the difficulties of ruling the South after 1865, to the incorporation or control of any community not anxious to be one with them and thoroughly in harmony with their own body. Although they might rejoice over so great an extension of territory and resources, they are well satisfied with the present size and progress of their own country, which, as some remark, is at least big enough for one Congress.

As respects Canada herself, her material growth might possibly be quickened by union, and had the plan of a commercial league or customs union formerly discussed been carried out, it might have tended towards a political union; but, the temper and feelings of her people, and the growth

---

[3] Tocqueville, for instance, says (vol. ii, ch. 10): "On ne saurait voir de haine plus envenimée que celle qui existe entre les Américains des États Unis et les Anglais." And very old men will tell you in America that their recollections are to the same effect.

of a vigorous national sentiment among them, have not been making for their union with the far larger mass of the United States, which they regarded with a jealousy that has declined only as they felt themselves to be rising to the stature of a nation holding an assured and respected place in the eyes of the world. Their life, and that not as respects politics only, may seem less intense than the life of their neighbours to the South. But it is free from some of the blemishes which affect the latter. Municipal governments are more pure. Party organizations have not fallen under the control of bosses. Public order has been less disturbed; and criminal justice is more effectively administered.

This is not the place for considering what are the interests in the matter of Great Britain and her other colonies, nor the prospects of the schemes suggested for a closer practical union between the mother country and her swiftly advancing progeny. As regards the ultimate interests of the two peoples most directly concerned, it may be suggested that it is more to the advantage, both of the United States and of the Canadians, that they should continue to develop independent types of political life and intellectual progress. Each may, in working out its own institutions, have something to teach the other. There is already too little variety on the American continent.

Fifteen hundred miles south of British Columbia the United States abuts upon Mexico. The position of Mexico offers a striking contrast to that of Canada. The people are utterly unlike those of the United States; they are Roman Catholics, more than half Indian in blood and preserving many Indian superstitions, easygoing, uncultured, making little advance in self-government, whether local or national, increasing but slowly in numbers,[4] making very slender contributions to literature or science. They have done little to develop either the mineral or agricultural wealth of their superb territory, much of which, in fact all the interior plateau, enjoys a climate more favourable to physical exertion than that of the southernmost states of the Union. The export and import trade of the ports on the Gulf and the Pacific is in the hands of German and English houses; the mines of the north are worked by Americans, who come across from Texas and Arizona in greater and greater numbers. Two railways cross Northern Mexico from United States to the Pacific and others traverse the great plateau from the Rio Grande as far as the city of Mexico. In the northernmost states of the Mexican federation the American interests are already large, for much of

---

[4] The population of Mexico is about 14,000,000, of whom I believe less than 10 per cent to be pure whites, perhaps 30 per cent of mixed race, and the rest Indians mostly quite illiterate.

the capital is theirs, their language spreads, their pervasive energy is everywhere felt. As the mines of Colorado and Arizona become less and less attractive, the stream of immigration may more and more set out of the United States across the border. It has long been feared that if American citizens should be killed, or their property attacked, the United States government would be invoked, and should the government of Mexico relapse into that weakness out of which Presidents Juarez and Diaz raised it, a difficult position would arise. American settlers, if their numbers grow, might in such a case be tempted to establish order for themselves, and perhaps at last some sort of government. In fact, the process by which Texas was severed from Mexico and brought into the Union might conceivably be repeated in a more peaceful way by the steady infiltration of an American population. Traveller after traveller used to repeat that it was all but impossible for a comparatively weak state, full of natural wealth which her people do not use, not to crumble under the impact of a stronger and more enterprising race. It was argued that all experience pointed to the detachment of province after province from Mexico and its absorption into the American Union; and that when the process had once begun it would not stop till, in a time to be measured rather by decades than by centuries, the petty republics of Central America had been also swallowed up and the predominant influence, if not the territorial frontier, of the United States advanced to the Isthmus of Panama.

If the United States were a monarchy like Russia, this might well happen, happen not so much from any deliberate purpose of aggression as by the irresistible tendency of facts, a tendency similar to that which led Rome to conquer the East, England to conquer India, Russia to conquer northwestern Asia. But the Americans are most unwilling that it should happen, and will do all they can to prevent it. They have none of that earth hunger which burns in the great nations of Europe, having already dominions which are still far from fully peopled. They are proud of the capacity of their present population for self-government. Their administrative system is singularly unfitted for the rule of dependencies, because it has no proper machinery for controlling provincial governors; so that when it found regions which were hardly fit to be established as states, it gave them a practically all but complete self-government as Territories. Administrative posts set up in a dependent country might be jobbed, and the dependent country itself maladministered. Hence the only form annexation can with advantage take is the admission of the annexed district as a self-governing state or Territory, the difference between the two being that in the latter the inhabitants, though they are usually permitted to administer their domestic affairs, have no vote in federal elections. If Chihuahua and Sonora were like Dakota, the temptation to annex these provinces and turn them into states or Territories would be strong. But the Indo-Spaniards of Mexico have not as yet shown much fitness for the exercise of political power. They would be not only an inferior and diverse element in the Union, but an element likely, if admitted to federal suffrage, to injure federal politics, to demoralize the officials who might be sent among them, and to supply a fertile soil for all kinds of roguery and rascality, which, so far as they lay within the sphere of state action, the federal government could not interfere with, and which in federal affairs would damage Congress and bring another swarm of jobs and jobbers to Washington.

One still finds in the United States, and of course especially in Arizona, New Mexico, and Texas, some people who declare that Mexico will be swallowed, first the northern provinces, and the whole in time. It is "manifest destiny," and the land and mining-claim speculators of these border lands would be glad to help destiny. But the feeling of the nation disapproves a forward policy, nor has either party any such interest in promoting it as the Southern slaveholders had long ago in bringing in Texas. The question, which had seemed remote, came suddenly to the front when the fall of President Diaz was succeeded by confusion, civil war, and brigandage in Mexico. Disorder was rampant when these pages were passing through the press, nor could the issue be foreseen. It was however clear that all the best opinion in the United States desired to avoid armed intervention, fearing to be thereby drawn into an occupation of the country which would throw upon the United States grave responsibilities and involve its government in many difficulties.

I have already observed that the United States government formerly desired and seemed likely to acquire some of the West India islands. The South had a strong motive for adding to the Union regions in which slavery prevailed, and which would have been admitted as slave states. That motive has long since vanished. The objections which apply to the incorporation of Northern Mexico apply with greater force to the incorporation of islands far less fit for colonization by the Anglo-American race than are the Mexican tablelands. Till the acquisition of Puerto Rico in 1898–99 one islet only, Navassa, between Jamaica and San Domingo, belonged to the United States.[5]

One spot there had long been shewn a disposition to in which the

---

[5] As to Puerto Rico, see next chapter.

Americans had, ever since 1843 (when there was for a time a risk of its being occupied by England), declared that they felt directly interested. This is the island group of Hawaii, which lies 2,000 miles to the southwest of San Francisco. They conceived that the position of these isles over against their own Western coast would be so threatening to their commerce in a war between the United States and any naval power, that they could not suffer the islands to be occupied by, or even to fall under the influence of, any European nation, and though no nation had of late years such an influence, the United States government was considering the purchase of land for a naval station at Pearl River in Oahu when the events of 1898 led to their annexing the whole of it.[6]

The fate of western South America belongs to a still more distant future. When capital, which is accumulating in the United States with extraordinary rapidity, is no longer able to find highly profitable employment in the development of western North America, it will seek other fields. When population has filled up the present territory of the United States, enterprising spirits will overflow into undeveloped regions. The nearest of these is western South America, the elevated plateaux of which are habitable by Northern races. The vast territories in Colombia, Ecuador, Peru, and Bolivia,[7] for which the Spaniards have done so little, and which can hardly remain forever neglected, offer a tempting field for the extension of the commercial and political influence of the United States, but the growth of Argentina, Brazil, and Chile into powerful states, and their jealousy of any action looking to such extension, have created a new factor in the situation. They already resent the too frequent references made by politicians and the press in the United States to the Monroe Doctrine as applicable to the southern continent; and the wisest among North American statesmen have now recognized that the less they dwell upon that doctrine, the better will be the relations of their own country with the great republics of the south, and the greater her influence for peace and progress in the Western Hemisphere.

[6] See next chapter.

[7] These four countries have a total area of about 1,580,000 square miles, with a settled population not exceeding 9,000,000, besides an unascertained number of uncivilized Indians.

The New Transmarine Dominions

The last preceding chapter, written in 1894, has been allowed to stand because it describes what was then the character of the foreign policy of the United States and the attitude of the nation towards other powers.

Much has happened since then—much which nobody expected—and in order to present a view of the facts as they stand in 1910, some important events that have befallen in and since 1898 must be briefly set forth but without the comments which might be proper if the events were more remote.[1]

For many years before 1898 the disturbed condition of the island of Cuba, where risings against the Spanish government occurred from time to time, had engaged the attention of the American public. Suggestions were often made, but always rejected, that the United States should, as the nearest neighbour, interfere to set things right. At last an insurrection which, sometimes smouldering and sometimes blazing out, had continued for many months, the Spanish troops being apparently unable to stamp it out, aroused public sentiment and led the United States government into a correspondence with Spain which ended in a war between the two nations. Hostilities began on April 21, 1898, and were virtually over in the July following.

During the campaign the United States forces had occupied the islands of Cuba and Puerto Rico, while the fleet had destroyed that of Spain in an engagement in the bay of Manila, and had occupied that town. Though neither the government nor the people of the United States had in April, 1898, the slightest idea of acquiring any of the dominions of Spain, a sentiment sprang up against abandoning a conquest that had been almost

[1] A comprehensive and thoughtful treatment of the political problems presented in the foreign relations of the United States may be found in a book by Mr. A. C. Coolidge, entitled *The United States as a World Power*, published in 1908.

accidentally achieved, and in particular against losing a port which would be serviceable as a naval station, so the administration, obeying this sentient, stipulated in the treaty of peace (signed in April, 1899), for the cession of the Philippine Islands. For this a sum of $20,000,000 was paid by the United States to Spain, which at the same time ceded the island of Guam in the Pacific Ocean and also the island of Puerto Rico, with a population of about a million. Moreover, at the very outbreak of the war the United States, by a joint resolution of both houses of Congress, annexed the Hawaiian Islands, in which a sort of republic had been set up by the American residents, who had five years before overthrown the native monarchy, then in the incompetent hands of Queen Liliuokalani. The self-constituted authorities of this republic had forthwith asked the United States government for annexation; and this, though it had been previously refused by President Cleveland, was in 1898 accorded with general approval, partly because the war with Spain had evoked a wish to have a naval station in the central part of the Pacific, partly because there had been a large influx of Japanese labourers into the isles, and the Americans feared that if they did not take the islands, Japan would.

Thus in 1899 the United States found itself suddenly and unexpectedly in the possession of three considerable pieces of transmarine tropical territory, inhabited by races diverse in blood, speech, and customs from its own people and from one another. A fourth bit of territory, extremely small, but serviceable from the excellent harbour it contains, is the island of Tutuila in the Samoan group. As far back as 1872 the United States had acquired a sort of interest in it; and this, by a treaty with Britain and Germany, was turned into sovereignty in 1899. Still later a fifth acquisition, small in extent but great in value, was made by the cession to the United States of a strip of land five miles wide on each side of the line to be followed by the interoceanic ship canal from the Atlantic at Colon to the Pacific at Panama. This grant, which under a right of administration practically amounts to sovereignty, was obtained from the little republic of Panama immediately after it had revolted and severed itself from the much larger republic of Colombia.

Each of these five acquisitions has been dealt with in a separate and distinct way. Hawaii has been erected into a Territory with a governor and legislature of two houses, much as if it were on the continent of North America. As its population of American and British stock is very small, the bulk of the inhabitants being Japanese and Chinese, with nearly 30,000 Hawaiian aborigines and almost as many Portuguese, there is no present likelihood of its being turned into a state of the Union. The Constitution of the United States is, however, in full force in Hawaii, as in other Territories, and it is for tariff purposes a part of the United States.

The island of Puerto Rico has received a sort of colonial organization, with a legislature, the lower branch of which is elected on a limited suffrage, while the upper is composed of a few officials and other persons appointed by the federal government. The inhabitants, though they did not object to annexation, and have gained by it in material prosperity, are far from satisfied with these arrangement, desiring a fuller autonomy, or even to be admitted as a state of the Union. Considering, however, that they speak Spanish only, and contain a Negro element amounting to nearly one-third of the whole population, in which only 17 per cent can read and write, these wishes may have to wait some time for fulfilment. The people are orderly, and education has begun to make rapid progress.

Guam and Tutuila are nothing more than naval coaling stations. But the Philippine group, with their area of 128,000 square miles and their population of nearly eight millions, much of it uncivilized or semi-civilized, while the rest consists of Malays who have received with a slight admixture of Spanish blood a Spanish Roman Catholic type of civilization, presents administrative problems of no small difficulty. Although there was in the islands much disaffection with Spanish rule, and an insurrection had broken out shortly before the American fleet appeared on the scene, there was no sort of wish to be transferred to the United States, and when the islanders found themselves ceded by their late masters, the insurgents quickly turned their arms against those whom they had at first regarded as deliverers. Resistance was stamped out after a guerrilla warfare of three years, and in the large island of Mindanao, as well as in Luzon, a regular administration has been created, but local troubles have from time to time occurred, and the risk of their recurrence may not be past. In Luzon great improvements have been effected in the way both of constructing roads and other public works, and of introducing sanitary reforms. Municipal councils have been set up, elected by the people; natives are being appointed to administrative posts, and the friars, who were large landowners and enjoyed great power, have been settled with on liberal terms.

Chinese immigration has been forbidden, and the taking up of land by incorporated companies restricted. It may fairly be said that the American authorities have exerted themselves in a worthy spirit for the benefit of all sections of the population irrespective of race or religion. Nevertheless the natives have so far shown themselves less grateful for benefits received than desirous of an autonomy for which neither their rulers nor impartial foreign observers deem them qualified. They are not the only people which apparently prefers governing itself badly to being well governed by strangers.

A sharp controversy arose in the United States over both the constitutionality and the wisdom of the annexation of the Philippines, most of the Democrats and a section of the Republican party arguing that the fundamental principles of the Constitution were being forsaken, and that these remote tropical territories, inhabited by a population diverse in blood and speech from their rulers, would be rather an encumbrance than a source of strength to the Republic. The subject was a prominent issue at the presidential election of 1900. This controversy has since then gradually subsided, and it played little part in subsequent elections. There has, however, continued to exist much difference of opinion as to the benefits derivable by the United States from the acquisition of the islands, and as to the action proper to be taken regarding them in the future. The absorption of men's minds in domestic questions and the fact that few have proposed to withdraw forthwith from the islands, leaving them "to sink or swim," has latterly reduced public interest in the matter, the discussion of which began to seem rather academical than practical when it appeared that feeling had so far cooled and opinions so far approximated that the one party no longer claimed any credit for the conquest and the other could not suggest how to get rid of it.

Large sums have been voted from the revenues of the United States to be expended in the islands, and the tariff upon their products entering United States ports was in 1909 lowered almost to the point of extinction. Were they deemed to be a part of the United States within the meaning of Article I, § 8, par. 1 of the Constitution, their products would of course be subject to no import duties at all. A legislature has been established, one house of which is elected on a property qualification, the other being composed of officials, as in some British Crown colonies. The progress made in the provision of instruction is very remarkable when the difficulties of the country are considered, for out of about 2,000,000 of children between the ages of five and eighteen, 529,660 were in 1912 enrolled, with an average attendance of 329,073. Provision has been made for the establishment of a university, and the medical school which is to form a part of it is already at work.

The Canal Zone (as it is called) at the Isthmus of Panama is important not for its area, only 474 square miles, but from its position, for it brings the United States into direct contact with Central America, while the future control of the Canal opens up a vista of closer relations with the commerce and possibly the politics of western South America. The strip of territory which has been ceded is administered by the War Department, and the legal status of its inhabitants under the federal Constitution does not seem to have been precisely determined. Great difficulty has indeed been found in adjusting to these new transmarine possessions the provisions of an instrument framed with no idea that it might ever have to be applied to remote countries inhabited by alien peoples and held by the sword. The overwhelming naval strength of the United States as towards the weak republics of Colombia and Costa Rica, and the still weaker new republic of Panama, makes the defence of the Zone an easy matter, for the great difficulty of former days— a high mortality due to frequent outbreaks of yellow fever and the constant presence of malarial fevers—has been removed by the sanitary measures carried out here, as previously in Cuba, by the American authorities with an admirable energy and skill which entitle them to the undying gratitude of mankind.

Cuba, the island whose troubles led the United States into the war which brought about these recent acquisitions, was not herself annexed, nor was even any protectorate established. But in 1901, at the time when the American forces were in occupation, though preparing to leave the island, Congress passed a statute the provisions of which were subsequently incorporated in an ordinance appended to the Cuban constitution and ultimately embodied in a treaty between the United States and the republic of Cuba in 1903. These provisions declare, *inter alia,* that the Cuban government shall never permit any foreign power to obtain lodgment in or control over any part of the island; that the United States may intervene for the preservation of Cuban independence and the maintenance of a government adequate for the protection of life, property, and individual liberty; that the Cuban government shall carry out sanitary measures such as will prevent the recurrence of epidemic and infectious diseases, and that it will also lease or sell to the United States lands for coaling or naval stations at points to be subsequently agreed upon. Under these provisions, commonly known as "the Platt amendment," the harbours of Guantanamo and Bahia Honda were subsequently leased to the United States. The closeness of the tie uniting Cuba with her powerful neighbour was ultimately further recognized by the special treatment extended by each country to the other in the framing of customs duties.

The stipulations above mentioned create a very peculiar relation between the United States and Cuba, although they neither amount to an alliance nor destroy the character of the island as a sovereign state, independent in general international relations. In 1906 effect was given to the clause providing for intervention. Disorders having arisen in Cuba, a small body of American troops was despatched thither. Having reestablished tranquillity and supervised the election of a new president, it withdrew early in 1909. It is generally believed that if similar difficulties were to recur, a similar intervention would follow. But the United States government has given every evidence of its honest desire to avoid the annexation of the island or the assumption of any further responsibilities in respect of it, nor is there reason to think that this policy, deliberately adopted, will be soon or lightly forsaken. Reciprocal reductions have been made in the respective tariffs of the two governments, and a good deal of American capital has now been invested in the island.

The notion that all the republics of the New World ought, simply because they are called republics, to stand closely together apart from the rest of the world—a notion as old as the early part of last century and savouring of those simple days—was revived, but with a view rather to business than to sentiment, when in 1899 a Pan-American Congress was invited to meet in Washington chiefly for the purpose of trying to arrange something approaching a general tariff system for the independent states of the Western Hemisphere. That project came to nothing, but three subsequent congresses have been held, in Mexico, in Rio de Janeiro, and in Buenos Aires, at the two latter of which various questions of common interest have been discussed, and a certain reciprocal interest is believed to have been awakened. Under the auspices of these gatherings, moreover, there has been established in Washington an institution called the Pan-American Union, which collects and supplies to all enquirers, information relating to the industry, products, commerce, and legislation of these states which promises to be of real value, and doubtless tends to bring the American countries into closer commercial touch with one another, each republic having a right to be represented in the organization of the Union. In other ways also the relations of the United States with Latin America have become closer and more frequent. On several occasions there have been pacific interventions by the former, sometimes in order to give protection against European powers, sometimes for the purpose of averting conflicts. In the case of Central America, where the independent states are the smallest, the most turbulent, the most bellicose, and the least advanced in point of civilization, efforts were made in 1907–1908 to take action in conjunction with Mexico, as being the republic not only the nearest to the disturbed area, but also more powerful under the rule of Diaz, than its petty neighbours to the south. Later, under the joint auspices of Mexico and the United States, there was set up a Central American Court of Arbitration, by whose action, if the rather irresponsible presidential dictators can be compelled to resort to it, it is hoped that the constantly recurring strife that has retarded progress in these countries may be prevented.

The temptation to intervene and either bring to reason or dethrone and expel the military adventurers who rule most of these states is often a strong one, especially to a nation which, eager to develop its trade on its own continent, perceives that till peace and order are secured, trade cannot advance. But the wisest statesmen of America feel that the temptation ought to be resisted. The example of other countries, and especially of Great Britain in India and of Russia in Central Asia, has shown how difficult it is for a strong power, when once it has interfered to put down one government and set up another, to withdraw and leave the new government to take its chances. Most of the advances of Russia in Central and Northern and of England in Southern Asia have arisen because an interference which seemed justifiable or even necessary led on to an annexation that was never intended, and in many cases never desired. With this lesson before them such statesmen have generally sought to restrain any popular impulse, whether ambitious or philanthropic, to step out of their own sphere. They have another sound reason in the fact that any action on their part that could seem aggressive or overbearing would rekindle all over Spanish America those suspicions of the too powerful sister republic which have been more or less felt ever since the Mexican war of 1846. To allay such suspicions ought to be a main aim of United States policy.

Americans have latterly been wont to speak of themselves as having become, through the events of 1898, a world power. So far as potential strength was concerned, they were a world power even before that year, for their material resources were at least equal to those of any other state. But it is true that the acquisition of transmarine dominions and the wider horizon which the control of these opened out before them, had led to their taking a larger part in the affairs of the planet as a whole than they had ever done before. To this tendency another cause also has contributed. The immense expansion of the productive and manufacturing industries of the country has induced a desire to have a larger share in world commerce and to increase the mercantile marine.[2] "New foreign markets for American goods" loom

---

[2] Mr. Coolidge observes that whereas in 1880 manufactured goods formed but $12\frac{1}{2}$ per cent of the total exports (in value) from the United States in 1906 these had risen to $36\frac{1}{2}$ per cent. (*The United States as a World Power*, p. 177.)

larger in the eyes of the mercantile class, and administrations have proclaimed the wish and purpose to do all that can be done to promote American enterprise abroad. This tendency, which seems likely to grow stronger in the years to come, has taken concrete shape not only in stimulating the effort to claim for the United States a sort of hegemony among the republics of its own hemisphere, but also in the adoption of a forward commercial policy in the Far East, where the doctrine of what is called "the Open Door" for trade in Manchuria and China has been repeatedly proclaimed as the watchword of the United States, and as the principle it seeks to urge upon other powers.

A question has been raised as to whether the traditional maxim that the United States should confine the assertion of its interests to the Western Hemisphere—a maxim correlative to the declaration in which Monroe and Adams stated their objection to any fresh establishment of European powers therein—applies to the eastern side of Asia as well as to the rest of the Old World.[3] Is or is not the Pacific Ocean to be the boundary of American action on the one side as the Atlantic is on the other? To this question no answer has so far been returned.

As after the Spanish war the regular army of the United States was more than doubled, so with the acquisition of territories beyond the sea and the assumption of wider responsibilities in the world, there came an even greater expansion of the navy, which had in 1910 become one of the three strongest afloat. In 1889 it had cost only $25,000,000 and in 1912 was costing $123,000,000.

What have been the broad results of these changes, and what future do they portend for the United States as a world power?

If ever there was a warning administered to overconfident prophets, that warning was given by the events of 1898. It was the unforeseen that happened. There was nothing in the world which the American people less expected when they went into the war against Spain than that they should come out of it the sovereigns of the Philippine Islands, four thousand miles from their own shores. Even the victory at Manila was won with no intent to acquire the isles. That was the result of a series of accidents. The Americans drifted into dominion, and were amazed to find whither they had drifted.

But without speculating about the future, a few remarks may be made on the present state of national opinion.

---

[3] See upon this subject the remarks of Mr. Coolidge *ut supra*, pp. 117–19.

The people have not been seized by any lust for further conquests. From 1903 till 1912 they appeared to be taking comparatively little interest in their new possessions, which were seldom mentioned even at election time, and regarding the administration of which no more controversy was arising in the national legislature than in the British parliament about Ceylon or Borneo. It is only tariff questions affecting these transmarine territories that have latterly given rise to debates in Congress.

Among statesmen, who must of course study the position both in its actualities and its possibilities, there is a difference of opinion as to the best mode of dealing with the possessions already acquired; for though no one proposes to give up Hawaii or Puerto Rico, the Democratic Convention of 1912 recommended the abandonment of the Philippines, while others, including the administrations in power from 1898 till 1913, have held that the islands ought to be retained, at least until their people can be pronounced fit for self-government. But as to future policy, all agree in the view that the United States ought to make no further conquests and, if possible, avoid the annexation of any more territory. Such territory, they observe, would lie within the tropics, for there is none to be had elsewhere, and therefore the population would not be of American or North European stock. It would either have to be governed as a subject colony or else admitted to the Union as a state. The objection to the former alternative is that not only the Constitution and frame of government, but the political habits of the American people, are not well fitted for ruling over distant subjects of another race. The thing may no doubt be done, and in the Philippines it is being done, and that in a worthy spirit. But it is not a welcome task. The Declaration of Independence is a plant ill fitted for transplantation to tropical lands inhabited by backward races. The latter alternative (admission to the Union) presents still greater difficulties, because a state composed of citizens speaking a different language, unused to constitutional self-government, imbued with quite other notions and traditions, would be detrimental to the political life of the American people, as a foreign substance lodged in the physical body injures or endangers its vital forces. Or, to put it shortly, democratic government requires for its success the equality and the homogeneity of the citizens.

Thoughtful Americans feel that the Republic has already a sufficiently heavy load to carry in ten millions of Negroes and four or five millions of recent immigrants, ignorant of its institutions. To add other millions of mixed Spanish-Indian or Spanish-Negro blood would be an evil not compensated by the gain of territory and possible growth of trade. The recognition of these facts and the dying down of the sudden imperialistic impulse of 1898–1900 make it probable that for some time to come American policy will aim at avoiding annexations, or interventions likely to lead to annexations. As to the more distant future—let us again remind ourselves of 1898 and beware of prophesying.

In realizing herself as a world power America has not become more arrogant or more combative. Relations with Mexico were during the prudent rule of President Diaz better than ever before, and still more noteworthy has been the growth of friendliness between the United States and Canada, evidenced by the conclusion (in 1908–11) of a group of treaties designed to remove, or provide means for the settlement of, all possible causes of controversy. Though there are in her people, as in all peoples, latent bellicose tendencies capable under excitement of bursting into a blaze, the better sentiment which desires peace and endeavours to substitute arbitration for war has gained strength; and all that recent administrations have done in concluding arbitration treaties, and in urging on other powers the desirability of establishing permanent courts of arbitration, has been heartily approved by the nation.

CHAPTER 98

Laissez Faire

An English friend of a philosophic turn of mind bade me, when he heard that I was writing this book, dedicate at least one chapter to the American theory of the state. I answered that the Americans had no theory of the state, and felt no need for one, being content, like the English, to base their constitutional ideas upon law and history.

In England and America alike (I pursued) one misses a whole circle and system of ideas and sentiments which have been potent among the nations of the European continent. To those nations the state is a great moral power, the totality of the wisdom and conscience and force of the people, yet greater far than the sum of the individuals who compose the people, because consciously and scientifically, if also by a law of nature, organized for purposes which the people indistinctly apprehend, and because it is the inheritor of a deep-rooted reverence and an almost despotic authority. There is a touch of mysticism in this conception, which has survived the change from arbitrary to representative government, and almost recalls the sacredness that used to surround the mediæval church. In England the traditions of an ancient monarchy and the social influence of the class which till lately governed have enabled the state and its service to retain a measure of influence and respect. No one, however, attributes any special wisdom to the state, no one treats those concerned with administration or legislation as a superior class. Officials are strictly held within the limits of their legal powers, and are obeyed only so far as they can show that they are carrying out the positive directions of the law. Their conduct, and indeed the decisions of the highest state organs, are criticised, perhaps with more courtesy, but otherwise in exactly the same way as those of other persons and bodies. Yet the state is dignified, and men are proud to serve it. From the American mind, that which may be called the mystic aspect of the state, and the theory of its vast range of action, are as conspicuously absent as they are from the English. They are absent, not because America is a democracy, but because the political ideas of the two branches of the race are fundamentally the same, a fact which continental observers of the United States constantly fail to appreciate. In America, however, even the dignity of the state has vanished. It seems actually less than the individuals who live under it. The people, that is to say, the vast multitude of men who inhabit the country, inspire respect or awe, the organism is ignored. The state is nothing but a name for the legislative and administrative machinery whereby certain business of the inhabitants is despatched. It has no more conscience, or moral mission, or title to awe and respect, than a commercial company for working a railroad or a mine; and those who represent it are treated in public and in private with quite a little deference.

Hereupon my friend rejoined that people in America must at least have some general views about the functions of government and its relations to the individual. "We are told," he continued, "that the whole American polity is more coherent, more self-consistent than that of England; it must therefore have what the Germans call 'ground ideas.' There is a profusion of legislation. Legislation must proceed upon these ideas, and by examining the current legislation of the federal government and of the states you will be able to discover and present the beliefs and notions regarding the state which the Americans cherish."

The term "ground-ideas" does not happily describe the doctrines that prevail in the United States, for the people are not prone to form or state their notions in a philosophic way. There are, however, certain dogmas or maxims which are in so far fundamental that they have told widely on political thought, and that one usually strikes upon them when sinking a shaft, so to speak, into an American mind. Among such dogmas are the following:

Certain rights of the individual, as, for instance, his right to the enjoyment of what he has earned, to the free expression of opinion, are primordial and sacred.

All political power springs from the people, and the most completely popular government is best.

Legislatures, officials, and all other agents of the sovereign people ought to be strictly limited by law, by each other, and by the shortness of the terms of office.

Where any function can be equally well discharged by a central or by a local body, it ought by preference to be entrusted to the local body, for a centralized administration is more likely to be tyrannical, inefficient, and impure than one which, being on a small scale, is more fully within the knowledge of the citizens and more sensitive to their opinion.

Two men are wiser than one, one hundred than ninety-nine, thirty millions than twenty-nine millions. Whether they are wiser or not, the will of the larger number must prevail against the will of the smaller. But the majority is not wiser because it is called the nation, or because it controls the government, but only because it is more numerous. The nation is nothing but so many individuals. The government is nothing but certain representatives and officials, agents who are here today and gone tomorrow.

The less of government the better; that is to say, the fewer occasions for interfering with individual citizens are allowed to officials, and the less time citizens have to spend in looking after their officials, so much the more will the citizens and the community prosper. The functions of government must be kept at their minimum.

The first five of these dogmas have been discussed and illustrated in earlier chapters. The last of them needs a little examination, because it suggests points of comparison with the Old World, and because the meaning of it lies in the application. It is all very well to say that the functions of government should be kept at a minimum; but the bureaucrats of Russia might say the same. What is this minimum? Every nation, every government, every philosopher has his own view as to the functions which it must be taken to include.

The doctrine of laissez faire, or noninterference by government with the citizen, has two foundations, which may be called the sentimental and the rational. The sentimental ground is the desire of the individual to be let alone, to do as he pleases, indulge his impulses, follow out his projects. The rational ground is the principle, gathered from an observation of the phenomena of society, that interference by government more often does harm than good—that is to say, that the desires and impulses of men when left to themselves are more likely by their natural collision and cooperation to work out a happy result for the community and the individuals that compose it than will be attained by the conscious endeavours of the state controlling and directing those desires and impulses. There are laws of nature governing mankind as well as the material world; and man will thrive better under these laws than under those which he makes for himself through the organization we call government.

Of these two views, the former or sentimental has been extremely strong in America, being rooted in the character and habits of the race, and seeming to issue from that assertion of individual liberty which is proclaimed in such revered documents as the Declaration of Independence and the older state constitutions. The latter view, incessantly canvassed in Europe, has played no great part in the United States; or rather it has appeared in the form not of a philosophic induction from experience, but of a common-sense notion that everybody knows his own business best, that individual enterprise has "made America," and will "run America," better than the best government could do.

The state governments of 1776 and the national government of 1789 started from habits and ideas, mental habits, and administrative practice generally similar to those of contemporary England. Now England in the eighteenth century was that one among European countries in which government had the narrowest sphere. The primitive paternal legislation of the later Middle Ages had been abandoned. The central government had not begun to stretch out its arms to interfere with quarter sessions in the counties, or municipal corporations in the towns, to care for the health, or education, or morals of the people. That strengthening and reorganization of administration which was in progress in many parts of the Continent, as in Prussia under Frederick the Great, and in Portugal under Pombal, had not spread to England, and would have been resisted there by men of conservative tendencies for one set of reasons, and men of liberal tendencies for another. Everything tended to make the United States in this respect more English than England, for the circumstances of colonial life, the process of settling the Western wilderness, the feelings evoked by the struggle against George III, all went to intensify individualism, the love of enterprise, the pride in personal freedom. And from that day to this, individualism, the love of enterprise, and the pride in personal freedom, have been deemed by Americans not only their choicest, but their peculiar and exclusive possessions.

The hundred years which have passed since the birth of the Republic have, however, brought many changes with them. Individualism is no longer threatened by arbitrary kings, and the ramparts erected to protect it from their attacks are useless and grass-grown. If any assaults are to be feared they will come from another quarter. New causes are at work in the world tending not only to lengthen the arms of government, but to make its touch quicker and firmer. Do these causes operate in America as well as in Europe? And if so, does America, in virtue of her stronger historical attachment to individualism, oppose a more effective resistance to them?

I will mention a few among them. Modern civilization, in becoming more complex and refined, has become more exacting. It discerns more benefits which the organized power of government can secure, and grows more anxious to attain them. Men live fast, and are impatient of the slow working of natural laws. The triumphs of physical science have enlarged their desires for comfort, and shown them how many things may be accomplished by the application of collective skill and large funds which are beyond the reach of individual effort. Still greater has been the influence of a quickened moral sensitiveness and philanthropic sympathy. The sight of preventable evil is painful, and is felt as a reproach. He who preaches patience and reliance upon natural progress is thought callous. The sense of sin may, as theologians tell us, be declining; but the dislike to degrading and brutalizing vice is increasing; there is a warmer recognition of the responsibility of each man for his neighbour, and a more earnest zeal in works of moral reform. Some doctrines which, because they had satisfied philosophers, were in the last generation accepted by the bulk of educated men, have now become, if not discredited by experience, yet far from popular. They are thought to be less universally true, less completely beneficial, than was at first supposed. There are benefits which the laws of demand and supply do not procure. Unlimited competition seems to press too hardly on the weak. The power of groups of men organized by incorporation as joint-stock companies, or of small knots of rich men acting in combination, has developed with unexpected strength in unexpected ways, overshadowing individuals and even communities, and showing that the very freedom of association which men sought to secure by law when they were threatened by the violence of potentates may, under the shelter of the law, ripen into a new form of tyranny. And in some countries, of which Britain may be taken as the type, the transference of political power from the few to the many has made the many less jealous of governmental authority. The government is now their creature, their instrument—why should they fear to use it? They may strip it tomorrow of the power with which they have clothed it today. They may rest confident that its power will not be used contrary to the wishes of the majority among themselves. And as it is in this majority that authority has now been vested, they readily assume that the majority will be right.

How potent these influences and arguments have proved in the old countries of Europe, how much support they receive not only from popular sentiment, but from the writings of a vigorous school of philosophical economists all the world knows. But what of newer communities, where the evils to be combated by state action are fewer, where the spirit of liberty and the sentiment of individualism are more intense? An eminent English statesman expressed the general belief of Englishmen when he said in 1883:

> How is it that while the increasing democracy at home is insisting, with such growing eagerness, on more control by the state, we see so small a corresponding development of the same principle in the United States or in Anglo-Saxon colonies? It is clearly not simply the democratic spirit which demands so much central regulation. Otherwise we should find the same conditions in the Anglo-Saxon democracies across the seas.[1]

This belief of Englishmen was then the general belief of Americans. Nine men out of ten told the stranger that both the federal government and the state governments interfered little, and many ascribed the prosperity of the country to this noninterference as well as to the self-reliant spirit of the people. So far as there can be said to be any theory on the subject in a land which gets on without theories, *laissez aller* is the orthodox and accepted doctrine in the sphere both of federal and of state legislation.

Nevertheless the belief was mistaken then and has since then become still more evidently groundless. The new democracies of America are as eager for state interference as the democracy of Britain, and try their experiments with even more light-hearted promptitude. No one need be surprised at this when he reflects that the causes which have been mentioned as telling on Europe, tell on the United States with no less force. Men are even more eager than in Europe to hasten on to the ends they desire, even more impatient of the delays which a reliance on natural forces involves, even more sensitive to the wretchedness of their fellows, and to the mischiefs which vice and ignorance breed. Unrestricted competition has shown its dark side: great corporations have been more powerful than in Britain, and more inclined to abuse their power. Having lived longer under a democratic government, the American masses have realized more perfectly than those of Europe that they are themselves the government. Their absolute command of its organization (except where constitutional checks are interposed) makes them turn more quickly to it for the accomplishment of their purposes. And in the state legislatures they possess bodies with which it is easy to try legislative experiments, since these bodies, though not of themselves disposed

---

[1] Mr. Goschen, in an address delivered at Edinburgh.

to innovation, are mainly composed of men unskilled in economics, inapt to foresee any but the nearest consequences of their measures, prone to gratify any whim of their constituents, and open to the pressure of any section whose self-interest or impatient philanthropy clamours for some departure from the general principles of legislation. For crotchet-mongers as well as for intriguers there is no such paradise as the lobby of a state legislature. No responsible statesman is there to oppose them, no warning voice will be raised by a scientific economist.

Thus it has come to pass that, though the Americans have no theory of the state and take a narrow view of its functions, though they conceive themselves to be devoted to laissez faire in principle, and to be in practice the most self-reliant of peoples, they have grown no less accustomed than the English to carry the action of the state into ever-widening fields. Economic theory did not stop them, for practical men are proud of getting on without theory.[2] The sentiment of individualism did not stop them, because state intervention has usually taken the form of helping or protecting the greater number, while restraining the few; and personal freedom of action, the love of which is strong enough to repel the paternalism of France or Germany, was at first infringed upon only at the bidding of a strong moral sentiment, such as that which condemns intemperance. So gradual was the process of transition to this new habit that for a long time few but lawyers and economists became aware of it, and the lamentations with which old-fashioned English thinkers accompany the march of legislation were in America scarcely heard and wholly unheeded. Now however the complexity of civilization and the desire to have things done which a public authority can most quickly do, and the cost of which is less felt by each man because it comes out of the public revenue, to which he is only one of many contributors—these causes have made the field of governmental action almost as wide as it is in Euoope, and men recognize the fact.

As ordinary private law and administration belong to the states, it is chiefly in state legislation that we must look for instances of governmental intervention. Recent illustrations of the tendency to do by law what men were formerly left to do for themselves, and to prohibit by law acts of omission and commission which used to pass unregarded, might be culled from the statute-books of nearly every commonwealth.[3] It is in the West,

---

[2] Till recently, there has been little theoretical discussion of these questions in the United States. At present the two tendencies, that of laissez faire and that which leans to state interference, are well represented by able writers.

[3] I have collected some instances in a note to this chapter.

which plumes itself on being preeminently the land of freedom, enterprise, and self-help, that this tendency is most active, and plays the strangest pranks, because legislators are in the West more impatient and self-confident than elsewhere.

The forms which legislative intervention takes may be roughly classified under the following heads:

Prohibitions to individuals to do acts which are not, in the ordinary sense of the word, criminal (e.g., to sell intoxicating liquors, to employ a labourer for more than so many hours in a day).

Directions to individuals to do things which it is not obviously wrong to omit (e.g., to provide seats for shopwomen, to publish the accounts of a railway company).

Interferences with the ordinary course of law in order to protect individuals from the consequences of their own acts (e.g., the annulment of contracts between employer and workmen making the former not liable for accidental injuries to the latter, the exemption of homesteads, or of a certain amount of personal property, from the claims of creditors, the prohibition of more than a certain rate of interest on money).

Directions to a public authority to undertake work which might be left to individual action and the operation of supply and demand (e.g., the providing of schools and dispensaries, the establishment of state analysts, state oil inspectors, the collection and diffusion, at the public expense, of statistics).

Retention, appropriation, or control by the state of certain natural sources of wealth or elements in its production (e.g., the declaration, made by Washington, Wyoming, Montana, and Idaho, that the use of all waters, whether still or flowing, within their respective bounds, is a public use, and forever subject to state control, the prohibition by Indiana of the wasteful use of natural gas).

In every one of these kinds of legislative interference the Americans, or at least the Western states, seem to have gone farther than the English Parliament. The restrictions on the liquor traffic have been more sweeping; those upon the labour of women and children, and of persons employed by the state, not less so. Moral duties are more frequently enforced by legal penalties than in England. Railroads, insurance and banking companies, and other corporations are, in most states, strictly regulated. Efforts to protect individuals coming under the third head are so frequent and indulgent that their policy is beginning to be seriously questioned.[4] Gratuitous elementary and secondary education is provided all over the Union, and in the West there are also gratuitous state universities open to women as well as to men. And although the state has not gone so far in superseding individual action as to create for itself monopolies, it is apt to spend money on some objects not equally cared for by European governments. It tries to prevent adulteration by putting its stamp on agricultural fertilizers, and prohibiting the sale of oleomargarine; it establishes dairy commissions and bureaux of animal industry, and boards of livestock commissioners armed with wide powers of inspection; it distributes seed to farmers, provides a state chemist to analyze soils gratuitously and recommend the appropriate fertilizers, subsidizes agricultural fairs, sends round lecturers on agriculture, and encourages by bounties the culture of beetroot and manufacture of sugar therefrom, the making of starch from state-grown potatoes, tree planting, and the killing of noxious animals—English sparrows in Massachusetts, panthers and wolves in Wyoming.[5] The farmer of Kansas or Iowa is as much the object of the paternal solicitude of his legislature as the farmer of any European country. And in the pursuit of its schemes for blessing the community the state raises a taxation which would be complained of in a less prosperous country.[6]

What has been the result of this legislation? Have the effects which the economists of the physiocratic or *laissez aller* school taught us to expect actually followed? Has the natural course of commerce and industry been

[4] "A numerous and ever-increasing list of possessions has been entirely exempted from execution for debt, starting with the traditional homestead, and going on through all the necessities of life, implements of trade, and even corner-lots and money, until, in some States, as in Texas, almost every conceivable object of desire, from a house and corner-lot to a span of fast horses, may be held and enjoyed by the poor man free from all claims of his creditors. Without going further into details it may be boldly stated that the tendency of democratic legislation on this subject has been to require the repayment of debts only when it can be made out of superfluous accumulated capital."—Mr. F. J. Stimson in a vigorous and thoughtful article on the "Ethics of Democracy," in *Scribner's Magazine* for June 1887.

I find in the latest constitution of Texas a provision that where a contractor becomes bankrupt, the labourers employed by him shall have a right of action against the company or person for whose benefit the work on which they were employed was done.

[5] In Kansas the gift of bounties for the heads of coyotes (prairie wolves) led to the rearing of these animals on a large scale in a new description of stockfarms!

[6] "Speaking broadly, and including indirect taxation, it may be stated that the laws now purport to give the State power to dispose of at least one-third the annual revenues of property. . . . Of course these taxes are largely, by the richest citizens, evaded, but upon land at least they are effectual. It is certainly understating it to say that the general taxation upon land equals one-third the net rents, *i.e.* Ricardo's margin of cultivation less expenses of management."—Stimson, *ut supra*.

disturbed, has the self-helpfulness of the citizen been weakened, has government done its work ill and a new door to jobbery been opened? It is still too soon to form conclusions on these points. Some few of the experiments have failed, others seem to be succeeding; but the policy of state interference as a whole has not yet been adequately tested. In making this new departure American legislatures are serving the world, if not their own citizens, for they are providing it with a store of valuable data for its instruction, data which deserve more attention than they have hitherto received, and whose value will increase as time goes on.

It is the privilege of these unconscious philosophers to try experiments with less risk than countries like France or England would have to run, for the bodies on which the experiments are tried are so relatively small and exceptionally vigorous that failures need not inflict permanent injury. Railroads and other large business interests complain, and sometimes not without reason, but no people is shrewder than the American in coming to recognize the results of overbold legislation and modifying it when it is found to tell against the general prosperity.

N O T E

I collect a few instances of legislation illustrating the tendency to extend state intervention and the scope of penal law:

New York provides that no guest shall be excluded from any hotel on account of race, creed (some had refused to receive Jews), or colour.

Wisconsin requires every hotel above a certain height to be furnished with fireproof staircases; and Michigan punishes the proprietors of any shop or factory in which the health of employees is endangered by improper heating, lighting, ventilation, or sanitarian arrangements.

Michigan compels railroad companies to provide automatic car couplings. Other states direct the use of certain kinds of brakes.

Georgia orders railway companies to put up a bulletin stating how much any train already half an hour late is overdue; Arkansas requires this even if the train is only a few minutes late.

Wyoming requires railroads passing within four miles of any city to provide, at the nearest point, a depot whereat all local trains shall stop; while Arkansas forbids baggage to the tumbled from cars on to the platform at a depot; and Ohio permits no one to be engaged as a train conductor unless he has had two years' previous experience as trainhand.

Massachusetts forbids the employment of colour-blind persons on railways, and provides for the examination of those so employed.

Ohio requires druggists to place on bottles containing poison a red label, naming at least two of the most readily procurable antidotes.

Several states order employers to find seats for women employed in shops, warehouses, or manufactories.

Several states forbid anyone to practise dentistry as well as medicine unless licensed by a state board.

Massachusetts, Rhode Island, and Illinois compel corporations to pay workmen weekly. (Massachusetts forbade employers to deduct fines from the sums payable by them for wages, but the supreme court of the state [by a majority] held the statute unconstitutional.)

Maryland institutes a "State Board of Commissioners of Practical Plumbing," and confines the practice of that industry to persons licensed by the same. New York provides boards of examiners to supervise plumber's work.

Kansas punishes as a crime the making any misrepresentation to or deceiving any person in the sale of fruit of shade trees, shrubs or bulbs; and New Jersey does the like as regards fruit trees or briars.

Mississippi punishes with fine and imprisonment any legislative, executive, judicial, or ministerial officer, who shall travel on any railroad without paying absolutely, and without any evasion whatever, the same fare as is required of passengers generally.

Many states offer bounties on the raising of various agricultural products or on manufactures, while California appropriates money for the introduction from Australia of parasites and predaceous insects, with a view to the extermination of a moth which injures orange trees.

Texas makes it a punishable misdemeanour to deal in "futures" or "keep any 'bucket shop' or other establishment where future contracts are bought or sold with no intention of an actual delivery of the article so bought or sold," while Massachusetts is content with making such contracts voidable.

Michigan prescribes a system of minority voting at the election of directors of joint stock corporations; Kentucky prescribes cumulative voting in like cases.

Pennsylvania forbids the consolidation of telegraph companies.

Ohio punishes by fine and imprisonment the offering to sell "options," or exhibiting any quotations of the prices of "margins," "futures," or "options." Georgia imposes on dealers in "futures" a tax of $500 a year.

New York forbids the hiring of barmaids, and Colorado permits no woman to enter a "wine room."

Colorado, Kansas, and North Carolina, make the seduction under promise of marriage of any chaste woman a felony.

New York punishes with fine and imprisonment any person "who shall send a letter with intent to cause annoyance to any other person."

Virginia punishes with death the destruction by dynamite or any other explosive of any dwelling, if at night, or endangering human life.

Kentucky makes it a misdemeanour to play with dice any game for money, and a felony to keep, manage, or operate any such game.

Washington punishes anyone who permits a minor to play at cards in his house without the written permission of the minor's parent or guardian.

Oregon prohibits secret societies in all public schools; and California also forbids the formation of "secret oath-bound fraternities" in public schools.

Maine requires every public school teacher to devote not less than ten minutes per week to instruction in the principles of kindness to birds and animals, and punishes any nurse who fails at once to report to a physician that the eye of an infant has become reddened or inflamed within five weeks after birth. Rhode Island in a similar statute fixes a fortnight from birth and allows six hours for the report.

Illinois and Arizona forbid marriages between first cousins.

Virginia punishes with a fine of $100 the sale to a minor, not only of pistols, dirks, and bowie knives, but also of cigarettes. Twenty-four other states have similar laws forbidding minors to smoke or chew tobacco in public. Arizona makes it penal to sell or give liquor to a minor without his parents' consent, or even to admit him to a saloon.

Several states have recently made the smoking of cigarettes a punishable offence.

Kentucky prohibits the sale of any book or periodical, "the chief feature of which is to record the commission of crimes, or display by cuts or illustrations of crimes committed, or the pictures of criminals, desperadoes, or fugitives from justice, or of men or women influenced by stimulants"; and North Dakota punishes the sale or gift to, and even the exhibition within sight of, any minor of any book, magazine, or newspaper "principally made up of criminal news or pictures, stories of deeds of bloodshed, lust, or crime."

Some states permit judges to hear in private cases the evidence in which is of an obscene nature.

Massachusetts compels insurance companies to insure the lives of coloured persons on the same terms with those of whites.

Oregon requires the doors of any building used for public purposes to be so swung as to open outwards.

Minnesota enacts that all labour performed by contract upon a building shall be a first lien thereon; and declares that the fact that the person performing the labour was not enjoined from so doing shall be conclusive evidence of the contract; while Iowa gives to all workers in coal mines a lien for the their wages upon all property used in constructing and working the mine.

Alabama makes it penal for a banker to discount at a higher rate than 8 percent.

Many states have stringent usury laws.

Pennsylvania forbids a mortgagee to contract for the payment by the mortgagor of any taxes over and above the interest payable.

Kentucky and some other states have been making strenuous (but imperfectly successful) efforts to extinguish lotteries. On the other hand, Nevada appears to have authorized one.

Some of the newer states by their constitutions, and many others by statutes, endeavour to destroy the combinations of capitalists called "trusts," treating them as conspiracies, and threatening severe penalties against those concerned in them.

Laws purporting to limit the hours of adult male labour have been passed by Congress and in many states. None, however, appear to forbid under penalty overtime work, except as respects public servants (under the federal government, and in Massachusetts, Maryland, Pennsylvania, Colorado), the limit being 8 or 9 hours, railway servants (Maryland, New Jersey, Michigan), 10 to 12 hours, and coal miners (Wyoming), 8 hours. These laws, in fact, amount to little more than a declaration that the number of hours mentioned shall (except as aforesaid) constitute a legal day's work in the absence of an agreement for longer service.

Congress and the legislatures of at least fourteen states have by statute created or provided for the creation of boards of arbitration in trade disputes, but have conferred very restricted powers for that purpose.

CHAPTER 99

Woman Suffrage

Although the question of admitting women to the right of voting has never been one of the foremost political issues in the United States, its history and present position are so illustrative of the way in which political proposals spring up, and are agitated and handled in that country, that it would deserve to be here noticed, even were it not a matter which has a present interest for at least one European country. All those who have speculated on the foundations of human society and government have long been confronted by the question how far differences of sex ought to imply and prescribe a distinction of civic rights and functions between men and women. Some of the bolder among philosophers have answered the question by simply ignoring the differences. Perceiving in women an intelligence and will, which, if never equal to that of the very strongest men, yet makes the average woman the equal for most purposes of the average man, inasmuch as she gains in quickness and delicacy of perception what she loses in force and endurance, they have found no reason why woman should not share the labours, duties, and privileges of man. This was Plato's view, pushed by him so far as to expunge marriage and domestic life altogether; and it has found expression in more than one religious movement in ancient as well as in modern times.

Christianity approached the problem from another side. Recognizing in woman an immortal soul equally precious with the soul of man, the New Testament and the usages of the primitive church opened to her a wide range of functions, virtues, and glories, in some of which she was fitted to surpass, and has in fact surpassed man; while the imagination of the Middle Ages, more intense and fervid than that of any other epoch in history, created an ideal of feminine sweetness, purity, and moral beauty infinitely surpassing that of the ancient world, and which the modern world may count as its noblest possession, an ideal on the preservation of which, more perhaps than of any other human conception, the welfare of the race depends.

The consecration of the spiritual equality of woman would doubtless have gone still farther than it did to secure for her a tangible equality in social and possibly even in political matters but for the rudeness of the times, in which physical force counted for much, and for the growth of a sacramental and sacerdotal system, which confined priesthood and the administration of certain life-giving sacraments to men. Thus, though the relations of the sexes were placed on a more wholesome basis than in Greek and Roman antiquity, though the standard of purity was raised and the conception of marriage dignified, the recognition of equality in the sphere of law, both private and public, was less complete than might have been expected. When sacramentalism and sacerdotalism were, in the peoples of northern Europe, shattered by the religious movement of the sixteenth century, the idea of a clerical order confined to men was nevertheless maintained, except in a few small sects; and though the law grew constantly more just and humane to women, scarcely a voice was raised to claim for them a share in the privileges of public life.

In the early days of the American Republic it seems to have occurred to no statesman, though it did occur to a few keen-witted women, that the principles of the Declaration of Independence might find application without distinction of sex; but as they were not to be applied to men of any other colour but white, this need the less be wondered at. However, the legal position of women was speedily improved. State legislation gave them fuller rights of property and a better social status than they had enjoyed under the English common law, and the respectful deference with which they were treated was remarked by travellers as a singular exception to the general imperfection of American male manners, and as in fact tending to affect inauspiciously the grace of female manners.

When Negro slavery began to excite the horror of sensitive minds, it became necessary to reexamine the foundations of society and find a theory which would, in asserting the ultimate similarity and equality of all men, condemn the ownership of one man by another. This was done by recurring to the New Testament and the Declaration of Independence. Two questions speedily suggested themselves. If all men of whatever race are equal, what of women? If equality be an absolute and, so to speak, indefeasible truth and principle, what does it import? Does it cover merely the passive rights of citizenship, the right to freedom and protection for person and property? Or does it extend to the active right of participating in the government of the commonwealth? "We demand freedom for the Negro. Do we also demand a share in the government? If we do, are not women at least as well entitled? If we do not, it is because we see that the Negro is so ignorant and altogether backward as to be unfit to exercise political power. But can this be said of women? The considerations which might apply to the case of the liberated Negro do not apply to her, for she is educated and capable. How, then, can she be excluded?"

This was an abstract way of looking at the matter, because there had not as yet been any substantial demand by women for political rights. But it was on the basis of abstract right that they were proceeding. Theory is potent with those who are themselves appealing from an actual state of things to theory and general principles. And in this instance a practical turn was given to the question by the fact that many of the most zealous and helpful workers in the Abolitionist movement were women. They showed as much courage in facing obloquy and even danger in what they deemed a sacred cause as Garrison or Lovejoy. They filled the Abolition societies and flocked to the Abolitionist conventions. They were soon admitted to vote and hold office in these organizations. The more timid or conservative members protested, and some seceded. But in an aggressive movement, as in a revolution, those who go farthest are apt to fare best. The advocates of women's claims were the bolder spirits who retained the direction of the anti-slavery movement. The women established their right to share the perils of the combat and the glories of the victory.

The claim of women to be admitted to the franchise and to public office would no doubt have been made sooner or later in America (as it had been made in England) had there been no anti-slavery agitation. But the circumstances of its origin in that agitation have tinged its subsequent course. They invested it in the eyes of one set of persons with a species of consecration, while providing it with a body of trained workers and a precedent inspiring hope and teaching patience. To minds of an opposite cast they gave it a flavour of sentimentalism, crotchetiness, and of what used to be called in America "radicalism."[1] While the struggle against slavery continued, the question was content to stand back, but since the end of the Civil War and the admission of the Negroes to the franchise, it has come to the front, and continues to be actively pressed. There are now woman suffrage societies in most parts of the North and West. An annual

---

[1] The word "radical," frequently applied outside the sphere of pure politics, e.g., to theology, seems in American use to denote rather a tendency than either a party or a set of doctrines.

convention of delegates from these societies is held, which stimulates the local workers and resolves on a plan of operations.[2] Proposals for the admission of women to this or that species of suffrage are sedulously urged on state legislatures. In many Congresses amendments to the federal Constitution recognizing women as voters have been submitted, but have always failed to secure a majority of either house. The chance three-fourths of the states would accept one is at present very small. Once or twice women have been nominated as candidates for the presidency, though none has ever put out a list of presidential electors pledged to support her candidature.

These efforts have borne some fruit, though less than the party counted on when the agitation began. So far as I have been able to ascertain the present state of the law in the different states and Territories of the Union, the political rights of women stand as follows:

In 1869 the legislature of the Territory of Wyoming conferred the suffrage on women for all purposes and when the Territory received statehood in 1890, this provision was retained.[3] Since then a like privilege has been given to women in Colorado and Idaho by amendments to their constitutions,

---

[2] The first women's convention was held in 1848.

[3] According to Governor Hoyt of Wyoming woman suffrage was carried there in 1869, by the arts of one man. His account is as follows: "One large-hearted legislator in Wyoming went and talked with other members of the legislature. They smiled. But he got one of the lawyers to help him draw up a short bill, which he introduced. It was considered and discussed. People smiled generally. There was not much expectation that anything of that sort would be done; but this was a shrewd fellow, who managed the party card in such a way as to get, as he believed, enough votes to carry the measure before it was brought to the test. Thus he said to the Democrats: 'We have a Republican Governor and a Democratic Assembly. Now then, if we can carry this bill through the Assembly, and the Governor vetoes it, we shall have made a point, you know; we shall have shown our liberality and lost nothing. But keep still; don't say anything about it.' They promised. He then went to the Republicans and told them that the Democrats were going to support his measure, and that if *they* didn't want to lose capital they had better vote for it too. He didn't think there would be enough of them to carry it; but the vote would be on record, and thus defeat the game of the other party. And they likewise agreed to vote for it. So when the bill came to a vote it went right through! The members looked at each other in astonishment, for they hadn't intended to do it, *quite*. Then they laughed, and said it was a good joke, but they had 'got the Governor in a fix.' So the bill went, in the course of time, to John A. Campbell, who was then Governor—the first Governor of the Territory of Wyoming—and he promptly signed it! His heart was right!"—Address delivered at Philadelphia in 1882. Sir Horace Plunkett, however, discredits this story, and assigns as the reasons for the passing of the bill the notion that it would serve to advertise Wyoming (which it did) and a sort of rough Western liking for a joke. (*The Working of Woman Suffrage in Wyoming*, Cheyenne, Wyo., 1890). In Colorado the amendment conferring the suffrage won the support of the Populist party, powerful in 1893, and of large sections of the working men, who are supposed to have been influenced by abstract doctrines of equality.

and in Utah by the first constitution, adopted in 1895.[4] In Colorado the proposal was (in 1893) carried by the "Populist" party, then for a brief space dominant. In several states including South Dakota and Oregon it has been subjected to popular vote, but rejected by large majorities, nor does it appear in the constitutions of the three newest states. In Washington Territory the law which conferred it in 1883 was declared invalid by the courts in 1887, because its nature had not been properly described in the title, was reenacted immediately afterwards, and was in 1888 again declared invalid by the U.S. Territorial Court, on the ground that the act of Congress organizing the Territorial legislature did not empower it to extend the suffrage to women. In enacting their state constitution (1889) the people of Washington pronounced against female suffrage by a majority of two to one; and a good authority declared to me that "few women took advantage of the privilege and most of them were greatly relieved that the responsibility was removed." But in 1910 it was carried on an initiative vote with little discussion, the people (it is stated) hardly understanding what they were doing, because a large number of questions were submitted to popular vote at the same time and this question was described on the ballot paper in a way which did not indicate the real issue.

In many states besides the ten which give full suffrage[5] women are allowed to vote at elections of school officers, or on some question connected with schools; and in several other states (nine at least), as well as in all of these already referred to, they may be chosen to fill school offices, such as that of school visitor, or superintendent, or member of a school committee. They also enjoy "school suffrage" sporadically in a few cities.

In several states they have the right of voting upon questions submitted to the vote of the taxpayers as such. This includes the question of granting licenses for the sale of intoxicants. A bill to confer the same right was lost in the Massachusetts legislature of 1888 by a majority of one vote only.

In Kansas in 1886 and in Michigan in 1893 women received the suffrage

---

[4] The territorial legislature had in Utah established woman suffrage, but a federal statute had abolished it, as believed to be employed by Mormon wives at the bidding of their polygamous husbands, to maintain polygamy.

[5] Arizona, Connecticut, North Dakoa, South Dakota, Nevada, Illinois, Indiana, Kansas, Kentucky, Massachusetts, Michigan, Minnesota, Montana, Nebraska, New Hampshire, New Mexico, New York, New Jersey, Oklahoma, Oregon, Vermont, Wisconsin. Women enjoy school and municipal franchise in the Canadian provinces of Ontario, Nova Scotia, Manitoba, and British Columbia.

in all municipal elections. In Michigan, however, the law was subsequently held unconstitutional.[6]

In those states where women possess the school suffrage it is reported that few vote; and this is ascribed partly to indifference, partly to the difficulty which women on the humbler class experience in leaving their homes to go to the poll. In Massachusetts the number of women going to the poll declined rapidly after the first few years. But there have been cases there, and also in Kansas at municipal elections, in which a heavy vote was cast by the female voters.

In Wyoming (while it was still a Territory) women served as jurors for some months till the judges discovered that they were not entitled by law to do so, and in Washington (while a Territory) they served from 1884 to 1887, when the legislature, in regranting the right of voting, omitted to grant the duty or privilege of jury service. Those whole opinions I have enquired inform me that the presence of women on juries was deemed a grave evil, and that in prosecutions for gambling or the sale of intoxicants a defendant had no chance before them. It is also stated that comparatively few went to the poll. In Wyoming, moreover, the women on juries are stated to have been more severe than men.

As respects the suffrage in Wyoming, the evidence I have collected privately is conflicting. One of the most trustworthy authorities wrote to me as follows:

"After the first excitement is over, it is impossible to get respectable women out to vote except every two or three years on some purely emotional question like Prohibition or other temperance legislation. The effect on family life seems to be *nil*; certainly not bad." Another highly competent witness wrote: "There are no large towns. In the larger places most of the women, who are chiefly married, vote; in the smaller and more rural places the women take little interest in it, as indeed the men do. As a rule, women are in favour of temperance and good schools, and so far as they have been able to cast their influence, it has been on the right side in those questions. Woman suffrage so far seems to work well, but the field of its operations is one presenting singular immunity from the evils which elsewhere might attach to it, the population being sparse and women in the minority."

Beside these and similar statements may be set the fact that no opposition was offered in the convention of 1889, which drafted the present constitution,

---

[6] Similar proposals have from time to time been defeated in a good many states, though often by small majorities. In several of the smaller cities of Kansas all the municipal offices, from the mayoralty and police judgeship downwards, have occasionally been filled by women.

to the enactment of woman suffrage for all purposes. The opinion of the people at large was not duly ascertained, because the question was not separately submitted to them at the polls, but there can be little doubt that is would have been favourable. The declarations of Wyoming officials may deserve no great weight, for they do not wish to offend any section of the voters, and every Western American feels bound to say the best he can and something more for the arrangements of his own state. But the whole proceedings of the convention of 1889 leave the impression that the equal suffrage in force since 1869 had worked fairly, and the summing up of the case by a thoughtful and dispassionate British observer (Sir H. Plunkett[7]) is to the same effect. Moreover, had the results been obviously bad in Wyoming, they would have been quoted against the adoption of the proposal by Colorado in 1893. In these new Western states, however, women have been in a minority. Comparatively few of them seem to have shown any eagerness to obtain the suffrage, and the laws affecting women are much the same there and in other parts of the West.

No evidence has been produced to show that politics are in the woman suffrage states substantially purer than in the adjoining states, though it is said that the polls are quieter. The most that seems to be alleged is that they are no worse; or, as the Americans express it, "Things are very much what they were before, only more so." The conditions of the small and scattered populations of most of these states—Utah and in a less degree Idaho, being moreover exceptional as still largely Mormon—render their experience of slight value for such communities as the Eastern and Middle states.

Colorado, with a population of nearly 800,000, and with one great city, Denver, offers a better field for observations, and a book by Miss Helen L. Sumner, published in 1909 under the title of *Equal Suffrage*, presents the results of a minute and careful study of the working of woman suffrage there in a spirit which strikes the reader as impartial and scientific.[8] The

---

[7] In the pamphlet already cited. He observes that his informants never attempted to connect the frequency of divorces in Wyoming with the political equality of the sexes, conceiving this to have exercised no influence on the family life, nor led to domestic discord. "Political differences constitute one of the few domestic troubles which no State or Territory (so far) recognizes as just cause for dissolution of matrimony."

[8] It would be impossible to abridge the facts and arguments without the danger of misrepresenting them; but two or three points may be worth noting. Miss Sumner thinks legislation has been improved by the voting of women, and cites instances, but remarks that the Prohibition cause does not appear to have substantially gained, nor the salaries paid to women to have been equalized with those paid to men, even in educational work. One of the gains has, however, been the general appointment of women as county superintendents of schools. Eleven women were between 1893 and 1909 elected to the state house of representatives, but none to the state senate.

It is stated that "the only occupation legally forbidden to women in Colorado is work in coal

conclusions reached are, on the whole, favourable to the experiment, though there is admittedly much difference of opinion in Colorado itself upon the subject, among women as well as among men. Such changes as there have been for good or for evil, are less marked than either advocates or opponent expected. Enquiries made in many quarters do not shew that woman suffrage has done any positive harm to politics in Colorado, and some say that it occasionally prevents men of bad character from being nominated for office. Whether, however, the state, or the women in it, have as a whole gained, the discrepant eivdence makes it hard to determine.

Wherever the suffrage or any other public right has been given, it is given equally to married and to unmarried women.[9] No one dreams of drawing any distinction between the claims of the single and the married, or of making marriage entail disfranchisement. To do so would be alien to the whole spirit of American legislation, and would indeed involve a much grosser anomaly or injustice than the exclusion of all women alike from political functions. This point, therefore, on which much controversy has arisen in England, has given no trouble in the United States; and, similarly, the Americans always assume that wherever women receive the right of voting at the election to any office, they become as a matter of course eligible for the office itself. In some cases eligibility for the office has preceded the gift of the suffrage. There are states in which women have no school suffrage, but are chosen to school offices; and states (Massachusetts, for instance) in which they have no vote at municipal or state elections, but where they are placed on the state board of education or the board of prison commissioners. It would be deemed in the last degree illogical to give women municipal suffrage, and not allow a woman to be chosen mayoress, to give state (and therewith congressional) suffrage and not allow a woman to be capable of holding any state or any federal office. In Wyoming, five votes out of thirty-five were once given for a woman candidate for the post of United States senator.[10]

---

mines, though in practice they are excluded from other mines also. By police order they have been prevented from serving as barmaids in Denver saloons" (*Equal Suffrage*, p. 162).

[9] In a few States, however (e.g., Indiana and Oregon), school suffrage is limited to women who are heads of families, because these only are deemed to be interested in respect of children; and in a few (e.g., Michigan, Indiana, and Oregon) there are property qualifications of small amount attached to the school suffrage in the case of women which are not required in the case of men. In Kentucky school suffrage is granted only to widows who have children.

[10] Women are not unfrequently appointed to posts connected with legislative bodies. I found in Washington Territory that they had been chosen to be clerks and messengers to one or other of the houses of the (Territorial) legislature. It appears to have been held in Connecticut that a

"What," it will be asked, "are the forces by which the women's rights movement is now pressed forward? What are the arguments used to support it? Are they of a theoretical or of a practical nature? Is it on the ground of abstract justice and democratic principle that the battle is being fought, or is it alleged that women suffer from positive disabilities and hardships which nothing but an equal share in political power will remove?"

Both sets of arguments are employed; but those of a theoretical order seem to hold the chief place. In all or nearly all states married women have complete rights to their property; and mothers have rights considerable, if not quite equal to those of fathers, in the guardianship of their children. Women enjoy the equal protection of the law and are admissible to professions and the training needed for professions, while the laws of divorce, whatever may be said of them in other respects, are not more indulgent to husbands than to wives. Although therefore the advocates of woman suffrage claim that some tangible legislative benefits will accrue to woman from her admission to the franchise, especially in the way of obtaining better protection for her and for children, the case on this side seems weak, and excites little feeling. No one who observes America can doubt that whatever is deemed to be for the real benefit of women in the social and industrial sphere will be obtained for them from the goodwill and sympathy of men, without the agency of the polticial vote. It is on grounds of abstract right, it is because the exclusion from political power is deemed in itself unjust and degrading, and is thought to place woman on a lower level, that this exclusion is resented. It seems to be supposed that a nobler and more vigorous type of womanhood would be developed by the complete recognition of her equality, a wider and grander sphere of action opened to her efforts. Perhaps the commonest argument is contained in the question, "Why not? What reason can you give, you whose forefathers revolted from England because representation was not suffered to go with taxation, you who annually repeat the Declaration of Independence as if it were the Nicene Creed, you who after the war enfranchised ignorant Negroes, for excluding from the suffrage women who pay taxes, who are within the reason and meaning of the Declaration of 1776, who are far more intellectually and morally competent than the coloured millions of the South?" This appeal, which becomes all the stronger as an *argumentum ad hominem* because the American man is exceptionally deferential to women, and the American

---

woman may be appointed pension agent and in Illinois that she may be master (or mistress) in chancery.

statesman exceptionally disposed to comply with every request which is urgently pressed upon him, is the kernel of the suffragist case. However, it derived for a time no small practical aid from a practical consideration. The one question of current politics which usually interests women is the question of restricting or prohibiting the sale of intoxicants. This is also the question which excites not perhaps the widest yet certainly the keenest interest in the minds of a great host of male voters. The enemies of the liquor traffic have therefore a strong motive for desiring to see their voting power reinforced by those whose aid would secure victory; and in fact Prohibitionist conventions almost always declare in favour of women's suffrage. For a different reason, the Socialist and Labour parties are, as were the Populists also, disposed to support it, as indeed the Socialists usually do in Europe.

Yet it must not be supposed that the sentimental arguments are all on one side. There is a widespread apprehension that to bring women into politics might lower their social position, diminish men's deference for them, harden and roughen them, and, as it is expressed, "brush the bloom off the flowers." This feeling is at least as strong among women as among men, and some judicious observers deem it stronger now than it was formerly. The proportion of women who desire the suffrage seems to be smaller in America than in England. Of the many American ladies whose opinion I have from time to time during forty years inquired, the enormous majority expressed themselves hostile; and in most of the states where the qeustion has come near to being a practical issue there have been formed women's anti-suffrage associations which conduct an active agitation, and present to the committees of state legislatures their arguments against the proposal. They support journals also, which press upon women the desirability of their continuing in the sphere they have hitherto occupied, and dwell upon the greater and better influence which, so it is thought, they may exert on legislation and administration if they remain "outside politics." It is remarkable that the movement has hitherto found comparatively little support among what may be called the "upper classes." Woman suffragism has been, though less so now than formerly, thought "bad form," and supposed to betoken a want of culture and refinement. The same reproach attached before the Civil War to Abolitionism. It was at one time an injury to the cause that some few of its prominent advocates, disavowed no doubt by the great bulk of the suffrage party, also advocated a general unsettlement of the relations between the sexes, and that a few others were too masculine in their manners and discourse. The sentimental aversion to seeing women immersed in politics is all the greater because "politics" have a technical meaning which is repellent to refined Americans; and it is felt that "politics" are more likely to soil women than women to purify "politics."

But one of the objections deemed gravest is this, that in this land where the suffrage is, as respects men, universal, the constituencies, which are already enormous—a member of Congress represents more than six times as many voters as an English member of Parliament—would be doubled in size, and all the difficulties which already attach to elections be immensely aggravated. Even those who desire to see the sale of intoxicants restricted doubt the expediency of attaining their object by the votes of women, because the difficulty of enforcing prohibitory legislation, already serious where the drinking minority is strong, would be much greater if a majority of men in favour of keeping bars and saloons open were overborne by a minority of men turned into a majority by the votes of women.

The extension, in recent years, of woman suffrage over some Western states does not seem to have been due to any marked increase in the number of women asking for the vote, for the great bulk of the sex in those states are reported to have remained indifferent, but to the following four causes.

One is the influence of the English propaganda of the scheme. Its advance in Europe stimulated the hopes and efforts of those who advocate it in America.

A second is the growth of the Socialist and Labour parties, the leaders of which believe that woman suffrage will promote their aims. The example of Australia, where the Labour party has been greatly strengthened by the woman vote, has encouraged this belief.

A third is the tendency to exalt direct popular sovereignty and disparage representative government. The advocacy of initiative, referendum and recall disposes men to favour extensions of the suffrage, and to be moved by abstract principles and a belief in the so-called "natural right" to vote rather than by considerations of practical expediency, i.e., of what are likely to be the tangible results of any measure on the good government of the community.

A fourth is the idea that the votes of women will further social reforms. In point of fact, such reforms have moved as fast in states that have not adopted woman suffrage as in states that have, and the influence of women in promoting useful legislation seems to have been no slighter. Nevertheless the idea subsists, and seems to have led to the support extended to woman suffrage by the new Progressive party at the election of 1912.

To these one might add the influence of what is called the "woman movement" as a whole, a movement too large to be entered on here, and one felt in Britain as well as in America.

To a European observer the suffrage question seems one rather of social than of political moment. If he sees no reason to expect an improvement in politics from the participation of women in elections and their admission to Congress and to high political office, neither does he find much cause for fear. The results of universal suffrage may not, so far as legislation is concerned, greatly differ from those of manhood suffrage. Such misgivings as he entertains are of a different nature. They are serious misgivings, and they are rendered not less serious by a study of the social changes which are passing upon the world in Europe as well as in America.

CHAPTER 100

The Supposed Faults of Democracy

The question which in one form or another every European politician has during the last half-century been asking about the United States, is the broad question, How does democracy answer? No other country has tried the experiment of a democratic government on so large a scale, with so many minor variations, for the state governments are forty-six autonomous democracies, or with such advantages of geographical position and material resources. And those who think that all civilized countries are moving towards democracy, even though they may not be destined to rest there, find the question an important one for themselves. The reader who has followed thus far the account I have tried to give of the federal Constitution and its working, of the state constitutions, of local government, of the party machinery, of the influence of public opinion as a controlling power over all the institutions of the country, will be content with a comparatively brief summary of the results to which the inquiries made under these heads point.

That summary naturally falls into three parts. We have to ask first, how far the faults usually charged on democracy are present in America; next, what are the special faults which characterize it here; last, what are the strong points which it has developed.

The chief faults which philosophers, from Plato downwards, and popular writers repeating and caricaturing the dicta of philosophers, have attributed to democratic governments, are the following:

Weakness in emergencies, incapacity to act with promptitude and decision;
Fickleness and instability, frequent changes of opinion, consequent changes in the conduct of affairs and in executive officials;
Insubordination, internal dissensions, disregard of authority, a frequent resort to violence, bringing on an anarchy which ends in military tyranny;

A desire to level down, and an intolerance of greatness;

Tyranny of the majority over the minority;

A love of novelty: a passion for changing customs and destroying old institutions;

Ignorance and folly, producing a liability to be deceived and misled; consequent growth of demagogues playing on the passions and selfishness of the masses.

I do not say that this list exhausts the reproaches directed against democracy, but it includes those which are most often heard and are best worth examining. Most of them are drawn from the history of the Greek republics of antiquity and the Italian republics of the Middle Ages, small communities where the conditions of social and political life were so different from those of a great modern country that we ought not to expect similar results to follow from political arrangements called by the same name. However, as this consideration has not prevented writers and statesmen, even in our own day, from repeating the old censures, and indeed from mixing together in one repulsive potion all the faults that belonged to small aristocratic republics with all that can belong to large democratic republics, it is worth while to examine these current notions, and try them by the light of the facts which America furnishes.

Weakness and Want of Promptitude. The American democracy is long-suffering and slow in rousing itself; it is often perplexed by problems, and seems to grope blindly for their solution. In the dealings with England and France which preceded the war of 1812, and in the conduct of that war, its government showed some irresolution and sluggishness. The habit of blustering in its intercourse with foreign powers, and the internal strife over slavery, led Europeans to think it lacked firmness and vigour. They were undeceived in 1861. While it seemed possible to avert a breach with the Southern slaveholders, the North was willing to accept, and did accept, a series of compromises whose inadequacy was soon revealed. The North was ill led in Congress, and the South was boldly if not wisely led. Yet when the crisis arrived, the North put forth its power with a suddenness and resolution which surprised the world. There was no faltering in the conduct of a struggle which for two long years French and English statesmen deemed hopeless. The best blood of the North freely offered itself to be shed on the battlefields of Virginia and Pennsylvania for the sake of the Union; while an enormous debt was incurred in equipping army after army. As everyone knows, the Southern people displayed no less vigour even when the tide had evidently began to turn against them, and the hope of European intervention died away. If want of force, dash, and courage in moments of danger is a defect generally chargeable on popular governments, it was not then chargeable on the United States. But the doctrine is one which finds little to support it either in ancient or in modern history, while there are many instances to the contrary: witness the war of the Swiss against Charles the Bold, and the defence of Florence against Charles V.

Fickleness and Instability. The indictment fails on this count also. The people are open to sudden impulses, and in particular states there have been ill-considered innovations and a readiness to try wild experiments, such as those I have described in California. But taking the nation as a whole, its character is marked by tenacity of beliefs and adherence to leaders once chosen. The opposite charge of stubbornness in refusing to be convinced by argument and to admit the failings of men who have established some title to gratitude, might more plausibly be preferred. Western farmers have been accustomed to suffer from the high price of the clothes they wear and the implements they use, but once they have imbibed the belief that a protective tariff makes for the general good of the country they remained Protectionists down till 1890; and of those who then wavered many have since reverted to that view. The blunders of President Grant's first administration, and the misdeeds of the knot of men who surrounded him, playing upon the political inexperience of a blunt soldier, scarcely affected the loyalty of the masses to the man whose sword had saved the Union. Congressmen and state officials are no doubt often changed, but they are changed in pursuance of a doctrine and a habit in which the interests of a class are involved, not from any fickleness in the people.[1]

Insubordination and Contempt for Authority. On this head the evidence is more conflicting. There are states and cities in which the laws are imperfectly enforced. Homicide is hardly a crime in some parts of the South—that is to say, a man who kills another is not always arrested, often not convicted when arrested and put on his trial, very rarely hanged when convicted.[2] One might almost say that private war is recognized by opinion

---

[1] See Chap. 20 in Vol. I.

[2] Thirty years ago a distinguished American lawyer said, "There is no subject within the domain of legislation in which improvement is so needed as in the law against murder. The practical immunity that crime enjoys in some sections of the country, and the delay, difficulty, and uncertainty in enforcing the law almost everywhere, is a reproach to our civilization. Efforts to save assassins from punishment are so strenuous, the chances of escape so numerous, and the proceedings so protracted, that the law has few terrors for those disposed to violate it."—Address of Mr. E. J. Phelps to the American Bar Association, 1881.

More recently President Taft observed, "I grieve to say that the administration of the criminal law is in nearly all the States of the Union a disgrace to our civilization" (address at Yale University), and in 1906 he repeated, "No one can examine the statistics of crime in this country and of successful prosecutions without realizing that the administration of the criminal law is a

in these districts, as it was in Europe during the earlier Middle Ages. In the mountainous country of eastern Kentucky, and the adjoining parts of Virginia and Tennessee, quarrels are kept up from generation to generation between hostile families and their respective friends, which the state authorities cannot succeed in repressing. In 1890, I was assured when passing the borders of that region, that in one such blood fued more than fifty persons had perished within the preceding ten years, each murder provoking another in revenge. When a judge goes into these parts it has sometimes befallen that a party of men come down fully armed from the mountains, surround the court house, and either drive him away or oblige him to abandon the attempt to do justice on slayers belonging to their faction. In the West, again, particularly in such Southwestern states as Missouri, Arkansas, and Texas, brigandage was for a time, and is still in some few places, regarded with a certain amusement, rising into sympathy, by a part of the peaceable population. Having arisen partly out of the border ruffianism which preceded the outbreak of the Civil War, partly among men who were constantly engaged in skirmishing with the Indian tribes, there was a flavour of romance about it, which ceased to gild the exploits of train robbers only when their activity threatened the commercial interests of a rising city. Jesse James, the notorious bandit of Missouri, and his brothers, were popular heroes in the region they infested, much like Robin Hood and Little John in the ballads of the thirteenth century in England. These phenomena are, however, explicable by other causes than democratic government. The homicidal habits of the South are a relic of that semi-barbarism which slavery kept alive long after the Northern free states had reached the level of European order. The want of a proper police is apparently the cause answerable for the train robberies which still, even in such states as Illinois and Ohio, sometimes occur, and these are detected and punished more frequently by the energy of the railroad or express (parcel delivery) companies and their skilled detectives than through the action of the state authorities. Brigandage is due to the absence of a mounted gendarmerie in the vast and thinly-peopled Farther West; and there is no gendarmerie because the federal government leaves the states to create their own, and unsettled Western communities, being well armed, prefer to take care of themselves rather

---

disgrace to our civilization, and without tracing to this condition as a moving and overwhelming cause for them, the horrible lynchings that are committed the country over, with all the danger of injustice and exhibition of fiendish cruelty which occurrences involve" (address to Pennsylvania State Bar Association, 1906).

Upon this whole subject see Professor Garner's article, *Crime and Judicial Inefficiency*.

than spend their scanty corporate funds on a task whose cost would, as they think, be disproportionate to the result.[3] In the western wilds of Canada, however, the mounted police secures perfect safety for wayfarers, and train robberies seem to be unknown.

Lynch law is not unknown in more civilized regions, such as Indiana and Illinois. A case occurred recently not far from New York City. Now lynch law, however shocking it may seem to Europeans and New Englanders, is far removed from arbitrary violence. According to the testimony of careful observers, it is not often abused, and its proceedings are generally conducted with some regularity of form as well as fairness of spirit. What are the circumstances? Those highly technical rules of judicial procedure and still more technical rules of evidence which America owes to the English common law, and which have in some states retained antiquated minutiæ now expunged from English practice, or been rendered by new legislation too favourable to prisoners, have to be applied in districts where population is thin, where there are very few officers, either for the apprehension of offenders, or for the hunting up of evidence against them, and where, according to common belief, both judges and juries are occasionally "squared" or "got at." Many crimes would go unpunished if some more speedy and efficient method of dealing with them were not adopted. This method is found in a volunteer jury, summoned by the leading local citizens, or in very clear cases, by a simple seizure and execution of the criminal.[4] Why not create an efficient police? Because crime is uncommon in many districts—in such a district, for instance, as Michigan or rural Wisconsin—and the people have deliberately concluded that it is cheaper and simpler to take the law into their own hands on those rare occasions when a police is needed than to be at the trouble of organizing and paying a force for which there is usually no employment. If it be urged that they are thus forming habits of lawlessness in themselves, the Americans reply that experience does not seem to make this probable, because lawlessness does not increase among the farming population, and has disappeared from places where the rudeness or simplicity of society formerly rendered lynch law necessary. Cases however occur for which no such excuse can be offered, cases in

[3] There is always a sheriff, whose business it is to pursue criminals, and hang them if convicted, but much depends on his individual vigour.
[4] The savageness which occasionally appears in these lynchings is surprising to one who knows the general kindliness of the American people. Not long ago the people of East Kentucky hunted for a murderer to burn him to death, and the White Cap and Night Riding outrages are sometimes accompanied by revolting cruelty.

which a prisoner (probably a Negro) already in the hands of justice is seized and put to death by a mob. Some years ago there was in several states, and notably in parts of southern Indiana—a rough, wooded country, with a backward and scattered population—a strange recrudescence of lynching in the rise of the so-called White Caps, people who seized by night men or women who had given offence by their immoral life or other vices, dragged them into the woods, flogged them severely, and warned them to quit the neighbourhood forthwith. Similar outrages are often reported from other states to the southwest of Indiana, as far as Mississippi. In Ohio they were promptly repressed by an energetic governor. In 1908–9 disputes connected with the alleged attempt by a powerful corporation to create a monopoly in the purchasing of tobacco for manufacture led to a series of nocturnal outrages by armed men who sought, by whipping or killing those farmers who refused to join them in their resistance to the attempts referred to, to coerce the tobacco growers into joining that organized resistance. These Night Riders gave great trouble in Kentucky and parts of Tennessee, though the governor took vigorous measures against them.

The so-called "Molly Maguire" conspiracy, which vexed and terrified Pennsylvania for several years, showed the want of a vigorous and highly trained police. A sort of secret society organized a succession of murders, much like the Italian Camorra, which remained undetected till a daring man succeeded in persuading the conspirators to admit him among them. He shared their schemes, and learnt to know their persons and deeds, then turned upon them and brought them to justice. This remarkable case illustrates not any neglect of law or tenderness for crime, but mainly the power of a combination which can keep its secrets. Once detected, the Molly Maguires were severely dealt with. The Pittsburg riots of 1877, and the Cincinnati riots of 1884, and the Chicago troubles of 1894 alarmed the Americans themselves, so long accustomed to domestic tranquillity as to have forgotten those volcanic forces which lie smouldering in all ignorant masses, ready to burst forth upon sufficient excitement. The miners and ironworkers of the Pittsburg district are rough fellows, many of them recent immigrants who have not yet acquired American habits of order; nor would there have been anything to distinguish this Pennsylvanian disturbance from those which happen during strikes in England, as, for instance, at Blackburn, in Lancashire and, later, during a coal strike at one or two places in Yorkshire and Derbyshire, or in times of distress in France, as at Decazeville in 1886, had there been a prompt suppression. Unfortunately there was in 1877 no proper force on the spot. The governor was absent; the mayor and other local authorities lost their heads; the police, feebly handled, were overpowered; the militia showed weakness; so that the riot spread in a way which surprised its authors, and the mob raged for several days along the railroads in several states, and over a large area of manufacturing and mining towns.

The moral of this event was the necessity, even in a land of freedom, of keeping a force strong enough to repress tumults in their first stage. The Cincinnati riot began in an attempt to lynch two prisoners who were thought likely to escape the punishment they richly deserved; and it would probably have ended there had not the floating rabble of this city of 300,000 inhabitants seized the opportunity to do a little pillage and make a great noise on their own account. Neither sedition had any political character, nor indeed any specific object, except that the Pennsylvanian mob showed special enmity to the railroad company.

In 1892 the same moral was enforced by the strike riots on some of the railroads in New York State and in the mining regions of Idaho, by the local wars between cattlemen and "rustlers" in Wyoming, by the disturbances at the Homestead works in Pennsylvania, and by the sanguinary conflict which arose at the convict-worked mines in Tennessee, where a mob of miners attacked the stockades in which were confined convicts kept at labour under contracts between the state and private mine owners, liberated many of the convicts, captured and were on the point of hanging an officer of the state militia, and were with difficulty at last repressed by a strong militia force. The riots at Chicago in 1894 and the more protracted strife between mine owners and striking miners in Colorado somewhat later are other instances. Such tumults are not specially products of democracy, but they are unhappily proofs that democracy does not secure the good behaviour of its worst and newest citizens, and that it must be prepared, no less than other governments, to maintain order by the prompt and stern application of physical force.[5]

It was a regrettable evidence of the extent to which public authorities have seemed to abnegate the function of maintaining order that the habit grew up among railroad directors and the owners of other large enterprises of hiring a private armed force to protect, at the time of a strike, not only the workmen they bring in to replace the strikers, but also their yards, works, and stock in trade. A firm which began business as a private detective

---

[5] There is a great difference between different states and cities as regards police arrangements. The police of New York City are said to be very efficient and indeed sometimes too promptly severe in the use of their staves; and in many cities the police are armed with revolvers.

agency was for years accustomed to supply for this purpose bodies of men well trained and drilled, who could be relied on to defend the place allotted to them against a greatly superior force of rioters. This firm used to keep not less than one thousand men permanently on a war footing, and sent them hither and thither over the country to its customers. They were usually sworn in as sheriff's deputies, on each occasion before the proper local authority. So frequent had been the employment of "Pinkerton's men," as they are called (though it is not always from Messrs. Pinkerton of Chicago that they are obtained, and the name, like "Delmonico," for a restaurant, seems to be passing from a proper into a common noun), that some new state constitutions (e.g., Wyoming, Idaho, Montana, Washington, Kentucky) and statutes in other states (e.g., Massachusetts) expressly prohibit the bringing of armed men into the state, and a committee of Congress was set to investigate the subject, so far without result, for it is going a long way to forbid a man by statute to hire persons to help him to protect his property when he finds it in danger. These strike cases are of course complicated by the reluctance of a state governor or a mayor to incur unpopularity by taking strong measures against a crowd who have votes. Here we touch a difficulty specially incident to a directly elected executive—a difficulty noted already in the cases of elected judges and elected tax officers, and one which must be taken into account in striking the balance between the good and the evil of a system of direct and pervading popular control. The remedy is in extreme cases found in the displeasure of the good citizens, who, after all, form the voting majority. But it is a remedy which may follow with too tardy steps. Meantime, many large employers of labour find themselves obliged to defend their property by these condottieri, because they cannot rely on the defence which the state ought to furnish, and the condottieri themselves, who seem to be generally men of good character as well as proved courage, are so much hated by the workmen as to be sometimes in danger of being lynched when found alone or in small parties.[6]

In some states not a few laws are systematically ignored or evaded, sometimes by the connivance of officials who are improperly induced to abstain from prosecuting transgressors, sometimes with the general consent of the community which perceives that they cannot be enforced. Thus some years ago the laws against the sale of liquor on Sundays in the city of Chicago were not enforced. The German and Irish part of the population

---

[6] It is probably this popular hostility to the employment of Pinkerton's men that has caused them to figure little if at all in the more recent strike troubles. They are now seldom heard of.

disliked them, and showed its dislike by turning out of the municipal offices those who had enforced them, while yet the law remained on the statute book because, according to the Constitution of Illinois it took a majority of two-thirds in the legislature to repeal an act; and the rural members, being largely Prohibitionists, stood by this law against Sunday dealing. When in Texas I heard of the same thing as happening in the city of San Antonio, and doubt not that it occurs in many cities. Probably more laws are quietly suffered to be broken in America than in either England or Germany. On the other hand, it is fair to say that the credit which the New Englanders used to claim of being a law-abiding people is borne out by the general security of property and person which, apart from the cases mentioned above, and especially from strike troubles, the traveller remarks over the rural parts of the Eastern and Middle states.[7] Political disturbances (other than occasional collisions between whites and Negroes) are practically unknown. Even when an election is believed to have been fraudulently won, the result is respected, because it is externally regular. Fights seldom occur at elections; neither party disturbs the meetings or processions of the other in the hottest presidential campaign. To Americans the habit of letting opponents meet and talk in peace seems essential to a well-ordered free government.

The habit of obedience to constituted authority is another test, and one which Plato would have considered specially conclusive. The difficulty of applying it in America is that there are so few officials who come into the relation of command with the people, or in other words, that the people are so little "governed," in the French or German sense, that one has few opportunities of discovering how they comport themselves. The officers of both the federal and the state governments, in levying taxes and carrying out the judgments of the courts, have seldom any resistance to fear, except in such regions as those already referred to, where the fierce mountaineers will not brook interference with their vendetta, or suffer the federal excisemen to do their duty. These regions are, however, quite exceptional, forming a sort of *enclave* of semi-barbarism in a civilized country, such as the rugged Albania was in the Roman Empire. Other authorities experience no difficulty in making themselves respected. A railroad company, for instance, finds its passengers only too submissive. They endure with a patience which astonishes Englishmen frequent irregularities of the train service and other discomforts,

---

[7] There is little use in comparing the aggregate of crimes reported and of convictions with the aggregates of European countries, because in disorderly regions many crimes go unreported as well as unpunished.

which would in England produce a whole crop of letters to the newspapers. The discipline of the army and navy in the war was nearly as strict as in European armies. So in universities and colleges discipline is maintained with the same general ease and the same occasional troubles as arise in Oxford and Cambridge. The children in city schools are proverbially docile. Except when strikes occur, employers never complain of any trouble in keeping order among their workpeople while at work. So far, indeed, is insubordination from being a characteristic of the native Americans, that they are conspicuously the one free people of the world which, owing to its superior intelligence, has recognized the permanent value of order, and observes it on every occasion, not least when a sudden alarm arises. Anarchy is of all dangers or bugbears the one which the modern world has least cause to fear, for the tendency of ordinary human nature to obey is the same as in past times, and the aggregation of human beings into great masses weakens the force of the individual will, and makes men more than ever like sheep, so far as action is concerned. Much less, therefore, is there ground for fancying that out of anarchy there will grow any tyranny of force. Whether democracies may not end in yielding greater power to their executives is quite another question, whereof more anon; all I observe here is that in no country can a military despotism, such as that which has twice prevailed in France and once in England, be deemed less likely to arise. During the Civil War there were many persons in Europe cultivating, as Gibbon says, the name without the temper of philosophy, who predicted that some successful leader of the Northern armies would establish his throne on the ruins of the Constitution. But no sooner had General Lee surrendered at Appomatox than the disbandment of the victorious host began; and the only thing which thereafter distinguished Generals Grant, Sherman, and Sheridan from their fellow citizens was the liability to have "receptions" forced on them when they visited a city, and find their puissant arms wearied by the handshakings of their enthusiastic admirers.

Caesarism is the last danger likely to menace America. In no nation is civil order more stable. None is more averse to the military spirit. No political system would offer a greater resistance to an attempt to create a standing army or centralize the administration.

Jealousy of Greatness, and a Desire to Level Down. This charge derives a claim to respectful consideration from the authority of Tocqueville, who thought it a necessary attribute of democracy, and professed to have discovered symptoms of it in the United States. It alarmed J. S. Mill, and has been frequently dwelt on by his disciples, and by many who have adopted no other part of his teachings, as an evil equally inevitable and fatal in democratic countries. There was probably good ground for it in 1830. Even now one discovers a tendency in the United States, particularly in the West, to dislike, possibly to resent, any outward manifestation of social superiority. A man would be ill looked upon who should build a castle in a park, surround his pleasure grounds with a high wall, and receive an exclusive society in gilded drawing rooms. One of the parts which prominent politicians, who must be assumed to know their business, most like to play is the part of Cincinnatus at the plough, or Curius Dentatus receiving the Samnite envoys over his dinner of turnips. They welcome a newspaper interviewer at their modest farm, and take pains that he should describe how simply the rooms are furnished, and how little "help" (i.e., how few servants) is kept. Although the cynics of the New York press make a mock of such artless ways, the desired impression is produced on the farmer and the artisan. At a senatorial election not long ago in a Northwestern state, the opponents of the sitting candidate procured a photograph of his residence in Washington, a handsome mansion in a fashionable avenue, and circulated it among the members of the state legislature, to show in what luxury their federal representative indulged. I remember to have heard it said of a statesman proposing to become a candidate for the presidency, that he did not venture during the preceding year to occupy his house in Washington, lest he should give occasion for similar criticism. Whether or not this was his real motive, the attribution of it to him is equally illustrative. But how little the wealthy fear to display their wealth and take in public the pleasures it procures may be understood by anyone who, walking down Fifth Avenue in New York, observes the superb houses which line it, houses whose internal decorations and collected objects of art rival those of the palaces of European nobles, or who watches in Newport, one of the most fashionable of summer resorts, the lavish expenditure upon servants, horses, carriages, and luxuries of every kind. No spot in Europe conveys an equal impression of the lust of the eyes and the pride of life, of boundless wealth and a boundless desire for enjoyment, as does the Ocean Drive at Newport on an afternoon in August.

Intellectual eminence excites no jealousy, though it is more admired and respected than in Europe. The men who make great fortunes—and their number as well as the scale of their fortunes increases—are regarded not so much with envy, as with admiration. "When thou doest good unto thyself, all men shall speak well of thee." Wealth does not, as in England, give its possessors an immediate entrée to fashionable society, but it marks them as the heroes and leaders of the commercial world, and sets them on a pinnacle of fame which fires the imagination of ambitious youths in dry goods stores or traffic clerks on a railroad. The demonstrations of hostility to wealthly "monopolists," and especially to railroad companies, and the magnates of trusts, are prompted, not by hatred to prominence or wealth, but by discontent at the immense power which capitalists exercise, especially in the business of transporting goods, and which they have frequently abused.

Tyranny of the Majority. Of this I have spoken in a previous chapter, and need only summarize the conclusions there arrived at. So far as compulsive legislation goes, it has never been, and is now less than ever, a serious or widespread evil. The press is free to advocate unpopular doctrines, even the most brutal forms of anarchism. Religious belief and practices are untouched by law. The sale of intoxicants is no doubt in many places restricted or forbidden, but to assume that this is a tyrannical proceeding is to beg a question on which the wise are much divided. The taxation of the rich for the benefit of the poor offers the greatest temptation to a majority disposed to abuse its powers. But neither Congress nor the state legislatures have, with a very few exceptions, gone any farther in this direction than the great nations of Europe. If such abstention from legislative tyranny be held due, not to the wisdom and fairness of the American democracy, but to the restraints which the federal and state constitutions impose upon it, the answer is, Who impose and maintain these restraints? The people themselves, who deserve the credit of desiring to remove from their own path temptations which might occasionally prove irresistible. It is true that the conditions have been in some points exceptionally favourable. Class hatreds are absent. The two great national parties are not class parties, for, if we take the country as a whole, rich and poor are fairly represented in both of these parties. Neither proposes to overtax the rich. Both denounce monopolism in the abstract, and promise to restrain capital from abusing its power, but neither is more forward than the other to take practical steps for such a purpose, because each includes capitalists whose contributions the party needs, and each includes plenty of the respectable and wealthy classes. Party divisions do not coincide with social or religious divisions, as has often happened in Europe.

Moreover, in state politics—and it is in the state rather than in the federal sphere that attacks on a minority might be feared—the lines on which parties act are fixed by the lines which separate the national parties, and each party is therefore held back from professing doctrines which menace the interests of any class. The only exceptions occur where some burning economic question supersedes for the moment the regular party attachments. This happened in California, with the consequences already described. It came near happening in two or three of the Northwestern states, such as Illinois and Wisconsin, where the farmers, organized in their Granges or agricultural clubs, caused the legislatures to pass statutes which bore hardly on the railroads and the owners of elevators and grain warehouses. Similar attempts were more recently made by the Populists and must from time to time be expected. Yet even this legislation could scarcely be called tyrannical. It was an attempt, however clumsy and abrupt, to deal with a real economical mischief, not an undue extension of the scope of legislation to matters in which majorities ought not to control minorities at all.

Love of Novelty; Passion for Destroying Old Institutions. It is easy to see how democracies have been credited with this tendency. They have risen out of oligarchies or aristocratic monarchies, the process of their rise coinciding, if not always with a revolution, at least with a breaking down of many old usages and institutions. It is this very breaking down that gives birth to them. Probably some of the former institutions are spared, are presently found incompatible with the new order of things, and then have to be changed till the people has, so to speak, furnished its house according to its taste. But when the new order has been established, is there any ground for believing that a democracy is an exception to the general tendency of mankind to adhere to the customs they have formed, admire the institutions they have created, and even bear the ills they know rather than incur the trouble of finding some way out of them? The Americans are not an exception. They value themselves only too self-complacently on their methods of government; they abide by their customs, because they admire them. They love novelty in the sphere of amusement, literature, and social life; but in serious matters, such as the fundamental institutions of government and in religious belief, no progressive and civilized people is more conservative.

Liability to Be Misled; Influence of Demagogues. No doubt the inexperience of the recent immigrants, the want of trained political thought among the bulk even of native citizens, the tendency to sentimentalism which marks all large masses of men, do lay the people open to the fallacious reasoning and specious persuasions of adventurers. This happens in all popularly governed countries; and a phenomenon substantially the same occurs in oligarchies, for you may have not only aristocratic demagogues, but demagogues playing to an aristocratic mob. Stripped of its externals and considered in its essential features, demagogism is no more abundant in

America than in England, France, or Italy. Empty and reckless declaimers, such as were some of those who figured in the Granger and Populist movements (for sincere and earnest men have shared in both), are allowed to talk themselves hoarse, and ultimately relapse into obscurity. A demagogue of greater talent may aspire to some high executive office; if not to the presidency, then perhaps a place in the cabinet, where he may practically pull the wires of a president whom he has put into the chair. Failing either of these, he aims at the governorship of his state or the mayoralty of a great city. In no one of these positions can he do permanent mischief. The federal executive has no influence on legislation, and even in foreign policy and in the making of appointments requires the consent of the Senate. That any man should acquire so great a hold on the country as to secure the election of two houses of Congress subservient to his will, while at the same time securing the presidency or secretaryship of state for himself, is an event too improbable to enter into calculation. Nothing approaching it has been seen since the days of Jackson. The size of the country, the differences between the states, a hundred other causes, make achievements possible enough in a European country all but impossible here. That a plausible adventurer should clamber to the presidential chair, and when seated there should conspire with a corrupt congressional ring, purchasing by the gift of offices and by jobs their support for his own schemes of private cupidity or public mischief, is conceivable, but improbable. The system of counter-checks in the federal government, which impedes or delays much good legislation, may be relied on to avert many of the dangers to which the sovereign chambers of European countries are exposed.

A demagogue installed as governor of a state—and it is usually in state politics that demagogism appears—has but limited opportunities for wrongdoing. He can make a few bad appointments, and can discredit the commonwealth by undignified acts. He cannot seriously harm it. Two politicians who seem to deserve the title recently obtained that honourable post in two great Eastern states. One of them, a typical "ringster," perpetrated some jobs and vetoed a few good bills. Venturing too far, he at last involved his party in an ignominious defeat. The other, a man of greater natural gifts and greater capacity for mischief, whose capture of the chief magistracy of the state had drawn forth lamentations from the better citizens, seems to have left things much as he found them, and the most noteworthy incident which marked his year of office—for he was turned out at the next election— was the snub administered by the leading university in the state, which refused him the compliment usually paid to a chief magistrate of an honorary degree of Doctor of Laws.

This inquiry has shown us that of the faults traditionally attributed to democracy one only is fairly chargeable on the United States; that is to say, is manifested there more conspicuously than in the constitutional monarchies of Europe. This is the disposition to be lax in enforcing laws disliked by any large part of the population, to tolerate breaches of public order, and to be too indulgent to offenders generally. The Americans themselves admit this to be one of their weak points. How far it is due to that deficient reverence for law which is supposed to arise in popular governments from the fact that the people have nothing higher than themselves to look up to, how far rather to the national easygoingness and goodnature, how far to the prejudice against the maintenance of an adequate force of military and police and to the optimism which refuses to recognize the changes brought by a vast increase of population, largely consisting of immigrants, these are points I need not attempt to determine. It has produced no general disposition to lawlessness, which rather tends to diminish in the older parts of the country. And it is sometimes (though not always) replaced in a serious crisis by a firmness in repressing disorders which some European governments may envy. Men who are thoroughly awakened to the need for enforcing the law, enforce it all the more resolutely because it has the whole weight of the people behind it.

The True Faults of American Democracy

We have seen that the defects commonly attributed to democratic government are not specially characteristic of the United States. It remains to inquire what are the peculiar blemishes which the country does show. So far as regards the constitutional machinery of the federal and of the state government this question has been answered in earlier chapters. It is now rather the tendency of the institutions generally, the disposition and habits of the governing people, that we have to consider. The word democracy is often used to mean a spirit or tendency, sometimes the spirit of revolution, sometimes the spirit of equality. For our present purpose it is better to take it as denoting simply a form of government, that in which the numerical majority rules, deciding questions of state by the votes, whether directly, as in the ancient republics, or mediately, as in modern representative government, of the body of citizens, the citizens being if not the whole, at least a very large proportion of the adult males. The enquiry may begin with the question, What are the evils to which we may expect such a form of government to be exposed? and may then proceed to ascertain whether any other defects exist in the United States government which, though traceable to democracy, are not of its essence, but due to the particular form which it has there taken.

It is an old maxim that republics live by virtue—that is, by the maintenance of a high level of public spirit and justice among the citizens. If the republic be one in which power is confined to, or practically exercised by, a small educated class, the maintenance of this high level is helped by the sense of personal dignity which their position engenders. If the republic itself be small, and bear rule over others, patriotism may be intense, and the sense of the collective dignity of the state may ennoble the minds of the citizens, make them willing to accept sacrifices for its sake, to forego private interests and suppress private resentments, in order to be strong against the outer world. But if the state be very large, and the rights of all citizens equal, we must not expect them to rise above the average level of human nature. Rousseau and Jefferson will tell us that this level is high, that the faults which governments have hitherto shown are due to the selfishness of privileged persons and classes, that the ordinary unsophisticated man will love justice, desire the good of others, need no constraint to keep him in the right path. Experience will contradict them, and whether it talks of original sin or adopts some less scholastic phrase, will recognize that the tendencies to evil in human nature are not perhaps as strong, but as various and abiding even in the most civilized societies, as its impulses to good. Hence the rule of numbers means the rule of ordinary mankind without those artificial helps which their privileged position has given to limited governing classes, though also, no doubt, without those special temptations which follow in the wake of power and privilege.

Since every question that arises in the conduct of government is either a question of ends or a question of means, errors may be committed by the ruling power either in fixing on wrong ends or in choosing wrong means to secure those ends. It is now, after long resistance by those who maintained that they knew better what was good for the people than the people knew themselves, at last agreed that as the masses are better judges of what will conduce to their own happiness than are the classes placed above them, they must be allowed to determine ends. This is in fact the essence of free or popular government, and the justification for vesting power in numbers. But assuming the end to be given, who is best qualified to select the means for its accomplishment? To do so needs in many cases a knowledge of the facts, a skill in interpreting them, a power of forecasting the results of measures, unattainable by the mass of mankind. Such knowledge is too high for them. It is attainable only by trained economists, legists, statesmen. If the masses attempt it they will commit mistakes not less serious than those which befall a litigant who insists on conducting a complicated case instead of leaving it to his attorney and counsel. But in popular governments this distinction between ends and means is apt to be forgotten. Often it is one which cannot be sharply drawn, because some ends are means to larger ends, and some means are desired not only for the sake of larger ends, but for their own sakes also. And the habit of trusting its own wisdom and enjoying its own power, in which the multitude is encouraged by its leaders and servants, disposes it to ignore the distinction even where the distinction is clear, and makes it refer to the direct arbitrament of the people matters which the people are unfit to decide, and which they might safely leave to their trained ministers or representatives. Thus we find that the direct government of the multitude may become dangerous not only because the multitude shares the faults and follies of ordinary human nature, but also because it is intellectually incompetent for the delicate business of conducting the daily work of government, i.e., of choosing and carrying out with vigour and promptitude the requisite executive means. The people though we think of a great entity when we use the word, means nothing more than so many millions of individual men. There is a sense in which it is true that the people are wiser than the wisest man. But what is true of their ultimate judgment after the lapse of time sufficient for full discussion, is not equally true of decisions that have to be promptly taken.

What are the consequences which we may expect to follow from these characteristics of democracy and these conditions under which it is forced to work?

Firstly, a certain commonness of mind and tone, a want of dignity and elevation in and about the conduct of public affairs, an insensibility to the nobler aspects and finer responsibilities of national life.

Secondly, a certain apathy among the luxurious classes and fastidious minds, who find themselves of no more account than the ordinary voter, and are disgusted by the superficial vulgarities of public life.

Thirdly, a want of knowledge, tact, and judgment in the details of legislation, as well as in administration, with an inadequate recognition of the difficulty of these kinds of work, and of the worth of special experience and skill in dealing with them. Because it is incompetent, the multitude will not feel its incompetence, and will not seek or defer to the counsels of those who possess the requisite capacity.

Fourthly, laxity in the management of public business. The persons entrusted with such business being only average men, thinking themselves and thought of by others as average men, with a deficient sense of their high responsibilities, may succumb to the temptations which the control of legislation and the public funds present, in cases where persons of a more enlarged view and with more of a social reputation to support would remain incorruptible. To repress such derelictions of duty is every citizen's duty, but for that reason it is in large communities apt to be neglected. Thus the very causes which implant the mischief favour its growth.

The above-mentioned tendencies are all more or less observable in the United States. As each of them has been described already in its proper place, a summary reference may here be sufficient to indicate their relation to the democratic form of government and to the immanent spirit or theory which lies behind that form.

The tone of public life is lower than one expects to find it in so great a nation. Just as we assume that an individual man will at any supreme moment in his own life rise to a higher level than that on which he usually moves, so we look to find those who conduct the affairs of a great state inspired by a sense of the magnitude of the interests entrusted to them. Their horizon ought to be expanded, their feeling of duty quickened, their dignity of attitude enhanced. Human nature with all its weaknesses does show itself capable of being thus roused on its imaginative side; and in Europe, where the traditions of aristocracy survive, everybody condemns as mean or unworthy acts done or language held by a great official which would pass unnoticed in a private citizen. It is the principle of *noblesse oblige* with the sense of duty and trust substituted for that of mere hereditary rank.

Such a sentiment is comparatively weak in America. A cabinet minister, or senator, or governor of a state, sometimes even a president, hardly feels himself more bound by it than the director of a railway company or the mayor of a town does in Europe. In order to avoid the assumption of being individually wiser or better than his fellow citizens, he has been apt to act and speak as though he were still simply one of them, and so far from magnifying his office and making it honourable, seems anxious to show that he is the mere creature of the popular vote, so filled by the sense that it is the people and not he who governs as to fear that he should be deemed to have forgotten his personal insignificance. There is in the United States abundance of patriotism, that is to say, of a passion for the greatness and happiness of the Republic, and a readiness to make sacrifices for it. The history of the Civil War showed that this passion is at least as strong as in England or France. There is no want of an appreciation of the collective majesty of the nation, for this is the theme of incessant speeches, nor even of the past and future glories of each particular state in the Union. But these sentiments do not bear their appropriate fruit in raising the conception of public office, of its worth and its dignity. The newspapers assume public men to be selfish and cynical. Disinterested virtue is not looked for, is perhaps turned into ridicule where it exists. The hard commercial spirit which pervades the meetings of a joint-stock company is the spirit in which most politicians speak, and are not blamed for speaking, of public business. Something, especially in the case of newspapers, must be allowed for the humorous tendencies of the American mind, which likes to put forward the absurd and even vulgar side of things for the sake of getting fun out of them. But after making such allowances, the fact remains that, although no people is more emotional, and even in a sense more poetical, in no country is the ideal side of public life, what one may venture to call the heroic element in a public career, so ignored by the mass and repudiated by the leaders. This has affected not only the elevation but the independence and courage of public men; and the country has suffered from the want of what we call distinction in its conspicuous figures.[1]

I have discussed in a previous chapter the difficulties which surround the rule of public opinion where it allows little discretion to its agents, relying upon its own competence to supervise administration and secure the legislation which a progressive country needs. The American masses have been obliged, both by democratic theory and by the structure of their government, to proceed upon the assumption of their own competence. They have succeeded better than could have been expected. No people except the choicest children of England, long trained by the practice of local self-government at home and in the colonies before their revolt, could have succeeded half so well. Nevertheless the masses of the United States as one finds them today show what are the limitations of the average man. They can deal with broad and simple issues, especially with issues into which a moral element enters. They spoke out with a clear strong voice upon slavery, when at last it had become plain that slavery must either spread or vanish, and threw themselves with enthusiasm into the struggle for the Union. Their instinctive dislike for foreign complications as well as for acquisitions of new territory have from time to time checked unwise attempts to incur needless responsibilities. Their sense of national and commercial honour has defeated more than one mischievous scheme for tampering with the public debt. But when a question of intricacy presents itself, requiring either keen foresight, exact reasoning, or wide knowledge, they are at fault. Questions relating to currency and coinage, free trade and protection, improvements in the machinery of constitutions or of municipal governments, the control by law of corporations and still more of trusts, the method of securing purity of elections, the reform of criminal procedure in the state courts, these are problems which long baffled, and some of which seem still to baffle them, just as the Free Soil question did before the war or the reconstruction of the revolted Southern states for a long time after it. In

---

[1] There are signs that the view here presented is becoming less true than it was when this paragraph was first written.

those two instances a solution came about, but in the former it was no so much effected by the policy of the people or their statesmen as forced on them by events, in the latter it has left serious evils behind.

Is this a defect incidental to all popular governments, or is there anything in the American system specially calculated to produce it?

A state must of course take the people as it finds them, with such elements of ignorance and passion as exist in masses of men everywhere. Nevertheless, a representative or parliamentary system provides the means of mitigating the evils to be feared from ignorance or haste, for it vests the actual conduct of affairs in a body of specially chosen and presumably specially qualified men, who may themselves entrust such of their functions as need peculiar knowledge or skill to a smaller governing body or bodies selected in respect of their more eminent fitness. By this method the defects of democracy are remedied, while its strength is retained. The masses give their impulse to the representatives: the representatives, directed by the people to secure certain ends, bring their skill and experience to bear on the choice and application of the best means. The Americans, however, have not so constructed or composed their representative bodies as to secure a large measure of these benefits. The legislatures are disjoined from the administrative offices. The members of legislatures are not chosen for their ability or experience, but are, two-thirds of them little above the average citizen, being in many places so chosen as to represent rather the local machine than the people. They are not much respected or trusted, and finding no exceptional virtue expected from them, they behave as ordinary men do when subjected to temptation. The separation of the executive from the legislature is a part of the constitutional arrangements of the country, and has no doubt some advantages. The character of the legislatures is due to a mistaken view of human equality and an exaggerated devotion to popular sovereignty. It is a result of democratic theory pushed to extremes, but is not necessarily incident to a democratic government. The government of England, for instance, has now become substantially a democracy, but there is no reason why it should imitate America in either of the points just mentioned; nor does democratic France, apt enough to make a bold use of theory, seem to have pushed theory to excess in these particular directions. I do not, however, deny that a democratic system makes the people self-confident, and that self-confidence may easily pass into a jealousy of delegated power, an undervaluing of skill and knowledge, a belief that any citizen is good enough for any political work. This is perhaps more likely to happen with a people who have really reached a high level of political competence; and so one may say that the American democracy is not better just because it is so good. Were it less educated, less shrewd, less actively interested in public affairs, less independent in spirit, it might be more disposed, like the masses in Europe, to look up to the classes which have hitherto done the work of government. So perhaps the excellence of rural local self-government has lowered the conception of national government. The ordinary American farmer or shopkeeper or artisan bears a part in the local government of his township or village, or county, or small municipality. He is quite competent to discuss the questions that arise there. He knows his fellow citizens, and can, if he takes the trouble, select the fittest of them for local office. No high standard of fitness is needed, for the work of local administration can be adequately despatched by any sensible man of business habits. Taking his ideas from this local government, he images Congress to himself as nothing more than a larger town council or board of county commissioners, the president and his cabinet as a sort of bigger mayor and city treasurer and education superintendent; he is therefore content to choose for high federal posts such persons as he would elect for these local offices. They are such as he is himself; and it would seem to him a disparagement of his own civic worth were he to deem his neighbours, honest, hard-working, keen-witted men, unfit for any places in the service of the Republic.

A European critic may remark that this way of presenting the case ignores the evils and losses which defective government involves. "If," he will say, "the mass of mankind possesses neither the knowledge nor the leisure nor the skill to determine the legislation and policy of a great state, will not the vigour of the commonwealth decline and its resources be squandered? Will not a nation ruled by its average men in reliance on their own average wisdom be overtaken in the race of prosperity or overpowered in a warlike struggle by a nation of equal resources which is guided by its most capable minds?" The answer to this criticism is that America has hitherto been able to afford to squander her resources, and that no other state threatens her. With her wealth and in her position she can with impunity commit errors which might be fatal to the nations of Western Europe.

The comparative indifference to political life of the educated and wealthy classes which is so much preached at by American reformers and dwelt on by European critics is partly due to this attitude of the multitude. These classes find no smooth and easy path lying before them. Since the masses do not look to them for guidance, they do not come forward to give it. If they wish for office they must struggle for it, avoiding the least appearance of presuming on their social position. I think, however, that the abstention of the upper class is largely ascribable to causes, set forth in a previous chapter, that have little to do with democracy, and while believing that the United States have suffered from this abstention, do not regard it as an inseparable incident of their government. Accidental causes, such as the Spoils System, which is a comparatively recent distemper, already partially eliminated, have largely contributed to it.

The Spoils System reminds us of the machine and the whole organization of rings and bosses. This ugliest feature in the current politics of the country could not have grown up save under the rule of the multitude; and some of the arrangements which have aided its growth, such as the number and frequency of elections, have been dictated by what may be called the narrow doctrinairism of an irreflective democratic theory. It is not, however, necessarily incident to popular government, but is in America due to peculiar conditions which might be removed without rendering the government less truly popular. The city masses may improve if immigration declines; offices may cease to be the reward of party victory; the better citizens may throw themselves more actively into political work.

The many forms in which wealth displays its power point to a source of evil more deep-seated than the last, and one which, though common to all governments, is especially dangerous in a democracy. For democracy, in relying on the average citizen, relies on two things, the personal interest which he has in good government and the public virtue which makes him desire it for the sake of the community. Wealth, skilfully used, can overcome the former motive, because the share of the average man in the state is a small one, less than the gain by which wealth may tempt him. As for virtue, the average man's standard depends on the standard maintained by the public opinion of other average men. Now the sight of wealth frequently prevailing over the sense of duty, with no punishment following, lowers this standard, and leads opinion to accept as inevitable what it knows to be harmful, till only some specially audacious offender stirs the public wrath. Under arbitrary governments one expects a low level of honour in officials, because they are not responsible to the people, and in the people, because they have no power. One looks for renovation to freedom, and struggles for freedom accordingly. If similar evils appear under a government which is already free, the remedy is less obvious and the prospect darker.

Such corruption as exists in the United States will not, however, be ascribed to its democratic government by anyone who remembers that corruption was rife in the English Parliament in the days of Walpole, in English constituencies very much later, and now prevails not only in an almost absolutist state like Russia but also (less widely) in some other European monarchies. There are diseases which attack the body politic, like the natural body, at certain stages of growth, but disappear when a nation has passed into another stage, or when sedulous experimentation has discovered the appropriate remedy. The corruption of Parliament in Sir Robert Walpole's days characterized a period of transition when power had passed to the House of Commons, but the control of the people over the House had not yet been fully established, and when, through a variety of moral causes, the tone of the nation was comparatively low. The corruption of the electorate in English boroughs appeared when a seat had become an object of desire to rich men, while yet the interest of the voters in public affairs was so feeble that they were willing to sell their votes, and their number often so small that each vote fetched a high price. The growth of intelligence and independence among the people, as well as the introduction of severe penalties for bribery, and the extinction of small constituencies, have now almost extinguished electoral corruption. Similar results may be expected in American constituencies from the better ballot and election laws now being enacted.

It is not, however, only in the way of bribery at popular elections that the influence of wealth is felt. In some places it taints the election of federal senators by state legislatures. In others it induces officials who ought to guard the purity of the ballot box to tamper with returns. It is always trying to procure legislation in the interests of commercial undertakings. It supplies the funds for maintaining party organizations and defraying the enormous costs of electoral campaigns, and demands in return sometimes a high administrative post, sometimes a foreign mission, sometimes favours for a railroad, sometimes a clause in a tariff bill, sometimes a lucrative contract. Titles and ribands it cannot, as in Europe, demand, for these the country happily knows not; yet these would be perhaps less harmful than the recompenses it now obtains. One thing alone it can scarcely ever buy— impunity for detected guilt. The two protections which the people retain are criminal justice, and the power, when an election comes, of inflicting condign chastisement not only on the men over whose virtue wealth has prevailed, but even over the party in state, or nation, which they have compromised. Thus the money power is held at bay, and though cities have suffered terribly, and national interests seriously, the general tone of public honour seems to be rather rising than falling. It would, I think rise faster but for the peculiar facilities which the last few years have revealed for the action of great corporations, wielding enormous pecuniary resources, but keeping in the background the personality of those who direct these resources for their own behoof.

Of the faults summarized in this chapter, other than the influence of wealth, those which might seem to go deepest, because they have least to do with the particular consitutional arrangements of the country, and are most directly the offspring of its temper and habits, are the want of dignity in public life, the prominence of inferior men, and the absence of distinguished figures. The people are good, but not good enough to be able to dispense with efficient service by capable representatives and officials, wise guidance by strong and enlightened leaders. There is too little of good serving and good leading.

If it were clear that these are the fruits of liberty and equality, the prospects of the world would be darker than we have been wont to think them. They are, however, the fruits not of liberty and equality, but of an optimism which has underrated the inherent difficulties of politics and failings of human nature, of a theory which has confused equality of civil rights and duties with equality of capacity, and of a thoughtlessness which has forgotten that the problems of the world and the dangers which beset society are always putting on new faces and appearing in new directions. The Americans started their Republic with a determination to prevent abuses of power such as they had suffered from the British Crown. Freedom seemed the one thing necessary; and freedom was thought to consist in cutting down the powers of legislatures and officials. Freedom was the national boast during the years that followed down till the Civil War; and in the delight of proclaiming themselves superior in this regard to the rest of the world they omitted to provide themselves with the other requisites for good government, and forgot that power may be abused in other ways than by monarchic tyranny or legislative usurpation. They continued to beat the drum along the old ramparts erected in 1776 and 1789 against George III, or those who might try to imitate him, when the enemy had moved quite away from that side of the position, and was beginning to threaten their rear. No maxim was more popular among them than that which declares eternal vigilance to be the price of freedom. Unfortunately their vigilance took account only of the old dangers, and did not note the development of new ones, as if the captain of a man-of-war were to think only of his guns and armour plating, and neglect to protect himself against torpedoes. Thus abuses were suffered to grow up, which seemed trivial in the midst of so general a prosperity; and good citizens who were occupied in other and more engrossing ways, allowed politics to fall into the hands of mean men.

The efforts which these citizens are now making to recover the control of public business would have encountered fewer obstacles had they been made sooner. But the obstacles will be overcome. No one, I think, who has studied either the history of the American people, or their present mind and habits, will conclude that there is among them any jealousy of merit, any positive aversion to culture or knowledge. Neither the political arrangements nor the social and economical conditions of the country tend at this moment to draw its best intellects and loftiest characters into public life. But it is not the democratic temper of the people that stands in the way.

The commonest of the old charges against democracy was that it passed into ochlocracy. I have sought to show that this has not happened, and is not likely to happen in America. The features of mob rule do not appear in her system, whose most characteristic faults are the existence of a class of persons using government as a means of private gain and the menacing power of wealth. Plutocracy, which the ancients contrasted with democracy, has shown in America an inauspicious affinity for certain professedly democratic institutions.

Perhaps no form of government needs great leaders so much as democracy. The fatalistic habit of mind perceptible among the Americans needs to be corrected by the spectacle of courage and independence taking their own path, and not looking to see whither the mass are moving. Those whose material prosperity tends to lap them in self-complacency and dull the edge of aspiration, need to be thrilled by the emotions which great men can excite, stimulated by the ideals they present, stirred to a loftier sense of what national life may attain. In some countries men of brilliant gifts may be dangerous to freedom; but the ambition of American statesmen has been schooled to flow in constitutional channels, and the Republic is strong enough to stand any strain to which the rise of heroes may expose her.

The Strength of American Democracy

Those merits of American government which belong to its federal Constitution have been already discussed:[1] we have now to consider such as flow from the rule of public opinion, from the temper, habits, and ideas of the people.

I. The first is that of stability. As one test of a human body's soundness is its capacity for reaching a great age, so it is high praise for a political system that it has stood no more changed than any institution must change in a changing world, and that it now gives every promise of durability. The people are profoundly attached to the form which their national life has taken. The federal Constitution is, to their eyes, an almost sacred thing, an Ark of the Covenant, whereon no man may lay rash hands. All over Europe one hears schemes of radical change freely discussed. There is still a monarchical party in France, a republican party in Italy and Spain, a social democratic party everywhere, not to speak of sporadic anarchist groups. Even in England, it is impossible to feel confident that any one of the existing institutions of the country will be standing fifty years hence. But in the United States the discussion of political problems busies itself with details, so far as the native Americans are concerned, and has assumed that the main lines must remain as they are.[2] This conservative spirit, jealously watchful even in small matters, sometimes prevents reforms, but it assures to the people an easy mind, and a trust in their future which they feel to be not only a present satisfaction but a reservoir of strength.

The best proof of the well-braced solidity of the system is that it survived the Civil War, changed only in a few points which have not greatly affected

---

[1] See Chaps. 27–30 in Vol. I.

[2] This attitude is however less general now than it was in 1880.

the balance of national and state powers. Another must have struck every European traveller who questions American publicists about the institutions of their country. When I first travelled in the United States, I used to ask thoughtful men, superior to the prejudices of custom, whether they did not think the states' system defective in such and such points, whether the legislative authority of Congress might not profitably be extended, whether the suffrage ought not to be restricted as regards Negroes or immigrants, and so forth. Whether assenting or dissenting, the persons questioned invariably treated such matters as purely speculative, saying that the present arrangements were far too deeply rooted for their alteration to come within the horizon of practical politics. So when a serious trouble arises, a trouble which in Europe would threaten revolution, the people face it quietly, and assume that a tolerable solution will be found. At the disputed election of 1876, when each of the two great parties, heated with conflict, claimed that its candidate had been chosen president, and the Constitution supplied no way out of the difficulty, public tranquillity was scarcely disturbed, and the public funds fell but little. A method was invented of settling the question which both sides acquiesced in, and although the decision was a boundless disappointment to the party which had cast the majority of the popular vote, that party quietly submitted to lose those spoils of office whereon its eyes had been feasting.

II. Feeling the law to be its own work, the people is disposed to obey the law. In a preceding chapter I have examined instances of the disregard of the law, and the supersession of its tardy methods by the action of the crowd. Such instances, serious as they are, do not disentitle the nation as a whole to the credit of law-abiding habits. It is the best result that can be ascribed to the direct participation of the people in their government that they have the love of the maker for his work, that every citizen looks upon a statute as a regulation made by himself for his own guidance no less than for that of others, every official as a person he has himself chosen, and whom it is therefore his interest, with no disparagement to his personal independence, to obey. Plato thought that those who felt their own sovereignty would be impatient of all control; nor is it to be denied that the principle of equality may result in lowering the status and dignity of a magistrate. But as regards law and order the gain much exceeds the loss, for everyone feels that there is no appeal from the law, behind which there stands the force of the nation. Such a temper can exist and bear these fruits only where minorities, however large, have learned to submit patiently to majorities, however small. But that is the one lesson which the American government through every grade and in every department daily teaches, and which it has woven into the texture of every citizen's mind. The habit of living under a rigid constitution superior to ordinary statues—indeed two rigid constitutions, since the state constitution is a fundamental law within its own sphere no less than is the federal—intensifies this legality of view, since it may turn all sorts of questions which have not been determined by a direct vote of the people into questions of legal construction. It even accustoms people to submit to see their direct vote given in the enactment of a state constitution nullified by the decision of a court holding that the federal Constitution has been contravened. Every page of American history illustrates the wholesome results. The events of the last few years present an instance of the constraint which the people put on themselves in order to respect every form of law. The Mormons, a community not exceeding 140,000 persons, persistently defied all the efforts of Congress to root out polygamy, a practice eminently repulsive to American notions. If they had inhabited a state, Congress could not have interfered at all, but as Utah was then only a Territory, Congress had not only a power of legislating for it which overrides Territorial ordinances passed by the local legislature, but the right to apply military force independent of local authorities. Thus the Mormons were really at the mercy of the federal government, had it chosen to employ violent methods. But by entrenching themselves behind the letter of the Constitution, they continued for many years to maintain their "peculiar institution" by evading the statues passed against it and challenging a proof which under the common law rules of evidence it has been usually found impossible to give. Declaimers hounded on Congress to take arbitrary means for the suppression of the practice, but Congress and the executive submitted to be outwitted rather than depart from the accustomed principles of administration, and succeeded at last only by a statute whose searching but strictly constitutional provisions the recalcitrants failed to evade. The same spirit of legality shows itself in misgoverned cities. Even where it is notorious that officials have been chosen by the grossest fraud and that they are robbing the city, the body of the people, however indignant, recognize the authority and go on paying the taxes which a ring levies, because strict legal proof of the frauds and robberies is not forthcoming. Wrongdoing supplies a field for the display of virtue.

III. There is a broad simplicity about the political ideas of the people, and a courageous consistency in carrying them out in practice. When they have accepted a principle, they do not shrink from applying it "right through," however disagreeable in particular cases some of the results may be. I am far from meaning that they are logical in the French sense of the word. They have little taste either for assuming abstract propositions or for syllogistically deducing practical conclusions therefrom. But when they have adopted a general maxim of policy or rule of action they show more faith in it than the English for instance would do; they adhere to it where the English would make exceptions; they prefer certainty and uniformity to the advantages which might occasionally be gained by deviation.[3] If this tendency is partly the result of obedience to a rigid constitution, it is no less due to the democratic dislike of exceptions and complexities, which the multitude finds not only difficult of comprehension but disquieting to the individual who may not know how they will affect him. Take for instance the boundless freedom of the press. There are abuses obviously incident to such freedom, and these abuses have not failed to appear. But the Americans deliberately hold that in view of the benefits which such freedom on the whole promises, abuses must be borne with and left to the sentiment of the people and the private law of libel to deal with. When the Ku Klux outrages disgraced several of the Southern states after the military occupation of those states had ceased, there was much to be said for sending back the troops to protect the Negroes and Northern immigrants. But the general judgment that things ought to be allowed to take their natural course prevailed; and the result justified this policy, for the outrages after a while died out, when ordinary self-government had been restored. When recently a gigantic organization of unions of working men, purporting to unite the whole of American labour, attempted to enforce its sentences against particular firms or corporations by a boycott in which all labourers were urged to join, there was displeasure, but no panic, no call for violent remedies. The prevailing faith in liberty and in the good sense of the mass was unshaken; and the result is already justifying this tranquil faith. Such a tendency is not an unmixed blessing, for it sometimes allows evils to go too long unchecked. But in giving equability to the system of government it gives steadiness and strength. It teaches the people patience, accustoming them to expect relief only by constitutional means. It confirms their faith in their institutions, as friends value one another more when their friendship has stood the test of a journey full of hardships.

---

[3] What has been said (Chapters 44 and 45) of special and local legislation by the state legislatures may seem to be an exception to this rule. Such legislation, however, is usually procured in the dark and by questionable means.

Looking both to the national and to the state governments, it may be said that, with a few exceptions, no people has shown a greater regard for public obligations, and that no people has

IV. American government, relying very little on officials, has the merit of arming them with little power of arbitrary interference. The reader who has followed the description of federal authorities, state authorities, county and city or township authorities, may think there is a great deal of administration; but the reason why these descriptions are necessarily so minute is because the powers of each authority are so carefully and closely restricted. It is natural to fancy that a government of the people and by the people will be led to undertake many and various functions for the people, and in the confidence of its strength will constitute itself a general philanthropic agency for their social and economic benefit. Of late years a current has begun to run in this direction.[4] But the paternalism of America differs from that of Europe in acting not so much through officials as through the law. That is to say, when it prescribes to the citizen a particular course of action it relies upon the ordinary legal sanctions, instead of investing the administrative officers with inquisitorial duties or powers that might prove oppressive, and when it devolves active functions upon officials, they are functions serving to aid the individual and the community rather than to interfere with or supersede the action of private enterprise. Having dwelt on the evils which may flow from the undue application of the doctrine of direct popular sovereignty, I must remind the European reader that it is only fair to place to the credit of that doctrine and the arrangements it has dictated, the intelligence which the average native American shows in his political judgments, the strong sense he entertains of the duty of giving a vote, the spirit of alertness and enterprise, which has made him self-helpful above all other men.

V. There are no struggles between privileged and unprivileged orders, not even that perpetual strife of rich and poor which is the oldest disease of civilized states. One must not pronounce broadly that there are no classes, for in parts of the country social distinctions have begun to grow up. But for political purposes classes scarcely exist. No one of the questions which now agitate the nation is a question between rich and poor. Instead of suspicion, jealousy, and arrogance embittering the relations of classes, good feeling and kindliness reign. Everything that government, as the Americans have hitherto understood the term, can give them, the poorer classes have already, political power, equal civil rights, a career open to all citizens alike, not to speak of that gratuitous higher as well as elementary education

---

more prudently and honourably refrained from legislation bearing hardly upon the rich, or indeed upon any class whatever.

[4] See Chapter 98.

which on their own economic principles the United States might have abstained from giving, but which political reasons have led them to provide with so unstinting a hand. Hence the poorer have had little to fight for, no grounds for disliking the well-to-do, no complaints to make against them. The agitation of the last few years has been directed, not against the richer classes generally, but against incorporated companies and a few wealthy capitalists, who are deemed to have abused the powers which the privilege of incorporation conferred upon them, or employed their wealth to procure legislation unfair to the public. Where violent language has been used like that with which France and Germany are familiar, it has been used, not by native Americans, but by newcomers, who bring their Old World passions with them. Property is safe, because those who hold it are far more numerous than those who do not: the usual motives for revolution vanish; universal suffrage, even when vested in ignorant newcomers, can do comparatively little harm, because the masses have obtained everything which they could hope to attain except by a general pillage. And the native Americans, though the same cannot be said of some of the recent immigrants, are shrewd enough to see that the poor would suffer from such pillage no less than the rich.

When I revised in 1894 the preceding part of this chapter, I left these words, which were written in 1888, to stand as they were. I leave them still in 1910, because they seem still to express the view which the most judicious Americans themselves then took and take now of their country. Looking at the labour troubles which have more than once occurred since 1888, including the great railroad strike riots of July 1894, that view may seem too roseate. But it must be remembered that strike riots are largely due to the passion of recent immigrants, whom American institutions have not had time to educate; and it must also be noted that the opinion of the native Americans, with little distinction of class, has usually approved the action, however, bold, of the executive, federal or state, whenever it puts forth all its legal powers to repress disorder. It is not wonderful that over the immense area of the country the public should be now and then disturbed, and that the force to preserve it should sometimes be wanting. But things, so far from getting worse, seem rather to be mending.

A European censor may make two reflections on the statements of this part of the case. He will observe that, after all, it is no more than saying that when you have got to the bottom you can fall no farther. And he will ask whether, if property is safe and contentment reigns, these advantages are not due to the economical conditions of a new and resourceful country, with an abundance of unoccupied land and mineral wealth, rather than to the democratic structure of the government. The answer to the first objection is, that the descent towards equality and democracy has involved no injury to the richer or better educated classes; to the second, that although much must doubtless be ascribed to the bounty of nature, her favours have been so used by the people as to bring about a prosperity, a general diffusion of property, an abundance of freedom, of equality, and of good feeling which furnish the best security against the recurrence in America of chronic Old World evils, even when her economic state shall have become less auspicious than it now is. Wealthy and powerful such a country must have been under any form of government, but the speed with which she has advanced, and the employment of the sources of wealth to diffuse comfort among millions of families, may be placed to the credit of stimulative freedom. Wholesome habits have been established among the people whose value will be found when the times of pressure approach, and though the troubles that have arisen between labour and capital may not soon pass away, the sense of human equality, the absence of offensive privileges distinguishing class from class, will make those troubles less severe than in Europe, where they are complicated by the recollection of old wrongs, by arrogance on the one side and envy on the other.

Some American panegyrists of democracy have weakened their own case by claiming for a form of government all the triumphs which modern science has wrought in a land of unequalled natural resources. An active European race would probably have made America rich and prosperous under any government. But the volume and the character of the prosperity attained may be in large measure ascribed to the institutions of the country. As Dr. Charles W. Eliot observes in a singularly thoughtful address:

> Sensible and righteous government ought ultimately to make a nation rich; and although this proposition cannot be directly reversed, yet diffused well-being, comfort, and material prosperity establish a fair presumption in favour of the government and the prevailing social conditions under which these blessings have been secured. . . .
>
> The successful establishment and support of religious institutions—churches, seminaries, and religious charities—upon a purely voluntary system, is an unprecedented achievement of the American democracy. In only three generations American democratic society has effected the complete separation of Church and State, a reform which no other people has ever attempted. Yet religious institutions are stinted in the United States; on the contrary, they abound and thrive, and all alike are protected and encouraged, but not supported, by the State. . . . The

maintenance of churches, seminaries, and charities by voluntary contributions and by the administrative labours of volunteers, implies an enormous and incessant expenditure of mental and moral force. It is a force which must ever be renewed from generation to generation; for it is a personal force, constantly expiring, and as constantly to be replaced. Into the maintenance of the voluntary system in religion has gone a good part of the moral energy which three generations have been able to spare from the work of getting a living; but it is worth the sacrifice, and will be accounted in history one of the most remarkable feats of American public spirit and faith in freedom.

A similar exhibition of diffused mental and moral energy has accompanied the establishment and the development of a system of higher instruction in the United States, with no inheritance of monastic endowments, and no gifts from royal or ecclesiastical personages disposing of great resources derived from the State, and with but scanty help from the public purse. Whoever is familiar with the colleges and universities of the United States knows that the creation of these democratic institutions has cost the life-work of thousands of devoted men. At the sacrifice of other aspirations, and under heavy discouragements and disappointments, but with faith and hope, these teachers and trustees have built up institutions, which, however imperfect, have cherished scientific enthusiasm, fostered piety, literature, and art, maintained the standards of honour and public duty, and steadily kept in view the ethical ideals which democracy cherishes. It has been a popular work, to which large numbers of people in successive generations have contributed of their substance or of their labour. The endowment of institutions of education, including libraries and museums, by private persons in the United States is a phenomenon without precedent or parallel, and is a legitimate effect of democratic institutions. Under a tyranny—were it that of a Marcus Aurelius—or an oligarchy— were it as enlightened as that which now rules Germany—such a phenomenon would be simply impossible. Like the voluntary system in religion, the voluntary system in the higher education buttresses democracy; each demands from the community a large outlay of intellectual activity and moral vigour.

VI. The government of the Republic, limited and languid in ordinary times, is capable of developing immense vigour. It can pull itself together at moments of danger, can put forth unexpected efforts, can venture on stretches of authority transcending not only ordinary practice but even ordinary law. This is the result of the unity of the nation. A divided people is a weak people, even if it obeys a monarch; a united people is doubly strong when it is democratic, for then the force of each individual will swells the collective force of the government, encourages it, relieves it from internal embarrassments. Now the American people is united at moments of national concern from two causes. One is that absence of class divisions and jealousies which has been already described. The people are homogeneous: a feeling which stirs them stirs alike rich and poor, farmers and traders, Eastern men and Western men—one may now add, Southern men also. Their patriotism has ceased to be defiant, and is conceived as the duty of promoting the greatness and happiness of their country, a greatness which, as it does not look to war or aggression, does not redound specially, as it might in Europe, to the glory or benefit of the ruling caste or the military profession, but to that of all the citizens. The other source of unity is the tendency in democracies for the sentiment of the majority to tell upon the sentiment of a minority. That faith in the popular voice whereof I have already spoken strengthens every feeling which has once become strong, and makes it rush like a wave over the country, sweeping everything before it. I do not mean that the people become wild with excitement, for beneath their noisy demonstrations they retain their composure and shrewd view of facts. I mean only that the pervading sympathy stirs them to unwonted efforts. The steam is superheated, but the effect is seen only in the greater expansive force which it exerts. Hence a spirited executive can in critical times go forward with a courage and confidence possible only to those who know that they have a whole nation behind them. The people fall into rank at once. With that surprising gift for organization which they possess, they concentrate themselves on the immediate object; they dispense with the ordinary constitutional restrictions; they make personal sacrifices which remind one of the self-devotion of Roman citizens in the earlier and better days of Rome.

Speaking thus, I am thinking chiefly of the spirit evolved by the Civil War both in the North and South. But the sort of strength which a democratic government derives from its direct dependence on the people is seen in many smaller instances. In 1863, when on the making of a draft of men for the war, the Irish mob rose in New York City, excited by the advance of General Robert E. Lee into Pennsylvania, the state governor called out the troops, and by them restored order with a stern vigour which would have done credit to Radetzsky or Cavaignac. More than a thousand rioters were shot down, and public opinion entirely approved the slaughter. Years after the war, when the Orangemen of New York purposed to have a 12th of July procession through the streets, the Irish Catholics threatened to prevent it. The feeling of the native Americans was aroused at once; young men of wealth came back from their mountain and seaside resorts to fill the militia regiments which were called out to guard the procession, and the display of force was so overwhelming that no disturbance followed. These Americans had no sympathy with the childish and mischievous partisanship which leads the Orangemen to perpetuate Old World feuds on New World soil. But processions were legal, and they were resolved that the law should be respected, and the spirit of disorder repressed. They would have been equally ready to protect a Roman Catholic procession.

Given an adequate occasion, executive authority can better venture to take strong measures, and feels more sure of support from the body of the people, than is the case in England. When there is a failure to enforce the law, the fault lies at the door, not of the people, but of timid or time-serving officials who fear to offend some interested section of the voters.

VII. Democracy has not only taught the Americans how to use liberty without abusing it, and how to secure equality; it has also taught them fraternity. That word has gone out of fashion in the Old World, and no wonder, considering what was done in its name in 1793, considering also that it still figures in the programme of assassins. Nevertheless, there is in the United States a sort of kindliness, a sense of human fellowship, a recognition of the duty of mutual help owed by man to man, stronger than anywhere in the Old World, and certainly stronger than in the upper or middle classes of England, France, or Germany. The natural impulse of every citizen in America is to respect every other citizen, and to feel that citizenship constitutes a certain ground of respect. The idea of each man's equal rights is so fully realized that the rich or powerful man feels it no indignity to take his turn among the crowd, and does not expect any deference from the poorest. Whether or no an employer of labour has any stronger sense of his duty to those whom he employs than employers have in Europe, he has certainly a greater sense of responsibility for the use of his wealth. The number of gifts for benevolent and other public purposes, the number of educational, artistic, literary, and scientific foundations, is larger than even in Britain, the wealthiest and most liberal of European countries. Wealth is generally felt to be a trust, and exclusiveness condemned not merely as indicative of selfishness, but as a sort of offence against the public. No one, for instance, thinks of shutting up his pleasure grounds; he seldom even builds a wall round them, but puts up only a low railing, so that the sight of his trees and shrubs is enjoyed by passers-by. That anyone should be permitted either by opinion or by law to seal up many square miles of beautiful mountain country against tourists or artists is to the ordinary American almost incredible. Such things are to him the marks of a land still groaning under feudal tyranny.

It may seem strange to those who know how difficult European states have generally found it to conduct negotiations with the government of the

United States, and who are accustomed to read in European newspapers the defiant utterances which American politicians address from Congress to the effete monarchies of the Old World, to be told that this spirit of fraternity has its influence on international relations also. Nevertheless if we look not at the irresponsible orators, who play to the lower feelings of a section of the people, but at the general sentiment of the whole people, we shall recognize that democracy makes both for peace and for justice as between nations. Despite the admiration for military exploits which the Americans have sometimes shown, no country is at bottom more pervaded by a hatred of war, and a sense that national honour stands rooted in national fair dealing. The nation has been often misrepresented by its statesmen, but although it has sometimes allowed them to say irritating things and advance unreasonable claims, it has seldom permitted them to abuse its enormous strength, as most European nations possessed of similar strength have in time past abused theirs.

The characteristics of the American people which I have passed in review though not all due solely to democratic government, have been strengthened by it, and contribute to its solidity and to the smoothness of its working. As one sometimes sees an individual man who fails in life because the different parts of his nature seem unfitted to each other, so that his action, swayed by contending influences, results in nothing definite or effective, so one sees nations whose political institutions are either in advance of or lag behind their social conditions, so that the unity of the body politic suffers, and the harmony of its movements is disturbed. America is not such a nation. There have, no doubt, been two diverse influences at work on the minds of men. One is the conservative English spirit, brought from home, expressed, and (if one may say so) entrenched in those fastnesses of the federal Constitution, and (to a less degree) of the state constitutions, which reveal their English origin. The other is the devotion to democratic equality and popular sovereignty, due partly to Puritanism, partly to abstract theory, partly to the circumstances of the Revolutionary struggle. But since neither of these two streams of tendency has been able to overcome the other, they have at last become so blent as to form a definite type of political habits, and a self-consistent body of political ideas. Thus it may now be said that the country is made all of a piece. Its institutions have become adapted to its economic and social conditions and are the due expression of its character. The new wine has been poured into new bottles; or to adopt a metaphor more appropriate to the country, the vehicle has been built with a lightness, strength, and elasticity which fit it for the roads it has to traverse.

Note to Edition of 1914

I have allowed this and the two last preceding chapters to stand substantially as they were written in 1888 and revised in 1894, because the picture they present seems to be still true in its general outlines, though one might qualify it in some of the details. However, in every country time brings certain changes, and of those to be noted as having come to pass since 1894, the following seem most noteworthy.

Respect for the law is less generally evident, as has appeared in the frequent disorders caused by labour disputes.

The administration of the criminal law is more conspicuously defective.

There is less faith in representative government, and less reverence for the federal Constitution.

The power of wealth, and especially the power of the great corporations, has begun to decline. It had gone so far as in 1900 to arouse fear and resentment, and has since then been curbed.

The spirit which makes for "good citizenship" is more generally diffused, and the educated class in particular are more disposed to discharge their civic duties with earnestness and perseverance. This phenomenon, full of promise for the future of democratic government, is due partly to that resentment against the undue influence of wealth already mentioned, partly to a growing interest in what are called "social reforms."

A reader who may think that some recent events point to conclusions more or less at variance with those stated in these chapters is requested to take the latter subject with the foregoing qualifications.

How Far American Experience Is Available for Europe

There are two substantial services which the study of history may render to politics. The one is to correct the use, which is generally the abuse, of the deductive or a priori method of reasoning in politics. The other is to save the politician from being misled by superficial historical analogies. He who repudiates the a priori method is apt to fancy himself a practical man, when, running to the other extreme, he argues directly from the phenomena of one age or country to those of another, and finding somewhat similar causes or conditions bids us to expect similar results. His error is as grave as that of the man who relies on abstract reasonings; for he neglects that critical examination of the premises from which every process of reasoning ought to start. The better trained any historical inquirer is, so much the more cautious will he be in the employment of what are called historical arguments in politics. He knows how necessary it is in attempting to draw any conclusion of practical worth for one country from the political experience of another, to allow for the points in which the countries differ, because among these points there are usually some which affect the soundness of the inference, making it doubtful whether that which holds true of the one will hold true of the other. The value of history for students of politics or practical statesmen lies rather in its power of quickening their insight, in its giving them a larger knowledge of the phenomena of man's nature as a political being and of the tendencies that move groups and communities of men, and thus teaching them how to observe the facts that come under their own eyes, and what to expect from the men with whom they have to deal. A thinker duly exercised in historical research will carry his stores of the world's political experience about with him, not as a book of prescriptions or recipes from which he can select one to apply to a given case, but rather as a physician carries a treatise on pathology which instructs him in the general principles to be followed in observing the symptoms and investigating the causes of the maladies that come before him. So, although the character of democratic government in the United States is full of instruction for Europeans, it supplies few conclusions directly bearing on the present politics of any European country, because both the strong and the weak points of the American people are not exactly repeated anywhere in the Old World, not even in such countries as France, Switzerland, and England. The picture given of the phenomena of America in preceding chapters has probably already suggested to the reader the inferences to be drawn from it, and such application as they may have to Europe. I shall therefore be here content with recapitulating in the most concise way the points in which the institutions of the United States and the methods employed in working them seem, if not quite directly, yet most nearly, to touch and throw light upon European problems. America has in some respects anticipated European nations. She is walking before them along a path which they may probably follow. She carries behind her, to adopt a famous simile of Dante's, a lamp whose light helps those who come after her more than it always does herself, because some of the dangers she has passed through may not recur at any other point in her path; whereas they, following in her footsteps, may stumble in the same stony places, or be entangled in the quagmires into which she has slipped.

I. *Manhood Suffrage.* This has been now adopted by so many peoples of Europe that they have the less occasion to study its transatlantic aspects. The wisest Americans, while appreciating the strength which it gives to their government, and conceiving that they could hardly have stopped short of it, hold that their recent experience does not invite imitation by European nations, unless at least Europeans adopt safeguards resembling those they have applied. With those safeguards the abolition of property qualifications has, so far as the native population is concerned, proved successful; but in the hands of the Negroes at the South, or the newly enfranchised immigrants of the larger cities, a vote is, and is now generally admitted to be, a dangerous weapon.

II. *The Civil Service.* To keep minor administrative offices out of politics, to make them tenable for life and obtainable by merit instead of by private patronage, is at present the chief aim of American reformers. They are laboriously striving to bring their civil service up to the German or British level. If there is any lesson they would seek to impress on Europeans, it is the mischief of allowing politics to get into the hands of men who seek to make a living by them, and of suffering public offices to become the reward of party work. Rather, they would say, interdict officeholders from participation in politics; appoint them by competition, however absurd competition may sometimes appear, choose them by lot, like the Athenians and Florentines; only do not let offices be tenable at the pleasure of party chiefs and lie in the uncontrolled patronage of persons who can use them to strengthen their own political position.[1]

III. *The Judiciary.* The same observation applies to judicial posts, and with no less force. The American state bench suffers both from the too prevalent system of popular election and from the scanty remuneration allotted. To procure men of character, learning, and intellectual power, and to keep them independent, ample remuneration must be paid, a life tenure secured, and the appointments placed in responsible hands. There is nothing in the English frame of government which thoughtful Americans so much admire as the maintenance of a high level of integrity and capacity in the judges; and they often express a hope that nothing will be done to lower the position of officials on whose excellence the well-being and commercial credit of a country largely depend.[2]

IV. *Character and Working of Legislatures.*[3] Although the rule of representative chambers has been deemed the most characteristic feature of well-ordered free governments, as contrasted with the impetuous democracies of antiquity which legislated by primary assemblies, it must be confessed that the legislative bodies of the United States have done something to discredit representative government. Whether this result is mainly due, as some think, to the disconnection of the executive from the legislature, or whether it must be traced to deeper sources of weakness, it is not without instruction for those who would in Europe vest in legislatures, and, perhaps, even in one-chambered legislatures, still wider powers of interference with administration than they now possess.

V. *Second Chambers.*[4] The Americans consider the division of every political legislature into two coordinate bodies to be absolutely necessary; and their opinion, in this respect, is the more valuable because several states tried for a time to work with one chamber, and because they are fully sensible of the inconveniences which the frequent collision of two chambers involves. Their view is, doubtless, tinged by the low opinion which they hold of the quality of their legislators. Distrusting these, they desire to place every possible check upon their action. In cities it does not appear that either the two-chambered or the one-chambered system shows any advantage

[1] See Chapter 65.
[2] See Chapters 42 and 102.
[3] See Chapters 14, 19, 41, 44, and 45.
[4] See Chapters 18, 40, and 50.

over the other; but it is now beginning to be seen that city government has altogether been planned too much on political lines, and is conducted too little according to business methods.

VI. *Length of Legislative Terms.*[5] The gain and the loss in having legislatures elected for short terms are sufficiently obvious. To a European, the experience of Congress seems to indicate that the shortness of its term is rather to be avoided than imitated. It is not needed in order to secure the obedience of Congress to the popular will: it increases the cost of politics by making elections more frequent, and it keeps a considerable proportion of the legislators employed in learning a business which they are dismissed from as soon as they have learnt it.

VII. *Indirect Elections.*[6] American experience does not commend this device, which, until the establishment of the present mode of choosing the French Senate, was chiefly known from its employment in the Republic of Venice. The choice of the president by electors, chosen for the purpose, has wholly failed to attain the object its authors desired. The election of senators by state legislatures give no better, and possibly worse, men to the Senate than direct popular election would give.

VIII. *A Rigid Constitution.*[7] Although several European states have now placed themselves under constitutions not alterable by their legislatures in the same way as ordinary statutes are altered, America furnishes in her state governments, as well as in her federal government, by far the most instructive examples of the working of a system under which certain laws are made fundamental, and surrounded not only with a sort of consecration, but with provisions which make change comparatively difficult. There is nothing in their system with whose results, despite some obvious drawbacks, the multitude as well as the wise are so well satisfied; nothing which they more frequently recommend to the consideration of those Europeans who are alarmed at the progress which democracy makes in the Old World.

IX. *Direct Legislation by the People.*[8] In this respect also the example of the several states—for the federal government is not in point—deserves to be well studied by English and French statesmen. The plan, whose merits seem to me in America to outweigh its defects, could hardly work as well in a large country as it does in communities of the size of the American states, and in the new form of initiative it offers an alluringly easy means of effecting radical changes. The method is useful less by its own merits

[5] See Chapters 19 and 40.
[6] See Chapters 5, 10, and 12.
[7] See Chapters 23, 31, 35, and 37.
[8] See Chapter 39.

than by comparison with the faults of the legislatures. The people are as likely to be right in judgment as are those bodies; and they are more honest and more independent, but in countries which have capable and trustworthy legislatures direct legislation might work ill by lowering the dignity and importance of such bodies. It would be an appeal from comparative knowledge to comparative ignorance. This consideration does not apply to its use in local affairs, where it stimulates the activity of the citizen without superseding the administrative body.

X. *Local Self-Government.*[9] Nothing has more contributed to give strength and flexibility to the government of the United States, or to train the masses of the people to work their democratic institutions, than the existence everywhere in the Northern states of self-governing administrative units, such as townships, small enough to enlist the personal interest and be subject to the personal watchfulness and control of the ordinary citizen. Abuses have indeed sprung up in the cities, and in the case of the largest among them, have become formidable, partly because the principle of local control has not been sufficiently adhered to. Nevertheless the system of local government as a whole has been not merely beneficial, but indispensable, and well deserves the study of those who in Europe are alive to the evils of centralization, and perceive that those evils will not necessarily diminish with a further democratization of such countries as Britain, Germany, and Italy. I do not say that in any of the great European states the mass of the rural population is equally competent with the American to work such a system; still it presents a model towards which European institutions ought to tend. Very different is the lesson which the American cities teach. It is a lesson of what to avoid. Nowhere have the conjoint influences of false theory, party cohesion, and the apathy of good citizens, together with a recklessly granted suffrage, rendered municipal government so wasteful, inefficient, and impure.

XI. *The Absence of a Church Establishment.* As the discussion of ecclesiastical matters belongs to a later part of this book,[10] I must be content with observing that in America everybody, to whatever religious communion he belongs, professes satisfaction with the complete separation of church and state. This separation has not tended to make religion less of a force in America as respects either political or social reform, not does it prevent the people from considering Christianity to be the national religion, and their commonwealth an object of the Divine care.

---

[9] See Chapters 48–52.
[10] See Chapters 110 and 111.

XII. *Party Machinery.*[11] The tremendous power of party organization has been described. It enslaves local officials, it increases the tendency to regard members of Congress as mere delegates, it keeps men of independent character out of local and national politics, it puts bad men into place, it perverts the wishes of the people, it has in some places set up a tyranny under the forms of democracy. Yet it is hard to see how free government can go on without parties, and certain that the strenuous rivalry of parties will not dispense with machinery. The moral seems to be the old one that "Eternal vigilance is the price of freedom," that the best citizens must, as the Americans say, "take hold," must by themselves accepting posts in the organization keep it from falling into the hands of professionals, must entrust as few lucrative places as possible to popular election or political patronage, must leave reasonable discretion to their representatives in the national councils, must endeavour to maintain in politics the same standard of honour which guides them in private life. These are moral rather than political precepts, but party organization is one of those things which is good or bad according to the spirit with which it is worked.

XIII. *The Unattractiveness of Politics.*[12] Partly from the influence of party machinery, partly from peculiarities of the federal Constitution, partly from social and economical causes, the American system does not succeed in bringing the best men to the top. Yet in democracy more perhaps than in other governments, seeing it is the most delicate and difficult of governments, it is essential that the best men should come to the top. There is in this fact matter for Europeans to reflect upon, for they have assumed that political success will always attract ambition, and that public life will draw at least enough of the highest ability. America disproves the assumption. Her example does not, however, throw much light on the way to keep politics attractive, for her conditions are dissimilar to those of European countries, where ambition finds less scope for distinction in the field of industrial enterprise, and rank is less disjoined from political eminence.

XIV. *The Power of Wealth.* Plutocracy used to be considered a form of oligarchy, and opposed to democracy. But there is a strong plutocratic element infused into American democracy; and the fact that constitutions ignore differences of property, treating all votes alike, makes it neither less potent nor less mischievous. Of the power of wealth democracies may say, with Dante, Here we find the great enemy.[13] Though it has afflicted all

[11] See Chapters 59–65.
[12] See Chapters 58 and 74.
[13] Quivi trovammo Pluto il gran nemico: *Inf.* VI, 115.

forms of government, it seems specially pernicious in a popular government, because when the disease appeared under despotisms and oligarchies, freedom was deemed the only and sufficient antidote. Experience, however, shows that in democracies it is no less menacing, for the personal interest of the average man in good government—and in a large democracy he feels himself insignificant—is overborne by the inducements which wealth, skilfully employed, can offer him; and when once the average man's standard of public virtue has been lowered by the sight of numerous deflections from virtue in others, great is the difficulty of raising it. In the United States the money power acts by corrupting sometimes the voter, sometimes the juror, sometimes the legislator, sometimes a whole party; for large subscriptions and promises of political support have been known to influence a party to procure or refrain from such legislation as wealth desires or fears. The rich, and especially great corporations, have not only enterprises to promote but dangers to escape from at the hands of unscrupulous demagogues or legislators. But whether their action has this palliation or not, the belief, often well grounded, that they exercise a secret power in their own interests, exasperates other sections of the community, and has been a factor in producing not only unwise legislation directed against them, but also outbreaks of lawless violence.

To these scattered observations, which I have made abrupt in order to avoid being led into repetitions, I need hardly add the general moral which the United States teach, that the masses of the people are wiser, fairer, and more temperate in any matter to which they can be induced to bend their minds than most European philosophers have believed it possible for the masses of the people to be; because this is the moral which the preceding chapters on public opinion have been intended to make clear. But the reader is again to be reminded that while the foregoing points are those in which American experience seems most directly available for European states, he must not expect the problems America has dealt with to reappear in Europe in the same forms. Such facts—to mention two only out of many—as the abundance of land and the absence of menace from other powers show how dissimilar are the conditions under which popular government works in the Eastern and in the Western Hemisphere. Instructive as American experience may be if discreetly used, nothing will be more misleading to one who tries to apply it without allowing for the differences of economic and social environment.

PART VI

SOCIAL INSTITUTIONS

CHAPTER 104

The Bar

Among the organized institutions of a country which, while not directly a part of the government, influence politics as well as society, the bar has in England, Scotland, and France played a part only second to that played by the church. Certainly no English institution is more curiously and distinctively English than this body, with its venerable traditions, its aristocratic sympathies, its strong, though now declining, corporate spirit, its affinity for certain forms of literature, its singular relation, half of dependence, half of condescension, to the solicitors, its friendly control over its official superiors, the judges. To see how such an institution has shaped itself and thriven in a new country is to secure an excellent means of estimating the ideas, conditions, and habits which affect and colour the social system of that country, as well as to examine one of the chief among the secondary forces of public life. It is therefore not merely for the sake of satisfying the curiosity of English lawyers that I propose to sketch some of the salient features of the legal profession as it exists in the United States, and to show how it has developed apart from the restrictions imposed on it in England by ancient custom, and under the unchecked operation of the laws of demand and supply.

When England sent out her colonies, the bar, like most of her other institutions, reappeared upon the new soil, and had gained before the revolution of 1776 a position similar to that it held at home, not owing to any deliberate purpose on the part of those who led and ruled the new communities (for the Puritan settlers at least held lawyers in slight esteem), but because the conditions of a progressive society required its existence. That disposition to simplify and popularize law, to make it less of a mystery and bring it more within the reach of an average citizen, which is strong in modern Europe, is of course still stronger in a colony, and naturally tended in America to lessen the corporate exclusiveness of the legal profession, and do away with the antiquated rules which had governed it in England. On the other hand, the increasing complexity of relations in modern society, and the development of many new arts and departments of applied science, bring into an always clearer light the importance of a division of labour, and, by attaching greater value to special knowledge and skill, tend to limit and define the activity of every profession. In spite, therefore, of the democratic aversion to exclusive organizations, the lawyers in America soon acquired professional habits and a corporate spirit similar to that of their brethren in England; and early last century they had reached a power and social consideration relatively greater than the bar has ever held on the eastern side of the Atlantic.

But the most characteristic peculiarity of the English system disappeared. In the United States, as in some parts of Europe, and most British colonies, there is no distinction between barristers and attorneys. Every lawyer, or "counsel," is permitted to take every kind of business: he may argue a cause in the Supreme Federal Court at Washington, or write six-and-eightpenny letters from a shopkeeper to an obstinate debtor. He may himself conduct all the proceedings in a cause, confer with the client, issue the writ, draw the declaration, get together the evidence, prepare the brief, and conduct the case when it comes on in court. He is employed, not like the English barrister, by another professional man, but by the client himself, who seeks him out and makes his bargain directly with him, just as in England people call in a physician or make their bargain with an architect. In spite, however, of this union of all a lawyer's functions in the same person, considerations of practical convenience have in many places established a division of labour similar to that existing in England. Where two or more lawyers are in partnership, it often happens that one member undertakes the court work and the duties of the advocate, while another or others transact the rest of the business, see the clients, conduct correspondence, hunt up evidence, prepare witnesses for examination, and manage the thousand little things for which a man goes to his attorney. The merits of the plan are obvious. It saves the senior member from drudgery, and from being distracted by petty details; it introduces the juniors to business, and enables them to profit by the experience and knowledge of the mature practitioner; it secures to the client the benefit of a closer attention to details than a leading counsel could be expected to give, while yet the whole of his suit is managed in the same office, and the responsibility is not divided, as in England, between two independent personages. However, the custom of forming legal partnerships is one which prevails much more extensively in some parts of the Union than in others. In Boston and New York, for instance, it is common, and I think in the Western cities; in the towns of Connecticut and in Philadelphia one is told that it is rather the exception. Even apart from the arrangement which distributes the various kinds of business among the members of a firm, there is a certain tendency for work of a different character to fall into the hands of different men. A beginner is of course glad enough to be employed in any way, and takes willingly the smaller jobs; he will conduct a defence in a police court, or manage the recovery of a tradesman's petty debt. I remember having been told by a very eminent counsel that when an old apple-woman applied to his son to have her market licence renewed, which for some reason had been withdrawn, he had insisted on the young man's taking up the case. As he rises, it becomes easier for him to select his business, and when he has attained real eminence he may confine himself entirely to the higher walks, arguing cases and giving opinions, but leaving most of the preparatory work and all the communications with the client to be done by the juniors who are retained along with him. He is, in fact, with the important difference that he is liable for any negligence, very much in the position of an English leader or King's counsel, and his services are sought, not only by the client, but by another counsel, or firm of counsel, who have an important suit in hand, to which they feel themselves unequal. He may however be, and often is, retained directly by the client; and in that case he is allowed to retain a junior to aid him, or to desire the client to do so, naming the man he wishes for, a thing which the etiquette of the English bar is supposed to forbid. In every great city there are several practitioners of this kind, men who only undertake the weightiest business at the largest fees; and even in the minor towns court practice is in the hands of a comparatively small group. In one New England city, for instance, whose population is about 50,000, there are, I was told, some sixty or seventy practising lawyers, of whom not more than ten or twelve ever conduct a case in court, the remainder doing what Englishmen would call attorney's and conveyancer's work.

Whatever disadvantages this system of one undivided legal profession has, it has one conspicuous merit, on which anyone who is accustomed to watch the career of the swarm of young men who annually press into the Temple or Lincoln's Inn full of bright hopes, may be pardoned for dwelling. It affords a far better prospect of speedy employment and an active professional life, than the beginner who is not "strongly backed" can look forward to in England. Private friends can do much more to help a young man, since he gets business direct from the client instead of from a solicitor; he may pick up little bits of work which his prosperous seniors do not care to have, may thereby learn those details of practice of which in England a barrister often remains ignorant, may gain experience and confidence in his own powers, may teach himself how to speak and how to deal with men, may gradually form a connection among those for whom he has managed trifling matters, may commend himself to the good opinion of older lawyers, who will be glad to retain him as their junior when they have a brief to give away. So far he is better off than the young barrister in England. He is also, in another way, more favourably placed than the young English solicitor. He is not taught to rely in cases of legal difficulty upon the opinion of another person. He does not see the path of an honourable ambition, the opportunities of forensic oratory, the access to the judicial bench, irrevocably closed against him, but has the fullest freedom to choose whatever line his talents fit him for. Every English lawyer's experience, as it furnishes him with cases where a man was obliged to remain an attorney who would have shone as a counsel, so also suggests cases of persons who were believed, and with reason believed, by their friends to possess the highest forensic abilities, but literally never had the chance of displaying them, and languished on in obscurity, while others in every way inferior to them became, by mere dint of practice, fitter for ultimate success. Quite otherwise in America. There, according to the universal witness of laymen and lawyers, no man who combines fair talents with reasonable industry fails to earn a competence, and to have, within the first six or seven years of his career, an opportunity of showing whether he has in him the makings of something great. This is not due, as might be supposed, merely to the greater opportunities which everybody has in a new country, and which make America the working man's paradise, for, in the Eastern states at least, the professions are nearly as crowded as they are in England. It is owing to the greater variety of practice which lies open to a young man, and to the fact that his patrons are the general public, and not, as in England, a limited class who have their own friends and connections to push. Certain it is that American lawyers profess themselves unable to understand how it can happen that deserving men remain briefless for the best years of their life, and are at the last obliged to quit the profession in disgust.

A further result of the more free and open character of the profession may be seen in the absence of many of those rules of etiquette which are, in theory at least, observed by the English lawyer. It is not thought undignified, except in the great cities of the Eastern states, for a counsel to advertize himself in the newspapers.[1] He is allowed to make whatever bargain he pleases with his client: he may do work for nothing, or may stipulate for a commission on the result of the suit or a share in whatever the verdict produces—a practice which is open to grave objections, and which in the opinion of more than one eminent American lawyer, has produced a good deal of the mischief which caused it to be seventeen centuries ago prohibited at Rome. However, in some cities the sentiment of the bar seems to be opposed to the practice, and in some states there are rules limiting it. A counsel can, except in New Jersey (a state curiously conservative in some points), bring an action for the recovery of his fees, and, *pari ratione*, can be sued for negligence in the conduct of a cause.

A lawyer can readily gain admission to practice in the federal courts, and may by courtesy practise in the courts of every state. But each state has its own bar, that is to say, there is no general or national organization of the legal profession, the laws regulating which are state laws, differing in each of the forty-eight commonwealths. In no state does there exist any body resembling the English Inns of Court, with the right of admitting to the practice of public advocacy and of exercising a disciplinary jurisdiction; and in few have any professional associations resembling the English Incorporated Law Society obtained statutory recognition. State law generally vests in the courts the duty of admitting persons as attorneys, and of generally excluding them if guilty of any serious offence. But the oversight of the judges is necessarily so lax that in many states and cities voluntary bar associations have been formed with the view of exercising a sort of censorship over the profession. Such associations can blackball bad candidates for admission, and expel offenders against professional honour; and they are said to accomplish some good in this way. More rarely they institute proceedings to have black sheep removed from practice. Being virtually an open profession like stockbroking or engineering, the profession has less of a distinctive character and corporate feeling than the barristers of England or France have, and I think rather less than the solicitors of England have. Neither wig, bands, gown, cap, nor any other professional costume is worn, and this circumstance, trivial as it may seem, no doubt contributes to weaken the sentiment of professional privilege and dignity, and to obscure the distinction between the advocate as an advocate, not deemed to be pledging himself to the truth of any fact or the soundness of any argument, but simply presenting his client's case as it is presented to him.

---

[1] California has passed a statute forbidding counsel to advertise for divorce cases.

In most states the judges impose some sort of examination on persons seeking to be admitted to practice, often delegating the duty of questioning the candidate to two or three counsel named for the purpose. Candidates are sometimes required to have read for a certain period in a lawyer's office, but this condition is easily evaded, and the examination, nowhere strict, is often little better than a form or a farce. Notwithstanding this laxity, the level of legal attainment is in some cities as high or higher than among either the barristers or the solicitors of London. This is due to the extraordinary excellence of many of the law schools. I do not know if there is anything in which America has advanced more beyond the mother country than in the provision she makes for legal education.[2] As far back as 1860, when there was nothing that could be called a scientific school of law in England, the Inns of Court having practically ceased to teach law, and the universities having allowed their two or three old chairs to fall into neglect and provided scarce any new ones, several American universities possessed well-equipped law departments, giving a highly efficient instruction. Even now, when England has bestirred herself to make a more adequate provision for the professional training of both barristers and solicitors, this provision seems insignificant beside that which we find in the United States, where, not to speak of minor institutions, all the leading universities possess law schools, in each of which every branch of Anglo-American law, i.e., common law and equity as modified by federal and state constitutions and statutes, is taught by a strong staff of able men, sometimes including the most eminent lawyers of the state.[3] Here at least the principle of demand and supply works to perfection. No one is obliged to attend these courses in order to obtain admission to practice, and the examinations are generally too lax to require elaborate preparation. But the instruction is found so valuable, so helpful for professional success, that young men throng the lecture halls, willingly spending two or three years in the scientific study of the law which they might have spent in the chambers of a practising lawyer as pupils or as

---

[2] Modern England seems to stand alone in her comparative neglect of the theoretic study of law as a preparation for legal practice. Other countries, from Germany at the one end of the scale of civilization to the Mohammedan East at the other end, exact three, four, five, or even more years spent in this study before the aspirant begins his practical work.

[3] This instruction is in most of the law schools confined to Anglo-American law, omitting theoretic jurisprudence, Roman law (except, of course, in Louisiana, where the Civil Law is the basis of the code), and international law. The latter subjects are, however, now beginning to be more frequently taught, though sometimes placed in the historical curriculum. In some few law schools educational value is attributed to the moot courts in which the students are set to argue cases, a method much in vogue in England two centuries ago.

junior partners. The indirect results of this theoretic study in maintaining a philosophical interest in the law among the higher class of practitioners, and a higher sense of the dignity of their profession, are doubly valuable in that absence of corporate organizations on which I have already commented.[4]

In what may be called habits of legal thought, their way of regarding legal questions, their attitude towards changes in the form or substance of the law, American practitioners, while closely resembling their English brethren, seem on the whole more conservative. Such law reforms as have been effected in England during the last century have mostly come from the profession itself. They have been carried through Parliament by attorneys general or lord chancellors, usually with the tacit approval of the bar and the solicitors. The masses and their leaders have seldom ventured to lay profane fingers on the law, either in despair of understanding it or because they saw nearer and more important work to be done. Hence the profession has in England been seldom roused to oppose projects of change; and its division into two branches, with interests sometimes divergent, weakens its political influence. In the United States, although the legislatures are largely composed of lawyers, many of these have little practice, little knowledge, comparatively little professional feeling. Hence there is usually a latent and sometimes an open hostility between the better kind of lawyers and the impulses of the masses, seeking probably at the instigation of some lawyer of a demagogic turn to carry through legal changes. The defensive attitude which the upper part of the profession is thus led to assume fosters those conservative instincts which a system of case law engenders, and which are further stimulated by the habit of constantly recurring to a fundamental instrument, the federal Constitution. Thus one finds the same dislike to theory, the same attachment to old forms, the same unwillingness to be committed to any broad principle which distinguished the orthodox type of English lawyers in the first half of last century. Prejudices survive on the shores of the Mississippi which Bentham assailed when those shores were inhabited by Indians and beavers; and in Chicago, a place which living men remember as a lonely swamp, special demurrers, replications *de injuria*, and various elaborate formalities of pleading which were swept away by the

---

[4] Some of the best American lawbooks, as for instance that admirable series which has made Justice Story famous, have been produced as lectures given to students. Story was professor at Harvard while judge of the Supreme Court, and used to travel to and from Washington to give his lectures. A few years ago there were several men in large practice who used to teach in the law schools out of public spirit and from their love of the subject, rather than in respect of the comparatively small payment they received.

English Common Law Procedure Acts of 1850 and 1852, flourish and abound to this day.

Is the American lawyer more like an English barrister or an English solicitor? This depends on the position he holds. The leading counsel of a city recall the former class, the average practitioners of the smaller places and rural districts the latter. But as every American lawyer has the right of advocacy in the highest courts, and is accustomed to advise clients himself instead of sending a case for opinion to a counsel of eminence, the level of legal knowledge—that is to say, knowledge of the principles and substance of the law, and not merely of the rules of practice—is somewhat higher than among English solicitors, while the familiarity with details of practice is more certain to be found than among English barristers. Neither an average barrister nor an average solicitor is so likely to have a good working all-round knowledge of the whole field of common law, equity, admiralty law, probate law, patent law, as an average American city practitioner, nor to be so smart and quick in applying his knowledge. On the other hand, it must be admitted that England possesses more men eminent as draftsmen, though perhaps fewer eminent in patent cases, and that much American business, especially in state courts, is done in a way which English critics might call lax and slovenly.

I have already observed that both in Congress and in most of the state legislatures the lawyers outnumber the persons belonging to any one other walk of life. Nevertheless, they have not that hold on politics now which they had in the first and second generations after 1783. Politics have, in falling so completely into the hands of party organizations, become more distinctly a separate profession, and an engrossing profession, which a man occupied with his clients cannot follow. Thus among the leading lawyers, the men who win wealth and honour by advocacy, comparatively few enter a legislative body or become candidates for public office. Their influence is still great when any question arises on which the profession, or the more respectable part of it, stands together. Many bad measures have been defeated in state legislatures by the action of the bar, many bad judicial appointments averted. Their influence strengthens the respect of the people for the Constitution, and is felt by the judges when they are called to deal with constitutional questions. But taking a general survey of the facts of today, as compared with those of the middle of last century, it is clear that the bar counts for less as a guiding and restraining power, tempering the crudity or haste of democracy by its attachment to rule and precedent, than it did then.

A similar decline, due partly to this diminished political authority, may be observed in its social position. In a country where there is no titled class, no landed class, no military class, the chief distinction which popular sentiment can lay hold of as raising one set of persons above another is the character of their occupation, the degree of culture it implies, the extent to which it gives them an honourable prominence. Such distinctions carried great weight in the early days of the Republic, when society was smaller and simpler than it has now become. But of late years not only has the practice of public speaking ceased to be, as it once was, almost their monopoly, not only has the direction of politics slipped in great measure from their hands, but the growth of huge mercantile fortunes and of a financial class has, as in France and England, lowered the relative importance and dignity of the bar. An individual merchant holds perhaps no better place compared with an average individual lawyer than he did forty years ago; but the millionaire is a much more frequent and potent personage than he was then, and outshines everybody in the country. Now and then a brilliant orator or writer achieves fame of a different and higher kind; but in the main it is the glory of successful commerce which in America and Europe now draws wondering eyes. Wealth, it is true, is by no means out of the reach of the leading lawyers; yet still not such wealth as may be and constantly is amassed by contractors, railway men, financial speculators, hotel proprietors, newspaper owners, and retail storekeepers. The incomes of the first counsel in cities like New York are probably as large as those of the great English leaders. I have heard firms mentioned as dividing sums of $300,000 a year, and individual lawyers as earning $200,000 or more. It is, however, only in two or three of the greatest cities that such incomes can be made, and possibly not more than thirty counsel in the whole country make by their profession more than $100,000 a year. Next after wealth, education may be taken to be the element or quality on which social standing in a purely democratic country depends. In this respect the bar ranks high. Most lawyers have had a college training, and are, by the necessity of their employment, persons of some mental cultivation; in the older towns they, with the leading clergy, form the intellectual elite of the place, and maintain worthily the literary traditions of the Roman, French, English, and Scottish bars. But education is so much more diffused than formerly, and cheap literature so much more abundant, that they do not stand so high above the multitude as they once did. It may, however, still be said that the law is the profession which an active youth of intellectual tastes naturally takes to, that a large proportion of the highest talent of the country may be found in its ranks, and that almost all the first statesmen of the present and the last generation have belonged to it, though many soon resigned its practice. It is also one of the links which best serves to bind the United States to England. The interest of the higher class of American lawyers in the English law, bar, and judges, is wonderfully fresh and keen. An English barrister, if properly authenticated, is welcomed as a brother of the art, and finds the law reports of his own country as sedulously read and as acutely criticized as he would in the Temple.[5]

I have left to the last the question which a stranger finds it most difficult to answer. The legal profession has in every country, apart from its relation to politics, very important functions to discharge in connection with the administration of justice. Its members are the confidential advisers of private persons, and the depositaries of their secrets. They have it in their power to promote or to restrain vexatious litigation, to become accomplices in chicane, or to check the abuse of legal rights in cases where morality may require men to abstain from exacting all that the letter of the law allows. They can exercise a powerful influence upon the magistracy by shaming an unjust judge, or by misusing the ascendency which they may happen to possess over a weak judge, or a judge who has something to hope for from them. Does the profession in the United States rise to the height of these functions, and in maintaining its own tone, help to maintain the tone of the community, especially of the mercantile community, which, under the pressure of competition, seldom observes a higher moral standard than that which the law exacts? So far as my limited opportunities for observation enable me to answer this question, I should answer it by saying that the profession, taken as a whole, seems to stand on a level with the profession, also taken as a whole, in England. But I am bound to add that some judicious American observers hold that since the Civil War there has been a certain decadence in the bar of the greater cities. They say that the growth of enormously rich and powerful corporations, willing to pay vast sums for questionable services, has seduced the virtue of some counsel whose eminence makes their example important, and that in a few states the degradation of the bench has led to secret understandings between judges and counsel for the perversion of justice. Strenuous efforts have of late been made by the bar associations to establish codes of legal ethics and etiquette, and much good is expected from their action.

---

[5] American lawyers remark that the English Law Reports have become less useful since the number of decisions upon the construction of statutes has so greatly increased. They complain of the extreme difficulty of keeping abreast of the vast multitude of cases reported in their own country, from the courts of all the states as well as federal courts.

As the question of fusing the two branches of the legal profession into one body has been of late much canvassed in England, a few words may be expected as to the light which American experience throws upon it.

There are two sets of persons in England who complain of the present arrangements—a section of the solicitors, who are debarred from the exercise of advocacy, and therefore from the great prizes of the profession; and a section of the junior bar, whose members, depending entirely on the patronage of the solicitors, find themselves, if they happen to have no private connections among that branch of the profession, unable to get employment, since a code of etiquette forbids them to undertake certain sorts of work, or to do work except on a fixed scale of fees, or to take court work directly from a client, or to form partnerships with other counsel. Attempts have also been made to enlist the general public in favour of a change, by the argument that law would be cheapened by allowing the attorney to argue and carry through the courts a cause which he has prepared for trial.

There are three points of view from which the merits or demerits of a change may be regarded. These are the interests respectively of the profession, of the client, and of the community at large.

As far as the advantage of the individual members of the profession is concerned, the example of the United States seems to show that the balance of advantage is in favour of uniting barristers and attorneys in one body. The attorney would have a wider field, greater opportunities of distinguishing himself, and the legitimate satisfaction of seeing his cause through all its stages. The junior barrister would find it easier to get on, even as an advocate, and, if he discovered that advocacy was not his line, could subside into the perhaps not less profitable or agreeable function of a solicitor. The senior barrister or leader might, however, suffer, for his attention would be more distracted by calls of different kinds.

The gain to the client is still clearer; and even those (very few) American counsel who say that for their own sake they would prefer the English plan, admit that the litigant is more expeditiously and effectively served where he has but one person to look to and deal with throughout. It does not suit him, say the Americans, to be lathered in one shop and shaved in another; he likes to go to his lawyer, tell him the facts, get an off-hand opinion, if the case be a simple one (as it is nine times out of ten), and issue his writ with some confidence; whereas under the English system he might either have to wait till a regular case for the opinion of counsel was drawn, sent to a barrister, and returned, written on, after some days, or else take the risk of bringing an action which turned out to be ill-founded. It may also be believed that a case is, on the whole, better dealt with when it is kept in one office from first to last, and managed by one person, or by partners who are in constant communication. Mistakes and oversights are less likely to occur, since the advocate knows the facts better, and has almost invariably seen and questioned the witnesses before he comes into court. It may indeed be said that an advocate does his work with more ease of conscience, and perhaps more sangfroid, when he knows nothing but his instructions. But American practitioners are all clear that they are able to serve their clients better than they could if the responsibility were divided between the man who prepares the case and the man who argues or addresses the jury. Indeed, I have often heard them say that they could not understand how English counsel, who rarely see the witnesses beforehand, were able to conduct witness causes satisfactorily.

The English plan is more conducive to the despatch of business, because in England the few leading counsel know the judges, and the judges know them, whereas in America, the absence of a small class to whom advocacy is restricted brings into court a number proportionately much larger of lawyers handling causes. Where the counsel and the judges are in constant contact, cases are more promptly dealt with. The counsel knows when he has said enough to the judge. The judge knows how far he can trust the counsel.

If asked whether the community has gained by the disappearance of a distinction between the small body of advocates and the large body of attorneys, I should reply that it has not. Society is interested in the maintenance of a high tone among those who can powerfully influence the administration of justice and the standard of commercial morality. It is easier to maintain such a tone in a small body, which can be kept under a comparatively strict control and cultivate a warm professional feeling than in a large body, many of whose members are practically just as much men of business as lawyers. And it may well be thought that the conscience or honour of a member of either branch of the profession is exposed to less strain where the two branches are kept distinct. The counsel is under less temptation to win his cause by doubtful means, since he is removed from the client by the interposition of the attorney, and therefore less personally identified with the client's success. He probably has not that intimate knowledge of the client's affairs which he must have if he had prepared the whole case, and is therefore less likely to be drawn into speculating, to take an obvious instance, in the shares of a client company, or otherwise playing a double and disloyal game. Similarly it may be thought that the attorney also is less tempted than if he appeared himself in court, and were not obliged, in carrying out the schemes of a fraudulent client, to call in the aid of another practitioner, amenable to a strict professional discipline. Where the advocate is also the attorney, he may be more apt, when he sees the witnesses, to lead them, perhaps unconsciously, to stretch their recollection; and it is harder to check the practice of paying for legal services by a share of the proceeds of the action.

Looking at the question as a whole, I doubt whether the result of a study of the American arrangements is calculated to commend them for imitation, or to induce England to allow her historic bar to be swallowed up and vanish in the more numerous branch of the profession. Those arrangements, however, suggest some useful minor changes in the present English rules. The passage from each branch to the other might be made easier; barristers might be permitted to form open (as they now sometimes do covert) partnerships among themselves; students of both branches might be educated and examined together in the professional law schools as they now are, with admittedly good results, in the universities.

The Bench

So much has already been said regarding the constitution and jurisdiction of the various courts, federal and state, that what remains to be stated regarding the judicial bench need refer only to its personal and social side. What is the social standing of the judges, the average standard of their learning and capacity, their integrity and fidelity in the discharge of functions whose gravity seems to increase with the growth of wealth and the complexity of society?

The English reader who wishes to understand the American judiciary ought to begin by realizing the fact that his conception of a judge is purely English, not applicable to any other country. For some centuries Englishmen have associated the ideas of power, dignity, and intellectual eminence with the judicial office; while a tradition, shorter no doubt, but still of respectable length, has made them regard it as incorruptible. The judges are among the greatest permanent officials of the state. They have earned their place by success, more or less brilliant, but generally considerable, in the struggles of the bar; they are removable by the Crown only upon an address of both houses of Parliament; they enjoy large incomes and great social respect. Some of them sit in the House of Lords; some are members of the Privy Council. When they traverse the country on their circuits, they are received by the High Sheriff of each county with the ceremonious pomp of the Middle Ages, and followed hither and thither by admiring crowds. The criticisms of an outspoken press rarely assail their ability, hardly ever their fairness. Even the bar, which watches them daily, which knows all their ins and outs (to use an American phrase) both before and after their elevation, treats them with more respect than is commonly shown by the clergy to the bishops. Thus the English form their conception of the judge as a personage necessarily and naturally dignified and upright; and, having formed it, they carry it abroad with them like their notions of land tenure and other insular conceptions, and are astonished when they find that it does not hold in other countries. It is a fine and fruitful conception, and one which one might desire to see accepted everywhere, though it has been secured at the cost of compelling litigants to carry to London much business which in other countries would have been dealt with in local courts. But it is peculiar to Britain; the British judge is as abnormal as the British Constitution, and owes his character to a not less curious and complex combination of conditions. In most parts of the Continent the judge, even of the superior courts, does not hold a very high social position. He is not chosen from the ranks of the bar, and has not that community of feeling with it which England has found so valuable. Its leaders outshine him in France; the famous professors of law often exert a greater authority in Germany. His independence, and even purity, have been at times by no means above suspicion. In no part of Europe do his wishes and opinions carry the same weight, or does he command the same deference as in England. The English ought not, therefore, to be surprised at finding him in America different from what they expect, for it is not so much his inferiority there that is exceptional as his excellence in England.

In America, the nine federal judges of the Supreme Court retain much of the dignity which surrounds the English Supreme Court of Judicature. They are almost the only officials who are appointed for life, and their functions are of the utmost importance to the smooth working of the Constitution. Accordingly great public interest is felt in the choice of a judge, and the post is an object of ambition. Though now and then an eminent lawyer may decline it because he is already making by practice five times as much as the salary it carries, still there has been no difficulty in finding first-rate men to fill the court. The minor federal judges are usually persons of ability and experience. They are inadequately paid, but the life tenure makes the place desired and it is usually respected.

Of the state judges it is hard to speak generally, because there are great differences between state and state. In six or seven commonwealths, of which Massachusetts is the best example among Eastern and Michigan among Western states, they stand high—that is to say, the post attracts a prosperous barrister though he will lose in income, or a law professor though he must sacrifice his leisure. But in some states it is otherwise. A place on the bench of the superior courts carries little honour, and commands but slight social consideration. It is lower than that of an English county court judge or stipendiary magistrate, or of a Scotch sheriff-substitute. It raises no presumption that its holder is able or cultivated or trusted by his fellow citizens. He may be all of these, but if so, it is in respect of his personal merits that he will be valued, not for his official position. Often he stands below the leading members of the state or city bar in all these points and does not move in the best society.[1] Hence a leading counsel seldom accepts the post, and men often resign a judgeship, or when their term of office expires do not seek reelection, but return to practice at the bar.[2] Hence, too, a judge is not expected to set an example of conformity to the conventional standards of decorum. No one is surprised to see him in low company, or to hear, in the ruder parts of the South and West, that he took part in a shooting affray. He is as welcome to be "a child of nature and of freedom" as any private citizen.

The European reader may think that these facts not only betoken but tend to perpetuate a low standard of learning and capacity among the state judges, and from this low standard he will go on to conclude that justice must be badly administered, and will ask with surprise why an intelligent and practical people allow this very important part of their public work to be ill discharged. I shrink from making positive statements on so large a matter as the administration of justice over a vast country whose states differ in many respects. But so far as I could ascertain, civil justice is better administered than might be expected from the character which the bench bears in most of the states. In the federal courts and in the superior courts of the six or seven states just mentioned it is equal to the justice dispensed in the superior courts of England, France, and Germany. In the remainder it is inferior, that is to say, civil trials, whether the issue be of law or of fact, more frequently give an unsatisfactory result; the opinions delivered by the judges are wanting in scientific accuracy, and the law becomes loose and uncertain.[3] This inferiority is more or less marked according to the general tone of the state. That it is everywhere less marked than a priori reasonings would have suggested, may be ascribed partly to the way shrewd juries have of rendering substantially just verdicts, partly to the ability of the bar, whose arguments make up for a judge's want of learning, by giving

[1] Years ago a prominent New Yorker said to me, speaking of one of the chief judges of the city, "I don't think him such a bad fellow; he has always been very friendly to me, and would give me a midnight injunction or do anything else for me at a moment's notice. And he's not an ill-natured man. But, of course, he's the last person I should dream of asking to my house."

[2] Most states are full of ex-judges practising at the bar, the title being continued as a matter of courtesy to the person who has formerly enjoyed it, and sometimes even extended to an elderly counsel who has never sat on the bench. For social purposes, once a judge, always a judge.

[3] State constitutions sometimes require the judges of the higher courts to give their decisions in writing and this seems to be the practice everywhere.

him the means of reaching a sound decision, partly to that native acuteness of Americans which enables them to handle any sort of practical work, roughly, perhaps, but well enough for the absolute needs of the case. The injury to the quality of state law is mitigated by the fact that abundance of good law is produced by the federal courts, by the highest courts of the best states, and by the judges of England, whose reported decisions are frequently referred to. Commercial men complain less of the inefficiency than of the delays of state tribunals, while the leading lawyers, whose interest in the scientific character of law makes them severe critics of current legislation, and opponents of these schemes for codifying the common law which have been dangled before the multitude in several states, blame the legislatures more than the judges for such faults as they discover.

Whatever the defects of civil justice, those of criminal justice are much more serious. It is accused of being slow, overtechnical, uncertain, and unduly lenient both to crimes of violence and to commercial frauds. Yet the blame is laid less on the judges than on the weakness of juries,[4] and on the facilities for escape which a cumbrous and highly technical procedure, allowing numerous opportunities for interposing delays and raising points of law, provides for prisoners.[5] Indulgence to prisoners is now as marked as harshness to them was in England before the days of Bentham and Romilly. Legislation is chiefly to blame for this procedure, though stronger men on the bench would more often overrule trivial points of law and expedite convictions.[6]

The European traveller must own his surprise that stronger and more

---

[4] There are places where the purity of juries is not above suspicion. New York has recently created a new office, that of Warden of the Grand Jury. As a distinguished lawyer observed in mentioning this, *Quis custodiet ipsum custoderm.*

[5] Even judges suffer from this misplaced leniency. Here is a case which happened in Kentucky. A decree of foreclosure was pronounced by a respected judge against a defendant of good local family connections. As the judge was walking from the court to the railway station the same afternoon the defendant shot him dead. It was hard to avoid arresting and trying a man guilty of so flagrant an offence, so arrested he was, tried, and convicted; but on an allegation of lunacy being put forward, the court of appeals ordered a new trial; he was acquitted on the ground of insanity, under instructions based on the opinion of an appellate court, and presently allowed to escape into Ohio from the asylum to which he had been consigned. There was, I was told, a good deal of sympathy for him.

[6] The message of President Taft of December 1909, in referring to "the deplorable delays in the administration of civil and criminal law," proceeded as follows: "A change in judicial procedure, with a view to reducing its expense to private litigants in civil cases and facilitating the despatch of business and final decision in both civil and criminal cases, constitutes the greatest need in our American institutions. Much of the lawless violence and cruelty exhibited in lynchings is directly due to the uncertainties and injustice growing out of the delays in trials, judgments and the execution thereof by our courts." See also note 3 to Chapter 100, page 1239.

persistent efforts have not been made long ago to secure the needed improvements in the administration of justice in state courts.

The causes which have lowered the quality of the state judges have been referred to in previous chapters. Shortly stated they are: the smallness of the salaries paid, the limited tenure of office, often for seven years only, and the method of appointment, nominally by popular election, practically by the agency of party wire-pullers. The first two causes have prevented the ablest lawyers, the last often prevents the most honourable men, from seeking the post. All are the result of democratic theory, of the belief in equality and popular sovereignty pushed to extremes. And this theory has aggravated the mischief in withdrawing from the judge, when it has appointed him, those external badges of dignity which, childish as they may appear to the philosopher, have power over the imagination of the mass of mankind, and are not without a useful reflex influence on the person whom they surround, raising his sense of his position, and reminding him of its responsibilities. No American magistrate, except the judges of the Supreme Court when sitting at Washington, and those of the intermediate federal Courts of Appeal, the judges of the New York Court of Appeals at Albany, and those of the Supreme Court of Pennsylvania, wears any robe of office or other distinctive dress, or has any attendant to escort him,[7] or is in any respect treated differently from an ordinary citizen. Popular sentiment tolerates nothing that seems to elevate a man above his fellows, even when his dignity is really the dignity of the people who have put him where he is. I remember in New York under the reign of Boss Tweed to have been taken into one of the courts. An ill-omened looking man, flashily dressed, and rude in demeanour, was sitting behind a table, two men in front were addressing him, the rest of the room was given up to disorder. Had one not been told that he was a judge of the highest court of the city, one might have taken him for a criminal. His jurisdiction was unlimited in amount, and though an appeal lay from him to the Court of Appeals of the state, his power of issuing injunctions put all the property in the district at his mercy. This was what democratic theory had brought New York to. For the change which that state made in 1846 was a perfectly wanton change. No practical object was to be gained by it. There had been an excellent bench, adorned, as it happened, by one of the greatest judges of modern times, the illustrious Chancellor Kent. But the convention of 1846 thought that the power of the

---

[7] Save that in the rural counties of Massachusetts and possibly of some other New England states, the sheriff, as in England, escorts the judges to and from the courthouse.

people was insufficiently recognized while judges were named by the governor and council and held office for life, so theory was obeyed. The convention in its circular address announced, in proposing the election of judges for five years by the voters of the district, that "the happiness of the people of this State will henceforth, under God, be in their own hands." But the quest of a more perfect freedom and equality on which the convention started the people gave them in twenty-five years Judge Barnard instead of Chancellor Kent.

The limited attainments of the bench in many states, and its conspicuous inferiority to the counsel who practise before it are, however, less serious evils than the corruption with which it is often charged. Nothing has done so much to discredit American institutions in Europe as the belief that the fountains of justice are there generally polluted; nor is there any point on which a writer treating of the United States would more desire to be able to set forth incontrovertible facts. Unluckily, this is just what from the nature of the case cannot be done as regards some parts of the country. There is no doubt as to the purity of most states, but as to others it is extremely hard to test the rumours that are current. I give such results as many questions in many districts enable me to reach.

The higher federal judges are above suspicion. I do not know that any member of the Supreme Court or any Circuit judge has been ever accused of corruption; and though the appointments made to district judgeships are sometimes freely criticised, the allegations made against these persons have not been, except in two or three instances, seriously pressed.

The state judges have been and are deemed honest and impartial in most parts of the Union. In a few states, such as Massachusetts, Vermont, Pennsylvania, and Michigan, the bench has within the last or the present generation included men who would do credit to any court in any country. Even in other states an eminent man is occasionally found, as in England there are some County Court judges who are sounder lawyers and abler men than some of the persons whom political favour has of late years raised to the bench of the High Court.

In some states, perhaps six or seven in all, suspicions have at one time or another since the Civil War attached to one or more of the superior judges and in a few other states they are deemed to be, although personally honest, subservient to powerful local influences. Sometimes these suspicions may have been ill-founded.[8] But though I know of very few cases in which

---

[8] An instance told me in the West shows how suspicions may arise. A person living in the capital of the state used his intimacy with the superior judges, most of whom were in the habit of

they have been substantiated, there can be little doubt that some improprieties have been committed. The judge may not have taken a bribe, but he has perverted justice at the instance of some person or persons who either gave him a consideration or exercised an undue influence over him. It would not follow that in such instances the whole bench was tainted; indeed I have never heard of a state in which more than two or three judges were the objects of distrust at the same time.[9]

In one state, viz., New York, in 1869–71, there were flagrant scandals which led to the disappearance of three justices of the superior court who had unquestionably both sold and denied justice. The Tweed Ring, when masters of New York City and engaged in plundering its treasury, found it convenient to have in the seat of justice accomplices who might check inquiry into their misdeeds. This the system of popular elections for very short terms enabled them to do; and men were accordingly placed on the bench whom one might rather have expected to see in the dock—barroom loafers, broken-down Tombs[10] attorneys, needy adventurers whose want of character made them absolutely dependent on their patrons. Being elected for eight years only, these fellows were obliged to purchase reelection by constant subservience to the party managers. They did not regard social censure, for they were already excluded from decent society; impeachment had no terrors for them, since the state legislature, as well as the executive machinery of the city, was in the hands of their masters. It would have been

---

occasionally dining with him, to lead litigants to believe that his influence with the bench would procure for them favourable decisions. Considerable sums were accordingly given him to secure his good word. When the litigant obtained the decision he desired, the money given was retained. When the case went against him, the confidant of the bench was delicately scrupulous in handing it back, saying that as his influence had failed to prevail, he could not possibly think of keeping the money. Everything was done in the most secret and confidential way, and it was not till after the death of this judicious dinner-giver that it was discovered that he had never spoken to the judges about lawsuits at all, and that they had lain under a groundless suspicion of sharing the gains their friend had made.

[9] For instance, there is a Western state in which a year or two ago there was one, but only one, of the superior judges whose integrity was doubted. So little secret was made of the matter, that when a very distinguished English lawyer visited the city, and was taken to see the courts sitting, the newspapers announced the fact next day as follows:

> Lord X. in the city,
> He has seen Judge Y.

A statute of Arizona prescribes a change of venue where an affidavit is made alleging that a judge is biased.

[10] The Tombs is the name of the city prison of New York, round which lawyers of the lowest class hover in the hope of picking up defences.

vain to expect such people, without fear of God or man before their eyes, to resist the temptations which capitalists and powerful companies could offer.

To what precise point of infamy they descended I cannot attempt, among so many discordant stories and rumours, to determine. It is, however, beyond a doubt that they made orders in defiance of the plainest rules of practice; issued, in rum shops, injunctions which they had not even read over; appointed notorious vagabonds receivers of valuable property;[11] turned over important cases to a friend of their own stamp, and gave whatever decision he suggested. There were members of the bar who could obtain from these magistrates whatever order or decree they chose to ask for. A leading lawyer and man of high character said to me in 1870, "When a client brings me a suit which is before —— (naming a judge), I feel myself bound to tell him that though I will take it if he pleases, he had much better give it to So-and-So (naming a lawyer), for we all know that he owns that judge." A system of client robbery had sprung up by which each judge enriched the knot of disreputable lawyers who surrounded him; he referred cases to them, granted them monstrous allowances in the name of costs, gave them receiverships with a large percentage, and so forth; they in turn either at the time sharing the booty with him, or undertaking to do the same for him when he should have descended to the bar and they have climbed to the bench. Nor is there any doubt that criminals who had any claim on their party often managed to elude punishment. The police, it was said, would not arrest such an offender if they could help it; the district attorney would avoid prosecuting; the court officials, if public opinion had forced the attorney to act, would try to pack the jury; the judge, if the jury seemed honest, would do his best to procure an acquittal; and if, in spite of police, attorney, officials, and judge, the criminal was convicted and sentenced, he might still hope that the influence of his party would procure a pardon from the governor of the state, or enable him in some other way to slip out of the grasp of justice. For governor, judge, attorney, officials, and police

---

[11] "In the minds of certain New York judges," said Mr. Charles F. Adams at that time, "the old-fashioned distinction between a receiver of property in a Court of Equity and a receiver of stolen goods at common law may be said to have been lost." The abuses of judicial authority were mostly perpetrated in the exercise of equitable jurisdiction, which is no doubt the most delicate part of a judge's work, not only because there is no jury, but because the effect of an injunction may be irremediable, whereas a decision on the main question may be reversed on appeal. In Scotland some of the local courts have a jurisdiction unlimited in amount, but no action can be taken on an interdict issued by such a court if an appeal is made with due promptness to the Court of Session.

were all of them party nominees; and if a man cannot count on being helped by his party at a pinch, who will be faithful to his party?

Although these malpractices diverted a good deal of business from the courts to private arbitration, the damage to the regular course of civil justice was much less than might have been expected. The guilty judges were but three in number, and there is no reason to think that even they decided unjustly in an ordinary commercial suit between man and man, or took direct money bribes from one of the parties to such a suit. The better opinion seems to be that it was only where the influence of a political party or of some particular persons came in that injustice was perpetrated, and the truth, I believe, was spoken by another judge, an honest and worthy man, who in talking to me at the time of the most unblushing of these offenders, said, "Well, I don't much like ——; he is certainly a bad fellow, with very little delicacy of mind. He'll give you an injunction without hearing what it's about. But I don't think he takes money down from everybody." In the instance which made most noise in Europe, that of the Erie Railroad suits, there was no need to give bribes. The gang of thieves who had gained control of the line and were "watering" its stock were leagued with the gang of thieves who ruled the city and nominated the judges; and nobody doubts that the monstrous decisions in these suits were obtained by the influence of the Tammany leaders over their judicial minions.

The fall of the Tammany Ring was swiftly followed by the impeachment or resignation of these judges, and no similar scandal has since disgraced the Empire State, though it must be confessed that some of the criminal courts of the city would be more worthily presided over if they were "taken out of politics." At present New York appoints her chief city judges for fourteen years and pays them a large salary, so she gets fairly good if not first-rate men.[12] Unhappily the magnitude of this one judicial scandal, happening in the greatest city of the Union, and the one which Europeans hear most of, has thrown over the integrity of the American bench a shadow which does great injustice to it as a whole.

Although judicial purity has of late years come to be deemed an indispensable accompaniment of high civilization, it is one which has been

---

[12] As to the recent introduction in some states of the recall of judges by popular vote, see Vol. I, Chap. 42 (State Judiciary). Although the recall is a significant evidence of distrust in the bench, that distrust springs not so much from suspicions of corruption as from the belief that judges are apt to be too much under the influence of financial interests, especially those of great corporations. The similar proposal for a recall (i.e., reversal) of judicial decisions by the people is grounded on the notion that in interpreting the state constitutions the judges are over technical, and are too much in sympathy with the sentiments of the wealthy class.

realized in very few times and countries. Hesiod complained that the kings who heard the cause between himself and his brother received gifts to decide against him. Felix expected to get money for loosing St. Paul. Among Orientals to this day an incorruptible magistrate is a rare exception.[13] In England a lord chancellor was removed for taking bribes as late as the time of George I. In Spain, Portugal, Russia, parts of the Austro-Hungarian monarchy, and, one is told, even in Italy, the judges, except perhaps those of the highest court, are not assumed by general opinion to be above suspicion. Many are trusted individually, but the office is not deemed to guarantee the honour of its occupant. Yet in all these countries the judges are appointed by the government, and hold either for life or at its pleasure,[14] whereas in America suspicion has arisen only in states where popular election prevails; that is to say, where the responsibility for a bad appointment cannot be fixed on any one person. The shortcomings of the bench in these states do not therefore indicate unsoundness in the general tone either of the people or of the profession from whom the offenders have been taken, but are the natural result of a system which, so far from taking precautions to place worthy persons on the seat of justice, has left the choice of them in four cases out of five to a secret combination of wire-pullers. When this system has been got rid of—and the current seems to be flowing against it—the quality of the bench will doubtless improve.

[13] Neither is he at all too common in Central and South America. In Egypt I was told in 1888 that there might be here and there among the native judges a man who did not take bribes, but probably not more than two or three in the whole country. Things have, however, mended since then.

[14] There is the important difference between these countries and England that in all of them not only is little or no use made of the civil jury, but public opinion is less active and justice more localized, i.e., a smaller proportion of important suits are brought before the supreme courts of the capital. The centralization of English justice, costly to suitors, has contributed to make law more pure as well as more scientific.

C H A P T E R   1 0 6

Railroads

No one will expect to find in a book like this a description of that prodigy of labour, wealth, and skill—the American railway system. Of its management, its finance, its commercial prospects, I do not attempt to speak. But railroads, and those who own and control them, occupy a place in the political and social life of the country which requires some passing words, for it is a place far more significant than similar enterprises have obtained in the Old World.

The United States are so much larger, and have a population so much more scattered than any European state that they depend even more upon means of internal communication. It is these communications that hold the country together, and render it one for all social and political purposes as well as for commerce. They may indeed be said to have made the West, for it is along the lines of railway that the West has been settled, and population still follows the rails, stretching out to south and north of the great trunk lines wherever they send off a branch. The Americans are an eminently locomotive people. Were statistics on such a point attainable, they would probably show that the average man travels over thrice as many miles by steam in a year as the average Englishman, six times as many as the average Frenchman or German. The New Yorker thinks of a journey to Chicago (900 miles) as the Londoner of a journey to Glasgow (400 miles); and a family at St. Louis will go for sea-bathing to Cape May, a journey of thirty-five or forty hours, as readily as a Birmingham family goes to Scarborough. The movements of goods traffic are on a gigantic scale. The greatest branch of heavy freight transportation in England, that of coal from the north and west to London, is not to be compared to the weight of cotton, grain, bacon, cattle, fruit, and ores which comes from the inland regions to the Atlantic coast. This traffic does not merely give to the trunk lines an enormous yearly turnover—it interests all classes, I might almost say all individuals, in railway operations, seeing that every branch of industry and every profession except divinity and medicine is more or less directly connected with the movements of commerce, and prospers in proportion to its prosperity. Consequently, railroads and their receipts, railroad directors and their doings, occupy men's tongues and pens to a far greater extent than in Europe.

Some of the great railway companies posses yet another source of wealth and power. At the time when they were formed, the enterprise of laying down rails in thinly peopled, or perhaps quite uninhabited regions, in some instances over deserts or across lofty mountains, seemed likely to prove so unremunerative to the first shareholders, yet so beneficial to the country at large, that Congress was induced to encourage the promoters by vast grants of unoccupied land, the property of the United States, lying along the projected line.[1] The grants were often improvident, and they gave rise to endless lobbying and intrigue, first to secure them, then to keep them from being declared forfeited in respect of some breach of the conditions imposed by Congress on the company. However, the lines were made, colonists came, much of the lands was sold to speculators as well as to individual settlers; but much long remained in the hands of two or three companies. These gifts made the railroads great landowners, gave them a local influence and divers local interests besides those arising from their proper business of carriers, and brought them into intimate and often perilously delicate relations with leading politicians.

No wonder, then, that the railroads, even those that held no land beyond that on which their rails ran, acquired immense power in the districts they traversed. In a new and thinly peopled state the companies were by far the wealthiest bodies, and able by their wealth to exert all sorts of influence. A city or a district of country might depend entirely upon them for its progress. If they ran a line into it or through it, emigrants followed, the value of fixed property rose, trade became brisk; if they passed it by, and bestowed transportation facilities on some other district, it saw itself outstripped and began to languish. If a company owned a trunk line it could, by raising or lowering the rates of freight on that line through which the products of the

---

[1] These grants usually consisted of alternate sections, in the earlier cases of five to the mile along the line. The total grant made to the Union Pacific Railway was 13,000,100 acres; to the Kansas Pacific 6,000,000; to the Central Pacific, 12,100,100; to the Northern Pacific, 47,000,000; to the Atlantic and Pacific, 42,000,000; to the Southern Pacific, 9,520,000. Enormous money subsidies, exceeding $60,000,000, were also granted by Congress to the first transcontinental lines.

district or state passed towards the sea, stimulate or retard the prosperity of the agricultural population, or the miners, or the lumbermen. That is to say, the great companies held in their hands the fortunes of cities, of counties, even sometimes of states and Territories.[2] California was for many years practically at the mercy of the Central Pacific Railway, then her only road to the Mississippi Valley and the Atlantic. Oregon and Washington were almost equally dependent upon the Oregon Railroad and Navigation Company, and afterwards upon the Northern Pacific. What made the position more singular was that, although these railroads had been built under statutes passed by the state they traversed (or, in the case of Territories, wholly or partially under federal statutes), they were built with Eastern capital, and were owned by a number, often a small number, of rich men living in New York, Boston, or Philadelphia, unamenable to local influences, and caring no more about the wishes and feelings of the state whence their profits came than an English bondholder cares about the feelings of Paraguay. Moreover, although the railroads held a fuller sway in the newer states, they were sometimes potent political factors in the older ones. In 1870 I often heard men say, "Camden and Amboy (the Camden and Amboy Railroad) rules New Jersey." In New York the great New York Central Railroad, in Pennsylvania the Pennsylvania Railroad under its able chief, exerted immense influence with the legislature, partly by their wealth, partly by the opportunities of bestowing favours on individuals and localities which they possessed, including the gift of free passes and sometimes influence exercised on the votes of their employees. Sometimes, at least in Pennsylvania and New York, they even threw their weight into the scale of a political party, giving it money as well as votes. But more commonly they have confined themselves to securing their own interests, and obliged, or threatened and used, the state leaders of both parties alike for that purpose. The same sort of power was at one time exerted over some of the cantons of Switzerland by the greater Swiss railway companies; though, since the Constitution of 1874, it was believed to have disappeared.[3]

In such circumstances conflicts between the railroads and the state governments were inevitable. The companies might succeed in "capturing" individual legislators or committees of either or both houses, but they could

---

[2] This was of course especially the case with the newer Western states; yet even in the older parts of the country any very large railway system had great power, for it might have a monopoly of communication; or if there were two lines they might have agreed to "pool," as it is called, their traffic receipts and work in harmony.

[3] The Swiss railways are now under the control of the federal government.

not silence the discontented cities or counties who complained of the way in which they were neglected while some other city obtained better facilities, still less the farmers who denounced the unduly high rates they were forced to pay for the carriage of their produce. Thus a duel began between the companies and the peoples of some of the states, which has gone on with varying fortune in the halls of the legislatures and in the courts of law. The farmers of the Northwest formed agricultural associations called "Patrons of Husbandry," or popularly "Granges," and passed a number of laws imposing various restrictions on the railroads, and providing for the fixing of a maximum scale of charges. But although the railroad companies had been formed under, and derived their powers of taking land and making bye-laws from, state statutes, these statutes had in some cases omitted to reserve the right to deal freely with the lines by subsequent legislation; and the companies therefore attempted to resist the "Granger laws" as being unconstitutional. They were defeated by two famous decisions of the Supreme Federal Court in 1876,[4] establishing the right of a state to impose restrictions on public undertakings in the nature of monopolies. But in other directions they had better luck. The Granger laws proved in many respects unworkable. The companies, alleging that they could not carry goods at a loss, refused to construct branches and other new lines, and in various ways contrived to make the laws difficult of execution. Thus they procured (in most states) the repeal of the first set of Granger laws; and when further legislation was projected, secret engines of influence were made to play upon the legislatures, influences which, since the first wave of popular impulse had now spent itself, often proved efficacious in averting further restrictions or impeding the enforcement of those imposed. Those who profited most by the strife were the less scrupulous among the legislators, who, if they did not receive some favour from a railroad, could levy blackmail upon it by bringing in a threatening bill.[5]

The contest, however, was not confined to the several states. It passed to Congress. Congress was supposed to have no authority under the Constitution to deal with a railway lying entirely within one state, because it carried intrastate commerce only, but to be entitled to legislate, under its power of regulating commerce between different states, for all lines (including

---

[4] See *Munn* v. *Illinois*, and *Peake* v. *Chicago, Burlington, and Quincy Railroad*, 94 U.S. Reports.

[5] Some time ago the legislature of Iowa passed a statute giving the state Railway Commission full powers to fix charges; and injunctions were obtained from the courts restraining the commission from imposing, as they were proceeding to do, rates so low as to be destructive of reasonable profits.

connecting lines which are worked together as a through line) which traverse more than one state there being agencies of interstate commerce. And of course it has always had power over railways situate in the Territories. As the federal courts decided some time ago that no state could legislate against a railway lying partly outside its own limits, because this would trench on federal competence, the need for federal legislation, long pressed upon Congress, became urgent; and after much debate an act was passed in 1887 establishing an Interstate Commerce Commission, with power to regulate railroad transportation and charges in many material respects. The companies had opposed it; but after its passage they discovered that it hurt them less than they had feared, and in some points even benefited them; for the prohibition of all discriminations and secret rebates, and the requirement to adhere to their published list of charges, although they could not "take care" of the commissioners as they often had state legislatures, gave them a ready answer to demands for exceptional privileges.[6] This momentous statute, which forbade the exaction of unreasonable charges and all discriminations between persons and places gave rise to a swarm of difficult legal questions, and while hampering the railroads did not at first do much to lessen the complaints of the farming and commercial classes. It has, however, been amended, and the act of 1906, while strengthening the Commission in its numbers and its powers, provided for it a more efficient procedure. The act of 1910 has still further extended its powers, which now cover telegraph and telephone companies so far as relates to interstate business, and also pipelines carrying oil. A court of commerce was also created, consisting of five judges to be selected from the federal Circuit judges.

That the railroads had exercised autocratic and irresponsible power over some regions of the country, and had occasionally abused this power, especially by imposing discriminations in their freight charges, is not to be denied.[7] They had become extremely unpopular, a constant theme for demagogic denunciations; and their success during some years in resisting public clamour by their secret control of legislatures, or even of the state commissioners appointed to deal with them, increased the irritation. All corporations are at present unpopular in America, and especially corporations

---

[6] Subsequent statutes have enlarged the functions of this commission and have, among other things, put an end to the bestowal of free passes for passengers, a form of preference which had assumed large proportions and given rise (especially where legislators were concerned) to some abuses.

[7] It would appear that the freight charges on American railways were, before 1887, generally lower than those in England and in Western Europe generally. They are now lower, and in some cases very much lower, than those of British railways. English third-class passenger fares are, however, as a rule slightly lower than those in the ordinary American cars.

possessed of monopolies. The agitation may continue, though the confidence felt in the Commission has done something to allay it, and attempts be made to carry still more stringent legislation. Some have proposed that all railways, as well as telegraphs, should be taken over by the nation, and that not merely for revenue purposes, but to make them serve more perfectly the public convenience. Apart from the question of amending the Constitution for this end, the objection which to most men seems decisive against any such arrangement is that it would not only encumber government with most difficult rate problems, affecting local interests, and therefore involving the certainty of local political pressure, but would also throw a stupendous mass of patronage and power into the hands of the party for the time being holding office. Considering what a perennial spring of bitterness partisan patronage has been, and how liable to perversion under the best regulations patronage always must be, he would be a bold man who would toss an immense number of places—the railroads employed in 1907, 1,672,000 persons and were paying them $1,072,386,427—into the lap of a party minister. Economic gain, assuming that such gain could be secured, would be dearly bought by political danger.

Their strife with the state governments has not been enough to occupy the pugnacity of the companies. They must needs fight with one another; and their wars have been long and fierce, involving immense pecuniary interests, not only to the shareholders in the combatant lines, but also to the inhabitants of the districts which they served. Such conflicts have been most frequent between the trunk lines competing for the carriage of goods from the West to the Atlantic cities, and have been conducted not only by lowering charges so as to starve out the weaker line,[8] but by attacks upon its stocks in the great share markets, by efforts to defeat its bills in the state legislatures, and by lawsuits with applications for injunctions in the courts. Sometimes, as in the famous case of the struggle of the Atchison Topeka and Santa Fe railway with the Denver and Rio Grande for the possession of the great canyon of the Arkansas River,[9] the easiest route into an important group of Rocky Mountain valleys, the navvies of the two companies fought with shovels and pickaxes on the spot, while their counsel were fighting in the law courts sixteen hundred miles away. A well-established company has

---

[8] In one of these contests, one railway having lowered its rates for cattle to a figure below paying point, the manager of the other promptly bought up all the cattle he could find at the inland terminus, and sent them to the coast by the enemy's line, a costly lesson to the latter.

[9] This so-called "Royal Gorge" of the Arkansas is one of the most striking pieces of scenery on the North American continent, not unlike the grandest part of the famous Dariel Pass in the Caucasus.

sometimes to apprehend a peculiarly annoying form of attack at the hands
of audacious adventurers, who construct a competing line where the traffic
is only sufficient to enable the existing one to pay a dividend on the capital
it has expended, aiming, not at the creation of a profitable undertaking, but
at levying blackmail on one which exists, and obtaining an opportunity of
manipulating bonds and stocks for their own benefit. In such a case the
railway company in possession has its choice between two courses: it may
allow the new enterprise to go on, then lower its own rates, and so destroy
all possibility of profits; or it may buy up the rival line, perhaps at a heavy
price. Sometimes it tries the first course long enough to beat down the
already small prospects of the new line and then buys it; but although this
may ruin the "pirates" who have built the new line, it involves a hideous
waste of the money spent in construction, and the shareholders of the old
company as well as the bondholders of the new one suffer. This is a form
of raid upon property which evidently ought to be prevented by greater care
on the part of state legislatures in refusing to pass special acts for unnecessary
railroads, or in so modifying their law as to prevent a group of promoters
from using, for purposes of blackmail, the powers of taking land and
constructing railroads, which general statutes confer.[10]

This atmosphere of strife has had something to do with the feature of
railway management which a European finds most remarkable; I mean its
autocratic character. Nearly all the great lines are controlled and managed
either by a small knot of persons or by a single man. Sometimes one man,
or a knot of three or four capitalists acting as one man, holds an actual
majority of the shares, and then he can of course do exactly what he pleases.
Sometimes the interest of the ruling man (or knot) comes so near to being
a controlling interest that he may safely assume that no majority can be
brought against him, the tendencies of many shareholders being to support
"the administration" in all its policy. This accumulation of voting power in

[10] "It is an extraordinary fact," says Mr. Hitchcock, "that the power of eminent domain which the
State itself confessedly ought never to use save on grounds of public necessity should be at the
command of irresponsible individuals for purposes of private gain, not only without any guarantee
that the public interest will be promoted thereby, but when it is perfectly well known that it may
be, and has been deliberately availed of for merely speculative purposes. The facility with which,
under loosely drawn railroad laws, purely speculative railroad charters can be obtained has
contributed not a little to develop the law of receiverships. In Missouri there is nothing to prevent
any live men whose combined capital would not enable them to build five miles of track on a
level prairie from forming a railroad corporation with power to construct a road five hundred
miles long, and to condemn private property for that purpose, for a line whose construction no
public interest demands, and from which no experienced man could expect dividends to accrue." —
Address to the American Bar Association, 1887.

a few hands seems to be due partly to the fact that the shares of new lines do not, in the first instance, get scattered through the general public as in England, but are commonly allotted in masses to a few persons, often as a sort of bonus upon their subscribing for the bonds of the company. In the United States shares do not usually represent a cash subscription, the practice being to construct a railway with the proceeds of the bonds and to regard the shares as the materials for future profit, things which may, if the line be of a speculative character, be run up in price and sold off by the promoters; or, if it be likely to prosper, be held by them for the purpose of controlling as well as gaining profits from the undertaking, the profits including those derivable from watering the stock.[11] It is partly also to be ascribed to the splendid boldness with which financial operations are conducted in America, where the leaders of Wall Street do not hesitate to buy up enormous masses of shares or stock for the purpose of some coup. Having once got into a single hand, or a few hands, these stock masses stay there, and give their possessors the control of the line. But the power of the railways, and the position they hold towards local governments, state legislatures, and one another, have also a great deal to do with the phenomenon. War used for a time to be, and in some parts of the country is still, the natural state of an American railway towards all other authorities and its own fellows, just as war was the natural state of cities towards one another in the ancient world. And as an army in the field must be commanded by one general, so must this latest militant product of an eminently peaceful civilization. The president of a great railroad needs gifts for strategical combinations scarcely inferior to those, if not of a great general, yet of a great war minister—a Chatham or a Carnot. If his line extends into a new country, he must be quick to seize the best routes—the best physically, because they will be cheaper to operate, the best in agricultural or mineral resources, because they will offer a greater prospect of traffic. He must so throw out his branches as not only to occupy promising tracts, but keep his competing enemies at a distance; he must annex small lines when he sees a good chance, first "bearing" their stocks so as to get them cheaper; he must

---

[11] The great Central Pacific Railway was constructed by four men, two of whom were, when they began, storekeepers in a small way in San Francisco, and none of whom could be called capitalists. Their united funds when they began in 1860 were only $120,000 (£24,000). They went on issuing bonds and building the line bit by bit as the bonds put them in funds, retaining the control of the company through the shares. This Central Pacific Company ultimately built the Southern Pacific and numerous branches, and became by far the greatest power in the West, owning nearly all the railways in California and Nevada. When one of the four died in 1878, his estate was worth $30,000,000, a vast sum for those days.

make a close alliance with at least one other great line, which completes his communications with the East or with the farther West, and be prepared to join this ally in a conflict with some threatening competitor. He must know the governors and watch the legislatures of the states through which his line runs; must have adroit agents at the state capitals, well supplied with the sinews of war, ready to "see" leading legislators and to defeat any legislative attacks that may be made by blackmailers or the tools of rival presidents. And all the while he must not only keep his eye upon the markets of New York, prepared for the onslaught which may be made upon his own stock by some other railroad or by speculators desiring to make a profit as "bears," and maintaining friendly relations with the capitalists whose help he will need when he brings out a new loan, but must supervise the whole administrative system of the railroad—its stations, permanent way, locomotives, rolling stock, engineering shops, freight and passenger rates, perhaps also the sale of its land grants and their defence against the cabals of Washington. No talents of the practical order can be too high for such a position as this; and even the highest talents would fail to fill it properly except with a free hand. Concentration of power and an almost uncontrolled discretion are needed; and in America whatever commercial success needs is sure to be yielded. Hence, when a group of capitalists own a railway, they commit its management to a very small committee among themselves, or even to a single man; and when the shares are more widely distributed, the shareholders, recognizing the necessary conditions of prosperity, not to say of survival in the struggle for existence, leave themselves in the hands of the president, who has little to fear except from the shares being quietly bought up by some syndicate of enemies seeking to dethrone him.

Of these great railway chieftains, some have come to the top gradually, by the display in subordinate posts of brilliant administrative gifts. Some have begun as financiers, and have sprung into the presidential saddle at a bound by forming a combination which has captured the railway by buying up its stock. Occasionally a great capitalist will seize a railroad only for the sake of manipulating its stock, clearing a profit, and throwing it away. But more frequently, when a really important line has passed into the hands of a man or group, it is held fast and developed into a higher efficiency by means of the capital they command.

These railway kings are among the greatest men, perhaps I may say are the greatest men, in America. They have wealth, else they could not hold the position. They have fame, for everyone has heard of their achievements; every newspaper chronicles their movements. They have power, more power—that is, more opportunity of making their personal will prevail—than perhaps anyone in political life, except the president and the Speaker, who after all hold theirs only for four years and two years, while the railroad monarch may keep his for life. When the master of one of the greatest Western lines travels towards the Pacific on his palace car, his journey is like a royal progress. Governors of states and Territories bow before him; legislatures receive him in solemn session; cities and towns seek to propitiate him, for has he not the means of making or marring a city's fortunes? Although the railroad companies are unpopular, and although this autocratic sway from a distance contributes to their unpopularity, I do not think that the ruling magnates are themselves generally disliked. On the contrary, they receive that tribute of admiration which the American gladly pays to whoever has done best what everyone desires to do. Probably no career draws to it or unfolds and develops so much of the characteristic ability of the nation; and I doubt whether any congressional legislation will greatly reduce the commanding positions which these potentates hold as the masters of enterprises whose wealth, geographical extension, and influence upon the growth of the country and the fortunes of individuals, find no parallel in the Old World.

It has already been shown how the task of regulating railroads by law, nowhere an easy one, is in the United States rendered more perplexing by the division of jurisdiction between the national government and the states, the control of the former having been deemed to be confined to traffic between the states. To adhere to and apply this distinction has become in practice more and more difficult with the increase not only of interstate traffic but of the demands made for regulating matters formerly untouched by legislation. Thus the tendency to enlarge the scope of national control is inevitable, and likely to go further. Little as the railroads relish regulation from either quarter, they prefer that which proceeds from Congress, because it is uniform, it hampers them less, it is less subject to frequent change, and it is exerted through a body, the Interstate Commerce Commission, whose members possess capacity and experience. People already ask whether the ultimate issue will not be the assumption by the national government of the sole power of controlling an agency of transportation of national magnitude which ought to be dealt with as a whole and which would, one can hardly doubt, have been assigned to that government by the framers of the Constitution had it existed in their day.

It may be thought that some of the phenomena I have described belong to an era of colonization, and that when the West has been filled up, and all the arterial railways made, when, in fact, the United States have become even as England or France, the power of railroads and their presidents will decline. No doubt there will be less room for certain bold ventures and feats of constructive strategy; and as the network of railways grows closer, states and districts may come to depend less upon one particular company. At the same time it must be remembered that the more populous and wealthy the country, so much the larger the business of a trunk line, and the number of its branches and its employees; while the consolidation of small lines, or their absorption by large ones, is a process evidently destined to continue. In 1910 six or seven financial groups controlled more than four-fifths of all the 250,000 miles of railroad in the United States; and it seemed probable that some of these groups might unite or make arrangements with one another, under which the vast systems which each group administered might be worked as one system. It may therefore be conjectured that the railroad will long stand forth as a great and perplexing force in the economico-political life of the country. It cannot be left to itself—the most extreme advocate of laissez faire would not contend for that, for to leave it to itself would be to make it a tyrant. It cannot be absorbed and worked by the national government as are the railways of Switzerland and many of those in Germany and the Austro-Hungarian monarchy. Only he most sanguine state socialist would propose to impose so terrible a strain on the virtue of American politicians, not to speak of the effect upon the constitutional balance between the states and the federal authority. Many experiments may be needed before the true mean course between these extremes is discovered. Meanwhile, the railroads illustrate two tendencies specially conspicuous in America—the power of the principle of association, which makes commercial corporations, skilfully handled, formidable to individual men; and the way in which the principle of monarchy, banished from the field of government, creeps back again and asserts its strength in the scarcely less momentous contests of industry and finance.

Wall Street

No invention of modern times, not even that of negotiable paper, has so changed the face of commerce and delighted lawyers with a variety of new and intricate problems as the creation of incorporated joint-stock companies. America, though she came latest into the field, has developed these on a grander scale and with a more refined skill than the countries of the Old World. Nowhere do trading corporations play so great a part in trade and industry; nowhere are so many huge undertakings in their hands; nowhere else has the method of controlling them become a political problem of the first magnitude. So vigorous, indeed, is the inventive genius of American commerce that, not satisfied with the new applications it has found for the principles of the joint-stock corporation, it subsequently attempted a further development of the arts of combination by creating those anomalous giants called trusts, groups of individuals and corporations concerned in one branch of trade or manufacture, which are placed under the irresponsible management of a small knot of persons, who, through their command of all the main producing or distributing agencies, intend and expect to dominate the market, force manufacturers or dealers to submit, and hold the consumer at their mercy.[1]

Here, however, I am concerned with the amazing expansion of joint-stock companies in America, only as the cause of the not less amazing activity in buying and selling shares which the people display. This is almost

---

[1] *Note to edition of 1914:* The question what is the legal status (if any) of these trusts, the first of which was created in 1869, has been much discussed by American jurists. When Congress legislated against them in 1890 there existed at least thirty, and their power grew thereafter.

During the last ten years many lawsuits have been brought by successive administrations, under the Sherman Act, to restrain the monopolistic action of trusts and great corporations, and considerable results have been thereby attained.

the first thing that strikes a European visitor, and the longer he remains the more deeply is he impressed by it as something to which his own country, be it England, France, or Germany, furnishes no parallel. In Europe, speculation in bonds, shares, and stocks is confined to a section of the commercial world, with a few stragglers from other walks of business, or from the professions, who flutter near the flame and burn their wings. Ordinary steady-going people, even people in business, know little or nothing about the matter, and seldom think of reading the share lists. When they have savings to invest they do as they are bidden by their banker or stockbroker, if indeed they have a stock broker, and do not get their banker to engage one.[2] In the United States a much larger part of the population, including professional men as well as businessmen, seem conversant with the subject, and there are times when the whole community, not merely city people but also storekeepers in country towns, even farmers, even domestic servants, interest themselves actively in share speculations. At such times they watch the fluctuations of price in the stocks of the great railroads, telegraph companies (or rather the Telegraph Company, since there is practically but one), and other leading undertakings; they discuss the prospects of a rise or fall, and the probable policy of the great operators; they buy and sell bonds or stocks on a scale not always commensurate with their own means.[3] In the great cities the number of persons exclusively devoted to this occupation is very large, and naturally so, because, while the undertakings lie all over a vast extent of country, the capital which owns them is mostly situate in the cities, and, indeed, six-sevenths of it (so far as it is held in America) in four or five of the greatest Eastern cities. It is chiefly in railroads that these Easterns speculate. But in the Far West mines are an even more exciting and pervasive interest. In San Francisco every-one gambles in mining stocks, even the nursemaids and the Chinese. The share lists showing the oscillations of prices are hung up outside the newspaper offices, and fixed on posts in the streets, and are changed every hour or two during the day. In the silver districts of Colorado and New Mexico the same kind of thing goes on.[4] It is naturally in such spots that

---

[2] There are, of course, simple folk in England who take shares on the faith of prospectuses of new companies sent to them; but the fact that it pays to send such prospectuses is the best proof of the general ignorance, in such matters, of laymen (including the clergy) and women in that country.

[3] In many country towns there are small offices, commonly called "bucket shops," to which farmers and tradesmen resort to effect their purchases and sales in the stock markets of the great cities. Not a few ruin themselves. Some states have endeavoured to extinguish them by penal legislation.

[4] In a mining town in Colorado the landlady of an inn in which I stayed for a night pressed me to bring out in London a company to work a mining claim which she had acquired, offering me

the fire burns hottest. But go where you will in the Union, except, to be sure, in the more stagnant and impecunious parts of the South, you feel bonds, stocks, and shares in the atmosphere all round you. *Te veniente die*—they begin the day with the newspaper at breakfast; they end it with the chat over the nocturnal cigar.[5]

This eager interest centres itself in New York, for finance, more perhaps than any other kind of business, draws to few points, and New York, which has as little claim to be the social or intellectual as to be the political capital of the country, is emphatically its financial capital. And as the centre of America is New York, so the centre of New York is Wall Street. This famous thoroughfare is hardly a quarter of a mile long, a little longer than Lombard Street in London. It contains the Sub-Treasury of the United States, and the Stock Exchange (which used to be in it) is quite close to it. In it and the three or four streets that open into it are situated the Produce Exchange, the offices of the great railways, and the places of business of the financiers and stockbrokers, together representing an accumulation of capital and intellect comparable to the capital and intellect of London, and destined before many years to surpass every similar spot in either hemisphere.[6] Wall Street is the great nerve centre of all American business; for finance and transportation, the two determining powers in business, have here their headquarters. It is also the financial barometer of the country, which every man engaged in large affairs must constantly consult, and whose only fault is that it is too sensitive to slight and transient variations of pressure.

The share market of New York, or rather of the whole Union, in "the Street," as it is fondly named, is the most remarkable sight in the country after Niagara and the Yellowstone Geysers. It is not unlike those geysers in the violence of its explosions, and in the rapid rise and equally rapid subsidence of its active paroxysms. And as the sparkling column of the geyser is girt about and often half concealed by volumes of steam, so are the rise and fall of stocks mostly surrounded by mists and clouds of rumour, some purposely created, some self-generated in the atmosphere of excitement,

---

what is called an option. I inquired how much money it would take to begin to work the claim and get out the ore. "Less than thirty thousand dollars" (£6,000). (The carbonates are in that part of Colorado very near the surface.) "And what is to be the capital of your company?" "Five millions of dollars" (£1,000,000)!

[5] Of course I am speaking of the man you meet in travelling, who is a sample of the ordinary citizen. In polite society one's entertainer would no more bring up such a subject, unless you drew him on to do so, than he would think of talking politics.

[6] The balances settled in the New York Clearing House each day are two-thirds of all the clearings in the United States.

curiosity, credulity, and suspicion which the denizens of Wall Street breathe. Opinions change from moment to moment; hope and fear are equally vehement and equally irrational; men are constant only in inconstancy, superstitious because they are sceptical, distrustful of patent probabilities, and therefore ready to trust their own fancies or some unfathered tale. As the eagerness and passion of New York leave European stock markets far behind, for what the Paris and London exchanges are at rare moments Wall Street is for weeks, or perhaps, with a few intermissions, for months together, so the operations of Wall Street are vaster, more boldly conceived, executed with a steadier precision, than those of European speculators. It is not only their bearing on the prosperity of railroads or other great undertakings that is eagerly watched all over the country, but also their personal and dramatic aspects. The various careers and characters of the leading operators are familiar to everyone who reads a newspaper; his schemes and exploits are followed as Europe followed the fortunes of Prince Alexander of Battenberg or the Dreyfus trial. A great "corner," for instance, is one of the exciting events of the year, not merely to those concerned with the stock or species of produce in which it is attempted, but to the public at large.

How far is this state of things transitory, due to temporary causes arising out of the swift material development of the United States? During the Civil War the creation of a paper currency, which rapidly depreciated, produced a wild speculation in gold, lasting for several years, whose slightest fluctuations were followed with keen interest, because in indicating the value of the paper currency they indicated the credit of the nation, and the view taken by the financial community of the prospects of the war. The reestablishment of peace brought with it a burst of industrial activity, specially directed to the making of new railroads and general opening up of the West. Thus the eyes that had been accustomed to watch Wall Street did not cease to watch it, for these new enterprises involved many fortunes, had drawn much capital from small investors, and were really of great consequence—the transcontinental railways most of all—to the welfare of the country. From time to time the work of railway construction slackens, when trade is depressed and loans are less easily raised, but it presently revives. In the five years from 1903 to 1907 inclusive the average number of miles annually added exceeded 6,000. Silver mines have been less profitable since the heavy fall in that metal; copper mines, however, continue subject to rapid variations, their value having greatly increased with the new applications of electricity. The price of United States bonds fluctuates, in ordinary times, less than does that of the public securities of the great

European countries. Times of commercial depression are comparatively quiet, yet even when transactions are fewer, the interest of the public in the stock markets does not greatly diminish. Trade and manufactures cover the whole horizon of American life far more than they do anywhere in Europe. They—I include agriculture, because it has been, in America, commercialized, and become really a branch of trade—are the main concern of the country, to which all others are subordinate. So large a part of the whole capital employed is in the hands of joint-stock companies,[7] so easy a method do these companies furnish by which the smallest investor may take part in commercial ventures and increase his pile, so general is the diffusion of information (of course often incorrect) regarding their state and prospects, so vehement and pervading is the passion for wealth, so seductive are the examples of a few men who have realized stupendous fortunes by clever or merely lucky hits when there came a sharp rise or fall in the stock market, so vast, and therefore so impressive to the imagination, is the scale on which these oscillations take place,[8] that the universal attention given to stocks and shares, and the tendency to speculation among the nonfinancial classes which reveals itself from time to time, seem amply accounted for by permanent causes, and therefore likely to prove normal. Even admitting that neither such stimulations as were present during the war period nor those that belonged to the era of inflated prosperity which followed are likely to recur, it must be observed that habits formed under transitory conditions do not always pass away with those conditions, but may become a permanent and, so to speak, hereditary element in national life.

So far as politics are concerned, I do not know that Wall Street does any harm. There is hardly any speculation in foreign securities, because capital finds ample employment in domestic undertakings; and the United States are so little likely to be involved in foreign complications that neither the action of European powers nor that of the federal government bears directly enough upon the stock markets to bring politics into stocks or stocks into politics.[9] Hence one source of evil which poisons public life in Europe, and is believed to have proved specially pernicious in France—the influence of

[7] The wealth of corporations has been estimated by high authorities at one-fourth of the total value of all property in the United States.

[8] The great rebound of trade in 1879–83 trebled within those years the value of many railroad bonds and stocks, and raised at a still more rapid rate the value of lands in many parts of the West.

[9] Of course the prospects of war or peace in Europe do sensibly affect the American produce markets, and therefore the railroads, and indeed all great commercial undertakings. But these prospects are as much outside the province of the American statesman as the drought which affects the coming crop or the blizzard that stops the earnings of a railway.

financial speculators or holders of foreign bonds upon the foreign policy of a government—is wholly absent. An American secretary of state, supposing him base enough to use his official knowledge for stock-jobbing operations, would have little advantage over the meanest broker in Wall Street.[10] Even as regards domestic politics, the division of power between Congress and the state legislatures reduces the power of the former over industrial undertakings, and leaves comparatively few occasions on which the action of the federal government tends to affect the market for most kinds of stocks, though of course changes in the public debt and in the currency affect by sympathy every part of the machinery of commerce. The shares of railroad companies owning land grants were, and to some slight extent still are, depressed and raised by the greater or slighter prospects of legislative interference; but this point of contact between speculators and politicians, which, like the meeting-point of currents in the sea, was marked by a good deal of rough and turbid water, has now ceased to exist, there being no more railroad lands which Congress has to deal with.

The more serious question remains: How does Wall Street tell on the character of the people? They are naturally inclined to be speculative. The pursuit of wealth is nowhere so eager as in America, the opportunities for acquiring it are nowhere so numerous. Nowhere is one equally impressed by the progress which the science and arts of gain—I do not mean the arts that add to the world's wealth, but those by which individuals appropriate an exceptionally large share of it—make from year to year. The materials with which the investor or the speculator has to work may receive no sensible addition; but the constant application of thousands of keen intellects, spurred by sharp desire, evolves new combinations out of these old materials, devises new methods and contrivances apt for a bold and skilful hand, just as electricians go on perfecting the machinery of the telegraph, just as the accumulated labours of scholars present us with always more trustworthy texts of the classical writers and more precise rules of Greek and Latin syntax. Under these new methods of business, speculation, though it seems to become more of a science, does not become less speculative. People seem to buy and sell on even slighter indications than in Paris or London. The processes of "bulling" and "bearing" are more constant and more skilfully applied. The whole theory and practice of "margins" has been more completely worked out. The stock market is worked in conjunction with the

---

[10] The secretary of the treasury, by his control of the public debt, has no doubt means of affecting the markets; but I have never heard any charge of improper conduct in such matters on the part of anyone connected with the Treasury Department.

stock markets of Europe, and the fact that the stock exchange in London opens four hours earlier than that of New York enables the former to be used so as to affect the latter. However, it is of less consequence for our present purpose to dwell on the proficiency of the professional operator than to note the prevalence of the habit of speculation: it is not intensity so much as extension that affects an estimate of the people at large.

Except in New York, and perhaps in Chicago, which is more and more coming to reproduce and rival the characteristics of New York, Americans bet less upon horse races than the English do. Horse races are, indeed, far less common, though there is a good deal of fuss made about trotting-matches. However, much money changes hands, especially in Eastern cities, over yacht-races, and plenty everywhere over elections.[11] The purchase and sale of "produce futures," i.e., of cotton, wheat, maize, bacon, lard, and other staples not yet in existence but to be delivered at some distant day, has reached an enormous development.[12] There is, even in the Eastern cities, where the value of land might be thought to have become stable, a real estate market in which land and houses are dealt in as matter for pure speculation, with no intention of holding except for a rise within the next few hours or days; while in the new West the price of lands, especially near cities, undergoes fluctuations greater than those of the most unstable stocks in the London market. It can hardly be doubted that the preexisting tendency to encounter risks and "back one's opinion," inborn in the Americans, and fostered by the circumstances of their country, is further stimulated by the existence of so vast a number of joint-stock enterprises, and by the facilities they offer to the smallest capitalists. Similar facilities exist in the Old World; but few of the inhabitants of the Old World have yet learned how to use and abuse them. The Americans, quick at everything, have learned long ago. The habit of speculation is now a part of their character, and it increases that constitutional excitability and high nervous tension of which they are proud.

Some may think that when the country fills up and settles down, and finds itself altogether under conditions more nearly resembling those of the Old World, these peculiarities will fade away. I doubt it. They seem to have already passed into the national fibre.

---

[11] The mischief has been thought sufficient to be specially checked by the constitutions or statutes of some states; and there has been a good deal of legislation against betting on races.

[12] It is stated that the Produce Exchange sells in each year five times the value of the cotton crop, and that the Petroleum Exchange has sometimes sold fifty times the amount of that year's yield.

I have referred in a note to a preceding chapter to some recent attempts to check by legislation this form of speculation (p. 1220 *ante*).

CHAPTER 108

The Universities and Colleges

Among the universities of America there is none which has sprung up of itself like Bologna or Paris or El Azhar or Oxford, none founded by an emperor like Prague, or by a pope like Glasgow. All have been the creatures of private munificence or denominational zeal or state action. Their history is short indeed compared with that of the universities of Europe. Yet it is full of interest, for its shows a steady growth, it records many experiments, it gives valuable data for comparing the educational results of diverse systems.

When the first English colonists went to America, the large and liberal mediæval conception of a university, as a place where graduates might teach freely and students live freely, was waxing feeble in Oxford and Cambridge. The instruction was given chiefly by the colleges, which had already become, what they long continued, organisms so strong as collectively to eclipse the university they had been meant to aid. Accordingly when places of superior instruction began to grow up in the colonies, it was on the model not of an English university but of an English college that they were created. The glory of founding the first place of learning in the English parts of America belongs to a Puritan minister and graduate of Cambridge, John Harvard of Emmanuel College,[1] who, dying in 1638, eighteen years after the landing of the Pilgrim Fathers, gave half his property for the establishment of a college in the town of Cambridge, three miles from Boston, which, originally organized on the plan of Emmanuel College, and at once taken under the protection of the infant

---

[1] Emmanuel was a college then much frequented by the Puritans. Of the English graduates who emigrated to New England between 1620 and 1647, nearly one hundred in number, three-fourths came from the University of Cambridge.

Commonwealth of Massachusetts, has now grown into the most famous university on the North American continent.[2]

The second foundation was due to the Colonial Assembly of Virginia. So early as 1619, twelve years after the first settlement at Jamestown, the Virginia Company in England voted ten thousand acres of land in the colony for the establishment of a seminary of learning, and a site was in 1624 actually set apart, on an island in the Susquehanna River, for the "Foundinge and Maintenance of a University and such schools in Virginia as shall there be erected, and shall be called Academia Virginiensis et Oxoniensis." This scheme was never carried out. But in 1693 the Virginians obtained a grant of land and money from the home government for the erection of a college, which received the name of the College of William and Mary.[3] The third foundation was Yale College, established in Connecticut (first at Saybrook, then at New Haven) in 1700; the fourth Princeton, in New Jersey, in 1746. None of these received the title of university: Harvard is called "a school or colledge"; Yale used the name "collegiate school" for seventeen years. "We on purpose gave your academy as low a name as we could that it might the better stand the wind and weather" was the reason assigned. Other academies or colleges in New England and the Middle states followed: such as that which is now the University of Pennsylvania, in 1749; King's, now Columbia, College in New York, in 1754; and Rhode Island College (now Brown University), in 1764; and the habit of granting degrees grew up naturally and almost imperceptibly. A new departure is marked after the Revolution by the establishment, at the instance of Jefferson, of the

---

[2] In 1636 the General Court of the colony of Massachusetts Bay agreed "to give Four Hundred Pounds towards a school or college, whereof Two Hundred Pounds shall be paid the next year, and Two Hundred Pounds when the work is finished, and the next Court to appoint where and what building." In 1637 the General Court appointed a commission of twelve "to take order for a college at Newtoun." The name Newton was presently changed to Cambridge. John Harvard's bequest being worth more than twice the £400 voted, the name of Harvard College was given to the institution; and in 1642 a statute was passed for the ordering of the same. Teaching began in 1650.

[3] The Virginians had worked at this project for more than thirty years before they got their charter and grant. "When William and Mary had agreed to allow £2000 out of the quit rents of Virginia towards building the college, the Rev. Mr. Blair went to Seymour, the attorney-general, with the royal command to issue a charter. Seymour demurred. The country was then engaged in war, and could ill afford to plant a college in Virginia. Mr. Blair urged that the institution was to prepare young men to become ministers of the gospel. Virginians, he said, had souls to be saved as well as their English countrymen. 'Souls!' said Seymour. 'Damn your souls! Make tobacco!' " —*The College of William and Mary*, by Dr. H. B. Adams. This oldest of Southern colleges was destroyed in the Civil War [1862] (it has recently received a national grant of $64,000 as compensation), but was restored, and has been reendowed by the legislature of Virginia in 1888.

University of Virginia, whose large and liberal lines gave it more resemblance
to the universities of the European continent than to the then educationally
narrow and socially domestic colleges of England.

At present most of the American universities are referable to one of two
types, which may be described as the older and the newer, or the private
and the public type. By the old or private type I denote a college on the
model of a college in Oxford or Cambridge, with a head called the president,
and a number of teachers, now generally called professors; a body of
governors or trustees in whom the property and general control of the
institution is vested; a prescribed course of instruction which all students
are expected to follow; buildings, usually called dormitories, provided for
the lodging of the students, and a more or less strict, but always pretty
effective discipline enforced by the teaching staff. Such a college is usually
of private foundation, and is almost always connected with some religious
denomination.

Under the term new or public type I include universities established,
endowed, and governed by a state, usually through a body of persons called
regents. In such a university there commonly exists considerable freedom
of choice among various courses of study. The students, or at least the
majority of them, reside where they please in the city, and are subject to
very little discipline. There are seldom or never denominational affiliations,
women are admitted, and very low charges are made for instruction.

There are, however, institutions which it is hard to refer to one or other
type. Some of these began as private foundations, with a collegiate and
quasi-domestic character, but have now developed into true universities,
generally resembling those of Germany or Scotland. Harvard in Massachusetts
and Yale in Connecticut are instances. Others have been founded by private
persons, but as fully equipped universities, and wholly undenominational.
Cornell at Ithaca in western New York is an instance; Johns Hopkins in
Baltimore is another of a different order. Some have been founded by public
authority, yet have been practically left to be controlled by a body of self-
renewing trustees. Columbia College in New York City is an instance. Still
if we were to run through a list of the universities and colleges in the United
States, we should find that the great majority were either strictly private
foundations governed by trustees, or wholly public foundations governed
by the state. That is to say, the two familiar English types, viz., the
university, which though a public institution is yet little interfered with by
the state, which is deemed to be composed of its graduates and students,
and whose self-government consists in its being governed by the graduates,
and the college, which is a private corporation, consisting of a head, fellows,

and scholars, and governed by the head and fellows—neither of them appear in modern America.[4] On the other hand, the American university of the public type differs from the universities of Germany in being placed under a state board, not under a minister. Neither in Germany nor in Scotland do we find anything corresponding to the American university or college of the private type, for in neither of these countries is a university governed by a body of self-renewing trustees.[5]

It is impossible within the limits of a chapter to do more than state a few of the more salient characteristics of the American universities. I shall endeavour to present these characteristics in the fewest possible words, and for the sake of clearness shall group what I have to say under separate heads.

Statistics. The United States Education Bureau received in 1912 reports from 596 universities and colleges and technological schools, i.e., institutions granting degrees and professing to give an instruction, higher than that of schools, in the liberal arts. Of these 144 were for men only and 343 for both men and women, while 109 were for women only. The total number of teachers was 30,034, 24,508 men and 5,524 women teachers, teaching in the 596 institutions. Of the total number, 80.2 per cent were men, 19.8 percent women.[6]

The total number of students in the undergraduate and graduate departments of the 596 institutions was 198,453, viz., 125,750 men and 72,703 women. In the 109 colleges for women only there were 21,423 undergraduate students. These numbers do not include those in the preparatory departments. The attendance has risen rapidly: it is double that of eighteen years ago. Besides these there are returned:

Schools of	theology	182	with	1,502	teachers	11,242	students
”	law	118	”	1,707	”	20,760	”
”	medicine[7]	115	”	7,572	”	18,542	”
”	dentistry and pharmacy			8,050	”	13,352	”

---

[4] As respects government the American university more resembles the newer type of university recently created in some great cities, which is governed by a council in which various elements are represented and, for some educational purposes, by its faculty.

[5] The Scotch universities (since the Act of 1858), under their university courts, present, however, a certain resemblance to the American system, inasmuch as the governing body is in these institutions not the teaching body.

[6] These figures are to some extent imperfect, because a few institutions omit to send returns, and cannot be compelled to do so, the federal government having no authority in the matter. The number of degree-giving bodies, teachers, and students is therefore somewhat larger than is here stated, but how much larger it is not easy to ascertain.

[7] Of these students 712 were women.

The total number of baccalaurate degrees conferred is returned as 22,354, 58 per cent on men, 42 per cent on women; of graduate degrees, 5,226, 83.4 per cent on men, 16.6 per cent on women.

General Character of the Universities and Colleges. Out of this enormous total of degree-granting bodies very few answer to the modern conception of a university. If we define a university as a place where teaching that puts a man abreast of the fullest and most exact knowledge of the time is given in a range of subjects covering all the great departments of intellectual life, not more than fifteen and possibly only ten or twelve of the American institutions would fall within the definition. Of these two-thirds are to be found in the Atlantic states. Next below them come some forty or more foundations which are scarcely entitled to the name of university, some because their range of instruction is still limited to the traditional literary and scientific course such as it stood fifty years ago, others because, while professing to teach a great variety of subjects, they teach them in an imperfect way, having neither a sufficiently large staff of highly trained professors, nor an adequate provision of laboratories, libraries, and other external appliances. The older New England colleges are good types of the former group. Their instruction is sound and thorough, well calculated to fit a man for the professions of law or divinity, but it omits many branches of learning and science which have grown to importance within the last fifty years. There are also some Western colleges which deserve to be placed in the same category. Most of the Western state universities belong to the other group of this second class, that of institutions which aim at covering more ground than they are as yet able to cover. They have an ambitious programme; but neither the state of preparation of their students, nor the strength of the teaching staff, enables them to do justice to the promise which the programme holds out. They are true universities rather in aspiration than in fact.

Below these again there is a third and much larger class of colleges, three hundred or more, which are for most intents and purposes schools. They differ from the gymnasia of Germany, the lycées of France, the grammar schools of England, and high schools of Scotland, not only in the fact that they give degrees to those who have satisfactorily passed through their prescribed course or courses, but in permitting greater personal freedom to the students than boys would be allowed in those countries. They are universities or colleges as respects some of their arrangements, but schools in respect of the educational results attained. This large group may be further divided into two subclasses, distinguished from one another partly by their revenues, partly by the character of the population they serve, partly by the personal gifts of the president and teachers. Some seventy or eighty, though comparatively small, are strong by the zeal and capacity of their staff, and while not attempting to teach everything, teach the subjects which they do undertake with increasing thoroughness. The remainder would do better to renounce the privilege of granting degrees and be content to do school work according to school methods. The West and South are covered with these small colleges. In Illinois I find 32 named in the Report of the United States Education Bureau, in Tennesse 25. Oklahoma has already 6, with nearly 2,000 students, but all are still in an early stage of development. In Ohio out of 35, or possibly more, scarce any deserves to be called a university. The number of teachers and students is sometimes large, but not very many are in the collegiate and far fewer in the graduate departments. Most of the students are to be found in the preparatory department.

The total number of students in Harvard University was, in 1913, 4,354, in Yale 3,262, in Columbia University, New York, 9,379, and in four great state universities as follows: Michigan 5,805, Illinois 5,054, Wisconsin 5,982, California 6,817. These numbers, which except in the first case include women, show a great increase during the last twenty years.

Revenues. Nearly all, if not all, of the degree-granting bodies are endowed, the great majority by private founders, but a good many also by grants of land made by the state in which they stand, partly out of lands set apart for educational purposes by the federal government. In most cases the lands have been sold and the proceeds invested. Many of the state universities of the West receive a grant from the state treasury, voted annually or biennially by the legislature, but a preferable plan, adopted by several states, is to enact a permanent statute giving annually to the university some fraction of a cent, or a mill ($\frac{1}{1000}$ of a dollar) our of every dollar of the total valuation of the state. This acts automatically, increasing the grant as the resources of the state increase. The greater universities are constantly being enriched by the gifts of private individuals, often their own graduates; but the complaint is heard that these gifts are too frequently appropriated to some specific purpose, instead of being added to the general funds of the university. Harvard, Yale, Columbia, Princeton, Cornell, and Johns Hopkins are now all of them wealthy foundations, and the stream of munificence swells daily.[8] Before long there will be universities in America with resources far

---

[8] Mr. Johns Hopkins gave £700,000 to the university he founded at Baltimore. In 1906–7 the State University of Wisconsin received from its state treasury $624,456, that of California $446,040, that of Illinois $350,000. The legislature of California has since further raised its grant. Some

surpassing those of any Scottish university, and exceeding even the collective income of the university and all the colleges in Oxford or in Cambridge. In some states the real property and funds of universities are exempt from taxation.

Government. As already remarked, no American university or college is, so far as I know, governed either by its graduates alone, like Oxford and Cambridge, or by its teaching staff alone, like the Scotch universities before the Act of 1858. The state universities are usually controlled and managed by a board generally called the regents, sometimes elected by the people of the state, sometimes appointed by the governor or the legislature. There are states with an enlightened population, or in which an able president has been able to guide and influence the regents or the legislature, in which this plan has worked excellently, securing liberal appropriations, and interesting the commonwealth in the welfare of the highest organ of its intellectual life. There have also been states in which the haste or unwisdom of the legislature seemed for a time to have cramped the growth of the university. On the whole the regents of late years have generally ruled well and the states have shown more and more interest in university work; though too apt to bestow their liberality almost wholly on the more directly practical branches of its work.

All other universities and colleges are governed by boards of governors or trustees, sometimes allowed to renew themselves by cooptation, sometimes nominated by a religious denomination or other external authority.[9] The president of the institution is often, but not always, an *ex officio* member of this board, to which the management of property and financial interests belongs, while internal discipline and educational arrangements are usually left to the academic staff. A visitor from Europe is struck by the prominence of the president in an American university or college, and the almost monarchical position which he sometimes occupies towards the professors as well as towards the students. Far more authority is vested in him, more

---

universities, such as Columbia (in New York), Harvard, and Chicago, have very large revenues derived from private endowments. A magnificent endowment was given by Mr. Leland Stanford, senator for California, to found a new university at Palo Alto in that state, and still more recently Mr. John D. Rockefeller bestowed immense sums on the new university (opened in 1891) he established in Chicago.

[9] In Harvard the government is vested in a self-renewing body of seven persons called the corporation, or technically, the President and Fellows of Harvard College, who have the charge of the property; and in a board of overseers, appointed formerly by the legislature, now by the graduates, five each year to serve for six years, with a general supervision of the educational system, educational details and discipline being left to the faculty.

turns upon his individual talents and character, than in the universities of Europe. Neither the German pro-rector, nor the vice-chancellor in Oxford and Cambridge, nor the principal in a Scottish university, nor the provost of Trinity College in Dublin, nor the head in one of the colleges in Oxford or Cambridge, is anything like so important a personage.[10] In this, as in not a few other respects, America is less republican than England.

Of late years there have been active movements to secure the representation of the graduates of each university or college upon its governing body; and it now frequently happens that some of the trustees are elected by the alumni. Good results follow, because the alumni are disposed to elect men younger and more abreast of the times, than most of the persons whom the existing trustees coopt.

The Teaching Staff. The faculty, as it is usually called, varies in numbers and efficiency according to the popularity of the university or college and its financial resources. The largest staff mentioned in the tables of the U.S. Bureau of Education is that of Harvard, with 731 professors, instructors, and lecturers; while Yale has 455, Columbia has 907, the University of Pennsylvania 553, Princeton 203, the University of Michigan 331, Johns Hopkins 225. Cornell returns 700, but apparently not all of these are constantly occupied in teaching.

In the colleges of the West and Northwest the average number of teachers is small, say twelve to fifteen in the collegiate, five to ten in the preparatory department. It is larger in the state universities, but in some of the Southern and ruder Western states sinks to five or six, each of them taking two or three subjects. I remember to have met in the Far West a college president— I will call him Mr. Johnson—who gave me a long account of his young university, established by public authority, and receiving some small grant from the legislature. He was an active sanguine man, and in dilating on his plans frequently referred to "the faculty" as doing this or contemplating that. At last I asked of how many professors the faculty at present consisted. "Well," he answered, "just at present the faculty is below its full strength, but it will soon be more numerous." "And at present?" I inquired. "At present it consists of Mrs. Johnson and myself."

---

[10] The president of a college was formerly usually, and in denominational colleges almost invariably, a clergyman, and generally lectured on mental and moral philosophy. (When a layman was chosen at Harvard in 1828 the clergy thought it an encroachment.) He is today not so likely to be in orders. However, of the forty Ohio colleges twenty have clerical presidents. The greater universities of the East and the Western state universities are now usually ruled by laymen. Even some of the denominational colleges have no longer clerical heads.

The salaries paid to professors seem small compared with the general wealth of the country and the cost of living. The highest known to me are those in Columbia College, a few of which exceed $5,000 a year, and in the University of Chicago, which pays some of $7,000. Even in Yale, Johns Hopkins, and Cornell, most fall below $4,000. A very few presidents receive $10,000, but over the country generally I should guess that a president rarely receives $4,000, often only $3,000 or $2,000, and the professors less in proportion. Under these conditions it may be found surprising that so many able men are to be found on the teaching staff of not a few colleges as well as universities, and that in the greater universities there are also many who have trained themselves by a long and expensive education in Europe for their work. The reason is to be found partly in the fondness for science and learning which has lately shown itself in America, and which makes men of intellectual tastes prefer a life of letters with poverty to success in business or at the bar, partly, as regards the smaller Western colleges, to religious motives, these colleges being largely officered by the clergy of the denomination they belong to, especially by those who love study, or find their talents better suited to the classroom than to the pulpit.

The professors seem to be always among the social aristocracy of the city in which they live, though usually unable, from the smallness of their incomes, to enjoy social life as the corresponding class does in Scotland or even in England. The position of president is often one of honour and wide influence.

The Students. It is the glory of the American universities, as of those of Scotland and Germany, to be freely accessible to all classes of the people. In the Eastern states a comparatively small yet an increasing number have been the sons of working men, because parents can rarely bear the expense of a university course, or dispense with a boy's earnings after he reaches fourteen. But even in the East a good many come from straitened homes, receiving assistance from some richer neighbour or from charitable funds belonging to the college at which they may present themselves; while some, in days when the standard of instruction was lower, and women were less generally employed as teachers, used to teach district schools for three months in winter. In the West, where there is little distinction of classes though great disparity of wealth, the state universities make a small or possibly no charge, and some other institutions require a merely nominal fee, or are ready to receive without charge a promising student. Thus the only difficulty in a young man's way is that of supporting himself during his college course; and this he frequently does by earning during one half the year what keeps him during the other half. Often he earns it by teaching school: many of the eminent men, including several presidents of the United States, from 1840 to 1890 thus supported themselves in some part of their earlier careers. Sometimes he works at a trade, as many a student has done in Scotland; and, as in Scotland, he is all the more respected by his classmates for it. The instruction which he gets in one of these Western colleges may not carry him very far, but it opens a door through which men of real power can pass into the professions, or even into the domain of learning and scientific research. In no country are the higher kinds of teaching more cheap or more accessible. There is a growing tendency for well-to-do parents to send their sons to one of the greater universities irrespective of the profession they contemplate for him, that is to say, purely for the sake of general culture, or of the social advantages which a university course is thought to confer. The usual age at which students enter one of the leading universities of the East is, as in England, from eighteen to nineteen, and the usual age of graduation twenty-two to twenty-three,[11] the regular course covering four years. In the West some students come at a more advanced age, twenty-four or twenty-five, their early education having been neglected, so the average in Western colleges is higher than in the East. In Scotland boys of fourteen and men of twenty-four used to sit side by side in university classrooms, and compete on equal terms, a pleasing relic of mediæval times which survives in the University of El Azhar in Cairo. The places of less note draw students from their immediate vicinity only; to those of importance boys are sent from all parts of the Union. The University of Michigan, the first among the state universities to develop on a large scale, used to be a sort of metropolitan university for the Northwestern states. Harvard and Yale, which used to draw only from the Atlantic states, now receive students from the West and even from the shores of the Pacific. Princeton has long drawn many from the South.[12] A student generally completes his four years' graduation course at the same institution, but some few leave a small college after one year to enter at a larger one. A man who has graduated in a college which has only an arts or collegiate department, will often, in case he designs himself for law or medicine, resort to the law or medical school of a larger university, or even, if he means to devote himself to science or philology, will pursue what is called

[11] President Eliot gives it for Harvard at 22 years and 7 months.
[12] Many students now come from Europe and Asia. In 1909 there were in 34 United States universities 1,467 from abroad, including 458 from Asia (including 158 Japanese and 193 Chinese, with 60 from the East Indies), 313 from Europe, 154 from South America, and 64 from Australia.

a "post-graduate course" at some one of the greatest seats of learning. Thus it may happen, as in Germany, that a man has studied at two or three universities in succession.

Buildings and External Aspect. Few of the buildings in any college or university are more than a century old,[13] and among these there is none of an imposing character, or with marked architectural merit. Many of the newer ones are handsome and well arranged, but I have heard it remarked that too much money is now being spent, at least in the West, upon showy buildings, possibly with the view of commanding attention. The ground plan is rarely or never that of a quadrangle as in England and Scotland, not because it was desired to avoid monastic precedents, but because detached buildings are thought to be better adapted to the cold and snows of winter. At Harvard and Yale the brick dormitories (buildings in which the students live) and classrooms are scattered over a large space of grass planted with ancient elms, and have a very pleasing effect. Rochester, too, has a spacious campus. Princeton, Amherst, Williams, and Dartmouth, being placed in small country towns and pleasing scenery, have even more attractive surroundings, and the situations of the Universities of Virginia, Wisconsin, and California are highly favoured by nature. Ample and agreeable pleasure grounds surround the women's colleges of Vassar, Wellesley, and Bryn Mawr.

Time Spent in Study. Vacations are shorter than in England or Scotland. That of summer usually lasts from the middle of June to the middle of September, and there are generally ten days or more given at Christmas and at least a week in April. Work begins earlier in the morning than in England, but seldom so early as in Germany. Hardly any students seem to work as hard as the men reading for high honours do at Cambridge in England.

Local Distribution of Universities and Colleges. The number of degree-granting bodies seems to be larger in the Middle and Northwestern states than either in New England or in the South. In the tables of the Bureau of Education I find New York, Pennsylvania, Ohio, Indiana, Illinois, Iowa, credited with 191, one-third of the total for the United States; but as many are small and indifferent, the mere number does not necessarily speak of an ample and solid provision of education. Indeed Ohio has no single institution to which a place in the front rank would be assigned. The fourteen Southern states (excluding Missouri, Maryland, and Delaware) stand in the tables as

---

[13] I remember one in Yale of 1753, called South Middle, which was venerated as the oldest building there.

possessing 191, but it may be doubted whether any of these, except the University of Virginia, attains the very first rank; and though some have been rising steadily, the great majority are undermanned and hampered by the imperfect preparation of the students whom they receive. In this respect, and as regards education generally, the South, though advancing, is still far behind the other sections of the country. There are several colleges, all or nearly all of them denominational, established for coloured people only.

System and Methods of Instruction. In 1860 it would have been comparatively easy to describe these, for nearly all the universities and colleges prescribed a regular four years' curriculum to a student, chiefly consisting of classics and mathematics, and leading up to a B.A. degree. A youth had little or no option what he would study, for everybody was expected to take certain classes in each year, and received his degree upon having satisfactorily performed what was in each class required of him.[14] The course was not unlike that followed (till 1892) in the Scottish universities: it began with Latin, Greek, and mathematics, and wound up with logic, mental and moral philosophy, and a tincture of physics. Instruction was mainly, indeed in the small colleges wholly, catechetical. About 1870 the simple uniformity of this traditional system began to vanish in the greater universities of the Eastern and Middle states, and in most of the state universities of the West. In most of the smaller colleges, however, there are still regular classes, a certain number of which every student must attend, but he is allowed to choose for himself between a variety of courses or curricula, by following any one of which he may obtain a degree. The freedom of choice is greater in some universities, less in others; in some, choice is permitted from the first, in most, however (including the great university of Yale), only after two years. In Harvard freedom reached its maximum. The controversies out of which the "elective system" emerged turned largely on the question whether Greek should be a compulsory subject. The change was introduced for the sake of bringing scientific subjects into the curriculum and enabling men to specialize in them and in matters like history and Oriental or Romance philology, and was indeed a necessary concomitant to such a broadening of universities as may enable them to keep pace with the swift development of new branches of study and research during the last forty years. It is defended both on this ground and as being more likely than the old strictly limited courses to give every

---

[14] The University of Virginia was an exception, having received from the enlightened views of Jefferson an impulse towards greater freedom.

student something which will interest him. It is opposed as tending to bewilder him, to disperse and scatter his mind over a too wide range of subjects, perhaps unconnected with one another, to tempt him with the offer of an unchartered freedom which he wants the experience to use wisely. One or two conspicuous universities, and many smaller colleges, have clung to the old system of two or three prescribed degree courses in which little variation is admitted.[15] An elective system is indeed possible only where the teaching staff is able to do justice to a wide range of subjects.

A parallel change has passed upon the methods of teaching. Lecturing with the interposition of few or no questions to the class is becoming the rule in the larger universities, those especially which adopt the elective system, while what are called "recitations," that is to say, catechetical methods resembling those of Scotland or of a college (not university) lecture in Oxford sixty years ago, remain the rule in the more conservative majority of institutions, and are practically universal in the smaller colleges. Some of the largest universities have established a system of informal instruction by the professor to a small group of students on the model of the German seminar. Private "coaching," such as prevailed largely in Oxford and still prevails in Cambridge, is almost unknown.

Requirements for Entrance. All the better universities and colleges exact a minimum of knowledge from those who matriculate. Some do this by imposing an entrance examination. Others allow certain schools, of whose excellence they are satisfied, to issue leaving certificates, the production of which entitles the bearers to be admitted without examination. This plan is said to work well.[16] Michigan led the way in establishing a judiciously regulated and systematized relation between the public schools and the state university, and other universities have now an excellent system for inspecting schools and admitting students on the basis of school certificates.

Degrees and Examinations. It is only institutions which have been

---

[15] The small colleges were the more unwilling to drop Greek as a compulsory subject because they think that by doing so they would lose the anchor by which they held to the higher culture, and confess themselves to be no longer universities. But Greek declines in them also.

[16] At Harvard I was informed that about one-third of the students came from the public (i.e., publicly supported) schools. The proportion is in most universities larger. There is a growing tendency in America, especially in the East, for boys of the richer class to be sent to private schools, and the number and excellence of such schools increases. The total number of endowed academies, seminaries, and other private secondary schools over the country in 1912 is returned as 2,044, with 12,110 pupils (7,646 boys and 4,464 girls) preparing for a college classical course; 8,575 pupils (7,679 boys and 896 girls) preparing for a scientific course. But these figures are far from complete.

chartered by state authority that are deemed entitled to grant degrees. There are others which do so without any such legal title, but as the value of a degree per se is slight, the mischief done by these interlopers can hardly be serious. B.A., M.A., (less frequently) Ph.D., D.D., and LL.D., the two latter usually for honorary purposes,[17] are the only degrees conferred in the great majority of colleges; but of late years the larger universities have, in creating new courses, created a variety of new degrees also.[18] Degrees are awarded by examination, but never, I think, as often in Europe, upon a single examination held after the course of study has been completed. The student, as he goes through the various classes which make up his course, is examined, sometimes at frequent intervals, sometimes at the end of each year, on the work done in the classes or on prescribed books, and the degree is ultimately awarded or refused on the combined result of all these tests. At no point in his career is he expected to submit to any one examination comparable, for the combined number and difficulty of the subjects in which he is questioned, to the final honour examinations at Oxford or Cambridge, even as now constituted, much less as they stood in the middle of last century.

There is indeed no respect in which the American system is more contrasted with that of Oxford and Cambridge than the comparatively small part assigned to the award of honours. In England the class list or tripos has for many years past, ever since the universities awoke from their lethargy of the eighteenth century, been the main motive power in stimulating undergraduates to exertion and in stemming the current which runs so strongly towards amusement and athletic exercises. Examinations have governed teaching instead of being used to test it. In the United States, although most universities and colleges reward with some sort of honourable mention the students who have acquitted themselves conspicuously well, graduation honours are not a great object of ambition; they win little or no fame within the institution, they are unnoticed beyond its walls. In many universities there is not even the stimulus, which acts powerfully in Scotland, of class prizes, awarded by examination or by the votes of the students. It is only a few institutions that possess scholarships awarded by competition.

---

[17] Honorary degrees are in some institutions, and not usually those of the highest standing, conferred with a profuseness which seems to argue an exaggerated appreciation of inconspicuous merit.

[18] Among the degree titles awarded in some institutions to women, the titles of Bachelor and Master being deemed inappropriate, are the following—Laureate of Science, Proficient in Music, Maid of Philosophy, Mistress of Polite Literature, Mistress of Music (*North American Review* for March 1885).

American teachers seem to find the discipline of their regular class system sufficient to maintain a reasonable level of diligence among their students, being doubtless aided by the fact that, in all but a very few universities, the vast majority of the students come from simple homes, possess scanty means, and have their way in life to make. Diligence—a moderate but fairly sustained diligence—was the tradition of the American colleges until the passion for athletic competitions became pronounced; and this is still true in most of those remote from the dissipating influences and social excitements of large cities. It is still the rule in post-graduate courses and in the professional schools, for students who have got so far feel the need for turning their opportunities to full account. Even the greater universities have never been, as the English universities avowedly were in the first half of the last century, and to some extent are still, primarily places for spending three or four pleasant years, only incidentally places of instruction. For the absence of a competitive system two merits have been claimed. One is that it escapes that separation which has grown up in Oxford and Cambridge between pass or poll men and honour men. The ordinary student supposes himself to have come to college for the purpose of learning something. In all countries, even in Switzerland and Scotland, there is a percentage of idle men in places of study; but the idleness of an American student is due to something in his own character or circumstances, and does not, as in the case of the English "poll-man," rest on a theory in his own mind, probably shared by his parents, that he entered the university in order to enjoy himself and form useful social connections. It is held to be another merit that the love of knowledge and truth is not, among the better minds, vulgarized by being made the slave of competition and of the passion for quick and conspicuous success. An American student is not induced by his university to think less of the intrinsic value of what he is learning than of how far it will pay in an examination; nor does he regard his ablest fellow students as his rivals over a difficult course for high stakes, rivals whose speed and strength he must constantly be comparing with his own. Americans who have studied in an English university after graduating in one of their own have told me that nothing surprised them more in England than the incessant canvassing of one another's intellectual capacities which went on among the undergraduates.[19] Much less work is got out of the better American students than the examination system exacts from the same class of men in Oxford and Cambridge. Probably the qualities of readiness and accuracy

---

[19] If this be true of England, the evil is probably no smaller under the class prize system of Scotland.

are not so thoroughly trained. Possibly it is a loss not to be compelled to carry for a few weeks a large mass of facts in one's mind under the obligation of finding any one at a moment's notice. Those who direct the leading American universities recognize in these points the advantages of English practice, but have not so far been disposed to alter their own traditional system, which relies on the interest the student has in turning to account his college years and doing work enough to secure his degree.

Nearly all American students do graduate, that is to say, as those who would be likely to fail drop off before the close of the fourth year, the proportion of plucks in the later examinations is small. As regards the worth of the degrees given, there is of course the greatest possible difference between those of the better and those of the lower institutions, nor is this difference merely one between the few great universities and the mass of small colleges or Western state universities, for among the smaller colleges there are some which maintain as high a standard of thoroughness as the greatest. The degrees of the very numerous colleges to which I have referred as belonging to the lower group of the third class have no assignable value, except that of indicating that a youth has been made to work during four years at subjects above the elementary. Those of institutions belonging to the higher group and the two other classes represent, on an average, as much knowledge and mental discipline as the poll or pass degrees of Cambridge or Oxford, possibly less than the pass degrees of the Scottish universities. Between the highest American degrees and the honour degrees of Oxford and Cambridge it is hard to make any comparison.

A degree is in the United States given only to those who have followed a prescribed course in the teaching institution which confers it. No American institution has so far departed from the old and true conception of a university, approved by both history and policy, as to become a mere examining board, awarding degrees to anybody who may present himself from any quarter. However, the evils of existing arrangements, under which places below the level of German gymnasia are permitted to grant academic titles, are deemed so serious by some educational reformers that it was proposed as far back as 1890 to create in each state a single degree-conferring authority to which the various institutions within the state should be, so to speak, tributary, sending up their students to its examinations, which would of course be kept at a higher level than most of the present independent bodies maintain. This is what physicians call a "heroic remedy"; it does not seem to have won favour, nor need this be regretted.

Notwithstanding these evils, and the vast distance between the standard of a university like Johns Hopkins at the one end of the scale, and that of the weakest Southern colleges at the other, a degree, wherever obtained, seems to have a certain social value. "It is," said one of my informants, "a thing which you would mention regarding a young man for whom you were writing a letter of introduction." This does not mean very much, but it is better than nothing; it would appear to give a man some sort of advantage in seeking for educational or literary work. In several states a man who can point to his degree obtains speedier entrance to the bar, and some denominations endeavour to secure that their clergy shall have graduated.

Post-graduate Courses. Several of the leading universities have lately instituted sets of lectures for students who have completed the regular four years' collegiate course and taken their B.A. or B.Sc., hoping in this way to provide for the special study of subjects for which room cannot be found in the regular course. Johns Hopkins University was among the first to devote itself especially to this object. Its aim was not so much to rival the existing universities as to discharge a function which many of them had not the means of undertaking—that of providing the highest special instruction, not necessarily in every subject, but in subjects which it could secure the ablest professors. It did much admirable work in this direction, and soon made good its claim to a place in the front rank of transatlantic seats of education. There are also many graduates who, desiring to devote themselves to some particular branch of science or learning, such as experimental physics, philology, or history, spend a semester or two at a German or to a less extent at a French university.[20] Fewer come to Oxford or Cambridge, but the number has increased since the foundation of the Rhodes scholarships provided funds for two from each state to proceed to Oxford. American professors, when asked why they send their men chiefly to Germany, considering that in England they would have the advantage of a more interesting social life, and of seeing how England is trying to deal with problems similar in many respects to their own, answer that the English universities make no provision for any students except those who wish to go through one of the regular degree courses, and are so much occupied in preparing men to pass examinations as to give, except in two or three branches, but little advanced teaching. There can be no doubt that if Oxford and Cambridge offered the advantages which Leipzig and Berlin do, the afflux to the two former of American graduates would soon be considerable.

Professional and Scientific Schools. Besides the very large number of

---

[20] In 1909 there were said to be 298 American students enrolled at the German universities.

schools for all the practical arts, agriculture, engineering, mining, and so forth, as well as for the professions of theology, law, and medicine, statistics of which have been already given, some universities have established scientific schools, or agricultural schools, or theological, legal, and medical faculties. The theological faculties are usually denominational; but Harvard, which used to be practically Unitarian, has now an unsectarian faculty, in which there are several learned divines belonging to Trinitarian denominations; and no difficulty seems to have arisen in working this arrangement. The law school is usually treated as a separate department, to which students may resort who have not graduated in the university. The course is usually of two, sometimes of three, years, and covers all the leading branches of common law, equity, crimes, civil and criminal procedure. Many of these schools are extremely efficient.

Research. Till recently no special provision was made for the promotion of research as apart from the work of learning and teaching; but the example set by Johns Hopkins and Harvard in founding fellowships for this purpose has now been largely followed, and in 1907 there were 664 fellowships, of which 115 were in Massachusetts, 114 in Illinois, and 85 in New York. The munificence of private benefactors may be expected to continue to supply the necessary funds. There is now, especially in the greater universities, a good deal of specialization in teaching, so an increasing number of professors are able to occupy themselves with research. The Institution for Research founded in Washington by Mr. Carnegie incidentally aids the universities by its grants of money to professors engaged in research work.

Aids to Deserving Students. In proportion to the number of colleges, not many have scholarships or bursaries open to competition like those of the colleges in Oxford and Cambridge and of the Scottish universities. The number has, however, been increasing.[21] But in a large number there exist funds, generally placed at the disposal of the president or the faculty, which are applicable for the benefit of industrious men who need help; and it is common to remit fees in the case of those whose circumstances warrant the indulgence. When, as occasionally happens, free places or grants out of these funds are awarded upon examination, it would be thought improper for anyone to compete whose circumstances placed him above the need of pecuniary aid. When the selection is left to the college authorities, they are said to discharge it with honourable impartiality. Having often asked whether

---

[21] The Report of the Bureau of Education for 1911–12 gives the total number of scholarships and fellowships at 13,989, but does not state how many are awarded by competition. Of these, 7,073 were reported from the North Atlantic states.

favouritism was complained of, I could never hear that it was. In some colleges there exists a loan fund, out of which money is advanced to the poor student, who afterwards repays it. President Garfield obtained his education at Williams College by the help of such a fund. The denominations often give assistance to promising youths who intend to enter the ministry. Says one of my most experienced informants: "In our country any young fellow of ability and energy can get education without paying for it."[22] The experiment tried at Cornell University in the way of providing remunerative labour for poor students who were at the same time to follow a course of instruction, seems to have proved unworkable, for the double effort is found to impose too severe a strain.

Social Life of the Students. Those who feel that not only the keenest pleasure, but the most solid moral and intellectual benefit of their university life lay in the friendships which they formed in that happy springtime, will ask how in this respect America compares with England. Oxford and Cambridge, with their historic colleges maintaining a corporate life from century to century, bringing the teachers into easy and friendly relations with the taught, forming between the members of each society a close and almost family tie which is not incompatible with loyalty to the great corporation for whose sake all the minor corporations exist, have succeeded in producing a more polished, graceful, and I think also intellectually stimulative, type of student life than either Germany, with its somewhat boyish frolics of duelling and compotations, or Scotland, where the youth has few facilities for social intercourse with his classmates and none with his professor. The American universities occupy an intermediate position between those of England and those of Germany or Scotland. Formerly all or nearly all the students were lodged in buildings called dormitories— which, however, were not merely sleeping places, but contained sitting rooms jointly tenanted by two or more students—and meals were taken in common. This is still the practice in the smaller colleges, and remains firmly rooted in Yale, Harvard, and Princeton, though in the two former for part only of the students. In the new state universities, and in nearly all universities planted in large cities, the great bulk of the students board with private families, or (more rarely) live in lodgings or hotels, and an increasing

---

[22] Fees, in the West especially, are low. In the University of Michigan a student belonging to the state pays $10 on admission and an annual fee of $30 (Department of Literature, Science, and the Arts), or $45 (other departments), students from without the state paying $25 (admission), $40 (Department of Literature, etc.), $55 (other departments), with special fees in law and laboratory courses.

number have begun to do so even in places which, like Harvard and Brown University (Rhode Island) and Cornell, have some dormitories. The dormitory plan works well in comparatively small establishments, especially when, as is the case with the smaller denominational colleges, they are almost like large families, and are permeated by a religious spirit. But in the larger universities the tendency is now towards letting the students reside where they please, though some state universities have dormitories. The maintenance of discipline gives less trouble; the poorer student is less inclined to imitate or envy the luxurious habits of the rich. Sometimes, however, as where there is no town for students to lodge in, dormitories are indispensable. The chief breaches of order which the authorities have to deal with arise in dormitories from the practice of "hazing," i.e., playing practical jokes, especially upon freshmen. In an American college the students are classed by years, those of the first year being called freshmen, of the second year sophomores, of the third year juniors, of the fourth year seniors. The bond between the members of each "class" (i.e., the entrants of the same year) is a pretty close one, and they are apt to act together. Between sophomores and freshmen—for the seniors and juniors are supposed to have put away childish things—there is a smouldering jealousy which sometimes breaks out into a strife sufficiently acute, though there is seldom anything more than mischievously high spirits behind it, to give the president and faculty trouble.[23] Otherwise the conduct of the students is generally good. Intoxication, gaming, or other vices are rare, those who come to work, as the vast majority do, being little prone to such faults; it is only in a few universities situate in or near large cities and resorted to by the sons of the rich that they give serious trouble. Of late years the passion for baseball, football, rowing, and athletic exercises generally, has become very strong in the universities last mentioned, where fashionable youth congregates, and the student who excels in these seems to be as much a hero among his comrades as a member of the university eight or eleven is in England.

The absence of colleges constituting social centres within a university has helped to develop in the American universities one of their most peculiar and interesting institutions—I mean the Greek letter societies. There are clubs or fraternities of students, denoted by two or three Greek letters, the initials of the secret fraternity motto. Some of these fraternities exist in one

---

[23] Sophomores and freshmen have a whimsical habit of meeting one another in dense masses and trying which can push the other aside on the stairs or path. This is called "rushing." In some universities the admission of women as students has put an end to it. Hazing has diminished of late years.

college only, but the greater are established in a good many universities and colleges, having in each what is called a chapter, and possessing in each a sort of clubhouse, with several meeting and reading rooms, and sometimes also with bedrooms for the members. In some colleges as many as a third or a half of the students belong to a fraternity, which is an institution recognized and patronized by the authorities. New members are admitted by the votes of the chapter; and to obtain early admission to one of the best is no small compliment. They are, so far as I know, always nonpolitical, though political questions may be debated and political essays read at their meetings; and one is told that they allow no intoxicants to be kept in their buildings or used at the feasts they provide. They are thus something between an English club and a German *Studenten Corps*, with a literary element sometimes thrown in. They are deemed a valuable part of the university system, not so much because they cultivate intellectual life as on account of their social influence. It is an object of ambition to be elected a member; it is a point of honour for a member to maintain the credit of the fraternity. Former members, who are likely to include some of the university professors, keep up their connection with the fraternity, and often attend its chapters in the college, or its general meetings. Membership constitutes a bond between old members during their whole life, so that a member on settling in some distant city would probably find there persons who had belonged to his fraternity, and would be admitted to their local gatherings.[24] Besides these there exist a few honorary societies into which students are elected in virtue of purely literary or scientific acquirements, as evidenced in the college examinations. The oldest and most famous is called the φ B K, which is said to mean φιλοσοφία βίου κυβερνήτης, and exists in many of the leading universities in some of the states.

Religion. I have already observed that a good many of the American universities, and indeed a majority of the smaller colleges, are denominational. This term, however, does not mean what it would mean in Europe, or at least in England. It means that they have been founded by or in connection with a particular church, and that they remain to some extent associated with it or influenced by it. Apart from the 81 state or municipal institutions, only 84 out of the 493 mentioned in the educational report state that they are unsectarian. The Methodists claim 77 colleges; the Presbyterians, 54; the Baptists, 39; the Roman Catholics, 52; the Congregationalists, 10;

---

[24] There are, of course, other students' societies and social clubs, sometimes expensive and exclusive, besides these Greek letter ones.

the Protestant Episcopalians, 2. But, except as regards the Roman Catholic institutions, there is seldom any exclusion of teachers, and never of students, belonging to other churches, nor any attempt to give the instruction (except, of course, in the theological department, if there be one) a sectarian cast; this indeed is apt to be expressly repudiated by them. Although it usually happens that students belonging to the church which influences the college are more numerous than those of any other church, students of other persuasions abound; nor are efforts made to proselytize them. For instance, Harvard retains a certain flavour of Unitarianism, and has one or two Unitarian clergymen among the professors in its theological faculty; Yale has always been Congregationalist, and has by its charter ten Congregationalist clergymen among the trustees; and moreover had formerly Congregationalist clergymen as its presidents, as Brown University has a Baptist clergyman.[25] Princeton is still more specifically Presbyterian, and the Episcopalians have several denominational colleges in which the local bishop is one of the trustees. But in none of these is there anything approaching to a test imposed upon professors; all are resorted to alike by students belonging to any church or to none.

In all the older universities, and in the vast majority of the more recent ones, there is a chapel in which religious services are regularly held, short prayers on the five weekdays and sometimes also a full service twice on Sundays. In most institutions every student, unless of course he has some conscientious objection, is expected to attend. The service seldom or never contains anything of a sectarian character, and arrangements are sometimes made for having it conducted by the clergy of various denominations in turn. Even among the professedly neutral new state universities, there are some which, like the University of Michigan, have daily prayers. There are of course persons who think that an unsectarian place of education cannot be a truly Christian place of education, and Cornell University in its early days had to face attacks directed against it on this score.[26] But the more

[25] Brown University, formerly called Rhode Island College (founded in 1764), is in the rather peculiar position of having by its regulations four denominations, Baptists, Congregationalists, Episcopalians, and Quakers, equally represented on its two governing bodies, the trustees and the fellows, the Baptists having a majority.

[26] At Cornell University there exists a Sunday preachership endowed with a fund of $30,000 (£6000), which is used to recompense the services of distinguished ministers of different denominations who preach in succession during twenty-one Sundays of the academic year. The founder was an Episcopalian, whose first idea was to have a chaplaincy limited to ministers of his denomination, but the trustees refused the endowment on such terms. The only students who absent themselves are Roman Catholics.

prevalent view is that a university ought to be in a general sense religious without being sectarian.[27] An interesting experiment in unsectarian religious worship has for some time past been tried at Harvard. Attendance at the college chapel, formerly compulsory, is now voluntary, and short morning daily services with extempore prayers are conducted by the chaplains, who are eminent ministers of different denominations, serving in turn for a few weeks each. The late Dr. Phillips Brooks was one of them; and his short addresses profoundly impressed the students.

The Provision of University Education for Women. The efforts made and experiments tried in this matter furnish material for a treatise. All I have space to mention is that these efforts have chiefly flowed in two channels. One is the admission of women to coeducation with men in the same places of higher education. This has gone on for many years in some of the denominational colleges of the West, such as Oberlin and Antioch in Ohio. Both sexes have been taught in the same classes, meeting in the hours of recreation, but lodged in separate buildings. My informants generally commended the plan, declaring that the effect on the manners and general tone of the students was excellent. The state universities founded of late years in the West are by law open to women as well as to men. The number of women attending is always smaller than that of men, yet in some institutions it is considerable, as for instance at the University of Michigan at Ann Arbor there were, in 1911–12, 810 women and 4,120 men, in that of California 1,710 women and 3,088 men, in that of Minnesota, 1,746 women and 3,143 men, while Oberlin had 1,064 women and 670 men and Chicago 3,611 women and 3,421 men. The students live where they will, but are taught in the same classes, generally, however, sitting on the opposite side of the classroom from the men. The evidence given to me as to the working of this system in the Universities of California and Michigan, as well as in Cornell University, was on the whole favourable, save that the

---

[27] This idea is exactly expressed in the regulations for the most recent great foundation, that of Mr. Leland Stanford in California. It is declared to be the duty of the trustees "to prohibit sectarian instruction, but to have taught in the University the immortality of the soul, the existence of an all-wise and benevolent Creator, and that obedience to His laws is the highest duty of man." The founders further declare, "While it is our desire that there shall be no sectarian teaching in this institution, it is very far from our thoughts to exclude divine service. We have provided that a suitable building be erected, wherein the professors of the various religious denominations shall from time to time be invited to deliver discourses not sectarian in character." On the other hand, the still more recent foundation of Mr. Rockefeller at Chicago prescribes that "at all times two-thirds of the trustees and also the president of the university and of its said college shall be members of regular Baptist churches—and in this particular the charter shall be for ever unalterable." All professorships, however, are to be free from any religious tests.

young men sometimes find the competition of the girls rather severe, and call them "study machines," observing that they are more eager, and less addicted to sports or to mere lounging.

In the Eastern states the tendency has been to establish universities or colleges exclusively for women, and cases are known to me in which institutions that received both sexes ended by having a distinct department or separate college for women. There are persons even in the East who would prefer the scheme of coeducation, but the more general view is that the stricter etiquette and what is called the "more complex civilization" of the older states render this undesirable.[28] The total number of colleges specially for women was given in the Education Report for 1909 at 113, at two grades. In Division A were 16 colleges, with 357 male and 568 female instructors and 8,610 students of whom 142 were in preparatory departments. The 97 colleges in Division B might more fitly be described as "upper schools" with 301 male instructors, 1,443 women, 12,211 "collegiate students" and 6,691 preparatory. The number of degrees conferred was 978. Among these colleges the best known, and apparently the most complete and efficient,[29] are Vassar, at Poughkeepsie, New York; Wellesley, Smith, and Mount Holyoke in Massachusetts; Bryn Mawr in Pennsylvania. In visiting three of these, I was much impressed by the earnestness and zeal for learning by which both the professors and the students seemed to be inspired, as well as by the high level of the teaching given. They have happily escaped the temptation to which some similar institutions in England were in danger of yielding, of making everything turn upon degree examinations. Harvard has established, in what was called its Annex, but is now more generally known as Radcliffe College, a separate department for women, in which the university professors lecture. I have no adequate data for comparing the quality of the education given to women in America with that provided by women's colleges, and especially by those in Cambridge and Oxford, in England, but there can be no doubt that the eagerness to make full provision for women has been keener in the former country, and that a much larger number avail themselves of what has been provided.

---

[28] As the late Mr. George William Curtis wrote: "It is now settled that Juliet may study, but shall she study with Romeo?—that is a question which gives even Boston pause."

[29] In 1913–14 Wellesley had 1,480 students, with 133 professors and teachers and an income from all sources of $716,000. Smith College had 1,548 students, 127 instructors and an income from all sources of $581,000. Vassar had 1,073 students, 115 instructors and an income of $1,176,108. Bryn Mawr had 469 students, 67 instructors and an income of $331,274. The proportion of men teachers to women teachers varied from one-third to two-thirds.

General Observations. The European reader will by this time have perceived how hard it is to give such a general estimate of the educational and social worth of the higher teaching in the United States as one might give of the universities of Germany, England, and Scotland. In America the universities are not, as they are in those countries, a well-defined class of institutions. Not only is the distance between the best and the worst greater than that which in Germany separates Leipzig from Rostock, or in England Cambridge from Durham, but the gradations from the best down to the worst are so imperceptible that one can nowhere draw a line and say that here the true university stops and the pretentious school begins.[30] As has been observed already, a large number present the external seeming and organization—the skeleton plan, so to speak—of a university with the actual performance of a rather raw school.

Moreover, the American universities and colleges are in a state of transition. True, nearly everything in America is changing, the apparently inflexible Constitution not excepted. But the changes that are passing in the universities are only to be paralleled by those that pass upon Western cities. The number of small colleges, especially in the Mississippi and Pacific states, has greatly increased since 1870. The character of the Eastern universities is being constantly modified. The former multiply, because under the federal system, every state likes to have its own universities numerous, and its inhabitants independent of other states, even as respects education; while the abundance of wealth, the desire of rich men to commemorate themselves and to benefit their community, and the rivalry of the churches, lead to the establishment of new colleges where none are needed, and where money would be better spent in improving those which exist. Individualism and laissez faire have, in this matter at least, free scope, for a state legislature is always ready to charter any number of new degree-giving bodies.[31] Meanwhile, the great institutions of the Atlantic states continue to expand and develop not merely owing to the accretion of wealth

---

[30] Even in Europe it is curious to note how each country is apt to think the universities of the other to be rather schools than universities. The Germans call Oxford and Cambridge schools, because they have hitherto given comparatively little professional and specialized teaching. The English call the Scotch universities schools because many of their students enter at fifteen.

[31] The New York legislature recently offered a charter to the Chatauqua gathering, one of the most interesting institutions in America, and one most thoroughly characteristic of the country, standing midway between a popular university and an educational camp meeting, and representing both the religious spirit and the love of knowledge which characterize the better part of the native American middle and poorer classes. It has been imitated in the West; there are many such gatherings called Chautauquas.

to them from the liberality of benefactors, but because they are in close touch with Europe, resolved to bring their highest education up to the European level and to keep pace with the progress of science, filled with that love of experiment and spirit of enterprise which are so much stronger in America than anywhere else in the world.

Not the least interesting of the phenomena of the last thirty years is the struggle which has gone on in the Middle and Western states between the greater, and especially the state universities, and the small denominational colleges. The latter, which used to have the field to themselves, are now afraid of being driven off it by the growth of the former, and not only redoubled their exertions to increase their own resources and students, but— in some states—to prevent the state university from obtaining larger grants from the state treasury. They alleged that the unsectarian character of the state establishments, as well as the freedom allowed to their students, made them less capable of giving a moral and religious training. But as the graduates of the state universities became numerous in the legislatures and influential generally, and as it was more and more clearly seen that the small colleges would not, for want of funds, provide the various appliances— libraries, museums, laboratories, and so forth—which universities need, the balance inclined in favour of the state universities. It is probable that while these will rise towards the level of their Eastern sisters, many of the denominational colleges will subside into the position of places of preparatory training.

One praise which has often been given to the universities of Scotland may be given to those of America. While the German universities have been popular but not free, while the English universities have been free[32] but not popular, the American universities have been both free and popular. Although some have been managed on too narrow a basis, the number has been so great that the community have not suffered. They have been established so easily, they have so fully reflected the habits and conditions of the people, as to have been accessible to every stratum of the population. They show all the merits and all the faults of a development absolutely uncontrolled by government, and little controlled even by the law which binds endowments down to the purposes fixed by a founder,[33] because new

---

[32] Free as regards self-government in matters of education, for they were tightly bound by theological restrictions till 1871.

[33] The law of most American states has not yet recognized the necessity of providing proper methods for setting aside the dispositions made by founders when circumstances change or their regulations prove unsuitable. Endowments, if they continue to increase at their present rate, will become a

foundations were constantly rising, and new endowments were accruing to the existing foundations. Accordingly, while a European observer is struck by their inequalities and by the crudeness of many among them, he is also struck by the life, the spirit, the sense of progress, which pervades them. In America itself educational reformers are apt to deplore the absence of control. They complain of the multiplication of degree-giving bodies, and consequent lowering of the worth of a degree. They point to such instances as the dissipation over thirty-five colleges in Ohio of the funds and teaching power which might have produced one first-rate university. One strong institution in a state does more, they argue, to raise the standard of teaching and learning, and to civilize the region which it serves, than can be done by twenty weak ones.

The European observer, while he admits this, conceives that his American friends may not duly realize the services which these small colleges perform in the rural districts of the country. They get hold of a multitude of poor men, who might never resort to a distant place of education. They set learning in a visible form, plain, indeed, and humble, but dignified even in her humility, before the eyes of a rustic people, in whom the love of knowledge, naturally strong, might never break from the bud into the flower but for the care of some zealous gardener. They give the chance of rising in some intellectual walk of life to many a strong and earnest nature who might otherwise have remained an artisan or storekeeper, and perhaps failed in those avocations. They light up in many a country town what is at first only a farthing rushlight, but which, when the town swells to a city, or when endowments flow in, or when some able teacher is placed in charge, becomes a lamp of growing flame, which may finally throw its rays over the whole state in which it stands. In some of these smaller Western colleges one finds today men of great ability and great attainments, one finds students who are receiving an education quite as thorough, though not always as wide, as the best Eastern universities can give. I do not at all deny that the time for more concentration has come, and that restrictions on the power of granting degrees would be useful. But one who recalls the history of the West during the second half of the last century, and bears in mind the tremendous rush of ability and energy towards a purely material development which has marked its people, will feel that this uncontrolled freedom of teaching, this multiplication of small institutions, have done for the country

---

very doubtful blessing unless this question is boldly dealt with. The difficulties of so dealing are complicated by the provisions of the federal Constitution.

a work which a few state-regulated universities might have failed to do. The higher learning is in no danger. The great universities of the East, as well as one or two in the West, are already beginning to rival the ancient universities of Europe. They will soon have far greater funds at their command with which to move towards the same ideal as Germany sets before herself; and they have already what is better than funds—an ardour and industry among the teachers which equals that displayed early in the last century in Germany by the foremost men of the generation which raised the German schools to their glorious eminence.

It may be thought that an observer familiar with two universities which are among the oldest and most famous in Europe, and are beyond question the most externally sumptuous and beautiful, would be inclined to disparage the corresponding institutions of the United States, whose traditions are comparatively short, and in whose outward aspect there is little to attract the eye or touch the imagination. I have not found it so. An Englishman who visits America can never feel sure how far his judgment has been affected by the warmth of the welcome he receives. But if I may venture to state the impression which the American universities have made upon me, I will say that while of all the institutions of the country they are those of which the Americans speak most modestly, and indeed deprecatingly, they are those which seem to be at this moment making the swiftest progress, and to have the brightest promise for the future. They are supplying exactly those things which European critics have hitherto found lacking to America: and they are contributing to her political as well as to her contemplative life elements of inestimable worth.

Further Observations on the Universities

As the many years that have elapsed since the last preceding chapter was written have brought many changes to the universities of the United States, it seems fitting to note here the more important among those changes, and thus convey more fully than can be done by insertions made here and there in that chapter the present state of the universities, the course which their development is taking, the reflections which a more intimate knowledge of them suggests.

I. Except in the newest parts of the West such as Oklahoma and parts of the Pacific slope, the founding of colleges or universities has almost stopped. It is generally felt all through the more populous and well-settled regions that there are already at least enough degree-giving institutions, and that it is more important to strengthen and improve those that exist than to create new ones. Nevertheless the desire of a rich man to perpetuate his name by a new foundation and the desire of a denomination to have the satisfaction of pointing to a college as its very own may be expected to cause new institutions to be from time to time, though less frequently than heretofore, established even in districts where they are not needed.

The development of the already existing universities and colleges goes on with undiminishing speed. It is seen in four directions: additions to the endowments, the creation of new departments, the raising of salaries paid to teachers, and an increase in the number of students. In 1913 the total gifts of money for the purposes of higher education amounted to \$24,983,090, and the number of students in institutions of higher education (including science schools) had risen from 55,687 in 1889 to 227,074, exclusive of those in preparatory departments.

In every civilized country the march of scientific discovery has led to an enormous increase in the applications of science to productive industry. This has been followed by a demand for men conversant with these applications, and to supply that demand the teaching of applied science has been provided on a scale undreamed of even a generation ago. Nowhere, perhaps not even in Germany, has this movement gone so fast or so far as in the United States. While the existing universities have been enlarged by the addition of scientific departments, a host of independent or affiliated scientific schools and technical institutes have sprung up. Most of these have been planted in the cities, but the agricultural colleges, perhaps the most numerous class, are often placed in rural areas. Of these latter many are really secondary schools, or are teaching engineering quite as much as agriculture, but some of the best have experimental farms attached to them. Many of the states, and especially the Western states, have been active in setting up and endowing such schools of agriculture either as parts of a state university or as independent institutions, and in the case of the best of these, such as those of Wisconsin and Illinois, the large sums spent in buildings and annual grants are deemed to have been amply repaid to the state by the increase in its production whether of tillage crops, or of fruit, or of milk and cheese, or of other forms of food. The classes in these best agricultural colleges are attended by crowds of students, some of them middle-aged or elderly farmers; while the universities also send their lecturers out through the country and supply from their head offices information and advice to those who apply for it. Thus one may say that the idea that agriculture in all its branches is a science, to be pursued with exact knowledge and by scientific methods, has now thoroughly laid hold of the American mind, and is, in the north and west, almost as fully realized by the farmers as by the men of science.[1]

These new developments, including the enlargement of the professional schools (medicine, dentistry, and law) attached to the universities, have of course led to large increases in the teaching staff. The number of professors and instructors of all kinds rose from 7918 in 1889 to 30,034 in 1912. There has also been a tendency to raise the salaries of the teachers, and in some few universities the full professor now receives $5,000 to $6,000 a year.[2] But as a rule the remuneration allotted to presidents and teachers of all grades remains small when compared on the one hand with the attainments now expected and on the other hand with the growing cost of living.[3]

[1] Though many of the so-called agricultural colleges are still far from having reached the level of those few mentioned above. Some trenchant remarks on this subject may be found in the Report of the Carnegie Foundation for 1909.

[2] In Harvard the maximum salary is in the Law School $7,500, in other departments $5,500, but this maximum is reached only after a number of years' service as full professor.

[3] In 1908 one-third of the degree-granting universities paid their full professors an average salary of less than $1,000 a year, and only 20 paid an average of $3,000 or over, only 5 paying an

The most considerable improvement in the position of the professor has come from a private source. Mr. Andrew Carnegie has created a fund with an annual income (in 1909) of $500,000 for the purpose of providing retiring allowances for professors in those universities and colleges in the United States, Canada, and Newfoundland that comply with certain conditions prescribed, the most important of which is that they are not to be under the control of any particular sect or denomination, the trustees of the fund having a discretionary power to determine how this principle is to be applied in each particular case.[4]

The recent development of the higher education is, however, most conspicuous in the enormous increase in the attendance of students. In 1889–90 the total number returned to the Bureau of Education as collegiate and resident graduate students was 44,926 men and 10,761 women. In 1910–11 the numbers were 169,026 men and 10,761 women. In 1910–11 the numbers were 169,026 men and 64,549 women, besides several thousand students in the collegiate and graduate departments of a different and much less advanced group of colleges for women. The actual number was larger, because there are colleges which make no return. But these figures are enough to show how rapid has been the growth in twenty years, a growth whose rate is far in excess of the rate at which the population has grown, and which is twice as large for women students as for the men. Of the total number of students who are receiving higher education no accurate record is attainable, for though the Bureau of Education Report gives a total enrolment of 308,163 in the preparatory, collegiate, graduate, and professional departments of the 606 universities, colleges, and technological schools that have made returns, it is quite impossible to say how many of these are receiving instruction of a true university type. The institutions that make up the 606 enumerated are of all kinds and descriptions. Many are not above the grade of secondary schools, and it is impossible to draw the line between them and those which give an instruction corresponding to that of universities in Europe. Still, without venturing to form any numerical estimate of the students in institutions of the latter class, it is safe to say that they bear a larger proportion to the population of the United States than

---

average salary of $3,500 or over. The salaries of assistant professors are much lower, those of instructors lower still.

[4] In 1913 the total number of retiring allowances in force was 315, and 83 widows' pensions, total annual distribution being $570,423.

The creation of this fund has had the incidental result of tending to establish, not without protests and complaints, a sort of unofficial standard of excellence for colleges, and this "by-product" is deemed valuable.

similar students do to the whole population in any other country. That is to say, universities and technical or professional schools of the university level are more numerous and attract more students, not merely absolutely, but relatively to the whole community, than in the most advanced of European countries.

Of the quality of the instruction given it is even more difficult to speak in general terms than it is to fix the type to which each institution belongs. But the fact remains that the institutions are there and the students are there. The revenues grow; the attendance grows. Quantity at least has been obtained. Of quality I shall speak later.

This striking growth in the number of students seems due to two causes. One cause, operative all over the country, but perhaps most operative in the Western states, is the sense that a knowledge of applied science has great practical value for many occupations, and especially for agriculture and for the various branches of engineering, and that it is therefore worth while "as a business proposition" to spend some years in acquiring that knowledge systematically rather than to begin practical life on leaving school at fifteen or sixteen years of age. The other cause is that university education has become fashionable,[5] and is more and more coming to be considered not a luxury for the few, nor a thing needed only by those who mean to enter one of the so-called "learned professions," but a preparation for life with which all those who can afford the money and the time ought to be furnished. Formerly young men intended for a business life seldom thought, except in two or three of the older states, of going to college. Now they are just as likely to go as are any others. This is the most noteworthy new feature of the last thirty years, and is also the most striking educational difference between America and Europe. A university education has in the United States ceased to be the privilege of the few. It is for all the world.

The change is itself largely due to two economic facts. One is the rapid increase in the number of persons with incomes large enough to make it easy for them to send sons and daughters to college. The other is the creation of state universities, especially in the Western states, in which instruction is provided at a very low charge. These have so much popularized the higher education that through their example and influence the afflux of students to all colleges has increased. It may be added that charges are everywhere moderate, and that in the smaller towns of the West, a student

---

[5] A degree conferred at one of the few oldest and most famous universities has even a social value, especially to a member of a "new rich" family which is, as people say, "on the make."

can lodge and board cheaply. Two other causes, however, must not be altogether omitted. Colleges have profited by the modern passion for athletic competition and the immense interest which the public take in football and baseball matches between the teams of different universities. Many a boy finds in these an incitement to university life which the desire for knowledge might have failed to provide. Nor can it be denied that the rivalry, not only of denominations but of particular places, even comparatively small places, has borne a part in this immense multiplication of teaching institutions. Each little city or even rural area thinks it a feather in its cap to possess a college, and those who own real estate believe that it raises the value of the land they have to sell. Once the college is established, its staff as well as the local people are concerned to "boom" and "boost" it. So the resources of advertising are called in, sometimes with a certain lack of the dignity which befits a seat of learning. Thus it happens, not only that colleges are established where they are not wanted, but that many students are drawn to them who ought to be preparing themselves at school, including some whom nature has not blessed with the gifts needed to profit by the higher branches of education.

This increase has tended to give the universities, and especially the larger ones, a much more prominent place in the life of the country than they formerly had. They have become objects of general interest. Questions affecting them are more amply discussed in newspapers and magazines, and appear to lay more hold on the attention of the community at large than is the case in England or perhaps in any European country. The alumni of the greater universities form associations, some few of which have branches in the chief cities of the country, while others are locally established. They meet from time to time; and when their *Alma Mater* celebrates an anniversary or opens a new building or inaugurates a new president, they flock to her, and give importance to the festivity. They are inclined—sometimes unduly inclined—to discourage innovations. The elder man was even in the days of Horace *laudator temporis acti, se puero,* and a reforming president sometimes finds the influence of the alumni to be a drag on his efforts. But they respond generously when the university asks them to contribute to some new object; indeed, it is largely through them that extension funds are raised. In one university the custom has grown up that each "class" shall on the completion of the twenty-fifth year from graduation offer not less than $100,000 (£20,000) to the university treasury.

With this rise in the importance of the American university its headship has come to be an office of enhanced dignity and influence. The man selected for it is usually a person of literary or scientific eminence, though he is also expected to possess administrative talents. He is now, in the larger universities, almost always a layman, and needs to have unusual energy and tact, for one of his chief duties is to travel hither and thither delivering public addresses, meeting the societies of the alumni of his university, and endeavouring, by a description of its desires and needs, to obtain further funds for its purposes. His powers in the management of the institution and the selection of professors are much greater than those of the head of an English or Scottish university. But he is often also a leading figure in the state, perhaps even in the nation. No persons in the country, hardly even the greatest railway magnates, are better known, and certainly none are more respected, than the presidents of the leading universities. Much of course depends on personal qualities. The place will not give strength to a weak man. But if he be strong, the place doubles his opportunities for exerting his strength, and ensures a wide and attentive hearing for anything he may have to say.

Although the terms "university" and "college" continue to be loosely used in the United States, and although it is still difficult to draw lines dividing into classes the various institutions which bear these names, still it may be said that three main types are now beginning to emerge, to one or other of which all may be referred.

The first includes the larger among the old degree-giving bodies of the Eastern states, such as Harvard, Yale, and Columbia, to which may be added some more recent institutions of private foundation, such as the University of Chicago, Cornell University in New York, Stanford University in California, and Washington University in St. Louis. All these were originally colleges giving instruction of the old-fashioned kind in classics, mathematics, and moral philosophy. They have now superadded to those subjects, formerly deemed to constitute a general liberal education, various professional and technical departments, as well as post-graduate courses in special but not professional subjects, the students in which, taken all together, exceed in number those pursuing the course for the regular academic arts or science degrees. In these institutions it is now the practice to use the term "university" to denote the aggregate of all the various aforesaid schools and to restrict the term "college" to that central department which prepares students for some regular degree in the liberal arts, science, or philosophy.

The institutions of this type are all (with minor differences in their constitutions) governed by bodies of trustees who perpetuate themselves by cooptation (with sometimes the addition of persons representing the alumni) and they are supported by endowments *plus* the sums which the students pay for instruction.[6]

The second type embraces universities founded and supported wholly or mainly by a state. There are several of these in the Eastern states, such as the Universities of North Carolina,[7] Virginia, Vermont, and Maine. But the largest and most characteristic examples occur in the West, such as the Universities of Michigan, Illinois, Wisconsin, Iowa, Minnesota, California. There are in all thirty-eight such state universities, including three in Ohio, and the youthful universities of New Mexico and Arizona. These resemble the first type in having an undergraduate department giving a general liberal education, round which cluster a number of professional and technical schools, the schools of medicine and agriculture being the most important. They differ from the first type in being governed by a body, usually called regents, appointed by the state government (generally by the legislature) and in being supported by annual or biennial grants from the revenues of the state, which has of course provided their buildings and apparatus. In a few of them instruction is gratuitous to citizens of the state; in all it is supplied very cheaply to citizens and cheaply to all comers. Women students are admitted on equal terms with men. As respects instruction, they differ little from the universities of the former type. Being state supported, they are of course absolutely undenominational.

The third type is less easy to describe, and is, indeed, rather a residual mass than a well-defined class. It includes those degree-granting bodies, most of them called colleges but some of them universities (there being seldom any distinction in fact corresponding to the difference in name), which confine themselves wholly or mainly to the giving of a general liberal education without providing either post-graduate courses or professional departments. To this division belong a very few Eastern colleges of high rank and a large attendance of students—Princeton, Dartmouth, and Brown (in Rhode Island) are examples—which have not yet set up professional schools. Johns Hopkins in Baltimore holds a peculiar position, for having begun with post-graduate and professional schools it has now engrafted

---

[6] Cornell, however, receives also a grant from the state of New York though not strictly a state university.

[7] The state university of North Carolina, founded in 1789, seems to be the oldest state institution of the modern type, though in several states, such as Massachusetts, Connecticut, and Pennsylvania, the legislatures had granted charters and money to colleges which were or subsequently became self-governing. See an interesting paper entitled *The Origin of American State Universities* by Dr. Elmer Elsworth Brown (Univ. of Calif. Publications, 1903).

thereon an academic department. Here too we must place those old New England colleges such as Williams, Amherst, and Bowdoin, which, situated in small country towns, have adhered to the older traditions and devoted themselves chiefly to the preparation of students for the B.A. degree, whether in literary or in scientific courses. These latte colleges have as a rule remained, and have wished to remain, comparatively small. They retain, and they well deserve, the credit of making their instruction thorough and of cultivating a strong social spirit among their alumni. From them have come many of the strongest intellects and characters of the last generation. In this division we must also place the large number of small colleges in the Middle, the Southern, and the Western states, most of which provide only the regular undergraduate course, though a very few have begun to develop special departments, especially of a technical kind. Most of these are connected with some denomination, those of the Roman Catholic, Methodist, Protestant Episcopal, Presbyterian, and Baptist bodies being the most numerous, but students of all persuasions are freely admitted to them. There are such great differences among them both as regards the size and qualifications of the staff, the attendance of students, and the standard of instruction that no general statements can be made. Comparatively few, however, have an attendance exceeding five hundred; many might be classed rather with upper secondary schools than with universities; some can scarcely be called efficient even as schools. Some few, such as the Iowa College at Grinnell, resemble the small colleges of New England, such as Amherst, in the thoroughness of their academic work; and it is to be desired that this useful order was more largely represented in the West. As has been already observed, colleges of this third type now spring up less frequently than formerly, and we may conjecture that in the West and South the weakest among them will either die out, or frankly admit thmselves to be no more than secondary schools, or possibly be affiliated to some strong state university, while the richest and strongest will grow into institutions of the first type. Denominational sentiment is a less powerful force now than it was fifty years ago, so the state university, with its conspicuous visibility and its command of money, begins to dwarf all but the best endowed universities of private foundation.

It was noted in the preceding chapter that the old system of prescribed courses for degrees limited to a few subjects, taken in regular order, had about 1880 begun to break up and disappear in nearly all the universities. The process went on briskly after 1890, until, in some institutions, a student might attend lectures and offer himself for examination in any one or more of the numberous sujects taught. The subjects need not have any relation to one another, the selection of a prescribed number among them being left entirely to his personal tastes. After a while a reaction set in against this "unchartered freedom." Much debate followed as to the desirability of prescribing a certain small number of regular curricula, either for the whole or at least for the first year, or first two years, of the students' four years of residence. Great diversity still exists, both in opinion and in practice; indeed, the present situation is, if not chaotic, yet evidently transitional. Only two things are pretty clear: the first that the general tendency is at present away from the extreme form of what is called the elective system; the second that nothing like the rigidity of the old curriculum will reappear. Probably, while some universities may continue to allow the widest freedom, the bulk will arrange some four, five, or six groups or curricula suited to different tastes and capacities, or will permit the student a choice, within certain limits, or subjects to the approval of some members of the faculty entrusted with the duty of advising.

Controversies, similar to those with which Europe is familiar, are carried on regarding the respective values of various subjects of study. But the main issue between the ancient classics versus the natural sciences and so-called "modern subjects" has been practically decided in favour of the latter. Latin and (still more) Greek are, especially in the West, vanishing quantities. Less than ten per cent of all the students in the universities and colleges acquire an effective knowledge of the former, less than two per cent of the latter language, understanding by "effective knowledge" the ability to read a previously unseen but easy Latin or Greek passage two years after graduation. If universities of the first type only were taken, the percentage would be larger, yet even in them small. Efforts are being made to restore the study of the ancient authors to their proper place in the scheme of a truly liberal education. But in America, as in Europe, the stream runs stong towards those branches of instruction deemed most directly useful for gainful occupations. Even in Europe, where traditions are more powerful than in America, it is hard to convince persons who have not themselves either a knowledge of the ancient languages or a taste for letters and for history, of what is called the "cultural value" of a knowledge of ancient literature. Philosophical courses have in American declined less than classical; and history, which does not usually require a knowledge of ancient languages, holds its own. It is indeed one of the subjects for which a comparatively ample provision is made in Universities both of the first and of the second of the above-mentioned types. The number of persons teaching it in all the

Universities and colleges must be reckoned by hundreds, indeed, by many hundreds. It is, however, towards scientific subjects, and especially towards applied science, that the drift is strongest. The same tendency prevails in Europe, and seems likely to continue for a good while to come.

The graduate schools mentioned in the preceding chapter as novelties have immensely expanded. Johns Hopkins has the honour of having led the way; and now such schools have been created in most of the great universities, a notable instance in which the educational spirit and enterprise of Americans have outstripped the conservatism or the poverty of English and Scottish seats of learning. It may, however, be doubted whether it would not have been better if some at least of the universities which have founded these schools had, instead of attempting to spread themselves over a large variety of subjects, each confined itself to a few only, on which its resources might have been concentrated. Some few universities may command revenues large enough to enable them to cover the whole field of knowledge, but in others the spirit of rivalry induces the spending, in efforts to do many things imperfectly, the money which might better have been employed in doing a few things thoroughly. The academic department must of course make full provision for all the general academic subjects; and to specialize a university, on its general teaching side, would be to narrow it, and to lose the benefit that comes from the mingling of minds pursuing different branches of scholarship or scientific enquiry. But more might be done for advanced study in particular subjects if one university devoted itself chiefly to one group of subjects, another to another, so that the graduate student might resort to an institution which had gathered together the most eminent teachers and investigators in the line he desired to follow, and had provided the most complete laboratory or apparatus. The country is so large that there would always be several universities dedicated to each group, so that none would enjoy a monopoly, yet the benefits incident to division of labour and specialization of function would follow. Nearly all the scientific work of the country, except that directly connected with inventions of practical commercial value, is done in the universities and the need for strengthening research departments begins to be more and more recognized.

It may be added that in this, as in some other respects, there is at present less diversity between American universities than the European visitor who sees the vastness of the country, the different economic conditions of its different parts, and the different elements in its population has been led to expect. Oxford and Cambridge are more unlike either the Scottish universities or the new universities in Manchester and Liverpool, than any American university is to any other, for although the appliances are generally (not always) inferior in the newer parts of the country, although the students are less well prepared and possibly rougher in externals in some districts than in others, still the educational habits and views of policy and methods of instruction are essentially similar all over the country. This is a natural result of the long course of historical development in Britain, as compared with the shorter time during which the higher education has been developing itself in the New World, but it suggests the wish that American universities may in time similarly differentiate themselves from one another, for there is in variety a sort of richness helpful to the thought and imagination of a great country.

The restless activity of our time has further displayed itself in the university extension movement, which, coming a little later than it did in England, has reached even larger proportions. It was felt that something ought to be done for those who could not spare the time to follow a regular degree course, as well as for those whose previous training had not qualified them to matriculate. Of the many institutions which are doing this work, twenty-three state universities offer general extension work, and fifteen of these have organized departments for the purpose. Correspondence study has been found valuable for students living in rural areas which lecturers cannot easily reach. Some universities, notably the great one at Chicago, have established summer schools to which great numbers of students resort who have not time for a regular four years' course. It is believed that these extension methods have been helpful to the elementary teachers and are serving to bring the teaching profession of a state into closer touch with the leading universities, a thing profitable to both.[8] They throw, however, a heavy burden on the university staff, which is already so hard worked as to have insufficient time for study and research.

The number of women students has increased faster than that of men and faster in the West than in the other parts of the country. In the University of Illinois the proportion of one-fourth is steadily maintained, but in Chicago the attendance of women bears a higher ratio. All state universities are coeducational, though fears are expressed that as these institutions become more fashionable places of resort it may prove less easy to maintain that spirit of hard work which has hitherto prevented questions of college discipline from causing trouble. There is even some talk of establishing

---

[8] The universities and colleges in and near Boston have organized a combined system of courses and offer the degree of A.A. to those who attain a certain standard.

separate departments for women in the state universities. In the East coeducation does not make way. Parents prefer to send their daughters to colleges for women only, and three colleges which taught men and women together have recently ceased to do so.[9] So far, the women are said to have shown more assiduity and zeal in their studies than the men. A sort of differentiation is visible in the fact that while men prefer science as practically serviceable, women favour the courses in languages and history, and keep going, in the West, the classes in Latin and Greek. As the public schools in the North and West are chiefly staffed by female teachers, who in some states are five-sixths or even more of the total number of instructors, this equal right of access to the universities does much for the teaching profession.

Among the minor changes of the last twenty years it is not without interest to note that the growth of an æsthetic spirit among the educated classes has led some universities to erect handsome buildings in mediæval or post-mediæval styles. Washington University at St. Louis has followed the types of English college architecture with felicity; the University of Chicago has reproduced the hall of Christ Church, Oxford and the tower of Magdalen College. Standford University, near San Francisco, has beautiful cloisters and lecture rooms of a colonial Spanish type; and the University of California has half erected, half carved out of the hillside, a Greek theatre modelled on that at Epidaurus which has preserved the admirable acoustic properties of the original. So too, the faculties of nearly all the greater universities have now blossomed out into a variety of gowns and a still richer and more brilliant variety of coloured hoods worn upon solemn academic occasions. The effect when a long procession, clad in all the colours of the rainbow, winds across the green spaces of the college campus under the shade of spreading trees has been such as to silence the cavils of those who condemned this departure from democratic simplicity. It is an innovation which even the alumni do not disapprove.

Three other questions besides that relating to curricula and the range of choice allowed to students, have of recent years begun to claim the attention of those who direct university policy.

One of these is the increased passion for athletic competitions, especially in football and baseball, and, to a much smaller extent, in rowing. The ordinary undergraduate plays games far less than does the ordinary English youth at Oxford or Cambridge, and as little as the ordinary youth in a Scotch or German university. But he is incomparably more interested in the

---

[9] One of these has provided a separate college for women.

performances of his college team when it competes with that of another university. The members of the team are the heroes of their time. The contests sometimes draw fifty or sixty thousand spectators and excite passionate curiosity over the country, among women not less than among men; and while the long list of hurts, not rarely fatal, received in their contests leads to protests against the roughness of the way in which football is played, some college presidents declare that the preoccupation of the undergraduate with these games has reduced the attention, not too great before, which is given to study. But these contests continue to be the most conspicuous, and to many the most attractive, feature of university life, especially in the Eastern states, where the rival claims of learning might be thought to have a better chance than in the strenuously practical and fiercely competitive West.

Another topic of discussion is the possibility of creating in those universities which have grown very large something in the nature of the residential colleges at Oxford and Cambridge. It is thought that these might furnish social groups of a size favourable to the formation of friendships and the creation of a sort of quasi-domestic life. The idea has not yet had time to strike root, but if it does, benefactors to give effect to it will be found, for the universities have now among their alumni a great many rich men who are on the lookout for means of spending their fortunes on purposes useful in themselves, and calculated to perpetuate their names.

The third question touches a more vital point. In the professional and scientific and post-graduate departments of universities, diligence and interest on the part of the students are the rule. They have entered in order to fit themselves for their future avocations, and they apply themselves steadily, throwing their force into work which they feel to be for their practical benefit. But in the so-called "college," or academic part of the institution, that which gives a general liberal education, whether in languages or philosophy or history or natural science, things are said to be otherwise. The average undergraduate, especially the son of well-to-do parents, is now described as being more absorbed in social life and its amusements than in the subjects in which he is lectured and on which he is examined. He does no more than is absolutely needed to get his degree. The man who enjoys his work and follows it *con amore* is the exception. That intellectual stimulation which a university ought to give is received by comparatively few; that atmosphere of keen and eager thought which ought to pervade all the more vigorous minds is, if not wanting, yet comparatively faint.

To these criticisms, those who know Oxford and Cambridge sometimes add another, viz., that there is not a sufficiently close relation between teacher and student whereby the latter is influenced and stimulated privately as well as in class lectures. Many of the teachers are young men—the instructors (as distinct from the full professors) are nearly all so. Yet it is alleged that the want of something resembling a college and something in the nature of a tutorial system prevents the teachers from getting into personal touch with the students as individuals as they do in the older English universities, though to be sure neither in Scotland nor in Germany.[10]

How far either of these allegations is true, I am not able to determine. But this at least seems certain, that in most universities, including the oldest and greatest in the Eastern states, intellectual distinction in the work of the college is little sought by ambitious spirits, and little valued by their companions. A prominent athlete is a far more brilliant and honoured figure than the man most distinguished in the studies of the place. Undergraduates declare that the assiduous student, even if there be nothing of the bookworm about him, is apt to be looked down upon as a dull and plodding fellow. And a further point of unlikeness to English and Scotch conditions appears in the fact that nobody seems to think he will get any better start in his profession by having done well at college; nor when references are made to men who have won success or fame in after life, does one hear anything said about their university careers, though statistical enquiries have shown that the proportion of successes in life is much larger among those who did in fact apply themselves to their studies.[11] In England there are of course many undergraduates, perhaps a half, who neglect their work, and others who, though they do study, are moved less by love of knowledge than for the sake of getting a degree sufficiently high to help them forward in their future profession. Still there are also many who are really interested, and care far more for their studies than they do for the amusements of the place. Among nearly all the men of talent the desire to achieve distinction is strong, and the men who achieve it are marked out among their fellows. Accordingly those who in the American universities regret what they think the deficient interest taken by undergraduates in their studies and the preponderating attraction of interuniversity contests in such games as football,

---

[10] Except of course in what is called in Germany the seminar.

[11] Distinction in a professional school (law and medicine) in a few of the greatest universities is, however, supposed to help a man in his start in professional life, and in some few universities there are honours to be won by competition. Harvard so awards scholarships, and the number of those who thought they obtain the honour do not receive, because they do not need, the emolument, practically equals that of those to whom the stipend is paid.

have begun to canvas the question whether the introduction of honour courses and of competitions for literary and scientific distinctions may not be needed. Observers from other countries have long expected that such a debate would some day arise, and await with curiosity its issue.

One who surveys the progess of the United States during the last fifteen or twenty years finds nothing more significant than the growth of the universities in number, in wealth, and in the increased attendance of students from all ranks of life. They have become national and popular in a sense never attained before in any country. This growth is not due to any set purpose; and in it the national government has had no hand.[12] For nearly a century it was a quite spontaneous growth, due to private liberality and denominational zeal, since it is only within the last few decades that the state legislatures have thrown themselves effictively into the work. Effective as their action has been, it has been done without concert, and seldom upon any fixed plan, so the state universities have enjoyed a large freedom of natural development and have, taking them all in all, suffered little more from governmental control than have those which depended on private liberality or on the payments made by students.

In some ways they would all, both state and private institutions, have profited by a little more, not indeed of uniformity, yet of systematic direction and regulation. There has been much waste of effort and of money in planting several weak colleges where one strong one would have rendereed better service. Weakness has meant acquiescence in a low standard of entrance requirements (hard anyhow to avoid in the newer states where secondary schools are still insufficient in number and quality), in imperfect teaching, in degrees which witness to no high level of attainment. This has been specially unfortunate as respects the profession of medicine, where the maintenance of a high level is essential for the safety of the whole community. Some of the American medical schools are equal to any in Europe, but some are far below the level of any recognized in England, France, or Germany.[13] The abundance of colleges and universities whose performances are obviously mediocre has naturally lowered among the people at large the conception of what a university ought to be and achieve, and the eagerness

---

[12] Except of course in respect of the land grants made by Congress to the states for university and agricultural education. Latterly, moreover, the Agricultural Department at Washington has rendered valuable help to agricultural state colleges.

[13] The Carnegie Foundation Report for 1909 observes, "There are in this country more medical schools than in all Europe, and these schools have turned upon the public a far larger number of physicians than are needed, the majority ill trained and educated, the imperative need being now not more medical schools but fewer and better ones," p. 91.

of rival institutions to secure students has led not only to superficiality but to a preference of the subjects most attractive to the practical mind and a corresponding undervaluing of those whose virtue lies in the general intellectual cultivation they give.

Nevertheless, with all these defects the universities and colleges have, taken as a whole, rendered an immense service. They have brought instruction within the reach of every boy and girl of every class. They receive a larger proportion of the youthful population than do any similar institutions in any other country. They are resorted to hardly less by those who mean to tread the paths of commerce or industry than by those who prepare themselves for a learned profession. They have turned a university course from being the luxury which it has been in the Old World into being almost a necessary of life. And they have so expanded their educational scheme as to provide (in the larger institutions) instruction in almost every subject in which men and women are likely to ask for it.

So far then as quantity goes, whether quantity and variety of attendance or quantity and variety of instruction, nearly all that the needs of the time and the country demand has been attained.

Quality is of course another matter. In education, improvements in quality do not always keep pace with increase in quantity, and often follow with sadly lagging steps. Nevertheless, they do generally tend to follow. No doubt the first and easier thing for an ambitious institution is to devote itself to material improvements, to enlarge its buildings and its library, its scientific apparatus, even its gymnasium.[14] When money is spent on these things the result can be seen, and even the least instructed visitors are impressed. To secure more able, more learned, more inspiring teachers, and by their help to improve the instruction given and the standard of attainment which a degree represents is a slower and more difficult task. Yet here, too, the natural tendency is upward, and the emulation of these numerous and aspiring bodies helps that tendency. When one university has made evident its excellence by the work of its teachers and by the kind of men it turns out, others feel they must try to reach its level by similar methods.

The thingjs which the most judicious friends of the universities (including many of their presidents) hold to be now most needed, would appear to be the following:

(1) The development in each region of the country—by which I mean in

---

[14] One university is reported to have recently mortgaged its campus for $400,000 to erect what is called a stadium, while paying its full professors an average yearly salary of $1,800 only.

each populous state or in each group of less populous states—of at least one university which may serve as a model to the others in that section, setting before them in a tangible form the organs of activity and the excellences of arrangement and method which a first-rate place of education, learning, and research ought to possess. In some parts of the country there are several universities so much ahead of others that they are already being taken as patterns. In other parts none such yet exist.

(2) As a means to the above end, there is required a higher scale of salaries for the teaching staff. This is no doubt needed in European countries also, but in those countries the attractions which other careers have for a man of energy are seldom so great as in the United States, and the cost of living is neither so high nor rising so rapidly.

(3) It is felt that there ought to be a stonger pulse of intellectual life among the undergraduates in the "college" or academic department. They are not generally idle or listless, but rather, like most young Americans, alert and active in temperament. Their conduct is usually good; in no country are vices less common among students. But those who are keenly interested either in their particular studies or in the "things of the mind" in general are comparatively few in number. Athletic competitions and social pleasures claim the larger part of their thoughts, and the university does not seem to be giving them that taste for intellectual enjoyment which ought to be acquired early if it is to be acquired at all.

(4) The conception of a general liberal education, the ideal of such an education as something which it is the function of a university to give in order to prepare men for life as a whole, over and above the preparation required for any particular walk of life, is described as being in some institutions insufficiently valued and imperfectly realized. Those whose views I am setting forth admit that professional and other special schools can give, and often do give, an effective training of the mental powers in the course of the special instruction they impart. What they miss is that largeness of view and philosophic habit of thought which the study of such subjects as literature, philosophy, and history is fitted to implant when these subjects are taught in a broad and stimualting way. In short, the pressure of the practical subjects and of the practical spirit in handling these subjects, is deemed to be unduly strong.

How far the criticisms summarized under the two last heads as made by competent American observers are generally applicable, I will not attempt to determine. They are given because they are made by persons entitled to be heard. This, however, may be said, that forces and tendencies are discernible all over the country which cannot but work for raising the level of instruction and diffusing more widely those educational ideals which the best representatives of university progress already cherish.

Foreign critics often say, and some domestic critics have echoed the censure, that what is chiefly admired in America is bigness, things being measured by their size or by what they cost. This quantitative estimate finds little place in the universities. With very few exceptions, the teaching staff are not thinking of size, nor of money, except so far as it helps to extend the usefulness of their institution. All the better men, and not merely the ablest men, but the good average men, feel that it is the mission of a university to seek and find and set forth the real values. It has been well said by one of the most acute and large-minded of all recent visitors to the United States[15] that nowhere in the world do university teachers feel more strongly that the first object of their devotion is truth. They are of all classes in the country that which is least dazzled by wealth, least governed by material considerations. No wealth-seeker would, indeed, choose such a profession. To one who looks back over the last twenty years, the universities seem to have grown not only in their resources and the number of their students, but also in dignity and influence. They hold a higher place in the eyes of the nation. They have almost entirely escaped any deletrious contact either with politics or with those capitalistic groups whose power is felt in so many other directions.[16] Through the always widening circle of their alumni they are more closely in touch than ever before with all classes in the community. The European observer can express now with even more conviction than he could twenty years ago the opinion that they constitute one of the most powerful and most pervasive forces working for good in the country.

[15] Professor Dr. Lamprecht of Leipzig in his *Amerikana*.

[16] The exceptions to this general statement are so rare as to emphasize the fact that it is almost universally true.

The Churches and the Clergy

In examining the national government and the state governments, we have never once had occasion to advert to any ecclesiastical body or question, because with such matters government has in the United States absolutely nothing to do. Of all the differences between the Old World and the New this is perhaps the most salient. Half the wars of Europe, half the internal troubles that have vexed European states, from the Monophysite controversies in the Roman Empire of the fifth century down to the Kulturkampf in the German Empire of the nineteenth, have arisen from theological differences or from the rival claims of church and state. This whole vast chapter of debate and strife has remained virtually unopened in the United States. There is no established church. All religious bodies are absolutely equal before the law, and unrecognized by the law, except as voluntary associations of private citizens.

The federal Constitution contains the following prohibitions:

Art. VI. No religious test shall ever be required as a qualification to any office or public trust under the United States.

Amendment I. Congress shall make no law respecting an establishment of religion or prohibiting the free exercise thereof.

No attempt has ever been made to alter or infringe upon these provisions. They affect the national government only, placing no inhibition on the states, and leaving the whole subject to their uncontrolled discretion, though subject to the general guarantees against oppression.

Every state constitution contains provisions generally similar to the above. Most declare that every man may worship God according to his own conscience, or that the free enjoyment of all religious sentiments and forms of worship shall be held sacred;[1] most also provide that no man shall be compelled to support or attend any church; some forbid the creation of an established church, and many the showing of a preference to any particular sect; while many provide that no money shall ever be drawn from the state treasury, or from the funds of any municipal body, to be applied for the benefit of any church or sectarian institution or denominational school. Thirty-three constitutions, including those of the six most recently admitted states, forbid any religious test to be required as a qualification for office; some declare that this principle extends to all civil rights; some specify that religious belief is not to affect a man's competence as a witness. But in several states there still exist qualifications worth noting. Vermont and Delaware declare that every sect ought to maintain some form of religious worship, and Vermont adds that it ought to observe the Lord's Day. Six Southern states exclude from office anyone who denies the existence of a Supreme Being. Besides these six, Pennsylvania and Tennessee pronounce a man ineligible for office who does not believe in God and in a future state of rewards and punishments. Maryland and Arkansas even make such a person incompetent as a juror or witness.[2] Religious freedom has been generally thought of in America in the form of freedom and equality as between different sorts of Christians, or at any rate different sorts of theists; persons opposed to religion altogether have till recently been extremely few everywhere and practically unknown in the South. The neutrality of the state cannot therefore be said to be theoretically complete.[3]

In earlier days the states were very far from being neutral. Rhode Island indeed, whose earliest settlers were seceders from Massachusetts, stood from the first for the principle of complete religious freedom and the detachment of Christian communities from all secular power or secular control. Roger Williams, the illustrious founder of this little state, was one of those few to whom this principle was revealed when the great mass of Christians were still in bondage to the ideas of the Middle Ages. But the other two states of old New England began with a sort of Puritan theocracy, and excluded from some civil rights persons who sood outside the religious community. Congregationalism was the ruling faith, and Roman Catholics,

---

[1] Four states provide that this declaration is not to be taken to excuse breaches of the public peace, many that it shall not excuse acts of licentiousness or justify practices inconsistent with the peace and safety of the state, and three that no person shall disturb others in their religious worship.

[2] Full details on these points will be found in Mr. Stimson's valuable collection entitled *American Statute Law*.

[3] Idaho disfranchises all polygamists or advocates of polygamy; but Mormonism is attacked not so much as a religion as in respect of its social features and hierarchical character.

Quakers, and Baptists were treated with great severity. The early constitutions of several states recognized what was virtually a state church, requiring each locality to provide for and support the public worship of God. It was not till 1818 that Connecticut in adopting her new constitution placed all religious bodies on a level, and left the maintenance of churches to the voluntary action of the faithful. In Massachusetts a tax for the support of the Congregationalist churches was imposed on all citizens not belonging to some other incorporated religious body until 1811, and religious equality was first fully recognized by a constitutional amendment of 1833. In Virginia, North and South Carolina, and Maryland, Protestant Episcopacy was the established form of religion till the Revolution, when under the impulse of the democratic spirit, and all the more heartily because the Anglican clergy were prone to Toryism (as attachment to the British connection was called), and because, at least in Virginia, there had been some persecution of Nonconformists, all religious distinctions were abolished and special eccle-siastical privileges withdrawn. In Pennsylvania no church was ever legally established. In New York, however, first the Dutch Reformed, and afterwards the Anglican Church, had in colonial days enjoyed a measure of state favour. What is remarkable is that in all these cases the disestablishment, if one may call it by that name, of the privileged church was accomplished with no great effort, and left very little rancour behind. In the South it seemed a natural outcome of the Revolution. In New England it came more gradually, as the necessary result of the political development of each commonwealth. The ecclesiastical arrangements of the states were not inwoven with the pecuniary interests of any wealthy or socially dominant class; and it was felt that equality and democratic doctrine generally were too palpably opposed to the maintenance of any privileges in religious matters to be defensible in argument. However, both in Connecticut and Massachusetts there was a political struggle over the process of disestablishment, and the Congregationalist ministers predicted evils from a change which they afterwards admitted to have turned out a blessing to their own churches. No voice has ever since been raised in favour of reverting—I will not say to a state establishment of religion—but even to any state endowment or state regulation of ecclesiastical bodies. It is accepted as an axiom by all Americans that the civil power ought to be not only neutral and impartial as between different forms of faith, but ought to leave these matters entirely on one side, regarding them no more than it regards the artistic or literary pursuits of the citizens.[4] There seem to be no two opinions on this subject in the

[4] There was however, for some time, a movement led I think by some Baptist and Methodist ministers, for obtaining the insertion of the name of God in the federal Constitution. Those who

United States. Even the Protestant Episcopalian clergy, who are in many ways disposed to admire and envy their brethren in England; even the Roman Catholic bishops, whose creed justifies the enforcement of the true faith by the secular arm, assure the European visitor that if state establishment were offered them they would decline it, preferring the freedom they enjoy to any advantages the state could confer. Every religious community can now organize itself in whatever way it pleases, lay down its own rules of faith and discipline, create and administer its own system of judicature, raise and apply its funds at its uncontrolled discretion. A church established by the state would not be able to do all these things, because it would also be controlled by the state, and it would be exposed to the envy and jealousy of other sects.

The only controversies that have arisen regarding state action in religious matters have turned upon the appropriation of public funds to charitable institutions managed by some particular denomination. Such appropriations are expressly prohibited in the constitutions of some states. But it may happen that the readiest way of promoting some benevolent public purpose is to make a grant of money to an institution already at work, and successfully serving that purpose. As this reason may sometimes be truly given, so it is also sometimes advanced where the real motive is to purchase the political support of the denomination to which the institution belongs, or at least of its clergy. In some states, and particularly in New York, state or city legislatures are often charged with giving money to Roman Catholic institutions for the sake of securing the Catholic vote.[5] In these cases, however, the money always purports to be voted not for a religious but for a philanthropic or educational purpose. No ecclesiastical body would be strong enough to obtain any grant to its general funds, or any special immunity for its ministers. The passion for equality in religious as well as secular matters is everywhere in America far too strong to be braved, and nothing excites more general disapprobation than any attempt by an ecclesiastical organization to interfere in politics. The suspicion that the Roman Catholic church uses its power over its members to guide their votes for its purposes has more than once given rise to strong anti-Catholic or (as they would be called in Canada) Orange movements, such as that which at

---

desired this appear to hold that the instrument would be thereby in a manner sanctified, and a distinct national recognition of theism expressed.

[5] In 1910 the Roman Catholic schools and charities of New York received more than $1,500,000; very few other denominational institutions received money, but those of some Hebrew, German, French, and similar societies received smaller amounts, of which the largest, $235,000, went to Hebrew charities.

the end of the nineteenth century figured largely in Ohio, Indiana, Michigan, and Illinois under the name of the American Protective Association. So the hostility to Mormonism was due not merely to the practice of polygamy, but also to the notion that the hierarchy of the Latter Day Saints constitutes a secret and tyrannical *imperium in imperio* opposed to the genius of democratic institutions.

The refusal of the civil power to protect or endow any form of religion is commonly represented in Europe as equivalent to a declaration of contemptuous indifference on the part of the state to the spiritual interests of its people. A state recognizing no church is called a godless state; the disestablishment of a church is described as an act of national impiety. Nothing can be farther from the American view, to an explanation of which it may be well to devote a few lines.

The abstention of the state from interference in matters of faith and worship may be advocated on two principles, which may be called the political and the religious. The former sets out from the principles of liberty and equality. It holds any attempt at compulsion by the civil power to be an infringement on liberty of thought, as well as on liberty of action, which could be justified only when a practice claiming to be religious is so obviously antisocial or immoral as to threaten the well-being of the community. Religious persecution, even in its milder forms, such as disqualifying the members of a particular sect for public office, is, it conceives, inconsistent with the conception of individual freedom and the respect due to the primordial rights of the citizen which modern thought has embraced. Even if state action stops short of the imposition of disabilities, and confines itself to favouring a particular church, whether by grants of money or by giving special immunities to its clergy, this is an infringement on equality, putting one man at a disadvantage compared with others in respect of matters which are not fit subjects for state cognizance.

The second principle, embodying the more purely religious view of the question, starts from the conception of the church as a spiritual body existing for spiritual purposes, and moving along spiritual paths. It is an assemblage of men who are united by their devotion to an unseen Being, their memory of a past divine life, their belief in the possibility of imitating that life, so far as human frailty allows, their hopes for an illimitable future. Compulsion of any kind is contrary to the nature of such a body, which lives by love and reverence, not by law. It desires no state help, feeling that its strength comes from above, and that its kingdom is not of this world. It does not seek for exclusive privileges, conceiving that these would not only create bitterness between itself and other religious bodies, but might attract persons who did not really share its sentiments, while corrupting the simplicity of those who are already its members. Least of all can it submit to be controlled by the state, for the state, in such a world as the present, means persons many or most of whom are alien to its beliefs and cold to its emotions. The conclusion follows that the church as a spiritual entity will be happiest and strongest when it is left absolutely to itself, not patronized by the civil power, not restrained by law except when and in so far as it may attempt to quit its proper sphere and intermeddle in secular affairs.

Of these two views it is the former much more than the latter that has moved the American mind. The latter would doubtless be now generally accepted by religious people. But when the question arose in a practical shape in the earlier days of the Republic, arguments of the former or political order were found amply sufficient to settle it, and no practical purpose has since then compelled men either to examine the spiritual basis of the church, or to inquire by the light of history how far state action has during sixteen centuries helped or marred her usefulness. There has, however, been another cause at work, I mean the comparatively limited conception of the state itself which Americans have formed. The state is not to them, as to Germans or Frenchmen, and even to some English thinkers, an ideal moral power, charged with the duty of forming the characters and guiding the lives of its subjects. It is more like a commercial company, or perhaps a huge municipality created for the management of certain business in which all who reside within its bounds are interested, levying contributions and expending them on this business of common interest, but for the most part leaving the shareholders or burgesses to themselves. That an organization of this kind should trouble itself, otherwise than as matter of police, with the opinions or conduct of its members would be as unnatural as for a railway company to inquire how many of the shareholders were Wesleyans or total abstainers. Accordingly it never occurs to the average American that there is any reason why state churches should exist, and he stands amazed at the warmth of European feeling on the matter.

Just because these questions have been long since disposed of, and excite no present passion, and perhaps also because the Americans are more practically easygoing than pedantically exact, the national government and the state governments do give to Christianity a species of recognition inconsistent with the view that civil government should be absolutely neutral in religious matters. Each house of Congress has a chaplain, and opens its proceedings each day with prayers. The president annually after the end of harvest issues a proclamation ordering a general thanksgiving, and occasionally appoints a day of fasting and humiliation. So prayers are offered in the state legislatures,[6] and state governors issue proclamations for days of religious observance. Congress in the crisis of the Civil War (July 1863) requested the president to appoint a day for humiliation and prayer. In the army and navy provision is made for religious services, conducted by chaplains of various denominations, and no difficulty seems to have been found in reconciling their claims. In most states there exist laws punishing blasphemy or profane swearing by the name of God (laws which, however, are in some places openly transgressed and in few or none enforced), laws restricting or forbidding trade or labour on the Sabbath, as well as laws protecting assemblages for religious purposes, such as camp meetings or religious processions, from being disturbed. The Bible is (in most states) read in the public state-supported schools, and though controversies have arisen on this head, the practice is evidently in accord with the general sentiment of the people.

The matter may be summed up by saying that Christianity is in fact understood to be, though not the legally established religion, yet the national religion.[7] So far from thinking their commonwealth godless, the Americans conceive that the religious character of a government consists in nothing but the religious belief of the individual citizens, and the conformity of their conduct to that belief. They deem the general acceptance of Christianity to be one of the main sources of their national prosperity, and their nation a special object of the Divine favour.

The legal position of a Christian church is in the United States simply that of a voluntary association, or group of associations, corporate or unincorporate, under the ordinary law. There is no such thing as a special ecclesiastical law; all questions, not only of property but of church discipline and jurisdiction, are, if brought before the courts of the land, dealt with as questions of contract;[8] and the court, where it is obliged to examine a question of theology, as for instance whether a clergyman has advanced opinions inconsistent with any creed or formula to which he has bound

---

[6] Though Michigan and Oregon forbid any appropriation of state funds for religious services.

[7] It has often been said that Christianity is a part of the common law of the states, as it has been said to be of the common law of England; but on this point there have been discrepant judicial opinions, nor can it be said to find any specific practical application. A discussion of it may be found in Justice Story's opinion in the famous Girard will case.

[8] Or otherwise as questions of private civil law. Actions for damages are sometimes brought against ecclesiastical authorities by persons deeming themselves to have been improperly accused or disciplined or deprived of the enjoyment of property.

himself—for it will prefer, if possible, to leave such matters to the proper ecclesiastical authority—will treat the point as one of pure legal interpretation, neither assuming to itself theological knowledge, nor suffering considerations of policy to intervene.[9] Questions relating to the union of two religious bodies are similarly dealt with on a basis merely legal.

As a rule, every religious body can organize itself in any way it pleases. The state does not require its leave to be asked, but permits any form of church government, any ecclesiastical order, to be created and endowed, any method to be adopted of vesting church property, either simply in trustees or in corporate bodies formed either under the general law of the state or under some special statute. Sometimes a limit is imposed on the amount of property, or of real estate, which an ecclesiastical corporation can hold; but, on the whole, it may be said that the civil power manifests no jealousy of the spiritual, but allows the latter a perfectly free field for expansion. Of course if any ecclesiastical authority were to become formidable either by its wealth or by its control over the members of its body, this easy tolerance would disappear; all I observe is that the difficulties often experienced, and still more often feared, in Europe, from the growth of organizations exercising tremendous spiritual powers, have in America never proved serious.[10] No church has anywhere a power approaching that of the Roman Catholic church in Lower Canada. Religious bodies are in so far the objects of special favour that their property is in most states exempt from taxation; and this is reconciled to theory by the argument that they are serviceable as moral agencies, and diminish the expenses incurred in respect of police administration.[11] Two or three states impose restrictions on the creation of religious corporations, and one, Maryland, requires the sanction of the legislature to dispositions of property to religious uses. But speaking generally, religious bodies are the objects of legislative favour.[12]

[9] The emperor Aurelian decided in a like neutral spirit a question that had arisen between two Christian churches.

[10] Occasionally a candidate belonging to a particular denomination receives some sympathetic support from its members. Once in a state election in Arkansas, as one candidate for the governorship had been a Baptist minister and the other a Methodist presiding elder, and four-fifths of the voters belonged to one or other denomination, each received a good deal of denominational adhesion.

[11] In his message of 1881 the governor of Washington Territory recommends the legislature to exempt church property from taxation, not only on the ground that "churches and schoolhouses are the temples of education, and alike conduce to the cultivation of peace, happiness, and prosperity," but also because "churches enhance the value of contiguous property, which, were they abolished, would be of less value and return less revenue."

[12] New Hampshire has lately taxed churches on the value of their real estate exceeding $10,000.

I pass on to say a few words as to the religious bodies of the country.[13]

In 1906 an attempt was made to obtain from each of these bodies full statistics regarding its numbers and the value of its property. The results, which I take from the bulletins and abstracts of that census, were, as respects the denominations whose membership exceeds 500,000 persons, as follows:

Roman Catholics	10,879,930[14]
Methodists (17 bodies)	6,551,891
Baptists (16 bodies)	5,241,841
Lutherans (23 bodies)	1,957,433
Presbyterians (12 bodies)	1,771,787
Disciples of Christ	1,264,758
Protestant Episcopalians	837,073
Congregationalists	694,923[15]

Besides these eight bodies the Jews are returned as having 143,000 members (only heads of families, however, being reckoned), the Friends 118,752, the Spiritualists 295,000, and eight communistic societies (including the so-called Shakers) only 3,084. The total number of persons returned as communicants or members of all the churches is 32,936,445.

Of the above-mentioned denominations, or rather groups, for most of them include numerous minor denominations, the Methodists and Baptists are numerous everywhere, but the Methodists especially numerous in the South, where they have been the chief evangelizers of the Negroes, and in the Middle states, New York, Pennsylvania, Ohio, Indiana, Illinois. Of the Congregationalists nearly one-half are to be found in New England, the rest in such parts of the Middle and Western states as have been peopled from New England. The Presbysterians are strongest in Pennsylvania, New York, Ohio, New Jersey, and in the older Southern states,[16] especially Virginia and North Carolina, states where many Scoto-Irish emigrants settled, but are well represented over the West also. Of the Lutherans nearly one-half are Germans and one-quarter Scandinavians, including Icelanders and Finns. The Protestant Episcopalians are strongest in New York (which supplies one-fourth of their total number), Pennsylvania, New Jersey, and Massachusetts.

---

[13] An interesting and impartial summary view of the history of the chief denominations in the United States may be found in Dr. George P. Fisher's *History of the Christian Church*, pp. 559–82.

[14] All baptized Roman Catholics over nine years of age are treated as members.

[15] The total number of ministers of all denominations is returned at 156,107, the total value of church sites and buildings (including many Chinese temples) at $1,257,575,867.

[16] The strength of Presbyterianism in the South is probably due in part to the immigration into those states of Ulstermen in the middle of last century, and of settlers from Holland at a still earlier date.

There are 65 dioceses and 94 bishops, but no archbishop, the supreme authority being vested in a convention which meets triennially. The Unitarians (in all 70,542 with 541 ministers) are few outside New England and the regions settled from New England, but have exercised an influence far beyond that of their numbers owing to the eminence of some of their divines, such as Channing, Emerson, and Theodore Parker, and to the fact that they include a large number of highly cultivated men. The Roman Catholics are, except in Maryland and Louisiana, nearly all either of Irish, German, Italian, Slavonic, or French-Canadian extraction. They abound everywhere, except in the South and some parts of the Northwest, and are perhaps, owing to the influx of Irish and French-Canadians, most relatively numerous in New England. The great development of the Lutheran bodies is of course due to German and Scandinavian immigration. Of all denominations the Jews have increased most rapidly, viz., at the rate of 160 per cent for the ten years 1880–90. The Jewish population of the U.S. was estimated to be in 1880, 230,257; in 1897, 937,800; and in 1907, 1,777,185. Of the Orthodox Jews (for there is also a large "Reformed" section), half are in New York.

All these phenomena find an easy historical explanation. The churches of the United States are the churches of the British Isles, modified by recent Roman Catholic, Lutheran, and Jewish immigration from the European continent. Each race has, as a rule, adhered to the form of religion it held in Europe; and where denominations comparatively small in England have, like the Methodists and Baptists, swelled to vast proportions here, it is because the social conditions under which they throve in England were here reproduced on a far larger scale. In other words, the causes which have given their relative importance and their local distribution to American denominations have been racial and social rather than ecclesiastical. No new religious forces have sprung up on American soil to give a new turn to her religious history. The breaking up of large denominations into smaller religious bodies seems to be due, partly to immigration, which has introduced slightly diverse elements, partly to the tendency to relax the old dogmatic stringency, a tendency which has been found to operate as a fissile force.

It need hardly be said that there exist no such social distinctions between different denominations as those of England. No clergyman, no layman, either looks down upon or looks up to any other clergyman or layman in respect of his worshipping God in another way. The Roman Catholic church of course stands aloof from the Protestant Christians, whom she considers schismatic; and although what is popularly called the doctrine of apostolic succession is less generally deemed vital by Protestant Episcopalians in

America than it has come to be by them of late years in England, the clergy of that church did not often admit to their pulpits pastors of other bodies (though they sometimes appear in the pulpits of those churches) until in 1908 a canon was passed expressly legalizing the admission of ministers of other Christian communions. Such exchanges of pulpit are common among Presbyterians, Congregationalists, and other orthodox Protestant bodies. In many parts of the North and West the Protestant Episcopal church has long been slightly more fashionable than its sister churches; and people who have no particular "religious preferences," but wish to stand well socially, will sometimes add themselves to it.[17] In the South, however, Presbyterianism (and in some places Methodism) is equally well regarded from a worldly point of view; while everywhere the strength of Methodists and Baptists and Roman Catholics resides in the masses of the people.[18]

Of late years proposals for union between some of the leading Protestant churches, and especially between the Presbyterians and Congregationalists and Lutherans, have been freely canvassed. They witness to a growing good feeling among the clergy, and a growing indifference to minor points of doctrine and church government. The vested interests of the existing clergy create some difficulties serious in small towns and country districts; but it seems possible that before many years more than one such union will be carried through.

The social standing of the clergy of each church corresponds pretty closely to the character of the church itself—that is to say, the pastors of the Presbyterian, Congregationalist, Episcopalian, and Unitarian bodies come generally, at least in the Northern states, from a higher social stratum than those of other more numerous denominations. The former are usually graduates of some university or college. As in Great Britain, comparatively few are the sons of the wealthy; and not very many come from the working classes. The position of a minister of the Gospel always carries with it some dignity—that is to say, it gives a man a certain advantage in the society, whatever it may be, to which he naturally belongs in respect of his family connections, his means, and his education. In the great cities the leading ministers of the chief denominations, including the Roman Catholic and

---

[17] The proposal which has been more than once made in the annual convention of the Protestant Episcopal church, that it should call itself "The National Church of America," has been always rejected by the good sense of the majority, who perceive that an assumption of this kind would provoke much displeasure from other bodies of Christians.

[18] The Methodists and Baptists are said to make more use of social means in the work of evangelizing the masses, and to adapt themselves more perfectly to democratic ideas than do the other Protestant bodies.

Protestant Episcopal bishops, whether they be eminent as preachers, or as active philanthropists, or in respect of their learning, are among the first citizens, and exercise an influence often wider and more powerful than that of any layman. Possibly no man in the United States, since President Lincoln, has been so warmly admired and so widely mourned as the late Dr. Phillips Brooks. Some of the Roman Catholic prelates are known and admired far beyond the limits of their dioceses. In cities of the second order, the clergymen of these denominations, supposing them (as is usually the case) to be men of good breeding and personally acceptable, move in the best society of the place. Similarly in country places the pastor is better educated and more enlightened than the average members of his flock, and becomes a leader in works of beneficence. The level of education and learning is rising among the clergy with the steady improvement of the universities. This advance is perhaps most marked among those denominations which, like the Methodists and Baptists, have heretofore lagged behind, because their adherents were mostly among the poor. So far as I could learn, the incomes of the clergy are also increasing, though not so fast as the cost of living, which, especially in cities, bears heavily upon members of a profession from which the maintenance of "a certain style" is expected. The highest salaries are those received by the Presbyterian and Congregationalist pastors in the great cities, which run from $8,000 up to $15,000, and by the Protestant Episcopal bishops ($3,300 up to $12,500). Roman Catholic bishops, being celibate and with poorer flocks, have from $3,000 to $5,000; Methodist bishops usually $5,000, with travelling expenses. In the wealthier denominations there are many city ministers whose incomes exceed $3,000, while in small towns and rural districts few fall below $1,000; in the less wealthy $1,500 for a city and $700 for a rural charge may be a fair average as regards the North and West. The average income of a Roman Catholic priest is given at $800. To the sums regularly paid must be added in many cases a residence, and in nearly all various gifts and fees which the minister receives.

These figures, which, however, must be a little reduced for the Southern states, compare favourably with the average incomes received by the clergy of all denominations in England or Scotland, and are above the salaries paid to priests in France or to Protestant pastors in Germany. Reckoning in the clergy of all denominations in Great Britain and in the United States, both the pecuniary and the social position of the American clergy may, so far as it is possible to strike an average, be pronounced slightly higher.

Although the influence of the clergy is still great it has changed its nature, yielding to the universal current which makes for equality. At the beginning of the century the New England ministers enjoyed a local authority not unlike that of the bishops in Western Europe in the sixth century or of the Presbyterian ministers of Scotland in the seventeenth. They were, especially in country places, the leaders as well as instructors of their congregations, and were a power in politics scarcely less than in spiritual affairs.[19] That order of things has quite passed away. His profession and his education still secure respect for a clergyman,[20] but he must not now interfere in politics; he must not speak on any secular subject *ex cathedra*; his influence, whatever it may be, is no longer official but can only be that of a citizen distinguished by his talents or character, whose office gives him no greater advantage than that of an eminence where shining gifts may be more widely visible. Now and then this rule of abstention from politics is broken through. Mr. Henry Ward Beecher took the field as a Mugwump in the presidential campaign of 1884, and was deemed the more courageous in doing so because the congregation of Plymouth Church were mostly "straight out" Republicans. The Roman Catholic bishops have sometimes been accused of lending secret aid to the political party which will procure subventions for their schools and charities, and do no doubt, as indeed their doctrines require, press warmly the claims of denominational education. But otherwise they also abstain from politics. Such action as is constantly taken in England by ministers of the Established Church on the one side of politics, by Nonconformist ministers on the other, would in America excite disapproval. It is only on platforms or in conventions where some moral cause is to be advocated, such as Abolitionism was before the war years or temperance is now, that clergymen can with impunity appear.

Considering that the absence of state interference in matters of religion is one of the most striking differences between all the European countries on the one hand and the United States on the other, the European reader

---

[19] In a few states clergymen are still declared ineligible, by the constitution, as members of a state legislature. They do not seem to have in the early days sat in these bodies; and they very rarely sit in Congress, but one finds them in conventions. One of the signers of the Declaration of Independence was John Witherspoon, a Presbysterian minister and president of Princeton College, who had come recently from Scotland. Some of the best speeches in the Massachusetts convention of 1788 which ratified the federal Constitution were made by ministers. In New England, they were nearly all advocates of the Constitution, and passed into the Federalist party.

[20] The clergy are the objects of a good deal of favour in various small ways; for instance, they used to receive free passes on railroads, and the Interstate Commerce Act of 1887, while forbidding the system of granting free passes, which had been much abused, specially exempted clergymen from the prohibition. Their children are usually educated at lower fees, or even gratis, in colleges, and storekeepers often allow them a discount.

may naturally expect some further remarks on the practical results of this divergence. "There are," he will say, "two evil consequences with which the European defenders of established churches seek to terrify us when disestablishment and disendowment are mentioned, one that the authority and influence of religion will wane if state recognition is withdrawn, the other that the incomes of the clergy and their social status will sink, that they will in fact become plebeians, and that the centres of light which now exist in every country parish will be extinguished. There are also two benefits which the advocates of the 'Free Church in a Free State' promise us, one that social jealousies and bitternesses between different sects will melt away, and the other that the church will herself become more spiritual in her temper and ideas, more earnest in her proper work of moral reform and the nurture of the soul. What has American experience to say on these four points?"

These are questions so pertinent to a right conception of the ecclesiastical side of American life that I cannot decline the duty of trying to answer them, though reluctant to tread on ground to which European conflicts give a controversial character.

I. To estimate the influence and authority of religion is not easy. Suppose, however, that we take either the habit of attending church or the sale of religious books as evidences of its influence among the multitude; suppose that as regards the more cultivated classes we look at the amount of respect paid to Christian precepts and ministers, the interest taken in theological questions, the connection of philanthropic reforms with religion. Adding these various data together, we may get some sort of notion of the influence of religion on the American people as a whole.

Purposing to touch on these points in the chapter next following, I will here only say by way of anticipation that in all these respects the influence of Christianity seems to be, if we look not merely to the numbers but also to the intelligence of the persons influenced, greater and more widespread in the United States than in any part of western continental Europe, and I think greater than in England. In parts of France, Italy, Spain, and the Catholic parts of Germany, as well as in German Austria, the authority of religion over the masses is of course great. Its influence on the best educated classes—one must include all parts of society in order to form a fair judgment—is apparently smaller in France and Italy than in Great Britain, and apparently smaller than in the United States. The country which most resembles America in this respect is Scotland, where the mass of the people enjoy large rights in the management of their church affairs, and where the interest of all classes has, ever since the Reformation, tended to run in ecclesiastical channels. So far from suffering from the want of state support, religion seems in the United States to stand all the firmer because, standing alone, she is seen to stand by her own strength. No political party, no class in the community, has any hostility either to Christianity or to any particular Christian body. The churches are as thoroughly popular, in the best sense of the word, as any of the other institutions of the country.

II. The social and economic position of the clergy in the United States is above that of the priesthood, taken as a whole, in Roman Catholic countries, and equal to that of all denominations taken together; Anglican and Nonconformist, in England. No American pastors enjoy such revenues as the prelates of England and Hungary; but the average income attached to the pastoral office is in America larger. The peculiar conditions of England, where one church looks down socially on the others, make a comparison in other respects difficult. The education of the American ministers, their manners, their capacity for spreading light among the people, seem superior to those of the seminarist priesthood of France and Italy (who are of course far more of a distinct caste) and equal to those of the Protestant pastors of Germany and Scotland.

III. Social jealousies connected with religion scarcely exist in America, and one notes a kindlier feeling between all denominations, Roman Catholics included, a greater readiness to work together for common charitable aims, than between Catholics and Protestants in France or Germany, or between Anglicans and Nonconformists in England. There is a rivalry between the leading denominations to extend their bounds, to erect and fill new churches, to raise great sums for church purposes. Viewed from the side of the New Testament, it may appear a foolish rivalry; but it is not unfriendly, and does not provoke bad blood, because the state stands neutral, and all churches have a free field. There is less mutual exclusiveness than in any other country, except perhaps Scotland. An instance may be found in the habit of exchanging pulpits, another in the comparative frequency with which persons pass from one denomination to another, if a particular clergyman attracts them, or if they settle in a place distant from a church of their own body. One often finds members of the same family belonging to different denominations. Some of the leading bodies, and especially the Presbyterians and Congregationalists, between whose doctrines there exists practically no difference, have been wont, especially in the West, to cooperate for the sake of efficiency and economy in agreeing not to plant two rival churches in a place where one will suffice, but to arrange that one denomination shall set up its church, and the other advise its adherents to join and support that church.

IV. To give an opinion on the three foregoing questions is incomparably easier than to say whether and how much Christianity has gained in spiritual purity and dignity by her severance from the secular power.

There is a spiritual gain in that diminution of envy, malice, and uncharitableness between the clergy of various sects which has resulted from their being all on the same legal level; and the absence both of these faults and of the habit of bringing ecclesiastical questions into secular politics, gives the enemy less occasion to blaspheme than he is apt to have in Europe. Church assemblies—synods, conferences, and conventions—seem on the whole to be conducted with better temper and more good sense than these bodies have shown in the Old World, from the Council of Ephesus down to our own day. But in America as elsewhere some young men enter the clerical profession from temporal motives; some laymen join a church to improve their social or even their business position; some country pastors look out for city cures, and justify their leaving a poorer flock for a richer by talking of a wider sphere of usefulness. One hears that in some bodies there is much intriguing to secure a post of eminence, and that men of great wealth exert undue influence, as they did in the days when the Epistle of St. James was written. The desire to push the progress of the particular church or of the denomination often mingles with the desire to preach the gospel more widely; and the gospel is sometimes preached, if not with "respect of persons" yet with less faithful insistence on unpalatable truths than the moral health of the community requires.

So far as I could ascertain, the dependence of the minister for his support on his congregation does not lower him in their eyes, nor make him more apt to flatter the leading members than he is in established churches. If he is personally dignified and unselfish, his independence will be in no danger. But whether the voluntary system, which no doubt makes men more liberal in giving for the support of religious ordinances among themselves and of missions elsewhere, tends to quicken spiritual life, and to keep the church pure and undefiled, free from the corrupting influences of the world, is another matter, on which a stranger may well hesitate to speak. Those Americans whose opinion I have inquired are unanimous in holding that in this respect also the fruits of freedom have been good.

The Influence of Religion

To convey some impression of the character and type which religion has taken in America, and to estimate its influence as a moral and spiritual force, is an infinitely harder task than to sketch the salient ecclesiastical phenomena of the country. I approach it with the greatest diffidence, and do not profess to give anything more than the sifted result of answers to questions addressed to many competent observers belonging to various churches or to none.

An obviously important point to determine is the extent to which the external ministrations of religion are supplied to the people and used by them. This is a matter on which no trustworthy statistics seem attainable, but on which the visitor's own eyes leave him in little doubt. There are churches everywhere, and everywhere equally: in the cities and in the country, in the North and in the South, in the quiet nooks of New England, in the settlements which have sprung up along railroads in the West. It is only in the very roughest parts of the West, and especially in the region of mining camps, that they are wanting, and the want is but temporary, for "home missionary" societies are quickly in the field, and provide the ministrations of religion even to this migratory population. In many a town of moderate size one finds a church for every thousand inhabitants, as was the case with Dayton, in Ohio, which, when it had 40,000 people, had just forty churches. The growth of churches is deemed an indication of prosperity, as I remember that the dweller in a new Oklahoma city, anxious to prove its swift progress, pointed to a corner lot and said, "A fifteen thousand dollar church is going up there."

Denominational rivalry has counted for something in the rapid creation of churches in the newly settled West and their multiplication everywhere else. So, too, weak churches are sometimes maintained out of pride when it would be better to let them be united with other congregations of the same body. Attendance is pretty good, though in some denominations the women greatly outnumber the men. In cities of moderate size, as well as in small towns and country places, a stranger is told that possibly a half of the native American population go to church at least once every Sunday. In the great cities the proportion of those who attend is very much less, but whether or no as small as in English cities no one could tell me. One sometimes finds the habit of churchgoing well formed in the more settled parts of the Far West where the people, being newcomers, might be supposed to be less under the sway of habit and convention. California is an exception, and is the state supposed to be least affected by religious influences. In the chief city of Oregon I found in 1881 that a person, and especially a woman of the upper class, who did not belong to some church and attend it pretty regularly, would be looked askance on. She need not actually lose caste, but the fact would excite surprise and regret; and her disquieted friends would put some pressure upon her to enrol herself as a church member. That would hardly happen in such a city today, and there are grounds for thinking that, taking the country as a whole, church attendance does not keep pace with the growth of population.

The observance of the Sabbath as it was, or the Sunday as it is now usually, called, furnishes another test. The strictness of Puritan practice has quite disappeared, even in New England, but there are still a few out of the way places, especially in the South, where the American part of the rural population refrains from amusement as well as from work.[1] It is otherwise with the Germans; and in some parts of the country their example has

---

[1] An interesting summary of the laws for the observance of Sunday may be found in a paper read by Mr. Henry E. Young at the Third Annual Meeting of the American Bar Association (1880). These laws, which seem to exist in every state, are in many cases very strict, forbidding all labour, except works of necessity and mercy, and in many cases forbidding also travelling and nearly every kind of amusement. Vermont and South Carolina seem to go farthest in this direction. The former prescribes, under a fine of $2, that no one shall "visit from house to house, except from motives of humanity or charity, or travel from midnight of Saturday to midnight of Sunday, or hold or attend any ball or dance, or use any game, sport, or play, or resort to any house of entertainment for amusement or recreation."

In Indiana, where all labour and "engaging in one's usual avocation" are prohibited, it has been held by the Courts that "selling a cigar to one who has contracted the habit of smoking is a work of necessity."

South Carolina winds up a minute series of prohibitions by ordering all persons to apply themselves to the observance of the day by exercising themselves thereon in the duties of piety and true religion. It need hardly be said that these laws are practically obsolete, except so far as they forbid ordinary and unnecessary traffic and labour. To that extent they are supported by public sentiment, and are justified as being in the nature not so much of religious as of socially and economically useful regulations. The habit of playing outdoor games and that of resorting to places of public amusement on Sunday have much increased of late years.

brought in laxity as regards amusement. Such cities as Chicago, Cincinnati, New Orleans, and San Francisco have a Sunday quite unlike that of New England, and more resembling what one finds in Germany or France. Nowhere however does one see the shops open or ordinary work done. On many railroads there are few Sunday trains, and museums are in many cities closed. But in two respects the practice is more lax than in Great Britain. Most of the leading newspapers publish Sunday editions, which contain a great deal of general readable matter, stories, gossip, and so forth, over and above the news of the day; and in the great cities theatres are now open on Sunday evenings.[2]

The interest in theological questions is less keen than it was in New England a century ago, but keener than it has generally been in England since the days of the Commonwealth. Much of the ordinary reading of the average family has a religious tinge, being supplied in religious or semi-religious weekly and monthly magazines. Till recently in parts of the West the old problems of predestination, reprobation, and election continued to be discussed by farmers and shopkeepers in their leisure moments with the old eagerness, and gave a sombre tinge to their views of religion. The ordinary man used to know the Bible better, and took up an allusion to it more quickly than the ordinary Englishman, though perhaps not better than the ordinary Scotchman. Indeed I may say once for all that the native American in everything concerning theology reminds one much more of Scotland than of England, although in the general cast and turn of his mind he is far more English than Scotch. One is told, however, that nowadays the knowledge of Scripture has declined. It is hard to state any general view as to the substance of pulpit teaching, because the differences between different denominations are marked; but the tendency has been, and daily grows alike among Congregationalists, Baptists, Northern Presbyterians, and Episcopalians, for sermons to be less metaphysical and less markedly doctrinal than formerly, and to become either expository or else of a practical and hortatory character. This is less the case among the Presbyterians of the South, who are more stringently orthodox, and in all respects more conservative than their brethren of the North. The discussion of the leading theological questions of the day, such as those of the authority of Scripture,

---

[2] One hears that it is now becoming the custom to make a week's engagement of an operatic or theatrical company—there are many traversing the country—begin on Sunday instead of, as formerly, on Monday night.

　Boston, Philadelphia, and New York have opened their public libraries, museums, and art galleries on Sunday.

the relation of natural science to the teachings of the Bible, the existence of rewards and punishments in a future state, goes on much as in England. Some of the leading reviews and magazines publish articles on these subjects, which are read more widely than corresponding articles in England, but do not, I think, absorb any more of the thought and attention of the average educated man and woman.

Whether scepticism makes any sensible advance either in affecting a larger number of minds, or in cutting more deeply at the roots of their belief in God and immortality, is a question which it is today extremely difficult for anyone to answer even as regards his own country. There are many phenomena in every part of Europe which appear to indicate that it does advance; there are others which point in the opposite direction. Much more difficult, then, must it be for a stranger to express a positive opinion as regards America on this gravest of all subjects of enquiry. The conditions of England and America appear to me very similar; whatever tendency prevails in either country is likely to prevail in the other and like changes of taste in theological literature have shown themselves. The mental habits of the people are the same; their fundamental religious conceptions are the same, except that those who prize a visible church and bow to her authority are relatively fewer among American Protestants; their theological literature is the same. In discussing a theological question with an American one never feels that slight difference of point of view, or, so to speak, of mental atmosphere, which is sure to crop up in talking to a Frenchman or an Italian, or even to a German. Considerations of speculative argument, considerations of religious feeling, affect the two nations in the same way: the course of their religious history is not likely to diverge. If there be a difference at all in their present attitude, it is perhaps to be found in this, that whereas Americans are more frequently disposed to treat minor issues in a bold spirit, they are more apt to recoil from blank negation. As an American once said to me—they are apt to put serious views into familiar words— "We don't mind going a good way along the plank, but we like to stop short of the jump-off."

Whether pronounced theological unbelief, which has latterly been preached by lectures and pamphlets with a freedom unknown half a century ago, has made substantial progress among the thinking part of the working class is a question on which one hears the most opposite statements. I have seen statistics which purport to show that the proportion of members of Christian churches to the total population rose in the Protestant churches from 1 in $14\frac{1}{2}$ in 1800 to 1 in 5 in 1880; and which estimated the number of com-

municants in 1880 at 12,000,000, the total adult population in that year
being taken at 25,000,000. So the census of churches of 1906 gives the
number of church members or communicants at 33,000,000 or 39.1 of the
total estimated population. But one also hears many lamentations over the
diminished attendance at city churches; and in ecclesiastical circles people
say, just as they say in England, that the great problem is how to reach the
masses. The most probable conclusion seems to be that while in cities like
New York and Chicago the bulk of the humbler classes (except the Roman
Catholics, who are largely recent immigrants) are practically heathen to the
same extent as in London, or Liverpool, or Berlin, the proportion of working
men who belong to some religious body is rather larger in towns under
30,000 than it is in the similar towns of Great Britain or Germany.

In the more cultivated circles of the great cities one finds a number of
people, as one does in England, who have virtually abandoned Christianity,
and a much larger number who seem practically indifferent, and seldom
accompany their wives or sisters to church. So also in most of the cities
there is said to be a knot of men who profess agnosticism, and sometimes
have a meeting place where secularist lectures are delivered. In the middle
of the last century the former class would have been fewer and more
reserved; the latter would scarcely have existed. But the relaxation of the
old strictness of orthodoxy has not diminished the zeal of the various
churches, nor their hold upon their adherents, nor their attachment to the
fundamental doctrines of Christianity.

This zeal and attachment happily no longer show themselves in intolerance.
Except perhaps in small places in the West or South, where aggressive
scepticism would rouse displeasure and might affect a man's position in
society, everybody is as free in America as in London to hold and express
any views he pleases. Within the churches themselves there is an unmistakable
tendency to loosen the bonds of subscription required from clergymen.
Prosecutions for heresy of course come before church courts, since no civil
court would take cognizance of such matters unless when invoked by
someone alleging that a church court had given a decision, or a church
authority had taken an executive step, which prejudiced him in some civil
right, and was unjust because violating an obligation contracted with him.[3]
Such prosecutions have latterly become uncommon, but the sympathy of
the public is usually with the accused minister, and the latitude allowed to

---

[3] Including the case in which a church court had disregarded its own regulations, or acted in
violation of the plain principles of judicial procedure.

divergence from the old standards becomes constantly greater. At present it is in the Congregationalist church pretty much the same as in that church in England; in the Presbyterian church of the North, and among Baptists and Methodists, slightly less than in the unestablished Presbyterian churches of Scotland. Most of the churches usually called orthodox have allowed less latitude in doctrine and in ritual than recent decisions of the courts of law, beginning from the "Essays and Reviews" case, have allowed to the clergy of the Anglican Establishment in England; but I could not gather that the clergy of the various Protestant bodies feel themselves fettered, or that the free development of religious thought is seriously checked, except in the South, where orthodoxy is rigid, and forbids a clergyman to hold Mr. Darwin's views regarding the descent of man.[4] A pastor who begins to chafe under the formularies or liturgy of his denomination would be expected to leave the denomination and join some other in which he could feel more at home. He would not suffer socially by doing so, as an Anglican clergyman possibly might in the like case in England. In the Roman Catholic church there is, of course, no similar indulgence to a deviation from the ancient dogmatic standards; but there is a greater disposition to welcome the newer forms of learning and culture than one finds in England or Ireland, and what may be called a more pronounced democratic spirit. So among the younger Protestant clergy there has been of late years a tendency, if not to Socialism, yet to a marked discontent with existing economic conditions, resembling what is now perceptible among the younger clergy in Britains.

As respects what may be called the everyday religious life and usages of the United States, there are differences from those of England or Scotland which it is easy to feel but hard to define or describe. There is rather less conventionalism or constraint in speaking of religious experiences, less of a formal separation between the church and the world, less disposition to treat the clergy as a caste and expect them to conform to a standard not prescribed for the layman,[5] less reticence about sacred things, perhaps less sense of the refinement with which sacred things ought to be surrounded. The letting by auction of sittings in a popular church, though I think very rare, excites less disapproval than it would in Europe. Some fashionable churches are supplied with sofas, carpets, and the other comforts of a

---

[4] Some while ago, a professor, not in the theological faculty, was removed from his chair in the University of South Carolina for holding Unitarian views.

[5] Although total abstinence is much more generally expected from a clergyman than it would be in Great Britain. In most denominations, including Baptists and Methodists, Congregationalists and Presbyterians, it is practically universal among the clergy.

drawing room; a well-trained choir is provided, and the congregation would not think of spoiling the performance by joining in the singing. The social side of church life is more fully developed than in Protestant Europe. A congregation, particularly among the Methodists, Baptists, and Congregationalists, is the centre of a group of societies, literary and recreative as well as religious and philanthropic, which not only stimulate charitable work, but bring the poorer and richer members into friendly relations with one another, and form a large part of the social enjoyments of the young people, keeping them out of harm's way, and giving them a means of forming acquaintances. Often a sort of informal evening party, called a "sociable," is given once a month, at which all ages and classes meet on an easy footing.[6] The Young Men's Christian Association movement which has attained vast dimensions does much to attract the young people by providing facilities for exercise and amusement as well by work of a more definitely religious character. Religion seems to associate itself better with the interests of the young in America, and to have come within the last forty years to wear a less forbidding countenance than it has generally done in Britain, or at least among English Nonconformists and in the churches of Scotland.

A still more peculiar feature of the American churches is the propensity to what may be called Revivalism which some of them, and especially the Methodist churches, show. That exciting preaching and those external demonstrations of feeling which have occasionally appeared in Britain were long chronic there, appearing chiefly in the form of the camp meeting, a gathering of people usually in the woods or on the sea shore, where open-air preaching goes on perhaps for days together. One hears many stories about these camp meetings, not always to their credit, which agree at least in this that they exercise a powerful even if transient influence upon the humbler classes who flock to them. In the West they have been serviceable in evangelizing districts where few regular churches had yet been established. Of late years they have tended to pass into mere summer outings, except in some parts of the South, where however it is now chiefly among the humbler classes, and of course still more among the Negroes, that they flourish. All denominations are more prone to emotionalism in religion, and have less

---

[6] Even dances may be given, but not by all denominations. When a Presbyterian congregation in a great Western city was giving a "reception" in honour of the opening of its new church building— prosperous churches always have a building with a set of rooms for meetings—the sexton (as he is called in America), who had come from a Protestant Episcopal church in the East, observed, as he surveyed the spacious hall, "What a pity you are not Episcopalians; you might have given a ball in this room!"

reserve in displaying it, than in England or Scotland. I remember in 1870 to have been a passenger by one of the splendid steamers which ply along the Sound between New York and Fall River. A Unitarian Congress was being held in New York, and a company of New England Unitarians were going to attend it. Now New England Unitarians are of all Americans perhaps the most staid and sober in their thoughts and habits, the least inclined to a demonstrative expression of their faith. This company, however, installed itself round the piano in the great saloon of the vessel and sang hymns, hymns full of effusion, for nearly two hours, many of the other passengers joining, and all looking on with sympathy. Our English party assumed at first that the singers belonged to some Methodist body, in which case there would have been nothing to remark except the attitude of the bystanders. But they were Unitarians.

European travellers have in one point greatly exaggerated the differences between their own continent and the United States. They have represented the latter as preeminently a land of strange sects and abnormal religious developments. Such sects and developments there certainly are, but they play no greater part in the whole life of the nation than similar sects do in Germany and England, far less than the various dissenting communities do in Russia. The Mormons drew the eyes of the world because they attempted to form a sort of religious commonwealth, and revived one ancient practice which modern ethics condemn, and which severe congressional legislation is supposed to have now stamped out. But the Mormon church is chiefly recruited from Europe. In 1881 I found few native Americans among the Mormons in Salt Lake City, and those few from among the poor whites of the South.[7] The number of recruits from all quarters began soon thereafter to decrease. The Shakers are an interesting and well-conducted folk, but there are very few of them, and they decrease—there were in 1906 only 516 persons in their eleven communities; while of the other communistic religious bodies one hears more in Europe than in America. Here and there some strange little sect emerges and lives for a few years;[8] but in a country

---

[7] There is a nonpolygamous Mormon church, rejecting Brigham Young and his successors in Utah, which returned itself to the census of 1906 as having 40,851 members. Some Southern states punish the preaching of Mormonism.

[8] Near Walla Walla in the state of Washington I came in 1881 across a curious little sect formed by a Welshman who fell into trances and delivered revelations. He had two sons, and asserted one of them to be an incarnation of Christ, and the other of St. John Baptist, and gathered about fifty disciples, whom he endeavoured to form into a society having all things in common. However, both the children died; and in 1881 most of his disciples had deserted him. Probably such phenomena are not uncommon; there is a good deal of proneness to superstition among the less

seething with religious emotion, and whose conditions seem to tempt to new departures and experiments of all kinds, the philosophic traveller may rather wonder that men have stood so generally upon the old paths.[9]

We have already seen that Christianity has in the United States maintained, so far as externals go, its authority and dignity, planting its houses of worship all over the country and raising enormous revenues from its adherents. Such a position of apparent influence might, however, rest upon ancient habit and convention, and imply no dominion over the souls of men. The Roman Empire in the days of Augustus was covered from end to end with superb temples to many gods; the priests were numerous and wealthy, and enjoyed the protection of the state; processions retained their pomp, and sacrifices drew crowds of admiring worshippers. But the old religions had lost their hold on the belief of the educated and on the conscience of all classes. If therefore we desire to know what place Christianity really fills in America, and how far it gives stability to the commonwealth, we must inquire how far it governs the life and moulds the mind of the country.

Such an enquiry may address itself to two points. It may examine into the influence which religion has on the conduct of the people, on their moral standard and the way they conform themselves thereto. And it may ask how far religion touches and gilds the imagination of the people, redeeming their lives from commonness, and bathing their souls in "the light that never was on sea or land."

In works of active beneficence no country has surpassed, perhaps none has equalled, the United States. Not only are the sums collected for all sorts of philanthropic purposes larger relatively to the wealth of America than in any European country, but the amount of personal interest shown in good works and personal effort devoted to them seems to a European visitor to exceed what he knows at home. How much of this interest and effort would be given were no religious motive present it is impossible to say. Not all, but I think nearly all of it, is in fact given by religious people, and, as they themselves suppose, under a religious impulse. This religious impulse is less frequently than in England a sectarian impulse, for all Protestants, and to some extent Roman Catholics also, are wont to join hands for most works of benevolence.

---

educated Westerns, especially the immigrants from Europe. They lead a solitary life in the midst of a vast nature.

[9] As regards new sects the most noticeable feature of recent years has been the growth of the body which calls itself by the name of "Christian Science." It is said to claim a million of adherents, many of them in New England.

The ethical standard of the average man is of course the Christian standard, modified to some slight extent by the circumstances of American life, which have been different from those of Protestant Europe. The average man has not thought of any other standard, and religious teaching, though it has become less definite and less dogmatic, is still to him the source whence he believes himself to have drawn his ideas of duty and conduct. In Puritan days there must have been some little conscious and much more unconscious hypocrisy, the profession of religion being universal, and the exactitude of practice required by opinion, and even by law, being above what ordinary human nature seems capable of attaining. The fault of antinomianism which used to be charged on high Calvinists is now sometimes charged on those who become, under the influence of revivals, extreme emotionalists in religion. But taking the native Americans as a whole, no people seems today less open to the charge of pharisaism or hypocrisy. They are perhaps rather more prone to the opposite error of good-natured indulgence to offences of which they are not themselves guilty.

That there is less crime among native Americans than among the foreign born is a point not to be greatly pressed, for it may be partly due to the fact that the latter are the poorer and more ignorant part of the population; and in parts of the South and West violence and even homicide are common enough among the native-born. If, however, we take matters which do not fall within the scope of penal law, the general impression of those who have lived long both in Protestant Europe and in America seems to be that as respects veracity, temperance, the purity of domestic life,[10] tenderness to children and the weak, and general kindliness of behaviour, the native Americans stand rather higher than either the English or the Germans.[11] And those whose opinion I am quoting seem generally, though not universally, disposed to think that the influence of religious belief, which may survive

---

[10] The great frequency of divorce in many states—there are districts where the proportion of divorces of marriages is 1 to 7—does not appear to betoken immorality, but to be due to the extreme facility with which the law allows one or both of a married pair to indulge their caprice. Divorce is said to be less frequent in proportion among the middle classes than among the richer and the humbler and is, speaking generally, more frequent the further West one goes, though it is unhappily frequent in some of the Middle states and in some Eastern also. It is increasing everywhere; but it increases also in those European countries which permit it. Some remarks on this subject, and a comparison of the conditions which prevailed in the Roman Empire may be found in an essay entitled "Marriage and Divorce in Roman and English Law" in my *Studies in History and Jurisprudence*.

[11] This cannot be said as regards commercial uprightness, in which respect the United States stand certainly on no higher level than England and Germany, and possibly below France and Scandinavia.

in its effect upon the character when a man has dropped his connection with any religious body, counts for a good deal in this. There is now a general feeling that the state judges administer in too lax and easy a way laws which are themselves too lax. The abuse of divorce procedure amounts in some states to a scandal.

If we ask how far religion exerts a stimulating influence on the thought and imagination of a nation, we are met by the difficulty of determining what is the condition of mankind where no such influence is present. There has never been a civilized nation without a religion; and though many highly civilized individual men live without one, they are so obviously the children of a state of sentiment and thought in which religion has been a powerful factor, that no one can conjecture what a race of men would be like who had during several generations believed themselves to be the highest beings in the universe, or at least entirely out of relation to any other higher beings, and to be therewithal destined to no kind of existence after death. Some may hold that respect for public opinion, sympathy, an interest in the future of mankind, would do for such a people what religion has done in the past; or that they might even be, as Lucretius expected, the happier for the extinction of possible supernatural terrors. Others may hold that life would seem narrow and insignificant, and that the wings of imagination would droop in a universe felt to be void. All that need be here said is that a people with comparatively little around it in the way of historic memories and associations to touch its emotion, a people whose energy is chiefly absorbed in commerce and the development of the material resources of its territory, a people consumed by a feverish activity that gives little opportunity for reflection or for the contemplation of nature, seems most of all to need to have its horizon widened, its sense of awe and mystery touched, by whatever calls it away from the busy world of sight and sound into the stillness of faith and meditation. A perusal of the literature which the ordinary American of the educated farming and working class reads, and a study of the kind of literature which those Americans who are least coloured by European influences produce, led one to think that the Bible and Christian theology altogether have in the past done more in the way of forming the imaginative background to an average American view of the world of man and nature than they have in most European countries.

No one is so thoughtless as not to sometimes ask himself what would befall mankind if the solid fabric of belief on which their morality has hitherto rested, or at least been deemed by them to rest, were suddenly to break up and vanish under the influence of new views of nature, as the ice fields split and melt when they have floated down into a warmer sea. Morality with religion for its sanction has hitherto been the basis of social polity, except under military despotisms. Would morality be so far weakened as to make social polity unstable? And if so, would a reign of violence return? In Europe this question does not seem urgent, because in Europe the physical force of armed men which maintains order is usually conspicuous, and because obedience to authority is everywhere in Europe matter of ancient habit, having come down little impaired from ages when men obeyed without asking for a reason. But in America the whole system of government seems to rest not on armed force, but on the will of the numerical majority, a majority most of whom might well think that its overthrow would be for them a gain. So sometimes, standing in the midst of a great American city, and watching the throngs of eager figures streaming hither and thither, marking the sharp contrasts of poverty and wealth, an increasing mass of wretchedness and an increasing display of luxury, knowing that before long a hundred millions of men will be living between ocean and ocean under this one government—a government which their own hands have made, and which they feel to be the work of their own hands—one is startled by the thought of what might befall this huge yet delicate fabric of laws and commerce and social institutions were the foundations it has rested on to crumble away. Suppose that all these men ceased to believe that there was any power above them, any future before them, anything in heaven or earth but what their senses told them of; suppose that their consciousness of individual force and responsibility, already dwarfed by the overwhelming power of the multitude, and the fatalistic submission it engenders, were further weakened by the feeling that their swiftly fleeting life was rounded by a perpetual sleep:

> Soles occidere et redire possunt:
> Nobis, quum semel occidit brevis lux
> Nox est perpetua una dormienda.

Would the moral code stand unshaken, and with it the reverence for law, the sense of duty towards the community, and even towards the generations yet to come? Would men say "Let us eat and drink; for tomorrow we die"? Or would custom, and sympathy, and a perception of the advantages which stable government offers to the citizens as a whole, and which orderly self-restraint offers to each one, replace supernatural sanctions, and hold in check the violence of masses and the self-indulgent impulses of the individual? History cannot answer this question. The most she can tell us is that hitherto civilized society has rested on religion, and that free government has prospered best among religious peoples.

America is no doubt the country in which intellectual movements work most swiftly upon the masses, and the country in which the loss of faith in the invisible might produce the completest revolution, because it is the country where men have been least wont to revere anything in the visible world. Yet America seems as unlikely to drift from her ancient moorings as any country of the Old World. It was religious zeal and the religious conscience which led to the founding of the New England colonies nearly three centuries ago—those colonies whose spirit has in such large measure passed into the whole nation. Religion and conscience have been a constantly active force in the American commonwealth ever since, not, indeed, strong enough to avert many moral and political evils, yet at the worst times inspiring a minority with a courage and ardour by which moral and political evils have been held at bay, and in the long run generally overcome.

It is an old saying that monarchies live by honour and republics by virtue. The more democratic republics become, the more the masses grow conscious of their own power, the more do they need to live, not only by patriotism, but by reverence and self-control, and the more essential to their well-being are those sources whence reverence and self-control flow.

The Position of Women

It has been well said that the position which women hold in a country is, if not a complete test, yet one of the best tests of the progress it has made in civilization. When one compares nomad man with settled man, heathen man with Christian man, the ancient world with the modern, the Eastern world with the Western, it is plain that in every case the advance in public order, in material comfort, in wealth, in decency and refinement of manners, among the whole population of a country—for in these matters one must not look merely at the upper class—has been accompanied by a greater respect for women, by a greater freedom accorded to them, by a fuller participation on their part in the best work of the world. Americans are fond of pointing, and can with perfect justice point, to the position their women hold as an evidence of the high level their civilization has reached. Certainly nothing in the country is more characteristic of the peculiar type their civilization has taken.

The subject may be regarded in so many aspects that it is convenient to take up each separately.

As respects the legal rights of women, these, of course, depend on the legislative enactments of each state of the Union, for in no case has the matter been left under the rigour of the common law. With much diversity in minor details, the general principles of the law are in all or nearly all the states similar. Women have been placed on an equality with men as respects all private rights. In some states husband and wife can sue one another at law. Married as well as unmarried women have long since (and I think everywhere) obtained full control of their property, whether obtained by gift or descent, or by their own labour. This has been deemed so important a point that, instead of being left to ordinary legislation, it has in several states been directly enacted by the people in the constitution. Women have in most, possible not yet in all, states rights of guardianship over their children which the law of England denied to them till the Act of 1886; and in some states the mother's rights are equal, where there has been a voluntary separation, to those of the father. The law of divorce is in many states far from satisfactory, but it always aims at doing equal justice as between husbands and wives. Special protection as respects hours of labour is given to women by the laws of many states, and a good deal of recent legislation has been passed with intent to benefit them, though not always by well-chosen means.

Women have made their way into most of the professions more largely than in Europe. In many of the Northern cities they practise as physicians, and seem to have found little or no prejudice to overcome. Medical schools have been provided for them in some universities.[1] It was less easy to obtain admission to the bar, yet several have secured this, and the number seems to increase. They mostly devote themselves to the attorney's part of the work rather than to court practice. One edited the *Illinois Law Journal* with great acceptance. Several have entered the Christian ministry, though, I think, only in what may be called the minor sects, not in any of the five or six great denominations, whose spirit is more conservative. Several have obtained success as professional lecturers, and not a few are journalists or reporters. One hears little of them in engineering. They are seldom to be seen in the offices of hotels, but many, more than in Europe, are employed as clerks or secretaries, both in some of the government departments, and by telegraphic and other companies, as well as in publishing houses and other kinds of business where physical strength is not needed. Typewriting work is largely in their hands. They form an overwhelming majority of the teachers in public schools for boys as well as for girls, and are thought to be better teachers, at least for the younger sort, than men are.[2] No class prejudice forbids the daughters of clergymen or lawyers of the best standing to teach in elementary schools. Taking one thing with another, it is easier for women to find a career, to obtain remunerative work of literary or of a commercial or mechanical kind, than in any part of Europe. Popular

[1] In 1909 there were 805 women returned as studying medicine in the medical schools, and 95 in the dentistry schools.

[2] The number of teachers in the common schools is given by the United States Bureau of Education Report for 1909 at 104,495 men and 390,988 women. As male teachers are in a majority in a very few Southern states (Tennessee, West Virginia, and Arkansas), and in New Mexico, the preponderance of women in the Northern states generally is very great. It has increased sensibly of late years over the whole country. In Massachusetts women teachers are ten and one-half times as numerous as men.

sentiment is entirely in favour of giving them every chance, as witness the constitutions of those Western states (including Washington, even while it refused them the suffrage) which expressly provide that they shall be equally admissible to all professions or employments. They have long borne a conspicuous part in the promotion of moral and philanthropic causes. They were among the earliest, most zealous, and most effective apostles of the anti-slavery movement, and have taken an equally active share in the temperance agitation. Not only has the Women's Christian Temperance Union with its numerous branches been the most powerful agency directed against the traffic in intoxicants, particularly in the Western states, but individual women have thrown themselves into the struggle with extraordinary zeal. Some time ago, during what was called the women's whiskey war, they forced their way into the drinking saloons, bearded the dealers, adjured the tipplers to come out. At elections in which the Prohibitionist issue is prominent, ladies will sometimes assemble outside the polls and sing hymns at the voters. Their services in dealing with pauperism, charities, and reformatory institutions have been inestimable. In New York when legislation was needed for improving the administration of the charities, it was a lady (belonging to one of the oldest and most respected families in the country) who went to Albany, and by placing the case forcibly before the state legislature there, succeeded in obtaining the required measure. Many others have followed her example with the best results. The charity organization societies of the great cities are largely managed by women; and the freedom they enjoy makes them invaluable agents in this work, which the inrush of new and ignorant immigrants renders daily more important. So too when it became necessary after the war to find teachers for the Negroes in the institutions founded for their benefit in the South, it was chiefly Northern girls who volunteered for the duty, and discharged it with single-minded zeal.

American women take far less part in politics than their English sisters, although more than the women of Germany, France, or Italy. That they talk less about politics may be partly ascribed to the fact that politics come less into ordinary conversation in America (except during a presidential election) than in England. But the practice of canvassing at elections, recently developed by English ladies with eminent success, seems unknown. Women have seldom been chosen members of either Republican or Democratic conventions. However, at the National Convention of the Prohibitionist party at Pittsburg in 1884 some presented credentials as delegates from local organizations, and were admitted to sit. One of the two secretaries of that convention was a woman. In 1912 women served as delegates to the Republican National Convention. So women have in some cities borne a useful and influential, albeit comparatively inconspicuous, part in movements for the reform of municipal government. Here we are on the debatable ground between pure party politics and philanthropic agitation. Women have been so effective in the latter that they cannot easily be excluded when persuasion passes into constitutional action, and one is not surprised to find the Prohibition party declare in their platform of 1884 that "they alone recognize the influence of woman, and offer to her equal rights with man in the management of national affairs." At some gatherings in the West which gave expression to the discontent of the farming class, women appeared, and were treated with a deference which anywhere but in America would have contrasted strangely with the roughness of the crowd. One of them signalized herself by denouncing a proposed banquet, on the ground that it was being got up in the interest of the brewers. Presidential candidates have often "receptions" given in their honour by ladies. Attempts have been, but with little success, to establish political "salons" at Washington, nor has the influence of social gatherings anywhere attained the importance it has often possessed in France, though occasionally the wife of a politician makes his fortune by her tact and skill in winning support for him among professional politicians or the members of a state legislature. There was another and less auspicious sphere of political action into which women found their way at the national capital. The solicitation of members of a legislature with a view to the passing of bills, especially private bills, and to the obtaining of places, has become a profession there, and the persuasive assiduity which had long been recognized by poets as characteristic of the female sex made them widely employed and efficient in this work.

I have already, in treating of the woman suffrage movement (Chapter 99), referred to the various public offices which have been in many states thrown open to women. It is admitted that wherever the suffrage has been granted the gift carries with it the right of obtaining those posts for which votes are cast.

The subject of women's education opens up a large field. Want of space obliges me to omit a description, for which I have accumulated abundant materials, and to confine myself to a few concise remarks.

The public provision for the instruction of girls is quite as ample and adequate as that made for boys. Elementary schools are of course provided alike for both sexes, grammar schools and high schools are organized for the reception of girls sometimes under the same roof or even in the same classes, sometimes in a distinct building, but always, I think, with an equally complete staff of teachers and equipment of educational appliances. The great majority of the daughters of mercantile and professional men, especially of course in the West,[3] receive their education in these public secondary schools; and what is more remarkable, the number of girls who continue their education in the higher branches, including the ancient classics and physical science, up to the age of seventeen or eighteen, is as large, in many places larger than, that of the boys, the latter being drafted off into practical life, while the former indulge their more lively interest in the things of the mind. In the Western universities the ancient classics are now more largely studied by women than by men, partly because the latter form a majority of the teachers. One sometimes hears it charged as a fault on the American system that its liberal provision of gratuitous instruction in the advanced subjects tends to raise girls of the humbler classes out of the sphere to which their pecuniary means would destine them, makes them discontented with their lot, implants tastes which fate will forever forbid them to gratify.

As stated in a previous chapter (Chapter 108), university education is provided for women in the Eastern states by colleges expressly erected for their benefit, and in the Western states by state universities, whose regulations usually provide for the admission of female equally with male students to instruction in all subjects. There are also some colleges of private foundation which receive young men and maidens together, teaching them in the same classes, but providing separate buildings for their lodging.

I must not attempt to set forth and discuss the evidence regarding the working of this system of coeducation, interesting as the facts are, but be content with stating the general result of the inquiries I made.

Coeducation answers perfectly in institutions like Antioch and Oberlin in Ohio, where manners are plain and simple, where the students all come from a class in which the intercourse of young men and young women is easy and natural, and where there is a strong religious influence prevading the life of the place. No moral difficulties are found to arise. Each sex is said to improve the other: the men become more refined, the women more manly. Now and then students fall in love with one another, and marry when they have graduated. But why not? Such marriages are based upon a better reciprocal knowledge of character than is usually attainable in the

---

[3] There are many private boarding schools as well as private day schools for girls in the Eastern states. Comparatively few children are educated at home by governesses.

great world, and are reported to be almost invariably happy. So also in the Western state universities coeducation is generally, if not quite invariably, well reported of. In these establishments the students mostly lodge where they will in the city, and are therefore brought into social relations only in the hours of public instruction; but the tendency of late years has been, while leaving men to find their own quarters, to provide places of residence for the women. Of late years a resort to them has become so fashionable that the authorities express some anxiety lest the interest in social enjoyments may with some women students be found to exceed their devotion to study. Should this happen to any great extent, difficulties might arise. But so far there has been little to do in the way of discipline or supervision, and the heads of the universities have raised few objections to the system of coeducation. I did find, however, that the youths in some cases expressed aversion to it, saying they would rather be in classes by themselves; the reason apparently being that it was disagreeable to see a man whom men thought meanly of standing high in the favour of women students. In these Western states there is so much freedom allowed in the intercourse of youths and girls, and girls are so well able to take care of themselves, that the objections which occur to a European have little weight. Whether a system which has borne good fruits in the simple society of the West is fit to be adopted in the Eastern states, where the conditions of life approach nearer to those of Europe, is a question warmly debated in America. The need for it is at any rate not urgent, because the liberality of founders and benefactors has provided in at least five women's colleges—one of them a department of Harvard University—places where an excellent education, surpassing that of most of the Western universities, stands open to women. These colleges are at present so efficient and popular, and the life of their students is in some respects so much freer than it could well be, considering the etiquette of Eastern society, in universities frequented by both sexes, that they will probably continue to satisfy the practical needs of the community and the wishes of all but the advocates of complete equality.

It will be seen from what has been said that the provision for women's education in the United States is ampler and better than that made in any European countries, and that the making of it has been far more distinctly recognized as a matter of public concern. To these advantages, and to the spirit they proceed from, much of the influence which women exert must be ascribed. They feel more independent, they have a fuller consciousness of their place in the world of thought as well as in the world of action. The practice of educating the two sexes together in the same colleges tends, in those sections of the country where it prevails, in the same direction, placing women and men on a level as regards attainments, and giving them a greater number of common intellectual interests. It is not deemed to have made women either pedantic or masculine, or to have diminished the differences between their mental and moral habits and those of men. Nature is quite strong enough to make the differences of temperament she creates persistent, even under influences which might seem likely to reduce them.

Custom allows to women a greater measure of freedom in doing what they will and going where they please than they have in any European country, except, perhaps, in Russia. No one is surprised to see a lady travel alone from the Atlantic to the Pacific, nor a girl of the richer class walking alone through the streets of a city. If a lady enters some occupation heretofore usually reserved to men, she is subject to much less censorious remark than would follow her in Europe, though in this matter the society of Eastern cities is hardly so liberal as that of the West.

Social intercourse between youths and maidens is everywhere more easy and unrestrained than in England or Germany, not to speak of France. Yet, there are considerable differences between the Eastern cities, whose usages have begun to approximate to those of Europe, and other parts of the country. In the rural districts, and generally all over the West, young men and girls are permitted to walk together, drive together, go out to parties, and even to public entertainments together, without the presence of any third person, who can be supposed to be looking after or taking charge of the girl. So a girl may, if she pleases, keep up a correspondence with a young man, nor will her parents think of interfering. She will have her own friends, who, when they call at her house, ask for her, and are received by her, it may be alone; because they are not deemed to be necessarily the friends of her parents also, nor even of her sisters. In the cities of the Atlantic states, it is beginning to be thought scarcely correct for a young man to take a young lady out for a solitary drive; and he would not in all sets be permitted to escort her alone to the theatre. But girls still go without chaperons to dances, the hostess being deemed to act as chaperon for all her guests; and as regards both correspondence and the right to have one's own circle of acquaintances, the usage even of New York or Boston allows more liberty than does that of London or Edinburgh. It was at one time, and it may possibly still be, not uncommon for a group of young people who know one another well to make up an autumn "party in the woods." They choose some mountain and forest region, such as the Adirondack wilderness west of Lake Champlain, engage three or four guides, embark with guns and fishing rods, tents, blankets, and a stock of groceries, and pass in boats up the rivers and across the lakes of this wild country through sixty or seventy miles of trackless forest to their chosen camping ground at the foot of some tall rock that rises from the still crystal of the lake. Here they build their bark hut, and spread their beds of the elastic and fragrant hemlock boughs; the youths roam about during the day, tracking the deer, the girls read and work and bake the corn cakes; at night there is a merry gathering round the fire or a row in the soft moonlight. On these expeditions, brothers will take their sisters and cousins, who bring perhaps some women friends with them; the brothers' friends will come too; and all will live together in a fraternal way for weeks or months, though no elderly relative or married lady be of the party.

There can be no doubt that the pleasure of life is sensibly increased by the greater freedom which transatlantic custom permits; and as the Americans insist that no bad results have followed,[4] one notes with regret that freedom declines in the places which deem themselves most civilized. American girls have been, so far as a stranger can ascertain, less disposed to what are called "fast ways" than girls of the corresponding classes in England,[5] and exercise in this respect a pretty rigorous censorship over one another. But when two young people find pleasure in one another's company, they can see as much of each other as they please, can talk and walk together frequently, can show that they are mutually interested, and yet need have little fear of being misunderstood either by one another or by the rest of the world.[6] It is all a matter of custom. In the West custom sanctions this easy friendship; in the Atlantic cities so soon as people have come to find something exceptional in it, constraint is felt, and a conventional etiquette like that of the Old World begins to replace the innocent simplicity of the older time, the test of whose merit may be gathered from the universal persuasion in America that the generally happy marriages in the society of

---

[4] I may be reminded of the prevalence and growing frequency of divorce, but think that this grave evil is due not to the comparative freedom of transatlantic matters. The cause is rather to be sought in the habit which men no less than women have formed of lightly, almost capriciously, entering into and dissolving the marriage tie. I have, however, discussed this subject in another book (*Studies in History and Jurisprudence*).

[5] The habit of smoking cigarettes which began to spread among English women of the richer class in the end of last century seems to be less frequent among American girls.

[6] Between fastness and freedom there is in American eyes all the difference in the world, but newcomers from Europe are startled. I remember to have once heard a German lady settled in a Western city characterize American women as "*furchtbar frei und furchtbar fromm*" (frightfully free and frightfully pious).

the rural districts, no less than the idyllic charm of the life of young people there, were due to the ampler opportunities which young men and women have of learning one another's characters and habits. Most girls have a larger range of intimate acquaintances than girls have in Europe, intercourse is franker, there is less difference between the manners of home and the manners of general society.

In no country are women, and especially young women, so much made of. The world is at their feet. Society seems organized for the purpose of providing enjoyment for them. Parents, uncles, aunts, elderly friends, even brothers, are ready to make their comfort and convenience bend to the girls' wishes. The wife's opportunities are circumscribed, except among the richest people, by the duties of household management, owing to the great difficulty of obtaining domestic "help." But she holds in her own house a more prominent, if not a more substantially powerful, position than in England or even in France. With the German *Hausfrau*, who is too often content to be a mere housewife, there is of course no comparison. The best proof of the superior place American ladies occupy is to be found in the notions they profess to entertain of the relations of an English married pair. They talk of the English wife as little better than a slave, declaring that when they stay with English friends, or receive an English couple in America, they see the wife always deferring to the husband and the husband always assuming that his pleasure and convenience are to prevail. The European wife, they admit, often gets her own way, but she gets it by tactful arts, by flattery or wheedling or playing on the man's weaknesses; whereas in America the husband's duty and desire is to gratify the wife and render to her those services which the English tyrant exacts from his consort.[7] One may often hear an American matron commiserate a friend who has married in Europe, while the daughters declare in chorus that they will never follow the example. Laughable as all this may seem to Englishwomen, it is perfectly true that the theory as well as the practice of conjugal life is not the same in America as in England. There are overbearing husbands in America, but they are more condemned by the opinion of the neighbourhood than in England. There are exacting wives in England, but their husbands are more pitied than would be the case in America. In neither country can one say that the principle of perfect equality reigns, for in America the balance inclines as much in favour of the wife as it does in England in favour of the husband.

[7] I have heard American ladies say, for instance, that they have observed that an Englishman who has forgotten his keys sends his wife to the top of the house to fetch them; whereas an American would do the like errand for his wife, and never suffer her to do it for him.

No one man can have a sufficiently large acquaintance in both countries to entitle his individual opinion on the results to much weight. Those observers who, having lived in both countries, favour the American practice, do so because the theory it is based on departs less from pure equality than does that of England. Such observers do not mean that the recognition of women as equals or superiors makes them any better or sweeter or wiser than Englishwomen; but rather that the principle of equality, by correcting the characteristic faults of men, and especially their selfishness and vanity, is more conducive to the concord and happiness of a home. This may be true, but I have heard others declare that there is, at least among the richer class, a growing detachment of the wife from the husband's life and interests, so that she is more disposed to absent herself for long periods from him; and some observers maintain that the American system, since it does not require the wife habitually to forego her own wishes, tends, if not to make her self-indulgent and capricious, yet slightly to impair the more delicate charms of character; as it is written, "It is more blessed to give than to receive."

It need hardly be said that in all cases where the two sexes come into competition for comfort, the provision is made first for women. Before drawing room cars had become common, the end car in railroad trains, being that farthest removed from the smoke of the locomotive, was often reserved for them (though men accompanying a lady could enter it), and at hotels their sitting room is the best and sometimes the only available public room, ladyless guests being driven to the bar or the hall. It is sometimes said that the privileges yielded to American women have disposed them to claim as a right what was only a courtesy, and have told unfavourably upon their manners. Instances, such as that of women entering public vehicles already overcrowded, are cited in support of this view, but I cannot on the whole think it well founded. The better bred women do not presume on their sex; and the area of good breeding is always widening. It need hardly be said that the community at large gains by the softening and restraining influence which the reverence for womanhood diffuses. Nothing so quickly incenses the people as any insult offered to a woman. Wife beating, and indeed any kind of rough violence offered to a woman, is far less common among the rudest class than it is in England. Field work or work at the pit-mouth of mines is seldom or never done by women in America; and the American traveller who in some parts of Europe finds women performing severe manual labour is revolted by the sight in a way which Europeans find surprising.

In the farther West, that is to say, beyond the Mississippi, in the Rocky

Mountain and Pacific states, one is much struck by what seems the absence of the humblest class of women. The trains are full of poorly dressed and sometimes (though less frequently) rough-mannered men. One discovers no women whose dress or air marks them out as the wives, daughters, or sisters of these men, and wonders whether the male population is celibate, and if so, why there are so many women. Closer observation shows that the wives, daughters, and sisters are there, only their attire and manner are those of what Europeans would call middle class and not working class people. This is partly due to the fact that Western men affect a rough dress. Still one may say that the remark so often made that the masses of the American people correspond to the middle class of Europe is more true of the women than of the men, and is more true of them in the rural districts and in the West than it is of the inhabitants of Atlantic cities. I remember to have been dawdling in a book store in a small town in Oregon when a lady entered to inquire if a monthly magazine, whose name was unknown to me, had yet arrived. When she was gone I asked the salesman who she was, and what was the periodical she wanted. He answered that she was the wife of a railway workman, that the magazine was a journal of fashions, and that the demand for such journals was large and constant among women of the wage-earning class in the town. This set me to observing female dress more closely, and it turned out to be perfectly true that the women in these little towns were following the Parisian fashions very closely, and were, in fact, ahead of the majority of English ladies belonging to the professional and mercantile classes.[8] Of course in such a town as I refer to there are no domestic servants except in the hotels (indeed, almost the only domestic service to be had in the Pacific states was that of Chinese), so these votaries of fashion did all their own housework and looked after their own babies.

Three causes combine to create among American women an average of literary taste and influence higher than that of women in any European country. These are, the educational facilities they enjoy, the recognition of the equality of the sexes in the whole social and intellectual sphere, and the leisure which they possess as compared with men. In a country where men are incessantly occupied at their business or profession, the function of keeping up the level of culture devolves upon women. It is safe in their hands. They are quick and keen-witted, less fond of open-air life and physical exertion than Englishwomen are, and obliged by the climate to

---

[8] The above, of course, does not apply to the latest immigrants from Europe, who are still European in their dress and ways, though in a town they become quickly Americanized.

pass a greater part of their time under shelter from the cold of winter and the sun of summer. For music and for the pictorial arts they do not yet seem to have formed so strong a taste as for literature, partly perhaps owing to the fact that in America the opportunities of seeing and hearing masterpieces, except indeed operas, are rarer than in Europe. But they are eager and assiduous readers of all such books and periodicals as do not presuppose special knowledge in some branch of science or learning, while the number who have devoted themselves to some special study and attained proficiency in it is large. They love society, and now there is hardly a village that has not its women's club where papers are read and all sorts of current questions discussed, often with the incidental result of enabling those of slender means but cultivated tastes to come into social contact with those of higher position. The fondness for sentiment, especially moral and domestic sentiment, which is often observed as characterizing American taste in literature, seems to be mainly due to the influence of women, for they form not only the larger part of the reading public, but an independent-minded part, not disposed to adopt the canons laid down by men, and their preferences count for more in the opinions and predilections of the whole nation than is the case in England. Similarly the number of women who write is infinitely larger in America than in Europe. Fiction, essays, and poetry are naturally their favourite provinces. In poetry more particularly, many whose names are quite unknown in Europe have attained widespread fame.

Someone may ask how far the differences between the position of women in America and their position in Europe are due to democracy, or if not to this, then to what other cause?

They are due to democratic feeling in so far as they spring from the notion that all men are free and equal, possessed of certain inalienable rights, and owing certain corresponding duties. This root idea of democracy cannot stop at defining men as male human beings, any more than it could ultimately stop at defining them as white human beings. For many years the Americans believed in equality with the pride of discoverers as well as with the fervour of apostles. Accustomed to apply it to all sorts and conditions of men, they were naturally the first to apply it to women also; not, indeed, as respects politics, but in all the social as well as legal relations of life. Democracy is in America more respectful of the individual, less disposed to infringe his freedom or subject him to any sort of legal or family control, than it has shown itself in continental Europe, and this regard for the individual enured to the benefit of women. Of the other causes that have worked in the same direction two may be mentioned. One is the usage of the Congregationalist, Presbyterian, and Baptist churches, under which a woman who is a member of the congregation has the same rights in choosing a deacon, elder, or pastor, as a man has. Another is the fact that among the westward-moving settlers women were at first few in number, and were therefore treated with special respect. The habit then formed was retained as the communities grew, and propagated itself all over the country.

What have been the results on the character and usefulness of women themselves?

On the whole favourable. Though critics dwell on some drawbacks, it is a gain that American women have been admitted to a wider life and more variety of career than is enjoyed in continental Europe. Thus there has been produced a sort of independence and a capacity of self-help which are increasingly valuable as the number of unmarried women increases. Many resources are now open to an American woman who has to lead a solitary life, not merely in the way of employment, but for the occupation of her mind and tastes; while her education has not rendered the American wife less competent for the discharge of household duties.

How has the nation at large been affected by the development of this new type of womanhood, or rather perhaps of this variation on the English type?

If women have on the whole gained, it is clear that the nation gains through them. As mothers they mould the character of their children, while the function of forming the habits of society and determining its moral tone rests greatly in their hands. But there is reason to think that the influence of the American system tells directly for good upon men as well as upon the whole community. The respect for women which every American man either feels or is obliged by public sentiment to profess has a wholesome effect on his conduct and character, and serves to check the cynicism which some other peculiarities of the country foster. The nation as a whole owes to the active benevolence of its women, and their zeal in promoting social reforms, benefits which the customs of continental Europe would scarcely have permitted women to confer. Europeans have of late years begun to render a well-deserved admiration to the brightness and vivacity of American ladies. Those who know the work they have done and are doing in many a noble cause will admire still more their energy, their courage, their self-devotion. No country seems to owe more to its women than America does, nor to owe to them so much of what is best in social institutions and in the beliefs that govern conduct.

C H A P T E R   1 1 3

Equality

The United States are deemed all the world over to be preeminently the land of equality. This was the first feature which struck Europeans when they began, after the peace of 1815 had left them time to look beyond the Atlantic, to feel curious about the phenomena of a new society. This was the great theme of Tocqueville's description, and the starting point of his speculations; this has been the most constant boast of the Americans themselves, who have believed their liberty more complete than that of any other people, because equality has been more fully blended with it. Yet some philosophers say that equality is impossible, and others, who express themselves more precisely, insist that distinctions of rank are so inevitable, that however you try to expunge them, they are sure to reappear. Before we discuss this question, let us see in what senses the word is used.

First there is legal equality, including both what one may call passive or private equality, i.e., the equal possession of civil private rights by all inhabitants, and active or public equality, the equal possession by all of rights to a share in the government, such as the electoral franchise and eligibility to public office. Both kinds of political equality exist in America, in the amplest measure, and may be dismissed from the present discussion.

Next there is the equality of material conditions, that is, of wealth, and all that wealth gives; there is the equality of education and intelligence; there is the equality of social status or rank; and there is (what comes near to, but is not exactly the same as, this last) the equality of estimation, i.e., of the value which men set upon one another, whatever be the elements that come into this value, whether wealth, or education, or official rank, or social rank, or any other species of excellence. In how many and which of these senses of the word does equality exist in the United States?

Not as regards material conditions. Till about the middle of last century there were no great fortunes in America, few large fortunes, no poverty. Now there is some poverty (though only in a few places can it be called pauperism), many large fortunes, and a greater number of gigantic fortunes than in any other country in the world. The class of persons who are passably well off but not rich is much larger than in the great countries of Europe. Between the houses, the dress, and the way of life of these persons, and those of the richer sort, there is less difference than in Europe. The very rich do not (except in a few places) make an ostentatious display of their wealth, because they have no means of doing so, and a visitor is therefore apt to overrate the extent to which equality of wealth, and of material conditions generally, still prevails. The most remarkable phenomenon of the last half century has been the appearance, not only of those few colossal millionaires who fill the public eye, but of a crowd of millionaires of the second order, men with fortunes ranging from $5,000,000 to $20,000,000. At a seaside resort like Newport, where one sees the finished luxury of the villas, and counts the well-appointed equipages, with their superb horses, which turn out in the afternoon, one gets some impression of the vast and growing wealth of the Eastern cities. But through the country generally there is little to mark out the man with an income of $100,000 a year from the man of $20,000, as he is marked out in England by his country house with its park, or in France by the opportunities for display which Paris affords. The number of these fortunes seems likely to go on increasing, for they are due not merely to the sudden development of the West, with the chances of making vast sums by land speculation, or in railway construction, but to the field for doing business on a great scale, which the size of the country presents. Where a merchant or manufacturer in France or England could realize thousands, an American, operating more boldly, and on this far wider theatre, may realize tens of thousands. We may therefore expect these inequalities of wealth to grow; nor will even the habit of equal division among children keep them down, for families are often small, and though some of those who inherit wealth may renounce business, others will pursue it, since the attractions of other kinds of life are fewer than in Europe. Politics are less exciting, there is no great landholding class with the duties towards tenants and neighbours which an English squire may, if he pleases, usefully discharge; the pursuit of collecting pictures or other objects of curiosity implies frequent visits to Europe, and although the killing of birds prevails in the Middle states and the killing of deer in the West, this rather barbarous form of pleasure is likely in time to die out from a civilized people. Other kinds of what is called "sport" no doubt remain, such as horse racing, eagerly pursued in the form of trotting matches,[1] "rushing round" in an automobile, and the manlier amusements of yacht racing, rowing, and baseball, but these can be followed only during part of the year, and some of them only by the young. To lead a life of so-called pleasure gives much more trouble in an American city than in Paris or Vienna or London. Accordingly, while great fortunes will continue to be made, they will be less easily and quickly spent than in Europe, and one may surmise that the equality of material conditions, almost universal in the eighteenth century, still general in the middle of the nineteenth will more and more diminish by the growth of a very rich class at one end of the line, and of a very poor class at the other end.[2]

As respects education, the profusion of superior as well as elementary schools tends to raise the mass to a somewhat higher point than in Europe, while the stimulus of life being keener and the habit of reading more general, the number of persons one finds on the same general level of brightness, keenness, and a superficially competent knowledge of common facts, whether in science, history, geography, or literature, is extremely large. This general level tends to rise. But the level of exceptional attainment in that small but increasing class who have studied at the best native universities or in Europe, and who pursue learning and science either as a profession or as a source of pleasure, rises faster than does the general level of the multitude, so that in this regard also it appears that equality has diminished and will diminish further.

So far we have been on comparatively smooth and easy ground. Equality of wealth is a concrete thing; equality of intellectual possession and resource is a thing which can be perceived and gauged. Of social equality, of distinctions of standing and estimation in private life, it is far more difficult to speak, and in what follows I speak with some hesitation.

One thing, and perhaps one thing only, may be asserted with confidence. There is no rank in America, that is to say, no external and recognized stamp marking one man as entitled to any social privileges, or to deference and respect from others. No man is entitled to think himself better than his fellows, or to expect any exceptional consideration to be shown by them to him. Except in the national capital, there is no such thing as a recognized order of precedence, either on public occasions or at a private party, save

---

[1] The trotting horse is driven, not ridden, a return to the earliest forms of horse racing we know of.

[2] How far exteme inequality of material conditions, coexisting with political equality, is likely to prove a source of political danger is a question discussed in other chapters. Hitherto it has not proved serious. Cf. Aristotle, *Polit.* V., 1, 2.

that yielded to a few official persons, such as the governor and chief judges of a state within that state, as well as to the president and vice-president, the Speaker of the House, the federal senators, the judges of the Supreme Federal Court, and the members of the president's cabinet everywhere, through the Union. In fact, the idea of a regular "rule of precedence" displeases the Americans,[3] and one finds them slow to believe that the application of such rules in Europe gives no offence to persons who possess no conventional rank, but may be personally older or more distinguished than those who have it.

What, then, is the effect or influence for social purposes of such distinctions as do exist between men, distinctions of birth, of wealth, of official position, of intellectual eminence?

To be sprung from an ancient stock, or from a stock which can count persons of eminence among its ancestors, is of course a satisfaction to the man himself. There is at present almost a passion among Americans for genealogical researches. A good many families can trace themselves back to English families of the sixteenth or seventeenth century, and of course a great many more profess to do so. For a man's ancestors to have come over in the *Mayflower* is in America much what their having come over with William the Conqueror used to be in England and is often claimed on equally flimsy grounds. The descendants of any of the revolutionary heroes, such as John Adams, Edmund Randolph, Alexander Hamilton, and the descendants of any famous man of colonial times, such as the early governors of Massachusetts from William Endicott downwards, or of Jonathan Edwards, or of Eliot, the apostle of the Indians, are regarded by their neighbours with a certain amount of interest, and their legitimate pride in such an ancestry excites no disapproval.[4] In the Eastern cities, and at fashionable summer resorts one begins to see carriages with armorial bearings on their panels, but most people appear to disapprove or ridicule this as a piece of Anglomania, more likely to be practised by a parvenu than by the scion of a really old family. Virginians used to set much store by their pedigrees, and the letters F.F.V. (First Families of Virginia) had become a sort of jest

---

[3] In private parties, so far as there is any rule of precedence, it is that of age, with a tendency to make an exception in favour of clergymen or of any person of special eminence. It is only in Washington, where senators, judges, ministers, and congressmen are sensitive on these points, that such questions seem to arise, or to be regarded as deserving the attention of a rational mind.

[4] In all the cases mentioned in the text, I remember to have been told by others, but never by the persons concerned, of the ancestry. This is an illustration of the fact that while such ancestry is felt to be a distinction it would be thought bad taste for those who possess it to mention it unless a necessity arose for them to do so.

against persons pluming themselves on their social position in the Old Dominion.[5] Since the war, however, which shattered old Virginian society from its foundations, one hears little of such pretensions.[6]

The fault which Americans are most frequently accused of is the worship of wealth. The amazing fuss which is made about very rich men, the descriptions of their doings, the speculation as to their intentions, the gossip about their private life, lend colour to the reproach. He who builds up a huge fortune, especially if he does it suddenly, is no doubt a sort of hero, because an enormous number of men have the same ambition. Having done best what millions are trying to do, he is discussed, admired, and envied in the same way as the captain of a cricket eleven is at an English school, or the stroke of the university boat at Oxford or Cambridge. If he be a great financier, or the owner of a great railroad or a great newspaper, he exercises vast power, and is therefore well worth courting by those who desire his help or would avert his enmity. Admitting all this, it may seem a paradox to observe that a millionaire has a better and easier social career open to him in England than in America. Nevertheless there is a sense in which this is true. In America, if his private character be bad, if he be mean, or openly immoral, or personally vulgar, or dishonest, the best society will keep its doors closed against him. In England great wealth, skilfully employed, will more readily force these doors to open. For in England great wealth can, by using the appropriate methods, practically buy rank from those who bestow it; or by obliging persons whose position enables them to command fashionable society, can induce them to stand sponsors for the upstart, and force him into society, a thing which no person in America has the power of doing. To effect such a stroke in England the rich man must of course have stopped short of positive frauds, that is, of such frauds as could be proved in court. But he may be still distrusted and disliked by the elite of the commercial world, he may be vulgar and ill-educated, and indeed have nothing to recommend him except his wealth and his willingness to spend it in providing amusement for fashionable people. All this will not prevent him from becoming a baronet, or possibly a peer, and thereby acquiring a position of assured dignity which he can transmit to his offspring. The

---

[5] An anecdote is told of the captain of a steamer plying at a ferry from Maryland into Virginia, who being asked by a needy Virginian to give him a free passage across, inquired if the applicant belonged to one of the F.F.V. "No," answered the man, "I can't exactly say that; rather to one of the second families." "Jump on board," said the captain; "I never met one of your sort before."

[6] Clubs have been formed in Eastern cities including only persons who could prove that their progenitors were settled in the state before the Revolution, and one widely spread women's association (the Colonial Dames) has a like basis.

existence of a system of artificial rank enables a stamp to be given to base metal in Europe which cannot be given in a thoroughly republican country.[7] The feeling of the American public towards the very rich is, so far as a stranger can judge, one of curiosity and wonder rather than of respect. There is less snobbishness shown towards them than in England. They are admired as a famous runner or a jockey is admired, and the talents they have shown, say, in railroad management or in finance, are felt to reflect lustre on the nation. But they do not necessarily receive either flattery or social deference, and sometimes, where it can be alleged that they have won their wealth as the leading spirits in monopolistic combinations, they are made targets for attack, though they may have done nothing more than what other businessmen have attempted, with less ability and less success.

The persons to whom official rank gives importance are very few indeed, being for the nation at large only about one hundred persons at the top of the federal government, and in each state less than a dozen of its highest state functionaries. For these state functionaries, indeed, the respect shown is extremely scanty, and much more official than personal. A high federal officer, a senator, or justice of the Supreme Court, or cabinet minister, is conspicuous while he holds his place, and is of course a personage in any private society he may enter; but less so than a corresponding official would be in Europe. A simple member of the House of Representatives is nobody. Even men of the highest official rank do not give themselves airs on the score of their position. Long ago, in Washington, I was taken to be presented to the then head of the United States Army, a great soldier whose fame all the world knows. We found him standing at a desk in a bare room in the War Department, at work with one clerk. While he was talking to us the door of the room was pushed open, and there appeared the figure of a Western sightseer belonging to what Europeans would call the lower middle class, followed by his wife and sister, who were "doing" Washington. Perceiving that the room was occupied they began to retreat, but the commander in chief called them back. "Walk in, ladies," he said. "You can look around. You won't disturb me; make yourselves at home."

Intellectual attainment does not excite much notice till it becomes eminent, that is to say, till it either places its possessor in a conspicuous position, such as that of president of one of the greatest universities, or till it has

---

[7] The English system of hereditary titles tends to maintain the distinction of ancient lineage far less perfectly than that simple use of a family name which prevailed in Italy during the Middle Ages, or in ancient Rome. A Colonna or a Doria, like a Cornelius or a Valerius, carried the glory of his nobility in his name, whereas any upstart may be created a duke.

made him well known to the world as a preacher, or writer, or scientific discoverer. When this kind of eminence has been reached, it receives, I think, more respect than anywhere in Europe, except possibly in Italy, where the interest in learned men, or poets, or artists, seems to be greater than anywhere else in Europe.[8] A famous writer or divine is known by name to a far greater number of persons in America than would know a similar person in any European country. He is one of the glories of the country. There is no artificial rank to cast him into the shade. He is possibly less famous than the railroad kings or manipulators of the stock markets; but he excites a different kind of sentiment; and people are willing to honour him in a way, sometimes distasteful to himself, which would not be applied to the millionaire except by those who sought to gain something from him.

Perhaps the best way of explaining how some of the differences above mentioned, in wealth or official position or intellectual eminence, affect social equality is by reverting to what was called, a few pages back, equality of estimation—the idea which men form of other men as compared with themselves. It is in this that the real sense of equality comes out. In America men hold others to be at bottom exactly the same as themselves.[9] If a man is enormously rich, or if he is a great orator, like Daniel Webster or Henry Ward Beecher, or a great soldier like Ulysses S. Grant, or a great writer like R. W. Emerson, or president, so much the better for him. He is an object of interest, perhaps of admiration, possibly even of reverence. But he is deemed to be still of the same flesh and blood as other men. The admiration felt for him may be a reason for going to see him and longing to shake hands with him, a longing frequent in America. But it is not a reason for bowing down to him, or addressing him in deferential terms, or treating him as if he was porcelain and yourself only earthenware.[10] In this

---

[8] In Germany great respect is no doubt felt for the leaders of learning and science; but they are regarded as belonging to a world of their own, separated by a wide gulf from the territorial aristocracy, which still deems itself (as in the days of Candide's brother-in-law) a different form of mankind from those who have not sixteen quarterings to show.

[9] Someone has said that there are in America two classes only, those who have succeeded and those who have failed.

[10] This is seen even in the manner of American servants. Although there is an aversion among native Americans to enter domestic service, the temporary discharge of such duties does not necessarily involve any loss of caste. Many years ago I remember to have found all the waiting in a large hotel in the White Mountains done by the daughters of respectable New England farmers in the low country who had come up for their summer change of air to this place of resort, and were earning their board and lodging by acting as waitresses. They were treated by the guests as equals, and were indeed cultivated and well-mannered young women. So college students sometimes do waiting, and do not feel humbled thereby.

respect there is, I think, a difference, slight but perceptible, between the sentiment of equality as it exists in the United States, and as one finds it in France and Switzerland, the countries of the Old World where (if we except Norway, which has never had an aristocracy) social equality has made the greatest progress. In France and Switzerland there lingers a kind of feeling as if the old *noblesse* were not quite like other men. The Swiss peasant, with all his manly independence, has in many cantons a touch of instinctive reverence for the old families; or perhaps, in some other cantons, a touch of jealousy which makes him desire to exclude their members from office, because he feels that they still think themselves better than he is. Nothing like this is possible in America, where the very notion of such distinctions excites a wondering curiosity as to what sort of creature the titled noble of Europe can be.

The total absence of rank and the universal acceptance of equality do not however prevent the existence of grades and distinctions in society which, though they may find no tangible expression, are sometimes as sharply drawn as in Europe. Except in the newer parts of the West, those who deem themselves ladies and gentlemen draw just the same line between themselves and the multitude as is drawn in England, and draw it in much the same way. The nature of a man's occupation, his education, his manners and breeding, his income, his connections, all come into view in determining whether he is in this narrow sense of the word "a gentleman," almost as they would in England,[11] though in most parts of the United States personal qualities count for rather more than in England, and occupation for hardly anything. The word is equally indefinable in both countries, but in America the expression "not quite a lady" seems to be less frequently employed. One is told, however, that the son of cultivated parents would not like to enter a retail store; and even in a Western city like Detroit the best people will say of a party that it was "very mixed." In some of the older cities society was, till the sudden growth of huge fortunes towards the end of last century, as exclusive as in the more old-fashioned English counties, the "best set" considering itself very select indeed. In such a city I remember to have heard a family belonging to the best set, which is mostly to be found in a particular quarter of the city, speak of the inhabitants of a handsome suburb

---

[11] On the New York elevated railroad smoking is not permitted in any car. When I asked a conductor how he was able to enforce this rule, considering that on every other railway smoking was practised, he answered, "I always say when any one seems disposed to insist, 'Sir, I am sure that if you are a gentleman you will not wish to bring me into a difficulty,' and then they always leave off."

two miles away just as Belgravians might speak of Islington; and the son of the family who, having made in Europe the acquaintance of some of the dwellers in this suburb, had gone to a ball there, was questioned by his sisters about their manners and customs much as if he had returned from visiting a tribe in Central Africa. On inquiry I discovered that these North Side people were as rich and doubtless thought themselves as cultivated as the people of my friends' quarter. But all the city knew that the latter were the "best set." People used to say that this exclusiveness spreads steadily from East to West, and that before long there would be such sets in all the greater cities. So indeed there are sets, but great wealth now so generally secures entrance to them that they can scarcely be called exclusive.

Europeans have been known to ask whether the United States do not suffer from the absence of a hereditary nobility. As may be supposed, such a question excites mirth in America; it is as if you were to offer them a court and an established church. They remark, with truth, that since Pitt in England and the Napoleons in France prostituted hereditary titles, these have ceased to be either respectable or useful. "They do not," say the Americans, "suggest antiquity, for the English families that enjoy them are mostly new; they are not associated, like the ancient titles, with the history of your nation; they are merely a prize offered to wealth, the expression of a desire for gilding that plutocracy which has replaced the ancient aristocracy of your country. Seeing how little service hereditary nobility renders in maintaining the standard either of manners, or morals, or honour, or public duty, few sensible men would create it in any European country where it did not exist; much less then should we to dream of creating it in America, which possesses none of the materials or conditions which could make it tolerable. If a peerage is purchaseable even in England, where the dignity of the older nobility might have suggested some care in bestowal, purchaseable not so openly as in Portugal or a German principality, but practically purchaseable by party services and by large subscriptions to public purposes, much more would it be purchaseable here, where there are no traditions to break down, where wealth accumulates rapidly, and the wealthy seek every avenue for display. Titles in this country would be simply an additional prize offered to wealth and ambition. They could not be respected. They would make us as snobbish as you are." A European observer will not quarrel with this judgment. There is a growing disposition in America, as everywhere else, to relish and make the most of such professional or official titles as can be had; it is a harmless way of trying to relieve the monotony of the world. If there be, as no doubt there is, less disposition than in England to run after and pay court to the great or the fashionable, this is perhaps due not to any superior virtue, but to the absence of those opportunities and temptations which their hereditary titles and other social institutions set before the English. It would be the very wantonness of folly to create in the new country what most thinking people would gladly be rid of in the old one.

Another question is more serious and less easily answered. What is the effect of social equality upon manners? Many causes go to the making of manners, as one may see by noting how much better they are in some parts of Europe than in other parts where nevertheless the structure of society is equally aristocratic, or democratic, as the case may be. One must therefore be careful not to ascribe to this source only such peculiarities as America shows.[12] On the whole, bearing in mind that the English race has less than some other races of that quickness of perception and sympathy which goes far to make manners good, the Americans have gained more than they have lost by equality. The upper class does not lose in grace, and the humbler class gains in independence. The manners of the "best people" are exactly those of England, with a thought more of consideration towards inferiors and of frankness towards equals. Among the masses there is, generally speaking, as much real courtesy and good nature as anywhere else in the world.[13] There is less outward politeness than in some parts of Europe, Portugal for instance, or Tuscany, or Sweden. There is a certain coolness or off-handedness which at first annoys the European visitor, who still thinks himself "a superior"; but when he perceives that it is not meant for insolence, and that native Americans do not notice it, he learns to acquiesce. Perhaps the worst manners are those of persons dressed in some rag of authority. The railroad car-conductor has a bad name; but personally I have always been well treated by him, and remember with pleasure one on a Southern railroad (an ex-Confederate soldier) who did the honours of his car with a dignified courtesy worthy of those Hungarian nobles who are said to have the best manners in Europe. The hotel clerk used to be supercilious, but when one frankly admitted his superiority, his patronage became friendly,

---

[12] It was an old reproach in Europe against republics that their citizens were rude: witness the phrases, "manières d'un Suisse," "civilisé en Hollande" (Roscher, *Politik*, p. 314).

[13] There are parts of the West which still lack polish; and the behaviour of the whites to the Chinese often incenses a stranger from the Atlantic states or Europe. I remember in Oregon to have seen a huge navvy turn an inoffensive Chinaman out of his seat in a railway car, and when I went to the conductor and tried to induce him to interfere, he calmly remarked, "Yes, I know those things do make the English mad." On the other hand, on the Pacific slope coloured people often sit down to table with whites.

and he would even condescend to interest himself in making your stay in the city agreeable. One finds most courtesy among the rural population of New England and the Middle states, least among the recent immigrants in the cities and the unsettled population of the West. However, the most material point to remark is the improvement of recent years. The concurrent testimony of European travellers, including both admirers and detractors of democracy, proves that manners must have been disagreeable in the days when Dickens and Lyell travelled through the country, and one finds nowadays an equally general admission that the Americans are as pleasant to one another and to strangers as are the French or the Germans or the English. The least agreeable feature to the visitors of former years, an incessant vaunting of their own country and disparagement of others, has disappeared, and the tinge of self-assertion which the sense of equality used to give is now but faintly noticeable.

CHAPTER 1 1 4

The Influence of Democracy
on Thought

Two opposite theories regarding the influence of democratic institutions on intellectual activity have found currency. One theory extols them because they stimulate the mind of a people, not only sharpening men's wits by continual struggle and unrest, but giving to each citizen a sense of his own powers and duties in the world, which spurs him on to exertions in ever-widening fields. This theory is commonly applied to Athens and other democracies of the ancient world, as contrasted with Sparta and the oligarchic cities, whose intellectual production was scanty or altogether wanting. It compares the Rome of Cicero, Lucretius, and Catullus, and the Augustan age, whose great figures were born under the Republic, with the vaster but comparatively sterile Roman world of Marcus Aurelius or Constantine, when freedom had long since vanished. It notes the outburst of literary and artistic splendour that fell in the later age of the republics of mediæval Italy, and dwells with especial pleasure on the achievements of Florence, the longest-lived and the most glorious of the free commonwealths of Italy.

According to the other theory, democracy is the child of ignorance, the parent of dulness and conceit. The opinion of the greatest number being the universal standard, everything is reduced to the level of vulgar minds. Originality is stunted, variety disappears, no man thinks for himself, or, if he does, fears to express what he thinks. A drear pall of monotony covers the sky.

> Thy hand, great Anarch, lets the curtain fall
> And universal darkness buries all.

This doctrine seems to date from the appearance of Tocqueville's book, though his professed disciples have pushed it much further than his words warrant. It is really an a priori doctrine, drawn from imagining what the consequences of a complete equality of material conditions and political powers ought to be. But it claims to rest upon the observed phenomena of the United States, which, in the middle of last century, were still the only great modern democracy; and it was with reference to the United States that it was enunciated by Mr. Robert Lowe in one of those speeches of 1866 which so greatly impressed his contemporaries.

Both these theories will be found on examination to be baseless. Both, so far as they are a priori theories, are fanciful; both, in so far as they purport to rest upon the facts of history, err by regarding one set of facts only, and ignoring a great number of concomitant conditions which have probably more to do with the result than the few conditions which have been arbitrarily taken to be sufficient causes. None of the Greek republics was a democracy in the modern sense, for all rested upon slavery; nor, indeed, can the name be applied, except at passing moments, to the Italian cities. Many circumstances besides their popular government combined to place the imperishable crown of literary and artistic glory upon the brows of the city of the Violet and the city of the Lily. So also the view that a democratic land is necessarily a land of barren monotony, while unsound even as a deduction from general principles, is still more unsound in its assumption of certain phenomena as true of America, and in the face it puts on the phenomena it has assumed. The theorists who have propounded it give us, like Daniel, the dream as well as their interpretation of it. But the dream is one of their own inventing; and such as it is, it is wrongly interpreted.

It is a common mistake to exaggerate the influence of forms of government. As there are historians and politicians who, when they come across a trait of national character for which no obvious explanation presents itself, set it down to "race," so there are writers and speakers who, too indolent to examine the whole facts of the case, or too ill-trained to feel the need of such examination, pounce upon the political institutions of a country as the easiest way to account for its social and intellectual, perhaps even for its moral and religious peculiarities. Few problems are in reality more complex than the relation between the political and the intellectual life of a country; few things more difficult to distinguish than the influences respectively attributable to an equality of political rights and powers on the one hand, and an equality of material and social conditions on the other. It is commonly assumed that democracy and equality go hand in hand, but as one may have popular government along with enormous differences of wealth and dissimilarities in social usage, so also one may have social equality under a despot. Doubtless, when social and political equality go hand in hand they intensify one another; but when inequality of material conditions becomes marked, social life changes, and as social phenomena become more complex their analysis becomes more difficult.

Reverting to the two theories from which we set out, it may be said that the United States furnish little support to either. American democracy has certainly produced no age of Pericles. Neither has it dwarfed literature and led a wretched people, so dull as not even to realize their dulness, into a barren plain of featureless mediocrity. To ascribe the deficiencies, such as they are, of art and culture in America, solely or even mainly to her form of government, is not less absurd than to ascribe, as many Americans of what I may call the trumpeting school do, her marvelous material progress to the same cause. It is not democracy that has paid off a gigantic debt and raised Chicago out of a swamp. Neither is it democracy that has denied her philosophers like Burke and poets like Wordsworth.

Most writers who have dealt with these matters have not only laid more upon the shoulders of democratic government than it ought to bear, but have preferred abstract speculations to the humbler task of ascertaining and weighing the facts. They have spun ingenious theories about democracy as the source of this or that, or whatever it pleased them to assume; they have not tried to determine by a wide induction what specific results appear in countries which, differing in other respects, agree in being democratically governed. Such speculations may have their use in suggesting to us what phenomena we ought to look for in democratic countries; but if any positive results are to be reached, they must be reached by carefully verifying the intellectual phenomena of more than one country, and establishing an unmistakable relation between them and the political institutions under which they prevail.

If someone, starting from the current conception of democracy, were to say that in a democratic nation we should find a disposition to bold and unbridled speculations, sparing neither theology nor morals, a total absence of rule, tradition, and precedent, each man thinking and writing as responsible to no criticism, "every poet his own Aristotle," a taste for strong effects and garish colours, valuing force rather than fineness, grandeur rather than beauty, a vigorous, hasty, impetuous style of speaking and writing, a grandiose, and perhaps sensational art: he would say what would be quite as natural and reasonable a priori as most of the pictures given us of democratic societies. Yet many of the suggested features would be the opposite of those which America presents.

Every such picture must be fanciful. He who starts from so simple and (so to speak) bare a conception as that of equal civil rights and equal political powers vested in every member of the community cannot but have recourse to his fancy in trying to body forth the results of this principle. Let anyone study the portrait of the democratic man and democratic city which the first and greatest of all the hostile critics of democracy has left us,[1] and compare it with the very different descriptions of life and culture under a popular government in which European speculation has disported itself since Tocqueville's time. He will find each theory plausible in the abstract, and each equally unlike the facts which contemporary America sets before us.

Let us, bidding farewell to fancy, try to discover what are now the salient intellectual features of the mass of the native population in the United States.

As there is much difference of opinion regarding them, I present with diffidence the following list:

1. A desire to be abreast of the best thought and work of the world everywhere, to have every form of literature and art adequately represented, and excellent of its kind, so that America shall be felt to hold her own among the nations.
2. A fondness for bold and striking effects, a preference for large generalizations and theories which have an air of completeness.
3. An absence among the multitude of refined taste, and disposition to be attracted rather by general brilliance than by delicacy of workmanship; a want of mellowness and inadequate perception of the difference between first-rate work in a quiet style and mere flatness.
4. Little respect for canons or traditions, accompanied by the notion that new conditions must of necessity produce new ideas.
5. An undervaluing of special knowledge or experience, except perhaps in the sphere of applied science and commerce, an idea that an able man can do one thing pretty much as well as another, as Dr. Johnson thought that if he had taken to politics he would have been as distinguished therein as he was in poetry.
6. An admiration for literary or scientific eminence, an enthusiasm for anything that can be called genius, with an undue eagerness to discover it.

---

[1] Plato indeed indulges his fancy so far as to describe the very mules and asses of a democracy as prancing along the roads, scarcely deigning to bear their burdens. The passion for unrestrained licence, for novelty, for variety is to him the note of democracy, whereas monotony and even obstinate conservatism are the faults which the latest European critics bid us expect.

7. A passion for novelties.
8. An intellectual impatience, and desire for quick and patent results.
9. An overvaluing of the judgments of the multitude; a disposition to judge by newspaper success work which has not been produced for the sake of success.
10. A tendency to mistake bigness for greatness.

Contrariwise, if we regard not the people generally but the most cultivated class, we shall find, together with some of the above-mentioned qualities, others which indicate a reaction against the popular tendencies. This class relishes subtlety of thought and highly finished art, whether in literature or painting. Afraid of crudity and vagueness, it is prone to devote itself to minute and careful study of subjects unattractive to the masses.

Of these characteristics of the people at large some may at first sight seem inconsistent with others, as for instance the admiration for intellectual gifts with the undervaluing of special knowledge; nevertheless it could be shown that both are discoverable in Americans as compared with Englishmen. The former admire intelligence more than the latter do; but they defer less to special competence. However, assuming for the moment that there is something true in these suggestions, which it would take too long to attempt to establish one by one, be it observed that very few of them can be directly connected with democratic government. Even these few might take a different form in a differently situated democracy. The seventh and eighth seem due to the general intelligence and education of the people, while the remainder, though not wholly uninfluenced by the habits which popular government tends to breed, must be mainly ascribed to the vast size of the country, the vast numbers and homogeneity of its native white population, the prevalence of social equality, a busy industrialism, a restless changefulness of occupation, and the absence of a leisured class dominant in matters of taste—conditions that have little or nothing to do with political institutions. The prevalence of evangelical Protestantism has been quite as important a factor in the intellectual life of the nation as its form of government.

Someone may say—I wish to state the view fairly though I do not entirely agree with it—that assuming the foregoing analysis to be correct, the influence of democracy, apart from its tendency to secure an ample provision of education, is discernible in two points. It produces self-confidence and self-complacency, national and personal, with the result both of stimulating a certain amount of thought and of preventing the thought that is so produced from being subjected to proper tests. Ambition and self-esteem will call out what might have lain dormant, but they will hinder a nation as well as a man from duly judging its own work, and in so far will retard its progress. Those who are naturally led to trust and obey common sense and the numerical majority in matters of state, overvalue the judgment of the majority in other matters. Now the judgment of the masses is a poor standard for the thinker or the artist to set before him. It may narrow his view and debase his style. He fears to tread in new paths or express unpopular opinions; or if he despises the multitude he may take refuge in an acrid cynicism. Where the masses rule, a writer cannot but think of the masses, and as they do not appreciate refinements he will eschew these, making himself at all hazards intelligible to the common mind, and seeking to attract by broad, perhaps coarsely broad, effects, the hasty reader, who passes by Walter Scott or Thackeray to fasten on the latest sketch of fashionable life or mysterious crime.

There is some force in this way of putting the case. Though democracy tends to produce a superficially active public, and perhaps also a jubilant and self-confident public, yet there may be a democratic people which shall be neither fond of letters nor disposed to trust its own judgment and taste in judging them. Much will depend on the other features of the situation. In the United States the cultivated public increases rapidly, and the very reaction which goes on within it against the defects of the multitude becomes an important factor. All things considered, I doubt whether democracy tends to discourage originality, subtlety, refinement, in thought and in expression, whether literary or artistic. Monotony or vulgarity under any and every form of government have appeared and may appear. The causes of these things lie deeper. Art and literature have been base and vulgar under absolute monarchies and under oligarchies. For two centuries the society of Vienna was one of the most polished and aristocratic societies in Europe. Yet what society could have been intellectually duller or less productive? Venice was almost the only Italian city of the first rank that contributed nothing to the literature of the Middle Ages and the Renaissance. Moreover, it must not be forgotten that the habits of popular government which open a career to talent in public life, open it in literature also. No man need lean on a faction or propitiate a coterie. A pure clear voice with an unwonted message may at first fail to make itself heard over the din of competitors for popular favour; but once heard, it and its message will probably be judged on their own merits.

Passing away from this question as to the supposed narcotic power of democracy, the further question may be asked, What is the distinctive note of democratic thought and art as they actually appear in the United States? What is the peculiar quality or flavour which springs from this political element in their condition? I cannot tell. I find no such note. I have searched for it, and, as the Americans say, it is hard work looking for what is not there. Some Europeans and many Americans profess to have found it, and will tell you that this or that peculiarity of American literature is due to democracy. No doubt, if you take individual writers, you may discover in several of them something, though not always the same thing, which savours of democratic feeling and tinges their way of regarding human life. But that is not enough. What must be shown is a general quality running through the majority of these writers—a quality which is at once recognized as racy of the soil, and which can be traced back to the democratic element which the soil undoubtedly contains. Has any such quality been shown? That there is a distinctive note in many—not, perhaps, in all—of the best American books may be admitted. It may be caught by ears not the most delicate. But is this note the voice of democracy? Is it even the voice of democracy and equality combined? There is a difference, slight yet perceptible, in the part which both sentiment and humour play in American books, when we compare them with English books of equivalent strength. The humour has a vein of oddity, and the contrast between the soft copiousness of the sentiment and the rigid lines of lingering Puritanism which it suffuses, is rarely met with in England. Perhaps there is less repose in the American style; there is certainly a curious unrestfulness in the effort, less common in English writers, to bend metaphors to unwonted uses. But are these differences, with others I might mention—and, after all, they are slight— due to any cause connected with politics? Are they not rather due to a mixed and curiously intertwined variety of other causes which have moulded the American mind during the last two centuries? American imagination has produced nothing more conspicuously original than the romances of Hawthorne. If anyone says that he finds something in them which he remembers in no previous English writer, we know what is meant and probably agree. But can it be said that there is anything distinctively American in Hawthorne, that is to say, that his specific quality is of a kind which reappears in other American writers? The most peculiar, and therefore I suppose the most characteristically American school of thought, has been what used to be called the Concord or Transcendental school of 1830 to 1860; among the writings produced by which those of Emerson and Thoreau are best known in Europe. Were the authors of that school distinctively democratic either in the colour of their thought, or in its direction, or in the style which expresses it? And if so, can the same democratic tinge be discerned in the authors of today? I doubt it; but such matters do not admit of proof or disproof. One must leave them to the literary feeling of the reader.

A very distinguished American man of letters once said to me that he hated nothing so much as to hear people talk about American literature. He meant, I think, that those who did so were puzzling themselves unnecessarily to find something which belonged to a new country, and a democratic country, and were forgetting or ignoring the natural relation of works of imagination and thought produced in America to books written by men of the same race in the Old World before and since 1776.

So far, then, as regards American literature generally, there may be discovered in it something that is distinctive yet little (if anything) specifically democratic. Nor if we look at the various departments of speculative thought, such as metaphysics and theology, or at those which approach nearer to the exact sciences, such as economics and jurisprudence, shall we find that the character and substance of the doctrines propounded bear marked traces of a democratic influence. Why should we be surprised at this, seeing that the influence of a form of government is only one among many influences, even where a nation stands alone, and creates a literature distinctively local? But can books written in the United States be deemed to constitute a literature locally American in the same sense as the literatures of France and Germany, of Italy and Russia, belong to those countries? For the purposes of thought and art the United States is a part of England, and England is a part of America. Many English books are more widely read and strike deeper to the heart in America than in England. Some American books have a like fortune in England. Differences there are, but differences how trivial compared with the resemblances in temper, in feeling, in susceptibility to certain forms of moral and physical beauty, in the general view of life and nature, in the disposition to revere and be swayed by the same matchless models of that elder literature which both branches of the English race can equally claim. American literature does not today differ more from English literature than the Scottish writers of the later eighteenth century—Burns, Scott, Adam Smith, Reid, in later eighteenth century Hume, Robertson— differed from their English contemporaries. There was a fondness for abstractions and generalizations in the Scottish prose writers; there was in the Scottish poets a bloom and fragrance of mountain heather which gave to their work a charm of freshness and singularity, like that which a faint touch of local accent gives to the tongue of an orator. But they were English as well as Scottish writers: they belong to English literature and make part of its glory to the world beyond. So Franklin, Fenimore Cooper, Hawthorne, Emerson, Longfellow, Lowell, and those on whom their mantle has fallen, belong to England as well as to America; and English writers, as they more and more realize the vastness of the American public they address, will more and more feel themselves to be American as well as English, and will often find in America not only a larger but a more responsive audience.

We have been here concerned not to discuss the merits and estimate the place of American thinkers and writers, but only to examine the relation in which they stand to their political and social environment. That relation, however, sets before us one more question. The English-speaking population of the United States is more than double that of the United Kingdom. The white part of it is a more educated population, in which a greater number of persons come under the influence of books and might therefore be stirred up to intellectual production. Why then does it not make more important contributions to the common literary wealth of the race? Is there a want of creative power? And if so, to what is the want due?

This is a question frequently propounded. I propose to consider it in the chapter which follows.

CHAPTER 1 1 5

Creative Intellectual Power

There is a street in Florence on each side of which stand statues of the famous Florentines of the fourteenth and fifteenth centuries—Dante, Giotto, Petrarch, Boccaccio, Ghiberti, Machiavelli, Michael Angelo, and others scarcely less illustrious, all natives of the little city which in their days had never a population of more than seventy thousand souls.[1] No one can walk between these rows of world-famous figures, matched by no other city of the modern world, without asking himself what cause determined so much of the highest genius to this one spot; why in Italy herself populous Milan and Naples and Venice have no such list to show; why the succession of greatness stopped with the beginning of the sixteenth century and has never been resumed? Questions substantially the same constantly rise to the mind in reading the history of other countries. Why did England produce no first-rate poet in the two stirring centuries between Chaucer and Shakespeare, and again in the century and a half between Milton's birth and Wordsworth's? Why have epochs of comparative sterility more than once fallen upon Germany and France? And why has music sometimes reached its highest pitch of excellence at moments when the other arts were languishing? Why does the sceptre of intellectual and artistic leadership pass now to one great nation, now to another, inconstant and unpredictable as are the shifting winds?

These questions touch the deepest and most complex problems of history; and neither historian nor physiologist has yet been able to throw any real light upon them. Even the commonplace remark that times of effort and struggle tend to develop an unusually active intellectual movement and

[1] Petrarch saw the light in Arezzo, but his family was Florentine, and it was by a mere accident that he was born away from his own city.

therewith to awaken or nourish rare geniuses, is not altogether true; for some of the geniuses have arisen at moments when there was no excitement to call them forth, and at other times seasons of storm and stress have raised up no one capable of directing the efforts or interpreting the feelings of his generation. One thing, however, is palpable: numbers have nothing to do with the matter. There is no average of a man of genius to so many thousands or millions of persons. Out of the seventy thousand of Florence there arise during two centuries more men of undying fame than out of huge London during the last three centuries. Even the stock of solid second-class ability does not necessarily increase with increasing numbers; while as to those rare combinations of gifts which produce poetry or philosophy of the first order, they are revealed no more frequently in a great European nation now than they were in a Semitic tribe or a tiny Greek city twenty-five or thirty centuries ago.

There is therefore no reason why the absence of brilliant genius among the ninety millions in the United States should excite any surprise; we might as well wonder that there is no Goethe or Schiller or Kant or Hegel in the Germany of today, so much more populous and better educated than the Germany of their birthtime. It is not to be made a reproach against America that men like Tennyson or Darwin have not been born there. "The wind bloweth where it listeth;" the rarest gifts appear no one can tell why or how. In broad France a century ago no man was found able to spring upon the neck of the Revolution and turn it to his will. Fate brought her favourite from a wild Italian island, that had but just passed under the yoke of the nation to which it gave a master.

The question we have to ask as regards the United States is therefore not why it has given us few men of the highest and rarest distinction, but whether it has failed to produce its fair share of talents of the second rank, that is, of men capable of taking a lead in all the great branches of literary or artistic or scientific activity, men who instruct and delight their own generation, though possibly future generations may not hold all of them in remembrance.

Have fewer men of this order adorned the roll of fame in the United States, during the years since 1776, than in England, or France or Germany during the same period? Obviously this is the fact as regards art in all its branches; and also, though less distinctly so, as regards physical and mathematical science. In literature there is less disparity, yet most candid Americans will agree with Englishmen that it is greater than those who know the education and intelligence of the younger people would have expected. I pass by oratory and statesmanship, because comparison is in these fields very difficult. The fact therefore being admitted, we have to endeavour to account for it.

If the matter were one of numerical averages, it would be pertinent to remark that of the total population of the United States about one-tenth are Negroes, at present altogether below the stratum from which production can be expected; that of the whites there may be four or five millions to whom English is virtually a foreign language, and that many millions are recent immigrants from Europe who are below the educational stratum in which literary gifts can be expected to germinate. This diminishes the contrast between numbers and intellectual results. But numbers have so little to do with the question that the point scarcely deserves a passing reference.

Those who have discussed the conditions of intellectual productivity have often remarked that epochs of stir and excitement are favourable, because they stimulate men's minds, setting new ideas afloat, and awakening new ambitions. It is also true that vigorous unremitting labour is, speaking generally, needed for the production of good work, and that one is therefore less entitled to expect it in an indolent time and from members of the luxurious classes. But it is not less true, though less frequently observed, that tranquillity and repose are necessary to men of the kind we are considering, and often helpful even to the highest geniuses, for the evolving of new thoughts and the creation of forms of finished and harmonious beauty. He who is to do such work must have time to meditate, and pause, and meditate again. He must be able to set his creation aside, and return to it after days or weeks to look at it with fresh eyes. He must be neither distracted from his main purpose, nor hurried in effecting it. He must be able to concentrate the whole force of his reason or imagination on one subject, to abstract himself when needful from the flitting sights and many-voiced clamour of the outer world. Juvenal said this long ago about the poet; it also applies, though possibly in a lower degree, both to the artist and to the serious thinker, or delicate workman, in any field of literature, to the metaphysician, the theologian, the philosophic historian, the economist, the philologist, even the novelist and the statesman. I have heard men who had gone from a quiet life into politics complain that they found their thinking powers wither, and that while they became far more expert in getting up subjects and speaking forcibly and plausibly, they found it harder and harder to form sound general views and penetrate beneath the superficialities of the newspaper and the platform. Interrupted thought, trains of reflection or imaginative conceptions constantly broken by a variety of petty transient calls of business, claims of society, matters passing in the world to note and think of, not only tire the mind but destroy its chances of attaining just and deep views of life and nature, as a wind-ruffled pool ceases to reflect the rocks and woods around it. Mohammed falling into trances on the mountain above Mecca, Dante in the sylvan solitudes of Fonte Avellana, Cervantes and Bunyan in the enforced seclusion of a prison, Hegel so wrapt and lost in his speculations that, taking his manuscript to the publisher in Jena on the day of the great battle, he was surprised to see French soldiers in the streets; these are types of the men and conditions which give birth to thoughts that occupy succeeding generations; and what is true of these greatest men is perhaps even more true of men of the next rank. Doubtless many great works have been produced among inauspicious surroundings, and even under severe pressure of time; but it will, I think, be almost invariably found that the producer had formed his ideas or conceived his creations in hours of comparative tranquillity, and had turned on them the full stream of his powers to the exclusion of whatever could break or divert its force.

In Europe men call this a century of unrest. But the United States is more unrestful than Europe, more unrestful than any country we know of has yet been. Nearly everyone is busy; those few who have not to earn their living and do not feel called to serve their countrymen, find themselves out of place, and have been wont either to make amusement into a business or to transfer themselves to the ease of France or Italy. The earning of one's living is not, indeed, incompatible with intellectually creative work, for many of those who have done such work best have done it in addition to their gainful occupation, or have earned their living by it. But in America it is unusually hard for anyone to withdraw his mind from the endless variety of external impressions and interests which daily life presents, and which impinge upon the mind, I will not say to vex it, but to keep it constantly vibrating to their touch. Life is that of the squirrel in his revolving cage, never still even when it does not seem to change. It becomes every day more and more so in England, and English literature and art show increasing marks of haste. In the United States the ceaseless stir and movement, the constant presence of newspapers, the eagerness which looks through every pair of eyes, even that active intelligence and sense of public duty, strongest in the best minds, which make a citizen feel that he ought to know what is passing in the wider world as well as in his own, all these render life more exciting to the average man than it is in Europe, but chase away from it the opportunities for repose and meditation which art and philosophy need, as growing plants need the coolness and darkness of night no less than the blaze of day. The type of mind which American conditions have evolved is quick, vigorous, practical, versatile; but it is unfavourable to the natural germination and slow ripening of large and luminous ideas; it wants the patience that will spend weeks or months on bringing details to an exquisite perfection. And accordingly we see that the most rich and finished literary work America has given us has proceeded from the older regions of the country, where the pulsations of life are slower and steadier than in the West or in the great commercial cities. It is from New England that nearly all the best books of the last generation came; and that not solely because the English race has been purest there, and education most generally diffused, for the New Englanders who have gone West, though they have carried with them their moral standard and their bright intelligence, seem either to have left behind their gift for literary creation, or to care to employ it only in teaching and in journalism.

It may be objected to this view that some of the great literary ages, such as the Periclean age at Athens, the Medicean age at Florence, the age of Elizabeth in England, have been ages full of movement and excitement. But the unrestfulness which prevails in America is altogether different from the large variety of life, the flow of stimulating ideas and impressions which marked those ages. Life is not as interesting in America, except as regards commercial speculation, as it is in Europe; because society and the environment of man are too uniform. It is hurried and bustling; it is filled with a multitude of duties and occupations and transient impressions. In the ages I have referred to men had time enough for all there was to do, and the very scantiness of literature and rarity of news made that which was read and received tell more powerfully upon the imagination.

Nor is it only the distractions of American life that clog the wings of invention. The atmosphere is over full of all that pertains to material progress. Americans themselves say, when excusing the comparative poverty of learning and science, that their chief occupation is at present the subjugation of their continent, that it is an occupation large enough to demand most of the energy and ambition of the nation, but that presently, when this work is done, the same energy and ambition will win similar triumphs in the fields of abstract thought, while the gifts which now make them the first nation in the world for practical inventions, will then assure to them a like place in scientific discovery. There is evidently much truth in this. The attractions of practical life are so great to men conscious of their own vigour, the development of the West and the vast operations of commerce and finance which have accompanied that development have absorbed so many strenuous talents, that the supply of ability available not only for pure science (apart from its applications) and for philosophical and historical studies, but even for statesmanship, has been proportionately reduced. But, besides this withdrawal of an unusually large part of the nation's force, the predominance of material and practical interests has turned men's thoughts and conversation into a channel unfavourable to the growth of the higher and more solid kinds of literature, perhaps still more unfavourable to art. Goethe said, "If a talent is to be speedily and happily developed the chief point is that a great deal of intellect and sound culture should be current in a nation." There is certainly a great deal of intellect current in the United States. But it is chiefly directed to business, that is, to railways, to finance, to commerce, to inventions, to manufactures (as well as to practical professions like law), things which play a relatively larger part than in Europe, as subjects of universal attention and discussion. There is abundance of sound culture, but it is so scattered about in divers places and among small groups which seldom meet one another, that no large cultured society has arisen similar to that of European capitals or to that which her universities have created for Germany. In Boston in 1860 a host could have brought together round his table nine men as interesting and cultivated as Paris or London would have furnished. But a similar party of eighteen could not have been collected, nor perhaps even the nine, anywhere except in Boston. At present, culture is more diffused: there are many cities where men of high attainments and keen intellectual interests are found, and associate themselves in literary or scientific clubs. Societies for the study of particular authors are not uncommon among women. I remember to have been told of a Homer club and an Æschylus club, formed by the ladies of St. Louis, and of Dante clubs in some Eastern cities. Nevertheless a young talent gains less than it would gain in Europe from the surroundings into which it is born. The atmosphere is not charged with ideas as in Germany, nor with critical *finesse* as in France. Stimulative it is, but the stimulus drives eager youth away from the groves of the Muses into the struggling throng of the marketplace.

It may be thought fanciful to add that in a new country one whole set of objects which appeal to the imagination are absent—no castles gray with age; no solemn cathedrals whose altering styles of architecture carry the mind up or down the long stream of history from the eleventh to the seventeenth century; few spots or edifices consecrated by memories of famous men or deeds, and among these none of remote date. There is certainly no want of interest in those few spots: the warmth with which Americans cherish them puts to shame the indifference of the English Parliament to the historic and prehistoric sites and buildings of Britain. But not one American youth in a thousand comes under the spell of any such associations. In the city or state where he lives there is nothing to call him away from the present. All he sees is new, and has no glories to set before him save those of accumulated wealth and industry skilfully applied to severely practical ends.

Someone may say that if (as was observed in last chapter) English and American literature are practically one, there is no need to explain the fact that one part of a race undivided for literary purposes leaves the bulk of literary production to be done by the other part, seeing that it can enter freely into the labours of the latter and reckon them its own. To argue thus would be to push the doctrine of the unity of the two branches rather too far, for after all there is much in American conditions and life which needs its special literary and artistic interpretations; and the question would still confront us, why the transatlantic branch, nowise inferior in mental force, contributes less than its share to the common stock. Still it is certainly true that the existence of a great body of producers, in England of literature, as in France of pictures, diminishes the need for production in America. Or to put the same thing in another way, if the Americans did not speak English they would evidently feel called on to create more high literature for themselves. Many books which America might produce are not produced because the men qualified to write them know that there are already English books on the same subject; and the higher such men's standard is, the more apt are they to overrate the advantages which English authors enjoy as compared with themselves. Many feelings and ideas which now find adequate expression through the English books which Americans read would then have to be expressed through American books, and their literature would be not only more individual, but more copious and energetic. If it lost in breadth, it would gain in freshness and independence. American authors conceive that even the nonrecognition of international copyright has told for evil on their profession. Since the native writer was undersold by reprints of English and French books, which, paying nothing to the European author, can be published at the cost of the paper and printing only, native authorship was discouraged, native talent diverted into other fields, while at the same time the intellectual standard of the public was lowered and its taste vulgarized. It might be thought that the profusion of cheap reprints would tend to quicken thought and diffuse the higher kinds of knowledge among the masses. But experience proves that by far the largest part of these reprints, and the part which is most extensively read, were novels, and among them many flimsy novels, which drove better books, including some of the best American fiction, out of the market, and tended to Europeanize the American mind in the worst way. One may smile at the suggestion that the allegiance of the working classes to their democratic institutions will be seduced by descriptions of English duchesses; yet it is probably true— eminent observers assure one of it—that the profusion of new frothy or highly-spiced fiction offered at ten or twenty-five cents a volume did much to spoil the popular palate for the enjoyment of more wholesome and nutritious food. And whatever injures the higher literature by diminishing the demand, may further injure it by creating an atmosphere unfavourable to the growth of pure and earnest native literary talent.

What then of the newspapers? The newspapers would need a chapter to themselves, and their influence as organs of opinion has been already discussed. The vigour and brightness of many among them are surprising. Nothing escapes them; everything is set in the sharpest, clearest light. Their want of reticence and delicacy is regretfully admitted by all educated Americans—the editors, I think, included. The cause of this deficiency is probably to be found in the fact that, whereas the first European journals were written for the polite world of large cities, American journals were, early in their career, if not at its very beginning, written for the bulk of the people, and published in communities still so small that everybody's concerns were already pretty well known to everybody else. They had attained no high level of literary excellence when towards the middle of last century an enterprising man of unrefined taste created a new type of "live" newspaper, which made a rapid success by its smartness, copiousness, and variety, while addressing itself entirely to the multitude. Other papers were almost forced to shape themselves on the same lines, because the class which desired something more choice was still relatively small; and now the journals of the chief cities have become such vast commercial concerns that they still think first of the mass and are controlled by its tastes, which they have themselves done so much to create. There are cities where the more refined readers who dislike flippant personalities are counted by tens of thousands, but in such cities competition is now too severe to hold out much prospect of success to a paper which does not expect the support of hundreds of thousands. It is not, however, with the æsthetic or moral view of the newspaper that we are here concerned, but with the effect on the national mind of the enormous ratio which the reading of newspapers bears to all other reading, a ratio higher than even in France or England. A famous Englishman, himself a powerful and fertile thinker, contrasted the value of the history of Thucydides with that of a single number of the *Times* newspaper, greatly to the advantage of the latter. Others may conceive that a thoughtful study of Thucydides, or, not to go beyond our own tongue, of Bacon, Milton, Locke, or Burke, perhaps even of Gibbon, Grote, or Macaulay, will do more to give keenness to the eye and strength to the wings of the mind than a whole year's reading of the best daily newspaper. It is not merely that the matter is of more permanent and intrinsic worth, nor that the manner and style form the student's taste; it is not merely that in the newspaper we are in contact with persons like ourselves, in the other case with rare and splendid intellects. The whole attitude of the reader is different. His attention is loose, his mind unbraced, so that he does not stop to scrutinize an argument, and forgets even valuable facts as quickly as he has learnt them. If he read Burke as he reads the newspaper, Burke would do him little good. And therefore the habit of mind produced by a diet largely composed of newspapers is adverse to solid thinking and dulling to the sense of beauty. Scorched and stony is the soil which newspaper reading has prepared to receive the seeds of genius.

Does the modern world really gain, so far as creative thought is concerned, by the profusion of cheap literature? It is a question one often asks in watching the passengers on an American railway. A boy walks up and down the car scattering newspapers and books in paper covers right and left as he goes. The newspapers are glanced at, though probably most people have read several of the day's papers already. The books are nearly all novels. They are not bad in tone, and sometimes they give incidentally a superficial knowledge of things outside the personal experience of the reader; while from their newspapers the passengers draw a stock of information far beyond that of a European peasant, or even of an average European artisan. Yet one feels that this constant succession of transient ideas, none of them impressively though many of them startlingly stated, all of them flitting swiftly past the mental sight as the trees flit past the eye when one looks out of the car window, is no more favourable to the development of serious intellectual interests and creative intellectual power than is the limited knowledge of the European artisan or peasant.

Most of the reasons I have hazarded to account for a phenomenon surprising to one who recognizes the quantity of intellect current in America, and the diffusion, far more general than in any other country, of intellectual curiosity, are reasons valid in the Europe of today as compared with the

Europe of last century, and still more true of the modern world as compared with the best periods of the ancient. Printing is by no means pure gain to the creative faculties, whatever it may be to the acquisitive; even as a great ancient thinker seems to have thought that the invention of writing in Egypt had weakened the reflective powers of man. The question follows, Are these causes, supposing them to be true causes, likely to be more or less operative in the America of next century than they now are? Will America become more what Europe is now, or will she be even more American?

I have elsewhere thrown out some conjectures on this point. Meantime it is pertinent to ask what are the most recent developments of American thought and research, for this will help us to see whether the tide of productive endeavour is rising or falling.

The abundant and excellent work done in fiction need be mentioned only for the sake of calling attention to the interest it has, over and above its artistic merit, as a record of the local manners and usages and types of character in various parts of the Union—types which are fast disappearing. The Creoles of Louisiana, the Negroes under slavery, with African tales still surviving in their memories, the rough but kindly backwoodsmen of early Indiana, the bosses of rural New England, the mountain folk of Tennessee, the humours of the Mississippi steamboat and the adventurous life of the Far West, were all made known to Europe through the tales of writers of the last or present generation, as the Indians of long ago became known through the romances of Fenimore Cooper. However, this is familiar ground to European readers, so I pass to work of a less generally attractive order.

In the middle of last century the standard of classical scholarship was low, and even the school commentaries on classical authors fell far short of those produced in Germany or England. Nowadays both in classical and in Oriental philology admirably thorough and painstaking work is produced. I have heard high European authorities observe that there is an almost excessive anxiety among American scholars to master all that has been written, even by third-rate Germans, and that the desire they evince to overtake Germany in respect of knowledge betrays some among them into the German fault of neglecting merits of form and style. In the sciences of nature, especially in those of observation, remarkable advances have been made. Dr. Asa Gray, was one of the two or three greatest botanists of his age, and Simon Newcomb one of the greatest mathematical astronomers. Much excellent work has been done in geology and palæontology, particularly in exploring the Rocky Mountain regions. Both for the excellence of their instruments and the accuracy of their observations, the astronomers stand in the front rank; nor has America fallen behind Europe in the theoretical part of this science. In some branches of physics and chemistry, such as spectrum analysis, American investigators have won like fame. Competent authorities award the highest praise to their recent contributions to biology and to medical science and are perhaps still more impressed by the achievements of their surgeons. In economics they seem to stand before either England or France, both as regards the extent to which the subject is studied in universities and as regards the number of eminent persons whom it occupies. In jurisprudence and law, American textbooks are of high excellence;[2] and one author, the late Mr. Justice Story, deserves, looking to the quantity as well as to the quality of his work, to be placed at the head of all who have handled these topics in the English tongue during the nineteenth century. Political science has begun to be studied more energetically than in England, where, to be sure, it is scarcely studied at all; and every year sees treatises and articles of permanent value added to the scanty modern literature which our language possesses on this subject. Similarly there is great activity in the field of both secular and ecclesiastical history, though as the work done has largely taken the direction of inquiries into local American history, and has altogether been more in the nature of research than of treatises attractive to the general public, its quantity and its merits have not yet been duly appreciated even at home, much less in Europe. Indeed, it is remarkable how far from showy and sensational is the bulk of the work now done in America. It is mostly work of a solid, careful, exact, and often rather dry type, not at all the sort of work which theorists about democracy would have looked for, since it appeals rather to the learned few than to the so-called general reader. One receives the impression that the class of intellectual workers, who until recently wanted institutions in which the highest and fullest training could be had, have now become sensible that their country, occupied in developing its resources and educating its ordinary citizens, had fallen behind Europe in learning and science, and that they are therefore the more eager to accumulate knowledge and spend their energy in minutely laborious special studies.[3]

I may be reminded that neither in the departments above mentioned, nor

---

[2] The number of legal journals and magazines in the United States is very much larger than in England, and the average level of workmanship in them equally high. Two journals are dedicated to political science, a subject only just beginning to be represented in the British press.

[3] The extreme pains taken in America to provide every library with a classified catalogue directing readers to the books on each subject, seem to illustrate this tendency.

in statesmanship, can one point to many brilliant personalities. Perhaps this is true of Europe also; perhaps the world is passing through an age with a high level of mediocrity in literature, art, and science as compared with the outstanding figures of last century. There have been periods in history when striking figures were lacking, although great events seemed to call for them. As regards America, if there be few persons of exceptional gifts, it is significant that the number of those who are engaged in scientific work, whether in the investigation of nature or in the moral, political, and historical sciences, is larger, relatively to the population of the country, than it was fifty years ago, the methods better, the work done more solid, the spirit more earnest and eager. Nothing more strikes a stranger who visits the American universities than the ardour with which the younger generation has thrown itself into study, even kinds of study which will never win the applause of the multitude. There is more zeal and heartiness among these men, more freshness of mind, more love of learning for its own sake, more willingness to forego the chances of fame and wealth for the sake of adding to the stock of human knowledge, than is to be found today in Oxford or Cambridge, or in the universities of Scotland. One is reminded of the scholars of the Renaissance flinging themselves into the study of rediscovered philology, or of the German universities after the War of Liberation. And under the impressions formed in mingling with such men, one learns to agree with the conviction of the Americans that for a nation so abounding in fervid force there is reserved a fruitful career in science and letters, no less than in whatever makes material prosperity.

The Relation of the United States to Europe

One cannot discuss American literature and thought without asking, What is the intellectual relation of the United States to Europe? Is it that of an equal member of the great republic of letters? Or is it that of a colony towards the mother country, or of a province towards a capital? Is it, to take instances from history, such a relation as was that of Rome to Greece in the second and first centuries before Christ? or of Northern and Western Europe to Italy in the fifteenth? or of Germany to France in the eighteenth? in all of which cases there was a measure of intellectual dependence on the part of a nation which felt itself in other respects as strong as or stronger than that whose models it followed, and from whose hearth it lighted its own flame.

To answer this question we must first answer another—How do the Americans themselves conceive their position towards Europe? And this, again, suggests a third—What does the American people think of itself?

The conceit of the people was at one time a byword. It was not only self-conscious but obtrusive and aggressive. Every visitor satirized it, Dickens most keenly of all, in forgiving whom the Americans gave the strongest proof of their good nature. Doubtless all nations are either vain or proud, or both; and those not least who receive least recognition from their neighbours. A nation could hardly stand without this element to support its self-reliance; though when pushed to an extreme it may, as happens with the Turks, make national ruin the more irretrievable. But American conceit has been steadily lessening as the country has grown older, more aware of its true strength, more respected by other countries.[1] There was less conceit

---

[1] Tocqueville complains that the Americans would not permit a stranger to pass even the smallest unfavourable criticism on any of their institutions, however warmly he might express his admiration of the rest.

after the Civil War than before, though the Civil War had revealed elements of greatness unexpected by foreigners; there is less now than there was at the close of the Civil War. An impartially unsparing critic from some other planet might say of the Americans that they are at this moment less priggishly supercilious than the Germans, less restlessly pretentious than the French, less pharisaically self-satisfied than the English. Among the upper or better-educated classes, glorification has died out, except of course in Fourth of July and other public addresses, when the scream of the national eagle must be heard. One sometimes finds it replaced by undue self-depreciation, with lamentations over the want of culture, the decline of faith, or the corruption of politics. Among the masses it survives in an exultation over the size and material resources of the country—the physically large is to them the sublime—in an overestimate of men and events in American history; in a delight, strongest, of course, among the recent immigrants, in the completeness of social equality, and a corresponding contempt for the "serfs of Europe" who submit to be called "subjects" of their sovereign, in a belief in the superior purity of their domestic life and literature, and in the notion that they are the only people who enjoy true political liberty, liberty far fuller than that of England, far more orderly than that of France.[2] Taking all classes together, they are now not more sensitive to external opinion than the nations of Western Europe, and less so than the Russians, though they are still a trifle more apt to go through Europe comparing what they find with what they left at home. A foreign critic who tries to flout or scourge them no longer disturbs their composure; his jeers are received with amusement or indifference.

Accordingly the attitude of thoughtful Americans to Europe has no longer either the old open antagonism or the old latent self-distrust. It is that of a people which conceives itself to be intellectually the equal of any other people, but to have taken upon itself for the time a special task which

[2] It must, however, be admitted that this whimsical idea is not confined to the masses. I find, for instance, in an address delivered by an eminent man to a distinguished literary fraternity in October 1887 the following passage: "They (i.e. 'the immortal periods of the Declaration of Independence') have given political freedom to America and France, unity and nationality to Germany and Italy, emancipated the Russian serf, relieved Prussia and Hungary from feudal tenures, *and will in time free Great Britain and Ireland also*"!

I have often asked Americans wherein they consider their freedom superior to that of the English, but have never found them able to indicate a single point in which the individual man is worse off in England as regards either his private civil rights, or his political rights, or his general liberty of doing and thinking as he pleases. They generally turn the discussion to social equality, the existence of a monarchy and of hereditary titles, and so forth—matters which are of course quite different from freedom in its proper sense.

impedes it in the race of literary and artistic development. Its mission is to reclaim the waste lands of a continent, to furnish homes for instreaming millions of strangers, to work out a system of harmonious and orderly democratic institutions. That it may fulfil these tasks it has for the moment postponed certain other tasks which it will in due time resume.[3] Meanwhile it may, without loss of dignity or of faith in itself, use and enjoy the fruits of European intellect which it imports until it sees itself free to rival them by native growths. If I may resort to a homely comparison, the Americans are like a man whose next-door neighbour is in the habit of giving musical parties in the summer evenings. When one of these parties comes off, he sits with his family in the balcony to enjoy the quartettes and solos which float across to him through the open windows. He feels no inferiority, knowing that when he pleases he can have performers equally good to delight his own friends, though for this year he prefers to spend his surplus income in refurnishing his house or starting his son in business.

There is of course a difference in the view of the value of European work as compared with their own, taken by the more educated and by the less educated classes. Of the latter some fail to appreciate the worth of culture and of science, even for practical purposes, as compared with the industrial success, though in this respect they are no more obtuse than the bulk of Englishmen; and they accordingly underrate their obligations to Europe. Others, knowing that they ought to admire works of imagination and research, but possessed of more patriotism than discernment, cry up second or third-rate fiction, poetry, and theology because it is American, and try to believe that their country gives as much to Europe as she receives. Taste for literature is so much more diffused than taste in literature that a certain kind of fame is easily won. There are dozens of poets and scores of poetesses much admired in their own state, some even beyond its limits, with no merit but that of writing verse which can be scanned, and will raise no blush on the most sensitive cheek. Yet the quality of the poetry publishing improves, and its quantity witnesses to the growing number of those who love letters and cultivate the imagination. Criticism is lenient, and for a time it could scarcely be said to exist, for the few journals which contained good reviews were little read except in four or five Northern Atlantic states, and several inland cities. A really active and searching criticism, which

---

[3] A Chicago man is reported to have expressed this belief with characteristic directness in the sentence "Chicago has had no time for culture yet, but when she does take hold she will make it hum." The time came; and Chicago has now set an example to many an older city in what it is doing for the adornment of its lake front and the establishment of art collections.

should appraise literary work on sound canons, not caring whether it has been produced in America or in Europe, by a man or by a woman, in the East or in the West, is one of the things which America needed, and the rise of which is a thing to be welcomed. Among highly educated men this extravagant appreciation of native industry used to produce a disgust expressing itself sometimes in sarcasm, sometimes in despondency. Some still deem their homegrown literature trivial, and occupy themselves with European books, watching the presses of England, France, and Germany more carefully than almost anyone does in England. Yet even these, I think, cherish silently the faith that when the West has been settled and the railways built, and possibilities of sudden leaps to wealth diminished, when culture has diffused itself among the classes whose education is now superficial, and their love of art extended itself from furniture to pictures and statuary, American literature will in due course flower out with a brilliance of bloom and a richness of fruit rivalling the Old World.

The United States are therefore, if this account be correct, in a relation to Europe for which no exact historical parallel can be found. They do not look up to her, nor seek to model themselves after her. They are too proud for a province, too large for a colony. They certainly draw from Europe far more thought than they send to her, and though they have produced several brilliant artists, no distinctively American school has arisen. Yet they cannot be said to be led or ruled by Europe, because they apply their own standards and judgment to whatever they receive.

Their special relations to the leading European countries are worth noting. In old colonial days England was everything. The revolt of 1776 produced an estrangement which might have been healed after 1783, had England acted with common courtesy and good sense, but which was embittered by her scornful attitude. Wounds which were just beginning to scar over were reopened by the war of 1812; and the hostility continued as long as the generation lived whose manhood saw that war. The generation which remembered 1812 was disappearing when the sympathy for the Southern Confederacy not indeed of the English people, but of a section of the English upper classes, lit up the almost extinguished flames. These were quenched, so far as the native Americans are concerned, by the settlement of the Alabama claims, which impressed the United States not merely as a concession to themselves, but as an evidence of the magnanimity of a proud country. There remained a certain amount of rivalry with England, and for a time a certain sensitiveness to the criticisms even of ignorant Englishmen. But these lingering touches of jealousy have all but vanished with the growing sympathy felt for "the old country," as it is still called. It is the only European country in which the American people can be said to feel any personal interest, or towards an alliance with which they are drawn by any sentiment. For a time, however, the sense of gratitude to France for her aid in the War of Independence was very strong. It brought French literature as well as some French usages into vogue, and increased the political influence which France exercised during the earlier years of her own Revolution. Still that influence did not go far beyond the sphere of politics: one feels it but slightly in the literature of the half century from 1780 to 1830.

During the reign of Louis Napoleon, wealthy Americans resorted largely to Paris, and there, living often for years together in a congenial atmosphere of display and amusement, imbibed undemocratic tastes and ideas, which through them found their way back across the ocean, and coloured certain sections of American society, particularly in New York. Although there is still an American colony in Paris, Parisian influence seems no longer to cross the Atlantic. French books, novels excepted, and these in translations, are not largely read. French politics excite little interest; France is practically not a factor at all in the moral or intellectual life of the country. Over art, however, especially painting and decoration, she has still great power. Many American artists study in Paris, indeed all resort thither who do not go to Rome or Florence; French pictures enjoy such favour with American dealers and private buyers as to make the native artists complain, not without reason, that equally good homemade work receives no encouragement;[4] and house decoration, in which America seems to stand before England, particularly in the skilful use of wood, is much affected by French designs and methods.

The enormous German immigration from about 1860 till 1900 might have been expected to do something in the way of Germanizing the American mind, giving it a taste for metaphysics on the one hand, and for minutely patient research on the other. It had neither the one result nor the other, nor indeed any result whatever in the field of thought. It enormously stimulated the brewing industry; it retarded the progress of Prohibitionism; it introduced more outdoor life than formerly existed; it increased the taste for music; it broke down the strictness of Sabbath observance; and has indeed in some

---

[4] The heavy import duty on foreign works of art did not benefit the native artist, for the men who buy pictures can usually buy notwithstanding the duty, while it prevented the artist from furnishing himself with the works he wished to have around him for the purposes of his own training. The Tariff Act of 1909 dropped the duty for works of art more than twenty years old.

critics produced what is commonly called "a Continental Sunday." But the vast majority of German immigrants belong to the humbler classes, and were but faintly influenced by their own literature. There have been among them extremely few *savants*, or men likely to become *savants*, nor have these played any conspicuous part in the universities or in literature.

Nevertheless the influence of Germany has been of late years powerfully stimulative upon the classes that follow after learning, for not only are German treatises largely read, but many of the most promising graduates of the universities proceed to Germany for a year or two to complete their studies, and there become imbued with German ideas and methods. The English universities have, by their omission to develop advanced instruction in special branches of knowledge, lost a golden opportunity of coming into relation with and influencing that academic youth of America in whose hands the future of American science and learning lies. This German influence on American work has however not tended towards the propagation of metaphysical schools, metaphysics themselves being now on the ebb in Germany. It appears in some departments of theology, and is also visible in historical and philological studies, in economics, and in the sciences of nature.

On the more popular kinds of literature, as well as upon manners, social usages, current sentiment generally, England and her influences are of course nearer and more potent than those of any other European country, seeing that English books go everywhere among all classes, and that they work upon those who are substantially English already in their fundamental ideas and habits. Americans of the cultivated order, and especially women, are more alive to the movements and changes in the lighter literature of England, and more curious about those who figure in it, especially the rising poets and essayists, than equally cultivated English men and women. I have been repeatedly surprised to find books and men that had made no noise in London well known, especially in the Atlantic states, and their merits canvassed with more zest and probably more acuteness than a London drawing room would have shown. The verdicts of the best circles were not always the same as those of similar circles in England, but they were nowise biased by national feeling, and often seemed to proceed from a more delicate and sympathetic insight. I recollect, though I had better not mention, instances in which they welcomed English books which England had failed to appreciate, and refused to approve American books over which English reviewers had become ecstatic.

Passing English fashions in social customs and in such things as games sometimes spread to America—possibly more often than similar American fashions do to England—but sometimes encounter ridicule there. The Anglomaniac is a familiar object of good-humoured satire. As for those large movements of opinion or taste or practical philanthropy in which a parallelism or correspondence between the two countries may often be discerned, this correspondence is more frequently due to the simultaneous action of the same causes than to any direct influence of the older country. In theology, for instance, the same relaxation of the rigid tests of orthodoxy has been making way in the churches of both nations. In the Protestant Episcopal church there has been a similar, though less pronounced, tendency to the development of an ornate ritual. The movement for dealing with city pauperism by voluntary organizations began later than the charity organization societies of England, but would probably have begun without their example. The university extension movement, and the establishment of "university settlements" in the poorer parts of great cities are further instances. The semi-socialistic tendency which I have referred to as now noticeable among the younger clergy and the younger teachers in some of the universities, although similar to that which may be discerned in England, does not seem traceable to direct English influences. So too the rapidly growing taste for beauty in house decoration and in street architecture is a birth of the time rather than of Old World teaching, though it owes something to Mr. Ruskin's books, which have been more widely read in America than in England.[5]

In political matters the intellectual sympathy of the two countries is of course less close than in the matters just described, because the difference between institutions and conditions involves a diversity in the problems which call for a practical solution. Political changes in England affect American opinion less than such changes in France affect English opinion, although the Americans know more and care more and judge more soundly about English affairs than the French do about English or the English about French. The cessation of bitterness between Great Britain and the Irish has made a difference in American politics; but no political event in England less serious than, let us say, the establishment of a powerful Socialist party, would sensibly tell on American opinion, just as no event happening beyond the Atlantic, except the rise and fall of the Southern Confederacy, has

---

[5] America has produced of late years several distinguished architects, and the art is cultivated with great energy and success. European artists and critics who saw the buildings erected for the Chicago Exhibition of 1893 were greatly impressed by the inventiveness and taste they displayed; nor can a traveller fail to be struck by the beauty and variety of design shown both by some of the newer public buildings and by the villas which surround the richer cities.

influenced the course of English political thought. However, the wise men of the West watch English experiments for light and guidance in their own troubles. A distinguished American who came a year or two ago to London to study English politics, told me that he did so in the hope of finding conservative institutions and forces from which lessons serviceable to the United States might be learned. After a fortnight, however, he concluded that England was in a state of suppressed revolution, and departed sorrowful.

On a review of the whole matter it will appear that although as respects most kinds of intellectual work America is rather in the position of the consumer, Europe, and especially England, in that of the producer, although America is more influenced by English and German books and by French art than these countries are influenced by her, still she does not look for initiative to them, or hold herself in any way their disciple. She is in many points independent; and in all fully persuaded of her independence.

Will she then in time develop a new literature, bearing the stamp of her own mint? She calls herself a new country: Will she give the world a new philosophy, new views of religion, a new type of life in which plain living and high thinking may be more happily blended than we now see them in the Old World, a life in which the franker recognition of equality will give a freshness to ideas and to manners a charm of simplicity which the aristocratic societies of Europe have failed to attain?

As regards manners and life, she has already approached nearer this happy combination than any society of the Old World. As regards ideas, I have found among the most cultivated Americans a certain cosmopolitanism of view, and detachment from national or local prejudice, superior to that of the same classes in France, England, or Germany. In the ideas themselves there is little one can call novel or distinctively American, though there is a kind of thoroughness in embracing or working out certain political and social conceptions which is less common in England. As regards literature, nothing at present indicates the emergence of a new type. The influence of the great nations on one another grows always closer, and makes new national types less likely to appear. Science, which has no nationality, exerts a growing sway over men's minds, and exerts it contemporaneously and similarly in all civilized countries. For the purposes of thought, at least, if not of literary expression, the world draws closer together, and becomes more of a homogeneous community.

A visitor doubts whether the United States are, so far as the things of the mind are concerned, "a new country." The people have the hopefulness of youth. But their institutions are old, though many have been remodelled or new faced; their religion is old; their views of morality and conduct are old; their sentiments in matters of art and taste have not greatly diverged from those of the parent stock. Is the mere fact that they inhabit new territories, and that the conditions of life there have trained to higher efficiency certain gifts, and have left others in comparative quiescence, is this fact sufficient so to transform the national spirit as to make the products of their creative power essentially diverse from those of the same race abiding in its ancient seats? A transplanted tree may bear fruit of a slightly different flavour, but the apple remains an apple and the pear a pear.

However, it is still too early in the growth of the United States to form any conclusions on these high matters, almost too soon to speculate regarding them. There are causes at work which may in time produce a new type of intellectual life; but whether or not this come to pass, it can hardly be doubted that when the American people give themselves some repose from their present labours, when they occupy themselves less with doing and more with being, there will arise among them a literature and a science, possibly also an art, which will tell upon Europe with a new force. It will have behind it the momentum of hundreds of millions of men.

The Absence of a Capital

The United States are the only great country in the world which has no capital. Germany and Italy were long without one, because the existence of the mediæval Empire prevented the growth in either country of a national monarchy. But the wonderfully reconstructive age we live in has now supplied the want; and although Rome and Berlin are by no means to their respective states what Paris and London are to France and England, what Vienna and Pesth are to the Dual Monarchy, they may in time attain a similar rank[1] in their respective nations. By a capital I mean a city which is not only the seat of political government, but is also by the size, wealth, and character of its population the head and centre of the country, a leading seat of commerce and industry, a reservoir of financial resources, the favoured residence of the great and powerful, the spot in which the chiefs of the learned professions are to be found, where the most potent and widely read journals are published, whither men of literary and scientific capacity are drawn. The heaping together in such a place of these various elements of power, the conjunction of the forces of rank, wealth, knowledge, intellect, naturally makes such a city a sort of foundry in which opinion is melted and cast, where it receives that definite shape in which it can be easily and swiftly propagated and diffused through the whole country, deriving not only an authority from the position of those who form it, but a momentum from the weight of numbers in the community whence it comes. The opinion

[1] Athens, Lisbon, Copenhagen, Stockholm, Brussels, are equally good instances among the smaller countries. In Switzerland, Bern has not reached the same position, because Switzerland is a federation, and, so to speak, an artificial country made by history. Zurich, Lausanne, and Geneva are intellectually quite as influential. So Holland retains traces of her federal condition in the relatively less important position of Amsterdam. Madrid being a modern city placed in a country more recently and less perfectly consolidated than most of the other states of Europe, is less of a capital to Spain than Lisbon is to Portugal or Paris to France.

of such a city becomes powerful politically because it is that of the persons who live at headquarters, who hold the strings of government in their hands, who either themselves rule the state or are in close contact with those who do. It is true that under a representative government power rests with those whom the people have sent up from all parts of the country. Still these members of the legislature reside in the capital, and cannot but feel the steady pressure of its prevailing sentiment, which touches them socially at every point. It sometimes happens that the populace of the capital, by their power of overawing the rulers or perhaps of effecting a revolution, are able to turn the fortunes of the state. But even where no such peril is to be apprehended, any nation with the kind of a capital I am describing acquires the habit of looking to it for light and leading, and is apt to yield to it an initiative in political movements.

In the field of art and literature the influence of a great capital is no less marked. It gathers to a centre the creative power of the country, and subjects it to the criticism of the best instructed and most polished society. The constant action and reaction upon one another of groups of capable men in an atmosphere at once stimulative to invention and corrective of extravagance may give birth to works which isolated genius could hardly have produced. Goethe made this observation as regards Paris, contrasting the centralized society of France with the dispersion of the elements of culture over the wide area of his own Germany.

> Now conceive a city like Paris, where the highest talents of a great kingdom are all assembled in a single spot, and by daily intercourse, strife, and emulation mutually instruct and advance each other; where the best works, both of nature and art, from all kingdoms of the earth, are open to daily inspection—conceive this metropolis of the world, I say, where every walk across a bridge or across a square recalls some mighty past, and where some historical event is connected with every corner of a street. In addition to all this, conceive not the Paris of a dull spiritless time, but the Paris of the nineteenth century, in which, during three generations, such men as Molière, Voltaire, Diderot, and the like, have kept up such a current of intellect as cannot be found twice in a single spot on the whole world, and you will comprehend that a man of talent like Ampère, who has grown up amid such abundance, can easily be something in his four-and-twentieth year.[2]

The same idea of the power which a highly polished and strenuously active society has to educe and develop brilliant gifts underlies the memorable

---

[2] *Conversations with Eckermann.*

description which Pericles gives of Athens.[3] And if it be suggested that the growth of such a centre may impoverish the rest of a country because the concentration of intellectual life tends to diminish the chances of variability, and establish too uniform a type, some compensation for any such loss may be found in the higher efficiency which such a society gives to the men of capacity whom it draws into its own orbit.

In the case both of politics and of literature, the existence of a capital tends to strengthen the influence of what is called society, that is to say, of the men of wealth and leisure who have time to think of other matters than the needs of daily life, and whose company and approval are apt to be sought by the men of talent. Thus where the rich and great are gathered in one spot to which the nation looks, they effect more in the way of guiding its political thought and training its literary taste than is possible where they are dispersed over the face of a large country. In both points, therefore, it will evidently make a difference to a democratic country whether it has a capital, and what degree of deference that capital receives. Paris is the extreme case of a city which has been everything to the national literature and art, and has sought to be everything in national politics also. London, since the decline of Dublin and of Edinburgh, has stood without a British rival in the domain of art and letters, and although one can hardly say that a literary society exists in London, most of the people who employ themselves in writing books and nearly all those who paint pictures live in or near it. Over politics London has less authority than Paris has exerted in France, doubtless because parts of the north and west of Britain are more highly vitalized than the provinces of France, while the English city is almost too populous to have a common feeling. Its very hugeness makes it amorphous.

What are the cities of the United States which can claim to approach nearest to the sort of capital we have been considering? Not Washington, though it is the meeting place of Congress and the seat of federal administration. It has a relatively small population (in 1910, 331,069, of whom one-third were Negroes). Society consists of congressmen (for about half the year), officials (including many scientific men in the public service), members of the diplomatic corps, and some rich and leisured people who come to spend the winter. The leaders of finance, industry, commerce, and the professions are absent; there are some journalists, but few men of letters, and scarcely any artists. What is called the fashionable society of Washington, which, being small, polished, and composed of people who constantly meet

[3] Thucyd. II, 37–41.

one another, is agreeable, and not the less agreeable because it has a peculiar flavour, is so far from aspiring to political authority as to deem it "bad form" to talk politics.[4] Its political society on the other hand has been so largely composed of officials, "professionals," and office-seekers, as to produce an atmosphere unlike that of the nation at large, and dangerous to those statesmen who breathe it too long without interruption.

Not New York, though it is now by far the most populous city. It is the centre of commerce, the sovereign of finance. But it has no special political influence or power beyond that of casting a large vote, which is a main factor in determining the thirty-nine presidential votes of the state. Business is its main occupation: and though the representatives of literature are now pretty numerous, few of them are concerned with politics, the journals, marked as is their ability, are, after all, New York journals, and not, like those of Paris, London, or even Berlin, professedly written for the whole nation. Next come Chicago, perhaps the most typically American place in America, and Philadelphia, the latter once the first city of the Union. Neither is a centre of literature or ideas for more than its own vicinity. Boston was for a time the chosen home of letters and culture, and still contains, in proportion to her population, a larger number of men and women capable of making or judging good work than any other city. But she can no longer be said to lead abstract thought, much less current opinion. Nor can one say that any of these cities is on the way to gain a more commanding position. New York will probably retain her preeminence in population and commercial consequence, but she does not rise proportionately in culture, while the centre of political gravity, shifting slowly to the West, will doubtless finally fix itself in the Mississippi Valley.[5]

It deserves to be remarked that what is true of the whole country is also true of the great sections of the country. Of the cities I have named, none, except possibly Boston and Chicago, can be said to be even a local capital, either for purposes of political opinion or of intellectual movement and tendency. Boston retains her position as the literary centre of New England;

---

[4] Washington, being situated in the federal District of Columbia, is not a part of any state, and therefore enjoys no share in the federal government. Its inhabitants vote neither for a member of Congress nor for presidential electors; and the city is ruled, greatly to its advantage, by a federal commission.

[5] A leading New York paper once said, "In no capital that we know of does the cause of religion and morality derive so little support against luxury from intellectual interest or activity of any description. This interest has its place here, but it leads a sickly existence as yet under the shadow of great wealth which cares not for it." This remark is, I think, less true today of New York or Chicago or St. Louis than it would have been in 1890.

San Francisco by her size has a preponderating influence on the Pacific coast. But no other great city is regarded by the inhabitants of her own and the adjoining states as their natural head, to which they look for political guidance, or from which they expect any intellectual stimulance. Even New Orleans, though by far the largest place in the South, is in no sense the metropolis of the South; and does little more for the South than set a conspicuous example of municipal misgovernment. Though no Paris, no Berlin stands above them, these great American cities are not more important in the country, or even in their own sections of the country, than Lyons and Bordeaux are in France, Hamburg and Cologne in Germany. Even as between municipal communities, even in the sphere of thought and literary effort, equality and local independence have in America their perfect work.

The geographical as well as political causes that have produced this equality are obvious enough, and only one needs special mention. The seat of federal government was in 1790 fixed at a place which was not even a village, but a piece of swampy woodland,[6] not merely for the sake of preventing the national legislature from being threatened by the mob of a great city, but because the jealousies of the states made it necessary to place the legislature in a spot exempt from all state influence or jurisdiction. So too in each state the seat of government is rarely to be found in the largest city. Albany, not New York, is the capital of New York State; Springfield, not Chicago, of Illinois; Sacramento, not San Francisco, of California; Harrisburg, not Philadelphia, of Pennsylvania. This seems to have been so ordered not from fear of the turbulence of a vast population, but partly to secure a central spot, partly from the jealousy which the rural districts and smaller cities feel of the place which casts the heaviest vote, and may seek to use the state resources for its own benefit.

It is a natural result of the phenomena described that in the United States public opinion crystallizes both less rapidly and in less sharp and well-defined forms than happens in those European countries which are led by the capital. The temperature of the fluid in which opinion takes shape (if I

---

[6] Congress, however, did not remove from Philadelphia to the banks of the Potomac until 1800. Thomas Moore's lines on Washington as he saw it in 1804 deserve to be quoted:

> An embryo capital where Fancy sees
> Squares in morasses, obelisks in trees;
> Where second-sighted seers the plain adorn
> With fanes unbuilt and heroes yet unborn,
> Though nought but woods and Jefferson they see,
> Where streets should run, and sages ought to be.

may venture to pursue the metaphor), is not so high all over a large country as in the society of a city, where the minds that make opinion are in daily contact, and the process by which opinion is made is therefore slower, giving a somewhat more amorphous product. I do not mean that a European capital generates opinion of one type only; but that each doctrine, each programme, each type of views, whether political or economic or religious, is likely to assume in a capital its sharpest and most pronounced form, that form being taken up and propagated from the capital through the country. And this is one reason why Americans were the first to adopt the system of conventions, mass meetings of persons belonging to a particular party or advocating a particular cause, gathered from every corner of the country to exchange their ideas and deliberate on their common policy.

It may be thought that in this respect the United States suffer from the absence of a centre of light and heat. Admitting that there is some loss, there are also some conspicuous gains. It is a gain that the multitude of no one city should be able to overawe the executive and the legislature, perhaps even to change the form of government, as Paris has so often done in France. It is a gain, for a democratic country, that the feeling of what is called society—that is to say, of those who toil not, neither do they spin, who are satisfied with the world, and are apt to regard it as a place for enjoyment—should not become too marked and palpable in its influence on the members of the legislature and the administration, that it should rather be diffused over the nation and act insensibly upon other classes through the ordinary relations of private life than take visible shape as the voice of a number of wealthy families gathered in one spot, whose luxury may render them the objects of envy and the target for invective. And although types of political view may form themselves less swiftly, though doctrines may be less systematic, programmes less fully reasoned out than when the brisk intelligence of groups gathered in a capital labours to produce them, they may, when they do finally emerge from the mind of the whole people, have a breadth and solidity proportioned to the slowness of their growth, and be more truly representative of all the classes, interests, and tendencies that exist within the nation.

How far the loss exceeds the gain as respects the speculative and artistic sides of intellectual effort, it is too soon to determine, for American cities are all the creatures of the last two centuries. That which Goethe admired in Paris is evidently impossible to the dispersed geniuses of America. On the other hand, that indraught of talent from the provinces to Paris which many thoughtful Frenchmen deplore, and which has become more unfortunate since Paris has grown to be the centre of amusement for the dissipated classes of Europe, is an experience which no other country need wish to undergo. Germany has not begun to produce more work or better work since she has given herself a capital; indeed, he who looks back over her annals since the middle of last century will think that so far as scholarship, metaphysics, and possibly even poetry are concerned, she gained from that very want of centralization which Goethe regretted. Great cities realize so vividly the defects of the system they see around them that they sometimes underrate the merits that go with those defects. It may be that in the next age American cities will profit by their local independence to develop varieties greater than they now exhibit, and will evolve diverse types of literary and artistic production. Europe will watch with curiosity the progress of an experiment which it is now too late for any of her great countries to try.

American Oratory

Oratory is an accomplishment in which Europeans believe that Americans excel; and that this is the opinion of the American themselves, although they are too modest to express it, may be gathered from the surprise they betray when they find an Englishman fluent before an audience. They had at one time the advantage (if it is an advantage) of much more practice than any European nation; but now, with democracy triumphant in England and France, the proportion of speeches and speaking to population is probably much the same in all three countries. Some observations on a form of effort which has absorbed a good deal of the talent of the nation, seem properly to belong to an account of its intellectual life.

Oratorical excellence may be said to consist in the combination of five aptitudes:

Invention, that is to say the power of finding good ideas and weaving effective arguments

Skill and taste in the choice of appropriate words

Readiness in producing appropriate ideas and words at short notice

Quickness in catching the temper and tendencies of the particular audience addressed

Weight, animation, and grace in delivery

Such excellence as the Americans possess, such superiority as they may claim over Englishmen, consists rather in the three latter of these than in the two former.

The substance of their speeches is not better than one finds in other countries, because substance depends on the intellectual resources of the speaker and on the capacity of the audience for appreciating worthy matter. Neither is the literary form better, that is to say, the ideas are not clothed in any choicer language. But there is more fluency, more readiness, more self-possession. Being usually nimbler in mind than an Englishman, and feeling less embarrassed on his legs, an American is apt to see his point more clearly and to get at it by a more direct path. I do not deny that American speakers sometimes weary the listener, but when they do so it is rather because the notions are commonplace and the arguments unsound than because, as might often happen in England, ideas of some value are tediously and pointlessly put. It is true that with the progress of democracy, and the growing volume of speeches made, the level of public speaking has in Britain risen within the last generations while the number of great orators has declined. Still, if one is to compare the two countries, the English race seems to have in America acquired a keener sensitiveness of sympathy. That habit of deference to others, and that desire to be in accord with the sentiments of others, which equality and democratic institutions foster, make the American feel himself more completely one of the audience and a partaker of its sentiments than an average English speaker does. This may have the consequence, if the audience be ignorant or prejudiced, of dragging him down to its level. But it makes him more effective. Needless to add that humour, which is a commoner gift in America than elsewhere, often redeems an otherwise uninteresting address, and is the best means of keeping speaker and audience in touch with one another.

A deliberate and even slow delivery is the rule in American public speaking, as it is in private conversation. This has the advantage of making a story or a jest tell with more effect. There is also, I think, less stiffness and hesitation among American than among English speakers, greater skill in managing the voice, because more practice in open-air meetings, greater clearness of enunciation. But as regards grace, either in action or in manner, the Teutonic race shows no more capacity on the other side of the Atlantic than it has generally done in England for rivalling the orators of Italy, Spain, and France.

The commonest American defect used to be a turgid and inflated style. The rhetoric was Rhodian rather than Attic, overloaded with tropes and figures, apt to aim at concealing poverty or triteness in thought by exaggeration of statement, by a profusion of ornament, by appeals to sentiments loftier than the subject or the occasion required. Too frequently the florid diction of the debating club or the solemn pomp of the funeral oration was invoked when nothing but clearness of exposition or cogency of argument was needed. These faults sprang from the practice of stump oratory, in which the temptation to rouse a multitude by declamation is specially strong. A man straining his voice in the open air is apt to strain his phrases also, and command attention by vehemence. They were increased by the custom of having orations delivered on certain anniversaries, and especially on the Fourth of July, for on these great occasions the speaker feels bound to talk "his very tallest." Public taste, generally good in the days after the Revolution, when it was formed by a small number of educated men, degenerated in the first half of the nineteenth century. Despite the influence of several orators of the first rank, incessant stump speaking and the inordinate vanity of the average audience brought a gaudy and inflated style into fashion, which became an easy mark for European satire. Of late years a reaction for the better set in, probably strengthened by the example of Abraham Lincoln, who was direct, clear, and sinewy. There are still those who imitate Macaulay or Webster without the richness of the one or the stately strength of the other. The newspapers, in acknowledging that a lecturer is fluent or lucid, still complain if he is not also "eloquent." Commemorative addresses, which are far more abundant than in Europe, usually sin by over-finish of composition. But on the whole there has been an improvement in the taste of listeners and in the style of speeches. Such improvement would be more rapid were it not for the enormous number of speeches by people who have really nothing to say, as well as by able men on occasions when there is nothing to be said which has not been said hundreds of times before. This is, of course, almost equally true of England, and indeed of all popularly governed countries. Profusion of speech is one of the drawbacks to democracy, and a drawback which shows no signs of disappearing.

As respects the different kinds of oratory, that of the pulpit is pretty much on the English level, the discourses not superior in substance, but perhaps less frequently dull in delivery. Even when the discourse is read, it is read in a less mechanical way, and there is altogether more sense of the worth of vivacity and variety. The average length of sermons is a mean between the twenty minutes of an Anglican minister and the fifty minutes of Scotland. The manner is slightly less conventional, because the American pastor is less apt than his European brother to feel himself a member of a distinct caste.

Forensic oratory has not of late years been cultivated with the ardour of former years. In the United States, as in England, there are many powerful advocates, but no consummate artist. Whether this is due to the failure of nature to produce persons specially gifted, or to the absence of trials whose issues and circumstances are calculated to rouse forensic ability to exceptional efforts, or to a change in public taste, and a disposition to prefer the practical to the showy, is a question which is often asked in England, and no easier to answer in America.

Congress, for reasons explained in the chapter treating of it, is a less favourable theatre for oratory than the great representative assemblies of Europe. The House of Representatives has at no period of its history shone with lights of eloquence, though a few of Clay's great speeches were delivered in it. There is some good short brisk debating in Committee of the Whole, but the set speeches are mostly pompous and heavy. The Senate has maintained a higher level, partly from the smaller size of its chamber, partly from its greater leisure, partly from the superior ability of its members. Webster's and Calhoun's greatest efforts were made on its floor, and produced an enormous effect on the nation. At present, however, the "full-dress debates" in the Senate are apt to want life, the great set speeches being fired off rather with a view to their circulation in the country than to any immediate effect on the assembly. But the ordinary discussions of bills, or questions of policy, reveal plenty of practical speaking power. If there be little passion and no brilliancy, there is strong common sense put in a plain and telling form.

Of the state legislatures not much need be said. In them, as in the House of Representatives, the bulk of the work is done in committees, and the opportunities for displays of eloquence are limited. They are good schools to form a practical business speaker, and they do form many such. But the characteristic merits and defects of transatlantic oratory are more fully displayed on the stump and in those national and state nominating conventions whereof I have already spoken. So far as the handling great assemblies is an art attainable by a man who does not possess the highest gifts of thought and imagination, it has been brought to perfection by the heroes of these mass meetings. They have learnt how to deck out commonplaces with the gaudier flowers of eloquence; how to appeal to the dominant sentiment of the moment; above all, how to make a strong and flexible voice the means of rousing enthusiasm. They scathe the opposite party by vigorous invective; they interweave stories and jokes with their declamatory passages so as to keep the audience constantly amused. They deliver contemptible claptrap with an air of hearty conviction. The party men who listen, because there are few present at a mass meeting, and still fewer at a convention, except members of the party which convoked the gathering, are better pleased with themselves than ever, and go away roused to effort in the party cause. But there has been little argument all through, little attempt to get hold of the reason and judgment of the people. Stimulation, and not instruction or conviction, is the aim which the stump orator sets before himself; and the consequence is that election campaigns have generally been less educationally valuable than those of England. It is worth remarking that the custom which in England requires a representative to deliver at least once a year an address to his constituents, setting forth his view of the political situation and explaining his own speeches and votes during the preceding session, does not seem to be general in the United States. In the campaign of 1896, however, the currency question was argued before the electors with a force and point which were both stimulative and instructive; and the habit of appealing to the intelligence as well as the feelings or prejudices of the voters has been since maintained. When an address meant to be specifically instructive has to be given, it takes the form of a lecture, and is usually delivered by some well-known public man, who receives a fee for it.

There are three kinds of speech which, though they exist in most European countries, have been so much more fully developed beyond the Atlantic as to deserve some notice.

The first of these is the oration of the occasion. When an anniversary comes round—and celebrations of an anniversary are very common in America—or when a sort of festival is held in honour of some public event, such for instance as the unveiling of a statue, or the erection of a monument on a battlefield, or the opening of a city hall or state capitol, or the driving the last spike of a great railroad, a large part of the programme is devoted to speaking. The chief speech is entrusted to one eminent person, who is called the orator of the day, and from whom is expected a long and highly finished harangue, the length and finish of which are wearisome to an outsider, though the people of the locality are flattered. Sometimes these speeches contain good matter—I could mention instances when they embody personal recollections of a distinguished man in whose honour the celebration was being held—but the artificial elevation at which the speaker usually feels bound to maintain himself is apt to make him pompous and affected.

Speeches of a complimentary and purely "epideictic" nature of the English public banquet type are very common. There is scarcely an occasion in life which brings forty or fifty people together on which a prominent citizen or a stranger from Europe is not called upon "to offer a few remarks." No subject is prescribed for him; often no toast has to be proposed or responded to. He is simply put on his legs to talk upon anything in heaven or earth which may rise to his mind. The European, who is at first embarrassed by this unchartered freedom, presently discovers its advantages, for it gives him a wider range for whatever he may have to say. In nothing does the good nature of the people stand revealed more than in the courteous patience with which they will listen to a long-winded after-dinner speaker, even when he reads a typewritten address at one o'clock A.M.

The third form of discourse specially characteristic of the United States is the lecture. It was less frequent and less fashionable, partly from the rise of monthly magazines full of excellent matter, partly because other kinds of evening entertainment have become more accessible to people outside the great cities, but it began to revive towards the close of last century. With the disappearance of Puritan sentiment the theatre is now extremely popular, perhaps more popular than in any part of Europe. There is hardly a new settlement in the West which strolling companies do not visit. But the lecture, even if dwarfed by the superior attractions of the drama, is still a valuable means of interesting people in literary, scientific, and political questions. And the art of lecturing has been developed in a corresponding measure. A discourse of this kind, whatever the merits of its substance, is usually well arranged, well composed to meet the taste of the audience, and above all, well delivered. It is listened to with an absence of laughter (where it is intended to amuse) and of applause which surprises European observers, but no audiences can be imagined more attentive or appreciative of any real effort to provide good matter.

This grave reserve in American listeners surprises Europeans,[1] especially those who have observed the excitability shown on presidential campaigns. It seems to arise from the practical turn of their minds as well as from their intelligence. In an election campaign it is necessary and expedient to give vent to one's feelings; in listening to a lecture it is not. One comes to be instructed or entertained, and comes with a critical habit formed by hearing many lectures as well as reading many books. Something may also be due to the large proportion of women in an American audience at lectures or other nonpolitical occasions.

Many Europeans think that the kind of oratory in which the Americans show to most advantage is neither the political kind, abundant as it is, nor the commemorative oration, assiduously as it is cultivated, but what may be called the lighter ornamental style, such as the after-dinner speech. The

---

[1] A story is told of Edmund Kean acting before an audience in New England which he found so chilling that at last he refused to come on for the next scene unless some applause were given, observing that such a house was enough to put out Vesuvius.

fondness (sometimes pushed to excess) of the people for anecdotes, and their skill in telling them, the general diffusion of humour, the readiness in catching the spirit of an occasion, all contribute to make their efforts in this direction more easy and happy, while furnishing less temptation for the characteristic fault of a straining after effect. I have already observed that they shine in stump speaking, properly so called—that is, in speaking which rouses an audience but ought not to be reported. The reasons why their more serious platform and parliamentary oratory has been, of course with brilliant exceptions, less excellent are, over and above the absence of momentous issues, probably the same as those which have affected the average quality of newspaper writing. In Europe the leading speakers and writers have nearly all belonged to the cultivated classes, and, feeling themselves raised above their audiences, have been in the habit of obeying their own taste and that of their class rather than the appetite of those whom they addressed. In England, for instance, the standard of speaking by public men has been set by parliamentary debate, because till within the last few decades the leading men of the country had all won their reputation in Parliament. They carried their parliamentary style with them into popular meetings, and aspirants of all classes imitated this style. It sometimes erred in being too formal and too prolix; but its taste was good, and its very plainness obliged the speaker to have solid matter. In America, on the other hand, stump oratory is older or at least quite as old as congressional oratory, and the latter has never gained that hold on the ideas and habits of the people which parliamentary debate held in England. Hence speaking has generally moved on a somewhat lower level, not but what there were brilliant popular orators in the first days of the Republic, like Patrick Henry, and majestic parliamentary orators like Daniel Webster in the next generation, but that the volume of stump speaking was so much greater than in England that the fashion could not be set by a few of the greatest men, but was determined by the capacities of the average man. The taste of the average man, instead of being raised by the cultivated few to their own standard, but tended to lower the practice, and to some extent even the taste, of the cultivated few. To seem wiser or more refined than the multitude, to incur the suspicion of talking down to the multitude, would have offended the sentiment of the country, and injured the prospects of a statesman. It is perhaps a confirmation of this view that, while pompousness has flourished in the West, and floridity still marks the South, the most polished speakers have generally belonged to New England, where the level of average taste and knowledge was exceptionally high. One of these speakers, the late

Mr. Wendell Phillips, was, in the opinion of competent critics, an opinion which those who remember his conversation will be inclined to agree with, one of the first orators of that time, and not more remarkable for the finish than for the transparent simplicity of his style, which attained its highest effects by the most direct and natural methods.

CHAPTER 119

The Pleasantness of American Life

I have never met a European of the middle or upper classes who did not express astonishment when told that America was a more agreeable place than Europe to live in. "For working men," he would answer, "yes; but for men of education or property, how can a new rough country, where nothing but business is talked and the refinements of life are only just beginning to appear, how can such a country be compared with England, or France, or Italy?"

It is nevertheless true that there are elements in the life of the United States which may well make a European of any class prefer to dwell there rather than in the land of his birth. Let us see what they are.

In the first place there is the general prosperity and material well-being of the mass of the inhabitants. In Europe, if an observer takes his eye off his own class and considers the whole population of any one of the greater countries, he will perceive that by far the greater number lead very laborious lives, and are, if not actually in want of the necessaries of existence, yet liable to fall into want, the agriculturists when nature is harsh, the wage earners when work is scarce. In England the lot of the labourer has been hitherto a hard one, incessant field toil, with rheumatism at fifty and the workhouse at the end of the vista; while the misery massed in such cities as London, Liverpool, and Glasgow is only too well known. In France there is less pauperism, but nothing can be more pinched and sordid than the life of the bulk of the peasantry. In the great towns of Germany there is constant distress and increasing discontent. The riots of 1886 in Belgium told an even more painful tale of the wretchedness of the miners and artisans there. In Italy the condition of the rural population of Venetia as well as of the southern provinces still gives cause for grave concern. Of Russia, with her ninety millions of ignorant peasants living in half barbarism, there is no need to speak. Contrast any one of these countries with the United States, where the working classes are as well fed, clothed, and lodged as the lower middle class in Europe, and the farmers who till their own land (as nearly all do) much better, where a good education is within the reach of the poorest, where the opportunities for getting on in one way or another are so abundant that no one need fear any physical ill but disease or the results of his own intemperance. Pauperism already exists and increases in some of the larger cities, where drink breeds misery, and where recent immigrants, with the shiftlessness of Europe still clinging round them, are huddled together in squalor. But outside these few cities one sees nothing but comfort. In Connecticut and Ohio the native American operatives in many a manufacturing town lead a life easier, and more brightened by intellectual culture and by amusements, than that of the clerks and shopkeepers of England or France. In cities like Kansas City or Chicago one finds miles on miles of suburb filled with neat wooden houses, each with its tiny garden plot, owned by the shop assistants and handicraftsmen who return on the electric cars in the evening from their work. All over the wide West, from Lake Ontario to the Upper Missouri, one travels past farms of one to two hundred acres, in every one of which there is a spacious farmhouse among orchards and meadows, where the farmer's children grow up strong and hearty on abundant food, the boys full of intelligence and enterprise, ready to push their way on farms of their own or enter business in the nearest town, the girls familiar with the current literature of England as well as of America. The life of the agricultural settler in the further West has its privations, but it is brightened by hope, and has a singular charm of freedom and simplicity. The impression which this comfort and plenty makes is heightened by the brilliance and keenness of the air, by the look of freshness and cleanness which even the cities wear, all of them except the poorest parts of those few I have referred to above. The fog and soot flakes of an English town, as well as its squalor, are wanting; you are in a new world, and a world which knows the sun. It is impossible not to feel warmed, cheered, invigorated by the sense of such material well-being all around one, impossible not to be infected by the buoyancy and hopefulness of the people. The wretchedness of Europe lies far behind; the weight of its problems seems lifted from the mind. As a man suffering from depression feels the clouds roll away from his spirit when he meets a friend whose good humour and energy present the better side of things and point the way through difficulties, so the sanguine temper of the Americans, and the sight of the ardour with which they pursue their aims, stimulates a European, and makes him think the world a better place than it had seemed amid the entanglements and sufferings of his own hemisphere.

To some Europeans this may seem fanciful. I doubt if any European can realize till he has been in America how much difference it makes to the happiness of anyone not wholly devoid of sympathy with his fellow beings, to feel that all round him, in all classes of society and all parts of the country, there exist in such ample measure so many of the external conditions of happiness: abundance of the necessaries of life, easy command of education and books, amusements and leisure to enjoy them, comparatively few temptations to intemperance and vice.

The second charm of American life is one which some Europeans will smile at. It is social equality. To many Europeans the word has an odious sound. It suggests a dirty fellow in a blouse elbowing his betters in a crowd, or an ill-conditioned villager shaking his fist at the parson and the squire; or, at any rate, it suggests obtrusiveness and bad manners. The exact contrary is the truth. Equality improves manners, for it strengthens the basis of all good manners, respect for other men and women simply as men and women, irrespective of their station in life. Probably the assertion of social equality was one of the causes which injured American manners fifty years ago, for that they were then bad among townsfolk can hardly be doubted in face of the testimony, not merely of sharp tongues like Mrs. Trollope's, but of calm observers like Sir Charles Lyell and sympathetic observers like Richard Cobden.[1] In those days there was an obtrusive self-assertiveness among the less refined classes, especially towards those who, coming from the Old World, were assumed to come in a patronizing spirit. Now, however, social equality has grown so naturally out of the circumstances of the country, has been so long established, and is so ungrudgingly admitted, that all excuse for obtrusiveness has disappeared. People meet on a simple and natural footing, with more frankness and ease than is possible in countries where everyone is either looking up or looking down.[2] There is no servility

---

[1] Volney, who at the end of last century commented on the "incivilité nationale," ascribes it "moins à un système d'intentions qu'à l'indépendance mutuelle, à l'isolement, au défaut des besoins réciproques."

[2] A trifling anecdote may illustrate what I mean. Long ago in Spokane, a small Far Western town, the stationmaster lent me a locomotive to run a few miles out along the railway to see a remarkable piece of scenery. The engine took me and dropped me there, as I wished to walk back, much to the surprise of the driver and stoker, for in America no one walks if he can help it. The same evening, as I was sitting in the hall of the hotel, I was touched on the arm, and turning round found myself accosted by a well-mannered man, who turned out to be the engine driver. He expressed his regret that the locomotive had not been cleaner and better "fixed up," as he would have liked to make my trip as agreeable as possible, but the notice given him had been short. He

on the part of the humbler, and if now and then a little of the "I am as good as you" rudeness be perceptible, it is almost sure to proceed from a recent immigrant, to whom the attitude of simple equality has not yet become familiar as the evidently proper attitude of one man to another. There is no condescension on the part of the more highly placed, nor is there even that sort of scrupulously polite coldness which one might think they would adopt in order to protect their dignity. They have no cause to fear for their dignity, so long as they do not themselves forget it. And the fact that your shoemaker or your factory hand addresses his employer as an equal does not prevent him from showing all the respect to which any one may be entitled on the score of birth or education or eminence in any walk of life.

This naturalness is a distinct addition to the pleasure of social life. It enlarges the circle of possible friendship, by removing the *gêne* which in most parts of Europe persons of different ranks feel in exchanging their thoughts on any matters save those of business. It raises the humbler classes without lowering the upper; indeed, it improves the upper no less than the lower by expunging that latent insolence which deforms the manners of so many of the European rich. It relieves women in particular, who in Europe are specially apt to think of class distinctions, from that sense of constraint and uneasiness which is produced by the knowledge that other women with whom they come in contact are either looking down on them, or at any rate trying to gauge and determine their social position. It expands the range of a man's sympathies, and makes it easier for him to enter into the sentiments of other classes than his own. It gives a sense of solidarity to the whole nation, cutting away the ground for all sorts of jealousies and grudges which distract people so long as the social pretensions of past centuries linger on to be resented by the levelling spirit of a revolutionary age. And I have never heard native Americans speak of any drawbacks corresponding to and qualifying these benefits.

There are, moreover, other rancours besides those of social inequality whose absence from America brightens it to a European eye. There are no quarrels of churches and sects. Judah does not vex Ephraim, nor Ephraim envy Judah. No Established Church looks down scornfully upon Dissenters from the height of its titles and endowments, and talks of them as hindrances in the way of its work. No Dissenters pursue an Established Church in a spirit of watchful jealousy, nor agitate for its overthrow. One is not offended

---

talked with intelligence, and we had some pleasant chat together. It was fortunate that I had resisted in the forenoon the British impulse to bestow a gratuity.

by the contrast between the theory and the practice of a religion of peace, between professions of universal affection in pulpit addresses and forms of prayer, and the acrimony of clerical controversialists. Still less, of course, is there that sharp opposition and antagonism of Christians and anti-Christians which lacerates the private as well as public life of France. Rivalry between sects appears only in the innocent form of the planting of new churches and raising of funds for missionary objects, while most of the Protestant denominations, including the four most numerous, constantly fraternize in charitable work. Between Roman Catholics and the more educated Protestants there is little hostility, and sometimes even cooperation for a philanthropic purpose. The sceptic is no longer under a social ban, and discussions on the essentials of Christianity and of theism are conducted with good temper. There is not a country in the world where Frederick the Great's principle, that everyone should be allowed to go to heaven his own way, is so fully applied. This sense of religious peace as well as religious freedom all around one is soothing to the weary European, and contributes not a little to sweeten the lives of ordinary people.

I come last to the character and ways of the Americans themselves, in which there is a certain charm, hard to convey by description, but felt almost as soon as one sets foot on their shore, and felt constantly thereafter. In purely business relations there is hardness, as there is all the world over. Inefficiency has a very short shrift. But apart from those relations they are a kindly people. Good nature, heartiness, a readiness to render small services to one another, an assumption that neighbours in the country, or persons thrown together in travel, or even in a crowd, were meant to be friendly rather than hostile to one another, seem to be everywhere in the air, and in those who breathe it. Sociability is the rule, isolation and moroseness the rare exception. It is not merely that people are more vivacious or talkative than an Englishman expects to find them, for the Western man is often taciturn and seldom wreathes his long face into a smile. It is rather that you feel that the man next you, whether silent or talkative, does not mean to repel intercourse, or convey by his manner his low opinion of his fellow creatures. Everybody seems disposed to think well of the world and its inhabitants, well enough at least to wish to be on easy terms with them and serve them in those little things whose trouble to the doer is small in proportion to the pleasure they give to the receiver. To help others is better recognized as a duty than in Europe. Nowhere is money so readily given for any public purpose; nowhere, I suspect, are there so many acts of private kindness done, such, for instance, as paying the college expenses of a promising boy, or aiding a widow to carry on her husband's farm; and these are not done with ostentation. People seem to take their own troubles more lightly than they do in Europe, and to be more indulgent to the faults by which troubles are caused. It is a land of hope, and a land of hope is a land of good humour. And they have also, though this is a quality more perceptible in women than in men, a remarkable faculty for enjoyment, a power of drawing more happiness from obvious pleasures, simple and innocent pleasures, than one often finds in overburdened Europe.

As generalizations like this are necessarily comparative, I may be asked with whom I am comparing the Americans. With the English, or with some attempted average of European nations? Primarily I am comparing them with the English, because they are the nearest relatives of the English. But there are other European countries, such as France, Belgium, Spain, in which the sort of cheerful friendliness I have sought to describe is less common than it is in America. Even in Germany and German Austria, simple and kindly as are the masses of the people, the upper classes have that *roideur* which belongs to countries dominated by an old aristocracy, or by a plutocracy trying to imitate aristocratic ways. The upper class in America (if one may use such an expression) has not in this respect differentiated itself from the character of the nation at large.

If the view here presented be a true one, to what causes are we to ascribe this agreeable development of the original English type, a development in whose course the sadness of Puritanism seems to have been shed off?

Perhaps one of them is the humorous turn of the American character. Humour is a sweetener of temper, a copious spring of charity, for it makes the good side of bad things even more visible than the weak side of good things; but humour in Americans may be as much a result of an easy and kindly turn as their kindliness is of their humour. Another is the perpetuation of a habit of mutual help formed in colonial days. Colonists need one another's aid more constantly than the dwellers in an old country, are thrown more upon one another, even when they live scattered in woods or prairies, are more interested in one another's welfare. When you have only three neighbours within five miles, each of them covers a large part of your horizon. You want to borrow a plough from one; you get another to help you to roll your logs; your children's delight is to go over for an evening's merrymaking to the lads and lasses of the third. It is much pleasanter to be on good terms with these few neighbours, and when others come one by one, they fall into the same habits of intimacy. Anyone who has read those stories of rustic New England or New York life which delighted those who were English children in 1850—I do not know whether they delight children still, or have been thrown aside for more highly spiced food—will remember the warm-hearted simplicity and atmosphere of genial goodwill which softened the roughness of peasant manners and tempered the sternness of a Calvinistic creed. It is natural that the freedom of intercourse and sense of interdependence which existed among the early settlers, and which have always existed since among the pioneers of colonization in the West as they moved from the Connecticut to the Mohawk, from the Mohawk to the Ohio, from the Ohio to the Mississippi, should have left on the national character traces not effaced even in the more artificial civilization of our own time. Something may be set down to the feeling of social equality, creating that respect for a man as a man, whether he be rich or poor, which was described a few pages back; and something to a regard for the sentiment of the multitude, a sentiment which forbids any man to stand aloof in the conceit of self-importance, and holds up geniality and good fellowship as almost the first of social virtues. I do not mean that a man consciously suppresses his impulses to selfishness or gruffness because he knows that his faults will be ill regarded; but that, having grown up in a society which is infinitely powerful as compared with the most powerful person in it, he has learnt to realize his individual insignificance, as members of the upper class in Europe never do, and has become permeated by the feeling which this society entertains—that each one's duty is not only to accept equality, but also to relish equality, and to make himself pleasant to his equals. Thus the habit is formed even in natures of no special sweetness, and men become kindly by doing kindly acts.

Whether, however, these suggestions be right or wrong, there is no doubt as to the fact which they attempt to explain. I do not, of course, give it merely as the casual impression of European visitors, whom a singularly frank and ready hospitality welcomes and makes much of. I base it on the reports of European friends who have lived for years in the United States, and whose criticism of the ways and notions of the people is keen enough to show that they are no partial witnesses.

The Uniformity of American Life

To the pleasantness of American life there is one, and perhaps only one, serious drawback—its uniformity. Those who have been struck by the size of America, and by what they have heard of its restless excitement, may be surprised at the word. They would have guessed that an unquiet changefulness and turmoil were the disagreeables to be feared. But uniformity, which the European visitor begins to note when he has travelled for a month or two, is the feature of the country which Englishmen who have lived long there, and Americans who are familiar with Europe, most frequently revert to when asked to say what is the "crook in their lot."

It is felt in many ways. I will name a few.

It is felt in the aspects of nature. All the natural features of the United States are on a larger scale than those of Europe. The four chief mountain chains are each of them longer than the Alps.[1] Of the gigantic rivers and of those inland seas we call the Great Lakes one need not speak. The centre of the continent is occupied by a plain larger than the western half of Europe. In the Mississippi Valley, from the Gulf of Mexico to Lake Superior, there is nothing deserving to be called a hill, though, as one moves westward from the great river, long soft undulations in the great prairie begin to appear. Through vast stretches of country one finds the same physical character maintained with little change—the same strata, the same vegetation, a generally similar climate. From the point where you leave the Alleghenies at Pittsburg, until, after crossing the Missouri, you approach the still untilled prairie of the West, a railway run of some twelve hundred miles, there is a uniformity of landscape greater than could be found along any one hundred

---

[1] The Alleghenies, continued in the Green and White Mountains; the Rocky Mountains; the Sierra Nevada, continued in the Cascade Range; and the Coast Ranges, which border the Pacific.

miles of railway run in Western Europe. Everywhere the same nearly flat country, over which you cannot see far, because you are little raised above it, the same fields and crops, the same rough wooden fences, the same thickets of the same bushes along the stream edges, with here and there a bit of old forest; the same solitary farmhouses and straggling wood-built villages. And when one has passed beyond the fields and farmhouses, there is an even more unvaried stretch of slightly rolling prairie, smooth and bare, till after three hundred miles the blue line of the Rocky Mountains rises upon the western horizon.

There are some extraordinary natural phenomena, such as Niagara, the Yellowstone Geysers, and the indescribably grand and solemn canyon of the Colorado River, which the Old World cannot equal. But taking the country as a whole, and remembering that it is a continent, it is not more rich in picturesque beauty than the much smaller western half of Europe. The long Allegheny range contains a good deal of pretty scenery and a few really romantic spots, but hardly anything so charming as the best bits of Scotland or southern Ireland, or the English Lake Country. The Rocky Mountains are pierced by some splendid gorges, such as that famous one through which the Arkansas River descends to South Pueblo, and show some very grand prospects, such as that over the Great Salt Lake from the Mormon capital. But neither the Rocky Mountains, with their dependent ranges, nor the Sierra Nevada, can be compared for variety of grandeur and beauty with the Alps; for although each chain nearly equals the Alps in height, and covers a greater area, they have little snow, no glaciers,[2] and a singular uniformity of character. One finds, I think, less variety in the whole chain of the Rockies than in the comparatively short Pyrenees. There are, indeed, in the whole United States very few quite first-rate pieces of mountain scenery rivalling the best of the Old World. The most impressive are two or three of the deep valleys of the Sierra Nevada (of which the Yosemite is the best known), and the superb line of extinct volcanoes, bearing snowfields and glaciers, which one sees, rising out of vast and sombre forests, from the banks of the Columbia River and the shores of Puget Sound.[3] So the Atlantic coast, though there are charming bits between

---

[2] There are a few inconsiderable glaciers in the northernmost part of the Rocky Mountains, and a small one on Mount Shasta.

[3] Want of space compels the omission of the chapters which were intended to describe the scenery of the United States and conjecture its probable future influence on the character of the people.

The Great West, from the eastern slope of the Rocky Mountains to the Pacific, has many striking and impressive pieces of scenery to show. Nevertheless its mountains are less beautiful than the Alps, just as the mountains of Asia Minor, even when equal or superior in height, are

Newport and the New Brunswick frontier, cannot vie with the coasts of Scotland, Ireland, or Norway; while southward from New York to Florida it is everywhere flat and generally dreary. In the United States people take journeys proportionate to the size of the country. A family thinks nothing of going twelve hundred miles, from St. Louis to Cape May (near Philadelphia), for a seaside holiday. But even journeys of twelve hundred miles do not give an American so much change of scene and variety of surroundings as a Parisian has when he goes to Luchon, or a Berliner to Berchtesgaden. The man who lives in the section of America which seems destined to contain the largest population, I mean the states on the Upper Mississippi, lives in the midst of a plain wider than the plains of Russia, and must travel hundreds of miles to escape from its monotony.

When we turn from the aspects of nature to the cities of men, the uniformity is even more remarkable. With eight or nine exceptions to be mentioned presently, American cities differ from one another only herein, that some of them are built more with brick than with wood, and others more with wood than with brick. In all else they are alike, both great and small. In all the same wide streets, crossing at right angles, ill-paved, but planted along the side walks with maple trees whose autumnal scarlet surpasses the brilliance of any European foliage.[4] In all the same shops, arranged on the same plan, the same Chinese laundries, with Li Kow visible through the window, the same ice-cream stores, the same large hotels with seedy men hovering about in the dreary entrance hall, the same streetcars passing to and fro with passengers clinging to the doorstep, the same locomotives ringing their great bells as they clank slowly down the middle of the street. I admit that in external aspect there is a sad monotony in the larger towns of England also. Compare English cities with Italian cities, and most of the former seem like one another, incapable of being, so to speak, individualized as you individualize a man with a definite character and aspect unlike that of other men. Take the Lancashire towns, for instance,

---

less beautiful, and largely for the same reaon. They are much drier, and have therefore fewer streams and less variety and wealth of vegetation, the upper zone of the Sierra Nevada and Cascade Range excepted; and the Rockies, as they run north and south, present less of a contrast between their two sides than do the northern and southern derivities of the Alps or the Caucasus. The deserts have a strange and weird beauty of their own, unlike anything in Europe.

[4] In the newer cities one set of parallel streets is named by numbers, the others, which cross them at right angles, are in some instances, as in New York, called avenues, and so numbered. In Washington the avenues are called after states, and of the two sets of streets (which the avenues cross obliquely), one is called by numbers, the other by the letters of the alphabet, a convenient but unpleasing system.

large and prosperous places. You cannot individualize Bolton or Wigan, Oldham or Bury, except by trying to remember that Bury is slightly less rough than Oldham, and Wigan a thought more grimy than Bolton. But in Italy every city has its character, its memories, its life and achievements wrought into the pillars of its churches and the towers that stand along its ramparts. Siena is not like Perugia, nor Perugia like Orvieto; Ravenna, Rimini, Pesaro, Fano, Ancona, Osimo, standing along the same coast within seventy miles of one another, have each of them a character, a sentiment, what one may call an idiosyncrasy, which comes vividly back to us at the mention of its name. Now, what English towns are to Italian, that American towns are to English. They are in some ways pleasanter; they are cleaner, there is less poverty, less squalor, less darkness. But their monotony haunts one like a nightmare. Even the irksomeness of finding the streets named by numbers becomes insufferable. It is doubtless convenient to know by the number how far up the city the particular street is. But you cannot give any sort of character to Fifty-third Street, for the name refuses to lend itself to any association. There is something wearisomely hard and bare in such a system.

I return joyfully to the exceptions. Boston has a character of her own, with her beautiful Common, her smooth environing waters, her Beacon Hill crowned by the gilded dome of the State House, and Bunker Hill, bearing the monument of the famous fight. New York, besides a magnificent position, has in the gigantic towerlike buildings which have since 1890 soared into her sky, as well as in the tremendous rush of men and vehicles along the streets, as much the air of a great capital as London, or Paris, or Berlin. Chicago, with her enormous size and the huge warehouses that line her endless thoroughfares, now covered by a dense smoke pall, leaves an impression which might be gloomy were it not for the stateliness of her lake front with the stretch of blue beyond. Richmond has a quaint old-world look which dwells in the memory; few cities have a prospect over shining waters finer than that which the heights of Cleveland command. Kansas City has shown how to use a noble situation, for she has laid out parks along the valleys and preserved the steep wooded slope of the bluff that rises above the broad flood of the Missouri. Washington, with its wide and beautifully graded avenues, and the glittering white of the Capitol, has become since 1880 a singularly handsome city. In April and May it has a woodland charm unequalled by any other great city in the world. Charleston has the air of an English town of last century, though lapped in a far richer vegetation, and with the shining softness of summer seas spread out before it. And New Orleans—or rather the Creole quarter of New Orleans, for the rest of the city is commonplace—is delicious, suggesting old France and Spain, yet a France and Spain strangely transmuted in this new clime. I have seen nothing in America more picturesque than the Rue Royale, with its houses of all heights, often built round a courtyard, where a magnolia or an orange tree stands in the middle, and wooden external staircases lead up to wooden galleries, the house fronts painted of all colours, and carrying double rows of balconies decorated with pretty ironwork, the whole standing languid and still in the warm soft air, and touched with the subtle fragrance of decay. Here in New Orleans the streets and public buildings, and specially the old City Hall, with the arms of Spain still upon it, speak of history. One feels, in stepping across Canal Street from the Creole quarter to the business parts of the town, that one steps from an old nationality to a new one, that this city must have had vicissitudes, that it represents something, and that something one of the great events of history, the surrender of the northern half of the New World by the Romano-Celtic races to the Teutonic. Quebec and (in some slight degree) Montreal, fifteen hundred miles away, tell the same tale; Sante Fe in New Mexico repeats it.

It is the absence in nearly all the American cities of anything that speaks of the past that makes their external aspect so unsuggestive. In pacing their busy streets and admiring their handsome city halls and churches, one's heart sinks at the feeling that nothing historically interesting ever has happened here, perhaps ever will happen. In many an English town, however ugly with its smoke and its new suburbs, one sees at least an ancient church, one can discover some fragments of a castle or a city wall. Even Wigan and Northampton have ancient churches, though Northampton lately allowed the Northwestern Railway to destroy the last traces of the castle where Henry II issued his assize. But in America hardly any public building is associated with anything more interesting than a big party convention; and, nowadays, even the big conventions are held in temporary structures, whose materials are sold when the politicians have dispersed. Nowhere, perhaps, does this sense of the absolute novelty of all things strike one so strongly as in San Francisco. Few cities in the world can vie with her either in the beauty or in the natural advantages of her situation; indeed, there are only two places in Europe—Constantinople and Gibraltar—that combine an equally perfect landscape with what may be called an equally imperial position. Before you there is the magnificent bay, with its far-stretching arms and rocky isles, and beyond it the faint line of the Sierra Nevada, cutting the clear air like mother-of-pearl; behind there is the roll of the ocean; to the left, the majestic gateway between mountains through which ships bear in commerce from the farthest shores of the Pacific; to the right, valleys rich with corn and wine, sweeping away to the southern horizon. The city itself is full of bold hills, rising steeply from the deep water. The air is keen, dry, and bright, like the air of Greece, and the waters not less blue. Perhaps it is this air and light, recalling the cities of the Mediterranean, that make one involuntarily look up to the top of these hills for the feudal castle, or the ruins of the Acropolis, which one thinks must crown them. I found myself so looking all the time I remained in the city. But on none of these heights is there anything more interesting, anything more vocal to the student of the past, than huge hotels or the sumptuous villas of railway magnates, who have chosen a hilltop to display their wealth to the city, but have erected houses like all other houses, only larger. San Francisco has had a good deal of history since 1846; but this history does not, like that of Greece or Italy, write itself in stone.

Of the uniformity of political institutions over the whole United States I have spoken already. Everywhere the same system of state governments, everywhere the same municipal governments, and almost uniformly bad or good in proportion to the greater or smaller population of the city; the same party machinery organized on the same methods, "run" by the same wire-pullers and "workers." In rural local government there are some diversities in the names, areas, and functions of the different bodies, yet differences slight in comparison with the points of likeness. The schools are practically identical in organization, in the subjects taught, in the methods of teaching, though the administration of them is as completely decentralized as can be imagined, even the state commissioner having no right to do more than suggest or report. So it is with the charitable institutions, with the libraries, the lecture courses, the public amusements. All these are more abundant and better of their kind in the richer and more cultivated parts of the country, generally better in the North Atlantic than in the inland states, and in the West than in the South. But they are the same in type everywhere. It is the same with social habits and usages. There are still some differences between the South and the North; and in the Eastern cities the upper class is more Europeanized in its code of etiquette and its ways of daily life. But even these variations tend to disappear. Eastern customs begin to permeate the West, beginning with the richer families; the South is more like the North than it was before the war. Travel where you will, you feel that what you have found in one place that you will find in another. The thing which hath been, will be: you can no more escape from it than you can quit the land to live in the sea.

Last of all we come to man himself—to man and to woman, not less important than man. The ideas of men and women, their fundamental beliefs and their superficial tastes, their methods of thinking and their fashions of talking, are what most concern their fellow men; and if there be variety and freshness in these, the uniformity of nature and the monotony of cities signify but little. If I observe that in these respects also the similarity of type over the country is surprising, I shall be asked whether I am not making the old mistake of the man who fancied all Chinese were like one another, because, noticing the dress and the pigtail, he did not notice minor differences of feature. A scholar is apt to think that all businessmen write the same hand, and a businessman thinks the same of all scholars. Perhaps Americans think all Englishmen alike. And I may also be asked with whom I am comparing the Americans. With Europe as a whole? If so, is it not absurd to expect that the differences between different sections in one people should be as marked as those between different peoples? The United States are larger than Europe, but Europe has many races and many languages, among whom contrasts far broader must be expected than between one people, even if it stretches over a continent.

It is most clearly not with Europe, but with each of the leading European peoples that we must compare the people of America. So comparing them with the people of Britain, France, Germany, Italy, Spain, one discovers more varieties between individuals in these European peoples than one finds in America. Scotchmen and Irishmen are more unlike Englishmen, the native of Normandy more unlike the native of Provence, the Pomeranian more unlike the Würtemberger, the Piedmontese more unlike the Neapolitan, the Basque more unlike the Andalusian, than the American from any part of the country is to the American from any other. Differences of course there are between the human type as developed in different regions of the country—differences moral and intellectual as well as physical. You can generally tell a Southerner by his look as well as by his speech. A native of Maine will probably differ from a native of Kentucky, a Georgian from an Oregonian. But these differences strike even an American observer much as the difference between a Yorkshireman and a Warwickshire man strikes the English, and is slighter than the contrast between a middle-class southern Englishman and a middle-class Scotchman, slighter than the differences between a peasant from Northumberland and a peasant from Dorsetshire. Or, to take another way of putting it: If at some great gathering of a political party from all parts of the United Kingdom you were to go round and talk to, say, one hundred, taken at random, of the persons present, you would be struck by more diversity between the notions and the tastes and mental habits of the individuals comprising that one hundred than if you tried the same experiment with a hundred Americans of the same education and position, similarly gathered in a convention from every state in the Union.

I do not in the least mean that people are more commonplace in America than in England, or that the Americans are less ideal than the English. Neither of these statements would be true. On the contrary, the average American is more alive to new ideas, more easily touched through his imagination or his emotions, than the average Englishman or Frenchman. I mean only that the native-born Americans appear to vary less, in fundamentals, from what may be called the dominant American type than Englishmen, Germans, Frenchmen, Spaniards, or Italians do from any type which could be taken as the dominant type in any of those nations. Or, to put the same thing differently, it is rather more difficult to take any assemblage of attributes in any of these European countries and call it the national type than it is to do the like in the United States.

These are not given as the impressions of a traveller. Such impressions, being necessarily hasty, and founded on a comparatively narrow observation, would deserve little confidence. They sum up the conclusions of Europeans long resident in America, and familiar with different parts of the country. They are, I think, admitted by the most acute Americans themselves. I have often heard the latter dilate on what seems to them the one crowning merit of life in Europe—the variety it affords, the opportunities it gives of easy and complete changes of scene and environment. The pleasure which an American finds in crossing the Atlantic, a pleasure more intense than any which the European enjoys, is that of passing from a land of happy monotony into regions where everything is redolent with memories of the past, and derives from the past no less than from the present a wealth and a subtle complexity of interest which no new country can possess.

Life in America is in most ways pleasanter, easier, simpler, less cumbered by conventions than in Europe; it floats in a sense of happiness like that of a radiant summer morning. But life in any of the great European centres is capable of an intensity, a richness blended of many elements, which has not yet been reached in America. There are more problems in Europe calling for solution; there is more passion in the struggles that rage round them; the past more frequently kindles the present with a glow of imaginative light. In whichever country of Europe one dwells, one feels that the other countries are near, that the fortunes of their peoples are bound up with the fortunes of one's own, that ideas are shooting to and fro between them. The web of history woven day by day all over Europe is vast and of many colours: it is fateful to every European. But in America it is only the philosopher who can feel that it will ultimately be fateful to Americans also; to the ordinary man the Old World seems far off, severed by a dissociating ocean, its mighty burden with little meaning for him.

Those who have observed the uniformity I have been attempting to describe have commonly set it down, as Europeans do most American phenomena, to what they call democracy. Democratic government has in reality not much to do with it, except in so far as such a government helps to induce that deference of individuals to the mass which strengthens a dominant type, whether of ideas, of institutions, or of manners. More must be ascribed to the equality of material conditions, still more general than in Europe, to the fact that nearly everyone is engaged either in agriculture, or in commerce, or in some handicraft, to the extraordinary mobility of the population, which in migrating from one part of the country to another brings the characteristics of each part into the others, to the diffusion of education, to the cheapness of literature and universal habit of reading, which enable everyone to know what everyone else is thinking, but above all to the newness of the country, and the fact that four-fifths of it have been made all at a stroke, and therefore all of a piece, as compared with the slow growth by which European countries have developed. Newness is the cause of uniformity, not merely in the external aspect of cities, villages, farmhouses, but in other things also, for the institutions and social habits which belonged a century ago to a group of small communities on the Atlantic coast, have been suddenly extended over an immense area, each band of settlers naturally seeking to retain its customs, and to plant in the new soil shoots from which trees like those of the old home might spring up. The variety of European countries is due not only to the fact that their race elements have not yet become thoroughly commingled, but also that many old institutions have survived among the new ones; as in a city that grows but slowly, old buildings are not cleared away to make room for others more suited to modern commerce, but are allowed to stand, sometimes empty and unused, sometimes half adapted to new purposes. This scarcely happens in America. Doubtless many American institutions are old, and were old before they were carried across the Atlantic. But they have generally received a new dress, which, in adapting them to the needs of today, conceals their ancient character; and the form in which they have been diffused or reproduced in the different states of the Union is in all those states practically identical.

In each of the great European countries the diversity of primeval and mediæval times, when endless varieties of race, speech, and faith existed within the space of a few hundred miles, has been more or less preserved by segregative influences. In America a small race, of the same speech and faith, has spread itself out over an immense area, and has been strong enough to impose its own type, not only on the Dutch and other early settlers of the Middle states, but on the immigrant masses who have been arriving since the middle of last century.

There are now in America more Irish people, and children of Irish people, than there are in Ireland; while large tracts in the country and some of the cities are in speech rather German than American, so much so that public documents are issued in both tongues.[5] Yet neither the Celtic nor the Teutonic incomers, much less the more recent Slavs and Italians, have as yet substantially affected the national character and habits.

May one, then, expect that when novelty has worn off, and America counts her life by centuries instead of by decades, variety will develop itself, and such complexities, or diversities, or incongruities (whichever one is to call them) as European countries present, be deeper and more numerous?

As regards the outside of things, this seems unlikely. Many of the small towns of today will grow into large towns, a few of the large towns into great cities, but as they grow they will not become less like one another. There may be larger theatres and hotels, more churches (in spite of secularist lecturers) and handsomer ones; but what is to make the theatres and churches of one city differ from those of another? Fashion and the immense facilities of intercourse tend to wear down even such diversities in the style of building or furnishing, or in modes of locomotion, or in amusements and forms of social intercourse, as now exist.

As regards ideas and the inner life of men, the question is a more difficult one. At present there are only two parts of the country where one looks to meet with the well-marked individualities I refer to. One of these is New England, where the spirit of English Puritanism, expressed in quite other forms by Emerson and his associates, did produce a peculiar type of thinking and discoursing, which has now, however, almost died out; and where one still meets, especially among the cultivated classes, a larger number than elsewhere of persons who have thought and studied for themselves, and are unlike their fellows.[6] The other part of the country is the Far West, where

---

[5] Even so far back as the presidential contest of 1892 "campaign documents" were published by the Democratic National Committee in German, French, Italian, Swedish, Norse, Polish, Dutch, Welsh, and Hebrew; and newspapers were distributed printed in Czech, Hungarian, and Spanish.

[6] The old-fashioned Puritan farmer has vanished from Massachusetts; when he went West, attracted by the greater richness of the soil, Irishmen, and now Poles also, have come in his place.

the wild life led by pioneers in exploration, or ranching, or gold-mining has produced a number of striking figures, men of extraordinary self-reliance, with a curious mixture of geniality and reckless hardihood, no less indifferent to their own lives than to the lives of others. Of preserving this latter type there was never much hope; the swift march of civilization has now almost expunged it. Before the end of the twentieth century the natural resources of the country will have been completely developed and some of them exhausted. Railway construction will have slackened. Few if any irrigation works will remain to be made. Some of the present opportunities for amassing vast fortunes will have vanished. When lines of work that are now open and stimulants to ambition that are now operative have become less numerous or less potent, upon what will the eager and restless energy of the American expend itself? Or will that eagerness itself abate when the present stimuli have become less insistent?

When one sees millions of people thinking the same thoughts and reading the same books, and perceives that as the multitude grows, its influence becomes always stronger, it is hard to imagine how new points of repulsion and contrast are to arise, new diversities of sentiment and doctrine to be developed. Nevertheless it may be hoped that as the intellectual proficiency and speculative play of mind which are now confined to a comparatively small class become more generally diffused, as the pressure of effort towards material success is relaxed, as the number of men devoted to science, art, and learning increases, so will the dominance of what may be called the business mind decline, and with a richer variety of knowledge, tastes, and pursuits, there will come also a larger crop of marked individualities, and of divergent intellectual types.

Time will take away some of the monotony which comes from the absence of historical associations; for even if, as is to be hoped, there comes no war to make battlefields famous like those of the Civil War, yet literature and the lives of famous men cannot but attach to many spots associations to which the blue of distance will at last give a romantic interest. No people could be more ready than are the Americans to cherish such associations. Their country has a short past, but they willingly revere and preserve all the memories the past has bequeathed to them.

The Temper of the West

Western America is one of the most interesting subjects of study the modern world has seen. There has been nothing in the past resembling its growth, and probably there will be nothing in the future. A vast territory, wonderfully rich in natural resources of many kinds; a temperate and healthy climate, fit for European labour; a soil generally, and in many places marvellously, fertile; in some regions mountains full of minerals, in others trackless forests where every tree is over two hundred feet high; and the whole of this virtually unoccupied territory thrown open to a vigorous race, with all the appliances and contrivances of modern science at its command— these are phenomena absolutely without precedent in history, and which cannot recur elsewhere, because our planet contains no such other favoured tract of country.[1]

The Spaniards and Portuguese settled in tropical countries, which soon enervated them. They carried with them the poison of slavery; their colonists were separated, some by long land journeys, and all by still longer voyages from the centres of civilization. But the railway and the telegraph follow the Western American. The Greeks of the sixth and seventh centuries before Christ, who planted themselves all round the coasts of the Mediterranean, had always enemies, and often powerful enemies, to overcome before they could found even their trading stations on the coast, much less occupy the lands of the interior. In Western America the presence of the Indians has done no more than give a touch of romance or a spice of danger to the

---

[1] *Note to the Edition of 1910:* This chapter, composed in 1887 after two visits to the Far West, has been left almost as it was then written, because it describes a phase of life which is now swiftly disappearing and may never be again seen elsewhere. Pioneer work in the Rocky Mountain and Pacific states is almost at an end; and these regions are becoming more like the older parts of the Republic. Yet the habits of those days have left their mark upon Western character.

exploration of some regions, such as Western Dakota and Arizona, while over the rest of the country the unhappy aborigines have slunk silently away, scarcely even complaining of the robbery of lands and the violation of plighted faith. Nature and time seem to have conspired to make the development of the Mississippi basin and the Pacific slope the swiftest, easiest, completest achievement in the whole record of the civilizing progress of mankind since the founder of the Egyptian monarchy gathered the tribes of the Nile under one government.

The details of this development and the statistics that illustrate it have been too often set forth to need restatement here. It is of the character and temper of the men who have conducted it that I wish to speak, a matter which has received less attention, but is essential to a just conception of the Americans of today. For the West is the most American part of America; that is to say, the part where those features which distinguish America from Europe come out in the strongest relief. What Europe is to Asia, what England is to the rest of Europe, what America is to England, that the Western states are to the Atlantic states, the heat and pressure and hurry of life always growing as we follow the path of the sun. In Eastern America there are still quiet spots, in the valleys of the Alleghenies, for instance, in nooks of old New England, in university towns like Ithaca or Ann Arbor. In the West there are none. All is bustle, motion, and struggle, most so of course among the native Americans, yet even the immigrant from the secluded valleys of Thuringia, or the shores of some Norwegian fjord, learns the ways almost as readily as the tongue of the country, and is soon swept into the whirlpool.

It is the most enterprising and unsettled Americans that come West; and when they have left their old homes, broken their old ties, resigned the comforts and pleasures of their former homes, they are resolved to obtain the wealth and success for which they have come. They throw themselves into work with a feverish yet sustained intensity. They rise early, they work all day, they have few pleasures, few opportunities for relaxation.[2] I remember in the young city of Seattle on Puget Sound to have found business in full swing at seven o'clock A.M.: the shops open, the streets full of people. Everything is speculative, land (or, as it is usually called, "real estate") most so, the value of lots of ground rising or falling perhaps two

---

[2] In the newer towns, which are often nothing more than groups of shanties with a large hotel, a bank, a church, an inn, some drinking saloons, and gambling houses, there are few women and no homes. Everybody, except recent immigrants, Chinese, and the very poorest native Americans, lives in the hotel.

or three hundred per cent in the year. No one has any fixed occupation; he is a storekeeper today, a ranchman tomorrow, a miner next week. I found the waiters in the chief hotel at Denver, in Colorado, saving their autumn and winter wages to start off in the spring "prospecting" for silver "claims" in the mountains. Few men stay in one of the newer cities more than a few weeks or months; to have been there a whole year is to be an old inhabitant, an oracle if you have succeeded, a byword if you have not, for to prosper in the West you must be able to turn your hand to anything, and seize the chance today which everyone else will have seen tomorrow. This venturesome and shifting life strengthens the reckless and heedless habits of the people. Everyone thinks so much of gaining that he thinks little of spending, and in the general dearness of commodities, food (in the agricultural districts) excepted, it seems not worth while to care about small sums. In California for many years no coin lower than a ten-cent piece (5d.) was in circulation; and even in 1881, though most articles of food were abundant, nothing was sold at a lower price than five cents. The most striking alternations of fortune, the great coups which fascinate men and make them play for all or nothing, are of course commoner in mining regions than elsewhere.[3] But money is everywhere so valuable for the purposes of speculative investment, whether in land, livestock, or trade, as to fetch very high interest. In Walla Walla (in what was then the Territory of Washington) I found in 1881 that the interest on debts secured on what were deemed good safe mortgages was at the rate of fourteen per cent per annum, of course payable monthly.

The carelessness is public as well as private. Tree stumps are left standing in the streets of a large and flourishing town like Leadville, because the municipal authorities cannot be at the trouble of cutting or burning them. Swamps are left undrained in the suburbs of a populous city like Portland, which every autumn were breeding malarial fevers; and the risk of accidents to be followed by actions does not prevent the railways from pushing on their lines along loosely heaped embankments, and over curved trestle bridges which seem as if they could not stand a high wind or the passage of a heavy train.

This mixture of science and rudeness is one of a series of singular contrasts which runs through the West, not less conspicuous in the minds of the people than in their surroundings. They value good government, and have a remarkable faculty for organizing some kind of government, but they

[3] In California in 1881 I was shown an estate of 600,000 acres which was said to have been lately bought for $225,000 (£45,000) by a man who had made his fortune in two years' mining, having come out without a penny.

are tolerant of lawlessness which does not directly attack their own interest. Horse-stealing and insults to women are the two unpardonable offences; all others are often suffered to go unpunished. I was in a considerable Western city, with a population of seventy thousand people, some years ago, when the leading newspaper of the place, commenting on one of the train robberies that had been frequent in the state, observed that so long as the brigands had confined themselves to robbing the railway companies and the express companies of property for whose loss the companies must answer, no one had greatly cared, seeing that these companies themselves robbed the public; but now that private citizens seemed in danger of losing their personal baggage and money, the prosperity of the city might be compromised, and something ought to be done—a sentiment delivered with all gravity, as the rest of the article showed.[4] Brigandage tends to disappear when the country becomes populous, though there are places in comparatively old states like Illinois and Missouri where the railways are still unsafe. But the same heedlessness suffers other evils to take root, evils likely to prove permanent, including some refinements of political roguery which it is strange to find amid the simple life of forests and prairies.

Another such contrast is presented by the tendency of this shrewd and educated people to relapse into the oldest and most childish forms of superstition. Fortune-telling, clairvoyance, attempts to pry by the help of "mediums" into the book of fate, are so common in parts of the West that the newspapers devote a special column, headed "astrologers," to the advertisements of these wizards and pythonesses.[5] I have counted in one issue of a San Francisco newspaper as many as eighteen such advertisements, six of which were of simple fortune-tellers, like those who used to beguile the peasant girls of Devonshire. In fact, the profession of a soothsayer or astrologer is a recognized one in California now, as it was in the Greece of Homer. Possibly the prevalence of mining speculation, possibly the existence of a large mass of ignorant immigrants from Europe, may help to account for the phenomenon, which, as California is deemed an exceptionally unreligious state, illustrates the famous saying that the less faith the more superstition.

All the passionate eagerness, all the strenuous effort of the Westerners is

---

[4] This makes plausible the story of the Texas judge who allowed murderers to escape on points of law till he found the value of real estate declining, when he saw to it that the next few offenders were hanged.

[5] Ohio in 1883 imposed a licence tax of $300 a year on "astrologers, fortune-tellers, clairvoyants, palmisters, and seers."

directed towards the material development of the country. To open the greatest number of mines and extract the greatest quantity of ore, to scatter cattle over a thousand hills, to turn the flower-spangled prairies of the Northwest into wheatfields, to cover the sunny slopes of the Southwest with vines and olives: this is the end and aim of their lives, this is their daily and nightly thought—

juvat Ismara Baccho
Conserere atque olea magnum vestire Taburnum.

The passion is so absorbing, and so covers the horizon of public as well as private life that it almost ceases to be selfish—it takes from its very vastness a tinge of ideality. To have an immense production of exchangeable commodities, to force from nature the most she can be made to yield, and send it east and west by the cheapest routes to the dearest markets, making one's city a centre of trade, and raising the price of its real estate—this, which might not have seemed a glorious consummation to Isaiah or Plato, is preached by Western newspapers as a kind of religion. It is not really, or at least it is not wholly, sordid. These people are intoxicated by the majestic scale of the nature in which their lot is cast, enormous mineral deposits; boundless prairies; forests which, even squandered—wickedly squandered—as they now are, will supply timber to the United States for centuries; a soil which, with the rudest cultivation, yields the most abundant crops; a populous continent for their market. They see all round them railways being built, telegraph wires laid, steamboat lines across the Pacific projected, cities springing up in the solitudes, and settlers making the wilderness to blossom like the rose. Their imagination revels in these sights and signs of progress, and they gild their own struggles for fortune with the belief that they are the missionaries of civilization and the instruments of Providence in the greatest work the world has seen. The following extract from a newspaper published at New Tacoma in Washington (then a Territory) expresses with frank simplicity the conception of greatness and happiness which is uppermost in the Far West; and what may seem a touch of conscious humour is, if humorous it be, nonetheless an expression of sincere conviction.

WHY WE SHOULD BE HAPPY

Because we are practically at the head of navigation on Puget Sound. Tacoma is the place where all the surplus products of the south and of the east, that are exported by way of the Sound, must be laden on board the vessels that are to carry them to the four corners of the world. We should be happy because being at the head of navigation on Puget Sound, and the shipping point for the south and the east, the centre from which shall radiate lines of commerce to every point on the circumference of the earth, we are also nearer by many miles than any other town on Puget Sound to that pass in the Cascade mountains through which the Cascade division of the Northern Pacific railroad will be built in the near future; not only nearer to the Stampede pass, but easily accessible from there by a railroad line of gentle grade, which is more than can be said of any town to the north of us.

We should be happy for these reasons and because we are connected by rail with Portland on the Willamette, with St. Paul, Chicago, and New York; because being thus connected we are in daily communication with the social, political, and financial centres of the western hemisphere; because all the people of the south and of the east who visit these shores must first visit New Tacoma; because from here will be distributed to the people of the north-west all that shall be brought across the continent on the cars, and from here shall be distributed to merchants all over the United States the cargoes of ships returning here from every foreign port to load with wheat, coal, and lumber. We should be and we are happy because New Tacoma is the Pacific coast terminus of a trans-continental line of railroad. Because this is the only place on the whole Pacific coast north of San Francisco where through freight from New York can be loaded on ship directly from the cars in which it came from the Atlantic side.

Other reasons why we should be happy are, that New Tacoma is in the centre of a country where fruits and flowers, vegetables and grain, grow in almost endless variety; that we are surrounded with everything beautiful in nature, that we have scenery suited to every mood, and that there are opportunities here for the fullest development of talents of every kind. We have youth, good health, and opportunity. What more could be asked?

If happiness is thus procurable, the Great West ought to be happy.[6] But there is often a malignant influence at work to destroy happiness in the shape of a neighbouring city, which is making progress as swift or swifter, and threatens to eclipse its competitors. The rivalry between these Western towns is intense and extends to everything. It is sometimes dignified by an unselfish devotion to the greatness of the city which a man has seen grow with his own growth from infancy to a vigorous manhood. I have known citizens of Chicago as proud of Chicago as a Londoner, in the days of

---

[6] Tacoma has one glory which the inhabitants, it is to be feared, value less than those dwelt on in the article: it commands the finest view of a mountain on the Pacific coast, perhaps in all North America, looking across its calm inlet to the magnificent snowy mass of Mount Tacoma (14,700 feet) rising out of deep dark forests thirty miles away.

Elizabeth, was proud of London. They show you the splendid parks and handsome avenues with as much pleasure as a European noble shows his castle and his pictures; they think little of offering hundreds of thousands of dollars to beautify the city or enrich it with a library or an art gallery. In other men this laudable corporate pride is stimulated, not only by the love of competition which lies deep in the American as it does in the English breast, but also by personal interest, for the prosperity of the individual is inseparable from that of the town. As its fortunes rise or fall, so will his corner lots or the profits of his store. It is not all towns that succeed. Some after reaching a certain point stand still, receiving few accessions; at other times, after a year or two of bloom, a town wilts and withers; trade declines; enterprising citizens depart, leaving only the shiftless and impecunious behind; the saloons are closed, the shanties fall to ruin, in a few years nothing but heaps of straw and broken wood, with a few brick houses awaiting the next blizzard to overthrow them, are left on the surface of the prairie. Thus Tacoma is harassed by the pretensions of the even more eager and enterprising Seattle;[7] thus the greater cities of St. Paul and Minneapolis have striven for the last twenty years for the title of Capital of the Northwest. In 1870 St. Paul was already a substantial city, and Minneapolis just beginning to be known as the possessor of immense water advantages from its position on the Mississippi at the Falls of St. Anthony. In 1883, though St. Paul contained some 135,000 inhabitants, Minneapolis with 165,000 had distanced her in the race, and had become, having in the process destroyed the beauty of her falls, the greatest flour-milling centre in America.[8] The newspapers of each of such competing cities keep up a constant war upon the other; and everything is done by municipal bodies and individual citizens to make the world believe that their city is advancing and all its neighbours standing still. Prosperity is largely a matter of advertising, for an afflux of settlers makes prosperity, and advertising, which can take many forms, attracts settlers. Many a place has lived upon its "boom" until it found something more solid to live on; and to a stranger who asked in a small Far Western town how such a city could keep up four newspapers, it was well answered that it took four newspapers to keep up such a city.

Confidence goes a long way towards success. And the confidence of these Westerner is superb. I happened in 1883 to be at the city of Bismarck in Dakota when this young settlement was laying the cornerstone of its capitol,

---

[7] Seattle has now (1910) distanced Tacoma, while St. Paul and Minneapolis have so expanded that they touch one another and are (though distinct municipalities) practically one city.

[8] In 1910 Minneapolis had 301,400 inhabitants and St. Paul 214,700.

intended to contain the halls of the legislature and other state offices of Dakota when that flourishing Territory becomes, as it soon must, a state, or perhaps, for they talk of dividing it, two states. The town was then only some five years old, and may have had six or seven thousand inhabitants. It was gaily decorated for the occasion, and had collected many distinguished guests—General U. S. Grant, several governors of neighbouring states and Territories, railroad potentates, and others. By far the most remarkable figure was that of Sitting Bull, the famous Sioux chief, who had surprised and slain a detachment of the American army some years before. Among the speeches made, in one of which it was proved that as Bismarck was the centre of Dakota, Dakota the centre of the United States, and the United States the centre of the world, Bismarck was destined to "be the metropolitan hearth of the world's civilization," there came a short but pithy discourse from this grim old warrior, in which he told us, through an interpreter, that the Great Spirit moved him to shake hands with everybody. However, the feature of the ceremonial which struck us Europeans most was the spot chosen for the capitol. It was not in the city, nor even on the skirts of the city; it was nearly a mile off, on the top of a hill in the brown and dusty prairie. "Why here?" we asked. "Is it because you mean to enclose the building in a public park?" "By no means; the Capitol is intended to be in the centre of the city; it is in this direction that the city is to grow." It is the same everywhere from the Mississippi to the Pacific. Men seem to live in the future rather than in the present; not that they fail to work while it is called today, but that they see the country not merely as it is, but as it will be, twenty, fifty, a hundred years hence, when the seedlings shall have grown to forest trees.

This constant reaching forward to and grasping at the future does not so much express itself in words, for they are not a loquacious people, as in the air of ceaseless haste and stress which pervades the West.[9] They remind you of the crowd which Vathek found in the hall of Eblis, each darting hither and thither with swift steps and unquiet mien, driven to and fro by a fire in the heart. Time seems too short for what they have to do, and result always to come short of their desire. One feels as if caught and whirled along in a foaming stream, chafing against its banks, such is the passion of these men to accomplish in their own lifetimes what in the past it took centuries to effect. Sometimes in a moment of pause, for even the visitor

---

[9] In the West men usually drop off the cars before they have stopped, and do not enter them again till they are already in motion, hanging on like bees to the end of the tail car as it quits the depot.

finds himself infected by the all-pervading eagerness, one is inclined to ask them: "Gentlemen, why in heaven's name this haste? You have time enough. No enemy threatens you. No volcano will rise from beneath you. Ages and ages lie before you. Why sacrifice the present to the future, fancying that you will be happier when your fields teem with wealth and your cities with people? In Europe we have cities wealthier and more populous than yours, and we are not happy. You dream of your posterity; but your posterity will look back to yours as the golden age, and envy those who first burst into this silent splendid nature, who first lifted up their axes upon these tall trees and lined these waters with busy wharves. Why, then, seek to complete in a few decades what the other nations of the world took thousands of years over in the older continents? Why do things rudely and ill which need to be done well, seeing that the welfare of your descendants may turn upon them? Why, in your hurry to subdue and utilize nature, squander her splendid gifts? Why allow the noxious weeds of Eastern politics to take root in your new soil, when by a little effort you might keep it pure? Why hasten the advent of that threatening day when the vacant spaces of the continent shall all have been filled, and the poverty or discontent of the older states shall find no outlet? You have opportunities such as mankind has never had before, and may never have again. Your work is great and noble: it is done for a future longer and vaster than our conceptions can embrace. Why not make its outlines and beginnings worthy of these destinies the thought of which gilds your hopes and elevates your purposes?"

Being once suddenly called upon to "offer a few remarks" to a Western legislature, and having on the spur of the moment nothing better to offer, I tendered some such observations as these, seasoned, of course, with the compliments to the soil, climate, and "location" reasonably expected from a visitor. They were received in good part, as indeed no people can be more kindly than the Western Americans; but it was surprising to hear several members who afterwards conversed with me remark that the political point of view—the fact that they were the founders of new commonwealths, and responsible to posterity for the foundations they laid, a point of view so trite and obvious to a European visitor that he pauses before expressing it— had not crossed their minds. If they spoke truly—as no doubt they did— there was in their words further evidence of the predominance of material efforts and interests over all others, even over those political instincts which are deemed so essential a part of the American character. The arrangements of his government lie in the dim background of the picture which fills a Western eye. The foreground is filled by ploughs and sawmills, ore-crushers and railway locomotives. These so absorb his thoughts as to leave little time for constitutions and legislation; and when constitutions and legislation are thought of, it is as means for better securing the benefits of the earth and of trade to the producer, and preventing the greedy corporation from intercepting their fruits.

Politically, and perhaps socially also, this haste and excitement, this absorption in the development of the material resources of the country, are unfortunate. As a town built in a hurry is seldom well built, so a society will be the sounder in health for not having grown too swiftly. Doubtless much of the scum will be cleared away from the surface when the liquid settles and cools down. Lawlessness and lynch law will disappear, saloons and gambling houses will not prosper in a well-conducted population; schools will improve and universities grow out of the raw colleges which one already finds even in the newer Territories. Nevertheless the bad habits of professional politics, as one sees them on the Atlantic coast, are not unknown in these communities; and the unrestfulness, the passion for speculation, the feverish eagerness for quick and showy results, may so soak into the texture of the popular mind as to colour it for centuries to come. These are the shadows which to the eye of the traveller seem to fall across the glowing landscape of the Great West.

The Future of Political Institutions

The task of forecasting the future is one from which a writer does well to turn away, for the coasts of history are strewn with the wrecks of predictions launched by historians and philosophers. No such ambitious task shall be essayed by me. But as I have described the institutions of the American commonwealth as they stand at this moment, seldom expressing an opinion as to their vitality or the influences which are at work to modify them, I may reasonably be asked to state, before bringing this book to a close, what processes of change these institutions seem to be at this moment undergoing. Changes move faster in our age than they ever moved before, and America is a land of change. No one doubts that fifty years hence it will differ at least as much from what it is now as it differs now from the America which Tocqueville described. The causes whose action will mould it are far too numerous, too complex, too subtly interwoven to make it possible to conjecture their joint result. All we can ever say of the future is that it will be unlike the present. I will therefore attempt, not to predict future changes, but only to indicate some of the processes of change now in progress which have gone far enough to let us see that they are due to causes of unmistakable potency, causes likely to continue in activity for some time to come.

I begin with a glance at the federal system, whose equilibrium it has been the main object of the federal Constitution to preserve. That equilibrium has been little disturbed. So far as law goes, it has suffered no change since the amendments to the Constitution which recorded and formulated the results of the Civil War. Before the war many Americans and most Europeans expected a dissolution of the Union, either by such a loosening of the federal tie as would reduce the Union to a mere league, or by the formation of several state groups wholly independent of one another. At this moment, however, nothing seems less likely than another secession. The states' rights spirit has declined. The material interests of every part of the country are bound up with those of every other. The capital of the Eastern cities has been invested in mines in the West, in iron works and manufactories in the South, in mortgages and railroads everywhere. The South and the West need this capital for their development, and are daily in closer business relations with the East. The produce of the West finds its way to the Atlantic through the ports of the East. Every produce market, every share market, vibrates in response to the Produce Exchange and Stock Exchange of New York. Each part of the country has come to know the other parts far better than was possible in earlier times; and the habit of taking journeys hither and thither grows with the always-growing facilities of travel. Many families have sons or brothers in remote states; many students come from the West and the South to Eastern universities, and form ties of close friendship there. Railways and telegraphs are daily narrowing and compressing the vast area between ocean and ocean. As the civilized world was a larger world in the days of Herodotus than it is now—for it took twice as many months to travel from the Caspian Sea to the Pillars of Hercules as it takes now to circumnavigate the globe; one was obliged to use a greater number of languages, and the journey was incomparably more dangerous—so now the United States, with their ninety millions of people, extending from the Bay of Fundy to the Gulf of California, are a smaller country for all the purposes of government, of commerce, and of social intercourse than before the purchase of Louisiana in 1803, for it took longer then to go from Boston to Charleston than it takes now to go from Portland in Maine to Portland in Oregon, and the journey was far more costly and difficult.

Even the Pacific states, which might have seemed likely to form a community by themselves, are being drawn closer to those of the Mississippi basin. Population will in time become almost continuous along the lines of the Northern and Southern Pacific Railways, and though the deserts of Nevada may remain unreclaimed, prosperous communities round the Great Salt Lake will form a link between California and the Rocky Mountain states and irrigation may create habitable oases along the courses of some of the rivers. With more frequent communication, local peculiarities and local habits of thought diminish; the South grows every day less distinctively Southern, and country-folk are more influenced by city ideas. There is now not a single state with any material interest that would be benefited, probably none with any sentiment that would be gratified, by separation from the body of the Union. No great question has arisen tending to bind states into groups and stimulating them to joint action. The chief problems which lie before the country wear an aspect substantially the same in its various sections, and public opinion is divided on them in those sections upon lines generally similar. In a word, the fact that the government is a federal one does not at this moment seem to make any difference to the cohesion of the body politic; the United States are no more likely to dissolve than if they were a unified republic like France or a unified monarchy like Italy.

As secession is improbable, so also is the extinction of the several states by absorption into the central government. It was generally believed in Europe, when the North triumphed over secession in 1865, that the federal system was virtually at an end. The legal authority of Congress and the president had been immensely developed during the struggle; a powerful army, flushed with victory, stood ready to enforce that authority; and there seemed reason to think that the South, which had fought so stubbornly, would have to be kept down during many years by military force. However, none of these apprehended results followed. The authority of the central government presently sank back within its former limits, some of the legislation based on the constitutional amendments which had extended it for certain purposes being cut down by judicial decision. The army was disbanded; self-government was soon restored in the lately insurgent states, and the upshot of the years of civil war and reconstruction has been, while extinguishing the claim of state sovereignty, to replace the formerly admitted states rights upon a legal basis as firm as they ever occupied before. At this moment states' rights are in question only so far as certain economic benefits might be obtained by a further extension of federal authority, nor has either party an interest in advocating the supersession of state action in any department of government. The conservatism of habit and well-settled legal doctrine which would resist any such proposal is very strong. State autonomy, as well as local government within each state, is prized by every class in the community, and bound up with the personal interest of those who feel that these comparatively limited spheres offer a scope to their ambition which a wider theatre might deny.

It is nevertheless impossible to ignore the growing strength of the centripetal and unifying forces. I have already referred to the influence of easier and cheaper communications, of commerce and finance, of the telegraph, of the filling up of the intermediate vacant spaces in the West. There is an increasing tendency to invoke congressional legislation to deal with matters, such as railroads, which cannot be adequately handled by state laws, or to remove divergences, such as those in the law of marriage and divorce, which give rise to practical inconveniences. So the various parties which profess to champion the interests of the farmers or of workingmen recur to the federal government as the only agency strong enough and wide-reaching enough to give effect to their proposals, most of which indeed would obviously be impracticable if tried in the narrow area of one or a few states. State patriotism, state rivalry, state vanity, are no doubt still conspicuous, yet the political interest felt in state governments is slighter than it was before the civil war, while national patriotism has become warmer and more pervasive. The role of the state is socially and morally, if not legally, smaller now than it then was, and ambitious men look on a state legislature as little more than a stepping-stone to Congress. Moreover, the interference of the federal executive to suppress by military power disorders which state authorities have seemed unable or unwilling to deal with has shown how great a reserve of force lies in its hands, and has led peace-loving citizens to look to it as their ultimate resort in troublous times. It would be rash to assert that disjunctive forces will never again reveal themselves, setting the states against the national government, and making states' rights once more a matter of practical controversy. But any such force is likely, so far as we can now see, to prove transitory, whereas the centripetal forces are permanent and secular forces, working from age to age. Wherever in the modern world there has been a centrifugal movement, tending to break up a state united under one government, or to loosen the cohesion of its parts, the movement has sprung from a sentiment of nationality, and has been reinforced, in almost every case, by a sense of some substantial grievance or by a belief that material advantages were to be secured by separation. The cases of Holland and Belgium, of Hungary and Germanic Austria, of the Greeks and Bulgarians in their struggle with the Turks, of Iceland in her struggle with Denmark, all illustrate this proposition. When such disjunctive forces are absent, the more normal tendency to aggregation and centralization prevails. In the United States all the elements of a national feeling are present, race,[1] language, literature,

---

[1] The immense influx of immigrants of various races speaking diverse languages has not greatly affected the sense of race unity, for the immigrant's child is eager to become, and does soon become, to all intents and purposes an American. Moreover, the immigrants are so dispersed over the country that no single section of them is in any state nearly equal to the native population. Here and there in the West, Germans tried to appropriate townships or villages, and keep English-speaking folk at a distance; and in Wisconsin their demand to have German taught regularly in the schools once caused some little bitterness. But these were transitory phenomena, and the very fact that the feeling of racial distinction produces no results more serious shows how far that feeling is from being a source of political danger.

pride in past achievements, uniformity of political habits and ideas; and this national feeling which unifies the people is reinforced by an immensely strong material interest in the maintenance of a single government over the breadth of the continent. It may therefore be concluded that while there is no present likelihood of change from a federal to a consolidated republic, and while the existing legal rights and functions of the several states may remain undiminished for many years to come, the importance of the states will decline as the majesty and authority of the national government increase.

The next question to be asked relates to the component parts of the national government itself. Its equilibrium stands now as stable as at any former epoch. Yet it has twice experienced violent oscillations. In the days of Jackson, and again in those of Lincoln, the executive seemed to outweigh Congress. In the days of Tyler, Congress threatened the executive; while in those of Andrew Johnson it reduced the executive to impotence. That no permanent disturbance of the balance followed the latter of these oscillations shows how well the balance had been adjusted. There is nothing now to show that any one department is gaining on any other, though whenever the president is personally a strong man, the executive may seem to be dominating Congress. The judiciary seemed in 1890 to have less discretionary power than they had exerted fifty years earlier, for by their own decisions they have narrowed the scope of their discretion, determining points in which, had they remained open, their personal impulses and views might have had room to play. But soon after new groups of questions arose, raising new issues for judicial determination, nor have the rulings of the Supreme Court ever involved larger interests or been awaited with more eager curiosity than were those delivered in 1908 and the immediately succeeding years. Congress has been the branch of government with the largest facilities for usurping the powers of the other branches, and probably with the most disposition to do so. Congress has constantly tried to encroach both on the executive and on the states, sometimes, like a wild bull driven into a corral, dashing itself against the imprisoning walls of the Constitution. But although Congress has succeeded in occupying nearly all of the area which the Constitution left vacant and unallotted between the several authorities it established, Congress has not become any more distinctly than in earlier days the dominant power in the state, the organ of national sovereignty, the irresistible exponent of the national will. In a country ruled by public opinion, it could hold this position only in virtue of its capacity for leading opinion; that is to say, of its courage, promptitude, and wisdom. Since it grows in no one of these qualities, it wins no greater ascendency;

indeed its power, as compared with that of public opinion, seems rather to decline. Its division into two coordinate houses is no doubt a source of weakness as well as of safety. Yet what is true of Congress as a whole is true of each house taken separately. The Senate, to which the eminence of many individual senators formerly gave a moral ascendency, has lost as much in the intellectual authority of its members as it has gained in their wealth. The House, with its far greater numbers and its far greater proportion of inexperienced members, suffers from the want of internal organization, and seems unable to keep pace with the increasing demands made on it for constructive legislation. Now and then the helplessness of the House when a party majority happens to be torn by internal dissensions, or the workings of self-interest visible in the Senate, when the animosities or personal aims of individual senators or groups retard or confuse its action, causes delays and leads to compromises or half measures which exasperate even this all too patient people. One is sometimes inclined to think that Congress might lose its hold on the esteem and confidence of the nation, and sink into a subordinate position, were there any other authority which could be substituted for it. There is, however, no such authority, for lawmaking cannot be given to a person or to a court, while the state legislatures have the same faults as Congress in a greater degree. We may accordingly surmise that Congress will retain its present place; but so far as can be gathered from present phenomena, it will retain this place in respect not of the satisfaction of the people with its services, but of their inability to provide a better servant.

The weakness of Congress is the strength of the president. Though it cannot be said that his office has grown in power or dignity since the days when it was held by Washington, there are reasons for believing that it has been rising to a higher point than it has occupied at any time since the Civil War. The tendency everywhere in America to concentrate power and responsibility in one man is unmistakable. There is no danger that the president should become a despot, that is, should attempt to make his will prevail against the will of the majority. But he may have a great part to play as the leader of the majority and the exponent of its will. He is in some respects better fitted both to represent and to influence public opinion than Congress is. No doubt he suffers from being the nominee of a party, because this draws on every act he does the hostility of zealots of the opposite party. But the number of voters who are not party zealots increases, increases from bad causes as well as from good causes; for as a capable president sways the dispassionately patriotic, so a crafty president can find means of playing upon those who have their own ends to serve. A vigorous personality attracts the multitude, and attracts it the more the huger it grows and the more the characteristic weakness of an assembly stand revealed; while a chief magistrate's influence, though his political opponents may complain of it, excites little alarm when exerted in leading a majority which acts through the constitutional organs of government. There may therefore be still undeveloped possibilities of greatness in store for the presidents of the future. But as these possibilities depend, like the possibilities of the British and German Crowns, perhaps one may add of the papacy, on the wholly unpredictable element of personal capacity in the men who may fill the office, we need speculate on them no further.

From the organs of government I pass to the party system, its machinery and its methods. Nothing in recent history suggests that the politicians who act as party managers, are disposed either to loosen the grip with which their organization has clasped the country, or to improve the methods it employs. Changes in party methods there will of course be in the future, as there have been in the past; but the professionals are not the men to make them changes for the better. The machine will not be reformed from within; it must be assailed from without. Three heavy blows have been lately struck at it. The first was the Civil Service Reform Act of 1883. If this act continues to be honestly administered, and its principle extended to other federal offices, if states and cities follow, as a few have done, in the wake of the national government, the Spoils System may be rooted out, and with that system the power of the machine will crumble. The Spoils System has stood since Jackson's days, and the bad habits it has formed cannot at once be unlearned. But its extinction will deprive professionals of their chief present motive for following politics. The tares which now infest the wheat will presently wither away, and the old enemy will have to sow a fresh crop of some other kind. The second blow has been the passing of secret ballot laws and other measures which have reduced the opportunities for tampering with elections, and have made them purer. And the third has been that uprising of independent citizens which has induced the enactment of the so-called Primary Laws, intended to take nominations out of the hands of the machine and place them in those of the voters as a whole. Whether these laws succeed or not, they testify to a new spirit among the better citizens, impatient of the perversion of republican institutions to selfish ends. There is now often seen in state and municipal elections, a strong group of independent men pledged to vote for honest candidates irrespective of party. The absence for a number of years past of genuine political issues dividing the two parties, if it has worked ill in taking moral and intellectual life out of the parties, and making their contests mere scrambles for office, has worked well in disposing intelligent citizens to sit more loose to party ties, and to consider, since it is really on men rather than on measures that they are required to vote, what the personal merits of candidates are. In and after 1840, at the time when the fruits of Jacksonism, that is to say, of wild democratic theory coupled with sordid and quite undemocratic practice, had begun to be felt by thoughtful persons, the urgency of the slavery question compelled the postponement of reforms in political methods, and made patriotic men fling themselves into party warfare with unquestioning zeal. When the winning of elections, no less than the winning of battles, meant the salvation of the Union, no one could stop to examine the machinery of party. For ten years after the war, the party which was usually in the majority in the North was the party which had saved the Union, and on that score commanded the devotion of its old adherents; while the opposite party was so much absorbed in struggling back to power that it did not think of mending its ways. But when the war issues had been practically settled and dismissed, public-spirited citizens at last addressed themselves to the task, which ought to have at last been undertaken in 1850, of purifying politics. Their efforts began with city government, where the evils were greatest, but have now become scarcely less assiduous in state and national politics.

Will these efforts continue, and be crowned by a growing measure of success?

To a stranger revisiting America at intervals, the progress seems to be steadily though very slowly upward. This is also the belief of those Americans who, having most exerted themselves in the struggle against bosses and spoilsmen, have had most misrepresentation to overcome and most disappointments to endure. The presidents of this generation are abler and more high-minded men than those of 1830–60, and neither the members of a knot of party managers nor its creatures. The poisonous influence of slavery is no longer felt. There is every day less of sentimentalism, but not less of earnestness in political discussions. There is less blind obedience to party, less disposition to palliate sins committed from party motives. The standard of purity among public men, especially in the Federal government, is higher. The number of able men who occupy themselves with scientific economics and politics is larger, their books and articles are more widely read. The press more frequently helps in the work of reform; the pulpit deals more largely with questions of practical philanthropy and public morals. That it should be taken as a good sign when the young men of a city throw themselves into politics, shows that the new generation is believed to have either a higher sense of public duty or a less slavish attachment to party ties than that whose votes ruled from 1870 till 1890. Above all, the nation is less self-sufficient and self-satisfied than it was in days when it had less to be proud of. In the middle of last century the Americans walked in a vain conceit of their own greatness and freedom and scorned instruction from the effete monarchies of the Old World, which repaid them with contemptuous indifference. No despot ever exacted more flattery from his courtiers than they from their statesmen. Now when Europe admires their power, envies their wealth, looks to them for instruction in not a few subjects, they have become more modest, and listen willingly to speakers and writers who descant upon their failings. They feel themselves strong enough to acknowledge their weaknesses, and are anxious that the moral life of the nation should be worthy of its expanding fortunes. As these happy omens have become more visible from year to year, there is a reasonable presumption that they represent a steady current which will continue to work for good. To judge of America rightly the observer must not fix his eye simply upon her present condition, seeking to strike a balance between the evil and the good that now appear. He must look back at what the best citizens and the most judicious strangers perceived and recorded seventy, forty, twenty years ago, and ask whether the shadows these men saw were not darker than those of today, whether the forecasts of evil they were forced to form have not in many cases been belied by the event. Tocqueville was a sympathetic as well as penetrating observer. Many of the evils he saw, and which he thought inherent and incurable, have now all but vanished. Other evils have indeed revealed themselves which he did not discern, but these may prove as transient as those with which he affrighted European readers in 1834. The men I have met in America, whose recollections went back to the fourth decade of last century, agreed in saying that there was in those days a more violent and unscrupulous party spirit, a smaller respect for law, a greater disposition to violence, less respect for the opinion of the wise, a completer submission to the prejudices of the masses, than there is today. No ignorant immigrants had yet arrived upon the scene, but New York was already given over to spoilsmen. Great corporations had scarcely arisen; yet corruption was neither uncommon nor fatal to a politician's reputation. A retrospect which shows us that some evils have declined or vanished while the regenerative forces are more numerous and more active in combating new mischiefs than they ever were before, encourages the belief that the general stream of tendency is towards improvement, and will in time bring the public life of the country nearer to the ideal which democracy is bound to set before itself.

When the Americans say, as they often do, that they trust to time, they mean that they trust to reason, to the generally sound moral tone of the multitude, to a shrewdness which after failures and through experiments learns what is the true interest of the majority, and finds that this interest coincides with the teachings of morality. They can afford to wait, because they have three great advantages over Europe—an absence of class distinctions and class hatred, a diffusion of wealth among an immense number of small proprietors all interested in the defence of property, an exemption from chronic pauperism and economical distress, work being at most times abundant, many careers open, the still undeveloped parts of the West providing a safety valve available in times of depression. With these advantages the Americans conceive that were their country now left entirely to itself, so that full and free scope could be secured to the ameliorative forces, political progress would be sure and steady; the best elements would come to the top, and when the dregs had settled the liquor would run clear.

In a previous chapter I have observed that this sanguine view of the situation omits two considerations. One is that the country is not being left to itself. European immigration continues, and though more than half of the immigrants make valuable citizens, the remainder, many by their political ignorance and instability, some few by their proneness to embrace anti-social doctrines, are a source of danger to the community, lowering its tone, providing material for demagogues to work on, threatening outbreaks like those of Pennsylvania in 1877, of Cincinnati in 1884, of Chicago in 1886 and 1894, of large districts in the West in 1893 and subsequently.

The other fact to be borne in mind is of still graver import. There is a part of the Atlantic where the westward speeding steam vessel always expects to encounter fogs. On the fourth or fifth day of the voyage, while still in bright sunlight, one sees at a distance a long low dark gray line across the bows, and is told this is the first of the fog banks which have to be traversed. Presently the vessel is upon the cloud, and rushes into its chilling embrace, not knowing what perils of icebergs may be shrouded within the encompassing gloom. So America, in her swift onward progress, sees, looming on the horizon and now no longer distant, a time of mists and shadows, wherein dangers may lie concealed whose form and magnitude she can scarcely yet conjecture. As she fills up her western regions with inhabitants, she sees the time approach when all the best land, even that which the extension of irrigation has made available, will have been occupied, and when the land now under cultivation will have been so far exhausted as to yield scantier crops even to more expensive culture. Although transportation may also have then become cheaper, the price of food will rise; farms will be less easily obtained and will need more capital to work them with profit; the struggle for existence will become more severe. And while the outlet which the West now provides for the overflow of the great cities will have become less available, the cities will have grown immensely more populous; pauperism, now confined to some six or seven of the greatest, will be more widely spread; wages will probably sink and work be less abundant. In fact the chronic evils and problems of old societies and crowded countries, such as we see them today in Europe, will have reappeared on this new soil, while the demand of the multitude to have a larger share of the nation's collective wealth may well have grown more insistent.

High economic authorities pronounce that the beginnings of this time of pressure lie years ahead. All of the best arable land in the West is already occupied; much even of the second and third best is already under cultivation; and unless agricultural science renders further aid, the exhaustion already complained of in farms which have been under the plough for three or four decades will be increasingly felt. It may be a time of trial for democratic institutions. The future of the United States during the next half century sometimes presents itself to the mind as a struggle between two forces, the one beneficent, the other malign, the one striving to speed the nation on to a port of safety before this time of trial arrives, the other to retard its progress, so that the tempest may be upon it before the port is reached. And the question to which one reverts in musing on the phenomena of American politics is this—Will the progress now discernible towards a wiser public opinion and a higher standard of public life succeed in bringing the mass of the people up to the level of what are now the best districts in the country before the days of pressure are at hand? Or will existing evils prove so obstinate, and European immigration so continue to depress the average of intelligence and patriotism among the voters, that when the struggle for life grows far harder than it now is, the masses will yield to the temptation to abuse their power and will seek violent, and because violent, probably vain and useless remedies, for the evils which will afflict them? Some such are indeed now proposed, and receive a support which, small as it is, is larger than any one would in 1870 have predicted for them.

If the crisis should arrive while a large part of the population still lacks the prudence and self-control which a democracy ought to possess, what result may be looked for? This is a question which no experience from similar crises in the past helps us to answer, for the phenomena will be new in the history of the world. There may be pernicious experiments tried in legislation. There may be—indeed there have been already—occasional outbreaks of violence. There may even be, though nothing at present portends it, a dislocation of the present frame of government. One thing, however, need not be apprehended, the thing with which alarmists most frequently terrify us: there will not be anarchy. The forces which restore order and maintain it when restored are as strong in America as anywhere else in the world.

While admitting the possibility of such a time of strife and danger, he who has studied America will not fail to note that she will have elements of strength for meeting it which are lacking in some European countries. The struggles of labour and capital, though they have of late years become more virulent, do not seem likely to take the form of a widely prevailing hatred between classes. The distribution of landed property among a great many small owners is likely to continue. The habits of freedom, together with the moderation and self-control which they foster, are likely to stand unimpaired, or to be even confirmed and mellowed by longer use. The restraining and conciliating influence of religion is stronger than in France or Germany, and more enlightened than in those continental countries where religion now seems strongest. I admit that no one can say how far the United States of fifty years hence will in these respects resemble the United States of today. But if we are to base our anticipations on the facts of today, we may look forward to the future, not indeed without anxiety, when we mark the clouds that hang on the horizon, yet with a hope that is stronger than anxiety.

C H A P T E R   1 2 3

Social and Economic Future

If it be hard to forecast the development of political institutions and habits, how much harder to form a conception of what the economic and social life of the United States will have become when another half century of marvellously swift material progress has quintupled its wealth and tripled its population; and when the number of persons pursuing arts and letters, and educated to enjoy the most refined pleasures of life, will have become proportionately greater than it is now. The changes of the last fifty years, great as they have been, may then prove to have been no greater than those which the next fifty will have brought. Prediction is even more difficult in this sphere than in the sphere of government, because the forces at work to modify society are more numerous, as well as far more subtle and complex, and because not only the commercial prosperity of the country but its thought and culture are more likely than its politics to be affected by the course of events in the Old World. All I can attempt is, as in the last preceding chapter, to call attention to some of the changes which are now in progress, and to conjecture whether the phenomena we now observe are due to permanent or to transitory causes. I shall speak first of economic changes and their influence on certain current problems, next of the movements of population and possible alterations in its character, lastly, of the tendencies which seem likely to continue to affect the social and intellectual life of the nation.

The most remarkable economic feature of the years that have elapsed since the war has been the growth of great fortunes. There is a passage in the *Federalist*, written in 1788, which says, "the private fortunes of the President and Senators, as they must all be American citizens, cannot possibly be sources of danger." Even in 1833, Tocqueville was struck by the equal distribution of wealth in the United States and the absence of

1508

capitalists. Today, however, there are more great millionaires, as well as more men with a capital of from $500,000 to $2,000,000, in America than in any other country; and before 1950 it may probably contain as many large fortunes as will exist in all the countries of Europe put together. Nor are these huge accumulations due to custom and the policy of the law, which in England keep property, and especially landed property, in the hands of a few by the so-called custom of primogeniture, whereas in the United States the influence of law has tended the other way. An American testator usually distributes his wealth among his children equally. However rich he may be, he does not expect his daughters to marry rich men, but is just as willing to see them mated to persons supporting themselves by their own efforts. And he is far more inclined than Europeans are to bestow large parts of his wealth upon objects of public utility, instead of using it to found a family. In spite of these dispersing forces, great fortunes grow with the growing prosperity of the country, and the opportunities it offers of amassing enormous piles by bold operations. Even an unspeculative business may, if skilfully conducted, bring in greater gains than can often be hoped for in Europe, because the scale of operations is in America so large that a comparatively small percentage of profit may mean a very large income. These causes are likely to be permanent; nor can any legislation that is compatible with the rights of property as now understood, do much to restrict them. We may therefore expect that the class of very rich men, men so rich as to find it difficult to spend their income in enjoying life, though they may go on employing it in business, will continue to increase.

It may be suggested that the great fortunes of today are due to the swift development of the West, so that after a time they will cease to arise in such numbers, while those we now see will have been scattered. The development of the West must, however, continue at least till the middle of the century; and though the wealthy do not seek to keep their wealth together after their death by elaborate devices, many are the sons of the rich who start with capital enough to give them a great advantage for further accumulation. There are as yet comparatively few careers to compete with business; nor is it as easy as in Europe to spend a fortune on pleasure. The idle rich of America, who, though relatively few, are numerous enough to form a class in the greatest Atlantic cities, are by no means the most contented class in the country.

The growth of vast fortunes has helped to create a political problem, for they become a mark for the invective of the more extreme sections of the Labour or Socialist parties. But should its Collectivist propaganda so far prosper as to produce legislative attacks upon accumulated wealth, such attacks will be directed (at least in the first instance), not against individual rich men, but against incorporated companies, since it is through corporations that wealth has made itself obnoxious. Why the power of these bodies should have grown so much greater in the United States than in Europe, and why they should be more often controlled by a small knot of men, are questions too intricate to be here discussed. Companies are in many ways so useful that any general diminution of the legal facilities for forming them seems improbable; but I conceive that they will be even more generally than hitherto subjected to special taxation; and that their power of taking and using public franchises will be further restricted. He who considers the irresponsible nature of the power which three or four men, or perhaps one man, can exercise through a great corporation, such as a railroad or telegraph company, the injury they can inflict on the public as well as on their competitors, the cynical audacity with which they have often used their wealth to seduce officials and legislators from the path of virtue, will find nothing unreasonable in the desire of the American masses to regulate the management of corporations and narrow the range of their action. The same remark applies, with even more force, to combinations of men not incorporated but acting together, the so-called trusts, i.e., commercial rings or syndicates. The next few years or even decades may be largely occupied with the effort to deal with these phenomena of a commercial system far more highly developed than the world has yet seen elsewhere. The economic advantages of the amalgamation of railroads and the tendency in all departments of trade for large concerns to absorb or supplant small ones, are both so marked that problems of this order seem likely to grow even larger and more urgent than they now are. Their solution will demand, not only great legal skill, but great economic wisdom.

Of the tendency to aggregation there are happily few signs so far as relates to agriculture. The only great landed estates are in the Far West, particularly in California, where they are a relic from Spanish days, together with some properties held by land companies or individual speculators in the Upper Mississippi states, properties which are being generally sold in small farms to incoming settlers. The census returns of 1900 and of 1910 did no doubt show an increase in the number of persons who hire from others the lands they till. While the increase in the number of farms cultivated by the owner during the decade ending with the latter year was only 8.1 per cent, that of farms rented for money by the cultivator was 9.9 per cent, and that of farms rented for a share of the products 20.0 per cent. This may, however, be due partly to the growth of small Negro farms in the South, partly to the disposition of many Western farmers to retire from active labour when old age approaches, letting their farms, and living on the rent thereof, partly also to the buying up of lands near a "boom town" by speculators for a rise. Taking the country as a whole, there is no indication of any serious change to large properties.[1] In the South, large plantations are more rare than before the war, and much of the cotton crop is raised by peasant farmers, as the increase in the number of farms returned in 1910 proves. It is of course possible that cultivation on a large scale may in some regions turn out to be more profitable than that of small freeholders: agriculture as an art may be still in its infancy, and science may alter the conditions of production in this highly inventive country. But at present nothing seems to threaten that system of small proprietors tilling the soil they live on which so greatly contributes to the happiness and stability of the commonwealth. The motives which in Europe induce rich men to buy large estates are here wholly wanting, for no one gains either political power or social status by becoming a landlord.

Changes in economic conditions have begun to bring about changes in population which will work powerfully on the future of society and politics. One such change has been passing on New England during the last twenty years. Its comparatively thin and ungenial soil, which has generally hard rock at no great depth below the surface, and has been cultivated in many places for nigh two hundred years, has been unable to sustain the competition of the rich and virgin lands of the West. The old race of New England yeomen have accordingly mostly sold or abandoned their farms and migrated to the upper valley of the Mississippi, where they make the prosperity of the Northwestern states. The lands which they have left vacant are frequently occupied by immigrants, sometimes French Canadians, but chiefly Irish, with some Poles and other Slavs and a few Italians, for comparatively few Germans settle in rural New England; and thus that which was the most purely English part of America is now becoming one of the least English, since the cities also are full of Irish, Jews, Slavs, and Canadians. In Massachusetts, for instance, the persons of foreign birth were in 1910 31.5 per cent of the population, while the foreign born and their children

---

[1] Of 6,361,502 farms returned in the census of 1910, 3,948,722 were cultivated by the owner and 2,354,676 rented by the farmer; and of those owned a little more than one-third (33.6) would appear to be subject to mortgages. The proportion to the whole number of dwellings not owned but hired by those who live in them is, of course, very much larger, viz., 53.5 per cent for the whole country, and 74.3 per cent for 160 cities with at least 25,000 inhabitants.

were more than half. In Rhode Island the percentages of foreigners are even higher. It is impossible not to regret the disappearance of a picturesquely primitive society which novelists and essayists have made familiar to us, with its delightful mixture of homely simplicity and keen intelligence. Of all the types of rustic life which imagination has since the days of Theocritus embellished for the envy or refreshment of the dwellers in cities, this latest type has been to modern Europe the most real and not the least attractive. It has now almost entirely passed away; nor will the life of the robust sons of the Puritans in the Northwestern prairies, vast and bare and new, reproduce the idyllic quality of their old surroundings. But the Irish squatters on the forsaken farms rear their children under better conditions than those either of the American cities or of the island of their birth, and they are replenishing New England with a vigorous stock.

Another change is now beginning to be seen, for immigration is already turning from the Northwest towards the Southern region, the far greater part of which has remained until now underdeveloped. Western North Carolina, Northern Georgia and Alabama, and Eastern Tennessee possess enormous mineral deposits, only a few of which have yet begun to be worked. There are also splendid forests; there is in many places, as for instance in the vast swamp regions of Florida, a soil believed to be fertile, much of it not yet brought under cultivation; while the climate is not, except in a very few low maritime tracts, too hot for white labour. As the vacant spaces of the West are ceasing to be able to receive the continued influx of settlers, even with the room which has been made by the migration of farmers into the Western provinces of Canada, these Southern regions will more and more attract settlers from the Northern and Western states, and these will carry with them habits and ideas which may further quicken the progress of the South, and bring her into a more perfect harmony with the rest of the country.

The mention of the South raises a group of questions, bearing on the future of the Negro and the relation she will sustain to the whites, which need not be discussed here, as they have been dealt with in preceding chapters (Chapters 93 to 95). The alarm which the growth of the coloured people formerly excited was allayed by the census of 1890, which showed that they increase more slowly than the whites, even in the South, and form a constantly diminishing proportion of the total population of the country. The Negro is doubtless a heavy burden for American civilization to carry. No problems seem likely so long to confront the nation, and so severely to tax the national character on its moral side, as those which his presence raises. Much patience will be needed, and much sympathy. The Negroes, however, are necessary to the South, which has not enough white workers; and their labour is helpful not only to the agriculturist but also to the mine-owners and iron-masters of the mining regions I have just referred to. Their progress since emancipation has been more rapid than those who saw them in slavery expected, for no section has relapsed into sloth and semi-barbarism, while in many districts there has been a steady rise in education, in intelligence, in thrift, and in the habit of sustained industry. The relation of the two races, though it presents some painful features, is not, on the whole, one of hostility, and contains no present elements of political danger. Though the great majority of the Negroes are now excluded from the exercise of the suffrage, their condition is not the same as though that gift had never been bestowed, for the fact that the Negro is legally a citizen has raised both the white's view of him and his own view of himself. Thoughtful observers in the South seem to feel little anxiety, and expect that for many years to come the Negroes, naturally a good-natured and easy-going race, will be content with the position of an inferior caste, doing the humbler kinds of work, but gradually permeated by American habits and ideas, and sending up into the walks of commercial and professional life a slowly increasing number of its most capable members. It might be thought that this elevating process would be accelerated by the sympathy of the coloured people at the North, who, as they enjoy greater educational opportunities, might be expected to advance more quickly. But the Negro race increases comparatively slowly to the north of latitude 40°, and does not make sufficient progress in wealth and influence to be able to help its Southern members.[2]

Two other questions relating to changes in population must be adverted to before we leave this part of the subject. There are Europeans who hold—and in this physiologically-minded age it is natural that men should hold—that the evolution of a distinctively American type of character and manners must be still distant, because the heterogeneous elements of the population (in which the proportion of English blood is smaller now than it was in 1850) must take a long time to become mixed and assimilated. This is a plausible view; yet I doubt whether differences of blood have the importance which it assumes. What strikes the traveller, and what the Americans themselves delight to point out, is the amazing solvent power which

---

[2] In 1790 the coloured people were 19.3 per cent of the total population of the United States, and in 1880 only 13.1. In 1900 the percentage had sunk to 11.6, in 1910 to 10.7, and is still on the decrease.

American institutions, habits, and ideas exercise upon newcomers of all races. The children of Irishmen, Germans, and Scandinavians are certainly far more like native Americans than the current views of heredity would have led us to expect; nor is it without interest to observe that Nature has here repeated on the Western continent that process of mixing Celtic with Germanic and Norse blood which she began in Britain more than a thousand years ago. The ratio borne by the Celtic elements in the population of Great Britain (i.e., the Picts and Gaels of Northern Britain and those of the Cymry of Middle and Western Britain who survived the onslaught of the Angles and Saxons in the fifth and sixth centuries) to the Teutonic (Low German and Norse) elements in that population as it stood in the seventeenth century, when England began to colonize North America, may probably be a ratio not much smaller than that which the Irish immigrants to America bear to the German immigrants; so that the relative proportions of Celtic and Teutonic blood, as these proportions may be taken to have existed in the Americans of a hundred years ago, have not been greatly altered by Irish and German immigration.[3]

On the whole, we may conclude that the intellectual and moral atmosphere into which the settlers from Europe come has more power to assimilate them than their race qualities have power to change it; and that the future of America will be less affected by this influx of new blood, even Italian and Slavonic blood, than anyone who has not studied the facts on the spot can realize. The influence of European immigration is so far to be traced, not in any tinging of the national character, but economically in the amazingly swift growth of the agricultural West, and politically in the unfortunate results it has had upon the public life of cities, in the outbreaks of savage violence which may be traced to it, particularly in the mining districts, and in the severe strain it has put on universal suffrage. Another possible source of evil has caused disquiet. The most conspicuous evidence of American prosperity has been hitherto seen in the high standard of living to which the native working classes of the North have risen, in the abundance of their food and the quality of their clothing, in the neatness and comfort of their homes, in the decent orderliness of their lives, and the fondness for

---

[3] The analogy may be carried one step farther by observing that the Scandinavians who now settle in the Northwestern states, as they have come to America later than Celts or Germans, so also have come in a proportion to Celts and Germans corresponding to that borne to the previous inhabitants of Britain by the Danes and Norwegians who poured their vigorous blood into the veins of the English race from the ninth century onwards. The larger and more obscure question of the influence of Slavonic, Jewish, and Italian immigrants has been dealt with in Chapter 92.

reading of their women. The Irish and German settlers of last century, though at first behind the native Americans in all these respects, have now risen to their level and, except in a few of the larger cities, have adopted American standards of comfort. Will the same thing happen with the new swarms of European immigrants who have been drawn from their homes in the eastern parts of Central Europe by the constant cheapening of ocean transit and by that more thorough drainage, so to speak, of the inland regions of Europe which is due to the extension of railways?[4]

Some have feared that possibly these immigrants, coming from a lower stratum of civilization than the German immigrants of the past, and, since they speak foreign tongues, less quickly amenable to American influences than are the Irish, retain their own low standard of decency and comfort, and menace the continuance among the white work people of that far higher standard which has hitherto prevailed. But experience has hitherto shown that these latest comers, though they live far more roughly than native Americans, soon cease to be content with lower wages, so if they do depress the average of decent living, it will not be through underbidding the older inhabitants.

The intrusion of these inauspicious elements is not the only change in the population which may cause anxiety. For many years past there has been an indraught of people from the rural districts to the cities. More than one-third of the whole population is now, it is estimated, to be found in cities with a population exceeding eight thousand, and the transfer of people from a rural to an urban life goes on all the faster because it is due not merely to economic causes, such as operate all the world over, and to the spirit of enterprise which is strong in the American youth, but also to the distaste which the average native American, a more sociable and amusement-loving being than the English or German peasant, feels for the isolation of farm life and the monotony of farm labour.[5] Even in 1844 R. W. Emerson wrote:

---

[4] The largest percentages of increase of foreign population, where absolute numbers were significant, were, in the decade of 1900–10 the following: Persons born in Hungary 240.1 per cent, in Russia 177.4 per cent, in Italy 177.5 per cent, in Austria 139.2 per cent. In the preceding decade these percentages had been 133, 132, 165, and 124, respectively.

[5] There is sometimes a scarcity of labour on farms in the Eastern states, while the cities are crowded with men out of work.

The percentage of urban to total population, which in 1790 was 3.35, was, in 1890, 29.12, in 1900, 33.1, and in 1910, 46.3. In the New England and Middle Atlantic states it was 83.3 and 71 per cent, respectively, of the population. The increase in these states was chiefly in Massachusetts, New Jersey, and Pennsylvania, and a part was of course due to the large increase of immigration into New York City.

"The cities drain the country of the best part of its population, the flower of the youth of both sexes goes into the towns, and the country is cultivated by a much inferior class." Since then the Western forests have been felled and the Western prairies brought under the plough by the stalwart sons of New England and New York. But now again, and in the West hardly less than in the East, the complaint goes up that native American men and women long for a city life, and gladly leave tillage to the newcomers from Germany and Scandinavia. To make rural life more attractive and so check the inflow to the cities, is one of the chief tasks of American statesmanship today. Fortunately, the introduction of the telephone, of electric car lines traversing the rural districts, of automobiles, and of a delivery of letters over the country are all tending to reduce the loneliness and isolation which have made country life distasteful.

Whether a city-bred population will have the physical vigour which the native rural population has shown—a population which in some of the Western states strikes one as perhaps more vigorous than any Europe can point to—is at least doubtful, for though American cities have sanitary advantages greater than those of most towns in Europe, the stress and strain of their city life is more exhausting. And it need scarcely be added that in the oldest and most highly civilized districts of the country, and among the more refined sections of the people, the natural increase of population is much smaller than it is among the poorer and the ruder.

We have been wont to think of the principle of natural selection as that which makes for the progress of the race in mankind, as it has done in the other families of animated creatures. But in the most advanced communities this principle is apt to be reversed, and the section of the population which tends to propagate itself most largely is that very section which is least fitted to raise, or even to sustain, the intellectual and moral level, as well as the level of physical excellence, already attained. Marriages are later and families smaller among the best nurtured and most cultivated class than they are among the uneducated and improvident; more children are born to the physically weak and morally untrained than to those among the rich whose natural gifts would in ages of violence, when men and families survived by physical and mental strength, have enabled them to prevail in the struggle for existence. Thus a force which once worked powerfully for the improvement of a national stock has now been turned the other way, and makes for a decline in the average capacities wherewith each man is born into the world. So in New England and the Eastern states generally, though there are a few families, historic by the number of eminent names they have produced, which still flourish and count their cousinhood by hundreds, it is nevertheless true that the original English stock, if it maintains its numbers (which seems in some parts of the country to be doubtful), grows less swiftly than do the immigrant stocks, and far less swiftly than it did a century ago.[6] Yet here also that assimilative power of which I have spoken comes to the help of the nation. Those who rise from the less cultivated classes, whether of native or foreign extraction, are breathed upon by the spirit of the country; they absorb its culture and carry on its traditions; and they do so all the more readily because the pervading sense of equality makes a man's entrance into a class higher than that wherein he was born depend solely on his personal qualities.

European readers may ask whether the swift growth not only of wealth but of great fortunes in the United States will not end in creating an aristocracy of rich families, and therewith a new structure of society. I see no ground for expecting this, not merely because the wealthiest class passes down by imperceptible gradations of fortune to a working class far better off than the working classes of Europe, but also because the faith in equality and the love of equality are too deeply implanted in every American breast to be rooted out by any economic changes. They are the strongest beliefs and passions of the people. They make no small part of the people's daily happiness; and I can more easily imagine the United States turned into a monarchy on the one hand or a group of petty republics on the other than the aristocratic ideas and habits of Germany established on American soil. Social exclusiveness there may be—signs of it are already discernible—but visible and overt recognitions of differences of rank, whether in the use of hereditary titles, or in the possession by one class of special privileges, or in the habit of deference by one class to another, would imply a revolution in national ideas, and a change in what may be called the chemical composition of the national mind, which is of all things the least likely to arrive.

I have left to the last the most difficult problem which a meditation on

[6] General F. A. Walker gave the rate of increase of the native whites generally in the United States at 31.25 per cent in the decade 1870–80, but that of native whites born of native parents at 28 per cent. The thirteenth census, 1910, gives the rate of increase in the years 1900–10 as 20.8 per cent of native whites, and of native whites born of native parents as 20.9 per cent. The average size of the family decreased in 1870–80 from 5.09 persons to 5.04. In 1900 it had further fallen to 4.7 and in 1910 to 4.5 and in some of the states where the population is most largely native born it was still lower, e.g., Maine (4.20), New Hampshire (4.20), Indiana (4.20), whereas in the South it was comparatively high, e.g., West Virginia (4.90), Texas (4.9), North Carolina (5.00).

the future of American society raises. From those first days of the Republic in which its people realized that they were Americans and no longer merely English colonists, it has been a question of the keenest interest for them, as it is now for the world, when and how and in what form they would develop a distinctively new and truly national type of character and genius. In 1844 Emerson said, addressing those who had lately seen the coincidence of two fateful phenomena—the extension of railways into the West and the establishment of lines of swift ocean steamers to Europe:

> We in the Atlantic States by position have been commercial and have imbibed easily a European culture. Luckily for us, now that steam has narrowed the Atlantic to a strait, the nervous rocky West is intruding a new and continental element into the national mind, and we shall yet have an American genius. We cannot look on the freedom of this country in connection with its youth without a presentiment that here shall laws and institutions exist on some scale of proportion to the majesty of nature. To men legislating for the area between the two oceans, betwixt the snows and the tropics, somewhat of the gravity of nature will infuse itself into the code.

Since these words were spoken, many events have intervened to delay that full expression of the national gifts in letters and arts, as well as in institutions, by which a modern people must reveal the peculiar nature of its genius. Emerson would doubtless have admitted in 1874 that the West had contributed less of a "new and continental element" than he expected, and that the majesty of nature had not yet filled Congress with its inspiration. Probably another generation must arise, less preoccupied with the task of material development than the two last have been, before this expression can be looked for. Europe, which used to assume in its contemptuous way that neither arts nor letters could be expected from commercial America— as Charles Lamb said that the whole Atlantic coast figured itself to him as one long counter spread with wares—Europe has now fallen into the opposite error of expecting the development of arts and letters to keep pace with and be immediately worthy of the material greatness of the country. And the Americans themselves have perhaps, if a stranger may be pardoned the remark, erred in supposing that they made, either in the days of the first settlements or in those when they won their independence, an entirely new departure, and that their new environment and their democratic institutions rendered them more completely a new people than the children of England, continuing to speak the English tongue and be influenced by European literature, could in truth have been expected to become. As Protestants have been too apt to forget the traditions of the mediæval church, and to renounce the glories of St. Anselm and St. Bernard and Dante, so the Americans of 1850—for this is a mistake which they have now outgrown—sought to think of themselves as superior in all regards to the aristocratic society from which they had severed themselves, and looked for an elevation in their character and an originality in their literature which neither the amplitude of their freedom nor the new conditions of their life could at once produce in the members of an ancient people.

What will be either the form or the spirit of transatlantic literature and thought when they have fully ripened is a question on which I do not attempt to speculate, for the forces that shape literature and thought are the subtlest the historian has to deal with. I return to the humbler task of pointing to causes whose already apparent power is producing a society such as has never yet been seen in Europe. Nowhere in the world is there growing up such a vast multitude of intelligent, cultivated, and curious readers. It is true that of the whole population a vast majority of the men read little but newspapers, and many of the women little but fiction. Yet there remains a number to be counted by millions who enjoy and are moved by the higher products of thought and imagination; and it must be that as this number continues to grow, each generation rising somewhat above the level of its predecessors, history and science, and even poetry, will exert a power such as they have never yet exerted over the masses of any country. And the masses of America seem likely to constitute one-half of civilized mankind. There are those now living who may see before they die three hundred millions of men dwelling between the Atlantic and the Pacific, obeying the same government, speaking the same tongue, reading the same books. A civilized society like this is so much vaster than any which history knows of, that we can scarcely figure to ourselves what its character will be, nor how the sense of its immensity will tell upon those who address it. The range of a writer's power will be such as no writers have ever yet possessed; and the responsibility which goes hand in hand with the privilege of moving so great a multitude will devolve upon the thinkers and poets of England hardly less than upon those of America.

The same progress which may be expected in the enjoyment of literature and in its influence may be no less expected in the other elements of what we call civilization. Manners are becoming in America more generally polished, life more orderly, equality between the sexes more complete, the refined pleasures more easily accessible than they have ever yet been among the masses of any people. And this civilization attains a unity and harmony which makes each part of the nation understand the other parts more perfectly, and enables an intellectual impulse to be propagated in swifter waves of light than has been the case among the far smaller and more ancient states of Europe.

While this unity and harmony strengthen the cohesion of the Republic, while this diffused cultivation may be expected to overcome the economic dangers that threaten it, they are not wholly favourable to intellectual creation, or to the variety and interest of life. I will try to explain my meaning by describing the impression which stamps itself on the mind of the stranger who travels westward by railway from New York to Oregon. In Ohio he sees communities which a century ago were clusters of log huts among forests, and which are now cities better supplied with all the appliances of refined and even luxurious life than were Philadelphia and New York in those days. In Illinois he sees communities which were in 1848 what Ohio was in 1805. In the newer states of Wyoming and Washington he sees settlements just emerging from a rudeness like that of primitive Ohio or Illinois, and reflects that such as Ohio is now, such as Illinois is fast becoming, such in a few years more will Wyoming and Washington have become, the process of development moving, by the help of science, with an always accelerated speed. "If I return this way twenty years hence," he thinks, "I shall see, except in some few tracts which nature has condemned to sterility, nothing but civilization, a highly developed form of civilization, stretching from the one ocean to the other; the busy, eager, well-ordered life of the Hudson will be the life of those who dwell on the banks of the Yellowstone, or who look up to the snows of Mount Shasta from the valleys of California." The Far West has hitherto been to Americans of the Atlantic states the land of freedom and adventure and mystery, the land whose forests and prairies, with trappers pursuing the wild creatures, and Indians threading in their canoes the maze of lakes, have touched their imagination and supplied a background of romance to the prosaic conditions which surround their own lives. All this is fast vanishing; and as the world has by slow steps lost all its mystery since the voyage of Columbus, so America will from end to end be to the Americans even as England is to the English. What new background of romance will be discovered? Where will the American imagination of the future seek its materials when it desires to escape from dramas of domestic life? Where will bold spirits find a field in which to relieve their energies when the Western world of adventure is no more? As in our globe so in the North American continent, there will be something to regret when all is known and the waters of civilization have covered the tops of the highest mountains.

He who turns away from a survey of the government and society of the United States and tries to estimate the place they hold in the history of the world's progress cannot repress a slight sense of disappointment when he compares what he has observed and studied with that which idealists have hoped for, and Americans have desired to establish. "I have seen," he says, "the latest experiment which mankind have tried, and the last which they can ever hope to try under equally favouring conditions. A race of unequalled energy and unsurpassed variety of gifts, a race apt for conquest and for the arts of peace, which has covered the world with the triumphs of its sword, and planted its laws in a hundred islands of the sea, sent the choicest of its children to a new land, rich with the bounties of nature, bidding them increase and multiply, with no enemies to fear from Europe, and few of those evils to eradicate which Europe inherits from its feudal past. They have multiplied till the sapling of two centuries ago overtops the parent trunk; they have drawn from their continent a wealth which no one dreamed of; they have kept themselves aloof from Old World strife, and have no foe in the world to fear; they have destroyed, after a tremendous struggle, the one root of evil which the mother country in an unhappy hour planted among them. And yet the government and institutions, as well as the industrial civilization of America, are far removed from that ideal commonwealth which European philosophers imagined, and Americans expected to create." The feeling expressed in these words, so often heard from European travellers, is natural to a European, who is struck by the absence from America of many of those springs of trouble to which he has been wont to ascribe the ills of Europe. But it is only the utterance of the ever-fresh surprise of mankind at the discovery of their own weaknesses and shortcomings. Why should either philosophers in Europe or practical men in America have expected human nature to change when it crossed the ocean? When history could have told them of many ideals not less high and hopes not less confident than those that were formed for America which have been swallowed up in night. The vision of a golden age has often shimmered far off before the mind of men when they have passed through some great crisis, or climbed to some specular mount of faith, as before the traveller when he has reached the highest pastures of the Jura, the line of Alpine snows stands up and glitters with celestial light. Such a vision seen by heathen antiquity still charms us in that famous poem of Virgil's which was long believed to embody an inspired prophecy. Such another rejoiced the souls of pious men in the days of Constantine, when the Christian church, triumphant over her enemies, seemed about to realize the kingdom of heaven upon earth. Such a one reappeared to the religious reformers of the sixteenth century, who conceived that when they had purged Christianity of its corrupt accretions, the world would be again filled with the glory of God, and men order their lives according to His law. And such a vision transported men just a century ago, when it was not unnaturally believed that in breaking the fetters by which religious and secular tyranny had bound the souls and bodies of men, and in proclaiming the principle that government sprang from the consent of all, and must be directed to their good, enough had been done to enable the natural virtues of mankind to secure the peace and happiness of nations. Since 1789 many things have happened, and men have become less inclined to set their hopes upon political reforms. Those who still expect a general amelioration of the world from sudden changes look to an industrial and not a political revolution, or seek in their impatience to destroy all that now exists, fancying that from chaos something better may emerge. In Europe, whose thinkers have seldom been in a less cheerful mood than they are today, there are many who seem to have lost the old faith in progress; many who feel when they recall the experiences of the long pilgrimage of mankind, that the mountains which stand so beautiful in the blue of distance, touched here by flashes of sunlight and there by shadows of the clouds, will when one comes to traverse them be no Delectable Mountains, but scarred by storms and seamed by torrents, with wastes of stone above, and marshes stagnating in the valleys. Yet there are others whose review of that pilgrimage convinces them that though the ascent of man may be slow it is also sure; that if we compare each age with those which preceded it we find that the ground which seems for a time to have been lost is ultimately recovered, we see human nature growing gradually more refined, institutions better fitted to secure justice, the opportunities and capacities for happiness larger and more varied, so that the error of those who formed ideals never yet attained lay only in their forgetting how much time and effort and patience under repeated disappointment must go to that attainment.

This less sombre type of thought is more common in the United States than in Europe, for the people not only feel in their veins the pulse of youthful strength, but remember the magnitude of the evils they have vanquished, and see that they have already achieved many things which the Old World has longed for in vain. And by so much as the people of the United States are more hopeful, by that much are they more healthy. They do not, like their forefathers, expect to attain their ideals either easily or soon; but they say that they will continue to strive towards them, and they say it with a note of confidence in the voice which rings in the ear of the

European visitor, and fills him with something of their own hopefulness. America has still a long vista of years stretching before her in which she will enjoy conditions far more auspicious than any European country can count upon. And that America marks the highest level, not only of material well-being, but of intelligence and happiness, which the race has yet attained, will be the judgment of those who look not at the favoured few for whose benefit the world seems hitherto to have framed its institutions, but at the whole body of the people.

A P P E N D I X   I

Note to Chapter 61

EXPLANATION (BY MR. G. BRADFORD) OF THE NOMINATING MACHINERY AND ITS PROCEDURE IN THE STATE OF MASSACHUSETTS[1]

1. By an Act of the Massachusetts legislature of 1909, the whole elective organization of the City of Boston was changed. The two branches of twelve aldermen elected at large and seventy-five councilmen elected by wards and precincts, as well as the system of ward primaries and ward and city committees, were abolished. In place of a mayor elected for two years, he was to be elected for four years, subject to recall at the end of two years by not less than a majority of all the voters in the city. The new city council was to consist of nine members elected at large for three years, renewable by three members elected in each year.

The sweeping character of the change may be best described by two Sections of the new Act:

SECTION 52. No primary election or caucus for municipal offices shall be held hereafter in the city of Boston, and all laws relating to primary elections and caucuses for such offices in said city are hereby repealed.

SECTION 53. Any male qualified registered voter in said city may be nominated for any municipal elective office in said city, and his name as such candidate shall be printed on the official ballot to be used at the municipal election: *provided,* that at or before five o'clock P.M. of the twenty-fifth day prior to such election nomination papers prepared and issued by the election commissioners, signed in person by at least five thousand registered voters in said city qualified to vote for such candidate at said election, shall be filed with said election commissioners, and the signatures on the same to the number required to make a nomination are subsequently certified by the election commissioners as hereinafter provided.

---

[1] In Mr. Bradford, who died since he revised this note (in 1910), Massachusetts lost a singularly thoughtful and public-spirited citizen.

The Act is mandatory in Boston, and its acceptance optional with other cities and towns of which thirteen have thus far been reported as voting in favor of it.

2. *County.* The county is much less important in New England than in any other part of the country. There are to be chosen, however, county commissioners (three in number, one retiring each year, having charge of roads, jails, houses of correction, registry of deeds, and, in part of the courts), county treasurer, registrar of deeds, registrar of probate, and sheriff. These candidates are nominated by party conventions of the county, called by a committee elected by the last county convention. The delegates are selected by ward and town primaries at the same time with other delegates.

3. *State.* First as to representatives to State legislature, 240 in number. The State is districted as nearly as may be in proportion to population. If a ward of a city, or a single town, is entitled to a representative, the party candidate is nominated in the primary, and must be by the Constitution (of the State) a resident in the district. If two or more towns, or two or more wards send a representative in common, the candidate is nominated in cities by a joint caucus of the wards interested called by the ward and city committee, and in towns by a convention called by a committee elected by the previous convention. The tendency in such cases is that each of these towns or wards shall have the privilege of making nomination in turn of one of its residents.

As regards senators the State is divided into forty districts. The district convention to nominate candidates is called by a committee elected by the preceding convention, and consists of delegates elected by ward and town primaries at the same time with those for State, county, and councillor conventions. Each senatorial district convention elects one member of the State central committee, and, among the Democrats, fifteen members at large are added to this central committee by the last preceding State convention.

The convention for nominating members of the governor's council (eight in number) also appoints a committee to call the next convention.

The State convention consists of delegates from ward and town primaries in proportion to their party votes at last elections, and is summoned by the State central committee, consisting of forty members, elected in October by senatorial convention, and taking office on 1st January. The State committee organizes by choice of chairman, secretary, treasurer, and executive committee, who oversee the whole State campaign. The State convention nominates the party candidates for governor, lieutenant-governor, secretary of state, treasurer, auditor, attorney-general.

4. *National.* First, representatives to Congress. Massachusetts is now (1910) entitled to fourteen, and is divided into fourteen districts. The convention in each district to nominate party candidates is called every two years by a committee elected by the last convention. The delegates from wards and primaries are elected at the same time with the other delegates. As United States senators are chosen by the State legislatures, no nominating convention is needed, though it has been suggested that the nominations might with advantage be made in the State convention, and be morally binding on the party in the legislature. Next are to be chosen, every four years, delegates to the National convention,—that is, under present party customs, two for each senator and representative of the State in Congress. For Massachusetts, therefore, at the present time, thirty-two. The delegates corresponding to the representative districts are nominated by a convention in each district, called in the spring by the same committee which calls the congressional representative nominating convention in the autumn. The delegates corresponding to senators are chosen at a general convention in the spring, called by the State central committee from wards and primaries, as always; and the thirty-two delegates at the meeting of the National convention choose the State members of the National committee.

The National convention for nominating party candidates for President, called by a National committee, elected one member by the delegates of each State at the last National convention. The National convention (and this is true in general of all conventions) may make rules for its own procedure and election—as, for example, that all State delegates shall be chosen at large instead of by districts. At the National conventions, especially of the Republicans, complaint has been frequently made, as in the case of city committees, that parts of the country in which there are very few members of the party have yet an undue share of representation in the conventions; but no successful plan has yet been devised for overcoming the difficulty. The National committee manage the party campaign, sending money and speakers to the weaker States, issue documents, collect subscriptions, and dispense general advice.

Note to Chapter 90

REMARKS BY MR. DENIS KEARNEY
ON "KEARNEYISM IN CALIFORNIA"

After the appearance of the first edition of this book I received a letter from Mr. Denis Kearney, taking exception to some of the statements contained in the chapter entitled "Kearneyism in California." This letter is unfortunately too long to be inserted as a whole; and it does not seem to me seriously to affect the tenor of the statements contained in that chapter, which my Californian informants, on whom I can rely, declare to be quite correct. I have, however, in a few passages slightly modified the text of the former edition; and I give here such extracts from Mr. Kearney's letter as seem sufficient to let his view of his own conduct be fairly and fully set forth. As he responded to my invitation to state his case, made in reply to his letter of remonstrance, I am anxious that all the justice I can do him should be done.[1]

Page 431.* "In September, 1877, immediately after the general State, municipal, and congressional elections, I called a meeting of working men and others to discuss publicly the propriety of permanently organizing for the purpose of holding the politicians up to the pledges made to the people before election. . . . I made up my mind that if our civilization—California civilization—was to continue, Chinese immigration must be stopped, and I saw in the people the power to enforce that 'must.' Hence the meeting. This meeting resolved itself into a permanent organization, and 'resoluted' in favour of a 'red-hot' agitation. I was, in spite of my earnest protests, elected President of this new organization, with instructions from the meeting to 'push the organization' throughout the city and State without delay. Our aim was to press Congress to take action against the Chinese at its next sitting. . . ."

Page 432.† "True I am not one of the literati, that is to say, a professor of degrees and master of languages, although I can speak more than one. For more than thirty years I have been a great reader and close student of men and measures. No *Chronicle* reporter ever wrote or dressed up a speech for me. They did the reverse; always made it a point to garble and misrepresent. It was only when the *Chronicle* saw where it could make a hit that it spread out a speech. To illustrate, if I attacked a monopoly whose rottenness the *Chronicle* shielded for money, it then would garble and misrepresent that speech; but if I attacked an institution the *Chronicle* wanted to blackmail, the speech would be given in full once or twice, or they would keep it up until 'seen.' "

Page 433.‡ (Meeting on Nob Hill.)

---

[1] *Note to Edition of 1910:* Mr. Kearney died in 1907.
* *Publisher's Note:* p. 1071 in the present edition.
† *Publisher's Note:* p. 1072 in the present edition.
‡ *Publisher's Note:* p. 1073 in the present edition.

"I did not use any such language as is imputed to me. Nob Hill is the centre of the Sixth Ward, and I advertised for the meeting there to organize the Sixth Ward Club. We had bonfires at all our meetings so as to direct the people where to go. . . . No such construction could have been put upon the language used in my speech of that evening. The police authorities had shorthand reporters specially detailed to take down my speeches verbatim. . . . I was not arrested on account of the Nob Hill meeting. I cannot now tell without looking up the matter how many times I was arrested. At last the authorities, finding their efforts to break up the movement of no avail, decided to proclaim the meetings *à la* Balfour in Ireland."

Page 435.* "Shortly after the election of the delegates I made a tour of the United States, speaking everywhere to immense audiences and urging that they petition Congress to stop Chinese immigration. . . . My trip was a brilliant success. In less than a year I had succeeded in lifting the Chinese from a local to a great national question. This also disputes the statement that my trip East was a failure."

Page 441.† ("Since 1880 he has played no part in Californian politics.")

"This is true to this extent. I stopped agitating after having shown the people their immense power, and how it could be used. The Chinese question was also in a fair way of being solved. The plains of this State were strewn with the festering carcasses of public robbers. I was poor, with a helpless family, and I went to work to provide for their comfort. Common sense would suggest that if I sought office, or the emoluments of office, I could easily have formed combinations to be elected either governor of my State or United States senator."

Page 436‡ ("hoodlums and other ragamuffins who formed the first Sand Lot meetings.")

"It was only when the city authorities, who while persecuting us, either hired all of the halls or frightened their owners or lessees into not allowing us to hire them, that we were driven to the Sand Lots. At these early meetings we sometimes had to raise from $500 to $1000 to carry on the agitation inside and outside the courts. If, then, the audiences were composed of hoodlums and ragamuffins, how could we have raised so much money at a single meeting?"

Page 440.§ "I also dispute some of the statements therein. All of the bills

---

* *Publisher's Note:* p. 1074 in the present edition.
† *Publisher's Note:* p. 1080 in the present edition.
‡ *Publisher's Note:* p. 1075 in the present edition.
§ *Publisher's Note:* p. 1079 in the present edition.

of the first session of the Legislature under the new Constitution were declared unconstitutional by the State Supreme Court on account of the little scheming jokers tucked away in them. The Anti-Chinese Bills that were passed—and all introduced were passed—were declared by the Federal judges as in conflict with the United States Constitution. I advocated the adoption of the new Constitution, and delivered one hundred and thirty speeches in that campaign. The San Francisco papers sent correspondents with me. The very prominence of the questions threw me into the *foreground*, so that I had to stand the brunt of the battle, and came very near being assassinated for my pains."

Page 443.* "I don't quite understand what you mean by the 'solid classes.' The money-lenders, land monopolists, and those who were growing rich by importing and employing Chinese labourers were against me, and did all in their power to kill both the movement and myself. . . . My only crime seems to have been that I opposed the Mongolization of my State in the interest of our own people and their civilization. I never received a dollar from public office or private parties for my services. They were gratuitous, and have secured me, I am sure, the esteem of the majority of my fellow-citziens, among whom I am still not without influence."

* *Publisher's Note:* p. 1081 in the present edition.

The Predictions of Hamilton and de Tocqueville

By James Bryce

A student of American institutions who desires to discover what have been the main tendencies ruling and guiding their development, may find that the most dramatic and not the least instructive method of conducting his inquiry is to examine what were the views held, and the predictions delivered, at different points in the growth of the Republic, by acute and well-informed observers. The contemporary views of such men as to the tendencies which prevailed in their own day and the results to be expected from such tendencies have a value that no analysis made by us now, with our present lights, our knowledge of what has actually followed, could possess, because we cannot help reading into the records of the past the results of all subsequent experience.

To do this with any approach to completeness would be a laborious undertaking, for one would have to search through a large number of writings, some of them fugitive writings, in order to gather and present adequate materials for determining the theories and beliefs generally prevalent at any given period. I attempt nothing so ambitious. I desire merely to indicate, by a comparatively simple example, how such a method may be profitably followed, disclaiming any pretensions to have sought to exhaust even the obvious and familiar materials which all students of American history possess.

For this purpose, then, I will take two famous books—the one written at the very birth of the Union by those who watched its cradle, and recording

Publishers Note: The Predictions of Hamilton and de Tocqueville by James Bryce originally appeared in the *Johns Hopkins University Studies in Historical and Political Science*, Vol. IX, 5th Series (September 1887).

incidentally, and therefore all the more faithfully, the impressions and anticipations of the friends and enemies of the infant Constitution; the other a careful study of its provisions and practical working by a singularly fair and penetrating European philosopher. I choose these books not only because both are specially representative and of rare literary merit, but because they are easily accessible to European readers, who may, by referring to their pages supply the omissions which want of space will compel me to make, and may thereby obtain a more complete and graphic transcript of contemporary opinion. One of these books is the *Federalist*—a series of letters recommending the new Constitution for adoption to the people of New York, written in 1788 by Hamilton, Madison, and Jay. The other, which falls almost exactly half-way between 1788 and our own time, is the *Democracy in America* of Alexis de Tocqueville.

I. The Ideas and Predictions of 1788

I begin by briefly summarizing the record which the *Federalist* preserves for us of the beliefs of the opponents and advocates of the draft constitution of 1787 regarding the forces then at work in American politics and the probable future of the nation.

To understand those beliefs, however, we must bear in mind what the United States then were, and for that purpose I will attempt to recall the reader's attention to some of the more salient aspects of the federal Republic at the epoch when its national life began.

In 1783 the last British soldier quitted New York—the last stronghold that was held for King George. In 1787 the present Constitution of the United States was framed by the Convention at Philadelphia and in 1788 accepted by the requisite number of states (nine). In 1789 George Washington entered on his presidency, the first Congress met and the machine began to work.[1] It was a memorable year for Europe as well as for America—a year which, even after the lapse of a century, we are scarcely yet ripe for judging, so many sorrows as well as blessings, πολλὰ μὲν ἐσθλὰ μεμιγμεν, πολλά δε λυγρά, were destined to come upon mankind from those elections of the States-General which were proceeding in France while Washington was being installed at Philadelphia.

---

[1] North Carolina did not ratify the Constitution till November, 1789; Rhode Island not till May, 1790.

All of the thirteen United States lay along the Atlantic coast. Their area was 827,844 square miles, their population 3,929,214, less than the population of Pennsylvania in 1880. Settlers had already begun to cut the woods and build villages beyond the Alleghenies; but when Kentucky was received as a state into the Union in 1792, she had a population of only 73,677 (census of 1790). The population was wholly of English (or Anglo-Scotch) stock, save that a few Dutch were left in New York, a few persons of Swedish blood in Delaware, and some isolated German settlements in Pennsylvania. But in spite of this homogeneity the cohesion of the states was weak. Communication was slow, difficult and costly. The jealousies and suspicions which had almost proved fatal to Washington's efforts during the War of Independence were still rife. There was some real conflict and a far greater imagined conflict of interests between the trading and the purely agricultural states, even more than between the slave states and those in which slavery had practically died out. Many competent observers doubted whether the new federal Union, accepted only because the Confederation had proved a failure and the attitude of foreign powers was threatening, could maintain itself in the face of the strong sentiment of local independence animating colonies which after throwing off the yoke of Britain, were little inclined to brook any external control. The Constitution was an experiment, or rather a bundle of experiments, whose working there were few data for predicting. It was a compromise, and its very authors feared for it the common fate of compromises—to satisfy neither party and to leave open rents which time would widen. In particular, it seemed most doubtful whether the two branches of the legislature, drawn from so wide an area and elected on different plans, would work harmoniously, and whether general obedience would be yielded to an executive president who must necessarily belong to and seem to represent one particular state and district. Parties did not yet exist, for there was as yet hardly a nation; but within a decade they grew to maturity and ferocity. One of them claimed to defend local self-government, the rights of the people, democratic equality; the other, the principle of national unity and the authority of the federal power. One sympathized with France, the other was accused of leaning to an English alliance. They were, or soon came to be, divided not merely on burning questions of foreign policy and home policy, but also—and this was an issue which mixed itself up with everything else—as to the extent of the powers to be allowed to the central government and its relations to the states—questions which the curt though apparently clear language of the Constitution had by no means exhausted, though by specifying certain powers as granted and certain others as withheld, it had supplied data for legal argument on points not expressly dealt with as well as on the general theory of the Constitution.

Slavery was not yet a leading question—indeed it existed to some slight extent in the Middle as well as in the Southern states, but the opposition of North and South was already visible. The Puritanism of New England, its industries and its maritime commerce gave it different sentiments as well as different interests from those which dominated the inhabitants of the South, a population wholly agricultural, among whom the influence of Jefferson was strong, and doctrines of advanced democracy had made great progress.

There was great diversity of opinion and feeling on all political questions in the America of those days, and the utmost freedom in expressing it. Over against the extreme democrats stood an illustrious group whose leader was currently believed to be a monarchist at heart, and who never concealed his contempt for the ignorance and folly of the crowd. Among these men, and to a less extent among the Jeffersonians also, there existed no small culture and literary power, and though the masses were all orthodox Christians and except in Maryland, orthodox Protestants, there was no lack of scepticism in the highest circles. One may speak of highest circles, for social equality, though rapidly advancing and gladly welcomed, was as yet rather a doctrine than a fact, and the respect for every kind of authority was great. There were neither large fortunes, nor abject poverty; but the working class, then much smaller relatively than it is now, deferred to the middle class, and the middle class to its intellectual chiefs. The clergy were powerful in New England; the great colonial families enjoyed high consideration in New York, in Pennsylvania, and above all in Virginia, whose landowners seemed to reproduce the later feudal society of England. Although all the states were republics of a hue already democratic, every state constitution required a property qualification for the holding of office or a seat in the legislature, and, in most states, a similar condition was imposed even on the exercise of the suffrage. Literary men (other than journalists) were rare, the universities few and unimportant, science scarcely pursued, philosophy absorbed in theology and theology dryly dogmatic. But public life was adorned by many striking figures. Five men at least of that generation, Washington, Hamilton, Franklin, Jefferson and Marshall, belong to the history of the world; and a second rank which included John Adams, Madison, Jay, Patrick Henry, Gouverneur Morris, James Wilson, Albert Gallatin, and several other gifted figures less familiar to Europe, must be mentioned with respect.

Everybody professed the principles of the Declaration of Independence and therefore held a republican form of government to be the only proper, or at any rate the only possible form for the central authority as well as for the states. But of the actual working of republican governments there was very little experience, and of the working of democracies, in our present sense of the word, there was really none at all beyond that of the several states since 1776, when they broke loose from the British Crown. Englishmen and Americans are more likely than Continentals to forget that in 1788 there was in the Old World only one free nation and no democracy.[2] In Europe now there remain but two strong monarchies, those of Russia and Prussia, while America, scarcely excepting Brazil and Canada, is entirely (at least in name) republican. But the world of 1788 was a world full of kings—despotic kings—a world which had to go back for its notions of popular government to the commonwealths of classical antiquity. Hence the speculations of those times about the dangers, the merits, the characteristic tendencies and methods of free governments under modern conditions, were and must needs be vague and fanciful, because the materials for a sound induction were wanting. Wise men when forced to speculate, recurred to the general principles of human nature. Ordinary men went off into the air and talked at large, painting a sovereign people as reckless, violent, capricious on the one hand, or virtuous and pacific on the other according to their own predilections, whether selfish or emotional, for authority or for liberty. Though no one has yet written the natural history of the masses as rulers, the hundred years since 1788 have given us materials for such a natural history surpassing those which Hamilton possessed almost as much as the materials at the disposal of Darwin exceeded those of Buffon. Hence in judging the views of the *Federalist* writers[3] and their antagonists, we must expect to find the diagnosis often inexact and the forecast fanciful.

Those who opposed the Constitution of 1787, a party both numerous and influential in nearly every state, were the men specially democratic and also specially conservative. They disliked all strengthening of government, and especially the erection of a central authority. They were satisfied with the system of sovereign and practically independent states. Hence they predicted

---

[2] The Swiss Confederation was scarcely yet a nation, and the few democratic cantons were so small as hardly to come into account.

[3] Of these writers Hamilton must be deemed the leading spirit, not merely because he wrote by far the larger number of letters, but because his mind was more independent and more commanding than Madison's. The latter rendered admirable service in the Philadelphia Convention of 1787, but afterwards yielded to the (in the main unfortunate) influence of Jefferson, a character with less purity but more vehemence.

the following as the consequences to be expected from the creation of an effective federal executive and legislature.[4]

1. The destruction of the states as commonwealths. The central government, it was said, would gradually encroach upon their powers; would use the federal army to overcome their resistance; would supplant them in the respect of their citizens; would at last absorb them altogether. The phrase "consolidation of the Union," which had been used by the Convention of 1787 to recommend its draft, was laid hold of as a term of reproach. "Consolidation," the consolidation of the states into one centralized government became the popular cry, and like other plausible catchwords, carried away the unthinking.

2. The creation of a despot in the person of the president. His legal authority would be so large as not only to tempt him, but to enable him to extend it further, at the expense of the liberties both of states and of people. "Monarchy," it was argued, "thrown off after such efforts, will in substance return with this copy of King George III, whose command of the federal army, power over appointments, and opportunities for intriguing with foreign powers on the one hand and corrupting the legislature on the other,[5] will render the new tyrant more dangerous than the old one. Or if he be more open to avarice than to ambition, he will be the tool of foreign sovereigns and the means whereby they will control or enslave America."[6]

3. The Senate will become an oligarchy. Sitting for six years, and not directly elected by the people, it "must gradually acquire a dangerous preeminence in the government, and finally transform it into a tyrannical aristocracy."[7]

---

[4] I take no account of those objections to the Constitution which may be deemed to have been removed by the first eleven amendments.

[5] See *Federalist*, No. 54.

[6] *Federalist*, No. 66, p. 667. "Calculating upon the aversion of the people to monarchy, the writers against the Constitution have endeavored to enlist all their jealousies and apprehensions in opposition to the intended President of the United States, not merely as the embryo but as the full grown progeny of that detested parent. They have to establish the pretended affinity, not scrupled to draw resources even from the regions of fiction. The authority of a magistrate in fewer instances greater, in some instances less, than those of a Governor of New York, have been magnified into more than royal prerogatives. He has been decorated with attributes superior in dignity and splendour to those of a King of Great Britain. He has been shewn to us with the diadem sparkling on his brow and the imperial purple flowing in his train. He has been seated on a throne surrounded with minions and mistresses, giving audience to the envoys of foreign potentates in all the supercilious pomp of majesty. The images of Asiatic despotism and voluptuousness have scarcely been wanting to crown the exaggerated scene. We have been taught to tremble at the terrific visages of murdering janizaries, and to blush at the unveiled mysteries of a future seraglio."

[7] *Federalist*, No. 62.

4. The House of Representatives will also, like every other legislature, aim at supremacy. Elected only once in two years, it will forget its duty to the people. It will consist of "the wealthy and well-born," and will try to secure the election of such persons only as its members.[8]

5. The larger states will use the greater weight in the government which the federal constitution gives them to overbear the smaller.

6. The existence of a strong central government is likely, not only by multiplying the occasions of diplomatic intercourse with foreign powers, to give openings for intrigues by them dangerous to American freedom, but also to provoke foreign wars, in which the republic will perish if defeated, or if victorious, maintain herself only by vast expenditure, with the additional evil of having created an army dangerous to freedom.

That some of these anticipations were inconsistent with others of them was no reason why the same persons should not resort to both in argument. Anyone who wishes to add to the number, for I have quoted but a few, being those which turn upon the main outlines of the Philadelphia draft, may do so by referring to the record of the discussions in the several state conventions which deliberated on the new Constitution, known as Elliott's Debates.

I pass from the opponents of the Constitution to its advocates. Hamilton and its friends sought in it a remedy against what they deemed the characteristic dangers of popular government. It is by dwelling on these dangers that they recommend it. We can perceive, however, that, while lauding its remedial power, they are aware how deep-seated such dangers are, and how likely to recur even after the adoption of the Constitution. It is plain from the language which Hamilton held in private that he desired a stronger and more centralized government, which would have approached nearer to that British Constitution which he regarded as being, with all its defects, the best model for free nations.[9] And in a remarkable letter written in February 1802, under the influence of disappointment with the course events were then taking, he calls the Constitution he was "still labouring to prop" a "frail and worthless fabric."

We may therefore legitimately treat his list of evils to be provided against by the new federal government as indicating the permanently mischievous tendencies which he foresaw. Some of them, he is obliged to admit, can not be wholly averted by any constitutional devices, but only by the watchful intelligence and educated virtue of the people.

[8] *Federalist*, Nos. 56 and 59.
[9] Though he, like other observers of that time had not realized, and might not have relished, the supremacy, now become omnipotence, which the House of Commons had already won.

The evils chiefly feared are the following:

1. The spirit and power of faction, which is so clearly the natural and necessary offspring of tendencies always present in mankind, that wherever liberty exists it must be looked for.[10]

   Its causes are irremovable; all you can do is to control its effects, and the best prospect of overcoming them is afforded by the representative system and the size of America with the diversities among its population.

2. Sudden impulses, carrying the people away and inducing hasty and violent legislative measures.[11]

3. Instability in foreign policy, due to changes in the executive and in public sentiment, and rendering necessary the participation of a comparatively small council or Senate in the management of this department.

4. Ill-considered legislation, "facility and excess of lawmaking,"[12] and "inconstancy and mutability in the laws,"[13] form the "greatest blemish in the character and genius of our governments."

5. The legislature is usually the strongest power in free governments. It will seek, as the example of the English Parliment shows, to encroach upon the other departments; and this is especially to be feared from the House of Representatives as holding the power of the purse.[14]

6. The states, and especially the larger states, may overbear the federal government. They have closer and more constant relations with the citizen, because they make and administer the ordinary laws he lives under. His allegiance has hitherto belonged to them and may not readily be acquired by the central authority. In a struggle, should a struggle come, state power is likely to prevail against federal power.

7. There is in republics a danger that the majority may oppress the minority. Already conspicuous in some of the state governments, as for instance Rhode Island, this danger may be diminished by the application of the federal system to the great area of the Union, where "society will be broken into so many parts, interests and classes of

---

[10] *Federalist*, No. 10 (written by Madison) and in other letters.

[11] *Federalist*, No. 62.

[12] *Federalist*, No. 61.

[13] *Federalist*, No. 72.

[14] "The Legislative Department is everywhere (*i.e.*, in all the States) extending the sphere of its activity and drawing all power into its impetuous vortex. . . . It is against the enterprising ambition of this department that the People ought to indulge all their jealousy and exhaust all their precautions." *Federalist*, No. 47.

citizens, that the rights of individuals or of the minority will be in little danger from interested combinations of the majority."[15]

8. Another source of trouble is disclosed by the rash experiments which some states have tried, passing laws which threaten the validity of contracts and the security of property. As there is unwisdom in these, so there are signs of weakness in the difficulty which state governments have found in raising revenue by direct taxation.[16] Citizens whose poverty does not excuse their want of public spirit refuse to pay; and the administration fears to coerce them.

Not less instructive than the fears of the *Federalist* writers are their hopes. Some of the perils which have since disclosed themselves are not divined. Some institutions which have conspicuously failed are relied on as full of promise.

The method of choosing the president is recommended with a confidence the more remarkable because it was the point on which the Convention had been most divided and had last arrived at an agreement.

"The mode of appointment of the Chief Magistrate of the United States is almost the only part of the system, of any consequence, which has escaped without severe censure, or which has received the slightest mark of approbation from its opponents. . . . If the manner of it be not perfect, it is at least excellent. It unites in an eminent degree all the advantages the union of which was to be wished for. . . . The process of election affords a moral certainty that the office of President will never fall to the lot of anyone who is not in an eminent degree endowed with the requisite qualifications. Talents for low intrigue, and the little arts of popularity may alone suffice to elevate a man to the first honors in a single State, but it will require other talents and a different kind of merit to establish him in the confidence and esteem of the whole Union, or of so considerable a portion of it as would be necessary to make him a successful candidate for the distinguished office of President of the United States. It will not be too strong to say that there will be a constant probability of seeing the station filled by characters preeminent for ability and virtue."[17]

---

[15] *Federalist*, No. 50.

[16] *Federalist*, No. 12.

[17] *Federalist*, No. 67. In 1800, twelve years after Hamilton wrote this passage, the contest for the presidency lay between Jefferson and Aaron Burr, and Hamilton was compelled by his sense of Burr's demerits to urge his party to vote (when the choice came before the House of Representatives) for Jefferson, his own bitter enemy. What he thought of Burr, who, but for his intervention, would certainly have obtained the chief magistracy of the nation, may be inferred from the fact that he preferred as president the man of whom he thus writes: "I admit that his (Jefferson's)

It is assumed that America will continue an agricultural and (to a less extent) a commercial country, but that she will not develop manufactures; and also that the fortunes of her citizens will continue to be small.[18] No serious apprehensions regarding the influence of wealth in elections or in politics generally are expressed.

The contingency of a division of the states into two antagonistic groups is not contemplated. When the possibility of state combinations is touched on, it is chiefly with reference to the action of small and of large states respectively. In particular no hint is dropped as to the likelihood of the institution of slavery becoming a bond to unite the Southern states and a cause of quarrel between them and the Northern.[19]

Although the mischiefs of faction are dwelt on, nothing indicates that its embodiment in highly developed party systems, whose organizations might overshadow the legal government, had occurred to anyone's mind. Still less, of course, is there any anticipation of the influence to be exerted on politics by the distribution of offices.

Let us now see which of these views and forecasts have been verified by the event.

Of those put forth by the opponents of the Constitution not one has proved true. The states are still strong, the president is not a despot, though for a time during the war he came near being one, nor has he ever fallen under the influence of any European power. The House does not consist of the "wealthy and well born"; the large states do not combine against nor press hardly on the smaller; no great country has so few wars or indeed foreign complications of any kind. Although persons are still found who call the Senate "an oligarchy," they only state the undeniable fact that it consists of comparatively few persons, most of them wealthy, and that it has a strong corporate feeling in favor of the personal interests of each of its members. It is really as dependent on public opinion as the House, perhaps even more

---

politics are tinctured with fanaticism; that he is too much in earnest in his democracy, that he has been a mischievous enemy to the principal measures of our past administration, that he is crafty and persevering in his objects, that he is not scrupulous about the means of success, nor very mindful of truth; and that he is a contemptible hypocrite. But, &c." (Letter to James A. Bayard, Jan. 16, 1801.)

After this it is superfluous, as it would be invidious, to dwell on the deficiencies of some recent presidents or presidential candidates.

[18] "The private fortunes of the President and Senators, as they must all be American citizens, cannot possibly be sources of danger." *Federalist*, No. 54.

[19] But as to the early emergence of the opposition of Northern and Southern men over slavery, see the first chapter of Dr. Von Holst's History.

afraid of public opinion, and almost as directly the offspring of popular election. One is in fact surprised to find that of the many arrows of accusation levelled at the Constitution, all should have flown wide of the mark.

The deeper insight and more exact thinking of Hamilton and Madison fastened upon most of the real and permanent weaknesses in popular government. Yet even they could not foresee the particular forms which those weaknesses would assume in the new nation. To examine in detail the eight points specified above would involve an examination of the whole of recent American history. I shall therefore simply indicate in a word or two the extent to which, in each case, the predictions of the *Federalist* may be deemed correct or the reverse.

1. The spirit of faction has certainly, as Madison expected, proved less intense over the large area of the Union than it did in the Greek republics of antiquity or in the several states from 1776 to 1789. On the other hand, the bonds of sympathy created by the federal system have at times enabled one state to infect another with its own vehemence. But for South Carolina, there would have been no secession in 1861. Today the "demon of faction" is less powerful in the parties than at any previous date since the so-called "Era of Good Feeling" in 1820.

2. Sudden popular impulses there have been. But finding a ready and constitutional expression in elections, they do not lead to physical violence, while the elaborate system of checks seldom allows them to result in dangerous federal legislation. In the states the risk of bad laws is greater, but it is largely averted by the provisions of the federal Constitution as well as by gubernatorial vetoes and the restrictions of recent state constitutions.

3. The early history of the Union furnishes illustrations of feebleness and inconstancy in foreign policy, yet not greater than those which mark most monarchies. Royal caprice, or the influence of successive favorites, has proved more pernicious in absolute monarchies than popular fickleness in republics. That of late years the foreign policy of the United States has been singularly consistent is due not so much to the Senate, nor even to the good sense of the people, as to the fact that the position and interests of the nation prescribe certain broad and simple lines.

4. On public matters, at least, Congress has not been prone to waste or excess in legislation. At present, it is more blameable for what it neglects or postpones than for what it enacts. The censure is more true of the states, especially the newer Western states.

5. The House of Representatives has doubtless sought to extend its sway at the expense of other departments. Whether it has succeeded is a question

on which good observers in America itself differ; but the fact of their differing proves that the encroachments have not been considerable. Whenever the president is weak or unpopular, Congress seems to be gaining on the executive chief. When the latter is presumably strong, he can keep the legislature at bay.

6. In the struggle which never quite ceases, though it is often scarcely noticed, between the states and the federal government, the states have rather lost than gained ground. Nor are the larger states more practically formidable than the small ones. No state would now venture to brave the federal judiciary as Georgia did, and did successfully, in the disgraceful case of the Cherokee Indians.

7. As regards the so-called tyranny of the majority, a question too large to be fully examined here, I must be content to remark that it has not hitherto proved a serious evil in America. This, however, is due rather to the character and habits of the people and their institutions generally than to the mere extent and population of the Union, on which the *Federalist* writers relied.

8. There is some foolish Congressional legislation, and, of course, much more foolish state legislation. But property is secure and the sense of civic duty seems, on the whole, to be improving.

It will appear from this examination and from the fact (noted a few pages back) that some remarkable developments which political life has taken never crossed the minds of the authors of the *Federalist*, that these wisest men of their time did not foresee what strike us now as the specially characteristic virtues and faults of American democracy. Neither the Spoils System nor the system of party nominations by wire-pullers crossed their minds. They did not foresee the inordinate multiplication of elections, nor the evils of confining eligibility for a seat in the legislature to a person resident in the electing district. No student of history will deem that this detracts from their greatness, for history teaches more plainly than the vanity of predictions in the realm of what we call the moral and political sciences, in religion, in ethics, in sociology, in government and politics. Deep thinkers help us when they unfold those permanent truths of human nature which come everywhere into play. Historians help us when, by interpreting the past, they demonstrate what are the tendencies that have so prevailed in recent years as to create the present. Observers keen enough to read the mind of the present generation may help us by rendering it probable that those tendencies, or some new ones just appearing, will be ruling factors in the near future. But beyond the near future—that is to say, beyond the lifetime of the generation which already holds power—no true philosopher will venture. He may indulge his fancy in picturing the details of the remoter landscape; but he knows that it is a region fit for fancy, not for science. In the works of great thinkers there are to be found some happy guesses about times to come; but these are few, indeed, compared with the prophecies whose worthlessness was so soon revealed that men forgot they had ever been made, or the dreams which, like those of Dante, idealized an impossible future from an irrevocable past.

As regards the views of Hamilton and Madison, who, be it remembered, do not present themselves as prophets but as the censors of present evils, it may be added that the Constitution which they framed and carried checked some of these very evils (e.g., the unjust lawmaking and reckless currency experiments of the state legislatures); and that it was obviously impossible till the federal government began to work to say how the existing forces could adapt themselves to it. Hamilton remarks in one of his letters that he holds with Montesquieu that a nation's form of government ought to be fitted to it as a suit of clothes is fitted to its wearer.[20] He would doubtless have added that it was difficult to make sure of the fit until the coat had been tried on.

The causes, moreover, which have affected the political growth of America are largely causes which were in 1788 altogether beyond human ken: the cotton gin, steam communications, Irish and German immigration have been supreme factors in that history; but even the first of these had not risen over the horizon in that year, and the last did not become a potent factor till half way through the present century.[21] What the sages of the Convention show us, are certain tendencies they discern in the contemporaries, viz.:

> Recklessness and unwisdom in the masses, producing bad laws;
> Unwillingness to submit to or support a strong government;
> Abuse by the majority of its legal power over the minority;
> Indifference to national as compared with local and sectional interests,
> 　and consequent preference of state loyalty to national loyalty.

That each of these tendencies then existed and might have been expected to work for evil, admits of no doubt. But if we ask American history what

---

[20] "I hold with Montesquieu that a government must be fitted to a nation as much as a coat to the individual; and consequently that what may be good at Philadelphia may be bad at Paris and ridiculous at Petersburgh." To Lafayette, Jan. 6th, 1799.

[21] The first cargo of cotton was sent from America to Europe in 1791 and the cotton gin invented in 1793.

it has to say about their subsequent course, the answer will be that the second and third tendencies have declined, and do not at present menace the public welfare, while the first, though never absent and always liable to marked recrudescence, as the annals of the several states prove, has done little harm in the sphere of national government. As to the fourth, which Hamilton seems to have chiefly feared, it ultimately took the form not of a general centrifugal force, impelling each state to fly off from the system, but of a scheme for the separation of the Southern or slaveholding states into a separate Confederacy, and in this form it received, in 1865, a crushing and apparently final defeat.[22]

II. Tocqueville and His Book

Fifty-one years after the recognition of the independence of the United States, fifty-three years before the present year, Alexis de Tocqueville published his *Democracy in America*, one of the few treatises on the philosophy of politics which has risen to the rank of a classic. His book, therefore, stands half way between our own days and those first days of the Republic which we know from the writings of the Fathers, of Washington, Hamilton, Jefferson, Adams, Madison. It offers a means of measuring the changes that had passed on the country during the half century from the birth of the Union to the visit of its most famous European critic, and again from the days of that critic to our own.

It is a classic, and because it is a classic one may venture to canvas it freely, without the fear of seeming to detract from the fame of its author. The more one reads Tocqueville, the more admiration does one feel for his acuteness, for the delicacy of his analysis, for the elegant precision of his reasonings, for the limpid purity of his style; above all for his love of truth and the elevation of his views. He is not only urbane, but judicial; not only noble, but edifying. There is perhaps no book of the generation to which he belonged which contains more solid wisdom in a more attractive dress.

We have here, however, to regard the treatise not merely as a model of art and a storehouse of ethical maxims, but as a picture and criticism of the government and people of the United States. And before using it as evidence

---

[22] When we come to Tocqueville, we shall find him touching but lightly on the two first of the above tendencies (partly, perhaps, because he attends too little to the state governments), but emphasizing the third and fearing from the fourth the dissolution of the Union.

of their condition fifty years ago, some observations must be made as to the reliance we may place upon it.

The first observation is that not only are its descriptions of democracy as displayed in America no longer true in many points, but that in certain points they were never true. That is to say, some were true of America, but not of democracy in general, while others were true of democracy in general but not true of America. It is worth while to attempt to indicate the causes of such errors as may be discovered in his picture, because they are errors which everyone who approaches a similar task has to guard against. Tocqueville is not much read in the United States, where the scientific, historical, and philosophical study of the institutions of the country, apart from the legal study of the Constitution, is of quite recent growth. He is less read than formerly in England and even in France. But his views of the American government and people have so passed into the texture of our thoughts that we cannot shake off his influence, and in order to profit by it are bound to submit his conclusions and predictions to a searching though respectful examination.

The defects of the book are due to three causes. He had a strong and penetrating intellect, but it moved by preference in the a priori or deductive path, and his power of observation, quick and active as it was, did not lead but followed the march of his reasonings. It will be found, when his method is closely observed, that the facts he cites are rather the illustrations than the sources of his conclusions. He had studied America carefully and thoroughly. But he wanted the necessary preparation for that study. His knowledge of England, while remarkable in a foreigner, was not sufficient to show him how much in American institutions is really English, and explainable only from English sources.

He wrote about America, and meant to describe it fully and faithfully. But his heart was in France, and the thought of France, never absent from him, unconsciously colored every picture he drew. It made him think things abnormal which are merely un-French; it made him attach undue importance to phenomena which seemed to explain French events or supply a warning against French dangers.

He reveals his method in the introduction to his book. He draws a fancy sketch of a democratic people, based on a few general principles, passes to the condition of France, and then proceeds to tell us that in Amercia he went to seek the type of democracy—democracy pure and simple—in its normal shape. *"J'avoue que dans l'Amérique, j'ai vu plus que l'Amérique: j'y ai cherché une image de la démocratie elle-même, de ses penchants, de son caractère, de ses préjugés, de ses passions."*

Like Plato in the *Republic,* he begins by imagining that there exists somewhere a type or pattern of democracy, and as the American Republic comes nearest to this pattern, he selects it for examination. He is aware, of course, that there must be in every country and people many features peculiar to the country which reappear in its government, and repeatedly observes that this or that is peculiar to America, and must not be taken as necessarily or generally true of other democracies. But in practice he underrates the purely local and special features of America, and often, forgetting his own scientific cautions, treats it as a norm for democracy in general. Nor does he, after finding his norm, proceed simply to examine its facts and draw inferences from them. In many chapters he begins by laying down one or two large principles, he develops conclusions from them, and then he points out that the phenomena of America conform to these conclusions. Instead of drawing the character of democracy from the aspects it presents in America, he arrives at its character a priori, and uses those aspects only to point and enforce propositions he has already reached. It is not democracy in America he describes, but democracy illustrated from America. He is admirably honest, never conceding or consciously evading a fact which he perceives might tell against his theories. But being already prepossessed by certain abstract principles, facts do not fall on his mind like seeds on virgin soil. He is struck by those which accord with, he is apt to ignore those which diverge from his preconceptions. Like all a priori reasoners, he is peculiarly exposed to the danger of pressing a principle too far, of seeking to explain a phenomenon by one principle only when it is perhaps the result of an accidental concurrence of several minor causes. The scholasticism we observe in him is due partly to this deductive habit, partly to his want of familiarity with the actualities of politics. An instance of it appears in his tendency to overestimate the value of constitutional powers and devices, and to forget how often they are modified, almost reversed in practice by the habits of those who use them. Though no one has more judiciously warned us to look to the actual working of institutions and the ideas of the men who work them rather than to their letter, he has himself failed to observe that the American Constitution tends to vary in working from its legal theory, and the name legislature has prevented him, like so many other foreign observers, from seeing in the English Parliament an executive as well as a lawmaking body.

In saying that he did not know England, I fully admit that his knowledge of that great free government was far beyond the knowledge of most cultivated foreigners. He had studied its history, had lived among and learnt the sentiments of its aristocracy. But he had little experience of the ideas and habits of the middle class, whom the Americans then more resembled, and he was not familiar—as how could a stranger be?—with the details of English politics and the working of the English courts. Hence he has failed to grasp the substantial identity of the American people with the English. He perceives that there are many and close resemblances, and traces much that is American to an English source. He has seen and described with perfect justness and clearness the mental habits of the English and American lawyer as contrasted with those of the French lawyer. But he has not grasped, as perhaps no one but an Englishman or an American can grasp, the truth that the American people is the English people, modified in some directions by the circumstances of its colonial life and its more popular government, but in essentials the same. Hence much which is merely English appears to Tocqueville to be American or democratic. The functions of the judges, for instance, in expounding the Constitution (whether of the federation or of a state) and disregarding a statute which conflicts therewith, the responsibility of an official to the ordinary courts of the land, the coexistence of laws of a higher and lower degree of authority, seem to him to be novel and brilliant inventions instead of mere instances of general doctrines of English law, adapted to the circumstances of a colony, dependent on a home government or a state partially subordinated to a federal government. The absence of what the French call "administration" and the disposition to leave people to themselves which strike him, would not surprise an Englishman accustomed to the like freedom. Much that he remarks in the mental habits of the ordinary American, his latent conservatism for instance, his indifference to amusement as compared with material comfort, his commercial eagerness and tendency to take a commercial view of all things, might have been just as well remarked of the ordinary middle-class Englishman, and has nothing to do with a democratic government. Other features which he ascribes to this last named cause, such as habits of easy social intercourse, the disposition to prize certain particular virtues, the readiness to give mutual help, are equally attributable to the conditions of life that existed among settlers in a wild country where few persons were raised by birth or wealth above their fellows, and everyone had need of the aid of others—conditions whose results remain in the temper of the people even when the community has passed into another phase, a phase in which inequalities of wealth have already begun to be marked, and temptations have appeared which did not beset the Puritans of the seventeenth century.

It is no reproach to Tocqueville that France formed to him the background of every picture whose foreground was the New World. He tells us frankly in the introduction that the phenomena of social equality, as they existed in France, and the political consequences to be expected from them, filled his mind when he examined the institutions of America; he hoped to find there lessons by which France might profit: "J'ai voulu y trouver des enseignements dont nous puissions profiter." But with this purpose before him, he could hardly avoid laying too much stress on points which seemed to have instruction for his own countrymen, and from fancying those things to be peculiar and abnormal which stood constrasted with the circumstances of France. Tocqueville is, perhaps of all eminent French writers, the least prone to assume the ways and ideas of his own country to be the rule, and those of another country the exception; yet even in him the tendency lurks. There is no more than a trace of it in his surprise at the American habit of using without abusing political associations, and at the disposition of legislatures to try experiments in legislation, a disposition which struck him chiefly by its contrast with the immutability which the Code of the First Empire seemed to have stamped upon the private law of France.

But this constant great reference to France goes deeper than the political philosophy of the book. It determines its scope and aim. The *Democracy in America* is not so much a political study as a work of edification. It is a warning to France of the need to adjust her political institutions to her social condition, and above all to improve the tone of her politics, to create a moral and religious basis for her national life, to erect a new fabric of social doctrine, in the place of that which, already crumbling, the Revolution had overthrown. We must not, therefore, expect to find in him a complete description and criticism such as a German would have given of the government of America in all its details and aspects. To observe this is not to complain of the book. What he has produced is more artistic, and possibly more impressive than such a description would have been, as a landscape gives a juster notion of scenery than a map. His book is permanently valuable, because its reflections and exhortations are applicable, not merely to the Frenchmen of fifty years ago, but to mankind generally, since they touch upon failings and dangers permanently inherent to political society. Let it only be remembered that in spite of its scientific form, it is really a work of art rather than a work of science, and a work suffused with strong, though carefully repressed emotion.

The best illustration I can give of these tendencies of Tocqueville will be found in a comparison of the first part of his work, published in 1834, and now included in the first and second volumes of recent editions with the second part published in 1840, and now forming the third volume. In the first part the author keeps close to his facts. Even when he has set out on the a priori road, he speedily brings his theory to the test of American phenomena: they give substance to, and (so to speak) steady the theory, while the theory connects and illumines them. But in the second part (third volume) he soars far from the ground and is often lost in the clouds of his own sombre meditation. When this part was written, the direct impressions of his transatlantic visit had begun to fade from his mind. With all his finesses and fertility, he had neither sufficient profundity of thought nor a sufficient ample store of facts gathered from history at large to enable him to give body and substance to his reflections on the obscure problems wherewith he attempts to deal.[23] Hence, this part of the book is not so much a study of American democracy as a series of ingenious and fine-spun abstract speculations on the features and results of equality on modern society and thought, speculations which, though they have been singled out for admiration by some high judges, such as Ampère and Laboulaye, will appear to most readers over fanciful, over confident in their effort to construct a general theory applicable to the infinitely diversified facts of human society, and occasionally monotonous in their repetition of distinctions without differences and generalities too vague, perhaps too hollow, for practical use.

How far do these defects of Tocqueville's work affect its value for our present purpose, that of discovering from it what was the condition, political, social, intellectual, of the United States in 1833 and what the forces that were then at work in determining the march of the nation and the development of its institutions?

It is but slightly that they impair its worth as a record of facts. Tocqueville is so careful and so unprejudiced an observer that I doubt if there be a single remark of his which can be dismissed as simply erroneous. There is always some basis for every statement he makes. But the basis is occasionally too small for the superstructure of inference, speculation and prediction which he rears upon it. To borrow an illustration from chemistry, his analysis is always right so far as it is qualitative, often wrong where it attempts to be quantitative. The fact is there, but it is perhaps a smaller fact than he thinks, or a transient fact, or a fact whose importance is, or shortly will be, diminished by other facts which he has not adequately recognized.

When we pass from description to argument he is a less safe guide. By

---

[23] Sainte Beuve says somewhere of him, "Il a commencé à penser avant d'avoir rien appris: ce qui fait qu'il a quelquefois pensé creux." Thiers once said, in the chamber, "Quand je considère intuitivement, comme dirait M. de Tocqueville."

the light of subsequent experience we can perceive that he mistook transitory for permanent causes. Many of the phenomena which he ascribes to democracy were due only to the fact that large fortunes had not yet grown up in America, others to the absence, in most parts of the country, of that higher education and culture which comes with wealth, leisure, and the settlement of society. I have already observed that he sometimes supposes features of American politics to be novel and democratic which are really old and English, that he does not allow sufficiently for the imprint which colonial life had left on the habits and ideas of the people, an imprint which though it partly wears off with time, partly becomes transformed into something which, while you may call it democratic, remains different from the democracy of an old European country, and is not an index to the character of democracy in general.

It need hardly be said that the worth of a book like his is not to be measured by the number of flaws which a minute criticism can discover in it. Even a sovereign genius like Aristotle cannot be expected to foresee which of the influences he discerns will retain their potency: it is enough if his view is more piercing and more comprehensive than that of his greatest contemporaries; if his record shows the high water mark of the learning and philosophy of the time. Had history falsified far more of Tocqueville's predictions than she has done, his work would still remain eminently suggestive and stimulating. And it is edificatory not merely because it contains precepts instinct with the loftiest morality. It is a model of that spirit of fairness and justice, that love of pure truth which is conspicuously necessary and not less conspicuously difficult in the discussion, even the abstract discussion, of the problems of political philosophy.

III. Tocqueville's View of the United States

Before we examine the picture of the social and political phenomena of America which Tocqueville has drawn, let us see what were the chief changes that had passed on the territory of the Union, on its material resources, on the habits and ideas of the people during the forty-six years that elapsed from the publication of the *Federalist* to that of the *Democracy in America*.

The territory of the United States had been extended to include the whole valley of the Mississippi, while to the northwest it stretched across the Rocky Mountains as far as the Pacific. All beyond the Missouri was still wilderness, much of it wholly unexplored, but to the east of the Mississippi there were now twenty-four states with an area of 2,059,043 square miles and a population of fourteen million. The new Western states, though rapidly increasing, were still so raw as to exercise little influence on the balance of national power, which vibrated between the free Northern and the Southern slave states. Slavery was not an immediately menacing question, for the first wound it made had been skinned over, so to speak, by the Missouri Compromise of 1820, but it was evidently pregnant with future trouble, for the number of slaves was rapidly increasing, and the slaveholders were already resolved to retain their political influence by the creation of new slave states. The great Federalist party had vanished, and the Republican-Democratic party, which had triumphed over it, had just been split up into several bitterly hostile factions. Questions of foreign policy were no longer urgent, for Europe had ceased to menace America, who had now no neighbors on her own continent except the British Crown on the north and the Mexican Republic on the south. The protective tariff and the existence of the United States Bank were the questions most agitated, but the main dividing party lines were still those which connected themselves with the stricter or looser interpretation of the federal Constitution—that is to say, they were questions as to the extent of federal power on the one hand, of the rights of the states on the other. New England was still Puritan and commercial, with a bias towards protection, the South still agricultural, and in favor of free trade. The rule of the masses had made its greatest strides in New York, the first among the other states which introduced the new methods of party organization and which thoroughly democratized in (1846) her constitution. Everywhere property qualifications for office or the electoral franchise were being abolished, and even the judges formerly nominated by the state governor or chosen by the state legislature, were beginning to be elected by universal popular suffrage and for terms of years. In fact a great democratic wave was passing over the country, sweeping away the old landmarks, destroying the respect for authority, casting office and power more and more into the hands of the humbler classes, and causing the withdrawal from public life of men of education and refinement. State feeling was still strong, especially in the South, and perhaps stronger than national feeling, but the activity of commerce and the westward movement of population were breaking down the old local exclusiveness, and those who saw steamboats plying on the Hudson and heard that locomotive engines were beginning to be run in England, might have foreseen that the creation of more easy, cheap, and rapid communications would bind the sections of the country together with a new and irresistible power. The time was one of great commercial activity and great apparent prosperity; but large fortunes were still few, while in the general pursuit of material objects science, learning, and literature had fallen into the background. Emerson was still a young Unitarian minister, known only to the circle of his own friends. Channing was just rising into note; Longfellow and Hawthorne, Prescott and Ticknor had not begun to write. Washington Irving was probably the only author whose name had reached Europe. How disagreeable the manners of ordinary people (for one must of course except the cultivated circles of Boston and Philadelphia) seemed to the European visitor may be gathered from the diaries of Richard Cobden and Sir Charles Lyell, who travelled in America a year or two after Tocqueville. There was a good deal of ability among the ruling generation of statesmen—the generation of 1787 was just dying out with Madison—but only three names can be said to have survived in the world's memory, the names of three party leaders who were also great orators, Clay, Calhoun, and Webster.[24]

In those days America was a month from Europe and comparatively little affected by Europe. Her people walked in a vain conceit of their own greatness and freedom, and scorned instruction from the effete monarchies of the Old World, which in turn repaid them with contemptuous indifference. Neither continent had realized how closely its fortunes were to be interwoven with those of the other by trade and the movements of population. No wheat, no cattle were sent across the Atlantic nor had the flow of immigration from Ireland, much less from Germany, as yet begun.

The United States of 1834 had made enormous advances in material prosperity from those of 1789. They had become a great nation, and could become a great power as soon as they cared to spend money on fleets and armies. Their federal government had stood the test of time and of not a few storms. Its component parts knew their respective functions, and worked with less friction than might have been expected. The sense of national unity, powerfully stimulated by the war of 1812,[25] was still growing. But the level of public life had not risen. It was now rather below than above that of average private society. Even in the realm of morality there were strange contrasts. A puritan strictness in some departments of conduct and

---

[24] To none of whom, oddly enough, does Tocqueville refer. He is singularly sparing in his references to individuals, mentioning no one except Jackson for blame, and Livingston (of the Louisiana Code and secretary of state, 1831–33) for praise.

[25] An interesting discussion of the effects in this respect of the war of 1812 is contained in Mr. N. M. Butler's paper in the *Johns Hopkins University Studies*, No. VII of the Fifth Series.

a universal recognition of the sanctions of religion coexisted in the North with great commercial laxity, while the semi-civilized South, not less religious and valuing itself on its high code of honor, was disgraced by the tolerance accorded to duels and acts of murderous violence, not to speak of the darker evils which slavery brought in its train. As respects the government of states and cities, democratic doctrines had triumphed all along the line. The masses of the people had now realized their power, and entered into the full fruition of it.[26] They had unlimited confidence in their wisdom and virtue, and had not yet discovered the dangers incidental to popular government. The wise elders, or the philosophic minds who looked on with distrust, were either afraid to speak out, or deemed it hopeless to stem the flowing tide. They stood aside (as Plato says) under the wall out of the storm. The party organizations had just begun to spread their tough yet flexible network over the whole country; and the class of professional politicians, at once the creator and the creature of such organizations, was already formed. The spoils of office had, three years before, been proclaimed to belong to the victors, but few saw to what consequences this doctrine was to lead. I will not say that it was a period of transition, for that is true of every period in America, so fast do events move even in the quietest times. But it was a period when that which had been democratic theory was passing swiftly into democratic practice, when the seeds sown long ago by Jefferson had ripened into a waving crop, when the forces which in every society react against extreme democracy were unusually weak, some not yet developed, some afraid to resist the stream.

IV. Tocqueville's Impressions

Let us see what were the impressions which the America of 1832 made on the mind of Tocqueville. I do not pretend to summarize his account, which every student ought to read for himself, but shall be content with presenting those more salient points to which our comparison of 1832 with 1788 on the one hand, and 1887 on the other, relates.

He is struck by the thoroughness with which the principle of the sovereignty of the people is carried out. Fifty-five years ago this principle was

---

[26] Dr. Von Holst gives at the beginning of the second part of his constitutional history a powerful picture of the democratic revolution, and inswarming of a new class of men, which accompanied the election and installation of Andrew Jackson.

far from having obtained its present ascendancy in Western Europe. In America, however, it was not merely recognized in theory, but consistently applied through every branch of local, state, and national government.

He is impressed by the greater importance to ordinary citizens of state government than of federal government, and their warmer attachment to the former than to the latter. The federal government seems comparatively weak, and in case of a conflict between the two powers, the loyalty of the people would be given rather to the state.[27]

The basis of all American government is to be found in the "commune," i.e., in local government, the ultimate unit of which is in New England the township, in the Southern and Middle states the county. It is here that the bulk of the work of administration is done, here that the citizens learn how to use and love freedom, here that the wonderful activity they display in public affairs finds its chief sphere and its constant stimulus.

The absence of what a European calls "the administration" is remarkable. Public work is divided up between a multitude of petty and unrelated local officials: there is no "hierarchy," no organized civil service with a subordination of ranks. The means employed to keep officials to their work and punish offences are two: frequent popular election and the powers of invoking the ordinary courts of justice to obtain damages for negligence or unwarranted action. But along with the extreme "administrative decentralization" there exists a no less extreme "governmental centralization," that is to say, all the powers of government are collected into one hand, that of the people, the majority of the voters. This majority is omnipotent; and thus authority is strong, capable of great efforts, capable also of tyranny. Hence the value of local self-government which prevents the abuse of power by a central authority; hence the necessity for this administrative decentralization, which atones for its want of skill in details by the wholesome influence it exerts on the character of the people.

The judges enjoy along with the dignity of their European brethren the singular but most salutary power of "declaring laws to be unconstitutional," and thus serve to restrain excesses of legislative as well as executive authority.

The president appears to our author to be a comparatively weak official. No person, no group, no party, has much to hope from the success of a particular candidate at a presidential election, because he has not much to

---

[27] Note the singular fact that he does not give any description of a state as a commonwealth, nor characterize the general features of its government.

give away. The elective system unduly weakens executive authority because a president who approaches the end of his four years' term feels himself feeble, and dares not take any bold step; while the coming in of a new president may cause a complete change of policy. His reeligibility further weakens and abases him, for he must purchase reelection by intrigue and an unworthy pandering to the desires of his party. It intensifies the characteristic fault of democratic government, the predominance of a temporary majority.

The federal Supreme Court is the noblest product of the wisdom of those who framed the federal Constitution. It keeps the whole machine in working order, protecting the Union against the states, and each part of the federal government against the aggressions of the others. The strength of the federation, naturally a weak form of government, lies in the direct authority which the federal courts have over the individual citizen; while their action, even against a state, is less offensive than might be expected because they do not directly attach its statutes, but merely, at the instance of an individual plaintiff or defendant, secure rights which those statutes may have infringed.

The federal Constitution is much superior to the state constitutions; the federal legislature, executive, and judiciary, are all of them more independent of the popular majority, and freer in their action than the corresponding authorities in the several states. Similarly the federal government is better than those of the states, wiser, more skilful, more consistent, more firm.

The day of great parties is past. There is now a feverish agitation of small parties and a constant effort to create parties, to grasp at some principle or watchward under which men may group themselves, probably for selfish ends. Self-interest is at the bottom of the parties, yet aristocratic or democratic sentiment attaches itself to each of them, that is to say, when a practical issue arises, the old antithesis of faith in the masses and distrust of the masses reappears in the view which men and parties take of it. The rich mix little in politics. Secretly disgusted at the predominance of the crowd, they treat their shoemaker as an equal when they meet him on the street, but in the luxury of their own homes lament the vulgarity of public life and predict a bad end for democracy.

Next to the people, the greatest power in the country is the press; yet it is less powerful than in France, because the number of journals is so prodigious, because they are so poorly written, because there is no centre like Paris. Advertisements and general news occupy far more of their space than does political argument, and in the midst of a din of opposing voices, the ordinary citizen retains his dull fixity of opinion, the prejudices of his sect or party.

A European is surprised, not only by the number of voluntary associations aiming at public objects, but at the tolerance which the law accords to them. They are immensely active and powerful, and do not threaten public security as they would in France, because they admit themselves, by the very fact of their existence, to represent a minority of voters, and seek to prevail by force of argument and not of arms.

Universal suffrage, while it gives admirable stability to the government, does not, as people in Europe expect that it will, bring the best men to the top. On the contrary, the governors are inferior to the governed,[28] the best men do not seek either office or a seat in the House of Representatives, and the people, without positively hating the "upper classes" does not like them; and carefully keeps them out of power. "Il ne craint point les grands talents, mais il les goûte peu."

The striking inferiority of the House to the Senate is due to the fact that the latter is a product of double election, and it is to double election that democracies must come if they will avoid the evils inseparable from placing political functions in the hands of every class of the people.[29]

American magistrates are allowed a wider arbitrary discretion than is common in Europe, because they are more constantly watched by the sovereign people, and are more absolutely at its mercy.[30]

Every office is, in America, a salaried office; nothing can be more conformable to the spirit of a democracy. The minor offices are, relatively to Europe, well paid, the higher ones ill paid. Nobody wears any dress or displays any insignia of office.[31]

Administration has both an unstable and an unscientific character. Few records are kept of the acts of departments, little information is accumulated, even original documents are neglected. Tocqueville was sometimes given

---

[28] This is a common remark of visitors to America, but it arises from their mistaking the people they see in society for the "governed" in general. They go with introductions to educated people: if they mixed with the masses they would form a different notion of the "governed," as Tocqueville rather oddly calls the ordinary citizens.

[29] It is remarkable that Tocqueville should have supposed this to be the chief cause of the excellence he ascribes to the Senate.

[30] The only instance given of this is in the discretion allowed to the officers of the New England townships, whose functions are, however, unimportant. I greatly doubt if the statement is or ever was generally true.

[31] Still true as regards public offices, save and except the judges of the Supreme Court when sitting at Washington.

such documents in answer to his queries, and told that he might keep them. The conduct of public business is a hand to mouth, rule of thumb sort of affair.[32]

Not less instability reigns in the field of legislation. Laws are being constantly changed; nothing remains fixed or certain.[33]

It is a mistake to suppose that democratic governments are specially economical. They are parsimonious in salaries, at least to the higher officials, but they spend freely on objects beneficial to the mass of the people, such as education, while the want of financial skill involves a good deal of waste. You must not expect economy where those who pay the bulk of the taxes are a mere fraction of those who direct their expenditure. If ever America finds herself among dangers, her taxation will be as heavy as that of the European monarchies.

There is little bribery of voters, but many charges against the integrity of politicians. Now the corruption of the governors is worse than that of the governed, for it lowers the tone of public morals by presenting the spectacle of prosperous turpitude.

The American democracy is self-indulgent and self-complacent, slow to recognize, still more slow to correct, its faults. But it has the unequalled good fortune of being able to commit reparable faults, of sinning with impunity (*la faculté de faire des fautes reparables*).

It is eminently ill-fitted to conduct foreign policy. Fortunately it has none.

The benefits which American society derives from its democratic government are summed up as follows:

As the majority make the laws, their general tendency, in spite of many errors in detail, is to benefit the majority, because though the means may sometimes be ill chosen, the end is always the same. Hence the country prospers.

Everyone is interested in the welfare of the country, because his own welfare is bound up with it. This patriotism may be only an enlarged egotism, but it is powerful nevertheless, for it is a permanent sentiment,

---

[32] This has ceased to be true in federal administration, and in that of the more advanced states.

[33] Tocqueville does not say whether he intends this remark to apply to state legislation only or to federal legislation also. He quotes dicta of Hamilton, Madison, and Jefferson to the same effect, but these testimonies all refer to a time anterior to the creation of the federal Constitution. Admitting that such instability did exist in 1832 as respects the states, one is tempted to believe that Tocqueville was unconsciously comparing America with France, where the Code has arrested legislation to an extent surprising to an English observer. During the last thirty years there have been more important changes in the ordinary law annually made by the English Parliament than by most American legislatures.

independent of transient enthusiams. Its character appears in the childish intolerance of criticism which the people display. They will not permit you to find fault with any one of their institutions or habits, not even if you praise all the rest.[34]

There is a profound respect for every political right, and therefore for every magistrate, and for the authority of the law, which is the work of the people themselves. If there be exceptions to this respect, they are to be found among the rich, who fear that the law may be made or used to their detriment.

The infinite and incessant activity of public life, the responsibilities it casts on the citizen, the sense of his importance which it gives him, have stimulated his whole nature, made him enterprising in all private affairs also. Hence, in great measure, the industrial prosperity of the country. Democracy effects more for the material progress of a nation than in the way of rendering it great in the arts, or in poetry, or in manners, or in elevation of character, or in the capacity for acting on others and leaving a great name in history.

We now come to the darker side of the picture. In democracies, the majority is omnipotent, and in America the evils hence flowing are aggravated by the shortness of the term for which a legislature is chosen, by the weakness of the executive, by the incipient disposition to elect even the judges, by the notion universally received that the majority must be right. The majority in a legislature being unchecked, laws are hastily made and altered, administration has no permanence, officials are allowed a dangerously wide range of arbitrary authority. There is no escape from the tyranny of the majority. It dominates even thought, forbidding, not indeed by law but through social penalties no less effective than legal ones, the expression of any opinion displeasing to the ordinary citizen. In theology, even in philosophy, one must beware of any divergence from orthodoxy. No one dare tell an unwelcome truth to the people, for it will receive nothing but incense. Such repression sufficiently explains the absence of great writers and of great characters in public life. It is not therefore of weakness that the free government in America will ever perish, but by excess of strength, the majority driving the minority to despair and arms.

There are, however, influences which temper the despotism of the majority. One is the existence of a strong system of local self-government, whereby

---

[34] Everyone knows how prominent this trait is among the observations which European visitors pass upon America. It is now much less noticeable than formerly. I can even say from experience that it had sensibly diminished between 1870 and 1883.

nearly all administration is decentralized. Another is the power of the lawyers, a class everywhere disposed to maintain authority and to defend that which exists, and specially so disposed in England and America because the law which they study and practice is founded on precedents and despises abstract reason. A third exists in the jury, and particularly the jury in its action in civil causes, for it teaches the people not only the regular methods of law and justice, but respect for law and for the judges who administer it.

Next we come to an enumeration of the causes which maintain republican government. They are, over and above the constitutional safeguards already discussed, the following:

The absence of neighboring states, and the consequent absence of great wars, of financial crises,[35] of invasions or conquests. How dangerous to republics is the passion for military glory is shown by the two elections of General Jackson to be president, a man of violent temper and limited capacity, recommended by nothing but the memory of his victory at New Orleans twenty years before.[36]

The absence of a great capital.

The material prosperity of the country, due to its immense extent and natural resources, which open a boundless field in which the desire of gain and the love of independence may gratify themselves and render the vices of man almost as useful to society as his virtues. The passions which really agitate America are commercial, not political.

The influence of religion. American Protestantism is republican and democratic: American Catholicism no less so; for Catholicism tends itself to an equality of conditions, since it treats all men alike. The Catholic clergy are as hearty republicans as any others.

The indirect influence of religion on manners and morality. Nowhere is marriage so much respected and the relations of the sexes so well ordered. The universal acceptance of Christianity, an acceptance which imposes silence even on the few sceptics who may be supposed to exist here as everywhere, steadies and restrains men's minds. "No one ventures to proclaim that everything is permissible in the interests of society. Impious maxim, which seems to have been invented in an age of liberty in order to give legitimacy to all tyrants to come."

---

[35] This observation seems strange indeed to anyone who has read the commercial history of the United States since the great crisis of 1838.

[36] Jackson's popularity began with his military exploit: but his hold on the people was due to other causes also. His election coincided with the rise of the great democratic wave already referred to.

The Americans themselves cannot imagine liberty without Christianity. And the chief cause why religion is so powerful among them is because it is entirely separated from the state.[37]

The intelligence of the people, and their education, but especially their practical experience in working their local politics. However, though everybody has some education, letters and culture do not flourish. They regard literature properly so called with disfavor; they are averse to general ideas. They have no great historian, not a single poet, legal commentators but no publicists, good artisans but very few inventors.[38]

Of all these causes, the most important are those which belong to the character and habits of the people. These are infinitely more important sources of well being than the laws, as the laws are in turn more important than the physical conditions.

Whether democracy will succeed in other parts of the world is a question which a study of America does not enable the observer confidently to answer. Her institutions, however suitable to her position in a world of her own, could not be transferred bodily to Europe. But the peace and prosperity which the Union enjoys under its democratic government do raise a strong presumption in favor of democracy even in Europe. For the passions and vices which attack free government are the same in America as in Europe, and as the legislator has overcome many of them there, combating envy by the idea of rights, and the presumptuous ignorance of the crowd by the practice of local government, he may overcome them here likewise.

One may suppose other institutions for a democracy than those the Americans have adopted, and some of them better ones. Since it seems probable that the peoples of Europe will have to choose between democracy and despotism, they ought at least to try the former, and may be encouraged by the example of America.

A concluding chapter is devoted to speculations on the future of the three races which inhabit the territories of the United States. (I need not transcribe what he says of the unhappy Indian tribes. Their fate was then already certain: the process which he saw passing in Alabama and Michigan is now repeating itself in California and Oregon.)

The presence of the blacks is the greatest evil that threatens the United States. They increase, in the Gulf states, faster than do the whites. They

---

[37] I do not profess to summarize in these few lines all that Tocqueville says of the character and influence of Christianity in the United States, for he devotes many pages to it, and they are among the wisest and most permanently true that he has written.

[38] Can this have been true even in 1832?

cannot be kept forever in slavery, the tendencies of the modern world run too strongly the other way. They cannot be absorbed into the white population for the whites will not intermarry with them, not even in the North where they have been free two generations. Once freed, they would be more from political rights. A terrible struggle would ensue. Hence the Southern Americans, even those who regret slavery, are forced to maintain it, and have enacted a harsh code which keeps the slave as near as possible to a beast of burden, forbidding him to be taught and making it difficult for him to be manumitted. No one in America seems to see any solution. The North discusses the problem with noisy inquietude. The South maintains an ominous silence. Slavery is evidently economically mischievous, for the free states are far more prosperous; but the South holds to slavery as a necessity.

As to the federal Union, it shows many signs of weakness. The states have most of the important powers of government in their hands; they have the attachment of the people; they act with vigor and promptitude, while the federal authority hesitates and argues. In every struggle that has heretofore arisen the federal government has given way, and it possesses neither the material force to coerce a rebellious state nor a clear legal right to retain a member wishing to dissolve the federal tie. But although the Union has no national patriotism to support it (for the professions of such patriotism one hears in America are but lip-deep), it is maintained by certain interests— the material interests which each part of the country has in remaining politically united with the rest. Against these one finds no strong interests making for material severance, but one does find diversities not indeed of opinion—for opinions and ideas are wonderfully similar over the whole country—but of character, particularly between Northern and Southern men, which increase the chance of discord. And in the rapid growth of the Union there lies a real source of danger. Its population doubles every twenty-two years. Before a century has passed its territory will be covered by more than a hundred million of people and divided into forty states. Now all partnerships are more difficult to keep together the more the number of partners increases.[39] Even admitting, therefore, that this hundred million of people have similar interests and are benefited by remaining united, still the mere fact that they will then form forty nations, distinct and unequally powerful, will make the maintenance of the federal government only a

---

[39] No proof is given of this proposition, which is by no means self-evident, and which has indeed all the air of a premiss laid down by a schoolman of the thirteenth century.

happy accident. "I cannot believe in the duration of a government whose task is to hold together forty different peoples spread over a surface equal to the half of Europe, to avoid rivalries, ambitions and struggles among them, and to unite the action of their independent wills for the accomplishment of the same plans."[40]

The greatest danger, however, which the Union incurs as it grows is the transference of forces which goes on within its own body. The Northern states increase more rapidly than the Southern, those of the Mississippi Valley more rapidly still. Washington, which when founded was in the centre of the Union, is now at one end of it. The disproportionate growth of some states menaces the independence of others. Hence the South has become suspicious, jealous, irritable. It fancies itself oppressed because outstripped in the race of prosperity and no longer dominant. It threatens to retire from a partnership whose charges it bears, but whose profits it does not share.[41]

Besides the danger that some states may withdraw from the Union (in which case there would probably be formed several federations, for it is highly unlikely that the original condition of state isolation would reappear), there is the danger that the central federal authority may continue to decline till it has become no less feeble than was the old Confederation. Although Americans fear, or pretend to fear, the growth of centralization and the accumulation of powers in the hands of the federal government, there can be little doubt that the central government has been growing steadily weaker, and is less and less able to face the resistance of a refractory state. The concessions of public territory made to the states, the hostility to the United States Bank, the (virtual) success of South Carolina in the nullification struggle, are all proofs of this truth. General Jackson (then president) is at this moment strong, but only because he flatters the majority and lends himself to its passions. His personal power may increase, but that of the president declines. "Unless I am strangely mistaken, the Federal Government of the United States tends to become daily weaker, it draws back from one kind of business after another, it more and more restricts the sphere of its action. Naturally feeble, it abandons even the appearance of force. On the other side, I think I perceive that in the United States the sentiment of independence becomes more and more lively in the States, and the tone of

---

[40] He has however nowhere proved that the states deserve to be called "peoples."

[41] The protective tariff was felt as a grievance by the South, being imposed in the interest of the Northern and Middle states. No doubt, the North got more gain out of the Union than the South did.

provincial government more and more pronounced. People wish to keep the Union, but to keep it reduced to a shadow: they would like to have it strong for some purposes and weak for the rest—strong in war and almost non-existent in peace—forgetting that such alternations of strength and weakness are impossible."

Nevertheless the time when the federal power will be extinguished is still distant, for the continuance of the Union is desired, and when the weakness of the Government is seen to threaten the life of the Union, there may be a reaction in its favor.

Whatever may be the future of the federation, that of republicanism is well assured. It is deeply rooted not only in the laws, but in the habits, the ideas, the sentiments, even the religion of the people. It is indeed just possible that the extreme instability of legislation and administration may some day disgust the Americans with their present government, and in that case they will pass rapidly from republicanism to despotism, not stopping by the way in the stage of limited monarchy. An aristocracy, however, such as that of the old countries of Europe, can never grow up. Democratic equality will survive, whatever be the form which government may take.

This brief summary, which gives no impression of the elegance of Tocqueville's reasonings, need not be pursued to include his remarks on the commercial and maritime greatness of the United States, nor his speculations on the future of the Anglo-American race. Still less shall I enter on the second part of the book, for (as has been observed already) it deals with the ideas of democracy and equality in a very abstract and sometimes unprofitable way, and would need a separate critical study.

But before passing on to consider how far the United States now differ from the republic which the French philosopher described, we must pause to ask ourselves whether his description was complete.

It is a salutary warning to those who think it easy to get to the bottom of the political and social phenomena of a nation, to find that so keen and so industrious an observer as Tocqueville, who has seized with unrivalled acuteness and described with consummate art many of the minor features of American politics, has omitted to notice several which had already begun to show their heads in his day, and have since become of the first importance. Among these are:

The system of party organization. It was full grown in some states (New York for instance), and spreading quickly through the rest.

The influence of commercial growth and closer commercial relations in binding together different states of the Union and breaking down the power of state sentiment. He does once refer to this influence, but is far from appreciating the enormous power it was destined to exercise, and must have exercised even without railways.

The results of the principle proclaimed definitely just before his visit, that public office was to be bestowed for political service alone, and held only so long as the party which bestowed it remained in power.

The rise of the Abolitionists (they had begun to organize themselves before 1830 and formed a National Anti-Slavery Society in 1833) and the intense hostility they aroused in the South.

The growth of the literary spirit, and the beginnings of literary production. The society which produced Hawthorne, Emerson, Longfellow, Channing, Thoreau, Prescott, Ticknor, Margaret Fuller—not to add some equally famous living names—deserved mention as a soil whence remarkable fruits might be expected which would tell on the whole nation. Yet it is not once referred to, although one can perceive that Tocqueville had spent some time in Boston, for many of his views are due to the conversations he held with the leading Whigs of that day there.

The influence of money on politics. It might have been foretold that in a country with such resources and among a people of such restless commercial activity, great piles of wealth would soon be accummulated, that this wealth would find objects which it might accomplish by legislative aid, would seek to influence government, and would find ample opportunities for doing so. But of the dangers that must thence arise we do not hear a word.

V. Examination of Tocqueville's Views and Predictions

Such were the United States in 1832, such the predictions which an unusually penetrating and philosophic mind formed of their future. I will not attempt to enquire whether his picture is in all respects accurate, because it would be unprofitable to contest his statements without assigning one's own reasons, while to assign them would lead me into a historical disquisition. A shorter and simpler course will be to enquire in what respects things have changed since his time, for thus we shall be in a position to discern which of the tendencies he noted have proved permanent, what new tendencies have come into being, what are those in whose hands the destinies of the Republic now lie.

I have noted at the end of last section the phenomena which, already existing in Tocqueville's time, he omitted to notice or to appraise at their due value. Let us see what time has brought forward since his day to alter the conditions of the problem as he saw it.

The great events that have befallen since 1834, are these:

The annexation of Texas in 1845.

The war with Mexico in 1846, leading to the enlargement of the United States by the vast territories of California, Nevada, Utah, Idaho, Arizona, and New Mexico.

The making of railways over the whole country culminating with the completion of three great transcontinental roads in 1869, 1881, and 1883, respectively.

The establishment of lines of swift ocean steamers between America and Europe.

The immigration from Ireland (immensely increased after the famine of 1846), and from Germany (beginning somewhat later).

The War of Secession, 1861–65.

The laying of submarine cables to Europe, and extension of telegraphic communication over the whole Union.

The settlement of the Alabama claims, an event scarcely less important in American history than in English, because it has immensely diminished the likelihood of a war between the two countries. In Tocqueville's time the hatred of Americans to England was rancorous.[42]

The growth of great cities. In 1830, only two had a population exceeding 100,000. There are now (census of 1880) twenty which exceed that population.

The growth of great fortunes, and of wealthy and powerful trading corporations: the stupendous development of speculation, not to say gambling, in stocks, shares, and produce.

The growth of the universities and of many kindred literary and scientific institutions.

These are events which have told directly or indirectly upon politics. I go on to enumerate the political changes themselves of the same fifty years:

. The democratization of state constitutions, total abolition of property qualifications, choice of judges by popular vote and for terms of years, restrictions on the power of state legislatures, more frequent use of the referendum.[43]

---

[42] "Il est impossible d'imaginer une haine plus venimeuse que celle des Americains contre les Anglais."

[43] In the form of the amendment of particular provisions of state constitutions.

Development of the Spoils System, consequent degradation of the increasingly large and important civil service, both federal, state, and municipal.

Perfection and hierarchical consolidation, on nominally representative, but really oligarchic lines, of party organizations; consequent growth of rings and bosses, and demoralization of city government.

Manumission and subsequent enfranchisement of the Negroes in the Southern states.

Intensification of the national (as opposed to state) sentiment consequent on the War of Secession; passion for the national flag; rejection of the dogmas of state sovereignty and right of nullification.

To these I add, as powerfully affecting politics, the development not only of literary, scientific, and historical studies, but in particular of a new school of publicists, who discuss constitutional and economic questions in a philosophic spirit; closer intellectual relations with Europe, and particularly with England and Germany; increased interest of the best class of citizens in politics; improved literary quality of the newspapers and of periodicals (political and semi-political) generally; growth of a critical and sceptical spirit in matters of religion and philosophy; diminished political influence of the clergy.

We may now ask which of Tocqueville's observations have ceased to be true, which of his predictions falsified. I follow the order in which they were presented in last chapter.

Although the powers of the several states remain in point of law precisely what they were (except as regards the constitutional amendments presently to be noticed) and the citizen depends as much on the state in all that relates to person and property, to the conduct of family and commercial relations, the national or federal government has become more important to him than it was then. He watches its proceedings more closely, and, of course, thanks to the telegraph, knows them sooner and more fully. His patriotism is far more national, and in case of a conflict between one or more states and the federal power, the sympathies of the other states would almost certainly be with the latter.

Local government has been maintained in its completeness, but it seems to excite less interest among the people. In the larger cities it has fallen into the hands of professional politicians, who have perverted it into a grasping and sordid oligarchy.

There is still, as compared with continental Europe, wonderfully little "administration." One is seldom reminded of the existence of a government.

But the influence of federal legislation on the business of the country is more considerable, for the tariff and the currency, matters of immense consequence ever since the war, are in its hands.

The dignity of the judicial bench has in most states suffered seriously from the system of popular election for comparatively short terms. In those states where nomination by the executive has been retained, and in the case of federal judges (nominated by the president) their position is perhaps the highest permanent one open to a citizen.

The president's authority received a portentous increase during the war, and although it has not returned to its normal condition, the sense of its importances has survived. His election is contested with increasing excitement, for his immense patronage and the magnitude of the issues he may influence by his veto power gives individuals and parties the strongest grounds for hope and fear. Experience has, on the whole, confirmed the view that the reeligibility of an acting president (i.e., the power of electing him for an immediately succeeding term) might be dispensed with.

The credit of the Supreme Court suffered somewhat from its proslavery decisions just before the war, and has suffered slightly since in respect to its treatment of the legal tender question. Nevertheless it remains respected and influential.

The state constitutions, nearly all of which have been reenacted or largely amended since 1834, remain inferior to the federal Constitution, and the state legislatures are, of course (possibly with a few exceptions in the New England states), still more inferior to Congress.

Two great parties reappeared immediately after Tocqueville wrote, and except for a brief interval before the war when the Whig party had practically expired before its successor and representative the Republican party had come to maturity, they have continued to divide the country, making minor parties of slight consequence. Now and then an attempt is made to start a new party as a national organization, but it rarely becomes strong enough to maintain itself. The rich and educated renewed their interest in politics under the impulse of the slavery and secession struggle. After an interval of subsequent apathy they seem to be again returning to public life. The secret murmurs against democracy, whereof Tocqueville speaks, are confined to a mere handful of fashionable exquisites less self-complacent now than they were in the days when they learnt luxury and contempt for the people in the Paris of Louis Napoleon.

Although the newspapers are much better written than formerly and those of the great cities travel further over the country, the multitude of discordant voices still prevents the people from being enslaved by the press. The habit of association by voluntary societies continues to grow.

The deficiencies of the professional politicians, a term which now more precisely describes those whom Tocqueville calls by the inappropriate European name of the governors, continue marked.

So, too, the House of Representatives continues inferior to the Senate, but for other reasons than those which Tocqueville assigns, and to a less degree than he describes. The Senate has latterly not maintained the character he gives it.

Whether American magistrates did ever in general enjoy the arbitrary power Tocqueville ascribes to them, may be doubted. They do not enjoy it now, but in municipalities there is a growing tendency to concentrate power in the hands of one or a few officers in order that the people may have some one person on whom responsibility can be fixed. A few minor offices are unsalaried; the salaries of the greater ones have been raised, particularly in the older states.

The methods of administration, especially of federal administration, have been much improved, but are still behind those of Europe, one or two departments excepted.

Government is far from economical. The war of the Rebellion was conducted in the most lavish way; the high protective tariff raises a vast revenue and direct local taxation takes more from the citizen than in most European countries.

Congress does not pass many statutes, nor do they greatly alter the law. Many legislative experiments are tried in the newer states, but the ordinary private law is in no such condition of mutability as Tocqueville describes. The law of England suffered more changes between 1868 and 1885 than either the common or statute law of the older states of the Union.

The respect for the rights of others, for the regular course of law, for the civil magistrate, remains strong; nor have the rich (at least till within the last year or two) begun to apprehend any attacks on them, otherwise than as stockholders in great railway and other corporations.

The tyranny of the majority does not strike one as a serious evil in the America of today, though to be sure people are always foretelling the mischief it will do. It cannot act through a state legislature so much as it may have done in Tocqueville's days, for the wings of these bodies have been generally clipped by the newer state constitutions. Faint are the traces which remain of that intolerance of heterodoxy in politics, religion, or social views whereon he dilates. Politicians on the stump still flatter the crowd, but many home truths are told to it nevertheless in other ways and places, and the man who ventures to tell them need no longer fear social proscription in the Northern or Western states, perhaps not even in the Southern.

The Republic has come scatheless out of a great war, and although the laurels of the general who concluded that war twice secured for him the presidency, they did not make his influence dangerous to freedom. There is indeed no great capital, but there are cities greater than most European capitals, and the Republic has not been imperilled by their growth. The influence of the clergy on public affairs has declined; whether or not that of religion has also been weakened it is more difficult to say. But everybody continues to agree that religion gains by its entire detachment from the state.

The Negro problem remains, but it has passed into a new and for the moment less threatening phase. Neither Tocqueville nor anyone else could have then foreseen that manumission would come as a war measure, and be followed by the grant of full political rights. It is no impeachment of his judgment that he omitted to contemplate a state of things in which the blacks have been made politically the equals of the whites, while immeasurably inferior in every other respect, and destined, apparently, to remain wholly separate from them. He was right in perceiving that fusion was not possible, and that liberation would not solve the problem, because it would not make the liberated fit for citizenship. His remark that the social repulsion between the races in the South would probably be greater under freedom than under slavery has so far been strikingly verified by the result.

All the forces that made for the maintenance of the federal Union are now stronger than they were then, while the chief force that opposed it, viz., the difference of character and habits between North and South, largely produced by the existence of slavery, tends to vanish. Nor does the growth of the Union make the retention of its parts in one body more difficult. On the contrary, the United States is a smaller country now when it stretches from the Bay of Fundy to the Gulf of California, with its sixty million of people, than it was then with its thirteen million, just as the civilized world was larger in the time of Herodotus than it is now, for it took twice as many months to travel from Persepolis or the Caspian Sea to the Pillars of Hercules as it does now to circumnavigate the globe, one was obliged to use a greater number of languages, and the journey was incomparably more dangerous.

Before steamboats plied on rivers, and trains ran on railways, three or four weeks at least were consumed in reaching Missouri from Maine. Now one goes in seven days of easy travelling from Portland in Maine to Portland in Oregon. Nor has the increased number of states bred more dissensions.

The thirty-eight states are not as Tocqueville assumes, and this is the error which vitiates his reasonings, thirty-eight nations. The differences in their size and wealth have become greater, but they work more harmoniously together than ever heretofore, because neither the lines which divide parties nor the substantial issues which affect men's minds coincide with state boundaries. The Western states are now, so far as population goes, the dominant section of the Union, and become daily more so. But their interests link them more closely than ever to the North, through which their products pass to Europe, and the notion once entertained of moving the capital from Washington to the Mississippi valley has been quietly dropped.

Before bidding farewell to Tocqueville, let us summarize his conclusions and his predictions.

He sees in the United States by far the most successful and durable form of democratic government that has yet appeared in the world.

Its merits are the unequalled measure of freedom, as respects action, not thought, which it secures to the ordinary citizen, the material and social benefits it confers on him, the stimulus it gives to all his practical faculties.

These benefits are likely to be permanent, for they rest upon the assured permanence of:

Social equality
Local self-government
Republican institutions
Widely diffused education

It is true that these benefits would not have been attained so quickly nor in such ample measure but for the extraordinary natural advantages of the New World. Nevertheless, these natural advantages are but subsidiary causes. The character of the people, trained to freedom by experience and by religion, is the chief cause, their institutions the second, their material conditions only the third; for what have the Spaniards made of like conditions in Central and South America?

Nevertheless, the horizon is not free from clouds.

What are these clouds?

Besides slavery and the existence of a vast Negro population they are:

The conceit and ignorance of the masses, perpetually flattered by their leaders, and therefore slow to correct their faults;

The withdrawal from politics of the rich, and inferior tone of the governors, i.e., the politicians;

The tyranny of the majority, which enslaves not only the legislatures, but
   individual thought and speech, checking literary progress, preventing
   the emergence of great men;
The concentration of power in the legislatures (federal and state), which
   weakens the executive, and makes all laws unstable;
The probable dissolution of the federal Union, either by the secession of
   recalcitrant states or by the slow decline of federal authority.

There is therefore warning for France in the example of America. But
there is also encouragement—and the encouragement is greater than the
warning.

Of these clouds one rose till it covered the whole sky, broke in a
thunderstorm and disappeared. Some have silently melted into the blue.
Some still hang on the horizon, darkening large parts of the landscape. But
how near may be the danger they threaten, and how serious, are questions
fitter to be discussed by Americans than by a European.

A P P E N D I X   I I I

Bryce's *American Commonwealth:* A Review

BY WOODROW WILSON

This is a great work, worthy of heartiest praise. Its strength does not lie in its style, although that, while lacking distinction, is eminently straightforward and clear; nor yet altogether in its broad scope of weighty topics—a scope wide almost beyond precedent in such objects, and rich in suggestion—but chiefly in its method and in its point of view. Mr. Bryce does not treat the institutions of the United States as experiments in the application of theory, but as quite normal historical phenomena to be looked at, whether for purposes of criticism or merely for purposes of description, in the practical, everyday light of comparative politics. He seeks to put American institutions in their only instructive setting—that, namely, of comparative institutional history and life.

It is of course inevitable to compare and contrast what Mr. Bryce has given us in these admirable volumes with de Tocqueville's great *Democracy in America*. The relations which the two works bear the one to the other are almost altogether relations of contrast, and the contrast serves to make conspicuous the peculiar significance of what Mr. Bryce has written. De Tocqueville came to America to observe the operation of a principle of government, to seek a well-founded answer to the question: How does

Publisher's Note: This review originally appeared in *Political Science Quarterly*, Vol. 4, No. 1 (March 1889). It is reprinted in *Bryce's "American Commonwealth"*: Fiftieth Anniversary, ed. Robert C. Brooks (New York: The Macmillan Company, 1939), pp. 169–88. "At the time of writing this review," Brooks notes, "Woodrow Wilson had just become professor of political science at Wesleyan University, Middletown, Connecticut. According to Ray Stannard Baker, his official biographer, Wilson 'pounced upon it [*The American Commonwealth*] with a kind of passion, characteristically underscored its significant passages, filled it with side notes, in short, tore the very vitals out of it and prepared a review for the *Political Science Quarterly*—as good a criticism of the work as was ever written.' (*Woodrow Wilson, Life and Letters*, Vol. 1, p. 310)."

democracy work? Mr. Bryce, on the other hand, came, and came not once but several times, to observe the concrete phenomena of an institutional development, into which, as he early perceived, abstract political theory can scarcely be said to have entered as a formative force. The question for which he sought an answer was this: What sort of institutions have the English developed in America? In satisfaction of his curiosity, his keen and elevated philosophical desire, de Tocqueville saw the crude and impatient democracy of Andrew Jackson's time. Mr. Bryce has seen the almost full grown, the measurably sobered America of today, and has seen, therefore, with a fairer chance of just proportion.

It will hardly be accounted a disparagement of Mr. Bryce's style to say that it is inferior to de Tocqueville's; the thoughts it has to convey, the meanings it has to suggest belong to quite another class than that to which de Tocqueville's judgments must be assigned: it is not meant to carry the illumination of philosophical conceptions into the regions of fact which it explores; its task is rather exposition than judgment. Mr. Bryce does not feel called upon to compete with de Tocqueville in the field in which de Tocqueville is possibly beyond rivalry. Something very different was needed, and that he has done to admiration: he has written a book invaluable to students of comparative politics—invaluable because of its fulness, its accuracy, its candor, its sane, perhaps I ought rather to say its sage, balance of practical judgment.

Mr. Bryce's qualifications for the great task he has thus worthily performed were probably equal to those of any other man of our generation. First of all, he is a Roman lawyer steeped in the legal and political conceptions of that race whose originative strength in the field of law and practical sagacity in the field of politics were as conspicuous and as potent in the ancient world as the legal capacity and political virility of the English race are in the modern world. His knowledge of Roman institutions constantly serves to remind him of the oldness and persistency of certain features of institutional development, to warn him against perceiving novelty where it does not exist. In the second place, he is a member of Parliament and an English constitutional statesman, knowing the parent stock from which our institutions sprang, not only through study, but also through having himself tasted of its present fruits. Perhaps no one can so readily understand our institutions as an English public man sufficiently read in our history and our constitutional law not to expect to find bishops in our Senate or prime ministers in the presidency. He has breathed the air of practical politics in the country from which we get our habits of political action; and he is so familiar with the machinery of government at home as to be able to perceive at once the most characteristic differences, as well as the real resemblances, between political arrangements in England and in the United States. He is prepared to see clearly, almost instinctively, the derivation of our institutions, at the same time that he is sure to be struck by even our minor divergences from English practice. But Mr. Bryce brought to the task of judging us a wider and more adequate preparation than even a schooling in Roman law and English practice could by itself have supplied. He is sufficiently acquainted with the history and practical operation of the present constitutions of the leading states of Europe to be able readily to discern what, in American practice, is peculiar to America, or to America and England, what common to modern political experience the world over. In brief, he has a comprehensive mastery of the materials of comparative politics, and great practical sagacity in interpreting them.

Mr. Bryce divided his work into six parts. In Part I he discusses "The National Government," going carefully over the ground made almost tediously familiar to American constitutional students by commentaries without number. But he gives to his treatment a freshness of touch and a comprehensiveness which impart to it a new and first-rate interest. This he does by combining in a single view both the legal theory and interpretation and the practical aspects and operation of the federal machinery. More than that, he brings that machinery and the whole federal arrangement into constant comparison with federal experiments and constitutional machinery elsewhere. There is a scope and an outlook here such as render his critical expositions throughout both impressive and stimulating. Congress, the presidency, and the federal courts are discussed in every point of view that can yield instruction. The forms and principles of the federal system are explained both historically and practically and are estimated with dispassionate candor. Perhaps the most emphasized point made in this part is one which is derived from comparative politics. It is the separation of the executive from Congress, a separation which deprives the executive of all voice in the formation of administrative and financial policy, and which deprives Congress of such leadership as would give its plans coherency and make available for its use that special and intimate knowledge of administrative possibilities without which much well-meant legislation must utterly miscarry. This is of course the particular in which our government differs most conspicuously from all the other governments of the world. Everywhere else there is one form or another of ministerial leadership in the legislature. A body of ministers constitutes, as it were, a nerve centre, or rather a sensitive presiding brain, in the body politic, taking from the nation such broad suggestions as public opinion can unmistakably convey touching the main ends to be sought by legislation and policy, but themselves suggesting in turn, in the light of their own special knowledge and intimate experience of affairs, the best means by which those ends may be attained. Because we are without such legislative leadership we remain for long periods of embarassment without any solution of some of the simplest problems that await legislation.[1] To this absence of cabinet government in America, and the consequent absence of party government in the European sense of the term, Mr. Bryce again and again returns as to a salient feature, full of significance both for much evil and for some good.[2] The evil consists in slipshod, haphazard, unskilled and hasty legislation; the good, so far as it may be stated in a single sentence, consists in delaying the triumphs of public opinion and thereby, perhaps, rendering them safer triumphs.

One chapter of this first part possesses conspicuous merit, namely, Chapter 23, on "The Courts and the Constitution." It brings out with admirable clearness the wholly normal character of the function of constitutional interpretation, as a function familiar from of old to English judicial practice in the maintenance of charter provisions, and of course necessary, according to English precedents and ideas, to the maintenance and application of charterlike written constitutions. In exposition of this view, now universally held but not always lucidly explained, he gives a prominence such as it has never before had to the very instructive fact that the Constitution does not grant the power of constitutional interpretation to the federal courts in explicit terms, but that that power, so marvelled at by Europeans, is simply a necessary inference (at least a necessary *English* inference) from its general provisions touching the functions of a federal judiciary. One point touching the action of the courts is, however, left perhaps a little too much to this same English inference. It is stated that cases involving questions of constitutionality must wait to be made up in the ordinary manner at the initiative of private parties suing in their own interest and are often, most often, decided at the instance and in behalf of private litigants; but it is left too much to inference—an inference easy of course to an American, but doubtless far from obvious to a foreigner—that a decision, when against the constitutionality of a law, is, not that the law is null and void, but is that the law *will not be enforced in that case*. Therefore other cases involving

---

[1] Bryce, *The American Commonwealth*, Vol. 3, Ch. 86, p. 146 [*Publisher's Note:* Vol. 2, p. 1004, of the present edition].

[2] Bryce, *op. cit.*, see particularly Vol. 1, Ch. 25, on "Comparison of American and European Systems."

the same points will not be made up, litigants knowing what to expect, and it is *thus*, indirectly, that the desired annulment is effected. This is not a matter of form merely or only of curious interest. For Mr. Bryce's purpose it is a point of importance. It illustrates the thesis he is trying to establish, namely, the normality of the whole principle and procedure: the entire absence from our system of any idea of a veto exercised by the courts upon legislation or of any element of direct antagonism between Congress and the judiciary, and the matter-of-course interpretation of the supreme law by those who interpret all law.

The appendix to Volume I adds to this first part, besides much other illustrative matter, a statement of the main features of the federal structure of the two great English universities* and the federal constitution of Canada.

Part II is devoted to "The State Governments." Here for the first time in any comprehensive treatise the states are given the prominence and the careful examination which they have always deserved at the hands of students of our institutions but have never before gotten. Under some seventeen heads, occupying as many close-packed chapters full of matter, the state governments (including of course local government and the virtually distinct subject of the government of cities), state politics, the territories, and the general topics in comparative politics suggested by state constitutions and state practice are discussed, so far as reliable materials serve, with the same interest and thoroughness that were in the first part bestowed upon the federal government. Mr. Bryce more than once urges upon European students of comparative politics, the almost incomparable richness of this well-nigh unexplored region of state law. If he can wonder that Mr. Mill "in his *Representative Government* scarcely refers to" our states, and that "Mr. Freeman in his learned essays, Sir. H. Maine in his ingenious book on *Popular Government*, pass by phenomena which would have admirably illustrated some of their reasonings," finding, as he does, in M. Boutmy and Dr. von Holst the only European discoverers in this field, it may profit American students to reflect in what light their own hitherto almost complete neglect of the constitutional history of the states ought to be viewed. This second part of Mr. Bryce's book ought to mark a turning point in our constitutional and political studies. In several of our greater universities some attention is already paid to state law and history; but it is safe to say that in no one of them are these subjects given the prominence they deserve; and it is safe to predict that our state history will some day be acknowledged a chief source of instruction touching the development of modern institutions. The states have been laboratories in

---

* *Publisher's Note:* This section of the appendix does not appear in the 1922 edition.

which English habits, English law, English political principles have been put to the most varied, and sometimes to the most curious, tests; and it is by the variations of institutions under differing circumstances that the nature and laws of institutional growth are to be learned. While European nations have been timidly looking askance at the various puzzling problems now pressing alike in the field of economics and in the field of politics, our states have been trying experiments with a boldness and a persistency which, if generated by ignorance in many cases and in many fraught with disaster, have at any rate been surpassingly rich in instruction.

Part III, on "The Party System," is the crowning achievement of the author's method. Here in a learned systematic treatise which will certainly for a long time be a standard authority on our institutions, a much used handbook for the most serious students of politics, we have a careful, dispassionate, scientific description of the "machine," an accurately drawn picture of "bosses," a clear exposition of the way in which the machine works, an analysis of all the most practical methods of "practical politics," as well as what we should have expected, namely, a sketch of party history, an explanation of the main characteristics of the parties of today, a discussion of the conditions of public life in the United States, those conditions which help to keep the best men out of politics and produce certain distinctively American types of politicans, and a complete study of the nominating convention. One can well believe that that not supersensitive person, the practical politician, much as he pretends to scorn the indignant attacks made upon him by "pious" reformers, would be betrayed into open emotion should he read this exact and passionless, this discriminating and scientific digest of the methods by which he lives, of the motives by which he is moved. And certainly those who are farthest removed from the practical politician's point of view will gain from these chapters a new and vital conception of what it is to study constitutions in the life. The wholesome light of Mr. Bryce's method shines with equal ray alike upon the just and upon the unjust.

Mr. Bryce very happily describes our system of nomination by convention as

> an effort of nature to fill the void left in America by the absence of the European parliamentary or cabinet system, under which an executive is called into being out of the legislature by the majority of the legislature. In the European system no single act of nomination is necessary, because the leader of the majority comes gradually to the top in virtue of his own strength.[3]

[3] Bryce, *op. cit.,* Vol. 2, Ch. 73, p. 596 [p. 884 of the present edition].

But what, in view of this, are we to say of his judgment that "a system for selecting candidates is not a mere contrivance for preventing party dissensions, but an essential feature of matured democracy"?[4] Clearly no system for nominating candidates can touch the leading places in a democracy, however matured that democracy may be, if those places be filled under the parliamentary or cabinet system, as they are in England and France. Mr. Bryce is able to show that the selection of candidates by local representative party associations has been coming more and more into vogue in England *pari passu* with the widening of the franchise, having in 1885 been behind almost every new Liberal candidate for the Commons;[5] but is it quite safe to argue *cum hoc ergo propter hoc?* Of course it needs no nominating convention in Midlothian to select Mr. Gladstone, and no caucus in any other constituency to choose for the voters a man who has made himself necessary because of mastery in Parliament, because of proof given there of a dominant mind in statesmanship. But, leaving parliamentary leaders apart, is not all nominating machinery a "separable accident" rather than an essential feature of democracy? Has it failed of construction in Switzerland merely because of the smallness of the Swiss constituencies? Have not the exceeding multiplicity of elective officers and that pernicious principle that no one may be chosen state or national representative except from the district in which he lives—a principle whose history runs back to insignificant Governor Phips of colonial Massachusetts—been more to blame than anything that can be regarded as essential to democracy? Above all is not that complete obscuration of individual responsibility which results from the operation of the "checks and balances" of our system chiefly chargeable? It prevents any man from selecting himself for leadership by conspicuous service and makes the active part of politics turn upon selecting men rather than selecting measures. Men are not identified with measures; there must, consequently, be some artificial way of picking them out.

In enumerating the causes why the best men do not enter politics,[6] Mr. Bryce seems to me to omit one of the most important, although he elsewhere repeatedly gives evidence that he is in full view of it, namely, the absence of all great prizes of legislative leadership to be won by sheer strength of persuasive mind and constructive skill. He sums up the reasons he does give with admirable point, however, by saying that "in America, while politics are relatively less interesting than in Europe, and lead to less, other

---

[4] Bryce, *op. cit.,* Vol. 2, Ch. 59, p. 416 [p. 752 of the present edition].
[5] Bryce, *op. cit.,* Vol. 2, Ch. 59, p. 418 [p. 753 of the present edition].
[6] Bryce, *op. cit.,* Vol. 2, Ch. 58, pp. 403–11 [pp. 743–48 of the present edition].

careers are relatively more interesting and lead to more'';[7] but he omits to state, in this connection, one of the most patent reasons why politics are relatively less interesting, why they lead to less, here than elsewhere.[8]

Part IV, on "Public Opinion," its American organs, its American characteristics, its American successes and failures, contains some of the author's best analytical work, but is less characteristic of his method than the preceding parts.

Part V contains "Illustrations and Reflections." It opens with an excellent chapter on the Tweed ring by one of the most lucid of our own writers, Professor Goodnow;* treats of other special phases of local ring government; of "Kearneyism in California," of laissez faire, of woman's suffrage, and of the supposed and true faults of democracy as it appears in America.

Part VI concerns "Social Institutions"—railroads, Wall Street, the bench, the bar, the universities, the influence of religion, the position of women, the influence of democracy on thought and on creative intellectual power, American oratory, etc.—and contains the author's cautious forecast of the political, social, and economic future of the United States.

All through, the work is pervaded with the air of practical sense, the air of having been written by an experienced man of affairs, accustomed to handle institutions as well as to observe them. Besides, this observer is an Englishman without English insularity, with views given elasticity by wide studies of institutions and extensive travel. He understands us with the facility of one who belongs to the same race; but he understands us also in our relations with the politics of the wider world of Europe.

The work, however, has the faults of its good qualities. If it is full of acute and sage observation and satisfying in its wonderfully complete practical analysis, it gains its advantage at a certain sacrifice. The movement of the treatment is irregular, and even hesitating at times, like the varied conversation of a full, reiterative talker; and the internal plan of each part is lacking in executive directness and consistency, is even sometimes a little confused, reminding one now and again of the political system the author is describing. So judicious and balanced is the tone, too, that it is also a little colorless. It is a matter-of-fact book in which, because of the prominence

---

[7] Bryce, *op. cit.,* Vol. 2, Ch. 58, p. 409 [p. 747 of the present edition].

[8] For Mr. Bryce's recognition of the readines of the people to receive and follow leaders whenever circumstances produce them, spite of institutions—an acknowledgement apparently not perfectly consistent with some other judgments of the book (e.g., that any arrogation of a right to consideration, greater than that accorded to the ordinary, the average man, is resented) . . . see Vol. 3, Ch. 87, pp. 169, 170 [Vol. 2, pp. 1019–20, of the present edition].

* *Publisher's Note:* Professor Goodnow's chapter on the Tweed Ring was rewritten by Bryce in later editions.

and multiplicity of the details, it is often difficult to discern the large proportions of the thought. It is full of thoughts, thoughts singularly purged of prejudice, notably rich in suggestion; but these thoughts do not converge towards any common conceptions. It is rather, one may imagine, like that lost book of Aristotle's which contained his materials of observation than like the *Politics.* It carries one over immense distances characteristic of its great subject; but this it does by carrying one in many directions, in order to do which, from substantially the same point of departure in each case, it repeatedly traverses the same ground. In brief, it is an invaluable storehouse of observations in comparative politics rather than of guiding principles of government inductively obtained. The facts, not the principles derivable from them, are prominent.

These underlying principles could not, indeed, have been made prominent without a much freer use, a much fuller use, of the historical method than Mr. Bryce has allowed himself; and it is in his sparing use of history that Mr. Bryce seems to me principally at fault. The other drawbacks to his treatment which I have mentioned are, no doubt, for the most part directly due to his purpose, clearly and consistently kept in view, to explore this rich field of politics in search of the facts only, not in search of generalizations. His method is that of thorough, exact, exhaustive analysis. But history belongs to the very essence of such a method; facts in comparative politics possess little value in the absence of clues to their development; and one cannot but wonder at the apologies which preface Mr. Bryce's occasional introduction of historical matter. Without more history than he gives there must be at least a partial failure to meet the demands of his own method. His work satisfies all who are in search of information, whether as to the existing facts or as to the formal historical derivation of our institutions. But its historical portions do not go beyond the formal history of measures and of methods to make evident the forces of national development and material circumstances which have lain behind measures and methods, and which, when once the nation gets past the youth of its continent, must work deep modification in its institutions and in its practical politics.

I can best illustrate what I mean by taking as points of departure Mr. Bryce's own clear statements of the views with which he approached our institutions. "America," he says, "is made all of a piece; its institutions are the product of its economic and social conditions and the expression of its character."[9] More pointedly and forcibly still does he express the same

---

[9] Bryce, *op. cit.,* Vol. 3, Ch. 96, p. 354. [This sentence appears with slight changes in Chapter 102 of the 1922 edition (Vol. 2, p. 1271. of the present edition).]

thing at page 404* of the same volume, in his chapter on laissez faire. He there reports himself as having said, to an English friend who bade him devote a chapter to the American theory of the state, "that the Americans had no theory of the state, and felt no need for one, being content, like the English, to base their constitutional ideas upon law and history." "No one doubts," he says, in another place, "that fifty years hence it [America] will differ at least as much from what it is now, as it differs now from the America which Tocqueville described";[10] and this difference, he is evidently ready to believe, may very possibly be a difference of institutions as well as a difference in material and social condition. Once again, in the chapters in which he discusses the influence of democracy on thought and on creative intellectual power, Mr. Bryce insists, assuredly with perfect justice, that political institutions have comparatively little to do with intellectual product and quality, certainly in the case of the United States. There is really, when American institutions are compared with English, nothing essentially novel in our political arrangements: they are simply the normal institutions of the Englishman in America. They are, in other words, English institutions as modified by the conditions surrounding settlements effected under corporate charters, in separate but neighbor colonies; above all as dominated by the material, economic, and social conditions attending the advance of the race in America. These conditions it is, not political principles, that have controlled our intellectual as well as our political development. Mr. Bryce has frequently to say of propositions of de Tocqueville's that, although possibly or even probably true when advanced, they are now no longer true; for example, certain "supposed faults of democracy." Many things supposed to be due to democracy, to political ideas, have turned out, under the test of time, to be due to circumstances. So disconnected with institutions, indeed, are actual national methods and characteristics that even what Mr. Bryce says of American public opinion in his very suggestive and valuable fourth part will doubtless be true only so long as our country is new. Americans, he says, are sympathetic, but they are unsettled and changeful. This cannot remain true of the people of an old and fully settled country, where sympathy will lead to cohesiveness and to the development of local types of opinion, where variety, consequently, will take the place of that uniformity of life and opinion which now leads to a too rapid transmission of impressions and impulses throughout the whole body of the

---

* *Publisher's Note:* This page number is incorrect; the correct page number is 266 (pp. 1210–22 of the present edition).]

[10] Bryce, *op. cit.*, Vol. 3, Ch. 115, p. 648 [Vol. 2, Chapter 122, p. 1496, of the present edition].

nation—the quick contagion of even transient impressions and emotions. America is now sauntering through her resources and through the mazes of her politics with easy nonchalance; but presently there will come a time when she will be surprised to find herself grown old—a country crowded, strained, perplexed—when she will be obliged to fall back upon her conservatism, obliged to pull herself together, adopt a new regimen of life, husband her resources, concentrate her strength, steady her methods, sober her views, restrict her vagaries, trust her best, not her average, members. That will be the time of change.

All this Mr. Bryce sees; his conspicuous merit consists, indeed, in perceiving that democracy is not a cause but an effect, in seeing that our politics are no explanation of our character, but that our character, rather, is the explanation of our politics. Throughout his work you feel that he is generally conscious of the operation of historical causes and always guided by a quick appreciation of the degree to which circumstances enter into our institutions to mould and modify them. A reader who is himself conscious of our historical make-up and tendencies can see that Mr. Bryce is also. But it is one thing for a writer to be conscious of such things himself and quite another thing for him to convey to readers not possessed of his knowledge adequate conceptions of historical development. If our politics are the expression of our character and if that character is the result of the operation of forces permanent in the history of the English race, modified in our case by peculiar influences, subtle or obvious, operative in our separate experience, the influences, namely, of a peculiar legal status and of unexampled physical surroundings, then it is to the explanation of these forces and influences that every means of exposition ought to be bent in order to discover the bases of our law and our constitutions, of our constructive statesmanship and our practical politics. A description of our institutions, even though it be so full and accurate as to call for little either of criticism or addition, like this of Mr. Bryce's, will not suffice unless backed by something that goes deeper than mere legal or phenomenal history. In legal history Mr. Bryce leaves little to be desired: nothing could be more satisfying than his natural history of our courts with their powers of constitutional interpretation. The course of constitutional amendment, too, he traces, and all such concrete phenomena as the growth and operation of nominating conventions, the genesis and expansion of the Spoils System, or of municipal rings and "bossdom," etc. But ouside of legal and phenomenal history he seldom essays to go. If his method were that which de Tocqueville too often followed, there would be little reason why he should look further than visible institutions; if a nation can be understood by the single light of its institutions, its institutions may be made to stand forth as itself. But if institutions be the expression of the national life, as Mr. Bryce rightly conceives, that national life must be brought constantly forward, even in its most hidden aspects, to explain them.

Some passages of Mr. Bryce's work, indeed, afford ground for suspecting that he does not himself always make sufficient private analysis even of the forces operative outside of our laws and acting in support and vivification of them. Thus he permits himself the old expression that we are "trying an experiment" in government. This is not true except in the same sense that it is true that the English are trying an experiment in their extensions of the franchise and in their extreme development of ministerial responsibility to the Commons. We are in fact but living an old life under new conditions. Where there is conservative continuity there can hardly be said to be experiment. Again, Mr. Bryce's statement—the old statement—that 1789 witnessed the birth of a national government could be made only by one who had not analyzed the growth of the national idea, which is coincident with the conscious development of the national experience and life. Its truth in juristic theory may be cogently maintained; but from the lay historian's point of view, and particularly from the point of view proper to English institutional and legal history, it is scarcely true at all. In the first place, no people can be a nation before its time, and its time has not come until the national thought and feeling have been developed and have become prevalent. Until a people thinks its government national it is not national. In the second place, the whole history—indeed the very theory—of judge-made law such as ours, whether it be equity or common law, bears witness to the fact that for a body of English people *the fundamental principles of the law are at any given time substantially what they are then thought to be.* The saving fact is that English (and American) thought is, particularly in the sphere of law, cautiously conservative, coherently continuous, not carelessly or irresponsibly spreading abroad, but slowly "broadening down from precedent to precedent" within a well-defined course. It is not a flood, but a river. The complete nationality of our law therefore, had to await the slowly developed nationality of our thought and habit. To leave out in any account of our development the growth of the national idea and habit, consequently, is to omit the best possible example of one of the most instructive facts of our politics, the development, namely, of constitutional principles outside the constitution, the thoroughly English accumulation of unwritten law. That there has been such an accumulation Mr. Bryce of course points out and illustrates; but because of his shyness touching the use of history, which he fears will be tedious or uninteresting, he leaves the matter, after all, without adequate analysis. For such an analysis is not supplied by his Chapter 34 on "The Development of the Constitution by Usage." That chapter contains a history of measures, of certain concrete practices, but no account of the national sentiment which has so steadily grown into a controlling, disposing, governing force, and which has really become a most tremendous sort of "usage." It is a sketch of the development of the government rather than of the influences which have made the government and altered the conceptions upon which it rests.

This must be taken to explain also the author's somewhat inadequate view of the constitutional effects of the war of secession. He seems to judge the effects of the war by the contents of the Thirteenth, Fourteenth, and Fifteenth Amendments.[11] A European reader, I believe, would get the impression that our civil war, which was a final contest between nationalism and sectionalism, simply confirmed the Union in its old strength, whereas it in reality, of course, confirmed it in a new character and strength which it had not at first possessed, but which the steady advance of the national development, and of the national idea thereby begotten, had in effect at length bestowed upon it.

If Mr. Bryce was obliged to exclude such historical analysis from his volumes, whose whole spirit and method nevertheless suggest such an analysis, and seem to await it, if not to take it for granted, why then much remains to be done in elucidation of the lessons of government to be learned in America. Those lessons can be fully learned only from history. There still remains to be accomplished the work of explaining democracy *by* America, in supplement of Mr. Bryce's admirable explanation of democracy *in* America. Comparative politics must yet be made to yield an answer to the broad and all-important question: What is democracy that it should be possible, nay natural, to some nations, impossible as yet to others? Why has it been a cordial and a tonic to little Switzerland and to big America, while it has been as yet only a quick intoxicant or a low poison to France and Spain, a mere maddening draught to the South American states? Why has England approached democratic institutions by slow and steady stages of deliberate and peaceful development, while so many other states have panted towards democracy through constant revolution? Why has democracy

---

[11] Thus he expresses surprise at the slightness of the changes wrought by the war in the Constitution— meaning, of course, the *formal* changes.

existed in America and Australia virtually from the first, while other states have utterly failed in every effort to establish it? Answers to such questions as these would serve to show the most truly significant thing now to be discovered concerning democracy: its place and office, namely, in the process of political development. What is its relative function, its characteristic position and power, in politics viewed as a whole?

Democracy is of course wrongly conceived when treated as merely a body of doctrine, or as simply a form of government. It is a stage of development. It is not created by aspirations or by new faith: it is built up by slow habit. Its process is experience, its basis old wont, its meaning national organic unity and effectual life. It comes, like manhood, as the fruit of youth: immature peoples cannot have it, and the maturity to which it is vouchsafed is the maturity of freedom and self-control, and no other. It is conduct, and its only stable foundation is character. America has democracy because she is free; she is not free because she has democracy. A particular form of government may no more be adopted than a particular type of character may be adopted: both institutions and character must be developed by conscious effort and through transmitted aptitudes. The variety of effects produced by democratic principles, therefore, upon different nations and systems, and even upon the same nation at different periods, is susceptible of instructive explanation. It is not the result of accident merely, nor of good fortune, manifestly, that the English race has been the only race, outside of quiet, closeted Switzerland, the only race, that is, standing forward amidst the fierce contests of national rivalries, that has succeeded in establishing and maintaining the most liberal forms of government. It is, on the contrary, a perfectly natural outcome of organic development. The English alone have approached popular institutions *through habit*. All other races have rushed prematurely into them through mere impatience with habit: have adopted democracy, instead of cultivating it. An expansion of this contrast would leave standing very little of the reasoning from experience which constitutes so large a part of Sir Henry Maine's plausible *Popular Government*, and would add to Mr. Bryce's luminous exposition of the existing conditions of life and the operative machinery of politics in the greatest of republics something which might serve as a natural history of republicanism.

Mr. Bryce has given us a noble work possessing in high perfection almost every element that should make students of comparative politics esteem it invaluable. If I have regretted that it does not contain more, it has been because of the feeling that the author of *The American Commonwealth*, who has given us a vast deal, might have given us everything.

A P P E N D I X   I V

Review of *The American Commonwealth*

By Lord Acton

"The American Commonwealth" cancels that sentence of Scaliger which Bacon amplifies in his warning against bookish politicians: *Nec ego nec alius doctus possumus scribere in politicis.*[1] The distinctive import of the book is its power of impressing American readers. Mr. Bryce is in a better position than the philosopher who said of another, *Ich hoffe, wir werden uns recht gut verständigen können; und wenn auch keiner den andern ganz versteht, wird doch jeder dem andern dazu helfen, dass er sich selbst besser verstehe.*[2] He writes with so much familiarity and feeling—the national, political, social sympathy is so spontaneous and sincere—as to carry a very large measure indeed of quiet reproach. The perfect tone is enough to sweeten and lubricate a medicine such as no traveller since Hippocrates has administered to contrite natives. Facts, not comments, convey the lesson; and I know no better illustration of a recent saying: *Si un livre porte un enseigement, ce doit être malgré son auteur, par la force même des faits qu'il raconte.*[3]

Publisher's Note: This review originally appeared in the *English Historical Review,* Vol. 4 (April 1889). It is reprinted in Bryce's *"American Commonwealth": Fiftieth Anniversary,* ed. Robert C. Brooks (New York: The Macmillan Company, 1939), pp. 189–203. John Emerich Edward Dalberg Acton (1834–1902) served in Parliament (1859, 1865) as a member of the Liberal Party, and was raised to the peerage by William Gladstone as Baron Acton of Aldenham. In 1895 he was appointed Regius Professor of History at Cambridge University. While at Cambridge he planned and partially completed *The Cambridge Modern History.* Readers interested in the works of Acton may consult *Selected Writings of Lord Acton,* ed. Rufus J. Fears, 3 vols. (Indianapolis: Liberty Fund, 1985–88).

[1] "Neither I nor any other learned person can write about politics."
[2] "I hope we will be able to understand each other quite well, and if neither understands the other wholly still each may be able to help the other to understand himself better."
[3] "If a book conveys a lesson it must do so in spite of the author, by the very force of the facts which it sets forth."

If our countryman has not the chill sententiousness of his great French predecessor, his portable wisdom and detached thoughts, he has made a far deeper study of real life, apart from comparative politics and the European investment of transatlantic experience. One of the very few propositions which he has taken straight from Tocqueville is also one of the few which a determined faultfinder would be able to contest. For they both say that the need for two chambers has become an axiom of political science. I will admit that the doctrine of Paine and Franklin and Samuel Adams, which the Pennsylvanian example and the authority of Turgot made so popular in France, is confuted by the argument of Laboulaye: *La division du corps législative est une condition essentielle de la liberté. C'est le seule garantie qui assure la nation contre l'usurpation de ses mandataires.*[4] But it may be urged that a truth which is disputed is not an axiom; and serious men still imagine a state of things in which an undivided legislature is necessary to resist a too powerful executive, whilst two chambers can be made to curb and neutralize each other. Both Tocqueville and Turgot are said to have wavered on this point.

It has been said that Tocqueville never understood the federal Constitution. He believed, to his last edition, that the opening words of the first section, "all legislative powers herein granted," meant *tous les pouvoirs législatifs déterminés par les représentants.*[5] Story thought that he "has borrowed the greater part of his reflections from American works [meaning his own and Lieber's] and little from his own observation." The French minister at Washington described his book as *intéressant mais fort peu exact;*[6] and even the *Nation* calls it "brilliant, superficial, and attractive." Mr. Bryce can never be accused of imperfect knowledge or penetration, of undue dependence upon others, or of writing up to a purpose. His fault is elsewhere. This scholar, distinguished not only as a successful writer of history, which is said to be frequent, but as a trained and professed historian, which is rare, altogether declines the jurisdiction of the *Historical Review*. His contumacy is in gross black and white: "I have had to resist another temptation, that of straying off into history." Three stout volumes tell how things are, without telling how they came about. I should have no title to bring them before this tribunal, if it were not for an occasional glimpse at the past; if it were not for a strongly marked and personal philosophy of American

[4] "The division of the legislative body is an essential condition of liberty. It is the only guaranty which insures the nation against the usurpation of its mandataries."

[5] "All the legislative powers determined by the representatives."

[6] "Interesting but not very exact."

history which looms behind the boss and the boom, the hoodlum and the Mugwump.

There is a valid excuse for preferring to address the unhistoric mind. The process of development by which the America of Tocqueville became the America of Lincoln has been lately described with a fulness of knowledge which no European can rival. Readers who thirst for the running stream can plunge and struggle through several thousand pages of Holst's *Verfassungs-geschichte*, and it is better to accept the division of labour than to take up ground so recently covered by a work which, if not very well designed or well composed, is, by the prodigious digestion of material, the most instructive ever written on the natural history of federal democracy. The author, who has spent twenty years on American debates and newspapers, began during the pause between Sadowa and Woerth, when Germany was in the throes of political concentration that made the Empire. He explains with complacency how another irrepressible conflict between centre and circumference came and went, and how the welfare of mankind is better served by the gathering than by the balance or dispersion of forces. Like Gneist and Tocqueville he thinks of one country while he speaks of another; he knows nothing of reticence or economy in the revelation of private opinion; and he has none of Mr. Bryce's cheery indulgence for folly and error. But when the British author refuses to devote six months to the files of Californian journalism, he leaves the German master of his allotted field.

The actual predominates so much with Mr. Bryce that he has hardly a word on that extraordinary aspect of democracy, the Union in time of war; and gives no more than a passing glance at the Confederate scheme of government, of which a Northern writer said: "The invaluable reforms enumerated should be adopted by the United States, with or without a reunion of the seceded states, and as soon as possible." There are points on which some additional light could be drawn from the roaring loom of time. In the chapter on Spoils it is not stated that the idea belongs to the ministers of George III. Hamilton's argument against removals is mentioned, but not the New York edition of *The Federalist* with the marginal note that "Mr. H. had changed his view of the Constitution on that point." The French wars of speculation and plunder are spoken of; but, to give honour where honour is due, it should be added that they were an American suggestion. In May 1790, Morris wrote to two of his friends at Paris: "I see no means of extricating you from your troubles, but that which most men would consider as the means of plunging you into greater—I mean a war. And you should make it to yourselves a war of men, to your neighbours a war of money. . . . I hear you cry out that the finances are in a deplorable situation. This should be no obstacle. I think that they may be restored during war better than in peace. You want also something to turn men's attention from their present discontents.'' There is a long and impartial inquiry into parliamentary corruption as practised now; but one wishes to hear so good a judge on the report that money prevailed at some of the turning-points of American history; on the imputations cast by the younger Adams upon his ablest contemporaries; on the story told by another president, of 223 representatives who received accommodation from the bank, at the rate of a thousand pounds apiece, during its struggle with Jackson.

America as known to the man in the cars, and America observed in the roll of the ages, do not always give the same totals. We learn that the best capacity of the country is withheld from politics, that there is what Emerson calls a gradual withdrawal of tender consciences from the social organisation, so that the representatives approach the level of the constitutents. Yet it is in political science only that Ameica occupies the first rank. There are six Americans on a level with the foremost Europeans, with Smith and Turgot, Mill and Humboldt. Five of these were secretaries of state, and one was secretary of the treasury. We are told also that the American of today regards the national institutions with a confidence sometimes grotesque. But this is a sentiment which comes down, not from Washington and Jefferson, but from Grant and Sherman. The illustrious founders were not proud of their accomplished work; and men like Clay and Adams persisted in desponding to the second and third generation. We have to distinguish what the nation owes to Madison and Marshall, and what to the army of the Potomac; for men's minds misgave them as to the Constitution until it was cemented by the ordeal and the sacrifice of civil war. Even the claim put forward for Americans as the providers of humour for mankind, seems to me subject to the same limitation. People used to know how often, or how seldom, Washington laughed during the war; but who has numbered the jokes of Lincoln?

Although Mr. Bryce has too much tact to speak as freely as the Americans themselves in the criticism of their government, he insists that there is one defect which they insufficiently acknowledge. By law or custom no man can represent any district but the one he resides in. If ten statesmen live in the same street, nine will be thrown out of work. It is worth while to point out (though this may not be the right place for a purely political problem) that even in that piece of censure in which he believes himself unsupported by his friends in the States, Mr. Bryce says no more than intelligent

Americans have said before him. It chances that several of them have discussed this matter with me. One was governor of his state, and another is among the compurgators cited in the preface. Both were strongly persuaded that the usage in question is an urgent evil; others, I am bound to add, judged differently, deeming it valuable as a security against Boulangism— an object which can be attained by restricting the number of constituencies to be addressed by the same candidate. The two American presidents who agreed in saying that Whig and Tory belong to natural history, proposed a dilemma which Mr. Bryce wishes to elude. He prefers to stand half-way between the two, and to resolve general principles into questions of expediency, probability, and degree: "The wisest statesman is he who best holds the balance between liberty and order." The sentiment is nearly that of Croker and De Quincy, and it is plain that the author would discard the vulgar definition that liberty is the end of government, and that in politics things are to be valued as they minister to its security. He writes in the spirit of John Adams when he said that the French and the American revolutions had nothing in common, and of that eulogy of 1688 as the true Restoration, on which Burke and Macaulay spent their finest prose. A sentence which he takes from Judge Cooley contains the brief abstract of his book: "America is not so much an example in her liberty as in the covenanted and enduring securities which are intended to prevent liberty degenerating into license, and to establish a feeling of trust and repose under a beneficent government, whose excellence, so obvious in its freedom, is still more conspicuous in its careful provision for permanence and stability." Mr. Bryce declares his own point of view in the following significant terms: "The spirit of 1787 was an English spirit, and therefore a conservative spirit. . . . The American constitution is no exception to the rule that everything which has power to win the obedience and respect of men must have its roots deep in the past, and that the more slowly every institution has grown, so much the more enduring is it likely to prove. . . . There is a hearty puritanism in the view of human nature which pervades the instrument of 1787. . . . No men were less revolutionary in spirit than the heroes of the American revolution. They made a revolution in the name of Magna Charta and the Bill of Rights." I descry a bewildered Whig emerging from the third volume with a reverent appreciation of ancestral wisdom, Burke's *Reflections*, and the eighteen Canons of Dort, and a growing belief in the function of ghosts to make laws for the quick.

When the last Valois consulted his dying mother, she advised him that anybody can cut off, but that the sewing on is an acquired art. Mr. Bryce feels strongly for the men who practised what Catharine thought so difficult, and he stops for a moment in the midst of his very impersonal treatise to deliver a panegyric on Alexander Hamilton. *Tanto nomini nullum par elogium.*[7] His merits can hardly be overstated. Talleyrand assured Ticknor that he had never known his equal; Seward calls him "the ablest and most effective statesman engaged in organising and establishing the Union"; Macmaster, the iconoclast, and Holst, poorly endowed with the gift of praise, unite in saying that he was the foremost genius among public men in the New World; Guizot told Rush that *The Federalist* was the greatest work known to him, in the application of elementary principles of government to practical administration; his paradox in support of political corruption, so hard to reconcile with the character of an honest man, was repeated to the letter by Niebuhr. In estimating Hamilton we have to remember that he was in no sense the author of the Constitution. In the convention he was isolated, and his plan was rejected. In *The Federalist,* written before he was thirty, he pleaded for a form of government which he distrusted and disliked. He was out of sympathy with the spirit that prevailed, and was not the true representative of the cause, like Madison, who said of him, "If his theory of government deviated from the republican standard, he had the candour to avow it, and the greater merit of co-operating faithfully in maturing and supporting a system which was not his choice." The development of the Constitution, so far as it continued on his lines, was the work of Marshall, barely known to us by the extracts in late editions of the Commentaries. "*The Federalist,*" says Story, "could do little more than state the objects and general bearing of these powers and functions. The masterly reasoning of the Chief Justice has followed them out to their ultimate results and boundaries with a precision and clearness approaching, as near as may be, to mathematical demonstration." Morris, who was as strong as Hamilton on the side of federalism, testifies heavily against him as a leader: "More a theoretic than a practical man, he was not sufficiently convinced that a system may be good in itself, and bad in relation to particular circumstances. He well knew that his favourite form was inadmissible, unless as the result of civil war; and I suspect that his belief in that which he called an approaching crisis arose from a conviction that the kind of government most suitable, in his opinion, to this extensive country, could be established in no other way. . . . He trusted, moreover, that in the changes and chances of time we should be involved in some war, which might strengthen our

---

[7] "To so great a name praise can add nothing."

union and nerve the executive. He was of all men the most indiscreet. He knew that a limited monarchy, even if established, could not preserve itself in this country. . . . He never failed, on every occasion, to advocate the excellence of, and avow his attachment to, monarchical government. . . . Thus, meaning very well, he acted very ill, and approached the evils he apprehended by his very solicitude to keep them at a distance.'' The language of Adams is more severe; but Adams was an enemy. It has been justly said that ''he wished good men, as he termed them, to rule; meaning the wealthy, the well-born, the socially eminent.'' The Federalists have suffered somewhat from this imputation; for a prejudice against any group claiming to serve under that flag is among the bequests of the French Revolution. *Les honnêtes gens ont toujours peur; c'est leur nature,*[8] is a maxim of Chateaubriand. A man most divergent and unlike him, Menou, had drawn the same conclusion: *En révolution il ne faut jamais se mettre du côté des honnêtes gens: ils sont toujours balayés.*[9] And Royer Collard, with the candour one shows in describing friends, said: *C'est le parti des honnêtes gens qui est le moins honnête de tous les partis. Tout le monde, même dans ses erreurs, était honnête à l'assemblée constituante, excepté le coté droit.*[10] Hamilton stands higher as a political philosopher than as an American partisan. Europeans are generally liberal for the sake of something that is not liberty, and conservative for an object to be conserved; and in a jungle of other motives besides the reason of state we cannot often eliminate unadulterated or disinterested conservatism. We think of land and capital, tradition and custom, the aristocracy and the services, the crown and the altar. It is the singular superiority of Hamilton that he is really anxious about nothing but the exceeding difficulty of quelling the centrifugal forces, and that no kindred and coæval towers divide his attachment or intercept his view. Therefore he is the most scientific of conservative thinkers, and there is not one in whom the doctrine that prefers the ship to the crew can be so profitably studied.

In his scruple to do justice to conservative doctrine, Mr. Bryce extracts a passage from a letter of Canning to Croker which, by itself, does not adequately represent that minister's views. ''Am I to understand, then, that you consider the king as completely in the hands of the tory aristocracy as his father, or rather as George II was in the hands of the whigs? If so,

---

[8] "Honest people are always afraid: that's their nature."

[9] "In a revolution one should never side with honest people: they are always swept out."

[10] "It is the party of honest people which is the least honest of all parties. Everyone, even in his errors, was honest in the Constituent Assembly except on the side of the [conservative] right."

George III reigned, and Mr. Pitt (both father and son) administered the government, in vain. I have a better opinion of the real vigour of the crown when it chooses to put forth its own strength, and I am not without some reliance on the body of the people.'' The finest mind reared by many generations of English conservatism was not always so faithful to monarchical traditions, and in addressing the incessant polemist of Toryism Canning made himself out a trifle better than he really was. His intercourse with Marcellus in 1823 exhibits a diluted orthodoxy: *Le système britannique n'est que le butin des longues victoires remportées par les sujets contre le monarque. Oubliez-vous que les rois ne doivent pas donner des institutions, mais que les institutions seules doivent donner des rois? . . . Connaissez-vous un roi qui mérite d'être libre, dans le sens implicite du mot? . . . Et George IV, croyez-vous que je serais son ministre, s'il avait été libre de choisir? . . . Quand un roi dénie au peuple les institutions dont le peuple a besoin, quel est le procédé de l'Angleterre? Elle expulse ce roi, et met à sa place un roi d'une famille alliée sans doute, mais qui se trouve ainsi, non plus un fils de la royauté, confiant dans le droit de ses ancêtres, mais le fils des institutions nationales, tirant tous ses droits de cette seule origine. . . . Le gouvernement représentatif est encore bon à une chose que sa majesté a oubliée. Il fait que des ministres essuient sans répliquer les épigrammes d'un roi qui cherche à se venger ainsi de son impuissance.*[11]

Mr. Bryce's work has received a hearty welcome in its proper hemisphere, and I know not that any critic has doubted whether the pious founder, with the dogma of unbroken continuity, strikes the just note or covers all the ground. At another angle, the origin of the greatest power and the grandest polity in the annals of mankind emits a different ray. It was a favourite doctrine with Webster and Tocqueville that the beliefs of the pilgrims inspired the revolution, which others deem a triumph of Pelagianism; while J. Q. Adams affirms that ''not one of the motives which stimulated the

---

[11] "The British system is only the final achievement of the long victories gained by the subjects against the monarch. Do you forget that kings ought not to establish institutions, but that institutions only should establish kings? . . . Do you know one king who deserves to be free, in the implicit sense of the word? And George IV, do you believe that I would be his minister if he had been free to choose? . . . When a king denies to the people the institutions which the people need what is the practice of England? It expels the king, and puts in his place a king of a related family no doubt, but one who finds himself thus no longer a son of royalty, trusting in the right of his ancestors, but the son of national institutions, drawing all his rights from this sole origin. . . . Representative government is still good for one thing which his majesty has forgotten. It is necessary that the ministers suffer without replying the epigrams of a king who seeks in this way to revenge himself for his impotence."

puritans of 1643 had the slightest influence in actuating the confederacy of 1774.'' The Dutch statesman Hogendorp, returning from the United States in 1784, had the following dialogue with the stadtholder: *La religion, monseigneur, a moins d'influence que jamais sur les esprits. . . . Il y a toute une province de quakers? . . . Depuis la révolution il semble que ces sortes de differences s'évanouissent. . . . Les Bostoniens ne sont-ils pas fort dévots?. . . . Ils l'étaient, monseigneur, mais à lire les descriptions faites il y a vingt ou même dix ans, on ne les reconnaît pas de ce côté-là.*[12] It is an old story that the federal Constitution, unlike that of Hérault de Séchelles, makes no allusion to the Deity; that there is none in the president's oath; and that in 1796 it was stated officially that the government of the United States is not in any sense founded on the Christian religion. No three men had more to do with the new order than Franklin, Adams, and Jefferson. Franklin's irreligious tone was such that his manuscripts, like Bentham's, were suppressed, to the present year. Adams called the Christian faith a horrid blasphemy. Of Jefferson we are assured that, if not an absolute atheist, he had no belief in a future existence; and he hoped that the French arms ''would bring at length kings, nobles, and priests to the scaffolds which they have been so long deluging with human blood.'' If Calvin prompted the revolution, it was after he had suffered from contact with Tom Paine; and we must make room for other influences which, in that generation, swayed the world from the rising to the setting sun. It was an age of faith in the secular sense described by Guizot: *C'était un siècle ardent et sincère, un siècle plein de foi et d'enthousiasme. Il a eu foi dans la vérité, car il lui a reconnu le droit de régner.*[13]

In point both of principle and policy, Mr. Bryce does well to load the scale that is not his own, and to let the jurist within him sometimes mask the philosophic politician. I have to speak of him not as a political reasoner or as an observer of life in motion, but only in the character which he assiduously lays aside. If he had guarded less against his own historic faculty, and had allowed space to take up neglected threads, he would have had to expose the boundless innovation, the unfathomed gulf produced by American independence, and there would be no opening to back the

---

[12] "Religion, sire, has less influence than ever over the minds [of men]. . . . There is a whole province of Quakers? . . . Since the Revolution it seems that differences of this sort are disappearing. . . . Are not the Bostonians very devout? . . . They were so, sire, but in reading descriptions of them written say twenty or even ten years ago one would not recognize them from this angle."

[13] "This was a century ardent and sincere, a century full of faith and enthusiasm. It had faith in the truth, for it recognized the right of truth to reign."

Jeffersonian shears against the darning-needle of the great Chief Justice. My misgiving lies in the line of thought of Riehl and the elder Cherbuliez. The first of those eminent conservatives writes: *Die Extreme, nicht deren Vermittelungen und Abschwächungen, deuten die Zukunft vor.*[14] The Genevese has just the same remark: *Les idées n'ont jamais plus de puissance que sous leur forme la plus abstraite. Les Idées abstraites ont plus remué le monde, elles ont causé plus de révolutions et laissé plus de traces durables que les idées pratiques.*[15] Lassalle says, *Kein Einzelner denkt mit der Consequenz eines Volksgeistes.*[16] Schelling may help us over the parting ways: *Der erzeugte Gedanke ist eine unabhängige Macht, fur sich fortwirkend, ja, in der menschlichen Seele, so anwachsend, dass er seine eigene Mutter bezwingt und unterwirft.*[17] After the philosopher, let us conclude with a divine: *C'est de révolte en révolte, si l'on veut employer ce mot, que les sociétés se perfectionnent, que la civilisation s'établit, que la justice règne, que la vérité fleurit.*[18]

The anti-revolutionary temper of the revolution belongs to 1787, not 1776. Another element was at work, and it is the other element that is new, effective, characteristic, and added permanently to the experience of the world. The story of the revolted colonies impresses us first and most distinctly as the supreme manifestation of the law of resistance, as the abstract revolution in its purest and most perfect shape. No people was so free as the insurgents; no government less oppressive than the government which they overthrew. Those who deem Washington and Hamilton honest can apply the term to few European statesmen. Their example presents a thorn, not a cushion, and threatens all existing political forms, with the doubtful exception of the federal Constitution of 1787. It teaches that men ought to be in arms even against a remote and constructive danger to their freedom; that even if the cloud is no bigger than a man's hand, it is their right and duty to take the national existence, to sacrifice lives and fortunes, to cover the country with a lake of blood, to shatter crowns and sceptres and fling parliaments into the sea. On this principle of subversion they erected their commonwealth, and by its virtue lifted the world out of its

---

[14] "Extremes, not their means and weaker sides, point out the future."

[15] "Ideas never have more power than when under their most abstract form. Abstract ideas have moved the world more, they have caused more revolutions and left more durable traces than have practical ideas."

[16] "No individual thinks with the consequence of the popular spirit."

[17] "A thought, once developed, is an independent power, working on for itself, yes, so growing in the human soul that it brings force to bear upon its own mother and reduces her to subjection."

[18] "It is by revolt after revolt, if one wishes to employ this word, that societies are perfected, that civilization is established, that justice reigns, that truth flourishes."

orbit and assigned a new course to history. Here or nowhere we have the broken chain, the rejected past, precedent and statute superseded by unwritten law, sons wiser than their fathers, ideas rooted in the future, reason cutting as clean as Atropos. The wisest philosopher of the old world instructs us to take things as they are, and to adore God in the event: *Il faut toujours être content de l'ordre du passé, parce qu'il est conforme à la volonté de Dieu absolue, qu'on connoît par l'évènement.*[19] The contrary is the text of Emerson: "Institutions are not aboriginal, though they existed before we were born. They are not superior to the citizen. Every law and usage was a man's expedient to meet a particular case. We may make as good; we may make better." More to the present point is the language of Seward: "The rights asserted by our forefathers were not peculiar to themselves, they were the common rights of mankind. The basis of the Constitution was laid broader by far than the super-structure which the conflicting interests and prejudices of the day suffered to be erected. The Constitution and laws of the federal government did not practically extend those principles throughout the new system of government; but they were plainly promulgated in the Declaration of Independence. Their complete development and reduction to practical operation constitute the progress which all liberal statesmen desire to promote, and the end of that progress will be complete political equality among ourselves, and the extension and perfection of institutions similar to our own throughout the world." A passage which Hamilton's editor selects as the keynote of his sysem expresses well enough the spirit of the revolution: "The sacred rights of mankind are not to be rummaged for among old parchments or musty records. They are written, as with a sunbeam, in the whole volume of human nature, by the hand of the Divinity itself, and can never be erased or obscured by mortal power. I consider civil liberty, in a genuine, unadulterated sense, as the greatest of terrestrial blessings. I am convinced that the whole human race is entitled to it, and that it can be wrested from no part of them without the blackest and most aggravated guilt." Those were the days when a philosopher divided governments into two kinds, the bad and the good, that is, those which exist and those which do not exist; and when Burke, in the fervour of early liberalism, proclaimed that a revolution was the only thing that could do the world any good: "Nothing less than a convulsion that will shake the globe to its centre can ever restore the European nations to that liberty by which they were once so much distinguished."

---

[19] "It is necessary always to be content with the order of the past, because it has conformed to the will of Almighty God, whom one recognizes in the event."

divided governments into two kinds, the bad and the good, that is, those which exist and those which do not exist; and when Burke, in the fervour of early liberalism, proclaimed that a revolution was the only thing that could do the world any good: "Nothing less than a convulsion that will shake the globe to its centre can ever restore the European nations to that liberty by which they were once so much distinguished."

Index

duties of, 180

election to: —constitutional provisions for, 352; customs regarding, 351; federal system and, 280; fraud and, 44–45; local feeling and, 44–45; number of terms, 176–77, 351; presidential elections compared with, 886–87; primaries and, 757; residential requirements, 171–75, 351

The Federalist and, 1540

foreign policy and, 324–27, 329, 330

judiciary and, 324–27, 329, 330

leadership in, 728: —lack of, 181–85, 269–70

legislation and, 150–51, 153–57, 1498–99: —constitutional interpretation, 348–49, 353; defence of system, 156; drafting of bills, 154; financial, 158–65; lack of responsibility for, 146, 155–56, 260; popular opinion's effect on, 1016–17; president's veto and, 157, 189–90; public vs. private acts, 150; reasons for maintaining system, 156–57; weakness of government based on popular opinion and, 1004–5

lobbying and, 146, 828

members of: —lawyers, 1290; payment of, 734, 735; personal characteristics, 70; as professionals, 736

models for, 30

oratorical skills of members of, 1463

political parties and, 182–86, 728: — caucuses, 183–85, 728–29

popular distrust of, 53

popular opinion's influence on, 924–25, 980

powers and duties of, 260: —cabinet members and, 189; constitutional interpretation, 349; as granted by Constitution, 338–42; nominating caucuses, 843, 844; president and, 189–90; war powers, 48, 338*n*, 340–42

president's relationship with, 49, 187–203: —conflicts, 83–84; financial legislation and, 190–92; future of, 1500–1502; impeachment and, 45, 190; independence and, 170; influence of president on Congress, 188–89; power of Congress over president,

189–90; Senate as balance in, 103, 111–12; veto power, 157, 201, 202

railroads and, 1309–11, 1315

reasons for division into two branches, 168–69

relations between Houses, 168–70

religion practiced in, 1375

salaries and, 175–76

size of, 178

state constitutions and, 382–84

state governments and, 171, 289–90

states' interests and, 167–68

term of office, 177–78

Tocqueville on, 1567

Congressional district conventions, 757

Congressional Government (Wilson), 146–47*n*, 163–64*n*

Congressional Record, 121, 124, 132

Congressmen: —status of, 181; use of term, 135*n*

Congress of the Confederation (1781–1788), 141*n*

Conkling, Roscoe, 56

Connecticut, 17, 222*n*, 297, 367, 1469

colleges and universities, 1358*n*

constitution of, 382, 384*n*, 406, 430, 433, 458, 1372

finances of, 461*n*: —property tax, 462–64

Fundamental Orders of, 380*n*

governor of, 427*n*, 428*n*

judiciary of, 451, 453, 454*n*, 458, 1285

legislature of, 430–31*n*, 433, 438, 482–83, 484

local government in, 530, 534, 535*n*, 536*n*, 555

political parties in, 720

popular opinion in, 963

primaries in, 762

religion and, 1372

voting rights in, 434, 1227*n*

women's rights in, 1227*n*, 1230–31*n*

Connolly, Richard B., 1030, 1031, 1035

Conservation of natural resources, 317, 444*n*

Conservatism, as national characteristic, 948, 949

Consistency, as strength of democracy, 1263–64

faith in, as national characteristic, 941
fatalism and, 992
fatalistic attitude and, 996–1002
mechanical difficulties of, 919–20
minorities and, 921, 922
national character and, 921–22
strength of, 920
Tocqueville on, 1556, 1557–58
as tyranny, 986–93, 1246–47, 1541,
  1567–68: —absence of intellectual
  freedom and, 991; Civil War's effect
  on, 992; constitutional limits on, 987;
  fatalistic attitude and, 998; religious
  issues, 989–90; social persecution and,
  989–92; state governments and,
  988–89
Malaria, 1102n
Male-female relations, 1224, 1231,
  1232–33
Managing committees, local party, 754–55
Manhattan, New York, 579
"Manifest destiny," 1198
Manual of Parliamentary Practice
  (Jefferson), 129n
Manufacturers, small, as class, 952–53
Manufacturing, 3, 1321. *See also* Industry
Manumission. *See* Negroes; Slavery
Marbury v. *Madison,* 335
Marcy, William Learned, 806, 1023
"Margins," 1322
Marriage, 306, 1516, 1558. *See also*
  Divorce
  immigrants and, 1113, 1117, 1119–21
  intermarriage (commixture) of races,
    1113–14, 1119, 1122, 1153, 1161–62,
    1164–65, 1176, 1180, 1182–83
  polygamy, 522, 525, 1111, 1263, 1371n,
    1393n
  state intervention in, 1220
  woman suffrage and, 1229n, 1230
  women and, 1230, 1399–1400, 1403–4,
    1406–8
Marshal, U.S., 212
Marshall, John, 56, 210–12n, 218–19, 335,
  337–38, 342–43, 354
Maryland, 17n, 22, 38, 39n, 175n, 367,
  368, 1532. *See also* Baltimore,
  Maryland
  after the Civil War, 1125
  capital of, 733n
  constitution of, 390n, 392–93, 1371

corruption in, 831
judiciary of, 453n, 1372
legislature of, 490
political parties in, 714, 715, 852
professional politicians in, 736
religion and, 1371, 1372, 1377
state intervention in, 1220
Massachusetts, 113n, 297, 367, 373, 401,
  428n, 1511–12. *See also* Boston,
  Massachusetts
birth rate in, 1119
city governments in, 594, 602
civil service in, 813
colleges and universities, 1358n (*see also
  specific universities*)
constitution of, 381, 382, 384, 392,
  398n, 399n, 406, 433, 1242, 1371,
  1372
corruption in, 830
criminal justice in, 1242
executive of, 428n, 442, 443, 446n
financial system of: —gross revenue,
  461; property tax, 465n, 466n
government of, 476n, 495
governor of, 478
judiciary of (the bench), 450–51, 453n,
  454n, 1300, 1301
legislature of, 431, 433, 435, 436, 437n,
  438, 439, 484, 503n, 1524–26
local government in, 533n, 534, 536,
  552n
political parties in, 515, 688, 720
popular opinion in, 963
primaries in, 768–69
professional politicians in, 736
religion and, 1372
rings and bosses in, 801–2
state intervention in, 1219, 1220, 1221
voting rights in, 434
women's rights in: —public office, 1230;
  suffrage, 1227n, 1228, 1230
Massachusetts Charter, 379–81
Massachusetts Convention of 1788, 177n
Maxims, 1211–12
Mayor, 560–62
  Boston example, 566–67
  description of office, 561
  election of, 561
Medical schools, 1400
Merchant guilds, charters of, 379–80
Merwin, H. C., 1040n, 1043–44

1006–7; solutions to, 1010; state government and, 1005–6; tolerance toward corruption and, 1008–9; on women, 1400–1401

Popular vote
effects of, 1243, 1244
expanded by state constitutions, 402
as illustrative of problems of democracy, 1252
legislation by (direct legislation), 412–26: —advantages of, 420, 421, 425; American experience applied to Europe, 1276–77; constitutional issues and, 417n; European precedents, 413–16; historical background, 413–14; as illustrative of problems of democracy, 1252; justification for, 421; methods by which legislative power is vested in the people, 417–19; the press and, 424; results of, 420–22; risks of, 412–13, 425–26; state legislatures and, 416–26
presidential election as, 37–39

Population
differences in, between states, 367–69
distribution of, 1099
growth of, 314, 317, 1497
movement of, 370

Populist party, 1086, 1138, 1247
woman suffrage and, 1226n, 1227

Portugal, 1486
immigrants from, 1069

Postmaster General, 76, 79

Post office regulations, 353n

Power of the purse. See Financial legislation

Prayers, 858, 1376

Predictions. See Forecasts

Presbyterians, 533n, 1378, 1378n, 1380, 1381, 1388, 1392n
party politics and, 715

President, the (the presidency), 34–75. See also specific topics
aspiring to, 62
character of, 40, 69–75
as commander-in-chief, 201
congressional addresses of, 51
Congress's relationship with, 83–84, 187–203: —Congress's power over president, 189–90; development of customs regarding, 350; financial

legislation and, 190–92; future of, 1500–1502; presidential influence, 188–89; Senate as balance in, 103, 111–12; veto and, 201, 202

Constitution and: —creation of office, 34; election, 36n, 41, 42, 43, 264–65, 270–71; powers granted, 52–54, 56, 57

corruption and, 826
creation of, 34–37
European rulers compared with, 59
impeachment of, 45, 100, 111, 118
inaugural address, 50
judiciary and, 205
number of terms, 35, 40: —development of customs regarding, 350; disruptions caused by, 63–64
party politics and, 728
party's relationship with, 188
policy statement of, 51
political life following, 73–74
powers and duties of, 47–61, 71–72, 83: —appointments, 54–58, 63, 99–100, 350; cabinet's actions and, 81; Congress and, 49; crises and, 59, 65; development of, 350, 357, 359, 360; domestic affairs and, 48–50; fear of abuse of, 60–61; foreign policy and, 48; legislative, 50–54, 58; removals from office, 56–57; veto, 52–54, 157, 189–90, 192, 350; war power, 48–49, 111, 360
problems of, in democracy, 65
public addresses of, 49–50
public opinion and, 60
reasons for, 34–35
religion and, 1375–76
removal of, 45–46
rotation in office notion not applied to, 843n
Senate's relationship with, 85: — development of, 357; executive functions of Senate, 48, 88, 96–100
as social concept, 66–68
state governments and, 291–92
as statesman, 74–75
strength of, 60
Tocqueville on, 1553–54
type of person chosen to be, 69–75

President, university or college, 1330–31, 1331n, 1332, 1356–57

The text of this book was set in Times Roman, a typeface designed by Stanley Morison for the *London Times* and introduced by that newspaper in 1932. The *Times* was seeking a typeface with an attractive, contemporary appearance, both readable and condensed enough to accommodate a substantial number or words per column. One of the most popular typefaces used for book work throughout the world, Times Roman can quite justly claim that it is the most important type design of the twentieth century. Stanley Morison, an influential figure in the design of typography, has served as typographical advisor to the English Monotype Corporation and as director of two distinguished English publishing houses. He is also a writer with sensibility, erudition, and a keen sense of practicality.

Book design by Hermann Strohbach, New York, New York
Editorial service by Dale Ramsey and Edward Ferraro,
New York, New York
Index by Riofrancos & Co., New York, New York
Typography by Monotype Composition Co., Inc., Baltimore, Maryland
Printed and bound by Worzalla Publishing Company,
Stevens Point, Wisconsin